International Directory of
COMPANY
HISTORIES

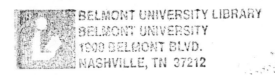

International Directory of
COMPANY
HISTORIES

VOLUME 62

Editor
Tina Grant

ST. JAMES
PRESS®

THOMSON
™
GALE

Detroit • New York • San Diego • San Francisco • Cleveland • New Haven, Conn. • Waterville, Maine • London • Munich

International Directory of Company Histories, Volume 62

Tina Grant, Editor

Project Editor
Miranda H. Ferrara

Editorial
Erin Bealmear, Joann Cerrito, Jim Craddock,
Stephen Cusack, Peter M. Gareffa,
Kristin Hart, Melissa Hill, Margaret
Mazurkiewicz, Carol A. Schwartz,
Michael J. Tyrkus

Imaging and Multimedia
Randy Bassett, Lezlie Light

Manufacturing
Rhonda Williams

LIBRARY OF CONGRESS CATALOG NUMBER 89-190943

ISBN: 1-55862-507-0

BRITISH LIBRARY CATALOGUING IN PUBLICATION DATA

International directory of company histories. Vol. 62
I. Tina Grant
33.87409

Printed in the United States of America
10 9 8 7 6 5 4 3 2 1

CONTENTS _____

Company Histories

PREFACE

The St. James Press series *The International Directory of Company Histories (IDCH)* is intended for reference use by students, business people, librarians, historians, economists, investors, job candidates, and others who seek to learn more about the historical development of the world's most important companies. To date, *IDCH* has covered over 6,650 companies in 62 volumes.

Inclusion Criteria

Most companies chosen for inclusion in *IDCH* have achieved a minimum of US$25 million in annual sales and are leading influences in their industries or geographical locations. Companies may be publicly held, private, or nonprofit. State-owned companies that are important in their industries and that may operate much like public or private companies also are included. Wholly owned subsidiaries and divisions are profiled if they meet the requirements for inclusion. Entries on companies that have had major changes since they were last profiled may be selected for updating.

The *IDCH* series highlights 10% private and nonprofit companies, and features updated entries on approximately 50 companies per volume.

Entry Format

Each entry begins with the company's legal name, the address of its headquarters, its telephone, toll-free, and fax numbers, and its web site. A statement of public, private, state, or parent ownership follows. A company with a legal name in both English and the language of its headquarters country is listed by the English name, with the native-language name in parentheses.

The company's founding or earliest incorporation date, the number of employees, and the most recent available sales figures follow. Sales figures are given in local currencies with equivalents in U.S. dollars. For some private companies, sales figures are estimates and indicated by the abbreviation *est.* The entry lists the exchanges on which a company's stock is traded and its ticker symbol, as well as the company's NAIC codes.

Entries generally contain a *Company Perspectives* box which provides a short summary of the company's mission, goals, and ideals, a *Key Dates* box highlighting milestones in the company's history, lists of *Principal Subsidiaries, Principal Divisions, Principal Operating Units, Principal Competitors,* and articles for *Further Reading.*

American spelling is used throughout *IDCH*, and the word "billion" is used in its U.S. sense of one thousand million.

Sources

Entries have been compiled from publicly accessible sources both in print and on the Internet such as general and academic periodicals, books, annual reports, and material supplied by the companies themselves.

Cumulative Indexes

IDCH contains three indexes: the **Index to Companies**, which provides an alphabetical index to companies discussed in the text as well as to companies profiled, the **Index to Industries**, which allows researchers to locate companies by their principal industry, and the **Geographic Index**, which lists companies alphabetically by the country of their headquarters. The indexes are cumulative and specific instructions for using them are found immediately preceding each index.

Suggestions Welcome

Comments and suggestions from users of *IDCH* on any aspect of the product as well as suggestions for companies to be included or updated are cordially invited. Please write:

The Editor
International Directory of Company Histories
St. James Press
27500 Drake Rd.
Farmington Hills, Michigan 48331-3535

AB	Aktiebolag (Finland, Sweden)
AB Oy	Aktiebolag Osakeyhtiot (Finland)
A.E.	Anonimos Eteria (Greece)
AG	Aktiengesellschaft (Austria, Germany, Switzerland, Liechtenstein)
A.O.	Anonim Ortaklari/Ortakligi (Turkey)
ApS	Amparteselskab (Denmark)
A.Š.	Anonim Širketi (Turkey)
A/S	Aksjeselskap (Norway); Aktieselskab (Denmark, Sweden)
Ay	Avoinyhtio (Finland)
B.A.	Buttengewone Aansprakeiijkheid (The Netherlands)
Bhd.	Berhad (Malaysia, Brunei)
B.V.	Besloten Vennootschap (Belgium, The Netherlands)
C.A.	Compania Anonima (Ecuador, Venezuela)
C. de R.L.	Compania de Responsabilidad Limitada (Spain)
Co.	Company
Corp.	Corporation
CRL	Companhia a Responsabilidao Limitida (Portugal, Spain)
C.V.	Commanditaire Vennootschap (The Netherlands, Belgium)
G.I.E.	Groupement d'Interet Economique (France)
GmbH	Gesellschaft mit beschraenkter Haftung (Austria, Germany, Switzerland)
Inc.	Incorporated (United States, Canada)
I/S	Interessentselskab (Denmark); Interesentselskap (Norway)
KG/KGaA	Kommanditgesellschaft/Kommanditgesellschaft auf Aktien (Austria, Germany, Switzerland)
KK	Kabushiki Kaisha (Japan)
K/S	Kommanditselskab (Denmark); Kommandittselskap (Norway)
Lda.	Limitada (Spain)
L.L.C.	Limited Liability Company (United States)
Ltd.	Limited (Various)
Ltda.	Limitada (Brazil, Portugal)
Ltee.	Limitee (Canada, France)
mbH	mit beschraenkter Haftung (Austria, Germany)
N.V.	Naamloze Vennootschap (Belgium, The Netherlands)
OAO	Otkrytoe Aktsionernoe Obshchestve (Russia)
OOO	Obschestvo s Ogranichennoi Otvetstvennostiu (Russia)
Oy	Osakeyhtiö (Finland)
PLC	Public Limited Co. (United Kingdom, Ireland)
Pty.	Proprietary (Australia, South Africa, United Kingdom)
S.A.	Société Anonyme (Belgium, France, Greece, Luxembourg, Switzerland, Arab speaking countries); Sociedad Anónima (Latin America [except Brazil], Spain, Mexico); Sociedades Anônimas (Brazil, Portugal)
SAA	Societe Anonyme Arabienne
S.A.R.L.	Sociedade Anonima de Responsabilidade Limitada (Brazil, Portugal); Société à Responsabilité Limitée (France, Belgium, Luxembourg)
S.A.S.	Societá in Accomandita Semplice (Italy); Societe Anonyme Syrienne (Arab speaking countries)
Sdn. Bhd.	Sendirian Berhad (Malaysia)
S.p.A.	Società per Azioni (Italy)
Sp. z.o.o.	Spólka z ograniczona odpowiedzialnoscia (Poland)
S.R.L.	Società a Responsabilità Limitata (Italy); Sociedad de Responsabilidad Limitada (Spain, Mexico, Latin America [except Brazil])
S.R.O.	Spolecnost s Rucenim Omezenym (Czechoslovakia
Ste.	Societe (France, Belgium, Luxembourg, Switzerland)
VAG	Verein der Arbeitgeber (Austria, Germany)
YK	Yugen Kaisha (Japan)
ZAO	Zakrytoe Aktsionernoe Obshchestve (Russia)

$	United States dollar	KD	Kuwaiti dinar
£	United Kingdom pound	L	Italian lira
¥	Japanese yen	LuxFr	Luxembourgian franc
A$	Australian dollar	M$	Malaysian ringgit
AED	United Arab Emirates dirham	N	Nigerian naira
ATS	Austrian schilling	Nfl	Netherlands florin
B	Thai baht	NIS	Israeli new shekel
B	Venezuelan bolivar	NKr	Norwegian krone
BD	Bahraini dinar	NT$	Taiwanese dollar
BFr	Belgian franc	NZ$	New Zealand dollar
C$	Canadian dollar	P	Philippine peso
CHF	Switzerland franc	PLN	Polish zloty
COL	Colombian peso	PkR	Pakistan Rupee
Cr	Brazilian cruzado	Pta	Spanish peseta
CZK	Czech Republic koruny	R	Brazilian real
DA	Algerian dinar	R	South African rand
Dfl	Netherlands florin	RMB	Chinese renminbi
DKr	Danish krone	RO	Omani rial
DM	German mark	Rp	Indonesian rupiah
E£	Egyptian pound	Rs	Indian rupee
Esc	Portuguese escudo	Ru	Russian ruble
EUR	Euro dollars	S$	Singapore dollar
FFr	French franc	Sch	Austrian schilling
Fmk	Finnish markka	SFr	Swiss franc
GRD	Greek drachma	SKr	Swedish krona
HK$	Hong Kong dollar	SRls	Saudi Arabian riyal
HUF	Hungarian forint	TD	Tunisian dinar
IR£	Irish pound	TRL	Turkish lira
ISK	Icelandic króna	VND	Vietnamese dong
J$	Jamaican dollar	W	Korean won
K	Zambian kwacha		

International Directory of

COMPANY

HISTORIES

AKG ACOUSTICS

AKG Acoustics GmbH

Lemboeckgasse 21-25
A-1230 Vienna
Austria
Telephone: (+43) 1-86654-1241
Fax: (+43) 1-86654-1205
Web site: http://www.akg.com

Wholly Owned Subsidiary of Harman International Industries Inc.
Founded: 1947
Employees: 576
Sales: EUR 90 million ($109.7 million) (2003)
NAIC: 334310 Audio and Video Equipment Manufacturing; 334419 Other Electronic Component Manufacturing

For more than five decades AKG Acoustics GmbH has enjoyed a reputation among professional recording engineers, sound men, and broadcasters for microphones and headsets of the highest quality. AKG manufactures more than 300 sound reinforcement products for both the professional and consumer markets, including dynamic and condenser microphones, wireless microphones, and cabled and wireless headphones. AKG also produces a large number of products for the original equipment manufacturer (OEM) market, in particular miniature transducers for mobile phones. More than 95 percent of AKG products are manufactured at its 17,000-square-meter state-of-the-art factory in Vienna Austria. The company has subsidiaries in Germany, the United States, and the United Kingdom, as well as joint ventures in Japan and India. AKG's stated philosophy is to be flexible regarding methods and techniques, while refusing to compromise on the quality of its products.

Entertaining War-torn Austria: 1945

AKG Acoustics was founded in Vienna soon after World War II. Dr. Rudolf Görike happened to meet an old prewar acquaintance, Ernst Pless, on the streets of Vienna. As they chatted, an idea for a business hatched: Viennese—indeed Euro-peans in general—were hungry for distraction from the hardships of postwar life. One of the most popular forms of popular entertainment was movies. Unfortunately, most of the movie theaters in Vienna had been destroyed or ransacked during the war, and it was almost impossible to find replacements for stolen or damaged projectors and sound systems. The two men set up a company that purchased old equipment from the stock of a closed factory in Hungary and sold it to the movie houses of Vienna. Görike and Pless were a perfect team. Görike's experience as an electrical engineer provided him with the technical expertise needed to repair and modify the machinery. Pless was a businessman who found customers and made deliveries. For smaller shipments, he used a backpack and bicycle, while larger ones required a wheelbarrow. The partners' first sale was more like a postwar, black-market deal than it was a conventional business exchange: unable to pay for Görike and Pless's wares in cash, the customer traded butter, cigarettes, and fresh meat for them.

Occupation authorities granted the partners their first permit to do business in July 1946. The new firm, with five employees and offices in a basement, was formally established the following year. Görike and Pless originally intended to call their company Photophon. Because the name was so similar to that of other companies at the time, they settled instead on Akustische u. Kino-Geräte, GesMBH—Acoustic and Film Equipment, Limited—which was abbreviated AKG. Görike was AKG's jack-of-all-trades. In addition to being a trained physicist and a skilled electrical engineer, he was also a talented violinist, painter, and draftsman. He designed AKG's first logo and was responsible for a stream of products that were soon to pour out of the Vienna headquarters.

In AKG's first year, under Görike's oversight, the company developed a varied array of products that included exposure meters, automobile horns, intercoms, and extra handsets for telephones. Almost immediately after the war, AKG began producing microphones, again thanks to Görike's expertise. In the 1930s, he had overseen the development of microphones for the Viennese company Henry Radio. AKG brought out the first of its innovative DYN Series microphones in 1946. Designed to amplify vocals and instruments, the DYN mics rapidly became popular at radio stations, music clubs, and theaters. The firm was able to produce about 500 DYN mics a year, each of them completely handmade. The C1, AKG's first condenser tube microphone, was introduced in 1947. Only six C1s were ever produced, but the design led to the CK12, a breakthrough microphone for the company. In 1949, with the release of the K120 DYN, the company's first headphone set, AKG launched another product line that would eventually become a pillar of the business.

Sound Innovations in the 1950s

By the early 1950s, AKG products were being distributed throughout Austria by Siemens/WSW. The company was also beginning to build a significant customer base in Eastern Europe. Product development also took off in the fifties. One of Görike's revolutionary developments in microphone technology was the moving coil transducer and mass-loaded diaphragm, which eliminated much of the shrillness characteristic of earlier microphones and extended frequency response deeper into the bass range. The first AKG microphone to make use of the new technology was the D12. Introduced in 1953, the D12 was the world's first dynamic cardioid mic, that is, it had a "unidirectional" design that served to reduce the amplification of extraneous sound and the production of feedback. The mic was an immediate success at radio stations, recording studios, and movie sets throughout the world. A number of other AKG microphones would be based on the D12, including the D20, D25, D30, D36, and the D45. The introduction of the D12 led AKG to modify its logo, replacing its three overlapping circles, representing omnidirectional polar diagrams, with three overlapping cardioid diagrams, a design the company still uses.

Around the same time, Konrad Wolf, a young AKG engineer, developed another classic mic design, the C12, the world's first remote-controlled, multi-pattern capacitor microphone. Designed on commission for Austria's national radio, RAVAG, C12's polar pattern could be switched noiselessly during operation without changing its output, thereby maintaining consistent volume levels. Major European makers of tape recorders, such as Philips, Grundig, Uher, Nordmende, Telefunken, and Saba, were relying increasingly on AKG microphones. To overcome the difficulties involved with exporting goods from occupied Austria, the company established its first foreign subsidiary in Germany in 1955. Located in Munich, it handled both production and distribution. At the same time, exports to Eastern Bloc countries expanded and AKG established itself for the first time in Asia and Latin America. In 1957, AKG expanded its Vienna facilities with the purchase of a larger building.

Beginning in the 1950s and extending into the following decade, standard studio equipment featured AKG's most successful product lines, including the BX10 E, the first portable reverb unit. In 1963, the company introduced a unique if unsuccessful reverb-microphone combo, the DX11. It was a dynamic microphone that contained a miniature reverb unit that gave the performer fingertip control of the reverb level during a performance.

Earning a Reputation for Quality in the 1960s

By the 1960s, AKG had established a solid reputation as a producer of high quality sound equipment. Many of the firm's sound products, notably its K58 lightweight headphones, were used at the 1964 Winter Olympics in Innsbruck, Austria. AKG engineers experienced a scare at the games opening ceremonies. When the welcoming speech began—spoken into an AKG microphone—the assembled athletes and dignitaries heard nothing. After a few frantic moments, the problem was traced to water from thawing snow that had seeped into a cable connection, causing a short circuit. The part was replaced and the games continued without further problems.

AKG made a major change in direction in 1965. Television had by then caused worldwide declines in movie theater attendance. In response, the company discontinued its production of film projectors and optical equipment, electing instead to focus completely on developing and producing audio transducers for microphones, headphones, and other audio products. Among the new products introduced in the latter half of the sixties were the D202 and D224, the first two-way cardioid microphones. They would become the standard against which reporters and public speakers measured their equipment. Other new items were the K141 and K240 studio headphones and the C414 condenser mic, which quickly established itself as a versatile studio microphone that could be used for either vocal or instrumental recording. The D1000 dynamic microphone was another innovation, one prized for its styling as much as for its technology. Compared to the bulky square mics frequently used at the time, the D1000 was so slender and elegant that in advertising AKG could boast that "it will not hide the face of the artist." The CMS modular microphone system enabled users to construct microphones from a variety of components for specific needs. The system eventually became a mainstay at the British Broadcasting Company (BBC), which came to rely on AKG mics to such an extent that in 1973, on the occasion of the broadcasting service's 50th anniversary, Britain issued a stamp with the BBC's standard microphones—all of which had been manufactured by AKG.

Growth and Change in the 1970s

AKG continued to expand in Europe in the late 1960s. In 1968, a Swiss subsidiary was founded in Zurich; a year later, AKG London was established. A Japanese affiliate began operations in 1979. The company's annual sales topped ATS 199 million for the first time in 1970. Four years later, the firm signed its 100th distributor and was awarded its 1000th patent. The year 1977 marked a second major turning point in the company's history. Cofounder Ernst Pless left AKG that year to establish a new plastics molding firm (his father had owned such a company some years before). Pless's new company, Vienna Plex, would become a major supplier to AKG of plastic parts. Pless's departure led to a major reorganization in the

Key Dates:

1945: Dr. Rudolf Görike and Ernst Pless begin supplying movie equipment to theaters in postwar Vienna.

1947: Görike and Pless found Akustische u. Kino-Geräte, GesMBH.

1953: AKG develops the D12, the world's first single diaphragm dynamic cardioid microphone.

1954: AKG Germany is founded.

1960: The first professional-quality small-sized capacitor microphone, the C60, is introduced.

1965: The company discontinues its production of movie equipment.

1966: The first two-way cardioid microphones, are introduced.

1970: The world's first portable reverb unit, the BX20, is introduced.

1974: AKG makes its 1,000th patent application.

1978: AKG launches the K340, the world's first dynamic/electrostatic headphones.

1984: AKG Holding AG is founded and goes public.

1988: AKG Acoustics (India) Ltd. is founded; Ernst Pless dies.

1994: Dr. Rudolf Görike dies.

1997: AKG Akustische und Kino-Geraete GesMBH is renamed AKG Acoustics GmbH.

2002: AKG equipment is used at the World Cup soccer tournament in South Korea.

ownership of AKG. Until Pless's resignation, he and Görike were AKG's sole owners. Beginning in 1975, however, Philips Austria and the Oesterreichische Laenderbank took over a 75 percent share in the firm.

By 1976, AKG had 105 representatives throughout the world. Its sales reached ATS350 million that year, with the German market accounting for 30 percent of that figure. Also in 1976, AKG held its first international product concept meeting, to which company representatives were invited to exchange ideas on new products. An unexpected result was a restructuring of the firm and the introduction of a new organizational scheme. In 1977, the reorganized firm had 800 employees and could turn out 20,000 microphones every week.

The seventies were also a period of innovation. In 1970, AKG introduced the BX20, the world's first portable studio reverb unit. Before its release, the BX20 had been under development for nine years, including a year's work on a suspension that would enable it to be safely shipped. The unit utilized helix springs with long time delays to create sounds that closely mimicked the reverberation characteristics of a large concert hall. It was a product that solidified and enhanced AKG's ever-growing reputation. The Libero, a set of wireless headphones that utilized infrared light to pick up the sound signal, was less successful. The futuristic device met with suspicion and resistance among consumers and was eventually withdrawn from the market. It would be more than a decade before AKG again marketed cordless headsets. The company introduced a line of phonograph cartridges in 1976.

Publicly Traded in the 1980s

In 1984, shares in a newly founded company, AKG Holding Allen Ginsberg, were publicly offered for the first time on the Vienna Stock Exchange. For the next ten years, AKG Holding would own a 75 percent interest in AKG GesMBH; the remaining 25 percent remained in the hands of founder Rudolf Görike. Following the public offering, however, majority ownership of AKG Holding changed frequently, as banks and other members of the finance industry bought and sold control. Once public, AKG began to take over other firms. In an effort to establish itself as a single source supplier for the sound industry, it concentrated on acquiring companies that also made audio parts or products. In the mid-1980s, AKG made major inroads in the United States, setting up an American subsidiary in 1985 and purchasing Ursa Major, a Boston company that was transformed into AKG's Digital Products Division. An affiliate in India, AKG Acoustics (India) Ltd. was established with its own factory and membership on the Indian Stock Exchange in 1989. The company expanded further in 1990. It acquired a 62 percent majority ownership in the Edge Technology of the United Kingdom while its Japanese subsidiary, AKG Japan, merged with SJC. In 1988, Ernst Pless, who had maintained close ties with the firm since his retirement in the middle seventies, passed away unexpectedly at the age of 73.

Continued Expansion, Challenges, and New Ownership: Late 1980s and 1990s

AKG continued to aggressively pursue acquisitions and expansion. In 1989, it acquired Acquisition of Orban and dbx Professional Products. The company also increased the percentage of some of its foreign holdings and at the same time acquired minority shares in CeoTronics, a German company, and the UK-based AMEK Technology Group PLC. That same year, AKG established a new French subsidiary, AKG Communications France. By 1992, AKG production warehousing had outstripped its buildings. The firm announced that it would consolidate its three Vienna properties at a single large facility in the city's suburbs. The first wing of the new structure was completed in 1993. AKG's rapid growth came at a cost. An early nineties recession, together with exchange rate fluctuations that dampened AKG's cash flow, sent the company into a downward spiral. In 1993, AKG reported a loss for the first time in its history.

In the wake of its losing year, AKG's majority shareholder GiroCredit inaugurated a search for a new partner/owner for AKG with the expertise and resources to ensure the company's future. Harman International Industries, Inc., a manufacturer of audio and electronic products for consumer and professional use, purchased a 76 percent interest in AKG in September 1993. AKG performed so well under Harman that the following July it exercised its option to acquire the remaining 24 percent from GiroCredit, thus assuming full ownership of AKG. With the assumption of the ownership, Harman ended trading in AKG shares on the Vienna Exchange and in 1994 liquidated AKG's former parent firm, AKG Holding AG, altogether. Harman closed the AKG subsidiaries in Japan, India, and the United Kingdom and substantially changed the ownership status of its United Stated and German subsidiaries. Under Harman, AKG returned to a sharp focus on microphones and headphones, along with industrial and telecommunication audio products. Harman relocated AKG's dbx Professional Products to Salt Lake City, Utah, put Orban under the management of its Lexicon unit, and sold some AKG-owned firms, such as CeoTronics and the French subsidiary. AKG manufacturing, research and development, and marketing and distribution continued to operate out of the company's Vienna headquarters.

The 1990s witnessed a burst of new product development at AKG. The CK77/C577, smaller than a thumbnail, was the world's smallest dual-diaphragm microphone. AKG also brought out its first cordless microphones and a variety of new headphone models, including the re-introduction of cordless, infrared headphones. In 1994, as AKG was moving into its newly completed facilities, Rudolf Görike passed away at age 87. The company celebrated its 50th anniversary in 1997 by producing a number of specially designed, collector's versions of popular AKG products, including the K240 and C414 B-ULS headphones. That same year, after studying the market carefully, AKG lowered the prices on three of its most popular and respected microphones, the C1000S, the C3000B, and the C535EB. The firm hoped the price cuts would lead to a fourfold increase in sales of these models. After the changes were implemented, however, sales leaped to eight to twelve times previous levels.

New Markets in the 2000s

The company, whose reputation had long been based on its expensive high-end products for recording studios, radio, television, movies, and concert amplification, launched its Emotion line of low-priced microphones in the early mid-1990s. Emotion mics were targeted to compete with cheap microphones being exported by Asian producers and marketed to entry-level musicians. Designed with AKG quality and the expertise gained over fifty years of product development, Emotion microphones sold for less than $200—a fifth or less of the price of many of AKG's famous microphones.

In the early 2000s, the explosion of new digital technologies—notably of inexpensive home recording studios—created a broad new market among musicians and home recording enthusiasts for mics that were affordable yet of good quality. To help finance the costs of entering this new market, the firm expanded its original equipment manufacturer business, in particular producing microphones for cell phones and global positioning systems. The OEM sector, which accounted for approximately 10 percent of AKG's revenues in 1997, had grown to more than 45 percent in 2000. In 1999 alone, it increased by 80 percent. That new business helped AKG's entrance into mass production

of lower-priced products. In October 2001, AKG's American subsidiary moved to a new, 60,000-square-foot facility in Nashville that doubled available warehousing and office space.

AKG continued to develop groundbreaking new headset and microphone systems in the 2000s. Its products were regularly honored with industry awards for achievement. The C3000B received the Musikmesse International Press Award in 2000 as the best large-diaphragm microphone. AKG received the Plasa and Mercur Awards in 2003. In 2002, AKG products were used for broadcasts of the World Cup soccer championships in South Korea. Looking to the future, the company hoped to use its high-end expertise to develop quality products across the price spectrum to double 2002 revenues by 2007.

Principal Competitors

Shure Inc.; Aiwa; Telex Communications, Inc.; Nady Systems Inc.; CAD Professional Microphones; RODE Microphones; BEHRINGER Spezielle Studiotechnik GmbH; Sennheiser Electronic GmbH & Co. KG; Audio-Technica Corporation; JVC Company of America; Pioneer Corporation.

Further Reading

"AKG Acoustics Buys Quested Monitoring Systems," *Broadcast*, October 26, 1990, p. 21.
"AKG Acoustics Reports 10% Fall in 1992 Turnover," *Die Presse*, May 6, 1993, p. 9.
"AKG Double Space with New U.S. Hdq.," *Music Trades*, October 1, 2001, Pg. 31.
"AKG Steps up Indian Stake," Reuters News, September 19, 1992.
AKG Vintage Products, Vienna: AKG International Press & Public Relations Office (CD-ROM).
"AKG zu Harman International," *Frankfurter Allgemeine Zeitung*, September 7, 1993, p. 25.
"Aphex Wins Patent Settlement," *PSN Europe*, February 1, 1997, p. 1.
"Austria's AKG Acquires 30% stake in AMEK Technology," *Die Presse*, July 3, 1991, p. 15.
Daley, Dan, "AKG Acoustics Finds Success through Low-End Expansion," *Billboard*, July 29, 2000, p. 42.
"Harman Audio Acquires Remaining Interest in AKG," *Pro Sound News Europe*, July 1, 1994, p. 1.
"Harman International Industries, Incorporated, Announces Acquisition Of AKG," *PR Newswire*, September 27, 1993.
History Report, Vienna: AKG International Press & Public Relations Office, 1997.
"The New AKG Acoustics," *Music Trades*, February 1, 2002, p. 202.

—Gerald E. Brennan

Alrosa Company Ltd.

6 Ul. Lenina
Mirny 678170
Republic of Sakha (Yakutia)
Russia
Telephone: +7 41136 227 717
Fax: +7 41136 304 517
Web site: http://www.alrosa.ru

Private Company
Incorporated: 1993
Employees: 40,250
Sales: $1.8 billion (2003 est.)
NAIC: 423940 Jewelry, Watch, Precious Stone, and
    Precious Metal Merchant Wholesalers; 212319 Other
    Crushed and Broken Stone Mining and Quarrying

Based in the frigid expanses of Russia's Far East, Alrosa Company Ltd. accounts for about 20 percent of the world's rough diamond output. The company has a near-monopoly on diamond mining in Russia and is also engaged in geological exploration, diamond cutting, and retail sales of diamonds. Its primary mines are located in the Republic of Sakha, an area about four times the size of Texas, which holds some of the coldest permanently inhabited communities in the world. The Soviets started a mining enterprise in the area after rich diamond deposits were discovered there in the 1950s. With the fall of communism, mining operations were privatized and transferred to a newly created company that became known as Alrosa. The federal and local governments, however, retain majority control of the company. As its original open-pit mines become depleted, Alrosa is starting to construct underground mines to access the remaining deposits. The company also is looking farther afield for rich deposits and has started operations in northwest Russia and in Angola. Alrosa has sold its diamonds through De Beers, the South African diamond monopoly, for more than four decades. More recently, Alrosa is selling more of its gems through its own contacts and is working on building a marketing network at home and abroad.

Mining Pioneers in the 1950s

The first deposit of the diamond-bearing mineral kimberlite was discovered in Russia's far eastern Republic of Sakha, also known as Yakutia, in 1954. It was given the name Zarnitsa or "Lightning." As later discoveries proved, kimberlite deposits were scattered throughout Yakutia in formations known as pipes. Two of the largest deposits in the world were discovered in 1955: the Mir ("Peace") Pipe and the Udachny ("Lucky") Pipe. Over the next year, an expeditionary force built a pilot ore processing facility at the Mir site. In 1957 the Soviet Ministry of Non-Ferrous Metallurgy adopted a resolution providing for the construction of diamond mining and processing facilities in the vicinity of the Mir Pipe. The Yakutalmaz ("Yakutia Diamond") Trust was established to manage the operations. Victor Tikhonov was the first director of Yakutalmaz.

The territory where the first mines were built was rich in minerals but inhospitable in almost every other way. Temperatures in the winter regularly dropped to around -60 degrees Celsius. The area was covered in permafrost hundreds of meters deep; only the top few meters thawed in the short summer, allowing some small trees to grow. The ground consisted mostly of sand and would have been unstable if not for the ice holding it together. As a result, dwellings had to be built on high concrete piles to keep them from melting the ground under them and collapsing. Nevertheless, the Soviet government was ready to meet any challenge necessary to access the valuable mineral resources. In 1958 several hundred young people from the southern parts of the republic were directed north to establish the mining town of Mirny. After a year, the town had a population of more than 5,000 and two more factories had been built. The town grew in size while the open pit mine on its outskirts grew deeper.

The U.S.S.R. sold its first lot of diamonds on the world market in 1959. From the beginning, Yakutalmaz marketed its diamonds through De Beers's Central Selling Organization (CSO). Until the emergence of Russia, the CSO had been dominated by southern African countries. But over the next few decades, the mines of Yakutalmaz became one of the most important sources of rough diamonds for De Beers. The trade relationship was threatened in the early 1960s when the United

Company Perspectives:

ALROSA Co. Ltd. was set up under Decree 158C of the President of the Russian Federation 'On the Establishment of the Almazy Rossii-Sakha Joint Stock Company' signed on 19 February 1992. It is Russia's largest diamond company engaged in exploration, mining, manufacture and sales of diamonds and one of the world's major rough diamond producers. ALROSA accounts for about 100% of all rough diamonds produced in Russia and for about 20% of the world's rough diamond output. In 1996 the company's rough diamond sales amounted to US $1.6 billion. Geological surveys indicate that the company has sufficient diamond reserves to maintain production at the current level for the next 50 years.

Nations imposed sanctions on South Africa related to apartheid. Publicly, Soviet leaders denounced apartheid while De Beers's 1963 annual report stated that trade with the U.S.S.R. was ended due to the boycott. But the two countries immediately cut a secret deal and the U.S.S.R. continued to sell all of its exports to the CSO through the next several decades.

Not only trade agreements, but most of the arrangements concerning diamond mining operations in the U.S.S.R. were kept secret under communism. The lucrative industry was a crucial source of hard currency for the regime, and decisions concerning it were made at the highest levels of government. The industry developed along branches that involved several different government organizations. Yakutalmaz was responsible only for diamond extraction. Gokhran, a division of the Finance Ministry, sorted the diamonds and the Almazyuvelirexport concern was responsible for marketing. Gokhran also stored a considerable amount of gems that were unable to be sold in a given year.

Investment and Production Growth: 1960–90

In 1961 the Aikhal mine, located about 450 kilometers north of Mirny, was established. Mining and processing facilities were fully developed there by the early 1970s. Factory No. 3, the largest mining facility yet, was completed at the Mir pipe in 1966. The next year Yakutalmaz was restructured into two separate organizations: Yakutalmaz and Aikhalalmaz. The two organizations were then reunited into a single production association in 1969 and Lev Soldatov was appointed director. Also that year, the Internatsionalnaya (''International'') Pipe was discovered near Mirny.

The Udachny Pipe began to be exploited in the mid-1970s. Processing Factory No. 11 extracted the first ore from the pipe in 1974 and by 1979 mining and processing facilities were fully developed. A powerful bucket excavator and a fleet of 120-ton dump trucks were first brought to the Far East to work in the Udachny pit. Over the decades, the mine produced more rough diamonds than any of the company's other sites.

Valeri Rudakov was appointed general director of Yakutalmaz in 1978. He was succeeded by Vladimir Piskunov in 1983. In the early 1980s, the extensive capital investments of the previous decades led to a considerable increase in diamond production. Yakutalmaz accounted for 10 percent of world rough diamond exports in 1985; by the end of the decade its annual exports of mostly rough diamonds were worth more than $2 billion. In addition, a domestic cutting industry had grown up around the Kristall concern in Moscow, Smolensk, and Barnaul and carried out exports of polished diamonds independently of Yakutalmaz. By this time, the town of Mirny had more than 30,000 residents. Because mining dominated the town, Yakutalmaz took on the responsibility of providing a range of amenities to workers, including a gym, a night club, a kindergarten, and a pool with a synchronized swimming team.

In 1987 the Ministry of Non-Ferrous Metallurgy reorganized Yakutalmaz into the Yakutsk Diamond Production and Research Association, or NPO ''Yakutalmaz.'' Development of the Yubileinaya (''Jubilee'') Pipe, which was discovered in 1975 near Aikhal, had just begun on a trial basis. By the early 1990s, however, the diamond business was faltering in the aftermath of the collapse of the Soviet regime. Production was expensive in the extreme Siberian conditions and the government was not making up for investments. Rough diamond exports in 1990 were only about $1 billion.

The U.S.S.R. signed a new five-year diamond trade agreement with De Beers in 1991. Under the deal, Yakutalmaz received $1 billion from De Beers against the collateral of gems stored by Gokhran; Yakutalmaz agreed to sell 95 percent of its export output through the Central Selling Organization. Over the next two years, however, diamond production fell about 40 percent due to the lack of funds from the federal government. Yakutalmaz threatened to withhold diamonds unless the federal government provided money for fuel, machinery, and food. Meanwhile, some officials in Moscow were suggesting that the contract with De Beers be terminated. Industry and government leaders also were debating how to reorganize the various sectors of the diamond industry now that the economy was no longer under Communist control.

Privatization: 1992

On February 19, 1992, President Boris Yeltsin signed a decree effecting the privatization of the diamond industry. The decree created a single entity, the Almazy Rossii-Sakha (ARS) Joint Stock Company, to be responsible for extraction, sorting, and marketing of diamonds. The company was the legal successor to NPO Yakutalmaz, the Almazjuvelirexport Foreign Trade Association, and the sorting division of the State Committee For Precious Metals and Gemstones (formerly Gokhran). The federal government and the Republic of Sakha shared control of the new entity with a 32 percent stake each. The remaining shares were divided among the company employee collective (23 percent), the eight local district authorities in Sakha (1 percent each), and a state pension fund (5 percent). At a July meeting, the company charter was adopted and Valeri Rudakov was appointed president. Yakutalmaz was liquidated and replaced by ARS at the start of 1993.

In August 1993 Andrei Kirillin replaced Rudakov as president. As the former deputy chairman of the Yakut parliament, Kirillin was expected to push for more independence from Moscow than his predecessor. He departed after two years and

Key Dates:

1954: The first diamond-bearing deposits are found in the Republic of Sakha.

1957: The Yakutalmaz Trust is established to manage mining and processing operations at Mirny.

1959: The first lot of rough diamonds is sold through De Beers.

1961: The Aikhal mine begins operation.

1974: The first ore is extracted from the Udachnaya Pipe.

1985: Yakutalmaz's share of world diamond exports reaches 10 percent.

1992: Almazy Rossii-Sakha (Alrosa) is formed as the diamond industry is privatized.

1996: The existing De Beers contract expires; renegotiation is disputed for two years.

1998: Federal law clarifies Alrosa's control of the diamond industry.

1999: The first underground mine begins operating at Internatsionalnaya.

2000: Brillianty Alrosa is founded to carry out diamond cutting.

2002: A new five-year contract with De Beers gives Alrosa greater freedom to market diamonds independently.

was replaced by Vyacheslav Shtyrov, the vice-president of the republic of Sakha, who was also likely to promote local control of the diamond industry. Meanwhile, diamond production rose slightly in 1994 for the first time in several years. Overall production, however, was not enough to meet De Beers export quotas, and the lack was made up by shipping diamonds from the stockpile maintained by the state committee Komdragmet (successor to Gokhran). In order to remain viable over the long term, ARS needed to improve production. Its major open pit mines were becoming so deep that the sides would soon start caving in. Investment in exploration led to the discoveries of the Botuobinskaya Pipe in 1994 and the Nyurbinskaya Pipe in 1996, both located in the new kimberlite field of Nakynskoye east of Mirny. But ARS had to ride out several rough years before it would be able to make real progress on its production problems.

Instability and Conflict in the Mid-1990s

The export contract with De Beers was due to expire at the end of 1995. Strained relations with the South African company, as well as disagreements between Moscow and Yakutsk on how to handle exports, caused the contract renewal process to drag on for nearly two years. De Beers was upset because an estimated $1 billion worth of diamonds was being leaked to international markets from Russia, depressing world prices and violating the terms of the 1991 contract. Russia also was accused of picking prime diamonds for the local cutting industry and leaving De Beers with the dregs. ARS president Shtyrov wanted the stability of a De Beers contract, but some industry overseers in Moscow were advocating for Russia to take a more independent route and develop its own diamond cutting and marketing capacities.

As part of the federal/regional conflict, Moscow accused ARS of tax fraud and raided its offices in early 1997. The instability caused international banks to freeze loans that had been granted to ARS. Meanwhile, the existing contract with De Beers was extended a month at a time until, at the end of 1996, De Beers cut off trade altogether. For the first three quarters of 1997, ARS did not export any diamonds. Finally, a one-year trade agreement was signed that October. It was extended for another three years in 1998. At the time, the Asian financial crisis was hurting worldwide diamond sales and ARS was inclined to look favorably on any deal that provided a reliable income. Under the agreement, De Beers would buy at least $550 of uncut Russian diamonds a year, and could buy up to 26 percent of its total sales from the Russian company. ARS was allowed to sell only 5 percent of international exports independently.

In 1998 the Almazy Rossii-Sakha company officially shortened its name to Alrosa Co. Ltd. The company had made some advances in production despite the upheaval of the last few years. In 1997 a technically sophisticated processing plant was put into operation at the Yubileinaya Pipe, where trial operations had first begun a decade earlier. Alrosa also began its first international venture at the Catoca deposit in Angola, one of the richest deposits in the world. Alrosa beat De Beers to win a 40 percent share in the operation and subsequently opened an office in the Angolan capital of Luanda.

In March 1998 Yeltsin signed legislation that codified Alrosa's control of the diamond industry. The legislation had been in the works for years; previous versions had been vetoed or stalled as Moscow used the diamond industry in an attempt to gain more control of the relatively autonomous Republic of Sakha. The final legislation was favorable to Alrosa. It granted the company a monopoly, prohibiting any smaller groups from mining and exporting diamonds. The government would still set export quotas. The law reinforced Alrosa's authority to sell diamonds; before this existing statutes could have been construed to prove that all diamonds were government property.

1999 and Beyond

With the most tumultuous years behind it, Alrosa moved ahead with plans to increase production and expand its activities in the areas of diamond cutting and marketing. The first underground diamond mine in Russia began operation at the Internatsionalnaya Pipe in 1999. The Anabar processing facility also was established that year to extract an alluvial deposit in the far northern city of Ebelyakh. Another new mining complex started on a pilot basis in Nyurba, at the Nakynskoye field, and began full-scale operations after a year. Total production in 1999 was $1.54 billion in rough and finished diamonds, $900 million of which was sold to De Beers. Alrosa reported a profit of several billion rubles, as it had for many years in a row, but 40 to 60 percent of profits was generally paid in taxes.

Alrosa made several advances related to its downstream activities in 2000. That year the subsidiary Brillianty Alrosa was founded to carry out diamond cutting and polishing. Cut diamonds could be worth almost ten times as much per carat as raw stones, so Alrosa was eager to increase exports of polished stones. Brillianty Alrosa opened a factory in Moscow in cooper-

10   Alrosa Company Ltd.

ation with Kristall, the longstanding Smolensk-based diamond cutting company. The factory used the highly regarded "Russian cut," which Kristall had introduced a few years earlier. Whereas diamonds were usually cut to retain as many carats as possible, the Russian cut sliced away all imperfections, with a wasteful yet stunning result. Alrosa opened offices in the diamond cutting centers of London, Antwerp, and Israel in order to develop marketing contacts. It also introduced the "Kristall-ALROSA" diamond brand in late 2001, a logo that would be stamped on all polished diamonds.

Alrosa entered the domestic jewelry retail market in 2000 with the opening of Almazny Dvor, or "Diamond Courtyard," just off Red Square in Moscow. At the grand opening, models walked the aisles wearing diamonds the size of golf balls. But the store's primary market, since Russian consumers were not particularly wealthy, would be small diamonds in the $100–$300 range.

These developments increased Alrosa's ability to market its production independently of De Beers. In the summer of 2000, De Beers had departed from its decades-old strategy of stockpiling diamonds to control prices. Instead, it would seek to increase demand through better marketing. The change raised a lot of questions about what sort of relationship Alrosa would maintain with De Beers once the current contract expired at the end of 2001. In the end, the two parties signed a five-year agreement that allowed Alrosa to market half of its output independently to the domestic cutting industry as well as companies in Israel and India. For the first time, Alrosa itself signed the agreement rather than the government. The deal could not be finalized, however, because it was being investigated by the European Commission for reasons of anti-trust regulation.

In the summer of 2001 open-pit mining stopped at the Mir Pipe because all the easily accessible ore had been extracted. Production was coming to a close at Aikhal and Udachny as well. Construction of underground mines had started at all those sites. Alrosa also was turning its attention to untapped deposits elsewhere in Russia. The so-called Lomonosov deposit had been discovered in the northwest region of Arkhangelsk in 1980. De Beers had started work on the site but backed out in 2000 because the local climate was not favorable to a foreign company. Over the next few years Alrosa acquired a more than 70 percent stake in Severalmaz, the company that had a tender to develop the field. In addition, Alrosa partnered with the Australian company Ashton Mining to explore for deposits in Karelia, the province bordering Finland.

Alrosa president Vyacheslav Shtyrov was elected president of the Republic of Sakha at the end of 2001. Vladimir Kalitin, Alrosa's chief engineer and a longtime employee, was appointed in 2002 to replace him. That year new legislation was passed regarding the diamond industry. Alrosa now was allowed to choose its own buyers and prices, although export quotas would still be set by the government. Alrosa also lost its monopoly as the export market was opened to other producers and diamond cutters.

In 2003 Alrosa finally was able to launch its first unsecured financing in the form of a $500 million Eurobond. The capital would help finance an investment plan that aimed to bring production to $2 billion worth of diamonds a year. The investment in the Angolan mine Catoca had already paid back, since production was much less expensive in Africa's warmer climate. Alrosa signed an agreement in late 2002 to develop the Luo deposit in Angola as well. Domestically, the company was moving ahead with the construction of underground mines and looking to start an open-pit mine at the more easily accessible Lomonosov deposit. Sales in 2003 were expected to reach $1.8 billion, $122 million of which came from polished stones. Alrosa estimated that it had sufficient reserves to maintain production at its current level for another 50 years.

Principal Subsidiaries

Udachninskii GOK; Mirninskii GOK; Aikhalskii GOK; Nyurbinskii GOK; Anabarskii GOK; Center for Diamond Sorting; Brillianty ALROSA.

Principal Competitors

De Beers Consolidated Mines Ltd.; Rio Tinto plc.

Further Reading

"Alrosa Signs $4 Billion Deal with De Beers," *Moscow Times,* December 18, 2001.
Aris, Ben, "A Diamond in the Rough," *Moscow Times,* September 11, 2001, p. 16.
Borisova, Yevgenia, "Alrosa Eyes Future, Sets Up Sales Force," *Moscow Times,* July 20, 2000.
Boulton, Leyla, "Veteran Diamond Chief Resigns 'Because of Ill Health,'" *Financial Times (London),* September 9, 1993, p. 36.
Daigle, Katy, "Bill Gives ARS Russia Gem Monopoly," *Moscow Times,* April 4, 1998.
"Diamond Dilemma," *East European Markets,* February 17, 1995.
"Diamond Market Liberalized," *Moscow Times,* December 6, 2002.
"Exhaustion of Diamond Deposits in Yakutia Makes Alrosa Develop Diamonds Production in Arkhangelsk Region and in Angola," *What the Papers Say (Russia),* February 3, 2003.
Farrelly, Paul, "Double Deals in Russia's New Stone Age," *Independent (London),* December 29, 1996, p. 7.
Gooding, Kenneth, "Diamond Deal Heralds a Retreat from the Abyss," *Financial Times (London),* February 26, 1996, p. 21.
Helmer, John, "Russia Looks for New Diamond Direction," *RusData DiaLine (Business World Weekly),* August 13, 1993.
———, "Yeltsin to Tighten Reins Over Diamond Industry," *Journal of Commerce,* July 17, 1996, p. 4A.
Ignatova, Mariya, "Craving for Diversity," *RusData DiaLine (Izvestia),* November 19, 2001.
Ivanova-Galitsina, Anna, "Alrosa Reviews De Beers Deal," *Financial Times (London),* July 20, 2000, p. 38.
Kazakov, Igor, "Diamonds and Gems: Time to Collect the Stones," *RusData DiaLine (Rossiiskiye Vesti),* January 5, 1993.
Khan, Alexandr, "The Diamond Side of the Law," *RusData DiaLine (Finansovaya Rossiya),* April 9, 1998.
Munter, Pavi, and Adrienne Roberts, "Alrosa Debut Dollar Deal Attracts Strong Demand," *Financial Times (London),* April 29, 2003, p. 47.
"Russia's Almazy Says Diamond Sales in Half Surpassed Its Forecast," *Wall Street Journal (Europe),* August 29, 1995.
Semenenko, Igor, "De Beers Abandons Diamond Project," *Moscow Times,* May 17, 2000.
Shchepotkin, Vyacheslav, "Diamond Company Launched in Russia," *RusData DiaLine (Izvestia),* August 6, 1992.

Teslenko, Vladimir, ''The Diamond Monopoly Has Lots of Things Coming Its Way,'' *RusData DiaLine (Kommersant-Daily),* July 1, 1997.

Thornhill, John, ''Diamonds Are No Longer Forever,'' *Financial Times (London),* December 20, 1996, p. 2.

Whalen, Jeanne, ''Alrosa to Feature Diamond Jewelry at Moscow Store,'' *Wall Street Journal (Europe),* November 22, 2000, p. 12.

——, ''Moscow Pursues Broader Influence on Diamond Mines,'' *Wall Street Journal (Europe),* December 21, 2001, p. 2.

——, ''Russia Wants to Double Output of Diamonds,'' *Wall Street Journal (Europe),* July 31, 2000, p. 11.

—Sarah Ruth Lorenz

Aral AG

Wittener Strasse 45
D-44789 Bochum
Germany
Telephone: (49) (234) 315-0
Fax: (49) (234) 315-3838
Web site: http://www.bpdeutschland.de

Wholly Owned Subsidiary of Deutsche BP AG
Incorporated: 1952 as B.V.-Aral AG
Employees: 1,974
Sales: EUR 1.09 billion ($965 million) (2001)
NAIC: 447110 Gasoline Stations with Convenience Stores

Aral AG, under the parentage of Deutsche BP AG, is Germany's largest operator of gas stations. With a network of roughly 2,500 gas stations in Germany, the company holds a market share of about 24 percent. Through sales at its convenience stores, Aral sees itself as Germany's fourth largest fast food chain and ranks 16th among the country's retailers. The Aral retail brand is present beyond Germany's borders in Luxembourg and the Czech Republic. In 2002 Aral became a wholly owned subsidiary of Deutsche BP AG, the German subsidiary of the British mineral oil group BP plc.

Brand Name Fuel Spurs Growth
in the Early 20th Century

The rise of Aral parallels that of the automobile in Germany in the first half of the 20th century. However, its history may be traced as far back as 1898, when automobiles were rare and 13 coal mines in the western German Ruhr region founded a marketing association for benzene—a by-product of producing coke from coal. The association, named Westdeutsche Benzol-Verkaufsvereinigung and headquartered in Bochum, sold benzene mainly to chemical and paint producers, as well as manufacturers of fuel for lighting fixtures. The 13 members companies agreed on annual production quotas and sold their product exclusively through the marketing association. After several reorganizations, the association was renamed Benzol-Verband (B.V.) in 1918. By that time, 75 benzene factories had joined the organization.

After World War I, Germany, like many countries, saw the rapid rise of the motor car. The number of motor vehicles in the country climbed from roughly 21,000 in 1906 to 300,000 in 1924. B.V. had tried marketing benzene as a substitute for imported gasoline before the war. Although the public endorsement of B.V.'s benzene fuel by the brother of the German Emperor and automobile-enthusiast Prince Heinrich von Hohenzollern helped garner attention, the endeavor failed. Motors at the time were simply not designed to smoothly absorb benzene's high-energy content. Meanwhile, chemist Walter Oswald was conducting experiments in B.V.'s laboratories, trying to formulate a new kind of gasoline that contained benzene. In 1924 he came up with a mixture of gasoline and benzene which he named Aral. The name combined the first two letters of the two groups of chemicals to which the ingredients belonged; Benzene was an ''aromatic'' chemical and gasoline was ''aliphatic.''

The highly-compressed B.V.-Aral gasoline was declared the world's first ''super fuel'' and soon developed into a brand product. Two years after the invention of Aral, B.V. established a research department to optimize and standardize the new gasoline and to assure a high product quality. In 1927, when Germany introduced new black-and-yellow traffic signs, B.V. switched its brand colors from black and yellow to blue and white, the colors of the city of Bochum. To distinguish B.V.-Aral from competing products, the company gave its branded gasoline a blue color. B.V. also formulated a special benzene-based high-energy fuel used in aviation. The product made headlines when used in the first motorized flight to cross the Atlantic from Europe to Canada in 1928.

After the creation of Aral fuel, B.V. focused on expanding its distribution network and product line. In the second half of the 1920s the company began to establish gas stations. At first attached to drugstores, restaurants or hotels, the facilities later became independent service stations. Within ten years the number of B.V. gas stations had risen sharply. There were about 200 gas stations in Germany in 1926; by 1937 the number of B.V. gas stations had reached 9,000. During this time, the company added motor oil and diesel fuel to its product line. Beginning in 1935, B.V. customers were also able to buy petroleum.

12

From Coal-Based to Oil-Based Gasoline: 1936–1967

In the late 1930s, after Adolf Hitler's National Socialist Party had achieved political power in Germany, the country began striving for economic self-sufficiency. One of the government's goals was to replace imported oil with an alternative fuel derived from domestic coal. In 1937, several B.V. members founded another association under the company's organizational umbrella, this one aimed at developing and selling coal-based gasoline.

During World War II Germany's fuel market was centrally administered by the government. Brand name fuels were abolished and replaced by a coal-based "standard" fuel. The prices were the same everywhere and the number of gas stations shrunk by two-thirds. In 1942 B.V. was integrated in a state-administered corporation of coal-based fuel producers—the Aktiengesellschaft der Kohlenwertstoffverbände.

After World War II B.V.'s future was uncertain. The company that owned Germany's largest distribution network for gasoline at a time of rapid mass motorization became the target of international oil giants, mainly American companies such as Mobil Oil. However, the authorities of the Allied Forces did not allow Mobil Oil or any other large oil company to acquire a majority share in B.V. The years of the centrally administered fuel market in Germany ended in 1951. Once again B.V. was able to sell its Aral-B.V. fuel. The following year, as a result of breaking up the former state-monopoly Kohlenwertstoff AG, B.V.-Aral AG was founded. At the same time, some large German mining companies in the Ruhr that were B.V.-members began refining imported raw oil and thereby supplied B.V. with the main ingredient of conventional gasoline, which had superceded coal-based fuel in postwar Germany. One of these B.V. members, the Gelsenberg mining operation, started refining raw oil supplied by Mobil Oil.

In 1955 B.V.-Aral began to expand beyond Germany's borders, founding its first subsidiary abroad, in neighboring Austria. Following German travelers to one of their favorite vacation destinations, the first B.V.-Aral gas station opened in Italy in 1959. Other target markets were Belgium and Luxembourg, where the company would become a market leader in the 1980s. At the same time Aral worked on expanding its domestic network of gas stations, improving their design, and expanding the range of services offered. In the 1960s the number of the company's gas stations surpassed prewar levels, reaching 11,000 by 1968.

As the importance of coal-based fuel in the gasoline market declined, B.V.-Aral outgrew its old organizational structure. The amounts of gasoline supplied to the company by its oil-refining members exceeded the volume of benzene provided by

the other members by far, a fact not reflected in the voting rights. In addition, new anti-trust laws introduced in Germany in 1958 called for a fundamental reorganization. Many options—including the breaking up of the company—were considered but abandoned. In 1962 the company withdrew from the B.V. and was renamed Aral AG. It took another five years for a new shareholder structure and accompanying agreement to be approved by the German cartel authorities.

Under the new agreement, ratified on March 1, 1967, all Aral shareholders signed individual long-term supply contracts with the company. The supplied amount of raw materials was reflected in the stakes each major Aral shareholder received in the company. The German oil refineries Hibernia Bergwerks AG—which later became part of Veba Oel AG—and Gelsenberg, as well as the American raw oil supplier Mobil Oil, held a 28-percent stake in Aral AG. Another 15-percent stake was held by Wintershall AG, another German mineral oil refiner. The benzene-manufacturers' combined share in Aral AG was just 1 percent. However, every major shareholder received the same voting power—regardless of his stake in the company's capital. The new shareholder agreement included a general clause that Aral was to remain a German enterprise. If any new developments in the market challenged this agreement, shareholders were obliged to consult each other.

New Directions After the Oil Crisis: 1973–1997

The 1970s opened a new chapter in Aral's history. The steady growth of the German market for gasoline came to a halt. Due to increased competition, gasoline prices came under pressure. Some smaller gas stations were not able to realize profits and were closed down. In 1970 for the first time since World War II, the number of Aral gas stations decreased. Three years later the so-called oil crisis hit Europe. In response to political crisis in the Middle East, the Organization of Petroleum Exporting Countries (OPEC) decided to sharply curtail their raw oil output. Consequently, oil prices jumped up by some 450 percent. To preserve oil reserves, Germans were not allowed to drive on Sundays. However, while that ban was ultimately lifted, the event triggered two new long-term trends that greatly affected Aral's business. First, consumers started cutting back on their gasoline use by driving less, and second, automakers instructed their research and development departments to focus on more fuel-efficient motors. Aral counteracted the new market trends by increasingly focusing on the expansion of its business beyond gasoline.

As a result of the oil crisis, a fundamental transformation in the company's gas stations, begun in the late 1960s, was accelerated. To lower costs for the company and for consumers, Aral introduced self-service to all of its gas stations. The company's first self-service gas station opened in 1969. By 1980, 77 percent of Aral's total fuel sales were generated by self-service stations. In 1968 the company began to extend the range of goods offered at its gas stations beyond the immediate needs of motorists. Besides gasoline and other fuels, motor oil, small replacement parts such as mirrors, light parts, windshield wipers, spark plugs and travel maps, the company started selling cigarettes, newspapers, candy bars and bottled beverages. Aral's new retail branch grew continuously throughout the 1970s and 1980s. The ever-expanding line of goods soon

Key Dates:

1898: Thirteen German benzene producers found West-deutsche Benzol-Verkaufsvereinigung.
1918: The benzene marketing association is transformed into Benzol-Verband (B.V.) and has 75 members.
1924: Chemist Walter Oswald invents "Aral" super fuel.
1937: The number of B.V. gas stations reaches 9,000.
1952: B.V.-Aral AG is founded.
1955: The company's first foreign subsidiary is established in Austria.
1962: The company withdraws from B.V. and is renamed Aral AG.
1968: The Aral network reaches its peak with 11,000 gas stations; the company introduces convenience products to its on-site stores.
1969: Aral's first self-service gas station opens.
1975: Veba Oel becomes Aral's majority shareholder.
1990: Aral begins to expand its network of gas stations to Eastern Europe.
2000: Aral becomes a wholly owned subsidiary of Veba Oel AG.
2002: After the acquisition of Veba Oel AG by BP plc, Aral becomes a subsidiary of BP's German unit, Deutsche BP AG.

outgrew the limited dimensions of the company's mini-markets. Over the years, shop areas were enlarged and modernized. Shelf space for auto-related articles was decreased, making room for convenience store items. By 1994, Aral shops contributed one-third to the total sales of the company's gas stations. Moreover, roughly 38 percent of sales was generated by such services as car washes, and oil and tire changes. Revenues generated by fuel and motor oil sales had shrunk from 41 percent of the total in 1984 to 29 percent ten years later.

Another hallmark of the period that followed the oil crisis was the increasing public concern over environmental pollution, as through auto emissions for example. Aral launched its own research program for environmentally friendly fuels in 1973. In 1984, when automobiles with catalytic converters entered the market in Germany, the company introduced unleaded regular gasoline, as leaded gasoline could not be used in cars equipped with catalytic converters. In the same year Aral launched a research program with German auto maker BMW exploring hydrogen as an alternative fuel. Between 1984 and 1988, ten models of BMW passenger vehicles filled their tanks with hydrogen gas at Aral's pilot hydrogen gas station in Berlin. For the world's first robot-controlled liquid hydrogen filling station at Munich Airport, which was opened in 1999, Aral developed the gas station infrastructure and contributed to the development of the robot that automatically filled up the tank.

In 1975, Veba Oel acquired a majority stake in Gelsenberg AG, taking over Gelsenberg's 28 percent stake in Aral and thereby becoming Aral's biggest shareholder. However, Veba Oel remained bound to the contract negotiated in 1967, which gave every major Aral shareholder a single vote, regardless of the size of their share in the company.

New Markets and Reorganizations: 1990 and Beyond

The reunification of the two German states in 1990 opened a rare window of opportunity for Aral to expand its market. In that year the first Aral gas station opened in the eastern German city of Leipzig. In the four years that followed the company established a network of gas stations in all of the new eastern German states. By 1995 Aral's market share in the German gas station business was about 20 percent, making it the country's market leader. However, despite the growing traffic volume, the German market for gasoline was shrinking. In 1994 fuel consumption decreased for the first time in 13 years. Besides new motors that used less gasoline, a significant raise in mineral oil taxes caused German consumers to cut back on driving. Aral decided to focus on the new markets in eastern Europe created by the fall of the Iron Curtain. The company established new networks of gas stations in Poland, the Czech Republic, Hungary and Slovakia. At the same time, Aral sold its network of gas stations in the Netherlands, Switzerland, and Belgium.

By 1998, the year of Aral's 100th anniversary, the company was firmly established as Germany's market leader in the gas station business. Aral's sales passed the DM 20 billion mark for the first time in that year, with almost 12 percent of sales generated outside of Germany. While the company was working hard to defend its leading position in a shrinking market, Aral's ownership structure changed fundamentally when a wave of mergers in the global mineral oil industry reached Germany.

In 1998 the American oil giant Exxon announced plans to merge with major Aral-shareholder Mobil Oil. The following year, Veba Oel's parent company merged with the Viag group, a major German electric power supplier, to form E.ON AG. A precondition of the Exxon-Mobil Oil merger was that the latter agree to sell its stake in Aral to Veba Oel, as did the other remaining major shareholder—Wintershall AG, which had meanwhile become a subsidiary of the German chemicals conglomerate BASF.

For an estimated DM 3.6 billion Aral became a wholly owned subsidiary of Veba Oel AG in 2000. That year was Aral's worst financially in some 15 years. A tough price war at Germany's gas stations resulted in losses from gasoline sales in the hundreds of millions for the market leader, which could not be fully made up for by the company's other branches. During his time, Veba became Aral's sole supplier of refined mineral oil products. The company was renamed Aral Aktiengesellschaft & Co. KG, and its subsidiaries were reorganized under a management holding.

In 2001 E.ON AG sold Veba Oel, including Aral, to the British mineral oil group BP plc, and Aral then came under the parentage of BP's German subsidiary, Deutsche BP AG. Two years later Aral's new parent company decided to re-brand its own gas stations in Germany under the Aral name, which was known by 98 percent of the German population. Expecting an increasingly fierce competition in the German gas station market, Aral was planning to defend its leading position through customer loyalty programs; through establishing large gas stations at busy locations that offered a variety of technical assistance services to motorists and with large, modern convenience shops on their premises; and through the introduction of innovative, environmentally friendly fuels such as natural gas and hydrogen.

Principal Competitors

Royal Dutch/Shell Group; Exxon Mobil Corporation; Conoco-Phillips; Total S.A.

Further Reading

Alles Super - And How It All Started, Bochum, Germany: Aral Aktiengesellschaft & Co. KG, 2001, 23 p.

''Aral - eine ganz und gar untypische AG; Rechtliche Grundverfassung in der 100jährigen Unternehmensgeschichte geprägt,'' *Börsen-Zeitung,* December 30, 1998, p. 9.

Hansen, Anne, ''Die Prämientanker,'' *Frankfurter Allgemeine Zeitung,* August 28, 2003, p. 7.

Reimann, Erich, ''Ein Nikolausgeschenk für die Veba,'' *Associated Press Worldstream - German,* December 6, 1999.

Reinking, Guido, ''100 Jahre Aral - vom Superbenzin zum Supermarkt,'' *Welt am Sonntag,* January 31, 1999.

Schwarz, Harald, ''Hintergrund: Aral,'' *Süddeutsche Zeitung,* September 2, 1999, p. 25.

—Evelyn Hauser

The Aristotle Corporation

---

96 Cummings Point Road
Stamford, Connecticut 06902
U.S.A.
Telephone: (203) 358-8000
Fax: (203) 358-0179
Web site: http://www.aristotlecorp.net

Public Company
Incorporated: 1986 as FFB Corporation
Employees: 1,010
Sales: $162.3 million (2003)
Stock Exchanges: NASDAQ
Ticker Symbol: ARTL
NAIC: 423450 Medical, Dental, and Hospital Equipment
   and Supplies Merchant Wholesalers

Originally formed as a bank holding company, The Aristotle Corporation is now involved in the manufacturing and distribution of a variety of education, health, and agricultural products through two primary subsidiaries: Nasco International, Inc. and Simuladids, Inc. Their products, mostly sold through catalogs, are divided between educational offerings and commercial offerings. Educational offerings include arts and crafts items for schoolchildren; classroom science equipment, as well as live and preserved specimens; math teaching aids for schoolchildren; healthcare training materials (such as manikins used for training in cardiopulmonary resuscitation) appropriate for nursing and medical school, emergency training professionals, and health teachers; teaching aids for family and consumer sciences, targeting dieticians, nutrition instructors, and family and consumer science teachers; fun learning activities for preschool children; and items for use by physical education professionals. Aristotle's commercial offerings include teaching aids for agricultural education to help farmers and ranchers with such tasks as breed identification, grooming, artificial insemination, and animal health; products for activity therapists in nursing homes and assisted living homes, including arts and crafts and games; resources that help in conducting an activity program in an assisted living home; and Whirl Pak sampling

bags for use by food and microbiology laboratories. With its headquarters located in Stamford, Connecticut, Aristotle maintains operations in California, Colorado, Michigan, New York, and Ontario, Canada. Although publicly traded on the NASDAQ, the company is 90 percent owned by Geneve Corporation, which is run by Aristotle's president Steven B. Lapin and board member Edward Netter.

Bank Holding Company Formed in 1986

The roots of Aristotle date back to 1986 when FFB Corporation was established as a holding company for New Haven-based First Federal Bank of Connecticut as part of an effort to take the federal thrift public. In 1988, the bank changed from a federal charter to a state chartered savings bank, in the process changing its name to First Constitution Bank. In turn, FFB Corporation changed its name to First Constitution Financial Corporation. At the time of the switch, the bank had assets of $1.8 billion, but some poor real estate investments in Connecticut soon put the institution in severe financial jeopardy when the bottom fell out of the local real estate market. Displeased shareholders, including Geneve Corp., forced the resignation of the chief executive officer of the bank and the holding company by threatening a proxy fight. The board was also enlarged to accommodate a director committed to the protection of shareholder interests. As loses mounted—during the first months of 1990 First Constitution lost $58.4 million—the bank was forced to cut staff and close three branch offices. The downward spiral continued over the next two years and in October 1992, when First Constitution was unable to complete a recapitalization plan it had filed with regulators, the Federal Deposit Insurance Corp. took preemptive action. Even before the bank was technically insolvent, it seized control and sold the bank to Webster Financial Corp., another Connecticut bank holding company.

First Constitution Financial Corporation wrote off its investment in the bank to the sum of $25.4 million. What was left was a corporate shell with no operating subsidiaries. Nevertheless, it did have $10 million in cash plus $120 million in tax credits. These tax credits, however, could not be used unless the company was actually engaged in a business. In April 1993, First Constitution changed its name to The Aristotle Corporation, and

Company Perspectives:

The Aristotle Corporation, founded in 1986 and headquartered in New Haven, Connecticut, is a leading manufacturer and global distributor of education, health, and agricultural products.

in September, nearly a year since the FDIC seizure, the holding company returned to active business, paying $4.5 million to acquire Strouse, Adler Company. 132-year-old Strouse designed, manufactured, and marketed women's intimate apparel in two categories: specialty brassieres and women's shapewear. Specialty brassieres were used with backless, strapless, and halter-top garments. The company's shapewear products provided abdominal support and control, much like a traditional girdle. Items included "body briefers," medium control panties, and control bottoms. Core Strouse brand names were Smoothie and Fleur de Lace. Customers included such major department stores as Macy's, Bloomingdale's, Nordstrom, Nieman Marcus, and Lord & Taylor. The company also marketed its wares through catalogs and provided private label goods to retailers, including Victoria's Secret, Dillard's, and JC Penney.

FDIC Suit Resolved in 1995

Aristotle was still not free of its previous banking experience, however. In April 1995, the FDIC sued the company in an effort to recover tax refunds paid and due to Aristotle. A class action lawsuit filed in 1990 also remained pending. Finally, in 1996 Aristotle was able to put these outstanding matters to rest. It signed a settlement agreement with the FDIC that allowed the company to retain $2 million of a $4 million tax refund; on its side, Aristotle agreed to relinquish further claims to another $1.7 million in tax refunds. In return, Aristotle and its former officers and directors, including those with First Constitution Bank, were absolved from any further claims connected to the 1992 failure of the bank. Furthermore, in August 1996, Aristotle reached a settlement on the 1990 class action suit when a Federal Court Judge approved a proposal. According to the company, the settlement presented no material financial impact on Aristotle. However, with the cloud of litigation removed, Aristotle had a chance to truly move beyond its banking roots, raise new capital, and concentrate on the task of growing shareholder value.

Although there were indications at the time of the Strouse acquisition that Aristotle might make further acquisitions in the apparel industry, management was disappointed with the performance of its lone subsidiary. In July 1998, Aristotle sold Strouse to Sara Lee Corporation for $21.5 million in cash plus the assumption of $8 million in debt. As a result, once again Aristotle was without an operating subsidiary. Nearly a year would pass before Aristotle settled on a new line of business: the fast growing for-profit education field. In April 1999, it acquired Woodstock, New York-based Simulaids, Inc. for approximately $8.7 million. Established in 1963, Simulaids manufactured health and medical education teaching aids. Products included manikins and simulation kits for training in CPR, emergency rescue, and patient care. Simulaid sold its products

internationally through distributors and catalogs. Primary end-users included nursing and medical schools as well as fire and emergency medical departments. In connection with the Simulaids acquisition, Aristotle established a relationship with Nasco International, Inc., a major manufacturer and distributor of educational materials which agreed to help Aristotle in adding more assets in the for-profit education field. Nasco was a unit of Aristotle's major shareholder, Geneve Corporation.

Aristotle's next move in the education field came the following year, in September 2000, when it bought an 80 percent stake in Safe Passage International, Inc. for an aggregate price of some $1.6 million. Management of Safe Passage retained the remaining 20 percent of the business. Operating out of Rochester, New York, Safe Passage was started in 1989 to develop computer-based training programs in conjunction with the airline industry and the Federal Aviation Agency for use in airport security. Aristotle hoped to create synergies between its two subsidiaries with the goal of transforming traditional medical manikins into computer-driven patient simulators. Moreover, Aristotle was interested in developing computer-based training programs that could provide online continuing education credits for healthcare professionals.

Aristotle soon veered away from the high-tech arena. In November 2001, majority shareholder Geneve engineered a reverse merger between Aristotle and Wisconsin-based Nasco, with Aristotle the surviving entity. Nasco was far larger than Aristotle, generating more than $150 million in annual revenues in fiscal 2001 compared to the $8.1 million posted by the combined efforts of Simulaids and Safe Passage. However, Aristotle still retained significant tax credits from its previous life as First Constitution Financial Corporation. By being folded into Aristotle, Nasco was able to enjoy a tremendous tax break, to the benefit of both Aristotle and Nasco shareholders. As a result of the merger, completed in 2002, Geneve increased its stake in Aristotle from 51 percent to more than 90 percent. While Aristotle's chief executive stayed on in that capacity, Geneve's president and chief operating officer, Steven B. Lapin, assumed these same positions in the much larger Aristotle Corporation.

Nasco was launched in 1940 by a Wisconsin agriculture teacher who, working out of his basement, created instructional books and assorted teaching aids. Over the next 60 years, the company branched off in numerous directions, ultimately selling more than 50,000 products through 25 specialty catalogs aimed at teachers, farmers, and industrialists. Nasco sold fake substances such as blubber, yogurt, crackers, and wheat bread. It also sold very real African clawed frogs, used by researchers around the world and raised in the company's own colonies as part of Nasco's lab supplies and kits sold to schools. Other educational products included a crying infant simulator and a realistic human head and torso dummy used to practice dislodging food and clearing blocked airways. Nevertheless, only three of the company's 25 catalogs served the healthcare market; the bulk of Nasco's business was devoted to the marketing of educational supplies for K-12 schoolchildren. The addition of Simulaids' proprietary mannequins and simulation kits were expected to greatly enhance Nasco's three healthcare catalogs. The combined business also hoped to use its greater breadth in Nasco's planned effort to expand into the Canadian healthcare business.

Key Dates:

1986: FFB Corporation is formed as a holding company for First Federal Bank.
1992: First Federal Bank is seized by FDIC.
1993: The company changes its name to The Aristotle Corporation.
1999: Simulaids is acquired.
2002: A merger is completed with Nasco International.

Safe Passage Interest Sold in 2002

In 2002, Aristotle made a pair of changes. In September, CEO John Crawford announced his retirement. Although he stayed on as a member of the board and the executive committee, responsibility for the day-to-day running of the business became the province of president and COO Lapin. In addition, Aristotle chief financial officer resigned, replaced by Dean Johnson, Nasco's CFO for the previous five years. Also in 2002, near the end of the year, Aristotle sold its 80 percent interest in Safe Passage, thus ending the company's foray into computer-driven educational products. Financially, the reverse merge between Aristotle and Nasco showed immediate results in fiscal 2002. While the two business had combined for $162 million in revenues for fiscal 2001, and income showed only modest growth in fiscal 2002, to $165.9, the impact on the bottom line of the balance sheet was hard to ignore. Net earnings increased from $8.8 million in fiscal 2001 to $30.3 million in fiscal 2002.

Aristotle continued to grow its for-profit educational business in 2003. It acquired Hann Crafts, an Otterbein, Indiana, company that produced and sold sewing kits used in middle-school family and consumer science classes. In order to fund further acquisitions to strengthen Aristotle's holdings, manage-ment announced in October 2003 that it had signed a five-year, $45 million credit agreement with Bank One, N.A. and Johnson Bank of Wisconsin. This revolving line of credit was a significant improvement over the company's prior $31 million credit capacity. Aristotle experienced a decline in revenues during fiscal 2003, to $163.2 million, but earnings before income taxes improved from $16.7 million in 2002 to $20.3 million in 2003. Business conditions were generally poor for the company, in large part due to many troubled state economies, which adversely impacted school budgets around the country and resulted in decreased sales for Aristotle. Nevertheless, the company, after making the transition from bank holding company to a for-profit educational concern, appeared well positioned to enjoy ongoing growth in the next phase of its corporate history.

Principal Subsidiaries

Simulaids, Inc.; Haan Crafts Corporation.

Principal Competitors

United Industrial Corporation; Vital Signs, Inc.

Further Reading

Bacon, Kenneth H., "FDIC Closes Banks by Using Low-Cost Plan," *Wall Street Journal*, October 5, 1992, p. B5.
Hawkins, Lee, Jr., "Nasco, A Wisconsin Catalog Firm, Markets Farm and Fitness Products," *Wisconsin State Journal*, February 29, 1996.
Miller, Paul, "Nasco to Merge With Aristotle," *Catalog Age*, January 2002, p. 5.
"Nasco to Be Acquired by Connecticut Firm," *Business Journal Serving Greater Milwaukee*, November 28, 2001.

—Ed Dinger

Atanor S.A.

Albarelloa 4914
Munro, Buenos Aires B1605AFR
Argentina
Telephone: (54) (11) 4721 3400
Fax: (54) (11) 4721 3413
Web site: http://www.atanorsa.com.ar

Public Company
Incorporated: 1943 as Atanor Compania Nacional para la
    Industria Quimica S.A.M.
Employees: 768
Sales: 618.17 million pesos ($183.43 million) (2002)
Stock Exchanges: Buenos Aires; Over the Counter (OTC)
Ticker Symbols: ATAN; ANOR
NAIC: 325110 Petrochemical Manufacturing; 325192
    Cyclic Crude and Intermediate Manufacturing; 325193
    Ethyl Alcohol Manufacturing; 325211 Plastics
    Material and Resin Manufacturing; 325320 Pesticide
    and Other Agricultural Manufacturing

Atanor S.A. is one of the leading manufacturers of chemicals, petrochemicals, and polymers in Argentina and is the largest producer and exporter of agrochemicals in Latin America, especially of herbicides. Indeed, most of the company's chemical products are used in the manufacture of its agrochemicals. Atanor is the only company in the world that manufactures all three of the leading types of herbicides: 2,4-D acids, triazines, and glyphosates. The company sells its goods to about 2,000 customers, many of them abroad. It is 51 percent-owned by Iowa-based herbicide manufacturer Albaugh Inc.

1938: 40 Years of Production
for Industry and Agriculture Begin

Atanor was founded by Argentine industrialists and technicians in 1938, its name taken from a small furnace used by ancient alchemists. With offices and a production facility in Munro, some 15 miles from Buenos Aires, the company began producing hydrogen peroxide. The company introduced oxygenated water to the market in 1940, followed the next year by

acetic acid and acetic aldehyde. In 1942, Atanor began exporting its products.

By 1944, with World War II well underway, the government took a share of the company as a security measure, providing about one-third of its capital through a military agency whose function was to assure that Argentina had the raw materials and finished products needed for its defense. As a result, Atanor began producing catalysts for the production of synthetic rubber and stabilizers for explosives. In 1948 the company opened a second plant in a military zone outside Rio Tercero, Cordoba. Its power supplied by hydroelectric energy, the facility began producing methanol there and assumed responsibility for oxygenated water in 1950.

The Postwar period was characterized by expansion. Atanor established a joint venture with Monsanto Chemical Co. in 1951 to manufacture, in Munro, molded phenolic powders and synthetic resins. Four years later, it acquired Monsanto's share of the enterprise and continued its activities under the name Atanor Plastics. The work there made possible the development of important industries dedicated to the manufacture of abrasives, foundry resins, laminated materials, paper, and textiles.

Atanor established a branch office in Rosario in 1953 and later added others covering almost the entire nation. From these offices agents sold and distributed Atanor products, while technical personnel provided support, especially to farmers. In 1956 the company installed, at Rio Tercero, a new plant to provide Argentina with four to six tons of pure DDT daily, as a joint venture with the Swiss pharmaceutical company Geigy. This was quickly followed by the development of other insecticides such as hexachlorocyclohexane and lindane and herbicides such as MCPA and 2,4-D acid. In 1957, with Olin Mathieson Chemical Corporation, Atanor established a joint venture to further these activities. In 1963 the company purchased Mathieson's share and founded Agroquimicos Atanor S.A.I.C., located in Munro. Atanor was Argentina's largest chemical company in the late 1950s and the only one of its kind that was totally Argentine-owned. Company shares were being traded on the Buenos Aires stock exchange by 1964.

Atanor formed a partnership with Hooker Chemical Corporation in 1960 to establish Duranor Industrias Quimicas S.A.I.C. as a manufacturer of phenol and monochlorobenzene at Rio Tercero. Atanor Plastics became part of Duranor in 1962. A new electrolytic plant at Rio Tercero in 1964 raised production of caustic soda, and in the same year the methanol plant was modified to take natural gas as its fuel. In 1971 the first oxygenated-water plant in Latin America using the autooxidation process was inaugurated at Rio Tercero with technology from the German firm of Degussa A.G. The previous plant was dismantled. Duranor was producing phenol, phenolic acids, and urea-formaldehyde glues in 1978, when Atanor purchased Hooker's 49-percent interest in the company. Duranor also had a cumene-based phenol plant under construction at this time and also was involved in a project to build a paranitrophenol plant in Argentina to supply feedstocks for malathion and parathion herbicide plants planned for Bolivia.

In the early 1970s industrial chemicals accounted for more than half of Atanor's sales. Agrochemicals comprised the vast bulk of the remainder, with home products making up the rest, about 10 percent, through an associated firm, Hoganor. Direccion General de Fabricaciones Militares, an agency under the control of the nation's ministry of defense, held a 21-percent stake in the company. In 1974 Atanor took a 51-percent share of Petroquimica Rio Tercero S.A., a new plant that initiated the nation's production of toluene diisocyanate (TDI), a prime material for urethane foam. The state-owned energy company YPF and Fabricaciones Militares were Atanor's partners. In 1982 Petroquimica Rio Tercero S.A. brought onstream a $170 million plant capable of producing 16,000 metric tons a year of TDI, 12,000 tons of liquid chlorine, and 13,000 tons of caustic soda.

As of 1978, Atanor's Munro and Rio Tercero complexes were producing not only a variety of final industrial and agricultural chemicals but also important intermediate materials for varnishes, resins, plastics, paints, textiles, hides, paper, metals, and pharmaceuticals. The principal intermediate products included ethyl acetates, butyl and isobutyl, acetic acid, oxygenated water, liquid chlorine, formol and its derivatives, phenol, caustic soda, phenolic resins, and vinyl emulsions. At Rio Tercero, work was underway on a new plant to produce chlorine and caustic soda, with the U.S. company Diamond Shamrock Corporation providing the basic engineering and electrolytic cells. Associated firms under the Atanor banner—besides Petroquimica Rio Tercero, Duranor, and Hoganor—included Fadecor (pyrethum insecticide powders, sprays, and spirals), Abetos Atanor (forestry and recuperation of arid lands), and Tecnor (engineering services).

Restructurings and Changes in Ownership: 1980–97

By 1980, however, it was clear that Atanor could not function profitably without scaling back in size. Accordingly, the com-

pany closed the only plant producing phenol in Argentina and eliminated other unprofitable lines, such as home products. A greater emphasis was then placed on exports such as solvents and herbicides. By the end of 1981 Atanor's workforce had been reduced by half, with many positions being eliminated and line managers assuming complete responsibility for decisions. The company now felt itself healthy enough to acquire Rhodia Argentina, a chemical complex at Baradero, located in the province of Buenos Aires about 90 miles from the capital. This facility was producing acetic acid, acetic aldehyde, acetic anhydride, ethyl acetate, butyl, isobutyl, ether, sorbitol, and triacetylene. In 1985 Atanor acquired the majority share of Dericel S.A., the only producer in Argentina of CMC (carboximethylcellulose). During 1987 the Rio Tercero facility opened the first Argentine unit for the production of 3,5 Dinitro, the principal material for the manufacture of trifluraline, used in certain herbicides. Shortly after, work was authorized for a new oxygenated-water plant. During this period Atanor was not only the sole Argentine producer of oxygenated water but also of acetic anhydride, acetic acid, ethyl acetate, and other acetates. Chemical products accounted for about 60 percent of its sales. The growing agrochemical range of products, accounting for 22 percent, included Ipersan, a herbicide for soybeans; EPTC, a herbicide for corn; and *monocrofotos*, a wide-spectrum insecticide.

In 1986 Argentinian President Raul Alfonsin pledged to relieve the government's budgetary problems by selling off some government holdings, beginning with petrochemicals. Atanor was one of the firms scheduled for privatization. The Bunge y Born group, a large food manufacturer and grain merchant in Argentina, anticipated the coming privatization by acquiring a 34-percent stake in the company from Grupo Roberts (a private holding company prominent in textiles). The purchase was made through Compania Quimica S.A., a Bunge y Born enterprise which was working with Atanor to produce herbicides and intermediate materials in the manufacture of fertilizers.

The 21-percent stake held by Fabricaciones Militares was sold in 1988 to Compania Quimica, giving it effective ownership. By this time Atanor was manufacturing a wide range of chemicals at three locations. The Munro plant was producing 35,000 metric tons a year of acetaldehyde, acetic acid, agrochemical formulations, ethyl butyl, formaldehyde, isobutyl acetates, phenolic resins, and other products. At Baradero, also in the province of Buenos Aires but about 90 miles from the capital, the company had the capacity to produce 15,000 tons a year of similar products, including sorbitol. The Rio Tercero complex had the means to turn out 80,000 tons a year of chloralkali, hydrogen peroxide, methanol, and other products. A distillery in Mendoza was producing 400,000 liters a month of ethyl alcohol.

The government sold its 40-percent share in Petroquimica Rio Tercero to Egerton Finance in 1992. Atanor continued to hold the majority stake in this enterprise, and a *Chemical Week* supplement in 1994 called Atanor's one of the most successful privatizations in Argentina, with a reduction in the workforce and an increase in manufacturing capacity. Rio Tercero was exporting about half of its output to Bolivia, Chile, Paraguay, and Uruguay. The parent company, however, was floundering, nearly going bankrupt in 1993 before refocusing its efforts on herbicide production. After modest improvement, Bunge y Born sold Petroquimica Rio Tercero to a bedding manufacture named Pieso in 1996 for $29 million. The 51-percent interest in the rest of Atanor was sold to Iowa-based Albaugh, Inc.—one of its clients—in 1997 for $58.6 million.

Late 1990s and Beyond

Atanor had five major production facilities and annual sales of $168 million by 1997. However, local authorities shuttered the Munro plant for a month that year when it was discovered that several people living near the plant were suffering severe health problems and were carrying unusually high levels of heavy metals in their bodies. In a statement presented to federal courts, the rector of the University of Quilmes, which had been contracted to design an environmental monitoring system, accused Atanor of tampering with the study. Atanor claimed it was complying with all environmental legislation but began shifting many of the factory's activities to the four other plants as part of a policy of transferring operations to non-urban areas.

Of Atanor's sales in 1999, chemicals accounted for 48 percent, agrochemicals for 28 percent, and petrochemicals for 24 percent. Seventy percent of the company's chemical products were being used in the production of its agrochemicals. Twenty-six percent of its sales were exported, and 81 percent of its exports were agrochemicals. Brazil and the United States were the chief markets. Atanor's labor costs fell from 22 percent of sales in 1993 to 13 percent in 1999.

At the end of 1999 Atanor added a plant in Pilar, Buenos Aires, that was producing the herbicide Glyphosate. Early the next year it purchased a sugar refinery in Marapa, Tucuman, converting it into a production plant for ethyl alcohol, with further production of acetic acid, anhydrous acetic, and acetates foreseen.

In 2003 Atanor purchased a company named Moonmate S.A. for $11 million, receiving two sugar plantations and a

sugar refinery with the goal of augmenting its production of ethyl alcohol. Atanor also was planning to build two new plants: one for chlorine and caustic soda, the other for a byproduct of these, hydrogen peroxide. Although Argentina passed through its third consecutive year of recession, Atanor's sales increased by 15 percent in 2000, and its net profit rose five-fold.

The economic crisis that gripped Argentina in 2001 and resulted in a devaluation of the peso at the beginning of 2002 proved greatly beneficial to Atanor, because the company's costs were now in cheaper pesos, enabling its products to be more competitive in export markets, with sales made in hard currencies. Wisely anticipating the devaluation of the peso, the company had pressed its clients to pay quickly while stretching out payments to its suppliers, thereby accumulating the funds it needed to pay $50 million in foreign debt before devaluation could make these debts even larger. Revenues rose by 70 percent in 2002, and net income tripled to 45.14 million pesos ($13.39 million). Production came to 245,081 tons, or 76 percent of capacity. Agrochemicals accounted for 77 percent of total sales. D.A. International, a company controlled by Albaugh president Dennis Albaugh, owned two-thirds of Atanor by the autumn of 2003, and made a tender offer of $57 million to purchase the remainder of the publicly traded outstanding shares of stock. Some 95 percent of these shares were tendered.

Atanor's agrochemicals in 2002 consisted of 11 herbicides, 3 insecticides, and a chemical for the treatment of worms in livestock. Two herbicides—2,4-D acid and Glyphoste—accounted for 35 percent and 34 percent, respectively, of its agrochemicals sales in 1999. Atanor's 23 chemical and petrochemical products in 2002 were ethyl acetate, butyl acetate, isobutyl acetate, acetic acid, hydrochloric acid, hydrogen peroxide, salicyclic acid, liquid chlorine, caustic soda, sorbitol, ethyl hexylacetate, isopropyl acetate, acetic anhydride, isobutylic alcohol, H-butylic alcohol, formaldehyde, phenol, concentrates of urea formaldehyde, hexamethylentetramine, sodium hypochlorite, methanol, and triacetin. The company's polymers were phenolic pure liquids and solids and modified resins, uric resins, uric-melaminic resins, phuramic resins, resorcinol-formaldehyde resins, and melamine-formaldehyde resins.

The Munro plant was producing formaldehyde, other methanol derivatives, phenolic resins, and uric glues. The Pilar plant produced glyphosates. The Baradero plant was the only one in Argentina producing the following six chemicals: ethyl acetate, butyl acetate, sorbitol, ethyl hexylacetate, acetic anhydride, and acetic acid. A plant in San Nicolas was producing triazines. The one in Rio Tercero was turning out numerous products.

As the company looked to the future, it sought to increase sales of products with higher added value, particularly herbicides. It also pledged to focus efforts on exports to Brazil and the United States, while seeking to keep abreast of technology and making further inroads in vertical integration.

Principal Subsidiaries

Atanor do Brasil Ltda. (Brazil); Atanor Uruguay S.A.; RAM Research Inc. (United States).

Principal Operating Units

Agrochemicals; Chemical-Petrochemical; Polymers.

Principal Competitors

Bayer S.A.; Dow Quimica Argentina S.A.; Grupo DuPont Argentina, S.A.; Monsanto Argentina S.A.I.C.; Solvay Indupa S.A.I.C.

Further Reading

"Albaugh Buys Agchem Business," *Chemical Market Reporter,* January 20, 1997, p. 3.

"El aporte de Atanor," *Mercado,* June 27, 1978, pp. 69–70.

"Argentina Getting Plant to Make DDT," *New York Times,* August 25, 1953, p. 34.

"Atanor Completes Purchase of Duranor," *European Chemical News,* November 17, 1978, p. 20.

"Atanor Expands H202 Capacity," *European Chemical News,* December 21/28, 1987, p. 8.

"Atanor: La llama que crece," *Mercado,* September 7, 1972, pp. 37–39.

Campbell, Andrea, "Illnesses Cast Shadow Over Argentine Agrochemical Plant," *Financial Times,* April 30, 1998, p. 6.

"Crecen las plantas de Atanor," *Mercado,* November 1, 1979, pp. 48–50.

"DA International Eyes Rest of *Atanor* Stake," *Asian Chemical News,* October 13, 2003, p. 4.

Garcia, Luis F., "Negocios con ritmo dispar," *Mercado,* September 26, 1985, pp. 88–90.

"Hooker Chemical Corp.," *New York Times,* August 2, 1961, p. 40.

Kessler, Richard, "Latin America's Chemical Industry Boom," *Chemical Week,* November 16, 1988, p. 42.

——, "Slow Going for 'Privatizations'," *Chemical Week,* October 21, 1987, p. 28.

"Medio siglo en la quimica," *Mercado,* March 30, 1989, pp. 51–58.

"La petroquimica de Atanor," *Mercado,* February 13, 1975, pp. 31–33.

"Por la buena senda," *Mercado,* March 31, 1988, pp. 73–74.

Salles, Flavio, and Andrew Wood, "Argentine Groups Shape Up," *Chemical Week,* November 16, 1994, pp. S12, S14.

Stok, Gustavo, "Rara avis," *America Economia,* June 6–19, 2003, p. 34.

"El turno de Atanor," *Mercado,* September 23, 1982, pp. 49–50.

—Robert Halasz

The Athletics Investment Group

Network Associates Coliseum
7000 Coliseum Way
Oakland, California 94621
U.S.A.
Telephone: (510) 638-4900
Fax: (510) 562-1633
Web site: http://oakland.athletics.mlb.com

Private Company
Founded: 1901
Employees:
Sales: $96 million (2002)
NAIC: 711310 Promoters of Performing Arts, Sports, and
   Similar Events with Facilities; 448150 Clothing
   Accessories Stores

The Athletics Investment Group owns the Oakland Athletics franchise, one of the most storied and controversial teams in major league baseball history. Located for 54 years in Philadelphia, and for 12 in Kansas City, Missouri, before moving to Oakland, California, the Athletics (A's) have won 14 divisional titles, 15 American League pennants, and nine World Series Championships. The team makes its home in Network Associates Coliseum (formerly the Oakland-Alameda Coliseum) although their future in Oakland remained uncertain. Sharing the relatively small Bay Area sports market with the National League's San Francisco Giants, the A's financial situation has long been unstable. For at least five years, The Athletics Investment Group has been searching for a buyer for the team. Still, the company realized an estimated $96 million in revenues in 2002.

The Connie Mack Era: 1901–54

While The Athletics Investment Group was formed in the 1990s, the history of the Athletics team may be traced to 1901, when the American League was formed as an upstart organization to compete with the long-established National League. A founding franchise was given to a Philadelphia consortium made up of a group of Philadelphia sportswriters, sporting goods manufacturer Benjamin F. Shibe, and Cornelius McGillicuddy, a manager and former ball player more familiarly known as Connie Mack. Mack brought into the new team his knowledge of baseball and players. He soon became virtually synonymous with the A's, who were often referred to as the Mack-Men. By the time he retired in 1951 at the age of 81, Mack and his family had a controlling interest in the Athletics, and he had become the longest serving manager in baseball history and one of the most beloved figures in the sport.

Mack assembled a team for the new franchise, finding players on the semi-pro and sandlot ball teams and also persuading seven established stars, most notably slugger Napoleon Lajoie, to jump their contracts with the local National League team, the Phillies. The Phillies sued and the Pennsylvania Supreme Court upheld their claim. Mack's response was canny. He traded the disputed players to the American League team in Cleveland, Ohio, outside the jurisdiction of the Pennsylvania court. Mack's baseball smarts brought the A's almost immediate success. The team won the American League pennant in 1902, a year before the first World Series. By the end of the decade, Mack had assembled the greatest powerhouse in the American League. Boasting future Hall of Famers such as Eddie Collins, Home Run Baker, Ed Plank, Rube Waddell, and Chief Bender, the A's won the American League pennant in 1910, 1911, 1913, and 1914, and the World Series every year but the last.

The 1914 loss was a bitter one. Heavily favored to defeat the underdog Boston Brave, the A's were swept in four games. That was the last straw. Suspecting that his players had thrown the Series for gamblers, and facing financial competition from the newly created Federal League, Mack launched a clearance sale of his championship players. It was not the last time a financially-strapped A's owner would dismantle his team, or try to. The A's immediately slipped into last place where they stayed for seven straight years. By the late 1920s, Mack had built another the premier club that the World Series in 1929 and 1930, and the league pennant in 1931. However, beset reportedly by stock market losses, Mack once again sold the core of his team, this time sending three players to the Chicago White Sox for $100,000. The sale sent the A's club into a downward economic spiral as angry fans stayed away from the park. Mack's financial woes increased

Key Dates:

1902: Athletics (A's) win American League pennant for the first time.

1929: A's win first of two consecutive World Series championships.

1932: After suffering severe losses in the stock market, manager Connie Mack once again sells off key A's players.

1951: Connie Mack retires after 50 years as A's manager.

1955: Connie Mack's sons, Roy and Earl sell A's to Arnold Johnson for more than $3 million; Johnson moves team to Kansas City.

1960: Arnold Johnson dies; A's are sold to Charles O. Finley for $4 million.

1968: Finley moves the A's to Oakland.

1972: The A's win first of three consecutive World Series.

1980: Walter A. Haas buys the A's for $12.7 million.

1990: The A's draw 2.9 million fans, more than any other northern California baseball team in history.

1994: Haas puts the A's up for sale on condition that the team remains in Oakland.

1995: New owners, partners Schott and Hofmann, begin turning the floundering organization around.

in 1933, and when the season ended—the A's finished third—he sold four more players, including future Hall of Famers Mickey Cochrane and Lefty Grove, for $225,000. The second gutting sent the A's into a tailspin. During the next ten years, the A's did not once win more than 68 games; they never again finished higher than fourth place during the Mack ownership.

In 1951 Connie Mack stepped down as A's manager, a job he had held uninterruptedly for 50 years, by far the longest tenure of any manager in major league history. Over the years he had bought out his sportswriter partners. In the early 1950s Mack's sons, Roy and Earl Mack, assumed a large mortgage to purchase shares from the Shibe family that gave them control of the team. It was a fateful decision. The huge debt weighed on a club already hurt by nearly three decades of second division finishes and the lack of an effective farm system. Across town, the greatly improved Philadelphia Phillies were drawing fans away from the A's. Adding to their difficulties, in a shortsighted attempt to raise funds, the owners lost a major source of income when they sold their rights to concession at Shibe Park. On the verge of financial collapse, the Mack family put the team up for sale. Philadelphia investors, including multimillionaire Jack Kelly, the father of actress Grace Kelly, tried to purchase the club, but the American League refused to approve the sale to a local buyer. It wanted to see the team move to the West where the populace was showing an increasing desire to spend money on major league baseball. In November 1954 the team was sold for $3 million to Arnold Johnson, a vending machine manufacturer from Chicago.

The Arnold Johnson Era: 1955–60

Johnson moved the team to Kansas City, Missouri. The new owner and venue did nothing to improve the performance of the Athletics, who continued to finish each season near the bottom

of the league standings. The A's did get their share of good players. By the time Arnold Johnson passed away in March 1960, the Kansas City Athletics had become a synonym for futility. In the five years of his ownership, the A's had not finished higher than sixth place. Hampered by the ball club's high costs, Johnson's family put the A's back on the sales block. In Kansas City, as in Philadelphia earlier, a local group was interested in purchasing the team, but circumstances conspired against them. By the time the group was able to mount a weak bid, Charles Finley had gone into Chicago probate court where Johnson's estate was and made a higher bid.

The Charles Finley Era: 1961–80

Charles O. Finley was one of the most colorful and controversial figures in the history of organized sports. By education an engineer, by avocation a talented semi-pro baseball player, Finley made his fortune in insurance and in the early 1950s set his sights on purchasing a major league ball club. As soon as he had the A's, Finley began grabbing headlines. He dressed the team in gaudy green and gold uniforms that contrasted boldly with the white or grey flannels worn by other teams. Instead of traditional black spikes, the A's wore white baseball shoes, supposedly made from kangaroo leather. Finley installed a mechanical rabbit that would pop up from the ground behind the plate with new balls for the umpire. In the late 1960s, when the rest of baseball kept up a clean-cut, all-American image, Finley paid his players $300 to grow moustaches.

He was not allowed to implement all of his ideas. When Finley moved in the right field fences by more than 40 feet and called it the "Pennant Porch," Commissioner Ford Frick ordered Finley to move it back. Major league baseball also nixed Finley's idea to introduce orange baseballs, which he claimed would be easier for batters to see. However, some of Finley's ideas changed baseball forever. He was one of the first advocates of the designated hitter rule, implemented by the American League in 1976. He was a strong proponent of World Series night games, an idea first tried in 1971.

When Finley assumed ownership in December 1960, the A's franchise was in disarray. Not only did it bear the weight of nearly 30 losing seasons, it was playing in Municipal Stadium, a ballpark better suited for minor league ball. In 1961 the club was so bad it managed to finish behind one of the two expansion teams that were added to the American League. Meager attendance dropped even more. From the start Finley was dissatisfied with everything about Kansas City and tried to get out of his Municipal Stadium lease to move the team somewhere else. He negotiated with a string of municipalities throughout the early and mid-1960s, including Dallas, Louisville, Kentucky, Washington, D.C., New Orleans, and Denver. At the end of the 1967 season, Finley finally reached an agreement with Oakland, California, and moved the A's there in time for the start of the 1968 season.

While still in Kansas City Finley's organization had nevertheless begun a major overhaul of the A's farm system. In 1966 a bumper crop of young talent that included the likes of Reggie Jackson and Jim Hunter was ready to be harvested. In its first year in Oakland, the team finished sixth. However, it had managed a significant achievement, finishing above .500 for only the fourth time since the early 1930s. The 1969 and 1970 seasons offered the first hints of the team that would soon be the most powerful and popular in baseball. In the first half of the 1970s, the A's would win five consecutive American League West divisional titles, three consecutive American League pennants, and at their peak, from 1972 to 1974, three consecutive World Series titles, a feat achieved previously only by the New York Yankees.

Unfortunately the A's field successes did not always translate into success at the turnstiles. In two of their championship years, 1972 and 1974, home attendance failed to top the one million mark. More disturbingly, the A's frequently failed to sell out their home games in the playoffs or even in the World Series, leading players to regularly disparage Oakland fans in the media. Dissatisfaction did not stop with fans. Just as frequently the players fought among themselves and with Charles Finley. Finley himself was personally responsible for much of the contentious feeling in the club house. He forced his players to accept oddball nicknames, such as "Catfish" and "Blue Moon," claiming they would increase popularity with fans. He flat out refused to give raises to players even after career seasons. He publicly humiliated players. After a game-losing error in the 1973 World Series, Finley pressured second baseman Mike Andrews into signing a public statement that he was not physically able to continue playing and wanted to be removed from the lineup. Two games later the A's players decided on their own to bring Andrews back, whether Finley approved or not.

The A's were at the forefront of free agency in the mid-1970s. In the middle of the 1974 World Series, pitcher Jim Hunter announced that Finley had reneged on $50,000 in payments. As a result, Hunter said, his A's contract would be null and void at the end of the season. The courts upheld Hunter's claims and the next season he signed as a million dollar free agent with the New York Yankees. After the 1975 season, when general free agency was introduced in baseball, nine of the A's core players, including Reggie Jackson, Vida Blue, and Rollie Fingers, were about to become free agents. Finley, a less well-to-do owner in a smaller media market, realized that he had little chance of competing for his star players on the open market. Like Connie Mack 35 years before him, Finley set about dismantling the team. He traded some players and sold others. When baseball commissioner Bowie Kuhn learned of the sales, however, he nullified them and ordered the three players to return to the Oakland club, claiming they threatened the competitive balance of the American League. Finley countered that he wanted *something* for his players rather than nothing when they signed with a new team. Seeking to overturn the commissioner's ruling, Finley sued Kuhn. The court ruled in Kuhn's behalf. A Finley-led effort to rouse other owners to depose Kuhn also failed. In the end, all the players except one signed with other teams.

Thanks to the lackluster team and competition from the San Francisco Giants across the bay, attendance dropped so badly in 1977 that the league pressured Finley to offer weekday tickets at half price. Facing a potential loss of $1 million for the year, Finley began exploring ways to move the team out of Oakland. He focused his efforts on moving the A's to Washington, D.C., where they would compete in the National League. The 20-year lease with the Oakland-Alameda Coliseum stood in the way of any move, however. An arrangement with major league baseball and the Giants to help buy out the stadium fizzled. Moreover, National League owners were loathe to bring Finley's contentious personality into their ranks and blocked the move. By the 1979 season, the A's had virtually stopped promoting themselves. The Coliseum sued, asking for $1.5 million for in lost earnings, as well as another $10 million in punitive damages for failing to maintain a team of "character and standing" as league rules stipulated. Personal woes added to Finley's business problems. His divorce was a costly one, and in September 1977 he underwent heart bypass surgery in Chicago.

The team reached rock bottom in 1979, posting a 54–108 record and attracting only 307,000 fans to the Coliseum. Finley's hiring of a manager as controversial as himself, Billy Martin, helped the A's recover slightly in 1980. Finley had, however, had enough. On August 24, 1980, he sold the club to Walter A. Haas for $12.7 million.

The Walter Haas Years: 1980–94

64-year-old Walter Haas was the chairman the Levi Strauss Company, based in San Francisco. He and his family lived in Oakland, and they brought to the team a strong commitment to keep the team there. Haas himself did not participate in the day-to-day operations of the A's; he knew next to nothing about baseball and later said he had only made the purchase as a gesture to Oakland. The A's organization was run by Haas' son, Walter J. Haas, and son-in-law, Roy Eisenhardt. The Haas family, though wealthier than Finley, learned to their chagrin that running a professional baseball club was not an inexpensive proposition, particularly in the tight Bay Area they shared with the San Francisco Giants. Between 1980 and 1987 Haas lost almost $30 million dollars, due in part to the refurbishing of the Coliseum, and the rebuilding of the A's farm system and promotional machinery. It was eight years before Haas was able scratch the first meager profit from his franchise.

By 1987, it seemed the investment might be about to pay off. The team developed a roster of promising young stars, including sluggers Jose Canseco and Mark McGwire. The greatly increased involvement of the A's organization in Oakland community affairs won the team new respect in the city—fans reportedly broke into spontaneous applause when they saw Haas at games. The A's finally resumed their winning ways in the late 1980s, winning the American League pennant in 1988 and 1990, and the World Series in 1989—the so-called Bay Bridge series against San Francisco that was delayed by the Loma Prieta earthquake. In 1990 the A's drew 2.9 million fans, a record for a Bay Area baseball team.

The days of high attendance and successful teams were short-lived. After winning the divisional title in 1992, the A's dropped out of contention for the rest of the decade. The financial problems returned immediately. In 1993, the club lost almost $5 million and was facing possible losses of $10 million in 1994. That April the team asked the Coliseum for a year-to-year lease and at the same time began a search for new owners. The team was formally put up for sale in May 1994. The asking price was $84 million, well below its appraised value. The only string attached to the bargain basement price was that the buyer keep the club in Oakland at least until 2001. If the team were eventually resold it had to be first offered to another local buyer at a reduced price. In early 1995, shortly before Walter Haas passed away at age 79, he sold the A's for $85 million to Northern California business partners Steven C. Schott and Kenneth Hofmann.

The Schott-Hofmann Years: 1995 and Beyond

When they took over the club, Schott and Hofmann had definite ideas about how a baseball club should be run, and they began putting their ideas in place immediately. Under their stewardship, the A's took an active role in the promotion and presentation of baseball in their home park, which had been renamed Network Associates Coliseum. They also took over as many ancillary money-making operations as possible, including parking, maintenance, and concessions at the stadium. At the same time, costs, especially player salaries, were to be kept as low as possible. As a result of their efforts, Schott and Hoffman made The Athletics Investment Group, and the A's, one of the finest organizations in the majors, one lauded as exemplary not only for its baseball but for its business acumen in general. The A's, especially under General Manager Billy Beane, rationalized the system of player selection, relying on statistical evidence rather than the anecdotal reports of human scouts that had been the norm in ball for the entire 20th century. As a result of its new philosophy, the team was able consistently to field teams that could over the course of a season challenge clubs with budgets three times greater.

Systematically cultivating its minor league organization and searching out talented players who for one reason or another were undervalued by the rest of baseball, the A's made it to post-season play every year between 2000 and 2003. Success not only boosted annual attendance six-fold between 1998 and 2003, it earned the A's organization back-to-back Organization of the Year honors in 1998 and 1999. The group was paid a much higher honor when other clubs started imitating the A's system. The Boston Red Sox went so far as to try to sign Beane away from Oakland—unsuccessfully.

After three losing seasons marked by poor attendance, the team finally turned the corner in 1998, finishing second. The return to success was welcome, but there were problems in Oakland, particularly with the Coliseum. In 1995 the stadium had been renovated to focus on serving professional football, and modifications interfered with the sight lines for baseball fans. In addition, each season brought the potential for losses in the millions. Schott and Hoffman considered various solutions, one of which to sell the team. The terms of their original purchase, however, required that an Oakland buyer be first given an opportunity to purchase the franchise at a reduced price. In 1999 an Oakland group that included broadcaster and ex-major leaguer Joe Morgan came close to acquiring the A's. The deal fell apart at the 11th hour, when organized baseball

postponed any action on the sale until its panel on the reorganization of baseball finished its work. Schott and Hofmann also explored moving the team to Santa Clara, where Schott's real estate business was based. In 2001, following rumors in the Bay Area press that a Las Vegas buyer was interested in the team, the city of Oakland took important first steps toward the construction of a brand new, baseball-only park. As the 2004 season began, the A's had agreed to play at the Coliseum at least through the 2007 season, with options to stay through 2010. Schott and Hofmann highlighted their commitment to the city with a series of community programs that included activities for underprivileged children, for minority children and seniors, as well as fundraising efforts for worthy charities. While new ownership loomed on the horizon, and its financial health was ever a challenge, The Athletics Investment Group and the Oakland A's had enjoyed an impressive turnaround and were poised for more success.

Principal Competitors

San Francisco Giants.

Further Reading

Anderson, Dave, "Why Charles O Finley Failed," *New York Times,* July 18, 1975, p. 23.

"A's Owners Talked Sale with D.C. Man," *Bay Business Times,* July 3, 2002.

"Battles in the Ball Park," *Economist,* July 10, 1976, p. 36.

DelVecchio, Rick, "With Nowhere Else to Go, A's Retrench," *San Francisco Chronicle,* September 29, 1997, p. A1.

Dickey, Glenn, *Champions: The Story of the First Two Oakland A's Dynasties and the Building of the Third,* Chicago: Triumph Books, 2002.

Dickey, Glenn, "Haas: The A's Bighearted Owner," *San Francisco Chronicle,* October 4, 1990, p. D3.

Dolgan, Bob, "Baseball's Demolition Man," *Cleveland Plain Dealer,* July 13, 2002, p. D2.

"Giants Shut Out Oakland in Media Revenue Game," *San Francisco Business Times,* December 21, 2001, p. 6.

"Is Charlie O. Throwing a Spitball at Oakland?," *Business Week,* May 21, 1979, p. 38.

Koppett, Leonard. "Solving the Bay Area's Baseball Problem," *New York Times,* February 16, 1986, p. E2.

Lieb, Frederick G., *Connie Mack: Grand Old Man of Baseball,* New York: G.P. Putnam's Sons, 1945.

Markusen, Bruce, *Baseball's Last Dynasty: Charlie Finley's Oakland A's,* Indianapolis, Ind.: Masters Press, 1998.

Povich, Shirley, "Finley Gets A's for His Final Marks on Game," *Washington Post,* February 21, 1996, p. F02.

Ross, Andrew, Janine DeFao, and Phillip Matier, "A's Zip Lips On Deal," *San Francisco Chronicle,* August 1, 2001, p. A1.

Scannell, Nancy, "Once-Dominant A's Near Collapse," *Washington Post,* March 3, 1977, p. D1.

Vass, George, "Competitive Balance," *Baseball Digest,* May 2000.

—Gerald E. Brennan

Bata

Bata Ltd.

59 Wynford Drive
North York, Ontario M3C 1K3
Canada
Telephone: (416) 446-2011
Fax: (416) 446-2175
Web site: http://www.bata.com

Private Company
Incorporated: 1931
Employees: 50,000
Sales: $2 billion (2002 est.)
NAIC: 316210 Footwear Manufacturing

Bata Ltd. is a privately owned global shoe manufacturer and retailer headquartered in Ontario, Canada. The company is led by a third generation of the Bata family. With operations in 68 countries, Bata is organized into four business units. Bata Canada, based in Toronto, serves the Canadian market with 250 stores. Based in Paris, Bata Europe serves the European market with 500 stores. With supervision located in Singapore, Bata International boasts 3,000 stores to serve markets in Africa, the Pacific, and Asia, Finally, Bata Latin America, operating out of Mexico City, sells footwear throughout Latin America. All told, Bata owns more than 4,700 retail stores and 46 production facilities. Total employment for the company exceeds 50,000.

Company Founded in 1894

The Bata family's ties to shoemaking span more than two dozen generations and purportedly date as far back as 1580 to the small Czech village of Zlin. However, it was not until 1894 that the family began to make the transition from cobblers to industrialists. In that year, Tomas G. Bata, Sr., along with his brother Antonin and sister Anna, took 800 florins, some $350, inherited from their mother and launched a shoemaking business. They rented a pair of rooms, acquired two sewing machines on an installment plan, and paid for their leather and other materials with promissory notes. They produced stitched, coarse-woolen footwear. Within a year, the business was successful enough to enable the Batas to employ ten people in their

factory, such as it was, as well as another forty who worked out of their own homes. In the same year, 1895, Antonin was drafted into the military and Anna quit the business to get married, forcing Tomas to assume complete control of the venture. He was just 19 years old.

In 1900, Bata moved the operation to a new building located close to Zlin's railway station and took the first major step in industrialization, installing steam-driven machines. The company enjoyed success producing light, linen footwear that appealed to a large portion of the population, who could not afford better-made leather shoes. Nevertheless, Bata came close to bankruptcy on more than one occasion and concluded that in order for his business to survive he needed to find more efficient ways to manufacture and distribute shoes. In 1904, he and three employees took a trip to the United States to learn firsthand the ways of mass production. Bata spent six months working as a laborer on a shoe assembly line in New England. On his way back to Zlin, he also took time to visit English and German factories. Upon his return home, Bata began to transform the family shoe business, not only by applying the latest production techniques—which would one day earned him the moniker, "the Henry Ford of the shoe industry"—but also by finding a way to preserve the role of workers, which all too often changed dramatically during the transition from an artisan to an industrial approach to commerce.

The Bata shoe business began to experience steady growth, so that by 1912 it was employing 600 full-time workers plus another few hundred who worked out of their homes in neighboring villages. Tomas Bata now began to exhibit another side to his personality, the social idealist. Because there was a shortage of housing in Zlin for his new workers, he constructed new homes, which he rented at cost. He also offered inexpensive meals in factory cafeterias and free medical care. He even built a new hospital to care for his workers. However, as soon as they began to earn higher incomes, area merchants raised prices. In answer, Tomas Bata opened his own less-expensive company stores to ensure that his employees were able to enjoy the fruits of their success. He also took steps to identify management talent among the ranks of his workers and instituted a training program that was ahead of its time.

Company Perspectives:

Shoemaking is one of the world's oldest crafts—shoes have been works of art and the stuff of legends. Around the world, the Bata brand is reserved for well-made and well-priced dress and casual footwear. We're devoted to designing, producing, and providing our customers with the best in commercial fashion footwear for the whole family.

World War I Boot Contract a Turning Point

Bata received a major boost in 1914, following the outbreak of World War I, when the company received a contract to produce boots for the Austro-Hungarian army. From the waste of these items, the company produced the uppers to a wooden shoe that it sold to the lower classes. Tomas Bata then invested the profits in new machinery, as well as in the opening of new retail shops, so that the business was well positioned to take advantage of the economic boom of the 1920s. Before the company could enjoy this strong period of growth, however, Tomas Bata and his employees were forced to take a major gamble together. In the years immediately following the end of World War I in 1918, an economic slump prevailed across the globe, leading to significant unemployment. Czechoslovakia, formed as part of the peace settlement of World War I, attempted to fight inflation, which had already devastated Germany, by adopting tight monetary controls. As a result, the country's currency lost three-quarters of its value, which in turn led to a drop in demand for products, a cutback in production, more unemployment, and even less consumer demand—developments that together threatened national economic devastation. In August 1922, a group of industrialists met to discuss their plight. Unlike the others, Tomas Bata did not simply throw up his hands and blame the government. Instead, he called on the industrialists to take decisive steps to stimulate market demand, and he shocked everyone by announcing that he was going to cut the price of Bata shoes in half. Once the surprise of the moment wore off, Bata's audience simply laughed at him.

Bata was able, however, to convince his workers that he had a plan, albeit a radical one, that would work. He believed that the company had to cut costs to the bone and work at peak efficiency in order to halve the price of Bata shoes. Workers, ignoring their union leadership, accepted a 40 percent reduction in wages across the board. Tomas Bata, in turn, provided food, clothing, and other necessities at half-price to mitigate the loss of wages. In addition, he introduced measures that were pioneering, including the creation of individual profit centers and incentive payments to both management and workers to spur productivity. With his operations lean and efficient, he then launched a national advertising campaign. The response from consumers was swift and dramatic, as Bata stores, which had been virtually empty for months, were now swamped with customers looking for inexpensive shoes. Bata was forced to increase production, and not only did the company maintain full employment, it began to hire. The decision to cut prices proved to be a turning point in the history of the company, which now grew at a tremendous pace.

Tomas Bata continued to innovate, improving on productivity primarily through the introduction of an assembly line approach. After five years, productivity improved 15-fold; after ten, the retail price of Bata shoes dropped by 82 percent. The employees' faith in Tomas Bata was also rewarded. After accepting a severe wage cut in 1922, by 1932 they had seen their salaries doubled. They were now working for the largest shoemaker in the world. According to company lore, in fact, in some developing countries "bata" gained currency where there was no word for "shoe." Moreover, Bata became involved in a variety of other industries, including socks, leatherwork, chemicals used in leather making, shoemaking machinery, wooden packing crates, tires and other rubber goods. The company launched its own film studio to produced advertising materials, and it soon evolved into a full-fledged enterprise that produced some of the earliest animated films. Because of the company's involvement in transportation, as Bata became the world's largest exporter of shoes, Tomas Bata even became involved in the manufacture of airplanes through the Zlin Air Company, which produced both sporting and business planes. He also became famous for housing his headquarters in the tallest reinforced concrete office building in Europe, which featured an elevator that housed his "floating office." With a push of a button, Bata was able to confer, and keep an eye on, his employees on every floor without leaving his desk.

Bata established operations in new markets, such as Singapore in 1930. The company, which in 1931 adopted a joint stock company form of organization, also established subsidiaries and shoe factories in a number of European countries as a way to circumvent tariffs that had been imposed in response to a worldwide economic depression. In mid-1932, Tomas Bata called together his team of executives and announced that in order for the company to weather increasingly difficult economic conditions and drive further growth, they would have to look to more distant markets, in particular North America. Just two days later, however, Tomas Bata was killed when an airplane he was in took off in a thick fog and crashed into a chimney of one of his buildings. He was 56 years old.

Bata left a 22-year-old son, Thomas J. Bata, whom he had groomed since childhood to one day head the business, but in the meantime Bata's half-brother Jan took over and continued the mentoring process. It was Thomas Bata who was to be dispatched to North America, to which the company was already exporting shoes, to establish a manufacturing operation. While most executives in the organization lobbied for the United States as the location for a plant, the young Bata was fixated on locating the business in Canada, a place he had romanticized since childhood after reading the works of Jack London. With the rise of Nazi Germany in the 1930s, the importance of organizing a North American operation took on increasing importance, as the company now made plans to relocate its headquarters to the West. In March 1939, with Germany on the verge of invading his country, Thomas Bata fled to Canada along with 180 Czechoslovakians. After being granted permission from the Canadian government, he started up operations in Frankford, Ontario, taking over a former Canadian Paper Company mill while a new factory was built. To aid in the Allied war effort, the company focused its personnel and equipment on the production of anti-aircraft equipment and machines used to inspect ammunition. For his part, Jan Bata moved his headquarters to the United States, but when blacklisted by the Allies he was forced to relocate to Brazil. The Bata Shoe Organization, as it was called, was now split between uncle and nephew, resulting in an eventual contest for management control and ownership. Thomas Bata essentially prevailed in 1949, but the contest continued to be played out in the courts of numerous countries until the end of 1966.

The return of Bata operations lost to the Nazis was short lived after World War II. In 1945, the communist government installed in Czechoslovakia by the Soviet Union had nationalized the country's industry, usurping the original Bata shoe factory in Zlin and the company's far-flung network of shops. (Even Zlin's name was changed, becoming known as Gottwaldov, a tribute to the country's first communist president.) Bata was further stripped of assets as other countries, including East Germany, Poland, and Yugoslavia, also nationalized their shoe industries. Now based in the West, Bata and its many Czechoslovakian expatriates began to rebuild the business, taking on an almost missionary zeal in the process. Rather than organizing in a centralized manner, the company established a structure based on autonomous operations, primarily in the new markets of developing countries. Also following the war, Thomas Bata married an aspiring architect named Sonja, a woman who would play an influential role in the success of the company, supplementing her husband's manufacturing and sales expertise with a sense of design and style. By the mid-1950s, Bata was operating 56 factories in 46 countries. Thirty years later, Bata was in 115 countries, selling close to $2 billion worth of footwear each year through 6,000 company-owned stores and 120,000 independent retailers.

Bata Shoes Returns to the Czech Republic in 1991

In the 1970s and 1980s, the manufacture of shoes began to shift increasingly to Pacific Rim countries, where lower labor costs provided a competitive edge that proved devastating to shoe companies around the world. With its widely cast operations and well-established distribution network, Bata was better able to compete, but it too suffered from a softening in its business.

With the fall of communism in the late 1980s, Bata was able to return to the country where the family business was founded. The company was not able to resume ownership of its prior assets, which has been combined with other Czech shoe operations, nor did Bata wish to be encumbered with facilities that the communists had neglected for more than 40 years. Nevertheless, Thomas Bata was committed to establishing a business in his native country. After some study, the management team elected to focus on a retail distribution business and a modest manufacturing facility, one that was not part of the old Bata operation. A small factory established by the communist regime was found acceptable, and the company then selected a number of retail locations, which would total a 20 percent market share, and presented the government with a joint venture proposal that was accepted in late 1991.

Thomas Bata, at the age of 80, elected to retire in 1994. His son, Thomas Bata, Jr., had been serving as president since 1985. According to *The Globe and Mail,* Thomas, Jr. "took over at a time when the international shoe maker was experiencing heightened competition from strong global marketers. The movement toward free trade challenged its network of quasi-autonomous national companies. Mr. Bata tried to make changes, but insiders says he lost the support of key members of the board." He was widely expected to succeed his father, but to the surprise of many, Stanley Heath, a Canadian with considerable executive experience with RJR Nabisco, took over as president and CEO to assume the day-to-day running of the business, while the younger Bata assumed the chairmanship, ostensibly charged with focusing on the "big picture." He soon left the family business and moved to Switzerland. His father, with a reputation as an autocrat, was slated to become honorary chairman, but the post proved to be far from ceremonial, as he continued to be involved in the company's operations on a day-to-day basis and was not reticent about letting management know his opinions. Little more than a year after coming to Bata, Heath resigned for "personal and family reasons." Taking over for Heath was a loyal company man, Rino Rizzo, who had been with the Bata organization since 1969. In 1999, Bata brought in Jim Pantelidis, an executive who had no experience in the shoe industry, to assume the CEO position. Pantelidis's background was in retail gasoline sales, and during his career he had worked for one of Canada's largest chains, Petro-Canada Corporation. Pantelidis instituted a plan to develop regional shoe lines, as opposed to lines created for individual countries. In addition, he wanted to create economies of scale by building regional infrastructures. The goal was to use the regional infrastructures to position the Bata brand on a global basis.

The tenure of Pantelidis lasted just two years. In late 2001, Thomas Bata, Jr. returned, gained control of the business, and was named chairman and CEO, while Pantelidis left to "pursue other challenges." Bata began to reorganize the company, essentially running the business out of Switzerland. It remained to be seen if he would be able to succeed where outsiders had failed in the effort to transform Bata from a federation of stand-alone local subsidiaries into a truly international company.

Principal Subsidiaries

Bata Canada; Bata Europe; Bata International; Bata Latin America.

Principal Competitors

Footstar, Inc.; Jimlar Corporation; Payless ShoeSource, Inc.

Further Reading

"Bata Going on Strong after 70 Years in the Business," *New Straits Times*, June 11, 2001.

Booth, Patricia L., and Alison C. Taylor, "Portrait of a Partnership: An Interview with Sonja Bata and Thomas J. Bata," *Canadian Business Review*, Autumn 1995, p. 6.

Lank, Alden G., "A Conversation with Tom Bata," *Family Business Review*, Fall 1997, p. 211.

Sender, Isabell, "The Bata Empire: A World Apart," *Footwear News*, July 3, 1995, p. S38.

Taylor, R.B., "The Bata Shoe Company of Canada, Ltd," *Quarter Review of Commerce*, Spring 1941, p. 240.

—Ed Dinger

Berger Bros Company

805 Pennsylvania Boulevard
Feasterville, Pennsylvania 19053
U.S.A.
Telephone: (215) 355-1200
Toll Free: (800) 523-8852
Fax: (215) 355-7738
Web site: http://www.bergerbros.com

Wholly Owned Subsidiary of Berger Holdings Inc.
Founded: 1874
Employees: 200
Sales: $44.6 million (2002)
NAIC: 332322 Sheet Metal Work Manufacturing

Berger Bros Company makes roof drainage products, including gutters and downspouts. The company maintains manufacturing facilities in Pennsylvania, Texas, and Georgia, and uses various techniques and materials (mainly copper, aluminum, steel, and zinc) to fabricate its products. In addition to gutters and downspouts, the company offers a selection of colored trim coils, roof flashings, roof edgings, snow guards, and the accessories needed for a complete roof-drainage system. Overall, more than 2,000 products are available to Berger's growing customer base of roofing distributors and building material centers and the individuals who shop there.

Early Years

The origins of Berger Bros may be traced to the late 1800s. William H. Berger was born in Milton, Pennsylvania, in 1841. He learned carpentry before enlisting as a private in the Union Army during the Civil War in 1862. After the war, Berger moved to Philadelphia and began his life's work as a builder and contractor. In 1874 he founded William Berger & Company, manufacturers of tinners' and roofers' supplies. He was soon joined in the business by his brother, and the company name was changed to Berger Bros Company.

William Berger's brother died in 1898, after which the business was formally incorporated with William H. Berger as president. The company grew steadily, becoming one of the largest concerns of its kind in the United States. Berger also introduced several new products to the marketplace, including Berger pipe and Berger roof grippers, used in the sheet metal industry. William Berger served as president of the company until his death in 1934.

Berger Bros continued to develop and manufacture roofing products, remaining family-owned until the 1970s. During this time, another company that would figure prominently in the future of Berger Bros was established. Life Care Communities Corporation was established in 1979 as a private company engaged in developing, marketing, and managing residential retirement life-care communities on a fee basis for non-profit ventures. By 1983, the company had begun shifting the scope of its operations to include developing and constructing the Life Care facilities. At this time its name was changed to Inovex Industries Inc.

Late 1980s Bankruptcy and Reorganization

Real change in the course of Berger's business did not occur until the late 1980s. In 1989, the company was acquired by Inovex, by then aiming to exit life-care communities all together. Thus, in 1989 Inovex entered the business of manufacturing and distributing roof drainage supplies, acquiring the stock of Berger Bros, which became an Inovex subsidiary. The following year, Inovex was renamed Berger Holdings, Ltd., a holding company for its major operating subsidiary, Berger Bros Company.

A sluggish economy in the early 1990s caused sales at Berger to slump. However, according to a 1991 story in the *Philadelphia Business Journal,* Berger's management placed the greatest share of blame for its failing financial health on its lending institution, Meridian Bank. The bank had over the past year cut off funding to Berger and called in its loans, forcing the company to file for protection under Chapter 11 of the Bankruptcy Code. To protect its asset base and ongoing operations, the Feasterville holding company's two subsidiaries—Berger Brothers (roof drainage products), and Graywood Products Co. Inc. (vinyl house siding)—also filed under Chapter 11 in order to reorganize their finances. At the time, based on 1990's revenues, Berger Holdings was the 143rd-largest company in the Philadelphia area, according to the *Philadelphia Business Journal*.

The company continued to operate during its reorganization period, laying off about 60 of its workforce. By 1993 Berger had modernized and modified its production facilities, machinery and equipment; it had also expanded existing product lines and publicized the quality of its aluminum-based roof drainage products (RDP). A plan for emerging from Chapter 11 was approved in 1993, and by 1994, under the reorganization, Berger had paid off its outstanding loans to Meridian, having been granted a loan by The CIT Group/Credit Finance Inc. Berger Holdings formed a new subsidiary, Berger Financial Corporation, which, in turn, became parent to Berger Bros. The company reported net sales of $15.6 million in 1995.

1996–99: Increased Marketing in a Stronger Economy

Having had new life breathed into it, Berger set about preparing for the future. In early 1996, Berger upgraded its Unix computer operating system, thereby improving order processing and advanced reporting capabilities. Berger manufactured its RDP product line—gutters, downspouts, trim coil, and associated accessories and fittings—at its Feasterville facility. RDP sales were made principally to wholesale distributors for resale directly to roofers and general contractors for repairs and replacements of roof drainage systems, mostly in residential buildings. To manufacture RDP products, Berger bought aluminum, copper, and galvanized and painted steel. The company strictly scrutinized all raw materials and all finished products for quality control based on industry and internal guidelines and standards.

Berger had to compete with both small and large manufacturers and fabricators, primarily in the Northeast/Mid-Atlantic region, its major market. Berger began to implement an advertising and marketing program to expand its business to a more national level. Record sales for fiscal 1996 were $19.75 million, compared to net sales of $11.94 million in 1993.

During February 1997, Berger completed the acquisition of Real-Tool Inc., thus gaining a complete line of commercial snow guards and a line of specialties for protecting and preserving metal roofs. On January 2, 1998, Berger acquired all the assets of Benjamin Obdyke Incorporated, Berger's single largest competitor as a manufacturer of roof drainage and aluminum soffit products. This transaction was beneficial for both companies: Berger became a one-stop source for all roof drainage needs and Obdyke could further expand its offering of quality

ventilation and other building products to a national market. The acquisition added approximately $14 million to Berger's revenue base in 1999, mostly from aluminum roof-drainage products. In December 1998, Berger acquired Sheet Metal Manufacturing Co., Inc. of Ridgewood, New York, and Waterbury, Connecticut—a manufacturer of roof drainage products and Berger's second-largest competitor. This Sheet Metal purchase was a major factor for an increase in sales from 1998–99. These acquisitions also Made it possible for Berger to penetrate the New York and New England markets.

Moreover, in an effort to grow the company and support future acquisitions, Berger arranged for additional financing and continued to search for immediately accretive acquisition candidates. The company built a solid infrastructure and increased the human resources needed to support future acquisitions. According to a 2003 article in the *Philadelphia Business Journal*, "A series of strategic acquisitions" broadened the company's "geographic reach and increased its manufacturing capacity." Berger believed that it had attained and could maintain a dominant position over many of the smaller manufacturers with whom it competed for business.

To assure that the company would always immediately fill special requests from the independent distributors who made up its core client base, President Joseph Weiderman continually bought new equipment and upgraded old equipment (investments ranging from $100,000 to $200,000 and up). This kind of service met with customer approval. By year-end 1999, Berger had expanded its product line to 2,000 individual items and posted higher revenues and income from operations than it had since it began to implement its 1996 acquisition strategy.

Once again, during this time, another company that would figure in Berger's future was planning to expand. United Kingdom-based Euramax International Ltd., a multinational company, completed a plan to establish headquarters in Norcross, Georgia. According to David Smith, president and chief executive officer of the American branch, Euramax International, Inc., Euramax required closer proximity to U.S. investors and capital markets.

2000 and Beyond

In 2000 Berger acquired CopperCraft, Inc., a manufacturer of high-end metal architectural products produced mainly at its suburban Dallas plant and sold directly to either distributors, major builders or general contractors for use in remodeling or renovating ornate sheet metal construction. This purchase gave Berger an internal source of specialty metal architectural products.

The company also completed the acquisition of Walker Metal Products, Inc., a manufacturer of roof drainage products with major business in the Southeast. Berger sold its products throughout the country, originally mostly in the Northeast/Mid-Atlantic region. With the acquisition of CopperCraft and Walker Metal Products, Berger gained greater national exposure in both the Southwest and the Southeast regions.

CopperCraft's and Walker Metal's sales contributed approximately $3 million of the $5.8 million increase in 2000 sales. Subsidiary Berger Bros' ongoing marketing efforts to increase its customer base contributed about $2.8 million.

Key Dates:

1874: William Berger & Company is founded as a manufacturer of roofing materials for builders.
1934: Company founder William Berger dies.
1979: Life Care Communities, later known as Inovex, is incorporated.
1989: Inovex Industries Inc. acquires Berger Bros.
1990: Inovex changes name to Berger Holdings, Ltd.
1991: Berger slips into Chapter 11 and reorganizes.
1996: Berger expands product line, intensifies marketing, begins era of acquisitions and geographic expansion.
2001: Berger's net sales peak at $51.13 million.
2003: Euramax International subsidiary Amerimax Pennsylvania merges with Berger Holdings.

Inclement winter weather and excessively hot and dry summers usually reduced the level of building activity in both the homebuilding and home improvement markets, thereby affecting reductions in the company's sales and profits. On the other hand, the absence of snow and other storms might also lessen the demand for the company's products by alleviating some of the consumer need to replace or repair Berger's roofing products. For example, due to severe weather experienced in Berger's core markets during the first quarter of 2001, sales fell by 8.7 percent, compared to sales for the first quarter of 2000. Nevertheless, because of steady sales from CopperCraft and Walker Metal, and of growth within the existing business, in 2001 net sales peaked at $51.13 million, rising from $45.4 million in 2000.

Over the years, Berger had rebounded successfully from bankruptcy and won investor loyalty through steadily increasing sales. However, during 2002 a mild winter, summer drought and recurring heat waves, a weak economy, rising costs for materials, and increased competition contributed to a 12.8 percent drop of net sales to $44.56 million. Despite these loss factors, President and Chief Executive Officer Weiderman said that year-end net income was the second-best in the company's history. By year-end 2002 Berger had used its strong cash flow to reduce funded debt from $21 million to $13.5 million.

Reorganization, nevertheless, ensued. In October 2003, Berger Holdings and Euramax International Inc., through its subsidiary Amerimax Pennsylvania, agreed to a Plan of Merger. Euramax, a leading producer of aluminum, steel, vinyl and fiber glass products, seemed a likely fit for Berger Bros. When all the transactions were completed on November 17, 2003, Berger Bros Company remained a subsidiary of Berger Holdings Ltd., which became a subsidiary of Euramax International. In the spirit of its intrepid founding family, Berger Bros had weathered enormous change yet remained poised to honor its heritage of "maximum customer satisfaction through superior service and competitive pricing."

Principal Competitors

Alcoa, Inc.; American Buildings Company; Lamb & Ritchie Co., Inc.; Owens Corning Fiberglass Corporation; Royal-Apex Manufacturing Company; Southeastern Metal Products, Inc.

Further Reading

Armstrong, Michael W., "Berger Holdings Slips Into Chapter 11," *Philadelphia Business Journal*, December 16, 1991, p. 1.
"Berger Bros Achieves Milestone 125 Years Supplying Quality Roof Drainage Products," *Building and Remodelng News,* October 1998, pp. 12–13.
"Berger to Be Bought by Georgia Firm Euramax," *Philadelphia Inquirer,* October 14, 2003.
"Euramax International, Inc. Completes Acquisition of Berger Holdings, Ltd.," *Financial News,* November 25, 2003.
Stone, Adam, "Berger Refocuses, Extends Its Geographic Reach," *Philadelphia Business Journal*, April 28, 2003.

—Gloria A. Lemieux

Black Diamond Equipment, Ltd.

2084 East 3900 South
Salt Lake City, Utah 84124
U.S.A.
Telephone: (801) 278-5552
Fax: (801) 278-5544
Web site: http://www.bdel.com

Private Company
Incorporated: 1989
Employees: 285
Sales: $36 million (2001)
NAIC: 339920 Sporting and Athletic Goods Manufacturing

Black Diamond Equipment, Ltd. (BDEL) specializes in designing and manufacturing mountaineering and backcountry skiing gear. It has broadened its markets somewhat by adding a popular line of headlamps, though it has eschewed such traditional brand extensions as clothing. The word ''passion'' is often associated with BDEL, and most of the company's employees are enthusiastic users of its products. In 1991, Black Diamond relocated from the California seaside to Salt Lake City, where the nearby Wasatch Mountains offer a great testing ground. Black Diamond pitches its goods through an elaborate catalog. Product lines include crampons, ice picks, ice screws, pitons, carabiners, backpacks, gloves, helmets, headlamps, telemark skis and bindings, and the AvaLung, an avalanche safety device.

Origins

Yvon Chouinard was born in French-speaking Lisbon, Maine, and moved with his family to California at the age of eight. Some years later, the young climber bought a book on blacksmithing, an anvil, and a coal-fired forge—spending less than $100—and soon after graduating from high school began making his own pitons (spikes for wedging into crevasses) out of hardened (chrome molybdenum) steel. Fellow climbers loved Chouinard's pitons because they could be reused repeatedly, allowing them to scale higher walls. In 1957, Chouinard visited top climbing spots around the country, selling pitons from the trunk of his car.

With $832 borrowed from his parents, Chouinard acquired aluminum forging equipment and began producing his own design of carabiner, a hooking link used to secure climbing ropes. Chouinard Equipment products were soon being distributed regionally via speciality stores such as the tiny North Face chain.

Forbes reported Chouinard was also working as a part-time detective for his brother, Jeff, who led Howard Hughes' security operation. After a tour of Korea in the Army, in 1966 Chouinard and his partner Thomas Frost set up shop in a tin shack next to a Ventura, California, slaughterhouse.

In 1969, Chouinard began making ice axes with curved picks, a popular innovation which increased their utility on different surfaces. Products were marketed to potential customers via a mailed list. At that time, Chouinard dominated the minuscule climbing gear market in the United States.

The corporate entity Great Pacific Iron Works Inc. was created by Chouinard in 1973. A line of clothing, Patagonia Outdoor Apparel, grew from the very successful import of some Scottish rugby shirts in 1974.

The cumulative effects of Chouinard's original product began to hammer at the company's environmental conscience, the result of numbers of the pitons being left behind in the rock. Consequently, Chouinard became an advocate of ''clean'' climbing that made use of such products as its Hexentrics and Stoppers nuts. The company introduced the first tubular ice screw in the late 1970s.

While Patagonia grew, Chouinard Equipment shrank to only six employees by 1982; sales were about $1 million a year. Peter Metcalf was hired as marketing and sales manager in 1982 and was made general manager within a year. Lost Arrow Corporation was created in 1984 as holding for the Chouinard-related businesses. Under Metcalf, sales reached $7 million by 1987, he told *Inc.*, and the company employed 60 people. By the end of the decade, annual revenues were $9 million.

Around this time, the company began hiring Beal Ropes of France to produce ropes under the Black Diamond brand. After

15 years, Black Diamond dropped its own brand of rope, becoming a distributor of Beal-branded ropes instead.

Climbing increased in popularity in the 1980s, bringing a number of novices into the sport. Chouinard Equipment was eventually forced into bankruptcy by lawsuits alleging not that it made defective equipment but that it failed to warn customers of the fact that rock climbing was dangerous. The company filed for Chapter 11 bankruptcy on April 17, 1989.

Black Diamond Created in 1989

Chouinard's former employees created Black Diamond Equipment, Ltd. on December 1, 1989, acquiring the assets of their one-time employer in a leveraged buyout. The Black Diamond name and symbol were reminiscent of Chouinard Equipment's diamond-C trademark. The buyout was structured along the lines of an employee ownership plan. Forty staffers bought in; financial support also came from rope supplier Michael Beal and Japanese distributor Naoe Sakashita.

One of the employees was Peter Metcalf, who had attained the position of general manager of Chouinard Equipment before the company went under. Unlike his old boss, Metcalf was not attached to California's surfing scene, and Black Diamond soon began looking for a new home. Access to an airport with customs capabilities was important.

In 1991, BDEL relocated from California to Salt Lake City. The company originally planned to move to Park City, on the other side of the nearby Wasatch mountain range, but the developer's financing collapsed. Subsequently, Metcalf decided to locate the company in a kitschy, abandoned shopping center that was styled in the fashion of Bavarian chalets and situated on the East Bench of the Salt Lake Valley. (It was formerly the home of Engh Floral.) Metcalf paid a little over $1 million for a seven-acre property that would include the company's offices, manufacturing, warehousing, and an outlet store. The new location offered a convenient testing ground for climbing and skiing gear, as well as a great location to find and recruit knowledgeable experts in relevant sports.

Black Diamond had 48 employees and revenues of $7 million in 1991, reported *Inc.* About one-third of sales at the time came from backcountry skiing products, reported the *Salt Lake Tribune*. In the first half of the 1980s, Chouinard had developed two new bindings for telemark skiing.

Most of Black Diamond's climbing equipment was produced at its Salt Lake City headquarters, while facilities in Italy supplied shoes, boots, and ropes, and a Texas subcontractor, Flatland Mountaineering, produced climbing harnesses. Black Diamond was the second-largest producer of carabiners in the world, noted the *Tribune*. The company hired another Utah firm, Chums Ltd., to install custom automation equipment to speed up its carabiner production in 1992. The company also had its own automated sewing operation.

Black Diamond developed a line of plastic telemark ski boots, called Terminator, in conjunction with SCARPA of Italy in 1992. International sales accounted for 15 percent of total revenues, with the fastest growth coming from Asia.

Continued Growth through Innovation and Acquisitions

Sales grew quickly in the early 1990s, exceeding $20 million in 1995, when the company had 200 employees. Metcalf was named "Utah Small Business Person of the Year" by the U.S. Small Business Administration. Recreational Equipment Inc. (REI) picked Black Diamond as its "Vendor Partner of the Year" over 1700 other companies. Metcalf wrote an inspirational article for *Inc.* magazine about how the value of training, teamwork, and commitment carried over from the world of climbing to the world of business. Chouinard had also written on the value of dedication, commitment, and confidence in both fields.

Todd Bibler sold the high altitude tent-making business he had founded to Black Diamond in 1996 in order to cope with competition from large companies. Bibler Tents was relocated from Boulder, Colorado, to Black Diamond's Salt Lake headquarters. Franklin Climbing Equipment, a small, eight-person maker of holds for climbing walls based in Seattle, merged with Black Diamond in 1998.

By the end of the decade, Metcalf told *Inc.*, Black Diamond had 250 employees and annual revenues of $30 million. Black Diamond began leasing a new warehouse in Salt Lake's Ninigret Park in 2000. BDEL also updated its electronic distribution systems and opened a branch office in Switzerland.

Through acquisitions, Black Diamond was expanding its range of products, particularly those related to backcountry skiing gear. It acquired the Ascension line of climbing skins (attached to skis to provide traction when scaling slopes). Skye Alpine Inc., a manufacturer of ski bindings and climbing skins, was acquired in the spring of 2002. In 2000, Black Diamond began selling LED headlamps designed for backpackers as well as climbers and skiers. These soon became one of the company's best-selling items.

Among Black Diamond's employees was Alex Lowe, whom *Outside Magazine* had dubbed the world's best climber. He died in an avalanche in October 1999. Lowe and other BDEL employees had been known to rise in the wee hours of the morning to hit the backcountry slopes before work.

```
┌─────────────────────────────────────────────┐
│                 Key Dates:                    │
│                                               │
│  1958:  Chouinard Equipment is formed in Ven-│
│         tura, California.                     │
│  1989:  Black Diamond (BDEL) is created from │
│         bankrupt Chouinard Equipment.        │
│  1991:  BDEL relocates to Salt Lake City.    │
│  1992:  Terminator ski boot is developed with│
│         SCARPA of Italy.                      │
│  1996:  Bibler Tents is acquired.            │
│  1998:  Franklin Climbing Equipment becomes  │
│         part of BDEL.                         │
│  2000:  LED headlamps are introduced; a new  │
│         warehouse is opened.                  │
│  2001:  AvaLung II is introduced.            │
│  2002:  Skye Alpine is acquired.             │
└─────────────────────────────────────────────┘
```

Several other Black Diamond employees had been lost to avalanches over the years, so it was natural that the company's next big product would be an avalanche safety device. The AvaLung was a vest with a network of porous tubes that deployed in the event of an avalanche, allowing the user to breathe air from the snowpack. It was invented by Denver psychiatry professor and backcountry skiing enthusiast Tom Crowley. Black Diamond spent a half million dollars making the design practical.

The first version retailed between $200 and $300. The lighter, smaller, and, at $100, cheaper AvaLung II was introduced in 2001. It was credited with saving a skier trapped for half an hour under five feet of snow in February 2002. Black Diamond was one of ten Utah companies honored with an Entrepreneur of the Year award in 2002.

Principal Subsidiaries

Black Diamond Equipment AG (Switzerland).

Principal Divisions

Ascension Enterprises; Beal Ropes; Bibler Tents; Franklin Climbing Equipment; Scarpa Mountain Boots.

Principal Competitors

Backcountry Access LLC; Entre Prises USA Inc.; Metolius Mountain Products; Petzl America; Voilé Mountain Equipment.

Further Reading

Aurand, Anne, "Couple Finds Success Making Climbing-Gym Holds," *Associated Press Newswires*, March 19, 1999.

——, "Climbing-Hold Business Is Looking Up," *Seattle Times*, April 3, 1999, p. C8.

Barker, Emily, "The Best Cities in America for Starting and Growing a Business," *Inc.*, December 1, 1999, p. 67.

Benson, Lee, "A Lifesaving Use for . . . Pantyhose?" *Deseret News* (Salt Lake City), February 1, 1999, p. B1.

——, "Mountaineer 'Reset the Standard,'" *Deseret News*, October 25, 1999, p. B1.

"Black Diamond Absorbs Skye Bindings, Skins," *Outdoor Retailer*, June 2002, p. 18.

"Black Diamond Born of a Shared Vision," *Deseret News*, June 9, 2002, p. M3.

Boulton, Guy, "AvaLung Ski-Safety Device Evolves into Lighter, More Affordable Product," *Denver Post*, October 13, 2002.

——, "Black Diamond No. 1 in Climbing Equipment; Salt Lake Company Growing Fast," *Denver Post*, October 13, 2002, p. K3.

Bryson, Robert, "At End of Rope, Climbing Firm Gets Chums' Help," *Salt Lake Tribune*, June 27, 1992, p. B5.

Carton, Barbara, "Spate of Avalanches Sparks Demand for Survival Gear," *Wall Street Journal*, April 5, 1999, p. B1.

Case, John, "Corporate Culture (How It Can Improve Company Performance)," *Inc.*, November 1, 1996, p. 42.

Dowell, T.R., "Outdoor-Gear Firm Happy with Move to Utah," *Salt Lake Tribune*, November 17, 1991, p. D12.

Edwards, Bob, "Profile: Patagonia Clothing Company and Founder Yvon Chouinard," *NPR: Morning Edition*, November 12, 2002.

Fahys, Judy, "S.L. President Helps Black Diamond Climb to Top of Equipment Summit; Mountains Are Moving for Black Diamond," *Salt Lake Tribune*, April 30, 1995, p. F1.

Foy, Paul, "Salt Lake City Mecca for Outdoor Gear," *Dayton Daily News* (Ohio), October 21, 2000, p. 1E.

Gorrell, Mike, "Avalanche-Safety Products Featured at Utah Winter Market," *Salt Lake Tribune*, February 1, 2003.

Groves, Martha, "The Rockies Are on a Roll as a Magnet for Business Enterprise," *Omaha World-Herald*, April 11, 1993, p. 1M.

Hansell, Craig, "Skiers Seek Backcountry Bindings," *Salt Lake Tribune*, January 20, 1992, p. C6.

Hawken, Paul, *Growing a Business*, New York: Fireside, 1988.

Hwang, Suein L., Christina Duff, and Christy Hobart, "Now Here's a Sport That's Got People Climbing the Walls," *Wall Street Journal Europe*, March 12, 1992, p. 1.

Jones, Lara, "Sports Equipment Firm to Undertake $3 Million Expansion," *Enterprise* (Salt Lake City), Sec. 1, July 25, 1994, p. 1.

——, "Black Diamond Equipment to Move Tent Maker's Operations to Utah," *Enterprise* (Salt Lake City), September 2, 1996, p. 3.

Knudson, Max B., "Black Diamond Equipment Owner Named Top Small-Business Person," *Deseret News*, April 26, 1995, p. D7.

——, "Black Diamond Carves Sizable Niche in World of Rocks, Mountainsides," *Deseret News*, May 21, 1995, p. M1.

"Labors of Love—with Mixed Results," *Inc.*, July 1, 1998, p. 21.

Lloyd, Jennifer, "Patagonia's Yvon Chouinard Scaled New Heights by Turning His Passion into a Business," *Investor's Business Daily*, May 9, 2001, p. A4.

McHugh, Paul, "The Retooling of Chouinard Equipment," *San Francisco Chronicle*, March 19, 1990, p. E1.

——, "Discipline, Courage, Tenacity, Concentration; When Outdoorsmen Go into Business, They Bring Along the Same Survival Skills," *San Francisco Chronicle*, December 22, 1985, p. 9.

McHugh, Paul, and Dan Giesin, "Insurance Woes Hit Climbing," *San Francisco Chronicle*, May 8, 1989, p. E1.

Maffly, Brian, "AvaLung's Maker Promises Life After Avalanche Burial," *Salt Lake Tribune*, February 19, 1999, p. B1.

——, "The Breath of Life," *Salt Lake Tribune*, March 11, 2002, p. D1.

——, "AvaLung Debut Yields Slow Sales, But Avalanche of Recognition," *Salt Lake Tribune*, June 6, 2000, p. B5.

——, "Anchors Aweigh! Climbers Tout Removable Bolts as Green Option," *Salt Lake Tribune*, August 8, 2000, p. C3.

——, "Avalanche Just Missed Salt Laker," *Salt Lake Tribune*, October 7, 1999, p. A1.

"Maker of Mountain Gear to Locate in Park City," *Salt Lake Tribune*, October 12, 1990, p. D5.

"Manufacturers Are Looking for Less Hostile Packaging," *Outdoor Retailer*, August 2002, p. 76.

Meeks, Fleming, "The Man Is the Message," *Forbes*, April 17, 1989, p. 148.

"Mention of Honor," *Salt Lake Tribune*, December 1, 1998, p. C2.

Metcalf, Peter, "Lessons Learned (How a Mountain Climbing Experience Helped Build a Business)," *Inc.*, April 1, 1995, p. 35.

Mitchell, Lesley, "Building Out of the Box," *Salt Lake Tribune*, August 24, 2003, p. E1.

Neal, Victoria, "Stayin' Alive," *Entrepreneur Magazine*, October 1, 1999.

O'Brien, Joan, "New Breed Puts Sporting Life into Utah Manufacturing," *Salt Lake Tribune*, May 23, 1993, p. E1.

Osborne, Steve, and Kristina Kunzi, "Adventure Capitalists," *Utah Business*, May 2001, p. 30.

"Picking the Right Alloy to Scale the Heights," *Materials World*, June 12, 1998, p. 332.

Van De Mark, Donald, and Susan Lisovicz, "Mt. Climbing Mogul," *CNNfn: Business Unusual*, February 10, 1998.

Venn, Tamsin, "Employees to Buy Chouinard," *STN*, August 1, 1989, p. 4.

"View from the Top," *World Trade*, August 1, 1994, p. 18.

Walzer, Emily, "Diamond in the Rough: Black Diamond Shines," *Sporting Goods Business*, March 1, 2000, p. 18.

Woolf, Marcus, "Black Diamond Ups Ante in Headlamp Market," *Outdoor Retailer*, August 2002, p. 78.

—Frederick C. Ingram

Bogen Communications International, Inc.

50 Spring Street
Ramsey, New Jersey
U.S.A.
Telephone: (201) 934-8500
Toll Free: (800) 999-2809
Fax: (201) 934-9832
Web site: http://www.bogen.com

Public Company
Incorporated: 1932 as David Bogen & Company, Inc.
Employees: 240
Sales: $59.1 million (2002)
Stock Exchanges: Over the Counter (OTC)
Ticker Symbol: BOGN
NAIC: 334210 Telephone and Telegraph Apparatus
Manufacturing; 334290 Communication Equipment,
Not Elsewhere Classified; 334310 Audio and Video
Equipment Manufacturing

With headquarters in New Jersey, Bogen Communications International, Inc., develops, manufactures, and markets telecommunications and audio products for offices, businesses, and schools. The company's product line includes amplifiers, speakers, background music equipment, sound processing equipment. Its European operations (through Speech Design GmbH, a German company with subsidiaries in Switzerland and Israel) develop, manufacture, and distribute voicemail systems as well as unified messaging digital voice-processing systems. Through these operations, in fact, Bogen holds a leading position in European telephony markets; in the United States, these product lines have gained a significant market share in the school intercom, signaling, and media-control segments.

Early History

Little has been published on the history of Bogen, making it a challenge to trace. The company was founded as David Bogen & Company in 1932 in New York by David Bogen, a pioneer in the burgeoning field of audio transmission. Among the company's first products were simple intercom systems and sound amplifiers.

By the early 1950s, the company had become well-known as a supplier of amplifiers and public address systems for schools. In 1956, Bogen was acquired by the Unitronics Corporation, a Long Island, New York-based leader in sound recording. During this time, Unitronics also bought the Presto Recording Corporation, opting to combine its new acquisitions as one division christened Bogen-Presto. From new adjacent facilities in Paramus, New Jersey, Bogen and Presto maintained their corporate autonomy but collaborated in order to tap each other's expertise. Presto was known primarily as the inventor of ''the record'', the black-lacquered recording disc, but the company also developed recording equipment such as turntables and amplifiers. For its part, Bogen and its engineering staff were pioneers in new amplifier and loudspeaker technologies. Assistant Chief Engineer Charles A. Wilkens explored ''damping'' effects on amplifiers, publishing widely on the subject, while colleague Herbert W. Sullivan received a patent on behalf of David Bogen & Co. in 1957 for his loudspeaker designs.

In 1957 Unitronics was acquired by Siegler Corporation, as the latter embarked on a rapid expansion program, acquiring numerous electronics-related companies. Five years later, Siegler merged with aerospace electronics manufacturer Lear to become Lear Siegler Inc.(LSI). Thereafter, the Presto name was dropped, and Bogen became known as LSI's Bogen Communications division.

LSI was involved in contract work for the U.S. military, and Bogen's technologies found a niche in that market. The company also continued to be well known for its amplifiers, particular the Challenger model. By the early 1970s, however, LSI had begun to falter under the weight of its numerous acquisitions, and new management began divesting noncore components. Bogen remained an LSI division, however, until 1987, when Memory Protection Devices Inc., merged with Bogen, paying LSI a reported $9.2 million in cash to assume Bogen's assets and liabilities. By 1991, Bogen had separated from Memory Protection Devices, the founders of which repurchased the company and relocated it to Farmingdale, New York. Bogen, meanwhile, was based in Ramsey, in northern New Jersey.

1990s: Focus on Product Development

In 1991, Bogen introduced the Telco product line, its first line of telecommunications peripherals. The first product was the MMT, a digital announcer with automatic microprocessor-controlled tape download for "on-hold" applications. The following year, Bogen introduced various other products in the digital telephone peripherals area, including the Automated Attendant and the Digital Announcer. These products were used in message/music on-hold and voice mail systems. During 1993, Bogen marketed its Office Automated Systems (OAS) to the retail and end-user markets. However, Bogen met with intense competition on several fronts: answering-service companies; local telephone companies, which offered central-voice mail services; and products with better brand-name recognition selling at lower retail prices. Bogen was forced to phase out OAS and concentrate on expansion of its traditional commercial and institutional customer base.

During this time, a German telecom equipment manufacturer called Speech Design GmbH was engaged primarily in selling peripherals equipment for cellular telephones used within an analog network. With the advent of the European GSM digital standard and the falling prices of ancillary subscriber equipment, Speech Design's management refocused its activities from the cellular market to the telephone peripherals market, and in 1992 introduced products for digital-telephone peripherals. "Friday The Personal/Office Receptionist" offered a competitive edge to small businesses, home offices, and such professionals as painters, roofers, plumbers, electricians, who worked away from their offices. Friday, an efficient version of the voice-mail system used by large corporations, could forward calls, route them to fax machines or computers, alert users to urgent messages, remind them of appointments, provide music-on-hold, as well as manage and screen calls.

In 1995, Bogen and Speech Design came together under a newly organized holding company, first registered in Delaware in 1993 as European Gateway Acquisition Corporation. The holding company acquired a 99 percent interest in Bogen and a 67 percent interest in Speech Design, and then made a public offering of 1.55 million shares, raising $8.12 million in net proceeds. The holding company was christened Bogen Communications International Inc. Speech Design's co-founders, Kasimir Arciszewski and Hans Meiler, retained managerial roles at Speech Design, eventually becoming directors at Bogen Communications.

Bogen's primary focus then shifted to long-term growth. In order to establish an international market presence, Speech Design signed distribution contracts with partners in ten European countries and gained approval in most major markets. This move constituted a coup against significant market-entry barriers to non-European and small European companies.

During the summer of 1996 a manufacturing subsidiary, Speech Design (Israel) Ltd., was opened in Israel to produce some of Speech Design's product line, thereby reducing manufacturing costs and taxes. In 2002, about 45 percent of all units manufactured by Speech Design were produced in the Israel factory.

In 1997, Bogen named Michael P. Fleischer president of the company. Fleischer, a graduate of Harvard's business school, came to Bogen from Ecko/Glaco Ltd. That year, Bogen acquired substantially all the net assets of New England Audio Resources, Inc. (NEAR), a leading manufacturer of high performance, all-environment speakers. NEAR became part of the company's Commercial Sound unit and its products were marketed with Bogen's product lines. During 1997 the company found new innovative solutions for the Telco paging market by developing the pro-Hold DRDX, a digitally produced, remote-downloadable MOH system. The Research and Development Department also developed a call-completion system that incorporated paging, voice messaging, and wireless messaging into one integrated system, the APS 2000.

The following year, Bogen Communications acquired the remaining equity interest in Speech Design, which immediately acquired all of Carrier Systems, located in northern Germany. Carrier Systems developed and manufactured LANs (local area networks) and Internet-based unified messaging products. In 1999 a newly formed Bogen subsidiary—Apogee Sound International LLC—acquired practically all the assets of Petaluma, California-based Apogee Sound Inc.

In the United States, Bogen Corporation developed, manufactured, and distributed commercial telecommunications and audio products and its two major subsidiaries: Bogen Communications, Inc., and Apogee Sound International LLC (Apogee). Although the majority of Bogen's sales were made through U.S. distributors, dealers, and contractors, the company also sold its products in Canada through a stocking representative with offices throughout that country.

Among Bogen's audio products were audio amplifiers and speakers as well as related sound and intercom systems equipment for professional, industrial, and commercial system applications. Other equipment was available for telephone paging systems and for background and foreground music applications. The company also marketed intercom and communications systems for the security and educational markets as well as a line of high-performance, all-environment speakers.

The company's Telco products, namely telephone-based paging systems and equipment and digital message/music-on-hold players, allowed installers to increase the value of their telephone systems by providing users with greater efficiency and convenience. For the 2000–02 fiscal years, Telco's net sales provided approximately 25 percent of the company's net sales. Some 100 distributors who operated 200 telecommunications distribution centers sold Telco products to thousands of

Key Dates:

1932: David Bogen & Co. Inc. is founded in New York.
1956: Bogen is acquired by Unitronics and facilities move to New Jersey.
1962: Bogen becomes a subsidiary of Lear-Siegler.
1991: Bogen Corporation introduces its Telco product line.
1993: A new holding company for Bogen Corporation and a majority share in Speech Design GmbH is formed and goes public.
1998: Bogen Communications acquires full ownership of Speech Design GmbH.

telecommunications installers (''interconnects'' or dealers) throughout North America.

The Commercial Audio product line included amplifiers, speakers, microphones, intercom systems and other sound equipment used in industrial public address systems, and background music in offices, restaurants, hotels, and stores. In 2002, Bogen introduced its new Power Vector modular amplifier series improved by the addition of higher-power and unique plug-in modules.

Apogee's pro audio product line consisted of speakers and speaker systems, amplifiers, processors, and system-balancing equipment for entertainment sound systems. Bogen's Engineered Systems featured custom-assembled, microprocessor-based intercom/paging.

Speech Design International, Inc. (SDI)—a Bogen subsidiary located in Germering (outside Munich), Germany; Wedel, Germany; Richterswil, Switzerland; and Kfar Saba, Israel—developed, manufactured, and marketed voice-mail systems, automated attendants, digital announcers, message-on-hold (MOH) systems and Unified Messaging (UMS) products and services. UMS products and services were part of the Telco product line.

Speech Design's Corporate Voice Processing (''CVP'') line of business focused on digital-voice processing systems for mid-sized Private Branch Exchanges (''PABX'') and was aimed at the European voice-processing market. With the late 1995 launch of a product family called ''Memo,'' Speech Design added innovative non-PC based voice mail systems to its existing line of telecommunication peripheral products: voice-mail, automated attendants, digital announcers, and message/MOH systems. In late 1998, Speech Design marketed the Teleserver Pro range of modular, higher-end (2–8 ports) voice and call-processing peripherals. Equipped with a higher capacity voice-mail than possible with Memo, Teleserver also offered LAN connectivity to PC networks and ACD (automatic call distribution). In 2000 and 2001, Speech Design ported the functions of its standard voicemail product on a single electronic board that thus became a major customer's PABX. In late 2002, the Teleserver family added MobilePro, thereby integrating mobile workers' cellular telephones with their office PABX.

In 1999, Speech Design added Unified Messaging products services to its flagship Thor (TM) series. This series improved communications within any enterprise and delivered value-added services to Internet Service Providers (ISPs) as well as to mobile and fixed-line network operators (carriers). Thor also could integrate fax and voice-mail into an existing e-mail environment, and integrate e-mail and fax into the mobile-phone environment.

The European voice-processing market for commercial and industrial end-users was the general market to which Speech Design offered its PABX products through leading European manufacturers. Most German clients were mid-size companies (50–200 employees) or major independent dealers outside Germany. Speech Design considered its sales network in Germany—Europe's largest telecommunication market—to be one of its best assets and a market-entry barrier to potential competitors. From 2001 and through 2003, several major international carriers implemented voice-mail platforms based on Thor's universal architecture: Deutsche Telekom, Europe's largest telephone company; TDC (formerly TeleDanmark), Denmark's leading telephone company; international operator Vodacom in South Africa; and the largest French wireless operator, Orange France.

2002 and Beyond

During 2002, Bogen introduced still more products, including the Power Vector (PV) family of modular input amplifiers adaptable for all Bogen divisions but aimed primarily at the commercial audio customer. This product line consisted of five amplifier power levels from 35 watts to 250 watts and 11 different input modules which could be installed into any of the eight input channels of the amplifiers. The PV amplifier models also could accommodate any of three specialized plug-in modules to eliminate expensive external-signal processing equipment.

In February 2002, Apogee finished development of a new high-powered amplifier, the CA-8000, also designed for fixed application. In April 2002, Bogen announced a new line of NEAR ceiling speakers—known as Orbit products and designed to satisfy the needs of higher-end business application of music for hospitality, restaurants, and retail stores. NEAR's ceiling speakers had a full-range pendant speaker for open space applications, a powered compact subwoofer, and a compact satellite speaker. Bogen began production of two members—the ceiling and pendant speakers—of the four-line concept family in preparation for sales in early 2003. The speakers used NEAR metal alloy cones and patented magnetic liquid suspension (MLS) technology that provided highly linear and accurate speaker response and superior speaker cooling for higher-power speakers. Both the Power Vector amplifier series mentioned above and the NEAR speakers were targeted to the medium/large segment of systems-contractors.

The company introduced its VHub teleconferencing device in late 2002 as another product of the Telco line. Over and above providing high quality and full duplex operation, the VHub had a LCD display and a 10-number speed dial. In February 2002 Vodacom, operator of the South African Cellular network, chose Speech Design Carrier Systems' Thor solution and Compaq Global Services to deliver mobile SMS to any traditional, fixed-line telephone; Thor software on Compaq's Telco servers called the fixed-line number and used text-to-speech technology to read the message.

By the end of fiscal 2002, Bogen Communications International, Inc. had survived almost two years of turbulence in the industries in which it competed, according to Bogen President and Chief Executive Officer Jonathan Guss. "2002 proved to be a pivotal year for Bogen," he stated in the company's *Annual Report*. However, "despite the general recession, sales increased over [those of] 2001, while costs were kept under tight control." He added that through a self-tender offer, 4.2 million shares of Bogen stock were bought back during the third quarter of 2002 and a major part of the cash borrowed to facilitate the tender offer was repaid. Demand for United States-based products began to recover but Speech Design's voicemail business continued "to suffer from the malaise affecting the European telecommunications sector."

On November 10, 2003, the Bogen Corporation announced the beginning of a tender offer for two million shares of its common stock at a price per share of $5.00. The purpose was to offer liquidity to stockholders who wanted to exit at a fair price and to create value for the stockholders who chose to keep their shares in Bogen. During a conference call, the company said that following the buyback (its third in three years), it would deregister and delist from NASDAQ. Bogen common stock would then cease to be quoted on the NASDAQ or the OTC Bulletin Board and probably be quoted only on the "pink sheets." This step reflected the hard fact that for Bogen, as for many other small companies, the advantages of NASDAQ registration were outweighed by the costs and the administrative burden.

Bogen continued to keep a very open eye on costs and tight control on overhead spending. During the third quarter, revenue increased in every domestic business, compared to the comparable quarter of the preceding year; there were improvements in the OEM business but, unfortunately, new products took a long time to penetrate the market. Engineered Systems revenues were up just slightly, compared to the those of the 2002 third quarter; a probable indication that state and local government spending was slightly loosening up.

In Europe, the telecommunications-equipment markets served by Speech Design were still depressed; both of the company's business lines,—corporate voice processing and Carrier Unified Messaging—reported a weak third quarter.

However, taking into account some large orders scheduled for fourth-quarter delivery, Speech Design hoped for major revenue improvement in the last quarter. Another source of hope was that Speech Design had established new relationships and installations with seven major carriers in six countries, including Deutsche Telecom, its flagship customer.

With new products, restructuring according to technological advances, and an established and efficient cost structure, Bogen was well positioned for profit—if 2003 business and economic conditions continued to improve, and if product revenues continued to increase.

Principal Subsidiaries

Apogee Sound International LLC; Bogen Communications (Barbados), Ltd.; Bogen Communications, Inc.; Bogen Communications LLC; Satelco AG (Germany); Speech Design (Israel) Ltd.; Speech Design Carrier Systems GmbH (Germany); Speech Design GmbH (Germany); Speech Design International, Inc.; Thor USA.

Principal Competitors

ADC Telecommunications, Inc.; Avaya Inc.; Cycos AG; Gores Technology Group; Nortel Networks Corporation; Polycom Inc.

Further Reading

"Apogee Sound Purchased by Bogen Communications," *Entertainment Design,* November 1999, p. 23.

"Bogen Communications International Inc. Buys Back Shares," *New York Times,* June 25, 2002, p. C4.

"Bogen Communications International Inc.," *Wall Street Journal,* January 19, 1996, p. B2.

Eng, Paul M., "An Electronic Receptionist for the Home Office," *Business Week,* May 24, 1993, p. 13.

"Geotek to Sell Its Bogen Communications Stake," *New York Times,* November 8, 1997, p. B3.

Laderman, Jeffrey M, "Big Noise on the Continent," *Business Week,* May 22, 2000, p. 181.

"TGIF," *Popular Mechanics,* June 1994, pp. 54–6.

—Gloria A. Lemieux

Bou-Matic

1919 South Stoughton Road
Madison, Wisconsin 53716-2259
U.S.A.
Telephone: (608) 222-3484
Fax: (608) 222-9314
Web site: http://www.bou-matic.com

Private Company
Incorporated: 1939
Employees: 380
Sales: $91.2 million (2002 est.)
NAIC: 333111 Farm Machinery and Equipment
Manufacturing

Headquartered in Madison, Wisconsin, Bou-Matic is a leading dairy equipment manufacturer that serves both domestic and international markets. The company's products include automated milking systems, bulk cooling tanks, integrated computerized management systems, and more.

Origins

Bou-Matic's history can be traced to 1939, when Lawrence Bouma established Bou-Matic Milkers, Inc. in Ontario, California. The new enterprise manufactured a line of milking machines for the dairy industry. According to the company, "the Bou-Matic milking system was scientifically designed for efficient milking while at the same time being gentle to the cow."

Bou-Matic quickly established a good reputation within the dairy industry. By 1956, the company operated from a location at 1126 West Mission Boulevard in Ontario, distributing equipment via its Bouma Distributor Agency. Bou-Matic continued operations from the site on Mission Boulevard until 1959, when it relocated to 12375 Euclid Avenue.

Bou-Matic's next move was significantly further afield. In 1961, the company was acquired by Madison, Wisconsin-based Dairy Equipment Company. As part of the acquisition, Bou-Matic relocated its manufacturing operations to Madison. A

Clintonville, Wisconsin, veterinarian named John C. Dahl, who would later become Bou-Matic's president, played a significant role in Dairy Equipment's acquisition of the small California firm. After learning about Bou-Matic Milkers at a seminar, Dahl became friends with founder Lawrence Bouma. Also during this time, he also served as a consultant to the Dairy Equipment Company. As columnist John Oncken explained in the April 25, 2002, issue of the *Capital Times*, Dahl's "interest and research into the new milking system was a major influence in the purchase of Bou-Matic Milkers." In addition, the Bou-Matic system was a complement to Dairy Equipment's existing Kari-Kool and Dari-Kool product lines. Dairy Equipment started to market Bou-Matic's equipment throughout the United States in 1962, and the solid reputation Bou-Matic had enjoyed in California spread accordingly.

Bou-Matic and the Dairy Equipment Company had similar histories. In addition to being in the same industry, both firms were founded in the late 1930s. Dairy Equipment was the brainchild of Gilmon F. Albrecht, a law graduate from the University of Wisconsin-Madison who worked for the James Manufacturing Company in Fort Atkinson, Wisconsin, before deciding to start his own company in 1938. His enterprise, a wholesale and retail distributorship, achieved rapid growth early on. The company expanded to serve customers in 11 states by 1947, at which time it was incorporated.

Albrecht was a true industry pioneer. As the Bou-Matic Web site noted: "Albrecht saw many problems and inefficiencies in the can system being used for handling milk at the time. Can-type milk coolers required the dairy farmer to lift a full can of milk over the sides of the cooler to place it inside the refrigerated compartment—a backbreaking job for even the strongest individual. Dairy Equipment Company designed a cooler with an open front so the milk can could be slid inside. This open-front can cooler was well received and the Dari-Kool line of milk cooling equipment was born." Albrecht proceeded to develop Dari-Kool bulk milk coolers in 1951, which made the use of milk cans unnecessary.

Following its acquisition of Bou-Matic, Dairy Equipment continued to grow and succeed. In 1969, it reorganized and formed a holding company called DEC International, Inc. Following the restructuring, Bou-Matic became a DEC International subsidiary.

New Directions in the 1970s

By 1970, the manufacture of Bou-Matic Milkers had been moved to the Truax Plant—a 60,000-square-foot airplane hanger leased from the City of Madison for ten years. In addition to Bou-Matic Milkers, Dari-Kool milk coolers also were manufactured in the plant. DEC obtained the new plant because of strong growth within its special products division, which made custom fabricated stainless steel products for a number of different industries. In 1971, John C. Dahl became Bou-Matic's president, a position he would retain until 1983.

In addition to Bou-Matic and the flagship Dairy Equipment Company, by the early 1980s DEC International had grown to include a number of other different enterprises, including Alkar; Berg Company; Bowman Dairy; Damrow Company; and Falls Dairy Company. Falls Dairy, which was at the time among the nation's largest producers of bulk cheese, accounted for approximately half of DEC's 1982 sales, which totaled $250 million.

By the early 1980s, technological advancements within the dairy sector had changed the industry significantly. DEC's Bou-Matic arm was at the forefront of producing computerized equipment that made farmer's lives easier and their operations more efficient. In the November 27, 1983, issue of the *Wisconsin State Journal*, columnist Joe Beck described the latest milking devices on the market, some of which used microprocessors to determine when a cow was finished milking and automatically detach from her udders. Beck explained: "Some of the newest systems now include computerized equipment that automatically checks, records and analyzes milk production. The computers record information on the production of each cow as it is milked and list cows in the herd in order of average individual production. A deviation report identified cows that have dropped below their average production. Eight other reports available from the new systems keep track of information, such as each cow's reproductive status, and summarize the day's total herd production."

Bou-Matic had evolved into a truly international business by the mid-1990s. By that time, the company attributed some 40 percent of its sales to international customers, a percentage that was expected to increase. As of late 1994, Bou-Matic had divisions in several different countries including Australia, England, France, Israel, Japan, and Saudi Arabia. At that time, the company was also pursuing markets in Korea and Taiwan.

Dairy cooperatives in Argentina represented an especially lucrative market for Bou-Matic, due to demand for the com-

pany's refrigerated milk tanks, which held anywhere from 600 to 2,000 gallons of milk and sold from $8,000–$17,000 apiece. Projections indicated that Bou-Matic would sell some 400 of its coolers to Argentina in 1995. Other South American countries, including Brazil, Chile, and Uruguay, also represented promising markets.

Despite its relatively strong international presence, Bou-Matic followed what some observers considered a conservative international expansion plan. As columnist Anita Weler explained in the December 29, 1994, issue of the *Capital Times*, the "company adds no more than three or four countries a year to its market base, in order to properly train distributors in installation, service and use of equipment."

By the late 1990s, Paul Thompson was serving as Bou-Matic's president. The company had made remarkable progress since the 1970s, benefiting from roughly 20 years of 10-percent annual sales increases. Sales were roughly $80 million in 1997, about 60 percent of which came from outside the United States. These revenues accounted for more than half of DEC International's sales, which were reported at $150 million that year.

By 1998, Bou-Matic employed 400 workers and held more than 200 patents related to dairy technology. This number continued to increase as Bou-Matic developed more high-tech products that helped farmers do their jobs more quickly and efficiently. One example was an electronic identification collar that transmitted such data as milking time and milk weight to the dairy manager's computer, where it could be stored in a database.

Another product developed during the late 1990s was actually a new attempt at something the dairy industry had tried during the 1920s, and again in the 1970s. In 1998 Bou-Matic was preparing to reintroduce rotary milking parlors, which involve cows lining up on a moving carousel for milking. Ranging in price from roughly $200,000 to more than $1 million, the best rotary parlors gave one or two technicians the ability to milk as many as 500 cows per hour.

Innovation at Bou-Matic continued into the 2000s. In mid-2000 the company was working in cooperation with a European firm to introduce robotic milking equipment to U.S. dairy farmers, once government regulations were met. Columnist Rick Barrett explained how the high-tech equipment worked in the July 29, 2000, issue of the *Wisconsin State Journal*: "With the equipment, cows will be able to milk themselves. The high-tech bovine, wearing a computer chip in her collar for identification, approaches a milking machine several times a day. A robot equipped with laser sensors preps the cow for milking by disinfecting her teats, and then does the milking—all in a few minutes." According to Barrett, one robot was capable of milking some 65 cows per day.

New product introductions continued during 2001. That year, Bou-Matic began distributing HydraFeed, a milk substitute produced by HYPRED/A&L Laboratories that was used to remedy dehydrated young calves. The company also introduced its Flo-Star Supreme Claw, a durable plastic milking unit intended for use in large dairy operations.

Headed by President Robert Kmoch, by the early 2000s Bou-Matic was widely recognized as an industry leader. In the

Key Dates:

1939: Lawrence Bouma establishes Bou-Matic Milkers, Inc. in Ontario, California.
1956: Bou-Matic operates from a new location in Ontario and distributes equipment via its Bouma Distributor Agency.
1961: Bou-Matic is acquired by Madison, Wisconsin-based Dairy Equipment Company and relocates to Madison.
1969: Bou-Matic becomes a subsidiary of the newly-formed holding company DEC International, Inc.
1997: Annual sales reach some $80 million, 60 percent of which derives from outside the United States.
2001: Bou-Matic parent DEC International files for Chapter 11 reorganization.
2002: DEC sells Bou-Matic to Houston businessman John P. Kotts for $32 million.

April 25, 2002, issue of the *Capital Times*, columnist John Oncken referred to the firm as "one of the 'big three' in terms of manufacturing and marketing of milking systems and bulk tanks to dairy farmers."

However, at the same time, Bou-Matic parent DEC International was in trouble, having filed for Chapter 11 reorganization in August 2001. Within the industry, many observers predicted that DEC would shed several of its 16 companies and retain Bou-Matic.

New Beginnings: 2002 and Beyond

Instead of rebuilding around Bou-Matic, DEC sold the company to Houston businessman John P. Kotts and his Madison One Holdings company for $32 million in 2002. According to *The Daily Deal*, after receiving the green light from Chief Judge Robert D. Martin of the U.S. Bankruptcy Court for the Western District of Wisconsin, Kotts paid $22 million in cash for Bou-Matic, along with a promissory note to cover the $10 million balance.

In Oncken's April 25, 2002, *Capital Times* article, DEC International Chairman Randal Albrecht, grandson of founder Gilmon F. Albrecht, commented on the circumstances that prompted the company's demise, explaining: "Mad cow disease in Europe brought the dairy business to a standstill. A currency devaluation and energy crisis brought the Brazil economy to a stop, and a period of very low milk prices in the U.S. in 2000 slowed dairy expansion. And a slowing economy hurt many of our subsidiaries. Banks get nervous when business

slows down and debt mounts. Even though we never missed a payment, the bank pulled the plug. It's a terrible financial blow for our family."

Kotts, who brought in a financial officer to address the company's challenges, was new to the dairy industry. His previous experience—as both an investor and business owner—was largely tied to the oil industry, especially in the Gulf of Mexico region. Following his purchase of Bou-Matic, Kotts became the company's chairman and CEO. According to various news accounts, Kotts bought the company because he was impressed with its products, employees, structure, market position, and potential for growth.

Bou-Matic continued introducing new products after Kotts took the helm, including software that dairy farmers could use to monitor herds via hand-held computers. In August 2003, Bou-Matic began marketing pulsation-monitoring equipment for dairy farmers under the brand name Pulse-O-Rater. According to *Feedstuffs*, the new equipment was "engineered to monitor dairy pulsation equipment around-the-clock and detect changes or malfunctions in pulsation systems." Under new leadership, Bou-Matic remained positioned for success. Despite challenging conditions that led to the demise of its once venerable parent company, the future appeared to be a bright one.

Principal Competitors

WestfaliaSurge, Inc.

Further Reading

Barrett, Rick, "Carousel for Cows Making a Comeback," *Wisconsin State Journal*, March 26, 1998.
Barrett, Rick, "Farmers Might Be Able to Catch Some More Zs," *Wisconsin State Journal*, July 29, 2000.
Beck, Joe, "Automation Eases Framstead Chores," *Wisconsin State Journal*, November 27, 1983.
Berke, Jonathan, "Kotts Wins DEC International," *Daily Deal*, September 5, 2002.
Kades, Deborah, "Bou-Matic Rebounds with New Owner," *Wisconsin State Journal*, October 4, 2002.
Oncken, John, "Bou-Matic Sale Marks End to Family's Reign," *Capital Times*, April 25, 2002.
Parkins, Al, "DEC International More Than a Name," *Capital Times*, April 9, 1982.
"Release of HydraFeed," *Feedstuffs*, September 3, 2001.
Weier, Anita, "Cowabunga! Madison Milk Tanks In Demand Globally," *Capital Times*, December 29, 1994.
Welch, Lynn, "New Era at Bou-Matic. New Texas Owner Promises Hands-Off Approach," *Capital Times*, October 4, 2002.
"What's New," *Feedstuffs*, August 25, 2003.
Wilcox, JoAnn, "Positive ID," *Successful Farming*, May-June 1998.

—Paul R. Greenland

Build-A-Bear Workshop Inc.

1954 Innerbelt Business Center Drive
St. Louis, Missouri 63114
U.S.A.
Telephone: (314) 423-8000
Toll Free: (888) 789-2327
Fax: (314) 423-8188
Web site: http://www.buildabear.com

Private Company
Incorporated: 1997
Employees: 1,800
Sales: 170 million (2002 est.)
NAIC: 451120 Hobby, Toy, and Game Stores

Located in upscale, family-oriented shopping malls, Build-A-Bear Workshop Inc. owns and operates more than 150 stores in 35 states in the United States and three provinces in Canada. Retail store developments in Europe and Asia occur through franchise agreement. Build-A-Bear Workshop offers a unique retail entertainment experience in providing children of all ages an opportunity to participate in the creation of a personalized teddy bear or other stuffed animal. Customers, referred to as Guest Bear-Builders, walk along The Bearway and stop at stations in a process of teddy bear construction. At the Choose Me station customers select a toy animal "skin" from a variety of colors and sizes. At the Hear Me station patrons can choose to have a sound microchip placed inside the stuffed animal. The next stop is the Stuff Me station where they decide on stuffing firmness or softness and use a foot pedal to operate a machine that the Master Bear Builder uses to stuff the plush animal. After choosing a small, heart-shaped, red satin pillow, customers are encouraged to rub and kiss the heart, make a wish, and then place it into the toy animal before the Master Bear Builder closes loosely embedded stitches. The stuffed animal can be fluffed and groomed under an air blower at the Huff Me station.

At the Name Me station, a childlike voice accompanies the process of entering the name of the new friend into a computer. Customers choose between a birth certificate signed by Chief Executive Bear Maxine Clark or a storybook about how the toy

is made. Personal information is used to track owners of lost teddy bears through a corresponding barcode placed inside each plush animal. At the Bear Boutiques shoppers can choose from a wide variety of teddy bear clothing and accessories, including formal and casual attire and clothing for specific activities or holidays. Choices range from tuxedos and wedding gowns, to denim skirts and pants, camouflage pants, sweaters, t-shirts, flannel shirts, underwear, and pajamas. Special interest clothing includes tutus, sports and cheerleader uniforms, and nurse, doctor, and firefighter uniforms. Accessories include miniature athletic equipment, shoes, hats, sunglasses, and "fur-niture." The new attire can be put on the stuffed animal at the Dress Me Station. Customers pay at the Take Me Home station where the toy is lodged in a Cub Condo, a cardboard house.

Inspiration and Early Success

Twenty-five years of experience in retail management prepared founder Maxine Clark for the creation and successful implementation of the Build-a-Bear Workshop concept. Her career began in 1972 when May Department Stores hired her as an executive trainee. She worked in numerous capacities at May, but found children's marketing to be her greatest strength. At Hecht's department store Clark created a children's department called the "The Land of Ahhs." As executive vice-president of marketing and merchandising for Venture Stores she assisted in the original development of children's character licensing for store merchandise. In 1992 Clark became president of Payless ShoeSource, another May subsidiary, and transformed the company into one of the leading providers of licensed children's footwear in the country, earning a place on Discount Store News' list of the "30 Most Powerful People In Discount Store Retailing" in 1995.

Clark resigned her position as president of Payless in January 1996 in order to establish her own retail business. In pursuing entrepreneurial success, Clark sought to bring creativity into the retail environment and to involve children in a fun, tactile, and interactive retail experience. The inspiration came from Clark's own childhood memories of the fun and magic she experienced at certain stores. For example, Burdines department store in Clark's hometown of Coral Gables, Florida, held

Company Perspectives:

Build-A-Bear Workshop Foundation is committed to improving communities and impacting lives through meaningful philanthropic programs that support causes for children and families. One focus of the Build-A-Bear Workshop Foundation's mission is to raise funds through Nikki's Bear programs to support children's cancer research and treatment programs. The Build-A-Bear Workshop Foundation and Nikki's Bear programs are driven by the inspiration and spirit of kids helping kids and the central messages of courage and hope. Courage for all kids who face cancer today. Hope for a brighter future tomorrow through cancer research and treatment.

fashion shows in the tea room, Christmas carnivals on the roof of the store, and other exciting events. Clark wanted to provide children with similar memorable experiences.

In the process of developing a retail entertainment concept for children, Clark visited toy factories and children's retail stores, put together a list of ideas, then consulted the experts: children. Clark consulted first with the children of a friend, then formed an advisory board of 20 children, ages six to 14, and showed them three of her ideas. The decision to pursue the Build-A-Bear concept emerged from the board's enthusiasm, combined with Clark's personal preference for teddy bears and the high profit margin for stuffed animals.

Clark then hired design consultant Adrienne Weiss Co. of Los Angeles, using 80 percent of her $750,000 personal savings investment, to develop the Build-A-Bear concept. Clark collaborated with consultants in developing every detail, including artwork, employee costumes, store design, and company logo. The logo features a teddy bear being measured, stitched, stuffed, and groomed. All lettering is similar to children's printing.

Every element of the store design was intended to delight children under the age of 12. The store entrance is flanked by two life-size bear figurines, a boy and a girl; they hold large sewing needles and wear thimbles for hats. Vibrant yellow-gold and red-orange colors dominate the store interior and bins holding the toy animal skins are shaped like spools of thread. At the Stuff Me station, children can see white stuffing being fluffed by a turning, open-spoke wheel and feel the downy texture of the extra stuffing stored in a canvas hamper. The store design was inspired in part by the Little Shop on Burdines' roof, featuring counters and displays at an appropriate height for children.

The first Build-A-Bear Workshop opened in the St. Louis Galleria in October 1997 with immediate success. The toys were popular with teenagers and young couples, as well as families with children. During the Christmas shopping season, the store was so busy children had to take a number and wait their turn. With each animal toy priced at $10 to $25 and clothing at $3 to $10, sales of $377,600 exceeded projections for 1997.

By providing numerous clothing options and other supplementary bear-themed merchandise, Clark hoped to attract repeat business. "Bearaphenalia" included greeting cards, sta-

tionery, candy, stickers, jewelry, and t-shirts stating, "Never settle for the bear necessities." At an in-store photo booth, customers could have their pictures taken and reproduced on a sheet of stickers.

Expansion in the Late 1990s

From the start Clark planned to implement the Build-A-Bear concept as a retail chain. To facilitate growth, she obtained all appropriate copyrights and trademarks before the first store opened, such as for Cub Condo and the company's slogan, "Where Best Friends Are Made." In developing Build-A-Bear into a national chain, Clark planned to open three to five stores in 1998, six to ten stores in 1999, and to operate 100 stores within five years. The St. Louis Galleria provided a model for market demographics, as a location with many families and a family friendly environment in an upscale regional mall. Clark considered prime family-oriented entertainment and tourist retail venues as other options.

The cost of opening a new store ranged from $500,000 to $700,000, but with annual sales estimated at $2 million per store, Clark easily found capital investment for expansion. Kansas City Equity Partners invested in the company, leading Build-A-Bear to open its second store in Overland Park near Kansas City, Kansas, in August 1998. A $4.5 million investment from Windsor Capital funded the opening of two stores in the Chicago area. With four stores in operation sales reached $3.3 million in 1998.

The charm of the Build-A-Bear concept coupled with its uniqueness earned Clark and the company industry recognition, including *Chain Store Age*'s Best New Retail Concept award. *Playthings Magazine,* the publication of the Toy Industry Association, gave the company a Merchandise Achievement Award for "Best Category Marketing."

Build-A-Bear continued to charm investors and the company found financial support for expansion through Walnut Capital Partners, which invested $5 million in 1999. Build-A-Bear Workshops opened in Indianapolis; Atlanta; Houston; Orlando, Palm Beach and Miami, Florida; McClean, Virginia, near Washington, D.C.; Myrtle Beach, South Carolina; and Scottsdale, Arizona. With 14 stores in operation, the company sold almost one million teddy bears and sales reached $18.6 million. Sales averaged $700 per square foot of retail space, an enormous success in contrast to national mall averages of $350 per square foot. While Clark expected to meet her operational goals, she did not expect immediate popularity with the public and the resulting sales.

One aspect of successful sales involved the company's responsiveness to customer feedback. Build-A-Bear learned about customer preferences and changed the product mix accordingly. New products focused more directly on the workshop experience, eliminating the greeting cards and the photo booth, and adding fresh choices to an expanded line of teddy bear-sized apparel and accessories. The company diversified its product selection by offering different animals, including horses, dogs, cats, and turtles, as well as limited-edition animals for holidays and nonprofit fundraising. A changing selection of prerecorded sound chips fit product offerings. In addition, the

Key Dates:

1996: Maxine Clark leaves position at Payless Shoe-Source to start her own business.

1997: The first Build-A-Bear Workshop opens in St. Louis; sales are near $400,000 in less than four months.

1999: The success of the retail concept attracts venture capital for expansion; Build-A-Bear opens ten new stores.

2001: The National Retail Federation names Build-A-Bear the Retail Innovator of the Year.

2002: Build-A-Bear Workshop celebrates the 100th anniversary of the teddy bear along with the opening of its 100th store.

2003: International expansion begins with new locations in Canada and England.

company introduced sound chips that allowed customers to record personal messages. Build-A-Bear released CDs with bear-themed music, including songs like ''Root Bear'' and ''Teddy Bear Boogie.''

The *Beary Newsworthy* newsletter kept customers abreast of new products and the BuyStuff program gave frequent buyers $10 off purchase after spending $100 on merchandise. The company web site, with a simulated trip through the Build-A-Bear assembly process, proved to be a very successful means of attracting new and repeat business.

The Cub Advisory Board played an important role in product development, holding meetings quarterly to discuss product ideas, making decisions about what animals to offer, fur colors, clothing styles, and accessories. Clark took the board's opinions seriously—if the board did not approve a product idea, the company did not use it.

Accelerating Expansion in 2000–01

With additional investment funds Build-A-Bear accelerated expansion, as Clark aimed to meet her goal of operating 100 stores in 2002. Walnut Capital Partners invested more than $60 million to fund new store development in 2000 and 2001. The St. Louis Galleria continued to provide a model for ideal store locations. Build-A-Bear opened units in New York, New Jersey, Connecticut, Massachusetts, Maryland, Alabama, Virginia, Tennessee, Michigan, Ohio, Pennsylvania, Colorado, Utah, Oregon, and California.

Although Clark's preference for premier, regional shopping malls directed expansion, Build-A-Bear expanded in an organic way as well. For instance, information obtained from the store in Myrtle Beach, a popular tourist destination, showed an unusually large number of visitors from Columbus, Ohio. While the company included Columbus in its long-term growth plan, the strong response from residents prompted the company to open a store in that area earlier, in April 2000. In addition, the company received an unusually large number of requests for a store from residents in the Dallas area, prompting Build-A-Bear to open a store in Arlington in May 2000, followed in late summer by stores in Frisco and Fort Worth.

The company's low-key marketing approach involved print advertising in community newspapers and parenting magazines, rather than television or major city newspapers. Promotion involved direct mail marketing to customers whose addresses were obtained at naming stations during visits to stores in other cities. Build-a-Bear used information from the Find-A-Bear ID program to promote Build-A-Party birthday party planning as well. The most successful marketing, for new and existing stores, occurred through the enthusiasm of children who told their friends about their memorable experience at Build-A-Bear.

Build-A-Bear continued to develop and change the merchandise mix at its stores and the clothing line expanded to more than 100 outfits. Build-A-Bear entered its first licensing partnership for co-branded products with Skechers footwear company. The Skechers for Bears line provided paw-shaped athletic footwear for teddy bears. The line was modeled on the company's Sportline of Energy joggers and featured metallic accents. With the purchase of bear footwear, customers received a coupon for $5 off a pair of Skechers adult or children's footwear.

During the company's new store expansion, Build-A-Bear obtained a space at one of the premier tourist locations for families, at the Downtown Disney District at Disneyland Resort in Anaheim, California. The store is located in a fee-free area outside the theme park, in a dining, entertainment, and shopping district. The store opened in fall 2001, the company's 32nd store opening that year, for a total of 72 stores in 30 states. Sales reached $107.3 million in 2001.

2002 Teddy Bear Centennial and Other Marketing Highlights

Throughout 2002 Build-A-Bear celebrated the Teddy Bear Centennial, the one hundredth anniversary of the creation of the teddy bear. The toy derived from a hunting trip taken by U.S. President Theodore ''Teddy'' Roosevelt, when he chose not to kill a bear cub. A *Washington Post* cartoonist immortalized the act, then a toy maker commemorated it with the creation of the first teddy bear. Centennial events included the Bearriffic Bear Story writing contest. Winners received a family trip to New York City for Thanksgiving, where Build-A-Bear debuted a float at Macy's Thanksgiving Day Parade.

Build-A-Bear coordinated centennial celebrations with new store openings. Children's parades, fashion shows, and charity events became regular features. Events culminated with the company's 100th store opening in Roosevelt Field, New York on September 19. Highlights of the Teddy Bear Centennial Charity Gala included live music, a Furry Fashions Show, and an auction of collectible teddy bears to benefit the Simon Youth Foundation. The next day a children's parade, led by company mascot Bearemy, took celebrants to the new store where Build-A-Bear held a birthday party.

After successful collaboration on fashion shows during the Teddy Bear Centennial, in late 2002 Build-A-Bear announced a licensing agreement with Limited Too, which created a line of bear clothing based on the popular styles found at Limited Too stores for girls. Several Build-A-Bear customers requested the clothing styles for their toy bears. New attire included shorts and matching tops.

Build-A-Bear formed a similar licensing partnership with the National Basketball Association and the Women's National Basketball Association. WNBA uniforms and t-shirts for seven teams and authentic NBA jerseys for 14 teams were available in markets appropriate to each team.

Through a master-license agreement with Hasbro, Build-A-Bear intended to expand its market beyond its retail stores and web site. Under the agreement Hasbro would develop and market a special kit for building teddy bears at home as well as a line of stuffed animals and clothing accessories. These products would extend Build-A-Bear sales to mass market retailers beginning in late 2004.

The excellence with which Build-A-Bear executed its retail formula attracted the attention of children's product marketers and authors of four books published in 2003 dedicated whole chapters to the company. Authors cited the company's attention to every detail of the retail experience as directed toward its target market. In *Brand Child* renowned marketing specialist Martin Lindstrom lauded Build-A-Bear for its effectiveness in meeting the needs of children between the ages of seven and 14 to express themselves, to be unique, to have fun, and to involve their friends. The authors of *Creating Customer Evangelists* credited Clark with creating a memorable retail experience that prompted word-of-mouth sales.

Although Clark intended to take the company global from its inception, concrete plans did not begin to take shape until late 2002. In November Build-A-Bear signed a franchise agreement with Japan, held by Tech R&DS Co. Ltd. The company also began a search for locations in the United Kingdom. These countries were chosen in response to requests from customers who had visited stores while in the United States or had visited the company's web site. A high number of addresses in the Find-A-Bear ID database for these countries indicated strong interest in the Build-A-Bear concept.

The opening of the company's first international locations occurred in Canada, however. In May 2003 Build-A-Bear opened at malls in Edmonton and Calgary, Alberta, with additional stores opening in Mississauga, Ontario, and Coquitlam, British Columbia, later that year.

In October 2003 the company signed a franchise agreement with Amsbra Limited for exclusive rights to open and operate Build-A-Bear Workshops in the United Kingdom and Ireland. The first overseas location opened in November in Sheffield. Amsbra prepared for a second store location to open in South London in spring 2004.

International franchisees planned several store openings in 2004, including a location in Tokyo and an undisclosed location in South Korea during the spring. In Europe plans called for

stores to open in Denmark and France, in spring and summer, respectively. In addition, a company-owned store was expected to open in Toronto, Ontario Canada, in fall 2004.

Expansion in the United States for 2004 involved new stores in Franklin, Tennessee; Wichita, Kansas; Hobart, Indiana; Dublin, Ohio; Sugarland, Texas; West Des Moines, Iowa; Poughkeepsie, New York; Little Rock, Arkansas; and its first store in Hawaii, in Honolulu. Build-A-Bear's goal is to operate 250 stores in the United States by 2007.

Principal Competitors

Applause LLC; The Boyds Collection Ltd.; The Basic Brown Bear Factory; Enesco Group, Inc.; Maine Bear Factory; Russ Berrie and Company; Ty, Inc.; Vermont Teddy Bear Company.

Further Reading

"Build-A-Bear Licensing Brand," *Home Accents Today,* December 2003, p. SS14.

"Build-A-Bear Workshop Inc.," *St. Louis Business Journal,* May 22, 2000, p. 32.

Del Vecchio, Gene, *The Blockbuster Toy! How to Invent the Next BIG Thing,* Gretna, La.: Pelican Publishing Co., 2003.

Grosse, Thomas K., "Teddy bear Tussle," *U.S. News & World Report,* November 11, 2002, p. 46.

Hemmer, Andy, "A Huge Bear Market? One Local Venture Capital Firm Hopes So," *Business Courier Serving Cincinnati-Northern Kentucky,* April 6, 2001, p. 3.

LaSalle, Diana, and Terry A. Britton, *Priceless: Turning Ordinary Products into Extraordinary Experience,* Boston: Harvard Business School Press, 2003.

Lindstrom, Martin, and Patricia B. Seybold, *Brand Child: Remarkable Insights into the Minds of Today's Global Kids and Their Relationships with Brands,* London: Kogan Page Ltd., 2003.

McConnell, Ben, and Jackie Huba, *Creating Customer Evangelists: How Loyal Customers Become a Volunteer Sales Force,* Chicago: Dearborn Trade Publishing, 2003.

Nelton, Sharon, "Build-A-Bear One Smile at a Time," *Success,* September 2000, p. 34.

Patten, Brad, "Teddy Bear Bonanza Run by Sweetheart of a System," *Washington Business Journal,* February 4, 2000, p. 53.

Showalter, Kathy, "Build-A-Bear Workshop Sets Paw in Easton Town Center," *Business First-Columbus,* March 24, 2000, p. 9.

Taylor, Lisa Y., "Build-A-Bear to Come to Arlington," *Dallas Business Journal,* December 17, 1999, p. 18.

Trollinger, Amy, "Build-A-Bear Retailer Hopes Concept Catches On in K.C.," *Kansas City Business Journal,* June 19, 1998, p. 3.

Tucci, Linda, "Retailer Maxine Clark Bets $750,000 on Bear Market," *St. Louis Business Journal,* July 14, 1997, p. 3A.

Vise, Marilyn, "Build-A-Bear Workshop," *St. Louis Business Journal,* May 4, 2001, p. 44.

Wilson, Marianne, "This Bear Market Toys with Success," *Chain Store Age,* January 1998, p. 50.

Zion, Lee, "Bear Necessities," *San Diego Business Journal,* November 18, 2002, p. 12.

—Mary Tradii

Bunge Ltd.

50 Main Street, 6th Floor
White Plains, New York 10606
U.S.A.
Telephone: (914) 684-2800
Fax: (914) 684-3499
Web site: http://www.bunge.com

Public Company
Incorporated: 1995 as Bunge Agribusiness Ltd.
Employees: 24,207
Sales: $14 billion (2002)
Stock Exchanges: New York
Ticker Symbol: BG
NAIC: 311222 Soybean Processing

With its corporate headquarters located in White Plains, New York, Bunge Ltd. is a global agribusiness and food company divided into three division. The agribusiness segment, which accounts for 56 percent of the company's operating profit in 2002, is comprised of three business lines: grain origination, oilseed processing, and international marketing. Bunge is a leading global soybean exporter. The fertilizer division serves the South American market, primarily Brazil, where Bunge is the only integrated fertilizer producer. Finally, Bunge's food products division takes advantage of the raw materials—soybeans, crude vegetable oils, wheat, and corn—available through the company's agribusiness operation to engage in four business lines: edible oil products, wheat milling and bakery products, soy ingredients, and corn products. Bunge employs some 24,000 people working out of more than 400 facilities located in 29 countries across four continents.

Roots Of Company Date to Early 1880s

The origins of Bunge Ltd. can be traced to 1818 and Amsterdam, where Johann Peter Gottlieb Bunge founded an import/export trading company, Bunge & Co. Some 40 years later, the company, led by Johann's grandson, Edouard Bunge, emerged as one of the world's top commodity trading firms. The relocation of Bunge's base of operations outside of The Netherlands began in 1884, when Edouard's brother, Ernst Bunge, moved to Argentina. He and his partners formed an affiliate, Bunge y Born, to become involved in the South American agricultural commodities market. Bunge itself began investing directly in South America 20 years later, targeting Brazil. Focusing initially on wheat exportation, the company eventually became involved in soybean crushing, the production of fats and oils, as well as the manufacture of paints, textiles, and cement.

In the 20th Century, Bunge became increasingly global, spreading its activities to Venezuela, the United States, the United Kingdom, Spain, Australia, and Asia. In 1938, the company became involved in the Brazilian fertilizer market, and ultimately became South America's leader in the category. The move to the United States occurred in 1918, when Bunge began to trade in agricultural commodities. The company formed Bunge North American Grain Corporation in 1923 to take advantage of the difference in seasons between the northern and southern hemispheres: farmers in South America would be harvesting their grain crops just as American farmers were planting theirs. The subsidiary built its first major grain facility in Midway, Minnesota, in 1935, after buying an old rail terminal in the community. Bunge North America became Bunge Corporation in 1943, as the company continued its efforts to expand beyond trading to add grain production and value-added processing capabilities. In keeping with this plan, Bunge bought two major grain companies in 1946: Hallet & Cary, Inc., with a number of midwestern elevators, and Gano Grain Company, with operations located mainly in Kansas. Over the next 15 years, Bunge continue to pick up grain elevators across the United States, in the process growing into one of America's top grain handling and exporting firms. Bunge made an even greater commitment to its export business in the 1960s when it began to focus its attention on the Mississippi River. In 1961, it opened the largest U.S. grain export facility of its day in Destrehan, Louisiana. In 1967, Bunge added to the facility by building its first soybean processing plant.

Over the next 20 years, Bunge expanded in a number of directions, creating a slate of value-added downstream businesses. The Lauhoff Grain Company (renamed Bunge Lauhoff Grain) was acquired in 1979, resulting in Bunge's emergence as

Company Perspectives:

Experience has proven that a decentralized approach to running our businesses works best for us. Over our 180-plus year history, we have grown Bunge by allowing our local teams to operate with the latitude to be entrepreneurial—to identify and capitalize on opportunities and trends before they become known to the broader market. Decentralization also allows us to remain close to our customers and to offer innovative services that match the particular needs of regions, market segments and individual customers. Operating with minimal bureaucracy requires that employees embrace teamwork, trust, openness and personal responsibility as a way of doing business. At Bunge we actively promote these values. We hire managers that possess these traits; we reinforce these criteria in our ongoing employee training; and we base acquisition and partnership decisions on these parameters.

the world's largest corn dry miller. A year later, Bunge, through its Bunge Foods subsidiary, established a shortenings and oils business when it acquired three edible oil refineries from Swift & Company. In 1987, Bunge Foods made another strategic acquisition, buying Carlin Foods Corporation and adding a range of bakery products for sale to retail and wholesale outlets, as well as to food processors and foodservice companies. During this period, Bunge also added more grain origination facilities, soybean processing plants, and corn dry milling operations. In 1988, management elected to focus on the grain origination assets it had accumulated on the Mississippi and its tributaries, and as a consequence sold a dozen interior grain elevators located in Texas and Oklahoma. To better manage its assets, Bunge moved its headquarters from New York City to more centrally located St. Louis in 1990. In that same year, the company picked up ten elevators located in Louisiana, five of which were on the Mississippi River. These assets acquired from the Great River Grain Corporation added some 12 million bushels in storage capacity. In 1992, Bunge Lauhoff Grain acquired the only corn dry mill in Canada, buying Ontario-based Kingroup, Inc. Furthermore in 1992, Bunge forged a joint venture with ContiQuincy Export Company to promote both companies' soybean operations.

Alberto Weisser Joins Company in 1993

Until the early 1990s, direct descendants of the Bunge and Born families ran Bunge y Born, a private company that was content to remain little known to the general public. It was not until 1988 that the company turned to public financing for the first time, issuing commercial paper in order to increase its credit and fund diversification efforts. Expansion and diversification, however, led to the need for more experienced executive talent. One of the managers Bunge recruited, Alberto Weisser, who joined the company in 1993 as chief financial officer, became Bunge's chairman and chief executive officer. Fluent in several languages, Weisser was well qualified to lead a global business. He also brought with him 15 years of experience in financial positions with the German chemicals conglomerate BASF. He was named a Bunge director in 1995, CEO in 1999, and ultimately rose to the chairmanship in 2001. Weisser was

also instrumental in Bunge hiring other executives from outside the grain trade business.

The management of Bunge y Born initiated a major restructuring of the business in the 1990s. In 1995, Bunge Foods bolstered its ability to serve the West Coast of the United States by acquiring the packaged edible oil business and other assets of Premier Foods Corporation. The operation was moved to Modesto, California, and increasingly began looking to agribusiness. In 1995, Bunge International spun off assets to create Bunge Agribusiness Ltd., which in 1999 would be renamed Bunge Ltd. In 1997, the company added to its milling capabilities by investing in one of the largest wheat mills in Mexico and also added nine midwestern grain elevators from Homer Grain Company. By 1998, however, Bunge decided to sell off its consumer product businesses in Argentina, Australia, and Venezuela in order to concentrate on such agribusiness areas as grain and oilseed origination, oilseed processing, export trading, feed, food ingredients, and fertilizers and phosphate-based nutrients. To support this vision, Bunge completed a number of initiatives in 1998. The grain division entered into an arrangement with Zen-Noh Grain Corporation to jointly manage their New Orleans-based export grain elevators. The company also expanded its Mexican operations. Subsidiary Lauhoff Grain acquired a Kellogg Company's corn dry operation located in Queretaro. In Mexico City, Bunge invested in a bakery mix facility to take advantage of the country's expanding in-store bakery market. In the United States, Bunge Foods bought a Missouri frozen dough production plant from Au Bon Pain, thereby entering the frozen bakery business. Included in the deal was a contract to supply frozen bakery products to some 300 Au Bon Pain bakery-cafes and another 70-plus St. Louis Bread Company restaurants. To gain a foothold in the frozen bakery products market in the West Coast, Bunge Foods also acquired a Tustin, California, production facility from Dansk Foods. On the agribusiness side of the business, in 1998 Bunge also opened a soybean crusher-refiner operation in Council Bluffs, Iowa, becoming the largest oil extractor in the country. In addition, the soybean processing division added an integrated refinery to its crushing facility located in Decatur, Alabama.

In order to better position itself as a global business, the company moved its headquarters from Sao Paulo, Brazil, to White Plains, New York, in 1999. Until this point in its history, according to a company spokesman quoted by *Global Finance,* Bunge had "always been a 'virtual' company. It didn't physically exist. There was just a holding company, not a real corporate center for all operations. Now we have the platform to fund the company on a centralized basis." A major component to Bunge's strategy was to take the company public. In 2000, management announced that it planned to take Bunge public within two years. In the meantime, subsidiary Bunge Global Markets was created to engage in export trade opportunities in bulk commodities; Bunge Foods opened a major new edible oil bottling plant in Illinois, serving the important private-label retail market in shortenings and oil; and sister company Bunge Corporation changed its name to Bunge North America.

Bunge Ltd. Goes Public in 2001

The parent company, Bunge Ltd., went public in August 2001, issuing 17.6 million shares at $16 each in an offering led

Key Dates:

1818: Bunge & Co. is founded by Johann Peter Gottlieb Bunge.
1884: Affiliated Argentine company, Bunge y Born, is founded.
1923: Bunge North American Grain Corporation is formed.
1995: Bunge Agribusiness Limited is formed.
1999: Bunge Agribusiness becomes Bunge Limited.
2001: Bunge Limited goes public and begins trading on the New Stock Exchange.

by Morgan Stanley and Credit Suisse First Boston, netting the company $281.6 million, much of which was earmarked to retire a portion of the company's $914 million in short-term debt. *Global Finance* explained why after 200 years of being privately held, Bunge now elected to become a public company: "Bunge's business is booming, the company can streamline its finances by consolidating the books of its far-flung international subsidiaries—and the 100-plus heirs of the founding Bunge and Born families can cash in some of their long-held ownership chips." The only member of the founding families to now hold a position of importance in the company was Jorge Born, Jr., a deputy chairman and director.

Bunge's global aspirations were greatly enhanced in 2002 when the company purchased a 55 percent controlling interest in Cereol SA, a French agribusiness competitor. Bunge paid approximately $830 million to Italian energy company Edison SpA and also assumed some $700 million in debt. (In April 2003 Bunge acquired all outstanding shares to become a 100 percent owner of Cereol.) As a result, Bunge greatly enhanced its capacity to process soybeans in the United States and Europe. Its North American operations were able to take advantage of Cereol's subsidiary, Central Soya Co., which operated six plants located in eastern farm-belt states, nicely complimenting Bunge's operations in Illinois, Iowa, Kansas, and Alabama. As for Europe, the world's top importer of soybeans, Bunge would now be able to process soybeans at Cereol-owned crushing facilities in Spain and Italy, rather than merely ship soybean byproducts to the region. Bunge also gained a strong presence in Central and Eastern Europe through the Cereol transaction. Overall, the acquisition was important on other levels. It provided more vertical integration, offering efficiencies and cost savings. Also, by adding European markets to its traditional strongholds in North and South America, Bunge was able to spread some of its risk, an important factor in light of South America's history of political instability. In addition, Cereol assets enabled Bunge to gain the size necessary to compete globally with the likes of Archer Daniels Midland and Cargill Inc. In a conference call conducted shortly after the deal was announced, Weisser commented, "This transaction

changes the industry landscape quite dramatically. By increasing our oilseed processing capacity from 20 million tons to nearly 34 million tons, we move ahead of Archer Daniels Midland Company (ADM) and Cargill. We will immediately become the market leader in regions such as Canada and Eastern Europe where we have no presence, while our position will be enhanced in countries where we already have operations, such as the US."

Although it remained open to additional acquisitions, Bunge made it clear that its top priority in the near term was to successfully integrate the Cereol operations. Nevertheless, Bunge was able in early 2003 to forge an important alliance with DuPont, creating an $800 million specialty food ingredients joint venture named Solae L.L.C. The business, based in St. Louis, was intended to be involved in the global production and distribution of specialty food ingredients, initially focusing on soy proteins and lecithins. DuPont, contributing its protein technologies food ingredients business, garnered a 72 percent stake in the Solae, while Bunge received $260 million in cash and a 28 percent minority interest in the new company in exchange for its soybean ingredients business. Furthermore, the deal called for DuPont and Bunge to use biotechnology to jointly develop and commercialize new strains of soybeans and other products for the farming industry. Another major area for growth targeted by management was the fertilizer market in Brazil, where farmers used about half as much fertilizer as those in more industrialized countries. Through its South American subsidiary, Bunge bought a number of small fertilizer companies and acquired large stakes in Brazilian phosphate mines. Little known for two centuries, the Bunge name appeared destined to receive greater recognition in the years to come.

Principal Subsidiaries

Bunge North America, Inc.; Cerco S.A.; Bunge Brazil S.A.

Principal Competitors

Archer Daniels Midland Company; Cargill, Incorporated; Con-Agra Foods, Inc.

Further Reading

Byrne, Harlan S., "To Market, to Market," *Barron's*, October 21, 2002, p. 20.
Kilman, Scott, "Bunge Increases Grain Position with Bid of $830 Million for Cereol," *Wall Street Journal*, July 22, 2002, p. C14.
Lee, Thomas, "Agribusiness Company Bunge Has Successful Year After Going Public," *St. Louis Post-Dispatch*, October 27, 2002.
McCrary, Ernest S., "Bunge Finally Lifts The Veil," *Global Finance*, September 1, 2001, p. 15.
Reeves, Amy, "Agribusiness Plants Seeds For Global Growth," *Investor's Business Daily*, October 28, 2002.
Willoughby, Jack, "Offerings in the Offing: Against the Grain," *Barron's*, July 30, 2001, p. 33.

—Ed Dinger

Butler Manufacturing Company

P.O. Box 419917
Kansas City, Missouri 64141
U.S.A.
Telephone: (816) 968-3000
Fax: (816) 968-3265
Web site: http://www.butlermfg.com

Public Company
Incorporated: 1901
Employees: 4,500
Sales: $796.17 million (2003)
Stock Exchanges: New York
Ticker Symbol: BBR
NAIC: 332311 Prefabricated Metal Building and
Component Manufacturing; 332999 All Other
Miscellaneous Fabricated Metal Product Manufacturing;
331316 Aluminum Extruded Product Manufacturing

Butler Manufacturing Company is a leading supplier of building systems, specialty components, and construction services for the nonresidential construction market. For more than 50 years, its "Butler Buildings," assembled onsite of metal parts made at Butler factories, have offered a quick solution to industrial, military, and commercial users seeking more space.

Founded 1901

Emanuel Norquist, along with brothers Charles and Newton Butler, founded Butler Manufacturing Company in Kansas City in 1901. A few years earlier, Charles and Emanuel had worked together on building an improved livestock watering tank, and, during the early 1900s, along with Newton Butler, the men designed and built several agricultural products, particularly grain storage bins. The company enjoyed success selling such merchandise locally. By 1908, Butler's headquarters included a staff of 14—six women and eight men. Sales boomed throughout the 1910s and 1920s.

Although Butler would become famous for its grain storage bins, or "Butler bins," during the early and mid-1900s, the company began branching out into new sideline businesses early in the century. For example, in 1909, the company erected its first metal building, an all steel garage. That simple structure would help to lay the foundation for what would eventually become Butler's bread-and-butter business. Other major ventures included metal farm implements and oil field equipment.

Among the company's most interesting early endeavors was the Butler Aircraft Corporation. Butler's founders started that subsidiary in the wake of the airplane craze prompted by Lindbergh's famed transatlantic flight in 1927. In 1929, in fact, more licenses were issued for planes than at any time in U.S. history. Butler designed and built the Blackhawk, a biplane typical of the many aircraft being produced across the nation at the time. The ship stood nine feet tall and 24 feet long, boasted a top speed of 130 miles per hour, and could travel 650 miles on a single tank of gas.

Drawing on expertise and materials it had garnered from its metal bin and building operations to construct the plane, Butler fashioned a three-building factory to manufacture the Blackhawks, which were priced at $7,995 each. Unfortunately, the Great Depression quashed Butler's airplane division after only 11 of its Blackhawks had been produced. Like other manufacturers at the time, Butler suffered during the Depression years as sales and profits declined dramatically.

Butler survived the 1930s, buoyed mainly by its oil equipment operations. Although it was the largest manufacturer of grain bins, Butler's farm equipment segment actually contributed the least revenue of its five divisions. The grain bin industry was susceptible to the cyclicality of the overall agriculture business: when crop yields were high, more storage was needed; when yields were low, demand for new bins would plummet. Butler's bin sales had languished during much of the early and mid-1930s. However, that would soon change as the result of an incident that would be highlighted in company annals throughout the century.

Government Work in 1939

The year 1938 turned out to be a very good one for crops, and 1939 was even better. As bumper crops were harvested, the nation's storage capacity was stressed. The U.S. Department of Agriculture (USDA), realizing the urgency of the situation, announced in July 1939 that it would accept bids on 30,666 steel storage bins. Incredibly, USDA officials required that all bids be submitted within 30 days and that the bins had to be delivered by the manufacturer within 60 days of receiving an order.

Butler's two plants in Kansas City and Minneapolis were already operating at full capacity, so Butler executives were split over whether or not to bid for the government work. They knew that failure to fulfill the contract terms could spell ruin for the company. Determined to capture a portion of the massive government job, nevertheless, managers embarked on a tenacious search for an abandoned plant that they could convert to build the bins. They found an acceptable, though dilapidated, plant in Galesburg, Illinois. As Butler scrambled to reclaim the facility, it also began preparing a bid to supply 14,500 bins, or about half of the entire contract.

Butler's bid was hand carried to Washington and opened on August 2, 1939. Butler, the low bidder, was awarded the job. "What occurred in Galesburg and throughout the company in the 60 days following that first contract is the stuff of legends," according to company archives. Indeed, Butler's work force launched a production campaign still unrivaled in its long history, churning out grain storage bins at an average rate of almost 250 per day. All 14,500 bins were delivered one day ahead of schedule. Furthermore, another 6,000 units that had been ordered in mid-contract were shipped 15 days later.

Butler used the government contract in 1939 as an opportunity to add a new production facility to its organization. The Galesburg plant was converted for year-round use in 1940 and began manufacturing steel buildings following World War II. Butler had been manufacturing metal buildings since the early 1900s, but it manufactured its first "rigid-frame" building design in 1939. Demand for its popular single-story, rigid-frame structures flourished during the postwar U.S. economic boom.

Postwar Construction

In the 1950s, the company stepped up its efforts in the metal building market. The shift to the production of metal buildings reflected management's desire to reduce Butler's susceptibility to volatile agricultural markets. Management completely eliminated the grain bin operations in the Galesburg plant, for example, converting it solely to the manufacture of pre-engineered, non-residential structures. Butler's goal was to create two major markets for its products—agricultural and construction—that would provide a more stable pattern of income. The scheme proved effective, and, although both industries were cyclical, Butler's construction and agricultural markets were rarely down at the same time through the 1960s and 1970s.

During this time, demand surged for Butler's expanding lines of agricultural and building products. Sales flourished, earnings rose, and the company posted profits virtually every year between the late 1950s and early 1980s.

1980s Slump

Butler's fortunes changed in the early 1980s, however, for several reasons. Most importantly, the U.S. agricultural market tailspinned into a long-term slump. Butler posted a loss in 1983 of $7.5 million, its first loss in more than 30 years. Moreover, the industrial and commercial construction markets were still struggling to recover from an ugly downturn that began in the late 1970s and lingered into the early 1980s.

Discouraged by its setbacks in agricultural markets, Butler management decided to begin downplaying that side of their business. They held onto their sporadically profitable grain bin operations (the storage bin business generally followed four or five year cycles, meaning that Butler could usually generate extremely high profits about one year in five) but jettisoned most of its other agricultural operations, which had less long-term potential. By 1986, Butler's agricultural holdings represented less than 15 percent of its total assets, down from about 25 percent just three years earlier.

Butler's decision to focus on pre-engineered buildings and related specialty products was made at an opportune time. The commercial and industrial real estate industry boomed during the mid- and late 1980s, bolstering demand for Butler's innovative pre-engineered buildings. Its structures ranged from airplane hangars, churches, and football practice facilitates to large steel mills and small commercial and industrial buildings. The structures were usually made to order in one of Butler's several factories and then assembled onsite.

To supplant revenue losses in its waning agricultural division, Butler acquired several companies that manufactured products related to its building division, such as exterior wall panels, windows, and electrical systems. Revenue from those acquisitions, combined with its core operations, allowed Butler to generate sales of more than $500 million annually by the mid-1980s. Earnings, however, remained in the $10 million range following the 1983 loss, despite strengthening construction markets.

In 1986, in an effort to improve the company's performance, Butler's directors placed Robert West at the helm of the organization as chairperson and named Donald Pratt as president. Both men had been with Butler since the mid-1960s. West oversaw the divestment of some of Butler's excess baggage, while seeking to integrate the company's newer acquisitions into its core building business. Unfortunately, he had his hands full with the latter task. Indeed, Butler was finding that many of its related subsidiaries were failing to perform as expected and were dragging down overall company gains.

For example, in mid-1986, Butler acquired Inryco, a manufacturer of exterior wall panels and accessories. Management hoped to integrate Inryco's product line and facilities into its pre-engineered building operations, and the Inryco plant was relocated from Minnesota to Kentucky at considerable cost. Only one year after the acquisition, however, West was having

```
┌─────────────────────────────────────────────────────┐
│                    Key Dates:                         │
│                                                       │
│  1901:  Butler Manufacturing is founded in Kansas City.│
│  1909:  The company constructs its first metal building.│
│  1939:  Butler wins a government contract for 14,500 grain│
│         storage bins.                                 │
│  1976:  Annville, Pennsylvania, plant opens.          │
│  1995:  A subsidiary is established in the People's Republic│
│         of China.                                     │
│  1996:  A Hungarian operation is acquired.            │
│  2002:  Butler sells its European business to Lindab AB.│
│  2004:  Australia's BlueScope Steel announces its acquisi-│
│         tion of Butler Manufacturing.                 │
└─────────────────────────────────────────────────────┘
```

doubts as to whether Butler would be able to keep the new subsidiary. Productivity and equipment reliability problems were proving much more acute than originally thought, and Butler stood to lose from the venture.

Moreover, Butler had made other acquisitions that it hoped would enhance its mainstay metal buildings, purchasing companies that would provide skylights, window walls, and exterior wall panels as well as handle other parts of the construction process. However, some of those additions also languished. Its Naturalite division, for instance, lost money and required a restructuring cost of about $4 million during the late 1980s.

West restructured or dispatched Butler's nonperforming divisions during the late 1980s and focused the company's efforts on its core metal building business. Despite stagnant earnings growth, its balance sheet was extremely healthy and the company enjoyed robust cash flow. Part of its financial health going into the early 1990s was attributable to West's strategy of plowing cash back into existing operations, rather than making risky acquisitions as the company had done in the past. In 1989, in fact, Butler surprised shareholders with a one-time, $20-per-share dividend.

Safer in the 1990s

Although Butler had made significant progress in restructuring its operations and shoring up its balance sheet since the early 1980s, commercial and industrial construction markets flopped beginning in the early 1990s, thus stifling opportunities for growth and tempering sales and profits for the company. Earnings hovered below the $10 million mark before the company posted the third loss in its history in 1991. Nevertheless, markets slowly began to improve in 1993 and 1994, and earnings eventually recovered.

While it repositioned its market stance during the 1980s, Butler also focused on improving the safety of its operations. The company had established a reputation for taking care of its employees, so when it recorded more than 130 major injuries in 1979, ranging from wrenched backs to broken bones, management decided to take action. Butler hired a safety director and initiated a 16-point safety program at its Galesburg plant. In fact, the program was so successful that it was implemented company-wide. By the early 1990s, Butler was leading the industry in safety with an injury rate of .32 per 100 workers, compared to the

industry average of 4.5 per 100. An added bonus was that Butler paid about half the workers' compensation insurance rates that most of its competitors paid. The company employed about 3,500 workers at the time.

Going into the mid-1990s, Butler was realizing the benefits of its restructuring efforts during previous five years. In addition, construction markets continued to improve, thus boosting sales of Butler's metal structures, while orders for grain storage systems also increased. Similarly, Butler enjoyed success with some of its subsidiaries. Its wood structure business, for example, which was acquired during the mid-1980s, was performing well and promised to represent an increasingly larger proportion of company revenues.

More importantly, Butler was making solid gains overseas. Already active throughout the world, with operations in Saudi Arabia and the United Kingdom, the company was also achieving strong growth in developing nations. Butler contracted with Wal-Mart to build stores in Mexico and South America, for example, and was engaged in a $6.7 million contract for an automobile plant in China in 1994; total sales to the Far East topped $28 million in 1994. Butler was also enjoying demand growth in Russia and other former Eastern Block countries. Foreign sales growth contributed significantly to Butler's 1994 revenue figure of $692 million and accounted for 15 percent of revenues. Operating earnings rose to $33 million in 1994, buoying Butler's stock price.

An interesting aside to the Butler story developed in the early 1990s and involved the old Butler Aircraft division of 60 years ago. Sometime after World War II, one of Butler's Blackhawk planes ended up in pieces in a barber's garage. LeRoy Brown, one of the barber's customers, purchased the pieces in the late 1960s for $250. Brown, a Pan American DC-10 pilot, spent 20 years restoring the plane. In 1980, Brown flew the plane for Butler executives, and the company purchased the aircraft in 1991. The plane, which Butler stored in a Kansas City hangar, continued to perform just as it had when the Butler brothers completed it in 1929.

On the Big Board in 1995

Butler achieved sales of $826 million in 1995. In November 1996, Butler's shares migrated to the New York Stock Exchange under the symbol "BBR." The next month, the company announced the purchase of 90 percent of Beker Kft, a manufacturer of building systems based in Nyiregyhaza, Hungary. Established in 1991, it had sales of about $2 million a year and employed 30 people. The purchase complemented Butler's existing plant in Kirkcaldy, Scotland. Butler planned to boost employment at Beker to 250 people as the unit took over the company's Central European business.

In 1995 and 1996, China and Brazil were Butler's largest export markets. A subsidiary, Butler (Shanghai) Inc. was established in the People's Republic in 1995. Within a couple of years, reported *China Daily,* local companies, rather than multinationals, would account for the bulk of Butler's business there.

Mexico was still important, and Butler developed a strategic partnership with a Guadalajara-based industrial construction firm, GVA Edifacaciones. After shutting down its plant in Kircaldy, Scotland, in 1999 Butler announced it was moving all European manufacturing to its base in Nyiregyhaza, Hungary, with plans to invest another $2 million in its facilities there.

Butler bolstered its Vistawall Architectural Products division in 1997 with the acquisitions of Rebco West Inc., a California manufacturer of entrance doors and storefront windows, and Modu-Line Windows, Inc. of Wisconsin. In the same year, the company sold its Grain Systems division to CTB, Inc. for $34 million.

Robert West retired as chairman and CEO in July 1999. He had held that position since 1986. John J. Holland succeeded him as CEO and also took the role of president while former president Donald H. Pratt became the next chairman.

Sales slipped from $973 million to $960 million in 2003; profits of $25.2 million were off only a little from the previous year. To try to get the company's profit margins, Butler was attempting to shift to a low-inventory production model. The company had about 5,000 employees at the time.

100 in 2001

In 2001, Butler Manufacturing celebrated its 100th anniversary, a rare achievement in the construction industry. The company was building a new $22 million headquarters near the Kansas City site where it had originally been founded. The 160,000-square-foot office complex housed 600 workers.

Butler celebrated another anniversary in 2001; its Annville, Pennsylvania, plant had been in business for 25 years. It had grown to 270 employees; the plant had doubled in size in 1995. One of its latest projects was building 42 hangars for Air National Guard jets.

Butler announced it was selling off its entire European operation, based in Hungary, in March 2002. Butler Europe Kft had had turnover between $19 million and $26 million a year but was not profitable. The buyer, Swedish building materials supplier Lindab AB, marketed Butler's products in Europe after taking over the Hungarian unit.

Butler continued to invest in other international markets. It invested $4 million in a 120,000-square-foot plant in Monterrey, Mexico, in 2003. In 2004, Butler was opening its third factory in the People's Republic of China, in Guangdong. It had added to its original Shanghai plant with another $25 million factory in Tianjin.

Butler posted sales of $796 million in 2003, down from $828 million, as its net loss widened from $1.8 million to $32.1 million. On the positive side, the company's backlog was up 21 percent to $319 million at the end of the year.

In February 2004, the Australian firm of BlueScope Steel Limited announced it was buying Butler for $204 million (A$260 million), including assumed debts of $60 million. BlueScope was interested in Butler as a way to expand its international business beyond its existing operations in Southeast Asia and North America.

Principal Subsidiaries

Butler Export, Inc. (Barbados); BMC Real Estate, Inc.; BUCON, Inc.; Butler Pacific, Inc.; Butler Real Estate, Inc.; Butler, S.A. de C.V. (Mexico); Butler (Shanghai) Inc. (China); Butler (Tianjin) Inc. (China); Global BMC (Mauritius) Holdings Ltd.; Butler Holdings, Inc.; Comercial Butler Limitada (Chile); ; Lester Holdings, Inc.; Liberty Building Systems, Inc.; Moduline Windows, Inc.

Principal Divisions

Construction Services; International Building Systems; North American Building Systems; Real Estate; Architectural Products Group.

Principal Competitors

Magnatrax Corporation; NCI Building Systems Inc.; VP Buildings Inc.

Further Reading

"A Better Process: Cooperation Facilitates Fast-Track Expansion of Toys 'R' Us DC," *Chain Store Age Executive*, June 2002, p. 111f.

Butcher, Lola, "Butler Steering for Smoother Road through Economic Cycle," *Kansas City Business Journal*, December 14, 1987, p. 2.

"Butler Investing Another USD 2m in Nyiregyhaza," *MTI Econews*, December 2, 1999.

"Butler Manufacturing Company to Invest USD 30 Million in Guangdong," *SinoCast China Business Daily News*, September 11, 2003.

"Butler Manufacturing Sets Up Production Base in Hungary," *MTI Econews*, December 9, 1996.

"Construction Company Has Plans for China," *China Daily*, September 28, 1999, p. 5.

Couch, Mark P., "Kansas City, Mo., Manufacturing Firm to Build New Headquarters," *Kansas City Star*, August 15, 2000.

Csir, Floyd J., "Connecticut Company to Buy Butler Manufacturing," *Parkersburg News*, November 6, 1993.

Cunningham, Norma, "Progress '92: Butler Plant Produces Array of Buildings," *Register-Mail* (Kansas City), September 14, 1992.

Forbes, Michael, "From the Ground Up; GVA Edifacaciones Sees New Possibilities for Run-Down Industry," *Business Mexico*, December 1, 1997.

Gose, Joe, "Butler Manufacturing Establishes New Low in Lost-in-Time-Injury Rate," *Kansas City Business Journal*, January 22, 1993, p. 11.

——, "Butler Plane, 63, Can Still Fly," *Kansas City Business Journal*, July 2, 1993, p. 1.

Grossman, Steve, "Butler Signs $6.7 million Deal with Chinese Carmaker," *Kansas City Business Journal*, July 29, 1994, p. 1.

——, "Butler Builds for Wal-Mart in Argentina," *Kansas City Business Journal*, August 5, 1994, p. 3.

Heaster, Randolph, "Kansas City, Mo.-Based Butler Manufacturing Elects New President," *Kansas City Star*, January 20, 1999.

——, "Kansas City, Mo.-Based Construction Company Celebrates Its 100th Anniversary," *Kansas City Star*, April 17, 2001.

Kaberline, Brian, "Butler Pre-Pays Debt, Impresses Market With Cash Flow," *Kansas City Business Journal*, September 10, 1990, p. 8.

Long, Victoria Sizemore, "Chairman of Kansas City, Mo.-Based Butler Manufacturing to Retire," *Kansas City Star*, June 17, 1998.

Miller, Barbara, ''Kansas City, Mo.-Based Building Maker Celebrates at Annville, Pa., Plant,'' *Patriot-News*, August 4, 2001.

——, ''Annville, Pa., Manufacturer Ships Hangars for Jet Fighters,'' *Patriot-News*, January 10, 2002.

Morse, Dan, ''Butler Manufacturing Aims to Rebuild Market Share—Metal-Building Company Gets a Bit Leaner as It Readies for Pickup in Business,'' *Wall Street Journal*, March 20, 2001, p. B2.

Pulliam, John R., ''Business Booming at Butler Manufacturing Plant Here,'' *Register-Mail* (Kansas City), September 20, 1994, p. C2.

Raine, Meredith, ''Walker's Path Brings Changes,'' *Parkersburg News*, July 15, 1994, p. S10.

—Dave Mote
—update: Frederick C. Ingram

Capezio/Ballet Makers Inc.

One Campus Road
Totowa, New Jersey 07512
U.S.A.
Telephone: (973) 595-9000
Fax: (973) 595-9120
Web site: http://www.capeziodance.com

Private Company
Incorporated: 1887
Employees: 400
Sales: $90 million (2003 est.)
NAIC: 424340 Footwear Merchant Wholesalers

Capezio/Ballet Makers Inc. is the leading U.S. manufacturer of dance and theatrical footwear. The respected brand has been around for over one hundred years, and scores of famous dancers have relied on Capezio shoes. Capezio specializes in ballet slippers and toe shoes, as well as costume shoes for jazz and modern dance and theatrical performances. Capezio also makes specialized footwear for circus performers and gymnasts. Along with shoes, the company produces dance and athletic clothing such as tights, leotards, and warm-up outfits. Capezio operates two factories, one in Fair Lawn, New Jersey, and one in Hialeah, Florida. Much of the shoe assembly is done painstakingly by hand. Capezio also contracts with factories in Brazil, Thailand, and China to make some of its shoes. Capezio runs ten retail stores in the United States, and its products are also sold in some 2,000 other retail outlets both in the United States and abroad. The company markets its shoes in Europe through a joint venture with Norwich Dancewear Ltd. called Ballet Makers-Europe Ltd. Capezio operates a large showroom in New York City which includes a dance studio and performance space. The company sponsors the Capezio Dance Award, which gives a cash prize to a significant dancer or choreographer each year. The award is overseen by the Capezio/Ballet Makers Dance Foundation, a charitable organization set up by the company in 1953. Capezio/Ballet Makers is a private company still run by descendants of the founder, Salvatore Capezio.

19th Century Roots

The company that became Capezio/Ballet Makers Inc. began as a tiny shoe shop in New York City run by a teenaged Italian immigrant. Salvatore Capezio was born in 1871 in the town of Bruno Lucania Potenza, Italy. Capezio trained as a cobbler and came to the United States as a youth. He set up shop on Broadway and 39th Street in New York in 1887, when he was only 17. His shop was called "The Theatrical and Historical Shoemaker." Though Capezio at first did not specialize in dance shoes, his shop was located kitty-corner to the Metropolitan Opera House, and the Met's singers and dancers began bringing him their shoes for repair. One day, he made an emergency pair of shoes for the danseur Jean de Reszke. Capezio's exemplary work for de Reszke consolidated his reputation with the Met crowd. Before long, he was not only repairing stage shoes but also making them himself, including crafting pointe shoes to order for ballerinas. In 1902, he married ballerina Angelina Passone, and this made the Capezio shop even more of a magnet for the New York dance community. The shop, and the Capezio name, earned indelible fame when the Russian ballerina Anna Pavlova visited in 1910. Pavlova was the most celebrated ballerina of her era and already world famous when she began her U.S. tour that year. She had Capezio make shoes for her and her whole company, thus giving the highest possible star endorsement to the brand. The Capezio company keeps a framed letter from Pavlova from 1915, in which she wrote that Capezio's theatrical shoes were "indeed the best I ever had."

The ballet pointe shoes that Capezio manufactured were extremely specialized footwear. Professional dancers required a custom-made shoe, fitted meticulously to their individual feet. The shoes needed to be elastic and flexible, yet stiff enough to hold the dancer's whole weight on the toe without crumpling. Dancers had their predilections for different strengths or thicknesses, and the shoemaker obliged. These shoes lasted for only one performance, so a professional ballet company needed hundreds of pairs at frequent intervals. Some European firms from the same era specialized in ballet and dance shoes, such as Romeo Niccolini in Milan, the London firm Gamba, and Ebermann in Berlin. With Pavlova's blessing, Capezio became the ballet shoemaker of New York. The shop named its standard toe shoe after her, the Pavlova brand.

Company Perspectives:

Ballet Makers is dedicated to the performer in dance, theater, and recreation. We are committed to providing exceptional service to our customers with innovative, quality products and services, while continuously advancing market research and technologies. Our total commitment to performance has been our source of inspiration for over 100 years. We believe our success is dependent upon the individual commitment of our customers, our suppliers, and each of our employees to continually set new standards of creativity and performance, while preserving our reputation for dependability and distinction. We maintain an ethical, healthy, and profitable environment in which each of our employees endeavors to provide excellence in our products and services, while promoting company growth. We pledge our support and dedication to the advancement of dance, theater, and recreation in communities worldwide.

New Markets from the 1920s to the 1960s

As the business grew in the 1920s, Capezio recruited family members to work for him. Capezio and his wife had no children of their own, but their nephews grew up working for the firm. Nicholas Terlizzi, Sr. was one nephew. He was known as a great craftsman. Another nephew, Ted Nelson, was an extremely effective salesman. In 1920, a teenager named Ben Sommers also joined the firm. Though he was not a relative, he became like a son to Capezio, and he later became president of the company. Capezio/Ballet Makers did more than make toe shoes and ballet slippers. New York was not only the center of ballet in the United States but also home to leading theater companies, musical revues, and innovative entertainment of all kinds. Capezio made shoes for the dancers of the famous Ziegfield Follies and the Radio City Music Hall Rockettes, as well as supplying footwear for the stars of numerous Broadway shows. In the 1920s, the firm made shoes for jazz dancers and also began making body wear such as tap dancer's skirts.

Capezio/Ballet Makers began experimenting with new styles and new marketing in the 1930s. In 1933, the company debuted a new ballet slipper it called the Teknik. The Teknik was a superior shoe based on years of research at the company, which had now been in business for almost 50 years. Capezio still sells the Teknik shoe. In 1934, Capezio branched out its retail operation, opening a store in Hollywood. This gave the company access to customers in the West Coast film industry. By the end of the 1930s, the company had brought out a full line of body wear, including skirts, leotards, dance pants, and tights. The company also brought out a separate fashion line of shoes in the 1930s.

Founder Salvatore Capezio died in 1940, leaving the company to four men—two blood relatives and two he looked upon as his sons. Nephews Nicholas Terlizzi and Ted Nelson ran the business, along with Ben Sommers and Nick Callan. They had all worked for the company since the 1920s. The Capezio line continued to consist of dance and theater shoes, but in the 1940s the brand gained more of a mainstream fashion following. American fashion designer Claire McCardell showed her 1941

clothing collection accompanied by Capezio shoes. Vaulted into haute couture by McCardell, Capezio shoes became fashionable footwear among women who were not dancers. The major department stores, including Bonwit Teller, Neiman Marcus, and Lord & Taylor began selling Capezios in their shoe departments. In 1949, Capezio style made the cover of the premiere women's fashion magazine, *Vogue*. Then, in 1952, the company was selected for the Coty Award, the highest prize in the world of fashion.

Capezio started a charitable arm, the Capezio Foundation, in 1953. This group began giving annual awards to individuals who made major contributions to the dance world. Capezio continued to provide shoes to Broadway stars and leading dancers in the 1950s and 1960s. It made shoes for the star of Broadway's *Can Can* in 1953 and for the hit *Hello, Dolly!* in 1964. In 1960, Capezio designed special shoes for the students of George Balanchine, the dean of ballet in New York. The Russian-born Balanchine established New York City Ballet in 1948, and he was the leading teacher of ballet toe work. He had Capezio make a toe shoe according to his instructions. For example, it was to have a longer sole and shorter pleats than other toe shoes. In addition, Balanchine wanted a shoe that made no noise. Capezio complied.

Capezio was still the hot brand of dance shoe in the American dance world in the 1950s and 1960s. In other respects, however, the company began to have problems. A third generation of management began to come into Capezio in the 1950s and early 1960s. Nicholas Terlizzi, Jr. joined the company in 1956. Over the next few years, two other grandnephews of founder Salvatore Capezio, Alfred and Donald Terlizzi, began working for the firm. The company was apparently in financial difficulty, and the older generation and the younger members could not quite agree on how to go forward. Capezio sold off its fashion line, which it had run since the 1930s, in 1964. Despite this divestiture, two years later the company was in dire straits. Alfred Terlizzi told *Dance Magazine* (October 1980), "In 1966, the company was broke; Capezio, the whole corporate structure."

Revival in the 1970s

The younger management group had plans to turn the company around, but Capezio was evidently slow to make changes. Fortunately, the dance world caught up with the struggling company and swept it forward on a new boom of dance popularity. New York had always been the center of the dance world in the United States, but in the 1970s more children across the nation began studying dance, and more regional dance companies opened. Dance was also made more popular by movies and television shows. Alfred Terlizzi credited dance programs on the public television network PBS for bringing dance to new audiences. Movies like *Nijinsky, Fame,* and *The Turning Point* also gave modern appeal to dance.

Between 1972 and 1976, Capezio's sales volume rose by 150 percent. Now the company could afford to expand. It moved into new offices and showrooms close to Lincoln Center in Manhattan and built a new manufacturing facility in Totowa, New Jersey. Capezio entered new markets in the late 1970s and early 1980s. Gymnastics was also growing in popularity, and the company brought out a new line of gymnastic wear, from

<table>
<tr><td colspan="2" align="center">**Key Dates:**</td></tr>
<tr><td>1887:</td><td>Salvatore Capezio opens a New York shoe shop.</td></tr>
<tr><td>1910:</td><td>Ballerina Anna Pavlova endorses Capezio shoes.</td></tr>
<tr><td>1934:</td><td>The company opens a Hollywood retail store.</td></tr>
<tr><td>1949:</td><td>Capezio fashions are featured on the cover of *Vogue*.</td></tr>
<tr><td>1964:</td><td>The company sells its fashion line in order to concentrate on its dance products.</td></tr>
<tr><td>1972:</td><td>The company's sales volume begins to rise sharply.</td></tr>
<tr><td>1987:</td><td>Capezio brings out a new fitness line.</td></tr>
<tr><td>1999:</td><td>The company forms a European joint venture with Norwich Dancewear Ltd.</td></tr>
<tr><td>2002:</td><td>The company opens a new showroom in New York.</td></tr>
</table>

shoes to leotards. Capezio also began making shoes for ballroom dancing. Serious ballroom dancers ordered their shoes from European makers, because they could not find what they needed in the United States. Capezio decided to manufacture ballroom shoes, and immediately drew customers.

Over the 1980s, the company introduced several new lines. It had a broad line of toe shoes, including its Pavlova brand, Duro Toes, Nicolinis, and Ultimos; its Tekniks slippers in several styles and materials; special shoes for children and for male dancers; jazz shoes; clogging shoes; and many other specialized dance shoes. In 1987, Capezio brought out a fitness line of shoes and clothing. This included the firm's first all-purpose sneakers. The company also sold a Dancer's Collection line of cotton clothing meant to be worn over dance gear. By the late 1980s, Capezio operated four manufacturing plants, including facilities in New Jersey and Florida. The company also ran ten retail stores and sold its goods through thousands of small retailers.

Competitive Landscape in the 1990s and After

Capezio/Ballet Makers moved into its fourth generation of management in the 1990s. Estelle Sommers, the widow of Ben Sommers, Salvatore Capezio's protégé, had worked with the company since the 1960s. She married Ben Sommers in 1961 and eventually ran the retail side of the business. She was also, like all Capezio's top management, a noted patron of the arts. Estelle Sommers died in 1994. Alfred Terlizzi, grandnephew of the founder, retired to Florida in 1997 and died a year later. He had been president of the company since 1977. The new chief executive was Paul Terlizzi. Other Terlizzi family members managed the company, as well as members of another Capezio family branch, the Giacoios.

Capezio sold much of its merchandise to dance students—children and teenagers. It continued to make its professional toe shoes by hand in its New Jersey factory. Its toe shoes sold for about $60 a pair, up from $7.50 in 1960. The company began to contract with factories abroad to make its less labor-intensive lines. Capezio had had four of its own manufacturing facilities in the 1980s. In the 1990s, it had two, as well as offices and showrooms in New York City, and employed about 400 people.

The company emphasized new fashion lines and new athletic markets in the 1990s. Ice-skating had become one of the

most-watched sports of the 1990s with the rise of many young American stars. Capezio introduced a line of skating gear in the late 1990s and had both Olympic medalists Tara Lipinski and Sarah Hughes as spokesmodels. Ballroom dancing became an Olympic exhibition sport in 2000, and Capezio introduced a new Dancesport line in time for the festivities. The company also sponsored a ballroom dancing competition, Dancesport Championship Limited. Capezio moved more heavily into European markets in 1999, forming a joint venture with Norwich Dancewear Ltd., a dance gear maker based in Norfolk, England. The two companies formed Ballet Makers-Europe, Ltd. The new company was expected to bring in roughly $3.5 million in sales in its first year. Capezio goods had previously been available in Europe only through independent distributors. The new company was expected to have much wider distribution, backed up by a significant investment in warehouse facilities and a knowledgeable, multilingual sales force.

In 2002, Capezio moved to new, larger quarters in Manhattan. Its new showroom on 39th Street also included a dance studio and housed retail sales and product development staff. The company had sales of about $90 million annually in the early 2000s. While Capezio remained the leading brand in American dancewear, it faced increasing competition from foreign firms. Freed of London was the world's largest ballet shoe manufacturer and had begun to make inroads into the U.S. market in the 1990s and early 2000s. Another new name in the U.S. market was the Australian firm Bloch, Inc. Bloch had started selling its dance shoes in the United States in the 1980s. Although it had far less name recognition than Capezio, the Australian maker was able to entice customers with its lower prices. Capezio vowed to stay ahead in the 2000s by continuing to focus on the world of dance. The company was a significant patron of dance through its foundation, and the supplier to many top stars as well as young performers.

Principal Subsidiaries

Ballet Makers-Europe, Ltd.

Principal Competitors

Bloch, Inc.; Freed of London, Ltd.; Chacott Co. Ltd.

Further Reading

"Alfred Terlizzi," *Dance Magazine*, May 1998, p. 40.
"Alfred Terlizzi, 58, Supporter of the Arts," *Star-Ledger* (Newark, N.J.), February 11, 1998, p. 58.
"Capezio Dances in Europe," *Dance Magazine*, July 1999, p. 23.
"Capezio Gets into Gear," *WWD*, March 14, 2002, p. 8.
Dalva, Nancy Vreeland, "Capezio Centenary," *Dance Magazine*, May 1987, pp. 90–94.
"Estelle Sommers," *Dance Magazine*, May 1994, p. 92.
Feitelberg, Rosemary, "Capezio Launches New Dancewear Line," *WWD*, April 12, 2001, p. 9.
Morley, Hugh R., "Capezio Still Tops in Ballet Slipper Business," *Knight Ridder/Tribune Business News*, January 12, 2002, p. ITEM02012049.
Stoop, Norma Mclain, "The Dancers They Serve: Capezio Ballet Makers," *Dance Magazine*, October 1980.

—A. Woodward

Charoen Pokphand Group

15/F CP Tower, 313 Silom Road
Bangkok 10500
Thailand
Telephone: (+66) 2 638 2000
Fax: (+66) 2 638 2139
Web site: http://www.cpfoods.net

Private Company
Incorporated: 1921
Employees: 100,000
Sales: $13 billion (2002 est.)
NAIC: 311119 Other Animal Food Manufacturing; 112320
Broilers and Other Meat-Type Chicken Production;
112511 Finfish Farming and Fish Hatcheries

Charoen Pokphand Group (CP) is one of Thailand's largest companies and one of the first true Asian multinationals. The group's operations span more than 250 companies in 20 countries—largely in Thailand and China but also in Indonesia, Malaysia, India, and Cambodia—with more than 100,000 employees and sales of $13 billion. These operations are placed under two main business divisions—that of Production and Processing and that of Service. CP has also made an effort, unusual among Asian conglomerates, to achieve a degree of financial transparency, including publicly listing a number of its key businesses. These included CP Feedmill, which groups most of the CP's core feedmill and livestock—poultry, pigs, and tiger shrimp—businesses in Thailand, and, in Hong Kong, CP Pokphand, which oversees the group's vast livestock and feedmill holdings (some 200 subsidiaries) on the Chinese mainland. Other key CP holdings include TelecomAsia, challenger to the government run phone company in Bangkok, which has built a network of 2.6 million fiber optic telephone lines for the city; Siam Makro, the group's discount retail chain; Ek Chor China Motorcycle, the New York Stock Exchange-listed maker of motorcycles for the Chinese market; and Vinythai, a maker of polyvinylchloride and other petrochemicals, developed in partnership with Belgium's Solvay. Other holdings comprise retail stores—including a share in the Tesco Lotus supermarket chain and the 7-11 convenience store franchise for Thailand—and restaurants, including the group's Bua Baan fast-food concept featuring CP's own processed foods. Despite its diversified activities, the Asian economic crisis of the late 1990s encouraged CP to restructure itself around a core focus of agribusiness and food operations through a new flagship company, Charoen Pokphand Foods. As such, the group has adopted a new slogan as the ''Kitchen of the World.'' CP has long been led by Dhanin Chearavanont, son of one of the company's founding brothers.

Sowing the Seeds of a Thai Feed Giant in the 1920s

In Thailand, as in most of the Asian region in the early 20th century, the arrival of Chinese expatriates transformed the country's economic and financial landscape. By the end of the century, the region hosted a large number of diversified conglomerates originated by Chinese businessmen, who took their place among the world's wealthiest people. Among them was Dhanin Chearavanont, who, at the turn of the 21st century, controlled a group producing more than $13 billion in revenues each year.

Chearavanont had built his fortune from the Charoen Pokphand Group, or CP Group. That company had originally been founded by two brothers, Chia Ek Chor and Chia Siew Whooy, who arrived in Thailand from China in 1919. The Chia brothers began importing seeds from China and in 1921 set up a small shop in Bangkok's Chinatown district. The original name of the business was Chia Thai Co.

The brothers expanded the operation, importing vegetables as well, to meet the demand of Bangkok's growing Chinese population. Before long, Chia Thai launched an export wing, sending pigs and eggs to Hong Kong. By the 1950s, the brothers' children had joined the business, and the company began looking for expansion opportunities. Chia Thai, which became known under the Thai name of Charoen Pokphand did not have to look far for its first attempt at diversification. Farmers formed the major part of CP's customers, and the extension into feedstuffs seemed a natural one. In this way, CP's seed customers became the suppliers for its new operation, animal feed. In 1954, the company launched its first subsidiary, Charoen Pokphand Feedmill. By the end of the decade, feed had become a major company focus.

CP expanded quickly and by 1960 had begun exporting feed to other markets, especially China. In that year, the company established its first foreign operation, opening a branch office in Hong Kong. At the same time, the company expanded its operations throughout Thailand, adding a growing number of farmer customers and feedmills. By the end of the 1960s, CP was already able to claim the position as Thailand's leading feed producer.

A major force behind the company's growth was Dhanin Chearavanont, son of Chia Ek Chor. Despite being the youngest of four brothers, all involved in the business, Dhanin Chearavanont clearly displayed the most energy, and by 1964, at the age of 25, had already begun to guide the company's development. In 1970, he became president of the firm.

Dhanin had recognized that poultry and feed industries in the West had been making a number of important developments since the 1950s, combining advances in breeding techniques with new feed formulas, including the use of growth hormones and antibiotics, as well as modern production line technologies to produce dramatic increases in poultry yields. Chickens were not only larger but their growth cycle had been cut by as much as half. In the early 1970s, Dhanin decided to extend CP's operations into the livestock arena.

For this, Dhanin displayed a willingness to engage foreign expertise, in the form of partnerships, a method that was to prove a company hallmark for much of its later growth. In 1970, the company set up its first joint-venture with U.S.-based Arbor Acres, which had been one of the pioneers in selectively breeding for the purpose of producing a meatier, faster-growing bird. CP imported its first chickens in 1973, launching the company's nursery operation. At the same time, the company hired foreign nutritionists to help it develop new, higher-yield feed formulas.

By the mid-1970s, CP had succeeded in developing a bird that reached maturity after only seven weeks—compared to up to four months for other breeds. At the same time, the company's improved feed formula meant that chickens could be brought to maturity with only half the amount of feed. CP then brought its chicks to Thai farmers, providing them with the feed, technology, and supplies needed to begin production of chickens. The company then bought the chickens back from farmers, who, encouraged by CP, quickly developed large-scale farms.

China Pioneer in the 1990s

Based on its success in livestock, CP stepped up its diversification, becoming a vertically integrated agribusiness, adding breeding farms, slaughterhouses, processed foods production,

and, later, its own chain of restaurants. CP had also gone international, launching feedmill operations in Indonesia in 1972, exporting chickens to Japan—the company soon challenged the giant U.S. companies that had previously been dominant as that country's leading supplier—in 1973, then moving into Singapore in 1976.

Yet CP's greatest overseas success was to come in China. At the end of the 1970s, that country instituted a series of economic reforms opening its economy to foreign investment for the first time since the Maoist revolution. CP's family ties with the mainland enabled it to become the first foreign company to establish itself in the newly created Shenzhen free trade zone, where the company set up its Chia Tai Co. subsidiary in 1979. While investment in China remained tentative in the early years of the decade, by the mid-1980s CP had gained valuable first-in experience in the market. The company stepped up its investment in the country, opening new feedmill and livestock operations. By the early 1990s, CP had launched some 200 subsidiaries in China.

CP had now become a highly sought-after partner for companies seeking entry into the Chinese market. The company's experience—and its prized political connections—made it the partner of choice for a variety of diversified ventures, one example being motorcycle manufacturing in partnership with Japan's Honda. In the meantime, CP's massive investment in poultry production on the mainland was credited with changing the country's dietary habits, as per-capita consumption more than doubled by the end of the decade.

Back home, CP continued to seek more markets for diversification. In 1980, the company partnered with another U.S. company, Avian Farms, to begin breeding ducks. The company also added pig breeding operations that year, importing livestock from Belgium, Holland, and the United States to develop its own pig hybrids. In 1986, the company spotted another food opportunity and launched a research center for the development of new breeds of shrimp that would be adaptable for fish-farming methods. The company's success in that area enabled it to become the world's leading supplier of black tiger shrimps.

Focusing on the New Century

By the end of the 1980s, the growing CP empire had already produced some $4 billion in revenues. Yet a significant part of that figure no longer came from the group's core food interests but from its increasingly diversified operations. The company's entry into the restaurant sector came in 1988 with the launch of Chester's Grill. That same year, CP launched its own supermarket group, Makro, which quickly became a leader in Thailand's retail sector. The following year, CP entered the dairy market, partnering with Japan's Meiji group to launch the CP Meiji line of dairy foods for the Thai market. The company also added convenience stores that year, gaining the Thai franchise for the 7-11 retail format. The company quickly began building that format into a national chain, adding as many as 20 stores each month and reaching a total of 1,000 by the end of the 1990s.

Yet the company's diversification went even further. In 1989, CP joined with Solvay of Belgium to launch Vinythai Co., a manufacturer of polyvinylchloride. The following year,

Key Dates:

1921: Chia Brothers, from China, set up a seed shop in Bangkok's Chinatown, then begin exporting poultry and pigs to Hong Kong.

1954: The company diversifies into animal feed production and launches a subsidiary, Charoen Pokphand Feedmill.

1964: Dhanin Chearavanont, son of one of the founders, takes over as company leader.

1970: The company launches a poultry breeding business in partnership with Arbor Acres of the United States.

1973: The company begins exporting poultry to Japan and becomes one of that market's leaders.

1979: The company becomes the first foreign firm to invest in the Chinese market, opening a feed subsidiary in the Shenzhen economic trade zone.

1986: The company diversifies into shrimp production and becomes the world's leader in this market.

1994: Lotus Supercenter retail network is launched in Thailand.

1998: The company restructures as a "focused" agribusiness.

2003: Dhanin Chearavanont is named one of *Fortune* magazine's "World's Most Powerful Business Leaders."

the company made an even bolder move, forming a partnership with the U.S. telecommunications firm of NYNEX (later Verizon) to launch TelecomAsia (TA) in a move to compete against the government's former telephone monopoly in Bangkok market. In 1993, TA went public on the Bangkok Stock Exchange and began construction of its own fiber-optic telephone network, which reached 2.6 million lines at the end of the decade.

TA was not the only one of CP's companies to be listed publicly, as the company brought Charoen Pokphand Feedmill, Siam Makro, and Vinythai to the Bangkok exchange, as well as its Hong Kong subsidiary, CP Pokphand to the Hong Kong exchange, a Shanghai-based animal feed and poultry group to the Shanghai exchange, a real estate development arm, Hong Kong Fortune, to the Hong Kong exchange, and Ek Chor China Motorcycle to the New York exchange. Investors seized the opportunity to purchase a stake in one of Asia's fastest-growing conglomerates. The public listings also represented a rare instance of financial transparency among the region's usually super-secret corporations. However, these publicly listed companies in fact represented only a small part of CP's total holdings.

Into the mid-1990s, CP continued to seek new means for diversifying its holdings. In 1994, the company launched its first Lotus Supercenter retail store, which it developed into a national chain in Thailand. CP also began nurturing an ambition to enter the semi-conductor market, beginning negotiations with Chinese officials to act once again as partner for foreign investors. By then, however, China had gained sufficient confidence in its dealings with foreign corporations and no longer needed CP to play the role of middleman. Instead, CP suddenly found

itself facing a new wave of competition in China as the international business world, including industry heavyweights operating on a global scale, rushed into what was fast becoming the world's largest single market.

The economic crisis that swept through the Asian region caught CP short as well. The company's fiber optic network went online concurrently with the country's financial collapse, and TelecomAsia was hard-pressed to find customers. Only half of the 2.6 million lines were rented by the end of the decade, forcing TA to default on payments and landing it $1.5 billion in debt. In return, the company's banks froze its line of credit across all of its operations.

CP, like many of the region's conglomerates, was forced to recognize that its diversification drive had been too ambitious. Unlike its counterparts, however, CP acknowledged its errors publicly, pledging to refocus its operations and at the same time simplify its structure in an effort to enhance the company's financial transparency.

CP began shedding a number of noncore businesses, such as its Thai-based Lotus Supercenter operation, the majority of which were acquired by the United Kingdom's Tesco and renamed Tesco Lotus. The company also sold off its Ek Chor Motorcycle subsidiary's Shanghai manufacturing stake and shut down a number of TA subsidiaries. Another feature of the company's restructuring was its willingness to turn down new joint-venture "offers," which typically involved the company taking on debt. If previously a number of the group's subsidiaries had built up debt-to-equity ratios of more than 1,000 percent, they were now under orders to pay down debt and balance their books.

Into the new century, CP decided to refocus itself as the "Kitchen to the World," looking to its core agribusiness holdings for future growth. As part of that effort, and in an attempt to increase its financial transparency, CP merged 11 of its Thai agribusiness subsidiaries into core group Charoen Pokphand Feedmill by 1999. Charoen Pokphand then became the main vehicle for the now "focused" CP.

The company's emphasis on gaining focus did not, however, prevent it from maintaining its diversified business interests, nor from entering new markets, such as the mobile telephone market in partnership with Orange in 2000, or an entry into the e-commerce market with the launch of Phantavanij and eMarketplace in 2001. CP had not abandoned the retail market either, and in 2002 the company began construction on a new style "super brand" Lotus mall in Shanghai, raising the number of the group's stores in China—where it maintained 100 percent control of the Lotus chain—to ten by 2003.

By then, Dhanin had been consecrated by *Fortune* magazine as one of its "World's Most Powerful Business Leaders" and the only corporate chief in the ASEAN economic zone to be featured on the list. As part of this recognition, Dhanin was credited with having built a fully vertically integrated agriculture-to-retail empire, including the world's largest producer of animal feed and one of the top producers of eggs, poultry, and other livestock. With some 250 companies, 100,000 employees, and more than $13 billion in revenues in 2002, the Charoen Pokphand Group represented a true success story.

Principal Subsidiaries

C.P. Feedmill Inc.; C.P. Pokphand (Hong Kong); Ek Chor China Motorcycle (United States); Hong Kong Fortune (Hong Kong); Shanghai Dajiang (Shanghai); Siam Makro; TelecomAsia.

Principal Competitors

Lajta-Hansag Rt; Nisshin Seifun Group; Hindustan Lever Ltd.; Nippon Flour Mills Company Ltd.; Unicharm Corp.; Nisshin Oillio Group; Uni-President Enterprises Corporation; Daesang Corporation.

Further Reading

"Back to School," *Far Eastern Economic Review*, April 8, 1999.

"Back to the Farm," *Far Eastern Economic Review*, December 28, 2000.

Biers, Dan, and Michael Vatikiotis, "Half Way There?," *Business Week*, May 28, 2001, p. 26.

"A Bruiser from Bangkok," *Economist*, November 26, 1994, p. 70.

Einhorn, Bruce, "CP's Challenge," *BusinessWeek Asian Edition*, October 6, 1997.

Lee, Josephine, "Chickens in Gloves," *Forbes*, March 31, 2003.

"Radicalism, Asian Style," *Economist*, March 24, 2001.

Tanzer, Andrew, "The Birdman of Bangkok," *Forbes*, April 13, 1992, p. 86.

—M.L. Cohen

Cherry Lane Music Publishing Company, Inc.

6 East 32nd Street, 11th Floor
New York, New York 10016
U.S.A.
Telephone: (212) 561-3000
Fax: (212) 683-2040
Web site: http://www.cherrylane.com

Private Company
Incorporated: 1960
Employees: 90
Sales: $26 million (2002 est.)
NAIC: 512230 Music Publishers; 511120 Periodical
    Publishers; 511190 Other Publishers; 711130 Musical
    Groups and Artists

Through its four divisions, Cherry Lane Music Publishing Company, Inc., publishes music in print, owns and administers publishing rights for a large catalog of music, transfers music from analog to digital form, and publishes such music industry trade journals as *Guitar* and *Home Recording*. Cherry Lane has business relationships with a host of songwriters, production companies, and other clients that include sports programming and children's programming companies. The company administers publishing rights for a wide array of songwriters including John Denver, Harry Belafonte, Lenny Kravitz, and the R&B/Hip-Hop group The Black Eyed Peas. In the 1990s, the company began aggressive efforts to expand is presence through new partnerships, joint ventures, and co-publishing relationships a variety of media, including television and film production companies; Latin and other minority songwriters, artists, and companies; sports entities; and children's programming.

1960s Origins

Cherry Lane was founded in 1960 by musicologist and composer Milton Theodore Okun. Born in Brooklyn in 1923, Okun became interested in music at a young age. He received his Bachelor of Music Education at New York University (NYU) in 1949, and then received a Master of Music Education at Oberlin Conservatory of Music in 1951. After graduation, he became a

singer and guitarist for record companies. When he founded Cherry Lane in Port Chester, New York, one of his earliest clients was John Denver, for whom he was a mentor. Other early musical credits included arranging and producing records for the Chad Mitchell Trio; Peter, Paul, and Mary; and Placido Domingo. He was also music director for the Brothers Four, Mary Travers, Peter Yarrow, the Starland Vocal Band, and Harry Belafonte.

Okun was the author of *Something to Sing About* (1968), and was editor for several *New York Times* song books, including the *New York Times Great Songs of the Sixties* (1970 & Volume 2, 1974); *New York Times Great Songs of Lennon and McCartney* (1973), *New York Times Country Music's Greatest Songs* (1978), and *New York Times Great Songs of the 70's* (1978). He was also an arranger and editor for the *New York Times Great Songs of Abba* (1980), and *The Complete Beatles* (1981) among other musical accomplishments. In all, Okun garnered 75 Gold and Platinum records and 16 Grammy nominations.

During Cherry Lane's early days, the company focused mainly on collecting royalties and copyright payments for songwriters. The company eventually developed unique proprietary systems called Income Trackers to oversee royalty statements and payments received from any number of sources, including mechanical rights and performance rights societies, co-publishers, sub-publishers, direct licensees, and record companies. Income Trackers handled shortfalls or delays in payments via a "collection" function, and the company maintained the services of such entities as Tribune Media Services and Essential Television Services to provide factual proof of broadcasts in order to track down any payment shortfalls.

Aggressive Expansion in the 1990s

Until the 1990s, Cherry Lane's primary work continued to be collecting royalties and payments for a roster of songwriting artists, from Mozart to Metallica. New management, however, would expand the scope of the operation. In 1986, Peter Primont, a graduate of the New York Institute of Technology, joined the company as president, eventually rising to the position of CEO. In 1990, Aida Gurwicz joined the company as

Company Perspectives:

We built our reputation, and an impressive list of credits, through careful cultivation of relationships within the music, film, and television communities. As an administrator, we have a record of unsurpassed meticulousness and diligence in the collection of income and protection of our clients' copyrights. We also work proactively to exploit our properties through our associations with producers, directors, music supervisors, record companies, commercial production companies, and trailer houses.

senior vice-president. Gurwicz, holding degrees from Temple University and NYU, accepted her first musical publishing job as head of the Foreign Department at Carl Fischer, Inc., a publisher of classical music. During the next ten years, she rose through the ranks to become senior vice-president of that firm. In 1990, she was approached by Peter Primont and was offered a position as the growing company's senior vice-president. Gurwicz accepted and rose to the office of president in 1998. Under her leadership, Cherry Lane began to aggressively pursue new musical business ventures and partnerships. In 1993, the company signed an agreement with Hal Leonard Publishing, the world's largest print music publisher, to distribute Cherry Lane's catalog worldwide. In 1998, the company moved its headquarters from Port Chester to Manhattan.

Gurwicz worked to develop a number of new relationships, among them partnerships with feature film and television producers. Acquisitions included owning and placing original music for both movies and TV, and exploiting the same for other uses. Cherry Lane also began efforts to create new music for a number of cable and network movies, including ''Movies of the Week'', a variety of televised sports programs and events, and children's programming.

In May 2001, Cherry Lane signed a worldwide co-publishing deal with Toronto-based Attack Records and Filmworks. The music deal allowed Cherry Lane to showcase the independent record and music publishing company's diverse roster of urban, pop, and rock acts while also promoting and protecting the music of flourishing Canadian artists and songwriters, including Sicboy, Hope Springs Eternal, Love/Candy, Kai Blackwood, and Blasternaut. President of Attack Records, Mark Berry, was nominated for Grammy and Juno productions and engineering and mixing credits for albums by Billy Idol, Boy George, David Bowie, Duran Duran, Voivoid, and Yes, among others. In all, he garnered more than 30 international Gold and Platinum records to his production and mixing credits. As a result of the co-publishing deal with Cherry Lane, Attack Records' roster would be part of the music publishing company's expanding catalogue.

Later that year, Cherry Lane announced another worldwide publishing deal, this one with Icon Productions. Founded by Mel Gibson and his business partner, Bruce Davey, Icon Productions was established in 1989. The Icon company had produced such film greats as *Hamlet, Maverick, Forever Young, The Man Without a Face, Immortal Beloved,* and the epic, *Braveheart,* which won Academy Awards in 1995 for Best Picture and Best Director (Mel Gibson). Icon also launched a record label called Icon Records, with releases that included soundtracks to the Icon films, *Anna Karenina, Fairy Tale: A True Story,* and *187.* The agreement allowed Cherry Lane to represent Icon's diverse catalogue of motion picture scores by composers that included James Horner, Alan Silvestri, and Stewart Copeland.

Also in 2001, Cherry Lane entered into an exclusive co-publishing agreement with Urbanworld Films. Stacy Spikes, former executive with Miramax and October Films, founded the Urbanworld Film Festival in 1997. Based in New York, the event became the largest display for minority films in the U.S., and presented a number of movie hits, including *Soul Food* and *How Stella Got Her Groove Back.* Drawing on the success of the festival, Urbanworld Films began releasing minority films that targeted African American, Asian, and Latin audiences. Titles from its 2001/2002 movies included *The Visit, King of the Jungle, Higher Ed,* and *Fidel.* Dan ''The Automator'' Nakamura, co-producer of *Gorillaz,* one of the biggest hit albums of 2001, wrote a score for *King of the Jungle.* The deal with Cherry Lane allowed the music publishing company to administer existing music and create new music for minority films from Urbanworld Films. Cherry Lane also became a creative partner, making it possible to share its catalogue of source music and extensive roster of composers with the film company.

Another agreement in 2001 was Cherry Lane's co-publishing deal with major Canadian film and television producer, Kevin Gillis. The deal gave Cherry Lane rights to promote and increase recognition for Gillis' works. Gillis was producer, creator, director, and head writer for the hit family television series, *The Raccoons,* shown in more than 180 countries. He also produced the animated theatrical feature, *The Nutcracker Prince,* with voices of Kiefer Sutherland and Peter O'Toole; and was producer of Jeff Healey's television documentary, *See the Light.* Gillis also collaborated with a number of other songwriters, including Joe Walsh of The Eagles.

Among other work, Gillis produced the animated series, *Eckhart,* and *I Was a Rat,* a family movie of the week based on the 1999 children's book of the same name by author Philip Pullman. Other children's and family projects included the feature film, *Larsonia;* an animated series; *Seaside Hotel;* and *KidsWorld Sports,* a show he co-produced with Clear Channel, WETA (Washington PBS affiliate), Canwest Global TV in Canada, Breakthrough Films, and Run With Us Productions. The latter show, with a focus on youth and sports around the world, allowed children with obstacles such as economic struggles, physical handicaps, cultural differences, or family pressures to participate in sports events. In addition, Gillis developed a feature film with the Canadian Broadcast Corporation (CBC) of *The Raccoons.* The exclusive agreement with Cherry Lane allowed the music publishing company the right to increase recognition of Gillis's large volume of work worldwide.

2002 and Beyond: New Media Opportunities

In January 2002, Cherry Lane created a joint marketing and publishing agreement with the Collections division of the AFMA (formerly known as the American Film Marketing Association). The deal was set to promote the services of both companies. The AFMA had long been known as one of the most prestigious trade associations for the independent film and television industry. AMFA member independent film and television companies crafted some of the most acclaimed and popular films of the late 20th and early 21st centuries, including *The Lord of the Rings: The Fellowship of the Ring; In the Bedroom; Monster's Ball; Pulp Fiction; Driving Miss Daisy; Four Weddings and a Funeral; Life is Beautiful; Shakespeare in Love; The Silence of the Lambs; Terminator 2: Judgment Day;* and *Traffic,* to name just a few. Under the joint agreement, Cherry Lane would promote the services of both companies, including collection of auto/video and music publishing royalties worldwide. Also under the agreement, AFMA members would receive licensing fees and music royalties for television and radio. In some markets, members would also receive music royalties for theatrical use of their products worldwide, and members would retain 100 percent ownership of the copyright for their music.

In September 2002, Cherry Lane and 4Kids Entertainment Music announced another partnership, this one for the release of *Yu-Gi-Oh! Music to Duel By* on DreamWorks Records. The new partnership would complement the highly popular *Yu-Gi-Oh!* card and video games from Konami, and toys from Mattel. 4Kids Entertainment, Inc., a company dedicated to the best in entertainment for children, had headquarters in New York City, and international offices in London.

The high-energy music for *Yu-G-Oh!: Music to Duel By* was the result of a collaboration between Norman Grossfeld, president of 4Kids Productions and John Siegler, 4Kids Music Supervisor, along with a group of established New York-based songwriters, composers, producers, studio musicians, and actors. The musical relationship between Cherry Lane and 4Kids had begun with the *Pokemon* phenomenon in November 1997. When *Yu-Gi-Oh!* was introduced, it became a cultural phenomenon, and a lifestyle that excited kids. The *Yu-Gi-Oh!* album was the result of this rising interest. The new partnership between Cherry Lane and 4Kids Entertainment Music would showcase the audio accompaniment to the popular 'dueling' card game that had generated a successful animated TV series, and a multitude of collectible merchandise.

In 2003, Cherry Lane added several partnerships, joint ventures, and agreements to its growing list. In January, Cherry

Lane and Tu Casa Entertainment (Your Home Entertainment) announced plans to create a joint venture company called Cherry Casa Music Publishing, to sign and develop Latin songwriters and artists. Cherry Lane also agreed to administer the company's compositions worldwide. Maribel Schumacher, founder and president of Tu Casa, represented and managed artists, and supervised film and television music and music publishing at the multi-level company. Her business history included launching Spain's first independent label, pioneering Latin rock music in the U.S., setting up Warner Latina's South American operations, and becoming VP of Marketing for Warner Music Latin America.

The joint venture helped both companies move forward to foster career development and create a roster of strong Latin singers and songwriters. Cherry Lane's administration, which also extended to film and television productions, would allow Cherry Casa to place the work of Latin artists in a large number of media projects. In the marketing arena, the company's involvement with contemporary Latin music would allow exposure in recordings, film, television, and commercials, and allow Cherry Lane to develop a large amount of work with appeal to an international market.

The Cherry Casa unit signed its first Latin songwriter and producer, Roberto Blades, in May 2003. Grammy winner and frequent nominee, Blades had earned songwriting credits for seven number one Latin singles, including Marc Anthony's hits, "Dimelo (I Need to Know)" and "Muy Dentro de Mi (You Sang to Me)". Blades had also worked with Gloria and Emilio Estefan, among other Latin artists.

Cherry Lane also entered into several partnerships with important sports entities. In February, the company announced plans to join forces with Professional Bull Riders (PBR). The partnership created Cherry Bull, a company dedicated to developing new music and recordings associated with PBR events. Because bull riding had become one of the fastest growing spectator sports in television ratings and stadium attendance, and because music was an important part of its sporting events, the relationship with Cherry Lane was designed to create new and exciting themes that would bring the music into a broader audience base.

PBR shows were broadcast on NBC Sports, Outdoor Life Network (OLN), and the Spanish-language station, Telemundo, in Australia, Canada, Sweden, and Russia. With Cherry Lane helping to present original music for its sports and entertainment properties, one of the first items on the Cherry Bull agenda was a new theme song. Composed by Guy Thomas, a writer with Cherry Lane who had worked previously with Carly Simon, Kenny Loggins, and Kenny Rogers, among other artists, the country tune created by Thomas made its TV debut on NBC in February. In addition, new music was composed for riders competing in the events. Music was even created for the bulls. Cherry Lane would also administer the company's compositions.

Cherry Lane also entered into a worldwide publishing and administration agreement with NFL Films for compositions and master recordings. NFL Films had set a standard for sports music for a generation, and had created a library of material instantly recognizable to a huge fan base. Cherry Lane's vision was for the NFL Films brand to be recognizable in various spheres of the music business. Because of the new relationship, long-time NFL fans and music lovers alike would be able to experience the musical results of this joint venture.

NFL Films had begun its operations in 1964 to provide excellence in sports filmmaking. It soon became the standard for providing outstanding cinematography and moving orchestral music to accompany poignant storytelling. In its 40+ year history, the company won 82 Emmy awards and became the most honored filmmaker in sports. During the 2003 season, NFL Films opened a new 200,000 square foot, high-tech television and film production facility in Mt. Laurel, New Jersey, where it began operating as one of the last self-contained, Hollywood-style studios. The production facility produced and distributed more than 400 hours of new NFL programming for broadcast and cable networks, NFL.com home videos, CD-ROMs, and DVDs.

The new partnership between NFL Films and Cherry Lane helped to create a series of musical compilation albums featuring songs from well-known hip-hop, rock, and pop musical artists. The recordings included NFL Films track remixes, along with new music created by NFL Films composers, Dave Robidoux and Tom Hedden. Use of the new NFL Films studio in New Jersey was part of the recording plan, with the albums released on NFL Records and launched along with major NFL events that included Training Camp, Draft Weekend, and the annual Super Bowl. Synchronization of efforts offered cross-promotional opportunities with recording artists and NFL sponsors, and gave even more avenues of exposure for NFL Records and the music.

In May 2003, Cherry Lane formed a relationship with the National Association for Stock Car Auto Racing (NASCAR). The partnership between Cherry Lane and NASCAR created Motor Music, a company designed to develop original music and sound recordings to identify and communicate the sounds of NASCAR. Motor Music offered complete services in music production and publishing to NASCAR's business partners, including sport teams, drivers, tracks, licensees, broadcast and video production partners, sponsors, and international television and entertainment projects. Cherry Lane administered the compositions and master recordings worldwide.

The first task of Motor Music was to create compositions for a complete catalogue of NASCAR-themed music that would express the excitement, drama, and thrill of NASCAR racing. Other projects would use commercial recordings to help extend the NASCAR brand into mainstream entertainment and wider audience recognition. In February 2004, Motor Music announced the debut of NASCAR's theme song, ''Thunder,'' composed by David Robidoux and mixed by Alan Meyerson.

Around this same time, Cherry Lane also made a deal with the World Wrestling Entertainment (WWE) to administrate and/or co-publish music for a variety of wrestling programs and events that included *Raw, SmackDown!, Heat,* and *After Burn,* to name just a few.

On the contemporary music scene, in June 2003, Cherry Lane made a worldwide co-publishing agreement with R&B/Hip-Hop band, the Black Eyed Peas. The deal covered musical rights to the groups' *Elephunk* album that was released on A&M Records. The Black Eyed Peas single, ''Where Is the Love?'' featuring Justin Timberlake, had risen quickly on the charts and was released overseas to excited fans. The success of the single, and the release of the *Elephunk* record, helped the group earn an opening slot on the 2003 Justified and Stripped tour, headlined by Timberlake and Christina Aguilera. The Peas also appeared on the debut broadcast of WB's ''Pepsi Smash.'' The deal helped Cherry Lane's efforts to diversify its client roster, and gave the band new opportunities via increased exposure from the record.

With its continuing efforts to create new and exciting co-publishing partnerships and administration agreements, its ongoing efforts to collect royalties and payments for standard and new releases, and its work to place old and new songs in innovative music for television and film, the company's future seemed secure.

Principal Divisions

Cherry Lane Music Publishing Company Inc.; Cherry Lane Licensing, LLC; Cherry Lane Digital LLC; Cherry Lane Magazines LLC; Cherry Lane Music Company (Print).

Principal Operating Units

Publishing, Print, Digital, Magazines.

Principal Competitors

Universal Music Publishing Company; EMI Music Publishing.

Further Reading

''Cherry Lane Commitment to Music Education,'' *Music Trades*, November 2000, p. 49.

''Hal Leonard to Distribute Cherry Lane,'' *Music Trades*, January 1993, p. 136.

Lichtman, Irv, ''Cherry Lane And OneHouse Form Alliance To Do Digital-Biz Consulting,'' *Billboard*, July 31, 1999, p. 47.

——, ''Cherry Lane, Peermusic Link in Deals,'' *Billboard*, November 14, 1998, p. 6.

——, ''Cherry Lane Takes Manhattan,'' *Billboard*, June 20, 1998, p. 101.

Marden, Lori, ''Home Recording (New Magazines),'' *Folio: The Magazine for Magazine Management*, March 15, 1998, p. 23.

—Nancy K. Capace

CJ Corporation

500 Namdaemunro 5-ka, Chung-ku
Seoul
South Korea
Telephone: +82 2 726 8114
Fax: +82 2 726 8089
Web site: http://www.cheiljedang.co.kr

Public Company
Incorporated: 1953 as Cheil Jedang
Employees: 3,506
Sales: KRW 2.27 trillion ($1.9 billion) (2002)
Stock Exchanges: KOSDAQ
NAIC: 311312 Cane Sugar Refining; 311119 Other
Animal Food Manufacturing; 311211 Flour Milling;
311225 Fats and Oils Refining and Blending; 311421
Fruit and Vegetable Canning; 311423 Dried and
Dehydrated Food Manufacturing; 312111 Soft Drink
Manufacturing; 325412 Pharmaceutical Preparation
Manufacturing; 325414 Biological Product (Except
Diagnostic) Manufacturing; 512110 Motion Picture
and Video Production; 512191 Teleproduction and
Other Postproduction Services

South Korea's largest food manufacturer, CJ Corporation, is also one of the world's leading producers of such food additives as monosodium glutamate, biotin, and vitamins, as well as amino acids, colorings and flavorings, and other Korean food ingredients, such as Dashida and Mipoong. The company's food production operations embrace the full spectrum of foods, including refined sugar, seasonings, cooking oil, canned and preserved foods, ready-cooked meals, instant noodles, fish products, confectionery, coffee creamer, soft drinks and other beverages, and fresh and processed meats, among others. CJ Corporation, formerly the Cheil Jedang division of the Samsung conglomerate, is also one of South Korea's top pharmaceutical groups, focusing on bulk actives for antibiotics—the company controls some 20 percent of the world's supply of 7-amino cephalosporanic acid, or 7-ACA—as well as the antibiotics themselves. CJ Corporation has diversified at the dawn of the 21st century, with a particular interest in the media and communications markets.

The company holds an 11 percent stake in the Steven Spielberg production vehicle Dreamworks SKG, and operates its own film production company, a record company, its own cable-based home shopping channel as well as m-net, the country's only cable music channel, and a national multiplex theater chain. The company is also present in the high-speed Internet market through its Dreamline and Dream Soft subsidiaries, and operates online shopping and logistics subsidiaries as well. CJ Corporation is led by the brother and sister team of Jay and Miky Lee, whose grandfather, Lee Byung Chull, founded Samsung in the 1950s. The company is listed on the Korea Stock Exchange and in 2002 posted sales of W 2.27 trillion ($1.9 billion).

Chaebol Origins in the 1950s

Son of a wealthy landowner, Lee Byung Chull took part of his inheritance and started a rice mill in the 1930s. That business failed, however, and instead, in 1938, Lee founded a trucking and real estate company, called Samsung, or "Three Stars." The Japanese invasion of Manchuria led to that company's bankruptcy as well. Yet this time Lee rebuilt his company, and by 1945 Samsung had begun its emergence as one of Korea's largest corporations. Samsung moved into international trading in the years following World War II. This placed the company in a strong position during the Korean civil war, and by the end of the war, Lee was one of Korea's richest men. Lee now decided to transform Samsung into the country's largest chaebol—a highly diversified conglomerate unique to Korea.

Although Samsung later re-oriented itself as an electronics and high-tech group, the company's growth during the 1950s and 1960s was led in large part by its food production. In 1953, Samsung set up a new subsidiary, Cheil Jedang (CJ, for "First Sugar"), and began construction of a sugar refinery in Pusan. That plant was opened in November 1953 and marked the start of Samsung's adventure as one of South Korea's leading manufacturing groups.

By the early 1960s, CJ had begun exporting its refined sugar. The company also had launched its own diversification, adding flour milling in 1958 and, in 1963, the production of the flavor enhancer monosodium glutamate. The company continued to

Company Perspectives:

CJ Corp. is a company that dares to dream and to pursue its dreams. Also, the company would like to see your dreams come true, to help you realize your hope for a better life. All of the company's business lines are created to improve the way we live—foods divisions come up with better tasting processed foods and more wholesome ingredients catered to your modern life; pharmaceutical division strives for overall improvement in the health of the global community; animal feeds division is constantly in search for more nutritional formula for cattle; entertainment division seeks to please all our senses by offering entertaining movies and animations. These are just some of the ways CJ Corp. has structured its business lines to help you reach for a better life.

focus on ingredients during the 1960s, beginning production of Mipoong, a seasoning, in 1964. CJ's rising production, and its growing list of products, led it to open a new manufacturing facility in Seoul in 1968. In 1970, the company added a second sugar refinery, in Inchon.

CJ, like the rest of the rapidly expanding Samsung empire, benefited from the government's protectionist trade policies, which placed high tariffs on imported goods. Lee's close relationship with the government—Lee, under threat of a corruption investigation, had agreed to use Samsung to implement the government's industrialization policies—also enabled CJ to garner leading positions in its product categories.

After establishing its position in basic foods during the 1960s, CJ began a drive to become a general food processor in the 1970s. The company entered the animal feed sector in 1973, opening a new facility in Pusan that year. The company then extended into the production of the seasoning Dashida in 1975, before adding nucleic acid seasonings in 1977. Other new food areas followed into the 1980s, including the start of cooking oils in 1979, meat processing in 1980, and flour-based products in 1985.

As part of its effort to impose itself on the food ingredients and seasonings sectors, as well as on the market for processed foods, CJ set up its own research and development laboratory in 1978. Yet that center quickly took on a new role for the company: an entry into the pharmaceuticals market. In 1984, CJ transferred its R&D department to new, larger quarters and applied to the Korean government for permission to begin pharmaceutical preparations.

CJ's earliest pharmaceutical products remained rooted in the food sector, such as its launch of aspartame and phenolanalin production in 1985. The company quickly targeted the broader pharmaceutical market, however, developing expertise particularly in the antibiotics and vaccines sectors. In 1986 the company began developed its own alpha interferon; that same year, the company began production of Heppacine-B, CJ's own hepatitis B vaccine.

Independence in the 1990s

CJ's expansion continued into the next decade with the construction of a new pharmaceuticals plant in Daeso in 1990.

The company then launched production of 7-amino acid cephalosporanic (7-ACA), a key bulk active in antibiotic preparations. CJ soon became one of the world's largest suppliers of 7-ACA, controlling more than 20 percent of the world supply by the beginning of the next decade.

During the 1980s, Lee Byung Chull had placed elder son Lee Maeng Hee as head of CJ—instead choosing a younger son, Lee Kun Hee, to head the Samsung empire itself. By then, CJ had become somewhat of a backwater among Samsung's major technology and industrial holdings. Worse, already Korea's largest food manufacturing business, CJ's future growth appeared modest at best.

In 1993, Lee Maeng Hee turned over direction of CJ to his children, Miky Lee and her younger brother Jay Lee. The pair—Jay Lee took over the company's day-to-day operations as CEO, while Miky Lee emerged as the company's idea person—quickly moved to emancipate CJ from the Samsung empire, severing its ownership ties with the company their grandfather had founded. Over the next three years, the company unraveled its holdings in Samsung and affiliated companies, and officially launched itself as Chiel Jedang Group in 1996.

CJ's new management sought not just to revitalize the company, but, recognizing the limited growth potential, transform it into a diversified powerhouse in its own right. In 1994, the company extended its food operations into a new area, the restaurant sector, launching the Foodvill restaurant chain. CJ also entered the catering market that year.

Yet Miky Lee had a new direction for the company in mind. Reasoning that CJ had succeeded in nourishing South Korea's bellies, Lee sought to nourish the country's minds as well. In 1995, CJ became one of the early investors in a new film production company then in the process of formation—Dreamworks SKG. Formed by Hollywood heavyweights Steven Spielberg, Jeffrey Katzenberg, and David Geffen, Dreamworks originally had been approached by Samsung, which proposed to put up $900 million to back the new company. When Samsung decided against the investment, Miky Lee took a chance, and CJ offered $300 million for an 11 percent stake in Dreamworks, as well as a seat on the company's board of directors.

The Dreamworks investment now became the cornerstone for CJ's entry into the media and entertainment market. In 1996, the company joined the CJ Golden Village joint venture ship, which included Australia's Village Roadshow as a partner, and began plans to roll out a national network of modern multiplex theaters. The following year, CJ bought up money-losing Music Network, which owned m.net, South Korea's only cable TV music station. That year, as well, the group acquired Dreamline, which had begun building a fiber optic network and providing high-speed Internet access services. The company also established its own film production house, CJ Entertainment, that year.

Food for the Body and Mind in the 20th Century

In 1998, CJ began developing a fourth branch of the group, logistics and online sales, setting up its own logistics group, CJ GLS. The following year, the company formed a food supply business as well, CJ Food System. On the entertainment side, CJ launched a new station, the Food Channel, and then entered

Key Dates:

1953: Samsung founds Cheil Jedang (First Sugar)(CJ), a sugar refiner, in its first move to enter the industrial sector.

1958: CJ begins milling flour.

1963: The company launches production of monosodium glutamate.

1968: The company builds a new plant in Kimpo, Seoul.

1970: Construction of a second sugar refinery at Inchon is completed.

1973: CJ begins production of animal feed.

1979: CJ begins production of food oils.

1985: CJ begins production of aspartame and phenolanalin.

1990: CJ builds a new pharmaceuticals plant in Daeso.

1993: Jay and Miky Lee take over the company, now separate from Samsung.

1995: CJ pays $300 million for an 11 percent stake in Dreamworks SKG.

1997: The company acquires a cable TV music channel, and a high-speed Internet company.

1999: CJ Food System, a food supplier, is launched.

2000: The company acquires a home shopping channel; the Food Channel cable channel is launched.

2001: CJ begins restructuring to focus on its core food, pharmaceuticals, entertainment, and logistics businesses.

the home shopping business with the acquisition of 39 Shopping, subsequently renamed as CJ 39 Shopping.

CJ also had continued investing in its foods and pharmaceuticals businesses, launching the Tous Les Jours bakery in 1997, and building a frozen bread dough factory that year as well. CJ also expanded its food operation internationally, opening production subsidiaries in Indonesia, the Philippines, Myanmar, and China in the late 1990s.

At the beginning of the 2000s, CJ launched a restructuring in order to focus itself on its four key business divisions: Food; Pharmaceuticals; Entertainment; and Logistics. As part of the restructuring process, which lasted more than three years, the company shut down or sold a number of its businesses, renaming some, such as Music Network, which became CJ Media

in 2002, while spinning off others, such as CJ Food System and CJ Entertainment, both of which went public with listings on the KOSDAQ board of the Korea stock exchange. The newly reborn company showed no signs of stopping in its drive to become a major conglomerate in its own right. In 2003, the company opened a new feed mill in Chengdu, in China. CJ also launched a new delivery service, bridging its foods and logistics businesses, in 2003. Dubbed Hetbahn, the new service brought in partner DHL to promise delivery of Korean foods to the Korean expatriate community worldwide. Climbing out from under the shadow of Samsung, CJ had successfully negotiated its transition from its reliance on foods to become a diversified, yet strongly focused group. Yet, far from taking a break from growth, CJ continued to seek out new opportunities to grow, such as its agreement to buy majority control of struggling rival Shindongbang in January 2004.

Principal Subsidiaries

MorningWell; CJ Food System; CJ Foodville; Samyang Oil & Feed; CJ Media; CJ Entertainment; CJ CGV; CJ CableNet; CJ Home Shopping; CJ Telenix; CJ GLS; CJ Investment & Securities; CJ Investment Trust Management; CJ Development; CJ Systems; CJ Indonesia; PT. Cheil Jedang Superfeed (Indonesia); PT. Cheil Jedang Indonesia; PT. Super Unggas Jaya (Indonesia); CJ Philippines Inc.; Myanmar Cheil Co., Ltd.; CJ Nutracon Inc. (U.S.A.); CJ Qingdao Foods Co., Ltd. (China); CJ Ord River Sugar Pty Ltd. (Australia); CJ Vina Agri Co., Ltd. (Vietnam); CJ Cambodia Co., Ltd.

Principal Competitors

Nong Shim Company Ltd.; Daesang Corporation; Dong Suh Foods Corporation; Samyang Foods Company Ltd.; TS Corporation; Tong Yang Confectionery Corporation; Pulmuone Company Ltd.

Further Reading

"CJ Consortium Buys Shindongbang," *Korea Herald,* January 30, 2004.

"CJ Starts 'Hetbahn' Delivery Service," *Korea Herald,* October 16, 2003.

"CJ Group Reborn Ahead of 50th Anniversary," *Business Korea,* October 2002, p. 28.

"Cheil Jedang Changes Name to CJ Group," *Korea Herald,* October 7, 2002.

—M.L. Cohen

Cleveland-Cliffs Inc.

1100 Superior Avenue
Cleveland, Ohio 44114-2589
U.S.A.
Telephone: (216) 694-5700
Fax: (216) 694-4880
Web site: http://www.cleveland-cliffs.com

Public Company
Incorporated: 1850 as The Cleveland Iron Mining
    Company
Employees: 3,956
Sales: $825.1 million (2003)
Stock Exchanges: New York
Ticker Symbol: CLF
NAIC: 212210 Iron Ore Mining

With six iron ore mines in Michigan, Minnesota, and Eastern Canada, Cleveland-Cliffs Inc. is North America's leading producer of iron ore pellets, which are used in the steelmaking process. The company's capacity stands at 36.9 million tons of ore, which represents nearly 28 percent of the continent's annual pellet capacity. Throughout its history, Cleveland-Cliffs has faced competition from imports, takeover attempts, shareholder revolts, ill-advised diversification efforts, and the vagaries of the cyclical steel sector. In the early years of the new century, the company focused on bolstering its assets while the industry restructured and consolidated.

Early History in the 1800s

Cleveland-Cliffs' predecessor, the Cleveland Iron Mining Company, was established in 1846 by a group of investors led by Samuel L. Mather. Mather, an attorney, had moved to Cleveland, Ohio, in 1843, just two years after iron ore was discovered in the Marquette Range of Michigan's Upper Peninsula. Although Mather was confident that, given time, the venture would prove profitable, it was for many years a losing proposition. Transportation costs were prohibitive until 1855, when the Sault Ste. Marie shipping canal was completed. A 1974 company history

noted that "it cost $200 a ton to smelt the ore and ship it down to Pittsburgh where [it] was selling at $80 per ton." Cleveland Iron Mining was only able to survive these difficult formative years through a "unique financial device" concocted by then-treasurer Mather and company president W.J. Gordon. They printed up scrip known as "Iron Money" in one-, two-, three-, and five-dollar denominations and met their financial commitments with these "IOUs" until the company's cash flow stabilized.

As the years went by and surface mines in the region were depleted, firms like Cleveland Iron Mining were forced to seek underground sources. Up to this time, mining was a fairly simple, but extremely labor-intensive, process. Below-ground mining necessitated the development of such specialized devices as power drills, hoisting and conveying machinery, pumps, and ventilation equipment. Cleveland Iron Mining in 1877 became one of the first firms to use these types of equipment to locate ore bodies. The company also pioneered the use of electricity at its mines, often establishing its own on-site hydroelectric and coal-fired generators. These one-time necessities grew into a profitable sideline in the early twentieth century.

During the late nineteenth century, Cleveland Iron Mining diversified into timber harvesting as a predictable adjunct to its mining efforts, since timber was used to support mine shafts and as fuel for blast furnaces. At its zenith, the mining company's lumber output topped 80 million feet of timber, and its timberland holdings peaked at 750,000 acres. As this property was cleared, it was often sold. After the turn of the century, the company formed a joint venture in paper production with the Munising Paper Company. It also acquired an interest in the Munising Woodenware Company, a manufacturer of wooden bowls, clothes pins, and rolling pins. The company divested itself of these timber sidelines in the 1930s.

The discovery of high-grade iron ore deposits at open-pit sites in Minnesota's Mesabi Range in the 1890s—and the new competitive front it opened—accelerated changes already underway in the Michigan-based segment of the iron mining industry. Between 1893 and 1905, many steel companies consolidated vertically through the acquisition of iron ore properties in the Lake Superior district. In order to protect their interests, several large mining companies merged and/or acquired their smaller competitors. This early shakeout formed the enduring structure of the industry.

A major transition at Cleveland Iron Mining reflected this change. In 1891, the company merged with the Iron Cliffs Mining Company to form the Cleveland-Cliffs Iron Company. Organized in 1864 by Samuel Tilden, the Iron Cliffs Company held broad mining interests but suffered from an aging and disinterested management.

The merger was spurred by Jeptha H. Wade, Sr., former co-founder and president of Western Union Telegraph Company, who purchased a controlling interest in Iron Cliffs in the late 1880s. He entered negotiations with Samuel Mather to unify the two mining companies, but before the merger could be concluded, both Wade and Mather died. Their sons, Jeptha Wade, Jr., and William G. Mather, consummated the deal, which gave the new business entity the fiscal wherewithal to be an effective competitor. Using their unified resources, Cleveland-Cliffs joined the Pittsburgh & Lake Angeline Iron Company to build a railroad from the mines to docks at Presque Isle in the late 1890s. (By the mid-1970s, the railroad transported over seven million tons of ore and one million tons of general freight each year.)

William Mather was elected president of Cleveland-Cliffs. Mather, who had started his career with Cleveland Iron Mining as a clerk in 1878, served as president for 42 years. Perhaps inspired by social reforms of the turn-of-the-century Progressive Era, the second-generation leader established a department that provided disability and death benefits to miners and their families, as well as educational assistance, a pension fund, and a worker safety program.

The ever-growing capital requirements of mining made it an increasingly venturesome proposition in the early twentieth century. In order to distribute the risk, Cleveland-Cliffs formed partnerships with steel companies to own and operate mines. The company established its first joint venture of this type in 1903 when it leased the Negaunee Mine to a company it co-owned with Bethlehem Steel Corporation. Cleveland-Cliffs' customer relationships were often strengthened through the exchange of ore for stock and equity positions in steel companies.

Surviving the Great Depression

This policy developed into a more coherent program in 1929, when Cleveland financier Cyrus Eaton hatched a plan to form a

top-ranking steel company through the union of several mid-sized competitors. In exchange for financing part of the venture, Cleveland-Cliffs would become its preferred supplier. The scheme called for Cleveland-Cliffs to establish a new entity, Cliffs Corporation, that would be jointly owned by Eaton and a group of steel magnates. For his part, Eaton traded a $40-million portfolio of dividend-paying steel stocks in Republic Steel Corporation, Inland Steel Company, and Youngstown Sheet and Tube. Meanwhile, Cleveland-Cliffs acquired a controlling interest in Corrigan-McKinney Steel Company, a Cleveland steelmaker, for $23 million in borrowed funds. The industrialists intended to merge these four steel companies into a new business called Midwest Steel Corporation. The onset of the Great Depression, however, squelched the plan. Cleveland-Cliffs was left with a heavy debt load in the midst of the world's deepest economic downturn. The company recorded a loss in 1932.

A company history published in 1974 called this low point "William G. Mather's finest hour." It was at this desperate time that he established Cleveland-Cliffs' policy of sacrificing all but domestic iron ore reserves to keep the mining concern alive. Despite his efforts, Cleveland-Cliff's financial condition continued to deteriorate. In 1933, local banker Edward B. Greene, an in-law of the Wade family, replaced Mather as president, who assumed the position of chairman. Greene reduced Cleveland-Cliff's debt through sale of some timberlands and steel stocks and the 1935 divestment of Corrigan-McKinney to Republic Steel. The financial reorganization brought about the 1947 reunion of Cleveland-Cliffs and the practically purposeless Cliffs Corporation. Mather retired in 1952 and was replaced by Greene. The position of president was briefly filled by Alexander C. Brown.

In the meantime, three forces converged on the iron industry and Cleveland-Cliffs to bring about fundamental changes in the business. World War II's military requirements had driven seemingly insatiable demand for high-quality iron ore. Given the high costs (and unpredictable payoff) of domestic underground exploration, iron and steel producers looked for alternative sources of high-grade ore through overseas exploration. Cleveland-Cliffs thus pursued options in eastern Canada, Venezuela, Colombia, Chile, and Peru, although it later scaled back its international operations to Canada and Australia.

At the same time, the U.S. steel market was inundated with high-grade, yet cheap, foreign ore. From 1953 to 1963, imports increased from 8 percent of domestic consumption to 36 percent. The combination of high costs, competition, and exhaustion of higher-grade domestic ore sources forced hundreds of American mines out of business in the postwar era.

Walter A. Sterling, who was elected president of Cleveland-Cliffs in 1953 and chief executive officer in 1955, instigated the company's transition to an emphasis on upgrading abundant low-quality ores into material useful to the steel industry. Over the course of the decade, Cleveland-Cliffs adopted the pelletizing process that later became the standard for the American steel industry. First developed in Europe in the early twentieth century, pelletization is a method of iron processing that upgrades low-quality iron ores through concentration (grinding and separating the unwanted materials from the desirable ore) and pelletization (moistening, forming, and firing the ore into spheres suitable for

---

Key Dates:

1846: Cleveland Iron Mining Company is established.
1891: The company merges with Iron Cliffs Mining Company to form the Cleveland-Cliffs Iron Company.
1929: Plans to form a top-ranking steel company through the union of several competitors fail during the onset of the Great Depression.
1947: A financial reorganization leads to the union of Cleveland-Cliffs and Cliffs Corporation.
1963: By now, imports have increased from 8 percent of domestic consumption to 36 percent.
1970: Cleveland-Cliffs purchases a majority interest in Detroit Steel in order to regain nearly one-third of its own stock.
1982: The company records its first loss since the Great Depression.
1987: Cleveland-Cliffs is forced to restructure during a financial crisis.
1994: Northshore Mining Company is acquired.
2001: The firm adds LTV Steel Mining Company's assets to its arsenal.

---

use in a blast furnace). By the time Sterling retired in 1961, Cleveland-Cliffs was poised for a decade of growth. Sterling was succeeded as president and chief executive officer by H. Stuart Harrison, a Cleveland-Cliffs veteran of 24 years.

Overcoming Problems in the 1970s and 1980s

Cleveland-Cliffs was not exempt from merger overtures during this era of heavy industry activity. By the late 1960s, Detroit Steel had accumulated nearly one-third of Cleveland-Cliffs' stock. Although heirs of the Mather, Wade, and Greene families owned a similar-sized stake in the company, many feared that a firm interested in acquiring Cleveland-Cliffs could launch a strong offensive through Detroit Steel. That apprehension came to fruition in 1970, when Cyclops Corporation, a steel company, bought 19 percent of Detroit Steel. In order to diffuse the situation, Cleveland-Cliffs essentially repurchased its own stock from Detroit Steel by acquiring the remaining shares of the latter company for $50 million, recovering its own 1.1 million shares, and turning over its majority interest in Detroit Steel to Cyclops.

Having repulsed this threat to its independence, Cleveland-Cliffs undertook a diversification program in the early 1970s in hopes of reducing its reliance on the cyclical steel industry. The strategy included re-entry into the timber market, as well as investment in shale oil, uranium, and copper mining. This tactic soon proved disastrous. In 1982, Cleveland-Cliffs experienced its first loss since the Great Depression. Cliffs executives blamed a 51 percent reduction in North American iron ore production and a 44 percent decline in iron ore shipments. Indeed, the U.S. iron mining industry took a beating throughout the 1980s, as increasing imports and two severe recessions forced the closure of one-third of America's iron ore mines. However, notwithstanding these inherent problems, analysts— and significantly, some Cleveland-Cliffs shareholders—

blamed the company's difficulties on its oil and gas operations, which experienced an 85 percent plummet in earnings in 1982. In recognition of this dreadful performance, *Fortune* indicated in 1991 that some Wall Street pundits dubbed the company's acquisition plan "de-worse-ification."

A second loss in 1986 brought the company perilously close to bankruptcy. By the end of 1987, Cleveland-Cliffs had $126 million in past due loans. As the company's stock declined, management instituted several anti-takeover measures, including a "poison pill" plan and "golden parachutes" that secured their own financial futures. The crisis—and the board's reaction to it—precipitated a battle with shareholders over the best way to restructure the company's debt. CEO M. Thomas Moore wanted to pay off the liability with the proceeds of a new stock issue, but dissident shareholders led by David Bolger, who held 6.8 percent of the company's stock, favored a more creative plan. According to a January 1988 *Forbes* article, Bolger proposed to "raise $144 million in new bank debt, toss in $221 million cash from the company treasury and the sale of a Michigan power plant, call in $53 million in preferred [stock] and make a hefty $168 million cash distribution to shareholders."

Moore tried his plan and floated four million shares in the fall of 1987. The company, however, was only able to earn $62.4 million on the $68 million offering. Within days of the scheme's failure, Bolger called for a special vote on the composition of Cleveland-Cliffs' upper echelon. The majority of shareholders elected to retain Moore and the board of directors, but only after the corporate leaders announced that they had adopted a plan to either recapitalize or sell the company.

The reorganization that ensued involved divesting the firm's peripheral holdings, closing two mines, paying down debt with the proceeds, and renegotiating contracts with customers, unions, and utilities. The restructuring culminated with a $175.9 million repurchase of over one-third of the company's stock.

Cleveland-Cliffs acquired a major rival, Pickands Mather, just in time for a late 1980s steel industry revival. Voluntary restraint agreements with importers also helped, giving U.S. iron miners time to retool. By the end of the decade, Cleveland-Cliffs was again garnering commendations. A 1990 article in the *Engineering & Mining Journal* asserted that "perhaps no mining company has been as successful as Cleveland-Cliffs." Indeed, from 1986 to 1992, the firm's stock rose 500 percent. In 1991, the company gave shareholders a special $4.00 cash dividend.

Steel Industry Woes in Early 1990s

Although Cleveland-Cliffs had recovered from its stumbling performance in the mid-1980s, in 1991 management again faced a shareholder revolt. This battle was initiated by Julian H. Robertson of Tiger Management Associates, which held 10 percent of Cleveland-Cliffs' stock. Robertson, who was characterized in a 1991 *Fortune* article as "one of Wall Street's hottest money managers," worried that Cleveland-Cliffs would use the over $115 million in cash and marketable securities it had built up to launch another "de-worse-ification." Robertson fomented a proxy vote and won the right to seat five directors (a minority) on an expanded board.

Even these new leaders, however, were powerless to prevent the problems that plagued Cleveland-Cliffs in the early 1990s. In 1992, two of Cliffs' major customers—Sharon Steel, which contributed 11 percent of annual operating revenues, and McLouth Steel Products, which chipped in an estimated 25 percent—encountered significant financial difficulties. Sharon Steel sought Chapter 11 bankruptcy protection that year, and McLouth stopped payments on its shipments. Cliffs was cited as the largest creditor of each of these two businesses. Fearful that it might never recover revenues lost to these two causes, Cleveland-Cliffs set aside $17.5 million in a contingency fund. This precaution contributed to the company's net loss of $7.9 million in 1992. A year later, in August 1993, labor problems bruised third quarter earnings. Finally, Cleveland-Cliffs faced threats from ever-present imports and new competition from ''mini-mills,'' which utilized electric arc furnaces to turn scrap metal into usable steel. By 1993, this new technology had captured 43 percent of total steelmaking.

Nonetheless, several industry observers expressed confidence that Cleveland-Cliffs' strengths would enable it to meet the challenges of the 1990s. They cited the company's position of dominance in the iron ore mining industry, its strong balance sheet, and its research into alternative production methods (including iron carbide and scrap metal substitutes) as evidence of its vigor. Industry factors, including the close accord of supply and demand, also boded well for the mining concern.

In the fall of 1994, Cliffs bolstered its top-ranking position with the acquisition of Cypress Amax Minerals Company's iron ore mine and power plant—Northshore Mining Company—in Minnesota for $66 million. The addition increased Cleveland-Cliffs annual production capacity by 69 percent, from 5.8 million tons to 9.8 million tons of standard pellets. The company netted $42.8 million on sales of $344.8 million that year, their highest levels for both figures since 1990. In 1995, the company launched a $6.1 million expansion project at Northshore Mining.

Facing Challenges in the New Century

As Cleveland-Cliffs headed into the late 1990s, the company shored up strong profits and was buoyed by a strong U.S. manufacturing sector. The firm was reminded of just how cyclical the industry can be however, as ore prices fell and imports increased in 1999. As such, the company was forced to temporarily shut down three of its mines—Empire, Hibbing Taconite, and Tilden—in order to balance out inventory levels. At the same time, problems were brewing at the company's new hot briquetted iron (HBI) plant in Trinidad. Cleveland-Cliffs was not able to overcome these difficulties and eventually shut down the plant in 2002.

The steel industry continued to struggle in the early 2000s. Nearly one-third of Cleveland-Cliffs' customers had declared bankruptcy by 2001, including its largest customer, LTV Steel Mining Company. The company saw this as a unique opportunity and began buying up assets. It acquired LTV's holdings in 2001 and converted them into a new company, International Steel Group (ISG). Cleveland-Cliffs secured a 15-year agreement to be the sole supplier pellets to the new firm in 2002.

During this time period, the company began bolstering its interests in taconite facilities. It increased its ownership in the Hibbing Taconite Company as well as the Tilden Mine and the Wabush Mine in 2002. In early 2003, it gained control of 79 percent of the Empire Mine in Michigan and landed a 12-year pellet sales contract with Ispat Inland Inc. The company also secured contract agreements with Algoma Steel Inc. and Rouge Industries Inc. Cleveland-Cliffs' actions appeared to pay off in the short-term. Sales increased by 39 percent over the previous year, and the company recorded an 82.6 percent improvement in net loss—the firm lost 188.3 million in 2002 and $32.7 million in 2003.

As consolidation in the steel industry promised to continue in the upcoming years, Cleveland-Cliffs remained optimistic. Chairman and CEO John Brinzo commented on the company's future in a February 2004 *American Metal Market* article, claiming that ''with solid steel demand and improved pricing, most integrated steel producers are operating their mills at high utilization rates. We anticipate the demand for iron ore will remain high and all of our operations are currently scheduled to run at or near capacity.'' He added, ''We are excited about 2004. We are at a point where our actions and a much stronger steel industry are expected to improve profitability for Cliffs.'' Indeed, it looked as though there may be a bright light at the end of Cliffs' tunnel. Only time would tell, though, just how long an upswing in the steel industry would last.

Principal Subsidiaries

CALipso Sales Company; Cleveland-Cliffs Ore Corporation; Cliffs and Associates Limited; Cliffs Biwabik Ore Corporation; Cliffs Empire, Inc.; Cliffs Erie L.L.C.; Cliffs IH Empire, Inc; Cliffs International Management Company LLC; Cliffs Marquette, Inc.; Cliffs MC Empire, Inc.; Cliffs Mining Company; Cliffs Mining Services Company; Cliffs Minnesota Mining Company; Cliffs Natural Stone, LLC; Cliffs Oil Shale Corporation; Cliffs Reduced Iron Corporation; Cliffs Reduced Iron Management Company (Cliffs Synfuel Corporation); Cliffs TIOP, Inc.; Cliffs Venezuela Technical Services Company LLC; Empire-Cliffs Partnership; Empire Iron Mining Partnership; Hibbing Taconite Company; IronUnits LLC; Lake Superior & Ishpeming Railroad Company; Lasco Development Corporation; Marquette Iron Mining Partnership; Marquette Range Coal Service Company; Minerais Midway Ltee-Midway Ore Company Ltd.; Northshore Mining Company; Northshore Sales Company; Pickands Hibbing Corporation; Republic Wetlands Preserve LLC; Seignelay Resources, Inc.; Silver Bay Power Company; Syracuse Mining Company; The Cleveland-Cliffs Iron Company; The Cleveland-Cliffs Steamship Company; Tilden Mining Company L.C.; United Taconite LLC; Wabush Iron Co. Ltd.; Wheeling-Pittsburgh/Cliffs Partnership.

Principal Competitors

BHP Billiton Ltd.; United States Steel Corporation; Companhia Vale do Rio Doce.

Further Reading

Ansberry, Clare, ''Seizing the Moment: Steelmakers' Troubles Create an Opening for an Iron-Ore Giant,'' *Wall Street Journal*, October 17, 2001, p. A1.

Bloomquist, Lee, "Cleveland-Cliffs Seeks Greater Role in Iron Ore Mining," *Duluth News-Tribune*, October 9, 2003.

Bradley, Hassell, "Cleveland-Cliffs' Moore Challenges Status Quo," *American Metal Market*, September 24, 1990, p. 24A.

Caney, Derek J., "Cliffs Completes Buy of Northshore Assets," *American Metal Market*, October 7, 1994, p. 3.

"Cleveland-Cliffs: 1st Loss in 50 Years, $30.2M Deficit," *American Metal Market*, February 4, 1993, p. 3.

"Cliffs Narrows Losses in 4th Qtr., Full Year; Brinzo Upbeat on 2004," *American Metal Market*, February 9, 2004, p. 4.

Furukawa, Tsukasa, "Mitsubishi, Cliffs Eye Plant for Iron Carbide," *American Metal Market*, June 4, 1993, p. 5.

Gerdel, Thomas W., "Problems Plague Cliffs' Trinidad Plant," *Plain Dealer* (Cleveland, Ohio), May 10, 2000, p. 3C.

Hardy, Eric S., "No Rust Here," *Forbes*, December 30, 1996, p. 164.

Harrison, H. Stuart, *The Cleveland-Cliffs Iron Company*, New York: Newcomen Society, 1974.

Hohl, Paul, "Cliffs Bolger Claims Victory after Vote," *American Metal Market*, December 17, 1987, p. 2.

——, "Cliffs Plans Stock Buy-back to Further Its Restructuring," *American Metal Market*, March 18, 1988, p. 3.

Lappen, Alyssa A., "Dilution Control," *Forbes*, January 11, 1988, p. 10.

Lazo, Shirley A., "Speaking of Dividends: Cleveland-Cliffs Steels Itself," *Barron's*, January 14, 2002, p. 30.

McGough, Robert, "High Iron," *Financial World*, April 14, 1992, p. 26.

Norton, Rob, "Who Owns This Company, Anyhow?" *Fortune*, July 29, 1991, p. 131.

Reingold, Jennifer, "Cleveland-Cliffs: A Bet on Upgrading Mini-mills," *Financial World*, March 29, 1994, p. 22.

Winter, Ralph E., "Cleveland-Cliffs Expects to Sell Less Ore in '99," *Wall Street Journal*, May 14, 1999.

Zaburunov, Steven A., "Cost Reduction at Cleveland-Cliffs," *EMJ—Engineering & Mining Journal*, September 1990, p. 29.

—April Dougal Gasbarre
—update: Christina M. Stansell

Commercial Federal Corporation

13220 California Street
Omaha, Nebraska 68154
U.S.A.
Telephone: (402) 554-9200
Toll Free: (800) 228-5023
Fax: (402) 554-9330
Web site: http://www.comfedbank.com

Public Company
Incorporated: 1887 as South Omaha Loan and Building
 Association
Total Assets: $12.19 billion (2003)
Employees: 2,800
Stock Exchanges: New York
Ticker Symbol: CFB
NAIC: 522120 Savings Institutions; 522292 Real Estate
 Credit; 52311 Investment Banking and Securities
 Dealing; 524210 Insurance Agencies and Brokerages;
 551111 Offices of Bank Holding Companies

Commercial Federal Corporation (ComFed) is the holding company for a leading thrift institution. Its major markets are Omaha, Nebraska; Denver, Colorado; and Des Moines, Iowa. Based in Nebraska, the company extended its operations to Colorado, Kansas, and Oklahoma during the 1980s. Following the period of economic malaise generally characterizing the savings and loan (thrift) industry as a whole in 1989 and 1990, Commercial Federal rebounded and again expanded its operations in the mid-1990s.

The second half of the 1990s was characterized by struggles to achieve sufficient profitability to prevent a takeover. ComFed made several acquisitions during this time and doubled in size in the late 1990s. It then underwent some consolidation before building new branch offices. At the end of 2003, ComFed had about $13 billion in assets and a network of about 200 offices in Arizona, Colorado, Iowa, Kansas, Missouri, Nebraska, and Oklahoma. As the company has grown, it has supplemented its traditional mortgage financial business with more commercial bank-type activities.

Origins

The history of Commercial Federal may be traced to the 1880s, when a group of Omaha businessmen bought land just south of the city limits, near the new Union Stockyards then under construction. In 1887, only a year after the village was incorporated, the South Omaha Loan and Building Association was opened. It was a mutual (depositor-owned) savings association, with voting privileges for all who subscribed for five shares at $200 a share. Customers paid for their shares through a regular savings plan and, to encourage regular saving, were fined if they missed a monthly payment. Once payments and interest reached $200 a share, the saver could then exchange the five shares for $1,000. A customer whose payments had reached one-quarter to one-third of the value of the shares could pledge them for a mortgage on a $2,000 home.

One of the savings and loan's early customers was an Irish immigrant named James J. Fitzgerald. In 1893, Fitzgerald was elected to the board of directors. Five years later, he quit his job in a packing plant to become secretary-manager of the association at a salary of $60 a month. By 1910, the association was prosperous enough to establish an office in downtown Omaha and changed its name to the Commercial Savings and Loan Association. When South Omaha was annexed by Omaha in 1915, however, the association closed the downtown office and used the savings to purchase its own three-story office building.

By 1929, Commercial's assets had grown from the original $10,000 to $4 million. Under the impact of the Great Depression, however, assets fell to $2.1 million in 1935. During this bleak period, the thrift institution made every effort to avoid foreclosing on the property of its borrowers. This was done in order to maintain good customer relations and because land sold after foreclosure typically went at a sharply reduced selling price. Commercial also refinanced mortgages at lower interest rates during this time, which meant smaller returns on its investments. Unlike some thrift institutions, Commercial did not go ''on notice''—meaning the institution was not required to have the cash to pay for all withdrawals. Fitzgerald's younger son William F. Fitzgerald, who became a teller in 1933, later recalled that sometimes, when a customer would come in to withdraw his funds, he ''would count the money very slowly to

Company Perspectives:

Many Perspectives. One vision. People make the difference at Commercial Federal. Each of our 2,800 employees plays a starring role in delivering the kind of service that has separated Commercial Federal from the competition. We pride ourselves on presenting an "opening night" performance to each customer we serve, every day. We take the business of banking personally at Commercial Federal. That might mean delivering an account application to a customer in a nursing home or visiting the construction site of one of our business customers. It's all about being there when and where we're needed. We know that elevating the customer experience from ordinary to extraordinary will enable us to achieve our vision to be: "The Bank of Choice in the communities we serve."

give them time to think. . . . Once they realized the cash was there and Commercial would be able to meet their withdrawal, they would decide to leave the money and let it continue to earn dividends."

Total assets did not begin to rise again until 1939, and by 1945 assets had again reached the 1929 level. By this time, James Fitzgerald was the company's president, with Williams serving as secretary-treasurer. Commercial, fifth in assets among the six Omaha savings and loan associations at the end of World War II, soon became the largest lender to veterans in Nebraska under the G.I. Bill. It was also aggressive in meeting the pent-up postwar demand for housing by financing tract developments.

Postwar Pioneering

Commercial placed the first television ad in Omaha, widely promoting its sixty-fifth anniversary in 1952, and in 1953 opened a drive-in teller window—Nebraska's first. In 1959, Commercial got into data processing, signing up other savings and loans institutions to help pay for a computer that more than met its own needs at the time.

Although James Fitzgerald retired in 1955, he continued to serve as board chairperson and went to the office nearly every day until his death the following year at the age of 87. William Fitzgerald became president in 1950, and his son, William A. Fitzgerald, joined the company in 1955. The younger William would rise in the corporate ranks, becoming president in 1974, chief executive officer in 1983, and board chairperson in 1994.

By 1960, Commercial had five locations, and a new home office was opened two years later, when assets reached $100 million. This three-story structure featured an 85-foot tower with carillon bells and served as the model for all later Commercial branches.

In 1967, the association moved outside the Omaha metropolitan area for the first time by merging with Allied Building and Loan of Norfolk, Nebraska. Soon Commercial had branches in other Nebraska communities as well, some started from scratch, others by merger with an established savings and

loan institution. By the end of 1974, Commercial was the largest savings and loan association in Nebraska, with 15 offices and $516 million in assets. In 1979, it became the first such thrift in its market to sell mortgage-backed bonds. Two years later, it was among the first savings and loans to offer checking accounts. Also in 1981, Commercial introduced automated teller machines and spun off its lending division into a separate mortgage-banking subsidiary. A full-service brokerage program was introduced in 1983.

Reincorporated 1983

Reincorporated in Nebraska on August 18, 1983, as Commercial Federal Savings & Loan Association, the company converted the next year from a depositor-owned federal mutual savings and loan to a publicly traded, investor-owned institution. A holding company, Commercial Federal Corporation, became the parent company of the savings and loan association. A national public offering of shares in Commercial Federal was completed before the end of 1984, with 1.76 million shares of common stock sold at $8.50 each.

Commercial Federal's business strategy in the 1980s was based on expansion, diversification, high-quality loans, and economies of scale achieved through computer technology. By early 1986, it was the largest depository financial institution in Nebraska, with assets in excess of $3 billion. On March 3, 1986, Commercial Federal opened its first depository institution outside the state, acquiring about $86 million in insured deposits of the insolvent Denver-based Sierra Federal Savings and Loan Association from the Federal Savings and Loan Insurance Corporation. Fitzgerald told *American Banker* that the acquisition was "part of an overall plan for targeted expansion in the Midwest," which would mean expanding into "four additional states within the next four years."

The company already had loan mortgage banking offices in surrounding states, was offering discount stock brokerage services, and was adding a full range of insurance products. By early 1988, it also had a subsidiary, Commercial Service Corporation, which acted as a vehicle for insurance sales, real estate developments and the marketing of pooled real estate investments, and other projects.

In September 1984, even before the holding company was formed, Commercial Federal had purchased an 81.3 percent interest in Systems Marketing Inc., a firm that primarily leased IBM peripheral computer equipment to Fortune 500 companies. It was also active in the mortgage market, buying fixed-rate mortgage loans and securities with long-term Federal Home Loan Bank borrowings. By March 1986, the company had realized substantial gains from these investments, while avoiding direct loans to agriculture, despite its location in the nation's farm belt. Its rate of nonperforming loans was less than 1 percent, and its stock had risen from the original $8.50 a share to about $27.

Soon thereafter, Commercial Federal acquired two failed thrift institutions. The first, purchased in August 1986, was Coronado Federal Savings and Loan Association of Kansas City, Kansas. One month later, it bought Denver's Empire Savings, Building and Loan Association from bankrupt Baldwin-United Corporation for $45 million in cash. The purchase price, about 57 percent of Empire's regulatory net worth, was considered a bargain. To help pay for the acquisition, Commercial Federal issued $60 million of preferred stock to El Paso Electric Co. The company then moved into its fourth state—Oklahoma—when it acquired insolvent Territory Savings and Loan Association of Seminole, Oklahoma, in January 1988 for $4.2 million.

The fourth leg of the company's strategy—computer technology—was represented by several efforts. In 1985, for example, Commercial Federal became the first financial institution in the nation to introduce personal banking machines (PBMs) in branch offices. By April 1988, it had 68 branches and was providing at least one product or service to 54 percent of the households in its home market of Omaha. To better understand its customer base, the company had created a Marketing Customer Information File, a database of its account relationships. One objective of this database was to increase revenues by repackaging and repricing products for specific customer segments. In addition, the paper records of the company's largest subsidiary, Commercial Federal Mortgage Corporation, were transferred to a microfilm-based computer-assisted retrieval system. By 1994, the company credited its computer-driven automation with allowing each agent to service 850 loans, compared to an industry average of about 600.

However, Commercial Federal faced some major challenges beginning in 1989. With Denver's economy in a serious slump, Empire Savings became a liability rather than an asset. Part of the problem was attributed to federal regulators, who had imposed tighter capital restrictions, making it harder for Commercial Federal to mark down Empire's bad loans as goodwill. The objective of the regulators, Fitzgerald later said in a 1994 interview published in *American Banker,* "was to see how many write-downs they could take to finally find the bottom in the value of a financial institution. Whether or not you agreed with them, it didn't matter."

Suddenly Commercial Federal was facing the same abyss that had swallowed so many of the savings and loans during this time. "They had one foot in the grave," a banking analyst recalled of Commercial Federal in an *American Banker* article, noting that "on a tangible net worth basis, they were bankrupt." Company executives responded by shedding nonperforming assets—mostly commercial loans—and cutting costs. Over a 15-month

period, they reduced assets from $6.8 billion to $4.8 billion, closed 20 branches, and laid off 400 employees. All lending was halted, and all assets were converted to mortgage-backed securities. The company's stock fell below $2 a share in 1990.

Federal Charter in 1990

Commercial Federal emerged by issuing a capital plan that was approved by the Federal Office of Thrift Supervision in May 1990. By then, the holding company had purchased Commercial Federal Savings and Loan's outstanding preferred stock, augmenting tangible capital by $61.4 million. The plan called for adding $70 million to its capital by mid-1991 and meeting the new federal capital guidelines about two years before the compliance deadline of December 31, 1994. Commercial Federal Savings and Loan Association converted its federal charter to a federal savings bank on July 30, 1990, changing its name to Commercial Federal Bank, FSB (the initials standing for Federal Savings Bank).

During a six-month period in 1992, the parent company sold all $3.3 billion of its mortgage-backed securities to several investors. In addition, the company sold $950 million in loan servicing rights to Source One Mortgage Services Corporation of Detroit in a single transaction. Then it offered about $40 million in equity and a similar amount in subordinated notes to improve its capital position and, in Fitzgerald's words, "get the regulators off our backs."

Commercial Federal also began bolstering its thrift holdings again in 1993, acquiring 19 thrift branches in Oklahoma and Kansas to reach a total of 67. In October 1993, the company paid $18.2 million to the Federal Deposit Insurance Corporation for 12 offices and the $567.9 million of deposits of Heartland Federal Savings and Loan Association of Ponca City, Oklahoma. In June 1994, it acquired four branches and about $255.7 million of deposits of the bankrupt Franklin Federal Savings Association in Kansas from the Resolution Trust Corporation, a federal bailout agency, for about $9 million. In July 1994, the company announced it had paid about $9 million for the two branch offices and $87.1 million of deposits of the Home Federal Savings & Loan of Ada, Oklahoma.

Growth and Independence in the 1990s

By 1993, Commercial Federal had recovered so well that it had become the subject of takeover talk. CAI Corporation, a Dallas-based investor group with a stake of nearly 10 percent in the company, campaigned for a sale, driving the stock price to over $23 a share in June. However, the offer was ultimately rejected. Over the course of the following year, the company's stock value ranged between $28 and $17.50 per share. Moreover, for fiscal 1994 (the year ended June 30), operating earnings had increased 20 percent and total assets had reached $5.52 billion on deposits of $3.36 billion. By the end of the calendar year, total assets had grown to $5.8 billion.

In April 1995, Commercial Federal announced that it had acquired the Provident Federal Savings Bank of Lincoln, Nebraska. In the transaction, Commercial Federal gained five offices in Lincoln with assets of around $95 million and deposits of $57 million. Also during this time, the company entered into an agreement to acquire Railroad Financial Corporation of Wichita, Kansas. In a press release, chairperson and CEO Fitzgerald noted that ''the acquisitions will immediately strengthen our retail franchise and our future earnings potential.''

A booming economy was helping the company, with unemployment below 4 percent in all four states where it maintained bank branches. ''The goal now,'' company vice-president Stan Blakey told *American Banker,* ''is to make yourself a little more profitable, to exceed the analysts' estimates by a little bit every quarter, and to do a little better than the rest of the guys out there.''

In 1995, Commercial Federal had $6 billion in assets and operated 72 branches in Nebraska (30 branches), Colorado (20), Oklahoma (17), and Kansas (5).

The company continued to grow by acquisition. It bought Railroad Savings Corporation of Wichita, Kansas, in October 1995. A few months later, Commercial acquired Conservative Savings Corporation, also based in Omaha, for about $44 million. Conservative had $380 million in assets and 113 employees.

Mid-Continent Federal Savings Bank of El Dorado, Kansas, was soon acquired in a stock swap worth $75 million. In late 1996, Commercial announced the acquisition of Liberty Financial Corporation of Arizona for $108.6 million, which owned seven independent banks having assets of $620 million. Liberty brought with it an array of business banking products.

Larger deals followed in 1998, including acquisitions of First Colorado Bancorp, with assets of $1.6 billion, and AmerUs Bank of Des Moines, with $1.5 billion in assets. AmerUs operated 37 branches, six of them in supermarkets, a new area for Commercial Federal. A smaller, $83 million purchase of Midland Bank, Missouri, was announced in August.

By the fall of 1998, reported *American Banker,* nine acquisitions had nearly doubled Commercial's assets to $11.7 billion in two years. It was the tenth-largest savings and loan in the United States. According to the *Omaha World-Herald,* the number of workers had doubled in one year to 3,300; the number of branches had also doubled, to 241.

Having attained the critical mass necessary to weather competition and cumbersome government regulation, CEO William A. Fitzgerald led the thrift into the traditional territory of commercial banks by offering financial products such as investment and trust services and small business loans.

A New Jersey-based investment group, Franklin Mutual Advisers Inc., acquired a significant (9.2 percent) shareholding and attempted to force the board to sell the company. Another group had attempted the same thing in 1995; however, ComFed was able to fend off both these threats to its independence.

Restructuring in 2000

In order to please Wall Street, ComFed brought in new executive management and set out on a $125 million restructuring program. The number of branch offices peaked at 259 in 1999; however, within a year ComFed had consolidated them down to 192. A new president and chief operating officer, Robert J. Hutchinson, was hired in April 2001. William A. Fitzgerald remained chairman and CEO.

Commercial Federal sold its namesake Omaha tower to Blue Cross Blue Shield of Nebraska in 1999. ComFed had occupied the building for 20 years and continued to use three floors in the tower while a planned $50 million office complex was put on for economic reasons. In August 2001, ComFed's offices in the tower were moved to three different buildings.

A wave of home mortgage refinancing inspired by lower interest rates helped ComFed post record net income of $108.5 million for 2002. The thrift ended the year with assets of $13.1 billion, including $6.4 billion in deposits.

ComFed was soon opening new branches again, including its technological showcase branch in western Omaha. Officials claimed features such as cash counting machines would allow two tellers to do the work of four while boosting security.

Commercial Federal ended 2003 with assets of $12.2 billion, down about $900 million from the previous year. Net income slipped form $107 million to $89 million. The company added five new locations in 2003.

Principal Subsidiaries

Commercial Federal Bank, F.S.B.

Principal Competitors

American National Bank; First National Bank of Omaha; U.S. Bancorp; Wells Fargo Co.

Further Reading

1887–1987: Milestones & Reflections—A Centennial Retrospective, Omaha, Neb.: Commercial Federal Savings and Loan, 1987.

Basch, Mark, ''Commercial Federal Moves West with Deal for Failed Denver S&L,'' *American Banker,* March 4, 1986, pp. 2, 22.

Bennett, Andrea, ''Nebraska Thrift Company Moves into Oklahoma,'' *American Banker,* February 2, 1988, p. 23.

Chase, Brett, ''Omaha CEO Remaking His Thrift in Bank's Image,'' *American Banker,* September 17, 1998.

——, ''Still Chewing on Two Deals, Neb. Thrift Hungry for More,'' *American Banker,* June 3, 1998, p. 5.

Engen, John R., ''Omaha's Commercial Federal Corp. Breathing Easy after Brush with Disaster,'' *American Banker,* September 30, 1994, pp. 4–5.

Helzner, Jerry, ''Canny Cornhusker,'' *Barron's,* June 23, 1986, p. 53.

Jordon, Steve, ''Commercial Fed Shareholders Say No to Sale Idea,'' *Omaha World-Herald,* Bus. Sec., November 19, 1996, p. 14.

——, ''Omaha, Neb.-Based Commercial Federal Turns Heads on Wall Street,'' *Omaha World-Herald,* October 5, 1998.

——, ''Omaha, Neb.-Based Bank Resists Investors' Push to Sell,'' *Omaha World-Herald,* August 6, 1999.

——, ''Workers Deal with Threat of Buyout,'' *Omaha World-Herald,* Bus. Sec., November 7, 1999, p. 1.

——, ''ComFed Preparing to Build Savings Bank; Company Says Land Purchase Clears the Way for Construction of a New Headquarters,'' *Omaha World-Herald,* Bus. Sec., December 21, 1999, p. 22.

——, ''ComFed to Cut Down Number of Offices,'' *Omaha World-Herald,* Bus. Sec., October 12, 2000, p. 18.

——, "Omaha, Neb.-Based Banking Firm Quietly Tries to Get Back on Its Feet," *Omaha World-Herald*, January 9, 2001.

——, "Omaha, Neb.-Based Bank Holding Company Hires New President," *Omaha World-Herald*, April 22, 2001.

——, "Commercial Federal's Offices Move Out of Omaha, Neb., Tower," *Omaha World-Herald*, August 20, 2001.

Katz, Martin, "Marketing CIF," *Bank Systems & Equipment*, April 1988, pp. 62–65.

Reilly, Patrick, "Commercial Federal Says Face-Lift Is Nearly Complete," *American Banker,* May 1, 2001, p. 4.

"Savings and Loan Creates Its Own Savings Plan," *Management Review*, March-April 1989, pp. 19–21.

Shim, Grace, "Cutting Edge: New Bank Branch Capitalizes on Technology Features," *Omaha World-Herald*, May 24, 2003, p. 1D.

Stieven, Joseph A., "Commercial Federal Corporation," *Wall Street Transcript*, July 21, 1986.

Taylor, John, "Omaha Thrifts' Deal Attracts Positive Reviews," *Omaha World Herald*, Bus. Sec., August 17, 1995, p. 21.

——, "Commercial Acquires Conservative," *Omaha World Herald*, Bus. Sec., February 2, 1996, p. 16.

—Robert Halasz
—update: Frederick C. Ingram

Crosman Corporation

Route 5 & 20
East Bloomfield, New York 14443
U.S.A.
Telephone: (585) 657-6161
Toll Free: (800) 724-7486
Fax: (585) 657-5405
Web site: http://www.crosman.com

Private Company
Incorporated: 1924 as Crosman Rifle Company
Employees: 300
Sales: $100 million (2002 est.)
NAIC: 332994 Small Arms Manufacturing; 332992 Small
    Arms Ammunition Manufacturing

Crosman Corporation is one of the leading manufacturers of air guns in the world and also produces related items like CO2 capsules, ammunition, and paintball equipment. The company sells its products under a variety of brand names, including Crosman, Benjamin, Sheridan, Copperhead, and Gameface, and also distributes Smith & Wesson, Beretta, Colt, Walther, and Logan air guns in North America. Its products are sold at gun shops as well as by mass-marketers like Wal-Mart and Dick's Sporting Goods in the United States and in more than 60 countries abroad. Crosman is owned by a group of investors that include senior members of management.

Beginnings

The present-day Crosman Corporation can trace its roots back to 1838, when Fred Crosman formed a seed company. Over time, its ownership passed down to new generations of Crosmans, and the name was changed to Crosman Brothers Company. In 1923, the firm began to make pellets for use in airguns and .22 caliber air rifles. The following year, the company was sold to Frank Hahn, who renamed the business Crosman Rifle Company. By 1940, the small firm had a total of six employees.

Following World War II, Crosman introduced a new line of air pistols, and as their sales took off it entered a period of rapid growth, with employment reaching 150 by 1952. The 1950s saw the company produce large numbers of air rifles under the brand names of major retail chains like Sears, Roebuck and Co., Montgomery Ward, and Western Auto.

Airguns were similar to full-fledged guns in many ways, but there were important differences. The ammunition was smaller, and rather than being propelled by an explosive charge, it was shot with compressed air. Some guns used a pneumatic system in which the air was compressed for each shot by "breaking" the gun in half at a hinge and then re-closing it in a pumping action to fill a chamber, while others used a spring mechanism or carbon dioxide (CO2) capsules to supply the air. In general, airguns were considered less dangerous because the ammunition was smaller and its velocity was lower, and as a result they were not subject to the same legal restrictions as actual firearms. They were also quieter, and the ammunition was less expensive, which made them popular for uses like small game hunting and target shooting. Airgun ammunition included metal or plastic pellets and tiny round copper-covered "BBs." Many airgun users were children or young adults who would later move on to real guns when they grew up.

In 1958, Crosman introduced its first BB gun, a CO2 powered, lever-action repeating rifle, and in 1961 the company brought out Powerlets, the first disposable CO2 containers. In 1966, the Model 760 Pumpmaster was unveiled. This short-stroke, compressed air BB rifle, which was sold under the Crosman brand name, retailed for under $30 and quickly proved a success with the public. It would go on to be one of the firm's signature products. The company had by now moved its ammunition and receiving and shipping departments into a new facility in East Bloomfield, New York, about 30 miles from Rochester, and it shifted manufacturing and assembly of guns there in 1970.

Sale to Coleman in 1971

In 1971, the firm was sold to the Wichita, Kansas-based Coleman Company, a manufacturer of camping equipment.

Company Perspectives:

Crosman Corporation has been dedicated to innovation and quality since 1923. Its mission is to design, produce, and market the best quality product at the most cost-effective price that fills both the wants and needs of the shooting public, while proactively advocating proper gun safety and proper gun etiquette.

Soon afterward, most of its remaining operations were moved from Rochester to East Bloomfield, New York. The year 1972 brought production of the one millionth Model 760 rifle, which the company presented to the National Rifle Association.

Growth continued during the 1970s and 1980s as Coleman helped Crosman win new accounts like Kmart and Wal-Mart. The year 1984 saw the recognition of air rifle shooting as an Olympic sport, and Crosman became the first American company to produce rifles that met Olympic specifications. The following year, Crosman moved its sales division and headquarters to East Bloomfield.

In 1989, the Coleman Company was acquired by Mac-Andrews & Forbes Holdings of New York, which sold off the Crosman subsidiary for an estimated $41 million in August of 1990. The buyer was Worldwide Sports and Recreation, a unit of the Tulsa, Oklahoma-based investment group Pexco Holdings, Inc. By this time, the firm had annual sales of approximately $40 million and employees numbering more than 280. The company now had a 44 percent share of the U.S. BB gun, pellet gun, and air pistol market.

In July of 1991, Crosman acquired Visible Impact Target Company, founded in Victor, New York, by Steve Lamboy, which made targets for gun enthusiasts. That same year saw the introduction of another major product, the Model 1008 RepeatAir, a semi-automatic pellet pistol that was powered by CO_2. It would go on to be a strong seller for the company.

In 1992, Crosman purchased the assets of Benjamin Sheridan Corporation, a 45-year old maker of pneumatic and CO_2 powered airguns, paintball equipment, slingshots, and related products. Crosman Premier Pellets, a new, highly accurate line of pellet gun ammunition, was introduced during 1992 as well. In 1994, the company closed Benjamin Sheridan's plant in Racine, Wisconsin, and moved its operations to the firm's facility in East Bloomfield. They year 1996 saw Crosman introduce the Copperhead line of entry-level, spring-air guns.

In January 1997, ownership of Crosman was acquired by an investment group led by Leonard Pickett, who was named president and CEO of the firm. During the year, the company also began working to expand distribution beyond mass merchandisers to smaller chains and dealers, started manufacturing steel shot, and made the CrosBlock trigger blocking safety device standard on all of its airguns. Crosman was a supporter of several organizations that promoted safe shooting, including the National Shooting Sports Foundation, the Boy Scouts of America, and 4-H, and distributed more than 500,000 copies of a pamphlet on shooting safety to participants of gun safety programs.

Sheridan Paintball Division Formed in 1998

In the late 1990s, sales of paintball equipment began growing at a rate of 25 percent per year. Interest in the sport, in which participants shot paint-filled markers at each other in mock battles, had grown beyond a small band of enthusiasts to become a relatively mainstream activity. As a result of this trend, Crosman began to boost its production of paintball gear, and in 1998 the company created the Sheridan Paintball division. The firm later tripled the number of paintball items it offered to become a full-line supplier for the sport. By this time, the company had also introduced its first camping accessory, the Pressuremate CO_2 canister for camp stoves and lanterns.

Growing regulation of the ownership and use of firearms had begun to help drive sales of high-end products in the $125 million airgun marketplace, as buyers began to see them as acceptable alternatives for certain applications. Crosman saw sales increasing as a result, especially in such places as Canada and the United Kingdom, where handgun ownership was much more restricted than in the United States.

During 1999, Crosman introduced a new line of bolt action guns and opened a stock manufacturing facility in Stover, Missouri. In October, the firm finalized a deal to secure $8 million in funding from American Capital Strategies, Ltd. and Stratford Capital Partners, L.P. to help continue its expansion. By this time, the company's offerings had grown to include about 50 different models of air rifles and pistols, marketed under the Crosman, Benjamin, Sheridan, and Copperhead brand names. The company also made a number of accessories, including pellet and BB ammunition, paintball markers, Visible Impact Targets, Copperhead brand slingshots, and shooting dart games. Crosman was now recognized as the leading U.S. airgun manufacturer, with an estimated 55 percent of the market, and was the dominant manufacturer of CO_2 cartridges for airguns, producing as many as 100,000 per day.

In 2000, Crosman added the Challenger 2000, a three-position CO_2-powered competition air rifle that was priced below similar offerings from its competitors. During the year, the firm also became a partner of USA Shooting, which organized shooting events in the United States. Crosman would contribute a portion of every airgun sale's proceeds to the organization. The company was now sponsoring such events as the Crosman International Airgun Grand Prix, held in Toronto, Canada.

In November 2000, Crosman's 44-year old CEO Leonard Pickett was killed in an automobile accident. Several months later, the company named a new president and CEO, Ken D'Arcy. During 2001, the firm also formed Diablo Marketing in partnership with Procaps to sell paintball products to mass merchandisers and upgraded its Web site to better facilitate online orders. In December, Crosman became the exclusive North American distributor of Walther and Smith & Wesson airguns.

Although the U.S. economy was in a downturn, especially after the September 11 terrorist attacks, Crosman's sales held relatively stable and in fact increased slightly after the attacks. During the year, the company also unveiled a new logo, which was based on one that had been first used in 1946, and announced a new line of spring-air guns.

Key Dates:

1838: Fred Crosman founds a seed company.
1923: Crosman Brothers Co. begins producing airgun pellets.
1924: Sale of firm to Frank Hahn, who changes the company's name to Crosman Rifle Company.
1945: Air pistols are introduced.
1950s: Employment tops 150 as Crosman makes air guns for Sears, Roebuck and Co., Montgomery Ward, and others.
1966: Model 760 air rifle is introduced and quickly becomes a top seller.
1971: Coleman Corp. buys Crosman.
1990: Crosman is acquired by Worldwide Sports and Recreation.
1991: RepeatAir CO2-powered semi-automatic pistol is introduced.
1992: Benjamin Sheridan Corporation, maker of airguns and paintball products, is bought.
1997: Investors led by Leonard Pickett acquire Crosman from Worldwide Sports.
2003: Deals are signed to make Remington air rifles and distribute Colt, Logan, Beretta airguns.

In 2002, Crosman began distributing Umarex and Walther products in North America, as well as the Gameface Paintball line. The company also introduced a new disposable four-ounce CO2 bottle, brought out the Soft Air line of recreational, low-impact target shooting pistols, and produced the ten millionth Model 760 rifle.

Crosman expanded its offerings again in 2003 by signing agreements to market Beretta, Colt, and Logan airguns in the United States and to manufacture a line of Remington brand airguns for North American sale. The firm also teamed with the NRA to sponsor a program that would promote safe sport shooting. Crosman would supply airguns, targets, and other equipment at a discount for use by NRA clubs and certified trainers. At the end of the year, the company introduced a new U.S.-made line of break barrel air rifles, the Benjamin Legacy 1000 and 1000X models, which were capable of 1000-foot-per-second velocity. They retailed for approximately $200. By now, Crosman was operating its plant round the clock, seven days a week, to produce more than one million airguns a year, along with large quantities of BBs, pellets, paint balls, and CO2 cartridges.

With more than 80 years of experience, Crosman Corporation had established itself as one of the leading manufacturers of airguns and accessories in the world. The firm offered such classic, attractively priced products as its Model 760 rifle and RepeatAir pistols, and had also successfully moved into other areas, including paintball equipment manufacturing.

Principal Divisions

Sheridan Paintball.

Principal Competitors

Daisy Manufacturing Company; Industrias El Gamo SA; Beeman Precision Airguns; Dynamit Nobel-RWS, Inc.

Further Reading

"Air Gun Manufacturer's CEO Killed in Car Crash," *Associated Press Newswires*, November 11, 2000.
"Crosman and NRA Join Forces," *Shooting Industry*, May 1, 2003, p. 49.
"Company History." Available from http://www.crosman.com.
"Crosman, Procaps Form Diablo Marketing," *Shooting Industry*, February 1, 2002, p. 10.
Eaton, John, "New York's Crosman to Buy Denver Maker of Gun Sights," *Denver Post*, December 17, 1992, p. 1C.
Elliott, Will, "While Others Go Splat, Crosman Paints a Rosy Picture," *Buffalo News*, December 16, 2001, p. C13.
Fletcher, D.T., *75 Years of Crosman Air Guns*, Portland, Ore., 1998.
Jacobson, Gary, "Hicks, Muse Group Buys Crosman for $41 Million," *Dallas Morning News*, November 22, 1989, p. 4D.
Kelly, J. Michael, "Airguns, Pellets Are Big Business," *Post-Standard* (Syracuse N.Y.), October 17, 2002, p. D4.
Levy, Mike, "Airguns Provide Sound Alternative," *Buffalo News*, November 23, 2003, p. C12.
"Okla. Investment Group Buys MacAndrews & Forbes Unit," *Dow Jones News Service*, August 29, 1990.
Rogers, Amy, "Crosman Aims for New Web Presence," *Computer Reseller News*, October 15, 2001, p. 45.

—Frank Uhle

CUNA MUTUAL GROUP

CUNA Mutual Group

5910 Mineral Point Road
Madison, Wisconsin 53705
U.S.A.
Telephone: (608) 238-5851
Toll Free: (800) 356-2644
Web site: http://www.cunamutual.com

Private Company
Incorporated: 1935
Employees: 5,000
Total Assets: $2.28 billion (2002)
NAIC: 524113 Direct Life Insurance Carriers; 524114
  Direct Health and Medical Insurance Carriers; 524126
  Direct Property and Casualty Insurance Carriers;
  524128 Other Direct Insurance (except Life, Health,
  and Medical) Carriers; 524130 Reinsurance Carriers;
  525190 Other Insurance Funds

Based in Madison, Wisconsin, CUNA Mutual Group provides financial services to credit unions. The company's industry leadership position is reflected in its massive offering of more than 300 credit-union-specific products. According to CUNA Mutual, its products fall under the categories of investment, insurance, and technology and are offered via a mix of strategic relationships and multiple service channels.

Officially organized under the CUNA Mutual Insurance Society (life, health, and accident insurance), the CUNA Mutual Group consists of CUNA Mutual Life Insurance Company (life insurance, long-term care insurance, and annuities); CUNA Brokerage Services, Inc. (investments and mutual funds); MEMBERS Capital Advisors (investment advice); CUNA Mutual Mortgage Corporation; CMG Mortgage Insurance Company; and CUNA Mutual Insurance Agency, Inc. (insurance and annuity products).

According to the organization, "The confidence and trust credit unions have in CUNA Mutual is reflected in the fact that it protects, with one or more coverages, nearly 95 percent of the 9,500-plus credit unions in the United States." CUNA Mutual belongs to its many policy owners, and the organization pro-

vides a variety of insurance and investment products to approximately nine million people.

Formative Years: 1934–58

CUNA Mutual's history dates back to August 10, 1934, when 52 credit union leaders from 21 states and the District of Columbia met in Estes Park, Colorado, and established the Credit Union National Association (CUNA). Prior to this historic event, North America's first credit union had been formed in Quebec, Canada, on January 23, 1901, and the Credit Union National Extension Bureau represented the credit union movement from 1921 to 1935. In addition, President Franklin D. Roosevelt had signed the landmark Federal Credit Union Act in 1934, allowing credit unions to be formed in any state.

The new association held its first meeting on January 27, 1935 in Kansas City, Missouri. Its headquarters were temporarily located in Madison, Wisconsin, where it rented a mansion that had been used for student housing at 142 East Gilman Street. This first location was dubbed Raiffeisen House after the German credit union pioneer Friedrich Wilhelm Raiffeisen. Roy F. Bergengren, a lawyer from Massachusetts, was elected as CUNA's first managing director.

It was not long before two affiliated organizations were established. In 1935, the CUNA Mutual Insurance Society (eventually named CUNA Mutual Group) was created with a $25,000 loan from Edward A. Filene, a Boston department store retailer, philanthropist, and credit union pioneer, to provide members with affordable credit insurance that covered loans in the event of a borrower's death. Its first claim totaled $40. In 1936, the CUNA Supply Cooperative was established to provide advertising materials and supplies to member credit unions.

Filene died in Paris in 1937 before the fruits of his efforts truly blossomed. However, he is widely recognized as the "father" of the credit union movement. In fact, President Franklin Roosevelt dubbed him a "prophet" for his foresight, according to the January 1, 1995 issue of the *Capital Times*.

In 1939, Madison became CUNA's permanent headquarters. In September of that year, the organization relocated to the

---

<blockquote>
Company Perspectives:

Our mission is creating financial security, and our vision is to be the best at serving credit unions and their members.
</blockquote>

Fuller and Johnson Building at 1342 East Washington Avenue. According to the January 3, 1959 issue of the <i>Wisconsin State Journal:</i> "The reasons given for Madison's selection were Wisconsin's position as a leader of progressive legislation, the central location of Madison, the fact that it is the home of the University of Wisconsin, the city's beautiful location on four lakes, and its friendly people."

During the 1940s, CUNA Mutual was forced to contend with the circumstances of World War II. As former CUNA Mutual Insurance Society President and CEO Charles F. Eikel, Jr. explained in <i>The Debt Shall Die with the Debtor: The CUNA Mutual Insurance Society Story</i>, the war "had its effect on the credit union movement just as it did on every segment of democracy. Key staff members, along with millions of credit union members, went to Europe and the Pacific. Other companies issued 'war policies,' limiting or canceling coverage for those in uniform. We did not. Moreover, we devised a plan where a serviceman's coverage could actually increase."

In 1950, CUNA relocated to new headquarters at 1617 Sherman Avenue. U.S. President Truman dedicated the new building by sealing its cornerstone and giving a 30-minute speech that was broadcast nationwide. Built at a cost of $350,000, the new facility was named Filene House. In its March 1954 newsletter, the Madison Chamber of Commerce and Foundation explained that Filene House was "a living memorial to the organization's founder—Edward A. Filene. Thousands of credit union members contributed their dimes and dollars to help finance the modern, two-story structure. It represents their tribute to the Boston businessman who spent so much of his time, efforts, and personal fortune promoting the credit union cause."

In 1956, Charles F. Eikel, Jr. was named president of CUNA Mutual. Born in New Orleans, Eikel joined the Credit Union National Association in 1938 as its southern field representative and later went to work for CUNA Mutual.

In <i>The Debt Shall Die with the Debtor</i>, Eikel noted that during the 1950s, the Credit Union National Association and CUNA Mutual Group became "physically separated" for the first time in the organization's history. While both entities remained headquartered in Filene House, differing organizational opinions and philosophies divided them. Despite this, Eikel explained that "As individuals, we were dedicated to the whole credit union idea— the comprehensive realization of economic security for all men and women through mutual efforts." Subsequently, each organization's leadership was able to make great strides toward resolving differences during the coming two decades.

Explosive Growth: 1959–94

By the late 1950s, CUNA Mutual had developed a more comprehensive offering of insurance coverage for its members. In addition to life savings and loan protection, by 1959 the organization's offerings included individual life, group life, league group life, home protection, family security, and major medical expense insurance. The previous year, total insurance-in-force reached $4.2 billion. With assets of $25 million, CUNA Mutual served more than seven million credit union members and paid out some 48,000 claims worth about $21 million.

Strong growth caused CUNA Mutual to outgrow Filene House. Some of the organization's staff was forced to rent office space off-site. With this in mind, CUNA Mutual broke ground on a new headquarters in May 1959. In September 1960, it relocated to a $1.5 million, three-story building at 5910 Mineral Point Road in Madison. Situated on an 18-acre campus, the new building had 55,000 square feet of floor space for CUNA Mutual's 250 employees. The move freed up space for the Credit Union National Association and CUNA Supply Cooperative to expand in Filene House.

In <i>The Debt Shall Die with the Debtor</i>, Charles Eikel explained: "We had almost outgrown the new building before we moved in, and by 1963, we found it necessary to build an addition which doubled the size of the structure." By the early 1970s, growth prompted CUNA Mutual to double the size of its facility once more.

In addition to moving into its new headquarters in 1960, CUNA Mutual also celebrated its 25th anniversary that year. It marked this milestone by becoming the nation's first life insurance company to have $5 billion of insurance-in-force. In addition, CUMIS Insurance Society, Inc. was formed to offer property and casualty coverage. By this time, CUNA Mutual served credit union members in Central and South America, the Caribbean, Ireland, and the Fiji Islands. Two years later, continued growth overseas led to the formation of a full-time department devoted to CUNA Mutual's international business.

As the 1960s progressed, CUNA Mutual continued to mark further achievements. The company's first billion-dollar year came in 1964, when total coverage amounted to $8.5 billion and assets totaled $53 million. In 1965, a Vietnam Provision pertaining to loan protection and life savings contracts was implemented to benefit veterans. According to <i>The Debt Shall Die with the Debtor</i>, the provision stated: "death and permanent disability claims paid for military personnel in combat zones are treated in the same way as catastrophic loss." In 1966, expansion caused CUNA Mutual to build an office in Pomona, California, to service the western United States, as well as a Canadian office in Burlington, Ontario.

By 1971, CUNA Mutual Insurance Society served roughly 45 countries, including credit unions in Great Britain, Hong Kong, Scotland, Peru, and New Zealand. The organization had actual offices in such far away locations as Tasmania, Bolivia, Trinidad, Ecuador, Antilles, Ireland, and Australia. Expansion plans included African countries like Kenya, as well as Japan and Korea. CUNA Mutual had evolved into North America's 15th largest life insurance company, insuring more than 23,700 of the world's credit unions and recording premium income of $117 million in 1970, with $15.5 billion of insurance-in-force.

Growth continued at CUNA Mutual throughout the 1970s. In 1973, Robert L. Curry succeeded Charles F. Eikel, Jr. as CUNA Mutual's CEO. A 1953 University of Wisconsin-

Madison Law School graduate, Curry was a senior member of law firm Boardman, Suhr, Curry and Field prior to joining CUNA Mutual. In the February 17, 1986 issue of the *Capital Times*, Rob Zaleski described Curry as "an astute, cordial, mild-mannered individual who looks the part of a Wall Street businessman, minus the glitter."

By 1974, CUNA Mutual's insurance-in-force reached $22.5 billion and assets totaled $207 million. The Credit Union National Association also continued to prosper, counting 29 million individuals among its membership at 22,950 credit unions. The organization then had $31 billion in assets, $24 billion in loans, and $27.5 billion in savings.

By the end of 1977, CUNA Mutual Group had grown to include the CUNA Mutual Insurance Society, CUNA Mutual Investment Corp., CUMIS Insurance Society Inc., CUDIS Insurance Society Inc., and CMCI Corp., as well as CUNA Services Group, ICU Services Corp., CUNA Supply Corp., CUNADATA Corp., Data Switch Corp., the International Association of Managing Directors, U.S. Central Credit Union, Credit Card Services Inc., CUNA Retirement Savings Fund, and CUNA Retirement Pension Plan. Insurance-in-force exceeded $34 billion that year, a $5 billion hike from 1976. Employees numbered 1,746, approximately 880 of whom were located in Madison.

At this time, CUNA was responsible for representing credit union leagues in all 50 states and some 36 million members at 22,000 U.S. credit unions. In 1978, CUNA CEO Herbert G. Wegner, the youngest top executive in the association's history, resigned after holding his post for seven years. Executive Vice-President of Administration Russell Notar stood in as CEO until a permanent replacement was made.

In June 1980, an exciting development occurred when CUNA Mutual's campus, which had grown to cover 30 acres, effectively became the credit union movement's international headquarters. The campus was appropriately renamed as the World Credit Union Center. In addition to CUNA Mutual's building, two new structures were added. One housed the Credit Union National Association and its affiliates, which relocated operations from Filene House after selling it to Wisconsin Physicians Service. The second structure, named the International Building, was home to an umbrella organization called the World Council of Credit Unions. Founded in 1970, it represented 67 countries and promoted credit unions around the world. The latter facility also housed a historical money museum, an 800-seat cafeteria, and a 175-seat theater. Together, the three buildings—owned by CUNA Mutual—housed some 1,500 employees of 16 different but related organizations. Approximately 1,000 people attended a dedication ceremony for the new campus, including U.S. House of Representatives member Robert Kastenmeier (D-Wis.).

As of 1984, CUNA Mutual had $58.3 billion of insurance-in-force and assets of $884 million. That year, the Credit Union National Association had grown to include 50.4 million members, with $111.5 billion in assets, $101.3 billion in savings, and $72.3 billion in outstanding loans.

A key leadership change unfolded at the Credit Union National Association in 1987 when Chief Operating Officer Ralph Swoboda was named president and CEO, succeeding Jim R. Williams. Swoboda also became the top executive for CUNA Service Group. Prior to joining the association in 1975, he was an attorney in Madison. By this time, the association had annual operating revenues of nearly $20 million. It faced rising competition from other financial service companies that marketed to credit unions, as well as competing trade organizations such as the National Association of Federal Credit Unions.

Important developments also were underway at CUNA Mutual during the late 1980s. Robert L. Curry retired as CUNA Mutual's CEO in October of 1988. During his tenure, the organization grew to a staff of more than 1,900 in Madison and 3,000 worldwide. A former professor named Richard "Doc" Heins succeeded Curry. Like Curry, Heins was a University of Wisconsin-Madison Law School graduate and his association with CUNA Mutual began in 1956. Finally, in May 1988, CUNA Mutual mourned the death of former CEO Charles Eikel, who passed away at the age of 80.

It was also in 1988 that a $14 million, four-story, 143,000-square-foot addition was made to the Credit Union National Association's building. The new structure, which included a 10,000-square-foot training and conference center, was built to house different departments of the association, CUNA Mutual, and the CUNA Mortgage Corp. The expansion corresponded to the overall growth of credit union membership, which had reached 57.1 million in the United States in 1987. From 1982 to 1987, credit union assets had exploded from $98.3 billion to $183.5 billion.

By the early 1990s, CUNA's Card Services subsidiary, which provided credit cards and related services to more than three million cardholders at 2,400 credit unions, was achieving healthy growth. Although CUNA had offered credit cards since 1978, volume began to increase significantly in 1984, when credit unions sought new ways to compete against no-interest loans offered by the auto industry.

Focus & Reorganization: 1995 and After

The mid-1990s brought more leadership changes to both CUNA Mutual and the Credit Union National Association. In March 1995, Michael Kitchen succeeded Richard Heins as CUNA Mutual's CEO. While Heins was at CUNA Mutual's helm, the organization's revenues had increased significantly, rising from $930 million in 1988 to $2.1 billion in 1994.

A Canadian native who had served as president and CEO of CUNA Mutual subsidiary CUMIS Canada, Kitchen placed an emphasis on cost cutting when he took office and guided the organization toward a goal of saving $16 million during his first year. In addition, he sought to increase productivity and increase the company's focus. In alignment with Kitchen's vision, the company reorganized in 1996. Without cutting any of CUNA Mutual's 4,700 employees, four new divisions were developed: Member Services, Lending, International, and Corporate Services. The new enterprise structure allowed CUNA Mutual to better concentrate on the delivery of its services.

At the Credit Union National Association, Ralph Swoboda resigned at the end of 1995. Temporarily replaced by Pete Crear, Swoboda was eventually succeeded in July 1996 by Daniel A. Mica, an insurance trade association executive and former Florida congressman.

CUNA Mutual entered the 21st Century on solid financial footing, with record 1999 revenues of $2.9 billion and a surplus of $870 million after all claims had been paid (also a record). The company had ventured into other financial services, including online servicing, brokerage, and lending, and employed 5,100 workers. Of CUNA Mutual's 2,600 employees in Madison, 1,600 were white-collar union workers represented by the Office & Professional Employees International Union Local 39.

Although relations between the union and CUNA Mutual Management had historically been very positive, by this time tension had emerged. In 2002, both sides agreed to a salary freeze, and a total of 122 workers, including 80 in Madison, lost their jobs. By late 2003, some union officials claimed that morale was low at CUNA Mutual, while the organization cited contrary results from employee satisfaction surveys.

Despite friction with its unionized workers and a $9 million capital-investment-related loss, in 2003 CUNA Mutual remained a powerful player in the insurance and financial services industry. With 2002 revenues of $2.3 billion, an increase of 12.5 percent from 2001, the firm had the resources and experience required for success in its second century of operations.

Principal Divisions

Member Services; Lending; International; Corporate Services.

Principal Competitors

The BISYS Group, Inc.; PrimeVest Financial Services, Inc.; U.S. Central Credit Union.

Further Reading

"CUNA Mutual Insurance Is Now 14th Largest U.S. Life Company," *Wisconsin State Journal*, January 22, 1972.

"CUNA Mutual Reorganizes; No Jobs Lost," *Wisconsin State Journal*, January 20, 1996.

"CUNA Names New Leader," *Wisconsin State Journal*, March 13, 1987.

"CUNA Will Mark Four Anniversaries in 1959," *Wisconsin State Journal*, January 3, 1959.

Eikel, Charles F., Jr., *The Debt Shall Die with the Debtor: The CUNA Mutual Insurance Society Story*, New York: Newcomen Society in North America, 1972.

Ivey, Mike, "With Mutual Interest: CUNA Mutual Faces Labor, Competitive Challenges," *Capital Times*, August 3, 2000.

Jaeger, Richard W., "CUNA Mutual Leader to Retire in October," *Wisconsin State Journal*, February 20, 1988.

Johnson, Paul, "Kitchen Named President, CEO of CUNA Mutual," *Wisconsin State Journal*, February 3, 1995.

——, "CUNA Head to Leave Job After 7 Years," *Wisconsin State Journal*, October 31, 1995.

Lueders, Bill, "Good CUNA, Bad CUNA," *Isthmus*, September 5, 2003.

McGlothren, Victoria, "CUNA Center Is Dedicated," *Wisconsin State Journal*, June 1, 1980.

Molvig, Dianne, "Passing the Baton at CUNA Mutual," *In Business*, May 1989.

——, "Richard Heins, Corporate Executive Professor," *In Business*, February 1992.

"New CUNA Chief, Ex-Rep, to Work, Lobby in D.C.," *Capital Times*, June 18, 1996.

"Over 20,000 Will Hear Truman, Take Part in CUNA Events Sunday," *Capital Times*, May 12, 1950.

Parkins, Al, "CUNA Credit Card Biz Growing," *Capital Times*, February 21, 1991.

Pfefferkorn, Robert, "22 Million CUNA Members Offer Challenge of Getting Things Done," *Wisconsin State Journal*, April 16, 1972.

Riddle, Jennifer, "CUNA Chief Uses Team Approach," *Wisconsin State Journal*, April 12, 1987.

Still, Thomas W., "CUNA President Wegner Resigns," *Wisconsin State Journal*, November 7, 1978.

Wendling, Patrice, "New Chief Puts CUNA on High-Profit, Low-Fat Diet," *Capital Times*, August 22, 1995.

Zaleski, Rob, "Low Profile Is Part of Curry's Game Plan," *Capital Times*, February 17, 1986.

—Paul R. Greenland

DANSKIN

Danskin, Inc.

530 Seventh Avenue
New York, New York 10018
U.S.A.
Telephone: (212) 764-4630
Toll Free: (800) 288-6749; (888) DANSKIN
Fax: (212) 764-7265
Web site: http://www.danskin.com

Public Company
Incorporated: 1882
Employees: 2,168
Sales: $81.8 million (2001)
Stock Exchanges: Over the Counter (OTC)
Ticker Symbol: DANS
NAIC: 315239 Women's and Girls' Cut and Sew Other
Outerwear Manufacturing

Danskin, Inc. is a leading maker and marketer of women's athletic and fitness wear. The company sells clothing to be worn during dance and exercise, and also offers hosiery. Founded in the late 19th century, Danskin made its name as a vendor of tights, tutus, and leotards, which became the standard for dancers across the United States. Although Danskin expanded its line of products to meet the needs of a much wider segment of the population, the company failed to capitalize on the women's fitness boom that began in the 1980s to the extent of up-and-coming rivals like Reebok and Nike. As CEO Carol Hochman told *Sporting Goods Business,* however, Danskin is the only leading women's fitness brand to have its roots in women's products. It has maintained a special place in the hearts of active women and girls by such gestures as sponsoring an educational tour by the Rockettes and by hosting the world's largest triathlon series, a women-only affair held in several cities. Danskin also continues to innovate, developing new fabrics such as Performance O2, which combines a layer of cotton cloth with one of CoolMax.

The Company's Founding in 1882

The company that became Danskin was founded in 1882 in New York City, when brothers Joel and Benson Goodman

opened a small dry goods store, which sold tights and hosiery that it imported from Europe. The store soon became popular with dancers, and, sensing a market opportunity, the Goodmans began to manufacture goods specifically for dancers' needs. From this start, Danskin soon came to dominate the market for clothing worn while dancing. The Goodmans introduced the first knit tights and leotards, and also pioneered the production of such dance standards as fishnet stockings. The company also popularized the use of the colors "ballet pink" and "theatrical pink" for dancers' tights.

Throughout the late 19th century and the first half of the 20th century, Danskin dominated the market for dancewear in the United States. Over time, the company's goods and products became synonymous with dance clothing. In addition to its tights and leotards for dancers of all sorts, the company introduced similar products for gymnasts and figure skaters.

Danskin is credited with producing the first nylon bodywear in the 1950s. In the late 1960s, the company broke out of the relatively restricted market consisting of dancers, gymnasts, and skaters when it marketed its first product for wear on the street by the general population. This innovative adaptation of its traditional product line was the bodysuit. The company added snaps for convenience to a conventional leotard, and also updated its styling to make it more fashionable. In this way, Danskin hoped to market its products to a broader range of consumers.

Following this innovation, Danskin entered a new market in the mid-1970s. In 1976, the company began to market swimwear, another extension of its basic leotard line. Using new technology, Danskin invented a shiny, stretchy fabric that was a blend of nylon and spandex. The company used this fabric in a maillot bathing suit, which, like the leotard, fit the wearer's body like a second skin. By the end of the decade, Danskin boasted an 80 percent share of the bodywear market overall.

Acquisition by Playtex/Esmark in 1980

At the start of the 1980s, Danskin ceased to be a privately held firm, when the company was sold to International Playtex, Inc., on April 29, 1980. Danskin's new owner had itself been purchased and become a subsidiary of a conglomerate called

Company Perspectives:

A combination of feminine styling and performance fabrics puts Danskin in a completely unique place for active women. From technically advanced fabrics like O2 Performance (a unique blend of CoolMax and cotton) and Supplex with Lycra to added product features for comfort and fit. Danskin is the only premier brand committed exclusively to addressing the multi-faceted needs of today's active women and girls from authentic sports to an active everyday lifestyle.

Esmark, Inc., in 1975. Esmark was founded in 1972 to take over the assets of the Swift & Company meatpacking business and since the early 1970s had grown by purchasing companies in a wide variety of fields, which were divided into four loose groupings: food divisions, leather and chemicals, insurance and financial services, and petroleum and oil.

With the purchase of Playtex, Esmark moved into the consumer goods area, and this unit's subsequent purchase of Danskin strengthened its holdings in the knit goods and hosiery fields. Playtex had first entered the market for women's hosiery in August 1977, when the company bought Pennaco Hosiery, Inc., which marketed women's stockings under the brand name "Round the Clock." Pennaco's history dated back to 1919. Playtex augmented its holdings in this field five months later, when it also acquired Virginia Maid Hosiery Mills, Inc.

In the early 1980s, Danskin saw the rapid expansion of another potential market for its products, as the popularity of aerobic exercise grew. As women flocked to dance and exercise classes, Danskin began to market a special line of athletic wear for use in fitness classes. The company's entry into the workout apparel market expanded its line of product offerings and its overall sales throughout the 1980s.

Four years after Danskin became a part of Esmark, the company's corporate parent was itself acquired by the Beatrice Companies, Inc., on August 7, 1984. Beatrice had grown through acquisitions into a wide-ranging and far-flung conglomeration of business interests, of which Esmark made up only a small part. As Beatrice moved into the mid-1980s, the company became caught up in the turmoil of the financial industry. By early 1986, efforts were under way to take Beatrice private in a leveraged buyout, as clearly the company's various parts would have to be broken apart and sold off in order to pay off part of the debt taken on when the company went private. As part of this process, Beatrice announced in October 1985 that it would sell its knitwear operations, including Danskin.

Spinoff in 1986

Preparatory to this effort, Beatrice set aside Esmark's apparel units, which consisted of Danskin and the Pennaco Hosiery Company, forming Esmark Apparel, Inc., on February 21, 1986. These operations recorded combined sales in 1985 of $100 million. Then, on April 17, 1986, the leveraged buyout of Beatrice was completed, as the company's outstanding shares were purchased by the BCI Holdings Corporation for $6.2 billion. Two months later, Beatrice announced the successful sale of its knitwear operations to Eaglewood Partners for just

$15 million, plus assumed debts of $12 million. Eaglewood Partners was an investor group put together by a private New York investment banking firm, Hero & Company. Eaglewood announced that its managing partner, Byron A. Hero, would be put in charge of Esmark. Danskin's general manager, Barbara Khouri, became the company's president. With this move, Esmark, with two divisions, Danskin and Pennaco Hosiery, once again became a privately held company.

At the time of its purchase by Eaglewood, Esmark Apparel held the largest portion of the fragmented women's exercise clothing market. Hero maintained that the company had missed opportunities to seize an even larger portion of this field, however, because it had not moved aggressively enough into the burgeoning fitness market. (Beatrice had been notorious, though, for distributing a cheap line of tights to discount stores under the "Playskin" brand name.) The company had not introduced enough new products to meet the growing demand in this sector of the market, according to Hero.

In addition, Hero felt that as a company on the auction block for nine months Esmark had been relegated to second-class status within the Beatrice organization, which had hampered Esmark's efforts to expand its product line more effectively. Therefore, Byron Hero planned to capitalize on the brand name recognition of Danskin and Pennaco, and to broaden the company's offerings of legwear and leotards. With Esmark as a privately held firm, Hero planned to reinvest the company's profits in expanding operations and market penetration. "The kinds of businesses that do well in the fashion industry are independently run and more sensitive to the market," Hero told the *Wall Street Journal.*

At the end of 1986, Esmark took its first steps toward expanding the company's line of goods, when it bought Dance France, Limited, another maker of dance apparel, from that company's French founder, Francois Greis. The operations of this company were merged into Danskin's existing structure. In the following year, Danskin further expanded its product offerings, introducing Danskin-Plus, a line of large-sized bodywear, in the fall of 1987.

Esmark announced that it would promote this new line, as well as its other products, with a $5 million advertising campaign. This campaign was slated to build on the $3 million campaign, which featured the slogan "all the world's a stage," which Danskin had used to promote a line of short, tight-fitting dresses. This effort boosted sales of the company's adult streetwear by more than one-third in 1987. In addition, Danskin saw sales of its dancewear for children grow by 40 percent over the course of 1987. "It seems that every little girl wants to be a ballerina," Rose Peabody ("Podie") Lynch, Danskin's new president, told *Forbes.*

In September 1987, Esmark made another strategic acquisition that strengthened its presence in the dancewear market. At that time, the company bought Repetto France, a French manufacturer of dancewear, which specialized in ballet shoes and tutus. Esmark also enhanced its standing in the hosiery market when it acquired the right to distribute the Givenchy Hosiery line of products in foreign markets.

By the start of 1988, Esmark's Danskin division boasted a 98 percent consumer recognition rating in its core bodywear

```
┌─────────────────────────────────────────────────────┐
│                    Key Dates:                         │
│                                                       │
│  1882:  The Goodman family opens a store selling Euro-│
│         pean hosiery.                                 │
│  1980:  The business is acquired by Esmark/International│
│         Playtex.                                      │
│  1984:  Beatrice acquires Esmark.                     │
│  1986:  Danskin goes private as a division of Esmark Ap-│
│         parel, Inc.                                   │
│  1992:  Danskin, Inc. goes public.                    │
│  1999:  New CEO Carol Hochman begins turnaround mea-  │
│         sures.                                        │
│  2001:  Danskin sponsors the Rockettes tour; Target begins│
│         carrying the product.                         │
│  2002:  A line of dance clothes is developed for the New│
│         York City Ballet.                             │
│  2003:  The Pennaco Hosiery division is sold off to a man-│
│         agement-led group.                            │
└─────────────────────────────────────────────────────┘
```

market, but its share of the market had shrunk to 35 percent, down from 80 percent at the start of the decade. Outside of its traditional dance product line, the company had become firmly identified in consumer's minds with Lycra-blend workout wear, a perception that held down sales of the company's non-dance-related clothing.

"We want to reposition Danskin products as young, vital and at the forefront of fashion," Lynch explained to *Forbes*. The company targeted women from the ages of 18 to 44, hoping to encourage customers to wear its clothes not just for workouts, but for everyday purposes as well. Surveys indicated that nearly half of Danskin's apparel buyers already saw the company's products in this versatile light, but Danskin hoped to increase this percentage even more. "Many of [our customers] like to exercise, but they all like to look good," Lynch maintained.

In addition to increasing sales, Danskin set out to hold down costs. The company reduced the work force at its York, Pennsylvania, knitting mill from 2,500 to 600. Eighty-five percent of the products Danskin sold were manufactured in York, and the other 15 percent were made in Taiwan and shipped to the United States. "Because of the weak dollar, we are bringing the concept of quality circles from Taiwan to our York plant to increase productivity," Lynch noted. All in all, as a result of these efforts, Danskin's sales had risen by 45 percent within two years of its sale by Beatrice.

Building on these gains, Danskin introduced a new line of tights made with Supplex nylon and Lycra in August 1989. Three months later, the company also rolled out Danskin Pro, a collection of athletic wear for women. This clothing was made for those participating in gymnastics, figure skating, track, volleyball, running, water sports, and other activities. To promote these products, Danskin recruited a group of female athletes, which it dubbed "Team Danskin," to serve as consultants, testers, and spokespersons. Among the members of "Team Danskin" were skater Katarina Witt, ballet dancer Darci Kistler, and Hero's own wife, water skier Camille Duvall-Hero.

Danskin continued its promotional efforts in 1990, when the company launched the "Danskin Women's Triathlon Series." This event was designed to meet the need for sports and fitness competitions among female non-career athletes. The triathlon started with events held in three cities, and soon spread to six locations, encompassing more than 10,000 first-time participants.

At the end of 1990, Danskin announced that it would introduce a new line of footwear the following spring. Overall, the company planned to diversify its product line and to further enhance its marketing effort. These efforts began to bear fruit in March 1991, when Danskin introduced a line of headbands and ponytail holders that matched its activewear. One month later, the company announced that it had seen a 50 percent rise in sales for items in its Danskin Plus line, an early attempt by the company to reach out to new customers.

1992 IPO

On July 2, 1992, Esmark Apparel changed its name to that of its most important operating unit, Danskin. Six days later, the company offered $3 million of stock to the public, in an effort to raise $36 million to fund further expansion. The company's initial public offering (IPO), however, was so successful that $39 million was raised.

While it sought capital in the market, Danskin outlined four strategies for further growth, which it had first elucidated in 1988. The first of these goals was to focus greater attention on expanding wholesale distribution of Danskin products. The company hoped to tailor its product lines to different segments of the market, defined as department stores, specialty shops, and sporting goods stores. Danskin hoped to hone marketing techniques that would push more Danskin goods onto the shelves of all of these retail outlets. In addition, Danskin planned to increase the number of retail stores selling its goods directly, by opening a chain of factory outlet stores, which would then be followed by more elaborate full-price stores.

To keep these stores supplied with as wide a range of merchandise as possible, Danskin plotted two strategies to broaden its product offerings. The company moved to license its brand names for use on products made by other manufacturers, and also moved to maximize its production capabilities, expanding the Danskin line of goods in every way possible, given the company's factory equipment. Finally, Danskin hoped to expand sales by increasing overseas marketing efforts.

Shortly after its first public stock offering, Danskin augmented its product offerings by adding a line of children's swimwear. At the end of the year, the company announced that it would push further into the activewear market, building on its strength in the workout gear segment of the apparel industry.

In the spring of 1993, Danskin stepped up its licensing activities. The company purchased rights to the "Shape" label from the Imagination Factory, which it used to launch a line of goods for sale in chain stores and mass merchandisers. One month later, Danskin's Pennaco division licensed its Round the Clock hosiery brand name to Paul Lavitt Mills.

Late in April 1993, Danskin introduced a collection of sportswear for the fall, as the company continued its quest to add market share in the women's apparel field. Although Danskin's sales and earnings showed improvement throughout the first nine months of 1993, the company ran into difficulty in the last quarter of the year, its most important segment for sales. Bad weather forced the company's factory in York, Pennsylvania, to close for 22 days of production in the winter of 1993, and the company's southern hosiery mills, located in Memphis, Tennessee, and Grenada, Mississippi, also were affected.

Although sales of Danskin products increased for the seventh year in a row, Danskin's hosiery division lost $6 million over 1993, as the stocking industry suffered from severe overcapacity. In an effort to stem the losses in this area, Danskin sought to expand into other, stocking-related products, such as socks and tights, and also to add new brand names, such as Christian Dior, a license acquired during the year.

In its effort to expand overall distribution channels, Danskin opened 15 new factory stores, bringing the company's total to 32. In addition, Danskin signed leases for full-service retail outlets in Manhattan and in Miami's trendy South Beach neighborhood. In these stores, Danskin planned to stock clothing for dance, exercise, and sports in a fashion environment. The company hoped that these flagship stores would give other Danskin retailers ideas about how best to present the company's merchandise. In addition, Danskin continued its push into international markets, signing an agreement with a retailer in Australia to market its apparel there. Although Danskin's initial year as a publicly held company proved a disappointment, the strength of its brand name and its firm establishment in its niche of the apparel market boded well for the company as it moved into the mid-1990s.

Former Jockey International Inc. president Howard Cooley was named CEO of Danskin in September 1994, succeeding Byron Hero, who retained the position of chairman for another 11 months. Cooley had helped develop Jockey's highly successful line of women's undergarments, Jockey for Her. He was named Danskin's chairman of the board in August 1995.

Mary Ann Domuracki was named the next CEO in April 1996; she had been the company's chief financial officer and president. At the time, sales were about $125 million a year and slipping as the company struggled under a massive $40 million debt. Observers traced the beginning of the company's crisis back to $6 million in loans made to help Esmark finance a fitness start-up company that had failed.

Renewed Focus in 1999

Sales fell 42 percent to $88 million in fiscal 1999. In the summer of 1999, Carol Hochman succeeded CEO Cathy Volker, formerly president and CEO of Hanes Hosiery, who had taken the position in early 1998. Hochman had been the head of Liz Claiborne Accessories. She set out to refocus Danskin on its core strengths in fitness and dancing. She steered the company away from courting department stores, reported *Sporting Goods Business,* back toward its traditional base of sporting goods and specialty stores. Within a couple of years, sporting goods, specialty, and department stores were each accounting for about a third of sales. In 2001, Danskin began shipping product to the Target chain of discount stores.

Hochman closed 11 of Danskin's own stores and scaled back seven others. The company had begun importing knit items from Turkey; it continued to produce certain lines at its plant in York, Pennsylvania. The product lineup included "Everywear," a hybrid of activewear and casualwear.

The Pennaco hosiery division was winning sales with niche-oriented specialty hosiery. Pennaco's advanced technology made it possible to incorporate new types of satin and lace detailing with these. The number of different hosiery offerings, however, was being reduced.

In the fall of 1999, Danskin brought out a line of yoga clothes in collaboration with distributor Spa Concepts Inc. Called Zen Sport, the clothes were made from earth-friendly materials like organic cotton and fibers from recycled soda bottles. Items included hoodies, Capri pants, drawstring pants, and tank tops with sewn-in bras.

Danskin partnered with two legendary names in the New York dancing world. Danskin helped the Radio City Rockettes celebrate their 75th anniversary in 2001 by sponsoring a multi-city tour offering dance lessons to girls aged 10 to 18. The next year, Danskin became the exclusive licensee for a line of contemporary dance apparel from the New York City Ballet. CEO Carol Hochman told *Sporting Goods Business* the company had spent a year developing seamless leotards in cotton Lycra for the troupe. Danskin also developed a unique cotton/CoolMax fabric called O2 Performance.

Fitness guru Denise Austin was signed up as a workout clothing endorsee in late 2001. For her, Danskin developed a line of fitness tights, which premiered on QVC, featuring figure-flattering mesh control panels. The company also brought out a zip-front bra. Moreover, Danskin continued to try fitness-related brand extensions, including a $150 weight bench for women in 2003, which retailed on QVC and in The Sports Authority retail stores.

In October 2003, Pennaco Hosiery was sold to a group (JBT Legwear LLC) led by that division's vice-president and general manager, Barry Tartarkin. The purchase included rights to sell hosiery under the Round the Clock, Ellen Tracy, Evan Picone, and Givenchy brands, plus private labels.

Principal Competitors

Adidas-Salomon AG; NIKE Corporation; Reebok, Ltd.; Sara Lee Branded Apparel; Weekend Exercise Company.

Further Reading

Botham, Peter, "Danskin Inc. Cuts Work Force," *York Daily Record* (Pennsylvania), April 13, 2000, p. E1.

Cuff, Daniel F., and Stephen Phillips, "Suitor of Esmark Plans to Broaden Its Lines," *New York Times,* June 11, 1986.

"Danskin Keeps on Dancin' Despite Financial Woes & Media Knocks," *Sporting Goods Business,* October 1996, p. 8.

"Danskin Targets Discount Crowd," *WWD,* March 23, 2001, p. 14.

Dolbow, Sandra, "Danskin Lassos Tartarkin in Bid to Boost Biz," *Brandweek,* May 29, 2000, p. 70.

Feitelberg, Rosemary, "Hochman Aims to Shape Up Pennaco," *WWD,* August 16, 1999, p. 16.

——, "Hochman Joins Danskin as CEO," *WWD,* June 2, 1999, p. 2.

——, "Hochman Takes New Steps at Danskin," *WWD,* August 3, 2000, p. 10.

Furman, Phyllis, "Exec's Grand Plan Unravels Danskin," *Crain's New York Business,* August 15, 1994, p. 1.

——, "Troubled Danskin Runs to Jockey for New CEO," *Crain's New York Business,* September 26, 1994, p. 35.

Grieves, Robert T., "Stretching the Image," *Forbes,* April 18, 1988, p. 99.

Grish, Kristina, "Danskin to a Different Beat," *Sporting Goods Business,* January 19, 2000, p. 20.

Hasty, Susan E., "Congrats, Danskin," *Apparel Industry Magazine,* April 1994.

Karimzadeh, Marc, "Tartarkin Buys Pennaco," *WWD,* October 27, 2003, p. 9.

McLaughlin, Patricia, "Designing Fashions for Tranquility," *Plain Dealer* (Cleveland), October 14, 1999, p. 5F.

Sullivan, Mark, "Danskin's New Choreography: Carol Hochman Is Returning Danskin to Its Heritage As a Core Supplier to Sports Stores," *Sporting Goods Business,* January 2002, pp. 46f.

Zuckerman, Laurence, "When a Good Name Falls Short; Debt and Executive Turmoil Keep Danskin Hobbling," *New York Times,* August 16, 1996, p. D1.

—Elizabeth Rourke
—update: Frederick C. Ingram

Dennis Publishing Ltd.

30 Cleveland Street
London W1P 5FF
United Kingdom
Telephone: (+44) 207-907-6000
Fax: (+44) 207-907-6020
Web site: http:// http://www.dennis.co.uk

Private Company
Incorporated: 1973
Employees: 335
Sales: £189 million ($302 million)
NAIC: 511120 Periodical Publishers; 511110 Newspaper
   Publishers

Dennis Publishing Ltd. is one of the United Kingdom's leading privately held magazine publishing groups. The company has long been a major player in the UK computer and trade magazine market, notably through *PC Pro,* the leading UK computer title. Yet since the mid-1990s, Dennis has repositioned itself as a lifestyle specialist—particularly through the successful and racy *Maxim* titles. That format, which targets an upwardly mobile 20- to 45-year-old men's market (the company claims a mean household income among its readership base of $60,000 per year) with a provocative editorial style and photographs of sexily posed, but not naked, women, has not only captured a leading position in the UK but has also enabled Dennis to take the U.S. market by storm. The company has also successfully licensed *Maxim* in 19 countries, including much of Western and Eastern Europe, an in South America as well, generating a total monthly circulation of more than 3.8 million copies, enough to allow the group to claim the position as publisher of the world's most popular general interest men's magazine. In addition to *Maxim,* Dennis publishes the gadget-oriented *Stuff,* news digest *The Week,* music magazine *Blender,* and other general interest titles that include *Men's Fitness, Shape, Auto Express, Bizarre, Jack, Fortean Times,* and computer magazines *Computer Buyer, C&VG, Computer Shopper, Custom PC, MacUser,* and *PCZone.* Dennis is also present on the Internet, operating the C&VG gaming portal and an IT-oriented portal through *PCPro* magazine. Led by founder, chairman (and poet) Felix Dennis, the company remains privately held. Dennis Publishing posted sales of £189 million ($302 million) in 2002.

Up from the Underground in the 1970s

Felix Dennis, a high-school dropout, part-time gravedigger, and occasional drummer, burst onto the UK publishing scene in the late 1960s as part of the editorial team behind the notorious *Oz* magazine. Originally produced in Australia, *Oz* had been brought to the United Kingdom in the mid-1960s and grew into one of the country's most-read counterculture-oriented "underground" magazines. With a circulation of some 50,000, the socially satirical, politically irreverent magazine ran afoul of the country's obscenity laws in the early 1970s.

After publishing a children's version of *Oz,* using children as part of the editorial staff—and featuring lewd cartoons of popular children's characters—Dennis, along with the magazine's publishers, were placed on trial, and ultimately jailed (although the decision was reversed several months later on appeal). During sentencing, Dennis himself received a more lenient sentence than his partners because, as the sentencing judge famously stated, Dennis was "very much less intelligent than his fellow defendants."

Oz remained in publication for another two years following the trial, while Dennis joined the others in launching a new mainstream title, *Ink.* However, by 1973, both ventures, like the hippie culture that had given them birth, had gone bankrupt. Subsequently, Dennis turned around and launched his own company, Dennis Publishing, built around £50 and some used printing equipment, including a floor-standing process camera. Dennis's new venture initially began publishing underground comics and by the end of its first year had run out of funds. Yet Dennis had already spotted a new opportunity in the form of the Kung Fu films featuring Bruce Lee that had become a huge success at the beginning of the decade.

After noticing the lines forming for Lee's and other Kung Fu films, Dennis recognized that fans would be willing to pay for a magazine devoted to the martial art. In 1974, Dennis Publishing launched *Kung Fu Monthly.* The new title not only gave Dennis its first success, it also brought the company into the industry mainstream. Dennis continued to prove the sentencing judge wrong when, by the end of the decade, he had parlayed *Kung Fu Monthly* into a world-wide title, with licensed editions in 14 countries, including a Cantonese edition for the Hong Kong market. Lee's sudden death brought Felix Dennis a new personal triumph when he published his successful biography of the actor. Dennis followed that book up the next year when he co-authored a biography of Muhammad Ali.

The company stuck close to the film world for its next magazine concepts, launching fan titles for the *Star Wars* and *ET* movies. At the same time, however, the group began to search for its first "real" titles to take over as the Kung Fu craze died down. Dennis Publishing began acquiring and launching a series of magazines, including *Hi-Fi Choice, Which Bike?,* and others.

More lasting success came with the group's acquisition of *Personal,* the first magazine in Europe devoted to the nascent personal computing market. The title proved the first of a series of trade titles, including *Auto Express* and *MacUser,* that enabled the company to build a solid, if less than flamboyant position in the UK magazine market. A crucial turning point for the company came when Dennis reorganized along more tradi-tional corporate lines, giving the company a more coherent and stable financial structure.

The company's early entry into the personal computing market enabled it to establish itself as the UK's pre-eminent computer magazine group, with a range of titles that grew to include *Windows* by the late 1980s; *PCPro,* launched in 1994; and computer gaming title *C&VG,* which covered all aspects of the consumer and professional computing market. Dennis was also successful in breaking into the U.S. magazine market, a rare event for the British publishing industry.

Racy Success in the 1990s

In addition to dominating the computer market, Dennis launched a number of general interest titles, such as *Men's Fitness* and *Shape,* which rode on the wave of health and fitness titles launched by rival *Men's Health* in the mid-1980s. The computer market, however, remained the company's ticket to sales revenues and provided for Felix Dennis's own high-profile lifestyle. Nevertheless, while Dennis himself remained chief of the group, the company's organizational structure

placed direct control of each title, including responsibility for editorial content, marketing, and advertising sales, under a dedicated "publisher."

Dennis Publishing continued to move closer to the magazine mainstream in the mid-1990s. In 1995, the company took the chance on a new magazine format—a general interest magazine targeting the male heterosexual market. Originally rejected by Dennis's larger UK competitors, the concept led the way to the launch of *Maxim.* Designed as a counterpart to the best-selling women's magazines titles, *Maxim* replaced those magazines' fashion spreads with photographs of scantily clad women, while styling its editorial content to appeal to the rising numbers of upwardly mobile, affluent 20 to 45 year olds.

Although not the first of the new "lads" titles to make it to the stands (a rival, *Loaded,* was launched the year before), *Maxim* quickly outstripped Dennis's original ambition of a 50,000-copy circulation and by the beginning of the new cen-tury had attained a circulation of more than 250,000 in the UK alone. Yet the title's strongest success came with the launch, in 1997, of a U.S. edition of *Maxim,* which by the end of the decade had gained first place in the men's magazine market, outpacing such industry stalwarts as *GQ* and *Esquire,* with a circulation of some 2.5 million.

General Interest Publisher for the New Century

The *Maxim* success attracted interest from around the world. By 2003, the company had licensed editions in 14 countries, including France, Germany, Holland, Italy, Belgium, Spain, Portugal, Russia, the Czech Republic, and the Ukraine, a Korean-language edition that provided an entry into the Asian market, Latin American titles published in Mexico, Chile, Co-lombia, and Venezuela, as well as a Spanish-language version for the U.S. market. With a circulation of more than 3.8 million worldwide, the company claimed the title had become the world's leading general interest men's magazine.

Although Dennis maintained its strong stable of niche and trade titles, the general interest market became the company's primary target for the new century. The company rolled out a new title, *Stuff,* to serve as a gadget and fashion-oriented com-panion to *Maxim.* Published six times a year, the title quickly achieved a circulation of more than 200,000 after its 1997 UK launch. The following year, Dennis brought its new format to the United States, and, by 2001, *Stuff*'s circulation in that market had topped one million. The company followed up that success with the launch of the bi-annual *Maxim Fashion.* In 2000, Dennis also attempted to break into the women's market, launching a home-shopping magazine, *PS.*

Dennis stretched further into the mainstream in 2001 with the launch of two new titles: music-oriented *Blender,* and the news review *The Week.* Both titles were well received, with *Blender* achieving circulation of more than 350,000, and *The Week* boasting a circulation of more than 100,000 by the end of their first year. At the close of 2002, the company's sales had topped £189 million ($300 million), making it the UK's largest privately held publishing group.

Dennis maintained its growth ambitions and, with its rising cash flow, announced plans to step up the pace of its expansion

Key Dates:

1973: Felix Dennis, formerly an editor for *Oz* magazine, launches his own publishing group, initially producing underground comics.

1974: Dennis Publishing incorporates and launches *Kung Fu Monthly,* its first mainstream success.

1979: *Personal,* the first European personal computing magazine, is acquired.

1995: The company's first general interest title, *Maxim,* is launched in the UK; *IT* magazine and *PC Pro* are introduced.

1997: Dennis Publishing successfully launches *Maxim* in the United States; *Stuff* begins publication.

2000: A home-shopping magazine, *PS,* is launched.

2001: The company begins publication of *The Week,* a news review; *Blender,* a music magazine; and *Maxim Fashion.*

2003: Dennis Publishing acquires I Feel Good and its titles, including *Jack, Viz, Bizarre,* and *Fortean Times.*

through targeted acquisitions. In 2003, the group reached an agreement to acquire smaller, publicly listed rival I Feel Good Ltd. for £5.1 million in cash. (Felix Dennis, with a 7 percent stake in IFG, had served as that company's chairman since 2000). That deal added a number of small but growing titles, including rival men's magazine *Jack,* two other titles targeting the men's market, *Viz* and *Bizarre,* and special interest magazine *Fortean Times.* Following the acquisition, Dennis began preparations to launch *Jack* and other IFG titles into the U.S. market. Nearly thirty years after its origins in the UK publishing counterculture, Dennis Publishing had matured into a leading member of the global publishing establishment.

Principal Competitors

Hearts Magazines Inc.; Conde Nast; Emap PLC; United Business Media Plc; Thomson plc; Modern Times Group; Wenner Media; Ziff-Davis Inc.

Further Reading

Brown, Maggie, "Felix and the Feelgood Factor," *Independent*, April 4, 1995, p. 22.

Buss, Dale, "The British Are Coming!," *Sales & Marketing Management*, August 2001, p. 32.

Darby, Ian, "Literary Schemer Offers Food Home for Fart Jokes and UFOs," *Campaign*, May 16, 2003, p. 16.

Granatstein, Lisa, "Growing Up," *Mediaweek*, April 8, 2002, p. 32.

Rothenberg, Randall, "Brit's Team Approach to Mag Management Makes Sense," *Advertising Age*, March 31, 2003, p. 14.

Silber, Tony, "Felix Dennis; Circus Maximus," *Folio*, June 1, 1999.

"The Biz—Dennis from Bikinis to Politics," *Advertising Age*, May 13, 2002, p. 71.

—M.L. Cohen

Djarum PT

Jl Aipda K S Tubun 2C/57
Jakarta
Indonesia
Telephone: +62 21 534 6901
Fax: +62 21 534 6892
Web site: http://www.djarum.com

Private Company
Incorporated: 1951
Employees: 30,000
Sales: $4.3 billion (2002)
NAIC: 312221 Cigarette Manufacturing

Djarum PT is one of Indonesia's top three producers of "kretek" cigarettes, the dominant form of tobacco in a country which ranks in the top ten among countries with the highest rates of smokers. Kretek cigarettes contain locally grown tobaccos blended with cloves—which typically represent about one-third of a cigarette, but can range as high as 50 percent of a kretek cigarette's content—and mixed with a special "saus" (sauce) specific to each brand. A sauce can contain up to 100 different ingredients, including flavorings, spices, fruits, coffee, and other seasonings. There are said to be more than 2,000 kretek brands, produced by as many as 500 different companies, in Indonesia, yet only a small handful approach the size of Djarum. The company produces a variety of kretek brands for the domestic market, including flagship Djarum Super, its best-selling brand, Djarum Coklat, Inspiro, LA Lights, and others. If Djarum continues to duke it out at home with chief rivals Gudang Garam and Sampoerna, it will have claimed the leading share of the international market for kretek cigarettes. The company's export brands, which include Djarum Original, Djarum Black, Djarum Bali Hai, LA Lights, and LA Lights Menthol, and fruit-flavored cigarettes such as Djarum Cherry, help it maintain market share positions as high as 70 percent, such as in the United States. At the beginning of the 21st century, Djarum has begun a diversification drive, fueled by the strong cash flow provided by its cigarette sales. In 2001, the company became a majority shareholder in the failing Suharto-controlled Bank Central Asia (BCA), then, in 2003, entered the property devel-

opment sector with the construction of a $100 million shopping complex. The company also has entered electronic appliance production, and in 2004 began a 30-year contract to upgrade and manage two prominent Jakarta hotels, the Hotel Indonesia and the Hotel Wisata. The company is wholly owned by the secretive Hartono family, and has been led by brothers Budi and Bambang Hartono since the beginning of the 21st century.

Birth of a Cultural Icon in the 19th Century

Perhaps more than any other product, kretek cigarettes represented the meeting of Western and Eastern cultures. The colonization of what later became known as Indonesia had introduced tobacco culture into the spice-rich region. Cultivation of higher-quality, higher-yield tobacco began in the 1860s under the influence of the Dutch colonial government. By the end of the century, tobacco had grown into a major crop—with many small farmers producing a wide range of tobacco varieties, which were in turn influenced by soil and climatic conditions. Yet cultivation of spices, and especially cloves, remained a vital part of the region.

The origin of kretek cigarettes traced to the late 19th century. At the beginning of the 1880s, Haji Jamahri, a native of the Kudus, had been suffering from chest pains brought on by asthma. Clove oil (also known as eugenol) had been used traditionally as a mild analgesic, and Jamahri initially had attempted to reduce the pain by rubbing the oil on his chest. While this provided some relief from the pain, Jamahri sought a means of bringing the clove oil in more direct contact with his lungs.

Smoking tobacco had by then increasingly become a central facet of Indonesian life, where tobacco was often rolled up as cigarettes using corn husks—which provided the additional benefit of waterproof protection during the rainy season. Jamahri wondered what would happen if he were to mix a bit of cloves with tobacco and smoked that blend.

The results surpassed Jamahri's hopes—the effect of the clove oil was immediate, and Jamahri's chest pains vanished. Word of Jamahri's clove cigarettes spread in the Kudus region. Jamahri began rolling his cigarettes for others, and made the first attempts to market the new cigarette commercially. Before long, the clove cigarettes—which became known as "kretek" cigarettes for the "kretek-kretek" popping sound made by the burning cloves—were available in pharmacies as a medicinal product.

Jamahri died in 1890 before he could fully commercialize his invention. Instead, a number of small, hand-rolling workshops sprang up, centered on the Kudus region—which later became synonymous with kretek. The 1890s saw the first effort to market kretek cigarettes, when Noto Semito (also spelled as Nitisemito; to whom a number of accounts ascribe the invention of kretek) developed his own blend of tobacco—itself blended from among the many varieties and qualities available—and clove, and began selling them under a brand name, Bal Tiga (Three Balls).

Bal Tiga grew into Indonesia's leading kretek brand, and Noto Semito became the islands' first tobacco millionaire, inspiring many others to begin preparing their own clove blends. Kretek cigarette makers—and smokers—had quickly discovered that a pure blend of clove and tobacco was too harsh to smoke. Instead, cigarette makers began experimenting with different ingredients—spices, fruits and other substances—to smooth out the tobacco-clove blend. These ingredients formed the basis of the third major part of a kretek cigarette—the "saus" (from the Dutch word for sauce), the recipes for which were jealously guarded in secret.

Hand-rolling remained the sole means of producing cigarettes, in part because the clove and other ingredients were too heavy for the cigarette-making machinery that was revolutionizing the tobacco industry elsewhere. The growing popularity of kretek cigarettes led to the development of an entire industry, and later became the nation's fourth largest industry and a primary source of tax revenues for the government. While the kretek industry remained centralized around Kudus, vast portions of the Indonesian economy came to depend on kretek. The industry employed millions of Indonesians, from the many small tobacco farmers, to the army of hand-rollers, typically women, capable of rolling thousands of cigarettes each day.

Modern Kretek Maker in the 1950s

New names began to appear in the years leading up to World War I, including Sampoerna, formed by Chinese immigrant Liem Seeng Tee, who was one of the first to begin marketing his own kretek blends. Yet for much of the 20th century, kretek cigarettes represented only a small part of the larger tobacco market, which came to be dominated by so-called "white" cigarettes, the standard tobacco cigarettes so named for the paper in which they were rolled.

A new generation of kretek cigarette makers appeared in the years following World War II. Many of the former businesses, including Noto Semito and his Bal Tiga brand, had not survived the turmoil of the war years and its immediate aftermath.

Competition for the kretek market became more and more fierce into the 1950s, as the numbers of kretek makers, and their brands, swelled.

Among the many smaller brands active in the Kudus region was one called Djarum Gramophon, which literally meant "gramophone needle." The needle remained the main symbol of the company as it developed over the following decades. Impetus for the company's growth came in 1951, when Oei Wie Gwan, another Chinese native, acquired the small business. Oei changed the company's name to Djarum and began developing his own kretek blend.

Starting with just 70 hand-rollers, Djarum began marketing its first brand, Djarum, during the 1950s. The company's spice blend proved quickly popular, and the company began adding new employees and new equipment. Djarum soon released a second, popular brand, Kotak Adjaib.

The Djarum company nearly ceased to be, after being destroyed by fire in 1963. The company rebuilt, however, and took the opportunity to modernize and upgrade its equipment. Djarum also continued adding new kretek blends and brands. In the late 1960s and early 1970s, Djarum recognized the need to modernize its management as well, and began hiring professional management. The company hired experts from overseas to train its personnel, and also began adopting modern marketing techniques.

In 1970, the company established its own research and development center to produce new kretek blends, but also to begin adapting the machinery used to produce white cigarettes for use with kretek blends. By 1976, Djarum had successfully launched its first machine-made brand, Djarum Filter. By then, the company had become among the first in Indonesia to recognize the potential of the international market—not only among the Indonesian expatriate community, but also among consumers in other markets receptive to the blend of spices used in kretek cigarettes. Djarum began exporting its brands—and creating blends and brands specifically for its export markets—in 1972.

By then, the domestic market had undergone a dramatic shift. Where previously tobacco sales had been dominated by white cigarettes, Indonesians now turned to kretek—in part because of protectionist policies adopted by the Suharto regime after it came to power in the 1960s. Another factor in kretek's growing popularity was the higher levels of nicotine present in a typical cigarette, which could deliver a nicotine charge as much as twice as high as a standard white cigarette. By the end of that decade, sales of kretek surpassed white cigarettes for the first time. By the 1990s, kretek accounted for more than 90 percent of all cigarette sales and had become nearly synonymous with Indonesian culture.

While the domestic market continued to support a large number of smaller cigarette makers, the era now gave rise to a handful of dominant groups. In the early 1980s, Djarum secured a place for itself among the country's top three kretek groups, in part due to the overwhelming success of its latest brand, Djarum Super, launched in 1981. By the end of the decade, that brand had become the strongest selling brand in the country, raising Djarum to the number one spot ahead of chief rivals Sampoerna, Bentoel, and Gudang Garam.

Key Dates:

1880: Clove cigarettes, later called kretek, are invented by Haji Jamahri.
1890: Noto Semito launches the first kretek brand, Bal Tiga.
1951: Oei Wie Gwan acquires a small kretek market in Kudus, Djarum Gramophon, which becomes Djarum.
1970: Djarum launches a research and development center.
1972: Djarum begins exporting kretek cigarettes.
1976: The first machine-made kretek brand, Djarum Filter, is launched.
1981: Djarum Super is introduced; Oei Wie Gwan's sons, Budi and Bambang Hartono, join the company.
1998: Djarum, now led by the Hartono brothers, acquires majority control of BCA, the largest bank in Indonesia.
2001: Djarum acquires a stake in Salim Oleochemicals.
2004: Djarum begins a 30-year contract to renovate and manage two Jakarta hotels.

Diversifying in the 2000s

Oei, joined by sons Budi and Bambang Hartono, continued to seek out new product opportunities. In 1984, the company began developing a new tobacco product, a kretek cigarillo. The company also continued to shift production to machinery. In 1988 the company launched a new machine-made brand, Exclusive, featuring a lighter flavor with a lower tar content (typical kretek cigarettes contained up to four times the tar levels of a standard tobacco cigarette). While that brand targeted especially the export market, Djarum launched another new brand in 1989, Filasta. Produced with a combination of hand-rolling and machine production, the new brand was added especially to appease workers' concerns over the company's rising reliance on machinery.

Despite its position as one of the top three kretek groups in Indonesia, the company—and the Hartono family that owned it—kept out of the spotlight, in part because of the family's distance from the Suharto regime. In the late 1990s, however, it became apparent that leadership of the company had passed to Budi and Bambang Hartono, who now faced into the severe economic climate of the period. The collapse of much of Indonesia's economy during the economic crisis that swept through much of Asia in the late 1990s toppled a number of great Indonesian fortunes. The kretek makers, including Djarum, managed to weather the worst of the crisis, in part because of the strong cash flows from cigarette sales. Indeed, kretek purchases continued to grow at a steady pace into the beginning of the 21st century—earning Indonesia the dubious honor of a place among the countries with the fastest-growing proportion of smokers.

The fall of Suharto in 1998 represented a new era of opportunity for the company, as many of the corporations, run by the circle of Suharto family, friends, and other "cronies," that had previously dominated much of the Indonesian economy were now shut down or sold off. Djarum's strong cash flow gave the company the resources to begin a new diversification drive—a rarity in the industry, where most of its competitors, like Djarum previously, had focused exclusively on the kretek market.

In 1998, the Hartonos joined a partnership to acquire majority control of Bank Central Asia (BCA), the largest private bank in Indonesia, previously owned by the Suharto and allied Salim families. The Hartonos, through Djarum, were said to have put up most of the $539 million for the 51 percent stake in BCA, giving the family effective control of the banking group and a place among the country's new generation of business "titans."

Djarum's interest in diversifying continued to grow into the 2000s—fueled in part by Indonesia's growing health concerns surrounding tobacco, particularly the high-tar and high-nicotine content of kretek cigarettes. In 2001, the company took part in the consortium, including Wings Group, that bought the Salim Oleochemicals in Surubaya, a producer of palm and coconut oils for shampoos.

Djarum also acquired interests in electronic appliances, then turned toward the real estate market. In 2002, the company launched construction of a $100 million shopping complex in Jakarta. The success of that venture encouraged the company to begin planning a second development project in North Jakarta. The following year, the company joined the bidding to acquire the management contract of two landmark Indonesian hotels, Hotel Indonesia and Hotel Wisata, both in downtown Jakarta. Djarum won the contract in 2004, after promising to spend more than $200 million renovating the two hotels. From a small kretek workshop just 50 years earlier, Djarum planned to build itself into one of Indonesia's most powerful 21st century conglomerates.

Principal Competitors

Sampoerna PT; Perusahaan Rokok Tjap Bentoel PT; Sumatra Tobacco Trading Company, N.V.; Gudang Garam Tbk PT; Hanjaya Mandala Sampoerna Tbk PT; BAT Indonesia Tbk, PT; KT&G Corporation.

Further Reading

Brace, Matthew, "Pragmatic Approach to Cigarette Tar Limits," *World Tobacco,* September 2003, p. 21.
Hays, Kathleen, Willis, Gerri, and Morris, Valerie, "Djarum Wins Bid to Manage Hotel Indonesia," *Jakarta Post,* October 14, 2003.
Hemmer, Bill, "Djarum to Invest in Hotels," *Worldsources,* September 18, 2003.
John, Glenn A., "Lighter Kreteks Likely for Export," *Tobacco International,* August 1, 1989, p. 18.
Kagda, Shoeb, "After BCA Takeover, Djarum Targets Property," *Business Times,* September 12, 2003.
Shari, Michael, "Jakarta's New Titans," *Businessweek,* July 15, 2002.

—M.L. Cohen

Dolce & Gabbana SpA

Via Goldoni, 10
20129 Milan
Italy
Telephone: +39 02 774271
Fax: +39 02 76020600
Web site: http://eng.dolcegabbana.it/main.asp

Private Company
Incorporated: 1982
Employees: 1,531
Sales: EUR 475 million ($524 million) (2003)
NAIC: 316214 Women's Footwear (Except Athletic)
    Manufacturing; 315233 Women's and Girls' Cut and
    Sew Dress Manufacturing; 315234 Women's and
    Girls' Cut and Sew Suit, Coat, Tailored Jacket, and
    Skirt Manufacturing; 315999 Other Apparel
    Accessories and Other Apparel Manufacturing

Dolce & Gabbana SpA cuts an independent swath in the international fashion scene. The Milan, Italy-based company is one of that country's most well-known fashion houses, boasting such high-profile clients as Madonna, Isabella Rossellini, Monica Bellucci, Tom Cruise, David Beckham, Kylie Minogue, and many others. Led by founders Domenico Dolce and Stefano Gabbana, who serve as company CEO and president, respectively, the company produces designs for women's and men's clothing, shoes, bathing suits, lingerie, and accessories. The company also designs a children's clothing line, and develops eyeglasses and fragrances produced under license. Products are grouped under two core brands: Dolce & Gabbana, and D&G Dolce & Gabbana. The company also further divides its designs under the "basic" White line and the more adventurous "Black" line. Dolce & Gabbana has been moving toward greater vertical integration in the 2000s, buying control of much of its own production, and bringing in-house most of its formerly licensed products. The company also has been buying up many of its previously franchised retail sites, and at the end of 2003 directly controlled some 60 stores. While remaining committed to its privately held status, in 2003 Dolce & Gabbana took the unusual step of publishing its first annual report—in part to highlight its impressive growth. By that year, the company's sales had risen to EUR 475 million ($525 million).

Partnering for Success in the 1980s

Domenico Dolce began his fashion career designing for his father's small clothing manufacturing business near Palermo, in Sicily. Dolce went on to study fashion design, then moved to Milan, where he became an assistant designer in a workshop in 1980. There, Dolce met Venice-born Stefano Gabbana, then just 18, who had entered the fashion business after starting out in graphic design. The pair quickly began working together, and by 1982 decided to enter into business for themselves, setting up their own studio in Milan that year with an initial investment of the equivalent of just $1,000.

Dolce and Gabbana worked as free-lancers, designing for other houses in the early 1980s. The partners' big break came in October 1985, when they were among a select group of just three young Italian designers chosen to present their designs in the "New Talents" section of that year's Milano Collezioni event. Dolce and Gabbana threw themselves into the preparations for the show, laying the foundations for the later Dolce & Gabbana look. The partners' irreverent and overtly sexual designs caused an immediate sensation, and Dolce & Gabbana left the event as an established brand name.

Dolce and Gabbana now set to work on creating their first full collection, and in March 1986 solidified their reputation with the presentation of their "Real Women" show. The Dolce & Gabbana look became synonymous with pinstripe suits, overtly worn lingerie, and extravagant prints—especially animal patterns—alternated with designs in black.

The company opened its first showroom in 1987, on Milan's Via Santa Cecilia. For the production of the line, the pair turned to Dolce's father, whose company, Dolce Saverio, became the group's primary manufacturer. That position was solidified when the two companies signed an agreement that turned over production of Dolce & Gabbana's ready-to-wear line to Dolce Saverio in 1988.

By then, Dolce & Gabbana were rising stars of the international fashion world. Their reputation was helped in large part

Company Perspectives:

It's not easy to circumscribe the Dolce & Gabbana universe within a definition. A world made up of sensations, traditions, culture and a Mediterranean nature.

Domenico Dolce and Stefano Gabbana have made a trademark of their surnames which is known throughout the world, easily recognizable thanks to its glamour and great versatility. Two Designers who have known how to make a flag out of their Italian character.

Two Designers who have known how to interpret and impose their sensual and unique style on a world-wide basis. Two young Designers who address themselves to young people and who draw inspiration from them. Two Designers adored by the Hollywood stars who have made the duo their favorites: two Designers who dress all of the rock stars of the moment and who have elected them as their unquestionable leaders. The Designers of Madonna, Monica Bellucci, Isabella Rossellini, Kylie Minogue and Angelina Jolie, amongst others.

by their success in dressing a number of top Hollywood names—such as Isabella Rossellini, who famously stated: "They find their way out of any black dress, any buttoned-up blouse. The first piece of theirs I wore was a white shirt, very chaste, but cut to make my breasts look as if they were bursting out of it."

Dolce & Gabbana's designs became steadily more sensual toward the end of the decade, as the pair heightened what was described as their celebration of womanhood. This "celebration" continued to attract celebrities to the young design team's creations. An important early customer was Madonna, who told *WWD:* "I like their designs because they make clothes for a womanly body. Most designers seem to be making clothes for girls with stick bodies who are flat-chested, but I always appreciate my own voluptuousness when I'm wearing their dresses."

Even as Dolce & Gabbana built a following in Hollywood, the company had begun to build sales in the Far East, specifically in Japan. In 1988, the company signed a distribution agreement with Onward Kashiyama, which opened the first Dolce & Gabbana franchise store in Tokyo the following year.

Fashion Stars in the 1990s

In 1989, Dolce and Gabbana expanded their collection, adding beachwear and the Intimo line of lingerie. In January 1990, the company expanded again, launching its first Men's collection. At the same time, Dolce & Gabbana signed on as the design team behind the Complice clothing line—previously designed by Versace and Claude Montana—marketed by Milan's Genny Group. In November 1990, the company backed up its growing U.S. sales with the opening of its first showroom in that country, in New York City. By then, the group's sales had topped the equivalent of $20 million.

Dolce and Gabbana continued adding to their collection of designs with the launch, in 1991, of a series of scarves, produced under license, followed by a second licensed product,

ties, in early 1992. These products were followed by other licensed products, including the first Dolce & Gabbana-branded perfume, produced and distributed by Euroitalia, and a men's beachwear collection, also launched in 1992. In 1993, the company added men's underwear, again manufactured under license. Footwear also became part of the Dolce & Gabbana portfolio during this period.

Dolce & Gabbana's growth maintained its rapid pace throughout the 1990s. The brand achieved new fame when Dolce & Gabbana were chosen to create costumes for Madonna's 1993 world tour. The immediate interest in the group's clothing following that tour led it to shift into high gear: in 1994, Dolce & Gabbana created a secondary line, D&G Dolce & Gabbana, designed for a broader, and younger, market. That line was launched in partnership with Iteria, which acquired a six-year production license.

The success of the new line quickly boosted the company's sales. From approximately $50 million at the beginning of 1994, Dolce & Gabbana's revenues jumped to nearly $125 million by the end of that year. First launched in Europe, the D&G collection was introduced to the U.S. market in 1996.

Dolce & Gabbana also began adding new large-scale "signature" boutiques, featuring the group's full collection. By 1997, the company operated 13 boutiques, in addition to a growing number of franchised locations. Adding to the company's sales was the 1995 launch of its D&G Jeans line. In that year, in addition, the group signed a license agreement with Italy's Marcolin to produce Dolce & Gabbana-branded eyewear.

Vertically Integrated and Independent in the 2000s

With retail revenues soaring past $200 million, Dolce & Gabbana began a restructuring effort in the late 1990s. A key feature of the group's new organization was a drive toward becoming a vertically integrated group with control of its own industrial operations. In 1999, the company bought up a 51 percent stake in Dolce Saveria, which, in addition to giving the company its own production component, brought Saveria's $58 million in revenues into the business. The acquisition also included a 100 percent stake in subsidiary DGS, which had handled distribution to the group's sales network. Dolce & Gabbana also bought a 6 percent stake in its eyewear licensee, Marcolin, which was then preparing its public offering.

Having acquired its own production capacity, Dolce & Gabbana now moved to further its vertical integration. In 2000, the company took over the manufacturing of many of its formerly licensed products, including ties, scarves, beachwear, and lingerie and underwear. Later that year, the company established its own Leather & Footwear division near the Italian shoe center of Florence, which began producing prototypes of the Dolce & Gabbana shoe designs.

In the meantime, the company continued to hone its product offering, dividing its clothing collections into two new labels: the more basic White and the more extravagant Black. The new labels first appeared in 2000. At the same time, the company launched its own collection of watches, D&G TIME. Another significant launch for the company came with the début of its line of children's clothing in 2001.

Key Dates:

1982: Domenico Dolce and Stefano Gabbana open their own studio in Milan.
1985: Dolce & Gabbana is selected as one of three "New Talents" for the Milano Collezioni.
1986: Dolce & Gabbana debuts its first full collection of women's clothing.
1991: The company launches a scarves collection, the first product to be made under license.
1995: D&G is launched in the United States.
2000: The company brings production of scarves, ties, and other accessories in-house.
2003: The company begins buying out franchise store owners, predicting sales of more than EUR 1 billion by 2005.

Dolce & Gabbana now began gearing up for even greater expansion in the 2000s. In 2003, the company continued in its vertical integration drive, opening a number of new, large-scale flagship stores, including in New York City and Las Vegas, as well as making its first entry into the Chinese market, with the opening of a store in Hong Kong. Dolce & Gabbana also moved to take firmer control of its retail network, beginning a program of buying out its franchisees, including the purchase of 20 stores from its Japanese partner that year. At the end of that year, the company's revenues had grown to EUR 475 million ($525 million).

By then, Dolce & Gabbana had matured into a fully vertically integrated and independent business. The company also was brimming with confidence. As Stefano Gabbana told the *Daily News Record:* "We're a strong company and right now we're at a significant period in our business. By 2005, we should reach the one-billion-euro mark." The company even began publishing its own annual reports—despite the fact that it had no plans to shed its status as a privately held company. From a company launched with just $1,000, Domenico Dolce and Stefano Gabbana had built one of the world's most respected fashion houses.

Principal Subsidiaries

Dolce & Gabbana Japan KK; DGS SpA; Dolce & Gabbana Industries SpA (51%).

Principal Competitors

Christian Dior SA; LVMH SA; Benetton SpA; Guess SpA.

Further Reading

Colavita, Courtney, "Dolce & Gabbana's Time Machine," *WWD*, April 7, 2003, p. 13.
"Dolce & Gabbana," *Hello Magazine,* February 2, 2004.
Forden, Sara Gay, "Dolce & Gabbana Grows Up and Out," *Daily News Record,* January 3, 1994, p. 28.
Kaiser, Amanda, "D&G Unveils Growth Plans," *WWD*, December 16, 2003, p. 2.
Kerwin, Jessica, "From Sicily to Hollywood," *WWD*, November 4, 2003, p. 8.
Lipke, David, "Dolce & Gabbana Men's: Pumping Up the Volume," *Daily News Record,* November 10, 2003, p. 8.
Murphy, Robert, "Dolce & Gabbana: Ready to Rise to the Next Level," *Daily News Record,* June 12, 2000, p. 16.
Wilson, Anamaria, and Conti, Samantha, "D&G Sets Sail for Expansion," *WWD*, March 12, 2002, p. 3.

—M.L. Cohen

Dollar Tree Stores, Inc.

500 Volvo Parkway
Chesapeake, Virginia 23320
U.S.A.
Telephone: (757) 321-5000
Fax: (757) 321-5111
Web site: http://www.dollartree.com

Public Company
Incorporated: 1986 as Only One Dollar, Inc.
Employees: 27,400
Sales: $2.32 billion (2002)
Stock Exchanges: NASDAQ
Ticker Symbol: DLTR
NAIC: 452990 All Other General Merchandise Stores

Dollar Tree Stores, Inc. is a leading discount variety store in the United States. With their merchandise priced at one dollar, the company's stores offer a wide assortment of general goods, including food, toys, housewares, cleaning supplies, health and beauty aids, hardware, books, stationery, paper products, and other consumer items. As of January 2004, Dollar Tree operated over 2,500 stores in 47 states. The company is able to offer its customers a wide variety of products for just one dollar because of its purchasing power—the company buys products in huge quantities. It also imports nearly 40 percent of its merchandise, purchases manufacturers' over-runs, and maintains a strong focus on controlling costs.

From Toy Store to Dollar Store: 1986–90

The founders of Dollar Tree, Inc. first worked together managing K&K Toys, Inc., building that company from one store to a 136-store toy retailer. In 1986, the three men, J. Douglas Perry, Macon F. Brock, Jr., and H. Ray Compton decided to diversify and established a new company, incorporating it in Virginia as Only One Dollar, Inc. "We had all started out in the variety store business, so it seemed a natural transition for us," Brock told *Chain Store Executive with Shopping Center Age.* The company opened with five stores in Virginia, Georgia, and Tennessee, and, typical of the dollar format, offered primarily closeout merchandise. Perry became chairman of the new com-

pany, Brock served as president, and Compton was executive vice-president and chief financial officer.

While the three men continued to manage K&K Toys, their new business grew to 171 stores over the next five years. In October 1991, they sold the toy chain, then one of the largest mall-based toy retailers in the country, to a subsidiary of Melville Corporation, and turned their full attention to their discount operation.

Changing Inventory and Locations: 1991–92

The company now began implementing two major strategic shifts in its efforts to expand. First, rather than continue to be a purveyor of closeout merchandise, Perry, Brock, Jr., and Compton moved to make their stores the modern equivalent of traditional variety stores, with a wide assortment of basic goods priced at no more than one dollar. To do this, they had to change their purchasing strategies, which had emphasized deals and novelties. Consequently, they started buying directly from foreign manufacturers and worked with manufacturers in the United States to offer customized packaging, a broader selection, and products that were larger. Management's aim was to "exceed its customers' expectations of the range and quality of products that can be purchased for $1.00" and to offer at that price items that other stores usually sold for more.

To underscore that value, they inaugurated a second change— the location of their stores. Until then, most of the stores were in enclosed malls, since that was what management knew from its operations of K&K Toys. Now they concentrated on opening stores in strip centers anchored by a large grocery store or a mass merchandiser such as Kmart, Target, or Wal-Mart that it could undersell. That strategy not only helped customers compare prices, it also saved the company money, because strip centers generally charged less rent and tended to generate higher operating margins than mall locations. By the end of 1992, the company had 256 stores. Net sales for the year grew by over 70 percent from $71.1 million to $120.5 million, with net income of $10.8 million.

A New Name and Continued Growth: 1993–95

During 1993, Macon Brock, Jr., was named CEO, the company changed its name to Dollar Tree Stores, Inc., and Dollar

Tree continued its expansion, gaining a net 72 new stores, all of which were located in strip shopping centers. Because management believed their stores had a relatively small shopping radius, they were able to open several locations in a single market without having the outlets compete with each other for customers. Most of the stores were located in mid-sized cities and small towns; the rest operated in major metropolitan areas. New stores historically were profitable within their first year of operation and that fact reinforced the company's expansion plans of opening new stores rather than growing through acquisition or merger.

The typical store was approximately 3,200 square feet, with 85 to 90 percent of that area devoted to selling space. Unlike many of its dollar competitors, Dollar Tree paid a lot of attention to the design of its stores and the physical presentation of its merchandise. The chain used the same layout plan in each of its stores, with merchandise organized by category and displayed in densely stocked bins and shelves. Carpeting, bright lighting, background music, and the use of vibrant colors such as red checkout stands made the stores attractive and comfortable. With an average purchase of $6.50 per customer, the chain did not accept credit cards, nor did it scan purchases at checkout. "We locate our stores where people are already shopping, hoping they will be curious enough to check us out," Brock explained to *Chain Store Executive with Shopping Center Age.* "And then we try and make the outlets as easy as possible for customers to get in and out of."

By the end of 1993, the chain had 328 locations, sales of $167.8 million, and net income of $9.5 million. The drop in income was due to $4 million in costs associated with a recapitalization. As part of the recapitalization, the founders and their spouses sold 50 percent of the outstanding stock to The SK Equity Fund, L.P. and four associates for a total of $23.6 million.

The company continued its successful formula in 1994, expanding to 409 stores, with sales topping the $200 million mark for the first time to reach $231.6 million. One of the key factors in the company's operations was its distribution system. Sharing space (186,000 square feet) at the Norfolk headquarters was one of the company's two distribution centers; the other, with 244,000 square feet, was located in Memphis, Tennessee. This capacity allowed the company to buy large quantities at good prices and to receive early shipment discounts, thus keeping prices within its one dollar range. Given the relatively small size of most of the stores, backup inventories were kept at the distribution centers, with stores receiving weekly shipments of merchandise from the centers. During the busy Christmas season, the company could make two weekly deliveries to high-volume stores.

The company began the year 1995 with the creation of two subsidiaries, Dollar Tree Management, Inc. and Dollar Tree Distribution, Inc. In March, management took Dollar Tree pub-

lic, and during the year the company opened its 500th store. Sales topped $300 million, with per share earnings of 76 cents.

Acquisition of Dollar Bills, Inc.: 1996

In January 1996, the company bought Dollar Bills, Inc. for approximately $52.6 million in cash and $2 million in inventory. The purchase moved the company into three new states (Iowa, Minnesota, and Wisconsin) and added 136 stores, increasing Dollar Tree's store base by 27 percent. A modern 250,000-square-foot distribution center and a wholesale division in the Chicago area completed the acquisition.

Most of the Dollar Bills stores were concentrated in urban areas, a different retail market than the existing Dollar Tree stores. The new additions were also typically larger (4,000 to 4,500 square feet), had higher average sales, and carried less inventory per square foot. They also had a higher proportion of low-margin items such as food, health and beauty aids, and household supplies. According to the company's 1996 annual report, the acquisition "taught us about urban marketing, intensified our commitment to variety merchandise, and showed us new ideas in warehousing and distribution." By the end of the year, the new acquisitions had been successfully integrated into the company. To help make sure that all locations followed the same operational procedures, the company instituted a new training program, "Dollar Tree University," at corporate headquarters.

In April 1996, the company initiated a stock dividend, with the effect of a 3-for-2 stock split, and in June it made a second stock offering to the public. While Asia continued to be the company's largest source of imported goods, the company added sources from Italy, Brazil, Argentina, and Mexico to its list of vendors. Imports made up over one-third of Dollar Tree's merchandise and around 40 percent of its sales. Closeout merchandise, which had been the company's initial concept, now made up less than 15 percent of its offerings.

In evaluating the overall merchandise mix, the company added more higher-margin inventory such as toys and gifts to the items available at the Dollar Bills locations and more consumable products on the shelves of the Dollar Tree stores. The integration was accomplished with little disruption to either the company's opening of 104 new Dollar Tree stores or the operations of the individual stores. Over 90 percent of the Dollar Tree stores that were opened the entire year had operating income profits of more than 15 percent, as did over 85 percent of the Dollar Bills stores. The company ended 1996 with 737 stores and sales up more than 64 percent, to $493 million. About half the increase was attributable to the Dollar Bills operations.

The mid-1990s were a tough period for many of Dollar Tree's competitors. Several, including Jamesway Corporation, Ben Franklin Retail Stores, 50-Off Stores, and Solo Serve Corporation were no longer publicly traded by the end of 1996. Others closed many of their stores or abandoned the dollar concept.

Late 1990s and Beyond

In January 1997, Dollar Tree began construction, at an estimated cost of $34 million, of its Store Support Center in Chesapeake, Virginia, ten miles from its Norfolk location. In

---

Key Dates:

1986: J. Douglas Perry, Macon F. Brock, Jr., and H. Ray Compton establish Only One Dollar Inc.

1991: The three men sell K&K Toys in order to focus their full attention on the discount operation.

1993: The company changes its name to Dollar Tree Stores, Inc.; Brock, Jr. is named CEO.

1995: Dollar Tree goes public.

1996: Dollar Bills Inc. is acquired.

1998: The company adds California-based 98 Cent Clearance Centers to its arsenal.

2000: Expansion continues with the purchase of Dollar Express Inc.

2003: Greenbacks Inc. is acquired.

April, Dollar Tree issued $30 million in unsecured notes to pay off some of its existing revolving credit facility so that the credit could be used to fund capital expenditures for the Store Support Center. In June, the founders, SK Equity Fund, and other shareholders offered four million shares of Dollar Tree stock for sale. While the company itself did not receive any of the proceeds of that sale, in July it issued a three-for-two stock split.

During 1997, the company continued to grow according to its expansion play, opening a net 150 new stores and reaching 887 locations. Many of the new locations fit the company's larger prototype for future Dollar Tree stores, which increased store space to between 3,500 and 4,000 square feet. The company hoped that by creating larger aisles, with more space for recently added shopping carts, customers would buy more. Net sales for the year rose nearly 29 percent to $635.5 million, with sales at stores open for a year up more than 7 percent. Net earnings increased from $33.8 million in 1996 to $48.6 million. This performance occurred as one of the company's variety store competitors, Woolworth's, closed its stores in the United States.

Staff moved into the new corporate headquarters at the Store Support Center before the year ended, and the new, automated distribution center began operating in January 1998. With an automated conveyor and sorting system, the new facility had the capacity to support up to 800 stores. Dollar Tree president and CEO Macon Brock, Jr., announced that the company was in the process of buying land in Olive Branch, Mississippi, for another distribution center to replace the nearby Memphis facility. The Olive Branch center, some 425,000 square feet in size, began operation in early 1999—the same year the company surpassed $1 billion in sales.

In March 1998, certain shareholders, including Brock and the other founders, along with SK Equity Fund, filed to sell 4.5 million shares of Dollar Tree stock. "There's nothing wrong with the dollar-store concept," Brock told *Chain Store Executive with Shopping Center Age.* "But the way you execute it can mean the difference between success and failure." By concentrating on finding a wide variety of merchandise it could sell for one dollar, by making its stores exciting and attractive, by closely watching costs, and by locating its stores in centers where their customers were already shopping, Dollar Tree obviously had found its niche. As Brock summed it up, "The failure of the traditional variety store, as seen in the recent closing of Woolworth's, and the dominance of the big-box retailers have left a huge gap that we can fill."

Indeed, Dollar Tree continued to strengthen its foothold in the industry through a series of strategic acquisitions it made in the late 1990s and in the early years of the new century. In 1998, the company purchased 98 Cents Clearance Centers, a California-based chain owned by Step Ahead Investments Inc. As a result, the firm expanded into California and Nevada that year, as well as moving into markets in Oklahoma, Connecticut, and Massachusetts. In 2000, Dollar Tree set its sights on Dollar Express Inc. The $306.8 million deal added over 100 stores in six mid-Atlantic states to the company's arsenal, bringing its total store count to 1,729 units by year-end. Perhaps its most important purchase however, was that of Greenbacks Inc. in 2003. The acquisition gave Dollar Tree a presence in Colorado, Arizona, Montana, New Mexico, Utah, and Wyoming, effectively positioning it as the first dollar store chain with a national reach.

While the company focused on growing both organically and through acquisition, it also made technology a cornerstone in its expansion platform. In 1999, the firm automated its distribution center in Chesapeake, Virginia, in order to simplify its supply chain flow operations. In 2001, Dollar Tree began implementing a point-of-sale (POS) scanning system in its stores, which allowed for better inventory control. By 2003, nearly 1,500 were utilizing POS systems.

To keep pace with its impressive growth, Dollar Tree opened additional distribution facilities with automation capabilities during this time period. In 2000, a facility went online in Stockton, California. Two additional warehouses were opened in Georgia and Pennsylvania the following year, while Oklahoma became home to yet another facility in 2003.

Dollar Tree broke the $2 billion mark in 2002 as sales and net income continued their upward trend. Bob Sasser took over as CEO in January 2004 while Brock continued on as chairman. An October 2003 *DSN Retailing Today* article commented on the management shift, reporting, "The change in leadership at Dollar Tree aligns with the way the company itself has matured and realized the importance of becoming a sophisticated retailer." Indeed, Dollar Tree's actions during the late 1990s and into the new century left it in an enviable position among its competitors. With an emphasis on increasing store size and utilizing cutting-edge technology to simplify operations, control cost, and maintain merchandise quality, the company appeared to be well positioned for growth well into the future.

Principal Subsidiaries

Dollar Tree Distribution Inc.; Dollar Tree Management, Inc.

Principal Competitors

99 Cents Only Stores; Dollar General Corporation; Family Dollar Stores, Inc.

Further Reading

''Automation Takes Root at Dollar Tree,'' *Transportation & Distribution*, February 1999.

Desjardins, Doug, ''Dollar Stores Outpace Industry by Pursuing New Market Penetration,'' *DSN Retailing Today*, September 17, 2001, p. 7.

''Dollar Tree Launches Operations at New Distribution Center,'' *Business Wire*, January 15, 1998.

''Dollar Tree Stores: Dollars and Sense,'' *Forbes*, January 8, 2001, p. 152.

''Dollar Tree Stores Inc.: Purchase of Dollar Express Closes in $306.8 Million Deal,'' *Wall Street Journal*, May 8, 2000, p. 1.

''Dollar Tree Stores, Inc. Reports Earnings Per Share of $1.13 for 1997,'' *Business Wire*, January 22, 1998.

Halverson, Richard, ''Dollar Tree Opens 1,000th Store, Acquires 98 Cents Clearance Centers,'' *Discount Store News*, August 24, 1998, p. 3.

Howell, Debbie, ''Dollar Tree to Toe $1 Billion Mark Following Store Expansion,'' *Discount Store News*, June 21, 1999, p. 2.

——, ''Five-and-Dime Stores May Be Dead, but Dollar Tree Keeps on Growing,'' *DSN Retailing Today*, December 16 2002, p. 2.

——, ''Dollar Tree to Acquire Greenbacks,'' *DSN Retailing Today*, June 9, 2003, p. 5.

——, ''New Dollar Tree CEO Stresses Technology,'' *DSN Retailing Today*, October 27, 2003, p. 8.

''Racking up Profit at Dollar Tree Stores,'' *Chain Store Age Executive with Shopping Center Age*, November 1997, p. 54.

—Ellen D. Wernick
—update: Christina M. Stansell

Drs. Foster & Smith, Inc.

2253 Air Park Road
Rhinelander, Wisconsin 54501
U.S.A.
Telephone: (715) 369-3305
Toll Free: (800) 381-7179
Fax: (715) 369-9419
Web site: http://www.drsfostersmith.com

Private Company
Incorporated: 1983
Employees: 600 (est.)
Sales: $170 million (2002 est.)
NAIC: 453910 Pet and Pet Supplies Stores

Based in Rhinelander, Wisconsin, Drs. Foster & Smith, Inc., is a leading seller of pet supplies through catalogs and a Web site. Founded by practicing veterinarians, the privately owned company has established a niche in the marketplace by providing professional advice and informative articles to help customers educate themselves about pet care. The Drs. Foster & Smith catalog, now mailed to 40 million addresses, contains an unusually large amount of editorial content. The company's Web site also contains a storehouse of educational material. Moreover, Drs. Foster & Smith funds the award-winning Web site PetEducation.com, which contains more than 1,500 in-depth articles written by the company's in-house staff of veterinarians. The site is used by pet owners and professionals around the world and is even accessed by some universities as a research resource for students and faculty. Originally devoted to medicines for dogs, Drs. Foster & Smith now offers a full range of products for dogs, cats, fish, birds, wild birds, reptiles, and small pets such as rabbits, guinea pigs, ferrets, and chinchillas.

Company Grows Out of Veterinarian Practice in the Early 1980s

The actual Drs. Foster and Smith were Dr. Marty Smith and Dr. Rory Foster, who ran four animal hospitals in Minocqua and Rhinelander, Wisconsin, located in a resort area of fishing lakes close to the Upper Peninsula region of Michigan. In the early 1980s, Foster was approached by a dog breeder asking for guidance on administering booster shots he bought from a mail order vaccine catalog. Because Foster and Smith were looking to supplement their income, due to a slowdown in business during the winter months, they seized on the idea of either publishing their own newsletter geared towards dog owners interested in home veterinary care or producing their own mail-order catalog selling dog medications. Although there were a number of catalogs serving the same market, they thought they could find a niche by being the only catalog produced by veterinarians. Not only would their business have credibility, it would be able to sell professional and pharmaceutical products that other catalogers would be unable to provide their target audience of breeders and kennel operators. Foster and Smith were already mailing a newsletter to their clients, so at first they simply dropped in a sheet of mail-order medications for sale. It was also during this time that Rory Foster was diagnosed with amyotrophic lateral sclerosis (commonly known as Lou Gerhig's disease) and had to give up practicing veterinary medicine. In 1983, Foster's brother, Race Foster, a recent graduate from Michigan State University, joined the practice.

The Foster brothers and Smith produced their first full-fledged mail-order catalog in 1983. It was a two-color, 16-page, digest-sized affair with simple production values. The partners wrote the copy and took all the photographs. From the outset they wanted their catalog to have a national distribution. For the first offering, they compiled their own mailing list by enlisting the help of family members. They scoured specialty dog magazines and wrote down the names of potential customers: breeders, kennel owners, fellow veterinarians, and hunters. After the addresses were all tracked down, the address labels were individually typed and applied to approximately 16,000 catalogs, which were then mailed out in February 1983. To answer the telephone and fill orders, the doctors employed two people, using a clinic waiting room as a makeshift warehouse and distribution center. Going up against 47 other pet catalogs, Drs. Forster & Smith generated $30,000 in sales during its first year.

Rory Foster Dies in 1987

To spur further growth, the partners began to rent mailing lists and advertised in publications that reached their target audience. As a result, the catalog business grew steadily, so that two years after its launch the operation outgrew the clinic space. With a loan from M&I Bank, they bought a separate building to meet their needs. Rory Foster died in 1987, leaving his brother Race and Smith to carry on both the veterinary practice and the catalog. In 1988, they expanded the catalog in several ways. It went from digest size to an 8½-by-11 inch format, doubled in length to 32 pages, and was now produced in full color, becoming the first four-color pet catalog. In addition, cat supplies were added and the target audience was shifted to ordinary pet owners. As a consequence, the catalog moved beyond medications and now featured toys, beds, furnishings, and other pet accessories. A limited number of horse products were also included.

Drs. Foster & Smith's catalog business enjoyed such steady growth that in 1989 the company added a partner, Mike Scrivener, to serve as chief financial officer. In the early 1990s, the partners decided the time had come to construct their own building to serve as headquarters, call center, and a locale for distribution and warehousing. Construction began in 1992 at a site located near the Rhinelander airport. (Additions followed over the course of the next ten years, increasing the size of the complex from 50,000 square feet to 240,000 square feet.) By this point, the catalog business overshadowed the veterinary practice, and Foster and Smith decided to cut back on their daily practice in order to grow the company. To reach the next level, however, they felt the need for a seasoned business partner with retail experience. They found it in John Powers, a former merchandising executive with the Boston-based Docktor Pet Centers chain (founded by Milton Docktor). The connection with Powers was actually a matter of chance. It was while visiting a Massachusetts kennel to buy an English setter that Dr. Smith met Powers, who happened to be there at the same time. They chatted and were impressed with each other, laying the groundwork for bringing Powers on board and taking advantage of his impressive knowledge of the pet industry. Powers would become Drs. Foster & Smith's chief executive officer and guide the company to even greater heights.

In 1993, the company launched the Drs. Foster & Smith brand of pet-care products, which after a year included more than 30 items, including dog beds and cat furniture, flea and tick shampoo, and dietary supplements. The next significant step in the company's development was the decision in 1997 to added more veterinarians to the staff to offer customers more advice and educational materials. The company was so committed to providing advice to customers that for some time both Dr. Smith and Dr. Foster regularly manned the phones. With the development of the Internet, Drs. Smith & Foster found an ideal way to store educational materials, in addition to giving customers another way to order the catalog products. Out of that

endeavor came the creation of PetEducation.com to provide a commercial-free site. The company's commercial site also continued to include a great deal of information that would help customers to choose appropriate products for their pets.

The year 1998 was also important to the pet supply industry because it marked the founding of Pets.com by Julie Wainwright. The idea of selling pet supplies via the Web attracted the attention of investors, who were lured by the size of the market, some $15 billion, into believing that an Internet retailer had only to capture a small share in order to become a profitable business. However, Pets.com, Petopia, and other attempts to sell pet supplies over the Web, became cautionary tales, emblematic of an era of irrational behavior surrounding e-commerce. Pets.com spent millions in advertising, managing to make a sock puppet famous, but in reality the business model was flawed at its core. What these Internet entrepreneurs failed to take into consideration was that half of the pet supply market was low-margin dog and cat foods that were relatively expensive to ship as small orders to remote locations. Moreover, while companies such as Pets.com may have been virtual supermarkets, they soon learned that clicks still needed bricks: even e-commerce ventures required a warehouse and shipping capabilities. Either they had to build their own system at great expense or contract someone else to do it, which cut deep into the bottom line. A year after going public, Pets.com went bankrupt.

Drs. Foster & Smith did not succumb to the temptation of trying to compete with Internet retailers on their terms. The company spent no money on advertising and continued to view its Web site as a mere adjunct to the catalog business. In addition, unlike their virtual competitors, Drs. Foster & Smith had established a reliable warehousing and distribution operation, allowing the company to be the first in the industry to promise that orders would be shipped within 12 hours. Furthermore, the business was not burning through venture capital with the vague hope of one day posting a profitable quarter. Drs. Foster & Smith earned a profit quarter after quarter, and when the dot-com pet supply stores went out of business, it enjoyed a spike in its Internet business, the result of others spending countless millions to promote the idea of buying pet supplies online. Many online customers of Pets.com and other sites redirected their business to catalogers like Drs. Foster & Smith who survived the Internet shakeout. Business also continued to grow on the catalog side, with the company now mailing more than 20 million catalogs each year. To meet this rising demand, Drs. Foster & Smith engaged in an on-going expansion project. A state-of-the art telecommunication center was added, as well as a new conveyor in the Order Fulfillment area.

Pet Warehouse Acquired in 2001

As Drs. Foster & Smith took their business into the new century, management began to consider expanding beyond cats and dogs into fish and birds. There was no thought to accomplishing this goal through acquisitions, but the company was presented with an opportunity for external growth when it was approached by two firms—LiveAquaria.com, specializing in fish supplies, and Pet Warehouse, which in addition to fish specialized in birds, reptiles, and other niche pet markets. Dayton, Ohio-based Pet Warehouse, like Drs. Foster & Smith, was a catalog operation, launched in 1986, and survived the Internet

Key Dates:

1983: A catalog business is established by Drs. Rory and Race Foster and Marty Smith.
1987: Rory Foster succumbs to Lou Gerhig's disease.
1989: Mike Scrivener becomes a partner and CFO.
1992: John Powers becomes a partner and CEO.
1998: The company launches a Web site.
2001: Pet Warehouse is acquired.

implosion in the pet supply category. The company generated annual sales in the $25 million range, compared to Drs. Foster & Smith $125 million. Pet Warehouse was then folded into the Rhinelander operations, with many of the company's employees making the move from Ohio to Wisconsin. Another 53,000 square feet was added to the warehouse to handle the increased number of stock-keeping units (some 7,000 new items) and increased order volume. An 18,000-square-foot call center was also added. For the time being, the Pet Warehouse catalog continued to be mailed. Integrating Pet Warehouse and LiveAquaria.com was not without difficulty, however. Drs. Foster & Smith quickly learned that fish owners were highly demanding consumers. Tropical fish owners, for example, were typically young males, technologically oriented and given to asking difficult questions of the company's telephone representatives, who were simply not prepared to provide answers. In order to maintain its reputation for having a knowledgeable staff, the company invested in a training program to shore up the phone representatives' knowledge of fish.

Another major step in the evolution of Drs. Foster & Smith came in July 2002, when the company signed the first advertising contract in its history, an effort to maintain an impressive five-year stretch of growth. Drs. Foster & Smith settled on Chicago's Martin/Williams, a shop with experience handling the account of another catalog merchandiser, L.L. Bean. The company also consolidated its catalog and Internet divisions and coordinated marketing efforts. Now featured catalog products were highlighted as well on the Web site. The databases of catalog and Internet customers were also integrated. In 2003,

the company introduced it own dog and cat food, a premium blend created by its veterinarian staff. Unlike Pets.com, Drs. Foster & Smith charged an appropriate amount for shipping heavy bags, but another innovation allowed customers to receive free shipping. Early in 2003, the company initiated an auto-replenishment program. Customers who signed up would have products they regularly bought—such as food and certain medicines—shipped automatically. An e-mail reminder would be sent a few days before a product was scheduled to ship. Also of note in 2003, Drs. Smith & Foster aired its first television spot, buying time on such cable networks as Animal Planet and Lifetime. At this point, Drs. Foster & Smith mailed more than 40 million catalogs a year and enjoyed a growing Internet business, recording annual sales of $170 million. It seemed likely that the four partners who owned the business might eventually seek an exit strategy, either through a sale or an initial public offering, but with the economy in the doldrums, that step appeared to be a distant possibility.

Principal Subsidiaries

Pet Warehouse Inc.; LiveAquaria.com.

Principal Competitors

PETCO Animal Supplies, Inc.; PetMed Express, Inc.; PETsMART, Inc.

Further Reading

"Drs. Foster & Smith Celebrates 20-Year Anniversary," *Rhinelander Daily News*, January 26, 2003, p. B3.
"Getting Personal . . . with Dr. Race Foster," *Catalog Age*, September 2001, p. 7.
Gomes, Lee, "Selling Strategies—Just Say No," *Wall Street Journal*, April 23, 2001, p. R33.
Hajewski, Doris, "Old Dog, New Market," *Milwaukee Journal Sentinel*, August 17, 2003.
Tedeschi, Bob, "The Pet Supply Business Is Finding That a Site May Serve Mostly to Guide Shoppers to Stores and Catalogs," *New York Times*, October 28, 2002, p. C7.

—Ed Dinger

Ecco Sko A/S

Industrivej 5
Bredebro
DK-6261
Denmark
Telephone: (+45) 74 91 16 25
Fax: (+45) 74 71 03 60
Web site: http://www.ecco.com

Public Company
Incorporated: 1963
Employees: 9,000
Sales: $493.9 million (2002)
NAIC: 316219 Other Footwear Manufacturing

Ecco Sko A/S is one of the world's top ten shoemakers and a worldwide leader in the "comfort" shoe segment. Based in Denmark, Ecco is also one of the few fully vertically integrated shoemakers, controlling the entire shoemaking process from tanning to design to manufacturing and even retail sales. The company produces casual, classic, and sportswear shoes for men, women and children, as well as clothing and accessories. Ecco's production takes place in a number of factories around the world, including Denmark, Portugal, Brazil, Indonesia, Thailand, China, and Poland. Together, the company's plants turn out some 12 million shoes each year. The company also operates sales and distribution subsidiaries around the world, including in the United States, Europe, and Australasia. In addition, Ecco has long played a pioneering role in the use of automated production techniques, and its robot-equipped production lines have been compared to those of the automotive industry. The automated production process enables the company to produce shoes exactly to its specifications, underscoring its commitment to quality. To complement its manufacturing base, Ecco operates research and development and design centers in Denmark and elsewhere. Its shoes are available at more than 1,000 retail stores worldwide, including some 500 franchised Ecco-branded stores. The company also owns and operates two flagship stores, one in London and the other in San Francisco, where it presents its full line of shoes, clothing, and accessories. These two stores also serve as test-marketing outlets. The United States, Germany, and Sweden are the company's major markets, and some 90 percent of its sales of approximately $500 million come from outside of Denmark. In the early 2000s, the company has been expanding its traditional markets—the 30- to 49 year-old segment—launching the Receptor sports shoe line, a children's shoe line, and other designs to attract more youthful segments. Founder Karl Toosbury remains at the head of the company, which is wholly owned by the Toosbury family.

A More Comfortable Shoe for the 1960s

Karl Toosbury sold his home and his car in order to set up a shoemaking business in Bredebro, in the Danish countryside. Joined by wife Birte and later by daughter Hanni, Toosbury set out to produce a new breed of more comfortable, high-quality shoe. Toosbury named his company Eccolet Sko and created the brand name Ecco. Production began in 1963 and found a ready market. By 1965, the company had already expanded its factory.

Toosbury himself played the major role in the company's fast-growing sales, traveling extensively to promote its brands and designs. Word of the new type of shoe quickly reached the other Scandinavian markets, and in 1966 Eccolet began exporting shoes to Sweden, Finland, and Norway. From there, the company extended its sales into the rest of Europe, with Germany providing a particularly receptive market for Ecco's "comfort" shoe styles.

From the start, Toosbury's emphasis on high quality and advanced design features led Eccolet into vertical integration. The company opened its own tannery, while investing in research and development and design initiatives. The latter played a role in the company's growing European sales. In 1968, for example, Eccolet produced its own version of the then fashionable knee-high boot.

Another strong success for the group came with the launch of a line of clogs in 1972. The clog collection remained a strong seller throughout that decade and was later revived at the beginning of the 2000s. The company's growing sales led it to expand its Bredebro factory again, stepping up production by some 20 percent in 1973.

Our business drive and thinking behind ECCO is the result
of continuous new ideas, dynamism, capability, and forward
movement—and about being part of our own movement.

Company Perspectives:

Toosbury had also laid plans to develop an international
manufacturing base, and in 1974 the company opened its first
foreign production facility in Brazil. In order to maintain strict
control of production quality, Eccolet adopted automated production techniques, becoming one of the first in the shoe industry to install CAD/CAM machinery and related equipment for
its shoe production.

Eccolet's expanded production capacity positioned the company for its first big-hit shoe design, the Joker, launched in
1978. That shoe put the company on the map as a top producer
of quality comfort shoes.

At the end of the decade, Ecco had become a fully international brand—more than 50 percent of its sales coming from
outside of Denmark, with Sweden and Germany providing the
strongest foreign markets. At the same time, Ecco had become
something of the national shoe at home.

New Markets in the 1980s and 1990s

The launch of a new shoe design, Free, gave Eccolet a new
hit in 1979. That design, a more youthful version of the Joker
shoe, also became the first of the company's designs to sell
more than a million pairs. The success of the Joker and Free
designs helped carry the Ecco brand still farther abroad, and in
1981 the company agreed to license its brand to Japanese
Achilles Corporation. The Japanese market proved highly receptive to the Danish shoe designs, and by the end of the decade
Japanese Achilles had sold more than ten million pairs.

Back at home, Eccolet entered the retail arena as well in a
bid to further its vertical integration. In 1983, the company
oversaw the launch of the first Ecco store in Denmark. From
there, the company expanded the chain worldwide to more than
500 franchised stores. Eccolet also developed an in-store boutique design, which was rolled out to department stores. At the
same time, the company carefully courted the independent shoe
retail channel.

In 1984, the company opened a new, larger production plant
in Portugal. With some 1,200 employees, the new factory was
capable of production levels as high as 18,000 shoes per day. The
factory also incorporated new robotics technology, as the company continued its drive to achieve full automated production.

In 1986, Eccolet set up a new, dedicated sales and distribution subsidiary in Sweden. By then, the company had already
begun to eye a new market: the United States. Eccolet's move
into the United States came slowly, as the company began
testing its designs in 1988.

Many European shoemakers had already attempted—and
failed—to crack the U.S. market. Eccolet, however, carefully

prepared its full-scale entry into the country. The company
recognized the importance of building a good relationship with
the independent retail channel, including providing strong sales
support. Eccolet also spent some time observing the market and
quickly reacted by adapting its own designs to match the U.S.
consumer's preference for sportier shoe styles.

In 1990, Eccolet launched its U.S. subsidiary, Ecco USA, in
Salem, Massachusetts. Marketing of the group's shoes was at
first limited to the more Euro-centric Northeast region, yet
California, with its openness to new styles and trends, became
another important early market for the company in the United
States.

Success was immediate, and just a year after its official
launch, Ecco USA had already placed the company's stores in
120 different retail channels. Eccolet now began preparing the
national rollout of the shoe brand, backed by new, sportier
designs created to appeal to American tastes, such as the new
Track outdoor shoe line launched in 1992.

Continued Success in the New Century

Eccolet's growing sales encouraged the company to add to
its manufacturing base, opening a new facility in Indonesia in
1991. That plant, with 3,500 employees, became the company's
largest. Two years later, Eccolet formed a new production and
distribution joint venture, this time with Bangkok Rubber Co, a
subsidiary of the Saha Group. Eccolet nonetheless controlled
the new company at 95 percent.

Eccolet continued to experience success with such offerings
as a line of sandals launched in 1994 and new classic women's
and men's business shoe designs at the end of the 1990s. By
then, Ecco—the company changed its name from Eccolet in
1999—had opened a new research center, called Futura, in the
town of Tonder in Denmark. The company had also opened new
production centers in Poland and in China.

Furthermore, Ecco made moves closer to consumers. In
1998, the company launched its first flagship store, on Oxford
Street in London. The large-scale store featured the complete
range of Ecco shoes, as well as accessories and clothing items,
and provided a testing ground for new designs, as well as a
means of generating feedback from the company's customers.
The success of that location led the company to open a second
flagship store in San Francisco.

By the turn of the 21st century, the United States had
become Ecco's single largest market. The company recognized that success in the United States would also translate into
higher sales elsewhere in the world. Therefore, Ecco was now
determined to take on the giants of another important shoe
category—sports shoes.

The company released a new line of mountain/hiking boots
in 2000. In 2001, Ecco unveiled a new sports shoe offering—
the Receptor series of athletic shoes. The Receptor series tuned
into the U.S. market's preference for casual shoes while maintaining the company's enhanced comfort features and high-
quality standards. The success of the line encouraged Ecco to
expand the series, adding golf shoes by 2003.

Key Dates:

1963: Karl Toosbury establishes Eccolet Sko to manufacture shoes in Bredebro, Denmark.
1966: The company begins exporting to Scandinavian markets.
1972: A successful line of clogs is launched.
1974: A production facility in Brazil is opened.
1981: The company introduces Free design, its first million-seller, and enters the Japanese market through a production license to Japanese Achilles Corporation.
1983: The first franchised Ecco retail store is opened.
1990: A full scale entry into the United States begins with the opening of a subsidiary in Massachusetts.
1993: A joint-venture manufacturing and distribution subsidiary in Thailand is created.
1999: The company changes its name to Ecco Sko.
2001: Receptor sports shoe line is launched.
2004: Ecco Sko signs a strategic alliance with sportswear maker Newline and begins construction on a new production site in India.

In 2004, the company prepared to take on industry leaders Nike, Reebok, and addidas with the launch of a new Receptor RXP series running shoe. Backing up that launch was a strategic alliance with sportswear maker Newline in January 2004. The company also announced plans to open a new manufacturing operation in India by September of that year. By then, the group had brought a new state-of-the-art tannery in Holland online. Ecco appeared set to step comfortably into the future as a global footwear leader.

Principal Subsidiaries

Ecco New Zealand Ltd.; Ecco Sweden AB; Ecco Thailand (95%); Ecco UK Ltd.; Ecco USA Inc.

Principal Competitors

Nike Inc.; adidas-Salomon AG; Reebok International Ltd.; Brown Shoe Company Inc.; C and J Clark Ltd.; Svit A.S.; Wolverine World Wide Inc.; Stride Rite Corp.; G.H. Bass and Company.

Further Reading

"Danish Shoe Maker Ecco to Launch in India," *Nordic Business Report*, January 20, 2004.
Dolley, Margaret, "Following in the Steps of the Shoe Man," *European*, November 5, 1993, p. 32.
"Ecco Steps up UK Retail Expansion," *In-store Marketing*, April 2001, p. 7.
Saeks, Diane Dorrans, "The Stir of Ecco," *Footwear News*, March 19, 2001, p. 8.
Schneider-Levy, Barbara, "A Quest for Youth," *Footwear News*, April 22, 2002, p. 14.

—M.L. Cohen

Edelman

200 East Randolph Drive, 63rd Floor
Chicago, Illinois 60601
U.S.A.
Telephone: (312) 240-3000
Fax: (312) 240-2900
Web site: http://www.edelman.com

Private Company
Incorporated: 1952 as Daniel Edelman Public Relations
Employees: 1,900
Sales: $220 million (2003 est.)
NAIC: 541820 Public Relations Agencies

Edelman, formerly known as Edelman Public Relations Worldwide, is counted among the world's leading public relations firms and is the largest to remain an independent private company. Its founder, Daniel J. Edelman, is regarded as the father of the public relations industry as well as one of its most innovative practitioners. From one office in Chicago, the firm evolved into a global entity, with outposts in 38 cities across the globe. Some 40 percent of Edelman's business is outside the U.S. Edelman's business is divided into several specialized practices, including public affairs, financial communications, consumer marketing, healthcare, and technology. Edelman's clients include many major corporations, such as Schering-Plough, United Parcel Service, Microsoft, Kraft, and Starbucks. The firm has crafted many key campaigns that have worked alongside of or in addition to advertising to alert consumers about products or problems. Edelman has promoted the sport of bowling, California wines, and landing rights for the Concorde supersonic jet. He also helped raise donations for the Vietnam Veterans Memorial, among many other projects. The private firm is headed by Richard Edelman, son of the founder.

Establishing an Industry in the 1950s

Daniel J. Edelman was born in Brooklyn, New York, in 1920. His father was a lawyer. The young Edelman showed a precocious interest in writing and communication skills. He claims to have written his first memo when he was five. At that age, Edelman was sick with the mumps and quarantined to a room off the kitchen in his family's home. So he typed notes to his mother, telling her what he wanted to eat. He produced a neighborhood newspaper when he was a little older and had moved with his family to Manhattan. Edelman graduated from high school at 15 and then enrolled at Columbia University. After he graduated, he took classes at Columbia's esteemed School of Journalism. He also worked as a reporter for a newspaper in Poughkeepsie, New York.

Edelman was drafted by the Army to serve in World War II. He took training as a communications specialist and was assigned to analyze German propaganda. After the war, Edelman returned to New York and began working as a news writer for the television network CBS. Through family connections, he found another job as a publicist for a small record company called Musicraft. Musicraft had several jazz stars under contract, including Duke Ellington and Dizzie Gillespie, as well as singer Mel Torme. The hair care company Toni sponsored a weekly radio spot for Torme. This gave Edelman the idea for a PR gimmick that led to the launching of his career. He packaged a Torme record to look like one of Toni's products and took it to disc jockeys at various radio stations. The gambit wowed radio men, who then talked up Toni. Subsequently, someone from Toni Co. contacted Edelman and got him a job working at the company's own public relations outfit.

Edelman's work for Toni set a precedent for the public relations industry. The company transferred him to its office in Chicago in 1949, where he continued working to promote Toni's home permanent wave kits. The home permanent kits threatened the salon industry, which was afraid its customers would stop frequenting beauty shops if they could do advanced processes for themselves. The bad feeling generated by beauty professionals had led to legislation that would have banned the home products or required a warning labeling the contents as poison. Edelman countered this mistrust and bad feeling with a road show highlighting the "Toni twins." Toni was already using twins in its magazine advertising. The campaign tag line was "Which twin has the Toni?" One woman had a professional salon permanent, the other the do-it-yourself job. Edelman took the Toni Twins beyond the magazine spread, hiring

Company Perspectives:

Our Mission: To provide public relations counsel and strategic communications services that enable our clients to build strong relationships and to influence attitudes and behaviors in a complex world. We undertake our mission through Convergence by integrating specialist knowledge of practices and industries, local market understanding, proprietary methodology, and breakthrough creativity. We are dedicated to building long-term, rewarding partnerships that add value to our clients and our people. Our clients are leaders in their fields who are initiating change and seeking new solutions.

six sets of twins to travel to 75 cities across the country so that consumers could see them up close. Edelman arranged for the twins to meet local dignitaries and engendered tremendous positive media coverage for the Toni home permanent. At the same time, Edelman successfully advocated for the packaging to carry a seal of safety rather than a warning label. Toni products sold well, and this kind of road show became a staple of public relations campaigns.

In 1952, Edelman decided he was ready to go into business for himself. When he told his boss of his plans, he was immediately fired. Edelman's boss soon repented his hasty treatment of the young man and allowed him to take the Toni account with him. Edelman opened Daniel Edelman Public Relations in October 1952. Beginning with a staff of three, the small company had little trouble finding clients in the booming postwar period. Many companies were introducing new kinds of consumer goods, and Edelman helped introduce these to the public. One early client was Sara Lee Co., whose signature product was frozen baked goods. Edelman worked to get coverage of Sara Lee products in leading women's magazines. He also helped place a story on the company in the leading daily business newspaper the *Wall Street Journal*. This story ran under the confident headline, "Sara Lee Builds Baking Bonanza on Heaping Slices of Quality." This kind of media coverage led to wide consumer acceptance of Sara Lee products. Edelman also worked with the lemon juice substitute ReaLemon in the 1950s. Like frozen desserts, ReaLemon was a new kind of convenience food that consumers were not sure they trusted. Edelman established the brand with home cooks and also got the food industry to try ReaLemon in various products.

By 1960, the firm had about 25 accounts. Around that time, some of Edelman's employees banded together and started their own public relations agency. To counteract this move, Daniel Edelman visited every company on his client roster, persuading them not to switch to the new firm. All the clients stayed, and the Edelman agency went on to do more signal work in the 1960s.

Edelman Public Relations took on the country of Finland as a client in 1962. Finnish international relations were suffering because of the perception in the United States that Finland was a satellite of the Soviet Union. Edelman founded the Finnfacts Institute to give out information about the country and sponsored Finland tours for VIPs and the media. The campaign

began to open U.S. markets to Finnish goods and companies. In 1966, Edelman began promoting California wines for the California Wine Institute. The domestic product did not have much of a reputation at that time, but Edelman worked to generate media coverage of the industry, getting articles in women's magazines as well as a spot on television's "Tonight Show." Consumption of California wines grew 70 percent through the 1960s. In 1969, Edelman began promoting the sport of bowling for the National Bowling Council. Edelman emphasized the fitness aspect of the sport, setting up a so-called "Bowl-A-Shape" tournament with former winners of the Miss America contest as participants. The company claimed 11 million people tried bowling over the 12 months of the National Bowling Council campaign.

Expanding beyond Chicago in the 1960s and 1970s

Edelman established an office in New York City in 1960, and another branch in Los Angeles in 1967. The next year, the firm opened a London office. Daniel Edelman had not expected to make his company an international player, but he met the right person at the right time. Toni had been bought by the Gillette Co., the world's leading manufacturer of shaving products, and Gillette did substantial business in England. While visiting the British Toni plant, Edelman met Michael Morley, who was a colleague of the head of public relations for Toni in the United Kingdom. Morley and Edelman hit it off, and after a single conversation the two men set up a British branch of Edelman Public Relations. Morley brought a strong British client base to the London office. He also oversaw Edelman's subsequent international expansion, including the opening of a branch in Frankfurt, Germany, in 1970. In 1972, the company opened two offices in Canada, one in Montreal and one in Toronto.

While most of Edelman's international expansion occurred in the late 1980s and after, especially as its operations moved into Asia, the firm had handled several cross-border accounts as early as the 1970s. One was its campaign to allow the Concorde jet landing rights in the United States. The Concorde was a superfast jet built by British and French interests and operated by British Airways and Air France. The United States had abandoned its own project to build an "SST," or supersonic transport, and allowing the Concorde to land became a contentious issue. When the advanced plane was finally ready for flights to the United States in 1976, it was permitted to land only at Dulles Airport, near Washington, D.C., where the Secretary of Transportation had jurisdiction. Other airports had banned the Concorde. Edelman's Michael Morley coordinated a campaign—run out of the company's London and Seattle offices—to change the public's perception of the Concorde. Edelman's work helped beat back six attempts by Congress to ban the plane, and the Concorde won general landing rights in the United States in 1977. Edelman handled another international issue in 1979, the promotion of African groundnut oils. The African Groundnut Council represented six African nations that depended on exports of the oils. Edelman's educational campaign successfully raised demand for the oils in Europe.

Breaking Ground in the 1980s

By 1979, Edelman was an established international public relations firm with billings of around $6 million. Much of the public was more familiar with the work of advertising agencies than public relations firms. Edelman's clients often worked in tandem with advertising agencies, but Edelman's slant was quite distinct. A good example is Edelman's work for ConAgra's Butterball turkey brand. Butterball's brand managers believed its sales were held back because American cooks had doubts about how to prepare a turkey. Rather than focusing on the brand name, as an advertiser might do, Edelman took on the underlying problem, and in 1981 established the Butterball "Turkey Talk Line." This was a toll-free telephone line consumers could use to find answers to questions about how to thaw a turkey, how to know if it was done, and so on. This was a unique approach to building sales for Butterball. It not only raised consumer confidence in the brand, but the talk line itself got media coverage, thus heightening Butterball's profile.

Edelman also broke new ground in the 1980s with its work for the broadcast network CBS. General William C. Westmoreland sued the network for libel after CBS aired a documentary in 1982 that claimed the general had misrepresented enemy troop strength in Vietnam in order to make it seem that the war was going better than it was. Edelman provided public relations to CBS in what is considered the first example of "litigation PR." An Edelman vice-president, John Scanlon, sat with the press corps each day of the trial. He provided documents to reporters, congratulated writers who covered the trial in a way favorable to CBS, and generally promulgated CBS's point of view. It was an extremely high-profile case, stirring up controversy about media bias and freedom of speech, as well as resurrecting unsettled issues of the Vietnam War itself. Immediately after the court heard testimony that damaged Westmoreland's case, the general dropped the suit. At that point, CBS and Westmoreland issued a joint statement saying that the case really needed to be decided in the court of public opinion. CBS had essentially won in that court already, due in part to Edelman's assiduous work. Litigation PR became a commonplace of highly publicized trials after this pioneering effort.

Edelman managed another significant example of crisis management in the 1980s when it worked with the H.J. Heinz company to bolster the image of its Starkist tuna brand. The late 1980s saw increasing media coverage of tuna fishing practices that ensnared and killed dolphins. Edelman helped Heinz find alternative fishing methods that did not endanger dolphins. It then made sure the public knew about it. Edelman managed Starkist's "Dolphin Safe" labeling effort, and by 1989 more than 80 percent of U.S. consumers were aware of the changes Starkist had made.

Continued International Expansion in the 1990s

In the late 1980s, Edelman began moving more strongly into international markets. At first, the company's overseas outposts were often the logical extension of U.S. offices working for global clients. Meanwhile, its competitors had pointedly bolstered their international business, buying up PR firms in other countries. Edelman's large competitors, Hill & Knowlton and Burson-Marstellar, had substantially more international clout than Edelman. Edelman caught up, however, when it acquired or opened PR shops in Europe and Asia, as well as expanding into more cities in the United States. Edelman had five international outposts in 1981. Over the next ten years, the company opened offices in Kuala Lampur, Beijing, Hong Kong, Sydney, Paris, and Singapore. This expansion continued over the 1990s. The company moved into Mexico City in 1994 and Sao Paulo, Brazil, and Buenos Aires, Argentina, in 1997. Edelman further bolstered its European presence in the 1990s with new offices in Frankfurt and Hamburg, Germany, and offices in Madrid and Brussels. By the early 2000s, Edelman was the fifth-largest public relations firm in Europe, with clients in all major national markets and European revenues of $45 million. Edelman moved into more Asian markets with new outposts in Seoul, Shanghai, and Taipei in the 1990s, enabling the company to help its domestic clients work in unfamiliar Asian territory. In 1997, Edelman worked for the Vidal Sassoon hair care company, putting on shows and conducting classes for Chinese stylists. Vidal Sassoon soon became a leading brand in the Chinese market.

In the United States, Edelman opened offices in more cities. It opened a Silicon Valley branch in 1992, putting it at the center of new technology developments. It also opened a branch in Sacramento, California, in 1994. Edelman went into the South in the 1990s, with a new branch in Atlanta, Georgia, in 1994 and a Miami, Florida, office in 1998. The company opened a Seattle, Washington, office in 1999. Edelman was also quick to see the potential of the Internet and in 1995 became the first public relations firm to operate a Web site. Over the next few years, the company put together Web-based PR projects for more than 300 clients.

During the 1990s, many public relations firms bought up competitors, creating an industry of huge international companies. The biggest players in the industry by 2000 were Omnicom Group, the Interpublic Group, and WPP Group. Burson-Marsteller and Hill & Knowlton, long-time competitors of each other and of Edelman, were both now owned by London-based WPP. WPP and Omnicom had revenues of around $700 million by 2000, and Interpublic brought in over $400 million. Edelman's revenue was $172 million for 1999 and around $210 for 2000, making it about half the size of Interpublic and less than a third the size of the other big two in the worldwide public relations industry. Daniel Edelman retired as chief executive in 1996, passing that job on to his son Richard. Two other Edelman children, John and Renee, also held high posts at the company. Daniel Edelman remained chairman of the board. In

1997, the company announced that it had considered offers from two competitors who wished to buy it. Daniel Edelman made it clear that he was opposed to selling the company, which gained revenue nicely in the late 1990s. By 2000, Edelman was the only independently owned public relations firm in the industry's top ten names worldwide.

New Challenges in the 2000s

Edelman saw its revenues rise through the boom years of the late 1990s. However, the early 2000s were a time of many difficulties for Edelman and for corporate America in general. The stock market had risen dramatically throughout the 1990s but contracted considerably in 2000. Especially hard-hit was the technology industry. Edelman had been at the forefront of the so-called dot-com boom, with an office in Silicon Valley and many high-tech clients. As the stock market collapsed, a wave of companies revealed either accounting misstatements, fraud, or executive malfeasance. These financial scandals hurt investors, who were then wary of returning to the stock market. Then the terrorist attacks in New York and Washington, D.C., on September 11, 2001 seemed to open a new and uncertain chapter in American history. In an article he wrote for *The Strategist* (Fall 2002), Daniel Edelman described these events as a "triple blow" that left PR executives "caught in a quagmire." Edelman saw the early 2000s as the most difficult time for the public relations industry since he founded his company 50 years earlier.

The company acknowledged that its billings fell in the early 2000s, but since Edelman was an independent firm it was not under as much pressure as some of its competitors to keep up profit levels. This difficult period brought some challenging assignments to the PR outfit. Edelman's client Cantor Fitzgerald was one of the companies most severely affected by the September 11 terrorist attacks after 700 of its employees died in the World Trade Center that day. Edelman took on the job of communicating with family members of those among Cantor Fitzgerald's employees who had been killed, as well as setting up a counseling center and a relief fund. Edelman also worked with the Red Cross in the aftermath of the attacks. The Red Cross raised more than $560 million after September 11 but was then criticized in the press when it revealed that not all of that money was earmarked for families of victims. The Red Cross hired Edelman to help explain what the relief agency had already accomplished and how its funds would be used.

In celebration of its 50th anniversary in 2002, the company changed its name. It had been doing business as Edelman Public Relations Worldwide, and it shortened that to simply Edelman. In 2003, the company set up a unit called First & 42nd to deal with issues of corporate social responsibility. Edelman had much experience dealing with issues of corporate citizenship, such as its campaign for Starkist tuna. With so many companies suffering tarnished reputations because of financial scandal,

Edelman felt it needed to create a specialized business devoted to these issues. Banana grower Chiquita Brands had already been using Edelman for several years to publicize its environmental work.

In the early 2000s, two-thirds of Edelman's work was still in consumer marketing. It helped Microsoft enter the computer games market in 2001, for example, promoting enthusiasm for the company's Xbox. Edelman had also developed several other major business areas. It worked with the healthcare industry, which was an increasingly complex and beleaguered market. In addition, Edelman ran a new division for financial communications. This sector grew by almost 40 percent in the few years after its founding in 1999. The company also operated a public affairs practice, principally out of its Seattle office. Edelman expected to grow more in international markets over the 2000s. The company also reiterated that it was not interested in selling but would remain a private firm.

Principal Subsidiaries

BioScience Communications; Blue; EIS; First & 42nd; P.R. 21; StrategyOne.

Principal Competitors

WPP Group plc; Interpublic Group of Companies; Omnicom Group, Inc.

Further Reading

Crain, Rance, "Edelman at 80 Enjoys Seeing PR out from Advertising's Shadow," *Advertising Age*, July 17, 2000, p. 36.
Edelman, Daniel J., "A Challenging Time, A Bright Future," *Strategist*, Fall 2002, pp. 1–3.
Farnham, Alan, "Twins of Genius," *Fortune*, June 20, 1988, p. 8.
Houston, Alan, "Dissent Sends Red Cross to Edelman," *PR Week*, November 12, 2001, p. 1.
Kaplan, Peter W., "Public Relations a Facet of Westmoreland Trial," *New York Times*, October 23, 1984, p. B5.
Kirk, Jim, "Edelman Savors Nearly 50 Years of Independence," *Knight Ridder/Tribune News Service*, June 20, 2002.
Lazarus, George, "Chicago Tribune Marketing Column," *Knight Ridder/Tribune Business News*, May 9, 2000, p. ITEM0013100C.
Londner, Robin, "Edelman/Cantor Fitzgerald Part Ways," *PR Week* (UK), February 8, 2002, p. 6.
McCarthy, Michael, "Edelman PR, Denying There Are Plans to Sell, Attracts Suitors," *Adweek*, June 9, 1997, p. 3.
Nicholas, Kate, "Analysis: 'Father of Modern Media Relations,'" *PR Week* (UK), November 1, 2002, p. 11.
"Pfizer Bids to Seize Control of Public Healthcare Issues," *PR Week*, August 12, 2002, p. 1.
Schrage, Michael, "Firm Footing," *Brandweek*, October 16, 2000, p. 24.
Van der Pool, Lisa, "PR Firms Catering to Do-Gooder Clients," *Adweek*, July 14, 2003, p. 12.

—A. Woodward

Educational Testing Service

Rosedale Road
Princeton, New Jersey 08541
U.S.A.
Telephone: (609) 921-9000
Fax: (609) 734-5410
Web site: http://www.ets.org

Nonprofit Company
Incorporated: 1947 as Educational Testing Service
Employees: 2,500
Sales: $620 million (2003)
NAIC: 541720 Research and Development in the Social
    Sciences and Humanities; 611710 Educational Support
    Services

Educational Testing Service (ETS) is the world's largest administrator of standardized tests and a leader in educational research. The company develops, administers, and scores achievement, occupational, and admissions tests, such as the Scholastic Aptitude Test (SAT) for The College Board, as well as tests for clients in education, government, and business. Through its five regional offices, including one in the Netherlands, ETS annually administers 20 million exams in the United States and 180 other countries.

Prewar Testing

ETS was created in 1947 by three nonprofit educational institutions, the American Council on Education, the Carnegie Foundation for the Advancement of Teaching (a part of the larger Carnegie Corporation), and The College Entrance Examination Board. Standardized tests had first been developed and distributed in the early 1930s. In 1930, the Cooperative Test Service of the American Council on Education began to conduct achievement tests at schools and colleges, administering 650 different exams. Six years later, the Educational Records Bureau began using the first test scoring machine, the IBM 805, to expedite the grading of standardized tests administered on a large scale by the Cooperative Test Service. In 1937, the Graduate Record Examinations (GRE) was introduced by the Carnegie Foundation, and the National Teacher Examinations followed shortly.

Although the president of Harvard University had publicly suggested a merger of the three test-giving services in 1937, the emphatic opposition of The College Board's associate secretary forestalled any further movement in this direction throughout the remainder of the 1930s. During World War II, the bulk of the standardized exams given by several test-giving bodies were administered to people enrolled in the military. In 1943, another Harvard administrator, Henry Chauncey, took an 18-month leave of absence from his job to run the Army-Navy College Qualifying Test, which was used to identify officer candidates. In 1945, Chauncey became director of The College Board's Princeton office.

In its prewar incarnation, The College Board had had a relatively simple and straightforward mission, but its activities had been transformed and greatly expanded during the war years. Instead of simply testing candidates for admission to select colleges, the organization had taken on such functions as making up exams for the State Department and the military.

This broadening of functions continued in the wake of the war, when the charitable Carnegie Foundation worked to transfer control of the GRE, which had started as an experiment but had grown to dwarf the rest of the Foundation, to The College Board. At the time of this proposal, The College Board was made up of 52 select member institutions. Absorbing the GRE necessitated a substantial restructuring of the organization and again raised the issue of a consolidation of test-giving organizations. A committee was formed to examine various proposals, and it began meeting in the fall of 1946. In October, this body recommended the creation of one central test-giving organization.

ETS Created 1947

By the end of 1946, the process of working out the actual details of a merger had begun in earnest among the three founding organizations of the tentatively-named Educational Testing Service. By June 1947, difficulties such as the composition of a Board of Trustees had been resolved, and ETS was set up for a trial five-year period. Each of the member groups

Company Perspectives:

Our mission is to help advance quality and equity in education by providing fair and valid assessments, research and related services. Our products and services measure knowledge and skills, promote learning and performance, and support education and professional development for all people worldwide.

turned over its testing operations and a portion of its assets. The Carnegie Foundation contributed the GRE and the Pre-Engineering Inventory. The American Council on Education added the National Teacher Examinations and the Cooperative Test Service, while The College Board turned over the Scholastic Aptitude Test, as well as the Law School Admission Test (LSAT) and several other programs. On December 19, 1947, the New York State Board of Regents chartered the new organization under the name Educational Testing Service.

The new organization set up operations in the old offices of The College Board at 20 Nassau Street in Princeton, New Jersey. Gradually, files, office equipment, and employees from the founding organizations of ETS arrived, until the organization had 212 employees. At the end of 1947, Chauncey was made president of the new organization, which had less than $2 million in initial capital. At the time, ETS elaborated a threefold goal: to develop and administer tests, to conduct research, and to advise educational institutions.

Among the first clients of the newly formed ETS were more than 50 colleges, the Association of American Medical Colleges, the U.S. Atomic Energy Commission, the U.S. State Department, and the Pepsi-Cola Corporation. The organization distributed a wide variety of tests for various assessment purposes. As the ranks of students at American colleges were swelled by soldiers returning from war and enrolling under the G.I. Bill, which promised a free college education to any soldier who had served in World War II, demand grew for ETS's services. In 1948, college admissions exams were taken by 75,000 students.

Postwar Growth

By 1950, ETS had begun to more fully understand and assess its role in society. In that year, Chauncey proposed in his annual report for ETS that a national census of abilities and talents be undertaken in order to assist the military and to strengthen educational and industrial planning. By 1954, ETS had already started to outgrow the building it had purchased on Nassau Street in Princeton, and Chauncey selected a new site for the organization, a 400-acre estate on Rosedale Road in Princeton that had formerly served as a working farm as well as the Stony Brook Hunt Club.

Throughout the decade, the activities and number of tests administered by ETS continued to grow. In 1958, ETS began to release students' scores on the SAT to their high schools, so that they could in turn be passed on to the students. By the beginning of the 1960s, nearly 25 percent of all American high school students were taking the SAT. By 1962, 15 years after its

inception, ETS had become not just a testing organization but a more broadly based educational entity.

In addition to expansion in the number of people taking ETS tests, the number of tests available also grew during the 1960s. The organization developed assessments to measure the abilities of people from secondary school right on through their professional career. Along with this growth in the number of tests given, the size and role of ETS expanded as well. On the occasion of the organization's 25th anniversary, ETS dedicated a $3 million conference center, named after Chauncey, its founding president, at its Princeton headquarters. During this time, ETS had also constructed a residence for its president on the Rosedale campus. This construction was made possible by the steady surge in growth ETS had experienced in the postwar years, as the organization's sales doubled every five years between 1948 and the early 1970s.

An American Institution in the 1970s and 1980s

By the mid-1970s, ETS had become, in effect, the nation's leading testing organization. The organization's tools for measuring ability—particularly the SAT, the GRE, and the LSAT—had become a standard feature of American educational life. In 1976, the institution was cited as a hot growth company in American business by *Forbes* magazine. The revenues generated by ETS's activities continued to expand throughout the late 1970s. The company suffered its first serious threat at the end of that decade, when, in response to growing criticism of its monopolistic power, New York state passed the Educational Testing Act, a disclosure law that required ETS to release certain test questions and graded answer sheets to students.

In the following year, 1980, ETS suffered its first fiscal deficit. In response, the company reduced its staff and commissioned a strategic plan from a management consulting firm in 1982. Following the enactment of the truth in testing law, ETS suffered further criticism in the early 1980s, as outsiders asserted that its tests were culturally biased to favor white members of the upper middle class and that they were poor predictors of actual performance.

ETS also took steps to protect its copyrighted materials from violation by entrepreneurs who offered courses to raise student's scores on its exams. In 1982, students who had prepared for achievement tests by taking a Princeton Review course reported that they had already seen some of the questions on the test. This violation of test security, along with others, caused ETS to remove several questions from active use on its exams. In May 1983, ETS sought and obtained an agreement with the Princeton Review that its workers would not retake the SAT again.

SATs Revised in 1990

In response to concerns over the format and scope of standardized tests, The College Board undertook a revision of the exams in 1990. ETS announced that the old SAT and achievement tests would, in the future, be known as Scholastic Assessment Tests. The new SAT-I, which measured verbal and mathematical skills, included longer reading passages and more questions to determine how well students had understood them. In the math sections, students were required to work out

```
┌──────────────────────────────────────────────────┐
│                  Key Dates:                        │
│                                                    │
│  1947:  Three testing services merge to form ETS.  │
│  1990:  SAT is revised; revenues are $300 million. │
│  1993:  A computerized version of GRE is introduced.│
│  1999:  E-rater software grades GMAT essays.       │
│  2001:  State-mandated K-12 testing and internat-  │
│         ional markets drive growth.                │
└──────────────────────────────────────────────────┘
```

some answers entirely on their own, with the use of a pocket calculator, rather than simply choosing from answers supplied to them. The SAT-II included a 20-minute essay. These changes, made at the direction of a committee headed by the president of Harvard, were designed to put a greater emphasis on problem solving.

Despite its somewhat embattled place in the culture of American education, ETS continued to thrive materially throughout the late 1980s. By 1990, it had solidified its place as by far the largest American private educational assessment service. The institution had a staff of nearly 3,000 employees, more than 270 clients, including the federal government, and gross revenues of nearly $300 million. Despite this impressive size, ETS sought, as it moved into the 1990s, to expand its activities even further. "Our traditional mission has been to place ourselves at the transitional points of education between high school and college, college and graduate school," ETS's president, Gregory Anrig, told *Time* magazine in 1990, adding that "now we are expanding into more and more programs that help kids to learn and teachers to teach more effectively."

Among the programs ETS began to offer at this time were educational tools making use of new technology. The company began to develop grammar school courses that used computers and interactive videos to foster critical-thinking skills. In addition, ETS used computers to re-configure the National Teachers Exam. This test was used in about two-thirds of the states to license teachers.

By 1991, ETS's gross revenues had grown to $311 million in revenues, of which 40 percent were derived from College Board activities. The company's roster of exams had ballooned to cover a wide variety of fields, from manicurists to shopping center managers. In addition, ETS had successfully expanded its geographic scope, offering tests in 170 foreign countries. By 1993, the company was administering nine million tests each year.

ETS continued to use new technology to update its tests throughout the early 1990s. In November 1993, the company introduced a computerized version of the GRE, which was slated to eventually replace the old paper-and-pencil version of the test. Rather than simply consisting of the old test on computer, the new exam was to be more adaptive, adjusting its level of difficulty to suit the aptitude of the student taking the test. Students who answered questions correctly were given successively harder questions; students who answered incorrectly prompted the computer to offer easier problems. In this way, ETS hoped to make testing more personalized for each student, provide easier and more frequent scheduling, and immediately provide scores upon conclusion of the test.

ETS began to offer the computerized GRE at 170 testing centers located around the country. In addition, the company was developing computerized testing for nurses, teachers, and architects. With the use of computers, the time needed to take an exam was shortened, but critics worried that the computer itself would prove a barrier to people unfamiliar with the use of machines.

In March 1994, ETS ran into difficulty implementing another new testing program when disabled students protested the limited number of dates available to them to take the new SAT-I test. After the U.S. Justice Department conducted an inquiry into the matter, ETS scheduled additional dates for disabled students to gain access to the exam. Later that year, ETS also encountered a snag in its admission of the new computerized GRE exam when employees of a test preparation course who took the new test were able to memorize and later recreate a large portion of the exam after the fact. Presented with this evidence that the repetition of questions had compromised test security, ETS suspended administration of the computerized test for a week in December 1994 in order to tighten a variety of security measures.

One month later, ETS announced that, in an effort to limit opportunities for theft, it would reduce the number of times the GRE would be offered by computer. The measure was taken in response to charges that some of the nearly half-million students who sat for the GRE each year were memorizing questions and using them to improve their scores when re-taking the test or passing them on to their friends who had not yet taken it. In an effort to prevent test preparation course employees from repeatedly trying to crack the test, ETS also filed suit against Kaplan Educational Centers, the largest such company, alleging copyright infringement and seeking to forbid its employees from retaking the test.

Despite such challenges, ETS remained an important part of American education in the 1990s. The company continued to design tests with input from educators and teachers and contributed policy and measurement research to help America meet its education goals.

In 1995, scoring for the SAT was recalibrated based on a new, larger sample of test-takers. Before the "recentering," a score of 500 on either the math or verbal section was equivalent to the average score of the original 1941 sample. The average scores in 1994 were 424 on the verbal and 479 on the math. A new scoring system was devised whereby a 500 on either test was the equivalent of the average score in 1990, when one million students took the test. A perfect score on either section was still 800.

A for-profit subsidiary of ETS, Chauncey Group International, was created in 1996. Its focus was assessment services for industry, government, and professions. (ETS had been doing this for 40 years.) This business was later named Capstar.

Computerized Testing for the New Century

By the late 1990s, ETS was losing nearly $20 million a year on revenues of about $500 million. This was attributed to heavy investment in computerized testing. In an effort to control costs, in 1998 ETS laid off 100 employees from its workforce of

2,500. Baltimore-based Sylvan Learning Systems held the contract to administer computerized versions of ETS's tests through 2003. ETS also partnered with the collegiate information publisher Peterson's and the Graduate Management Admissions Council to form GradAdvantage, an online system for applying to business colleges.

ETS also developed a computer application, called e-rater, for grading the essay questions on the Graduate Management Admission Test (GMAT). E-rater evaluated answers on the basis of vocabulary, syntax, and logic; its scores were compared with those of one or two professors for a final grade. It was first used in February 1999.

In September 2000, ETS created a for-profit subsidiary, ETS Technologies Inc., for the purpose of developing online learning technologies, beginning with its Criterion Online Writing Evaluation, based on e-rater. This was sold to schools on an annual subscription basis. Another new subsidiary, ETS K-12 Works, developed scholastic testing for individual states. ETS also used IntelliMetric software developed by Vantage Laboratories to score its online placement programs AccuPlacer and WritePlacer.

By this time, ETS was administering 11 million tests in 181 countries. In 2001, computer-based tests were available at more than 380 locations in the United States. For all its size and innovation, ETS was having a difficult time avoiding monetary losses. ETS was able to post a net operating profit of $18 million in fiscal 2000. However, both revenues and employment figures had been in decline since the late 1990s. To reverse this trend, the nonprofit brought in Kurt M. Landgraf, former CEO and chairman of DuPont Pharmaceuticals, to be its new president and CEO in August 2000.

Landgraf's turnaround strategy, according to *The Record* of Bergen County, New Jersey, was to control costs while expanding European operations (the goal was to have seven European offices) and pushing the new writing-evaluation software. New state-mandated testing of elementary and high school students was creating another important growth market. Landgraf told *The Record* he aimed for ETS to be a $1 billion company with 5,000 employees by 2006. Reports of revenues ranged from $600 million to $700 million in 2002.

The People's Republic of China, opening to the west due to acceptance into the World Trade Organization and landing the 2008 Olympics in Beijing, contracted ETS to develop testing programs to evaluate the English skills of native Chinese speakers. In 2000, ETS sued a test preparation school in China, charging that it improperly used old GRE, GMAT, and Test of English as a Foreign Language exams. ETS K-12 Works Inc. was itself sued by Psychological Corp., developer of the Stanford Achievement Test, which alleged its trade secrets were stolen by an executive who left to head the newly formed ETS subsidiary.

The standardized testing business continued to grow more crowded. ETS eliminated about 350 jobs in 2001 as a result of competition. The next year, it phased out computer-based testing (CBT) at 84 of 195 international centers. The affected test centers had been processing low volumes of tests and accounted for only 15 percent of international test takers. ETS's international CBT centers were run by Prometric, a unit of Thomson Corporation.

After nearly 50 years of administering the Graduate Management Admission Test (GMAT), ETS was replaced by Pearson VUE, which was assigned a $200 million, seven-year contract by the Graduate Management Admission Council (GMAC) in December 2003.

ETS acquired The Pulliam Group of Redlands, California, in January 2004. Pulliam, established five years earlier, had 60 employees and specialized in improving standards-based performance in elementary schools.

A written section was being added to the SAT for 2005. This would raise the total possible score from 1600 to 2400. The existing verbal section was being modified and renamed "critical reading."

Principal Subsidiaries

Capstar; ETS Global BV (Netherlands); ETS K-12 Works; ETS Pulliam; ETS Technologies Inc.

Principal Competitors

ACT Inc.; CTB/McGraw Hill; Harcourt Assessment, Inc.; Pearson VUE.

Further Reading

Bickerstaffe, George, "Students Without IT Need Not Apply," *Financial Times* (London), October 26, 1998, p. 17.

Brennan, Lisa, "ETS, Kaplan in Legal Skirmish over Test Security," *New Jersey Law Journal*, January 23, 1995, p. 3.

Celis, William, III, "Computer Admissions Test Found to Be Ripe for Abuse," *New York Times*, December 16, 1994.

Elson, John, "The Test That Everyone Fears," *Time*, November 12, 1990.

Honan, William, "Computer Admissions Test to Be Given Less Often," *New York Times*, January 4, 1995.

Johnson, Linda, "Testing Firm Wants Black Pencil on Bottom Line," *Record* (Bergen County, N.J.), February 19, 2001, p. A3.

——, "ETS Branching Out; Overseas Expansion Part of Plan," *Record* (Bergen County, N.J.), March 6, 2001, p. L5.

Kladko, Brian, "Computer Technology Passes Judgment on Students' Essays," *Record* (Bergen County, N.J.), July 9, 2001.

——, "New Jersey Students Prosecuted over Cheating," *Record* (Bergen County, N.J.), March 1, 2003.

Merritt, Jennifer, "Why the Folks at ETS Flunked the Course," *Business Week*, December 29, 2003, p. 48.

Nairn, Allan, *The Reign of ETS: The Corporation That Makes Up Minds*, New York: Ralph Nader, 1980.

Nissimov, Ron, "SAT Officials to Stop Flagging Disabled Students' Tests," *Houston Chronicle*, July 22, 2002.

Nowlin, Sanford, "Standardized Test Giants Lock Horns in Court over Allegedly-Stolen Secrets," *San Antonio Express-News*, April 8, 2001.

Owen, David, *None of the Above: Behind the Myth of Scholastic Aptitude*, Boston: Houghton Mifflin, 1985.

"SAT Maker Cutting Staff by 15 Percent," *Record* (Bergen County, N.J.), January 2, 2002, p. A3.

"SAT Numbers Reshuffled, and Students Look Brighter," *Record* (Bergen County, N.J.), May 18, 1995, p. A5.

Sidener, Jonathan, ''Educational Testing Service of Princeton, N.J., Develops New Grading System,'' *Arizona Republic*, February 1, 1999.

Tabor, Mary B.W., ''Disabled to Get an Extra Chance for S.A.T.s,'' *New York Times*, April 1, 1994.

''Testing Company Claims State's Bidding Process Is Unfair,'' *Associated Press State & Local Wire*, January 6, 2003.

Toch, Thomas, ''A Stunning Second Lap,'' *U.S. News & World Report*, May 18, 1992.

Toppo, Greg, ''English Teachers Encouraged by Proposed SAT Changes,'' *Associated Press State & Local Wire*, July 3, 2002.

Vickers, Marcia, ''Hate Exams? Here's a Chance to Profit from Them,'' *New York Times*, Bus. Sec., October 5, 1997, p. 4.

Weinstein, David, ''ETS to Create Standardized English Test for Chinese Government,'' *Associated Press State & Local Wire*, July 9, 2002.

Williams, Dennis A., ''Testers V. Cram Courses,'' *Newsweek*, August 12, 1985.

Winerip, Michael, ''No. 2 Pencil Fades as Graduate Exam Moves to Computer,'' *New York Times*, November 15, 1993.

—Elizabeth Rourke
—update: Frederick C. Ingram

Environmental Systems Research Institute Inc. (ESRI)

380 New York Street
Redlands, California 92373-8100
U.S.A.
Telephone: (909) 793-2853
Toll Free: (800) 447-9778
Fax: (909) 793-5953
Web Site: http://www.esri.com

Private Company
Incorporated: 1969
Employees: 2,750
Sales: $497 million (2002 est.)
NAIC: 541611 Administrative Management and General
   Management Consulting Services; 541910 Marketing
   Research and Public Opinion Polling; 541990 All
   Other Professional, Scientific and Technical Services

Headquartered in Redlands, California, Environmental Systems Research Institute Inc. (ESRI) is a privately held software company specializing in the development of geographic information systems (GIS), which allow users to see visual depictions of their data by incorporating it into maps. ESRI prides itself on its independence and the fact that it carries no debt. In addition to its headquarters, which includes research and development facilities, ESRI serves customers in 220 countries worldwide via 11 U.S. regional offices and 75 international distributors. ESRI's customers span virtually every industry and include all levels of government and business. Its clients include the Central Intelligence Agency, all U.S. Military branches, the Department of Homeland Security, hospitals and healthcare systems, *Fortune* 500 companies, and many small businesses. With its many applications, ESRI's software can guide military troops; locate lost hikers; find space shuttle debris; document public health concerns; study the effects of global warming; determine where to place schools, roads, fire stations, and restaurants; calculate the most efficient routes for emergency and delivery vehicles; visualize water districts and utility systems; display crime statistics; map the bodies of humans and animals to treat disease; develop effective building floor plans; and more.

1960s–70s: Origins and Early Years

ESRI is the brainchild of Jack Dangermond, considered by many as the father of commercial GIS. A native of Redlands, California, Dangermond earned a Master's degree in urban planning from the University of Minnesota, followed by a Master's degree in landscape architecture from the Harvard School of Design. In the December 16, 2003, issue of *The Press-Enterprise*, writer Phil Pitchford highlighted a few significant points about Dangermond's academic career: ''While at Cal Poly, Jack Dangermond pondered how computers that filled a room could help landscape architects with plant selection, his brother said. He fancied that a computer programmed to understand soil conditions in certain areas could produce a list of plants that would grow there. At Minnesota, he researched how computers could aid in planning, especially in regard to the environment.''

At Harvard, Dangermond became more intimately involved with computers. In the mid-1960s, he landed a job keying consumer survey data onto punch cards and entering them into a mainframe computer. Ultimately, he was inspired to create a software tool for depicting data in a visual way.

In a 1996 article in *Forbes*, Dangermond said: ''The idea was to display data in spatial relationships. Think of this as routing—finding the best, and worst, and any other paths through a given universe of data. And seeing it change in front of you as you change variables.'' Even though he was a poor math student in high school, Dangermond read math books on his own and enlisted a mathematician to help him develop a software program for merging data with digital maps. This monumental step led to the birth of ESRI.

In 1969, Jack Dangermond and his wife, Laura, established the Environmental Systems Research Institute (ESRI) with $1,100 of their own savings. ESRI first operated from the Dangermond's historic home, which was surrounded by orange groves. Eventually, an office building was purchased in Irvine, California, and transported back to Redlands.

ESRI initially focused on the organization and analysis of geographic information. In its first year, ESRI participated in a

Company Perspectives:

We at ESRI believe that better information makes for better decisions. Our reputation is built on contributing our technical knowledge, our special people, and valuable experience to the collection, analysis, and communication of geographic information.

project to develop an interstate from Milwaukee to Green Bay, Wisconsin. The company's first software customer was the Puerto Rico Planning Board. During these early years, ESRI became involved in several highly challenging projects. The company helped Mobil Oil to choose a location for the new town of Reston, Virginia, and also helped the City of Baltimore, Maryland, with redevelopment efforts.

During the 1970s, ESRI quickly found itself engaged in a wide variety of interesting projects with government agencies at the local, state, and federal levels. In 1970, San Diego County, California, chose the company to develop the Polygon Information Overlay System (PIOS). The following year, ESRI was involved in designing the Land Use Planning and Management System for the City of Los Angeles. After incorporating in 1973, ESRI continued to receive lucrative contracts, including one for developing the Maryland Automated Geographic Information System—the first commercially developed statewide GIS system.

Heading into the mid-1970s, ESRI pioneered a map-based information system for water resource management in Delaware. In addition, the U.S. Army Corps of Engineers praised the company as the only U.S. vendor capable of meeting its technical specifications related to land use and environmental studies. In 1976, ESRI applied GIS technology to the Mississippi River by working with the Great River Environmental Action Team, which consisted of the U.S. Army Corps of Engineers; the Fish and Wildlife Service; and the Department of Fish and Game in Iowa, Wisconsin, and Minnesota.

Commercial GIS Pioneer in the 1980s

During the 1980s, ESRI took its software applications to a new level when it released its first commercial GIS application in 1981. Called ARC/INFO, ESRI explained that the application "combined computer display geographic features, such as points, lines, and polygons, with a database management tool for assigning attributes to these features. Originally designed to run on minicomputers, ARC/INFO offered the first modern GIS. As the technology shifted to UNIX and later to the Windows operating systems, ESRI evolved software tools that took advantage of these new platforms. This shift enabled users of ESRI software to apply the principles of distributed processing and data management."

In tandem with ARC/INFO's release, ESRI hosted its first user conference in 1981, which was attended by a mere 18 people. The following year, ESRI performed its first commercial installation of ARC/INFO at the New Brunswick Department of Natural Resources. The application's first academic license was granted to the University of Maryland in 1983.

During the 1980s, ESRI became involved in projects of greater size and scope. In 1983–1984, the company worked with the United Nations Environmental Programme (UNEP) on several projects, including the development of high-resolution digital world maps. Around the same time, the State of Alaska Department of Natural Resources tasked ESRI with building an automated geographic database for the entire state.

In 1989, ESRI received a $10 million contract from the United States Defense Mapping Agency (DMA) to build the Digital Chart of the World (DCW). According to ESRI, the DCW was "the first 1:1,000,000–scale digital basemap of the world."

In addition to working on projects of a larger scale, ESRI's domestic and global market reach also was growing during the 1980s. In 1984, ESRI Canada Ltd. was established. Expansion unfolded at a rapid pace in the second half of the decade. Regional offices were established in Olympia, Washington, and Charlotte, North Carolina, in 1987, and ESRI France was established the following year along with another regional office in Minneapolis. The company concluded the decade with a bang, opening regional offices in Boston; Washington, D.C.; Denver; and Austin, Texas in 1989.

One of the decade's most important developments occurred in 1986, when ESRI unveiled a second product called PC ARC/INFO—a version of its software designed for individual personal computers. According to the company, PC ARC/INFO was a major milestone in that its release set the stage for future innovation at ESRI. Other noteworthy milestones included the establishment of ESRI's Instructor Certification Program for international distributors and its Business Partner Program in 1988.

Expansion and Modernization in the 1990s

During the 1990s, ESRI continued to experience phenomenal growth. In addition to doubling the size of its employee base, the company continued to open new offices. After establishing ESRI Italia in Rome during 1990, ESRI opened regional offices in St. Louis and California in 1991 and 1992, respectively. In 1995, offices were opened in Chicago, New York, Philadelphia, and Pennsylvania, along with another international office in Rotterdam, The Netherlands.

That year, ESRI employed about 1,200 people and was in the process of constructing new headquarters in Redlands—an X-shaped building spanning about 80,000 feet. The company held 28 percent of the GIS market and served major municipal clients including Los Angeles, Miami, Phoenix, Pittsburgh, and Seattle, and was helping countries like Japan to design entire towns. By this time, its ARC/INFO product had been updated 14 times since its 1981 release.

ESRI's strong growth during the 1990s was fueled by innovative new product introductions, as well as enhancements to existing applications. These included ArcCAD, as well as a new desktop mapping program called ArcView, which sold 10,000 copies in the first six months of 1992 alone. This was followed by the introduction of the ArcData GIS program. ArcData eventually became the Geography Network, which the company described as "a collaborative, multiparticipant system for publishing, sharing, and using geographic information on the Internet."

Key Dates:

1969: Jack Dangermond and his wife, Laura, establish the Environmental Systems Research Institute (ESRI) with $1,100 of their own savings.
1973: ESRI is incorporated.
1981: ARC/INFO, ESRI's first commercial GIS application, is released.
1989: A $10 million contract is received from the United States Defense Mapping Agency (DMA) to build the Digital Chart of the World (DCW).
1996: Sales reach approximately $170 million.
1997: *GIS World* names ArcView GIS and ARC/INFO as the world's two most widely used GIS software applications.
2001: ESRI plays an important role in the cleanup, rescue, and recovery operations following the September 11 terrorist attacks.
2002: ESRI Business Information Solutions is formed.

In 1994, ESRI's sales reached $150 million, supported by the release of applications for the business-to-business and business-to-consumer markets. The suite of available ESRI applications, which strengthened the company's market share, continued to expand during the mid-1990s, including programs like ArcInfo for Windows NT.

ESRI's sales reached approximately $170 million in 1996. That year, the company completed a new research and development facility and acquired Atlas GIS from Claritas. In 1997 ESRI initiated a project to reengineer all of its GIS software. Subsequently, *GIS World* named ArcView GIS and ARC/INFO as the world's two most widely used GIS software applications.

By 1998, ESRI employed approximately 1,800 workers and had sales of $278 million. That year, the company entered into a partnership with Bellcore to develop telecommunications software, as well as a software agreement valued at more than $20 million with the National Imagery and Mapping Agency (NIMA).

Other important developments during the 1990s included various enhancements and improvements in customer service, an arrangement with Oracle to resell the company's database products, and the formalization of the ESRI Conservation Program (ECP), which provided free software and training to worthy organizations. ESRI also started a national scholarship competition for high school students called GeoChallenge and co-sponsored the first GIS Day to increase awareness about the technology.

Mapping a New Millennium

At the dawn of the 21st century, ESRI served some 500,000 customers worldwide, including 2,000 city governments. The company's Redlands campus spanned 16 buildings. ESRI employed about 2,500 workers, including 1,000 at its California headquarters. It operated from 15 international offices and marketed products through distributors in 290 countries. Among the interesting projects at ESRI in 2000 was a $112 million initiative with Microsoft to incorporate mapping technology into different consumer products.

When the United States withstood devastating terrorist attacks on September 11, 2001, ESRI played an important role in the cleanup and rescue operations, earning recognition from the American Geographical Society (AGS). In addition to providing manpower and other resources to rebuild New York City's GIS infrastructure, ESRI helped to form the Emergency Mapping and Data Center, which used GIS technology to create maps of command posts, first aid stations, and continuing dangers, such as fires and debris.

At the time, ESRI led the industry with a market share of nearly 35 percent and 2001 revenues of approximately $427 million. In July 2002, the company purchased a two-story, 40,000-square-foot office building in Broomfield, Colorado. Situated on nearly 18 acres, 12 of which were undeveloped, the facility was formerly home to a traveling performance firm called Up With People.

ESRI acquired the Marketing Systems Group of CACI International, Inc., in 2002, leading to the formation of ESRI Business Information Solutions (ESRI BIS). The new group was devoted to serving ESRI's business and private sector clients. It also was in 2002 that ESRI partnered with Pasco Corporation to form ESRI Japan. That year, ESRI Hong Kong Ltd. was renamed ESRI China (Hong Kong), and ESRI China (Beijing) was formed.

Topping off 2002 were accolades from two government organizations, including a Certificate of Special Recognition from the National Association of Counties (NACO) for ESRI's role in the September 11 recovery efforts, as well as a Distinguished Public Service Award for Jack Dangermond from the U.S. Department of State's Open Forum for his positive role in domestic and world affairs.

By 2003, some 60 percent of U.S. counties used ESRI software. That year, approximately 12,000 people attended the company's annual user conference, hailing from 135 countries. This represented a significant increase from the 18 people who attended the conference in its first year. With 23 offices throughout the world, ESRI employed 2,750 people, about 1,400 of who worked at its headquarters.

In early 2003, ESRI acquired Alida, a French digital mapping company founded in 1996 by Marc Oliver Briat and Theirry Kressmann. ESRI announced plans to incorporate aspects of Alida's DataDraw application into its ArcGIS system.

It also was in 2003 that ESRI's technology was employed in southern Iraq and Kuwait, as part of a pilot project involving the U.S. Agency for International Development's Disaster Assistance Response Team. The project allowed humanitarian workers to collect data with laptop computers and create maps showing the location of residents who needed food and buildings requiring repair. Late that year, ESRI's software was used to map and fight wildfire outbreaks in the western United States.

ESRI achieved revenues of $497 million in 2003, capturing approximately 40 percent of the more than $1 billion GIS software market. Its nearest competitor, Intergraph, held about 10 percent market share in the early 2000s. With $1,100 and a clear vision of how GIS could benefit humankind, Jack and Laura Dangermond propelled a mere idea into a global software powerhouse that was poised for continued success well into the 21st century.

Principal Operating Units

ESRI Business Information Solutions; ESRI Japan; ESRI China (Hong Kong); ESRI China (Beijing).

Principal Competitors

Intergraph Corporation; Geographic Data Technology Inc.; MapInfo Corporation; Autodesk, Inc.

Further Reading

Bylinsky, Gene, "Managing with Electronic Maps," *Fortune*, April 24, 1989.

"ESRI Creates a Global Community in San Diego," *GEO World*, August 2001.

"Geographic Information Systems Center Maps a Future for Inland California," *Press-Enterprise* (Riverside, Calif.), March 7, 2001.

Newman, Morris, "The Great Connector," *Planning*, July 1995.

"One-to-One," *GEO: connexion*, November 2002.

Pitchford, Phil, "Founders of California-Based Software Firm Maintain Low Profile," *Press-Enterprise* (Riverside, Calif.), December 16, 2003.

Rothman, Matt, "Plotting Profits with Maps," *California Business*, September 1991.

Smith, Tom, "Oracle, ESRI Team Up for Spatial Data," *Computer Reseller News*, September 18, 1995.

Tucker, Darla Martin, "Redlands, Calif., Research Institute's Technology Puts Software Firms on Map," *Business Press* (San Bernardino, Calif.), December 18, 2000.

Tucker, Darla Martin, "Software Partnership Puts Redlands, Calif., Business School on Map," *Business Press* (San Bernardino, Calif.), August 4, 2003.

Young, Jeffrey, "Treasure Maps," *Forbes*, November 18, 1996.

—Paul R. Greenland

Epic Systems Corporation

5301 Tokay Boulevard
Madison, Wisconsin 53711-1027
U.S.A.
Telephone: (608) 271-9000
Fax: (608) 271-7237
Web Site: http://www.epicsys.com

Private Company
Incorporated: 1979
Employees: 910
Sales: $105 million
NAIC: 511210 Software Publishers

Based in Madison, Wisconsin, Epic Systems Corporation is one of the healthcare industry's leading information technology companies, serving many of the world's largest hospitals and healthcare systems. The company's software applications fall into a number of broad categories, including e-health and hand-helds, enterprise foundation, clinical, decision support, access, revenue cycle, health plan, and connectivity. Epic's product trademarks include Analyst, Bridges, Cadence, Chronicles, Clarity, Cohort, EpicCare, Epicenter, EpicLink, EpicOnHand, EpicRx, EpicWeb, Identifier, Identity, MyChart, MyEpic, Op-Time, Prelude, Resolute, Revenue Guardian, SmartForms, and Tapestry. According to Epic, its software applications help healthcare providers to "improve the patient experience, provide more effective care, streamline administrative tasks, and strengthen their financial health." Epic puts a premium on remaining independent. To maintain its focus and organic culture, the company has avoided public stock offerings, mergers, and the acquisition of other firms. Some 90 percent of Epic's staff is devoted to customer service or research and development initiatives.

A Healthy Start: 1979–89

Epic owes its start to Judith Faulkner, a computer programmer who came to Madison, Wisconsin in the 1970s to pursue graduate studies in computer science after earning a mathematics degree in her native Pennsylvania. Following graduate school, Faulkner worked as a consultant and taught computer science at the University of Wisconsin-Madison during the 1970s and early 1980s.

In the August 1998 issue of *Health Data Management,* Dan Balaban wrote of Faulkner: "During this time, she led the design of clinical records systems for various departments serving the university's hospital and for the Milwaukee County mental health department. To commercialize the systems, Faulkner and about a dozen other programmers and information managers at the university and other institutions pooled about $70,000 in 1979 to start Epic."

Initially known as Human Services Computing, Inc., Faulkner's new database and time-sharing firm "mostly did number crunching for medical researchers and state and government agencies," according to the March 7, 1990 issue of the *Capital Times.* During the 1970s, Faulkner developed what eventually became an Epic database product called Chronicles. Unlike competing products, Chronicles incorporated proprietary technology and was written in a 30-year-old programming language called "M" (formerly called MUMPS).

In *Epic Systems Corporation: A Brief History,* the company described its Chronicles data repository, explaining: "Based on the single, longitudinal patient record and designed to handle enterprise-wide data from inpatient, ambulatory, and payer environments, this database became the foundation of Epic's integrated application suite. Our earliest development efforts focused on fine-tuning this infrastructure, ensuring that all of our applications would provide organizations with the scalability, rapid response times, and seamless data-level integration required to manage large volumes of enterprise information in a single system. Building from the central data repository, we developed an integrated suite of clinical, patient access, revenue cycle, and e-health products to cover every point in the care process."

During its first decade, Epic found a considerable market for its practice management software. Cadence Enterprise Scheduling was first released in 1983. The application helped clients to improve the efficiency of resource utilization and manage patient access. Cadence eventually became one of the industry's leading scheduling applications.

In the mid-1980s, Human Services Computing changed its name to Epic. It was at this time that the company's focus shifted toward software applications used to track inventory and medical labor costs. In 1987, Epic released another new application called Resolute Professional Billing, which also evolved into an industry-leading program. According to Epic, Resolute helped users to connect patient access and scheduling functions on the front end with billing functions on the back end.

Epic ended the decade by securing a deal with Cambridge, Massachusetts-based Harvard Community Health Plan in 1989. Epic beat a large sea of competitors to provide the Harvard HMO, which operated 12 medical centers, with its Cadence system. By this time, the company had other large clients, including the Ontario Ministry of Health in Canada and a 490-bed hospital constructed by the Sultan of Brunei. In fact, Epic's bookkeeping software was used by approximately 100 hospitals in Asia, Canada, and the United States.

Explosive Growth: 1990 and Beyond

In 1990, Epic was conducting business from a site at 5609 Medical Circle in Madison. However, it soon relocated to a former elementary school at 5301 Tokay Boulevard. At this time, the company employed approximately 30 workers. While Epic specialized in general database, public health, and scheduling applications, it offered clients more than 50 different products, ranging in price from about $10,000 to several million dollars.

Epic reached a milestone in 1992 when it introduced a Windows-based electronic medical record (EMR) product called EpicCare. An industry first, the application quickly found acceptance among healthcare organizations and would go on to receive high marks from independent raters. EpicCare helped the company to complete its suite of ambulatory practice management software.

As the 1990s progressed, Epic continued to prosper and grow. The company's employee base, which numbered 49 in 1993, mushroomed to 125 in 1995. By this time, Epic's customer base included even more of the healthcare industry's major players, including Kaiser Permanente, Johns Hopkins University, and Prudential.

By early 1997, Epic's employee base was 200 and rising. The company, which devoted approximately 40 percent of its annual budget to research and development, soon began bringing in scores of college seniors to identify prospective new employees. To accommodate this explosive growth, Epic needed more space. Construction was soon underway on a $10 million, 72,000-square-foot addition to its Tokay Boulevard

headquarters. Epic's addition to the 40,000-square-foot building included an underground parking garage for 200 cars.

In 1997, Epic earned net income of $6.6 million on sales of $30.9 million. Its offerings had grown to include software applications in the areas of scheduling, billing and accounts receivable, managed care, and computerized medical records. By this time, the company's EpicCare product had evolved into the nation's largest EMR system, with some 18,000 licenses sold. In fact, Epic attributed more than half of its revenues to EpicCare in 1997.

It also was in 1997 that Epic introduced its first e-health product. Called EpicWeb, the new application became the foundation for an entire suite of Web-based healthcare IT systems. At first, EpicWeb allowed a client's healthcare professionals to access documentation, scheduling, and other information from any Internet-connected PC. However, this Web-based access eventually extended to both affiliated caregivers and patients.

Epic ended the 1990s with another new product introduction when it released the first EpicCare Inpatient Clinical System modules in 1999. By doing so, the company explained that it allowed healthcare providers ''to integrate their inpatient and ambulatory care facilities, combining full EMR access with special features for inpatient providers.'' Epic also announced that it planned to integrate speech recognition technology into EpicCare. It also was in 1999 that Epic sued competitor MedicaLogic, claiming the company copied a key component of its software, known as a text expander, used for physician notation.

In 2000, Epic's sales reached $50 million and employees numbered 550—up from 370 in 1999. This growth came on the heels of more new product introductions. In 2001, the company introduced Hyperspace, which it described as ''an intuitive, role-based GUI that improves enterprise wide workflows by integrating features from your entire Epic suite and presenting them as a single, comprehensive system. Users no longer have to move from application to application to perform tasks, and organizations have the opportunity to streamline workflows as opposed to simply automating manual tasks.'' It also introduced MyChart, which allowed patients to access their medical records, schedule appointments, request prescription refills, and more via the Internet.

By the early 2000s, Epic was receiving recognition for outstanding customer service. In 2001, KLAS Enterprises, an independent medical software rater, named Epic the industry's top vendor in the area of healthcare IT performance. In addition, KLAS also gave Epic an award for being the leading outpatient software vendor. These awards were evidence of the premium Epic put on its relationships with customers. In fact, the firm played ''The Wedding March'' over its PA system after securing a new client.

Epic soon outgrew its headquarters on Tokay Boulevard. In September 2001, the company announced plans to build a new headquarters in nearby Verona when it was unable to find a suitable site in the city of Madison. With an estimated price tag of $100 million, the new campus was expected to include 500,000 square feet of space and 1,200 offices spread across six buildings. According to Epic, its new 340-acre campus would support the local economy and preserve the natural beauty of

Key Dates:

1979: Judith Faulkner and others establish Human Services Computing, Inc., which becomes Epic.
1990: With 30 employees, Epic offers clients more than 50 different products.
1992: Epic introduces a Windows-based electronic medical record (EMR) product called EpicCare.
1997: EpicWeb, the company's first e-health product, is released.
2000: Sales reach $50 million and employees number 550.
2002: KLAS Enterprises names Epic the "best overall vendor of healthcare information technology" for the seventh straight year.

the land while accommodating the company's explosive growth. However, critics argued that Epic's move would have a negative impact on the environment by increasing traffic-related pollution at the rural site.

As the 2000s progressed, growth and success at Epic continued to unfold at an unprecedented pace. The company projected that it would double its employee base by 2005 and have as many as 2,000 workers by 2011. By this time, more healthcare industry heavyweights were among Epic's client base, including the Cleveland Clinic Foundation, Sutter Health, Northwestern Memorial Hospital, and the Sloan-Kettering Cancer Center.

As Epic grew, the company continued to keep its workforce happy by offering an environment that, by most standards, was both progressive and unconventional. In the June 8, 2003 issue of the *Wisconsin State Journal,* Judy Newman described Epic's facility this way: "There are giraffe sculptures 'nibbling' at indoor trees; sculptures of dancing figures; frog tables; a bust of Star Wars' Yoda. There are kites of butterflies, bats, and pterodactyls hanging from a skylit ceiling—the favorite of Epic founder Judith Faulkner. It's that touch of whimsy that helps define Epic as a non-traditional place to work—along with extras like free coffee, milk, juice, and popcorn and Candinas chocolates for employees on their birthdays and a welcome mat for pets on weekends. Employees can dress as they please; most wear jeans."

In 2002, sales reached $105 million and Epic's employee base swelled to 850. The company received good news in October when it settled a legal battle that had been in progress with competitor IDX Systems Corporation and the University of Wisconsin Medical Foundation for 19 months. The suit against Epic, the foundation, and two foundation employees involved the theft of trade secrets (a charge that had been dismissed earlier) and the improper sharing of proprietary information. IDX claimed that an improper disclosure made it possible for the foundation to revoke a new contract it had awarded to IDX and give it to Epic instead.

Other good news at Epic in 2002 came in the form of more awards. At the Medical Records Institute's annual conference that year, the company received top honors in the Clinical Documentation Challenge and also won five other awards in a competition against 145 other firms. In January of the following year, Epic outdistanced 200 competitors to receive KLAS Enterprises' designation as "best overall vendor of healthcare information technology" for the seventh year in a row.

In 2003, Epic secured a $1.8 billion deal with Kaiser Permanente that promised to catapult the company to new heights. Beating competitor Cerner Corporation, Epic secured a contract "to implement within three years a full electronic medical records system—supported by physician order entry, clinical decision support, scheduling, billing and Web portal software, along with a data repository—at 29 hospitals and 423 offices employing some 11,000 physicians," according to the April 2003 issue of *Health Data Management.*

Kaiser reportedly chose Epic over Cerner due to Epic's track record with seamless implementations and because the company's products were better in the areas of user friendliness and workflow functionality. In the February 10, 2003 issue of *Computerworld,* Bob Brewin said the new system "would be the largest healthcare IT system ever developed outside the federal government in terms of cost, scale, and scope."

In the February 5, 2003 issue of the *Capital Times,* Epic CEO Judith Faulkner said that because of Kaiser's size and the fact that it involved 8.4 million patients, the project could have a major impact on moving the larger healthcare industry toward electronic medical records. The deal also received praise from Dr. Carolyn Clancy, acting director of the Agency for Healthcare Research and Quality, U.S. Department of Human Services, who said: "This new initiative is a wonderful example of how the power of information technology can be harnessed to make the kind of achievable improvements in healthcare quality that the American people want and deserve."

By June of 2003, Epic's employee base had grown to 910, up from 850 the previous month. As ground was broken on the company's new headquarters, Epic prepared itself for a new era in its history—one in which it would likely make significant impacts on healthcare information technology. One example was the company's Care Everywhere technology, which would allow patients to essentially take their medical records with them to different healthcare providers. According to the company, "Independent healthcare organizations will not only be able to view patient information, but update it as well. This will create a secure 'virtual' electronic record, and insure that patients receive the best possible care no matter where they're seen."

Principal Competitors

Cerner Corporation; GE Medical Systems; Information Technologies; IDX Systems Corporation.

Further Reading

Balaban, Dan, "No Longer the Quiet Company," *Health Data Management,* August 1998.
Brewin, Bob, "$1.8B IT Rollout Is RX for Kaiser," *Computerworld,* February 10, 2003.
"Changes," *Wisconsin State Journal,* January 29, 2003.
Eisen, Marc, "Epic Decision," *Isthmus,* May 17, 2002.
"Epic Gets Harvard Order for Its Software," *Capital Times,* December 15, 1989.
"Epic Sues MedicaLogic," *Health Data Management,* January 2000.

Epic Systems Corporation: A Brief History, Madison, WI: Epic Systems Corp., 2003.

Epic Systems Corporation Product Catalog 2003, Madison, WI: Epic Systems Corp., 2003.

Goedert, Joseph, "Can Epic Handle the Epic Kaiser Contract?," *Health Data Management*, April 2003.

Hawkins, Lee, Jr., "Health Care without Paperwork," *Wisconsin State Journal*, December 14, 1995.

"IDX, Epic, Foundation Settle Suit," *Health Data Management*, October 2002.

Ivey, Mike, "Growing Epic Determined to Stay Local," *Capital Times*, September 7, 2001.

Johnson, Paul, "Software Success Story," *Wisconsin State Journal*, March 27, 1997.

Manning, Joe, "Madison, Wis.-Based Software Firm to Add Several Hundred New Jobs," *Milwaukee Journal Sentinel*, February 5, 2003.

Newman, Judy, "Non-Corporate Style. Epic Is Building an Elaborate and Unique Headquarters in Verona," *Wisconsin State Journal*, June 8, 2003.

Parkins, Al, "Local Software Firm Finds Cure for Medical Record-Keeping Woes," *Capital Times*, March 7, 1990.

"Physicians Get Web Interface to Records," *Wisconsin State Journal*, December 4, 1997.

Richgels, Jeff, "No One Does Medical Data Quite Like Epic," *Capital Times*, March 16, 2001.

——, "Epic Deal Means Jobs," *Capital Times*, February 5, 2003.

Schuetz, Lisa, "Software Company to Leave Madison, Wis.," *Wisconsin State Journal*, September 7, 2001.

Silver, Jonathan D., "Software Package Will Help Doctors," *Capital Times*, February 27, 1992.

—Paul R. Greenland

FAG—Kugelfischer Georg Schäfer AG

Georg-Schäfer-Strasse 30
D-97421 Schweinfurt
Germany
Telephone: (49) (9721) 91-0
Fax: (49) (9721) 91-3375
Web site: http://www.fag.de

Wholly Owned Subsidiary of INA-Holding Schaeffler KG
Incorporated: 1891 as Automatische Kugelfabrik
  Friedrich Fischer
Employees: 18,007
Sales: EUR 2.2 billion ($2.3 billion) (2001)
NAIC: 332991 Ball and Roller Bearing Manufacturing

FAG—Kugelfischer Georg Schäfer AG is one of the world's largest manufacturers of bearings. FAG bearings are used in cars, railway cars, airplanes, and industrial machinery. The company's bearings division operates production facilities in Western Europe, Asia, Brazil, the United States, and Canada. FAG's other divisions make industrial sewing machines and automated handling systems for the upholstery and apparel industries. The company is owned by German industrial bearings manufacturer INA-Holding Schaeffler KG.

Inventor Lays Groundwork in the 1870s

Company founder Friedrich Fischer was born in 1849 in the German town of Schweinfurt in Franconia, between Frankfurt and Nuremberg. His father, a musical instrument maker, had built himself a new kind of bicycle that he used to visit his clients. At a time when bicycles were propelled by the rider's feet pushing against the ground, the new device, which used foot pedals attached to a rotating rod to turn the wheels, caused a sensation in Schweinfurt. The young Friedrich Fischer, who inherited his father's technical talent and creative abilities, became an apprentice mechanic and, after some years of gaining experience elsewhere in Germany, returned to his hometown. In 1872, Fischer opened a repair shop for sewing machines and bicycles. Soon he also started a retail business that sold new bicycles and sewing machines, a combination that was common

at the time, since many sewing machine manufacturers had started making bicycles when they became popular in the later decades of the 19th century. Finally, Fischer took on the manufacture of his own bicycles.

A new, technically improved generation of bicycles created a rising demand for these vehicles in the 1870s, and thus there was also a demand for the ball bearings used in the wheels and sprockets. In order to make these ball bearings, Fischer depended on imported steel balls from England. However, they were expensive and of low quality, that is, they varied in size and their surface was not perfectly smooth. Convinced that he could do better, Fischer opened a mechanical workshop in 1875. After relentless experimentation, the young man—then age 34—built his first metal-ball grinding machine in 1883. Fischer's machine made it possible to produce at one time a large number of hardened steel balls that were of the exact same size—they varied by no more than two hundredths of a millimeter—and geometrically perfect in shape. The growing demand for high-quality bearings resulted in increasing sales for Fischer, who was soon called Kugel-Fischer or "Ball-Fischer." During the 1880s, Fischer's enterprise grew significantly. By 1887, his operation included six ball grinding machines. Three years later, production capacity was doubled again. Beginning in the mid-1880s, exports began to increase.

In July 1890, Fischer received a German patent for an improved version of his machine. In the following year, he founded his own company, which he named Automatische Kugelfabrik Friedrich Fischer—Automatic Ball Factory Friedrich Fischer. In 1892, Fischer moved his enterprise to a large building, a former cotton-spinning plant. However, it soon outgrew the new location. By 1896, Germany's bicycle industry was putting out 200,000 bicycles a year, and its future looked bright. In that year, Fischer sold his retail business and purchased a large property near the city's train station, where a brand-new factory with a capacity of more than five million steel balls a week was built. To raise the capital for his undertaking, Fischer transformed his enterprise into a public stock corporation in 1897 and renamed it Erste Automatische Gußstahlkugel-Fabrik, vorm. Friedrich Fischer AG (FAG). A banker from nearby Bamberg became the company's majority

Company Perspectives:

Our vision is the further development of FAG into a high-tech enterprise in the area of precision and bearings technology, internationally oriented, with persuasive innovative ability and strength of earnings.

shareholder and Fischer its technical director. However, the company founder died only two years later at age 50 and left the enterprise with no capable successor.

After Fischer's death in 1899, when the company employed about 400 workers, operations were continued under constantly changing management and ownership and took a downward turn. The new leadership proved unable to further enhance the company's position in a highly volatile market with a growing number of competitors, including mass imports of cheap bicycles from the United States. Ten years after Fischer's death, the number of staff working at FAG had dropped to 150.

Growth under New Leadership after 1909

Beginning in the 20th century, the automobile gradually replaced the bicycle as the most popular form of personal transportation and further increased the demand for high quality ball bearings. Ball and roller bearings became major components for rotating parts in motors as well as in many other kinds of machinery. This growing demand in turn attracted more manufacturers to enter the market. The town of Schweinfurt evolved as the center of the German bearings industry, with a number of major manufacturers locating there.

One of them was Georg Schäfer & Cie., a Schweinfurt-based company that started making ball bearings in 1904 and two years later moved into the same former cotton-spinning plant that Fischer's company had leased before building the new factory near the train station. In 1909, the company's ball bearings department, which employed more than 200 workers, needed more space for its operations. The owner, Georg Schäfer, acquired FAG and moved his operation to the Fischer factory. He merged his ball bearings division with FAG but kept the name of the oldest ball bearings manufacturer in the town. In order to have unlimited control over his enterprise, Schäfer transformed the new business into a private company with a number of silent partners. He invested in the modernization of equipment and organized the work flow more efficiently. While it took about three hours to manufacture an average ball bearing at Schäfer's operation, FAG needed nine to ten hours for the same job. The takeover also enabled Schäfer to use Fischer's patents for which he used to pay high license fees. The legal insecurity in connection with the many incomparable patents led Schweinfurt's many ball bearing manufacturers to pool all their patents into the so called "ball bearings convention" that helped overcome costly legal battles. The group was also formed to negotiate prices and technical standards among its members.

Until 1914, FAG's business soared, partly due to the dynamic growth of Germany's automobile industry. At the same time, Georg Schäfer systematically expanded the company's international reach. By 1914, exports—mainly to western Eu-

rope and the United States—accounted for more than half of FAG's output, and the company employed more than 800 workers. After the outbreak of World War I in the summer of 1914, normal operations were interrupted. The newly formed German war ministry now administrated the country's economy. To combat the spreading scarcity of lubricants, the ministry ordered the use of only ball bearings in transmissions and other rotating parts. During the war, FAG manufactured mainly replacement ball bearings for vehicles but also produced other war goods.

After the war ended in late 1918, FAG's situation was anything but rosy. Development work had been ceased and technical equipment was outdated. Many nations protected their national markets through high import duties. Most importantly, the company's clients abroad had switched to international competitors. While the company's orders were still low, Georg Schäfer had his workers repair and update machinery and produce a back stock of goods. The insecurity during the first year after the war led Schäfer's business partners to renege on their commitments. Schäfer bought them out and together with his son-in-law, Hermann Barthels, became FAG's sole owner by December 31, 1919.

The early 1920s brought more political and economic turmoil. Many workers lost their jobs. As inflation picked up speed, the cost of everyday goods became too expensive for most people. Worker's strikes disrupted the company's production for many days and sometimes weeks. Food and fuel became more and more scarce. Despite these difficulties, FAG managed to further expand its product range. For example, it was during this time that the company introduced roller bearings. FAG tried to gain lost ground by focusing on replacement parts while slowly and persistently reviving its international distribution channels at the same time. However, exports never reached the level of importance they had before the war. After hyperinflation was stopped by a currency reform in 1924, FAG experienced a short upturn that peaked in 1925. When Georg Schäfer died in May 1925, his company employed almost 2,000 workers.

Growth in Difficult Times after 1925

After Georg Schäfer's death, the ownership of FAG was transferred to his widow, Alwine Schäfer, his son-in-law Hermann Barthel, and his oldest son, Georg Schäfer, Jr., who each received a one-third interest in the company. Georg Schäfer, Jr. had joined the family business in 1919 at age 23 and became FAG's executive director three years later. Determined to follow his father's strong belief in independence, he successfully led the company through its most difficult times. During the second half of the 1920s, Germany's position in the world market for bearings weakened significantly. While important export markets became almost inaccessible due to high customs rates—the United States imposed a 30-percent custom rate on their value—Germany charged comparatively low rates of between 5 and 8 percent. Consequently, German bearings exports dropped from 40 percent in 1914 to 10 percent during the 1920s. At the same time, foreign competitors gained a significant market share in Germany with bearings imports increasing tenfold between 1925 and 1928. The fierce competition between German manufacturers pushed many of them into the red and resulted in the disintegration of the ball bearings convention. Finally, the Swedish firm

Key Dates:

1883: Friedrich Fischer invents his first metal-ball grinding machine.

1891: Automatische Kugelfabrik Friedrich Fischer is founded in Schweinfurt.

1905: The FAG trademark is officially registered.

1909: The company is merged with Georg Schäfer & Cie.

1933: FAG takes over Wuppertal-based manufacturer of bearings for railway vehicles G.u.J. Jaeger.

1939: FAG established its first production subsidiary abroad in the British city of Wolverhampton.

1945: Eighty-five percent of the company's facilities are destroyed.

1947: FAG's remaining machinery is dismantled.

1950: The company buys back the international rights to the FAG brand name.

1955: The company's reconstruction program is completed.

1953: FAG's first production subsidiary overseas is established in Canada.

1962: FAG takes over Dürrkoppwerke in Bielefeld.

1985: The company goes public.

1990: East German bearings manufacturer Deutsche Kugellagerfabriken (DKF) is acquired.

1993: FAG launches a tough restructuring program that saves the company from bankruptcy.

2001: Competitor INA-Holding Schaeffler KG acquires FAG in a hostile takeover.

SKF acquired seven major German manufacturers, which were merged into Vereinigte Kugellagerwerke AG. Five of the acquired firms were closed down or sold, and 7,850 jobs were cut. Georg Schäfer turned down SKF's attractive offer and FAG remained the only major German bearings manufacturer besides Vereinigte Kugellagerwerke, which moved the headquarters of its operations to Schweinfurt in 1932. In that year, FAG's workforce was 2,800, while Vereinigte Kugellagerwerke employed about 2,900 workers.

By 1933, the worldwide economic depression reached its climax in Germany. Six million Germans were without a job, and machine manufacturing was down to 50 percent compared with 1928. Georg Schäfer, however, managed to expand the company. He successfully focused on markets abroad and was able to secure major contracts in the Soviet Union when he traveled to Moscow in 1930. In early 1933, FAG took over the Wuppertal-based manufacturer of bearings for railway vehicles G.u.J. Jaeger, which soon became the company's division for large bearings. Beginning in 1935, the domestic demand for bearings picked up again, partly caused by the economic recovery program the National Socialists (Nazis) had launched after they came into power in 1933. However, the National Socialists also began to impose their will on German enterprises. In 1936, the year when Nazi leader Adolf Hitler demanded that Germany's manufacturers prepare for another war, FAG established its first production subsidiary abroad in Wolverhampton, the center of the British automobile and machine-building industries. With the German war industry gaining momentum and

mass motorization on the way, the demand for bearings followed suit. However, with war becoming a real possibility, Germany isolated itself more and more from the international community. FAG built two new plants near Schweinfurt and evolved into a major supplier of bearings to the German automobile industry. After 1937, Georg Schäfer, Jr. jointly managed the company with his brother Otto, who had set up FAG's British subsidiary. Two years later, their brother-in-law Hermann Barthel left the company. With Barthel's death in 1941, the company was renamed Kugelfischer Georg Schäfer & Co. After the war had begun, FAG's subsidiary in Britain was expropriated.

After World War II had begun, FAG still exported part of its output. Even in 1942, the third war year, exports accounted for 10 percent of total sales. At the same time, FAG became a major vendor to the German air force. However, the company's strategic importance to the German war industry made FAG, which employed up to 12,000 workers during the war, a primary target of air attacks by the Allies. The company's main plant in Schweinfurt was bombed heavily 15 times between summer 1943 and spring 1945. As a result, 85 percent of the plant was destroyed.

Regaining International Importance after World War II

After the war, FAG was put on the Allied Forces' reparations list and over 4,000 machine units were dismounted. However, the American military administration soon realized that the German economy could not be rebuilt without bearings. In September 1947, they concluded that because of a worldwide bearings shortage FAG had to be rescued and rebuilt as soon as possible. Following the currency reform in western Germany in June 1948, Georg and Otto Schäfer took over FAG's management again, after they had been removed in 1945 and 1946 respectively by the military occupation forces. It took seven years to rebuild the basic production facilities and administrative buildings. Until then, it was not uncommon for some FAG departments to work outdoors. By 1955, the number of FAG employees had grown to 8,300 and the production facilities were state-of-the-art once more.

Beginning in the 1950s, FAG focused on winning back markets abroad. However, during the war the company's former British subsidiary had taken over the international rights to FAG's brand name and kept producing bearings under the FAG label. The company was able to buy back the international rights and a sales office was set up again in Wolverhampton in 1951. Two years later, the first production subsidiary abroad was erected in Stratford, Canada. In 1957, FAG took over Swiss bearings manufacturer SRO Kugellagerwerke J. Schmid-Roost AG. By the beginning of the 1980s, FAG production subsidiaries were operating in Italy, Brazil, Portugal, India, Austria, and the United States, and about 20 sales offices had been established on all continents. During the same decade, the company expanded into China and Korea.

Beginning in the 1950s, the company also ventured into new markets, including measuring instruments, hydraulic brake systems for automobiles, and textile machine components. In 1962, the company acquired the Dürrkoppwerke in Bielefeld, the German manufacturer of industrial sewing machines and bearings that the family of Georg Schäfer, Sr.'s son-in-law had taken over in 1939, when the company got into financial difficulties.

The reconstruction years of the 1950s and the economic boom of the 1960s were followed by a period of stagnating and fluctuating world markets and an increasingly fierce international competition in the 1970s and 1980s. FAG focused on opening new markets for bearings, which were now used in earth-moving equipment, satellites and space stations, offshore installations, wind power generators, and robotics industries. In 1971, FAG's top management team was expanded to include Georg, Jr.'s son Georg, Otto Schäfer's son Otto G. Schäfer, some division managers, and the CEOs of Jaeger and Dürrkopp. After Georg Schäfer, Jr.'s death in 1975, his youngest son Fritz became a co-owner and joined the executive management team. In 1979, the company was renamed FAG Kugelfischer Georg Schäfer & Co. FAG's legal form was changed two times, in 1978 and in 1983, before the company finally went public in 1985. After its initial public offering, the Fischer family still held 51.5 percent of the common stock.

Struggles and Loss of Independence in the 1990s

After the fall of the communist regime in eastern Germany, FAG took over Deutsche Kugellagerfabriken (DKF), a major East German bearings manufacturer with eight production plants. However, following the introduction of West German currency into East Germany, DKF's eastern European markets disappeared over night. On the other hand, many factories in East Germany were shut down or taken over by West German firms, greatly diminishing the number of DKF's domestic clients. Consequently, DKF slipped deeply in the red. For business year 1992, FAG reported DM300 million in losses and DM2 billion in bank debt. By early 1993, the situation had grown into a serious financial crisis that brought FAG to the verge of bankruptcy. A crisis manager from outside was brought in who drafted a restructuring program that was approved by all stakeholders and implemented immediately. While many of FAG's assets were taken as collateral by banks, to whom the Schäfer family had to give up their voting rights, the company sold off business divisions such as hydraulic brakes, textile machine components, and measuring technology—together worth DM1 billion in annual sales, with about 6,500 employees—that were not defined as FAG's core business. Four market-oriented divisions remained:

automotive technology, industrial bearings, aircraft and spacecraft technology (including precision bearings), and the components division. DKF finally declared bankruptcy.

With its 1992 workforce of 31,000, bank debt and annual losses roughly cut in half, FAG was on its way to recovery in the second half of the 1990s. Between 1998 and 2000, FAG's pre-tax profits more than tripled. By the end of the decade, the company had regained its strong market position but was looking for strategic partners and negotiating with the world's number three bearings maker, Japanese NTN. However, in the fall of 2001, FAG, by then number four in the world's bearings market, fell victim to a hostile takeover by major competitor INA Holding Schaeffler KG, worldwide number six. After five weeks of arm-wrestling between the two companies, FAG's top management gave up their resistance. INA agreed to FAG remaining an independent subsidiary with its management holding based in Schweinfurt. However, INA delisted FAG from public trading.

Principal Subsidiaries

FAG Industrial Bearings AG; FAG Komponenten AG; FAG Automobiltechnik AG; FAG Sales Europe GmbH; FAG Hanwha Bearings Corporation (Korea; 70%); FAG Bearings Ltd. (Canada); Dürrkopp Adler AG (93.76%); FAG Aircraft/Super Precision Bearings GbmH; FAG Bearings Corporation (United States); FAG Corporate Services GmbH; FAG International Sales and Serivce GmbH; Rolamentos FAG Ltda. (Brazil).

Principal Competitors

Aktiebolegat SKF; The Timken Company; NSK Ltd.

Further Reading

1883–1983: 100 Jahre industrielle Kugelfertigung, Schweinfurt, Germany: FAG Kugelfischer Georg Schäfer KG, 1983, 28 p.
"Franconian Fistcuffs; Takeovers in Germany," *Economist*, October 6, 2001.
Goslich, Lorenz, "Die Schweinfurter leiden leise unter der Monostruktur," *Frankfurter Allgemeine Zeitung*, April 7, 1993, p. 20.
Was war wann? Daten aus der Werksgeschichte, Schweinfurt, Germany: FAG Kugelfischer Georg Schäfer KG auf Aktien, 1983, 19 p.

—Evelyn Hauser

Family Dollar Stores, Inc.

10401 Old Monroe Road
Matthews, North Carolina 28105
U.S.A.
Telephone: (704) 847-6961
Fax: (704) 847-0819
Web site: http://www.familydollar.com

Public Company
Incorporated: 1959
Employees: 37,000
Sales: $4.75 billion (2003)
Stock Exchanges: New York
Ticker Symbol: FDO
NAIC: 452990 All Other General Merchandise Stores

Family Dollar Stores, Inc., is a chain of discount stores that offer inexpensive merchandise for family and home needs to customers in 43 states located in mainly in the northeastern, southeastern, southwestern, and northwestern regions of the United States. The first Family Dollar store was opened in Charlotte, North Carolina, in 1959. Since that time, the company has grown to more than 5,000 units with $4.75 billion in annual sales. Family Dollar stocks its stores with a wide variety of products, ranging from food and housewares to apparel and linens—most priced at less than $10. Founder Leon Levine retired in 2003, handing over company reigns to his son, Howard Levine.

Company Origins

Company founder, Leon Levine, learned the retail business from his father. In fact, when his father Harry Levine died in 1947, Leon and his brother Al took over the store their father began; Leon was 13 years old at the time. The store, in Rockingham, North Carolina, billed itself as a department store, but was really more closely allied to the old-fashioned general store. By 1959, Leon was ready to strike out on his own, and he opened the first Family Dollar store in Charlotte. His target customer was the lower middle-income family who could not afford fancy name brands and was not a slave to high fashion, but did need good clothing and durable shoes.

The Family Dollar store proved popular among value shoppers, and soon new outlets were opened. By the early 1970s, the company had gone public and had opened its 100th store in Brevard, North Carolina. Although it was not the first in the self-service, discount variety field, Family Dollar secured a leading spot.

Overcoming Difficulties in the 1970s

One difficulty in targeting lower income consumers was that they were often the first hit during bad economic weather—whether due to inflation or recession—and were quickly forced to cut back on spending. Thus, whereas Family Dollar expanded and achieved record sales in the early 1970s, the mid-1970s presented a particular challenge. Clustered in the southern states, the chain was hard hit by fallout from the traumatized textile industry in 1974. Many of Family Dollar's customers in that region were textile workers; many others worked in the tobacco and furniture industries, and were similarly hard hit. Family Dollar saw its profits fall by as much as 50 percent in 1974 and 1975, which was especially shocking given the company's growth rate in the years before; earnings in the early 1970s had shot up 24 percent annually, on average.

To offset the effects of this economic downturn, the company began targeting some of its weaknesses, seeking to improve marketing and merchandising, as well as to diversify geographically. It also dropped its policy of pricing all merchandising at $3 or less, which, while it had appealed to shoppers, had proved too hard on store margins. Family Dollar also tightened inventory controls, adding an electronic data processing system. Although the economy continued to be volatile in the late 1970s, Family Dollar was able to exceed $100 million in sales in fiscal year 1978, and hit a record $151 million in sales in 1979. Same-store sales remained fairly flat around that time, however.

Family Dollar was operating about 400 outlets in eight states, all in the South, by 1980. Most of the sales gains over the

---

Company Perspectives:

We strive to grow our base of loyal and satisfied customers by offering convenience and great values, to grow our assortment of nationally advertised name brand merchandise, and to improve quality standards to bring greater value to our customers.

---

next few years were from additional stores. In 1979, Family Dollar acquired 40 Top Dollar stores from Sav-A-Stop. That same year, it also opened 36 new units of its own, putting it ahead of its own expansion schedule.

Family Dollar's draw at the time was its bargain-priced goods—such items as toys, automotive equipment, and school supplies—all displayed within 6,000 to 8,000 square feet of store. Much of the company's merchandise had come from vendors or suppliers who had overbought, so the company's savings on those underpriced goods could be passed on to its customers. Another winning strategy was to gather up manufacturer's overruns. Size and strategy helped as well. When Procter & Gamble refused to give Levine a deal on Pampers disposable diapers, figuring he would have to stock them anyway, Levine stocked more Kleenex disposable diapers, as well as a Family Dollar brand, and soon Pampers became less necessary.

Another ingredient in Family Dollar's success was its efficient distribution system, handled entirely out of Charlotte, from which the company was able to make bulk deliveries to its stores. In 1980, the size of the distribution center was doubled so that the company could take further advantage of discounts on single, bulk deliveries, as well as open new stores without concern about stock shortages.

Although Family Dollar was branching out geographically at this time, with 70 to 80 outlets in Georgia, it was still primarily a Carolina chain. Soon, the company began investigating further opportunities in Alabama, Tennessee, the Virginias, Florida, Kentucky, and Mississippi. Because the company had no long-term debt—despite the recent Top Dollar stores acquisition—the cash flow freed Family Dollar to expand without too much risk in borrowing. In fact, it opened 33 new stores between September 1979 and September 1980, and was boasting a growth of about 30 percent per year since 1975. Family Dollar stores generally operated in leased buildings, which saved the company on capital investment. In March 1982, the company's 500th store opened, in Brunswick, Georgia.

Battling Competition in the 1980s

Family Dollar continued to thrive through the early 1980s, ringing up more record profits—in fact, it had a nine-year streak of them—and opening more than 100 new stores a year between 1982 and 1987. But while the company was becoming a more national presence, it failed to keep a close eye on increasing competition from Wal-Mart Stores. Suddenly, sales growth in recently opened stores tripped from 9 percent in 1984, to a dull 2 percent in 1985, then came to a dead halt the following year, and dropped 10 percent in 1987.

At the time, and, indeed, since the company's inception, Family Dollar shoppers were families making less than $25,000 a year. Most stores were rooted in rural areas, usually in towns of less than 15,000, often within walking distance or a very short drive from home. The average Family Dollar customer shopped there at least once a week, spending about $8 on average. The stores were about one-tenth the size of a Wal-Mart or Kmart, so product lines had to be meticulously selected and limited. Even though the bigger stores could offer more merchandise, the draw of Family Dollar stores was often location. Wal-Marts typically were planted outside or on the edge of town, while Family Dollars were downtown. The real problem arose when Family Dollar management, preoccupied with expansion, stopped checking on the competition's pricing. When it did check, only after sales slipped enough to cause alarm, it found that Wal-Mart was pricing sometimes as much as 10 percent below Family Dollar—often on such things as health and beauty products that Family Dollar was advertising heavily as on sale.

Therefore, in 1987, Family Dollar instituted a new pricing policy: they would not be undersold. Within two months, same-store sales were up 10 percent. Clearly, the lower prices wounded margins somewhat, but the company compensated by scaling back its expansion. It had been expanding as far north as Michigan, and as far west as Texas, and right into Sam Walton's Wal-Mart territory. In 1986, there were 1,107 Family Dollar stores in 23 states. At the same time, Wal-Marts were infiltrating Family Dollar's stronghold, the rural southeast. Wal-Mart was using its buying power to plunge prices while Family Dollar was using its profits to open more stores.

After catching itself and lowering prices to boost sales, the company faced another challenge in the form of a management shakeup. In the mid-1980s, Leon Levine was the company's chairman and chief executive; Leon's first cousin, Lewis E. Levine, served as president and chief operating officer; and Leon's son Howard Levine was senior vice-president of merchandising. In September of 1987, just as Family Dollar reported its fourth consecutive quarter of lower earnings, Lewis Levine abruptly resigned, and Howard Levine left as well. Lewis had been with the company for 17 years and was reportedly upset by salary differentials (CEO Leon Levine made an estimated $1.84 million in 1986, while Lewis made slightly more than $260,040). Moreover, the cousins had disagreed over strategy; Lewis felt that Leon was not responding quickly enough to changes necessary to defend against the encroaching Wal-Mart. Essentially, it come down to a standoff, in which Lewis asked for more control and the board asked for Lewis's resignation. Leon served as president until a successor was named, capping his own salary at $350,000 for 1987 and 1988. Leon's son, Howard Levine, the heir-apparent, seemed to have left the company for more personal reasons.

Meanwhile, the battle with Wal-Mart grew heated. Family Dollar's new "everyday-low-price" strategy was still hard on the margins. In 1987, the company was spending $2 million to renovate its 1,272 stores, to make the most of their compact size. When Family Dollar first began matching or beating Wal-Mart on prices for items like health and beauty aids and automotive supplies, same-store sales rose 9 percent for a few months, but then fell back to the levels of the year prior. Still,

Key Dates:

1959: Leon Levine opens the first Family Dollar store in Charlotte, North Carolina.
1970: The company goes public.
1979: The company acquires 40 Top Dollar stores.
1982: Family Dollar opens its 500th store.
1987: The company launches a new pricing policy: they will not be undersold.
1992: Sales surpass $1 billion.
2002: Family Dollar becomes a member of the *Fortune 500*.
2003: The company's 5,000th store is opened in Jacksonville, Florida.

Family Dollar felt that it had two advantages: it could squeeze into urban store spaces without fear of a large Wal-Mart moving in next door, and Family Dollar was still virtually debt-free.

Back to Basics in the Late 1980s

After an intense headhunting mission, Levine appointed Ralph Dillon the new president and CEO of Family Dollar. Formerly the head of Coast American Corporation, Denver's retail franchise, Dillon joined Family Dollar in summer of 1987. Faced with rising sales, given the new store expansions, but essentially flat earnings, Dillon's strategy was simple: return to the basics that built Family Dollar in the first place, particularly in regard to pricing. The previous management's efforts at aggressive markdowns were pushed even further; a policy was now instituted requiring that any item tagged at more than $15 gain approval first from top management.

To assist margins, the company began stocking more of its own labeled products, as well as manufacturer's overruns and closeouts, practices that had been scaled back in the 1980s when the stores had tried to upscale merchandise. Also stocked were irregular brand-name goods, meaning jeans and sweaters that were slightly flawed. Other high-margin goods such as seasonal candies and costume jewelry were pushed. Coupled with an ad blitz stressing the chain's return to ''everyday low prices,'' Family Dollar felt confident of a comeback. The cuts would bite into the company's overall margin for a couple of years. Still, because of its healthy cash flow and minimal debt, the company had the equipment to ride out a recession and get through its own changes.

Indeed, despite the tough economic weather of the late 1980s, Family Dollar was thriving again and, by 1991, was reporting another record year. Significantly, same-store sales were up, overall sales exceeded the $1 billion mark for the first time, and revenues increased 18 percent in 1992 alone. That same year, the company planned to open 150 new stores, concentrating in New England, where existing store sales were above average. By year-end, Family Dollar had opened 175 new stores and closed 25.

Meanwhile, the management concentrated on improving gross margins. A new point-of-sale (POS) system was installed, which gave detailed information on apparel styles, colors, and sizes selling well in each store. The POS system also helped stores track regional competition on certain products. During this time, Peter Hayes became the new president of Family Dollar.

By 1992, as Wal-Mart captured 26 percent of the discount store market and many smaller discounters were sent into bankruptcy, Family Dollar seemed to have survived by concentrating on its core strengths of convenience, solid stock, and low prices. Family Dollar stores were on average within three miles of shopper's homes and were still about one-tenth the size of Wal-Mart stores. Moreover, because its stocks were smaller per store, the price of staples such as toothpaste and laundry detergent at Family Dollar were often slightly more than one might pay at Wal-Mart. Nevertheless, many customers seemed willing to pay slightly higher prices in exchange for convenience of location and getting around more quickly in a smaller store. Family Dollar had faced the superstore threat head-on, and was, by 1992, even posting a better net margin than Wal-Mart.

Apparel represented about 45 percent of the Family Dollar stock in 1993, and ''hard'' goods made up the remainder. The company spread out its search for merchandise and took advantage of downtime in factories—contracting them to manufacture merchandise at cut rates during times they would usually be fallow. About 10 percent of the company's overall business was attributable to private-label sales, and most store merchandise was priced lower than $18. The company also was sprucing up its distribution system, installing a building in Memphis, Arkansas, of more than 550,000 square feet, which when combined with the North Carolina center, totaled about 1.3 million square feet of space. Both centers were fully automated.

In 1994, having regained its sales strength, Family Dollar focused on fine-tuning its strategy of centering itself as a neighborhood convenience store with low prices. It began phasing out low-margin items like tools, paints, and motor oils, replacing them with more popular, higher-priced items like toys and portable stereos. The pricing policy began allowing for items up to $25. Expansion was also a focus; 165 new units were added to the Family Dollar chain in 1993, and the same number was planned for 1994. Indeed, the rash of bankruptcies among regional discount chains provided Family Dollar with opportunities for growth.

In the spring of 1994, Hayes resigned as president and chief operating officer of Family Dollar Stores, taking a position as president of a Florida-based jewelry company. He was replaced by John Reier, who had been with the company since 1987, having been senior vice-president in charge of Family Dollar's merchandising and advertising. Leon Levine remained board chair and CEO. Given the highly competitive nature of the industry, Family Dollar sales and earnings failed to meet expectations in 1994. In the 1994 annual report to shareholders, Levine remained optimistic, however, noting that the company would continue its aggressive expansion plans and continue to pursue price reductions at Family Dollar stores.

Growth in the Mid-1990s and Beyond

A major focus for Family Dollar continued to be store growth throughout the 1990s. Howard Levine returned to the company in 1996 and became president the following year. His intentions to aggressively increase store count proved evident as the company opened its 3,000th location in 1998. As the company made its move into Arizona in March 1999, a *Discount Store News* article reported, "Family Dollar stores have been opening at a steady, methodical pace in recent years, quietly cropping up in cities and rural towns across the country." Indeed, the company's impressive growth coupled with its successful financial record put it in an enviable position among its competitors.

To keep up with product demand, Family Dollar opened a new distribution center in Virginia in 1998 and an additional facility went online in Oklahoma in 1999. That year the company celebrated its 40th anniversary by posting record sales and profits.

Family Dollar entered the new millennium on solid ground. The company focused on putting additional brand names on its shelves while cutting back on its apparel line, decreasing it to just 15 percent of its product mix. In 2000, sales broke the $3 billion mark and by 2001 the 4,000th Family Dollar store had opened its doors. The company's success caught the eye of industry observers and in 2002, the firm was named to the *Fortune 500* list.

Family Dollar's successful business strategy appeared to be paying off handsomely. Overall, nearly 3,000 stores had been added to its arsenal over the past ten years and the company was operating in 43 states. By fiscal 2003, the firm could boast 30 consecutive quarters of record sales and earnings. Howard Levine—named CEO in 1998—took on the additional role of chairman in 2003. Under his leadership, Family Dollar continued its growth streak, opening its 5,000th store on August 28, 2003, in Jacksonville, Florida.

During 2004, the company planned to open more than 500 new stores as well as its eighth distribution center. It continued to focus on strengthening its supply chain, improving the quality of its apparel and housewares offerings, and bolstering its brand name product line. Although the firm had indeed come a long way from its start in 1959, the company's management team eyed continued expansion in the years to come. Levine firmly believed in Family Dollar's ability to succeed in the future, evident in the theme of the company's 2003 annual report—"We've still got a long way to grow!"

Principal Subsidiaries

Family Dollar, Inc.; Family Dollar Holdings, Inc.; Family Dollar Services, Inc.; Family Dollar Operations, Inc.; Family Dollar Trucking, Inc.; Family Dollar Merchandising, L.P.; Family Dollar Distribution, L.P.

Principal Competitors

Dollar General Corporation; Dollar Tree Stores, Inc.; Wal-Mart Stores Inc.

Further Reading

Clune, Ray, "Family Dollar Sticks to Its Niche," *Daily News Record,* December 6, 1993, pp. 4–5.

D'Innocenzio, Anne, "Building the Family Image," *Women's Wear Daily,* January 26, 1994, p. 18.

"Family Dollar Quietly Invades Northeast," *Discount Store News,* December 7, 1992, pp. 4–5.

"Family Dollar Succession," *Home Textiles Today,* January 20, 2003, p. 27.

Foust, Dean, "The Family Feud at Family Dollar Stores," *Business Week,* September 21, 1987, pp. 32–33.

Greene, Richard, "The Leon and Al Show," *Forbes,* September 29, 1980, pp. 52–54.

Grover, Mary Beth, "Tornado Watch," *Forbes,* June 22, 1992, pp. 66–69.

Halverson, Richard, "Leadership at Family Dollar Moves to the Next Generation," *Discount Store News,* May 19, 1997, p. 3.

Howell, Debbie, "Family Dollar Continues Record Pace, Will Surpass 5,000 Stores," *DSN Retailing Today,* July 21, 2003, p. 1.

——, "Family Dollar Posts Record Earnings, Celebrates 40th Anniversary," *Discount Store News,* February 7, 2000, p. 5.

——, "Family Dollar to Open Ariz. Units in Slow, Steady March West," *Discount Store News,* March 8, 1999, p. 3.

Johnson, Jay L., "Face to Face with Howard Levine," *Discount Merchandiser,* December 1999, p. 11.

Keefe, Lisa, "Guess Who Lost," *Forbes,* September 7, 1987, pp. 60–61.

Lillo, Andrea, "Family Dollar Grows Sales, Stores," *Home Textiles Today,* October 16, 2000, p. 21.

Palmer, Jay, "Back to Basics," *Barron's,* August 29, 1988, pp. 20–21.

Tronell, Thomas, "Bucking a Slump," *Barron's,* January 21, 1980, pp. 39, 41.

—Carol I. Keeley
—update: Christina M. Stansell

Farley's & Sathers Candy Company, Inc.

1 Sather Plaza
Round Lake, Minnesota 56157
U.S.A.
Telephone: (507) 945-8181
Fax: (507) 945-8343
Web site: http://www.farleyandsathers.com

Private Company
Incorporated: 2002
Sales: $250 million (2003 est.)
NAIC: 311340 Nonchocolate Confectionery
Manufacturing

Farley's & Sathers Candy Company, Inc. manufactures and distributes a wide variety of non-chocolate confections and snacks. The company's headquarters is housed in a packaging and distribution center located in the small town of Round Lake, Minnesota. Of Round Lake's 450 residents, 350 are employed by the candy maker. In addition, Farley's & Sathers runs a packaging and distribution center in Chattanooga, Tennessee, and a manufacturing plant in Des Plaines, Illinois, and maintains a fleet of some 80 semitrailer trucks. The company owns or has licensed the rights to a number of well-known brands, including Chuckles, Hot Dog!, JuJyfruits, Now and Later, RainBlo, Super Bubble, and Wunderbeans. Products are sold in a variety of sizes in bags, tubs, and boxes and are also produced in variety mixes. Farley's & Sathers is privately owned by Catterton Partners, a Greenwich, Connecticut, private equity firm.

Roots of Company Date to 1800s

The Farley's and Sathers' names boasted separate legacies until the two candy companies were combined in 1996. The older of the two is Farley's, which dates back to 1870, when Gunther Farley and two brothers established the Gunther Chocolate Company in Illinois. In 1891, the business was merged with a candy company owned by a relative, creating Farley Candy Company. A third generation of the Farley family, Preston Farley, took over in 1951, when the company moved to Skokie, Illinois. Majority control passed out of the hands of the

Farley family in 1968, when it was sold to Raymond Frank Underwood, a Nebraska native who held an MBA from Harvard Business School. Underwood worked in sales management for Farley before assuming the presidency in 1962. He held that post until 1974, when he sold the business to William H. Ellis. Under the guidance of Ellis, Farley enjoyed 20 years of strong growth, concentrating on the children's confection market. In 1981, the company acquired a Chicago Peter Paul-Cadbury plant, where it made a full line of chocolate candies, a variety of candy coated peanut treats, and gummi, jell, and starch confections. Other operations were added so that by the mid-1990s Farley operated four Chicago-area manufacturing facilities, plus distribution centers located in Illinois and on the West Coast. In 1996, Ellis sold the business to Lincolnshire, Illinois-based Favorite Brands International. He took a 15 percent equity stake in Favorite Brands and stayed on for a short while to run the unit. Under his leadership, Farley had grown from annual sales of $3.8 million to more than $300 million.

At the same time, it acquired Farley, Favorite Brands also picked up Sathers Inc., founded in Round Lake in 1936 by John Sather after his grocery store burned down. He started out by bagging cookies that he bought by the trainload and sold to other grocers in southwestern Minnesota. In 1946, he was joined by his son Ken, who had just finished a stint as a bomber pilot in World War II. Ken was instrumental in the company, adding almond bark and other candies to the bagging operation and expanding distribution to five Minnesota counties. A major turning point for the company came when its sales force quit en masse over low salaries. In addition to taking orders, the salesmen were also required to deliver the products and stock the shelves. Sathers responded by contacting customers and offering a discount if they would order by phone and stock their own shelves. The response was favorable, leading to the creation of one of the first telemarketing systems in America. Another innovation, credited to Ken Sather, was the introduction of the packaged ''pegboard'' from which Sathers' bags of treats were hung. The system became an industry standard for the selling of general-line candy. By the 1960s, Sathers was selling to a territory that encompassed five states, and by 1970 the company's reach doubled in size to ten states. It was at this time that Sathers experience a major breakthrough, becoming a supplier to Kmart, which at the time was

Company Perspectives:

We are "A New Company with a Long History."

rapidly expanding across the country and was permitting local managers to make many of their own buying decisions. Ken Sather was able to convince some Kmart managers to give the pegboard candies a try, retailing at the attractive price of two bags for $1. The ploy was a success and caught the attention of Kmart's corporate headquarters. In 1972, Sathers began to distribute to Kmart on a national basis, gaining half of the retailer's national account. Sathers picked up the rest of the account in 1983 by purchasing Chattanooga, Tennessee-based Kitchen Fresh.

In the mid-1980s, Sathers became involved in manufacturing as a way to secure sources of supply. (Earlier, during the 1960s, it acquired a nut-roasting operation.) At that time, the major supermarket chain A&P closed a candy plant, opting instead to buy from outside suppliers. Re-baggers like Sathers were now in an uncertain position, fearful that their suppliers might drop them in favor of serving A&P. In what was essentially a defensive move, Sathers bought the Bayou Candy unit from New Orleans-based The American Candy Co. in 1985, followed by the 1991 acquisition of Powells Candy Co., a Hopkins, Minnesota, candy maker. Also in 1991, Sathers added a Rogers, Minnesota, packaging company. Now, Sathers was capable of producing half of its product line. By the end of 1991, with plants in five cities, the company was generating revenues in the range of $130 million a year. It remained a family-owned business until 1996 when the Sathers agreed to sell the company to Favorite Brands.

Favorite Brands Created in 1995

Favorite Brands was created in late 1995 to acquire the branded caramel, marshmallow, peanut brittle, and dinner mints business of Philip Morris subsidiary Kraft Foods. Favorite Brands was launched by private equity group Texas Pacific Group—which itself was founded in 1992 by David Bonderman, James Coulter, and William Price—along with a smaller private equity firm, InterWest Partners. Favorite Brands paid a reported $200 million for the Kraft product lines, which were no longer a good fit for Kraft. As part of the deal, Favorite brands was allowed to sell caramels under the Kraft label for two years. Because Kraft caramels was the undisputed leader in the category, Favorite Brands enjoyed some immediate success. However, the new company was overly ambitious and too eager to grow the business, despite a lack of expertise in the candy field. Favorite Brands' chief executive officer was Al Bono, formerly the CEO of Gardenia Foods and California Gold Dairy; his head of sales and marketing came from the health and beauty industry. Bono told *Crain's Chicago Business,* "Business is business, whether it's dairy or chocolate or confections or selling lamps." Bono and his management team, however, would soon learn that the candy business operated under its own peculiar set of rules.

After adding Sathers and Farley in 1996, at a total cost of $400 million, Favorite Brands over the course of the next year acquired Dae Julie Inc., an Illinois seller of candy in bulk; Kidd's, a marshmallow manufacturer; and Trolli, a gummi candy manufacturer. In a very short time, Favorite Brands became the number four candy company, with $800 million in annual sales, trailing only the likes of Hershey Foods Corp.; Mars, Incorporated; and Nestlé USA, Inc. Texas Pacific hoped to take the company public, but it became apparent that Favorite Brands rollup strategy was fundamentally flawed. For one, the company paid too much for its assets and took on too much debt. Next, the acquisitions did not fit well together—featuring different operations, different products, and different customers—thus leading to severe difficulties in integrating the operations and achieving any benefits from the company's size. Moreover, when executives from acquired companies left, Favorite Brands lost an incalculable amount of trade relations and knowledge of the candy business, which had a debilitating effect on business. Some orders were now delivered late or only partially filled, providing an opening for competitors to seize all-important shelf space.

Losing the Kraft label for caramels also hurt. Farley's Original Chewy Caramels simply lacked the same brand appeal, and competitors such as Hershey and Brach's Confection's increased their marketing efforts to gain product share. Revenues for the company fell off, dropping to $764 million in fiscal 1998. Texas Pacific brought in turnaround specialist Steven F. Kaplan, but in March 1999 Favorite Brands filed for Chapter 11 bankruptcy protection. According to its filing, the company had assets of $805 million and $699 million in debts. Management attempted to line up new financing, but Texas Pacific soon put the business up for sale. Although Brach was reported to be interested in Favorite Brands, it was Nabisco that landed the company, paying $475 million in cash.

Kraft Foods acquired the Favorite Brands division from Nabisco in 2000, thereby regaining its marshmallow and caramel lines as well as the Farley's and Sathers companies, which were overlooked and undermanaged by the huge conglomerate. In March 2002, Kraft agreed to sell the unit to Catterton Partners, a Connecticut private equity firm focused on consumer industries. It was founded in 1990 by J. Michael Chu and Frank M. Vest, Jr. Just as Texas Pacific attempted to do with Favorite Brands, Catterton hoped to use Farley's & Sathers as a rollup vehicle for neglected brands, but unlike Texas Pacific it brought in management with experience in the field. Former Nestlé and Famous Amos executive Keith Lively was hired as the company's CEO.

Hershey Brands Acquired in 2002

Farley's & Sathers wasted little time adding to its business. In May 2002, it acquired the rights to Chuckles and bought several Hershey brands that originated with Henry Heide, Inc. The best known were Gummi Bears, Jujubees, JuJyfruits, Mexican Hats, Wunderbeans, and Red Hot Dollars. Like many candy makers, Heide boasted a long history. The founder of the business, Henry Heide, was born in Germany in 1846, emigrated to New York City 20 years later, and started the Henry Heide Candy Company in 1869. He would run the business until his death in 1931, after which one of his sons, Andrew Heide, assumed control. The company first started producing Jujubes and JuJyFruits in the 1920s. Red Hot Dollars debuted

Key Dates:

1891: Farley Candy Company is established.
1936: Sathers Inc. is founded.
1996: Favorite Brands International acquires Farley & Sathers.
1999: Favorite Brands is acquired by Nabisco.
2000: Kraft Foods acquires Nabisco division.
2002: Farley's & Sathers Candy Company Inc. becomes independent.

during the Great Depression of the 1930s. The company enjoyed particular success selling its products in movie theaters and five-and-dime stores. A third generation of the Heide family, Philip Heide, joined the company in the 1960s. He would be the last family member to own the business, which he sold to Hershey in 1995.

Also in 2002, Farley's & Sathers bought the three brands of Kraft's taffy business: Mighty Bite, Intense Fruit Chews, and Now and Later. As was the case with Heide, Now and Then possessed a proud heritage, with roots that reached back to Italian immigrant Charles Cari. Cari learned to make toffee at W.F. Schrafft's & Sons in Boston and then moved to New York to launch his own candy business, concentrating on taffy products. In 1953, he sold his company to a father and son partnership, Harry and Joseph Klein, who named the enterprise Phoenix Candy Company. They enjoyed some success producing Atlantic City-style Salt-Water Taffy, peanut brittle, and Halloween candy. Because the business was too seasonal, centering on Halloween, the Kleins in 1962 decided to make a product that could be sold year-round. The result was Now and Later taffy candy bars, which proved popular enough to allow the company to enjoy steady growth over the next 15 years. (The intent of the name was to suggest to children that they could eat some of the candy now and save some for later.) In 1978, the Kleins sold out to Beatrice Foods, which five years later sold the business to Finnish company Huhtomaki Oy. In January 1986, Huhtomaki Oy merged it with Leaf, Inc., which later in the year sold off the unit to a Finnish investment firm, Korui Capital. Now known as Phoenix Confections, Inc., the Brooklyn-based company operated independently until December 1992, when Nabisco acquired it and folded the assets into its LifeSavers division. Shortly after Kraft's taffy lines were sold to Farley's & Sathers, Now and Later's Brooklyn plant was closed down.

Farley's & Sathers continued to rollup candy brands in 2003. From Hershey it bought four gum brands—Fruit Stripe, Hot Dog!, Rain-Blo, and Super Bubble—adding $30 million in annual sales. These lines were also long-time favorites. Fruit Stripe was established in the early 1960s as Fruit Stripe Zebra, part of the Beech Nut gum line. RainBlo bubble gum was created by Leaf Confectionery in 1940; featuring an unusual hollow center, it was the first gumball to have flavoring inside. RainBlo proved to be an enduring product in the ever-changing gum category. Along with several other Leaf brands, it was sold in 1967 to W.R. Grace, then was reacquired by Lead in 1983. Huhtamaki Oy acquired RainBlo when it bought Leaf in 1983. Hershey then bought Leaf in 1996. Supple Bubble was developed by the Thomas Weiner Company shortly after World War II in the 1940s. The five-cent product was a huge success, but in the face of increased competition the company brought out a one-cent version in 1948. General Mills picked up Super Bubble in 1969. The gum line was later sold to Leaf and was acquired by Hershey in the 1996 acquisition of Leaf.

In a matter of just 18 months, Farley's & Sathers had grown into a company generating a quarter of a billion dollars in annual sales and was listed as number 36 on Candy Industry's roster of Global Confectionery companies. The company's goal was both ambitious and simple: to become the largest non-chocolate candy sales and manufacturing company in America. Given that the non-chocolate market was estimated to be as large as $2 billion, Farley's & Sathers was involved in a promising business. It was also proving successful in bringing resources to develop orphan brands and squeezing out greater results than larger corporate owners had been able to achieve. The company was very likely to add more brands to its portfolio and create even greater synergies.

Principal Competitors

Hershey Food Corporation; Mars, Inc.; Nestlé S.A.

Further Reading

DePass, Dee, ''Serious Jujubes,'' *Star Tribune*, October 29, 2003, p. 1D.

Fink, Laurie, ''Sweet Success,'' *Corporate Report-Minnesota*, March 1992, p. 28.

''It's in the Bag,'' *U.S. Distribution Journal*, July 15, 1994, p. 42.

Mehegan, Sean, ''Favorite Brands' Grab Bag,'' *Brandweek*, April 14, 1997, p. 36.

Rewick, C.J., ''Uphill Battle in Candyland: How Life Soured For Favorite Brands,'' *Crain's Chicago Business*, April 12, 1999, p. 3.

Tiffany, Susan, ''Sathers Secures Nice as Manufacturer,'' *Candy Industry*, Jul 1995, p. 51.

—Ed Dinger

# FileNet Corporation

3565 Harbor Boulevard
Costa Mesa, California 92626
U.S.A.
Telephone: (714) 327-3400
Toll Free: (800) FileNet (345-3638)
Fax: (714) 327-9835
Web site: http://www.filenet.com

Public Company
Incorporated: 1982
Employees: 1,778
Sales: $364.5 million (2003)
Stock Exchanges: NASDAQ
Ticker Symbol: FILE
NAIC: 511210 Software Publishers; 334112 Computer
    Storage Device Manufacturing; 33411 Computer and
    Peripheral Equipment Manufacturing

Since the mid-1980s, FileNet Corporation has been helping paperwork-heavy enterprises efficiently track and store digitized documents. The company has reoriented itself more than once in order to stay alive amid rapid changes in technology. In its early years, FileNet pioneered the use of optical disks to store digital images of documents. Later, it changed its focus from hardware to software, marketing programs that helped companies manage the flow of documents using their existing hardware. Now FileNet refers to its services as "enterprise content management," or ECM. The company's "P8" software allows organizations to store, track, and retrieve information in almost any format, from images to spreadsheets to e-mails. FileNet's typical clients are large financial services concerns such as insurance companies and government agencies. The company has a network of offices across the United States to provide technical support and consulting services. In addition, about 25 percent of its sales are in Europe, and it has subsidiaries in Asia and Australia as well.

Developing Optical Storage Systems: 1982–91

In 1981, Ted Smith had just gotten fired from his job as president of minicomputer maker Basic Four over a policy dis-

agreement. Smith had over two decades' experience in the computer industry. After earning a bachelor's degree in aeronautical engineering in the 1950s, he had learned about electronics in the Air Force and then worked for several different technology enterprises. When his stint at Basic Four came to an end, Smith took a few months to ponder his next step. He considered running an existing company, but none of the job offers he received was sufficiently enticing. So, as he told *Forbes* in 1988, "I decided that I wanted something over the horizon."

It did not take him long to find that something. A handful of U.S. laboratories and Japanese companies were working on something called optical disk storage. Unlike the magnetic disks common at the time, which stored information by magnetizing and demagnetizing parts of the disk, optical disks had data burned into them with a laser. A 12-inch disk could hold ten times more information than the highest-density hard disks then in use. The only drawback was that they could only be written on once. Who would want to use a disk that could not be modified?

Smith knew that many companies needed to keep exact replicas of documents such as loan applications, personnel records, and tax files. These documents needed to be stored as images rather than text files so that signatures and other unique elements would be preserved. However, images files were far too large to be stored conveniently on regular computers, so companies relied either on paper files or on expensive microfilm and microfiche systems for document storage and retrieval. Since this information was not digitized, it could not be integrated with the company's computerized operations. An optical storage system had the potential to increase productivity at paperwork-intensive businesses by allowing documents to be stored and exchanged electronically.

In 1982, Smith created FileNet Corp. in Costa Mesa, California, with the goal of commercializing optical disk technology. He raised $4 million in venture capital from investors and recruited Edward Miller from Xerox as his chief engineer. However, optical storage systems were far from being ready for the marketplace. The technology was still in the development stage at laboratories, and the supporting hardware needed to be designed and built. It took a year and a half of work before a complete optical storage and retrieval system was ready for

Company Perspectives:

FileNet Corporation helps organizations make better decisions by managing the content and processes that drive their business. FileNet's Enterprise Content Management (ECM) solutions allow customers to build and sustain competitive advantage by managing content throughout their organizations, automating and streamlining their business processes, and providing the full spectrum of connectivity needed to simplify their critical and everyday decision-making.

commercialization. While the laboratories refined optical disk technology, Smith worked with his engineers to develop a large piece of hardware they called a "jukebox," which was able to stack and retrieve over 200 optical disks using a robotic arm. To provide for the digital conversion of paper documents, FileNet had a scanner custom-built in Japan. In addition, the company was the first U.S. customer for Hitachi's new desktop laser printer, which would allow clients to print a copy of the image they saw on their screen.

After investing $30 million in the venture, FileNet installed its first system at Security Pacific Bank in 1985. The sale included all the hardware, wiring, scanners, jukeboxes, and PC consoles that were needed to work with optical document images. In addition to the hardware, FileNet's "WorkFlo" software provided for interface with the optical storage system. WorkFlo eventually developed beyond a mere document-viewing interface into a structured tool for regulating the way paperwork moved through an enterprise. "Workflow" became a generic term for this concept when the rest of the software industry developed similar programs.

FileNet's 1986 sales totaled $30 million; by the end of 1987, FileNet had sold about 120 systems, priced between $500,000 and $1.5 million, to clients such as Chase Manhattan, Citibank, Merrill Lynch, and the U.S. Air Force. Several of its clients were in Europe, so FileNet launched a division to market systems there. The company went public on the NASDAQ in July 1987 and raised $25 million for business development.

In 1989, FileNet had a large contract with the State of California turn sour. The secretary of state's office had installed a $4.1 million FileNet system to keep track of commercial borrowers and the assets they pledged as collateral. However, bugs with the new system led to a two-month backlog in requests for document searches. FileNet claimed the state would have avoided problems if, as advised, it had run the new system alongside the old system for a transition period of a few months. FileNet worked with the state to restart the system but eventually defaulted on the contract when the state demanded an earlier startup date than what FileNet believed was feasible. While the company lost a few million dollars in the deal, it nevertheless retained a largely positive reputation and remained able to convince potential clients of its reliability.

By the end of the decade, competitors were challenging FileNet's early dominance in the document image-processing industry. Small startups, including EastTek Corp. in New Jersey and Plexus Computer Inc. in California, as well as giants such as Kodak, Wang Laboratories, and 3M were able to develop

their own systems as optical storage technology became more well-known. In 1988, IBM entered the market as well and captured the largest share of clients by the early 1990s. FileNet was also hurt by the fact that the corporate world was not embracing the new technology as enthusiastically as predicted. The company posted its first loss in the third quarter of 1988. Smith responded with more energetic marketing, including new territories such as Japan, and made sure the FileNet's clients were led step by step through the conversion to optical storage technology. FileNet's superior customer support and its Work-Flo software gave the company a competitive edge, and it posted a $3.8 million profit in 1990 on sales of $102.9 million.

Reorientation from Hardware to Software: 1991–97

In 1991, FileNet introduced a new version of WorkFlo that was compatible with Microsoft's Windows interface. Unlike earlier versions, the software could be used on computers that were not directly supplied by FileNet. However, customers still needed to buy the scanner manufactured by FileNet. The incompatibility of FileNet's systems with less expensive off-the-shelf hardware was becoming an increasing burden to the company. Many of FileNet's competitors offered document storage solutions that allowed clients to use their existing hardware or buy workstations and scanners from the vendor of their choice, but FileNet was still shipping full systems of proprietary hardware to its customers.

In response, FileNet shifted its focus from hardware to software in 1992. The company discontinued many of its manufacturing operations and began buying file servers from IBM. New software known as FolderView came out that year; it was more flexible than WorkFlo, allowing people with less structured work routines to sort through documents and find what they needed. FileNet's software reorientation, as well as slower orders and economic problems in Europe, led to an $8 million loss in 1992. The company was also facing a few lawsuits that claimed it had misled investors with overly optimistic predictions.

FileNet laid off about 150 of its 1000 employees in 1993 after stopping production of customized computers. The company's selling point now was software that helped establish processes for moving work through an organization. At $100,000 to $250,000 for a software package, FileNet's products were much less expensive than they had been a few years earlier. The company also began marketing through resellers instead of using only its own sales force. In 1993, software sales accounted for about half of revenue, up from 5 percent at the start of the decade. FileNet posted profits in 1993, 1994, and 1995 and started hiring again. Net revenue was up to $215.5 million in 1995.

Now that it had successfully reinvented itself as a software company, FileNet began seeking acquisitions that would enhance its product line. In 1995, it acquired Watermark Software for $61 million in stock. Watermark was a two-year-old Massachusetts-based company that made document imaging systems for smaller companies than the clients FileNet generally targeted. The next year, FileNet acquired Saros, a Seattle-based software company, and International Financial Systems Limited, a New York developer of archiving software. The acquisitions gave FileNet a broader product range without requiring extensive research and development investment.

```
┌─────────────────────────────────────────────────────┐
│                    Key Dates:                         │
│                                                       │
│ 1982:  Ted Smith founds FileNet to develop optical    │
│        disk storage technology.                       │
│ 1985:  FileNet ships its first document storage and   │
│        retrieval system.                              │
│ 1987:  FileNet goes public on the NASDAQ.             │
│ 1992:  FileNet changes its focus from hardware to     │
│        software amid declining sales.                 │
│ 1997:  Lee Roberts takes the helm at FileNet and      │
│        revamps its sales force and product line.      │
│ 2000:  FileNet reports record sales and profits as    │
│        Internet-based content management grows.       │
│ 2003:  The company introduces P8 software, a          │
│        framework for managing information in many     │
│        formats.                                       │
└─────────────────────────────────────────────────────┘
```

Nevertheless, the acquisitions turned out to be difficult to integrate. Sales teams at the various companies did not function together well, and FileNet hit another rocky period. It lost $9.4 million in the first three months of 1997, sales fell 29 percent, and the company laid off 150 of its 1,650 employees. The Watermark subsidiary was shut down, and customers were saying they found the company "slow and stodgy."

Refining Internet Capabilities under Lee Roberts: 1997–2004

Amid the turmoil, Smith recruited Lee Roberts, a former IBM executive, to take over as FileNet's president and chief operating officer starting in the summer of 1997. Roberts became chief executive a year later. One of his first efforts was to replace many of the sales executives with an ambitious new team charged with revamping the entire sales force. Roberts also adopted a new motto, "To put the right information in the hands of the right person at the right time to make the right decisions," as well as a new FileNet logo featuring a window reminiscent of Microsoft. Software development was also in need of revival, so Roberts hired about 40 new engineers. A major goal of the new generation of programs was to make it possible to query and retrieve documents over the Internet or a corporate network. Engineers were also working on something called "integrated document management." This would allow users to access both documents and images using one program instead of the two separate programs that were necessary at the time.

By the end of 1997, sales were already picking up. At the start of 1998, FileNet launched Panagon, a set of integrated document management and workflow products that provided some Internet functionality. However, in the first stumble since Roberts took over, FileNet reported a loss in the third quarter of 1998. The company laid off about 6 percent of its workforce. Nevertheless, the new products and sales team were successful over the long term. After a small profit in 1998, FileNet had profits of $19.7 million in 1999.

Internet-based management of documents was the strongest trend in 2000. The simple storage of static documents was no longer an impressive service. In the electronic age, information could be stored in dynamic paperless form. E-commerce, for example, could be conducted using electronic documents with digital signatures. Flexible content management would also help firms provide more responsive customer service. These emerging applications gave FileNet a wider market for its products. The company refined its Panagon software to work more seamlessly with the Internet and mesh with a wider variety of Microsoft programs. FileNet had a record profit in 2000 of $38.5 million on revenues of nearly $400 million. Near the end of that year, Ted Smith resigned his chairmanship to Lee Roberts.

FileNet's high-flying performance came to an end with the economic downturn of 2001. Once again, the firm was cutting employees, and it reported a net loss of $16.6 million that year. Times were tight into 2002, and the company instituted mandatory vacations around Thanksgiving and Christmas to keep costs down without cutting more employees. Still, FileNet moved ahead with product development. In April 2002, it bought eGrail Inc., a small company making software to manage content on Web sites. Sales rose slowly toward the end of 2002.

January 2003 brought FileNet's largest product launch ever. Its "P8 architecture," which had been under development for several years, integrated the three previous programs—Panagon, Acenza and Brightsphere. P8 provided a uniform framework that clients could use to access more than 200 types of content, including PowerPoint presentations, photographs, streaming video, legal forms, and word-processing documents. The software had several parts, including a business process manager, a Web content manager, a document manager, a records manager, and an image manager. Customers could buy one or all parts for a cost of about $125,000 to $500,000 and scale the program to fit their needs. FileNet expected its clients to gradually shift to the new program over the next few years. In the spring of 2003, FileNet acquired Shana Corporation, an Edmonton, Canada-based company that made software for managing electronic forms. Shana's software was integrated into the P8 architecture.

As FileNet entered 2004, it was marketing its products as a solution for legal compliance in the wake of several corporate governance scandals. By helping enterprises keep track of information, FileNet promised to make it easier to follow newer, more stringent regulations. Meanwhile, the content management industry was going through a period of consolidation. FileNet was largely steering clear of the merger game and relying on organic growth and small acquisitions. The content management field was projected to grow over the next several years. Roberts expressed confidence that FileNet would keep a step ahead of the competition and remain standing through the consolidation shakeout.

Principal Subsidiaries

FileNet Corporation Pty. Limited (Australia); FileNet GesmbH (Austria); FileNet Canada, Inc.; FileNet S.A.R.L. (France); FileNet Hong Kong Limited; FileNet Company Limited (Ireland); FileNet Italy, S.R.L.; FileNet Japan; FileNet Corporation Korea; FileNet Corporation BV (Netherlands); FileNet Poland Sp. zo.o.; FileNet Corporation (Singapore); FileNet Iberia S.L. (Spain); FileNet Sweden AB; FileNet Switzerland GmbH; FileNet Limited (United Kingdom).

Principal Competitors

IBM Corporation; Oracle Corporation; Microsoft Corporation; Documentum Corporation; OpenText Corporation; Interwoven Inc.

Further Reading

Bonasia, J., ''Big Boys Muscle into ECM Software Field,'' *Investor's Business Daily*, December 12, 2003.

Campbell, Ronald, ''FileNet Lays off 107 in Cost-Cutting Move,'' *Orange County Register*, November 20, 1998.

Farnsworth, Chris, ''FileNet, Profits Go from Dull to Dazzling,'' *Orange County Register*, July 14, 2000.

''FileNet Introduces Software Package to Broaden Its Markets,'' *Los Angeles Times*, March 10, 1992, p. 7.

Flint, Jerry, ''The Cadillac-to-Chevrolet Strategy,'' *Forbes*, June 6, 1994, p. 94.

Galvin, Andrew, ''Bursting with Anticipation: FileNet Expects Explosion of Demand for Its Content-Management Software,'' *Orange County Register*, February 2, 2003, p. 1.

Huffstutter, P.J., ''FileNet Unveils New Software Product Line,'' *Los Angeles Times*, January 14, 1998, p. 10.

Kerber, Ross, ''Profits up, FileNet Buying Software Firm to Expand Product Line,'' *Los Angeles Times*, July 19, 1995, p. 6.

Rose, Frederick, ''FileNet to Switch Strategy in Wake of 4th-Period Woes,'' *Wall Street Journal*, February 3, 1993, p. B4.

Simons, Andrew, ''FileNet Cuts Workers; Sales Inching Upward, but 2003 Looks Tough,'' *Orange County Business Journal*, November 25, 2002, p. 3.

Takahashi, Dean, ''FileNet Sales May Top $100 Million in '90 for a Record,'' *Los Angeles Times*, January 11, 1991, p. 5.

Vernon, Mark, ''Why a Successful Company Must Reinvent Itself,'' *Financial Times*, October 4, 2000, p. 16.

Vranizan, Michelle, ''FileNet's New Vision: Image-Processing Pioneer Is Regaining Its Momentum,'' *Orange County Register*, July 30, 1989.

——, ''FileNet Makes and Image Recovery,'' *Orange County Register*, July 30, 1989.

——, ''FileNet Defaults on Contract,'' *Orange County Register*, October 20, 1989.

——, ''FileNet Sued Over Allegedly Inflated Stock,'' *Orange County Register*, January 13, 1993.

Wiegner, Kathleen K., '' 'We Had No Role Models','' *Forbes*, January 25, 1988, p. 103.

Williams, Elisa, ''FileNet Announces $8 Million '92 Loss,'' *Orange County Register*, February 12, 1993.

—Sarah Ruth Lorenz

FRED'S

Fred's, Inc.

4300 New Getwell Road
Memphis, Tennessee 38118
U.S.A.
Telephone: (901) 365-8880
Fax: (901) 365-8865
Web site: http://www.fredsinc.com

Public Company
Incorporated: 1947 as Baddour, Inc.
Employees: 7,850
Sales: $1.3 billion (2003)
Stock Exchanges: NASDAQ
Ticker Symbol: FRED
NAIC: 452990 All Other General Merchandise Stores

Fred's, Inc. is a discount retailer with stores in 14 states in the southeastern United States. Typically serving small and medium-sized towns, Fred's stores offer housewares, pharmaceuticals, clothing and linens, health and beauty aids, paper and cleaning supplies, food, and tobacco products, including a wide variety of items with the proprietary Fred's label. Fred's operates approximately 500 discount general merchandise stores, including 26 franchised locations. Nearly half of its stores have full-service pharmacies, which account for nearly one-third of company revenues. The company has grown at a steady clip in recent years, buoyed by strong sales and profits.

1947–88: Founding as Baddour, Inc.

The history of Fred's, Inc. may be traced to the mid-1940s founding of Baddour, Inc. Paul Baddour and his two brothers, sons of Lebanese immigrants, started the family-owned retail business in 1947, with one "Good Luck" store in Coldwater, Mississippi. Paul incorporated the company as Baddour, Inc., but as he expanded the chain throughout the Southeast, he began naming the individual stores after one of his brothers, Fred.

Fred's stores were located in such small towns as Stamps, Arkansas, and Iuka, Mississippi, and offered mostly closeout items that could be sold at discounted prices. By 1953, there were 53 stores in operation. The company grew in its niche market, opening franchised units as well as its own new stores for nearly 20 years, until a major upheaval occurred on the discount store scene with the arrival of Sam Walton and his Wal-Mart stores. Beginning in 1962, Walton moved into rural areas, first in Arkansas and Missouri, and then across the South, opening stores that were much larger than those already serving a town and stocking a much wider variety of discount-priced merchandise.

Paul M. Baddour took over the presidency of Baddour, Inc. from his father in the early 1970s, determined to compete head-on with Wal-Mart. He built bigger stores, increasing the size of the average Fred's from 5,000 square feet to 30,000 square feet, and ordered a broader inventory of merchandise, including products with the "Fred's" label. In 1980, he created a subsidiary, Retail Consulting Services, Inc., to provide advice and services to other retailers. One of its first projects, developed originally for the rapidly growing Fred's, was an integrated inventory management system called SWORD (Store, Warehouse, Ordering, Replenishment and Distribution). Among the customers for at least certain aspects of the program were G.C. Murphy Co. and Grand Central in Salt Lake City.

By the mid-1980s, Fred's company had more than 200 locations, but the expansion had left Baddour $56 million in debt, and its banks wanted their money. At this time, the Memphis Retail Investors Limited Partnership (MRILP) entered the scene, lending Baddour, Inc. $15.3 million at an interest rate of 8.95 percent in 1986. This allowed the company to pay back its more expensive debt. In return, MRILP got the right to convert its note into 51 percent of the company's equity.

One of the major players in MRILP was Michael Hayes, who had just left Wall Street's Oppenheimer & Co., where he had been head of corporate finance. According to William Stern's article in *Forbes,* Hayes thought that with an infusion of money, Paul M. Baddour would be able to get the company back on track, and then MRILP would convert the note into shares, take the company public, and sell its equity at a big profit. Hayes, along with his partner, David Gardner, were elected to the board of directors in January 1987.

144

But things did not work out as Hayes hoped. Instead, the company lost $27 million over the next three years. MRILP went to court in Tennessee and, in the autumn of 1989, received 51 percent of the company under a court settlement. Paul M. Baddour resigned immediately, and Hayes and Gardner took over as managing directors in October, with Hayes also serving as chief executive.

1989–91: New Management and a New Name

Hayes and Gardner quickly moved to improve profitability, adopting five goals: 1) recapture traditional Fred's customers; 2) focus management, store managers, buyers, and pharmacists on profitability; 3) reduce employee turnover; 4) reduce corporate operating expenses; and 5) increase pharmacy and related products sales.

To accomplish these, Hayes revised the merchandise mix, eliminating expensive items such as microwaves and color TVs and concentrating on inexpensive household goods. He standardized store size and layout around a 13,000-square-foot model and closed several unprofitable locations. He also put into place a bonus incentive plan for all salaried employees and started a management training program. Finally, Hayes changed the company's advertising strategy, eliminating direct mail circulars, adding coupon books, and using television and radio advertising, with an actor playing the role of ''Fred'' in the television ads.

Hayes's strategy was to make the smaller size of his stores a strength by appealing to customers who wanted to buy between five and ten specific items at a competitive price, in a friendly, familiar environment. He targeted customers who were not interested in roaming a huge superstore to find things they might need, and the company made the differentiation between ''buying'' at Fred's and ''shopping'' at larger, less conveniently located stores.

The changes quickly improved Fred's financial picture. In 1990, comparable store sales rose by 6 percent, and for the first time in four years, the company earned a profit. In 1991, net income tripled to $3.8 million on sales of $291 million. Moreover, the bonus incentive and training programs helped reduce the turnover among store management personnel, from 75 percent in 1988 to less than 25 percent in 1991. For store managers alone, turnover dropped from 55 percent to less than 20 percent in the same period.

Fred's stores were typically located in a shopping center or ''strip mall'' (anchored by a high-traffic grocery store) in small to medium-sized towns. According to the 1993 *Forbes* article, Fred's could be profitable in a town with only 1,500 citizens, compared with Wal-Mart, which targeted towns with a population of 10,000 or more. Customers were generally low, middle, and fixed income families.

Fred's stores offered some 12,000 items, primarily merchandise that people purchased frequently. Stores with pharmacies stocked an additional 600 items. By 1991, the 45 in-store pharmacies accounted for 12.1 percent of store sales, up from 7.2 percent in 1988.

Fred's discount prices were typically lower than those at drug or smaller variety/dollar stores. In 1991, household goods made up slightly more than a quarter of store sales, followed by health and beauty aids (17.5 percent), apparel and linens (17 percent), paper and cleaning supplies (15.2 percent), pharmaceuticals (12.1 percent), and food and tobacco products (11.4 percent). The company's private-label products included pet foods, disposable diapers, paper products, beverages, household cleaning supplies, and health and beauty aids. In 1991, these products constituted about 4 percent of total sales.

In May 1991, Hayes was named company president, and the shareholders voted to change the company name from Baddour, Inc. to Fred's, Inc. The change, according to the company prospectus, reflected the company's focus on its store operations and away from the family name of the founders and former management.

1992–95: Emphasizing Pharmacies

In 1992, Hayes took the company public, selling 39 percent of the shares for $52 million and using proceeds to pay off most of the bank debt. At the time, Fred's operated in eight states and had 144 company-owned stores and 43 franchise stores.

During the year, Hayes opened 12 new stores, reaching 156 company-owned locations, while the number of franchised stores dropped to 39. As a result, in both 1991 and 1992, wholesale sales to franchisees and others declined as a percentage of total sales. Hayes also added pharmacies in 15 stores, bringing the total to 60. At the end of the fiscal year, the company, which was now operating in nine states, paid its first quarterly cash dividend, $.04 per share.

In 1993, Hayes began exploring the possibilities of significantly increasing the company's size. In March, the company announced plans to buy Bill's Dollar Stores. Bill's, a privately held discount retailer based in Jackson, Mississippi, had 530 stores in 13 southern states. If the two chains had joined, they would have had total sales of more than $540, but the merger did not happen. Three years later, on March 1, 1996, the company announced that it had reached an agreement in principle to merge with Rose's Stores, Inc. But the acquisition of Rose's, which had 105 retail stores in 10 southeastern states, was canceled later that year.

Although Fred's management had concluded that merging with these other discount store chains would not be as beneficial as originally anticipated, the company did acquire a drug store chain. In 1995, Fred's paid Southern Wholesale Co. $3 million in cash for 18 Super D stores in Alabama, Georgia, North Carolina, and Tennessee. The company also acquired one independent pharmacy that year. Five of the purchases were established as stand-alone Fred's Xpress pharmacies. That concept, with locations ranging in size from 1,000 to 6,000 square feet and selling pharmaceuticals and other health and beauty items, allowed Fred's to enter a new market less expensively than if it

Key Dates:

1947: Paul Baddour and his two brothers start a family-owned retail business.
1953: By now, there are 53 stores in operation.
1980: Subsidiary Retail Consulting Services Inc. is created to provide advice and services to other retailers.
1986: Memphis Retail Investors L.P. lends Baddour $15.3 million in exchange for 51 percent of the company's equity.
1989: After several money-losing years, Paul M. Baddour resigns from the company.
1991: Under Michael Hayes's leadership, the company changes its name to Fred's Inc.
1992: Fred's goes public.
1995: Fred's acquires 18 Super D stores in Alabama, Georgia, North Carolina, and Tennessee.
2000: Fred's operates 320 stores.
2003: Sales surpass $1 billion.

were to open a new store. The company's plan was to expand these locations into a full-size Fred's when business warranted. At the end of 1995, in addition to the five Fred's Xpress units, the company had 87 stores with full-service pharmacies.

Prescriptions and other pharmacy products were an increasingly important part of Fred's merchandise mix. In 1995, pharmaceuticals accounted for nearly 18 percent of sales, the second largest sales category, behind household goods. This performance occurred amid the growth in alternative sources for prescriptions resulting from the managed care movement. Third-party firms, such as health maintenance organizations, hospitals, and mail-order houses, paid 70 percent of all prescription drug bills in 1995, up from four percent in 1960.

As more employers shifted their employees' health coverage to managed care or health maintenance organizations, pharmacies and drugstore chains were under great pressure. That pressure led to consolidation in the drugstore business and helped Fred's strategy of expanding its pharmacy activities by acquiring established independent pharmacies. The company either employed the pharmacists whose operation the company bought or purchased customer lists from retiring independent pharmacists.

The Mid-1990s and Beyond

Fred's continued to increase the number of pharmacies in its stores, reaching 101 by the end of 1996, more than double the number of pharmacies there had been five years before. The importance of this segment of products to the company was reflected in its portion of sales, which reached nearly 20 percent in 1996. The company also implemented a new pharmacy management system that provided centralized control of its chain of pharmacies.

Still, the company was not ignoring its other merchandise categories. It expanded its selection of garden supplies and established lawn and garden centers. By 1996, 89 of the stores had such centers, and 26 were full-line centers complete with greenhouses, a wide selection of garden equipment and tools, and live plants. During the year, Fred's also introduced moder-

ately priced videos and pre-paid telephone calling cards as well as new items with the Fred's label.

During this period, the company restructured its management ranks and revised its pricing strategy, introducing everyday low prices in 1994. The process involved reducing prices for many key items and eliminating four sale events in 1995 and two in 1996. Initially, this resulted in a significant drop in net income in 1995. But by 1996, customers began to shop at Fred's more regularly, not just during sale events. Although the average customer in 1996 spent 10 cents less each time she shopped at Fred's ($11.15), there were one million more customer transactions (34 million) than there were in 1995.

The year 1997 proved to be a very good one for the company, with record sales and growth. Sales for the year increased 17.7 percent to $492.2 million, up from $418.3 in 1996. Sales in stores that had been operating for at least 12 months rose 8.3 percent from the prior year. In November, Fred's bought 17 drugstores from CVS Corporation, expanding the company's presence in Georgia, Mississippi, and Tennessee and continuing its growing presence in the pharmacy business. That presence was further enhanced when Hayes announced in February 1998 that Fred's had opened a mail-order pharmacy facility and had signed its first national contract with participants in all 50 states.

As the new millennium approached, Fred's good fortune began to change. In 1998, the company experienced problems with its new distribution system. As a result, its inventories fell short and sales began to suffer. By May 1999, stock price had fallen from $27 per share to a mere $9. As a possible bankruptcy loomed in the distance, Hayes tapped John Reier to orchestrate a turnaround. Reier, a retail industry veteran, took over as president and immediately set plans in motion to get the company back on track. He began to examine the company's merchandise mix, making sure the stores were well stocked with their best-selling items, while products that did not sell well were eliminated from inventory. Store manager jobs were simplified, pricing was revamped, and products were added to Fred's private-label line. Overall, Reier implemented swift changes that appeared to pay off. In fiscal 2000 the company secured record sales, which had grown by 15 percent over the previous year to $781.3 million.

With Hayes and Reier leading Fred's management team, the company enjoyed success in the new decade. In 2001, the company launched a share offering designed to fund store and pharmacy growth, which it pursued steadily over the next several years. Since the late 1990s, sales from its pharmaceutical operations had been climbing by nearly 30 percent each year and had come to account for nearly one-third of the company's total revenue. As such, approximately half of its stores were equipped with pharmacies and the firm planned to include pharmaceutical services in all of its new stores.

In 2003, sales surpassed $1 billion. Company stores, which averaged 16,000 square feet, continued to pop up in the South as Fred's stepped up its expansion plans. The firm opened its second distribution center in Dublin, Georgia, signaling its commitment to strengthen its foothold in Georgia and the surrounding states. Hayes confirmed this in a September 2003 *Investor's Business Daily* article, claiming, "We haven't even begun to saturate the U.S. market."

Meanwhile, negative publicity began to surround Fred's when it became entangled in a battle with workers at its Memphis distribution facility who were attempting to unionize. During 2003, the company came under fire for claims of unfair labor practices as well as for importing goods from Myanmar, a country known for violating human rights. Despite the bad press, Fred's was well positioned for future growth as sales and income continued their upward climb. While many industry observers believed the company's good fortune would tumble as the economy strengthened, Hayes disagreed. In the aforementioned article, the CEO and chairman reported, "Customers in the shaky economy have become more aware of value. Once they get into a value store, they don't want to go back."

Principal Subsidiaries

Fred's Stores of Tennessee, Inc.; Fred's Capital Management Company, Inc.; Fred's Equipment Management and Leasing, Inc.; Fred's Capital Finance, Inc.; Insurance Value Protection Group, LTD.

Principal Competitors

Dollar General Corporation; Walgreen Co.; Wal-Mart Stores, Inc.

Further Reading

Alva, Marilyn, "This Discount Retailer Is Whistling Dixie All the Way to the Bank," *Investor's Business Daily,* September 16, 2003, p. A9.

"At Baddour: How Fred's Is Flourishing with Its SWORD," *Stores,* March 1983, p. 56.

Duff, Mike, "Fred's Nears $1bil. Mark," *DSN Retailing Today,* March 25, 2002, p. 3.

"Fred's Reports Record Sales for Fiscal 2000," *Memphis Business Journal,* February 16, 2001, p. 20.

Lee, Georgia, "UNITE Attacks Fred's Citing Labor Practices," *WWD,* June 19, 2003, p. 17.

Lofton, Dewanna, "Memphis, Tenn.-Based Discount Chain's New President to Lead Turnaround," *Knight Ridder/Tribune Business News,* June 16, 1999.

Robertshaw, Nicky, "Shifting Strategy Paid Off; Changes at Fred's Results in Dividends," *Memphis Business Journal,* June 9, 1997, p. 1.

Stern, William, "From Wall Street to Nowhere Street," *Forbes,* November 8, 1993, p. 116.

Troy, Mike, "Niche Players Prove Viable in Shadow of Mega-Retailers," *DSN Retailing Today,* January 1, 2001, p. 1.

—Ellen D. Wernick
—update: Christina M. Stansell

Funai Electric Company Ltd.

7-7-1 Nakagaito Daito City
Osaka 574-0013
Japan
Telephone: (+81) 72-870-4303
Fax: (+81) 72-871-1112
Web site: http://www.funai.co.jp

Public Company
Incorporated: 1961
Employees: 18,343
Sales: ¥280.44 billion ($2.77 billion)(2003)
Stock Exchanges: Tokyo
Ticker Symbol: 6839
NAIC: 423620 Electrical and Electronic Appliance,
    Television, and Radio Set Merchant Wholesalers;
    423420 Office Equipment Merchant Wholesalers;
    423430 Computer and Computer Peripheral
    Equipment and Software Merchant Wholesalers;
    423690 Other Electronic Parts and Equipment
    Merchant Wholesalers

Funai Electric Company Ltd. is the unsung hero of the global electronics industry. The Osaka, Japan-based company is the world's leading manufacturer of VCRs and TV/VCR combos and holds a leading position in a number of other key electronics segments, including DVD players, computer printers, and telephones and fax machines. Funai also produces large-screen LCD-based televisions, projectors, and DVD-RW and CD-RW devices, among other products. While the company distributes many of its products under the Funai brand name, a major share of its sales have long come under its brand names, which include Sylvania, Emerson, and Symphonic brands. Yet the company, one of the few fully integrated operations capable of producing nearly all of the parts and components of its products in-house, is also one of the world's leading original equipment manufacturers (OEM) in its product sectors. As such, Funai produces part or all of products sold by Toshiba, Hitachi, Matsushita, Mitsumi, Murata, Alps, Kaga, Rohm, Nichican, Philips, and Lexicon. Funai operates several manu-

facturing plants in China, as well as facilities in Malaysia and Thailand. The company also operates a number of sales and marketing subsidiaries, including the U.S.-based Funai Corporation. At the turn of the 21st century, the company has made a special target of the mass-market retail channel and has become an important supplier to the Wal-Mart chain. Funai has also begun shifting its product line away from analog technologies to focus its future product development on the digital market. Listed on the Tokyo Stock Exchange, Funai Electric continues to be led by founder Tetsuro Funai.

Pioneering the Consumer Transistor Market in the 1960s

Tetsuro Funai grew up in Kobe, Japan, the son of a manufacturer of sewing machines. At the age of 18, Funai left school and went to work as an apprentice at a rival sewing machine maker before rejoining the family firm in the early 1950s. While one of Funai's brothers led that company, Funai himself went to work as a salesman for the company. That position brought Funai into contact with the United States, as the company began supplying machines for the U.S. retail market.

Funai struck out on his own at the end of the 1950s. By then, the introduction of a new technology, the transistor, had begun to change the face of the electronics market. Funai quickly recognized the importance the transistor would play in developing a whole new home appliance sector and in 1961 founded his own company, Funai Electric Company, based in Osaka City, to begin manufacturing products based on transistor technology. Funai's first products were transistor radios.

From the start, Funai avoided a direct entry into the branded product market, preferring to produce as an OEM supplier before later developing a series of brand names. With Japan's economy still recovering from the devastation of World War II and the heavy reparations of its aftermath, Funai's sales were targeted exclusively at the U.S. market.

As an early entrant, Funai quickly gained a key share of the market and by 1964 opened its second manufacturing plant in Fukayusa-gun (later Fukuyama). The new facility enabled Funai to extend its product range to include popular consumer

Company Perspectives:

The digital revolution continues throughout the world, and in the years ahead we will continue to promote the digital sector and work to attain a secure position for the Funai Group in the global marketplace. The Funai Group will continue to work together to maximize corporate value. We earnestly seek the support and understanding of our shareholders in this ongoing effort.

devices as eight-track tape players. By the end of the decade, the company had established two more manufacturing subsidiaries, Nakagawa Electronics Company, in Naka-gun, in 1968, and Okayama Funai Electric Company, in Tsuyama, in 1969.

Funai's growth slowed however in 1970, as Tetsuro Funai explained to *Forbes*, "when the work force got infiltrated by Communists." Labor unrest caused by the Communist-inspired labor union forced Funai to end investment in new manufacturing facilities in Japan. Funai continued to seek additional product categories, including a early version of the video recorder in the early 1970s. Yet the company had lost its momentum during a period that saw the rise of Japan's giant electronics manufacturers, including Sony, Toshiba, and Matsushita.

The growth of these groups forced increasing numbers of Japan's smaller electronic makers out of business. Another factor in the transformation of the Japanese appliance sector was the appearance of new retail models. In the past, Japanese appliance sales were typically made through small vendors, which tended to stock a single brand. However, a new form of larger, multi-branded retail appliance store had begun to appear offering lower prices and wider choices. Companies that had relied on small vendors quickly found themselves squeezed out of the market as cheaper imports from Korea and elsewhere began to appear on Japanese store shelves.

Funai's manufacturing expertise and its focus on export sales enabled the group to survive in the increasingly competitive market. By controlling its own manufacturing—rather than outsourcing for parts and components as did its larger competitors—Funai matched the major groups' market clout with greater responsiveness to its customers' needs. This enabled the company to enter a number of key markets in the early 1980s, especially, the new market for video-cassette recorders. An early entrant, Funai quickly became one of the largest suppliers of VCR systems in the 1980s.

The company had also begun exploring other markets, adding a European manufacturing and sales subsidiary in 1980. Funai quickly became a major OEM producer of appliances for the major European brands. The export market remained the company's sole focus into the mid-1980s. At the same time, the company continued to turn its product development and manufacturing muscle to new products, and, in 1984, made its first preparations for entering the domestic appliance market, registering a new subsidiary, Tokyo Funai Company, later named Funai Sales Company. The company then began developing an entirely new product—an automatic bread baker. Launched in 1987, the Rakuraku Panda, as the machine was called, became

one of the year's most success consumer appliance launches, selling more than 100,000 units in its first year alone.

While the bread-making machine quickly inspired competing models, Funai swiftly capitalized on its new name recognition in its home country, bringing to Japan its line of VCRs and other products, which included microwave ovens, telephones, fax machines, satellite antennas, and set-top boxes. By 1988, with domestic sales now representing 10 percent of the group's total—up from zero the year before—Funai began plans to launch a wider array of 30 new products, nearly all of which were specially developed for the Japanese market. In this endeavor, the company was helped by the Japanese consumer's growing passion for all things electronic.

International Manufacturing Group in the 1990s and Beyond

At the end of 1988, the company's sales had reached $103 million. Two years later, the company had already begun projecting sales of more than $250 million, as consumer demand for its core products, especially videocassette recorders, swelled at the end of the decade. By then, Funai had found a solution to its labor problems. In 1989, the company established its first foreign manufacturing subsidiary, Funai Electric Malaysia, taking advantage of that country's lower labor costs.

While Funai's larger competitors clung to the Japanese labor market, Funai turned more and more to the foreign market for its manufacturing needs in the 1990s. The liberalization of the Chinese economy presented a particularly strong opportunity, and in the early years of the 1990s Funai began construction on its first factories in China in order to take advantage of that country's vast labor pool and extremely low wages. In 1992, the company established a new subsidiary, Highsonic Industrial Ltd., in Hong Kong to provide management oversight for the group's mainland production facilities. The first of these began operations in April 1992 in Dong Guan, in the Guand Dong province. By December of that year, the group's second Chinese plant opened, in Chang Ping. Moving closer to its core American market, the company also opened a manufacturing base in Mexico. In 1994, the company added its third Chinese plant, in Zhong Shan, also in Guand Dong province.

Funai not only pioneered the use of foreign manufacturing resources among Japanese companies, it also instituted highly efficient manufacturing techniques, including a Toyota-inspired just-in-time delivery system. These moves helped the company control its costs and thereby maintain a low pricing policy. The company's low prices helped attract a growing number of discount retailers, such as the United States' Sam's Club, which turned to Funai for its VCRs in 1990.

In the meantime, Funai's product offering continued to grow through the 1990s, particularly with the group's entry into OEM manufacturing of notebook and desktop computer systems. The company's computer market focus then came to bear on the printer market, and by the end of the 1990s Funai had become one of the world's leading manufacturers of OEM printer systems.

VCRs nevertheless remained the group's core product into the next decade. By the 2000s, Funai was responsible for producing as much as 30 percent of the VCRs sold around the

Key Dates:

1961: Tetsuro Funai sets up Funai Electric Company in Osaka, Japan and begins manufacturing transistor radios.

1964: Funai opens a second manufacturing plant in Fukayama.

1968: The company opens a factory in Naka-gun.

1969: A fourth factory is opened in Tsuyama.

1980: The company launches a sales and manufacturing subsidiary in Germany.

1987: The company launches the Rakuraku Panda bread machine in Japan, marking its entry into the domestic market.

1991: A U.S. sales subsidiary is established in New Jersey.

1992: The company opens its first two manufacturing plants on the Chinese mainland.

1999: Funai goes public on the Osaka Stock Exchange, switching to the Tokyo exchange soon thereafter.

2002: Funai becomes a strategic vendor for Wal-Mart's home electronics section.

world. Part of the reason for the group's dominance of the sector was the increasing willingness of major appliance groups to abandon manufacturing of certain products in favor of OEMs like Funai. In this way, the company picked up a new major customer, Philips Electronics, which turned over its Electrovoice and Philips brands to the company. The United States market, supported by a dedicated U.S. sales subsidiary established in 1991, remained the group's core market, especially for its VCR and growing television/VCR combo set sales marketed under the Sylvania and Symphonic brands. Since the late 1980s, however, Funai had begun developing a higher-end line of appliances for the U.S. market which were sold directly under its own name.

Tetsuro Funai, who turned 70 in the late 1990s, continued to lead the company's day-to-day operations into the new century. In 1999, Funai began preparing for his succession, taking the company public on the Osaka Stock Exchange. The following year, the group's listing was moved to the Tokyo main board. Funai then took his place among Japan's electronic tycoons, as the company he had founded became valued at more than $3 billion.

While Funai's growth was based on analog technology, the company recognized the growing importance of new digital technologies, particularly DVD players and recorders. Thus, the company began developing its competence in digitally based appliances, with a special interest in LCD-based televisions, projectors, and DVD players. By 2002, the company had begun to shift its product mix ahead of a future exit from analog technologies altogether.

Funai also began adapting its supply model as well, extending its focus from the specialized retail appliance channel to broader mass-market retailers. Funai had recognized that the retail market had begun to change in the late 1990s, particularly with the emergence of a smaller number of dominant retailers as exemplified by Wal-Mart. In the late 1990s, Funai succeeded in gaining a placement on Wal-Mart's shelves, but only twice per year.

In 1999, however, Wal-Mart asked Funai if it could deliver one million VCRs in time for a Wal-Mart "Early Bird" promotion. Funai did and bought the Emerson brand name—Emerson itself had gone out of business in 1993—to place on the VCRs. The promotion was a success, with Wal-Mart selling out all one million VCRs in just a matter of hours. That success helped Funai, and, after helping to redevelop Wal-Mart's home electronics department in 2000, the company was named one of Wal-Mart's strategic vendors for six of its products—including its VCRs, televisions, and DVD players—in 2002.

Funai continued adding new products in the new century, forming a partnership, in 2001, with Ricoh to develop and produce a new range of CD-RW and DVD-RW devices. In 2003, the group decided to expand its production of large-screen, LCD-based screens, setting up its first manufacturing subsidiary in Thailand. The new facility was already operational by the end of that year, with its capacity expected to reach 150,000 units per month. Funai's proven record of flexibility and production expertise made it one of the lasting fixtures in the global home appliance industry.

Principal Subsidiaries

Chugoku Funai Electric Company, Ltd.; Funai Electric(H.K) Ltd. Hong(Kong); Zhong Yue Highsonic Electron Company (China); Dong Guan Highsonic Electronic Products Company (China); Dong Guan Jia Xiang Highsonic Electronic Company(China); H.F.T. Industrial Ltd. (Hong Kong); Dong Guan Highsonic Electron Company (Hong Kong); Funai Electric (Malaysia) Sdn. Bhd.; Funai Electric (Europe) GmbH (Germany); Funai Mexico, S.A. De C.V.; Funai Sales Company Ltd. (Japan); F. Enterprise Company Ltd. (Japan); Funai Corporation, Inc. (United States); Funai Electric Trading (Europe) GmbH (Germany); Funai Asia Pte. Ltd. (Singapore); Funai Electric Research Institute Company Ltd. (Japan).

Principal Competitors

Siemens AG; Hyundai Corporation; Electrolux AB; Hitachi High-Technologies Corporation; Pioneer Corporation; Sony Corporation; Sharp Corporation; Sanyo Electric Shekou Ltd.; Samsung Corporation; Thomson S.A.

Further Reading

Fulford, Benjamin, "Japan's Last Electronics Tycoon," *Forbes*, July 3, 2000, p. 166.

"Funai Electric to Make Televisions in Thailand," *Knight Ridder/Tribune Business News*, September 5, 2003.

"Funai Electric to Set up R&D Centre," *RDSL Asia/Africa*, November 6, 2002.

Greenberg, Manning, and Inaba, Minoru, "Funai's Determined Approach," *HFD*, November 26, 1990, p. 6.

Greenberg, Manning, "Funai's Suwa: Street-smart," *HFD*, September 21, 1992, p. 155.

—M.L. Cohen

Future Shop Ltd.

8800 Glenlyon Parkway
Burnaby, British Columbia V5J 5K3
Canada
Telephone: (604) 435-8223
Fax: (604) 412-5237
Web site: http://www.futureshop.ca

Wholly Owned Subsidiary of Best Buy Company Inc.
Incorporated: 1983
Employees: 7,100
Sales: $1.3 billion (2002)
NAIC: 443112 Radio, Television, and Other Electronics
    Stores

Future Shop Ltd. is Canada's largest retailer of consumer electronics, with more than 100 superstores selling computers, televisions, home audio equipment, home office equipment, major appliances, and cellular phones. In 2001 the company was purchased by American retailer Best Buy, which has maintained the Future Shop brand with great success.

Founding and Early Success: 1982–93

Future Shop was founded in 1982 by Iranian entrepreneur Hassan Khosrowshahi, who left Iran to settle in Vancouver. Khosrowshahi, who had graduated from the University of Tehran with a degree in law and economics, was a member of the family that owned the Minoo Industrial Group, a large Iranian manufacturer of pharmaceuticals, cosmetics, and food products. Described by industry observers as "driven," Khosrowshahi recognized the potential of consumer electronics and set out to create a chain that would dominate the Canadian market. His longtime associate Mohammad Kiabakhsh took on the role of president and CEO of the company, while Khosrowshahi himself served as chairman.

By the end of 1983 Future Shop had opened three retail outlets in British Columbia selling computers, software, games, videocassette recorders, audio equipment, and other items. Two of these emulated the superstore concept popularized in the United States, carrying a huge range of products and stacking boxes of merchandise in a warehouse atmosphere. Brand names including Panasonic, Atari, Sanyo, Mitsubishi, and RCA provided customers with enough choices to discourage comparison shopping elsewhere. The company discounted its products heavily and spent aggressively on advertising. As Marketing Director Bill Jamieson told the *Vancouver Sun,* "We spend, in proportion to sales, double what our nearest competitor does. And the reason we do that is because the market is growing so fast and we're out to grab market share." He added: "We will not be undersold."

In December 1983, the first month that all three stores were in operation, Future Shop's revenues reached $2.8 million. Ten years later, Future Shop was Canada's largest retailer of computers and consumer electronics, with 38 stores and revenues of $334 million—in the midst of an economic recession that had devastated other retailers. Sales per square foot surpassed $1,000, considered exceptional by industry analysts, and net earnings reached $5 million.

Going Public in 1993

In August 1993 Future Shop went public on the Toronto Stock Exchange, raising $30 million (at $11.25 per share) to be used for expansion and to pay down long-term debt. Khosrowshahi—who was extremely media-shy and refused interviews—maintained a controlling interest. Sales boomed, with six-month revenues up 65 percent over the previous year. Only two months after its initial public offering, Future Shop's share price had doubled to $22, and the company forecast sales of $500 million for fiscal 1994.

In the fiercely competitive field of electronics retailing, Future Shop had a principal Canadian rival in A&B Sound. Both chains purchased in volume at low prices, offered deep discounts (sometimes below cost), and advertised aggressively in a competition that frequently turned ugly. A&B disputed Future Shop's claim that it offered "Canada's lowest prices," running an ad that featured a man with a six-inch Pinocchio nose and the headline "We'd like to point out a few things about Future Shop." Future Shop sued to protect its good name, and A&B countersued in an attempt to end the advertising claims. The feud dragged on for several years, as A&B alleged

Company Perspectives:

As part of its overall strategy, Future Shop offers its products at the lowest price in Canada . . . provides customers with a well-trained sales staff; generates and maintains a high level of consumer awareness through extensive advertising and frequent promotional sales events; offers a full-service, discount style store format, featuring easy to locate display groupings and a wide selection of name brand products; offers a wide range of price points in each product category, with the greatest selection in moderately priced products; offers customers both manufacturers' and extended warranty protection for most of its products and after sales service at over 250 locations throughout Canada; controls operating and overhead costs in various ways, including through the use of fully integrated point-of-sale and advanced management information systems; and cooperates with its suppliers in various initiatives to generate greater sales.

that Future Shop employees bought out A&B's loss-leader stock during sales, wasted their employees' time, and otherwise sought to disrupt business—and Future Shop threw the same allegations back at A&B. In an out-of-court settlement, Future Shop ultimately amended its low-price claim (offering a guarantee that it would match any competitor's price), while A&B agreed to stop running the Pinocchio ad. Both parties agreed that disruptive practices would cease.

Financial Challenges in the Mid-1990s

Commentators noted that the fierce competition between the two chains and other rivals hinged on the issue of volume purchasing, and that the chain that expanded the fastest would be able to secure the best deals on merchandise, offer the lowest prices, and ensure further growth. Profit margins were slim across the industry, and retailers bolstered their bottom lines by selling such higher-margin services as extended warranties and credit plans. By 1995 Future Shop's sales had reached the $1 billion mark, but increases were attributable solely to aggressive expansion, while sales at the chain's established stores began to plateau and even decline. The *Globe & Mail* wrote that Future Shop, "appears to have hit a brick wall." Future Shop's share price dropped to $16.

Analysts predicted that the coming of Incredible Universe megastores to Toronto would provide stiff competition and further impede sales at Future Shop. Analyst John Williams told the *Globe & Mail,* "This industry is brutally competitive, and this certainly raises the bar at least another notch," while analyst George Hartman voiced concern that Future Shop was "intent on the all-out pursuit of market share, sometimes at the expense" of profit. By 1996, Future Shop shares had dropped to $11.37 and analysts began removing their "buy" recommendations. The drop was attributed to a drop in demand for personal computers, declining overall sales at the chain's stores, and strong competition from U.S. retailers like Circuit City Stores. At the same time, Future Shop was expanding aggressively into the northwestern United States, opening eight stores in 1996 (for a total of 22) and laying plans for 15 more in the next few years.

Early in 1997 Future Shop announced a change in upper management, with Mohammad Kiabakhsh leaving the company. Khosrowshahi took on the roles of president and CEO in addition to serving as chairman. A number of other management executives were dismissed shortly afterward. "The intent is to evolve into a more professionally managed organization," said CFO Gary Patterson.

Future Shop began to show signs of a rebound. At the end of the fiscal year in March, Future Shop's Canadian operations had produced record sales and earnings; however, the company's net earnings were down 20 percent from the previous year, in part due to losses suffered by its U.S. outlets. Patterson announced that Future Shop would not expand further in the United States until the existing U.S. stores improved their performance, but that Future Shop would open 25 to 40 new stores in Canada.

Focus on Core Markets in the Late 1990s

In 1998 Future shop purchased seven Computer City stores for an undisclosed amount, only three months after the entire Computer City franchise had been purchased by CompUSA from Tandy Corporation. Within 18 months two of the outlets—deemed hopelessly unprofitable—had been shuttered. South of the border, the U.S. arm of Future Shop was suffering, with $53 million in losses over two years, and another $30 million in losses projected for 1999. In March 1999 the company announced that it would discontinue U.S. operations, leaving it with 81 stores in Canada. Analysts applauded the move, maintaining that Future Shop was wise to concentrate on its core market. Phil Boname told the *Vancouver Sun* that the divestiture would make Future Shop "lean and mean." He added: "Other retailers are going to have a real tiger to contend with as the company tries to make up for lost U.S. business at home." Future Shop's share price jumped on the news, to $14.50.

By 2000, Future Shop owned 83 Future Shop stores and five Computer City outlets. In January Kevin Layden, COO, was appointed president and CEO, and in June Future Shop announced plans to open flagship stores in downtown Vancouver, Toronto, and Montreal. Patterson told the *Vancouver Sun:* "Vancouver, Toronto and Montreal are all vibrant, downtown cities with large populations living in the downtown area. We always felt we could better serve those downtown cores, so we decided to take this step."

At the end of the fiscal year in March, Future Shop reported net earnings of $23.7 million, realizing a strong recovery from the $82.2 million loss the previous year. CEO Kevin Layden attributed the improvement to a new focus on Canadian markets, store renovations, and a booming retail market with strong demand for digital products. Future Shop's most popular products included digital cameras, DVD players, and wireless Internet devices. When U.S. giant Best Buy Company Inc. announced its intention to move into Canada, analysts predicted a huge battle for market share. "Future Shop has basically had something of a monopoly on these kinds of stores until now, but that is going to change," said retail consultant Blake Hudema in an interview with the *Vancouver Sun.* Future Shop claimed to welcome Best Buy, maintaining that competition would serve a positive purpose by expanding the market for consumer elec-

Key Dates:

1982: Future Shop is launched in Vancouver, B.C.
1993: The company goes public.
1998: Computer City stores are acquired.
1999: Future Shop's U.S. stores are closed.
2001: Future Shop is acquired by Best Buy.

tronics. Said Layden to the *Sun,* "We see being face to face with a national player on a big scale as a good thing." Nevertheless, in December Future Shop sued Best Buy for stealing trade secrets by hiring away a Future Shop senior executive and the company's real estate brokerage firm. Future Shop sought an injunction to prevent the broker, Northwest Atlantic, from working for Best Buy. The courts, however, held that Future Shop was unable to prove that a breach of confidence had occurred.

2001 and Beyond

In February 2001 Future Shop announced the closing of its five remaining Computer City stores, noting that the increasingly competitive retail market for computer equipment had taken its toll on profit margins. The company took a $4 million charge against earnings, which was more than offset by a $7.8 million fee received following an unsuccessful bid to take over the Chapters Inc. bookstore chain. Future Shop accelerated its expansion plans, aiming for 120 stores by 2005, and announced plans to relocate or completely renovate at least half of its existing stores during this period. The average Future Shop store was 27,000 square feet, but the chain operated four distinct store sizes from 18,000 to 32,000 square feet depending on the location.

By March 2001, Future Shop had posted double digit sales growth for 15 consecutive months and was exuding confidence it could face down any competition from Best Buy. Instead, the two chains announced in September that Best Buy had agreed to purchase Future Shop, for $387 million in cash. The company was to be run as a wholly owned subsidiary, and while Khosrowshahi would step down, Layden and other executives would remain in place. Best Buy COO Brad Anderson noted the value of the "added human capital," stating that the knowledgeable management team would be an asset both in Canada and as the chain expanded globally. The initial takeover plan stipulated that Future Shop would eventually take on the name of its larger parent; however, as time passed, Best Buy concluded that continuing to operate Future Shop as a distinct brand would the most profitable course. Tom Healey, president of Best Buy International, said, "The customers love Future Shop. Shutting it down would be a loss of brand equity." Furthermore, noted Layden, fewer than half of Future Shop stores were large enough to justify the cost of converting them to the Best Buy format, which was estimated at $3.5 million per store. He added, "We believe there is room in the market for two national players." The two brands set a goal of commanding 30 to 35 percent of the Canadian market for consumer electronics. The goal did not seem unreasonable, as sales for Future Shop alone had surpassed $2 billion.

Principal Competitors

Sears Canada Inc.; InterTAN, Inc.; Amazon.com Inc.; Staples, Inc.

Further Reading

Aarsteinsen, Barbara, "Future Shop Withdrawal from US Draws Raves from Analysts, Investors," *Sun,* March 11, 1999, p. F6.

Allard, Christian, "My Price Is Lower than Your Price," *BC Business,* December 1994, p. 38.

Berner, Robert, "Best Buy? Maybe Not for Investors," *Business Week,* November 11, 2002, p. 122.

"Category-Killer Shop's Low Prices Sock It to Competition," *Province,* November 8, 1992, p. 39.

Constantineau, Bruce, "Future Shop Launches Legal Battle Against US Retail Giant," *Sun,* December 15, 2000, p. C9.

——, "Future Shop Plans to Close Five Weakest Stores in US," *Sun,* September 11, 1998.

——, "Future Shop Records 20% Dip in Earnings," *Sun,* May 28, 1988.

——, "Future Shop's Restructuring, Exit from US Paying Off," *Sun,* November 13, 1999.

Gayle, Marlaina, "Pinocchio's Nose Sparks Court Fight," *Province,* January 7, 1994, p. 49.

Greenberg, Manning, "Canada's Future Shop Heads South to Grow," *HFD—The Home Furnishings Newspaper,* September 20, 1993, p. 94.

Heller, Laura, "Future Shop Accelerates Growth," *DSN Retailing Today,* March 5, 2001, p. 3.

Ingram, Mark, "The Future of Future Shop," *Globe & Mail,* May 19, 1997, p. B2.

Ingram, Mathew, "What's In Store for Future Shop?," *Globe & Mail,* April 20, 1995.

Kidded, Kenneth, "Future Shop Wins at Pricing Game," *Globe & Mail,* June 24, 1991.

Lamphier, Gary, "Future Shop Battles Bad Times," *Sun,* April 10, 1996, p. E1.

——, "Sales Dive at Established Future Shop Stores," *Globe & Mail,* October 13, 1995.

Lancit, Carla, "Computer City Closes," *Computer Dealer News,* March 2, 2001.

Lazarus, Eve, "Future Shop Has a Hand in Granada," *Sun,* August 13, 1994.

Lewis, Brian, "Share Offering to Help Finance Future Growth," *Province,* June 27, 1993, p. 49.

McDonald, Jonathan, "Keep Out, Future Shop Told," *Province,* July 11, 1995.

O'Brien, Jennifer M., "Future Shop Closes U.S. Stores," *Computer Dealer News,* March 19, 1999, p. 8.

"Outlasting the Newcomers: Future Shop and A&B Sound Prepare for the Entry of U.S. Retail Rivals," *Marketing Magazine,* May 20, 1996, p. 16.

Sasges, Michael, "Future Shop Makes Noises," *Sun,* February 17, 1984.

Scally, Robert, "Canada's Future Shop Invades Pacific Northwest CE Market," *Discount Store News,* October 7, 1996, p. 6.

Schick, Shane, "Future Shop Buys Computer City," *Computer Dealer News,* November 2, 1998, p. 8.

Sinoski, Kelly, "Burnaby's Future Shop Closes American Stores Due to Losses," *Sun,* March 9, 1999.

Smith, Dave, "Buoyant Electronics Seller Says Future Shock Not in Store," *Sun,* August 26, 1994.

—June Campbell and Paula Kepos

Global Berry Farms LLC

2241 Trade Center Way, Unit A
Naples, Florida 34109
U.S.A.
Telephone: (239) 591-1664
Fax: (239) 591-8133
Web site: http://www.globalberryfarms.com

Private Company
Incorporated: 2000
NAIC: 111333 Strawberry Farming; 111334 Berry
   (except Strawberry) Farming

Global Berry Farms LLC is a Naples, Florida-based joint venture of three major berry producers: MBG Marketing; Hortifrut, S.A.; and Naturipe Berry Growers. MBG operates out of Grand Junction, Michigan, and is North America's leading grower/shipper of fresh blueberries, packaged under the "Great Lakes" and "Great Sunbelt" labels. Hortifrut is the top grower/shipper of fresh blueberries, raspberries, and blackberries in Chile (where the company is based), Mexico, and Spain. Because of its unusual geography, Chile is comprised of six distinct climatic regions stretching some 1,200 kilometers. Relationships with growers in five of these areas allow Hortifrut to harvest blueberries from early November to late March, raspberries from November until early June, and Blackberries from late November until late March. In addition, Hortifrut also draws on production in Mexico and Guatemala to provide berries from as early as late September and as late as May. Hortifrut berries are marketed under the "Southern Sun" brand. The third participant in Global Berry is Naturipe, a major California grower/shipper of strawberries, packaging it products under the Naturipe name. Because the partners operate in a wide range of climatic regions in both the northern and southern hemisphere, Global Berry is able to provide retail food outlets with berries year round. For most areas of the United States, fresh berries were traditionally available during a few weeks in the summer. Now with the advent of global sourcing, as practiced by concerns like Global Berry, food retailers have access to berries all months of the year. Supermarkets, for instance, are able to set up permanent "Berry Patch" sections. Even with berries available year round, however, dis-tributing them to customers is a major logistical feat, especially because berries have a brief shelf life, lasting just a week. Nevertheless, Global Berry is so successful that many consumers now take it for granted that whenever they want fresh berries the supermarket will have them.

Roots of Naturipe Date to 1870s

A Watsonville, California, farmer named James Water is credited with planting Central California's first commercial strawberry crop in 1877 when he devoted 14 acres to cultivating Cinderella strawberries. When he took that crop to San Francisco, it sold for 20 cents a pound, a remarkable price that caught the attention of other farms who joined Water in planting strawberries. After 40 years, California strawberries grew in popularity, as did the number of growers. At this point, in 1917, area growers decided to band together to form a marketing cooperative, the Central California Berry Grower Association. In this way, strawberry growers were able to improve crops by sharing their knowledge. They were also able to bargain as a group to achieve higher prices and pool their resources to promote their product. In 1922, the association adopted the Naturipe trademark. These growers were simply following a path blazed by California's citrus growers decades earlier. The gold rush of the 1840s brought a large number of prospectors to California as well as the disease of scurvy. Citrus fruits were known to prevent the disease, and because of Southern California's mild climate, farmers quickly introduced lemons and oranges to the region. The railroad eventually made nationwide distribution possible, but growers were at the mercy of middlemen. To coordinate their marketing and maximize profits, groups of Southern California growers formed local associations. In 1893, the local associations were united into one organization, the Southern California Fruit Exchange, which set the standard for all cooperatives to follow, such as Naturipe. The Exchange began advertising in the early 1900s, and in 1908 its ad agency coined the name "Sunkist," which was soon printed on stickers placed on the highest grade of lemons and oranges marketed by the organization. Decades later, the Exchange would become known by its present-day name, Sunkist Growers. Thus, strawberry growers followed this time-tested approach, creating the Naturipe name in hopes of duplicating the success of Sunkist.

MBG Marketing Founded in 1936

The history of MBG Marketing dates back to 1936, when Michigan blueberry growers decided to try the marketing cooperative model pioneered by Sunkist and refined by the New Jersey blueberry and cranberry cooperatives. The organization was named the Michigan Blueberry Growers Association. The man instrumental in establishing the organization was horticulturist Stanley Johnston, who worked for the Michigan Agricultural Experiment Station (founded in 1888 as part of a government-funded, nationwide network of stations dedicated to conducting research and development projects for farmers). Johnston and 13 blueberry growers held the first meeting of Michigan Blueberry Growers on November 21, 1936. Within two years, the group established packaging standards and created the MBG logo for labeling, although at this stage they packed under the "Tru-Blu" brand created by the New Jersey Blueberry Growers Association. It was not until 1945 that MBG built its first warehouse, located in Grand Junction, Michigan. A year later, MBG formed its own sales organization rather than rely on private marketers. Later in the decade, Northern Indiana growers began to join the association, as blueberries became a popular crop in that nearby area. Annual sales topped the $1 million mark by the start of the 1950s, at which point MBG hired its first full-time general manager. By the middle of the decade, sales exceeded $2 million, as MBG ascended to a dominant position in the North American blueberry industry. In the 1960s, MBG continued its efforts to promote blueberries and now looked to market overseas. In order to extend the number of months the association could provide blueberries, MBG began in 1983 to extend membership to growers in Georgia and Florida. Now MBG offered blueberries as early as April. By this stage, annual sales totaled more than $18 million. To supplement its supply of blueberries, the association later in the decade began to establish sales agreements with non-member growers in Arkansas, Mississippi, North Carolina, and Louisiana. Gaining access to North Carolina blueberries was especially important because it opened up East Coast markets for MBG. Growth continued in the 1990s, with further expansion into southern states. MBG also opened The Blueberry Store, a retail operation located in South Haven, Michigan, that sold a variety of blueberry gift and novelty items, as well as gourmet food products. The store was eventually supplemented with a catalog operation and a Web site. Another important development during this period was the establishment of a marketing agreement with a South American berry producer, Hortifrut, S.A.

Hortifrut Founded in 1980

Hortifrut was founded in 1980 by Chilean entrepreneur Victor Moller, who developed the idea for the company while attending Oregon State University and observing the berry growers of that region. He recognized that Chile offered ideal growing conditions for blueberries and could take advantage of

its varied climatic regions. He was also a visionary, from the outset setting an ambitious goal of serving all the world markets and ultimately serving them year-round. He was also not content to limit Hortifrut to blueberries and became involved in blackberries, strawberries, currants, cherries, and asparagus. The company was at the forefront of Chile's rapidly growing export of blueberries. In 1990, the country exported 13,000 boxes. That number reached 567,000 boxes by the middle of the decade and soared to 2 million by 2000. A significant factor in Hortifrut's ability to make inroads in the American market was a marketing venture established with MBG in 1991.

In 2000, MBG and Hortifrut decided to establish a deeper tie between the two companies. In June of that year the parties signed an agreement creating Global Berry Farms, although word of the deal was withheld until Michigan's blueberry harvest was completed in October. The companies were simply responding to the year-round demand from food retailers for berries. Not only did they want a reliable supply, they wanted to be assured that the fruit met quality, food safety, and electronic record-keeping requirements. According to John Shelford, named Global Berry's president, "Our view of the future was that we could not afford to provide all these services as individual companies. And we didn't have the supply."

With more than 25 years of experience in produce, Shelford was well suited for his new position, having worked for both MBG and Hortifrut. A graduate of Cornell University, where he earned an undergraduate degree and MBA, Shelford served as a district manager for MBG from 1976 to 1983 and then was named general manager of MBG from 1983 to 1994, during which time annual revenues grew from $10 million to $40 million. After a stint as director of berry marketing for Gargiulo, Inc., he became president of Hortifrut, a position he held for four years before taking over Global Berry.

Because of their seasonal compatibility, MBG and Hortifrut were natural partners. Under the terms of their agreement, both parties retained their status as separate companies, but all of Hortifrut's importing, distribution, and sales functions were absorbed by Global Berry. MBG continued to market its own processing fruit while contracting fresh sales to Global Berry. The products would also be labeled under each company's existing labels. The new entity set up its headquarters in Naples, Florida. Staffed by a combination of Hortifrut and MBG personnel, sales offices were located in Dallas, Texas; Tampa, Florida; and Grand Junction, Michigan. Global Berry's stated goal was to become the world's top supplier of fresh blueberries, blackberries, golden raspberries, raspberries, and red currants. The company was also interested in becoming a year-round supplier of strawberries, by far the most popular item in the berry category and a key to future growth.

Global Berry enjoyed a successful launch. After a year in business, Shelford told the publication *Grocery Headquarters,* "Our produce buyers like the way we do business; they like having the ability to develop a relationship with one person as their berry source. Plans for the future are to service customers the best way possible. We're convinced that execution is more important than strategy sometimes. A lot of people have great strategies, but great strategies poorly executed are not as good as consistent strategies executed well."

Key Dates:

1917: Central California Berry Grower Association is formed.
1922: Central California Berry Grower Association adopts the Naturipe trademark for its strawberries.
1936: Michigan Blueberry Growers Association is formed.
1980: Hortifrut, S.A. is established in Chile.
2000: MBG and Hortifrut create Global Berry Farms.
2002: Naturipe Berry Growers becomes a partner of Global Berry.

In 2002, Hortifrut took steps to dramatically increase blueberry production over the next several years. The plan was to add new plantations so that the company could produce more than three million trays from 1,000 hactares of land. While this was an important development for Global Berry, it was overshadowed in significance in September 2002, when it was announced that Naturipe Berry Growers would become an equal partner in the joint venture. As a result of adding Naturipe strawberries, Global Berry was in a position, in the words of Shelford, "to offer a year-round of supply of the entire berry category." According to Hortifrut's Moller, Global Berry "will now be capable of providing promotional volumes with creative cross promotional opportunities so that we may better serve our customers." The importance of strawberries was reflected in the group's 2002 sales numbers for berries in America. Strawberries accounted for $939.7 million in volume, followed by blueberries with $141 million, raspberries with $80.9 million, and blackberries with $21.2 million. The future for Global Fruit

also appeared promising because of consumers' greater awareness of the health benefits of incorporating berries into their daily diet, supermarkets' creating permanent "Berry Patch" sections in their produce departments, the development of new varieties of berries able to survive in a variety of climates (thus allowing for greater availability of berries year-round), and innovations in shipping that provided reliable "cold chain" management to insure that a highly perishable product like berries could be reliably delivered at the highest quality. In order to better serve retailers and focus the company's marketing efforts, Global Berry began to move all of its products to the Naturipe brand in 2003.

Principal Competitors

Chiquita Brands International, Inc.; Dole Food Company, Inc.; Fyffes plc.

Further Reading

"Hortifrut Seeks Bigger Bite of Cherry," *Financial Times*, January 4, 1996, p. 19.
Howe, Peter J., "A Miracle at the Produce Counter for Shoppers," *Boston Globe*, February 19, 1997, p. A1.
Ladage, Megan, "The Impact of Global Produce," *Grocery Headquarters*, October 2001.
McLaughlin, Molly, "Profiting From the Berry Patch," *Grocery Headquarters*, April 1, 2003, p. 77.
Mark, Imogen, "Chilean Firm Fine-Tunes Art of Exporting Berries," *Financial Post*, January 9, 1996, p. 45.
Read, Richard, "Chile's Own Fast Track," *Portland Oregonian*, November 16, 1997, p. C1.

—Ed Dinger

Gold Fields Ltd.

24 St. Andrews Road
Parktown, 2193
Postnet Suite 252
Private Bag X30500
Houghton, 2041
South Africa
Telephone: (+11) 644 2400
Fax: (+11) 484 0626
Web site: http://www.goldfields.co.za

Public Company
Incorporated: 1887 as the Gold Fields of South Africa
  Ltd.
Employees: 48,000
Sales: $1.53 billion (2003)
Stock Exchanges: South Africa New York London Paris
  Brussels Swiss
Ticker Symbol: GFI
NAIC: 212221 Gold Ore Mining

Gold Fields Ltd. is one of the world's largest producers of gold, with operations in South Africa, West Africa, and Australia. During 2003, the company's annual attributable gold production reached more than 4.3 million ounces of gold, while its attributable mineral reserves level stood at 81.5 million ounces. Gold Fields' wholly owned mines include Driefontein, Kloof, and Beatrix. Its international arm overseas includes Ghanaian and Australian mines, along with the Arctic Platinum Partnership in Finland. Gold Fields was created in 1998 after the merger of Gold Fields of South Africa Ltd. and Gencor Ltd.

History of Gold Fields of South Africa

Gold Fields of South Africa was formed in 1887 by Cecil Rhodes and Charles Rudd to hold properties they had acquired on the Transvaal's Witwatersrand gold fields. The first of the financial groups that were to characterize the South African mining industry's organization, it generally remained heavily dependent on one or two profitable South African mines, while

going on to become a major international mining finance house. The company as it stood in the 1980s was formed to take over the African assets of Consolidated Gold Fields and was not included in that group's acquisition by Hanson PLC in 1989.

Reorganized as Consolidated Gold Fields of South Africa (Consgold) in 1892, it was plagued by uncertainties and found itself on a really firm footing only in the 1930s, when it took the lead in opening up the Western Rand—often referred to as the West Wits Line—in conjunction with, among others, the Anglo American Corporation. West Witwatersrand Areas Ltd. was formed in 1932 to work the new field. In 1959, as part of a major restructuring exercise, the name ''Gold Fields of South Africa'' was revived for a South African rather than a British domiciled company, a wholly owned subsidiary to take over the management of the parent company's southern African assets. In 1971, West Wits took over all of Gold Fields of South Africa's assets as well as its name.

In 1886, when gold was discovered on the Witwatersrand, Cecil Rhodes was skeptical because of earlier disappointments in the eastern Transvaal and was still very much preoccupied with De Beers Consolidated. Most of the properties acquired by Rhodes and his partner Charles Rudd when they finally joined the Rand rush were valueless, at least for the time being, due both to chance and to Rhodes' lack of firm commitment. He and Rudd formed Gold Fields of South Africa Ltd. on February 9, 1887 to hold their Transvaal interests but quickly turned their attention to the area further north, later known as Rhodesia, where they hoped to recoup some of their Transvaal losses and to further Rhodes' political and imperial ambitions. In 1889, the British South Africa Company (BSAC) was formed with a charter from the British government to administer the territory and with the right to a share in all mining operations that took place there. Rhodes, as joint managing director of Gold Fields, with wide personal power and freedom, was able to use that company to finance the BSAC through its early days, which were even less profitable than those of Gold Fields.

Although some of Rhodes' decisions had led to disastrous consequences for Gold Fields, it, like all other groups on the Rand, had to face difficulties caused by the fact that the Witwatersrand's gold-bearing reefs tilted sharply, with outcrops

Company Perspectives:

Our vision is to be the leading, value-adding, globally diversified, precious metals producer through the responsible, sustainable, and innovative development of quality assets.

that tended to be depleted at relatively shallow levels. Sinking shafts necessary to work the reef at greater depths required capital that investors were reluctant to provide. In 1892, Alfred Beit, Rhodes' close colleague in De Beers and other ventures, supported by Rudd, persuaded Rhodes to involve Gold Fields in a company that would work deep levels, Rand Mines Ltd. To finance the venture, Gold Fields brought several Rand companies together in 1892 to form Consolidated Gold Fields of South Africa. Deep levels produced more gold and new problems.

The weathered, oxidized outcropping ores could be treated relatively easily and cheaply by crushing and amalgamation, essentially the same technique used by the Spanish in Mexico in the 16th century. Ores found below about 100 feet were pyritic—containing sulphides—and therefore required more complex, expensive treatment. The 50 percent recovery rate of the chlorination process which was first used was too low for profit. The MacArthur-Forrest cyanide process, introduced into the Transvaal in 1889, solved the problem, ultimately convincing even the most pessimistic of the Rand gold fields' long-term viability.

Gold Fields acquired several new properties and began to change its management structure and style in the aftermath of the 1895 Jameson Raid, reducing Rhodes' unrestricted personal power. Substantial dividends were declared in 1895 and 1896 on profits derived from dividends paid on the company's holdings in De Beers Consolidated rather than from its own operational profits. Subsequent dividends were low or non-existent. Despite shareholder protests, this situation enabled the company to survive depression and accumulate reserves.

In 1908, using its reserves, Gold Fields began expanding investment outside Rhodesia and South Africa. Gold mines in Ghana—the Gold Coast—were not profitable; Nigeria's Ropp tin mines were. The gold of Siberia's Lena River basin also held considerable promise. When the Russian company operating there sought more advanced U.S. and British technology, Gold Fields became the largest single shareholder in Lena Goldfields Ltd., formed in 1908.

By 1911, Gold Fields had quietly disposed of its Lena share, using the profit on the sale to help replenish the reserves depleted by purchases in the Americas and elsewhere. Encouraged by its consulting engineer, John Hays Hammond, Gold Fields bought shares in U.S. gold and other mines, U.S. power companies, Mexican and Trinidadian oil, and American Telephone & Telegraph (AT&T), among others. In 1911, a new company, Gold Fields American Development Company (GFADC), was formed to administer holdings in the United States. These and other expansionist moves made at about the same time did not live up to expectations, in part perhaps because of American hostility to foreign investors who took an interest in mining enterprises but did not control them. However, not all of Gold Fields' investments were total failures. Investments outside

mining, such as AT&T and Trinidad Oil, in activities in which they had no prior experience or expertise, tended to be more profitable than those in mining.

Throughout most of its history, Gold Fields was sustained by one or two particularly successful operations. During the period 1904–20, for example, these operations were two Transvaal mines, the Robinson Deep and the Simmer and Jack, whose profitable working protected the company from the burdens of developing and working less profitable mines, old and new. Nonetheless, by 1918 the Gold Fields' reserves and its Lena profits had disappeared, and the company faced hard times. Temporary relief was obtained in 1919 when all South African mining companies were allowed to sell their output on the free market, earning a premium of about 16 shillings per ounce. Reliance on gold mines—a wasting asset in any case as they were finite and would eventually be exhausted—was now seen as a fundamental weakness and diversification as essential for salvation.

Since Gold Fields' Articles of Association limited the company's activities to mining and kindred ventures, New Consolidated Gold Fields was created, a wholly owned subsidiary with the same directors; in effect, it was the same company but with greater freedom than its parent. The new company acquired a range of interests, including property, cement, and carpets, but the benefits of diversification were elusive.

The company hit its lowest depths in 1922, as even Robinson Deep and Simmer and Jack profits declined, and the entire industry was affected by the major white miners' strike, the Rand Rebellion. The rebellion was quelled by Prime Minister Smuts's politically disastrous use of the army, while financial rescue came from the Sub Nigel mine in the East Rand. Gold Fields had bought property in the Nigel district before the Boer War, but work there did not begin until 1909, reaching the commercial production stage in the early 1920s and continuing to produce gold into the 1990s, as did the Simmer and Jack and Robinson Deep, albeit at rather lower yields.

In Western Australia, Gold Fields moved from a profitable share in the Wiluna mine in 1926 into the rich Kalgoorlie field and secured a controlling interest in Gold Mines of Australia, formed by the Australian financier W.S. Robinson in 1930. Gold Fields also participated in Bulolo Gold Dredging, formed in 1930 to work alluvial gold in Papua New Guinea. This company produced about $60 million worth of gold by the time it stopped dredging in 1965, while New Guinea Goldfields, which had a less promising start in 1929, benefited from the late 1970s rise in gold prices. Gold Fields' Australasian interests were brought under the administration of a holding company, Gold Fields Australian Development Company, in 1932.

A relatively little-known and not particularly successful Australian venture was the Gold Exploration and Finance Company of Australia (GEFCA), established in 1934. In this venture, Gold Fields joined with two South African mining groups, Central Mining and Investment Corporation and Union Corporation, and an Australian consortium led by Robinson. Initially, GEFCA operated primarily in eastern Australia, with mixed success. There was considerable friction between the main London board and the Australian committee, in part because the Australians seemed to regard Gold Fields' finances as unlimited and in part because Gold Fields was reluctant to allow GEFCA to move into Western Australia. In 1949, GEFCA was transferred to Australia and absorbed by the Western Mining Corporation, previously a GEFCA subsidiary.

American, Australian, and other expansions were financed largely by the recovered Robinson Deep, the Simmer and Jack, and the Sub Nigel. Help also came from the sale of the American Potash and Chemical Corporation, originally the Trona Corporation, which extracted salt from Searles Lake in California's Mojave Desert. GFADC had helped rescue the undertaking as part of its early U.S. acquisitions. By 1929, it was sufficiently attractive for a European group to offer to buy up all the issued shares, and Gold Fields and GFADC made a profit on the deal. GFADC retained managerial control but lost it in 1942 for violating the Sherman Antitrust Act by the sale, including allegations of a secret sale to Germans.

As Gold Fields fell prey to the worldwide depression of the 1930s, it was once again Witwatersrand gold that provided a foundation for recovery. In December 1930, Gold Fields financed a magnetometer survey of the West Rand, which was separated from the central fields by a major fault that had taken the gold-bearing reefs to substantially greater depths. The Rand strata were known to be very regular, however, and a layer of iron-bearing shales lay about 400 feet below the gold reef. The magnetometer survey, confirmed by subsequent boreholes, traced the reefs very accurately.

Earlier attempts to work these deposits had been defeated by uncontrollable flooding. An effective cementation or grouting process developed subsequently by a Belgian, Albert Francois, initially in connection with coal mining, solved the problem. In November 1932, Gold Fields formed West Witwatersrand Areas Ltd. (West Wits) to begin developing the West Rand. Several of the Rand mining groups were unable or unwilling to participate in financing the new company. The Anglo American

Corporation of South Africa and the General Mining and Finance Corporation were among those who agreed to take part. Gold Fields had to retain 30 percent of the shares, unhappily at first but ultimately to its great advantage. By October 1939, when the first West Rand ores were being milled, Gold Fields was once again on a sound financial footing. In the 1950s, when further development was going on in the West Rand fields, Gold Fields was unable to participate as fully as it would have liked because of heavy financial commitments elsewhere. Anglo American took the lead here as it had already done in the Orange Free State.

Gold Fields and Anglo American worked together in other ventures as well, some in South Africa, notably in the Far East Rand, and some in other countries, including the United States. The most important area in which the two companies did not work together was in the Orange Free State gold fields. Geologically very different from the Rand, the Free State gold deposits lay at considerable depth and were not susceptible to magnetometer investigation. Prospecting there was very costly, with boreholes frequently proving the absence of gold rather than providing confirmation of its presence, as was the case in the West Rand.

In a manner reminiscent of the company's 19th-century Witwatersrand acquisitions, Gold Fields came late to the Orange Free State, although this time for financial reasons rather than lack of interest. When it did begin to acquire claims, most proved worthless. The Saaiplaas mine seemed a good proposition in 1955 but failed to live up to its promise. Earlier, Gold Fields had attempted to participate in the areas which ultimately proved to include the most profitable Free State mines but were rebuffed by the claim holders, African and European Investment, whose major shareholder was the Lewis and Marks group. Anglo American bought up enough African and European shares to take control of it, using it as the basis of its subsequent dominance of Free State gold mining. Gold Fields did have a share in the Harmony mine, but its involvement in the field was very limited. In 1990, the company anticipated that the next gold mine it opened would be in the southern Free State.

Although West Wits did not pay its first dividends until 1954, its success helped strengthen Gold Fields generally. Further support came from Rustenberg Platinum, the result of a series of mergers in the 1920s and 1930s, which began paying dividends in 1942. Gold Fields itself was able to pay dividends throughout the war.

The postwar period saw new mines coming into production, with profits flowing in from Venezuelan oil and the sale of the Trinidad Oil company. By the mid-1950s, Gold Fields had again built up substantial reserves and again began diversifying. In order to decrease dependence on gold, mining, and Africa—which by then appeared to be becoming less stable—it began investing in a variety of industries, concentrating more on the United States, Canada, Australia, and New Zealand.

In 1956, New Consolidated Canadian Exploration Company was established in Toronto and New Consolidated Gold Fields (Australasia) in Sydney. The same year, Gold Fields and Central Mining and Investment Corporation discussed, but did not complete, a merger. Gold Fields continued its own takeover and diversification program, however, acquiring some other African mining companies and some British manufacturers as well. One takeover included a wine firm.

In 1959, a major restructuring led to the re-emergence of the name Gold Fields of South Africa, reorganized as a Johannesburg-based company which controlled all the company's African assets. Apart from any financial and administrative advantages that might have accrued from this restructuring, it also met the South African desire to have domestic companies, rather than London-based ones, exploiting the country's natural resources.

It is not likely that the decision to set up a separate South African company was specifically motivated, at the time, by political considerations. That separation did give Consolidated Gold Fields an excuse—not necessarily accepted—to distance itself from its South African ''associate'' when the mining industry in general, and Gold Fields of South Africa in particular, began to come under fire as opposition to apartheid, domestic and international, strengthened after 1960. In addition to widespread general enthusiasm for the independence of Black African colonies at the time, there was a tremendous wave of revulsion against the South African regime because of the Sharpeville Massacre that year.

Before the growth of that opposition began to impinge seriously on Gold Fields, the company continued to work its mines in different parts of the Rand. These remained generally profitable, but the fact that Gold Fields was not participating in the Orange Free State field limited the extent to which it could expand. The older Rand mines were moving towards depletion, requiring working at greater depth and consequently greater cost. Only by keeping labor costs very low was it possible to maintain profitability.

Working through its subsidiary, Gold Fields Mining and Development Corporation, Gold Fields also attempted to widen its asset base. Though not entirely failing in this endeavor, it was unable to compete successfully either with the Anglo American group, which came to have a substantial role, direct or indirect, in virtually every sector of the South African economy, or with that country's other major mining/industrial/financial conglomerate, Barlow Rand. Gold Fields did move into other minerals in South Africa, but, even as late as 1990, stated company policy was to concentrate on minerals in southern Africa. While newspapers reported that the group was about to embark on a foreign investment program, the company was officially willing to move only with considerable caution and to focus on the opening-up of new mineral fields rather than portfolio investment in existing operations.

Throughout the 1970s and 1980s, Gold Fields did indeed invest in a variety of other minerals, including zinc, lead, silver, and tungsten. The most important of these was platinum, which, with gold, accounted for 55 percent of the group's income in 1990 but constituted 74 percent of assets. In contrast, other minerals were responsible for 17 percent of group income against only 7 percent of its assets. However, these figures did not take account of the Northam platinum mine, which was expected to begin producing in 1991. The major producers of gold continued to be sufficiently successful to enable Gold Fields to rank as South Africa's second most important gold producer. There was also some involvement in engineering,

generally related to mining; in mineral treatment; and, in a fairly small way, in property. Limited diversification did not alter the company's basic orientation.

During the 1980s, Gold Fields—and Consgold—came under particularly strong pressure from anti-apartheid groups and from supporters of the black trade union movement in South Africa. The group was criticized on the grounds of its safety record; accident and death rates, it was argued, were worse than in the industry as a whole. Gold Fields was also attacked because of its reluctance to recognize trade unions and for its relatively lower rates of pay. There was some justification in these claims. Gold Fields argued that its continued profitability—and therefore its ability to employ people—required it to remain a low-cost producer. Many of its mines were older and were worked at greater depth, and therefore higher cost, than those of other groups. Gold Fields also maintained that most of its workers were happy with their pay and conditions and appreciated the company's policy of training unskilled workers and employing the children of people it had employed previously. Unrest among the workers, the company argued, had been stirred up by a small number of militants.

Whether or not workers did in fact appreciate some aspects of the group's employment policies, the first and last of these arguments could not be sustained. Strikes of varying duration continued to affect Gold Fields' operations. The group followed rather than led as the South African gold mining industry moved towards the full recognition of the National Union of Mine Workers, the elimination of the color bar in job allocation and training, and in general improvement of housing and health provision for black workers. These changes took place against a background of political and social unrest, a declining real gold price, and retrenchment throughout the mining industry.

In 1989, Consolidated Gold Fields was taken over by Hanson PLC after Minorco, an arm of Anglo American, had attempted a strongly opposed takeover bid. Consgold's remaining 38 percent stake in Gold Fields was sold. In August 1989, 30 percent was acquired by Gold Fields of South Africa Holdings, in which the Rembrandt Group held a 40 percent interest, as did Asteroid, a company owned equally by Remgro and Gold Fields, with the insurance company Liberty Life holding the remaining 20 percent. Before the end of the year, Hanson had also disposed of the remaining 8 percent. Gold Fields was more than ever a South African company, firmly rooted in the Witwatersrand but still looking for other opportunities, expecting the next gold mine it opened to be in the southern Orange Free State.

History of Gencor Ltd.

Gencor was the product of a 1980 merger between General Mining and Finance Corporation and Union Corporation, both of which were founded in the 19th century. General Mining was founded on December 30, 1895 by two Germans, George and Leopold Albu, who controlled a number of gold mines. In the same year, they changed the name of their firm from G&L Albu to General Mining and Finance Corporation.

In its early years, the company's activities were focused primarily on developing new gold mines and managing existing ones. In 1910, the company had seven mines under its management, including such well-known names as Meyer and Charlton, Van Ryn Gold Mines Estate, and West Rand Consolidated Mines, and was developing another two.

World War I was a difficult time for the industry; a flat gold price was accompanied by flagging productivity and rising costs on all fronts. The shortage of unskilled labor was a major issue, and its costs increased as contractors, who had to recruit and deliver the workers to the mines, became involved. The mines also had problems during this period with labor unrest, principally among white miners. The best-known example was the 1922 General Strike, during which two months of production were lost. In 1919, activities were diversified with the formation of Transvaal Silver and Base Metals to mine the lode outcrops and lead-bearing ore which the company owned. After six years, this venture was closed owing to its poor prospects. More successful was General Mining's acquisition of a large stake, during the 1920s, in Phoenix Oil and Transport Company, which had major interests in Romanian oil companies.

The mining houses were equally hard hit by World War II, which resulted in shortages of all forms of labor, lack of machinery, and delays in plant and machinery delivery. Good news came soon after, however, with the discovery of the Free State gold fields, which General Mining, together with other mining houses, had the right to develop. It also participated in the opening of gold mines on the Far West Rand. General Mining achieved some notable firsts: it was the first mining house to use the cyanide process for the extraction of gold and, through West Rand Cons, it was the first mining house in the country to produce uranium.

During the 1950s, the company's activities were boosted when it gained control of the Consolidated Rand-Transvaal Mining Group. This control brought with it a substantial interest in the gold mine Geduld, platinum (through Lydenburg), pipe fabrication, and sugar.

In 1964, the company merged with Strathmore Consolidated Investments and came to control two mines on Klerksdorp gold field—Stilfontein and Buffelsfontein. A major change took place during the 1960s when the Afrikaner-dominated mining house Federale Mynbou took control of General Mining. This was effected with the assistance of Anglo American, and its chairman Harry Oppenheimer in particular, who wished to assist the Afrikaans business community in attaining a better foothold in the mining industry. This aim had a political purpose: to counteract government policies which sought to separate Afrikaners from the English and whites from blacks by showing that these groups could cooperate in the same spheres of interest.

The outcome was that Federale made the takeover while Anglo took a substantial minority interest. Later, in 1965, it was decided to merge Federale and General Mining with Federale gaining effective control.

The merger resulted in the creation of the Federale Mynbou/General Mining group, the country's largest producer of uranium, accounting for more than one-third of output, and also the producer of approximately 7.25 percent of the country's gold. ''Federale Mynbou'' was dropped from the group's name in 1965. The group's ten collieries produced 10 percent of the country's output, and it had further mineral interests—asbestos fiber production, platinum, and copper. It was also involved in oil production, exploration, and marketing and managed the petroleum company Trek.

The late 1960s saw a program of diversification. It was the era of conglomerates and the prospects for gold were not exciting. However, many new projects pursued, particularly in the industrial field, were not compatible with the company's expertise and eventually failed. The turnaround came in 1970 with the arrival of Dr. Wim De Villiers as chief executive. He instituted a rationalization of activities which led to improved profitability. The major changes he implemented concerned decentralized management, strategic planning, and better utilization of labor. On the industrial side, De Villiers sold off the consumer interests of General Mining.

The other company involved in the eventual 1980 merger, Union Corporation, had been active about the same length of time as General Mining. It was founded in 1897 by a German, Adolf Goertz, the local representative of Deutsche Bank, and was initially known as A. Goertz and Co. Goertz became involved in the gold rush and staked 326 claims on the Modderfontein farm on the East Rand, from which emerged the Modder Deep Levels mine, ''the jewelbox of the Reef,'' in Goertz's words.

In 1902, Goertz and Co., with the assistance of U.K. and French investors, who took up shares, became the first Transvaal finance house to obtain a London listing. During World War I the company changed its name to Union Corporation.

There was much uncertainty in the early days, with financing for the Modderfontein mine being obtained literally hours before war broke out. After the declaration of war, all transactions with Germany were frozen.

Beginning in 1908, Union Corporation pioneered the Far East Rand, and in 1938 it discovered the Orange Free State gold fields. The first shaft was sunk at St. Helena, which became the first mine to produce gold in the Orange Free State, in 1947. In 1951 came the discovery of the Evander gold field, over which Union Corporation had sole control. It established four mines there: Bracken, Kinross, Leslie, and Winkelhaak.

Later mining ventures included involvement in Impala Platinum in 1969. Impala was the first platinum concern in the world to provide an integrated operation from the mining of the ore to the marketing of high purity platinum group metals. The gold mine Unisel was developed in 1974, and in 1978 Beisa, the first mine in the country to be established as a primary uranium producer, was opened.

Union Corporation also owned the original interest in Richards Bay and helped put together Richards Bay Minerals, which mines heavy mineral deposits from sand dunes north of the harbor, recovering ilmenite, rutile, zircon, and titanium. General Mining's rights in Richards Bay were later merged with these.

Union Corporation's diversification into the manufacturing industry started in earnest in 1936–37 with the formation of the paper company Sappi in the East Rand town of Springs. It was a long-term grassroots project which did not become significantly profitable until the 1970s.

During the 1960s, investments were acquired in the packaging company Kohler Brothers; African Coasters, forerunner of Unicorn Shipping Lines; and engineering companies Darling and Hodgson and Evelyn Haddon. At the time of the 1980 merger, Union Corporation had a 58 percent stake in Sappi, 74 percent of Kohler Brothers, 55 percent of Darling and Hodgson, 17 percent of Haggie—a wire rope manufacturer—and 27 percent of Kanhym. It also held a stake in Capital and Counties, the U.K. property concern which later became the major investment of First International Trust, the overseas arm of the Liberty Life group, a major player in the South African insurance field.

In 1978, 56 percent of Union Corporation's assets were in minerals, including 33 percent in gold. It was operating seven gold mines—Marievale, Bracken, Kinross, St. Helena, Winkelhaak, Leslie, and Grootvlei—in addition to developing the Unisel gold mine. Approximately 50 percent of net income came from industrial interests in the fiscal year 1977–78.

Although the General Mining/Union Corporation merger was not consummated until 1980, the courtship began in 1974 when General Mining acquired a 29.9 percent stake in Union Corporation after a battle with Gold Fields of South Africa. A further step was taken in 1976 when Union Corporation became a subsidiary of General Mining; the takeover, which is known as the country's most bitterly contested hostile bid, was completed four years later.

The decade under De Villiers had been a golden one for General Mining, whose earnings per share increased at an average rate of 26.2 percent per annum over the period. Prior to De Villiers's arrival, the company had paid a maintained dividend that was unchanged for the ten years up to 1968, with the dividend becoming only marginally higher in 1969. At the time of the merger, Union Corporation and General Mining were the fourth- and fifth-largest mining houses in South Africa, ranked by equity capitalization. More than one-third of each company's income derived from manufacturing.

The major reason for the merger was General Mining's need to create an improved capital base from which to undertake new investments, such as the first phase of Sappi's Ngodwana mill, the Beatrix mine, which was initially funded from within, and the Beisa uranium mine. There were also the additional benefits of manpower rationalization and, with the exception of gold, the two groups' activities supplemented each other rather than overlapping. It was also felt that Union Corporation's growth prospects would be improved through closer links with the ruling Afrikaner power bloc.

Given the hostile nature of the bid, it was inevitable that merging the two corporations would take time. Initially they remained separate operating entities, merging their corresponding product divisions whenever conditions were favorable. The process was apparently more complex than anyone imagined, and the period 1980–86 was to prove difficult for the group. In 1982, the two major stakeholders, Sanlam and Rembrandt, clashed over Gencor. Sanlam, the second-largest South African life insurer, had been a major shareholder in the two companies

that joined to form Federale Mynbou, thus becoming involved in General Mining and subsequently Gencor. The result of the clash was the replacement of De Villiers—later a member of the cabinet—as chief executive by former Union Corporation managing director Ted Pavitt. This change of guard followed a conflict between De Villiers and Dr. Andries Wassenaar, head of Sanlam, about the management of Gencor.

The perception that all was not well within the group was compounded in 1983 by the group's failure to find a new chief executive to succeed De Villiers. It settled instead for management by its five most senior executives: Johan Fritz, George Clark, Basil Landau, Tom de Beer, and Hugh Smith. Pavitt had relinquished executive responsibilities in August 1984.

Over the course of that year, manufacturing interests were underperforming; there was massive foreign loan exposure, and Gencor appeared to be something of a rudderless ship. The executive committee was thought to be concerning itself too much with operational issues and not enough with strategy and planning. Investor confidence waned. To some extent, this perception was unfair. Steps were being taken to address problems, such as the 1984 reorganization of mining and industrial interests in line with a policy of greater divisional autonomy.

While the 1984–85 period was a difficult one for the South African economy, Gencor's particular difficulties were compounded by an identity crisis. Staff had not outgrown their previous allegiances and still tended to see themselves as Union Corporation or General Mining employees. The two corporate cultures were very different. Union Corporation had a reputation for good engineering and exploration and General Mining for financial engineering.

Gencor's failings were analyzed in 1986 in a report commissioned by Federale, at that time controlling company of Gencor, and produced by Arthur D. Little, the U.S.-based management consultants. The report contained some strong criticisms, accusing the group of lack of focus and direction, weak leadership, and of failing to inspire corporate loyalty among its employees. The report served as a spur to change, but the man to whom it fell to implement this, Derek Keys, appointed executive chairman in April 1986, had no background in mining, having come from the industrial group Malbak. The appointment was not universally popular and caused Johan Fritz to resign and Basil Landau to take early retirement.

Keys made a number of important moves, one of which was to separate Gencor's manufacturing interests. He brought Malbak into the group and then sold into it all the manufacturing interests—Sappi, which was much too large, and Trek, which later found a home in Engen. Thus, at one stroke the manufacturing interests were separated from the mining interests, and Malbak was given the task of managing them. Previously, the manufacturing interests had been managed in true mining house style—from the center. Keys and Grant Thomas, managing director at Malbak, introduced a new decentralized structure.

The period from Keys's arrival was one of considerable expansion and growth, both organic and through acquisitions. On the mining side, the Oryx gold mine was developed as well as the smaller Weltevreden mine near Klerksdorp, and Impala

Platinum developed the Karee mine. In 1989, Gencor bought a 30.7 percent controlling interest in Alusaf, the Richards Bay aluminum smelter, from the Industrial Development Corporation for R270 million. A R1.47 billion rights issue in 1989 helped fund these developments and acquisitions. Other acquisitions included Sappi's purchase of Saiccor, which specializes in the productions of chemical cellulose pulp, and of a 49 percent interest in the Usuthu pulp mill in Swaziland. In mid-1990, Sappi also bought five paper mills in the U.K. subsidiary Malbak, while Abercom Holdings bid £42 million for the U.K.-quoted packaging group MY Holdings.

Another important event was the publication in 1988 of the Gencor mission, a brief statement of the group's fundamental corporate goals, which went a long way toward clarifying to the public and to its employees what Gencor stood for. In Keys' words, "Now they know that Gencor has only two businesses—to start or to acquire major businesses and to accelerate the development of those businesses which it already has."

Two major developments took place within Gencor in 1989. The first was the formation of General Mining Metals and Minerals Limited (Genmin) in March 1989. Genmin was made responsible for managing the group's mining, metals, and minerals interests, which comprise some 60 operations. These included 14 gold mines, the base metals group Samancor, the platinum producer Impala, the coal group Trans-Natal, and the minerals division.

The second major development was the formation of Engen, the company responsible for the group's energy interests, which included exploration and refining of crude oil and marketing of the final products. General Mining had first become involved in the petroleum sector back in 1968, when it participated in a joint venture launching the country's first petrol marketing company, Trek Beleggings (Trek Investment). The key event in the formation of Engen took place in July 1989 with Gencor's purchase, for $150 million, of Mobil Southern Africa from its disinvesting parent company. Its major assets were a refinery in Durban, the Mobil management team, and a country-wide network of approximately 1,150 service station sites.

Engen's other major interests included the Trek network of petroleum outlets, 20 percent interest in the oil and gas exploration outfit Soekor, and a 30 percent stake in, as well as the management contract for, Mossgas, a synthetic fuels venture.

The decade since Gencor's formation was a time of upheaval for the group. In the first half of the 1980s there was a lack of direction at Gencor, but this had changed under the leadership of Derek Keys. Keys was succeeded by Brian Gilbertson, who presided over Gencor at a time when politicians viewed the pyramid organization of such conglomerates with suspicion. Unbundling these complicated structures would also tend to increase share prices, which were traditionally undervalued in this system. Subsequently, Gencor divested itself of Engen, Genbel, Malbak, and Sappi.

Gencor bought Billiton International from Royal Dutch Shell in 1994 for £780 million, giving Gencor the opportunity to operate as an aluminum trader as well as producer. However, Billiton was not to remain very long under Gencor's umbrella.

In 1995, Alusaf began operating the mammoth Hillside Aluminum Smelter, which, when combined with the upgrade of a smaller Alusaf facility, nearly doubled Africa's production of the metal. The company planned an even larger smelter in Mozambique. Rangold bought some of Gengold's less profitable mines in 1995, while Gengold acquired some new mines of its own.

The European Commission scuttled Gencor's plans to merge Implats with Lonrho's platinum interests on anti-competition grounds. The only other competitor in South Africa, the EC reasoned, would have been Amplats (the platinum interests of Anglo American Corp.), and Russia was the only other external supplier. Gencor already owned a 27 percent share in the Lonrho operations Western Platinum and Eastern Platinum.

Steel and ferroalloys contributed most (31.7 percent) to revenues in 1996; aluminum accounted for the next largest share (27 percent). Other operations each contributed less than a tenth of total revenues. Approximately half the company's revenues came from abroad.

In 1997, Gencor's base metals and non-gold interests were split off as a separate company, Billiton, to be based in London. Alusaf, titanium producer Richards Bay Minerals, and the steel and ferroalloys division remained part of Billiton after the transition. The company had a market capitalization of £4.6 billion ($7.7 billion). The new Gencor would henceforth specialize in precious metals.

Gold Fields and Gencor Unite in 1998

By the time Gold Fields and Gencor made the decision to merge in the late 1990s, the South African gold mining industry was faltering. Gold production had fallen due to declining ore grades, higher mining costs, unhappy laborers, and overall industry restructuring. In 1997, gold production bottomed out, reaching its lowest level since 1956. In 1998, the gold assets of both Gencor and Gold Fields were merged, bringing together three of South Africa's most significant mines—Driefontein, Kloof, and Beatrix. The deal created Gold Fields Ltd., the country's second-largest gold concern and one of the largest in the world. At the same time, competitor Anglo American consolidated all of its gold assets into Anglogold, creating the world's largest producer of gold. Both transactions proved that the landscape of South Africa's mining industry was indeed experiencing considerable change.

"The challenge for the new Gold Fields is to bring the three core mines to peak operating efficiency, and to extend substantial improvements in operating costs and cash flows to shareholders," reported an April 1998 *African Business* article. Indeed, profits appeared hard to come by as a result of the gold price hovering at an 18 year low. While Gold Fields worked to bolster profits during the merger integration process, it made several purchases. In 1999, it bought the remaining shares of St. Helena Gold Mines Ltd. that it did not already own. In November 2001, St. Ives and Agnew Gold Mines was added to the company's holdings. Abosso Goldfields Ltd. was acquired the following year.

During the early years of the new century, Gold Fields had to deal with remaining competitive in the gold mining industry while facing changes in South Africa's political system that

Gold Fields Ltd. — 164

brought about the Broad Based Socio-Economic Charter for the South African Mining Industry—known as the Mining Charter. According to the company, the Charter allowed the Mineral and Petroleum Resources Development Act of South Africa to take effect. Its goal was to remedy the imbalances previously found in the mining industry and was designed to create a "globally competitive industry that will reflect the promise of a non-racial South Africa." As part of the charter, mining companies were required to transfer 15 percent ownership of their South African mining assets to historically disadvantaged South Africans (HDSAs) within five years, and then 26 percent over the next ten years. In June 2003, Gold Fields enacted its first Black Economic Empowerment transaction when it allowed Mvelaphanda Resources Ltd., an empowerment consortium representing HDSAs, to acquire a 15 percent beneficial interest in its South African assets.

By 2003, gold production as well as revenue had climbed from its 1999 levels. Net earnings had also increased, reaching $326 million (the company had reported losses in both 1999 and 2001). Gold Fields remained focused on diversification and acquisitions, exploration, and increasing worker safety. The company also pledged to fulfill the criteria of the Mining Charter, which included human resource development, employment equity, community upliftment, improved housing and living conditions, procurement, beneficiation, and ownership. Gold Fields faced challenges in its future, however, that ranged from changing legislation and cost pressures to South Africa's aging gold ore reserves and mining infrastructure. Nevertheless, company management appeared optimistic that a bright future lay ahead for Gold Fields.

Principal Subsidiaries

African Eagle Resources plc (23.3%); Abosso Goldfields Ltd. (71.1%); Agnew Gold Mining Company (Pty) Ltd.; Beatrix Mines Ltd.; Beatrix Mining Ventures Ltd.; Driefontein Consolidated (Pty.) Ltd.; GFL Mining Services Ltd.; Gold Fields Guernsey Ltd. (Guernsey); Gold Fields Ghana Ltd. (71.1%); Kloof Gold Mining Company Ltd.; Orogen Holdings (BVI) Ltd.; Oryx Gold Holdings Ltd.; St. Ives Gold Mining Company (Pty) Ltd.

Principal Competitors

AngloGold Ltd.; Barrick Gold Corporation; Newmont Mining Corporation.

Further Reading

"All That Glitters: Gencor," Economist, March 9, 1996.

Benjamin, Paul, "Mining Stands on the Brink of New Era," Business Day, September 20, 1996.

Beresford, Belinda, "Gencor to Separate Gold, Other Interests," Business Day, June 2, 1997.

"Business: Panned," Economist, February 7, 1998, p. 65.

Cartwright, A.P., Gold Paved the Way: The Story of the Gold Fields Group of Companies, London: Macmillan, 1967.

Consolidated Gold Fields, London: Counter Information Services, 1973.

Consolidated Gold Fields PLC: Partner in Apartheid, London: Counter Information Services, 1986.

Dhliwayo, Dominic, "Mega Aluminum Smelter for Maputo?" African Business, January 1997, pp. 27–28.

"Empowerment Deal for Gold Fields," Mining Journal, June 13, 2003, p. 393.

Freimond, Chris, "Rob Angel—Driving Engen," Executive, May 1990.

"Gencor to Shed Base Metals and Buy Australian Nickel," New York Times, June 19, 1997.

"Gold Fields Looks to Expand Abroad," Platt's Metals Week, November 24, 2003, p. 4.

Green, Timothy, The New World of Gold, New York: Walker and Co., 1981.

Johnson, Paul, Consolidated Gold Fields: A Centenary Portrait, London: Weidenfeld & Nicolson, 1987.

Jones, J.D.F., Through Fortress and Rock: The Story of Gencor 1895–1995, Johannesburg: J. Ball, 1996.

Kilalea, Des, "Gencor Looks Ahead," Finance Week, April 27–May 3, 1989.

McKay, David, "Gencor, Australian Firm in Indonesian Deal," Business Day, October 23, 1996.

——, "Gencor to Revise Mozambique Plan," Business Day, February 26, 1997.

McNulty, Andrew, "Man of the Year—Gencor's Derek Keys," Financial Mail, December 25, 1987.

Ross, Priscilla, "Implats' Impasse," African Business, June 1996, p. 22.

——, "Birth of a New Giant," African Business, April 1998, p. 14.

Ryan, Brendan, "GFSA-Gencor Gold Merger," Financial Mail, October 17, 1997, p. 32.

Scudder, Brian, "Tiny Shouts, But Nobody Listens," African Business, January 1996, p. 23.

"South African Conglomerates: The Unbundling Begins," Economist, May 15, 1993.

"South African Gold: A New Vein," Economist, September 27, 1997.

"South African Gold Giants to Combine," New York Times, October 11, 1997, p. D14.

"Unbundling: Restructuring the Corporate Scene," Barron's, October 11, 1993, p. 72.

—Philip Gawith and Simon Katzenellenbogen
—updates: Frederick C. Ingram and Christina M. Stansell

Graham Corporation

20 Florence Avenue
Batavia, New York 14020
U.S.A.
Telephone: (585) 343-2216
Fax: (585) 343-1177
Web site: http://www.graham-mfg.com

Public Company
Incorporated: 1936 as Graham Manufacturing Company
   Inc.
Employees: 281
Sales: $49.4 million (2003)
Stock Exchanges: American Stock Exchange
Ticker Symbol: GHM
NAIC: 333911 Pump and Pumping Equipment
   Manufacturing

Graham Corporation is a Batavia, New York-based, publicly traded, maker of vacuum and heat transfer equipment, with operations in both the United States and the United Kingdom. The U.S. segment designs and manufactures steam jet ejector vacuum systems, surface condensers for steam turbines, liquid ring vacuum pumps and compressors, dry pumps, and heat exchangers. Graham's engineers are able to package these components to create customized systems for customers in such industries as oil refining, chemical, petrochemical, metal refining, heating, ventilating, air conditioning, pharmaceuticals, power, processed food, pulp and paper, and shipbuilding. The company's wholly-owned U.K. subsidiary, Graham Vacuum & Heat Transfer Ltd., which in turn owns subsidiary Graham Precision Pumps Ltd., makes liquid ring vacuum pumps, rotary piston pumps, oil sealed rotary vane pumps, atmospheric air operated ejectors, condensers, seals, as well as complete vacuum pump systems. Applications include chemical, food, furnace, packaging, pharmaceutical, plastic and rubber, and printing and paper. Graham relies on company sales engineers and independent reps around the world to sell its products.

Origins

The foundation of Graham can be traced to 1936 when engineer Harold M. Graham created Graham Manufacturing Co., Inc. in New York State. In 1941, another engineer, Frederick D. Berkeley, joined forces with Graham. Both men had worked for Ross Heater Manufacturing Company and gained valuable experience in their area of expertise. Graham Manufacturing started out by designing steam ejector equipment and surface condensers and soon began manufacturing heaters in a plant located in Oswego, New York. In short order, new facilities were bought in Batavia, which became operational in 1942. As was the case for most American companies during this period, Graham played a part in the effort to fight World War II, concentrating almost exclusively on the manufacture of surface condensers and heat exchangers for shipboard applications. It was during the war that Harold Graham invented the Heliflow heat exchanger used for boiler sample cooling, a product still manufactured today and used in various applications.

After World War II ended in 1945, Graham was free to continue its efforts to develop commercial applications for its products and broaden its offerings. The company added a full range of shell and tube heat exchangers, surface condensers, barometric condensers, evaporators designed for power plants, vertical marine evaporators, deaerating feedwater heaters, steam jet ejectors, and steam vacuum refrigeration systems.

Postwar Expansion

Harold Graham headed the company until his death in 1956, at which point Berkeley took over. Most notably, he expanded the company beyond its New York base, in 1957 forming a Canadian subsidiary to service, market, and later manufacture the company's products in Canada. However, Berkeley would only remain in charge until 1962, when he too passed away and was succeeded by his son, Frederick D. Berkeley III, who had joined the company in the early 1950s. He proved to be a strong and ambitious leader—while committed to keeping the company located in Batavia and remaining independent. He took the company public in 1968 but retained a controlling interest.

Company Perspectives:

Graham recognizes the importance of engineering answers to users of our equipment. We are constantly striving to improve the manufacturing capabilities and engineering resources of our company to add value to and improve the efficiency of your customer's process.

The younger Berkeley oversaw an extended period of expansion and diversification. In 1969 Graham established Gramex S.A., a Mexico City-based subsidiary to sell and service the company's products throughout Latin America. A year later, in September 1970, a United Kingdom subsidiary was formed, Graham Process Equipment Ltd. Moreover, in early 1972 Graham Export, Inc. was created to handle export sales from U.S. operations. Berkeley also grew the business through external means. In October 1971 Graham completed the purchase of a company located in Abercarn, Wales, Heat Transfer Limited, paying nearly $160,000 in cash and assuming more than $1 million in debt.

Berkeley launched another phase of aggressive growth in the early 1980s, but the attempt to digest two acquisitions in a single year proved too difficult. First, in August 1983 he formed Graham Corporation to serve as a holding company for the growing roster of subsidiaries, then in November of that year paid nearly $1.85 million in cash and notes for L&A Engineering & Equipment, Inc., a California food processing equipment company. Only a few weeks later, in December 1983, Graham added Therma Technology, Inc. at the cost of $650,000 in cash. Therma was a Tulsa, Oklahoma, company that served the oil and gas industries. In 1985 Therma would record sales on a par with Graham Manufacturing, but oil and gas encountered a prolonged slump that proved devastating for many companies involved in this sector. Although Graham began to lose money in fiscal 1984, it was still in expansion mode well into 1985. In July of that year the company paid $864,000 in cash for Hobal Engineering Ltd., a United Kingdom-based company that mostly made equipment for use in nuclear energy generation.

A downturn in petroleum and other processing industries, exacerbated by management problems at Hobal, led to a string of loses in the mid-1980s. Graham suffered net losses of $1.19 million in 1984, $4.18 million in 1985, and $1.19 in 1986. Management looked forward to a return to profitability in fiscal 1987. One attempt at diversification, the move into power—providing equipment for cogeneration and geothermal power plants—proved to be a lifesaver in some respects. Despite strong results from the Batavia operation, however, matters grew only worse for the company as a whole and the balance sheet showed another loss of more than $1 million, forcing drastic action. Therma, with the oil industry still far from recovering, had already been the first casualty, shuttered in the fall of 1986. Next, Hobal came under the gun. During its first six months of operation in 1985, the subsidiary had turned a profit, but then its primary customer, British Nuclear Fuel Ltd., tightened quality control procedures, and the Hobal's management team was simply unable to adapt to the sudden change. To make matters worse, Hobal booked more orders than the company

could handle, resulting in late penalties and excessive levels of overtime pay. (Graham's other British subsidiary also booked an excessive number of orders, and together the two units lost a total of nearly $2 million for the year). In July 1988, Graham announced its intention to close down Hobal, but at the last minute a buyer surfaced and in October the business was sold at a price that Berkeley portrayed as a virtual giveaway, but management was happy to unload it and preserve the jobs. As a result, Graham also cut its debt by $3 million. Finally, in May 1989, Heat Transfer was cut loose, sold to Hoval Farrar, Ltd.

The measures adopted by management had the desired effect, so much so that in the second quarter of fiscal 1989, Graham recorded net income of $1.2 million, compared to a loss of $364,000 during the same period a year earlier. This surge caught the attention of Wall Street, which bid up the price of the company's stock by 100 percent in less than two weeks, increasing from $7 to $14. For the entire year Graham would earn $4.2 million, becoming the top stock on the American Stock Exchange in terms of growth in 1989. The stock price peaked in the fall of 1989 at $41, well above the company's previous historic high in the $16 range. A major reason for the dramatic spike in price, however, was related to the company's relatively small number of shares in circulation, because company insiders owned about 43 percent of the stock, with Berkeley himself owning 37 percent. Due to such a thin float the company was subject to a sudden collapse in price, should conditions suddenly change and, indeed, Graham's days as a Wall Street darling were brief. Once again, British operations were at the core of the problem. As had been the case in 1987, management overbooked orders, leading to delays that cost money. Instead of meeting projected earnings, the subsidiary produced an operating loss, and the price of Graham's stock steadily declined, so that by January 1991 it dipped below $12.

Challenges in the 1990s

During the early 1990s, Graham endured another difficult stretch. Management instituted cost-cutting measures and took other steps to improve profitability, but trimming staff was not one of the more readily available options. Because Graham's work force was highly skilled and costly to train, management was reluctant to sacrifice its investment in its people. But management did cut wages by 5 percent in 1993. Another step that could be taken was to unload L&A Engineering, which was sold off in February 1992. Since its acquisition in 1983, the subsidiary had only been profitable twice. Graham was forced to take a $1.3 million charge, but the company could now focus on its core markets, which now included the chemical, petrochemical, petroleum refining, and electric power generating industries.

Later in 1992 Graham was beset by yet another problem, this time in the form of litigation. A major customer, Mississippi-based Ingalls Shipbuilding, sued the company in November 1992, alleging that Graham breached the warranties on the condensers supplied to U.S. Navy Ships. According to *Buffalo News*, Graham maintained that "the troubles were caused because Ingalls subjected the condensers during testing to temperatures that were higher than both Ingalls' design limit and the maximum level Graham set for the equipment. When the condensers developed problems, Graham said it fixed them by modifying the design specifications." But addressing the prob-

Key Dates:

1936: Harold Graham establishes the Graham Manufacturing Company.
1941: Frederick D. Berkeley joins the enterprise.
1956: Harold Graham dies and is succeeded as president by Berkeley.
1962: Berkeley dies, succeeded by son, Frederick D. Berkeley III.
1968: Company goes public.
1998: Frederick D. Berkeley III dies, succeeded by CEO Alvaro Cadena.

lem came at a cost, and as a result the company suffered a $3.5 million operating loss for fiscal 1992. To make matters worse, "Graham's bankers also imposed tighter restrictions on its credit facility, which had a lasting impact on the company"—and Ingalls still proceeded with its litigation. On trial in U.S. District Court in Mississippi, Graham, a New York company, felt it was at a decided disadvantage. When the case finally went to trial, a jury, in January 1995, ruled against Graham on the most significant of three counts, leading to $1.2 million judgment. Although management believed it had a stronger case than Ingalls, it opted to pay the money rather than risk an even greater judgment being rendered in a second trial. "You just can't win against a company that's many, many times bigger," Berkeley told *Buffalo News,* adding "A New York company can't go down and win in court in Mississippi . . . We'd like to move on to a new chapter in Graham and forget Ingalls ever existed." The loss capped a highly disappoint year for Graham in fiscal 1994, when the company lost $8.4. In addition to the money paid to Ingalls, Graham also continued to be plagued by losses at its Graham Manufacturing Ltd. subsidiary in England, the poor health of which threatened the well-being of its profitable British sister company, Graham Precision Pumps Ltd. Faced with the choice of putting the business into receivership or making a quick sale, Graham opted for the later course, selling the operation in January 1995.

Distractions continued in 1995, this time by an attempt of the International Association of Bridge, Structural and Ornamental Iron Workers to organize 162 of the Batavia plant's 429 workers. A month before the union drive, management restored the 5 percent wage cut imposed in 1993, but did not threaten to relocate the business. In the end, a majority of the workers voted against the union. Although pleased by the results, management was still upset about the procedure, which because of the time lost to meetings with workers and workers discussing the vote among themselves adversely impacted productivity. This factor, coupled with extra legal fees and administrative costs, was key, in the opinion of management, to a quarterly loss of $137,000. But with its legal and labor problems in the past, the company was able to post $1.3 million in income from continuing operations for fiscal 1995. That number would more than double to $3.1 million in fiscal 1996.

The Late 1990s and Beyond

Diagnosed with cancer, Berkeley, aged 68, took the first step toward transferring power in July 1997 by naming 53-year-old Alvaro Cadena, a long-time Graham executive, to the presidency of the firm. Later in October 1997 Jerald D. Bidlack, president of a local firm, Griffin Automation Inc., was named vice-chairman. When Berkeley died in April 1998 Bidlack became chairman, and Cadena became chief executive officer and the primary architect of Graham's future. Cadena was born in Colombia and as the eldest of four sons was expected to one day take over the running of the family business, a prosperous distributorship for American Standard Cos. Inc. He came to the United States in 1965 to study engineering at New York University's Bronx campus. He first became involved with Graham in 1969 when he took a part-time job at the company's Long Island sales office. Liking the work, he took a full-time position and relegated his schools to night-time courses. He still intended to return to Colombia, but each time he was on the verge of moving he received a promotion and stayed. In 1975 he became manager of Latin American sales, which at least afforded him an opportunity to make periodic visits to family and friends at home. He later became manager of international sales, then vice-president of international sales. When he and his Colombian-born wife both became U.S. citizens in 1982, the thought of returning home to run the family business began to fade. Instead, he continued to climb the ranks at Graham, eventually becoming president and chief operating officer at the Batavia subsidiary.

As Graham embarked on a new phase in its history under the guidance of Cadena, it was a leaner operation, having shed all but two of its operating subsidiaries. Because the holding company structure no longer made sense, in January 1999 Graham Manufacturing Co., Inc. and parent company, Graham Corporation, merged, leaving a newly constituted Graham Corporation. The company closed the 1990s with some strong years, posting profits of $3.8 million in 1998 and $2.4 million in 1999. Business fell off because of a poor economy during the early years of the new century, but the company remained a profitable concern and well established and respected in its field.

Principal Subsidiaries

Graham Vacuum and Heat Transfer Ltd.; Graham Precision Pumps Ltd.

Principal Competitors

Dover Corporation; Haskel International, Inc.; Pfeiffer Vacuum Technology AG.

Further Reading

Astor, Will, "The Deep Roots of Graham's Chief Executive," *Rochester Business Journal,* December 17, 1999, p. 10.

Johnston, Phil, "Graham on Track to End 1988 in the Black," *Rochester Business Journal,* June 6, 1988, p. 1.

——, "Subsidiary Takes Blame for Graham's Bad Year," *Rochester Business Journal,* January 21, 1991, p. 4.

Robinson, David, "Graham Upbeat After 'Very Disappointing Year'," *Buffalo News,* May 12, 1995, p. A-10.

Whiskeyman, Dolores, "The Road to Recovery," *Rochester Business Journal,* July 3, 1989, p. 40.

—Ed Dinger

Hankyu Department Stores, Inc.

8-7 Kakuda-cho
Kita-ku
Osaka 530-8350
Japan
Telephone: (+06) 361 1381
Fax: (+06) 367 2943
Web site: http://www.hankyu-dept.co.jp

Public Company
Incorporated: 1947
Employees: 6,501
Sales: ¥395 billion ($3.68 billion) (2003)
Stock Exchanges: Tokyo
Ticker Symbol: 8242
NAIC: 452110 Department Stores

Hankyu Department Stores, Inc. is one of Japan's leading department store chains. The company's stores can be found in the Japanese cities of Osaka, Toyonaka, Kawanishi, Kyoto, Kobe, Takarazuka, Tokyo, and Yokohama. Hankyu and its peers in the retail industry were hit hard by Japan's sluggish economy and drop-off in consumer spending during the 1990s. The company launched a major restructuring effort in 2000 that included selling off subsidiaries, cutting costs, and developing a new management system in order to bolster sales and profits.

Early History

Although the first Hankyu Department Store did not open until 1929, the history of the company dates back to 1907, when Japanese entrepreneur Ichizo Kobayashi helped found the Mino-Arima Electric Railway Company, the forerunner to the Hankyu Corporation. To promote the use of the railway, Kobayashi developed a number of leisure facilities at sites along the track. The foremost of these was the Takarazuka Resort, famous for its Girl's Revue, an all-women theater troupe whose international reputation gained the company much valuable publicity. In 1918, Kobayashi attempted to expand the Mino-Arima railway company to run trains from Mino-Arima to Kobe. Unable to acquire permission to do so, he had to settle

for a line from Osaka to Kobe. It was at this time that the company changed its name to Hankyu Corporation. The name Hankyu derived from a combination of the Chinese characters for Osaka, which can be read as the words "Han" and "Kyu," the latter of which means express.

To promote the use of the railway further, Kobayashi opened the first Hankyu department store at Umeda railway station in the city of Osaka in 1929. It became the first railway terminal department store, designed to serve several hundred thousand daily commuters, and as such heralded a new movement among Japanese retailers. This movement was characterized by the opening of department stores by railroad companies on prime sites along the railway lines, in particular at important terminals and main interchange stations, using capital from their parent companies. The railway lines often originated within the stores themselves.

Hankyu Department Stores opened its second store in 1936 in Kobe, but growth soon came to a virtual standstill because of World War II. During the war, the company was enlisted to help the cause of the Japanese army. It donated money, and the escalators and lifts of the stores were stripped to provide the army with much-needed metal. During World War II, the department stores also became focal points for control and distribution of all consumer goods by the government. The store in Osaka was damaged by an Allied bombing raid.

Postwar Growth

After the war, the American forces who were now occupying Japan also used Hankyu and other department stores as distribution points for food and clothing, which were in short supply. In 1947, the Hankyu Corporation was reorganized into two smaller companies on the instructions of the U.S. occupying forces who were looking to reduce the power of Japan's big conglomerates in the wake of the war. The transport group became Hankyu Corporation and the retail business became Hankyu Department Stores, Inc. This breakup was seen to be in Hankyu Department Stores' favor, as the transport side of the company was facing a series of strikes by railwaymen demanding better conditions. This industrial action might have affected the department stores had they remained within the same group.

It was not until Japan's postwar boom years that Hankyu Department Stores really began to prosper. This was a time when Japan was experiencing rapid growth in income levels, personal consumption, and its general standard of living. Together with the system of floating exchange rates and the resultant appreciation of the yen, which made imported goods cheaper and therefore more competitive, Japan's retail industry expanded, opening it to a wider variety of consumer goods, including imports. Between 1953 and 1959, Hankyu Department Stores opened three more stores: Tokyo Oi in 1953, Sukiyabashi Hankyu in 1956, and, in the United States, Los Angeles Hankyu in 1967.

The Tokyo Oi store was a landmark in the company's development, taking the reputation of Hankyu Department Stores out of the suburbs and placing it firmly in the city. This standing was enhanced by the opening of a second Tokyo store in 1956.

Los Angeles Hankyu was originally a retail store, but because of the appreciation of the yen it became too expensive to maintain import goods from Japan. Los Angeles Hankyu therefore became a buying center for the Japanese stores and remained as such. The next boom in Hankyu Department Stores' history took place in the 1970s, when additional stores were opened: Senri Hankyu in Senri, a satellite town of Osaka, in 1970 and Shijo-Kawaramachi Hankyu in Kyoto in 1976.

Each store Hankyu Department Stores opened exploited its strategic location. The Umeda Main Store was situated in the commercial area which surrounds Umeda, in the city of Osaka. Umeda was one of the largest railway terminals in Japan, and Hankyu Department Stores expected good sales growth from this store as Osaka became one of the nation's major international cities with the completion of Kansai International Airport.

Expansion in the 1980s and Early 1990s

Senri Hankyu was created to cater to families in the nearby housing development district, providing locally oriented goods and services. It was also the pioneer store in the metropolitan suburbs. The store in the international port of Kobe was conveniently located for the users of Sannomiya terminal station. The Kyoto and Sukiyabashi stores both targeted young Japanese women who were starting to enjoy an increase in status and jobs. The early 1980s, however, saw a downturn in sales due to the worldwide recession, and in fiscal year 1983 the Japan Economic Journal reported that sales by Japan's 200 leading retailers rose by only 5.3 percent. The department stores' slowed growth was also due in part to changing lifestyles in Japan. Despite Japanese women's greater disposable income, they began to look more toward convenience stores and supermarkets, which grew rapidly. Department stores responded to this switch by implementing a range of measures designed to woo back consumers. They commissioned market research to discover what consumers

wanted, and they extended shopping hours so that working women could shop after work. Hankyu Department Stores and other department store retailers transformed their shops, making them not only places to shop but also entertainment and cultural centers encompassing restaurants, recreational areas for children, golf ranges and tennis courts, educational facilities, theaters, and art exhibitions. They also invested in sponsoring events. Hankyu Department Stores regularly sponsored cultural events. The company put particular emphasis on introducing the traditional crafts and cultures of foreign countries, illustrated by its "British Fair" and "French Fair," as well as its "Wonders of China" and "9,000 year-old Art and Culture of Jordan" exhibitions. Hankyu Department Stores also supported Japanese baseball and was one of the many major retailers that owned a team, Hankyu's being the Hankyu Braves.

Hankyu Department Stores continued to expand, opening another two stores, Yurakucho in 1984 and Kawanishi Hankyu in 1989. Meanwhile, the company responded to the increasing popularity of the Western-style department store by adopting the decoration, fittings, and look of the modern department stores of the United States and Europe. In the Ginza shopping area, which catered to 200,000 shoppers per day, the company used this theme in its Yurakucho store, complementing the more traditional-style store, Sukibayashi Hankyu.

In 1988, the company's pretax profits rose by 14.3 percent thanks to the longer shopping hours and increased sales in high-profit items, including accessories, handbags, and imported clothes such as American jeans. Imported products, or those seen to have a Western flavor, were particularly popular with Japanese consumers, and Hankyu Department Stores responded to this by developing its own brand of children's clothing, Potato Chips, which was highly successful and was even sold in other major department stores. In its Yurakucho store in central Tokyo, the company exclusively stocked overseas labels.

During this time period, the company was also known for its high quality foodstuffs. It responded to changes in eating habits, especially the trend toward gourmet food, by introducing a wide assortment of value-added products and more ready-to-serve products.

In 1989, the success of Hankyu Department Stores attracted the interest of the American retailer Bloomingdale's, and in November of that year the company approached Hankyu Department Stores with an invitation to participate in a buy-out of the chain. Hankyu Department Stores' president Shoji Fukumitsu met with Bloomingdale's chairman Marvin Traub but turned down a reported financing of $250 million out of the $1.2 billion to $1.3 billion needed for the buy-out.

Profitability of department stores throughout Japan and for Hankyu Department Store fell as a result of the Japanese government's introduction of a consumption tax on April 1, 1989. A large increase in sales volume in March 1989, just prior to the introduction of the tax, was followed by a slump in April. The slump was short lived, however, mainly due to the fact that the tax only had a slight impact on commodity prices. Consumer spending recovered soon after.

In the early 1990s, Hankyu Department Stores appeared to be entering one of its strongest periods of growth, with a large

Key Dates:

1907: Ichizo Kobayashi helps to establish the Mino-Arima Electric Railway Company.
1929: The first Hankyu Department Store opens.
1936: The company opens its second store.
1947: The firm is reorganized as Hankyu Department Stores Inc.
1953: The Tokyo Oi store opens.
1970: Senri Hankyu is established.
1976: A store is launched in Kyoto.
1989: The Japanese government introduces the consumption tax.
2000: The company opens its tenth department store.

number of developments planned for the next few years. However, Hankyu, like other Japanese department stores, faced a challenge from the relaxation of legal limitations on large-scale retail stores, triggered by Japan-U.S. Structural Impediments Initiative talks. This led to intensified competition in Japan's distribution and retail industries in the coming years.

In preparation, the company looked to develop a variety of management measures, including entering new markets and expanding its business base. The company set plans in motion to open a store in Kobe Harbor Land, one of Japan's largest waterfront development projects. The new store had a sales floor of approximately 30,000 square meters and opened to the public in 1992. Adjoining the store was a restaurant comparable in size.

Further expansion included plans to open a new store in Takarazuka, a place of symbolic significance for the Hankyu and Toho Group because of its associations with the first store. The company hoped to deepen its market through the formation of a store network encompassing a large part of the commercial sphere in northern Hanshin (Osaka-Kobe) area at sites centered on the Hankyu Railways' service area. Takarazuka Hankyu opened in 1993.

A new affiliated merchandising company, Hankyu Ings Company, Ltd., was also established and was separate from the merchandising function of Hankyu Main Store (Umeda). There was a strong emphasis on further product development of attractive, economical overseas brands and materials which the company saw as essential if it was to survive the retail wars of the future.

The company expanded overseas with the development of a food business in Bangkok, Thailand, through a joint venture with Central Department Store, the leading local operator. The new company, Central Hankyu Ltd., had a capital of 20 million bahts, 51 percent provided by Central and 49 percent by Hankyu. Hankyu occupied one floor of the Thai store, selling foodstuffs.

Facing Problems in the 1990s and Beyond

Hankyu began to face distinct challenges as Japan's economy bottomed out in the 1990s. In 1993, the company reported a decline in sales and recurring profit for the first time in its history. Net profit fell by 76.5 percent over the previous year's

results. As the company struggled to regain its footing, disaster struck. The January 1995 Kobe earthquake caused significant damage, leaving Hankyu with estimated costs totaling over ¥2.3 billion. The firm was forced to start making serious changes to its operating strategy and announced that it would cut nearly 60 percent of its managerial staff—approximately 1,000 jobs. It also began to promote and give salaries based on merit rather than seniority. This was a fairly new practice for Japanese companies as business culture traditionally held seniority high above other factors.

Hankyu was dealt another blow in April 1997 when Japan raised its consumption tax from 3 to 5 percent. This tax increase, along with the crisis in Asia's financial sector, weakened consumer confidence. Sure enough, the company reported its first ever after-tax loss during fiscal 1998. Department stores across Japan began to feel the crunch as sales continued to dwindle. Many of these companies had expanded significantly during the 1980s and early 1990s and were now left with too much floor space. According to a 1999 *Nikkei Weekly* report, sales per square meter of floor space declined by more than 30 percent from 1990 to 1999.

Hankyu and its competitors continued to face problems in the early years of the new century. A May 2000 *Nikkei Weekly* article reported, "Not only have operators been hemmed in by a stagnant market amid depressed personal consumption, but they have been forced to compete with new segments of retail commerce such as a growing number of suburban shopping malls, the rise of a new breed of vendors such as so-called 'category killers,' and domestic and foreign discount retailers." In response to these industry conditions, Hankyu launched a major restructuring effort that including selling off unprofitable subsidiaries, cost cutting measures, and the launching of a new management system designed to respond more efficiently to trends in the marketplace.

Overall, Hankyu fared better than many of its peers during this time period. The company opened its tenth department store in Tsuzuki, Yokohama in 2000. By fiscal 2003, it reported a profit of $73 million, in contrast to a loss the previous year. Restructuring efforts appeared to have paid off for the company, leaving it able to focus on an intense marketing strategy in hopes of shoring up store sales. While Hankyu's future remained dependent on an economic turnaround in Japan, it stood well positioned to battle the problems that may come its way.

Principal Subsidiaries

Kobe Hankyu Company Ltd.; Takarazuka Hankyu Company Ltd.; Hankyu Tomonokai Company Ltd.; Tasukara Company Ltd.; Hankyu Department Stores Europe B.V. (Netherlands); Hankyu Seisakusho Company Ltd.

Principal Competitors

The Daimaru Inc.; Seibu Department Stores Ltd.; Takashimaya Company Ltd.; Mitsukoshi Ltd.

Further Reading

"Consumer Spending May Have Bottomed Out," *Nikkei Weekly*, June 1, 1998, p. 3.

''Hankyu Department Stores' Group Net Profit Down 76.5%,'' *Japan Economic Newswire*, June 25, 1993.

''Hankyu Department Stores' Profits, Sales Drop in FY '97,'' *Jiji Press Ticker Service*, May 25, 1998.

''Hankyu Dept. Faces 1st After-Tax Loss,'' *Jiji Press Ticker Service*, March 25, 1999.

''Hankyu Incurs First-Ever Sales, Profit Drop,'' *Jiji Press Ticker Service*, May 18, 1993.

''Hankyu Names New President,'' *Nikkei Weekly*, April 25, 1994, p. 12.

''Hankyu Review May Bring Boost to Stores Sector,'' *Financial Times*, June 7, 2003, p. 6.

''Management in Japan: Salariless Man,'' *Economist*, September 16, 1995, p. 79.

''More Pain for Major Department Stores,'' *Nikkei Weekly*, February 22, 1999, p. 7.

Oshima, Atsuko, ''Department Stores Get Lean to Survive,'' *Nikkei Weekly*, May 1, 2000, p. 14.

''Quake Ravage Trims Hankyu Dept Stores Profits,'' *Japan Economic Newswire*, April 19, 1995.

Sato, Makoto, ''Department Stores Trim Goods, Staff,'' *Nikkei Weekly*, September 18, 1995, p. 8.

—Rachel Loos
—update: Christina M. Stansell

Hanwha Group

1 Changgyo-dong, Chung-ku
Seoul
South Korea
Telephone: (+82) 2 729 3581
Fax: (+82) 2 752 3475
Web site: http://www.hanwhacorp.co.kr

Public Company
Incorporated: 1953
Employees: 2,887
Sales: $6 billion (2002)
Stock Exchanges: Korea
Ticker Symbol: 0880
NAIC: 325920 Explosives Manufacturing; 325320
    Pesticide and Other Agricultural Chemical Manufac-
    turing; 551112 Offices of Other Holding Companies

Hanwha Group is one of South Korea's top ten *chaebol*s—
or conglomerates—with diversified holdings stretching from
explosives to retail to financial services and beyond. The group
operates through a complex network of subsidiaries, many of
which are publicly listed entities, including flagship company
Hanwha Energy Corporation. Hanwha's operations are grouped
under five major divisions: Manufacture/Construction, Distri-
bution/Leisure, Finance/Trade, SI/Communication, and Sports.
Manufacture/Construction includes Hanwha Corporation's explosives production; Hanwha Chemical Corporation, which
produces PVC; Hanwha L&C, which produces PVC-based
products; H-Pharm Company, which produces non-prescription
drugs and health and beauty products; and Hanwha Advanced
Materials, a partnership with Solvay, which produces materials
for the automobile and other industries. Distribution/Leisure
comprises the company group's Hanwha Stores, which operates
the seven-store Galleria Department Store chain, and Hanwha
Resort Company, the largest leisure company in South Korea.
Since 2002, Hanwha has made a push into the financial services
market, grouping its 51 percent stake in former state-owned
insurance group Korea Life under its Finance/Trade division.
The company also operates asset management and other insur-

ance subsidiaries. The two remaining divisions, SI/Communi-
cation and Sports, include operations in the advertising and
e-commerce sectors and ownership of the Hanwha Eagles professional baseball team. Hanwha, which emerged somewhat
humbled from the economic debacle of the late 1990s, is led by
chairman Kim Seung Yeon, son of the company's founder.

Success in the 1950s

The division of Korea following World War II, and especially after the outbreak of the Korean War in 1950, left South
Korea in economic ruin. Most of the country's infrastructure,
including the majority of its power plants and other important
installations, lay in the region now claimed by communist North
Korea. Yet the aftermath of the war also created an era of
opportunity for a new breed of entrepreneurs.

Among them was Kim Jong-Hee, who recognized that the
ongoing political tensions between North and South Korea
made the development of a weapons industry a national priority.
In 1952, Kim established a new company, Hyun Am, or the
Korea Explosives Corporation, becoming the first and only
privately held producer of explosives in South Korea.

Demand rose quickly, and the company began the expansion
that was to rank it among the country's top ten companies by the
end of the century. In 1955, the company added operations in
Inchon, buying up the power plant operated by that city's
Chosun Oil and Fat. By the end of the 1950s, Korea Explosives
had added two new explosive types, nitroglycerin, starting in
1957, and dynamite, starting in 1958. The company also began
producing fireworks.

The rebuilding of Korea's economy, as well as its civil and
industrial infrastructure, began in earnest in the 1960s. Hyun
Am's strong cash flow from its explosives business allowed it to
become one of the driving forces behind the country's industrialization. By the mid-1960s, Kim started buying up other businesses.
One of the company's first diversification moves came in 1964,
when it acquired Shinhan Bearing Industrial Company, which
later formed the basis of the group's Hanwha Machinery division.

Other diversified operations followed quickly, including an
entry into petrochemicals market and the manufacturing of PVC

Company Perspectives:

Hanwha was founded in 1952 in the ruins of industrial devastation. Built as an explosives company with the spirit of full-hearted contribution to the nation and society, Hanwha has walked along almost half a century since the start-up. During this half-century period, Hanwha has overcome lots of difficulties and crisis, with the "YOU CAN DO" spirit. Hanwha is now trying to emerge as a new image company.

Hanwha will establish an ideal management system, putting Hanwha's basic spirit, Trust and Justice, into the efficient management and new personnel system that can flexibly cope with the management environment of the 21st century.

and PVC-based products, starting in 1966, with the launch of Korea Hwasung Industrial Corporation. Under government insistence, however, that company was merged into the Korea Plastics Industrial Company in 1972, which led the company to begin developing other plastics holdings, such as Hankook Plastics in 1972 and Dongwon Industrial, acquired in 1974.

The company had by then entered the international trading arena, acquiring Taepyng Trading Corporation, later known as Golden Bell Trading Corporation, in 1966. In 1969, the group joined in the creation of Kyungin Energy Company, later renamed Hanwha Energy Corporation, which built and operated South Korea's sole privately held thermal power station. That operation soon developed into what the company described as its flagship business. In the meantime, Korea Explosives had begun exporting fireworks, especially to the Japanese market.

In the 1970s, Kim's range of business interests continued to expand as rapidly as the company itself. Over the next decade, the group entered a variety of industries, many of which had little to do with the its core explosives operation. Such was the case with its takeover of Daeil Dairy Industry Company in 1973 and the creation of Kimpo Ceramics Corporation the following year. The company also added shipping interests through the purchase of Sungwoon Trading Company in 1975 and made its first venture into the financial sector with the acquisition of Sungdo Securities Company in 1976. In that year, the company listed Korea Explosives on the Seoul Stock Exchange.

International Conglomerate in the 1980s

Kim Jong Hee died in 1981, and the chairmanship of the company was turned over to his son, Kim Seung Yeon, then just 29 years old. While his father had built up the company around a core manufacturing base, the younger Kim began transforming the family business into one of Korea's leading chaebols—known for their willingness to expand across a striking array of industries, as well as for their organizational and financial complexity. While the group continued to seek new manufacturing opportunities, such as its acquisition of Dow Chemical Korea in 1982 and the establishment of Hangyang BASF Urethane Corp in 1988, Hanwha now sought to impose itself on a variety of new business sectors.

Resorts development became a one of the group's first growth targets at the beginning of the 1980s, starting with the opening of the 768-room Seolak Hanwha Resort Hotel in 1981. The company's Hanwha Resorts began building a string of condominiums and resort complexes and soon grew to become Korea's leading leisure group.

In 1986, Hanwha entered the retail market as well, acquiring the Galleria Department Stores. That operation, targeting the high-end retail segment, grew into a chain of seven stores throughout Korea and formed the basis of the group's Hanwha Stores subsidiary. Later, Hanwha also began developing a discount retail format, Hanwha Mart, which grew into a nine-store chain by the end of the 1990s.

Yet any chaebol worthy of the name required still more diversified holdings, particularly in Korea's financial sector. The company launched its own bank, Hanwha Merchant Bank, and became the single largest shareholder in another, Chungkong Bank. The ownership of banks, a common practice among Korea's chaebols in the 1980s and into the 1990s, gave the group increased access to loans in order to fuel its ambitious growth. The company also founded Hanwha Investment Trust Management Company, entering the assets management field, in 1988.

In 1989, Hanwha purchased a newspaper, the Kyung Hyang Newspaper Company. By then, the company had also bought a baseball team, backing the formation of the Bingrae Eagles, later renamed the Hanwha Eagles, which became Korea's seventh professional baseball team.

In the 1990s, Hanwha's growth kept pace with Korea's emergence as both a regional and global economic powerhouse. Hanwha itself began to approach the top ranks of the country's corporations, finally cracking the top ten non-government owned companies by the middle of the decade. At this time, the company became implicated in the corruption that seemed to pervade South Korea's corporate and financial elite, and Kim Seung Yeon was jailed for 54 days in 1994 after being convicted for illegally smuggled foreign exchange currency worth nearly $6 million out of the country.

Restructured for the New Century

Hanwha entered the second half of the 1990s with high hopes for transforming itself into a high-technology contender. The company, which had already been involved in manufacturing telecommunications equipment, announced plans to step up its holdings in that sector. At the same time, it also entered the pharmaceuticals industry, acquiring Central Pharmaceutical Company, which formed the core of its new H-Pharm subsidiary in 1995.

The collapse of Korea's economy, and the implosion of its banking industry, brought Hanwha up short. Hanwha's policy of financing its unbridled expansion through debt had seen the company build up a debt-to-equity ratio of a whopping 1,200 percent. Both the Hanwha Merchant Bank and the Chungkong Bank folded, forcing a Korean government bailout. Hanwha itself now faced into a government-imposed breakup.

Kim rushed to restructure the company, selling off more than a dozen of its most profitable businesses, including its flagship Hanwha Energy and the manufacturing groups Hanwha

Key Dates:

1952: Kim Jong-Hee establishes Korea Explosives (Hyun Am) Corporation.
1955: The company purchases Inchon Power Plant.
1957: Korea Explosives begins production of nitroglycerin.
1958: The company begins producing dynamite.
1964: Korean Explosives begins diversifying with the acquisition of Shinhan Bearing Industrial Company.
1969: Korean Explosives backs the construction of the first privately held electrical power generating plant, which later becomes the company flagship as Hanwha Energy Corporation.
1976: Korea Explosives goes public on the Seoul Stock Exchange.
1979: Korea Plastics Industrial Corporation is acquired.
1981: Kim Jong-Hee dies and son Kim Seung Yeon takes over as group chairman.
1985: The company expands into retail sector with the acquisition of Galleria Department Store group.
1990: Hanwha acquires Kyung Hyang Newspaper Company.
1992: The company changes its name to Hanwha Group.
1994: Kim Seung Yeon is convicted of currency smuggling and sentenced to 54 days in jail.
1997: Amidst an economic crisis in Korea, Hanwha begins a companywide restructuring.
2002: The company acquires a 51 percent stake in Korea Life, restructuring itself as a financial and high-technology company.
2003: Hanwha faces three separate charges as part of a government crackdown on corporate corruption.

Bearing and Hanwha Precision. At the same time, the company began consolidating its other holdings, while shutting down others, such as its newspaper operation in 1998, which had lost more than $350 million since becoming part of the group. Perhaps most painful for the Hanwha Group was the sale of its control of Hanwha Energy to Hyundai in 1999, which deprived the group of what it had come to consider as its core business. However, as Kim told the *Korea Herald:* "I was actually bitter about selling flagship companies, but I just emptied my mind of any desire for managerial rights, while turning a blind eye to all dignities as a tycoon."

By the end of the decade, Hanwha had completed its restructuring and now found itself held up as an example for the rest of Korea's chaebols. The company now set out to identify its growth objectives for the new century, targeting a return to the financial market, on the one hand, and a new role in the high-technology sector on the other.

As the Korean government prepared to privatize its Korea Life insurance business, Hanwha stepped up as a potential buyer, only to be rebuffed by the government. In 2002, however, the company tried again, raising its offer and agreeing to a three-year moratorium on arranging any part of Hanwha's financing through Korea Life. At last, in September 2002, the government agreed to sell a 51 percent stake to Hanwha for more than KW 1 trillion ($770 million), which beat out a rival bid from MetLife. The addition of Korea Life raised the group's ranking among Korea's top companies, giving it the eighth place position by the end of 2003.

Reborn as one of Korea's top financial services groups, Hanwha began development of the second wing of its growth strategy in 2001. In that year, the company, in partnership with the city of Daejon and the Korea Development Bank, launched construction of Daedeok Techno Valley. A grandiose scheme involving the construction of an entire city devoted to developing businesses in the high-technology sector, the company hoped that Daedeok would grow to rival California's Silicon Valley as a force in the world technology market. Construction was scheduled to proceed in five phases, with the final phase to be completed in 2007.

While a number of observers remained skeptical about the long-term viability of the Daedeok project, others had begun to question whether Hanwha truly represented a "new" kind of Korean company. In 2003, as the Korean government launched a crackdown on the corruption that remained rampant throughout the country's top corporations, Hanwha found itself accused of misrepresenting its profits by as much as $800 million in order to secure its Korea Life bid. That charge was followed by a fresh accusation, that Korea Life had agreed to rollover a pre-existing loan to Hanwha into preferential interest rates, violating terms of the acquisition agreement.

Corruption probes had by then resulted in the arrest of a number of top Korean business leaders, and the government's focus was said to be targeting Hanwha in the later part of 2003. Indeed, the company returned to the spotlight again in September of that year, accusing Hanwha of being part of a slush-fund scandal between Daewoo Construction and Kangwon Casino.

Despite its legal problems, Hanwha remained a respected force among the Korean and worldwide business communities. In April 2003, for example, *Forbes* magazine named the company among its highly coveted "A-List" of the world's best big companies. With annual sales of more than $6 billion and more than 50 years among Korea's top companies, Hanwha now turned to the future with its new look as a Korean financial and high-technology force.

Principal Subsidiaries

DAEDUK Techno Valley Company Ltd.; Dong Yang Department Store Company; FAG Hanwha Bearings Corporation; Galleria Shooting Team; Han Comm Inc.; Hanwha Advanced Materials Company Ltd.; Hanwha Chemical Corporation; Hanwha Chemical Corporation R&D Center; Hanwha Company/Trading; Hanwha Corporation; Hanwha Corporation/Explosive Division; Hanwha Development Company Ltd.; Hanwha Eagles Professional Baseball Club; Hanwha Engineering & Construction Company Ltd.; Hanwha Finance Company Ltd.; Hanwha Investment Trust Management Company Ltd.; Hanwha L&C Corporation; Hanwha Land Development Company Ltd./FS Business Part; Hanwha Machinery Company Ltd.; Hanwha Polymer Company Ltd.; Hanwha Resort Company Ltd; Hanwha S&C Company Ltd.; Hanwha Securities Company Ltd.; Hanwha Station Development Company Ltd; Hanwha Stores Company Ltd.; Hanwha Tourmall Company Ltd.; Hanwha VC Corporation; H-Pharm Company, Ltd.; Korea Independent Energy Corporation; Korean Life Insurance Company Ltd.; SHINDONGAH Fire & Marine Insurance Company, Ltd.

Principal Competitors

Samsung Electronics Corporation; SK Corporation; Hyundai Motor; POSCO; Kookmin Bank; SK Telecom.

Further Reading

''Hanwha, Daewoo Accused of Stashing Secret Funds,'' *Korea Times*, September 19, 2003.

''Hanwha Energy to Secede from Parent Group,'' *Korea Herald*, May 10, 2000.

''Hanwha's Chaebol Ranking Rises to 8th,'' *Korea Herald*, September 25, 2002.

''Hanwha Sets Stage for Decisive Restructuring,'' *Korea Times*, June 15, 1999.

''Korea's Hanwha Faces Scrutiny,'' *CNN.com*, February 25, 2003.

''7 Korean Companies Rank among World's Best,'' *Korea Herald*, April 12, 2003.

Ward, Andrew, ''S. Korea Accepts Offer for Life Assurer,'' *Financial Times*, September 24, 2002, p. 22.

Yoo Cheong-mo, ''Hanwha Chairman Kim Dubbed Restructuring Magician,'' *Korea Herald*, April 17, 1999.

——, ''Hanwha Sets Sights on Financial Empire,'' *Korea Herald*, January 14, 2002.

—M.L. Cohen

Hilton Hotels Corporation

9336 Civic Center Drive
Beverly Hills, California 90210
U.S.A.
Telephone: (310) 278-4321
Fax: (310) 205-7678
Web site: http://www.hilton.com

Public Company
Incorporated: 1946
Employees: 74,000
Sales: $3.85 billion (2003)
Stock Exchanges: New York
Ticker Symbol: HLT
NAIC: 721110 Hotels (Except Casino Hotels) and Motels

Hilton Hotels Corporation is a leading hospitality company that owns, manages, and franchises over 2,000 hotels across the country. The company's international arm, Conrad Hotels, has locations in Australia, England, Ireland, Egypt, Belgium, Turkey, Hong Kong, and Singapore. Though publicly traded, the chain was for most of its history led by members of the Hilton family from 1919, when founder Conrad Hilton bought his first hotel. By the late 1940s, Hilton owned a worldwide chain of premium hotels. In the 1960s, Hilton sold its international operations and concentrated on management contracts and franchising. The company created innovative joint-venture arrangements that became standard industry practice. It then entered what would become a prime source of revenue for the company: casino-hotels. Hilton expanded into gaming in 1971; by 1989, gaming provided 44 percent of the company's income. In 1996, Barron Hilton relinquished day-to-day management of the chain to Stephen F. Bollenbach. Asserting that "Big companies do big things," Bollenbach revitalized the company with bold actions. He spun off the company's gaming operations as Park Place Entertainment Corporation in 1998. One year later he orchestrated the $3.7 billion acquisition of Promus Hotel Corporation, which added the Doubletree, Embassy Suites, Hampton Inn, Homewood Suites, and Harrison Conference Centers brand names to its line-up.

Early 20th-Century Origins

Conrad Nicholson Hilton was born in San Antonio, New Mexico, the second of eight children. Before he was 18, Conrad had worked as a trader, a clerk, a bellboy, and a pianist. By age 25 he had also worked in politics and banking. In 1919, following the death of his father, Hilton left the army and went to Texas. He had intended to take advantage of the oil boom by buying a small bank. Instead, he found bank prices prohibitive and hotels so overbooked he could not find a place to sleep. When one owner in Cisco, Texas, complained he would like to sell his property in order to take advantage of the oil boom, Hilton struck a deal. Hilton pulled together an investment group and the funds were transferred within a week. The Mobley, in Cisco, became Hilton's first hotel.

The hotel was booked solid, and Conrad and his partner, L.M. Drown, rented their own beds and slept on chairs in the office. They also converted much of the hotel's public space into additional guest quarters. Making use of wasted space became a hallmark of the Hilton chain. With the Mobley running smoothly, Hilton bought two more Texas properties in 1920; the Melba, in Fort Worth, and the Waldorf in Dallas—named after the prized New York hotel. In 1925 Conrad Hilton built the first hotel to carry his name, in Dallas.

With expansions well underway, Hilton consolidated his properties into Hilton Hotels, Incorporated, in 1929, when the stock market crashed. The El Paso Hilton was completed in November 1930 and opened with a fanfare. A year later, Hilton owned eight hotels and was more than half a million dollars in debt when a young bellboy slipped him $300—his life savings—so Hilton could feed himself and his family.

Depression-Era Wrangling over Corporate Ownership

In 1931 the Moody family of Galveston, Texas, from whom Hilton had borrowed, took possession of his hotels when he defaulted on a $300,000 loan. The Moodys then hired Hilton to manage their own and his hotels, now known as the National Hotel Company. Nine months later, in 1932, Hilton and the Moodys decided to part. The separation, however, was in no way peaceful. The Moody family and Hilton sued and coun-

Company Perspectives:

By providing the best service, value and amenities, along with a wide variety of hotel products and price points, we are focused on our mission of being the first choice of the world's traveler.

tersued each other regarding the terms of their agreement for separation, which Hilton claimed allotted him one-third of the hotels and one-third of the stock if the arrangement failed to prove satisfactory. In 1933, while Hilton continued to battle the Moodys in court, the Moodys defaulted on the loan for the El Paso Hilton, and Conrad Hilton managed to raise the necessary $30,000 to buy back that hotel. In 1934 Hilton settled with the Moodys, who lent him $95,000 and returned the Lubbock, Dallas, and Plainview hotels. According to Conrad Hilton, while Depression-era hotel owners saved less than one hotel out of five, Hilton emerged with five of his eight hotels, and he met his debts by the summer of 1937.

In 1938, Hilton bought his first hotel outside of Texas, the Sir Francis Drake in San Francisco. He sold it two years later at a $500,000 profit to raise capital to purchase the Stevens in Chicago, then the largest hotel in the world.

Although U.S. entry into World War II spawned caution, Hilton acquired three new properties, one in Los Angeles and two in New York. Thus, in 1942, his name stretched from coast to coast. The New York properties included the Roosevelt and the Plaza. Hilton claimed he was practicing for New York's Waldorf-Astoria, a picture of which he had clipped from a magazine and carried with him since the hotel opened in 1931.

Postwar Expansion

In 1945, Hilton traveled to Chicago to complete the purchase of the Stevens, which he had initiated in 1940, and ended up acquiring the Palmer House as well. In May 1946, Hilton Hotels Corporation was formed. It made history the next year as the first hotel company to have its stock listed on the New York Stock Exchange. Conrad N. Hilton was president and the largest stockholder.

Despite its reputation, the Waldorf-Astoria was not a profitable hotel. While negotiations to lease that hotel were taking place, Hilton worried his board members with his interest in international hotels in a postwar climate uncertain for international business. Nevertheless, Conrad Hilton pursued the venture that would become the Caribe Hilton in San Juan, Puerto Rico. An agreement was made to form a wholly owned subsidiary— Hilton Hotels International—for which Hilton formed a separate board. In 1949 Conrad Hilton bought the lease on the Waldorf-Astoria. The Waldorf made a $1 million profit in its first year under Hilton management. The first European Hilton was opened in Madrid in 1953.

The largest hotel merger in the industry took place in 1954 when Hilton Hotels purchased the Statler Hotel Company for $111 million. The Statler chain consisted of eight hotels, with two more under construction. Statler was noted for its fine properties

and solid reputation. The chain was about to be sold to a New York realty firm when Hilton made a plea to Statler's widow. She agreed to sell to Hilton, in order to keep the hotels in "the hands of hotel people." Earnings per share nearly doubled between 1953 and 1955, largely as a result of this acquisition. In 1955, another overseas Hilton was opened, in Turkey, and the Continental Hilton of Mexico City opened the following year. In 1964 Hilton International was spun off and became a public company with Conrad Hilton as its president. Hilton was made chairman of the board of Hilton Hotels that same year.

Second Generation of Management Introduces Casino-Hotels

The late 1960s saw significant changes, beginning with the 1965 formation of Statler Hilton Inns, a corporate franchising subsidiary, and a change of presidents. In 1966 Hilton's son, William Barron Hilton—known as Barron—assumed the presidency. Barron Hilton's conservative fiscal strategies set a decidedly different course for the company his father had built. The following year, Barron Hilton persuaded his father, as the largest shareholder of Hilton International, to swap his stake in the overseas operation for shares of Trans World Airlines (TWA). Hilton remained chairman of Hilton International. The expectation had been that TWA stock would rise, but its value halved over the next 18 months. Meanwhile, foreign travel boomed, and Hilton lost the rights to his name overseas.

In 1970, Barron Hilton engineered the $112 million purchase that would generate the largest percentage of the company's revenues within a decade: two casino-hotels in Las Vegas, Nevada. While Conrad Hilton had dabbled in gaming via a Puerto Rican casino in the late 1940s, the acquisition of the Las Vegas Hilton and the Flamingo Hilton marked the launch of a consistent strategy. This move paid for itself, particularly during the late 1970s and early 1980s, when the occupancy rate at both hotels remained steady in contrast to industry-wide trends.

Barron Hilton then concentrated on franchising the Hilton name and managing other hotels. In 1973, the company launched a computerized hotel reservation dubbed "HILTRON." The system served not only the Hilton chain but was also employed by other chains in the industry, providing yet another source of revenue. In 1975 Hilton sold a 50 percent interest in six major hotels to Prudential Life Insurance Company of America for $85 million. Hilton continued to manage the properties in exchange for a percentage of room revenues and gross profits. This was one of the first management leaseback deals in the industry. Joint-venture arrangements later became standard industry practice.

In 1977 the purchase of the Waldorf-Astoria's building and land was finalized for $35 million. The decade closed with the death of Conrad N. Hilton in 1979, at age 91. Barron Hilton became chairman of the board. During the 1980s Hilton continued to make its money primarily though casino gambling, leasing and management, and franchise fees. These were sound measures during recession years: while revenues for owned hotels increased an average of 4 percent in 1980 and 1981, management contract fees increased by 6 percent in 1980 and 14 percent in 1981. Overall earnings for Hilton increased by 6 percent during these years, and the company grew rich in liquid

Key Dates:

1919: Conrad Hilton buys his first hotel.
1925: The first hotel carrying the Hilton name is constructed in Dallas.
1946: Hilton Hotels Corporation is formed.
1947: Becomes the first hotel company to have its stock listed on the New York Stock Exchange.
1949: Hilton buys the lease on New York's Waldorf-Astoria.
1953: The first European Hilton opens in Madrid.
1964: Hilton International is spun off as a public company.
1970: The company buys two casino hotels in Las Vegas.
1982: Subsidiary Conrad International Hotels is formed to oversee international growth.
1996: Stephen F. Bollenbach becomes the first non-Hilton to guide the company; Hilton merges with Bally Entertainment Corporation.
1998: Hilton spins off its gaming operations as Park Place Entertainment Corporation.
1999: Hilton acquires Promus Hotel Corporation for $3.7 billion.

assets. It put this capital to use in hotel improvements and in 1981, the $34.4 million purchase of another casino-hotel in Nevada, the Sahara Reno. Barron Hilton maintained a no-partnership policy for the company's casino-hotels. Although the hotels suffered from the loss of convention bookings during the recession, an addition to the Las Vegas Hilton in 1982 made it the largest hotel in the world, and further convention facilities were added in 1985.

Having sold the international rights to the Hilton name, the corporation resumed international growth in 1982 under a new subsidiary, Conrad International Hotels. Construction began on a casino-hotel in Australia the following year. Over the course of the next decade, this division established hotels (many of them joint ventures) in Turkey, Egypt, Hong Kong, Uruguay and New Zealand.

By 1985 gaming was providing 40 percent of the company's operating income, and earnings had increased 20 percent annually since Hilton's entry into that industry. In 1985, however, after spending $320 million to build a casino in Atlantic City, New Jersey, Hilton was denied a license to operate. The New Jersey Casino Control Commission's primary objection was Hilton Hotel's longstanding relationship with Chicago labor attorney Sidney Korshak, who had been linked with organized crime figures and who the New York Times in 1976 had labeled "a behind-the-scenes fixer." Hilton severed its ties with Korshak, who had acted as a labor consultant for the company, and the gaming commission granted a new hearing. In April 1985, before the rehearing took place, however, the hotel-casino was sold to Donald Trump at cost.

While Hilton focused on the casino-hotels, Marriott and Hyatt were expanding in the luxury-hotels market. To keep pace with its competitors, Hilton pledged $1.4 billion to renovate older properties during the late 1980s. Barron Hilton also concentrated on solving the problem of his father's will.

Dispute over Founder's Will Spans 1980s

When Conrad Hilton died, he had bequeathed the bulk of his holding—a 27 percent block of Hilton shares—to the Conrad N. Hilton Foundation. This foundation, incorporated in 1950, gives aid to Roman Catholic nuns. This provision left Barron Hilton with 3.6 percent of Hilton Hotels, but he claimed to have exercised an option on the foundation's shares immediately, buying their portion at the market rate of $24. Ownership of the stock was contested for the next decade. At issue was the interpretation of an option Conrad Hilton had allotted Barron Hilton in his will: Barron Hilton claimed the will allowed him to buy the entire stock from the foundation at the 1979 price. The estate's executor, who was Conrad's personal attorney, claimed the will intended that Barron Hilton be entitled to no more than 7 percent of the shares. Meanwhile, Hilton and ex-wife Zsa Zsa Gabor's daughter also contested the will. The attorney general's office of California joined the case, arguing that the foundation was entitled to the shares at market value, or $225 million, in 1985. To complicate the issue further, Golden Nugget casino's chairman Steve Wynn attempted to buy the disputed shares in 1985 at their current market price—$72 a share—in order to launch a takeover of Hilton.

A November 1988 settlement gave Barron Hilton four million of the disputed shares, a stake valued at $204 million. The foundation kept 3.5 million shares, worth $178 million at the time, and six million shares, a $306 million stake, went into a trust with Barron Hilton serving as executor. Perhaps most significant, the agreement gave the CEO the trust's voting privileges, for a total voting presence of 25 percent. In addition, Hilton was to receive 60 percent of the trust's share dividends until 2008, after which they would revert to the foundation.

The chain closed the decade enjoying a 70 percent occupancy rate in its newly rejuvenated domestic hotels, greater international expansion, and properties totaling an estimated $4 billion to $6 billion. In May 1989, Chairman Barron Hilton solicited bids for the chain. By December 1989, however, the company had not received a satisfactory bid, and Hilton decided not to sell.

The 1990s and Beyond

After three decades of leadership, Barron Hilton relinquished the chief executive office of the corporation in 1996. While his final years at the helm were criticized as indecisive and overly conservative, the fact remained that its revenues increased from less than $1 billion in 1989 to $1.6 billion in 1995. Net income increased at an average annual rate of 19.6 percent, from $84.3 million in 1991 to $172.8 million in 1995.

In 1996 53-year-old Stephen F. Bollenbach became the first non-Hilton to guide the company. He came to the job with incontrovertible credentials, having engineered both a debt restructuring for the Trump empire and Walt Disney's $19 billion acquisition of Capital Cities/ABC. A spate of high-profile deals quickly ensued. Within five months, the new CEO had merged Hilton with Bally Entertainment Corporation via a stock swap valued at $2 billion. In one move, the deal created the world's largest gaming concern and made casino gambling Hilton's largest business. However, in the interest of equilibrium,

Bollenbach also executed several key moves to expand the hotel chain. First, he repurchased the Prudential Insurance Company's stake in six Hiltons for $433 million. He also pledged to increase via franchising Hilton's budget Garden Inns chain by 50,000 rooms over the remaining years of the decade.

Before 1996 had ended, Bollenbach had also pulled off a reunification of the global Hilton presence. By the mid-1990s, ownership of Hilton International (and the overseas rights to the Hilton name) had passed to London's Ladbroke Group plc. Hilton purchased a 3 percent stake in Ladbroke and in return the British concern agreed to invest in future Hilton enterprises. The two companies planned to create cooperative marketing programs (including honoring each other's frequent stay plans) and develop new hotels together.

On January 27, 1997, Hilton bid $55 per share for New York-based ITT Corporation, aiming primarily to acquire its ITT Sheraton subsidiary's 415 hotels and 14 casinos. The company's hostile takeover attempt eventually failed when Starwood Lodging Trust outbid Hilton in a very public and heated battle. Bollenbach was undeterred by the failure and forged ahead with his strategy to take Hilton into the next millennium. Believing that Hilton's hotel and casino operations could achieve a higher stock value if they became separate entities, Bollenbach set plans in motion to spin off the firm's gaming arm. Shareholders agreed with the plan and in 1998, Park Place Entertainment Corporation—now known as Caesar's Entertainment Inc.—began operating as a public company. Bollenbach was named chairman of the new firm.

Hilton Hotels' next big move came one year later when it made a $3.7 billion play for Promus Hotel Corporation. A September 1999 Wall Street Journal article summed up the company's reasoning for the deal claiming, "The transaction is designed to launch Hilton into a competitive triumvirate of top hotel companies with Marriott International Inc. and Starwood Hotels & Resorts Worldwide Inc." Indeed, as a result of the deal Hilton increased its portfolio to over 1,800 hotels located in all 50 states and added Doubletree, Embassy Suites Hotels, Hampton Inn, Hampton Inn & Suites, Homewood Suites, and Harrison Conference Centers to its hotel arsenal.

With the Promus deal under its belt, Hilton stood on solid ground as it entered the new millennium. During 2000, the company formed a joint venture with Hilton Group plc to strengthen and expand its Conrad Hotels unit overseas. The company signed an agreement the following year with Hoteles Camino Real S.A. de C.V. The partnership added the Camino Real hotels and resorts in Mexico and Texas to Hilton's brand portfolio. Bollenbach hinted at the company's future acquisition strategy in a 2001 *Hotel and Motel Management* article stating, "A lot of changes have occurred at Hilton in the last five years, going from a company that was about half gambling company and a half hotel company to today being focused on the hotel business. We have a company that is forever one of the major competitors in the hotel business." He went on to claim, "Hilton is what you think of as a strategically complete company. It means we don't need to add anything to what we have in our collection of businesses."

While Hilton digested its Promus purchase, it faced challenges due to a weak economy as well as a slowdown in travel as a result of the September 11, 2001, terrorist attacks. In fact, Hilton's stock fell to its lowest point in ten years during 2001. Revenues dropped in both 2001 and 2002, however net income increased by 19 percent in 2002. While net income fell in 2003, sales increased by nearly 51 percent over the previous year—a sure sign that the company had a solid business strategy in place. With Bollenbach at the helm, Hilton appeared to be well positioned for future growth in the years to come.

Principal Subsidiaries

Conrad International (Belgium) Corporation; Conrad International Corporation; Doubletree Corporation; Doubletree Hotels Corporation; Grand Vacations Realty LLC; Grand Vacations Title LLC; Hilton Chicago Corporation; Hilton Grand Vacations Club LLC; Hilton Grand Vacations Company LLC; Hilton Holdings Inc.; Hilton Hotels Partners I LLC; Hilton Hotels Partners II LLC; Hilton Hotels U.S.A. Inc.; Promus BPC Corporation; Promus Hotel Corporation; Promus Hotel Services Inc.; Promus Hotels Florida Inc.; Promus Hotels Minneapolis Inc.; Promus Hotels Inc.

Principal Competitors

Hyatt Corporation; Marriott International Inc.; Starwood Hotels & Resorts Worldwide Inc.

Further Reading

Binkley, Christina, "Hilton Shareholders Approve the Spinoff of Gambling Unit," *Wall Street Journal*, November 25, 1998, p. 1.

Binkley, Christina, and Neal Templin, "Hilton Agrees to Pay $4 Billion for Promus," *Wall Street Journal*, September 8, 1999, p. A4.

Gibbs, Melanie F., "Hilton Hotels Corp.: The Sleeping Giant Wakes," *National Real Estate Investor*, February 1997, pp. 40–41.

Goldgaber, Arthur, "Honeymoon Hotelier: Hilton's Stock Quickly Doubled after Stephen Bollenbach Took Over as CEO," *Financial World*, January 21, 1997, pp. 34–37.

Higley, Jeff, "Bollenbach: Hilton's Portfolio Set for Long Haul," *Hotel and Motel Management*, February 19, 2001.

Hilton, Conrad N., *Be My Guest,* New York: Prentice-Hall Press, 1957.

Lee, Daniel R., "How They Started: The Growth of Four Hotel Giants," *Cornell Hotel & Restaurant Administration Quarterly*, May 1985, pp. 22–32.

Liou, Su-Lan Bethany, *Hilton Hotels Corporation: A Strategic Analysis,* 1993.

Lubove, Seth, "Hilton's Head," *Forbes*, March 8, 1999, p. 50.

Moore, Thomas, "Barron Hilton Fights for Hilton Hotels," *Fortune*, May 27, 1985.

Picker, Ida, "Saying Good-bye to ITT," *Institutional Investor*, January 1998, p. 91.

Whitford, Marty, and Robert Selwitz, "A Deal in the Cards?," *Hotel and Motel Management*, October 4, 1999.

Wrubel, Robert, "Rumors at The Inn: The Wall Street Sharks Are Circling Hilton Hotels, Eager to Break Up the Family Dynasty," *Financial World*, April 4, 1989, pp. 32–33.

—Carol I. Keeley
—updates: April Dougal Gasbarre and
Christina M. Stansell

Holden Ltd.

241 Salmon Street
Port Melbourne Victoria 3207
Australia
Telephone: +61 03 9647 1111
Fax: +61 03 9647 2550
Web site: http://www.holden.com.au

*Wholly Owned Subsidiary of General Motors
    Corporation*
Incorporated: 1856 as JA Holden & Co.
Employees: 8,950
Sales: A $5.94 billion (2002)
NAIC: 336111 Automobile Manufacturing; 336399 All
    Other Motor Vehicle Parts Manufacturing

Holden Ltd. is one of Australia's leading automobile manufacturers. A subsidiary of General Motors Corporation (GM) since the early 1930s, Holden has nonetheless earned a reputation as an innovative automaker in its own right. The company has long dominated Australian automotive sales with its range of high-powered cars and sports utility vehicles, including the Commodore line of cars and the company's "Ute" trucks—a smaller, two-door, two-seat version of a sport utility vehicle. Holden designs, develops, and builds its own cars and engines, and also manufactures a variety of designs from other parts of the General Motors empire, including models from direct parent Opel, and others. While Holden remains tiny compared with the world's automotive greats, producing less than 150,000 cars and barely more than 35,000 light commercial vehicles per year, it is highly profitable, and flexible, capable of building some eight different automobile platforms on a single line. In 2003, the company's design and engineering prowess was recognized when GM announced its intention to export Holden's Monaro model to the United States to be marketed under the famed Pontiac GTO name. The Middle East remains the largest foreign market for the company's muscle cars, accounting for more than 75 percent of exports; New Zealand and the Pacific Southeast are also important markets for the group. Holden produces revenues of nearly A $6 billion per year, including more than A $1.2 billion in export sales.

Early 20th Century Origins

Holden's origins traced back to the mid-19th century, when James Alexander Holden emigrated from Staffordshire in England to Australia at the age of 17. Holden came from a family of leatherworkers, and in 1856, he set up his own saddlery and leather shop, JA Holden & Co., in Adelaide. Then just 21 years old, Holden quickly built up his business, and by 1865 had moved to larger quarters in the growing city. Holden was joined by son Henry James Holden in 1879 and the company then became known as JA Holden & Son.

Holden had by then expanded its business to include upholstery and other fittings for horse-drawn carriages. The arrival of a new business partner, Henry Frederick Frost from Germany, enabled the company to extend its range of operations to include iron and other metalwork, under the name of Holden & Frost. The company then began offering carriage repair services as well.

James Holden died in 1887 and son Henry James turned the company more fully toward its metalwork and repair business, before leading Holden & Frost into the production of carriages and coaches themselves. As such, the company was well prepared for the arrival of the new "horseless" coaches, and at the beginning of the 20th century began offering repair and upholstery services for the new automobiles as well. In the meantime, the company's leatherworking wing continued to prosper, particularly after it won a contract to supply saddles and bridles during the Boer War in South Africa.

Frost died in 1909 and Holden, now joined by son Edward Wheewall Holden, became sole owner of the company. Holden & Frost had by then become a supplier to the automobile industry, manufacturing hoods and fenders, starting in 1908. In 1913, the company began producing the bodies for motorcycle sidecars, and by 1914 had produced its first handmade automobile body.

World War I offered new opportunity as imports slowed dramatically. The Australian government, in an effort to conserve available shipping space, restricted automobile imports mainly to just the chassis. The government created legislation requiring that two-thirds of the chassis imported into the country be fitted with bodies built in Australia itself.

On the advice of a distributor, who reckoned that the Adelaide market alone would require some 5,000 auto bodies each year, Holden borrowed pounds 50,000 to launch a new company, Holden Motor Body Builders (HMBB). That operation distinguished itself by becoming the first in Australia to adopt the new mass production techniques pioneered by Henry Ford. During the war, the company had completed two prototype bodies, and in 1917 débuted its first finished body, fitted to a Dodge platform.

That same year, the company bought another local auto body builder, FT Hack Ltd. By year's end, the larger company had produced nearly 100 car bodies. Yet the company quickly ramped up its production, and by the end of its first full year in 1918, HMBB had built nearly 600 bodies. The company continued investing in new machinery, dramatically improving its efficiency—which dropped from 160 man-hours per car body to just five by the beginning of the 1920s.

HMBB quickly became Australia's leading automotive body producer, fitting not only Dodge vehicles, but also Ford, Chevrolet, and others. Production continued to rise, topping 500 car bodies per month in the early 1920s. By the end of 1923, the company was capable of building some 12,000 car bodies per year. The construction of a new plant in 1924, in the town of Woodville, gave HMBB the capacity to supply nearly half of the total Australian market. The following year, the company began producing closed automobile bodies for the first time. With the ramp up to full production at the Woodville site, HMBB now became the world's largest automobile body producer outside of the United States and the European continent.

By then under Edward Holden's leadership, the company began its relationship with the United States' General Motors during this period. GM had begun importing to Australia in the years following World War I, and had begun preparing to build its own bodybuilding plant in Australia. When he learned of this, Edward Holden traveled to Detroit and instead convinced GM to turn over its bodybuilding requirements to Holden. GM agreed, and backed by a contract for 9,500 car bodies per year, Holden invested in expanding its plant, adding hydraulic presses to the Woodville site. With assistance from GM, HMBB now became one of the world's most modern body plants, with production rising to more than 35,000 car bodies per year.

Merging for Survival in the Depression Era

GM entered Australia in 1926, forming GM Australia (GMA) and building car assembly facilities throughout Austra-

lia. Holden's fortunes continued to grow as GMA developed into one of the country's leading carmakers. Holden invested heavily in expanding its production through the end of the decade. The company also developed its own trademark, a Lion and Stone motif evoking the legend that a lion rolling a stone had given the inspiration for the invention of the wheel.

Yet both GMA and Holden were hit hard by the economic collapse of 1929. While Holden had concentrated on expanding its capacity, GMA had focused on production—but as sales dried up, Holden's production lines ground to a halt, while GMA found itself burdened with a huge stock of cars. By 1931, as both companies faced bankruptcy, they decided to merge, forming General Motors-Holden (Holden). The larger company was then able to arrange the loans needed to keep it afloat through the worst of the depression years.

Yet Holden continued to suffer at the start of the 1930s, as the company's sales slumped below 4,000 cars in all of 1932. Holden's future remained doubtful—in 1934, GM sent troubleshooter Laurence Hartnett with the mission of restoring Holden's profits, or shutting the company down altogether.

Hartnett's efforts paid off quickly, and by 1935, Holden once again posted a profit. By then, too, the Australian government had begun attempts to stimulate interest among the country's automakers for designing and producing the first all-Australian car. Hartnett decided to lead Holden into the race. As part of that effort, Holden transferred its headquarters to a newly built facility, including assembly plant, at Fishermen's Bend, in Melbourne. The company also continued to invest in new manufacturing equipment, and by 1937 was capable of producing all-steel cars for the first time. Local content by then accounted for 65 percent of the cars produced by Holden, which now had some 6,000 employees turning out more than 32,000 bodies per year.

The company began testing automotive designs in the years leading up to World War II. At the same time, Holden expanded its range of production expertise, so that by 1939 it had successfully constructed a complete vehicle, the Vauxhall 14.

The outbreak of World War II temporarily suspended Holden's work on its own car. Instead, the company turned its production capacity toward supporting the war effort, manufacturing aircraft frames, bomb cases, weapons and artillery, and armored vehicles and other transporters. Holden launched the production of aircraft engines, the first Australian company to mass-produce an internal combustion engine. As such, Holden built engines for aircraft, boats, and torpedoes. In support of its war production, the company installed its own foundry operations.

The First All-Australian Carmaker in the 1950s

Now capable of producing engines and precision mechanical components, Holden revived its quest to build the first all-Australian car. Design work began again in 1942 and by 1943 the company succeeded in building its first prototype, dubbed Project 2000. The following year, parent company GM gave Holden the go-ahead to proceed with the development of a full-fledged production model.

Following the war, Holden returned to its automotive body and assembly operations, turning out Vauxhalls, and then other

Key Dates:

1856: James Alexander Holden establishes JA Holden & Co. as a saddler and leathermaker in Adelaide, Australia.

1879: Company is renamed Holden & Son.

1885: Company (now Holden & Frost) begins repairing then building coaches and carriages.

1908: Holden & Frost begins upholstery repair for automobiles and begins producing car hoods and fenders.

1913: The company begins producing bodies for motorcycle sidecars.

1914: The first Holden-produced automobile body is launched.

1924: A new state-of-the art production plant helps support a contract to supply bodies for GM cars.

1931: Holden and GM Australia merge to form GM-Holden.

1936: Holden moves its headquarters to Melbourne and begins developing its own car.

1940: Holden shifts production to support the war effort, and begins building engines.

1948: The company launches the 48-215, known as the FX, the first all-Australian car.

1955: The company begins exports to New Zealand.

1972: The two millionth Holden automobile is produced.

1988: The company merges with Toyota Australia to form a UAAI joint venture.

1995: Holden exits from the UAAI joint venture and begins producing Opel-based car designs.

2003: Holden begins exporting its Monara model, to be marketed as the new Pontiac GTO in the United States.

members of the GM brand family, including Chevrolets, Buicks, and Pontiacs. In the meantime, Holden sent a team of engineers to Detroit to develop prototypes of the final model, as well as the manufacturing process to be used to produce it. Testing on the prototypes began in Melbourne in 1947.

In 1948, Holden officially launched the first all-Australian car—the 48-215, which later became known as the FX. Unlike competing models, the car was designed specifically for Australian driving conditions, including a rugged frame with a powerful yet fuel-efficient engine. The car, which benefited from trade tariffs put into place to encourage the domestic auto industry, also featured an attractive sales price.

Success of the new car was immediate, with a waiting list stretching well into the following year. By 1953, the company had already sold 100,000 cars. That year saw the launch of a new model, the FJ. Available in three levels, as well as a panel van, the FJ quickly outsold its predecessor, and became an icon in the Australian automotive market.

Over the next decades, Holden regularly launched new models. Exports of the company's designs started in 1955, to New Zealand, before spreading to include much of Africa, Asia,

and the Middle East. By 1957, the company had completed its 1,000,000th car body, and topped one million cars with the EJ model launched in 1962.

While Holden became synonymous with large-sized, powerful cars, in the mid-1960s the company extended its range with a small car, the Torana, introduced in 1967. The following year, the company launched Australia's answer to the American muscle car, with a sports coupe called the Monara. That launch was backed up the following year by the first V8 engine built in Australia. By the early 1970s, Holden's automobile production had topped three million total cars.

Reemergence as a Leader in the New Century

The 1970s marked the début of another significant Holden vehicle: the Commodore, launched in 1978. The car quickly became adopted as an official vehicle, used by the police and by the Australian government. Yet the company was hit hard by the oil crisis, as Australian consumers flocked to buy more fuel-efficient—and often better built—foreign cars.

By the early 1980s, Holden had lost its position as Australia's leading car seller, as the Australian automotive industry entered a new period of crisis. The Australian government stepped in, launching the so-called Button Plan, in which the country's automobile makers began building cars based on each other's platforms. As such, Holden began producing the Astra, based on a Nissan design. Yet into the mid-1980s, Holden sales continued to slip, and in a move engineered by the Australian government, the company finally merged with the equally troubled Australian branch of the Toyota Motor Company. The new joint venture company was named United Australian Automobile Industries (UAAI) in 1988.

Development of new Holden models ended, and the company instead began producing Toyota models. At the same time, Holden began focusing its own engineering efforts on producing engines for the export market. The company's Commodore line remained popular, however, and by 1990 helped the company's own automobile production top the five million mark. The launch of the VN Commodore line also helped the company win back the Australian consumer, and in 1991 Holden once again had become the top-selling automobile company in Australia.

By 1995, Holden had regained its confidence, and in that year the company pulled out of the UAAI joint venture. Holden, placed under direct control of GM's Opel branch, now began sourcing its production models from the GM brand pool, and especially from Opel's popular European models.

Holden's years of difficulty had enabled the company to develop an extremely lean organization. Despite its relatively small size—with total production below 200,000 vehicles at the beginning of the 21st century, the company's production remained tiny compared with the more than five million vehicles produced by GM's U.S. operation each year—Holden was able to produce strong profits.

Part of the company's success was its growing focus on building high-powered automobiles, including the highly popular "Ute," a sort of small sports utility vehicle that had become highly popular in Australia. By the beginning of the 21st century,

Holden had captured the attention of parent company GM itself. That company had abandoned production of the fabled Pontiac GTO in an effort to rescue its struggling Pontiac division. In 2002, GM turned to Holden for a replacement, starting imports of Holden's muscular Monaro—rebranded as a GTO—into the United States in 2003. Holden remained a flagship for the Australian automobile industry in the new century.

Principal Divisions

Holden Vehicle Manufacturing Operations; Holden Engine Manufacturing Operations; Holden Service Parts Operations; Holden Learning; Holden Innovation.

Principal Competitors

Toyota Motor Corporation Australia Ltd.; Mitsubishi Motors Australia Ltd.; DaimlerChrysler Australia/Pacific Holding Proprietary Ltd.; JGL Investments Pty.; BMW Australia Ltd.; ADI Ltd.; Sumitomo Australia Ltd.; Mitsubishi Australia Ltd.; Auto Group Ltd.

Further Reading

Corbett, Brian, and Tom Murphy, ''Holden Pattern,'' *Ward's Auto World,* May 1, 2002.

Guilford, Dave, ''Holden, GM's Current Darling, Could Send a 2nd Car to US,'' *Automotive News,* May 6, 2002, p. 3.

Kable, Mike, ''On the Road: Holden 50th Anniversary,'' *Weekend Australian,* November 14, 1998.

Lewis, Anthony, ''Ambitious Australia,'' *Automotive Industries,* April 2003, p. 46.

Wielgat, Andrea, ''Holden Is Golden,'' *Automotive Industries,* July 2002, p. 20.

Wright, John, *Heart of the Lion,* Adelaide: Allen & Unwin, 1999.

—M.L. Cohen

Hollinger International Inc.

Hollinger International Inc.

10 Toronto Street
Toronto, Ontario M5C 2B7
Canada
Telephone: (416) 363-8721
Fax: (416) 364-2088
Web site: http://www.hollinger.com

Public Subsidiary of Hollinger Inc.
Incorporated: 1990
Employees: 5,335
Sales: $1.05 billion (2002)
Stock Exchanges: Toronto
Ticker Symbol: HLG.C
NAIC: 511110 Newspaper Publishers

Hollinger International Inc. is best known for its ownership of newspapers such as London's *Daily Telegraph,* the *Chicago Sun-Times,* and the English-language *Jerusalem Post.* It also has built up holdings in more than 100 smaller publications. Struggling under a massive debt, Hollinger International began selling off regional publications in the late 1990s. Conrad Black, controlling shareholder of parent company Hollinger Inc., was forced out as Hollinger International CEO in late 2003 by angry shareholders. A U.S. judge later blocked the sale of his holding in Hollinger Inc. to London's Barclay twins, opening Hollinger International's assets to a field of dozens of prospective bidders.

Building a Global Media Empire in 1985

Conrad Black was born on August 25, 1944 in Montreal, Quebec. His father, George Montegu Black, Jr., was a prominent businessman who managed Canadian Breweries, a division of the Argus Corporation, in the 1950s. Conrad Black grew up dreaming of becoming the chairman of Argus Corporation, a dream made remarkable by the fact that he accomplished it in 1978. Conrad and his older brother, Montegu, were able to gain a controlling interest in Argus in July 1978 by combining the block of shares their father had left them upon his death in 1976 with shares purchased from the heirs of the company's founding partners for about $18.4 million. For this remarkable accom-

plishment, Conrad Black was named "Man of the Year" in 1978 by the *Toronto Globe and Mail,* while *Fortune* magazine called him "the boy wonder of Canadian business."

From 1978 to 1985, Black set about dismantling Argus, which controlled five corporations, including farm machinery manufacturer Massey-Ferguson, and selling off its assets. By June 1985, he had bought out his brother's interest and those of other minority shareholders. He then purchased a 14 percent interest in the *Daily Telegraph,* which was England's leading circulation broadsheet newspaper and the newspaper of choice of the country's ruling Conservative party. Black had begun building his global media empire.

By the end of 1985, Black had acquired a 50.1 percent interest in the *Daily Telegraph* for $43 million, a bargain basement price. Later acquisitions would follow a similar model, with Black stepping in and acquiring financially troubled newspapers. He also created Hollinger Inc. as a holding company for his interests. Hollinger was initially headquartered in Toronto, Ontario, but Black moved the company's headquarters to Vancouver, British Columbia, in 1990.

Acquiring U.S. Newspapers in 1986

Fearful of the costs associated with big-city newspapers, Black was also interested in small-market newspapers that focused on local news. Through his U.S. subsidiary, American Publishing Co., Black acquired a large number of smaller newspapers in the United States. American Publishing Co. was formed as a privately held, U.S.-based subsidiary of Hollinger Inc. in late 1986. Its first acquisition involved 16 small-town U.S. newspapers. Through a series of acquisitions, it grew to rank as the second-largest newspaper publisher in the United States in 1995 by number of titles and the 12th in terms of circulation. It owned 393 newspapers, including 96 dailies, by 1996.

In March 1994, American Publishing completed its acquisition of the *Chicago Sun-Times,* which at the time was the ninth-largest circulation metropolitan daily newspaper in the United States. With a daily circulation of 535,000, it was Chicago's number two newspaper. The cost of the *Sun-Times* was approximately $180 million. In April 1994, American Publishing

Key Dates:

1985: Conrad Black acquires a 50.1 percent holding in the *Daily Telegraph.*
1992: Hollinger acquires a 21.5 stake in Southam Inc.
1986: American Publishing Co. subsidiary is formed.
1994: American Publishing acquires the *Chicago Sun-Times,* goes public, and is renamed Hollinger International.
1996: Hollinger increases its Southam holding, acquires the rest of the *Daily Telegraph,* and goes public.
1998: A 40 percent interest in a U.S. community newspaper group is sold.
2003: Black is forced to resign as Hollinger International CEO.
2004: Hollinger begins auctioning off its assets.

launched an initial public offering (IPO) to raise money to pay for the acquisition. American had reported net losses in 1993 and 1994. At the time of its IPO, it owned 340 newspapers and was the fifteenth-largest U.S. newspaper group based on circulation. The IPO was expected to raise $101 million, and American's shares were traded on the NASDAQ. According to Security and Exchange Commission (SEC) filings, American Publishing Company was renamed Hollinger International Inc. in February 1994.

Venture into Australian Publishing in the Early 1990s

In late 1991, a group led by Conrad Black's Telegraph plc bought Australia's John Fairfax Holdings Ltd. out of receivership by purchasing a 25 percent interest in the Australian newspaper publisher. Fairfax published the *Sydney Morning Herald, Melbourne's Age,* and the *Australian Financial Review,* among other publications. Australian law prevented Black as a foreigner from owning more than 25 percent of the firm. Although Black's 25 percent interest gave him effective control of Fairfax, he was concerned about the possibility of an Australian media mogul acquiring controlling interest. Black appealed to the Australian government to allow him to increase his ownership to 35 or 50 percent, but permission was never granted. As a result, Black agreed to sell his holdings to a New Zealand investment firm at the end of 1996 for $513 million. Although disappointed, Black's group reportedly made $300 million on its investment. While happy with his profit, Black could not resist a parting shot at Australia, telling the *Financial Post,* ''It's not a politically mature jurisdiction and foreigners should understand what they're getting into there. . . . [The prime minister] is basically an old-time Australian nationalist.'' In his letter to shareholders in 1996, he again complained about ''Australia's capricious and politicized foreign ownership rules'' and complained that foreigners were ''treated with official bad faith and insurmountable suspicion.''

In 1992, Hollinger purchased a 21.5 percent stake in Southam Inc., Canada's leading newspaper publishing company. By 1996, Black was unhappy with the way Southam was being managed, and Hollinger was seeking to boost its ownership of Southam to

41 percent by buying out the co-controlling minority interest of the Power Corporation for $294 million. Black planned to replace most of Southam's independent directors.

Black obtained an advance ruling from Canada's Bureau of Competition Policy, which reviewed the proposed Southam acquisition for any overlap of ownership of newspapers competing for advertising in any one market. The Federal Court of Canada subsequently dismissed a motion by the Council of Canadians opposing Black's acquisition of Southam. During 1996, Hollinger International increased its interest in Southam to 50.7 percent. As Canada's largest publisher of daily newspapers, Southam published 32 daily newspapers and 58 non-daily newspapers. Its principal publications included the *Gazette* (Montreal), the *Ottawa Citizen,* the *Calgary Herald,* the *Vancouver Sun,* the *Province* (Vancouver), and the *Edmonton Journal.*

Going Private in 1996

In mid-1994, the *Daily Telegraph* was being challenged by Rupert Murdoch's *Times* for market leadership in England. When the *Daily Telegraph* lowered its cover price from 48 pence to 30 pence, the *Times* immediately dropped its cover price from 30 pence to 20 pence. In September 1993, the *Times* had lowered its price from 45 pence to 30 pence. The price cuts had boosted the *Times'* circulation from less than 400,000 copies a day in mid-1993 to average daily sales of 517,000. With its latest price cut, the *Times* expected its daily circulation to climb above 600,000. The price war was having an effect on the *Daily Telegraph*'s readership, the figure that was used to set advertising rates. For the period from December 1993 to May 1994, the *Daily Telegraph*'s readership declined 9.9 percent to 2.49 million, while the *Times'* readership increased 10.6 percent to 1.32 million, according to the National Readership Survey. The *Telegraph*'s CEO Dan Colson told the *Financial Post,* ''The *Telegraph* remains the undisputed market leader in the quality segment.''

Between October 1995 and August 1996, The Telegraph Group Ltd. became a wholly owned subsidiary of Hollinger International, which paid a total consideration of approximately $455.1 million for all of The Telegraph Group's outstanding shares. By taking The Telegraph Group private, Black was following the advice of investors who warned that it would be difficult to raise equity capital in London markets. Share prices of the *Telegraph* had fallen dramatically in 1994 as a result of the price war with Rupert Murdoch's *Times.* Subject to lingering criticism in the British press and government, Black's comment to the *Financial Post* was, ''Never underestimate the conservatism or xenophobic tendencies of the British.''

In July 1995, Hollinger Inc. announced it would sell its interests in the *Daily Telegraph* and Southam Inc. to its U.S. subsidiary, American Publishing Co. Analysts saw it as a move to strengthen American Publishing's shares, which were traded on the NASDAQ market. American owned the company's U.S. flagship newspaper, the *Chicago Sun-Times,* along with other newspaper chains. The move would also mean a transfer of assets out of Canada and into the United States, where Hollinger felt they would have a higher value.

By September 1995, the plan had changed somewhat. It now involved more of a corporate reorganization of American Publishing and Hollinger Inc., with the Canadian company Hollinger Inc. creating a $1 billion newspaper company with headquarters in Chicago. The Canadian-based Hollinger Inc. would still sell its interests in British Telegraph plc and in the Canadian company Southam Inc. to American Publishing, thereby more than doubling American Publishing's annual revenues of $422 million in 1994.

At the same time, Hollinger International Inc. would be established in Chicago as a new umbrella company over American Publishing Co. F. David Radler, chairman of APC and president and chief operating officer of Hollinger Inc. told *Crain's Chicago Business,* "We're consolidating our assets into one group with greater access to U.S. capital markets, which are the best capital markets in the world. We're de-Canadianizing ourselves and creating an American company."

Conrad Black was named Hollinger International's chairman of the board and CEO. Radler assumed the duties of president and COO. Black's strategy of entering the U.S. capital markets paid off in February 1996, when Hollinger International went public with an IPO that raised $380 million. As described in the company's annual report, "For most of our stockholders, Hollinger International Inc. is a new creation grouping a unique collection of high quality international newspaper assets. For other stockholders, it is a relaunch on a very broad basis of American Publishing Company, which continues as a core asset of Hollinger International."

As Conrad Black prepared to address shareholders at Hollinger International's annual meeting in May 1996, the company was under two credit reviews for having too much debt. Both the U.S.-based Standard & Poor's Corporation and Canada's Dominion Bond Rating Service put Hollinger International on credit watch. Standard & Poor said that a downgrade was inevitable "in the absence of Hollinger taking significant steps to ease its debt burden." The company had about $445 million of debt outstanding, plus debt it had taken on to increase its stake in Southam and debt it might take on to complete its purchase of the Telegraph. Moody's debt-rating service soon followed with an announcement that it, too, was reviewing its rating of Hollinger's debt. At the time, Hollinger International was the third largest newspaper chain in the world behind Gannett Co. Inc. and Rupert Murdoch's News Corp.

In August 1996 Hollinger International completed its acquisition of the minority shares of Telegraph plc, taking the company private and making it a wholly owned subsidiary called Telegraph Group Ltd. In addition to publishing various editions of the Telegraph, the Telegraph Group published *Spectator* magazine and owned 24.7 percent of Australia's John Fairfax Holdings Ltd., which would be sold later in the year for $513 million. As part of the financing of the acquisition, Hollinger International sold 11.5 million shares of its Class A common stock and 20.7 million shares of preferred stock to raise $301.1 million. Those proceeds, together with related bank financing, were used to pay for the acquisition.

Moving to the United States in 1997

Black began to implement his strategy of moving ownership of his newspaper assets into the United States, where they would be valued higher. In January 1997, Hollinger Inc. announced it would sell almost all of its Canadian publishing assets to its U.S.-based subsidiary Hollinger International for $342 million, excluding working capital of about $181 million. Those assets included Hollinger's interest in Southam and the Sterling Newspapers Company, which owned 26 daily and 49 non-daily newspapers in Canada.

Hollinger Inc.'s other assets included a 20 percent stake in the *Financial Post;* about 5 percent of Key Publishing, which published *Toronto Life* magazine; an interest in Toronto's SkyDome; and part of Gordon Capital Corp., a Toronto securities firm.

In March 1997, Hollinger International's stock hit a two-year low, and the company announced it intended to repurchase up to three million of its Class A common shares as well as some of its preferred stock. Since reaching a high of $13.125 in May 1996, the stock dropped to just under $9 in March 1997 before closing at $9.25.

One analyst explained that the company's complex transactions of 1996 and early 1997 turned off a lot of investors, who wanted companies that were easy to follow. John Reidy of Smith Barney Inc. told the *Financial Post,* "They don't want to talk about EBITDA (earnings before interest, taxes, depreciation, and amortization) or cash flow. Hollinger is an EBITDA and cash flow story, rather than an earnings story." Reidy admitted that Hollinger had a complex capital structure and that the company went through a radical transition in 1996, referring to taking The Telegraph Group private, Hollinger International's IPO, the sale of its interest in Fairfax, and the transfer of assets from its Canadian parent in early 1997.

In April 1997, Hollinger International established a new subsidiary, Hollinger Digital, with offices in the Soho district of New York City. Hollinger Digital would be responsible for managing and making investments in new media properties. One of its management functions would be to coordinate the 90 Web sites of Hollinger's more than 350 newspapers. The subsidiary's chairman and CEO was Richard Perle. Perle was also a director of Hollinger International and former assistant secretary of defense for international security during the Reagan administration. He was known as the architect of Reagan's Star Wars defense program.

In November 1997, Hollinger International announced it was selling about 40 percent of its U.S. community newspaper group. These included 160 weekly, small daily, and free circulation newspapers in 11 states with a combined circulation of approximately 900,000. The buyer was the Los Angeles-based Leonard Green and Partners LP, a firm which specialized in leveraged buyouts. The sale price was $310 million, which Hollinger International would use to reduce debt and finance the previously announced purchase of the *Post-Tribune* in Gary, Indiana. The sale was completed on January 27, 1998.

During December 1997, Black also told the *Financial Post* that Hollinger International would probably be cutting back on its acquisitions because prices were too high. He expected to use the $310 million from the sale of 160 small U.S. newspapers to reduce debt, not make acquisitions. As if to calm investors, he promised a more conservative financial approach in the future. "We will not issue stock at silly prices," he told the *Financial*

Post. ''We will not issue non-investment grade paper again. It's a much more conservative company.'' In the past, Hollinger had relied on high-yield junk bonds to finance its acquisitions. Hollinger's financial executives never seemed overly concerned about the company's debt level, though, because of the company's strong cash flows.

Black noted that circulations were increasing among the company's Canadian newspaper publishing group. The *Vancouver Sun* was leading with an average weekly increase of 10 percent. ''I think we've earned our spurs,'' he told the *Financial Post.* ''The whole theory of the inexorable decline of newspapers, I still say, is bunk.''

For 1997, Hollinger International reported earnings of $104.5 million. Operating income was up, but overall earnings declined from the previous year's levels due to higher taxes, interest payments, and other expenses not directly related to operations. The company benefited from improved advertising revenues in a good business environment. It also took steps to allay investor fears by reducing costs and making other improvements.

In April 1998, the *Jerusalem Post* announced it would buy 49 percent of the *Jerusalem Report,* its competitor. It was expected that the two English-language publications would merge their administrative, advertising, and circulation departments while remaining independent editorially. The twice-monthly *Jerusalem Report* was established by former *Post* reporters and financed primarily by Canadian businessman Charles Bronfman, chairman of the Seagram Company. The newspaper had lost money steadily since it began publishing in 1990.

Complex Transactions in the Late 1990s

By the end of 1997, Hollinger International owned or had an interest in 167 paid daily newspapers. Its major newspapers were the *Chicago Sun-Times,* the *Daily Telegraph,* and the *Ottawa Citizen.* It also owned or had an interest in 361 non-daily newspapers as well as other magazines and publications. For the past ten years, the company had pursued a strategy of growth through acquisitions. Since 1986, the company had acquired some 400 newspapers and other publications (net of those sold) in the United States, the *Daily Telegraph* in the United Kingdom, the *Jerusalem Post* in Israel, and had made significant investments in newspapers in Canada, including a controlling interest in Southam Inc., Canada's largest newspaper publisher. In 1997, it acquired the Canadian Newspapers division of its parent company, Hollinger, Inc.

Hollinger International's history, including that of its Canadian parent, had been characterized by complex financial transactions and an aggressive acquisitions strategy. Since Conrad Black successfully entered the U.S. capital markets with Hollinger International's IPO in 1996, he has sought to calm investor fears and simplify the company's financial structure. In 1996, the company divested itself of its 25 percent interest in John Fairfax Holdings Ltd., increased its stake in Southam Inc., and took 100 percent control of The Telegraph Group Ltd. The following year, it addressed investor concerns by accomplishing three financial goals: 1) it steeply improved operating and net profit; 2) it repurchased some of the company's un-

derpriced stock; and 3) it sold non-strategic assets at advantageous prices. The company also increased its stake in Southam to 58.6 percent. Enjoying a cleaner balance sheet and circulation gains at its major newspapers, Hollinger International appeared ready to consolidate its gains and embark on a more conservative acquisitions and financial program for the future.

Hollinger International sold off 160 newspapers representing 40 percent of its U.S. community newspapers group (American Publishing Co.) in late 1997. A Los Angeles investment group, Leonard Green & Partners, paid $310 million for them. The rest of the community papers were sold to four buyers (Bradford Publications Company, Newspapers Holdings, Inc. of Alabama, Paxton Media Group, Inc., and Forum Communications Company) in August 2000 for $215 million. In July 1998, Hollinger International had acquired two small dailies in West Virginia and Pennsylvania from Thomson Newspapers.

In 1998, after failed efforts to acquire the market-leading *Globe & Mail,* Hollinger Group founded a national Canadian daily, the *National Post of Toronto.* CanWest Global Communications acquired a 50 percent stake in the *National Post* in 2000, along with most of the other Southam papers, for $2.1 billion. It bought the remaining 50 percent stake in August 2001. The *Post* then had a circulation of 300,000 copies a day.

Conrad Black was awarded UK citizenship in 1999. He renounced his Canadian citizenship after Prime Minister Jean Chrétien refused to allow him to accept a British peerage. The UK then dubbed him Lord Black of Crossharbour.

Black Out in 2003–04

While Black was gaining a peerage from Britain, he would soon be giving up the titles of CEO and chairman at Hollinger International. Shareholders were angered over $200 million in payments to Conrad Black and four other directors. They questioned the reporting of some of these payments, including $73 million in non-compete fees paid by companies that had acquired Hollinger titles, and called for an SEC investigation.

Black was forced to step down as CEO of Hollinger International in November 2003. He and other executives agreed to repay some of the unauthorized payments, though the board was still suing them for $200 million. Black remained nonexecutive chairman, as well as chairman of parent company Hollinger Inc., for a few more months. Black remained the controlling shareholder of Hollinger Inc.

Hollinger International's debts then amounted to more than $700 million. The investment bank Lazards was called in to possibly sell off some of the company's properties.

In early 2004, the Barclay brothers, Sir David and Sir Frederick, bid $326.5 million (£259 million) through their Press Holdings International Ltd. for Conrad Black's holding in parent company Hollinger Inc., which held a 30 percent shareholding in Hollinger International, which carried 73 percent voting rights. If successful, they would assume $140 million in debt.

A Delaware court blocked this sale in February 2004, however. According to the *International Herald Tribune,* an array of 50 prospective bidders instantly materialized for a chance to acquire assets such as London's *Daily Telegraph,* the *Chicago Sun-Times,* and more than 100 smaller publications.

Principal Subsidiaries

American Publishing Company; Chicago Sun-Times, Inc.; Hollinger International (Canada) Holdings Co.; Hollinger International Publishing Inc.; Hollinger UK Holdings Limited (England); Jerusalem Post Publications Limited (Israel); Midwest Suburban Publishing Inc.; The Palestine Post Limited (Israel); Pioneer Newspapers Inc.; The Post-Tribune Company; The Spectator (1828) Limited (England); The Sun-Times Company; Telegraph Group Limited (England).

Principal Divisions

Canadian Newspaper Group; Chicago Group; Community Group; U.K. Newspaper Group.

Principal Competitors

Associated Newspapers; Daily Mail and General Trust; Express Newspapers; Gannett; Tribune Co.

Further Reading

Dalglish, Brenda, "Black Bites Back," *Maclean's,* November 15, 1993, p.24.

——, "Black Wants All of Telegraph," *Financial Post,* April 25, 1996.

——, "How Black Plans to Finance Southam Purchase," *Financial Post,* May 28, 1996.

——, "Debt, Competition Issues Dog Hollinger," *Financial Post,* May 29, 1996.

——, "Black Pulls out of Fairfax," *Financial Post,* December 17, 1996.

——, "Analysts Support Hollinger Move," *Financial Post,* January 9, 1997.

Darby, Ian, "Hollinger Looks at Alternative Bids," *Campaign,* January 23, 2004, p. 2.

Fitzpatrick, Peter, "Third Debt-Rating Agency Puts Hollinger Under Review," *Financial Post,* June 5, 1996.

Greising, David, "Pursuer of Hollinger International Displays Shrewd Deal-Making Skills," *Chicago Tribune,* February 1, 2004.

Hughes, Duncan, "New Newspaper to Begin Rolling off Presses in New York," *Sunday Business* (London), April 7, 2002.

"Jerusalem Post Buys 49 Percent of Jerusalem Report," *Reuters Limited,* April 6, 1998.

Kirbyson, Geoff, "TD's US$650M Loan Will Allow Hollinger to Make Telegraph Bid," *Financial Post,* July 2, 1996.

Laver, Ross, and David Estok, "Face to Face with Black," *Maclean's,* June 10, 1996, p. 44.

McGugan, Ian, "Publish and Flourish," *Canadian Business,* August 1994, p. 31.

Miller, James P., "Public Will Find Few Easy Answers in Sale of Complicated Hollinger Empire," *Chicago Tribune,* January 2, 2004.

Morgan, Richard, "Sale Possible for Hollinger," *Daily Deal,* November 18, 2003.

Nisse, Jason, "Lord Black Isn't Ready to Sail Off Into the Sunset . . . But Then Neither Was Napoleon," *Independent on Sunday* (London), November 23, 2003, p. 7.

Reguly, Eric, "Telegraph Faces Long War with Murdoch," *Financial Post,* July 6, 1994.

Siklos, Richard, "Hollinger Takes Telegraph Private," *Financial Post,* August 1, 1996.

Simon, Bernard, "Longtime Publisher Ends Era in Canada," *New York Times,* August 25, 2001, p. C3.

Sorenson, Jean, "The Paper Chaser," *BC Business,* August 1991.

Steinberg, Jacques, and Andrew Ross Sorkin, "A Swarm of Potential Bidders Emerges for Hollinger Assets," *International Herald Tribune,* March 8, 2004.

Theobald, Steven, "Hollinger Sells Batch of Community Papers, Plans to Use $440 Million to Pay Down Debt," *Toronto Star,* November 25, 1997.

"Two Jerusalem Newspapers to Merge," Associated Press, April 5, 1998.

—David Bianco
—update: Frederick C. Ingram

Home Hardware Stores Ltd.

34 Henry Street West
St. Jacobs, Ontario N0B 2N0
Canada
Telephone: (519) 664-2252
Fax: (519) 664-2865
Web site: http://www.homehardware.com

Private Company
Incorporated: 1963 as Hollinger Hardware Limited
Employees: 25,000
Sales: C$2.9 billion (est.)
NAIC: 421710 Hardware Wholesalers

Home Hardware Stores Ltd., is an Ontario, Canada-based dealer-owned cooperative, supplying more than 1,000 independently operated stores located in every Canadian province and territory. Member stores operate under four banners: Home Hardware, Home Building Centre, Home Hardware Building Centre, and Home Furniture. Home Hardware stores offer typical hardware supplies as well as painting supplies, automotive and farm supplies, sporting goods, and lawn and garden supplies. Home Building Centres sell all the materials needed for home renovation and repair projects. Home Hardware Building Centres combine the product lines of Home Hardware and Home Building Centre stores. Home Furniture stores sell furniture for every room in the house, plus accessories and home electronics.

Roots of Home Hardware Date to Late 1800s

Although Home Hardware was formed in 1963, the heritage of the company can be traced to the 1880s and the village of St. Jacobs, Canada. There, a tin-smithing business was established in a two-story brick building that was once a hotel. A German immigrant named Henry Gilles bought out the owner and opened a combination blacksmith shop and hardware store, which was managed by his son, Alfred Gilles. In 1933, Henry Sittler, who grew up on a farm and had worked as a clerk at a local general store, took over the management of the hardware business. When the elder Gilles died the following year and the store was sold to Gordon Hollinger, Sittler stayed on. Hollinger

added a wholesale hardware operation in 1936 to supplement his retail business. This wholesale business would one day form the basis of Home Hardware. Two years later, in 1938, Walter J. Hachborn—the driving forced behind the foundation and growth of Home Hardware—would come to work for Hollinger Hardware as a teenager. The son of a millwright, Hachborn grew up in a house behind the hardware store, so it was not surprising that Gordon Hollinger would ask the young man to come work for him after high school graduation. Moreover, Hachborn was bilingual, able to speak both English and the Pennsylvania Dutch favored by most of the store's customers, Mennonite farmers.

Hollinger made Hachborn his assistant and pupil, but Hachborn's education in the hardware business was interrupted by a stint in the military during World War II, an experience that would serve him later in his career. As a staff sergeant with the Royal Canadian Ordnance Corp, he acted as a warehouse foreman. Not only did he gain general knowledge about warehousing that he could apply to Hollinger's growing wholesale business, he was able at the close of the war to give Sittler the heads up on surplus military items that could be bought cheaply and converted to civilian use. A notable example were metal mortar cases that Hollinger Hardware bought by the thousands and converted into tool boxes.

Hollinger died of a heart attack in 1948, leaving Hachborn and Sittler to carry on running the business for Hollinger's wife. After she died in 1949, the business was put up for sale by the couple's daughter, who had married and moved away from St. Jacobs. After some difficult negotiations, Hachborn, Sittler, and a lawyer named Alfred Zilliax, who would act as a silent partner, bought Hollinger Hardware. The partners grew the business at a steady pace during the 1950s, so that after several years the company was in desperate need of additional space. In 1958, an adjacent property was purchased, and three years later a modern new warehouse, located on King Street in St. Jacobs, was added.

1960s Origins

The early 1960s was a time of transition for hardware retailers in Canada. Large chains able to command greater purchasing

---

Company Perspectives:

Home has four kinds of stores to serve you. Each store offers a distinctive array of products and services designed to meet your needs in different ways.

---

power and offer significant discounts—retailers such as Kmart, Woolco, and Zellers of Montreal—had eaten up market share in the hardware business, so much so that an estimated 1,000 local, independent hardware stores would close their doors during the period between 1955 to 1965. At Hollinger's, change was also in the air following a serious heart attack suffered by Zilliax (he would die in 1968). Hachborn, Sittler, and several of their dealer customers met in the fall of 1962 to discuss the future of both Hollinger and the hardware business in general. Out of this meeting grew the idea that independent hardware dealers needed to find a way to join forces in order to eliminate the wholesaler and pool their buying power to better compete against the big box chains. An exploratory meeting was then held in February 1963 at the St. Jacobs Fire Hall, where 25 dealers met. A month later, 122 Ontario hardware dealers convened at the Flying Dutchman Motel in Kitchener and created a steering committee to further develop the idea of a dealer-owned organization. Hachborn and Sittler were two of the nine members of the steering committee. A number of possibilities were explored, but in the end the steering committee recommended that the dealers acquire Hollinger Hardware. Each dealer bought 15 $100 shares of the new corporation, Hollinger Hardware Limited. No more than 15 shares could be purchased, and upon retirement dealers would be repaid. In September 1963, the new company received its charter, and at the close of the year the purchase was completed.

Hachborn became general manager of the enterprise, which started modestly in January 1964, owning but a single half-ton Ford pickup truck to make deliveries. By the end of the year, however, business was so brisk that the King Street warehouse went to three shifts. The extra hours would be needed in large part because in 1965 Home Hardware published its first consumer catalog, 100 pages in length, and the company began shipping to dealers in the Atlantic provinces. Plans were also underway to further increase Hollinger Hardware's purchasing power, an idea that originated with Hachborn and was brought to fruition by him. In 1965, United Hardware Wholesales Limited was created. Hollinger and three other Canadian dealer-owned hardware wholesalers—Edmonton-based Link Hardware Co. Limited; Winnipeg-based Falcon Hardware Ltd.; and Montreal-based Les Marchands RoNa Inc.—formed the super-wholesaler. In addition to acting as high volume buyer for its four members, United Hardware provided coordinating functions for promotion and inventory control. In reality, the company was just an office housed in Hollinger Hardware's St. Jacob's headquarters. Hachborn would serve ten years as the company's president before devoting himself exclusively to the running of Home Hardware.

In 1967, the company underwent a name change. Although Hollinger Hardware benefited from name recognition, Gordon Hollinger had been dead for nearly 20 years and there seemed no reason to attach his name to what was essentially a new

venture. Hachborn commissioned a friend to create potential names and logos, suggesting that the word "home" be incorporated. He been inspired by an annual sale, "Happy Home Value," held by in the United States by the National Retail Hardware Association. Out of the ideas offered to him, Hachborn chose Home Hardware Stores Limited. The logo featured back-to-back H's, which had the added advantage of being able to stand for Hollinger Hardware as well as Home Hardware. Hachborn also had in mind that one day the name could be shortened further, becoming Home Stores—an indication on his part that the concept of hardware was malleable and that he was willing to branch in any number of directions.

In 1969, Home Hardware sowed the seeds for a new division, Homeland Furniture. Furniture and hardware had coexisted in a number of member stores. In fact, the Hollinger Hardware retail operation had always carried a furniture line. As a result, some members were eager to pool their buying power on furniture in the same way they did with hardware, and in 1969 a buying group was established. To spur sales volume, part of Home Hardware's downtown St. Jacob's warehouse was turned into a furniture showroom, with the upper floors serving as warehouse space. In 1978, the Home Hardware board approved the creation of a separate furniture division.

Also in 1969, Home Hardware unveiled its first television commercial, aired on 20 Ontario stations. In addition, the company created radio jingles that dealers could use in local buys. By the end of 1970, Home Hardware consisted of 324 dealers and 334 stores; shipments totaled C$16 million. An even greater rate of growth would follow in the decade to come, causing an ever-increasing need for new warehouse space, as well as the introduction of an electronic order entry system for its dealers. In 1973, 140,000 square feet of warehouse space was opened, but just a year later the company initiated the addition of another 100,000 square feet. In 1978, ground was broken on a 260,000-square-foot warehouse to be built in Nova Scotia, and later in the year the board approved 130,000 square feet of multi-purpose space to be built in St. Jacobs to handle large bulk shipments, a special orders and relay shipments department, a truck wash and maintenance area, and an educational and conference center. By this point, annual shipments were in the C$115 million range.

Home Hardware established a building supply division in 1972, in keeping with Hachborn's belief that hardware and building supplies would one day find common ground. His vision would be born out with the emergence of the home center concept, epitomized by the likes of Home Depot and Lowes. Home Hardware's entry into building supplies took time to gain traction. Not only were dealers uncertain that the company was committed to the program, but the large suppliers of building products dismissed Home Hardware as a viable customer until 1975. With the advent of competition from home centers, and the obvious demand for affordable products from do-it-yourselfers, the Home Hardware's building supply business began to accelerate. In 1978, the division adopted the HomeAll trade name for the business, which began to produce its own catalog and develop its own advertising program.

Struggles and Expansion: 1970s–Early 2000s

Difficult economic conditions during the 1970s, in particular inflation (which ran as high 20 percent), hurt the business of

---

Key Dates:

1934: Hollinger Hardware is formed.
1936: Hollinger adds a hardware wholesale operation.
1963: Hollinger Hardware Limited is formed as a dealer-owned wholesaler.
1967: Hollinger Hardware changes its name to Home Hardware Stores Limited.
1969: A furniture division is launched.
1972: A building supply business is added.
1990: Home Hardware Building Centres name is adopted.
1999: Beaver Lumber is acquired.

---

many Home Hardware dealers, some of whom went out of business. A number of applicants to the Home Hardware network were also turned away because of poor finances. By late 1977, however, the economy began to rebound, and the number of acceptable applicants began to grow once again. By the end of 1980, the number of Home Hardware stores topped the 800 mark.

Home Hardware launched several initiatives in the 1980s. It opened its own paint factory in 1980 and also formed its own insurance division, Programmed Insurance Brokers Inc. Prior to 1965, Home Hardware acquired insurance from a number of brokers and companies, then switched to a collective insurance program put together by an army friend of Hachborn, Herbert Farrow. Dealers were able to save money on their general insurance needs, and over the years group, auto, disability, and life insurance coverage were added. When Farrow sold his agency in 1980, Hachborn decided to have Home Hardware own and operate its own insurance entity. In a similar manner, the company became involved in the travel business. As Home Hardware grew into a national enterprise, Hachborn found himself traveling a great deal and relying on several local travel agencies. One of those agencies began to experience financial problems, and in 1982 Hachborn arranged for Home Hardware to acquire a half-interest in the business. The result was an agency called Link With Home Travel Agency, which handled the travel arrangements for the growing number of Home Hardware staff and dealers.

One venture that did not pan out for the company was the launch in 1985 of the Home Circle Division, run by an executive named Dave Rodgers. The intent of the business was to provide dealers, particularly in small towns, with small wares. After Rogers retired, however, the division was closed down. A more positive develop took place in 1985 when Home Hardware launched its own credit card, the Homecard, supplementing the Visa and MasterCard program that had been established for dealers in 1977. In 1987, Home Hardware expanded its presence in western Canada by acquiring 55 Revelstoke building supply stores, which were then incorporated into the HomeAll division. A major milestone occurred in July 1988

when Hachborn announced his retirement. On January 1, 1989, a new general manager, Paul Straus, succeeded him.

In 1990, the HomeAll name was replaced by the Home Hardware Building Centres name, and in 1992 Home Furniture replaced the Homeland banner. In addition, in 1992 Home Hardware improved its purchasing power by forging a purchasing alliance with U.S.-based Do-It Best Corp., the joint venture named Alliance International LLC. New warehouse space was added on a regular basis in order to keep pace with the expanding number of members dealers and mounting sales. At the end of 1996, the company topped the C$1 billion threshold in annual sales.

A major addition to the Home Hardware business came in 1999 with the purchase of 138 Beaver Lumber Stores, improving buying power as well as increasing sales. Retail sales for Home Hardware stores topped C$2.2 billion, while Beaver sales totaled C$747 million. The Beaver stores, jointly owned by corporate parent Molson Inc., were subsequently converted to the dealer-owner format of Home Hardware. Also of interest during the decade, Home Hardware, in 1994, began publishing its own hardware magazine, *Home at Home*. At the close of the 1990s, Hachborn was named "Retailer of the Century" by *Hardware Merchandising* magazine. In 2000, he received an even greater honor when he was named a member of the Order of Canada. On a more somber note, Hachborn's long-time partner Henry Sittler died in January 1999. By the end of the year, the organization he was instrumental in founding would record shipping totals in excess of C$1.2 billion.

To keep up with its steady growth, Home Hardware continued to add warehouse and distribution space, so that by early 2001 it passed the two-million-square-foot mark. By the end of 2003, the company boasted retail sales of C$3.8 billion from more than 1,000 members. It offered 55,000 different products distributed by four regional centers, shipped on more than 100 leased power units and 350 trailers. Despite the ongoing growth and might of big box retailers, Home Hardware's local dealers, by pooling their resources, were still able to flourish in a competitive market.

Principal Competitors

Canadian Tire Corporation, Ltd.; The Home Depot, Inc.; RONA Inc.

Further Reading

Dewey, Martin, "How an Idea Revived the Hardware Business," *Globe and Mail*, May 7, 1979, p. B1.
Home of the Handyman, St. Jacobs, Ontario: Home Hardware Stores Ltd., 2001, 256 p.
Petty, Gary, "The Little Store That Could," *Fleet Owner*, February 2003, p. 32.

—Ed Dinger

Horseshoe Gaming Holding Corporation

9921 Covington Cross Drive
Las Vegas, Nevada 89144
U.S.A.
Telephone: (702) 932-7800
Toll Free: (800) 895-0711
Web site: http://www.horseshoegaming.com

Private Company
Incorporated: 1993 as Horseshoe Entertainment
Employees: 7,562
Sales: $826.3 million (2003 est.)
NAIC: 551120 Offices of Other Holding Companies;
713210 Casinos (Except Casino Hotels); 721120
Casino Hotels

Horseshoe Gaming Holding Corporation is one of the largest privately held gaming companies in the United States. The company owns and operates three river-based casinos: the Horseshoe Bossier City on the *King of the Red* riverboat across from downtown Shreveport in Louisiana; the Horseshoe Casino Center in Robinsonville, in northern Mississippi; and the Horseshoe Casino Hammond, in Hammond, Indiana, southeast of Chicago. With more than 137,000 square-feet of gaming space at the three casinos, Horseshoe Gaming offers patrons more than 5,000 slot and video poker machines, and over 185 game tables, including craps, blackjack, Caribbean stud, roulette, baccarat, and poker. Company founder Jack Binion attributes the success of Horseshoe Gaming casinos to his philosophy of presenting customers with exciting gaming opportunities by providing "the best odds, the highest limits, and the biggest jackpots." The company operates hotels at the Bossier City and Robinsonville properties, providing luxury accommodations and amenities, as well as meeting facilities and banquet rooms. All properties provide dining at American and Asian restaurants, at an international buffet, and at a Jack Binion's Steak House. In late 2003, the company announced that it had agreed to be acquired by Harrah's Entertainment for $1.45 billion.

The Founder's Family Legacy

When Jack Binion founded Horseshoe Entertainment in 1993, he brought a lifetime of experience in the gaming business to his ventures outside of Las Vegas. Binion grew up in the gaming business, being groomed for it from a young age by his infamous father, Lester "Benny" Binion. A Dallas mule-trader, Benny gained notoriety as a bootlegger and the operator of a floating craps game. In 1947, when Jack was ten years old, the election of a new sheriff prompted Benny to leave Texas with his wife and five children. According to legend, Benny left Dallas for Las Vegas with two suitcases containing $2 million in cash.

In 1951 Benny purchased the El Dorado Casino Hotel, known for its display of $1 million cash pasted into a glass case. Located in downtown Las Vegas' "Glitter Gulch," the casino was renamed Binion's Horseshoe Club. Benny Binion operated the casino in a casual, freewheeling style, managing the club from a table in the coffee shop on the casino floor. He emphasized providing pure gambling for serious gamblers, offering no entertainment but providing "good food, good service and a good gamble." He offered excellent gaming odds and accepted all bets without limit. Thus the Horseshoe Club attracted high-rolling, professional gamblers and became one of the most profitable casinos in Las Vegas.

In 1953 relentless Texas authorities convicted Benny Binion for income tax evasion. In addition to serving more than three years in a federal prison, Benny lost his casino license. He sold the Horseshoe Club to a group of investors. A few years later Jack Binion obtained a loan from his mother and bought an interest in the group, eventually restoring ownership of the Horseshoe Club to the Binion family. Jack Binion became president of the company in 1960, at the age of 22. He handled the finances while his more outgoing, younger brother, Ted, managed the casino floor. Benny Binion provided oversight unofficially from his table in the coffee shop.

The Horseshoe Club continued to be among the more profitable casinos in Las Vegas as the Binions invested in providing good gambling, rather than entertainment. In 1970 the Binions initiated the World Series of Poker, an annual event for which

Company Perspectives:

Jack Binion has been a casino operator for 45 years so he has a pretty good idea what makes a gambler tick. It's nothing sophisticated and it's no great secret: Jack puts the customer first. His personal approach to all his guests is unique in the gaming industry. You see, the bottom line for Jack is not calculated in dollars and cents, but rather by satisfied gamblers who feel the same rush from big action that he does. When you're at a Horseshoe Casino, you're a guest of Jack Binion and he wants to make sure his guests are having a great time, and a great game. Jack doesn't stop there. At Horseshoe, you will find a variety restaurants to suit your tastes, luxurious accommodations, nightly entertainment, gift shops, and specialty shops. You'll find Jack, too. His hands-on style creates friendly and familiar atmosphere that is a welcomed feature at each Horseshoe Casino.

the Horseshoe Club became famous. Like the free-wheeling atmosphere of the Horseshoe Club, the event attracted professional gamblers from around the world. While the prize money was collected from players who paid fees to compete, money won at the poker table often surpassed the value of the prize. Large bets and psychological maneuvering added suspense and intrigue to the event. Though the tournament evolved to include a variety of poker games, the variation known as Texas Hold 'Em determined the winner. After the ante, betting began when the first two cards were dealt, face-down, and continued with each additional card dealt, face-up, for a five-card hand.

During the late 1980s, Benny's health declined, and Ted Binion lost his gaming license amidst allegations of drug use. The Mint Casino next-door to the Horseshoe Club was acquired during this time, thereby doubling the size of the Binion's operation. When Benny died in 1989, Jack Binion held more than half of the shares in the Horseshoe Club, with the balance owned by his mother and his brother Ted. In 1994, Binion's mother died, and her interest in the casino passed to daughter Becky Binion Behnan. After some problems, including a $1 million regulatory fine in 1993 and financial losses in 1994, a dispute over management of the Horseshoe Club arose between Jack and Becky. After a two-year legal battle, Jack decided to sign over his interest in the Horseshoe Club to Becky in 1998. By that time, new gaming venues outside the Las Vegas market held his attention.

Growth Outside of Vegas in the Early 1990s

As legalized gambling expanded outside of Las Vegas, Jack Binion pursued business opportunities in these new markets. In 1993 he had founded Horseshoe Entertainment (later Horseshoe Gaming LLC) for the purpose of operating a riverboat gaming facility in Bossier City, Louisiana. While he used the Horseshoe name (acquiring rights in 1995 before the family dispute), Jack operated the company independently from the family business in Las Vegas. Funded in part by local investors, Horseshoe developed a four-story, 46,000 square-foot paddleboat designed in Victorian style, providing 30,000 square foot gaming area, with 1,060 slot machines and 42 gaming tables, including

blackjack, craps, roulette, and Caribbean stud. The *Queen of the Red*, named for the Red River on which the boat floated, carried 2,200 passengers. A land-based pavilion adjacent to the riverboat offered patrons a choice of a steakhouse or buffet dining, a sports lounge, an ice cream parlor, and a gift shop. The company purchased and refurbished the nearby LeBossier Hotel, which provided 202 guest rooms, an outdoor swimming pool, and the 240-seat Atrium Restaurant. The *Queen of the Red* opened for business on July 9, 1994, attracting much of its customer base from Dallas/Ft. Worth, Texas, less than 200 miles west.

In February 1995, Binion opened the Horseshoe Casino Center in Robinsonville, Mississippi, on the Mississippi River about 35 miles southwest of Memphis, Tennessee. The first floor of the barge held a casino, also designed in the Victorian style, with 1,022 slot machines, 39 table games, and 10 poker tables. On the top two floors, a hotel provided 200 guest rooms positioned in a horseshoe around a courtyard and swimming pool.

Wherever he opened a casino Binion carried the family legacy of exciting gaming. In August 1994, before opening its Mississippi casino, Horseshoe's outdoor advertising offered the ''loosest slots and biggest jackpots.'' Another ad promoted ''single deck 21'' for blackjack play with only one deck of cards, rather than the usual practice of play from multiple decks. On craps tables the Horseshoe purported to offer the ''best odds and highest limits.'' The Horseshoe Casino Center stirred competition with established casinos in the Tunica County gaming district with the offer of ''10x odds'' on craps. This meant that a player could place a bet ten times the amount of the original bet, a major benefit to players at the craps table where the odds of winning are 50–50. Other casinos met the 10x odds, prompting the Horseshoe to offer 20x odds; some competitors followed. The competition over odds generated excitement and attention to gaming in Tunica County, a benefit to all the casinos as the gaming market grew with greater volume of business.

From the beginning Horseshoe Gaming operated the most profitable casinos in their markets. At Bossier City, the *Queen of the Red* led Louisiana riverboat gaming with $151.2 million in gross casino revenues. Horseshoe recorded $160.7 million in net revenues, including hotel and food and beverage sales, less promotional allowances. Open 322 days in 1995, Horseshoe Casino Center recorded $137.5 million in net revenue. Overall, Horseshoe Gaming LLC, which owned 91 percent of Horseshoe Bossier City and 100 percent of Horseshoe Casino Center, collected $298.2 million in net revenues and earned $53.7 million in pretax income.

During 1996 the company initiated expansion projects at both the Mississippi and Louisiana properties. At Bossier City the company built a 26-story hotel, providing 606 luxury suites with king or queen size beds and marble bathrooms, many with Jacuzzi tubs. The $58 million project included an indoor pool, a health club and spa, retail shops, and three restaurants, including Jack Binion's Steak House.

In August Horseshoe purchased a second riverboat casino for the Bossier City location for $4 million, including land in Chalmette, Louisiana. The company acquired the unfinished riverboat from Circus Circus, which terminated its development project. The cost to finish the project was estimated at $35 million, including moving the boat to Bossier City, with completion expected in one year. Rather than adding a second riverboat casino, Horseshoe decided to replace the existing boat with the new boat, named *King of the Red*, which provided slightly more gaming space and passenger carrying capacity.

Expansion at Robinsonville involved development of the Bluesville entertainment complex, dedicated to the celebration of blues music. The complex included a 15,000 square-foot casino, housing more than 400 slots and 15 game tables and a 14-story hotel, holding 312 deluxe guest rooms, a health spa, conference rooms and banquet facilities, a 1,100-space parking garage, and a Jack Binion's Steak House and other dining options. The 61 Crossroads Café served southern and Cajun cuisine in a jukejoint atmosphere; an audio and video system played blues music and showed clips about blues musicians. The 1,000-seat Bluesville Performance Club provided space for live musical performances, including local, national, and internationally acclaimed acts in rock, pop, country, as well as blues music. The Blues and Legends Hall of Fame Museum recounted the historical development of blues music and featured guitars, harmonicas, and other memorabilia of renowned blues musicians.

Expanding to the Midwest in 1999

As expansion projects at existing properties came to completion, new projects came to fruition, specifically the pursuit of gaming opportunities in the Midwest. In September 1998 Horseshoe Gaming signed an agreement to acquire Empress Entertainment, operator of riverboat gaming operations in Hammond, Indiana, near Chicago, and in Joliet, Illinois. The *Empress Hammond* riverboat provided 43,000 square-feet of gaming space, with gambling available at 1,677 slots machines, 55 table games, and 8 poker tables. The *Empress Joliet*, with 30,000 square-feet of gaming space, housed 1,072 slot machines, 46 game tables, and 7 poker tables. Land-based pavilions at each site housed restaurants and a banquet room. The Joliet site included a 102-room hotel and an 80-space recreational vehicle park.

In preparation for the *Empress* acquisition, Horseshoe Gaming LLC incorporated in early 1999 as Horseshoe Gaming Holding Corporation, combining and acquiring various interests in the company. In May Horseshoe Gaming obtained funding for the acquisition of Empress Entertainment through a private placement of $600 million in 8⅝ percent senior subordinated notes. Upon approval of the acquisition by gaming regulators in Indiana and Illinois, Horseshoe acquired *Empress* for $629 million on December 1, 1999.

In an unexpected turn of events, however, in June 2000 the Illinois Gaming Board (IGB) refused to grant a gaming license to Jack Binion for operation of the *Joliet Empress*, noting several regulatory issues and questioning certain business practices. Binion was stunned as the IGB had approved the acquisition on condition that Horseshoe Gaming move its headquarters to Joliet, which the company did, relocating several key employees and their families. A ripple effect threatened the legal viability of other Horseshoe properties, as well; IGB forwarded a letter about the decision to the Louisiana Gaming Control Board which was considering Horseshoe among several gaming companies bidding for the 15th and final gaming license in that state. Binion asked a judge to give an opinion on the IGB decision before seeking a legal appeal.

In another unexpected change, the *Empress Joliet* casino rose in value rather dramatically. A law passed in June 1999 permitted gambling at riverboat casinos when docked, not strictly while traveling. The extended gaming time served to increase casino revenues by more than 30 percent. The acquisition of Empress Entertainment nearly doubled Horseshoe revenues to $1 billion in 2000, compared to $525.6 million in 1999. Bossier City accounted for $268.7 million in net revenues in 2000, Robinsonville accounted for $250.6 million, Empress Hammond for $245.5 million, and Empress Joliet for $247.6 million. Revenues were hampered somewhat by disruption from construction, increased competition, and adverse weather conditions.

In January 2001, Binion agreed to sell the Joliet facility and to pay a $2 million fine in Illinois for practices initiated after the acquisition. Argosy Gaming Company purchased the Empress Casino and Hotel in Joliet for $465 million, completing the transaction in August 2001.

Improvements in the Early 2000s

To meet increased competition as well as consumer demand for gaming opportunities, Horseshoe Gaming sought to improve its gaming services. In spring 2000 Horseshoe Casino Center, along with the Gold Strike Casino Resort, introduced the First Annual Jack Binion World Poker Open. The event offered several kinds of tournaments, such as satellites or mini-tournaments, and super satellites, the latter being required play for entrance into the Championship tournament. The play at super satellite events continued until a player at each table won all tournament chips at that table. Winners from different tables then played against each other until one person won at the final round of play.

Improvements at Horseshoe Casino Center involved additional gaming space and upgraded dining options. The company relocated central engineering and a buffet in the casino area to an adjacent building, opening space for 475 slot machines and ten table games in the casino. The buffet was converted to an international theme and expanded to accommodate 650 patrons. The addition of a piano bar and an American grill, called Café Sonoma, completed the improvements. The company also built infrastructure for the possibility of building a 1,000-room hotel tower.

In April 2001 Horseshoe Gaming completed an $11.5 million renovation at the Hammond casino and pavilion and renamed it Horseshoe Casino Hammond. The casino catered to the high-end Chicago market with a luxurious gaming space, featuring marble and wood grain accents and shades of terra cotta, cream, and black. The VIP room provided security personnel outfitted in tuxedos, a private hors d'oeuvre buffet, as well as high limit slots, and a $20,000 per hand limit at blackjack, the highest bet available in the Midwest gaming market. Also, Horseshoe Casino Hammond allowed bets up to $100,000 on Baccarat and 100x odds on craps. The company spent $2.5 million in employee training to improve customer service at the casino. On May 4, 2001, Horseshoe Gaming celebrated the renovation and new name with a grand opening gala event for VIPs and the media, featuring a variety of headline entertainment from around the world. Changes at the Hammond site resulted in a significant increase in revenues at the casino, particularly after dockside gaming opened in August 2002.

Horseshoe Gaming obtained license renewals for all of its properties. In Mississippi, where Horseshoe Casino Center remained the most profitable of 29 casinos in the state, the company was granted license renewal in September 2000. The Indiana Gaming Commission renewed the license for the Horseshoe Casino Hammond in August 2001. The Louisiana Gaming Control Board renewed the gaming license for Horseshoe Bossier City in early 2003.

Horseshoe Gaming casinos continued to operate in the Binion family tradition of providing ''good food, good service, and good gaming.'' In 2003 all of the Horseshoe Gaming properties won recognition in a *Casino Player* magazine's annual ''Best of Gaming'' issue. Horseshoe Casino Hammond was named for Best Blackjack, Best Craps, Best Roulette, and Best Baccarat. The Mississippi property was recognized for the Best Hotel Casino, Best Rooms, and Best Suites. Horseshoe Bossier City retained its positions in the Best Hotel, Best Rooms, and Best Hosts categories. That property was named as the Best Table Game Tournaments, Best Shopping, and for two dining categories, Best Seafood, at Jack Binion's Steak House, and Best Chinese, at Four Winds restaurant.

On September 12, 2003, Horseshoe Gaming signed an agreement to be acquired by Harrah's Entertainment, Inc. Several gambling companies expressed interest in acquiring Horseshoe Gaming, such as Ameristar Casinos which sought financing for its offer of $1.3 billion. Harrah's offered $1.45 billion to purchase outstanding stock and assume debt, with no financing required. Completion of the acquisition required approval of gaming boards in Mississippi, Louisiana, and Indiana, as well as a waiting period required by antitrust law. In January 2004, Harrah's announced that it also intended to acquire the troubled Horseshoe property in Las Vegas owned by Binion's sister. As the likely new owner of the Horseshoe properties, Harrah's hoped to profit from that company's good reputation and World Series of Poker tournament renown. The Binions' role in the company's future, however, was uncertain.

Principal Competitors

Boyd Gaming Corporation; Harrah's Entertainment, Inc.; Mandalay Resort Group; Park Place Entertainment Corporation; Pinnacle Entertainment, Inc.

Further Reading

Binkley, Christina, ''Royal Flush: Gambling's Binion Clan Finds Highest Stakes Aren't at the Tables,'' *Wall Street Journal,* August 24, 1998, p. A1.

Flaum, David, ''New President Is Named for Joliet, Ill.-Based Gaming Company,'' *Knight Ridder/Tribune Business News,* January 11, 2001.

''Gaming Company to Move to Las Vegas,'' *Knight Ridder/Tribune Business News,* February 15, 2003.

Hollis, Kerissa, ''Casino's Hotel Expansion Towers Over Delta Landscape,'' *Memphis Business Journal,* December 1, 1997, p. 18.

——, ''Lucky 13? Horseshoe Counting on Mature Market,'' *Memphis Business Journal,* February 20, 1995, p. 3.

——, ''Rising Tide: Horseshoe's Presence Improves Tunica Casino Market,'' *Memphis Business Journal,* May 15, 1995, p. 16.

''Indiana's Riverboat Gamble Pays Off,'' *United Press International,* August 26, 2003.

Johnson, Bill, ''A Las Vegas Casino Welcomes Customers Its Competitors Shun,'' *Wall Street Journal,* July 2, 1985, p. 1.

Lubove, Seth, ''All in the Family,'' *Forbes,* July 28, 1997, p. 48.

Richardson, Patricia, ''A Losing Hand for Binion?,'' *Crain's Chicago Business,* July 31, 2000, p. 1.

——, ''Bidders Balk at Binion's Asking Price,'' *Crain's Chicago Business,* March 12, 2001, p. 3.

Turni, Karen, ''Bossier Move is OK'd For Boat; Big Plans Made For New Casino,'' *Times-Picayune,* August 31, 1996, p. A1.

Valin, Tom, ''Playing Texas Hold 'Em for the World Poker Crown,'' *Wall Street Journal,* October 25, 1988, p. 1.

Wolfe, Frank, ''Inherited Talents,'' *Forbes,* October 17, 1994, p. 76.

Yerton, Stewart, ''LA. Seeks Illinois' Aid In Casino Permit OK,'' *Times-Picayune,* July 21, 2000, p. A01.

—Mary Tradii

The Kansai Electric Power Company, Inc.

3-22 Nakanoshima 3-chome
Kita-ku
Osaka 530-8270
Japan
Telephone: (+06) 6441-8821
Fax: (+06) 6447-7174
Web site: http://www.kepco.co.jp

Public Company
Incorporated: 1951
Employees: 35,554
Sales: $21.8 billion (2003)
Stock Exchanges: Tokyo Osaka Nagoya
Ticker Symbol: 9503
NAIC: 221110 Hydroelectric Power Generation; 221112
     Fossil Fuel Electric Power Generation; 221113 Nuclear
     Electric Power Generation; 221119 Other Electric
     Power Generation; 221122 Electric Power Distribution

The Kansai Electric Power Company, Inc. operates as one of Japan's ten regional power companies supplying electricity to over 13 million customers in the Kansai region. The company services the central part of the main island of the Japanese archipelago, covering an area of 28,643 square kilometers—about 8 percent of the nation's total land mass. It includes the three major cities of Osaka, Kyoto, and Kobe as well as the industrial region along the coast of Osaka. Relatively small in land area, Kansai accounts for nearly 16 percent of the nation's gross domestic product. As of March 2003, Kansai Electric's generating capacity was 35,434 megawatts (mW), which included its thermal, nuclear, and hydro-generating operations. Japan partially deregulated its retail electric power sector in March 2000, leaving the company's market open to competition. As such, Kansai Electric is focused on strengthening its core operations while branching out into new business areas.

Early History

Kansai Electric was formed as a company on May 1, 1951, when the General Headquarters of the Allied Powers (GHQ) under General MacArthur approved a plan submitted by the Japanese government to reorganize and rationalize the electrical power industry. Under the scheme, which was developed in 1948, the nation was divided into nine blocks, each with its own privately owned electric power company (EPC). In 1972, the Okinawa EPC was added as a tenth company.

Although immediately after World War II there was a sharp decrease in demand for electricity, since the bulk of electricity prior to this had been allocated to munitions production, the speed of reconstruction gathered pace so quickly that by the time of its inauguration the most pressing need for Kansai Electric was to build up its generating capacity to meet a critical power shortage. Despite booming demand, however, national pricing policies kept electricity rates so low that even costs could not be covered. Over the next three years, therefore, three rates reviews were allowed. In 1951, the average rates of the EPCs rose by 30 percent; in 1952, they rose by 28 percent; in 1954, they rose by 11 percent. In July 1952, the Electric Power Development Promotion Law was enacted to further the construction of generating plants and transmission and transformation facilities. The law created the Electric Power Development Coordination Council under the prime minister's office, which enabled the Electric Power Development Co. Ltd. (EPDC)—a government-owned corporation which could use government funds to promote power generation and transmission development—to begin operations in September 1952 using authorized capital totaling ¥100 billion.

With its share of this money, and with its financial situation improved by the three rates reviews, Kansai Electric was able to commence construction of the 125mW Maruyama hydroelectric power plant, which was then the largest in Japan and which pioneered large-scale hydroelectric power development. In 1954, with the completion of the Maruyama hydroelectric power plant, the power supply situation began to stabilize, and the shortage was gradually met.

In 1956, the company began the Kurobegawa No. 4 hydroelectric power project, an unprecedentedly arduous and large-scale civil engineering undertaking. Kurobegawa No. 4 was finally completed in 1963. However, from the mid-1950s, hydroelectric power had begun to take a back seat to thermal power in Japan. This was due to four major factors: 1) most of the good

Company Perspectives:

To achieve the company's sustainable growth in the current era, when the electric power industry is undergoing major transformations precipitated by deregulatory initiatives, we pledge to devote our full resources to the creation of optimum value for our customers and further fortification of our management base. We will create value for our customers not only through the development of enhanced services and rate schedules in our electricity operations, but also by mustering the comprehensive resources of our group network, which encompasses a broad palette of operations, including gas provision, amenities meeting life cycle needs, and IT services.

sites for hydroelectric power generation had already been developed; 2) rapid progress in thermal power technology had improved efficiency and made large-scale plants possible; 3) thermal construction costs per kilowatt (KW) had fallen; 4) fossil fuel costs were lower. Following this trend, in the mid-1950s Kansai Electric began replacing its worn-out fossil-fired generating capacity by constructing new high-performance plants using the latest technology from the United States. The first such plant was Tanagawa, with two units of 75mW. With the completion of Osaka Unit No. 1, by 1959 the system's total fossil-fired generating capacity had exceeded its total hydro-generating capacity.

Although all through the period of high economic growth in Japan—1961 to 1973—oil remained the principal source of electrical energy, accounting for 43 percent of fuels used for generation by the EPCs in 1963 and 87 percent in 1973, it was in 1954 that the first inroads into research and development on nuclear power were made. Albeit not without hindrances, this was a trend which was to develop substantially over the next four decades.

The 1950s had seen a general settling into the new system for the EPCs in Japan. This had been encouraged in part by the establishment of various regulatory bodies. The Public Utility Bureau, established in 1952, took the place of the abolished Public Utilities Commission as part of the Ministry of International Trade and Industry (MITI). The Federation of Electric Power Workers Unions was formed in May 1954 in response to labor disputes that had led to blackouts and serious disruptions of industry in the early 1950s. It was also part of an attempt to reconcile labor with the Law for the Regulation of Strike Activities in Electric Utility and Coal Industries, enacted in August 1953, which prohibited strikes that interrupted service. The Research Committee on Electricity Rate System was created in December 1957 in order to examine the existing rates and adjust them, through MITI, to a level more in line with actual conditions. The Japan Electric Power Information Center, Inc. was created in May 1958 to encourage the free flow of information within the industry on an international basis.

Impressive Growth in the 1960s

The 1960s saw the development of the electric power industry in Japan on an impressive scale. With many of its initial problems ironed out in the 1950s, flourishing industry and rising living standards led to an ever-booming market for the EPCs

during the 1960s and a chance to build on the foundations they had already laid.

Between 1961 and 1973, Japan's EPCs experienced an average annual increase in demand of 10.7 percent. This was due not only to Japan's booming economy but also to technological advances made by the industry during the period. Fossil fuel was the chief generator of energy in this period, and technological advancement in this area was impressive. Innovation in this area was also encouraged by the low price of oil. Crude oil, which cost $2.30 per barrel in 1960, went down to as little as $1.80 in 1971. Conversely, with improved technology, steam pressure increased from 60 kilograms per square centimeter (kg/cm2) to 246kg/cm2. Steam temperature went from 450C to 566C, and unit generating capacity from 53mW to 600mW. Heat efficiency also went up from 32 percent to 38 percent. As experience was gained in constructing these new super-plants, costs were cut and capacity per unit was increased. Also, the introduction of computers made possible the rationalization of personnel.

Fuel was also switched, initially from coal to heavy oil, and then from heavy to crude oil, which was more cost-efficient as well as more environmentally friendly. Also with a view to pollution problems, plants fired by liquified natural gas (LNG) began to be introduced in an effort to reduce sulfur emissions as well as to remove dependence on oil, all of which had to be imported. Tokyo Electric took the lead in this area from 1963 to 1973, and from 1964 to 1971 Kansai Electric commissioned two LNG/oil-fired plants, one at Himeji 2 and one at Sakaiko.

In December 1966, the company started to construct its first nuclear power plant, Mihama Unit No. 1—rated at 340mW—which employed a pressurized water reactor imported from the United States. In August 1970, the first nuclear-generated power from the unit was sent to the site of the EXPO '70 exhibition of industry, technology, and commerce held in Osaka. The unit itself was completed in November 1970.

Technological advances in transmission and distribution were also made during this period. Building on foundations laid in the mid-1950s, in 1960 Kansai Electric and Chubu Electric linked up utilities with Tokyo and Tohoku Electric Power companies. In 1962, Kansai Electric commissioned an Economic Load Dispatching System. This led to the starting of an automatic load dispatching operation in 1968, which made possible centralized control of unmanned hydroelectric power plants and substations. In 1964, Kansai Electric launched a campaign to provide a more reliable service to customers. In 1967, a Technical Research Center was established to strengthen the organization's research and development.

Thicker cables, adoption of multiconductors, allowing pylons to carry more than one transmission line, and improved pylons helped with the linking of systems. In addition, after Tokyo Electric boosted its Boso line in the Chiba prefecture to 500 kilovolts (kV), Kansai Electric completed its first 500kV trunkline, the Wakasa Line, in 1969. In 1970, the company's first large-scale pumped storage hydro plant, Kisenyama (466mW), was completed.

Dealing With Environmental Concerns

However, industrial development was to take its toll on the Japanese environment. The problem was particularly severe in

Key Dates:

1951: Kansai Electric Power Co. Inc. is established.
1963: The Kurobegawa No. 4 hydroelectric power facility is completed.
1969: Kansai Electric completes the Wakasa Line, its first 500kV trunkline.
1970: The company's first nuclear plant, Mihama Unit No. 1, begins operation.
1984: Kansai Electric is awarded the prestigious Demming Prize by the Association of Quality Control in the United States and Japan.
1991: Unit No. 2 at the Mihama plant is shut down after a problem with a steam generator.
1995: Japan partially liberalizes its electricity market.
2000: Deregulation begins in the retail sector of Japan's electric power industry.

comparison to other countries, and the electric power industry was involved. As the use of oil increased in the effort to meet demand for electricity, sulfur oxide emissions rose, causing bronchial problems and noise pollution. In the face of mounting public anger in the second half of the 1960s, the EPCs, along with other industrial sectors, began to take steps toward pollution control. These included the desulfurization of crude oil, a shift to the use of crude oil and LNG, using higher chimneys, and efforts to reduce particle emissions.

After years of hedging the issue owing to its links with the industrial sector, the government was eventually moved to tackle the problem, and a number of pollution control laws were finally forced through the Diet, Japan's parliamentary branch of government. These included in 1967 the Basic Law for Environmental Pollution Control, and in 1968 the Air Pollution Control Law and Noise Control Law. In 1970, the Diet made these laws more stringent and added the Water Pollution Control Law so that now the electric power stations acted under a strict set of pollution regulations. The result of this was that by the mid-1970s Japan had begun to lead the world in terms of pollution control. Also during this period, in 1966, owing to the rapid increase of the use of air-conditioning units, system peak demand changed from winter to summer.

In the 1970s, after enjoying a boom for many years, the electric power industry in Japan was plunged into an acute slump. The major reason for this was the fourth Middle East conflict, which broke out in autumn 1973, upsetting the world oil market. Two sharp increases in the price of oil ensued, in 1973–74 and in 1978–79, which profoundly changed the shape of the Japanese economy. Since oil was the prime source of fuel for electricity generation up until the first oil shock, accounting for 87 percent of fuels used, the electric power industry was hit particularly hard by the steep price increases. Kansai Electric was forced to revise its electricity rates in 1974 for the first time in 19 years, so that between 1970 and 1980 the price per unit of electric power for Kansai rose from ¥4.74 to ¥19.58 per kilowatt-hour.

The oil crises led to two main changes in the Japanese economy which affected the electricity industry directly. First,

demand for electricity within the industrial sector nosedived as higher energy costs forced smokestack industries out of business and encouraged a shift to high technology and service sectors. Energy conservation measures also contributed to declining demand.

Second, owing to increases in the price of oil, the EPCs were forced to seek alternative fuels for generation. Between 1973 and 1975, the percentage of oil-fired thermal generation was virtually halved in terms of total generation. The shortfall was made up largely by nuclear generation and liquefied natural gas.

In 1974, 1976, and 1980, the EPCs sought major rate increases to counteract the soaring price of oil. After the third increase in 1980, the cost of electricity was 3.5 times higher than it had been before the first oil shock. The average rise on each occasion was 56.8 percent in 1974, 23.1 percent in 1976, and 52 percent in 1980.

By 1977, because of these hikes, and also because of the rising value of the yen, the EPCs' profits began to improve again. In 1977, Kansai Electric's sales were 23.2 percent higher than in the previous year, and post-tax profits were 21.3 percent higher. Originally, the EPCs had marked out new rate increase margins far in excess of those actually enforced, in anticipation of a 5 percent increase in the price of crude oil and fuel oil in 1976.

Judging that no oil markup would take place, however, MITI cut down the original proposals. In approving the increases, MITI also set the value of the yen against the dollar at ¥299/$1.00, which was important to the EPCs as they procured all of their oil supplies from abroad. The yen subsequently continued to rise, reaching ¥272 against the dollar in the second half of 1977. In six months, the foreign exchange gains of Kansai Electric rose by ¥10 billion. Operation costs during the same period increased by ¥5 billion.

Thus, despite further oil price hikes by the Organization of Petroleum Exporting Companies (OPEC) in 1979, leading to the 1980 rate hike, the EPCs did not fare as badly as they might have done, or indeed as they seem to have expected, partly due to the rising value of the yen. With decreases in the price of oil beginning in late 1985, the companies temporarily and tentatively cut their rates—in 1986 for seven months and in 1987 for one year. In 1988, MITI approved a further cut, bringing the average reduction in rates for the industrial and residential sectors of the EPCs to about 17 percent.

The Development of Nuclear Power Leads to Problems

Because of its heavy dependence on imported oil, and because of the two oil shocks, Japan developed nuclear and other alternative energy sources. Nuclear power assumed an important position in Japan's energy policy.

Kansai Electric started its research and study of nuclear power in the 1950s and completed its first nuclear reactor in 1970. At one time, the company owned and operated nine reactors, with nuclear plants making up just over a quarter of its capacity and about 45 percent of its power needs. The development of nuclear power, however, was challenging.

A total of 36 legislative acts and 66 different legal procedures were required before construction of a nuclear-power plant could proceed. The process could take 7 to 15 years from the announcement of construction to the start of operation. Approval for construction was granted by the Electric Power Development Adjustment Council, which was chaired by the prime minister. After approval, the plan was then subjected to strict examinations by the Nuclear Safety Commission. After the government procedure, two public hearings needed be held to reflect the interests of local residents. These hearings were sponsored by MITI. The system was established in 1978.

Another problem with nuclear power generation was the non-nuclear proliferation policy followed by the United States. Following this policy, nations buying nuclear fuel from the United States needed to get case-by-case U.S. government permission to reprocess spent uranium. In 1988, the U.S. Congress refused to ratify a Japanese-U.S. nuclear cooperation agreement signed by Tokyo and Washington in November 1987, which would have allowed Japan to reprocess spent fuel for a 30-year period.

Especially in the early 1980s, in the light of President Ronald Reagan's massive arms build-up, demonstrations against the use of nuclear power were widespread in Japan. In 1980, the venue for the public hearings regarding Kansai Electric's plans to build the No. 3 and No. 4 reactors at Takahama were surrounded by demonstrators.

Public outcry was exacerbated and construction of nuclear reactors was further set back by a number of accidents around the world in the late 1970s, the 1980s, and the early 1990s. Repercussions of the Three Mile Island accident in the United States in March 1979 were keenly felt in Japan, resulting in the suspension for one year of all plans to build nuclear power plants. This delayed the construction of Kansai's 3 and 4 reactors at Takahama for a year and partly accounted for the public demonstrations when the hearings eventually began. Public confidence in nuclear power was not improved by the leaking of nuclear waste at Tsuruga nuclear plant, which was intentionally left unannounced by the Japan Atomic Power Co. The Chernobyl accident in the Soviet Union again shook public confidence. However, it should be noted that Japan developed technology to prevent accidents due to tubing stress corrosion and steam generator tubing pit holing. Although accident prevention was extremely expensive, the EPCs had no alternative but to follow a safety-first nuclear program because of public concern.

Accidents still happened in Japan, however, and in February 1991 Unit No. 2 at Kansai Electric's Mihama plant had to be closed down after a problem with a steam generator led to a leak of radioactive steam. This incident indicated that despite a waning of public opposition to nuclear fuel in the light of global warming, and despite the safety measures followed by the EPCs, nuclear power generation was still unlikely to be free of problems for the foreseeable future.

Partly as a response to environmental pollution, several non-nuclear alternatives to oil had been developed by the EPCs since 1970, when Tokyo Electric opened the world's first LNG-fired plant at Minami-Yokohama. During the early 1990s, a little less than one-fifth of Kansai Electric's capacity was LNG-fired, or LPG (liquified petroleum gas)-fired, accounting for about 25 percent of thermal power generation.

In 1984, partly due to an industrial move into a high-technology environment and partly in order to exploit their utilities more fully, the EPCs began diversifying into the telecommunications business. While this was to remain a peripheral aspect of the industry, the EPCs became major rivals of NTT (Nippon Telegraph and Telephone Ltd.). At this time Kansai Electric planned to continue its exploitation of the telecommunications industry, as well as launching into cogeneration and other local heat supply business.

Continuing its diversification, as well as contributing to various regional projects such as the construction of the 24-hour Kansai International Airport in Osaka Bay and the Kansai Science and Research Park, Kansai Electric was producing new businesses that were being incorporated as the company's subsidiaries and affiliates. As of March 1991, the company had a direct equity participation of 20 percent or more in 40 corporations.

In 1984, Kansai Electric was awarded the prestigious Demming Prize by the Association of Quality Control in the United States and Japan for the performance of its Total (company-wide) Quality Control program. Kansai Electric was the first EPC ever to be awarded the prize and the company intended to develop its quality improvement activities further.

Since the first oil crisis, the EPCs had been developing power-saving electrical devices. Paradoxically, this development led to a boost in demand for power. Kansai Electric expected a continued rise in demand for electricity and so continued to construct generating plants.

Kansai Electric continued to take an interest in environmental issues and in April 1991 organized a Global Environment Project Development Conference, chaired by the president of the company. The conference adopted a four-point plan to continue tackling the environmental issue and also made some headway in the field of reducing emissions from thermal-fired plants.

In the early 1990s, the breakdown of the company's energy sources was as follows: nuclear—7,408mW (24 percent); oil-fired—11,519mW (37 percent); LNG-fired—6,062mW (19 percent); combustion turbines—360mW (1 percent); conventional hydro—3,109mW (10 percent); and pumped storage hydro—2,920mW (9 percent). Its long-range plan, ''Kansai Electric Power in the Year 2030,'' released in 1988, envisaged a generating capacity mix of 40 percent nuclear, 33 percent oil and LNG, 18 percent hydro, and 9 percent coal.

Facing Deregulation: 1990s and Beyond

Kansai Electric entered a new era of challenges in the years leading up to the new century due to the liberalization in Japan's energy sectors. Indeed, by the mid-1990s the electricity industry in Japan was undergoing significant change. In 1995, adjustments to the Electricity Utilities Industry Law allowed competition to enter into the electricity generation and supply market. Then, in 1996, a wholesale electric power bidding system enabled non-electric power companies to sell electricity to electric power companies. Finally, in March 2000, the retail sale of electricity was partially deregulated, allowing large-lot customers—those demanding large amounts of electricity—to choose their power supplier. Nearly 30 percent of Kansai Electric's total sales volume came from this type of customer.

One of the goals of deregulation was to foster competition, which in turn would lower the electricity costs in the country. The deregulation was slow to change the Japanese industry, however, and during 2001 Kansai Electric and the nine other regional companies still controlled 99 percent of the market. In fact, only six Japanese-based companies—other than the original ten—supplied power to large customers, including retail stores and office buildings. This accounted for a .2 percent share of the overall market.

Despite the apparent slow arrival of competition, Kansai Electric made changes to its business strategy in response to deregulation. In 1998, for example, the company became the first Japanese power concern to become involved in an overseas venture when it acquired a 7.5 percent interest in a hydraulic power facility project in the Philippines. Kansai Electric established a new subsidiary to oversee its expansion in foreign markets. In 2001, the company announced its entrance into the retail gas market, becoming Japan's second EPC to land a contract to supply gas directly to retail customers.

During Japan's deregulation process, the nation as a whole was suffering due to an economic downturn. Demand for electric power fell, leaving Kansai Electric scrambling to shore up profits. In 2001, the company announced that plans to construct five new power plants had been temporarily shuttered as a result of faltering sales and profits. In 2002, it reported that over 10 percent of its workforce would be cut by 2005 and that capital investment would be cut by 15 percent. Revenues at all ten of Japan's EPCs fell in 2002. Profits at Kansai Electric fell by 37.3 percent over the previous year, mainly due to the termination of its power plant project.

While Kansai Electric focused heavily on changes brought about by deregulation, public sentiment in Japan remained hostile towards the development of nuclear power. According to a March 2000 *Business Week* article, however, nuclear power accounted for nearly 35 percent of Japan's electricity. In fact, for much of the 1990s, Japan's industry had aggressively focused on shifting from expensive and polluting coal-fired plants to nuclear power. Due to concerns over the safety of these nuclear facilities, Japan's government was forced to rethink its expansion efforts, cut back on its nuclear development plans, and find alternative sources of power.

Despite public opposition to nuclear power, Kansai Electric began to develop a plan to use reprocessed spent nuclear fuel in power reactors. After delays in 1999, the company received governmental permission to used mixed uranium-plutonium ox-

ide (MOX) fuel at its Takahama nuclear facility. According to *Japan Economic Newswire* (2004), Kansai Electric intended to use MOX fuel for plutonium-thermal, or pluthermal, nuclear power generation starting in 2007. While supporters of MOX claimed it could be a reliable source of power in Japan's energy sector, safety concerns and general public malaise regarding nuclear power threatened to undermine Kansai Electric's plans.

In the early 2000s, the company faced the promise of increased competition, future deregulation, and uncertainty regarding Japan's economy. As such, it launched a management plan focused on the following measures: increasing its competitive nature; improving its overall customer service; developing new products, including new electric appliances; and continuing its emphasis on global environmental issues, emission control, green power, and recycling. As one of Japan's original regional electric utilities, Kansai Electric stood well positioned to face future obstacles head on.

Principal Operating Units

Electricity; Information Technology; Energy-Related Business; Lifecycle-Related Business; Other Business.

Principal Competitors

The Tokyo Electric Power Company Inc.; Chubu Electric Power Company Inc.

Further Reading

"All Ten Power Companies See Revenues Fall in FY 2002," *Japan Economic Newswire*, May 21, 2003.

Bremner, Brian, "Tokyo's Nuclear Dilemma," *Business Week*, March 15, 2000.

Goto, Yasuhiro, "No Single Recipe for Deregulation of Utilities," *Nikkei Weekly*, March 5, 2001.

Ishizawa, Masato, "Japan's Power Producers Try to Tap Into Asian Growth," *Nikkei Weekly*, May 4, 1998.

"Kansai Electric to Cut Workforce by 10% Over 3 Yrs," *Japan Economic Newswire*, January 9, 2002.

"Kansai Electric to Enter Retail Gas Business," *Japan Economic Newswire*, January 26, 2001.

"Kansai Electric Power to Freeze New Power Plant Projects," *Japan Economic Newswire*, March 8, 2001.

"KEPCO Given Formal Nod to Pioneer MOX Fuel Use in Japan," *Japan Economic Newswire*, March 20, 2004.

Miller, Karen Lowry, "Is Nuclear Power Losing Steam in Japan?," *Business Week*, March 18, 1991, p. 47.

"Power Utilities Facing First Competitors," *Nikkei Weekly*, February 7, 2000, p. 7.

—Julian Kinsley
—update: Christina M. Stansell

Kellogg Brown & Root, Inc.

601 Jefferson Street
Houston, Texas 77002
U.S.A.
Telephone: (713) 753-2000
Fax: (713) 753-5353
Web site: http://www.halliburton.com

Wholly Owned Subsidiary of Halliburton Company
Incorporated: 1929 as Brown & Root, Inc.
Employees: 64,000
Sales: $9.27 billion (2003)
NAIC: 541330 Engineering Services; 23493 Industrial Nonbuilding Structure Construction; 23499 All Other Heavy Construction

Kellogg Brown & Root, Inc. (KBR) operates as the engineering and construction arm of Halliburton Company. The group designs, builds, and provides maintenance services for liquefied natural gas plants, refining and processing plants, production facilities, and onshore and offshore pipelines. Its non-energy business provides engineering and construction services to governments and civil infrastructure customers. KBR plays a large role as a private military company (PMC) and has been contracted to provide a host of military support services in Iraq. Because of a $4 billion asbestos settlement, parent Halliburton has placed KBR under bankruptcy protection. The company's government services business is not included in the filing.

Origins

With the financial backing of his brother-in-law Dan Root, Herman Brown started a road building company named Brown & Root in 1919 with mortgaged wagons and mules. Indeed, it was a meager beginning for a man who would ultimately spearhead some of the largest and most difficult construction projects in modern history and create one of the world's largest construction and engineering firms.

In considerable debt from setting up his business, Brown found work where he could before landing his first road build-

ing job in Freestone, Texas. This opportunity led to other road building and earth-moving work elsewhere as Brown gradually tried to make enough money to pay for the mules and wagons which he later described as a ''worn-out . . . three-fresno and plow outfit.'' Despite Brown's modest equipment, three years after commencing business he was able to win the contracts to rebuild four bridges that had been washed out by a flood in Central Texas. This project represented the fledgling company's first big break, but it also posed a formidable challenge. One of the bridges would require underwater blasting to set its piers, a task for which Brown had no experience; nevertheless, he was commissioned with superintending its execution. This project proved to be the first of many such challenges for Herman Brown and his company.

At many times in Brown & Root's history, the company's employees and management would find themselves either initially lacking the experience to complete a task or being the first group to undertake a certain endeavor. However, cast in the role of pioneer, Brown & Root rose to the occasion in an overwhelming majority of these situations, successfully navigating through uncharted waters and completing what theretofore had been considered improbable. For Brown, the solution to this first problem came from his younger brother George.

Possessing a degree in mining from the Colorado School of Mines, George Brown was home convalescing from a mining accident when his brother approached him about Brown & Root's contracts to rebuild the four bridges. The elder Brown convinced his brother to head the project, thereby resolving the underwater blasting issue and bringing George Brown into the Brown & Root fold. Beginning in 1922, the two brothers would work together for the next 40 years, taking Brown & Root to new heights in each succeeding decade and using their contrasting personalities to steward the company through the many challenges that lay waiting ahead. In meeting these challenges, Herman Brown would be remembered as a ''working man's man,'' personally visiting job sites throughout the year, wherever they were, often more inclined to spend time with his employees than with his fellow executives. His brother George was just the opposite, despite his practical experience in mining. George Brown functioned best as Brown & Root's salesman, able to negotiate over the telephone and influence others with his outgoing personality, talents that

Company Perspectives:

Service quality is referred to at KBR as performance excellence. A different name, but the meaning is the same: innovation and knowledge management, excellent execution, predictable results, and customer value.

were best applied to pursuing Brown & Root's business opportunities. With these two complementary styles, George and Herman Brown successfully concluded the reconstruction of the four bridges in Central Texas, opened an office in Houston in 1926, and then spent the remainder of the decade slowly expanding their business largely through work obtained from building contracts awarded by the State of Texas.

Securing Contracts in the 1930s and 1940s

Despite the promising beginning that Brown & Root had shown during the 1920s, two calamities struck at the end of the decade which had a profound effect on the company. In 1929, Dan Root, Herman and George Brown's brother-in-law, died, the same year that the stock market crash precipitated the Great Depression, sending the country into a deleterious decade-long economic slide. The death of Root, who had been instrumental in the formation of the company ten years earlier, caused the company to take stock of its situation. The Brown brothers purchased Root's interest in the company and then incorporated as Brown & Root, Inc. that same year, marking a new beginning for the company on the eve of the devastating economic climate of the 1930s.

With the onset of the depression, the number of state-funded construction projects slowed to a trickle, forcing the two brothers to pursue other work, including hauling garbage for the city of Houston. However, Brown & Root was able to escape from the grip of the depression in a relatively short time, securing a contract in 1934 for the construction of a board road for Humble Oil Company in Roanoke, Louisiana. The contract was significant for two reasons: first, it extended the company's geographic presence from Texas into Louisiana, and second, it formed the first connection with a company that 30 years later would purchase Brown & Root. Humble Oil, the client for Brown & Root's board road contract, was one of seven major oil companies that owned a company then known as Halliburton Oil Well Cementing Company. This business was later renamed the Halliburton Company, and it would become the parent company of Brown & Root in the 1960s.

Of more immediate significance to the two brothers, though, was a project awarded to the company in 1936, when Brown & Root secured the construction contract for the Marshall Ford Dam. This venture marked the company's entry into heavy construction and the power industry and proved to be a defining moment in the company's history. Located west of Austin, the Marshall Ford Dam, later renamed the Mansfield Dam, would become the largest structure of its kind in Texas, measuring nearly a mile wide and standing 25 stories high. This project, which lasted five years and took two million tons of concrete to complete, elevated Brown & Root's status from that of a constructor of moderately sized projects to a company capable of taking on the largest types of construction projects in the world.

The success of the Marshall Dam project led to more large-scale, government-funded work four years later when Brown & Root was awarded a contract to help build a $90-million naval air station at Corpus Christi, Texas, in 1940. The construction of the Corpus Christi Naval Air Station was prompted by the looming threat of World War II, and as the United States took steps toward entering the conflict, Brown & Root unexpectedly found itself at the center of the government's plans for armament. In addition to the Corpus Christi project, the U.S. Navy approached George Brown in 1941 about taking over the contract to build four submarine chasers, a venture that would pay the company $640,000 for each vessel. Similar to the company's early years, Brown & Root was faced with a project that called for skills that it did not possess.

With no previous experience in ship building, the Brown brothers formed Brown Shipbuilding Company and began work on the four submarine chasers stipulated in the Navy contract. Their marked success with the first four led to a contract for four additional submarine chasers, then 12 more, finally resulting in an order in early 1942 for a medium-sized fleet of destroyer escorts which yielded Brown & Root $3.3 million for each ship. By the end of the war, George and Herman Brown's uncertain foray into ship building had resulted in 359 combat ships, 12 pursuit craft, 307 landing craft, 36 rocket-firing boats, and four salvage boats being constructed for the U.S. Navy, a production total worth $500 million.

Brown & Root emerged from the war as a major U.S. construction company. Its success with the Marshall Ford Dam, the Corpus Christi Naval Station, and its impressive wartime work had propelled the company into the upper echelon of the country's construction firms, a remarkable achievement for a business that as recently as 20 years earlier was subsisting on constructing wooden roads to support oil field work.

Postwar Expansion

During the postwar period, Brown & Root continued to increase the magnitude and scope of its construction and engineering projects, pioneering a string of industry firsts. In 1946, the company received its first overseas assignment when it was selected as managing partner for the reconstruction of Guam, which had incurred severe damage during World War II. Also in that year, Brown & Root began work on its first major engineering project, a contract for a chlorine caustic plant on the Houston Ship Canal for Diamond Alkali, and was awarded its first paper-mill construction contract from Southland Paper in Lufkin, Texas. The following year, Brown & Root secured a contract from Kerr-McGee to design and build the world's first commercial out-of-sight-of-land oil drilling platform, a pivotal and historic step for a company that would become heavily involved in enabling the off-shore development of oil and gas.

During the 1950s, Brown & Root began to increase its presence outside the United States, laying a foundation for international expansion that would become an integral component of the company's future growth. In 1951, the company opened an office near Edmonton, Alberta, to facilitate the construction of a petrochemical and synthetic fiber plant. One year later, Brown & Root expanded to the southern hemisphere when it began building a series of gas injection plants on Lake

Key Dates:

1919: Herman Brown starts a road building company named Brown & Root with start-up money from Dan Root.
1929: Root dies; brothers Herman and George Brown incorporate as Brown & Root Inc.
1941: The U.S. Navy begins contracting with the firm.
1961: The company becomes the architect-engineer for NASA's Manned Spacecraft Center.
1962: Halliburton Company acquires Brown & Root.
1998: M.W. Kellogg Company merges with Brown & Root to form Kellogg Brown & Root (KBR).
2002: Halliburton forms two distinct business groups with KBR overseeing its engineering and construction business.
2003: Halliburton places KBR into bankruptcy as a result of a $4 billion asbestos settlement.

Maracaibo, Venezuela. After extending its presence into Canada and Venezuela, Brown & Root tackled two enormous projects in 1958, building the Bhumiphol Dam in Thailand and the Tantangara Dam and Tunnel for the Snowy Mountains Hydroelectric Authority in Australia. The company ended its first decade of international expansion by opening an office in London with the expectation of gaining contracts from anticipated oil and gas exploration in the North Sea.

In the meantime, Brown & Root also continued to augment the scope of its domestic operations. In 1951, the company designed and built a major petrochemical facility for the Celanese Corporation; one year later, it was awarded its first $100-million contract when it constructed a polyethylene plant in Seadrift, Texas, for Union Carbide. This venture expanded Brown & Root's diversification into petroleum and chemical activities and added customers such as Ciba Giegy and DuPont to the company's growing list of clients.

Going into the 1960s, Brown & Root had gained the reputation of an engineering and construction firm able to take on the largest of construction projects. As the company prepared for the challenges of the 1960s, it would enhance this reputation by becoming highly regarded for its technical expertise. Two projects in particular greatly contributed to this perspective. In 1960, the company became involved in a government project for the National Science Foundation dubbed Project Mohole, the objective of which was to drill in 14,000 feet of water and penetrate 21,000 feet below the earth's crust. The following year, Brown & Root followed up this ambitious foray into marine engineering technology by being selected by the National Aeronautics and Space Administration (NASA) as architect-engineer for the Manned Spacecraft Center in Houston.

The Halliburton Purchase: 1962–63

While Brown & Root was taking on these two signal projects, the company's founder was suffering from serious health problems. Herman Brown had undergone heart surgery in 1960, and in its aftermath his prognosis grew increasingly bleak,

causing concern over the company's future. A tightly held private firm up to this point, executives resolved to find a company to purchase a controlling interest in Brown & Root as Brown's health worsened in 1961 and 1962. Against this backdrop, Brown & Root was approached by Halliburton Company, an oil field services concern that brought companies with expertise in the oil and gas industry under its corporate umbrella. Since Brown & Root fit Halliburton's acquisition criteria and the company itself was agreeable to becoming part of Halliburton, acquisition negotiations between the two companies commenced in autumn 1962. The deal was completed in November, shortly after Brown's death, with Halliburton paying $32.6 million for roughly 95 percent of Brown & Root up front, then acquiring the remaining 5 percent in June 1963.

George Brown was elected to Halliburton's board of directors concurrent with Brown & Root's sale, and he continued as the company's president and chief executive officer for another year. In this new era, the company fared as well as it had during its past, becoming, like its parent company, increasingly involved in construction and engineering projects for the oil and gas industry. In 1966, Brown & Root laid the first marine pipeline in the North Sea; two years later, the company laid and buried the world's first 48-inch pipeline in offshore Kuwait.

During the 1970s, Brown & Root would use the talents it had first gained during the construction of the Marshall Ford Dam between 1936 and 1941 to build power generating plants. In 1977 alone, the company placed five electric plants into operation, part of Brown & Root's decade-long effort to meet the rising demand for electric power. Among the decade's other highlights were the design and construction in 1972 of two fabrication facilities, Highland Fabricators in Nigg, Scotland, and Sunda Straits Fabrication Yard in Indonesia. These projects positioned Brown & Root for offshore platform work and the design of Chahbahar Baval Port for the Iranian Imperial Navy in 1975.

Struggles and Success: Late 1970s to the Mid-1990s

After decades of remarkable success, Brown & Root's fortunes began to change in the late 1970s. In January 1977, the company announced that its documents pertaining to offshore oil platform activities had been subpoenaed by a Federal grand jury to investigate possible antitrust charges. Nine days after the announcement, Foster Parker, George Brown's hand-picked successor to the post of president and chief executive officer of Brown & Root, was discovered dead in his bedroom with a bullet wound in his right temple. No confirmed connection between the grand jury's inquiry and Parker's apparent suicide was immediately made, but nearly two years later, in December 1978, Brown & Root pleaded no contest to antitrust charges and paid $90 million to settle related civil claims. The allegations of price fixing, led, a short time later, to a protracted legal battle with the proprietors of the South Texas Nuclear Project, ending in a $750 million settlement paid by Brown & Root in 1985.

While it was embroiled in legal turmoil, Brown & Root continued to benefit from large construction and engineering projects, completing the Eisenhower Tunnel at Loveland Pass, Colorado, in 1979 and installing the world's first guyed tower platform in 1,200 feet of water in the Gulf of Mexico in 1984. In

Kellogg Brown & Root, Inc.

1986, Brown & Root completed a $475 million joint-venture project to build a military base for the U.S. Navy and Air Force on the island of Diego Garcia in the Indian Ocean. The same year, it formed Brown & Root Services Corporation to obtain government operations and maintenance work.

As Brown & Root maneuvered through the late 1980s, it strengthened its construction and engineering abilities with the acquisition of two companies: Howard Humphreys, a civil consulting company with expertise in water, dams, roads, bridges, buildings, and tunneling, in 1987, and CF Braun, a process engineering firm, in 1989. Entering the 1990s, Brown & Root extended its presence into Eastern Europe, completed its first major project off the shore of China, and participated in the reconstruction of Kuwait following the Persian Gulf War.

After strengthening its position in Eastern Europe in 1993 by forming Brown & Root Skoda in the Czech Republic through a joint venture, the company entered the mid-1990s intent on increasing its operations in the region, where opportunities in oil and gas development abounded. The company's future called for Brown & Root personnel to engage in large-scale, sophisticated construction and engineering projects across the globe. As Brown & Root moved toward this future, its remarkable rise from a small company boasting no more than mortgaged mules and wagons to one of the largest construction and engineering concerns in the world instilled confidence that the years ahead would represent a continuation of its storied past.

Problems Arise in the Late 1990s and Beyond

The years leading into the late 1990s and beyond, however, proved to be perhaps the biggest test of the company's resolve as it was catapulted into the public spotlight due to its relationship with Halliburton. Brown & Root's parent had been growing significantly over the past several years through a series of acquisitions made under the leadership of Dick Cheney, who was named chairman, CEO, and president of Halliburton in 1995. He had served as U.S. Secretary of Defense under President George H.W. Bush and would eventually leave Halliburton in 2000 to join running mate George W. Bush on the Republican ticket in the upcoming presidential election. During his tenure at Halliburton, Cheney orchestrated a number of deals, including a multi-billion dollar merger with Dresser Industries Inc., the parent company of M.W. Kellogg Company. Founded in 1900, Kellogg was acquired by Dresser in 1988 and since that time had made a name for itself in the construction of petroleum and petrochemical facilities. The Halliburton/Dresser union brought Kellogg and Brown & Root together in 1998, forming Kellogg Brown & Root (KBR).

The new KBR proved an instant success, shoring up a host of contract agreements worth billions, including a $1.5 billion contract to expand Malaysia's Bintulu liquefied natural gas complex. While the company remained focused on expanding its business, its parent company began to experience a host of problems related to asbestos claims and investigations into its accounting practices.

Overall, Halliburton had been involved in asbestos-related litigation for years—since 1976 there had been 474,500 claims against the firm for its use of asbestos in certain products.

During 2001 and 2002 however, the company faced an onslaught of new claims. Halliburton finally put the litigation to rest in 2002 by agreeing to pay approximately $4.2 billion to settle all outstanding claims. That same year, the Securities and Exchange Commission (SEC) began an investigation into Halliburton's accounting practices. During 1998, when Cheney was in office, the company changed how it booked revenue related to cost overruns on billion-dollar contracts. While the change itself was legal, the firm neglected to report it to shareholders and the SEC for over a year. By making the change, Halliburton was able to meet earnings expectations for 1998—the year of the Dresser merger. Without it, earnings would have fallen short. The SEC began its investigation in May, forcing Halliburton to hand over nearly 200,000 accounting documents to prove that it had not inflated cost overrun claims. The investigation came to a close and Halliburton eventually settled the case with shareholders for $6 million.

As a result of losses brought on by industry conditions and litigation, Halliburton restructured itself in 2002. The company realigned its businesses into two major groups—Halliburton Energy Services Group and KBR, the engineering and construction group. As part of its asbestos settlement, Halliburton placed KBR under bankruptcy protection in 2003. The filing did not include KBR's military and government services business.

While Halliburton struggled under a mountain of negative publicity, KBR also came under fire for its military services role in Iraq. A 2003 *Business Week* article reported, "The company's high-profile success in winning contracts, coupled with its intimate ties to the White House, has aroused suspicions that it is a beneficiary of political favoritism." Acting as a private military company (PMC), KBR had billed the U.S. government approximately $950 million by 2003 for contracts related to the invasions of Iraq and Afghanistan. The cap on those contracts was set at $8.2 billion. Most of its military-related work came under the Logistics Civil Augmentation Program, or LOGCAP, contract secured in 2001.

A separate contract—capped at $7 billion—was drawn up for KBR in late 2002. As part of the deal, KBR created a contingency plan to handle the possible burning of Iraq's oil fields during a U.S. invasion. KBR was awarded the contract without a bidding process which resulted in outcries of political favoritism that led to an investigation by the General Accounting Office of the U.S. Congress. To make matters worse, Halliburton and its KBR unit, along with other PMCs working in Iraq, were facing criticism from Pentagon officials as well as the Justice Department by early 2004 for quality of work issues and billing and pricing matters. While KBR would no doubt continue to play a significant role supporting the U.S. military, it faced a long and perhaps bumpy road ahead in the years to come.

Principal Competitors

Bechtel Group Inc.; Stolt Offshore S.A.; Technip.

Further Reading

Brown & Root, Inc., Brownbuilder (75th anniversary edition), 1994.
"Brown & Root Settles," *New York Times*, May 31, 1985, p. D3.
"B&R Executive Sees Busy Future for Marine Work," *Oil and Gas Journal*, November 16, 1970, pp. 217–18.

"Halliburton to Buy Brown & Root from Foundation," *Wall Street Journal*, December 13, 1962, p. 32.

"Halliburton Files KBR Bankruptcy," *Houston Chronicle*, December 17, 2003.

"Halliburton Is Said to Discuss Merger with Brown & Root," *Wall Street Journal*, December 11, 1962, p. 16.

"Halliburton Reshuffles Its Brown & Root Cards," *ENR*, September 30, 1996, p. 5.

"Halliburton Unit Plans Venture," *Wall Street Journal*, October 26, 1994, p. B5.

"Kellogg Brown & Root Gets More Competitive as Identity Emerges," *ENR*, February 21, 2000, p. 63.

King, Neil, "Halliburton's Iraq Costs Examined," *Wall Street Journal*, March 12, 2004, p. A8.

Korman, Richard, "Profit Push at 'New' Brown & Root," *ENR*, October 21, 1996, p. 10.

Lindsey, Robert, "Puzzle of Executive's Death Stuns Texas," *New York Times*, February 7, 1977, p. 35.

"Outsourcing War: An Inside Look at Brown & Root," *Business Week*, September 15, 2003, p. 68.

Stringer, Kortney, "Halliburton to Organize Structure as Two Separate Business Units," *Wall Street Journal*, March 20, 2002, p. A4.

"U.S. General Criticizes Halliburton," *Wall Street Journal*, March 15, 2004, p. A3.

—Jeffrey L. Covell
—update: Christina M. Stansell

VENDEXBB

Koninklijke Vendex KBB N.V. (Royal Vendex KBB N.V.)

De Klencke 6
1083 HH Amsterdam
Netherlands
Telephone: 31 20 549 0500
Fax: 31 20 646 1954
Web site: http://www.vendexkbb.com

Public Company
Founded: 1887
Sales: EURO 4.4 billion ($5.1 billion) (2003)
Employees: 43,900
Stock Exchanges: Amsterdam
Ticker Symbol: VDX
NAIC: 551120 Offices of Other Holding Companies;
  452110 Department Stores

Koninklijke Vendex KBB N.V., or Royal Vendex KBB N.V., is the leading non-food retailer in the Netherlands. The Vendex empire is vast, with nearly 1,700 retail outlets operating under 15 different store formats. The company's holdings span the Netherlands, Belgium, Luxembourg, Denmark, Germany, France, and Spain. The firm's department stores include Bijenkorf, HEMA, and Vroom & Dreesmann. Its other business areas include do-it-yourself, fashion, and consumer electronics. Vendex underwent a series of changes during the late 1990s, spinning off its food and temporary employment agency businesses, and merging with competitor Koninklijke Bijenkorf Beheer (KBB) to gain its number one market position. The company adopted its current name in 2000.

Origins

The founders of the company that eventually became Vendex Willem Vroom and Anton Dreesmann, had extensive retail experience, having clerked in various food stores and dry goods stores for years. After the two young men met they formed a close friendship; ambitious and energetic, they decided to open a department store of their own. When the first Vroom & Dreesmann retail store opened in downtown Amsterdam in 1887, bundles of soap and candles, swatches of clothing material, and brooms were just some of the items sold by the new company to the general public.

From that date to the beginning of World War I, Vroom & Dreesmann department stores expanded throughout The Netherlands. Both of the founders came from close-knit families, and the two men were able to convince their relatives to operate each new store that was opened. The stores were typically co-owned by Vroom & Dreesmann and the chosen relative, but individually managed by the relative, who was given a great deal of autonomy. Vroom & Dreesmann relied heavily on the idea of familial responsibility to assure the success of each new store.

The world wars hurt the company not only in loss of revenue but also in loss of personnel to the tragedies of both conflicts. Yet Vroom & Dreesmann continued to grow. People still needed soap, shoes, and toilet paper, and Vroom & Dreesmann stores were there to provide these necessities, although without the direction of the founders, who had passed away some time before.

Throughout the 1950s and into the 1960s, Vroom & Dreesmann department stores operated within a highly decentralized corporate structure. During the early 1960s, the Vroom & Dreesmann group decided to impose some order on the company by organizing the stores by region, in a first step toward a more centralized and more efficient operational structure. In 1973 the regional groups merged to form a united Vroom & Dreesmann Group. Anton Dreesmann's grandson, who was also named Anton Dreesmann, became chairman of the newly restructured company.

With a Ph.D. in economics and law, and having taught as a professor at the University of Amsterdam, Anton Dreesmann was well prepared to assume the leadership of Vroom & Dreesmann. He immediately began to overhaul the organization and administration of the firm, implemented standardized operating procedures, and initiated a bold expansion strategy. Seeking to diversify from the traditional department store business, Dreesmann moved into the fields of food retail, fashion, banking, hardware retail, jewelry retail, maintenance services, mail order services, employment services, catering services, and electronic retail. The acquisitions of such well-known firms as Kreym-

206

borg, Claudia Strater, Edah, Staal Bankiers, Vedior, Vedelectric, Siebel, and Nederlands Talen Institut were financed mostly through debt.

International Expansion Begins in the Late 1970s

During the late 1970s, the government in The Netherlands revised the corporate tax structure as a means of financing social programs, and companies such as Vroom & Dreesmann were faced with a significant increase in their taxes. In response, Dreesmann began seeking overseas partners and acquisitions. He established a U.S. subsidiary, Vendamerica, to analyze trends in American retailing, and in 1978 he negotiated a major agreement with Dillard's department stores. According to the agreement, Vroom & Dreesmann paid approximately $24 million for more than one million non-voting shares of stock; in return, Dreesmann was made a member of Dillard's Board of Directors. In 1979 Dreesmann purchased Ultralar, a major Brazilian department store chain.

During the 1980s, Dreesmann continued to pursue an aggressive expansion strategy, although at a somewhat slower pace. In 1980 he attempted to acquire 50 percent of W.R. Grace's retailing operations. Grace, one of the largest conglomerates in the United States, was initially receptive to Dreesmann's overtures, but after months of intense negotiations, the two companies could not reach a mutually satisfactory agreement. During the same year, Dreesmann expanded into the Far East by purchasing a 3 percent interest in UNY, one of Japan's largest retailers, which operated numerous superstore and specialty store outlets. Other notable purchases during this time included a 50 percent stake in the Brazilian branch of the Sears department store chain and the acquisition of Perry Sports, one of the largest and most successful sports retail store chains in The Netherlands.

From 1982 through the remainder of the decade, the company focused on implementing a comprehensive reorganization plan. This involved organizing the company's businesses into separate operating divisions, with the retail trading division comprising food stores, department stores, specialty fashion, specialty hard goods, and specialty home furnishings, and the business services division comprising maintenance services, employment services, and miscellaneous services. The divisions were under the direction of the holding company, which changed its name to Vendex International N.V. in 1985. Throughout these changes, Anton Dreesmann remained firmly in control of the company, especially since the Dreesmann family retained a majority of the firm's stock.

Revenues and profitability continued to grow as a result of Dreesmann's expansion strategy. In 1987 Vendex acquired a 50

percent interest in B. Dalton, a huge bookstore chain in the United States, and a 32 percent stake in the College Book Stores of Barnes & Noble, another large American retail bookseller. Vendex also acquired numerous European companies in unrelated industries, including a Belgian furniture store chain and a Dutch travel agency.

Late 1980s–Early 1990s: Meeting Challenges

By the late 1980s, however, Vendex was experiencing serious financial problems. Having concentrated for years on its highly successful expansion strategy, the company failed to adapt to changes in the domestic market, especially in the retailing industry. This, combined with a slowdown in the Dutch economy, led to declining sales. The company's heavy debt load and high interests rates also contributed to significant losses in certain sectors of its business. Compounding these problems was the poor health of Dreesmann, who suffered a series of debilitating strokes.

In 1988 Dreesmann appointed Arie Van der Zwan to take his place as chairman of Vendex. Van der Zwan, also an economics professor, began to improve the company's operational efficiency by taking drastic measures, which included layoffs of almost 18 percent of the company's retail employees. Dreesmann was furious. Highly regarded for his employee relations policies—and called ''Uncle Anton'' by his workers—Dreesmann returned to Vendex despite his failing health. He immediately fired Van der Zwan, and implemented his own reorganization and revitalization strategy.

In 1990 Dreesmann selected Jan Michiel Hessels to succeed him as chairman of Vendex. Hessels had obtained a law degree from the University of Leiden and had extensive administrative experience in companies such as Akzo, Delimaatschappij, and Deli Universal. Hessels' assignment was to revitalize the company through a three-pronged strategy: divest unprofitable, non-core businesses; restructure the retail department store division by concentrating on improved profitability and domestic acquisitions; and reduce corporate debt.

In 1990 Vendex discontinued almost all of its operations in Brazil, including its retail department store operations, banking operations, and hard goods retail operation, primarily due to declining profits and the instability of the Brazilian economy. The company also disposed of some holdings in banking, mail order services, and real estate operations within The Netherlands and reduced its interest in Barnes & Noble, the U.S. bookstore chain. In 1991, after its American home center retail store chain, Mr. Goodbuys, filed for Chapter 11 bankruptcy, Vendex ceased all operations of the company. Vendex sold its shares in Dillard's department stores, reaping a healthy profit from its investment, and reduced its share in Software, Etc., another American investment.

Hessels' strategic moves paid off handsomely. Vendex International's total income increased from NLG 164 million in 1990 to more than NLG 340 million in 1995. Part of this improvement resulted from an increase in profits reported by Vroom & Dreesmann department stores, which shot up from NLG 7 million in 1990 to NLG 86 million in 1995, and by an improvement in the

---

Key Dates:

1887: The first Vroom & Dreesmann retail store opens in downtown Amsterdam.
1973: The regional stores unite to form the Vroom & Dreesmann Group.
1978: The company begins international expansion as a result of changes in corporate tax structure.
1985: The firm changes its name to Vendex International N.V.
1998: Vendex spins off its food and temporary employment agency businesses.
1999: The company merges with Koninklijke Bijenkorf Beheer (KBB) to form Vendex KBB N.V.
2002: FAO Schwarz is sold.

---

company's debt-to-equity ratio, which decreased from 234 percent at the end of 1991 to just 48.4 percent in 1995.

In 1995 Vendex reported that approximately 72 percent of net sales and nearly 75 percent of its operating income came from its retail division, while the remainder was derived from the business services division. The company operated a total of 655 food stores and 121 franchise pet food retail stores, and had more than 11 percent of the total food retail market in The Netherlands. Edah, the company's largest retail food store chain, which operated medium-sized supermarkets, was listed as the third-largest food retail store in the country in 1995.

Vendex International's department store operation was led by Vroom & Dreesmann, which had a 40 percent share of the total department store market in The Netherlands. With 62 stores across the country, Vroom & Dreesmann department stores sold a wide variety of merchandise, including clothing, toys, and telecommunications equipment. The company's specialty store operations were equally diverse, with product lines including lingerie, camping accessories, jewelry, and home furnishings. Companies within the Vendex specialty retail family included such well-known names as Kreymborg, Kien, America Today, Perry Sport, the Siebel Group, and Kijkshop/Best-Sellers.

Vendex's business services operation was led by Cemsto, the largest cleaning service firm in the country, which had more than 11,000 employees. Most of Cemsto's cleaning services were contracted by large buildings, housing corporations, and other business enterprises. Vendex's Employment services sector operated 474 offices throughout The Netherlands, Belgium, Luxembourg, France, and Germany. Vedior International, which provided employment services such as helping people find temporary jobs or training the long-term unemployed to find work, was considered one of the most innovative firms in the field. With Hessels firmly in control, Vendex International's future looked bright. The company continued to grow within a small geographical area by adapting to the changing conditions of the European marketplace.

Late 1990s and Beyond

The European retail industry did in fact experience change, which brought about significant restructuring during the late 1990s. Modifications in business-related laws allowed large conglomerates like Vendex to spin off certain holdings. The company took advantage of the relaxed regulations and began to position itself as the leading Dutch nonfood retailer. In 1998, the firm spun off Vedior to Vendex shareholders. It then merged its food interests with De Boer Unigro to create supermarket giant Laurus. Having shed its business and food holdings, the company was left to focus on its department store and retail activities.

To this end, Vendex made a play for competitor Koninklijke Bijenkorf Beheer (KBB) in early 1998. The deal would unite the leading department store chains in the Netherlands under single ownership, creating the leading nonfood retailer in the country. The complicated merger process faced scrutiny not only by regulators, but shareholders as well that felt Vendex's bid for KBB was too low. A hostile battle ensued when a counter-offer was made by privately-held WE International—a move not often seen in the Dutch business arena. By October, Vendex had increased its offer price to thwart WE's attempts. Vendex eventually won out, completing the merger process in 1999.

The new Vendex KBB controlled 11 percent of the Dutch market, leaving room for further expansion. According to competition laws, a company was limited to a 20 percent market share which meant Vendex KBB could bolster its holdings. It did just that by acquiring electronics retailer It's in 2000. It added do-it-yourself retailer Brico to its arsenal in 2002 in a deal worth US$440.8 million. As part of its strategy to focus on its core businesses, Vendex sold its financially troubled FAO Schwarz toy stores in 2002.

While Vendex appeared to be well positioned to compete in the nonfood retailing sector, it began to face a host of challenges in the early years of the new millennium. Market conditions were less than stellar with consumer confidence falling to its lowest levels since 1983. Flat consumer spending, price wars, and heightened competition left Vendex's major department store operations—Vroom & Dreesmann and de Bijenkorf—struggling to shore up profits. By 2003, company shareholders were demanding changes and recommended that management either take Vendex private or break up the company. Vendex chairman Ed Hamming recognized the severity of the situation, claiming in a September 2003 *Financial Times* article, ''If we do not quickly put our house in order our credibility will suffer.'' Sure enough, rumors began to circulate about a possible takeover of Vendex KBB as earnings continued to falter in early 2004. At this time the company reported that it would consider offers made by certain parties that were interested in the company as whole and that would maintain its corporate strategy. Vendex's future was indeed up in the air, leaving it subject to speculation about its success in the years to come.

Principal Subsidiaries

Vroom & Dreesmann; Claudia Straeter; Hunkemoeller; Dixons; Hema; de Bijenkorf; It's; Modern Electronics; Prijstopper; Dynabyte; Scaap & Citroen; M&S Mode; Praxis; Formido; Brico.

Principal Competitors

AVA AG; Metro AG; Otto Versand Gmbh & Co.

Further Reading

Bradley, Sandrine, "Vendex Becomes Benelux Player," *Acquisitions Monthly*, May 2002, p. 44.

Cramb, Gordon, "Merger Mania Takes Hold," *Financial Times*, November 5, 1998, p. 3.

——, "Vendex and DBU in Foods Merger," *Financial Times*, May 26, 1998, p. 29.

——, "Vendex and KBB Act to Secure Merger," *Financial Times*, October 6, 1998, p. 34.

——, "Vendex Spins Off Recruitment Arm," *Financial Times*, June 25, 1998, p. 28.

"CVC Emerges as a Possible Bidder for Vendex KBB," *Financial Times*, February 7, 2004, p. 9.

"Losses Force Vendex KBB to Seek Help," *Financial Times*, September 10, 2003, p. 18.

Miller, Paul, "FAO Acquisition Rounds Out Right Start," *Catalog Age*, January 2002.

"Shoppers Circle KBB in Dutch Retail Takeover Battle," *Financial Times*, October 5, 1998, p. 28.

Smit, Barbara, "Vendex Bids to Take Over Rival KBB," *Financial Times*, February 10, 1998, p. 30.

"Vendex International NV," *Wall Street Journal*, April 8, 1998.

"VendexKBB Says 'Well Positioned' for European Non-food Sector Consolidation," *AFX News*, September 7, 1999.

—Thomas Derdak
—update: Christina M. Stansell

KORET®

Koret of California, Inc.

505 14th Street
Oakland, California 94612
U.S.A.
Telephone: (510) 622-7000
Fax: (510) 622-7110
Web site: http://www.koretsf.com

Wholly Owned Subsidiary of Kellwood Company
Incorporated: 1938
Employees: 300 (est.)
Sales: $300 million (1998, est.)
NAIC: 315232 Women's and Girls' Cut and Sew Blouse
and Shirt Manufacturing; 315999 Other Apparel
Accessories and Other Apparel Manufacturing

Koret of California, Inc., has been making moderately priced apparel for women since 1938. Over the decades, the company has passed through stages as a private family-owned concern, an acquisition-oriented public company, and a subsidiary of larger apparel enterprises. Koret is now a subsidiary of Kellwood Company, a $2.4 billion concern that markets a host of brand names in men's and women's wear. Koret first achieved widespread recognition in the early 1960s when it invented a permanent press process that was widely adopted in the apparel industry. Royalties from the process fueled a period of reckless expansion through acquisitions, after which Koret regained solid footing by focusing on its core women's wear operations. Koret now produces and distributes sportswear for women under the Koret, Beliza, and Napa Valley brand names. Its primary customers are department stores, where Koret is a leading label in the moderately priced range. The company also has factory outlet stores in 27 states. Headquartered in Oakland, California, it has sales offices in Los Angeles and New York and a distribution center in northern California. Koret's product lines, which included coordinated pants, blazers, and blouses, are mainly targeted at women over 45.

A Skirt-and-Sweater Partnership: 1938–66

In 1938 a husband-and-wife team, Joseph and Stephanie Koret, founded Koret of California in a small loft in San Fran-

cisco. Joseph was a sweater salesman at the time, while Stephanie was taking classes in fashion design at a local school. She began making skirts to go with Joseph's sweaters, and the two launched the Missy line of coordinated women's apparel. Joseph played the role of salesman and promoter at the young company, and Stephanie was in charge of design and human resources. Over the next two decades, the company made a name for itself as a small but successful producer of coordinated skirts and sweaters. The Koret Trickskirt pleated skirt, which sold 3.5 million pieces, was introduced in 1946.

Koret made a major breakthrough in 1961 when it developed the Koratron permanent press process, which it used to put pleats in its skirts. Specifically, Koratron was a "post-curing" process: fabric received a chemical pretreatment and, once made into a finished garment, heat was applied to activate the permanent press properties. The resulting garment was better able to hold its shape and resist creases. Koret executives had developed the process as a marketing ploy and started running ads across the nation announcing that they had emancipated women.

Koret began licensing the Koratron process around the world. A whole new permanent press market developed and royalties began pouring in. Levi Strauss was the first company to license the process in 1963. Over the next few years, about 400 other companies licensed the process and paid Koret a 1 percent royalty on sales of permanent press garments. By 1966, royalty revenues were twice as much as clothing sales; net sales that year were $33 million.

Investment bankers began encouraging the royalty-rich company to go public. Stephanie was uneasy with the idea, but Joseph saw it as an opportunity for his wife to be able to retire and for him to be able to afford a boat and other luxuries. Koret went public in May 1966 and raised $11.5 million. Soon afterwards, Stephanie retired and the company changed its name to Koracorp Industries, Inc.

Patent Battles and Ill-Advised Acquisitions in the 1970s

The company ran into difficulties soon after the initial public offering. As Joseph Koret told *Forbes* magazine in 1975, Stephanie's departure was a turning point. "The worst thing I ever

Company Perspectives:

Mission: Design, produce, and distribute moderate-to-bridge price women's sportswear and separates with focus on classic through modern lifestyles.

did was let my wife retire,'' he said. She had always been the ''voice of reason,'' according to Joseph. ''She was the restraining spirit. I tended to be too aggressive, too ruthless. My wife was the one who prevented me from going too far.'' Stephanie had also been in charge of hiring, and many of the people she employed stayed at Koret for decades. However, her health declined quickly after her retirement, leaving Joseph on his own to guide Koracorp through a series of new challenges.

Patents on the Koratron permanent press process were due to expire in 1978, so the company needed to find a way to replace royalty revenue. In fact, royalty revenues started to decline drastically a decade before the patent expiration as companies developed their own permanent press procedures. In 1967, several hundred licensees stopped paying royalties to Koret, contending that the Koratron patent did not cover their own permanent press fabrics and processes. Koracorp charged companies such as Deering Milliken, Inc., Blue Bell Inc., and Levi Strauss & Co. with patent infringement. In turn, many apparel companies started legal proceedings against Koracorp, alleging fraud of the Patent Office, breach of antitrust laws, and other violations. Royalty income plunged, accounting for only 10 percent of earnings in 1971.

The apparent way out was for Koracorp to acquire new sources of revenue by using its considerable store of funds to purchase other companies. Joseph's forte, however, was marketing, so he sought someone else who could carry out an acquisition strategy. In the late 1960s, he hired Jeré Helfat, a management consultant who had advised the Korets several years earlier on taking the firm public. Helfat became president, and Koret stayed on as Koracorp's chairman.

Helfat's vision was a company structured into several different operating centers, including men's apparel, women's apparel, venture capital, and international divisions. He embarked on an acquisition spree in the late 1960s, but many of his purchases turned out to be poor choices. Helfat bought men's and women's apparel makers whose operations were unprofitable and had to be discontinued. He acquired two unprofitable hat makers on the conviction that hats were coming back. He also bought a French maker of infant clothing before discovering that financing was unavailable to him. Koracorp's venture capital division, known as Koratec, invested in a direct mail magazine called *Homemaking with a Flair* that contained coupons for household products. The magazine reported profits, and the core Koret women's apparel operations were still doing well. The company reported a profit of $2.1 million in 1971 on sales of $92 million.

By 1973, however, an accumulation of money-losing acquisitions was dragging Koracorp into the red. Long-term debt that year reached $37 million. Nevertheless, company management delayed refinancing in the hope that better times were just around the corner. Finally, Koracorp's bankers insisted that the

company liquidate its receivables, many of which were in the coupon magazine operation. Yet when Koracorp started to take action, it discovered that most of the magazine's receivables existed only on paper, and most of the division's profits had been fabricated. The disastrous situation pushed Koracorp to the brink of bankruptcy.

Joseph Koret fired Helfat but did not want to take the helm himself, disheartened as he was by his company's nosedive. He took the post of ''chairman emeritus'' and persuaded Thaddeus Taube, a board member and real estate consultant, to take over as chief executive. Taube and the company treasurer Joseph Berghold dumped most of Koracorp's subsidiaries and took an $11 million loss. The banks decided to give Koracorp a chance and provided $50 million in credit and fresh capital, with Joseph and Stephanie Koret's 37 percent stake in the company acting as collateral. Koracorp gradually recovered value in the mid-1970s by relying on its dependable women's apparel label. The company produced a moderately priced velvet blazer in 1973 that sold over a million pieces and introduced coordinated denim sportswear in 1977 under the City Blues label. In 1976, the Koret label also moved into special sizes when it initiated a ''women's size'' or plus-size division. Net income was $7.8 million in 1978 on sales on $185 million. Koracorp had acquired a solid reputation among retailers by this point. ''Nobody is better than Koret in dealing with customers,'' William Hansen, the president of Los Angeles-based Buffums' chain, told *Business Week* in 1979.

A Levi Strauss Subsidiary: 1979–86

Levi Strauss & Co. bought Koracorp Industries in 1979, giving CEO Taube the chance to go back to the real estate business. Besides the Koret label, the Koracorp acquisition also included Oxxford Clothes, a maker of men's suits, the hat maker Byer-Rolnick, and men's sportswear maker Himalaya. This was Levi Strauss's first major acquisition and its first venture outside jeans manufacturing. The Koret label eventually became part of Battery Stressed Enterprises, Levi Strauss's non-jeans division. Koret further developed its women's wear line under Levi Strauss. A petite division was started in 1981. In 1982, the label moved into production of separates with Koret Separate Impressions, a line of coordinated garments that were in stock year-round. The next year, Koret introduced its Flatter Fit pant, featuring a Lycra spandex panel that held in the stomach. The pants were a great success and sold millions, contributing to a period of record growth for Koret in the mid-1980s.

Richard Banks was Koret's chief executive at Levi Strauss. He led a campaign to encourage department stores to devote more attention to moderately priced apparel. An excessive amount of space was assigned to high-end apparel, Banks contended, even though moderately priced labels like Koret contributed more reliably to sales. Koret implemented several promotions, including a gift-with-purchase program and a point-of-sale fixture called the Multiplier that demonstrated how shoppers could coordinate Koret clothes. In addition, the label introduced supplementary product lines called ''satellites'' that contained about 15 styles instead of the 60 in major groups. The satellites took a so-called ''fashion forward'' approach, demonstrating that Koret was aware of what was happening in the fashion world even as the company's overall

Key Dates:

1938: Joseph and Stephanie Koret found a sweater and skirt business in San Francisco.
1946: The Koret Trickskirt pleated skirt is introduced.
1961: Koret develops the Koratron permanent press process and earns royalties by licensing it to other apparel manufacturers.
1966: Koret goes public and changes its name to Koracorp; Stephanie Koret retires.
1967: Koracorp hires Jeré Helfat to manage an acquisition strategy as legal proceedings challenge Koratron patents.
1973: Helfat is fired; the company takes an $11 million loss as unsuccessful acquisitions are dumped.
1979: Koracorp is acquired by Levi Strauss.
1983: The Flatter Fit pant is a success and contributes to a growth period.
1986: Koret management and other investors acquire the company from Levi Strauss in a leveraged buyout.
1994: Koret buys Mr. Jax Fashions of Canada.
1999: Koret is acquired by Kellwood Company.

operations remained centered on less edgy styles for the 45-and-up demographic. In the early 1980s, Koret also started a division to market its products in Canada. The division became profitable around 1985 after a few years of losses.

By 1986, Levi Strauss was ready to drop its diversified apparel operations and refocus on jeans. Koret CEO Banks signed a leveraged buyout agreement that summer but later backed out of the deal and stayed in a position at Levi Strauss. Instead, the investment banking firm Oppenheimer & Co., which had been involved in arranging the management buyout, stepped in and formed KNA Acquisition Corp. to buy Koret. In November of that year, Levi Strauss sold its Koret of North America subsidiary, which included Koret of California and Koret of Canada, to a group of investors that included Oppenheimer executives, Koret management, and other individuals. Marty Granoff, a major investor in the buyout and the owner of a New York knitwear manufacturer, was named chairman. The new president was Richard Einstein, who had been with Koret since 1967. KNA Acquisition Corp. changed its name to Koret, Inc. in 1987.

Development as a Private Company in the 1990s

As an independent private company, Koret continued its reliable women's wear line and also expanded through a few apparel and accessory acquisitions. In 1989, the company formed the subsidiary Counterparts Sportswear, Inc. to acquire the assets of two women's apparel companies manufacturing under the Counterparts label. The following year, Koret closed its sewing factory in San Francisco, laying off about 300 workers, and shifted manufacturing to Guatemala, where labor costs were much lower. The company also contracted with domestic manufacturers. In 1992, Steven Rudin replaced Richard Einstein as president of Koret. Previously, Rudin had been Koret's chief financial officer for four years. Koret earned $20 million

in 1994 through a private placement of three million shares of common stock and used some of the funds to retire debt carried over from the leveraged buyout.

Later in 1994, Koret's Canadian subsidiary paid about $7 million for Mr. Jax Fashions, Inc. of Vancouver. Mr. Jax was a designer and manufacturer of upscale sportswear and one of Canada's leading apparel makers. The company had been posting losses and cutting back on operations; Koret planned to work with the company's existing designers and product lines to bring the label back to profitability. The acquisition of Mr. Jax gave Koret an entry into the upscale apparel market. Koret also bought MJF Imports, Inc., an American company that sold the Mr. Jax line in the U.S. market. In 1995, Koret Canada, Inc. and Mr. Jax Fashions merged to form West Coast Apparel, Inc.

Further acquisitions came in the spring of 1995, when Koret bought Campaign Inc. and Pheasant Inc. of Norfolk, Virginia, two separate companies that shared a factory making belts, wallets, and other leather goods for men and women. The two companies were the exclusive licensees for Ralph Lauren leather accessories and had combined sales of about $30 million. They were merged to form the Koret subsidiary New Campaign Inc. This was Koret's first licensing deal. Three years later, Koret won a license from Connecticut-based Carolee Designs to make handbags, belts, and other small leather goods.

Koret introduced a stain-resistant line of clothing, dubbed Korapel, in 1995. The garments were made of Dacron polyester and wool crepe and treated with Du Pont's Teflon fabric protector. Koret also updated its line for 25 to 46 year olds in the mid-1990s, but older women were still the company's major customers. With its petite and plus-size divisions, Koret had a tradition of making garments for specialized fits. The company used newly available data to adopt a new set of measurement standards for women over 55, replacing standards that dated from 1940. The company also introduced an ''insta-fit'' program in 1994, featuring pants with a mechanism on a track that let the wearer adjust the waistband by three inches.

Koret sold its Counterparts label to Tabah Family Enterprises of Montreal in 1998 in order to focus more attention on the Koret line. That year, the company also considered transferring product distribution from a company-owned center in Chico, California, to a third-party facility and changing its contract to do sewing in nonunion shops. Union organizers, however, handed out leaflets at Koret outlet stores, which brought the company to the bargaining table. Koret agreed to retain domestic production in union shops and keep distribution at the Chico center. Many orders at the center were being filled incorrectly, so Koret implemented an incentive system that allowed workers to earn more for accurate work.

A Kellwood Subsidiary: 1999 and Beyond

In 1999, Koret determined that it could improve its competitive position in the increasingly consolidated garment industry through a merger with a larger group. In April, it pooled shares with Kellwood Company, an apparel manufacturer and marketer with a suite of men's and women's wear brands. The merger included Koret's subsidiaries Koret of California, New

Campaign, and the Canadian branch West Coast Apparel. Koret's annual sales at the time were around $300 million.

Rudin remained chief executive through the merger but was eventually replaced by Fred Smeyne, who had a 30-year history at Koret. Later in 1999, Koret moved its headquarters from San Francisco to Oakland. This allowed it to put its administrative offices and product development operations under one roof; the administrative offices had been moved out of the nearly century-old Mission Street building after the 1989 earthquake.

As a Kellwood subsidiary, Koret of California continued making moderately priced sportswear and career apparel in its Koret Francisca, Koret City Blues, and Career Dressing lines. It also made apparel exclusively for Dillard's department stores under the Napa Valley label and clothing with "modern styling" under the Beliza label. Jax Canada and New Campaign Inc. also continued operations as Kellwood subsidiaries. Harold S. Brooks took over the chief executive position at Koret of California from Fred Smeyne in 2003. Brooks had a 30-year retail background and most recently had been president of a division of May Department Stores in St. Louis, Missouri. At the time, Koret of California was the second largest of about a dozen womenswear businesses at Kellwood and was considered one of the company's core brands.

Principal Competitors

Ellen Tracy, Inc.; Jones Apparel Group Inc.; McNaughton Apparel Group Inc.; Tarrant Apparel Group; Marisa Christina Inc.

Further Reading

"Adding Koracorp to Levi's Wardrobe," *Business Week*, June 4, 1979, p. 69.

Behbehani, Mandy, "Koret Looks for Growth in Moderate-Price Area," *WWD*, July 31, 1985, p. 64.

"Behind Every (Great) Man . . ." *Forbes*, March 1, 1975, pp. 17–18.

Carlsen, Clifford, "Rag Firm Sews up Pair of Acquisitions," *San Francisco Business Times*, March 10, 1995, p. 9.

"Carolee Bags It," *WWD*, February 9, 1998, p. 8.

D'Innocenzio, Anne, "Moderate Firms Push Fashion Limit Past 55," *WWD*, June 4, 1997, p. 1.

——, "Tabah Buys Counterparts," *WWD*, April 1, 1998, p. 19.

"Kellwood's Koret Deal Completed," *WWD*, April 30, 1999, p. 2.

"Koracorp Sweats Out a Patent Tangle," *Business Week*, September 30, 1972, pp. 70–71.

"Koret Names Granoff and Einstein," *WWD*, December 11, 1986, p. 10.

"Koret Names Steve Rudin President," *WWD*, October 22, 1992, p. 9.

"Koret Warming up for Oakland Move," *San Francisco Chronicle*, October 14, 1998, p. B2.

"Levi's Inks Koret LBO Agreement," *WWD*, June 23, 1986, p. 1.

Motamedi, Beatrice, "Inside SF's $5 Billion Garment Industry," *San Francisco Chronicle*, June 11, 1990, p. C1.

Socha, Miles, "Koret Takes over Mr. Jax Fashions," *WWD*, December 1, 1994, p. 3.

"Teflon Collection," *WWD*, May 18, 1995, p. 9.

Wilson, Eric, "Unite Holds Lunch-Hour Protest in Chinatown against Sweatshops," *WWD*, August 31, 1998, p. 14.

—Sarah Ruth Lorenz

KSB AG

Johann-Klein-Str. 9
D-67227 Frankenthal
Germany
Telephone: (49) (6233) 86 29 05
Fax: (49) (6233) 86 34 01
Web site: http://www.ksb.com

Public Company
Incorporated: 1871 as Frankenthaler Maschinen-&
    Armatur-Fabrik Klein, Schanzlin & Becker
Employees: 12,252
Sales: EUR 1.18 billion ($1.47 billion) (2003)
Stock Exchanges: Frankfurt Dusseldorf
Ticker Symbol: KSB
NAIC: 333911 Pump and Pumping Equipment
    Manufacturing; 332919 Other Metal Valve and Pipe
    Fitting Manufacturing

KSB AG is Europe's leading manufacturer of pumps, valves, and related control systems for use in construction and housing, the chemical industry, energy generation, public water works, and mining. The company also engineers complete water supply, drainage, and waste water systems for municipal and industrial clients. Headquartered in Frankenthal, Germany, KSB operates 24 production subsidiaries in 19 countries on six continents and maintains sales offices in 35 additional countries. Pumps account for about two-thirds of KSB's total sales, and some 60 percent of the group's revenues derive from Europe. The nonprofit foundation KSB Stiftung, which is controlled by the Kühborth family, owns a 74-percent majority stake in KSB AG.

19th Century Groundwork

Company founder Johannes Klein was born in 1845, the first of seven children on a farm in western Germany. Eschewing both farming and his parents' hope that he become a craftsman, the intelligent young man successfully applied for a stipend to attend the technical school in Munich. After two years in Munich

he added another year of studies at the technical school in Karlsruhe. The 20-year-old Klein then worked for two different machine manufacturers, where he gained a special interest in the design of steam boilers. In 1870 he introduced his own design for a boiler feed apparatus which was first installed at a brewery in Frankenthal, a small town 60 miles South of Frankfurt/Main.

The brewery owner, Friedrich Schanzlin, believed that Klein's apparatus had commercial potential and offered Klein help in obtaining funds to start a new enterprise based on his invention. After Klein had received a patent in June 1871, Schanzlin convinced a wealthy friend, Jakob Becker, to invest a significant sum in the new venture. In early August 1871, the new company—called Klein, Schanzlin & Becker—applied for a concession to build a machine building factory, which was granted about a month later. However, the endeavor encountered serious difficulties from the beginning.

As it turned out, Klein's patented novelty was not able to function for long periods of time; he had underestimated the effects of the calcium content in the so-called ''pure'' water. The growing deposits caused by calcium carbonate, gypsum, iron oxide, and magnesium silicate threatened to interfere with the secure functioning of his invention at a time when water purification technologies were yet to be invented.

Still, two manufacturing halls had already been erected and 12 workers hired for Klein's boiler feed apparatus, so Johannes Klein and his business partners decided to shift to producing specialty plumbing fixtures and installations used in commercial water supply systems. The time for starting such a new venture were far from ideal. The stock market crash in Vienna in May 1873 triggered a wave of bankruptcies throughout Europe. Industrial enterprises in the newly-founded German Empire went out of business. and price levels were dropping constantly for six consecutive years. However, despite these trying times, with a mixture of perseverance, business sense, conservative financing. and vision, Klein managed not only to stay afloat but to grow his business and lay the foundation for long-term future success.

Klein focused on improving and redesigning specialty plumbing fixtures and installations for steam engines and larger water supply systems, such as specialty faucets, security valves, and pumps. At a time when selling these articles was the hardest part of the business, Klein constantly adjusted his product line to meet the market's needs. Instead of using sales brochures with lots of technical details, he carried with him small models of the fixtures his company made—some attached like charms to his watch chain—to explain their advantages to potential customers. For several years production was sporadic and sometimes chaotic. Still, Klein's workforce had grown to 40 by 1874.

While Klein avoided large experiments and costly development projects, he constantly refined his company's product line, gradually focusing on a variety of pumps. Among Klein's major customers was the coal mining company Saargruben, which he supplied with custom-made water systems, including pipelines.

During this time Klein took two important steps to secure the future growth of his enterprise. First, he established a broad financial basis, restructuring Klein, Schanzlin & Becker as a joint stock company. Then, throughout the 1890s, he expanded the factory grounds more than five-fold by way of land exchanges and purchases. By 1911 the company's real estate holdings had again tripled. The workforce had grown from about 500 in 1893 to 1,200 at the turn of the century.

Leadership through War and Depression

In 1901 Johannes Klein contracted a serious case of the flu and asked his youngest brother Jacob to help him out. At that time Jacob Klein—24 years younger than his brother—was selling the company's products in England. Johannes Klein had financed Jacob's mechanical engineering studies and had named him the company's director in 1894. In practice, however, Johannes Klein still ran every step of the business, and in 1896 had sent Jacob to establish the company's first foreign subsidiary, in England. At the ailing Johannes's request, Jacob returned to Frankenthal to become executive director of Klein, Schanzlin & Becker. Yet, as soon as Johannes had regained his strength, he returned to running his company, a situation that led to conflict between brothers, particularly in the areas of finances and sales. This rivalry did not end until Johannes Klein's death at the age of 72 in 1917. By that time, however, Jacob Klein had already been the company's main driving force for ten years.

When World War I began in 1914, the company—by now known simply as KSB—was suddenly cut off from its export markets, including England and France, and some 1,000 of the company's 1,600 workers were called up for military duty. Under these circumstances Jacob Klein decided to focus exclusively on the manufacture of such war-related products as ammunition, torpedo parts, and pumps and plumbing fixtures

for military ships and submarines. As a result, KSB's workforce soon swelled to over 4,000 during the war.

However, heavy taxation consumed most of the company's profits. Left with a workforce consisting primarily of women and prisoners of war and having almost no funds to replace the run-down machinery, Klein and KSB had to look to the future and peacetime production strategies. Moreover, the trouble had just begun. After Germany's defeat in 1918, the country's currency collapsed under the heavy load of war bonds and reparation obligations. In January 1923, when inflation was nearing its peak, French and Belgian troops occupied the western German Ruhr. After German railroad workers went on strike in March, shipping KSB products became almost impossible. The French had already arrested many industrial leaders of the region, but Jacob Klein fled to Mannheim, about ten miles east, on the other side of the river Rhine, where he had moved KSB headquarters in 1921. Due to hyperinflation, wages were paid out daily, while business operations became more and more chaotic and had to be shut down completely at times. In the fall of 1923 a separatist movement demanded the establishment of an independent republic west of the Rhine. The attempt was finally defeated in January 1924. One month later KSB headquarters were moved back to Frankenthal.

In the midst of political and economic turmoil, Jacob Klein pursued his vision of KSB as a network spanning Germany and all of Europe. Klein's vision had several more components: to broaden KSB's product line of specialty pumps without the effort of costly research and development; to enlarge production capacity without investing in costly new buildings in Frankenthal; and to cut costs by acquiring a foundry of its own.

Between 1924 and 1934 KSB established and acquired several new production subsidiaries. Scouting a location in the French-occupied Saar to revive export business with France, Klein decided to set up another production plant, the Pumpen-AG, in the small town of Homburg. In mid-October 1929, just before the onset of the Great Depression, KSB acquired machine manufacturer Maschinenfabrik Oddesse GmbH in Oschersleben, west of the city Magdeburg. One year later, in a hostile takeover, the company gained a majority stake in Nuremberg-based Armaturen- und Maschinenfabrik, vormals S.A. Hilpert (AMAG), a major competitor roughly the size of KSB and founded in 1854. Now more than doubled in size, the KSB group bought its own iron and steel foundry, Leipzig-based Eisen- und Stahlgießerei Max. Jahn, in 1930. Four years later the company acquired another manufacturer of pumps based in the northern German city Bremen, L.W. Bestenbostel & Sohn GmbH. The various KSB subsidiaries started specializing in certain types of pumps. Jacob Klein's vision had become reality. In 1931, at age 62, he stepped down as KSB's executive director and handed the leading position over to his chosen successor and long-time right-hand man Otto Kühborth.

1930s–60s: Building an International Presence

Shortly after the 25-year-old business and law school graduate Otto Kühborth had joined KSB in 1921, Jakob Klein asked him to move from a technical position into the bookkeeping department. Three years later Klein made Kühborth responsible for the management of the newly established KSB subsidiary in

Key Dates:

1871: Three entrepreneurs found the Klein, Schanzlin & Becker.
1909: A presence in London is established.
1924: Production subsidiary is established in Homburg/ Saar.
1930: KSB acquires major competitor AMAG in a hostile takeover.
1939: Jacob Klein gains a majority stake in KSB.
1942: Otto Klein-Kühborth becomes Jacob Klein's heir.
1949: French administration of the company ends, and dismantling after World War II is prevented.
1960: Otto Klein-Kühborth transfers his majority stake in the company to the nonprofit foundation KSB Stiftung.
1971: Wolfgang Kühborth takes over as CEO.
1986: KSB acquires a majority share in French pump manufacturer Pompes Guinard S.A.
1988: The company moniker is shortened to KSB AG.
1992: KSB gains a majority stake in Georgia-based GIW Industries Inc.
1995: KSB acquires a majority share in Chinese pump manufacturer Shanghai Pump Works.
2003: The company takes over Dutch pump maker DP industries B.V.

Homburg in the Saar. Soon Kühborth, who married Klein's grandniece, became the man who set Klein's ideas and visions into practice. He helped acquire the majority share in AMAG before anyone even took notice. When Kühborth took over as CEO in 1931, the Great Depression was nearing its peak in Germany. KSB's workforce had shrunk to 749, about of half of 1927's workforce. Two years after Adolf Hitler's National Socialist Party came to power, the people in the Saarland voted to join the German Empire, and KSB's plant in Homburg became a domestic subsidiary. To counteract the increasing isolation of Germany in Europe, KSB focused on exports overseas and invested significantly in new product development in areas such as shipbuilding and fuel production. Jacob Klein celebrated his 70th birthday on July 3, 1939, three months before the outbreak of World War II; he was KSB's majority shareholder.

Without hesitation Otto Kühborth followed the call to military duty in fall 1939. However, he remained the company's leading executive and used his leave to deal with business matters. Once again KSB started making war goods, including fuel system parts for V2 rockets, which were produced in Frankenthal under high secrecy, the workers themselves not knowing what the parts they were making would be used for. During the war the company maintained its pump production, which continued to account for most of the output in Frankenthal. KSB employees who were drafted in the military were kept informed about the latest developments at KSB through a special newsletter; more and more of the work was being performed by women.

Two years into the war, Jacob Klein began to ponder the fate of his enterprise after his death. Unmarried and childless like his older brother Johannes before him, he decided to formally adopt

Otto Kühborth and make him the sole heir of his company. Kühborth agreed and became Klein's adopted son in January 1942, changing his name to Otto Klein-Kühborth. During the heavy bombings by the Allied Forces between 1942 and 1944, KSB's plants in Bremen and Nuremberg were completely destroyed. After the Frankenthal plant was hit in the fall of 1943, manufacturing operations were split up and distributed among 39 towns across the Palatinate region. In May 1944 Otto Klein-Kühborth returned to Frankenthal and took over KSB's management again. In March 1945, when American troops occupied the region, Jacob Klein was killed in an accident. During the last weeks of the war, Klein-Kühborth transferred his inherited majority share in KSB to Kleinschanzlin Pumpen AG in Homburg (a former subsidiary which he had sold to a friend in the Saar when Jacob Klein was still alive). This step was meant to protect KSB from a takeover by the French who—the two men correctly anticipated—would treat enterprises based in the Saar less strictly than companies in the Palatinate.

In mid-June 1945 the American military administration allowed the Kleinschanzlin Pumpen AG to resume operations. Despite the fact that the plant in Frankenthal never received such an official permit, workers there began to take on repair work and later started making hand-pumps which became so popular that they were used as a barter currency. KSB's two production plants in central Germany were seized by the Russian authorities and later expropriated. In 1947 KSB came under the administration of the French occupation forces. A trustee from outside the firm was appointed as chief executive officer, and he submitted every decision the company made to the French authorities for approval. In addition KSB found itself on a list of companies to be dismantled as a war reparation. In a long, tough, bureaucratic fight, the dismantling was prevented. By the time the foreign administration ended in February 1949, KSB had shrunk to three production plants.

After the death of one of the three surviving members of KSB's advisory board, Otto Klein-Kühborth became the board's president in 1949 and led the company through the postwar reconstruction period. The company profited from the conversion of big parts of the German economy from coal as a major fuel to mineral oil and natural gas, a transition which created an increasing demand for pipeline installations, including pumps and related fixtures. However, Klein-Kühborth's major focus was on KSB's international expansion. In 1947 a small subsidiary was established in Luxembourg, through which the company expanded into Belgium and the Netherlands. Between then and 1959 KSB sales offices sprung up in France, Italy, England, Switzerland, Austria, Greece and Spain. In the 1950s and 1960s KSB expanded its reach overseas. Sales offices and production plants were established in Pakistan, India, Argentina, Brazil and South Africa and a joint venture was set up in Japan.

Meanwhile, KSB's German subsidiaries were merged into Klein, Schanzlin & Becker AG in 1959. Five years later Otto Klein-Kühborth transferred his majority stake in the company to the nonprofit foundation KSB Stiftung which had been founded earlier by Jacob Klein. In 1971 he was succeeded as CEO by his son Wolfgang Kühborth.

1970s–90s: Dynamic Growth

The early 1970s were a period of dynamic growth for KSB with sales increasing by more than 12 percent annually. By 1970 KSB's export business accounted for 37 percent of the company's total sales of DM 385 million. Its foreign subsidiaries contributed an additional DM 110 million to the group's revenues. With 16 production subsidiaries, four of them in Germany and seven overseas, the company had again become a considerable presence.

Wolfgang Kühborth had been a member of KSB's executive management team for 12 years when he took over as CEO in 1971. He combined the technical knowledge of a machine tool engineer with his Swiss business school know-how. At KSB he oversaw the Frankenthal production plant in the late 1950s, took over responsibility for the company's foreign subsidiaries in 1962, and became KSB's Executive Technical Director one year later. After his father's death in 1976, Wolfgang Kühborth became president of the company's advisory board. However, when an economic downturn resulted in a severe crisis for KSB in the early 1980s, he resumed the responsibilities of CEO and led the company through a five-year period of cost consolidation and rationalization.

Under Wolfgang Kühborth's leadership the KSB group of companies developed from an export-oriented German enterprise into a truly global player. The number of foreign production subsidiaries, as well as the company's international distribution network, were considerably strengthened. The main event that marked this transformation was KSB's acquisition of the French market leader for industrial pumps, Ets. Pompes Guinard S.A., which was founded in 1919. The close contacts Otto Klein-Kühborth had established with the company's founding family were further developed by Wolfgang Kühborth who had a personal interest in France. Beginning in 1983, the two companies mutually supplemented their product ranges to compete against other pump manufacturers from overseas. Three years later KSB acquired a majority stake in the French company with four domestic production plants and 1,450 employees. Pompes Guinard was also the market leader in Africa. In the years following the acquisition, the French and German KSB branches were integrated, as were two other French manufacturers with about 800 employees that the company had acquired. French became the company's second language, and two of the five global business divisions created in 1989 were headed by French managers. In the late 1980s KSB group also ventured into the United States, focusing on waste water systems and power generation for industrial clients. In 1992 KSB acquired a majority stake in Georgia-based GIW Industries Inc., the world market leader for heavy duty pumps used in mining and for dredging pumps. In the late 1980s to mid-1990s joint ventures were set up in Turkey, Saudi Arabia, Thailand, Indonesia, and China. After entering into a joint venture with Shanghai Pump Works, one of China's leading industrial pump manufacturers, in 1992, KSB acquired a majority share in the Chinese partner firm three years later and renamed it KSB-Shanghai Pumps Co.

At the beginning of the 1990s KSB was Europe's largest pump manufacturer with over DM 2 billion in sales. However, growing pressure on prices from an increasing number of global competitors, stagnating markets in Western Europe, and economic crises in Latin America presented the company with new challenges. After the two German states were reunited in 1990, KSB acquired the pump manufacturing unit of eastern German VEB Kombinat Pumpen und Verdichter in February 1991. However, after West Germany's strong currency replaced the East German Mark, the Eastern European customers of the Halle-based company were no longer able to afford its products. The company slipped deeply into the red, and KSB decided to move its environmental engineering unit from Pregnitz to Halle. At the same time, shrinking markets in Germany and France and cheaper competition from overseas began to threaten KSB's core business with industrial pumps. In 1993 the company's French and Mexican subsidiaries produced losses. A major problem was that the company had taken on too many large projects in the energy sector which were financed by loans and did not cover all the cost. In 1995—the year of the company's 125th anniversary—KSB found itself on the verge of bankruptcy.

Retooling for a New Century

In February 1996, 71-year-old Wolfgang Kühborth was back in the trenches as president of the company's board of directors. KSB's management team was replaced, and the company launched a rigorous cost-cutting and restructuring program. The pump business was split into three divisions for standard, serial, and customized pumps, while the production of plumbing fixtures, the foundry, and the repair and service operations were spun off into independent subsidiaries. Between 1995 and 2002 KSB cut its workforce by roughly one-fifth, mainly in Germany and France. The foundry in Frankenthal was closed down, and the Bremen subsidiary was transformed into a service center. Production facilities in Europe were downsized, while the ones overseas—especially in India, Pakistan, Brazil and China—were expanded. Although the company was back in the black by 1997, KSB's sales were negatively affected by the economic crises of the late 1990s in Asia, Russia, and Latin America.

Since 1993, Wolfgang Kühborth's two sons, Klaus and Gerd, had headed Klein-Pumpen GmbH, the financial holding company for the KSB group. After Gerd Kühborth died in 2003, Klaus Kühborth—as a member of KSB's advisory board—was the last family member actively involved in the company.

Looking toward the future of KSB, CEO Josef Gerstner set his sights on new geographic markets, such as Poland and the United States, as well as new product markets such as technology for the desalinization of sea water. The company was planning to launch new products, such as the leak-free pump for chemical plants and high speed trains. Long-term contracts with major clients such as water utility companies Vivendi and Lyonnaise des Eaux were seen as future assets for KSB. Another path the company intended to pursue was to add value by designing, building, and running complete pumping stations for water works.

Principal Subsidiaries

KSB S.A.S. (France); PAB Pumpen- und Armaturen-Beteiligungsgesellschaft mbH (Germany; 51%); KSB Pumps Limited (India; 40.54%); KSB Bombas Hidráulicas S.A. (Brazil); KSB Pumps (S.A.) (Pty.) Ltd. (South Africa; 50%); GIW Industries

Inc. (United States); KSB Inc. (United States); KSB Chile S.A. (Chile); KSB Italia S.p.A. (Italy); AMRI Inc. (United States; 89.97%); KSB-Pompa, Armatür Sanayi ve Ticaret A.S. (Turkey; 76.48 %); KSB Finanz S.A. (Luxembourg); N.V. KSB Belgium S.A. (Belgium); KSB America Corporation (United States); KSB Pompy I Armatura Sp. z o.o. (Poland); KSB LIMITED (United Kingdom); Rotary Equipment Services Ltd. (United Kingdom); AMVI S.A. (Spain; 99.8%); KSB Österreich Ges. mbH (Austria); KSB Shanghai Pump Co. Ltd. (China; 51%); Techni Pompe Service S.A. (France); KSB-AMVI S.A. (Spain); MIL Controls Limited (India; 51%); KSB Nederland B.V. (Netherlands); KSB Pumps Co. Ltd. (Pakistan; 58.89%); KSB Moerck AB (Sweden; 55%); KSB Comp. Sudamericana (Argentina); KSB de Mexico, S.A.; Canadian Kay Pump Ltd. (Canada); KSB Zürich AG (Switzerland); Hydroskepi GmbH (Greece); KSB A/S (Denmark).

Principal Competitors

Ebara Corporation; IMI plc; ITT Industries, Inc.

Further Reading

"KSB: Schlechtestes Ergebnis der Unternehmensgeschichte," *Frankfurter Allgemeine Zeitung*, April 30, 1996, p. 24.

Schiele, Otto H. (ed.), *Die Goldene Mitte II,* Frankenthal, Ger.: Klein, Schanzlin & Becker Aktiengesellschaft, 1996, 287 S.

—Evelyn Hauser

KT&G Corporation

100 Pyongchon-dong, Daeduk-ku
Daejun
South Korea
Telephone: (+82) 42 939 5000
Web site: http://www.ktg.co.kr

Public Company
Incorporated: 2002
Employees: 4,635
Sales: KW 1.8 trillion ($1.57 billion) (2002)
Stock Exchanges: Korean
Ticker Symbol: KTG
NAIC: 312221 Cigarette Manufacturing; 424590 Other
    Farm Product Raw Material Merchant Wholesalers

KT&G Corporation is the new name for the former Korean government-controlled Korea Tobacco & Ginseng Corporation. Since its privatization, completed in 2002, and the spin off of Korea Ginseng Corporation, KT&G has focused on defending its nearly 80 percent market share at home and stepping up its cigarette export sales. By 2003, exports of KT&G-branded cigarettes have topped 10 percent of the group's total sales. KT&G, the world's seventh largest tobacco company, expects to crack the top five before the end of the decade. The company's impending entry into the huge Chinese market is slated to increase the share of exports to as high as 25 percent of KT&G's total revenues by 2005. The Middle East and other Asian markets presently form the largest share of the group's exports, at 80 percent; the company generates some 17 percent of its sales in the North and South American markets. KT&G has also risen to the challenge of foreign competition at home, where the final trade barriers were lowered at the turn of the century. As part of its effort to maintain its share of the Korean market, where more than 70 percent of men and a rising percentage of women smoke, KT&G has been rolling out a new line of premium tobacco brands, including Seasons, Humming Time, Lumen, Esse Lights, and the ultra low-tar Raison, all launched in 2002. Taking part in the thaw in relations between North and South Korea, KT&G formed a cigarette manufactur-

ing joint-venture outside of Pyongyang. In South Korea, the company operates five cigarette production plants and two leaf processing facilities, as well as its own printing plant. In 2003, the company began plans to build a foreign production facility in Turkey. While remaining committed to growth in its tobacco business, in 2003 KT&G launched a diversification drive, targeting expansion into the biotech sector. KT&G is listed on the Korean Stock Exchange. In 2002, the company posted revenues of KW1.8 trillion ($1.6 billion).

Ginseng and Tobacco Monopoly in the 20th Century

The use of ginseng as an herbal remedy goes back some 5,000 years. Modern usage of the root began in the 19th century, and by the beginning of the 20th century demand had outstripped supply. By then, Korean red ginseng had gained a reputation as being among the finest grown in the world; at the turn of the century, the country became the first to cultivate red ginseng for sale. The Korean royal government quickly exerted its control over the crop, establishing the Samjeongkwa, or Ginseng Management Division, which took over monopoly control of ginseng cultivation and sale, both in the domestic and export markets.

In 1980, the newly established Bureau of Taxation, part of the Ministry of Finance, took over the Ginseng Division, a move that was supported by the passage of legislation, the Red Ginseng Monopoly Law, that officially gave the Korean government oversight over all of the country's ginseng operations and development. That monopoly was to remain in effect until the late 1980s. By then, Korea had become the world's largest supplier of cultivated ginseng, which was marketed under the brand name adopted in 1940, Cheong-Kwan-Jang.

Parallel to its control of the country's ginseng sector, the Korean government also took over operations of another important crop and product group, tobacco, passing the Tobacco Taxation Law in 1908. Tobacco also was brought under the authority of the Bureau of Taxation, which became the sole conductor of tobacco growing and cigarette production in the country.

The country's tobacco and ginseng interests were transferred to the Department of Monopoly, under the Ministry of Finance, in 1948. The importance of both crops to the Korean economy was underscored in 1952 when they were placed under a separate entity, the Office of Monopoly. In the years following the Korean War, as South Korea rebuilt its economy into one of the region's powerhouses, tobacco sales grew strongly. The Office of Monopoly responded by increasing its area of cultivation and building a network of leaf processing and cigarette manufacturing facilities throughout the country. The Office of Monopoly also became responsible for developing a vast network of sales points—some 170,000—throughout the country.

By the mid-1960s, the country's production of tobacco and cigarettes had risen sufficiently to enable it to begin exporting cigarettes. Korea's proximity to other Asian markets gave it an edge in the region. As in South Korea itself, tobacco consumption throughout Asia was extremely high. Korea also entered a number of other markets, including the Middle East.

Facing Competition in the 1980s

Into the 1970s, tobacco remained the Office of Monopoly's major revenue source. Nonetheless, the company's ginseng operation had also grown strongly, building on its control of the world's largest supply of cultivated ginseng and successfully maintaining the reputation of Korean red ginseng as the world's highest quality ginseng. In 1976, the ginseng division launched construction of the Korea Ginseng Factory. Completed in 1978, the facility enabled the Monopoly Office to increase both its supply of ginseng and range ginseng-based products.

Into the 1980s, the Korea Tobacco & Ginseng Corporation Office of Monopoly lived up to its name, controlling 100 percent of South Korea's tobacco market. Indeed, the Korean government had added new legislation as a means of supporting its monopoly, passing laws that made the possession of foreign-made cigarettes and other tobacco products illegal. Western tobacco companies, reacting to sharp declines in tobacco consumption in their traditional territories, began lobbying for increased access to Asian markets, many of which, like Korea, had long kept out the far-larger U.S. and European groups.

In the early 1980s, pressure from the U.S. government began forcing open the Asian market. By 1986, Korea, fearful of losing trade in the United States, agreed to allow foreign cigarettes to enter its market. Imports, however, were limited to just 1 percent of the total domestic market. In addition, sales of foreign cigarettes were initially restricted to just 500 locations.

That provision was dropped in 1987 when foreign cigarettes became available at all of the country's tobacco stores.

Nonetheless, the high price of foreign cigarettes—at three times the price of domestic brands—helped the monopoly to maintain its grip on the home market. At the same time, a boycott movement, led by the country's tobacco farmers, kept foreign cigarettes from making significant inroads into the market.

At this point, the monopoly recognized that it would have to restructure in order to face the future, if only because of the increasing competition in its export markets, where sales of Western cigarette brands jumped nearly 100 percent by the end of the 1980s. The company had already received a preview of the coming competition when it attempted to enter the Japanese market in 1985 with two brands, Pine Tree and Ararang. Japanese consumers, who had been introduced to the milder flavored U.S.-style cigarettes, balked at the heavier taste of the Korean brands, and the company was forced to end the experiment in 1989. By then, the Office of Monopoly had begun restructuring, leading to the creation of Korea Tobacco & Ginseng Corporation in 1989.

The new structure now adopted a true customer service orientation, abandoning its former indifference to product quality, at least as far as its cigarette production was concerned. The company also began stepping up its export sales initiatives. In 1990, the company succeeded in entering the soon-to-collapse Soviet Union, where cigarette shortages had led to riots that summer, securing a contract for a shipment of five million packs of cigarettes.

Privatized and Diversified in the New Century

By the mid-1990s, Korea Tobacco & Ginseng's new emphasis on quality had begun to pay off. At home, the company was able to minimize the impact of the entry of the new foreign brands, which appealed especially to the country's youth, by launching its own Western-style brands. The company was then able to launch its new range of products on the export market, and in 1992 opened an overseas liaison office in Hong Kong. That office was converted to a full sales subsidiary, Korea Tobacco & Ginseng Hong Kong Ltd., in 1994. The following year, the company re-entered Japan, signing an agreement with that country's Mikuni to import one million packs of cigarettes.

In the late 1990s, Korea Tobacco & Ginseng stepped up its preparations for the coming abolition of its domestic monopoly, slated for 2001. The company began restructuring, announcing a plan to trim its payroll, which neared 9,000 employees, and shut down some of its most inefficient factories. That process got underway in 1996, when the company announced its intention to eliminate more than 400 jobs. Although criticized for dragging its feet, the company ultimately succeeded in slashing its payroll to less than 5,000 jobs by the beginning of the new century.

A major part of the privatization process was that Korea Tobacco & Ginseng's had restructured itself as a joint-stock company in 1997. The company then spun off its ginseng operations—which had lost its own monopoly in 1996—as a separate company, Korea Ginseng Corporation, in 1999. Korea Ginseng nonetheless remained a wholly owned subsidiary of Korea Tobacco & Ginseng, which went public on the Korea Stock Ex-

---

Key Dates:

1899: Ginseng Management Division is created under the royal government of Korea.
1908: Ginseng Division is placed under the Ministry of Finance, which also takes over the tobacco monopoly.
1952: The Office of Monopoly, which takes over ginseng and tobacco monopolies, is created.
1965: Cigarette exports begin.
1986: The Korean market is opened to foreign cigarette brands for the first time.
1989: The Office of Monopoly becomes Korea Tobacco & Ginseng Corporation.
1996: The Korean government ends its ginseng monopoly.
1999: Korean Tobacco & Ginseng spins off Korea Ginseng Corporation as a subsidiary and goes public on the Korean exchange.
2001: The tobacco monopoly ends.
2002: Korean Tobacco is fully privatized, changes its name to KT&G, and enters into a joint venture with Celtrion biotech.

---

change at the end of 1999. As part of the public offering, the Korean government agreed to allow as much as 25 percent of the company to be owned by foreign corporations.

KT&G began preparing for the full opening of its market to foreign competition in 2001, making continued improvements to the efficiency of its manufacturing facilities. The company also began developing a new range of brands designed to enable it to reposition itself in the premium cigarette market, where margins were higher but where competition was the most intense. At the same time, KT&G began negotiating an entry into the crucial Chinese market, which, with its huge population and rapid growth of cigarette consumption, promised to be one of the world's top tobacco markets in the future.

KT&G's entry into China occurred by the way of North Korea. In 1999, the company began talks to form a joint-venture agreement in order to construct a cigarette manufacturing facility outside of Pyongyang. In 2000, the two sides launched two jointly developed brands, and in 2001 they reached an agreement, hailed as a sign of a thaw between the two Koreas, to build a plant with a capacity of two billion cigarettes per year. The agreement gave KT&G access to the rail link between North Korea and China, which also extended into Russia and Central Asia, including Uzbekistan and Afganistan. KT&G's access to the rail link not only gave it the promise of additional markets but also far lower transportation costs for its other Asian and Middle Eastern markets.

KT&G met the abolition of its monopoly in 2001 head on with the launch of a new brand, Cima, a premium-priced brand featuring a high-end filter, mild flavor, and low nicotine content.

This marked the first of a whole range of new premium brands, which by the end of 2002 included Seasons, Humming Time, Lumen, Esse Lights, and the ultra low-tar Raison. In that year, the company was fully privatized as the government sold the rest of its stake in the company. The company then adopted a new name, KT&G Corporation.

KT&G's new brands helped it defend its market; by 2003, however, foreign brands had gained a 20 percent share of the Korean cigarette market. The company expected to counter this development with its increasing export sales, which were set to explode as the KT&G finalized agreements with the Chinese government to allow its brands into that country. KT&G's plans now called for exports to reach as high as 25 percent of the company's sales by 2005 and for the company, by then ranked as number seven among the world's tobacco companies, to crack the global top five. As part of that effort, KT&G announced its intention to build a new factory in Turkey in 2003.

As KT&G expanded its tobacco sales, it had already begun to diversify its operations. The biotech sector held particular interest for the company. In 2002, KT&G paid KW18.8 billion to join the Celtrion joint venture with VaxGen, which had been working to develop an AIDS vaccine. Then, in August 2003, KT&G announced that it had agreed to pay KW14.6 billion to acquire Youngjin Pharmaceutical. The company intended to use the acquisition in conjunction with the research efforts conducted at Korea Ginseng in order to impose itself as a new major player on the pharmaceutical market. KT&G turned with fresh confidence into the new century.

Principal Subsidiaries

Celtrion (50%); Korea Ginseng Corporation; Youngjin Pharmaceutical.

Principal Competitors

Philip Morris Australia Ltd.; British American Tobacco; Djarum PT; Ben Thanh Tobacco Company; Japan Tobacco Inc.; Shanghai Tobacco Group Corporation; Etsong Tobacco Group Company Ltd.; Perusahaan Rokok Tjap Bentoel PT.

Further Reading

"Former Monopoly Finds Opportunity in Changing Market Conditions," *Business Korea*, December 19, 2001.
"Korea's Tobacco Expensive by Global Standard," *Korea Times*, August 13, 2003.
"KT&G Stubs out Pessimists and Helps Korea Save Face," *Euroweek*, October 18, 2002, p. 18.
"Korea Tobacco & Ginseng Corp.: Tightly Managed Firm Readies for Privatization," *Business Korea*, November 1, 1999.
"Korea Tobacco & Ginseng to Market New Premium Cigarette," *AsiaPulse News*, July 22, 2002.
"Korea Tobacco Sale Saved by Share Buy Back," *Financial Times*, October 14, 2002.

—M.L. Cohen

Lanoga Corporation

17946 N.E. 65th Street
Redmond, Washington 98052
U.S.A.
Telephone: (425) 883-4125
Fax: (425) 882-2959
Web site: http://www.lanogacorp.com

Private Company
Incorporated: 1883 as Laird, Norton Company
Employees: 7,000
Sales: $1.45 billion (2002 est.)
NAIC: 551120 Offices of Other Holding Companies;
   444190 Other Building Material Dealers

Lanoga Corporation is one of the largest retailers of lumber and building materials in the United States, with about 240 stores in 14 states. Owned by roughly 300 Laird and Norton family heirs, Lanoga operates through regional subsidiaries and divisions, each of which has significant autonomy. Lanoga goes to market through its five divisions: United Building Centers, which has 180 lumberyards and component facilities in the upper Midwest and Rocky Mountain regions; Spenard Builders Supply, which serves Alaska with 13 lumberyards and component parts; Home Lumber, which serves the Front Range of Colorado through five large facilities; Lumbermens, which serves Washington, Oregon, Idaho, and Arizona with 70 yards and plants; and Dixieline in Los Angeles, California.

The First 50 Years

In April 1855, brothers William, James, and Matthew Laird purchased roughly $1,000 in lumber products from a firm in Eau Claire, Wisconsin. After rafting their purchase down the Chippewa and Mississippi Rivers to the frontier town of Winona, Minnesota, they used the lumber to start Laird & Brothers. In October 1856, brothers Matthew and James Norton, cousins of the Lairds, joined the company, and the firm changed its name to Laird, Norton & Company. Over the next two decades, the new company expanded to include a sawmill with 400 employees, numerous lumberyards along the Winona & St.

Peter Railroad, and thousands of acres of timber holdings throughout the pinelands of Minnesota and Wisconsin.

As settlers moved west from Minnesota, particularly after the Civil War, Laird, Norton & Company expanded its operations westward as well, setting up sawmills in Idaho and Washington along railroad routes. By 1883, the company had outgrown its original partnership model, and Matthew Norton, James Norton, and William Laird incorporated their business in the state of Minnesota as Laird, Norton Company.

In accordance with common business practices of the time, Laird, Norton established separate companies for each of its various business undertakings, a practice that left its long-term influence upon the organization of the company. After incorporation, two companies, the Hayes-Lucas Lumber Company and the Botsford Lumber Company, assumed management of retail yards operated by Laird, Norton. After half a century of steady growth, Hayes-Lucas Lumber Company and Botsford Lumber Company merged to form United Building Centers in 1962.

1980s: Serving Multiple Markets

In 1978, Laird, Norton merged its United Building Centers company with its newly acquired, four-store Spenard Building Supply chain to form a holding company called Lanoga (an acronym for Laird, Norton and Galco Distributing, Spenard's original parent company). Norton Clapp, a prominent timber and real estate financier, became the company's first chairman, a position he filled until 1986, while Booth Gardner, later governor of Washington from 1985 to 1993, became Lanoga's first president, a position he filled until 1981.

Spenard's history could be traced to 1952, when George A. Lagerquist and A.J. Johnson opened the first Spenard Builders Supply store with three employees in Anchorage, Alaska. In the 1950s and 1960s, Anchorage experienced a boom period in both the public and private sectors as the military expanded its presence in south central Alaska; Spenard Builders Supply grew along with the boom. The company withstood a devastating earthquake in 1964, as well as a fire that destroyed its facilities three years later.

In 1980, Lanoga purchased Lumberman's Building Centers, which it set up as a third division (United Building Centers being its first and Spenard's its second). Lumberman's also had a rich history that could be traced to the 1890s.

During its first year in operation, Lanoga generated sales of $140 million. Throughout the early 1980s, management had worked to centralize buying, but these efforts were eventually abandoned, due to cultural and logistical challenges among the holdings. Daryl Nagel, who became president of the company in 1987, credited the company's success in part to decentralization. In a 1993 *Puget Sound Business Journal* article he stated, "It's a retail business and you've got to be close enough to the customer to respond."

Nagel had spent almost his entire career working for Lanoga and had a legendary network of contacts; he became one of Lanoga's greatest assets, formulating a strategy of placing stores away from city centers, favoring suburban and rural areas where competition was less stiff, and beating others to the punch in making acquisition deals. He preferred to locate stores in rural "county seat markets" in cities with populations between 5,000 to 100,000.

With the advent of such building superstores as Home Depot, Lanoga faced stiff competition in the building materials market. In response, the company shifted from selling lumber and building supplies exclusively to also offering a broad range of home improvement supplies, including plumbing, electrical, and lawn and garden supplies. The company targeted for expansion fringe metro areas undergoing waves of new construction and remodeling. In these markets, the presence of warehouse retailers skewed Lanoga's customer mix toward the professional.

The Acquisitive 1990s

Relying on earnings to fuel growth in the 1990s, Lanoga embarked on a path of steady acquisition. Preferring to buy an established chain rather than introduce new concepts, Lanoga would identify a potentially lucrative market and then buy out the top-tier player. Good acquisition prospects were stores in non-metro areas that would fit nicely into one of the company's three divisions.

Business was good for Lanoga in the early 1990s. Its aggressive acquisition strategy provided the company with 51 percent volume growth from 1991 to 1994. In 1992, Lanoga generated gross revenues of $556 million. In 1993, with stores in 12 states,

that figure increased to $657 million. By this time, the company ranked near the top of Washington's largest private companies and was the 13th largest chain of its kind in the country. *BSHC* magazine named Lanoga its Generalist Retailer of the Year for 1993. At the time, approximately 40 percent of Lanoga's customer base were individual consumers, while 60 percent were building professionals.

Despite its growing renown, the company's headquarters, with its staff of five, was located in small offices in an unremarkable business park in Redmond, Washington. According to Nagel in a 1994 *BHSC* article, the company's small administration was consistent with its philosophy of micro-marketing, making decisions at the individual store and regional level. Each division had its own president, as well as its own departments for human resources, advertising, and marketing. Benefits programs and holding company finances were administered from the corporate headquarters. With such a high degree of autonomy among its holdings, Lanoga hoped to achieve the buying power of a large chain with the flexibility of a small regional player. Moreover, each store within a division determined its own product mix beyond a core mix of products. "Instead of merchandising and marketing driving product and forcing it into stores, it's really the reverse. Stores are finding out what's necessary in that market, and they pull the goods into the store," Nagel remarked in *BHSC*. Nevertheless, Lanoga's divisions did collaborate frequently. Marketing executives met quarterly to discuss market trends, company strategies, and pricing issues. In 1994, the company with stores in a multitude of markets launched a company-wide advertising campaign.

During the last years of the 20th century, Lanoga's overall sales continued to grow. In 1997, Lanoga hit the $1 billion mark in sales, an increased of almost 7 percent over 1995 sales. In 1998, Lanoga's sales again rose slightly more than 4 percent, taking the company over the $1 billion mark for the first time. Sales reached $1.25 billion in 1999. The company now wavered between positions as 10th- or 11th-largest home improvement company in the country.

2000 and Beyond

The 1999 acquisition of the Home Lumber Company brought Lanoga into the Denver and Yakima markets. Home Lumber was so large a company that Lanoga created a fourth division simply to accommodate it. Home Lumber had begun in 1954 in Littleton, Colorado, as a business focused on serving professional builders.

Daryl Nagel retired in 2000, and Paul W. Hylbert, Jr., became president and chief executive of the company, which by then was reporting annual sales of more than $1.3 billion and was firmly positioned among the nation's ten largest companies in the retail lumber and building material industry. Additional purchases in Utah, Missouri, Wisconsin, Oregon, and Iowa during this time bolstered Lanoga's presence considerably. Part of management's plan was to insulate Lanoga from the impact of regional downturns by having chains in different parts of the country. During this time, Lanoga also joined with six other building materials distributors to launch an online marketplace.

In 2003, Lanoga purchased the assets of Dixieland Lumber Company of San Diego, creating a fifth operating division.

Key Dates:

1855: William, James, and Matthew Laird found Laird & Brothers.
1856: Brothers Matthew and James Norton join the lumber firm, which is renamed Laird, Norton & Company.
1883: The company incorporates as Laird, Norton Company.
1952: Spenard Builders Supply begins operations in Anchorage, Alaska.
1954: Home Lumber and Supply Company is established in Littleton, Colorado.
1962: Hayes-Lucas Lumber Company and Botsford Lumber Company merge to form United Building Centers.
1978: The company acquires Spenard Builders Supply (aka Galco Distributing) and becomes Lanoga Corporation.
1980: Lanoga acquires Lumbermen's Building Centers.
1999: Home Lumber Company becomes Lanoga's fourth division.
2003: Dixieline becomes Lanoga's fifth division.

Dixieline had been founded as Dixie Lumber in 1913 as a branch of another lumber business. It was acquired by Weyerhauser in 1979 and Nortek in 1985, and then reacquired by the founding Cowling family in 1994. Dixieline served a customer base that was 80 percent professional contractors and 20 percent consumers. The acquisition well suited the company's estab-lished strategy of targeting industry leaders with a strong focus on contractor business in the Midwest and western states.

As it looked to the future, Lanoga anticipated additional growth from its established strategies as well as from fine-tuning the merchandise and marketing plans for its existing stores with the goal of increasing its market share at its established locations. With revenues at $1.8 billion in 2003, the prognosis for Lanoga's continued growth was good.

Principal Divisions

United Building Centers, Lumbermens Building Centers, Spenard Builders Supply, Home Lumber Company; Dixieline.

Principal Competitors

84 Lumber Company; Building Materials Holding Corporation; Lowe's Companies Inc.; The Home Depot Inc.;

Further Reading

McDowell, Bill, "The Quiet Giant," *BSHC*, June 1994, p. 48.
Park, Clayton, "Low-Profile Lanoga One of Area's Best-Kept Secrets," *Puget Sound Business Journal*, June 18, 1993, p. 46.
Tice, Carol, "Lanoga's Big Buy," *Puget Sound Business Journal*, November 8, 2002, p. 1.
——, "Lumber Retailer Responds to Changing Market," *Puget Sound Business Journal*, June 23, 2000, p. 42.
——, "Slow and Steady Tack Pays Offs for Lanoga Corp.," *Puget Sound Business Journal*, June 25, 1999, p. 45.
Wood, Chris, "Group Effort: With a Focus on People and an Eye on Expansion," *Prosales*, January 2003, p. 32.

—Carrie Rothburd

Ledesma

Ledesma Sociedad Anónima Agrícola Industrial

Avenida Corrientes 415
Buenos Aires, C.F. C1043AA3
Argentina
Telephone: (54) (11) 4378 1155
Fax: (54) (11) 4378 1688
Web site: http://www.ledesma.com.ar

Public Company
Incorporated: 1914 as Nueva Compania Azucarera y
    Refineria Ledesma
Employees: 5,000
Sales: 790.45 million pesos ($266.14 million) (2003)
Stock Exchanges: Buenos Aires; OTC
Ticker Symbols: LEDE; LMSA F
NAIC: 112111 Beef Cattle Ranching and Farming;
    111310 Orange Groves; 111320 Citrus (Except
    Orange) Groves; 111334 Other Noncitrus Fruit
    Farming; 111930 Sugarcane Farming; 311311
    Sugarcane Mills; 311312 Cane Sugar Refining;
    311411 Frozen Fruit, Juice and Vegetable Processing;
    322121 Paper (Except Newsprint) Mills; 322233
    Stationery, Tablet and Related Product Manufacturing;
    325193 Ethyl Alcohol Manufacturing

Ledesma Sociedad Anónima Agrícola Industrial, Argentina's largest sugar producer, is a model of stability: it has had only four presidents in nearly 100 years. It is also one of the few large Argentine companies that remains in Argentine hands. Ledesma is a diversified company that also produces and sells cereals, meats, fruits and fruit juices, and paper products, sells electrical energy, and explores, develops, and exploits gas fields. These activities are closely tied to its original business as a sugarcane grower and sugar producer.

First Sugar, Then Fruit and Paper: 1830–1970

The history of sugar producer Ledesma may be traced back to the 19th century. Jujuy is the name of an Argentine province located in the extreme northwest of the country, and Ledesma is a department of that province, named for the Spanish general and governor who built a fort there. Around 1700, another provincial governor introduced sugarcane and sugar manufacture in Jujuy's San Francisco river valley. Members of the Ovejero family had established a mill in the department by 1830, and by 1864 that property was yielding 69,000 kilograms (759 tons) of sugar a year. In 1876 English machinery was brought in by oxcart from Tucuman and installed by an English mechanic, Roger Chadwick Leach.

The business did not really begin to flourish, however, until the railroad came to Jujuy in 1891. In 1908, David Ovejero and Angel Zerda founded Compania Azucarera Ledesma (The Ledesma Sugar Company), which they sold three years later to Enrique Wollmann and Carlos Delcasse, who incorporated in 1914 as Nueva Compania Azucarera y Refineria Ledesma. Wollmann was president until 1928, when he was succeeded by Delcasse's son Jorge. In 1938, Herminio Arrieta, an engineer with the company, was named president.

Some 40 years later, Ledesma had increased its production of sugar and alcohol—a byproduct of sugar production—sixfold. Much of this expansion resulted from the purchase, in the early 1960s, of a company called Calilegua, which consisted of the nearby La Esperanza sugar plantation and mill.

La Esperanza was founded in 1882 by the Englishman Roger Chadwick Leach and partners. The operation consisted of 2,500 hectares (about 6,175 acres) and a channel for irrigation water. In 1895 Leach and his five brothers bought out the last of the partners. For the harvest they imported indigenous Indian tribes from the remote Chaco region to work the fields. A community named La Esperanza flourished, with schools, hospitals, and sports facilities. Sugarcane production under the Leaches reached a peak of 67,865 metric tons in 1959, perhaps as much as Ledesma's own output. The property also included orchards—chiefly of oranges and pomelos—planted as early as 1916. At some point Ledesma also acquired a smaller plantation, El Palmer de San Francisco, in another department of Jujuy.

In 1956, the company adopted its present name, Ledesma Sociedad Anónima Agrícola Industrial. Ledesma added a third sugar mill in 1963, increasing its capacity to refine sugarcane by

40 percent. The company opened a cellulose and paper mill in 1965, using as raw material bagasse, the residue from sugarcane. This made it one of the six larger paper producers that dominated the industry. In addition, some of the molasses obtained in refining sugarcane was converted to ethyl alcohol. The company's energy needs were being met by waterpower, natural gas, and burning its own bagasse. Mechanical equipment for the sugarcane harvest was introduced in 1967. Ledesma's goal was to process 2.4 million metric tons of sugarcane a year in order to yield 300,000 tons of sugar, 90,000 tons of bagasse pulp, 100,000 tons of paper, and 30 million liters of ethyl alcohol. (The company also had established by this time juice-concentrate and fruit-packing plants.)

However, these plans were frustrated by the perennial problem of sugarcane overproduction and the consequent low price of sugar that threatened the economic survival of small plantation and mill owners and thousands of field hands. The Argentine government first offered export subsidies, then established barriers to entry such as prohibiting new mills. Production caps began in 1967, to Ledesma's dismay, since smaller sugarcane crops meant not only less sugar production but also less bagasse for the paper mill that the company was planning to expand.

Vertical Integration: 1970–2000

Carlos Pedro Blaquier became the company's president in 1970. Ledesma now had 30,000 hectares (almost 75,000 acres) of sugar plantations and fruit orchards. It obtained over half of the sugarcane it milled from its own plantations. Since Jujuy did not receive enough rainfall to meet its crop needs, the plantations and orchards were irrigated by 120 kilometers (about 75 miles) of principal canals—mostly concrete and covered to avoid evaporation—and more than 1,000 kilometers (620 miles) of secondary canals, the water being diverted from four rivers. The company employed 6,300 full-time workers and hired 7,000 more for the harvest, since the process still was only partly mechanized.

During the early 1970s the government raised sugar production quotas, but Ledesma's paper production did not benefit until fiscal 1977, when labor-union problems were finally overcome and machinery put in place for the planned expansion of the mill. Ledesma had record sugar production in 1976 and 1977 (263,362

metric tons in the latter year), but then quotas were cut because of low internal demand and export curbs which were imposed by a group of exporting countries. An important reason for low demand was competition from non-caloric sweeteners such as saccharine and cyclamates and corn-derived fructose for use in such products as snacks and soft drinks. Combined, these products had taken 30 percent of the sweetener market by the 1980s.

In the early 1980s Ledesma opened a milling plant in Villa Mercedes, San Luis, for converting wet corn to fructose, glucose, and other corn-based products. Challenges continued in the mid-1980s, when a new law intended to support prices prohibited new fructose plants, banned imports of the product, and put production caps on corn syrup. Seeking to diversify its operations, Ledesma established a factory on its Villa Mercedes property for making notebooks and other stationery from the company's paper mill. The alcohol plant had been modified in 1983 to produce anhydrous alcohol for combination with naptha into a motor fuel. In 1985, when Ledesma reported annual sales of about $110 million, 63 percent was derived from sugar, 32 percent from paper, and 4 percent from alcohol. Ledesma later acquired four farming/ranching tracts in the provinces of Buenos Aires and Entre Rios for the cultivation of grain crops and the raising of cattle. In addition, the company took a small share in an enterprise seeking to develop Argentina's abundant deposits of natural gas.

The free-market reforms urged by the administration of President Carlos Menem and enacted by legislation during 1991 and 1992 had profound effects on Argentine sugar producers in the 1990s. Fixed sugarcane prices, production quotas, and export taxes were eliminated. Capital goods such as machinery were allowed entry without tariffs until 1996. These changes resulted in a 15-percent growth in sugarcane production between 1993 and 1998, even though land devoted to sugarcane fell by one-fifth. Since domestic sugarcane consumption (four-fifths of the total) remained flat (while consumption of other sweeteners grew ten-fold between 1980 and 1999), the 1999 price was 70 percent lower than it had been in 1976. As a result, marginal producers were forced out of business. The number of cane producers fell by one-third in the 1990s, and 5 percent of the remaining growers were producing 70 percent of the crop.

2001 and Beyond

In the early 2000s, Ledesma's main agricultural complex at Libertador General San Martin included 35,000 hectares (about 87,000 acres) planted in sugarcane, and 2,000 hectares (about 5,000 acres) planted in oranges, lemons, pomelos, avocados, and mangos, plus the juice-concentrate and fruit-packing plants. Ledesma had become Argentina's chief producer and exporter of oranges. The complex also included factories for the production of sugar, alcohol, paper, and cellulose, facilities to generate more than 49,000 kilowatts of energy, 600 kilometers (about 370 miles) of roads, and 1,400 kilometers (almost 900 miles) of irrigation canals.

In 2001 this complex milled 3.14 million metric tons of sugarcane—about half from its own plantations, the rest purchased—and manufactured 333,899 metric tons of sugar, more than 20 percent of the national total. Some 61,175 metric tons were exported. Ledesma retained about half of the rest and sold

Key Dates:

1908: The Ledesma sugar mill and plantation assumes a company structure.
1911: Enrique Wollmann becomes president of Ledesma.
1959: Record sugar production realized at La Esperanza, a plantation purchased by Ledesma soon after.
1965: Ledesma adds a cellulose and paper mill, with sugarcane residue as the raw material.
1970: Carlos Pedro Blaquier assumes the presidency.
1982: Ledesma adds a wet-corn mill to produce sweeteners other than sugar.
2001: Ledesma is producing about one-fifth of Argentina's sugar.

the remainder to commercial customers. The sugar was packed in bags ranging from the "classic" one kilo (2.2 pounds) found in supermarkets to the "Big Bags" of 1,100 to 1,250 kilograms (2,420 to 2,750 pounds) for the industrial sector. The molasses obtained in manufacturing sugar yielded 29.21 million liters of alcohol, some one-fifth of the Argentine total. About one-tenth was exported. Fruit production came to 70,613 metric tons, of which about half was exported and one-third converted to concentrated juices. Paper production, in rolls, sheets, cut-size, and continuous printer paper, came to 69,848 metric tons, making Ledesma one of Argentina's leading paper producers, accounting for 30 percent of national output of printing and writing paper. This production consisted of bobbins and large reams for the graphic industry; small reams for photocopies, photoduplication, offset printing, and ink-jet and laser printers; and rolls for offset, dot-matrix, and laser printing.

Glukovil, Ledesma's factory at Villa Mercedes for processing wet corn, was yielding corn syrup, corn starch, glucose and other such products. Fructose, in syrup form, was being produced as a substitute for sugar in carbonated soft drinks, juices, liquors, and industrial processes requiring liquid sugar. Glucose, in syrup form, was being used in the manufacture of caramels, nougats, milk chocolate, and other confections. Mixed syrups were being used generally in the manufacture of sweets, marmalades, preserved fruits, and other confections. Malt syrup was destined primarily for the beer industry. Corn starch was being produced for use in the paper, textile, food, and petroleum industries. Gluten feed and gluten meal were being produced as additives in cattle fodder and poultry feed, respectively. Corn germ was being produced as an ingredient in the production of corn oil. Also at this location was the Grafex San Luis factory, producing school notebooks, notepads, loose-leaf paper, and office stationery from the company's paper.

La Biznaga S.A. was the name of Ledesma's agricultural enterprise that comprised 52,000 hectares (almost 130,000 acres) in four farms and ranches—one in the province of Entre Rios, the other three in the province of Buenos Aires. These facilities had a combined storage capacity of 53,000 metric tons of grain. La Biznaga beef was said to be enjoying a high level of acceptance in supermarket and hypermarket chains. Ledesma also held a 4-percent stake in U.T.E. Aguarague, a company dedicated to the exploration, development, and distribution of deposits of petroleum and natural gas in the province of Salta. Ledesma was receiving from Aguarague 80 million cubic meters of gas a year for use in its industrial plants.

Sales rose 23 percent between 2002 (fiscal year ending March 31, 2002) and 2003, reaching 790.45 million pesos ($266.14 million) in the latter year. As Argentina's economic crisis deepened, the net profit margin of only a little more than 1 percent in 2002 disappeared entirely the following year, which ended with a net loss of 12.9 million pesos ($4.34 million). Ledesma's small long-term debt indicated that it was not in serious financial difficulty, however. Blaquier was still president of the company in 2003.

Principal Subsidiaries

Bridgeport Investments L.L.C. (62%; United States); Calilegua, S.A.

Principal Competitors

Alto Parana S.A.; Celulosa Argentina S.A.; Ingenio y Refineria San Martin del Tabacal S.A.; Massuh S.A.; Witcel, S.A.

Further Reading

Craviotti, Clara, *Azucar y conflictos en el Norte argentino,* Buenos Aires: Centro Editor de America Latina, 1992.
''El gigante de Jujuy,'' *Mercado,* November 30, 1972, pp. 41–44.
Garcia, Luis F., ''El papel de la discordia,'' *Mercado,* November 26, 1987, pp. 122–23.
——, ''La accion del mes,'' *Mercado,* March 21, 1985, pp. 71–73.
Sierra e Iglesias, Jubino P., *Un tiempo que se fue,* San Pedro de Jujuy: Universidad Nacional de Jujuy, 1998.
Moyano, Julio, ed. *The Argentine Economy.* Buenos Aires: J. Moyano Comunicaciones, 1997, pp. 468–69.
Rece, Lucio G., and Gabriel H. Pavellada, *El sector agropecuario argentino.* Buenos Aires: Editorial Facultad Agronomia, 2001.
Schleh, Emilio J., *Noticias historicas sobre el azucar en la Argentina.* Buenos Aires: Centro Azucarero Argentino, 1945, pp. 265–69.
Silveti, Edgardo A., ''Ledesma: Tecnologia y produccion,'' *Mercado,* June 7, 1973, pp. 30–31.

—Robert Halasz

Les Boutiques San Francisco, Inc.

50 de Lauzon Street
Boucherville, Quebec J4B 1E6
Canada
Telephone: (450) 449-1313
Fax: (450) 449-1317
Web site: http://www.bsf.ca

Public Company
Incorporated: 1978
Employees: 3000
Sales: $182.7 million (2003)
Stock Exchanges: Toronto
Ticker Symbol: SF.A
NAIC: 448120 Women's Clothing Stores; 452110
   Department Stores

Les Boutiques San Francisco, Inc. is a leading Canadian chain of clothing stores, with approximately 140 stores in the provinces of Quebec and Ontario. Though little known outside Quebec, Les Boutiques San Francisco (BSF) is an innovative retailer that reinvigorated the department store concept in the late 1990s with luxurious megastores called Les Ailes de la Mode (The Wings of Fashion). These large department stores, which emphasize extraordinary customer service, were a bright spot in the slumping North American department store industry. The unique Les Ailes de la Mode chain, with four stores, make up one division of the Les Boutiques San Francisco company. The other division is composed of the company's various boutique chains. These are San Francisco, with 40 stores in Quebec, and the first in the BSF family; San Francisco Maillots, a chain of sports and activewear specialty shops; the swimwear vendor Bikini Village, with 46 units in Quebec and Ontario; and two chains of lingerie shops, Moments Intimes and Victoire Delage. The company restructured under bankruptcy protection in 2003 and sold off its chains of menswear and children's clothing specialty shops. The company aimed to hold onto Les Ailes de la Mode and its swimwear boutiques. The company was founded by Paul Delage Roberge in the late 1970s.

Building a Retail Network in the 1980s

The company that became Les Boutiques San Francisco, Inc. began as a women's clothing store founded in 1978 by Paul Delage Roberge and his wife Camille. Roberge was born to retail. He grew up near Quebec City, where his father was a clothing representative and his grandfather ran a general store. Roberge worked at his grandfather's establishment as a youth, and by the age of 15 he was working in a department store. In 1967, he earned a marketing degree at the University of Sherbrooke. After graduation, he worked as a buyer for a Montreal department store, Morgan, which was later acquired by the Hudson's Bay Co. chain.

After six years at Morgan, Roberge decided to go into business for himself. With a friend from college, Roberge opened a clothing store that catered to young women, called Boutique 20 Ans. Founded in 1973, by 1978 Boutique 20 Ans had grown to a chain of five stores. By 1978, Roberge had married Camille, a nurse by training and evidently a great influence on his sense of women's fashion (he referred to her as the ''Queen Beauty of Quebec''). That year, Roberge sold his share of the Boutique 20 Ans chain, and with savings coming to about $40,000 the couple launched a new boutique in the Montreal suburb of St. Bruno. The new store was called San Francisco, a name that worked in both French and English for its evocation of the healthy lifestyle of the California city. San Francisco did so well that the Roberges opened two more stores within a year.

The new chain grew very quickly and soon had more than 20 locations. In 1985, the Roberges took their young company public on the Montreal Stock Exchange. Les Boutiques San Francisco consisted of 22 women's clothing boutiques. Quebec citizens were able to buy stock in the firm and receive a tax deduction as part of a government Quebec Stock Savings Plan that encouraged investment in Quebec companies. After the stock sale, BSF began to grow in a new way. Not only did it add more locations to its San Francisco chain, but the company launched other boutiques for different market segments. In 1986, BSF brought out San Francisco Maillots (also known as San Francisco Beach Club) stores, which specialized in swim gear and beach wear. By the early 1990s, San Francisco Maillots had close to 40 locations. Also in 1986, BSF began a chain of stores catering to fashions for businesswomen called L'Officiel. This grew to 20 stores by the early 1990s. In 1988, BSF debuted a chain of children's clothing stores, Frisco. The next year saw the firm enter the men's clothing market with a chain of stores called West Coast. Then, in 1991, BSF brought out Victoire Delage, a chain of lingerie shops.

For the most part, the new boutiques did well, though the company made a few avowed mistakes. In the late 1980s, BSF began manufacturing and franchising jeans, a venture that failed. This led the company to post a loss in 1988. BSF also had trouble moving into English-speaking markets. After some expensive and apparently ill-planned store openings in Ontario and Michigan, BSF pulled back to Quebec. The company's president, Guy Charron, told *Canadian Business* (June 26, 1998) that Boutiques San Francisco, to its disadvantage, had been "talking to Ontario in French." The company put together a team to craft a strategy for moving beyond Quebec in the future. Meanwhile, Camille Roberge began publishing a fashion magazine in Quebec that eventually became the best-selling fashion journal in the province.

By 1993, Boutiques San Francisco was running 60 of its namesake stores, and under its other five banners ran more than a hundred stores. The Quebec company had been remarkably successful at a time when other Canadian retailers were struggling. The company took advantage of strategic mall locations, where it often had several of its banner stores side by side. This encouraged customers to move from one to the other. Because the company had stores in several market segments, it was able to do well as a whole even when one area, children's clothing, for example, had an off year. The stores also did well selling BSF's own private label goods alongside designer labels. As well as clothing, the boutiques stocked private label skin care products and shampoo, and the beachwear stores sold suntan lotions. Sales grew nicely, hitting just over $93 million for 1993, and then growing to $109 million the next year.

Reinventing the Department Store in the Mid-1990s

The early 1990s were poor times for the retail sector in North America. The industry underwent a wave of consolidations as old-line department stores made way for newer vendors with discounted lines. While BSF's rivals aimed to cut costs, the boutique chains did well and remained profitable throughout the early 1990s recession. Paul Roberge, however, thought about quitting retail altogether. He was bored. He and his wife had

hoped to do well with their boutiques but had apparently not imagined the business growing to this size. The strategic operations of the company's financial empire were overseen by president Guy Charron, whereas Roberge was more of a hands-on salesman who liked to walk the store floor. Instead of abandoning the company he had built up so far, Roberge began an ambitious new plan. BSF's stores had up to this point been small, specialized boutiques. Now Roberge imagined building huge new department stores, bigger and more luxurious than anything else in North American retailing. This was Les Ailes de la Mode.

The first Les Ailes de la Mode opened in Brossard, Quebec, in 1994. The inspiration for Les Ailes was the Seattle, Washington-based chain Nordstrom's. Roberge had studied Nordstrom's history, and he was sure a similarly upscale chain would do well in Canada. The Canadian market had several mid-market department chains, including Hudson's Bay and Eaton's. At the upper end, there was Holt Renfrew. The market seemed to lack an upper-middle niche, and that was what Les Ailes aimed to fill. At the same time, Les Ailes was also a remarkable break with current trends in department store retailing. Where other stores had cut costs and trimmed back, Les Ailes was awash in customer service and extraordinary amenities. The Brossard store was originally supposed to be 45,000 square feet but then went to 65,000 square feet. It cost $12.6 million to build, having gone over its original budget by 50 percent and taken six months longer than expected before it was ready to open. The store was dotted with leather-upholstered piano lounges, gourmet concession areas, notable original artwork, and private lounges where mothers could nurse their babies. In a palatial environment, the store's employees went to extremes to satisfy customers. Les Ailes de la Mode aimed to be a shopping destination where customers took pleasure in plonking down money rather than in scouring racks for bargains. Though this seemed to be the antithesis of trends in retail, Les Ailes de la Mode was a success from the start. In its first year of business, the Brossard store did just shy of $25 million in sales, very close to what Roberge had predicted. Though the cost of running the store was high, Les Ailes was very profitable. It brought in about $450 per square foot in sales, which was more than twice the average of its nearest rival, and three times that of the mid-level Eaton's and Hudson's Bay stores. Les Ailes also did well by selling a high proportion of private label goods. Its profit margin was well above that of any comparable store.

By 1998, there were three Les Ailes de la Mode stores in Quebec, all built along the same extravagant lines. The company advertised primarily in its fashion magazine, then added a weekly television show that featured shopping advice and celebrity interviews. The stores' customers could take advantage of a Les Ailes credit card, which racked up bonus points redeemable at the store. This was the first so-called chip-based or "smart" credit card in Canada. It gave BSF an abundance of data about its shoppers and brought them into the store at least once a month to redeem points. BSF also brought shoppers to Les Ailes by chartering special buses and trains. Les Ailes de la Mode wowed shoppers and industry analysts alike. Roberge talked about having reinvented the department store—not just in Quebec, not just in Canada, but in North America. For a very limited number of stores in the distant north of the continent, his claims may have seemed hyperbolic. Yet Les Ailes truly stood

Key Dates:

1978:   The first San Francisco boutique opens.
1985:   The company goes public.
1986:   L'Officiel and San Francisco Maillot chains begin.
1991:   Victoire Delage shops open.
1994:   The first Les Ailes de la Mode opens.
2003:   The company restructures under bankruptcy protection.

out as a shopping experience and seemed to have the financial results to prove Roberge's point.

However, the greatest challenge of BSF's new shopping experience was moving it beyond French-speaking Quebec. The first three Les Ailes stores were all in suburban locations, and intense planning was necessary to move its next store into the very different big-city environment of Montreal. The company hoped to open stores in Toronto and then Vancouver following the Montreal opening. In 1999, the venerable T. Eaton Co., Ltd., a once-leading chain of 64 department stores, filed for bankruptcy. BSF beat out other competitors for space in what had been Eaton's flagship store in downtown Montreal, and in 2002 the company opened what was its fifth Les Ailes de la Mode. (The fourth Les Ailes opened in 2001 in Bayshore, Ottawa.) Les Ailes took up 258,000 square feet of the cavernous building, and the company spent some $40 million on renovations that included building a spectacular floating staircase. The Montreal Les Ailes de la Mode also featured a karaoke lounge, sushi bar, French café, and a Berlitz language school.

The opening of the Montreal store did not go as well as planned, as sales over the summer fell short of expectations. In the meantime, the boutique side of the business was not performing as well as it once had. In 2001, BSF split into two divisions, with the boutiques comprising one side of the business and Les Ailes de la Mode making up its own separate division. BSF posted a loss in the second quarter of 2001, but things seemed better for the same period the next year, when the company increased sales and posted a moderate profit. For the next quarter, however, the company was in the red again. At that point, president Guy Charron resigned. He had been praised as the steady man at the helm, while Roberge was the more visionary leader. Now Roberge temporarily took on Charron's duties.

The company attempted to cut costs in 2003, but this move was unsuccessful. BSF sold off its menswear chain, West Coast, as well as its children's wear stores and its L'Officiel chain of women's businesswear. The Les Ailes de la Mode store in Ottawa did not last long and closed in 2003. In December of that year, the company filed for bankruptcy, asking for court protection from creditors while it restructured. Its stores remained open. Meanwhile, BSF decided to cut down the square footage of its Montreal store, and revamping this

flagship location led the company to take a third quarter write-down of close to $40 million.

The company blamed intense competition for its poor showing. With the court's approval, BSF decided to concentrate its business on its four Les Ailes de la Mode stores and on its swimwear boutiques. These were San Francisco Maillot, with 21 stores, and its 39-store chain called Bikini Village. The company trimmed jobs and shut down boutiques. In 2004, it sold 33 of its 36 San Francisco stores, its original boutique chain, for about $2.4 million to Groupe Marie Claire. Marie Claire ran several chains of fashion stores, and it planned to keep the San Francisco name on its new acquisition. Even with all this seemingly bad news for BSF, the company maintained that its Les Ailes de la Mode stores remained among the most successful in Canada. The company hoped to return to its growth in the near future.

Principal Divisions

Les Ailes de la Mode; Boutiques San Francisco.

Principal Competitors

Groupe Marie Claire; Le Chateau Inc.; Hudson's Bay Company.

Further Reading

"Boutiques Get Court Approval for Plan," *Toronto Star*, January 16, 2004, p. E2.
"Boutiques San Francisco President Resigns," *Toronto Star*, December 12, 2002, p. D8.
Dougherty, Kevin, "Quebec Clothing Chain Makes Most of Recession," *Financial Post*, March 28, 1992, p. 19.
Fortin, Claude, "Credit/Smart Cards Creates New Marketing Vehicle," *Chain Store Age*, January 1998, p. 116.
Kucharsky, Danny, "Exotic Ailes Aims to Seduce Shoppers," *Marketing Magazine*, May 27, 2002, p. 2.
——, "Mtl. Department Stores Do Battle," *Marketing Magazine*, August 19, 2002, p. 2.
"Marie Claire Buys Boutique SF Stores," *Daily Deal*, January 28, 2004.
"Montreal Retailer Takes Writedown," *Toronto Star*, December 24, 2003, p. C5.
Peason, Kali, "On the Wings of Wow," *Profit*, November 1, 2002, p. 40.
"The Personal Touch," *Canadian Packaging*, March 1993, pp. 17–18.
"Results Soar at Two Clothing Chains," *Toronto Star*, September 14, 2002, p. C11.
Silcoff, Sean, "Super Shoppers," *Canadian Business*, February 27, 1998, p. 21.
——, "Move Over, Timothy Eaton," *Canadian Business*, June 26, 1998, p. 58.
——, "Life after Eaton's," *Canadian Business*, September 10, 1999, pp. 30–32.

—A. Woodward

Little Tikes Company

2180 Barlow Road
Hudson, Ohio 44236
U.S.A.
Telephone: (330) 650-3000
Fax: (330) 287-2864
Web site: http://www.littletikes.com

Wholly Owned Subsidiary of Newell Rubbermaid Inc.
Incorporated: 1970
Employees: 2,000
Sales: $2.59 billion (2002)
NAIC: 339932 Game, Toy, and Children's Vehicle
   Manufacturing

The distinctive, brightly colored plastic toys produced by the Little Tikes Company are a staple for kids around the world. The company manufactures a variety of children's products, including foot-to-floor vehicles, playhouses, basketball sets, activity gyms, and furniture. Its most famous product—the red and yellow Cozy Coupe Car—celebrated its 20th anniversary in 1999 with over six million units sold since its launch. While the company experienced stellar growth from the 1980s into the early 1990s, it faced challenges in the new century due to a slowing economy. As a wholly owned subsidiary of Newell Rubbermaid Inc., Little Tikes operates as the largest rotational molder in the world with manufacturing facilities in Ohio and California, as well as international locations in Europe and Asia.

Origins

Little Tikes was founded in 1970 by Thomas G. Murdough. Murdough became interested in the toy business in 1968 when his then-employer, Wilson Sporting Goods, asked him to run marketing for its Wonder Products subsidiary. The late 1960s saw the toy industry undergo a period of intense transformation, as smaller companies and distributors found themselves being swallowed up by the big manufacturers. Murdough was reportedly appalled by the increasing shoddiness of toys. According to an article in *Fortune*, Murdough felt that the toy manufacturers' sole aim had degenerated into bringing toys to market at

ever-cheaper prices. This trend was exacerbated by the huge new discount retailers who often sold popular toys at a loss in order to bring people into their stores. Murdough was determined to buck this trend. He quit his marketing job at Wilson and set out to start his own company. Murdough saw a need for well-made plastic toys, as only the cheapest fabrication processes and forms of plastic raw materials were being used in toy manufacture at that time. In 1970, he formed the Little Tikes Co. and, with nine employees, began to manufacture large plastic outdoor play equipment, toy boxes, and children's furniture in an old barn in Aurora, Ohio.

Murdough's Personal Approach Leads to Success:
1970s and 1980s

Little Tikes pioneered the use of rotational molding, an industrial process for molding plastic that had formerly been used mainly to produce large products like agricultural tanks and chemical containers. Rotational molding could produce larger, more durable products than the traditional blow molding that had been widely used in the toy industry. By allowing for a large variety of shapes with large surface areas, fewer parts were needed to create each large toy. Fewer parts meant not only less assembly time on the factory floor but also a more durable final product. In addition, the new process permitted the production of a variety of colors at the same time, adding versatility to the production process.

From the start, Murdough insisted on maintaining his own personal approach towards toy marketing. He was convinced that by restricting distribution of his products to independent toy stores and toy supermarkets he could avoid the deep discounting that had eventually forced other toy manufacturers to lower production costs and quality. Large discount stores like Kmart tended to "cherry-pick" the hottest items out of a given manufacturer's line and then sell them at or under cost in order to draw parents in. Small retailers were then faced with lowering their prices in order to compete. As their profit margins shrunk to unmanageable levels, they then put pressure on manufacturers to further lower wholesale costs. Murdough avoided this pattern by simply declining to distribute through large discount stores. "Murdough had a good understanding of how not to go to market. He was very careful not to flood the market

Company Perspectives:

Our common goal is to create and supply innovative children's products that provide fun that lasts to customers and consumers around the world. To reach that goal, Little Tikes' associates' actions are guided by the principles of Customer Satisfaction, Teamwork, Innovation, Marketing, and Continuous Improvement.

with merchandise,'' said one retailing executive in a 1989 *Business Week* article. Murdough carefully nurtured his relationship with the small toy retailers. By discouraging deep discounting of its most popular toys, Little Tikes kept profit margins high for all its retailers. In exchange, the company insisted that retailers stock the full range of the Little Tikes line.

In addition to keeping retailers happy, Murdough's approach to marketing allowed Little Tikes to create an up-scale, ''boutique'' image for its products. This was important because Little Tikes relied almost exclusively on word-of-mouth to promote its large, and often pricey, plastic play equipment. Murdough was convinced that advertising to kids was not only morally questionable but was also not good business sense. Little Tikes toys were almost exclusively designed for pre-schoolers, an age when pressure to conform to fads is at a minimum. The preschool market had always shown much more brand loyalty than other segments of the toy industry. Parents tended to choose toys they felt would be durable and safe for the younger child, and they relied on a manufacturer's reputation to ensure this kind of quality.

The giants of the pre-school toy industry, Fisher-Price and Playskool, had relied heavily on building brand equity to achieve their dominance of this sector, and it was clear that Little Tikes had to build a stellar reputation if it wanted to succeed. Advertising on television was a very expensive and not particularly effective way of communicating a message of reliability to new parents. For this reason, Murdough chose to forego all television advertising and concentrate instead on creating a reputation for superb customer service. Little Tikes became one of the first companies to mold a toll-free telephone number into all its products and to hire and train specialized staff to respond promptly to customer queries and complaints. The company enclosed a catalogue displaying the Little Tikes line with all of its toys in order to encourage a feeling of buying into a brand instead of just a single toy. With much lower advertising costs, Little Tikes could also afford to charge less for its products than the heavily advertised competition, which further encouraged parents to try the Little Tikes plastic play equipment.

Murdough's approach to the internal management of Little Tikes was as unconventional as his marketing philosophy. From the start, when all of the employees of Little Tikes could easily fit into his office, Murdough held monthly no-holds-barred meetings to discuss company strategy. As the company grew, Murdough retained this open style of management. He introduced profit-sharing, subsidized on-site child-care, and offered tuition reimbursement for employees furthering their education. In an industry that was known for a cut-throat approach to personnel management, Little Tikes commanded impressive staff loyalty. Murdough was also committed to keeping jobs in the United States. When most toy makers were transferring the bulk of their manufacturing overseas, 99 percent of Little Tikes products sold in the United States were made and assembled there.

The Little Tikes product marketing approach was an overwhelming success. As the baby-boom generation began to have kids of their own, the pre-school toy industry boomed. Little Tikes' image as a sort of parents' toy club encouraged word-of-mouth advertising, and sales soared. The company quickly outgrew the old barn that had served as its headquarters and manufacturing plant and in the mid-1970s moved its operations to a much larger plant in Macedonia, Ohio. Within the next decade, Little Tikes would also open manufacturing plants in Ireland and Canada and begin distribution of its toys outside the United States. By the end of the 1970s, Little Tikes' sales had grown to about $15 million and its product line had expanded to include ride-on toys. In 1979, the company introduced its first major hit toy, the Cozy Coupe ride-in car. This red and yellow foot-powered vehicle was enclosed, unlike the time-honored tricycle, and seemed to give kids a sense of security about venturing forth in the world. By the early 1990s, the Cozy Coupe was the best-selling car in North America, beating both Ford's Taurus and Honda's Accord, which prompted Ford's marketing director to quip that they'd ''have to give those kids a good trade-in on a Taurus.''

The Rubbermaid Purchase: 1984

With its Cozy Coupe and a variety of very popular playhouses and outdoor play equipment, Little Tikes entered the 1980s in a position to begin competing seriously with the large, established pre-school toy manufacturers. In 1982, during a period of decline for the toy industry as a whole, Little Tikes sales increased by 28 percent to $23.1 million, which was followed by an astounding 73 percent rise to $42.9 million in 1983. It was clear that Little Tikes toys were more than just a passing fad. During the same period the giant housewares company Rubbermaid Inc. was undergoing a major restructuring and was searching for new acquisitions. The fledgling toy company, with its emphasis on plastic and its family image, was a good match for Rubbermaid and an offer was made. Murdough was reluctant to give up control of Little Tikes, but he felt that the company needed Rubbermaid's capital if it was to continue to expand. Rubbermaid acknowledged that Murdough and his management team had been fundamental to the success of the toy company. In 1984, Rubbermaid bought Little Tikes for about $50 million, with the agreement that Murdough would stay on as president, and his approach towards management and marketing would be retained.

With new capital from Rubbermaid and a brand new manufacturing plant and headquarters in Hudson, Ohio, Little Tikes was set to begin an intensive expansion of its product line and distribution. It added a ''spring-summer'' line of outdoor play equipment that included climbing and sliding sets as well as plastic sports equipment. The company also began to depart from its exclusive reliance on rotational molding by having a line of small injection-molded toys manufactured for it at other facilities. With its new products and increased manufacturing

Key Dates:

1970: Thomas G. Murdough establishes the Little Tikes Co.
1979: The company introduces the Cozy Coupe ride-in car.
1983: Sales rise by 73 percent to $42.9 million.
1984: Rubbermaid Inc. acquires Little Tikes.
1989: Disagreements over marketing strategies lead to Murdough's resignation.
1999: Newell Inc. purchases Rubbermaid.
2002: Little Tikes launches its first national television advertising campaign.

capabilities, Little Tikes sales grew at a rate that far exceeded the toy industry as a whole. By 1987, the company's sales had topped $100 million, and then they more than doubled in the following two years to reach about $270 million in 1989. Little Tikes accounted for 28 percent of its parent company's profits by the late 1980s, prompting one analyst to comment in the *Wall Street Journal* that Little Tikes was the "star" of Rubbermaid's stable of companies.

Throughout the growth period of the 1980s, Murdough managed to retain the approach to marketing that had been so successful for the toy company. Only 6 percent of sales were spent on advertising, compared to an industry average of about 20 percent. Little Tikes also continued to resist television advertising or any ads directed at children. In 1985, Murdough even canceled Little Tikes' membership in the Toy Manufacturers of America because of the trade association's support of marketing to children. The customer service branch of the company was expanded and catalogue mailings continued to grow.

Murdough's Departure: 1989

In spite of this seemingly steady course, friction began to develop between the managers of Little Tikes and Rubbermaid over the retail distribution of Little Tikes toys. Large discounters like Kmart and Ames were the linchpin of Rubbermaid's approach to selling its popular housewares, and senior management at Rubbermaid began to put pressure on Little Tikes to end its policy of selling only through toy and specialty stores. Murdough felt that to allow discounters to carry only the best-selling Little Tikes products would be unfair to Little Tikes' full-line retailers, who had to make considerable commitments of floor and stockroom space to accommodate the large playsets. Murdough insisted that selling through discount chains would lead to short product life spans. "You saturate the marketplace," Murdough told the *Wall Street Journal* in 1989. "That's a big part of the reason the toy industry is flat on its back."

By the fall of 1989, it became clear that Murdough and parent Rubbermaid's positions on marketing could not be reconciled, and Murdough resigned his position with the company. "It turns out we never needed Rubbermaid's money," said a frustrated Murdough in a 1993 *Forbes* article. "I was spending all my time just keeping them [Rubbermaid executives] out of my hair." Rubbermaid chairman Stanley C. Gault, however, insisted that the dispute was not so much about retail relation-

ships as Murdough's management style. Gault told the *Wall Street Journal* after the resignation that Murdough "is unable to work for a boss, regardless of the autonomy he has. He won't take criticism."

Rubbermaid quickly appointed Gary Baughman, who had headed up its Evenflo division, as the new president of Little Tikes. Under Baughman, Little Tikes began to experiment with broader advertising, even conducting an ad agency review, but test marketing surveys revealed that 30-second television spots were ineffective at conveying the Little Tikes message and the campaign was dropped. Instead, the course that Murdough had set was strengthened and a new 6,000-square-foot center was built to house the company's growing customer service department. Baughman chose to concentrate on increasing the efficiency of the production end of the company, and five additional manufacturing plants were opened in the United States over the course of the following five years.

The early 1990s saw Rubbermaid making intensive efforts to increase its international presence, which at that time accounted for only about 15 percent of total sales. To this end, Little Tikes manufacturing and distribution centers were built in Luxembourg and Korea to serve the European and Asian markets. In spite of increased foreign manufacturing, about 80 percent of Little Tikes toys sold in the United States were still manufactured in North America.

Little Tikes' policy of growth took on a new direction in the 1990s as the company acquired three small commercial playground equipment companies: Iron Mountain Forge (Missouri), Ausplay (Australia), and Paris Playground Equipment (Canada). In conjunction with these companies, Little Tikes began to produce large commercial playground equipment suitable for child care centers and community playgrounds. The large plastic and steel PlayCenters were designed to sell at about $3,000, some two to five times less than the more traditional wood and steel structures. Although the longevity of these plastic play systems was only one-third that of the more traditional steel playgrounds, Little Tikes felt that the significantly lower cost would be attractive to child care centers, which tended to replace equipment every few years. In spite of president Baughman's 1994 defection to rival toy company Tyco, Little Tikes seemed poised to continue its rapid growth in the last half of the 1990s.

Overcoming Problems in the Late 1990s and Beyond

The company began to experience problems, however, as high material costs and slowing demand began to take their toll on Rubbermaid's profits. As such, Little Tikes bolstered its research and development activities, revamped its retail product displays, and increased the number of new product launches. As the company was setting these strategies in place, Newell Inc. announced its $5.6 billion acquisition of Rubbermaid. The deal, completed in 1999, left Little Tikes exposed to a new management style. As a 1998 *St. Louis Post-Dispatch* article reported, "After buying a company, Newell uses its formula—called 'Newellization'—of cutting overhead and production costs, improving service, and trimming product lines." The Little Tikes' plant in Shippensburg, Pennsylvania, became the first victim in the "Newellization" process. The company announced in early spring 1999 that it would close the facility in order to reduce excess manufacturing and streamline the firm's distribution network.

Instead of trimming its product lines, Little Tikes entered the new century focused on bolstering its merchandise mix. During 2000, the company launched its spring line that included over 30 new products. Since the Newell purchase, Little Tikes had focused heavily on consumer research—finding out what parents wanted or expected from toys. The firm's research found that consumers looked for products that stimulated role-play and imagination in their children. Many of the new products offered that year were based on the firm's new weather-resistant technology that allowed electronic toys to be left outside. One such product, the Imagine Sounds Playhouse, was designed to enhance imaginary play by using motion sensors to set off various sounds, including a knock at the door or the sound of rain falling on the roof.

The company strengthened its foothold in several new product categories in 2001 when it teamed up with Thinkway International Inc., Team Concepts North America, and Prestige Toy Corp. in licensing agreements that would market interactive, educational, and plush toys under the Little Tikes brand name. Despite the company's efforts, however, Little Tikes continued to face problems as a result of dwindling sales. The company's largest customer, Toys "R" Us Inc., began cutting its inventory. To make matters worse, an August 2001 *Crain's Chicago Business* article reported that "other retailers, intent on maximizing sales per square foot in a slowing economy, are allocating less space for Little Tikes' plastic playground sets and other bulky offerings." In response to these problems, the company revamped its packaging and merchandising strategies and began to investigate selling more of its products online. It also set plans in motion to launch its first national television advertising campaign during the 2002 holiday season. The commercials featured voice-overs by Christie Brinkley, Wolfgang Puck, and John Cleese.

As Little Tikes worked to regain its financial footing, rumors of a possible sale began to surface. Nevertheless, the company continued to strengthen its holdings, adding licensed character items, bath toys, and wood furniture to its product arsenal. It also signed 20 new licensing agreements in February 2003. Regardless of its future ownership, Little Tikes' products would no doubt continue to be found in homes across the world for years to come.

Principal Competitors

Koala Corp.; Mattel Inc.; SMOBY.

Further Reading

Fitzgerald, Kate, "Disney Aids Mattel Surge in Two-Legged Toy Race," *Advertising Age*, September 28, 1994, p. 41.

Flax, Steven, "The Christmas Zing in Zapless Toys," *Fortune*, December 26, 1983, pp. 98–103.

Gallun, Alby, "Kids Biz Paddling Newell Rubbermaid," *Chain's Chicago Business*, August 20, 2001, p. 4.

Grimm, Matthew, "Little Tikes with a Grown-up Dilemma," *Adweek's Marketing Week*, September 10, 1990, p. 18.

Lavin, Douglas, "Ford's Taurus No. 1? That's Bull Says Car Maker with Cozy Niche," *Wall Street Journal*, January 11, 1993, p. B1.

Mallory, Maria, "Why Little Tikes Managers Picked Up Their Toys and Left," *Business Week*, November 27, 1989, p. 33.

Mortland, Shannon, "Little Tikes Line to Weather the Elements," *Crain's Cleveland Business*, October 30, 2000, p. 18.

——, "Little Tikes Takes to the Tube," *Crain's Cleveland Business*, January 21, 2002, p. 6.

Murray, Teresa Dixon, "Little Tikes Plant Becomes 1st Victim of 'Newellization,'" *Plain Dealer*, April 1, 1999, p. 1C.

"Newell Buys Rubbermaid for $5 Billion," *St. Louis Post-Dispatch*, October 22, 1998, p. C1.

Palmeri, Christopher, "Back in Charge," *Forbes*, January 18, 1993, pp. 102–03.

Pierson, John, "Form and Function," *Wall Street Journal*, August 5, 1994, p. B1.

Rakoczy, Christine, "Quality Isn't Kid Stuff," *Quality in Manufacturing*, November-December 1992.

Swasy, Alecia, "Corporate Focus: Rubbermaid Moves beyond the Kitchen," *Wall Street Journal*, February 3, 1989.

Verespej, Michael, "A New Age for Little Tikes," *Industry Week*, April 16, 1990, pp. 11–13.

"Who's News: Rubbermaid Names Evenflo's Baughman President of Its Little Tikes Co. Toy Unit," *Wall Street Journal*, December 5, 1989.

Yerak, Becky, "Rubbermaid Profits Dip in 4th Quarter; Little Tikes Toy Unit Performance Is Still a Problem," *Plain Dealer*, February 6, 1997, p. 1C.

Zapanta, Melissa, "Little Tikes Sells Product with Reputation, Few Ads," *Crain's Cleveland Business*, August 31, 1992, p. 17.

—Hilary Gopnik
—update: Christina M. Stansell

Maid-Rite Corporation

2951 86th Street
Des Moines, Iowa 50322
U.S.A.
Telephone: (515) 276-5448
Toll Free: (866) JUST RITE
Fax: (515) 276-5449
Web site: http://www.maid-rite.com

Private Company
Incorporated: 1926
Employees: 15
Sales: not available
NAIC: 722110 Full-Service Restaurants; 533110 Owners
 and Lessors of Other Non-Financial Assets

Maid-Rite Corporation's franchise restaurants have been serving their signature "loose meat" ground beef sandwiches since 1926. While at one time there were as many as 400 Maid-Rite restaurants in small midwestern towns, only some 60 to 80 stores now remain in business. They are something of an institution in eastern Iowa and Illinois, with a few locations in Missouri, Nebraska, Wisconsin, and Minnesota as well. The chain was a fast food pioneer decades before McDonald's entered the scene, but it did not have the centralized effort and resources to partake in the franchising boom of the 1960s and 70s. The Maid-Rite franchise was loosely managed during this period and, as a result, Maid-Rite restaurants differ significantly from one another in their menus, decor, and store hours. Most of the franchises are locally owned and have a strong local flavor. The parent company owns only two locations. Although the restaurants are little known outside their home territory, many people who grew up near a Maid-Rite developed a strong attachment to the restaurant. One store even operates a mail-order business that ships frozen sandwiches as far away as Texas and Florida. In 2002, a group of investors purchased the chain with ambitious plans to tighten operations and open hundreds of new Maid-Rites across the Midwest.

An Early Fast Food Operation: 1926 to World War II

Iowa butcher Fred Angell created the first Maid-Rite sandwich in 1926. Legend has it that he served a crumbly beef sandwich with a special seasoning blend to a passing delivery man, who proclaimed that it was "made just right." Angell thereafter dubbed the sandwich "Maid-Rite," a name that he regarded as conveying a wholesome and pure aura. He opened his first restaurant in Muscatine, an Iowa river town just across the Mississippi from Illinois. Angell sold his sandwiches at a walk-up window, an innovation that would eventually develop into the familiar fast food drive-up window. The only other fast food franchise existing at the time was White Castle, which had been founded five years earlier.

As a franchise, the Maid-Rite concept spread largely through word of mouth. In 1927, Angell sold franchise rights to a woman in the town of Newton, about 25 miles east of Des Moines in central Iowa. Clifford Taylor, a resident of Newton, bought rights for Marshalltown, Iowa, in 1928 and opened Taylor's Maid-Rite Hamburger Shop. Taylor's contract was signed by a certain Floyd Angell, whose relationship to Fred Angell remains unknown. The contract had no stipulations related to royalties; Taylor simply paid $300 to use the Maid-Rite name and operated his store independently. He baked pies at home, bought pickles from the local vinegar works, and got his hamburger buns from the bakery down the street. Another early restaurant was located in Springfield, Illinois. This location had been started in 1921 by Arthur Knippenburg, who gave it to his friend Clyde Holbrook. After Maid-Rite was founded, the Springfield store adopted the chain's name but remained independent.

The chain continued to expand using an owner-operator strategy, so that most franchisees owned a single restaurant and had strong local roots. Maid-Rite's first logo was a friendly-looking maiden who adorned the top of most restaurants opened in the early years of the franchise. The classic Maid-Rite sandwich was made of ground beef cooked in a special steamer and served on a hot bun with a spoon to scoop up the filling that fell out. Angell developed a special seasoning for the filling and began to require that all franchises use it. However, Taylor's Maid-Rite in Marshalltown never adopted the seasoning; Angell respected the original terms of Taylor's contract, which was drawn up before the seasoning was created. In addition, some franchises stopped using the seasoning during World War II because of rationing and never switched back, since their communities had gotten used to the unseasoned sandwich. The original sandwich came with only three condiments: mustard, pickles, and onions.

Decentralized Growth: 1950–82

Franchising and distribution continued to be handled out of Muscatine as the Maid-Rite chain grew. The Maid-Rite Franchise Association estimates that the chain had between 300 and 400 stores at its high point. There were locations in nearly 20 states. Fred Angell's son Francis and his wife Bea became involved in the business. Over the decades, the Angell family sold franchises to people in Missouri, Nebraska, Minnesota, Wisconsin, and Michigan, but the largest concentration of Maid-Rites continued to be in eastern Iowa and western Illinois. Store owners began to vary the menu as they saw fit, adding such items as French fries and milk shakes. Without a strongly centralized chain identity, the development of the Maid-Rite franchise was largely determined by the steps individual locations took to respond to customer demand in their area.

For example, Nina Scudder bought a restaurant in downtown Toledo, Iowa, in 1946 and converted it into a Maid-Rite. Ten years later, she moved the restaurant to a new location on the recently built U.S. Highway 30. Her sons Bob and Gene joined the business; in 1972, it was sold to Dick Ridout. Ridout remodeled the interior and added menu items such as broasted chicken, fresh-baked donuts, and breakfast foods. In the 1980s, he built an addition for more table space. The store attracted customers with a Sunday breakfast special and a Saturday dinner special. In 2002, local residents Brad and Robin Crawford took over the operation. Robin had started as a waitress at the Toledo Maid-Rite in 1975 and subsequently acted as their bookkeeper for 25 years. They planned to carry on with the store's decades-old method of operation.

A location in Rolla, Missouri, opened in 1955. Bill Smith was the original owner. He bought an ice cream shop with a walk-up window and converted it into a Maid-Rite. For two decades, the restaurant had no interior seating. Larry Sherrell bought it in 1973 and added indoor tables, expanding even

further in the 1980s when people began having trouble finding a place to sit. Maid-Rite stores were free to adopt whatever operating hours they desired. Sherrell opted to close his store for a full two weeks every Christmas, and regular customers eagerly anticipated its reopening every new year.

Meanwhile, the original Maid-Rite restaurant in Muscatine was still in operation, along with a second location that had opened along the river in 1928. In 1973, after the site of the original store was condemned and converted to a parking lot, the restaurant moved to a new downtown location. Francis Angell died a few months after the move, and his son Bill began to operate the Muscatine stores and oversee the whole chain. Larry Meyer, a childhood friend of Bill Angell who had helped out at Maid-Rite as a child, bought the two Muscatine stores in 1997. He closed the ailing downtown location but retained the riverside store, which had survived two fires and a car crash through its wall. Meyer diversified the menu with breakfast items and a regular hamburger.

Taylor's Marshalltown Maid-Rite, on the other hand, stuck firmly to the traditional menu. Founder Clifford Taylor had died in 1944, and his son Don took over. Don built a cooler in the basement so that they could freshly grind hamburger daily and in 1958 moved across the street to a new state-of-the-art location with all stainless steel equipment and two cash registers. A Marshalltown native told the *Des Moines Business Record* in 1999, "Every Saturday night, this place was the big deal. We'd stop here and get two Maid-Rites and a malt and take them to the races with us. Every Saturday night." After Don died, his wife Polly operated the store. In 1985, she asked Clifford's great-grandson Don Taylor Short to help out. While other Maid-Rites were enlarging their menus, the Marshalltown franchise did not even provide ketchup: they honored the original contract, which stipulated that mustard, onions, and pickles were to be the only seasonings. Furthermore, Short did not add French fries to the menu because he did not want to have to bother cleaning a fryer. The Maid-Rite sandwich alone was enough to keep the customers coming in Marshalltown.

Gillotti Ownership: 1982–2002

In the 1970s, the food service industry began getting more and more competitive. McDonald's stores and other franchises were starting to blanket the nation. While the competition pushed many Maid-Rites out of business, others reported that the McDonald's phenomenon improved business, since it got people in the habit of eating out more frequently. Stores with a strong local following survived, but the Maid-Rite chain as a whole was left behind in the franchise boom. The Angell family did not have the money to expand nationally but at the same time it became increasingly difficult to run all the distribution out of Muscatine. Consequently, stores were allowed to buy their own supplies. Bill Angell continued to sign franchise agreements but did not conduct any centralized marketing.

In 1982, Angell went into the financial advising business and sold the Maid-Rite chain to Clayton Blue. Blue's partner John Gillotti provided most of the money for installment payments on the chain, and when Blue eventually defaulted on the contract Gillotti acquired all the assets of business. Blue remained involved in selling franchise contracts. A publicly held company

Key Dates:

1926: Fred Angell opens the first Maid-Rite in Muscatine, Iowa.
1970s: Fast food franchising takes off, but Maid-Rite remains loosely managed.
1982: Clayton Blue and John Gillotti acquire the chain.
1993: The Marshalltown, Iowa, location begins to offer frozen mail-order Maid-Rites.
2002: Bradley Burt takes control of the chain with plans to expand and tighten its operations.

called Maid-Rite Ventures, Inc., headed by Larry Meurlott and Brad Schoech, was formed around 1985. Gillotti was also on the board of directors. Schoech had a string of bankruptcy filings in his background and a history of questionable business dealings. Maid-Rite Ventures announced that it had acquired a chain of stores that expanded the franchise into Texas, Colorado, Nebraska, Kansas, Arkansas, Oklahoma, South Carolina, California, New Jersey, Pennsylvania, Washington, Oregon, Florida, and the greater Chicago area. However, the company is not known to have actually opened any stores, and it eventually changed its name and pursued unrelated business opportunities. Under the Gillottis, the Maid-Rite chain continued to be loosely managed. They did invest quite a bit of money into the business and hired a consulting firm from Chicago to present recommendations on franchise development. In the end, however, they did little more than open a few company-owned stores in Des Moines. The chain had a total of about 150 stores in the mid-1980s.

The largest Maid-Rite franchise to actually operate stores started in 1982 in the Quad City area of Illinois. Dave Collins, Joe Montenguise, and Larry Selser, three partners with a background at McDonald's, bought two stores in the cities of Milan and Moline. They dubbed their enterprise CSM Holding Company. Over time, they bought other locations and opened new stores until they had about a dozen locations in all. Their efforts greatly improved the chain's reputation in the Quad City area. They began remodeling stores to a 1950s theme in the late 1980s and added dinner items such as roast beef, pork chops, meat loaf, and spaghetti. In 1993, CSM Holding opened a store in Springfield, Illinois, where the 1921 Maid-Rite was still operating in its original location, a distinctive wood-framed tugboat-shaped building. In fact, the site had been put on the National Register of Historic Places and the owner, Clarence Donley, claimed it had the world's first drive-up window. Donley sued successfully to have the new Maid-Rite closed, claiming he had the original right to the Maid-Rite name, and CSM pulled out of Springfield.

Marlo Gillotti was running the Maid-Rite chain by the mid-1990s. After John Gillotti died in 1991, Clayton Blue produced a contract indicating that the business should pass to him. Following a legal battle, the court ruled in favor of the Gillotti estate, noting that the contract showed signs of tampering.

Maid-Rite got some unexpected publicity around 1993 thanks to the television show Roseanne, starring Roseanne Barr and Tom Arnold. Arnold happened to be a native of Iowa. On the show, Roseanne opened a diner serving a "crumbly burger from Iowa," and Midwesterners who knew about Maid-Rite picked up on the reference. The Maid-Rite mail order business started up around the same time, when a one-time Marshalltown resident asked Don Taylor Short to freeze a few sandwiches and mail them in an overnight box. After the customer reordered, Short began advertising mail order service, and by the late 1990s the store was sending out about 1,000 shipments a year. The service was advertised on the Marshalltown store's own web site.

A New Owner and Ambitious Plans: 2002–04

Late in the 1990s, the total number of Maid-Rite stores fell under 100. The Gillotti family hired Bradley Burt, a former Des Moines banker with his own marketing firm, to help them develop the chain. Burt ended up buying the chain in 2002 with a group of 13 other investors and afterward became the company's president and CEO. He had ambitious plans to revive the Maid-Rite franchise by standardizing operations, increasing promotional support for stores, and providing intensive training for franchisees. The new owners developed operating manuals, quality standards, and a seven-day "Maid-Rite University" for new store owners. Building on the successful formula of some franchisees, the new management came up with a 1950s style store design and an enhanced menu featuring mini-donuts, a pork sandwich, fresh-ground gourmet coffee, and cinnamon rolls for breakfast. "We have what I think is a treasure chest that just needs to be opened and given what it needs to be successful," Burt told the *Nation's Restaurant News* in 2002.

However, Burt's plans clashed with existing stores that had been operating successfully for decades in their own idiosyncratic way. Stores that ground their own beef, for example, did not want to use the precooked product provided by the Des Moines headquarters. The new management put the pressure on by starting to strictly enforce contracts that had been handled lackadaisically for years. Some stores closed, worried they would have to construct a new building and adopt a new menu when the time came for contract renewal. Other stores banded together to form the Maid-Rite Franchise Association, with Dave Collins of CSM Holding acting as president. After the Franchise Association found legal representation, the Maid-Rite headquarters toned down its approach and gave the existing restaurants more leeway. Meanwhile, Burt planned to opened 35 new stores by 2006 and hundreds more over the next several years. Neal Schuerer and Herbert Neubauer of Amana, Iowa, opened a local store conforming with the new style and also acquired a franchise for the Kansas City, Missouri, area, with plans to build 19 stores there. In Des Moines, company stores that had adopted the new menu reported improved business. The chain was also negotiating development agreements for Arizona, Florida, and parts of Chicago. Burt was doing his best to transform the underdeveloped chain into a consistent and widely recognized brand.

Principal Competitors

McDonald's Corporation; White Castle System Inc.; Subway; Burger King Corporation.

Further Reading

Bakke, Dave, "Springfield Maid-Rite Is Not Sold," *State Journal Register* (Springfield, Ill.), April 23, 2003, p. 11.

Butcher, Lola, "Questions Pile Up on Fast Food Franchiser," *Kansas City Business Journal*, April 22, 1985.

——, "Head of Maid-Rite Leaves Bankruptcy Trail," *Kansas City Business Journal*, April 29, 1985.

"Court Rejects Claim over Maid-Rite," *Omaha World-Herald*, August 23, 1997, p. 13.

Edgington, Denise, "Frozen In Time," *Des Moines Business Record*, February 1, 1999, p. 10.

Gardyasz, Joe, "Maid-Rite Growing Quality, Number of Franchises," *Des Moines Business Record,* October 20, 2003, p. 8.

Lovell, Michael, "Maid-Rite's Next Step," *Des Moines Business Record*, April 8, 2002, p. 1.

Lucas, Marlene, "Diner-Style Maid-Rite Super Store Is Coming to Amana, Iowa, Business Area," *The Cedar Rapids Gazette*, December 4, 2003.

Meyer, Karen, "A Diner out of the '50s Makes Burgers the Rite Way," *Chicago Tribune*, February 28, 1993, p. 5.

Pope, Steve, "Maid-Rite Holds the Ketchup, of Course," *Des Moines Register*, November 25, 2001, p. 2.

"Slice of History Roadside Restaurant Boasts Oldest Drive-in Service," *Fort Lauderdale Sun Sentinel*, April 2, 1990, p. 3A.

Speer, John, "Big T Maid-Rite Has New Operators," *Tama News Herald*, January 10, 2002.

Walkup, Carolyn, "New Maid-Rite Owners Seek to Make Chain's Menu Even Better," *Nation's Restaurant News*, April 29, 2002, p. 8.

—Sarah Ruth Lorenz

Marshall

Marshall Amplification plc

Denbigh Road, Bletchley
MK1 1DQ
United Kingdom
Telephone: (+44) 1908 375-411
Fax: (+44) 1908 376-118
Web site: http://www.marshallamps.com

Private Company
Founded: 1960
Employees: 400
NAIC: 335999 All Other Miscellaneous Electrical

Marshall Amplification plc manufactures one of the most recognized product lines in rock music. Since the early 1960s, Marshall amplifiers have produced what many musicians believe to be the sound that defines rock guitar. Succeeding generations of rock, blues, and heavy metal musicians have discovered and embraced Marshall equipment. Marshall produces a line of 120 products that include amp heads, speaker cabinets, combo amps, and stacks at prices that range from under $100 to about $2000. Over 70 percent of Marshall's sales are made to the low price end of the market. A workforce of more than 400 produces thousands of amplifiers every week at Marshall's state-of-the-art factory in Milton Keynes, England, for sale in more than 65 countries.

Jack of All Musical Trades

James Charles Marshall, the founder of Marshall Amplification, was born on July 29, 1923 in the English working-class town of North Kensington. At the age of five, he was diagnosed with tubercular bones, a condition that can leave the bones fragile and hypersensitive to pressure. As a result, he was confined to a full body cast in a local hospital for all of his childhood. When he emerged from the cast nine years later at age 14, Marshall rejected the idea of working in his father's fish-and-chips shop, opting instead for better paying jobs in local factories. At the same time, he took up tap dancing and singing and was soon performing in local music halls almost every night of the week. He later told Rick Maloof, ''I was earning as much money at 14 as any adult.'' Ineligible for

military service during World War II, Marshall sang with a jazz septet. When the group's drummer went off to the war, Marshall was persuaded to take his place.

It was a fateful decision. By the end of the 1940s, he had become one of the United Kingdom's top singers *and* drummers. During the 1950s, he began to teach drumming, in particular drumming for the upstart rock and roll music that was beginning to capture the imagination of young people in England. His lessons attracted so many students that Marshall was soon making more money as a teacher than from all his other work combined. By the end of the 1950s, Marshall had given up performing altogether to concentrate on teaching. In July 1960, he opened a drum shop, Jim Marshall & Son, in suburban London. The shop was an immediate success. He already had a loyal clientele composed of his drum students, some of whom would soon play a critical role in sixties rock. His drum students soon began to introduce him to guitarists. Drummer Keith Moon, for example, brought in Pete Townsend and bass player John Entwhistle, the three of whom, along with singer Roger Daltrey, would soon form The Who. Townsend began to badger Marshall to add guitars and amplifiers to his stock. ''We'd prefer to come to you than go to West End where we're treated like absolute idiots,'' Townsend told Marshall. Marshall added guitars and basses to his stock and was soon catering to the burgeoning London rock scene.

Developing the Marshall Sound

Players like Townsend and Deep Purple guitarist Ritchie Blackmore wanted more than mere amplifiers—they wanted a new sound. They were looking for amplifiers that were louder than others on the market, and they wanted a dirtier, more aggressive sound from these amps. For this, they turned to Jim Marshall. For one thing, Marshall had experience with amplification. He had built his own PA system while he was still singing, and during the war he had worked as an engineer. ''These players got onto me about building them an amplifier,'' Marshall told Rick Maloof, ''so I went to [service manager] Ken Bran, and said, 'Let's have a go at it.' '' Bran was willing but felt he did not have the specialized know-how that amplifier design required. However, he had heard of a young man working at the record label EMI, Dudley Craven, who had a reputation as an electronic whiz kid. Jim hired Craven immediately and the three men set to work creating a new guitar amp.

The bulk of the design of the amp was not original with Marshall's crew. Its starting point was the Fender Bassman amp, a popular model at the time. Craven and Bran tinkered with the Bassman's electronics. They experimented with various components purchased from cut-rate electronics surplus stores. Marshall's ears determined the course of what his team produced. "The players had told me what they wanted quite specifically, such that I could hear it in my mind what it should sound like," he told *Guitar Player*. Between July and September 1960, Marshall's team produced a series of prototypes. After each prototype was created, Marshall had rock guitarists—the musicians for whom he was designing the amp—put it through its paces. The first five models failed to reproduce the sound Marshall heard in his head. The sixth, however, was exactly what he had been hoping for and was christened the JTM45. It had a modest 45-watts of peak power, but after the first day in the window of Marshall's store he had 23 orders. This occurred at a time when it took nearly a week to build a single amplifier.

Business boomed. Six months after the first amp hit the market, Marshall's store moved to a larger space. For almost two years, Marshall amps were manufactured in a large empty room separate from the store. It was only in June 1964 that the firm moved its 15-man production staff into a Marshall-owned factory, a 30,00-square-foot facility in Hayes, Middlesex. Marshall's amps evolved rapidly. The original JTM45 consisted of two parts: the head, or electronic amplifier component, included an instrument input, tone and volume controls, and a power switch; the speaker cabinet housed two 12-inch speakers. Those two speakers were blown out repeatedly by the powerful 45-watt head. Worse still, they did not consistently produce the sound Marshall wanted. He modified the cabinet, stocking it with four 12-inch speakers that more efficiently used the amp's wattage and at the same time better projected the sound.

The next innovation came in 1964 when Eric Clapton, another guitarist on the cusp of superstardom, asked Marshall to build him a special amp. Clapton wanted the Marshall sound but in a smaller, more compact combo amp—an amp with the head and speakers in a single unit—that could be easily transported in the trunk of his car. Marshall responded with the Bluesbreaker. Its portability, its warm-yet-rough sound, and its price—the Bluesbreaker was half the price of comparable Fender amps—made the amp arguably the most important in the company's history.

Bigger and Louder Amps

In 1965, Pete Townsend came to Marshall with a new request. The Who were driving the volume of rock to previously unheard levels. Townsend asked Marshall for a 100-watt amplifier capable of producing sounds louder than anything Marshall

and his team had ever considered building. With it, Townsend asked for a cabinet with eight 12-inch speakers. Marshall said such a cabinet would be too heavy to move and offered to construct two four-speaker cabinets instead. Townsend insisted on the larger model. That was what roadies were for, he told Marshall. The Who's roadies, however, were anything but pleased with the monstrously heavy piece of equipment. Just weeks after he took delivery, Marshall recalled, Townsend returned the cabinet, asking if it could be cut in half. " 'I told him look, Pete, I can't do that because the bloody things will fall apart.' So I ended up doing what I wanted to do in the first place, which was the straight fronted cab with the angled one sitting on top." It was the birth of the stack, two 4 × 12 speaker cabinets, one on top of the other. It may be Marshall's most famous contribution to rock.

If Townsend and Clapton were the driving forces behind Marshall's innovations in amplifier technology, it was another icon—Jim Marshall's namesake—who put the Marshall name on the map in the United States and the rest of the world. Around 1966, Mitch Mitchell, another of Marshall's drum students, brought a young guitarist named James Marshall Hendrix—Jimi Hendrix—to the shop. Although he was still unknown at the time, Hendrix told Marshall that one day he would be the greatest name in the music world. Marshall thought it was a con. "I thought 'Cor, another Yank who wants something for nothing,' " Marshall told *The Australian*. In fact, Hendrix wanted to pay full list price for all his Marshall amps. What he insisted on was service whenever he needed it, wherever he was. Marshall responded by giving Hendrix's road crew a course in amp maintenance and repair at the Marshall factory. Throughout Hendrix's too-brief career, his roadies were able to deal with any problem with his amps. Hendrix was so committed to Marshall that he bought full rigs for North America, Europe, and Asia, so he would not have to transport a sound system overseas when he toured. Hendrix's use of Marshall equipment would soon make the brand legendary around the world.

Booming Business in the 1960s

By 1966, rock and roll was booming and so was Marshall's amplifier business. The company continued to develop new and improved products, such as a series of new amp heads that drove the Marshall sound harder than ever before. To cope with increased orders, a new factory was opened that doubled the firm's production capacity. That same year, Marshall's son Terry left to pursue a career as a musician, and the company was renamed Marshall Amplification. Business was so good that in 1996 the Rose Morris Agency approached Marshall about becoming the exclusive distributor of the company's goods. Marshall agreed to a 15-year pact. The contract barred the company from distributing amplifiers under the Marshall name. To continue to provide products to one of its loyal former distributors, Marshall launched a new brand—Park. Park amps, which were identical to the Marshall brand, except for the nameplate and price, remained in production until 1982. The company later developed another side brand, Kitchen-Marshall, for Kitchen's, a retail chain in the English city of Leed's. Kitchen's, who provided sound and lighting rigs for clubs and other venues in Leeds, asked Marshall to produce a Kitchen-brand PA system. Marshall offered a compromise, putting both firms' names on the system. The brand was on the market until about 1969.

Key Dates:

1923: Jim Marshall is born.
1937: Jim Marshall begins his career in music as a tap dancer and singer.
1949: Marshall begins offering drum lessons.
1960: The first Marshall music shop opens in London.
1962: Marshall produces his first amps.
1964: Marshall opens its first factory.
1965: Marshall produces the Bluesbreaker combo, the first 100-watt head, and the first stack amplifier.
1970: For a short time, Marshall offers its amps in a range of colors, including purple and orange.
1981: Marshall launches the JCM800 series.
1984: Marshall is awarded the Queen's Award for Export.
1987: Marshall releases the 25/50 silver Jubilee amp to celebrate Jim Marshall's 50th anniversary in the music business.
1991: Marshall introduces the hybrid Valvestate line of amps.
1992: Marshall Amplification celebrates its 30th anniversary; Marshall is awarded its second Queen's Award for Export.
1994: Jim Marshall becomes the second recipient of *Guitar Player* magazine's Leo Award for innovation in guitar equipment design.
2000: The AVT series is introduced.
2002: Marshall Amplification celebrates its 40th anniversary at the NAMM (National Association of Music Merchants) show in Anaheim, California.
2003: Jim Marshall celebrates his 80th birthday.

Jim Marshall soon regretted his alliance with Rose Morris. The distributor boosted the price of Marshall equipment so high—by approximately 55 percent—that it became prohibitively expensive for most musicians, especially in export markets like the United States. Over time, those artificially high process substantially depressed Marshall's amp business. To supplement the lost income Jim Marshall expanded into other areas, including the establishment of non-music shops and department stores in London. Even in this area, Marshall proved to be an able businessperson. In the late 1970s when the Rose Morris contract was about to expire, he sold the shop leases. "When I sold them in 1979," he told Rich Maloof, "I made far more money selling leases than I ever did from amplifiers."

A Growth Surge in the 1980s

The 1980s were a period of renewed growth for Marshall Amplification. With the expiration of the distribution contract with the Rose Morris Agency in 1981, Marshall was able to lower the retail prices of his amps to levels that made them affordable not only for headline acts but also for garage bands and hobby musicians. The company's sales surged. In the United States, in particular, sales increased 360 percent in a three-year period. The remarkable upswing earned Marshall the Queen's Award for Export in 1984. So successful was the firm during the 1980s that it was only natural it would be targeted for a takeover. In 1989, Harmon Instruments, a manufacturer of

musical instruments, offered £100 million in cash for the company together with a fifteen-year personal contract for Jim Marshall at £1 million a year. Marshall, who owned 100 percent of the business, refused the offer, and the company remained in Marshall's hands.

In the late 1980s, to meet growing international economic uncertainties, Marshall introduced a new emphasis on research and development. One result was a series of new amps for players of more modest means. Particularly noteworthy was the Valvestate line, a collection of hybrid amps that enabled Marshall to lower costs—and prices—by replacing the tubes in the power section with solid state circuitry while at the same time retaining much of the trademark Marshall sound. Other new products around that time included the JCM900 series and the JMP-1 MIDI pre-amp.

In the early 1990s, the company refurbished its factories with state-of-the art manufacturing systems that replaced hand-soldering and individual testing of products with a fully automated production system that also enabled Marshall to make all of its chassis in-house for the first time. The new equipment led to a quantum leap in the quality of finished goods and cut returns of defective merchandise to next to nothing. The changes made an impact. Between 1987 and 1994, sales increased by a remarkable 400 percent, winning Marshall a second Queen's Award for Export in 1992. In 1994, the company expanded its production once again, investing over $8 million in a new 60,000-square-foot factory next to its existing facility. Although the United States was the firm's largest market, Marshall told *Music Trades* he would never consider producing his amps there. "I've always wanted total control of manufacturing . . . under one roof . . . under my direction. . . . Rest assured, you will never see a Marshall product come from anywhere other than our plants in Milton Keynes." By 1995, Marshall's 350 employees were producing about 4000 cabinets every week with annual sales in more than 85 nations over $50 million.

As the years passed, Marshall amps have acquired a reputation that is legendary. The amps it built in the 1960s now sell for thousands of dollars. In the mid-1990s, to obtain three old models for the company museum, Jim Marshall had to spend approximately $20,000 for amps that originally sold for about $250 each. Marshall continued to refine its products in the 2000s. In 2002, the year Marshall celebrated its 40th anniversary, the company introduced a reissue series of its classic amps from the past, including the 2203ZW Zakk Wylde Signature model based on Marshall's JCM800 head. It also refined older technologies. The AVT series, introduced in 2000, represented the latest stage of the solid state power amp technology begun with Marshall's Valvestate amps. The company released a variety of new amps as well, most notably the MODE FOUR series, which combined tube, solid state, and digital technologies. It was a hit from the outset, winning high praise from guitar publications on both sides of the Atlantic.

Jim Marshall celebrated his 80th birthday in 2003. Despite his advanced age, he continued to be deeply involved in the day-to-day operations of the business and remained committed to maintaining full ownership of the company he built. "What would I do with the millions? You can only live in one house, drive one car, and eat one good meal a day. Anyway, I'm happy working. I'm a workaholic—been that way since the age of 14.'' he told the *Queensland Sunday Mail*. Marshall is actively involved in several charities, including Variety Club and the London Federation of Boys Clubs. Looking ahead to the future, Jim Marshall indicates that he intends to keep the firm growing as he moves through his eighties and nineties. As 2004 began, he was looking for ways to penetrate the African market.

Principal Competitors

Peavey Electronics Corporation; Fender Musical Instrument Corporation; Crate Amplifiers; Randall Amplifiers; Hughes & Kettner GmbH; Line 6, Inc.

Further Reading

Akbar, Arifa, ''Guitar Men Flock to Wembley for Festival Of Sound—But the Amp Man Steals the Show,'' *Independent*, May 12, 2003, p. 7.

Doyle, Michael, and Jon Eiche, *The History of Marshall: The Illustrated Story of ''The Sound of Rock,''* Milwaukee, Wis.: Hal Leonard Publications, 1993.

Holmes, Peter, ''Still Crankin' It Up,'' *Sydney Sun Herald*, May 9, 1999, p. 17.

Jinman, Richard, ''Amp Guru the Big Noise in Rock,'' *Australian*, June 27, 1996.

Maloof, Rich, *Jim Marshall: The Father of Loud: The Story of the World's Most Famous AMP Designer*, London: Backbeat Books, 2004.

''Marshall Doubles Production,'' *Music Trades*, October 1994, p. 97.

Molenda, Michael, ''Jim Marshall's 80th Birthday,'' *Guitar Player*, November 1, 2003, p. 26

Murray, Peter, ''Interview with Jim Marshall,'' *Canadian Musician*, October 1997, p. 26.

Perry, Andrew, ''Big Noise in Pop's Ear-splitting Quest,'' *Daily Telegraph*, August 2, 2003, p. 9.

''Pocket Timeline: Jim Marshall,'' *Guitar Player*, November 2003, p. 27.

''Rock 'n' roll Icon Jim Marshall Turns 80,'' *Music Trades*, September 2003.

Thompson, Art, ''The Second Annual Leo Award,'' *Guitar Player*, January 1994, p. 68.

Yorke, Ritchie, ''Jim's Past Speaks Volumes,'' *Queensland Sunday Mail*, April 25, 1999, p. 64.

—Gerald E. Brennan

O|O| MARUI CO., LTD.

Marui Company Ltd.

4-3-2 Nakano
Nakano-ku
Tokyo 164-8701
Japan
Telephone: (+03) 3384 0101
Fax: (+03) 5343 6640
Web site: http://www.0101.co.jp

Public Company
Incorporated: 1937
Employees: 10,517
Sales: ¥558.8 billion ($4.69 billion) (2003)
Stock Exchanges: Tokyo
Ticker Symbol: 8252
NAIC: 452110 Department Stores

Marui Company Ltd. is one of the largest department store chains in Japan, operating stores near major railroad stations in Tokyo. The chain's customers are predominantly fashion-conscious women and wealthy young Japanese in their late teens to early 30s. The company's stores sell a wide variety of merchandise, ranging from men's and women's apparel and accessories to furniture. Marui pioneered the use of credit shopping in Japan, and its store credit card is used by millions. During 2003, the company acquired full ownership of Virgin Megastores Japan and opened the first Marui department store in the Kansai region.

Origins

Marui's history dates back to 1931, when founder Chuji Aoi opened a store selling household utensils and furniture in the downtown Tokyo district of Nakano. Aoi was an energetic young retailer who saw a market opportunity and acted on it. Born in Toyama prefecture on the west coast of Japan in 1904, he graduated from the Takaoka Technological High School at the age of 18 and joined a Tokyo trading and retailing company, Maruni. The company was part of Zenshiro Tasaka's Maruzen group which, as a retailing chain, still existed in the early 1990s. The stores within the group were the first in Japan to allow customers to buy goods on monthly installment plans. Tasaka

had pioneered credit sales in Japan on the southern island of Kyushu in 1895 by selling lacquerware to customers on monthly installment plans. Chuji Aoi stayed with Maruni in Tokyo for nine years. Using savings and borrowed money, he then used his credit retailing experience to open his own store. The time seemed right for such an operation. The Tokyo region had been devastated in 1923 in the Great Kanto Earthquake. Although the city had largely been rebuilt, there was a high demand for furniture, and the prospect of credit sales was attractive to customers. The store was initially called Maruni, reflecting the initial capital provided by his old company. Aoi's venture flourished, and he increased his stock range to include clothes, shoes, electrical goods, and suitcases. By 1935, he had opened another store in nearby Asagaya. At the same time, the company name changed to Marui. In 1936, the business had expanded to such an extent that an adjacent building was acquired and the entire Nakano store renovated. The following year, in order to open a third store in the Tokyo district of Shimokitazawa, Aoi sold part of his share in the stores and formed Marui Co., Ltd., raising ¥50,000.

Postwar Growth

By 1939, Aoi had opened two more Marui stores in Tokyo. Although Japan's wartime economy boomed, it was not geared toward consumers. During the period 1941 to 1946, all Marui stores ceased business and were destroyed in the subsequent saturation bombing of Tokyo by the Allies. In August 1946, however, Aoi began selling furniture from the site of his old Nakano store. He was in effect starting again, and by 1947 he had rebuilt and reopened the store, with 1,190 square meters of sales space. Aoi had raised ¥200,000 in capital. Furniture was in high demand again in postwar Japan and the store flourished. By 1950, the number of stores had risen to five, and in that year four high school graduates joined the company as management trainees. The monthly payment schemes being offered by the company to customers were used to advertise Marui and differentiate it from its competitors. In 1951, many new products were stocked, such as baby clothes and bedding. A fleet of trucks was purchased for supplying and distributing goods to the stores, which by 1952 numbered eight. The first neon sign appeared over Marui's Shinjuku store in this year. In 1953,

Key Dates:

1931: Chuji Aoi opens a store in the downtown Tokyo district of Nakano.
1937: In order to expand, Aoi sells part of his shares in the stores and forms Marui Co. Ltd.
1947: Aoi rebuilds his Nakano store and reopens for business.
1959: The predecessor to advertising subsidiary AIM Create Co. Ltd. is established.
1960: The first Marui credit card is issued.
1975: The Red Card is launched.
1984: M&C Systems is established.
1990: Virgin Megastores Japan is created as a joint-venture.
2003: Marui acquires full ownership of Virgin Megastores Japan.

Japan's economic recovery began. Marui began advertising on the radio and selling gift vouchers that were valid in all eight stores. The company had become a chain with annual sales of more than ¥1 billion and 260 employees who had their own union. In 1955, customers were offered a ten-month payment scheme for selected goods. Opening hours were extended by instituting a shift system among the women counter sales staff—men counter staff did not participate.

Tadao Aoi, the son of the founder, joined the company in 1956 and was anxious to observe how credit sales chains operated in the United States. In 1957, he went on an inspection tour to look for new ideas. In 1959, Marui Advertising—now AIM Create Co., Ltd.—was formed to attend to the company's promotional needs. In the same year, Aoi established Maruishinpan to provide credit services to consumers. The following year saw the issue of the first Marui credit card and the establishment of Marui Transport—now Moving Co., Ltd.—which provided house-moving services.

The year 1961 was the 30th anniversary of the opening of Aoi's first store. There were by then 18 branches around Tokyo and sales totaled ¥5.7 billion. In 1962, the largest Marui branch was established by the renovation of the Shinjuku store. More than 2,000 square meters were added to the site, and the nine-story structure became one of the largest stores in the installment retail industry. The early 1960s marked a consumer boom in Japan and a time of expansion for Marui. In the period 1960 to 1967, sales floor space trebled to 35,000 square meters. A listing of Marui on the Tokyo Stock Exchange followed in 1963. In 1965, Aoi's son Tadao Aoi was promoted to vice-president in preparation for his eventual succession to the helm of Marui. The year 1966 was important for Marui as the company implemented its "scrap and build" policy of redeveloping its sites into large-scale stores that were cost-efficient and comfortable for customers. Most stores were affected.

Major capital investments were made in the operation of the stores with the introduction of an IBM 360 mainframe computer to handle the company's accounts and customers. To organize Marui's work force of 2,900, training schemes were introduced primarily for sales staff. By 1969, Japan had the second-largest gross national product in the world. A key part of this success lay in the high percentage of earnings that the average Japanese saved. The Japanese consumer at the time did not generally buy on credit. Marui's slogan at the time, "Play now, pay later," seemed to contradict this trend, but Marui provided for the young and not so cautious consumer who expected to be fairly well off in the near future. In 1971, the Marui Computer Centre was founded to centralize computer operations. Real estate and travel services began to be sold through Marui stores. An overseas trade department was set up within the company to handle imports of goods.

Success Continues in the 1970s and 1980s

An organizational change occurred in the company in 1972, with Chuji Aoi becoming chairman, allowing his son Tadao to take over the running of Marui as president. Tadao's brother Chuzaburo remained on the board of directors. In a 1974 cover story on world leaders, *Time* magazine featured Tadao Aoi along with the crown prince of Japan as representative of the country's rising leaders. In 1975, the Red Card, a house credit card, was offered to all Marui customers. The new cards had an initial interest rate charge of 9 percent, substantially higher than base rates, but the difficulty in arranging small consumer loans in Japan at the time attracted customers to Marui. In 1974, the company introduced on a trial basis a point-of-sales computer system to monitor transactions. The system was installed in all stores in 1977, linking them together and speeding up transaction time. This system greatly increased the number of Marui card holders. During this time, the number of Marui stores remained constant at 33, while the floor space was increased annually to reach 183,000 square meters in 1978. Constant renovation and the opening of specialty stores within existing stores accounted for the increase. Marui began to advertise its Red Card heavily and this, as well as the card's innovative nature, accounted for its success. The television and press advertisements were aimed primarily at the youth market and often won awards for their wit and originality. By the end of 1980, the number of card holders had reached four million. In the following year, Marui began offering consumer loans in the form of cash-dispensing services to customers.

At the company's 50th anniversary in 1981, it had annual sales of ¥260 billion and almost 7,000 employees. The company had by now developed expertise in the development of retail and credit control software. In 1984, Marui established the company M&C Systems to sell this knowledge to other retailers. Card holders could now withdraw money from all branches of Marui. Within a year, this feature had increased the number of holders to six million. Branches of Marui also had online information on exchange rates and other financial indicators.

In 1985, a new management division was added to the company to cope with the expanding work force. On the retail side, Marui continued the policy of expansion within existing sites and the opening of specialty boutiques within the stores. This strategy continued to be successful. By 1988, the combined membership figure for all card holders exceeded ten million. In 1990, Marui formed a joint venture with Richard Branson's Virgin Group in the United Kingdom in the establishment of Virgin Megastores Japan. The ownership of the company was split equally between Virgin and Marui, and the pilot plan was the opening of a small version of Virgin's UK megastores in Marui's Shinjuku branch.

The deal gave Marui excellent international publicity and increased its prestige among young Japanese consumers. For Virgin, it provided a foothold in the lucrative Japanese retail market while avoiding the excessive costs of renting or buying prime floor space in Tokyo.

Financially, Marui continued to grow steadily, increasing profits even in the wake of Japan's market crash in fiscal year 1990. During this time period, Marui had 464 cash-dispensing machines in operation, 69 of them outside Marui stores. Recently established service centers, separate from the stores, offered a wide range of financial services. The policy of developing specialty boutiques, such as the "In The Room" store in the Shibuya branch of Marui, was successful. In 1991, the company continued its slow but steady opening of new stores and set its sights on expand to the residential areas around Tokyo and possibly Osaka.

Overcoming Problems in the 1990s and Beyond

Tadao Aoi remained at the helm of Marui during the 1990s and into the early years of the new century. His leadership skills were put to the test, however, when Japan's economy bottomed out in the early 1990s. Consumer spending slowed and sales began to dwindle. Sure enough, the company reported a fall in pretax profits in fiscal 1992—the first time profits had dropped off since it went public in 1963. Sales and profits continued to wane as many customers spent their dollars at discount stores, leaving Japan's department stores in a pinch.

Marui and its peers faced yet another challenge in April 1997 when Japan raised its consumption tax from 3 percent to 5 percent. This tax increase, along with the crisis in Asia's financial sector, further weakened consumer confidence. Tadao Aoi commented on industry conditions in a 1997 *Nikkei Weekly* article, claiming, "I don't think consumer spending will pick up for some time. The situation will be even harsher next year than this year because the Japanese economy has several structural problems that it must address. It will take time for financial institutions to resolve the bad load problem and for the government to put its fiscal house in order."

Indeed, the dilemmas facing Japan's retail sector continued into the new century. Marui, however, was undeterred. The company set a strict strategy in place and continued to restructure certain business operations in an attempt to shore up sales. It fared better than many of its competitors, securing an increase in revenues during fiscal 2001 along with a significant jump in net profit, which rose by 78.9 percent over the previous year.

As part of its plan to penetrate new markets, Marui opened its first store in the Kansai region in 2003. The six-floor Kobe store featured 7,000 meters of floor space and included over 70 different retail vendors. The company announced that it planned to open a new store in Osaka as well. The location was slated to open in autumn 2006. Marui also acquired the remaining shares of its Virgin Megastores joint venture in 2003.

Along with its slow expansion plans, Marui also streamlined certain operations. It began to shut down its consumer electronics and home appliances departments in 2003 after they failed to meet profit expectations. The firm also announced that it would transfer a significant portion of its employees to specific subsidiaries. Overall, job count at company headquarters would fall to about 300 management-level employees, while approximately 5,500 personnel would be moved to 11 different subsidiaries. Seven hundred Marui employees opted for an early retirement package. The restructuring was designed to elevate customer service by allowing employees to specialize in one particular business area.

By November 2002, Japan's consumer price index had declined for 38 consecutive months. In a January 2003 *Nikkei Weekly* article, an analyst from UBS Warburg Japan Ltd. claimed, "For the first time in a decade or so, both income and consumer sentiment are simultaneously declining. We expect sales of luxury and durable goods to decline, which will negatively impact segments of the sector, such as department stores and discount electronic retailers." This news did not bode well for Marui; however, the company remained optimistic about its future. While its growth remained dependent on a turnaround in the Japanese economy, Marui had proved in recent years that it could overcome the problems brought on by sluggish sales and weak consumer spending.

Principal Subsidiaries

AIM Create Co Ltd.; Moving Co Ltd.; M&C Systems Co Ltd.; CSC Service Co Ltd.; Zero First Co Ltd.

Principal Competitors

The Daimaru Inc.; Seibu Department Stores Ltd.; Takashimaya Company Ltd.; Mitsukoshi Ltd.

Further Reading

Boyd, John, "Give Credit to Marui," *InformationWeek*, November 20, 1995.

Ishibashi, Asako, "Foreign Retailers Ignore Slump," *Nikkei Weekly*, January 6, 2003.

"Japan's Marui to Open First Osaka Store in 2006," *Asia Pulse*, October 9, 2003.

"Marui Exiting Home Electronics," *Nikkei Weekly*, August 25, 2003.

"Marui Opens Store in Kobe, its 1st Outlet in Kansai Region," *Japan Economic Newswire*, October 2, 2003.

"Marui's Recurring Profit Slips on Weak Sales," *Jiji Press Ticker Service*, March 24, 1998.

"Marui Reports 78.9% Jump in Consolidated Net Profits," *Japan Economic Newswire*, March 22, 2002.

"Marui Sees Lower Profit for '94 Amid Weaker Sales," *Japan Economic Newswire*, March 24, 1995.

"More Pain for Major Department Stores," *Nikkei Weekly*, February 22, 1999, p. 7.

"Retailer Leader Blames Taxes, Angst for Spending Slowdown," *Nikkei Weekly*, November 10, 1997, p. 3.

"Retailer Marui to Cut 95% of Workforce at Parent Firm," *Japan Economic Newswire*, August 12, 2003.

Terazono, Emiko, "Discounters Hurt Marui Profit," *Financial Times*, March 23, 1994, p. 34.

Thomson, Robert, "Marui Turns in First Loss since Stock Listing," *Financial Times*, March 25, 1992, p. 26.

—Dylan Tanner
—update: Christina M. Stansell

Monnaie de Paris

11, quai de Conti
75270 Paris Cedex 06
France
Telephone: (+33) 1 40 46 56 66
Fax: (+33) 1 40 46 57 00
Web site: http://www.monnaiedeparis.com

Government-Owned Agency
Employees: 9,673
Sales: EUR 2.3 billion ($$2.2 billion)(2002 est.)
NAIC: 339911 Jewelry (Including Precious Metal)
  Manufacturing

Monnaie de Paris is one of Europe's top money-issuing authorities. The French Mint, as the agency is also called, is attached to France's Ministry of Economy, Finance, and Industry, and is responsible for the production and issuing of the country's supply of euros. Monnaie de Paris manufactures coins and bills at two facilities—one in Paris and the other in Pessac, in the Gironde region near Bordeaux. The latter facility is a fully integrated site, with operations spanning metal production to packaging. Between 1998 and 2002, that facility produced more than nine billion coins for the launch of the euro. The state-run agency also manufactures foreign currency coins and bills. Through the Direction of Coins and Medals (DCM), Monnaie de Paris produces a wide range of commemorative coins (not just for the French government but also for the private and business sectors) and has extended its range to include art bronzes and even jewelry. In support of these activities, Monnaie de Paris began to hold thematic design compositions in 2003. The DCM is also responsible for the production of civil and military medals and related honor decorations for the French and other governments. In 2002, Dov Zerah was appointed as director of the Monnaie de Paris.

History of the French Franc

Charles the Bald became the first French monarch to assert control over the country's currency, proclaiming in 864 that the minting of coins was to be the exclusive province of the palace.

In 1358, the palace's minting powers were modified when oversight of the country's financial administration and the manufacture of its currency were separated. Production of coins was then given over to small workshops, which nonetheless acted under the authority of the crown.

The first record of a monetary unit known as the "franc" goes back to 1360. Captured by the English four years earlier in the midst of the Hundred Years War, John the Good had agreed to pay a ransom. In order to pay the ransom, the monarch ordered the creation of a new coin known as the "golden franc." The new coin served additional purposes, commemorating on the one hand that John the Good had been "franc'd" (freed) by the English, and, on the other, emphasizing the monarch's claim to sovereignty over France.

John the Good's franc, which continued to be minted for some 25 years, was just one of many currencies then in circulation in the country. Other versions of the franc appeared over the next two centuries, including a silver franc minted under Henri III starting in 1575. While that particular franc was withdrawn from circulation a decade later, the franc as a unit of common currency in France remained in circulation as half- and quarter-franc coins until 1642, when it was replaced by the livre (pound).

The next appearance of the franc proved more long-lasting. The French Revolution at the end of the 18th century brought about a call for a new French currency. The new government—which had not only adopted the metric system but also developed an entirely new calendar—officially established the franc as the country's monetary unit in 28 Thermidor Year III (August 15, 1795). The new coin was also placed under the metric system, subdivided into the decime, worth $\frac{1}{10}$th of a franc, and the centime, worth $\frac{1}{100}$th of a franc. At the same time, the weight of the full franc coin was fixed at 5 grams of .900 silver for a final weight of 4.5 grams, making the new coin roughly equivalent in value to the pound. Oversight of the new currency was given to a newly created body, later to be known as the Direction of Coins and Medals.

In 1803, the French government inaugurated a full-fledged coinage system based on the Franc Germinal, which officially

Company Perspectives:

The Direction of Coins and Medals' objective is to become a leading monetary institute of reference at the European level by building upon, on the one hand, its quality systems and industrial performance, and, on the other hand, its services to individual private and institutional clienteles, and by deploying a dynamic commercial strategy in the corporate gift and collector coin market segments.

established the weight of the French franc in silver. At that time, the range of issued coins included 50 and 25 cent pieces, as well as coins valued at two and five francs. The government also established larger currencies, 20 franc and 40 franc coins, which were minted in gold. This new monetary system, which linked the currency to both the silver and gold standards, proved the country's first modern currency and remained in effect until the outbreak of World War I.

The new franc resisted the many political upheavals in France, remaining the country's currency long after the end of the Revolution. While the portraits on the coins underwent a number of changes, the principle of the franc itself remained unchallenged. The strength of the French currency, at least in the first half of the 20th century, led a number of the country's neighbors to align their own currencies to the franc, starting with the Italian lire piemontaise in 1816 and including the Belgian and Swiss francs, the Greek drachma, and, finally the Spanish peseta in 1859.

A first attempt at European monetary union took place under Napoléon III with the creation of the Latin Union among France, Switzerland, Belgium, and Italy in 1865. Two years later, at the Universal Exposition, Napoléon proposed to extend that monetary alliance with the creation of an international currency. The idea failed to catch on, however, and the Latin Union succeeded in attracting only one other member, Greece, in 1868. In the meantime, the Union's use of both gold and silver standards compromised the franc. Dramatic increases in the production of silver had vastly lowered its value, leading to a flood of counterfeit silver coins into the Union's member nations. The silver standard remained in effect in France until 1928, when it was finally abandoned and gold became the de facto currency standard.

An important result of the currency crises resulting from silver's loss in value was the move by the French government to take control of the production of the country's currency. The first step was taken in 1876, when the government took over all production of silver franc coins, a move that was extended throughout the Latin Union two years later. Then, in 1879, the French government passed new legislation establishing the production of currency as the exclusive province of the state. This date marked the birth of the modern French Mint, the Monnaie de Paris.

Industrial production techniques enabled the Mint to increase its output. By the end of the century, the French Mint had reached production capacities of more than 22 million gold, silver, and bronze coins each year. The Mint had also become a major producer of foreign currencies as well, counting customers among a growing number of states, including Indo-China, Greece, Bolivia, Haiti, and Morocco.

New Franc in the 1950s

World War I not only put France's gold reserves under pressure, it made the manufacture of coins more costly as well. The Mint responded to the metal shortage, and to the war in general, by issuing a new series of bills featuring patriotic themes. The country also issued a new series of coins, made from nickel, featuring holes in the center in order to save on raw materials. The economic upheavals of the postwar period led to a rapid devaluation of paper-based currency in France and elsewhere. By 1926, the Latin Union was officially disbanded, and the franc itself was in danger of collapse.

The appointment of Raymond Poincaré as Finance Minister led, in 1928, to the stabilization of the country's currency around a devalued French franc—worth less than 20 percent of the former Franc Germinal. The currency reform meant that silver and gold-based coins were taken out of circulation and replaced by coins made of less valuable metals, particularly nickel, and a new series of designs. The Poincaré reforms rescued the franc, if only temporarily.

The Depression era revived the production of "pierced" coins, which were now made from a nickel-bronze alloy. By the end of the decade, zinc had been added to the mix. The occupation of France during World War II forced a new issue of coins, which replaced the slogan "Liberté, Fraternité, Egalité" with the Nazi-inspired "Work, Family, Country." These new coins, especially those of low value, were increasingly produced from zinc. One coin was even struck in iron.

Following the French liberation, the country issued a new set of currency. The French Mint also became responsible for the production of a new currency, the Franc CFA. During the war, France's colonial possessions had been placed under the French currency system. In 1948, the French government created the new currency for use throughout its zone of influence. The name CFA originally stood for Colonies Françaises d'Afrique. With the independence of nearly all of the countries within the CFA zone, the initials came to refer to "Communauté Financière Africaine."

In the meantime, France's rising postwar economy led to a new devaluation of the franc. In 1950, the French Mint began issuing a new series of coins featuring higher denominations. The new series included 10, 20, and 50 franc coins. These were supplemented with a 100 franc coin issued in 1954.

In 1958, the French government, under Charles de Gaulle, moved to reform the country's currency system as part of its commitment to economic stability. In that year, the government announced its intention to replace the existing currency with a "new" franc. The new currency system called for the emission of a revised range of coins and bills, which came into full circulation in the mid-1960s.

In 1973, the Monnaie de Paris decided to concentrate its coin production into a single facility, in Pessac, near Bordeaux. The new production plant gave the Mint a fully vertically integrated

Key Dates:

864: Charles the Bald asserts the French monarchy's control of production of currency.

1360: John the Good, after being ransomed from British captivity, introduces the first franc coin.

1795: The franc is adopted as France's official currency.

1803: A full-scale currency system based on the franc is developed; this action includes the creation of what will become the Monnaie de Paris.

1879: The French government passes legislation placing minting activities under the government's exclusive control.

1958: The French government, under Charles de Gaulle, announces creation of a "new" franc to replace the devalued old franc.

1973: The Monnaie de Paris builds a fully integrated coin production site in Pessac, near Bordeaux.

1979: The European Monetary System, a first step toward a common European currency, is adopted.

1998: Monnaie de Paris ends its production of the franc and launches full-scale production of euro coins, producing nine billion coins over four years.

1999: The euro becomes the officially monetary unit of the European Union.

2002: The euro begins circulation; Monnaie de Paris launches a restructuring program.

facility, from foundry operation to packaging. The site also took over production of medals and commemorative coins and developed into one of the world's major coin-production centers, enabling the Monnaie de Paris to continue producing coins for other countries. By the beginning of the new century, the Monnaie de Paris was responsible for the coin production for more than 30 countries.

New Currency for a New Century

The passage from the old to new franc gave France valuable experience for the next major revolution in the European currency market: the adoption of the euro. The creation of the European Common Market (EC) inspired new efforts to limit the fluctuation among European currencies. By the late 1970s, the EC countries had agreed to a first link among their currencies, launching the European Monetary System in 1979 and establishing a common unit of exchange, the "ecu."

Movement toward the creation of a truly common currency picked up speed with the passage of the Maastricht Treaty of 1992, which replaced the Common Market with the European Union and abolished trade barriers among member countries. The new union now turned toward creating its own currency, which, in 1995, was given the name "euro."

The euro was slated to become the official European monetary standard in 1999, with actual circulation of the new currency to begin on January 1, 2002. In the meantime, Monnaie de Paris turned its attention toward the herculean task of producing the bills and coins needed to replace the more than 12 billion

banknotes and seven billion coins then in circulation. The Department of Currency and Coinage began ramping up to that challenge in the mid-1990s, adopting a production strategy dubbed "Currency 2000," which included efficiency improvements at the Pessac facility.

The Monnaie de Paris was given the task not only of putting into place a production schedule for the euro but also of ensuring that the franc remained in full supply until the end of 2001. Indeed, as one of the world's most popular tourists destinations, hosting close to 100 million visitors each year, many coins fell out of circulation at the bottom of tourists' pockets. In preparation for the switch to the euro, the Pessac plant boosted its production output of franc coins.

At last, after striking a final, commemorative franc designed by Philippe Starck, the Monnaie de Paris converted its production to euro coins in May 1998. In 1999, the euro became the official currency of the European Union, although the use of euros took place only in the corporate and governmental sectors. By 2001, the government began preparing consumers for the "big bang." The first euro packs became available for purchase at the end of the year, allowing consumers to familiarize themselves with the new coins and leading up to the full-scale launch of the euro on January 1, 2002.

The Monnaie de Paris had successfully overseen production of more than nine billion coins in less than four years. The Mint and the Direction of Coins and Medals then began a restructuring program within a wider reorganization of France's Ministry of Economy, Finance, and Industry. The new strategy, launched at the end of 2002 and continued throughout 2003, involved a reorganization of the Mint's production facilities in Paris and Pessac in an effort to cut costs and enhance efficiency. An important part of the Monnaie de Paris' future strategy centered on its development as a design house for commemorative coins and medals, not only for government use but also for the corporate and consumer markets. As part of that effort, in 2003 the Monnaie de Paris launched the first of its design competitions, which were open to engravers, graphic designers, illustrators, and artists.

Principal Divisions

Direction of Coins and Medals; Department of Currency and Coinage.

Principal Competitors

Royal Mint; Royal Canadian Mint; U.S. Mint; Deutsche Bundesbank; De Koninklijke Nederlandse Munt; Fabrica Nacional de Moneda y Timbre.

Further Reading

Blume, Mary, "History Prepares France for the Daunting Euro," *International Herald Tribune*, April 4, 1998, p. 20.
"French Mint Forges ahead with Euro coin," *Metallurgica*, July 1999, p. 2.
Johnson, Jo, "Franc to Go out with a Bang," *Financial Times*, October 5, 2001, p. 12.

—M.L. Cohen

Norddeutsche Affinerie AG

Hovestrasse 50
D-20539 Hamburg
Germany
Telephone: (49) (40) 7883-0
Fax: (49) (40) 7883-2255
Web site: http://www.na-ag.com

Public Company
Incorporated: 1866 as Norddeutsche Affinerie-
   Gesellschaft AG
Employees: 3,612
Sales: EUR 1.9 billion ($2 billion) (2002)
Stock Exchanges: Frankfurt
Ticker Symbol: NDA
NAIC: 331411 Primary Smelting and Refining of Copper;
   331423 Secondary Smelting, Refining, and Alloying
   of Copper; 331421 Copper Rolling, Drawing, and
   Extruding

Norddeutsche Affinerie AG (NA) is the world's largest recycler of scrap copper and the fifth-largest producer of refined raw copper (copper cathodes). Based in Hamburg, Germany, the company ranks number three in the European market for copper wire rod, the material from which copper wire is produced. As a smelter that does not own ore mines, NA processes a great variety of copper-containing raw materials from different sources, concentrating mainly on copper concentrate made from ore, and charges a processing or refinement fee. NA is also a major producer of sulphuric acid (a by-product of copper production), iron silicate stone, and precious metals. NA's subsidiary Prymetall is a major manufacturer of half-finished copper products and holds a 50-percent stake in Schwermetall Halbzeugwerk, a leading producer of sheet copper. Copper accounts for roughly four-fifth of NA's metal sales, while the rest is derived from selling by-products of copper production, including lead, silver, and gold. The majority of the company's common stock is widely spread among institutional and private investors.

Smelting Silver and Gold in the 18th Century

Founded in 1866, Norddeutsche Affinerie AG is one of Germany's oldest joint stock corporations. However, the company's roots reach almost a whole century further back. In 1770, Hamburg's Senate approved the application of Marcus Salomon Beit to operate a small silver and gold smelting operation. The application of the 36-year-old Jewish-Portuguese entrepreneur came at a time when the value of money was fluctuating a great deal and many citizens—as well as banks—called for a new, stable silver currency. Although it took another 20 years until such a currency was finally introduced, Beit's smelter got enough business from its main client—Hamburger Bank—to survive. Around 1790, Marcus Salomon's brother Raphael Salomon joined as a business partner. At that time, Hamburg evolved as Europe's center for trading in silver, Hamburger Bank became the main institution for regulating the city's currency exchange, and the Beit brothers' smelter was the most important of its kind in Hamburg. Raphael Salomon Beit carried on the business after the founder's death and introduced new technology for separating the precious metals with the help of sulfuric acid, which was refined by his two sons John Raphael and Lipmann Raphael and later by their nephews, physician and chemist Ferdinand Beit and his brother Siegfried.

A new chapter of the Beit company—then called L.R. Beit & Co.—began in the middle of the 19th century, when the rise of industrialization brought about an increased demand for copper. The Beits already had some experience with copper as a by-product from smelting old coins and metal ore from a number of small southwestern German copper mines they owned. Together with entrepreneur Johann Caesar Godeffroy, who owned an ocean shipping business, and merchant Siegmund Robinow, a relative, the Beits founded a copper smelter on the Steinwerder, an island in the river Elbe in Hamburg's harbor in 1846. The following year, the *Elbkupferwerk*—the "Elbe copper plant"—started smelting South American copper ore, which was shipped there by Godeffroy; later, the plant began smelting ore from Swedish and Australian mines. The company made profits almost right away and developed into a healthy business.

The gold rushes in California and Australia and the discovery of new deposits of silver and silver-enriched copper around

Company Perspectives:

We stand for customer value, technological advantage, strong earnings, innovative power, and a leading position in environmental protection. The combination of copper production and the further processing into copper products and customized special solutions makes the NA-Group unique: two segments, fitted perfectly to one another. Our subsidiaries and shareholdings complement them ideally. Thus we occupy central market segments on the copper value chain. We guarantee our partners the best service and greatest value possible at every stage.

1850 resulted in a massive influx of precious metal into the European economy. The sudden economic boom inspired the owners of the *Elbkupferwerk*. In 1853, they decided to expand the plant and include a larger gold and silver smelter. However, a number of unfavorable circumstances doomed the endeavor to failure. It took three years to get the new facility approved by the city authorities—with many strings attached, for smelting was a "dirty business" that involved a great deal of chemicals, fumes, and toxic waste. When the approval finally came in 1856, the *Elbkupferwerk* was merged with the Beit business and transformed into a public stock corporation to finance the expansion. An outside investor, the Leipzig-based Allgemeine Deutsche Kreditanstalt, was won over by Ferdinand Beit's father-in-law, a banker in Frankfurt am Main. Allgemeine bought half of the shares of the new Elbhütten-Affinier- und Handelsgesellschaft, while Godeffroy and Beit held 25 percent each. After the necessary capital was secured, the completion of the new plant was greatly delayed because the machines needed were not delivered on time. Meanwhile, the Crimean War—in which France, England, and Turkey were allied against Russia—came to an end in 1856, after which there occurred an economic downturn that resulted in a decline in copper prices and demand. A financial crisis followed that brought Godeffroy to the verge of bankruptcy before he was bailed out by a wealthy aunt. At the same time, the stream of immigrants he had shipped to Australia began to slow down and diminished the number of trips his ships took there to bring back Australian copper ore. As the supply of copper ore dried up, the *Elbkupferwerk* ran out of raw material and was finally shut down in 1865.

A Second Start in 1866

One year before the economic crisis of 1857, Johann Caesar Godeffroy was one of the co-founders of a new bank in Hamburg, Norddeutsche Bank, which later became Germany's largest bank. Godeffroy became president of the bank's advisory board and Ferdinand Beit, then technical director of Elbhütten-Affinier- und Handelsgesellschaft, also joined the board. When the plant had to be closed in 1865, Godeffroy and Beit looked for a way to rescue the Beit family's smelter and asked Norddeutsche Bank for financial help. The bank saw a chance to obtain direct access to precious metals, which could be traded or used as a financial asset, and went along with Godeffroy and Beit's plan. Beit's smelter was taken out of the formally still existing Elbhütten-Affinier- und Handelsgesellschaft and re-founded as a joint stock corporation. On April 28, 1866, the

new entity was officially registered as Norddeutsche Affinerie AG. Norddeutsche Bank held roughly three-quarters of the company's share capital, Allgemeine Deutsche Creditanstalt held one-fifth, and the rest was held by four advisory board members of Norddeutsche Bank.

Despite political turmoil—mainly Prussia's war against Austria in 1866 and the Franco-Prussian War of 1870–71—the Breit family's smelter (now called Norddeutsche Affinerie, or simply NA) continued to reap healthy profits. Once again, the introduction of a new currency gave the business a major boost. After the German Empire had been formed in 1871, a new gold-based currency replaced the old silver-based one. The new German government assigned NA to smelt all outdated coins, most of which contained a significant proportion of copper along with about 30 percent silver. This contract was so large that the company had to expand its capacity. New smelting facilities were built on two newly purchased properties. In addition, NA took over a precious metal smelter with two sites, H.A. Jonas, Soehne & Co., in 1874. Ferdinand Beit's death in 1870 ended the Beit family's involvement in NA.

The development of a new technology—the separation of precious metals with the help of an electrical current, which was called electrowinning—contributed to NA's financial success and dynamic growth in the late 19th century. It was principally due to the efforts of chemist Emil Wohlwill, who began experimenting with this technology in 1871, that NA gained a significant competitive advantage for several decades. When Wohlwill, who was contracted to run the company's research laboratory, saw the first dynamo machine at the World Exhibition in Vienna in 1873, he had it shipped to Hamburg and used it for his experiments. Wohlwill focused his experiments on finding a better way to separate the copper and silver contained in the old German coins, because conventional mechanical separation was not very economical for this task. In 1875, NA ordered a larger dynamo machine for Wohlwill's experiments. One year later, the first installation for electrowinning copper started operations, producing about 21 kilograms of copper per hour.

With the help of this new technology, NA processed old silver coins worth 1.8 billion marks, yielding 11.5 million pounds of fine silver, until the end of 1879. Through the new process, NA's profits skyrocketed, enabling the company to pay between 36 and 55 percent in dividends to its shareholders.

A New Location and a New Leader in the Early 1900s

Until the end of the 19th century, smelting silver and gold remained NA's most important business, and the company established a reputation for high quality. However, as industrialization progressed, NA transformed itself from a smelter of precious metals into a supplier of raw materials for industry, specifically metals and related chemicals.

After all attempts to revive the production facilities of the former *Elbkupferwerk* on Steinwerder eventually failed, Elbhütten-Affinier- und Handelsgesellschaft was liquidated in 1884. More than 100 years old, the Beit family smelter remained NA's main production facility. However, the plant in Hamburg's Elbstrasse was not only run down and technically

Key Dates:

1770: Marcus Salomon Beit opens a silver smelter in Hamburg.
1866: Norddeutsche Affinerie AG is founded and acquires the Beit family business.
1876: The company pioneers copper-electrowinning.
1910: Metallgesellschaft and Degussa become NA shareholders.
1913: The company moves its operations to the Peute industrial park.
1920: Felix Warlimont becomes NA's CEO.
1924: NA begins the mass-production of sulphuric acid.
1926: British Metal Corporation becomes a major NA shareholder.
1928: The company takes over pesticide manufacturer Chemische Fabrik von J.E. Devirent A.G.
1932: The company starts making copper powder.
1949: NA's new facility for the continuous casting of copper goes into operation.
1963: The company takes over local competitor Zinnwerke Wilhelmsburg.
1972: NA's continuous cast wire rod production begins.
1985: A major investment program for modernization and environmental protection is launched.
1988: Major shareholder Metallgesellschaft becomes NA's sales agent.
1994: Metallgesellschaft's industrial leadership of NA ends.
1998: The company goes public on the Frankfurt Stock Exchange.
1999: NA acquires a majority stake in German competitor Hüttenwerke Kayser AG.
2002: The company takes over Prymetall GmbH & Co. KG and sells its chemicals and metal powder subsidiaries.

outdated, it had also been a constant nuisance for the people living in the neighborhood and offered no space for expansion. Therefore, plans for a brand-new larger production facility were developed in 1907. It soon became clear, though, that NA's financial resources were not sufficient to realize such a project. Two strategic partners and investors were found in Frankfurt-based metal trading firm Metallgesellschaft (MG) and in gold and silver smelter Deutsche Gold- und Silberscheideanstalt vorm. Roessler (Degussa), which financially backed the erection of a brand-new smelter in Hamburg's Peute industrial park, another island in the Elbe river. In the spring of 1910, NA's share capital was increased to include the two new shareholders, with MG and Degussa holding a 25 percent stake and Norddeutsche Bank holding about 39 percent. The remaining shares were held by private shareholders. Three months later, a brand-new copper-electrowinning facility started operations at the new location. Over the next four years, more and more facilities were added. Finally, in 1913, the old Elbstrasse plant was shut down.

Less than two years after the move, World War I broke out. During the five-year duration of the war, metal production and distribution was administered by the German War Ministry. In 1915, NA received a large contract from the ministry and agreed to double its production capacity for copper. The expansion was subsidized by the German government. In 1916, Norddeutsche Bank gave up its stake in NA and MG and Degussa became the company's major shareholders. During the war, NA workers who served in the army were replaced by prisoners of war. In 1919, NA shut down its silver smelting operations and transferred the silver-containing materials from the copper electrolysis to Degussa, where it was refined. The agreement lasted until 1923, but NA was not able to regain its earlier importance as a silver smelter.

As a result of World War I, Metallgesellschaft and Degussa lost an important metal smelter in the Netherlands near Antwerp. This turned out to be advantageous for NA, which was further expanded to take its place. In 1920, MG sent one of its executive directors, Felix Warlimont, to Hamburg to evaluate NA's future prospects. Warlimont, a metal-refining specialist, was appointed NA's CEO in the same year. Under his leadership, the existing facilities were expanded and modernized and new facilities were added to the Peute plant. To make NA competitive on the world market, Warlimont paid special attention to employing a mix of smelting processes, thus enabling the company to process a great variety of raw materials. He also focused on creating a modern, more efficient transportation system on NA's premises. By the mid-1930s, the company's product range had greatly expanded. Besides electrolytically purified copper, silver, gold, and platinum, it produced, nickel, tin, antimony, selenium, lead, and other metals, as well as alloys, copper powder, metal salts, and sulphuric acid. Slag from the smelting process was sold as construction material. By that time, NA also owned the ground on which the new facilities were built and was able to purchase additional land.

Growth and Destruction During and After World War II

After NA had survived the galloping inflation of the early 1920s and the economic depression that started in the fall of 1929, the company again became a crucial supplier to Germany's war industry during World War II. Again, metal became a major ingredient for the war economy. When raw material supplies from abroad began to dry out, the German government launched a national campaign asking the German people to donate metal. Everything from frying pans to church bells was shipped to Hamburg and melted and refined by NA. The company also produced aluminum powder that was used for making ammunition. Soon NA was not able to find enough workers and started employing forced labor from France, Belgium, the Netherlands, and Russia. Until the last few months of the war, NA's production facilities remained undamaged by the many Allied bombings of Hamburg. However, on November 4, 1944, an American bombing attack during work hours destroyed a number of facilities. Miraculously, only two NA employees were killed during the attack. However, two-thirds of NA's workforce was left without a roof over their heads. It was the scarcity of workers, fuel, and electricity that finally led to the shutdown of NA's last working facilities in February 1945. Two months later, British Allied troops marched into Hamburg.

After the war, NA's management fought fiercely for the company to be taken off the war reparations list and finally succeeded in mid-1946. The company's close connection with one of England's leading metal firms, the British Metal Corporation Ltd. (BMC), which became a major NA shareholder in 1928 when MG and Degussa each sold a 13-percent share, helped secure NA's first postwar contracts. At the same time, NA entered the pesticides and fertilizers market when the company started producing Dichlorodiphenyltrichloroethane (DDT), the basic chemical ingredient for many pesticides, in mid-1947. In 1928, NA had acquired a majority stake in pesticide manufacturer Chemische Fabrik von J.E. Devirent A.G., located in the southern German town Zwickau, and moved its production facilities to NA's Peute location. Devirent, which was later integrated into NA as a separate business division, used NA's DDT for making different kinds of pesticides.

After the currency reform in 1948, NA's smelting operations were back into full swing. Fortunately, the company was able to protect its reserves of metal concentrate from the attempts of different authorities to reallocate them. At the same time, the continuous repair work during and after the war paid off, and many facilities were in working condition by that time. In 1949, NA's new facility for the continuous casting of copper went into operation. Instead of mold-casting, the new technology allowed the final copper product to be put out in a continuous strand. The main advantage of this process was that the copper could be shaped according to a customer's specifications, including different forms such as round and square bars, sheets, strips and foils, as well as different dimensions.

While the chronic shortage of workers NA had been struggling with during World War II and in the first years after the war ended with the currency reform of 1948, the relief was short-lived. With standards of living constantly rising during the 1950s and 1960s, NA found it more and more difficult to recruit workers who were willing to work under the tough conditions of a metal and chemicals processing plant that required round-the-clock shifts. In 1958, the company established a shuttle bus for workers from Hamburg's surrounding areas. When that measure proved insufficient, NA started hiring workers from abroad. The first 228 foreign contract workers from Spain, Italy, and Greece were employed by NA in 1960. Five years later, the number of foreign workers, so-called *Gastarbeiter,* or guest workers, had roughly doubled. By 1973, the number of such workers was approaching 40 percent of the company's total production personnel.

In the 1960s, NA laid the groundwork for further expansion in the decades that followed. In 1963, the company took over Zinnwerke Wilhelmsburg GmbH, a smaller Hamburg-based copper smelter that nonetheless competed with giant NA. Within 12 months, NA closed down the former competitor's production plants and moved part of them onto its own grounds. By 1966, the size of NA's premises had grown more than sevenfold compared with the area the company occupied when it first moved to the *Peute*. One year later, that area doubled again when NA was able to acquire a large property nearby. This step enabled the company to build even bigger and more modern production facilities throughout the 1970s and 1980s.

Continuous Improvements after 1970

For NA, the 1970s were a decade of further expansion and modernization. A brand-new integrated copper foundry and smelter with an added-on sulphuric acid plant started operations in 1972. In the same year, NA took on the manufacture of continuous copper cast wire rod, a semi-finished product used to make copper wire. The company also became a major recycler of scrap copper after it had acquired a stake in Hamburg-based CABLO GmbH fuer Kabelzerlegung, a company that recycled copper cable and wire, in 1968. The recycling capacity for copper was further expanded during the 1990s through the construction of new recycling plants. By 1993, NA's ''secondary'' copper production from recycled scrap copper accounted for roughly one-third of the company's total copper output.

With environmental concerns mounting, NA focused on decreasing the environmental impact of its production facilities throughout the 1980s and 1990s. A major program to achieve that goal was launched in 1985. The company invested in new installations that purified process, waste, and rain water and reduced harmful emissions of toxic dust and gases into the air. Another area in which the company invested was recycling, including the re-use of process energy and the further processing of former waste products into saleable materials. The environmental program was accompanied by the continuous modernization of NA's production processes in terms of technology and efficiency. Altogether, the company invested about DM1 billion from the late 1980s until the end of the 1990s.

Beginning in 1987, NA's shareholder structure underwent major changes. In that year, the Australian international mining and metal processing conglomerate Mount Isa Mines Holdings (MIM) acquired 30 percent of NA's share capital. The company took over British Metal Corporation's 20 percent share and bought another 10 percent from Degussa. One year later, Metallgesellschaft took over control of the sale of NA's products. In September 1993, MG transferred its share in NA to one of its subsidiaries, Canadian copper producer Metall Mining Corporation (MMC), which became independent from MG in 1994 and was later renamed Inmet Mining Corporation. The year 1994 marked NA's independence from long-term shareholder MG. In 1998, major shareholder Degussa founded a joint venture with NA that focused on the refining and selling of precious metals. The new company was called Degussa-NA Edelmetall GmbH. In June of the same year, NA went public. By February 1999, the shares of MIM, Inmet Mining, and Degussa had shrunk to 10 percent each, while institutional investors held 30 percent; the remaining 40 percent was widely spread among private investors. One month later, Dresdner Bank acquired the stakes from MIM and Inmet Mining. By 2002, the bank's share had shrunk to 8 percent, while Hüttenwerke Kayser's parent company, L. Possehl & Co., held a 10 percent stake.

Throughout the 1990s and in the first years of the 21st century, market conditions remained extremely volatile. In the early 1990s, NA profited from the construction boom in the eastern German states that had joined the Federal Republic of Germany. However, for most of the decade Germany's economy grew only moderately and went into a recession in 2001. With Germany's construction industry being NA's single biggest market, the smelter's sales were closely linked to its development. Another significant factor that impacted NA's earnings was the world market prices for copper. Even as a ''smelter for hire''—one that does not own ore mines and therefore gets paid refinement charges for the service of smelting by the owner of the raw material—it depended on the demand for copper, which is closely connected with its price. A third major influence on NA's revenues was the value of the U.S. dollar—the currency in which the smelter is paid—which dramatically fluctuated between 1991 and 2003. As a result, NA's growing output, made possible by a copper smelting capacity expansion of more than one-third, often failed to translate into higher sales or profits. In an attempt to cut costs, the company laid off almost one-third of its workers in the second half of the 1990s.

Until the late 1990s, NA grew mostly internally. Further growth now became problematic due to limitations of physical space and the increasing hostility of Hamburg's inhabitants and its "green lobby" towards the company, which was seen as a major polluter. In the late 1990s, NA began to focus on external growth through acquisitions. In 1999, the company took over Germany's second largest copper producer, Hüttenwerke Kayser AG (Kayser) in Lünen, NA's main competitor in the area of scrap copper recycling. Kayser, which employed about 700 workers, slipped deeply into the red in 1998 when copper prices dropped sharply.

The 1990s also confronted NA with mounting energy costs, which were attributable in part to such factors as additional production capacity, environmentally friendly installations which required more energy, and, late in the decade, by rising taxes on the use of primary energy and fuels. When Germany's government launched a new law that significantly raised NA's energy cost, the company announced that it would spin off all of its less energy-intensive activities with about half of the company's employees into an independent business division.

A major slump in sales and profits hit NA in 2001 and worsened in 2002 and 2003, mainly because of severe losses in the copper products division. However, despite worldwide copper production overcapacities, NA's CEO since 1994, Werner Marnette, saw the company's future as promising. NA's raw material supply was secured by long-term contracts until about 2010. Marnette projected a strong demand from worldwide investments in infrastructure projects and telecommunications—two copper-intensive industries—with North America and Asia being important growth regions. He also saw NA well positioned geographically by its proximity to one of the world's major ports and to several of the most industrially developed countries on the global scene. To further enhance NA's position in the copper value chain, he was looking for strategic partners in the copper products industry. A major step in that direction was the acquisition of Prymetall GmbH & Co. KG, a major

manufacturer of unfinished copper products, in 2002. The acquisition also gave NA access to Schwermetall Halbzeugwerk GmbH & Co. KG, a leading manufacturer of sheet copper, in which Prymetall held a 50-percent stake. Also in 2002, NA sold its subsidiaries in the field of chemicals and metal powder, MicroMet GmbH Pulvertechnologie and Spiess-Urania Chemicals GmbH, which the company had spun off into independent units in 1999, to focus on its core business: the production of copper and copper products.

Principal Subsidiaries

Hüttenwerke Kayser AG; Retorte Ulrich Scharrer GmbH; CABLO Metall-Recycling & Handel GmbH; Prymetall GmbH & Co. KG; Schwermetall Halbzeugwerk GmbH & Co. KG (50%); Deutsche Giessdraht GmbH (60%).

Principal Competitors

Freeport-McMoRan Copper & Gold Inc.; Generale Industrie Metallurgiche S.p.A.; n.v. Umicore s.a.

Further Reading

Asendorf, Manfred, *125 Jahre Norddeutsche Affinerie Aktiengesellschaft*, Hamburg, Germany: Norddeutsche Affinerie AG, 1991, 131 p.

"Aus 50 Milliarden alten Muenzen entstehen bald neue Produkte," *Frankfurter Allgemeine Zeitung*, August 14, 2001, p. 14.

"Billiges Kupfer drueckt den Umsatz," *Sueddeutsche Zeitung*, March 14, 1992.

"Der Dollar verhagelt das Ergebnis," *Frankfurter Allgemeine Zeitung*, March 25, 1995, p. 14.

"Der Preisverfall bei Kupfer belastet das Ergebnis," *Frankfurter Allgemeine Zeitung*, March 10, 1994, p. 22.

"Die Huette am Markt soll schon bald Boersenwert warden," *Frankfurter Allgemeine Zeitung*, March 20, 1998, p. 29.

"Der Kupferabsatz bleibt auf hohem Niveau," *Frankfurter Allgemeine Zeitung*, March 8, 1993, p. 18.

"Die Metallgesellschaft ordnet ihr Kupfergeschaeft neu," *Frankfurter Allgemeine Zeitung*, August 19, 1993, p. 12.

"Die Norddeutsche Affinerie fuehlt sich gut geruestet," *Frankfurter Allgemeine Zeitung*, March 13, 1996, p. 28.

Prior, Karl, *100 Jahre Norddeutsche Affinerie*, Hamburg, Germany: Norddeutsche Affinerie AG, 1966, 109 p.

"Das Unternehmergespraech," *Frankfurter Allgemeine Zeitung*, April 29, 1996, p. 18.

—Evelyn Hauser

Olan Mills, Inc.

4325 Amnicola Highway
Chattanooga, Tennessee 37422-3456
U.S.A.
Telephone: (432) 622-5141
Fax: (432) 629-8128
Web site: http://olanmills.com

Private Company
Founded: 1932
Employees: 3,700 (est.)
Sales: $290 million (2001 est.)
NAIC: 541921 Photographic Studios, Portrait

Olan Mills, Inc. is one of the largest portrait photography operations in the United States and also operates in the United Kingdom. The Chattanooga, Tennessee-based, privately owned company divides its business into two divisions: Studio Portraits and Church Directories. At one time, Olan Mills operated 1,000 free-standing studios, but in recent years, to keep pace with the competition, it has opted instead to place studios in Kmart stores. Kmart's bankruptcy has complicated this shift in strategy, as Olan Mills has been forced to close studios in many Kmart locations. It continues to operate 125 free-standing studios in the United States and Puerto Rico and another 100 in the United Kingdom. The company is now starting to open studios in the stores of other retailers, such as Meijer's, Value City, and Toys 'R' Us. Olan Mills is owned by its chairman, Olan Mills II, the son of the company's founder.

Business Founded in 1932

Olan Mills, Sr., a former real estate salesman, and his wife Mary launched their business in Selma, Alabama, in 1932. Working out of an old woodshed they had converted into a darkroom, they started out in the photo restoration business. However, the couple had more ambitious plans—to make studio-quality photographic portraits available to the average person. At first, they took the studio to the customers, with the processing done at a bankrupt studio in Tuscaloosa, Alabama, they

were able to pick up. Both went door-to-door, selling their concept throughout the South, with Olan Mills also serving as the photographer. Mary Mills, an artist in her own right, divided her time between selling and work in Tuscaloosa, where she added color and other distinctive touches to give a more refined look to their black and white photographs. She would later be the driving force in the training of the artists that would come to work for the studios. By 1935, the Mills had settled on a look that would become forever associated with the photographs produced by Olan Mills Studios and portraits in general from this period: a black and white bust vignette set against an airbrushed background. A hand-signed logo on each picture helped to build the Olan Mills brand name. Despite the depression of the 1930s, Olan Mills was able to land enough business so that in 1938 the company opened its first permanent studio, located in Pine Bluff, Arkansas. It was soon followed by another operation in Terre Haute, Indiana. By the end of the decade, Olan Mills studios and its growing stable of photographers would be serving 29 states.

During the 1940s, the company grew on a number of fronts. In 1940, it opened its first plant in Springfield, Ohio. It also began to change its marketing approach, supplementing its door-to-door efforts with a bond program mailing. A more significant shift in the way the company reached new customers would follow later in the decade, but in the meantime Olan Mills had to contend with the difficulties of doing business during World War II. With the military commandeering so many raw materials, the company's salespeople were hard put to find enough gasoline, not to mention tires and auto repair parts, in order to travel their routes. Film and chemicals for development were also in short supply. In fact, film became so scarce during this time that Olan Mills was forced to innovate. A new film was developed, four-way sliding backs, which allowed one piece of 5 × 7 film to accommodate four separate shots. In this way, a photographer could shoot a complete sitting of four poses on a single piece of film. Olan Mills also took advantage of the war to open studios near the military bases that were established across the country, filling the vast need for photographs for service men and their loved ones, who were often separated for extended periods of time. The com-

Company Perspectives:

Olan Mills knows the key to a great portrait is making sure you and your family feel comfortable and look natural.

pany also built up a trained staff, hiring a number of military wives, who would then be needed during the postwar growth years as the Baby Boom generation began to have their lives chronicled on film.

In 1948, Olan Mills became involved in telemarketing—essentially by chance. One of the company's salesmen overheard someone pitching their product over the telephone and decided on his own to give selling photographs by phone a try. It worked: his weekly sales improved by an impressive 400 percent. Olan Mills, Sr. seized on the idea and had additional telephone lines installed and hired telephone solicitors. The method proved effective and was further refined over the years. In order to maintain the personal touch, key to making sales, each Olan Mills studio would be limited to contacting potential customers in their area. Moreover, the telemarketers were also local, selling to people who lived in their own community. While competitors would eventually attempt to emulate Olan Mills' success with phone sales, none possessed the same level of commitment to telemarketing in spite of its high employee turnover rate and other drawbacks.

Although telemarketing was a great help in growing the business, Olan Mills still faced a problem of seasonality. Customers were eager to have photographs taken during the holiday season in December, but business was slow at other times of the year, and even if the company laid off people during slack periods, it still had to pay for the fixed costs such as rent. To address this cash flow problem, Olan Mills, Sr. conceived of an innovative solution in 1952. Telemarketers began to sell a package deal, what would become known as a Club Plan. For three dollars, customers received three sittings that could be taken at any time during a 12-month period (40 years later the price for the plan would be just $15). Because most customers would order more pictures after their second or third sittings, Olan Mills was able to generate cash flow throughout the year. The 1950s also saw the company adopt some significant technical advances, such as the Battie camera and speed lights. Other equipment helped the company deal with the large volume of pictures its photographers were now taking. Centrifugal film dryers, for instance, were a vast improvement over the days of using clothes pins to hang film from a wire stretched across the darkroom. To generate large numbers of prints in a short period of time, equipment that was used to make blue prints was converted to fill the needs of the Olan Mills studios.

More technical advances followed in the 1960s, in particular the switch to all-color photographic work. The company took the old four-way sliding back approach of the 1940s and applied it to a new two-way camera, which could use a 70-millimeter film magazine split between black and white and color film. The results were proofs in both black and white and color. However, the color results from the camera proved to be so outstanding

that the company chose to the drop black and white and devote itself entirely to color photography.

A second generation of the Mills family—brothers Olan Mills II and Charles George Mills—began to assume greater control of the business in the 1960s. The elder son, Olan Mills II, was born in 1930 and went to work for the family business after graduating from Princeton University in 1952. Charles was born seven years later, graduated from Auburn University, and served in the military before joining his brother at Olan Mills, Inc. They assumed complete control of the business in 1972. Ownership would be split between the two, with Olan Mills II controlling 51 percent and his brother 49 percent. By this point, Olan Mills was generating an estimated $20 million a year, but with a new generation in charge the company was poised for even greater growth.

Olan Mills moved its headquarters to Chattanooga, and new studios sprouted up across the country, virtually one or two every week. They were situated in major cities as well as such small towns as Opelika, Alabama; Puyallup, Washington; and Xenia, Ohio. In addition, new plants were opened and the service departments were upgraded. As had been the case throughout its history, Olan Mills embraced new technology, adding computers and laser scanners to its operations. Second generation ownership also targeted new markets. While the company got its start by focusing on baby pictures, it faced increased competition in the family segment and as a result branched into new areas. It became involved in the school and yearbook business, the lucrative church directory business, and later moved into glamour photography, an upper-end product for people who wanted a more glossy magazine look for themselves. In 1981, Olan Mills expanded overseas, establishing a business in the United Kingdom, transferring the same techniques that proved so successful in the United States. The company's national competition focused on the pre-school market, a segment which now accounted for less than 30 percent of Olan Mills' business. Where Olan Mills prospered was in the follow-up business as customers grew up. In the adult portrait market, no rival could match Olan Mill's name recognition, and the company held numerous advantages over the local mom-and-pop studios that served as its competition in this segment. Having given up on copying Olan Mill's telemarketing program, larger competitors elected to open small studios in retailers like Sears, JC Penney, and Wal-Mart.

Some 20 years after the Mills brothers took charge of the business, Olan Mills was generating approximately $475 million in annual sales, controlling about 10 percent of the $5 billion portrait photography business. Its closest competitor, CPI Corporation, had just half as much market share. However, starting in the mid-1990s, the conservatively run Olan Mills began to lose its grip on the market as the dynamics of the industry changed and the affiliation between studios and big box retailers became a key factor. Olan Mills' top three rivals had such deals: CPI Corporation with Sears, Lifetouch with JC Penney and Target stores, and PCA International Inc. with Kmart and Wal-Mart. With business falling off from more than 30 percent in revenues from its record year, Olan Mills shut down a Waco, Texas, plant and closed some 300 freestanding studios around the country. Then, in August 1998, the company took the plunge and signed a deal with Kmart to start opening studios in some of the retailer's stores, replacing the more downscale PCA operation. For Kmart, adding Olan Mills was part of a strategy to revitalize its business in the wake of the tremendous growth of Wal-Mart. Research indicated that Kmart was attracting customers with much less income than those who shopped at Wal-Mart, on average $10,000 to $20,000 less. To attract customers with more disposable income, Kmart decided to incorporate signature product lines, such as Martha Stewart, Disney, and Sesame Street. The Olan Mills' name was in keeping with this strategy.

The year 1998 was also a time of change for Olan Mills on another front. In January of that year, Charles Mills died, leaving his older brother in charge, although the chief executive responsibilities had been handled by a non-family member since 1990, with Olan Mills II serving as chairman. None of the children of the two brothers were actively engaged in the company's business with their involvement essentially limited to a "cousin's council," which received regular briefings on the state of the business from senior management.

Changes at Olan Mills continued in the final years of the 1990s. Wholly owned subsidiary Olan Mills School Portraits, Inc. was sold in early 1999 to Lifetouch National School Studios. Olan Mills had been involved in this segment since the 1960s but now management decided it would be wiser to focus its attention and resources on the more lucrative church directory business and its Kmart initiative. In addition, Olan Mills eliminated its telemarketing promotions and closed scores of freestanding studios to concentrate on its Kmart studios, leaving

just 125 freestanding operations. According to the press, Olan Mills suffered through a poor year in 2001, although business rebounded in 2002.

When Kmart filed for bankruptcy early in 2002, Olan Mills was quick to assert that its portrait business would not be adversely impacted. While Kmart planned on closing several hundred of its more than 2,100 stores, most of these units were performing poorly, and Olan Mills had establishments located primarily in the more successful Big K superstores and other high-volume locations. All told, Olan Mills operated about 850 studios in the Kmart chain. Although losses were generally offset by the opening of new studios in surviving Kmart locations, problems at the giant retailer continued to worsen, and by early 2003 Olan Mills had lost close to 250 Kmart studios. To make up for this loss in business, Olan Mills began opening studios in Meijer's, Value City, and Toy 'R' Us locations. It also made other changes, including the elimination of a Springfield, Ohio, processing plant, the operations of which were consolidated with the main Chattanooga facility. With no third generation of the Mills family willing or ready to take over, and Olan Mills II well into his 70s, the future of the company faced a number of challenges.

Principal Divisions

Church Directories; Studio Portraits.

Principal Competitors

CPI Corporation; Lifetouch Inc.; PCA International, Inc.

Further Reading

Flessner, Dave, "Photography Company Olan Mills Plans to Continue Relationship with Kmart," *Chattanooga Times/Free Press*, January 24, 2002.

——, "Portrait Chain Cuts Chattanooga, Tenn., Staff by 44 Workers," *Chattanooga, Times/Free Press*, February 21, 2003.

Payne, Melanie, "Olan Mills Reportedly to Put Portrait Studios in Kmart Stores," *Knight-Ridder/Tribune Business News*, August 19, 1998.

" 'We Got on the Phone,' " *Forbes,* March 1, 1993, p. 94.

—Ed Dinger

Omaha Steaks International Inc.

11030 O Street
Omaha, Nebraska 68137
U.S.A.
Telephone: (402) 597-3000
Toll Free: (800) 960-8400
Fax: (402) 597-8277
Web site: http://www.omahasteaks.com

Private Company
Founded: 1917 as Table Supply Meat Company
Employees: 1,800
Sales: $353 million (2003)
NAIC: 424470 Meat and Meat Product Merchant
   Wholesalers

Based in Omaha, Nebraska, Omaha Steaks International Inc. manufactures, markets, and distributes premium cuts of beef, as well as pork, lamb, poultry, seafood, desserts, and kosher items. It also markets food seasonings and a series of cookbooks. Best known for its mail order business, Omaha Steaks has always been quick to embrace new technologies, such as the Internet, which the company began to use as early as 1990. The company has 1.6 million active customers. Meats are flash frozen, shrink wrapped, and then shipped in insulated coolers packed with dry ice. Omaha Steaks also sells its products to food service customers (high-end restaurants and hotels), to corporations through an incentive program, and in more than 70 retail stores bearing the Omaha Steaks name. In addition, the company sells entire meals through its A La Zing subsidiary, a separate Web business, and licenses its name to six restaurants, dubbed Omaha Steakhouses. Omaha Steaks is owned and operated by the fourth and fifth generation of the Simon family.

Company Founded in 1917

Like many immigrants, the first two generations of the Simon family, J.J. Simon and his son, B.A., came to America to escape religious persecution. They arrived in 1898 and after passing through Ellis Island took a train west in search of a place to settle. They chose Omaha because it reminded them of the farmland they had left behind in Riga, Latvia. Experienced butchers, they worked for nearly 20 years for other people. Then, in 1917, they struck out on their own, buying a carpentry shop in downtown Omaha to house a business that cut cattle carcasses. Sheer frugality led them to name their venture ''Table Supply Meat Co.'' The prior establishment had been called ''Table Supply Company.'' By abbreviating ''Company'' to ''Co.,'' they were able to insert ''Meat,'' thus avoiding the cost of adding an entirely new sign to the front of the building. The area restaurants and grocers could not have cared less about the name of the business, as long as the Simons were able to them with high quality, grain-fed cuts of beef—loin, ribs, boneless strips, and rib eyes.

Table Supply grew steadily, and by 1924 the Simons were able to move their operation to larger accommodations, although they opted to retain the name inherited from the old carpentry shop. They were also able to establish their own cattle-breaking operation to further ensure quality, allowing a crew to cut full cattle carcasses on the spot. The result was uniform cuts of meat that Table Supply was then able to sell to higher-end hotels, restaurants, and other institutional customers, as well as to the national grocery chains that were beginning to take shape across the country. In 1929, a third generation of the Simon family, B.A.'s son Lester, became involved in the business. He took over as president in 1946 and guided Table Supply through the next stage of its development.

Union Pacific Railroad Spurs Growth in the 1940s

A major development during the 1940s was the decision of the Union Pacific Railroad to serve Table Supply beef in its dining and private cars that traveled from Omaha to the West Coast. Leaving nothing to chance, Lester Simon personally selected the cuts to be sold to Union Pacific. As a result, Table Supply's reputation for providing top quality beef was spread ever wider, so that soon hotels and restaurants around the country were inquiring about becoming customers. The focus of the company now shifted from cutting to marketing, as the Simons recognized that consolidation was taking place in the beef breaking business and it was time to change strategies. In 1952, the first mail order operation was launched to serve distant customers. The meat was shipped in wax-lined cartons filled with dry ice. It was not until the early 1960s that polystyrene shipping coolers and vacuum packaging became available. The rise of direct parcel shipping was also a boon to the marketing efforts of Table Supply. Moreover, the company's reputation for quality continued to grow. In 1961, Nebraska Governor Frank B. Morrison sent steaks from Table Supply to President Kennedy and all of the governors in the United States. In that same year, Table Supply was honored to be involved in the Culinary Olympics held in Frankfurt, Germany, at which the United States team won the Grand Gold Prize with a dish that featured aged prime ribs of beef provided by Table Supply, thereby earning an international reputation for the Omaha company. Table Supply's cuts of beef would be shipped around the world to be enjoyed at the dinner tables of heads of states and other dignitaries.

Table Supply mailed its first direct mail flyers and catalogs in 1963. After just a year, the catalog was enhanced from simple black and white to color and presented an expanded offering of the company's products. In 1965, Table Supply launched an incentive division and began to build a nationwide network of representatives to help businesses create and implement promotion and reward programs. Eventually the division would publish its own catalog and, with the rise of the Internet, create its own Web presence. This market proved so lucrative that in time one-quarter of the company's business would take place in December, the month when many corporations gave food to their employees as holiday gifts. Business was so strong that in 1966 Table Supply built a new headquarters and plant that attracted visitors from around the world interested in the state-of-the-art facilities. The company also took the opportunity in 1966 to renamed itself, becoming Omaha Steaks International Inc..

To fuel further growth in its mail order and catalog business, Omaha Steaks was always in the vanguard of adopting the latest technology. In 1975, it opened an inbound call center, offering a toll-free telephone number to take catalog orders. Three years later, an outbound telemarketing operation was launched to contact current customers. The company did not, however, engage in cold calling. In 1979, a toll-free customer service line was added to the system. Then, in 1987, an automated order entry system was implemented. Omaha Steaks' catalog and telephone system was finely honed in the years to come. A complete catalog would be mailed to customers three times a year and solo mailers were sent out as often as once a month. Order forms came pre-addressed and coded to increase the efficiency of processing orders. Telephone representatives were given a full week of training on the products Omaha Steak had to offer, making them ''steak experts'' who were able to explain to customers the difference between various cuts of meat. During the rush of a holiday season, in fact, everyone at the headquarters would be commandeered to work the phones and take orders.

Omaha Steaks first became involved in retail operations in 1976, when it opened a store in Omaha at 79th and Dodge Streets. Over the next several years, other stores opened in Nebraska. It was not until 1985, though, that the company ventured beyond the state, opening a retail store in Houston. Over the next 20 years, more than 60 additional stores opened in Arizona, Connecticut, Florida, Georgia, Illinois, Maryland, Michigan, New Jersey, New York, Ohio, Pennsylvania, and Virginia. Texas had the most with 11 (three in Houston alone), followed by California and Florida with nine each.

As was the case with telecommunications, Omaha Steaks was an early user of electronic marketing, starting in 1990 before the creation of the graphic interface and the resulting emergence of the Internet. At that time, the company worked through CompuServe to provide customers with yet another way to place orders. In 1995, Omaha Steaks began to sell on America Online and also launched its own web page, offering an abridged version of its catalog to online customers. The company became part of the Microsoft Network in 1998 and a year later even launched a Japanese web site.

Because of strong growth during the 1990s, Omaha Steaks continually outgrew it facilities. In 1990, a new distribution center was created in a building bought in South Omaha. A 60,000-square-foot facility was built in 1993 to accommodate a number of departments, including human resources, marketing, information technology, and a call center. A building of similar size was opened nearby in 1999 to house the company's corporate and executives offices as well as administrative and marketing functions. In 1994, a new manufacturing plant was built in Snyder, Nebraska. Additional cold storage facilities were added in 1998 and 2000.

In the 1990s, Omaha Steaks made efforts to build on its brand and to achieve some diversification. In 1996, it teamed with HSC Hospitality Inc. to launch restaurants bearing the Omaha Steaks name. HSC was founded in 1990 by Peter Grace III, the son of W.R. Grace, a businessman involved in such restaurant chains as Houlihan's and Del Taco. HSC managed the food service operations at 14 hotels across the country and looked to place the new Omaha Steakhouses in hotels. Under a licensing agreement with Omaha Steaks, HSC would have complete operational control of the restaurants but would use the products of Omaha Steaks' food service division. The first Omaha Steakhouse opened in a Phoenix hotel in the fall of 1996. A larger restaurant would follow in an Embassy Suites Hotel in Charlotte, North Carolina. In 2001, the Kingston Plantation, a Myrtle Beach resort, opened an Omaha Steakhouse. A year later, a unit opened in a Sheraton Suites Hotel in Houston. Two more Omaha Steakhouses opened in 2003, at Embassy Suites' hotels in Jacksonville and Orlando, Florida.

Focus on Corporate Business in the Mid-1990s

Another area where Omaha Steaks focused on growing was its corporate sales unit, which it began beefing up in the mid-1990s. The corporate gift market was appealing, given that the average order ranged from $150 to $500, as opposed to $75 to $125 from the consumer food catalog. However, applying the company's consumer marketing expertise to corporate customers was not an easy task, primarily because corporate gift

Key Dates:

1898: The Simon family emigrates to America.
1917: The Simons start a company in an old carpentry shop.
1952: The company's first mail-order venture is launched.
1966: The name Omaha Steaks is adopted.
1976: Omaha Steaks' first retail store is opened.
1995: The company launches a Web site.
2003: Pet treats are introduced.

buyers tended to do business with vendors they had been working with on a long-term basis. Omaha Steaks created a separate corporate catalog, but unlike its consumer counterparts such publications were not geared toward establishing customer relationships. Rather, they were intended to serve the corporate buyers who were already customers. Another difference was that Omaha Steaks had to produce reminder notices, including a list of prior gift purchases, which was standard operating procedure in the market. These notices had to be periodically mailed from August through October to make sure that Omaha Steaks remained in the minds of corporate buyers when it came time for them to actually place their holiday orders. The effort soon began to pay off for Omaha Steaks. In just two years, the company was able to grow its corporate sales by 50 percent.

Omaha Steaks opted to voluntarily recall some 22,000 pounds of ground beef in October 2000 due to possible *E. coli* contamination, although it was more than likely that all the product from the lots in question had already been consumed without incident. Because it was so dependent on its reputation for quality, however, the company opted to err on the side of caution. It also took steps to ensure safety by introducing irradiation to its production process, whereby the foods were exposed to enough ionized radiation to kill such harmful bacteria as *E. coli* and salmonella. Omaha Steaks' trumpeting of the irradiation procedure awakened the fears of radioactivity in some consumers. When there was a rash of recalls of ground beef and deli meats across the country in 2002, however, many supermarkets eagerly sought irradiated products to assuage the fears of customers.

Despite poor economic conditions in the early years of the new century, Omaha Steaks continued to grow its business. In 2001, it launched a spin-off Web enterprise named A La Zing to become involved in the growing home meal replacement market. In 2003, the company added 42,000 square feet to its warehouse, greatly expanding its freezer capacity. At the same time, a cold-storage and ground beef processing facility was converted into a second distribution center. Omaha Steaks also continued in its efforts to exploit the power of its brand name, sometimes pursuing unusual avenues. In 2003, for example, it introduced all-beef ''snack treats'' for cats. In all likelihood, this was the first time that a human food product lent its brand name to a pet item. The company that had been launched in a former carpentry shop, unable to afford a new sign, was now generating more than $350 million a year in revenues and possessed a well known and respected brand name. There was every reason to expect that Omaha Steaks would find even more ways to exploit its brand and achieve even greater growth in the years to come.

Principal Subsidiaries

A La Zing.

Principal Competitors

Amazon.com, Inc.; Stock Yards Packing Company; Sutton Place Gourmet Inc.

Further Reading

Finney, Daniel P., ''Name Says Everything for Nebraska's Omaha Steaks,'' *Omaha World-Herald*, March 5, 2002.
Miller, Paul, ''Omaha Steaks Cooks up Corporate Sales,'' *Catalog Age*, October 1998, p. 18.
Orr, Alicia, ''Oh, the Possibilities,'' *Target Marketing*, December 1997, p. 30.
Rosenfeld, James R., ''In the Mail,'' *Direct Marketing*, September 1994, p. 49.

—Ed Dinger

Orleans Homebuilders, Inc.

One Greenwood Square, Suite 101
3333 Street Road
Bensalem, Pennsylvania 19020
U.S.A
Telephone: (212) 245-7500
Fax: (215) 633-2352
Web site: http://www.orleanshomes.com

Public Company
Incorporated: 1959 as Palm-Aire Corporation
Employees: 367
Sales: $388.5 million (2003)
Stock Exchanges: American
Ticker Symbol: OHB
NAIC: 236115 New Single-Family Housing Construction
(Except Operative Builders)

With its headquarters in the Philadelphia suburb of Bensalem, Pennsylvania, Orleans Homebuilders, Inc. develops residential communities in the Pennsylvania and New Jersey counties surrounding Philadelphia, as well as in the metropolitan areas of Richmond, Virginia; Charlotte, Greensboro, and Raleigh, North Carolina; and central Florida. The public company, trading on the American Stock Exchange, is majority-owned and operated by the third generation of the Orleans family.

Orleans' Founder Emigrates from Czarist Russia

Orleans was founded by Alfred P. Orleans, who was born in a Russian village in the 1890s. He was deemed a good prospect for becoming a doctor, but because Orleans was Jewish he was not allowed to attend medical school in Russia. Instead, he was sent to Philadelphia, Pennsylvania, for his education, with the understanding that he would one day return to his village to practice medicine. However, the pogroms that took place in his Russia, which led to the killing and exile of thousands of Jews, made it dangerous for him to return home. In addition, the revolution that swept the czar from power during World War I in Russia made life in Philadelphia seem to Orleans to be far more desirable than that in under the new Soviet regime.

Orleans earned money by selling insurance and real estate on street corners, a common practice of the day. He was able to parlay his success in these trades to set himself up as a homebuilder by 1918. He bought parcels of land in Philadelphia's Logan neighborhood and built row houses that cost around $1,200. From the outset, he was devoted to building affordable housing and to making maximum use of the space he purchased. His move into homebuilding proved fortuitous, as the economy boomed during the Roaring Twenties, leading to a greater amount of money available to the middle class for mortgages and more funding for homebuilders like Orleans to buy land and construct houses.

Orleans had the good sense to continue his insurance business, which proved to be his salvation when the stock market crash of 1929 brought on the Great Depression of the 1930s and a collapse in the housing business. Orleans had taken on considerable debt, but because he was still making commissions on insurance he was able to stay current on payments to the Frankford Trust Co. Frankford's president was impressed and offered Orleans new financing so that by 1933 he was able to resume building houses. Orleans not only earned a good reputation with bankers, he gained widespread recognition for being conscientious. He never lost sight of his goal of building affordable yet livable housing, and he also paid regular visits to his job sites, as well as to those of his competitors. Being a hands-on builder was a practice he passed on to succeeding generations of his family. As a result of the owners being on the job, Orleans' houses incorporated a number of spontaneous changes, sometimes to projects that were already completed, such as adding windows and square footage—whatever feature was needed to make the home more livable. This penchant for quality would be appreciated by realtors and homeowners who would benefit from the premium the Orleans name brought to a property when it came time to sell.

Postwar Move to the Suburbs

Orleans scraped by during the remaining years of the 1930s and into World War II by taking partners, most of whom were relatives. A typical Orleans product circa 1940 was a three-bedroom, one-bathroom row house that could be bought in the

$3,500 range. During this period, he concentrated on row houses and duplexes, while constructing the occasional apartment building. Orleans recognized that the end of World War II would lead to a housing boom, and to prepare for this time he began to buy up land in the communities surrounding Philadelphia. Meanwhile, he continued to fill out the city neighborhood of East Mount Airy, then made initial forays into Cheltenham Township and Montgomery County, where he was convinced the future lay. As he anticipated, it was after World War II that his business really took off. He was now joined by his son Marvin, who had served as a captain in the Army Air Corps. It was a period that saw veterans return home, get married, and give birth to the Baby Boom generation. With the help of financial benefits provided by the GI Bill, these middle-class veterans were able to attend college and buy homes in record numbers. The demand for housing was strong across the country. In the Philadelphia area, Orleans completed against the likes of William Levitt, who became a legend for applying assembly-line techniques to home building, creating "Levittowns"—cookie-cutter suburban communities that featured street after street of identical houses. The other major Philadelphia builder was the Korman family, which would be the area's top builder for a generation. Orleans was content to be the number two Philadelphia-area homebuilder, constructing 1,000 homes year after year. In the late 1940s, he too turned his attention to the suburbs, concentrating first on Montgomery County. He again displayed a knack for anticipating where people would eventually choose to live. During the late 1940s, for instance, he began to buy up cheap land in Philadelphia's Torresdale neighborhood. Thirty years later, when the demand he envisioned materialized, he began to build houses in the area.

Orleans' son Marvin, wanting to strike out on his own, set up a business in Florida. Backed by his father, he formed Florida Palm-Aire Corporation in June 1959 and built the Palm Aire master planned community that featured five golf courses in the Pompano Beach area. Over the next 25 years, he built 25,000 housing units in Florida. The business was reincorporated in Delaware in 1969 as FPA Corporation and taken public, trading on the American Stock Exchange. In the meantime, during the 1960s, Marvin's son, Jeffrey P. Orleans, went to work for the family business while attending college at Drexel University. Alfred Orleans exhausted his opportunities in Philadelphia by 1968 and focused all his attention on the city's suburbs. As a result, the company's headquarters was moved to Huntingdon Valley and then to its present location in Bensalem. His grandson focused his attention on southern New Jersey, across the Delaware River, where many Pennsylvanians increasingly turned for housing.

Alfred Orleans remained active in the business he founded until he was 92 years old. He died in 1981 at the age of 93. Marvin Orleans died in 1986, leaving his son Jeffrey as the lone shareholder of Orleans Construction Corporation, as well as chairman, president, and chief executive officer of FPA Corpo-

ration. For a time, he attempted to run both the Pennsylvania and Florida operations, but poor market conditions in Florida took its toll on FPA, which began to experience severe losses and distracted Jeffrey Orleans from his more successful Bensalem operation. As a result, Orleans lost its number two position among Philadelphia builders, falling as low as number five—well off the pace set by the new market leader, Toll Brothers, whose founder once worked as a subcontractor for Alfred Orleans. To refocus his attention on the Philadelphia market, Jeffrey Orleans began to exit the Florida market. In 1988, he sold the Palm-Aire Hotel and Spa, along with three golf courses, for $28.75 million. In 1990, he sold FPA's real estate brokerage firm, Palm-Aire Properties, to Linda L. Bosley, a vice-president and broker with the company.

FPA Becomes Orleans Homebuilders in 1998

The late 1980s and early 1990s were a difficult stretch for the real estate and home building industries, but by consolidating its efforts Orleans was able to weather the storm and begin regaining market share in the Philadelphia area. In 1993, Jeffrey Orleans reorganized the two companies, with Orleans Construction becoming a wholly owned subsidiary of FPA. In 1998, FPA changed its named to Orleans Homebuilders, Inc. After several losing years in the early 1990s, the company, starting in 1995, recorded several consecutive years of earnings growth. Revenues grew from $108 million in fiscal 1995 to $179 million in fiscal 2000, while income from continuing operations during this period increased from $1.2 million to more than $7.5 million.

As the new century dawned, the diminishing availability of land in the Philadelphia area became a concern. As Jeffrey Orleans explained to *Professional Builder,* "There's not a lot of building opportunity in the Delaware Valley. Ground is at a critical point. We have a backlog for at least the next five years and we hope to maintain that, but it's getting harder and harder. We're doing infill; we're going farther out. We're spreading into central New Jersey." In an effort to prepare for the future and venture into new markets, Orleans in October 2000 acquired Parker & Lancaster Corporation, a Richmond, Virginia-based residential home builder, paying approximately $6 million in cash and 300,000 shares of common stock. Parker & Lancaster, which generated some $87 million in revenues in 1999, operated in the major North Carolina metropolitan areas of Raleigh and Charlotte, as well as in the state's Triad section and parts of Virginia and South Carolina. The company was renamed Parker Lancaster of Orleans but the subsidiary continued to be run by its current management team with input from Orleans.

Orleans was able to bolster its business in the Philadelphia market in 2001 when it paid $14.7 million in cash and notes payable within one year to acquire the New Jersey subsidiary of Minneapolis-based Ruttlund Co. The assets of Ruttlund Homes of New Jersey comprised 300 lots on three parcels of land. In addition to developing single-family communities in the Philadelphia market, Orleans built townhouse and so-called adult communities, which appealed to empty nesters who no longer wanted the responsibilities of maintaining a large house. The Baby Boom generation, which had once precipitated the move of Alfred Orleans to the suburbs, now prompted his grandson to build suitable housing for this graying population.

Key Dates:

1918: Alfred Orleans begins building homes in Philadelphia, Pennsylvania.
1959: Palm-Aire Corporation is established in Florida.
1969: Palm-Aire becomes FPA Corporation and is taken public.
1981: Alfred Orleans dies at age 93.
1986: A third generation of the Orleans family heads the business.
1993: Orleans Construction becomes a subsidiary of FPA.
1998: FPA changes its name to Orleans Homebuilders, Inc.
2000: Parker & Lancaster is acquired.

Due in large part to the acquisition of Parker & Lancaster, Orleans recorded a major jump in revenues and net income for fiscal 2001. Sales reached $287.2 million and earnings topped $10.5 million. The company continued to prosper in 2002, benefiting a great deal by the poor showing of the stock market and low interest rates. Investing in new homes became a highly desirable alternative to investing in stocks. As a result, in fiscal 2002 Orleans again posted record results, with revenues totaling $354.6 million and net income improving to $17.7 million. Because of these impressive results, the company was recognized by the media. It was listed as the one of the top 50 fastest-growing homebuilders in America by *Builder* magazine. In 2002, *Forbes* ranked Orleans third on its list of the 200 Best Small Companies. In addition, *Fortune* ranked the company number 33 on its list of the 100 Fastest Growing Companies. Orleans ability to maintain its growth also looked strong. Entering fiscal 2003, the company owned some 1,700 lots in the Philadelphia market with another 3,600 under agreement. In Virginia, North Carolina, and South Carolina, Orleans owned approximately 700 lots with an addition 2,200 lots under agreement.

Orleans enjoyed another strong year in fiscal 2003. Although revenues did not grow at the rate experienced in the previous few years, they still improved by 10 percent, to nearly $388.5 million. Net income, on the other hand, increased from $17.7 million in 2002 to more than $27 million. Less than a month after the fiscal year ended on June 30, Orleans took another step in preparing for the future. Once again, it looked to the Florida market, acquiring the outstanding stock of Masterpiece Homes, a residential builder in the central Florida market. In calendar 2002, Masterpiece built 213 homes and generated revenues of $26.3 million. During the first six months of 2003, Masterpiece built 142 homes with revenue of approximately $20 million. In addition, Masterpiece boasted a backlog of 278 homes that were sold but not yet delivered; these comprised an aggregate revenue of approximately $39 million. In the foreseeable future, given low interest rates and continuing demand for housing in the company's primary market of Philadelphia, Orleans' prospects appeared bright. Houses were being sold before the company was able to complete them. Even if the housing market in the Philadelphia area grew tight, the company, with its growing southern division, was well positioned to prosper for many years to come.

Principal Subsidiaries

A.P. Orleans, Inc. of New Jersey; A.P. Orleans, Inc. of Pennsylvania; Parker Lancasters & Orleans, Inc.

Principal Competitors

Centex Corporation; Pulte Homes, Inc.; Toll Brothers, Inc.

Further Reading

Abueva, Jobert E., "Orleans Stays Flexible, Focused in Downturn," *Philadelphia Business Journal*, October 5, 2001, p. 22.
Bady, Susan, "Movers and Shakers," *Professional Builder*, April 2001, p. 118.
Heavens, Alan J., "Master Builder for 80 Years," *Philadelphia Inquirer*, June 7, 1998, p. R01.
O'Malley, Sharon, "Birthplace of a Builder," *Builder*, September-October 1999, p. 18.

—Ed Dinger

PCA International, Inc.

815 Matthews-Mint Hill Road
Matthews, North Carolina 28105
U.S.A.
Telephone: (704) 847-8011
Toll Free: (800) 438-8868
Fax: (704) 847-8010
Web site: http://www.pcainternational.com

Private Company
Incorporated: 1967 as Photo Corporation of America
Employees: 7,000
Sales: $296.60 million (2003)
NAIC: 541921 Photographic Studios, Portrait; 551112
Offices of Other Holding Companies

PCA International, Inc. operates photography studios in roughly 2,500 retail stores, primarily those owned by Wal-Mart Stores, Inc. PCA takes portraits, processing its prints at a 121,000-square-foot laboratory and customer care center in Matthews, North Carolina. The company targets children, schools, the military, and churches. PCA also operates stand-alone retail stores operating under the name Go Portraits Digital Destination, which sell digital photography equipment and portraits and prints on both film and CD-ROM.

Origins

In the early 1960s, PCA's founder, Bud Davis, designed a camera that helped launch a quarter-billion-dollars-in-sales company. Davis's so-called ''Framatic'' camera greatly increased the number of exposures a photographer could take without changing a roll of film, yielding cost advantages that his company would exploit. Davis incorporated his company, originally named Photo Corporation of America, in Charlotte in May 1967. The company began by offering photographic portrait services in a single S.S. Kresge store, where 5×7-inch color portraits were sold for 38 cents. The company employed a small group of itinerant photographers who set up shop inside a store for a week or so before moving on to a different location, with the number of the company's traveling photographers increasing as the number of its retail accounts increased. Although PCA allied itself with numerous discount chains and department stores during its formative years, no business tie was more important than the company's relationship with the discount chain Kmart. PCA operated its first temporary studio in a Kmart store in Atlanta, Georgia, in 1968, taking portraits of 1,200 children within a five-day period. The popularity of the service led to other temporary studios in Kmart stores and prompted other chains to sign up with PCA, fueling the company's early growth.

PCA expanded rapidly during the 1970s. The company spread its presence geographically at a robust pace, dispatching its roving photographers throughout the country to take portraits of children. Annual sales eclipsed $10 million by 1972. By 1975, the company's revenue had swelled to $53 million. In December 1976, the company completed an initial public offering (IPO) of stock and began trading on the NASDAQ, using the proceeds from the IPO to finance its expansion. In 1978, the company opened a processing center in Matthews, North Carolina, the same year it posted a record $6 million in profit. By the end of the decade, the company operated more than 8,000 temporary studios, pushing sales past the $100-million mark, but the years of dramatic growth soon ended. PCA maintained a presence throughout the United States and had branched out into Canada and Mexico, as well as into Europe and Japan, but it began to suffer from the extent of its expansion. Evidence of the problems stemming from over-expansion began to become apparent at the end of the 1979, as PCA concluded a decade of dramatic growth.

Problems in the 1980s

The halcyon years of the 1970s gave way to the gradual deterioration of PCA's financial health during the 1980s. The company's forays abroad met with a lukewarm reception from retailers and a diversification into family portraits in the United States failed. It soon became apparent that the company's problems were rooted in its own success. In a September 1997 interview with *Business North Carolina,* a former PCA chief financial officer explained the situation. ''PCA grew by just expanding the market,'' he said, ''but after you grow so far geographically, you've covered the market, and then you've

Company Perspectives:

In portrait photography, PCA International has staked out a position as a provider of high-quality family portraits at affordable prices. That strategy has led to successful partnerships with major retailers, notably Wal-Mart Stores, Inc. Industry changes and digital technology have enabled us to expand our retail portrait business and explore new and exciting venues for photography.

saturated it.'' From a high of $6 million in 1978, profits began a downward spiral, falling to $3.5 million the following year. In 1982, when the company was forced to lay off 110 employees, it posted a profit of $1.2 million. In 1986, the company lost money, recording a deficit of nearly $5 million. Shareholders, once gleeful about their investment in the company's robust growth, grew disgruntled.

Waning profitability and shareholder dissatisfaction led to a management change. In 1987, the company hired John Grosso as its new president and chief executive officer. A graduate of George Washington University, Grosso spent ten years working for Polaroid Corp., eventually serving as the company's director of marketing. After leaving Polaroid in 1981, Grosso joined Atlanta, Georgia-based Nimslo International Ltd., which owned a portrait business that operated out of Sears, Roebuck & Co. stores in the northeastern United States. When Grosso was hired by PCA's board of directors in 1987, the company's escalating costs had saddled it with debt, as had the ill-fated expansion overseas. Grosso restructured PCA's debt and reduced costs once he took the helm, which began to relieve the company's financial predicament. Grosso retreated from PCA's position overseas, and, domestically, he decided to winnow the company's focus as well. By the late 1980s, PCA had allied itself with more than 100 retail chains, but Grosso felt the company's best interests would be served by focusing on one client. He severed ties with many of PCA's retail accounts and focused on making Kmart the company's primary client. The changes worked, enabling PCA to post a $2.5 million profit in 1989, a year that saw the company generate $123.7 million in sales. The revenue total was substantially less than the nearly $180 million in sales produced at the beginning of the decade, but the changes directed by Grosso had restored profitability, a paramount concern of any commercial enterprise.

As PCA entered the 1990s, Grosso's salubrious touch led to greater and greater gains for the company. Aping the practices of his closest rivals, Grosso started converting to permanent studios within Kmart stores, replacing his network of roving photographers with fixed locations attended by ever-present photographers and salespeople. The quick conversion to permanent studios—PCA had 461 fixed locations in Kmart stores by the end of 1990—produced positive results. By 1992, profits swelled to more than $7 million, exhibiting the same luster of the late 1980s before the strains of too-rapid expansion manifested themselves. The greatest contribution to PCA's financial well-being occurred in 1992 as well, with an innovation that helped the company decimate one of its rivals and marked the highlight of the Grosso era.

Innovation and a Merger in the 1990s

As part of its operations, PCA employed a 25-member research and development team. In 1992, the group developed a digital-proofing system that greatly reduced the costs of unwanted prints and sped up delivery to customers. Between 1992 and 1994, PCA invested $64 million into incorporating its digital system into its network of 1,350 studios located in Kmart stores. The transition in technology delivered profound results, proving to be the death knell of a competitor with incestuous ties to the Matthews-based company. Buoyed by the introduction of a digital-proofing system, the operating profit of PCA's studios nearly tripled between 1991 and 1995, the leap arising from a decline in costs and a surge in sales. For American Studios, a company founded by three former PCA employees, the success of the digital-proofing system proved devastating.

In 1970, when PCA was just beginning to expand rapidly, three new employees arrived, Randy Bates, Kent Smith, and Norman Swenson, Jr. Bates and Swenson worked as salesmen, while Smith traveled the country as one of PCA's roving photographers. The trio eventually grew dissatisfied at PCA and, in 1982, with a $50,000 Small Business Administration loan, founded American Studios. Patterned after PCA, American Studios flourished during the 1980s, aided greatly by its affiliation with Bentonville, Arkansas-based Wal-Mart Stores, Inc., Smith's account while at PCA. At the time, PCA was reeling, which prompted Wal-Mart to give the new start-up a chance to distinguish itself at 19 stores. Within five years, American Studios was operating in more than 500 Wal-Mart stores, its resounding success in sharp contrast to PCA's beleaguered condition at the time.

After Grosso implemented the changes that gave PCA renewed vitality for the 1990s, he set his sights on beating back the threat posed by American Studios. The introduction of the digital-proofing system in 1992 served as Grosso's weapon, delivering a blow American Studios was unable to counter. In a September 1997 interview with *Business North Carolina*, an analyst explained what happened. ''Obviously,'' he said, ''American Studios had the premier retailer, but they didn't have the technology. They made a decision, initially, to wait it out, let technology prices drop. That didn't work. By then, they started having some difficulties. Their later stores weren't matching the success of earlier stores. PCA, with good technology, had shot ahead.''

After American Studios began to falter, Grosso was able to pursue a prize he coveted. American Studios lost nearly $6 million in 1995, igniting shareholder furor similar to the anger expressed by PCA shareholders a decade earlier. Grosso approached American Studios in November 1996, offering to buy the company and thereby secure its enviable association with Wal-Mart. Negotiations ensued, leading to the completion of the deal in February 1997, when PCA acquired American Studios for $66 million. The merger gave PCA 2,200 Wal-Mart locations, 850 of which operated as permanent studios. In the wake of the transaction, PCA began to close its Kmart locations, shuttering more than 400 of its 1,350 outlets during the first six months of 1997 and ending the year as a $240 million-in-sales company.

The next significant event in PCA's history occurred a year after the American Studios acquisition. In April 1998, PCA's

Key Dates:

1967: Photo Corporation of America (PCA) is founded.
1976: PCA completes its initial public offering of stock.
1987: John Grosso is hired as PCA's chief executive officer.
1992: PCA introduces a digital-proofing system.
1997: PCA acquires American Studios.
1998: PCA is taken private through a buyout led by Jupiter Partners II.
2001: PCA opens its first stand-alone retail store.

board of directors agreed to a buyout led by a New York-based investment firm named Jupiter Partners II and a group of PCA managers that included Grosso. The $276 million buyout returned PCA to private ownership, ending the company's 22-year-long status as a publicly traded concern.

After the buyout was completed, Grosso's 11-year tenure as PCA's chief executive officer ended. The company's new owners hired Barry Feld in August 1999 as PCA's new president and chief executive officer. A Baltimore native, Feld was a graduate of Essex College in 1976 who spent ten years as an acquisition and turnaround specialist for acquired optical retail companies for Pearle Health Services. After leaving Pearle in 1987, Feld helped build a chain of retail eye-care stores in California that operated under the name Frame-n-Lens Optical, Inc. In a June 8, 2001 interview with *The Business Journal Serving Charlotte and Metropolitan Area*, Feld described his arrival at PCA. "It was a legacy business that had to be reinvented," he stated. "I was brought in by a capital group to revamp it and look for ways to transform it into something more appropriate for the future."

Under Feld's stewardship, PCA began to diversify it product offerings. The company started adding portrait work for schools, churches, and the military. The most significant addition to PCA's business scope was the company's expansion into stand-alone retail sales, a move that for the first time took the company out of the shelter of another retailer. In 2001, PCA opened its first prototype outlet at a mall in North Carolina, a store named Go Portraits Digital Destination. Inside the store, the company sold digital photography equipment and portraits and prints on both film and CD-ROM.

As PCA prepared for the future, the company expected to greatly expand its stand-alone retail business. Feld was excited about Go Portraits Digital Destination's potential, envisioning the opening of hundreds of new stores each year. If successful, the addition of the stand-alone stores promised to add to PCA's already considerable strength. The company served more than five million customers nationwide through roughly 2,500 retail locations in the United States, Canada, and Mexico, producing more than 100 million prints annually. In the years ahead, further expansion was expected, as PCA promised to build on its leadership position in the portrait business.

Principal Subsidiaries

Wal-Mart Portrait Studio.

Principal Competitors

CPI Corporation; Lifetouch Inc.; Olan Mills, Inc.

Further Reading

Bailey, David, "What's Wrong with This Picture?," *Business North Carolina*, September 1993, p. 16.
Gibson, Ashley M., "PCA Exec Makes Things Click," *Business Journal Serving Charlotte and the Metropolitan Area*, June 8, 2001, p. 3.
Speizer, Irwin, "Photo Finish," *Business North Carolina*, September 1997, p. 48.
Weiner, Daniel P., "PCA International Inc.," *Fortune*, June 23, 1986, p. 52.

—Jeffrey L. Covell

Perusahaan Otomobil Nasional Bhd.

Kawasan Perindustrian HICOM, Bat
Selagor
Malaysia
Telephone: (+60) 3 511 1055
Fax: (+60) 3 511 1252
Web site: http://www.proton.com

Public Company
Incorporated: 1983
Employees: 6,000
Sales: RM 10.31 billion ($2.8 billion)(2002)
Stock Exchanges: Kuala Lumpur Stock Exchange
Ticker Symbol: PROT
NAIC: 336111 Automobile Manufacturing; 423110
Automobile and Other Motor Vehicle Merchant
Wholesalers

Perusahaan Otomobil Nasional Bhd., better known as Proton, is Malaysia's largest manufacturer of automobiles, commanding as much as 65 percent of the domestic market. The company produces a full range of vehicle styles, from its popular Wira sedan to its own mini-van and sport utility models. While most of the company's car designs were previously based on re-branded models from its long-standing technical partner, Mitsubishi, in the 2000s Proton has begun developing its own technology in partnership with its 80 percent-controlled subsidiary Lotus, of U.K. sports and racing car fame. The addition of Lotus engineering and design technology has enabled Proton to reposition itself, at least for the export market, as a niche market player with a focus on the sporty, higher-end segment. Founded in 1985 under the auspices of Malaysian prime minister Mahathir Mohamad, Proton has long enjoyed protective trade barriers in its domestic market, with foreign imports taxed as high as 300 percent. With those barriers slated to come down at the beginning of 2005 as part of the AFTA free trade agreement, Proton has taken steps to boost its efficiency, including building a new, highly automated production facility with a capacity of up to 150,000 cars per year. The company is also looking to establish international manufacturing facilities, targeting Syria, Iran, and China. In addition to its domestic dominance, Proton has proven itself a strong competitor on the international scene as well, with sales in 50 countries, including much of Asia, the Middle East, the United Kingdom, and parts of continental Europe. Proton is listed on the Kuala Lumpur Stock Exchange. In 2003, the company's sales topped RM10 billion ($2.8 billion).

Homegrown Carmarker in the 1980s

Malaysia, like most of its neighbors, began a drive toward industrial development at the beginning of the 1980s in an effort to reduce the country's reliance on foreign-made imported products. Among the sectors targeted by Prime Minister Mahathir Mohamad for development was that of a domestic automobile industry. Rather than creating a domestic industry from scratch, however, Mahathir sought a partner with an established auto maker. In 1981, during a visit to the country by executives from Japan's Mitsubishi Corporation, Mahathir proposed the creation of a joint-venture to produce Mitsubishi-designed automobiles in Malaysia.

The drafting of the joint-venture project was turned over to government-owned Heavy Industries Corporation of Malaysia (HICOM), which began negotiations with Mitsubishi at the beginning of 1982. The government in the meantime drafted legislation, known as the National Car Project, which, in addition for providing for the creation of a new, domestic automotive industry, also put into place protective trade barriers, including import duties that reached as high as 300 percent on some foreign makes and models. By the end of that year, HICOM had reached a joint-venture agreement with Mitsubishi that gave the Japanese car maker a 30 percent stake in the new company.

Perusahaan Otomobil Nasional Bhd. was officially launched in May 1983. Construction began on the company's manufacturing facility, located at HICOM's Industrial Area in Shah Alam, in August that year. Completed in 1984, the plant, which used largely manual labor production techniques, boasted a capacity of 80,000 vehicles per year. The company took the country's symbol, the tiger, as its own, while adopting Proton as its brand name.

By May 1984, Proton had begun testing of a prototype, and, after holding a ''Name the National Car'' contest, gave its first car the name of Saga. That model was based on Mitsubishi's

Lancer. While terms of the joint-venture agreement involved the transfer of technology that would enabled Proton to begin developing its own cars, the company's output in the mid-1990s remained based on Mitsubishi designs.

Proton launched the Saga commercially in July 1985, and, backed on the one hand by subsidized pricing policies and the other by the heavy trade barriers, quickly imposed itself as Malaysia's top car brand, with a 47 percent share of the market. Sales of Proton cars were handled primarily through a sister company, EON (Edaran Otomobil Nasional), formed in 1984. As EON built up its sales and marketing networks, Proton ramped up production. By 1987, the company had already built more than 50,000 automobiles.

Almost from the start, Proton targeted an international market. In 1986, it took a modest step toward this goal by exporting 25 cars to Bangladesh. In 1987, the company stepped up its export operation, with a focus on introducing the Proton name to the United Kingdom. A distribution subsidiary, Proton Cars (UK) Ltd., was formed the same year. Despite winning a number of awards at the International Exhibition in Birmingham the following year, actual sales to the United Kingdom were delayed until 1989.

In the meantime, Mitsubishi had stepped in to take over management of the Proton plant in 1988, helping to boost the facility's reliability record. In 1989, the Shah Alam site took over production of Proton's engines. At the end of that year, the company rolled its 150,000th car off its assembly line. By then, the group's domestic market share had already reached its peak, at 73 percent of all new Malaysian car purchases.

Retooling for the New Century

Sales continued to pick up into the 1990s, as the group completed its 300,000th car by mid-1991. The group had also begun expanding its range, launching the Megavalve Proton Saga in 1990, followed by a 12-valve version in 1991. In addition, production capacity was expanded with the opening of the company's Engine Assembly and Transmission factory in July 1991 followed by a new line stamping production unit the following year.

Proton went public in 1992, listing on the Kuala Lumpur Stock Exchange. In that year, the company at last added its second model, the Iswara. Matathir sought to step up the pace at Proton, which was hampered by its dependence on imported Japanese parts for much of its production, and in 1993 the prime minister turned to former classmate and leading Malaysian industrialist Yahaya Ahmad for help.

As one of the country's most influential businessmen, Yahaya had also developed his own automobile operation, among many others, assembling Isuzu, Mitsubishi, and Tata cars for the domestic market since the late 1970s. With Yahaya on board, the company launched its own research and development facility in 1993, which joined in the development of a new model for Proton, the sporty Wira, launched in 1993. The new car helped rejuvenate Proton and enabled the company's total production to top the half-million mark that year. In September 1993, Yahaya's Diversified Resources Berhad was awarded the contract to produce a new three-door vehicle for Proton.

Proton's exports had been increasing strongly, topping 10 percent of its total production by mid-decade. In 1994, the company began exports to Indonesia, followed by the creation of a subsidiary, Proton Philipinas Corporation, bringing the company's designs to that market as well.

Proton also went in search of additional partners, with France's Citroen agreeing to provide engines and technological assistance for new Proton models. These started to come more quickly and included the launch of the Wira Aeroback in October 1992, the Satria in 1994, and the Perdana in 1995. Also in 1995, Matathir rewarded Yahaya's work with Proton by allowing Diversified Resources to acquire the government's majority stake in Proton. The following year, the company released the Putra, a two-door coupe.

The year 1996 saw a major landmark in Proton's growth when the company agreed to pay more than $100 million, including a $20 million working capital commitment, to acquire an 80 percent stake in British sports car legend Lotus Automobiles. Although greeted with some skepticism, the purchase was intended to give Proton its own in-house development expertise as part of the group's effort to create its first, truly Malaysian design. The addition of Lotus also signaled the group's intention to extend its range into the higher-end of the automotive market, especially for its export vehicles. At the same time, the company pledged to maintain Lotus's engineering and design staff—including their work for third-party car makers—and to continue production of the company's elite Elise sports car.

Proton entered 1997 with high hopes and in that year launched a major expansion of its Shah Alam manufacturing site, nearly tripling its production capacity with the installation of a second facility. By 2000, the company's production annual production neared 200,000 cars.

Yet 1997 also marked the beginning of a difficult period for the company. In that year, Yahaya was killed in a helicopter accident. At the same time, the company tumbled headlong into the economic collapse that affected much of Asia. Having extended its finances both with the acquisition of Lotus and the

Key Dates:

1981: Malaysian Prime Minister Matathir begins plans to establish the first Malaysian automaker.

1983: Perusahaan Otomobil Nasional Bhd. (Proton) is launched as a joint-venture with Mitsubishi.

1985: The company begins distribution of its first model, the Saga, Malaysia's first national car, which captures a 47 percent share of the domestic market.

1986: The company begins operating internationally by exporting automobiles to Bangladesh.

1987: A U.K. subsidiary is established as Saga captures a 73 percent share of the domestic market.

1992: Proton goes public on the Kuala Lumpur Stock Exchange.

1995: DRB, controlled by industrialist Yahaya Ahmad, buys the Malaysian government's majority stake in Proton.

1996: Proton buys 80 percent of U.K. sports and racing car maker Lotus.

2000: Waja, the company's first in-house developed automobile, is launched.

2003: The company reaches an agreement to begin automobile production in Syria and applies for a manufacturing license in China.

extension of its manufacturing base, Proton was all the more vulnerable to the sudden drop in car purchases both at home and abroad. On the domestic front, the company was forced to bow to the government's insistence that it not raise its car prices. Meanwhile, the company found itself edged out on the international front by its wealthier and more aggressive competitors from Korea and Japan.

With its finances in a precarious position, Proton faced an uncertain future. The situation became more problematic, when Malaysia agreed to join the ASEAN region's AFTA free trade agreement. As part of that pact, the country assented to lower and even abolish most of its protective trade barriers, including the heavy duties on foreign cars and parts. Proton now braced itself for a new era of competition, initially scheduled to start in 2003.

Proton successfully lobbied, however, to push back the end of the government's protection to the beginning of 2005, which allowed the company to begin retooling. In 1999, the company began automating its production line, adding its first robots that year. Proton also intensified the development of its first in-house models, incorporating Lotus technology for the first time. By 2000, the company was ready to launch the Waja (''steel'' in Malay), which, with its sleek, racy design clearly displayed the influence of Lotus's design and engineering expertise. The project had cost some $250 million to develop, including the cost of launching the group's research and development center.

While the company was making great strides on the design front, Proton's production facilities, which continued to rely in large part on manual labor, were now out-of-date, leaving it ill-equipped to face the fast-approaching competition. As part of its drive for greater efficiency, the company began subcontracting

a larger number of components to third parties. At the same time, Proton encouraged its components suppliers to set up manufacturing facilities in closer proximity to the company. In 2001, Proton began construction of an entirely new facility in the newly built Proton City development in the town of Tanjung Malim. The state-of-the-art facility would have a production capacity of 150,000 cars per year and an automation level of 60 percent, enabling the company to slash nearly one-third off its production costs. The new site, which included space nearby for the company's growing list of components-producing partners, cost $400 million.

Completed in late 2003, the new facility formed the centerpiece of a renewal of Proton, which, having produced few new models at the beginning of the decade, had seen its market share slip by some 27 percent by the end of that year. Proton then began preparing the launch of an entirely new line of vehicles for 2004. As the date for the lowering of the country's automotive trade barriers approached, Proton began searching for new, foreign manufacturing opportunities, reaching an agreement to being producing cars in Syria and negotiating for manufacturing licenses in Iran and China. Observers, however, had already begun to question Proton's ability to survive as an independent in an era of rapid consolidation that pitted the company against the world's global automotive giants. With growing design and production confidence, and continued backing from Matathir, Proton prepared to put up a good fight to remain a Malaysian flagship enterprise in the years to come.

Principal Subsidiaries

Distribution Centre Sdn. Bhd.; Group Lotus plc (UK; 80%); Lotus Cars Ltd. (UK; 80%); Lotus Cars USA Inc. (80%); Lotus Cars USA Inc. (80%); Lotus Engineering Inc. (USA; 80%); Lotus Group International Ltd. (England; 80%); Lotus Motorsports Ltd. (United Kingdom; 80%); Marco Acquisition Corporation (United States); Proton Cars (UK) Ltd.; Proton Cars Australia Pty. Ltd.; Proton Direct Ltd. (UK); Proton Edar Sdn. Bhd.; Proton Engineering Research; Proton MC Metal Sdn. Bhd. (75%); Proton Parts Centre Sdn. Bhd. (55%); Proton Properties Sdn. Bhd.; Research Technology Sdn. Bhd.; Technology Sdn. Bhd.

Principal Competitors

Toyota Motor Corporation; Honda Motor Company Ltd.; Shenyang Brilliance Automotive Company Ltd.; Mitsubishi Motors Corporation; Yuejin Motor Group Corporation; Hyundai Motor Company Ltd.; Mazda Motor Corporation; Daewoo-FSO Motor S.A.; Isuzu Motors Ltd.; Kia Motors Corporation; Toyota Astra Motor PT.

Further Reading

Feast, Richard, ''Malaysia's Little-Known Proton Buys Lotus,'' *Automotive Industries*, December 1996, p. 40.

Fletcher, Matthew, and Poh, Steven K.C., ''Proton's Worldly Ambitions,'' *Asiaweek*, April 11, 1997.

Ramsay, Randolph, ''Proton Strives to Become 'Niche,' '' *Business Asia*, July 19, 1999, p. 13.

Shari, Michael, ''Can Proton Deliver?,'' *Business Week*, February 3, 2003, p. 16.

—M.L. Cohen

The Pillsbury Company

1 General Mills Boulevard
Minneapolis, Minnesota 55426
U.S.A.
Telephone: (763) 764-7600
Fax: (763) 764-7384
Web site: http://www.pillsbury.com

Wholly Owned Subsidiary of General Mills Inc.
Incorporated: 1869 as the Pillsbury Flour Mills
    Company
Employees: 27,300
Sales: $7.4 billion (2003 General Mills' U.S. Retail
    business segment)
NAIC: 311412 Frozen Specialty Food Manufacturing

The Pillsbury Company is one of the oldest and most recognized firms in American food retailing. From its beginnings in flour milling in the late 1800s, Pillsbury has grown into the leading refrigerated dough brand in the United States, with a product arsenal that includes a variety of biscuits, breadsticks, cookies, pie crusts, crescent rolls, and bread. Pillsbury also manufactures and sells frozen breakfast pastries, frozen pancakes and waffles, and the Jeno's and Totino's brands of frozen pizza products. In 1989, Pillsbury was acquired by Grand Metropolitan plc, a diversified British beverage company. General Mills Inc. became one of the largest food companies in the world after buying Pillsbury for $10.4 billion in 2001.

Pillsbury Gets Its Start in 1869

In 1869, after working in his uncle's hardware supply company in Minneapolis, 27-year-old Charles A. Pillsbury bought one-third of a local flour mill for $10,000 and began what would become the Pillsbury Company. Pillsbury and a competitor, the Washburn Crosby Company, formed the Minneapolis Millers Association that same year.

Pillsbury's improvements in milling machinery included the early incorporation of modern equipment for milling the very hard local wheat. These improvements and the purchase

of two additional mills allowed him to produce 2,000 barrels of flour a day by 1872. That year, he reorganized the company as C.A. Pillsbury and Company, making his father and uncle partners. In addition, he registered the trademark Pillsbury's Best XXXX in 1872.

During the 1880s, Pillsbury added six more mills, including one that was then the largest flour mill in the world. This mill was equipped with state-of-the-art machinery that more than tripled the company's output. Weakened by three mill fires in 1881, Pillsbury had just begun to recover and was buying grain elevators to cut storage costs, when, in 1889, it sold the Pillsbury mills to an English financial syndicate. The syndicate also purchased competing Minnesota mills, elevators, and bordering water-power rights. Charles Pillsbury remained as managing director of the new outfit, which was called the Pillsbury-Washburn Flour Mills Company Ltd. The company put its water-power rights to use, and in 1896 the company passed the 10,000-barrels-per-day mark. Pillsbury-Washburn eventually grew, under Pillsbury's leadership, into the world's largest milling company.

During the 1890s, the company focused on vertical integration. It began selling flour directly to retailers and stepped up advertising. Pillsbury-Washburn struggled with freight rates and the depressed agricultural economy during the first few years of the 20th century. In 1907, following a poor harvest, it became impossible for the company to mill profitably. Unmet financial obligations forced it into receivership. Charles S. Pillsbury, Charles A. Pillsbury's son, was one of the three men appointed to reorganize the firm, which became the Pillsbury Flour Mills Company.

The new company overhauled the mills and the organization that ran them. In addition, Pillsbury became a pioneer in product research by building its own laboratory. The firm rebounded and, on June 27, 1923, the Pillsbury Flour Mills Company purchased all remaining assets from the shareholders of Pillsbury-Washburn.

Expansion and Diversification: 1920s to the 1950s

During the 1920s, the Pillsburys opened several new plants and began to diversify. By 1932, Pillsbury had expanded into specialized grain products like cake flour and cereals. Expan-

Company Perspectives:

We are guided by our values—they are the source of our strength and the heart of who we are. We reinforce our values everyday through our people, our brands, our performance, and our innovation. Our values define us—and serve as the foundation of our promise to consumers, to our customers, to investors, and to ourselves.

sion continued through 1940 with deals like the $3 million purchase of the Globe Grain and Milling Company and its various plants. The purchase helped Pillsbury set a new flour-milling record of 40,000 barrels a day. Pillsbury also continued manufacturing Globe's line of pancake mixes, biscuit mixes, and pasta.

In 1944, the company changed its name to Pillsbury Mills, Inc. Throughout this period, Pillsbury family members had run the company, and in 1940 Philip W. Pillsbury, Charles S. Pillsbury's son, became president. The company limited itself to kitchen staples through the 1940s but expanded its offerings in that line. Pillsbury began to export its flour, introduced food products for hotels and restaurants, and manufactured food products for U.S. troops during World War II, developing dry soup mixes in addition to its grains.

In the late 1940s, Pillsbury ventured into higher-margin convenience products to meet growing consumer demand. Cake mixes were introduced in 1948, and over the next ten years Pillsbury increased the varieties it offered. The company expanded its product line with yet another acquisition, in 1951, of Ballard & Ballard Company and its line of refrigerated foods.

Pillsbury invested heavily in market research and development during the 1950s and by the end of the decade had broadened beyond baking-related products. The company also continued its vertical integration efforts during the decade, opening milling plants in Canada and increasing its grain storage capacity. The company grew so quickly that by 1963 the Pillsbury name appeared on 127 different products. As the company's marketing and development continued to accelerate throughout the 1950s, so did its interest in a bigger market.

In 1959, Pillsbury began purchasing flour mills abroad, including units in Venezuela, El Salvador, Guatemala, Ghana, the Philippines, and Trinidad. In successive years, international operations increased to include food companies in France, Australia, and Germany. Fast growth continued, and in 1960 Pillsbury made its first nonfood purchase, Tidy House Products Company, a manufacturer of household cleaners.

Growth through Acquisition Begins in 1967

Robert J. Keith, who became president in 1966, brought Pillsbury into a new phase of food production. The postwar convenience era culminated in 1967 with the purchase of Burger King, the fast-food restaurant chain. By 1968, Pillsbury also owned interests in a variety of companies, including a computer time-sharing business, publishing concerns, and a life insurance company.

At the end of its first 100 years, the Pillsbury Company had become highly diversified and decentralized in order to handle the variety of management decisions involved with producing flours and instant foods, as well as running restaurant, computer, and publishing operations. Terrance Hanold, who became president in 1967, planned to continue diversifying and increasing independence for managers in the 1970s.

In 1973, William H. Spoor became CEO, and Pillsbury entered an era of increasing sales and earnings. Spoor valued growth through acquisition, but he wanted Pillsbury to focus on food products, and he quickly stripped the company of businesses unrelated to that industry. Under Spoor, Pillsbury purchased Totino's Finer Foods, following this venture into frozen foods with the 1979 purchase of Green Giant, a packager of frozen vegetables. Steak & Ale, Pillsbury's first full-service restaurant chain, was acquired in 1976; the purchase of HäagenDazs ice cream came in 1983; and Van de Kamp, the seafood company that produced Chicken of the Sea canned tuna followed in 1984. A few weeks after Spoor retired in 1984, Pillsbury announced the purchase of two more restaurant companies: Diversifoods Inc. and QuikWok Inc.

Pillsbury's business boomed during the 1970s, as Spoor solidified Pillsbury's strategy and made several smart purchases. Green Giant and other frozen-food companies gave Pillsbury a much larger share of the food industry and more consistent earnings. Profits in 1976 were divided almost evenly between three groups: consumer foods, agricultural products, and restaurants. By 1984, the agriproducts group had shrunk to only 4 percent and restaurants provided 53 percent.

The agriproducts group had long been run by Fred C. Pillsbury, Charles S. Pillsbury's brother, who developed cattle feeds from mill byproducts before the turn of the century. The division grew to become responsible for the collection, milling, storage, trading, and distribution of grain and feed ingredients. Pillsbury continued to provide about 10 percent of U.S. flour into the 1980s, and the division became one of the largest U.S. purchasers of grains and dry beans.

Consumer foods, the company's largest division, marketed Pillsbury's supermarket products. In addition to its domestic subsidiaries, Pillsbury sold grocery items through H.J. Green and Hammond's in the United Kingdom, Erasco and Jokisch in West Germany, Gringoir/Brossard and Singapour in France and Belgium, and Milani in Venezuela. Pillsbury also owned similar operations in Mexico, Guatemala, Jamaica, and the Philippines. In the United States, Pillsbury's line of refrigerated dough, for products such as pastries and cookies, was distributed by Kraft Foods for many years. These products accounted for about 10 percent of the company's sales.

Pillsbury owed much of the credit for its extraordinary growth to its restaurants. By expanding Burger King's operations and hiring Donald Smith from McDonald's, it became the second largest fast-food chain operator. The purchase of Diversifoods—at $390 million Pillsbury's biggest acquisition—included nearly 400 additional Burger King outlets as well as Godfather's Pizza, Chart House, and Luther's BarBQ. Pillsbury decided to compete with McDonald's not in size but in per unit sales. As Burger King continued to grow, franchising became

Key Dates:

1869: Charles A. Pillsbury establishes the Pillsbury Flour Mills Company.
1872: Pillsbury's Best XXXX becomes a registered trademark.
1889: The company is purchased by an English financial syndicate, merges with a competitor, and is renamed the Pillsbury-Washburn Flour Mills Co. Ltd.
1923: Pillsbury severs all ties with its English parent.
1951: Ballard & Ballard Company is acquired.
1965: Poppin' Fresh, the Pillsbury Doughboy, makes his first appearance.
1967: Pillsbury purchases fast-food chain Burger King.
1979: Frozen vegetable brand Green Giant is added to the company's arsenal.
1989: Pillsbury is acquired by Grand Metropolitan plc.
2001: General Mills Inc. acquires Pillsbury.

more common and only 20 percent of the restaurants remained company owned.

John M. Stafford inherited a healthy company when he was appointed president in 1984. Each year between 1972 and 1986, the company set records for both sales and earnings. Pillsbury had a reputation for quiet, conservative growth, despite nearly doubling its earnings between 1980 and 1985, from $100 million to $190 million. Pillsbury finally surpassed its chief competitor and future suitor, General Mills, during Stafford's first full year. Because Stafford, who came to Pillsbury through Green Giant, expected growth through increased demand for products from the agriproducts and restaurant groups, company structure remained unchanged.

Pillsbury, however, had dramatically changed its position internationally. The company no longer exported flour, since local mills could produce it more efficiently. Instead, the international division began marketing prepared foods and restaurants overseas. By 1984, Pillsbury sold over 200 products in 55 countries and Burger King had restaurants in 22 countries.

Unchecked growth continued in 1985. Cash dividends increased for the 27th consecutive year. Earnings were up 13 percent over the previous year, setting another record, and over 400 percent higher than the 1976 level. Pillsbury focused on consumer foods abroad through acquisitions and subsidiary product development. In 1986, the company's international subsidiaries reported a 6 percent increase in sales, and Pillsbury prepared to market its domestic labels, like HäagenDazs, in Japan and Europe. International sales increased 18 percent the next year.

A Reversal of Fortune in 1989

The mid-1980s, however, saw the company's progress beginning to slow. Sectors of agriproducts reported losses, and the company spent heavily on concept development for its restaurants. The success of its Bennigan's restaurant chain covered its start-up costs, but sales for chains like Steak & Ale failed to increase.

Stafford began to shift priorities, albeit conservatively. Bennigan's and Burger King were squeezed to make up for decreasing returns on the smaller restaurant chains. Consumer foods showed a profit gain of 22 percent between 1985 and 1987, and Stafford planned to continue development of Pillsbury's frozen foods and its microwave line, first introduced in 1979.

The corporation continued to have problems second guessing the fast-paced restaurant industry. Total sales increased 5 percent, but earnings declined for the first time in 16 years, down 13 percent. Consumer foods and agriproducts remained strong, but the decline in profits prompted further evaluation.

Although acquisitions overseas and in Canada continued, the company announced early in 1988, after a nine-month review, that it would reduce its restaurant division. While it kept Burger King, Bennigan's, Godfather's, and Steak & Ale, the corporation sought to rid itself of company-run units by selling them to franchisers. It also planned to refurbish 145 Burger King units. These modest reductions disappointed some analysts and takeover rumors began to circulate.

Such rumors gained momentum when the board asked William Spoor to return as CEO. Then, the chairman of Steak & Ale and the president of the U.S. foods division left the company, creating the perception of a lack of leadership. In 1988, earnings plummeted to $6.9 million, less than half the level of the year before. Management attributed much of this decline to restaurant-related restructuring changes.

Philip L. Smith, formerly of the General Foods Corporation, became CEO in August 1988. He held the post for five months as he tried to fight off a takeover attempt that had begun in October, when the British distiller Grand Metropolitan plc first made a $60-per-share bid for Pillsbury. For nearly three months after GrandMet's initial offer, Pillsbury fought the takeover. The company tried to arrange a poison pill defense and to spin off Burger King, but it was prevented from doing so by court order.

In 1989, Pillsbury became a part of Grand Metropolitan after shareholders accepted a $66 per share offer. GrandMet was one of the world's leading consumer goods companies, specializing in branded food and drink businesses. The deal, worth $5.75 billion, made GrandMet the eighth largest food manufacturing company in the world. GrandMet's branded consumer foods businesses were organized into two main groups: Pillsbury and GrandMet Foods-Europe. Pillsbury's consumer foods business was organized along major brand groups, including Pillsbury, Green Giant, and HäagenDazs. Burger King became a separate entity within the food sector.

Operations Improve in the Early to Mid-1990s

Pillsbury's operations and sales improved following the acquisition. GrandMet's restructuring reduced expenses by about $150 million and eliminated about 3,550 jobs by the middle of 1990. In May of that year, GrandMet released an impressive financial report for the first six months of the fiscal year. Pre-tax profits were up 36 percent and earnings per share increased 25 percent. Furthermore, the company predicted it would turn a profit on the Pillsbury acquisition in its first full fiscal year and would have no problem meeting the corporate goal of 15 percent annual earnings growth.

Pillsbury, under the management of CEO Paul Walsh, planned to move away from commodity products such as flour and focus on products with established brand names, while expanding into the international market. Toward that end, the company made several significant acquisitions during the 1990s. The company's February 1992 acquisition of McGlynn Bakeries' frozen products division enhanced Pillsbury's bakery division through its marketing of frozen dough products to food service and convenience outlets, as well as bakery mixes to in-store bakeries. The McGlynn products were given the more recognizable Pillsbury brand name.

In November 1993, Pillsbury purchased Roush Products Company, a manufacturer of variety and specialty bread mixes for food service and wholesale bakers. The acquisition also included Country Hearth, a market-leading brand of bread. In 1994, Pillsbury purchased Rudi Foods Inc., a leading producer of partially baked breads for food service and supermarket bakeries. The operations were combined with Pillsbury Bakeries and Foodservice Inc., an entity with annual sales of about $500 million. That same year, Pillsbury acquired Martha White brand baking mixes and flours. Perhaps one of the most notable acquisitions was Pillsbury's February 1995 acquisition of food conglomerate Pet Inc. for $2.6 billion. The purchase gave Pillsbury such popular brand names as Old El Paso, Progresso, Pet-Ritz, and Downyflake. Moreover, the Pet line enabled Pillsbury to create a more diverse product line, so that the Pillsbury name spanned across supermarket shelves.

In 1994, Pillsbury introduced over 80 new products, including Totino's Select Pizza, Pillsbury Cream Cheese Toaster Strudel, HäagenDazs Sorbet, and Hungry Jack Microwave Syrups. Internationally, Pillsbury products were sold in more than 55 countries. In Japan, Green Giant achieved a market-leading position in the frozen vegetable market, and HäagenDazs became the leading brand of premium ice cream. The company planned on expanding its Pillsbury, Green Giant, and HäagenDazs brands into Russia, India, Asia, and Latin America.

By now, Pillsbury had created and marketed some of the best-known brands and products for over 125 years, making the Pillsbury Doughboy—created in 1965 by the Leo Burnett advertising agency—and Jolly Green Giant familiar figures to American consumers. Under GrandMet, Pillsbury remained a prominent leader in the food industry and was positioned as a powerful competitor in world markets.

A Change in Ownership for the New Century

By the late 1990s, GrandMet's focus had changed. In 1997, it merged with Guinness plc to form Diageo plc. The new company's main area of operations became its profitable spirits business, which included Smirnoff vodka, Johnnie Walker scotch whiskey, and Gordon's gin. With an eye on purchasing additional brands in this category, it soon became apparent that Pillsbury's operations, along with the rest of Diageo's food-related business, were taking a back seat. Nearly 34 percent of Diageo's investment capital had been earmarked for Pillsbury and its brands. Pillsbury, however, was generating just 9 percent growth in return on investment. Indeed, its U.S. sales were falling, which prompted Diageo management to put Pillsbury up for sale.

In July 2000, Diageo announced that General Mills Inc. had made a play for Pillsbury. For Diageo, the sale would mark its exit from the food business, leaving it well positioned to pursue additional beer and liquor brand purchases. General Mills stood to gain handsomely from the sale as well. By adding Pillsbury to its arsenal, the company would nearly double in size, become the third-largest food concern in North America, and stand as the fifth-largest food company in the world. General Mills also felt pressure to make a bold move as a result of recent consolidation in the food industry. Other mergers in the works at this time included ties between Unilever and Bestfoods and between Philip Morris and Nabisco Group Holdings. General Mills eyed its purchase of Pillsbury as necessary to keep pace with changing industry conditions.

The deal, worth $10.5 billion in stock and cash, underwent a long period of intense scrutiny by the Federal Trade Commission (FTC). Both General Mills and Pillsbury were forced to sell off certain brands in order to gain FTC approval. In a complex deal, Multifoods Corp. agreed to buy the Pillsbury and Martha White dessert operations, the Hungry Jack brand, various Pillsbury bake-mix products, and General Mills' Robin Hood flour brand. The FTC finally gave its authorization, and in October 2001 Pillsbury became part of General Mills' portfolio.

Pillsbury's integration, however, did not go as smoothly as planned. By spring 2002, General Mills was under fire from analysts when profits began to soften. "Clearly, over the past six months we have been getting our first real operating experience with businesses that we haven't lived with before, so our predicting capabilities haven't been as good," remarked General Mills CEO Steve Sanger in an April 2002 Minneapolis *Star Tribune* article. Meanwhile, the company faced slowing sales, intense competition, and a growing debt load. To make matters worse, General Mills was forced to pay out $273 million in April 2003 to Diageo plc. According to a February 2004 *Star Tribune* article, Diageo was given 141 million shares of the company's stock and a promise of a payment if General Mills stock did not reach $49 per share by April 30, 2003. Unfortunately, General Mills stock was only in the mid-$40s at that time, which forced the cash payout.

Despite these problems, Sanger and his management team continued to be optimistic about the purchase, claiming it would indeed pay off in the long term. In fact, by 2003 the company reported a sales increase of 32 percent over the previous year, while net earnings doubled. Pillsbury continued to hold its leading position in the refrigerated dough segment, with sales in that category reached $1.6 billion in 2003. By that time, General Mills had experienced $350 million in cost savings as a result of the Pillsbury acquisition. While only time would tell how much success Pillsbury would experience under its new ownership, its products would no doubt line grocery store shelves for years to come.

Principal Competitors

Nestlé S.A.; Sara Lee Bakery Group; Interstate Bakeries Corp.

Further Reading

Calian, Sara, "Discussions on Pillsbury Confirmed," *Wall Street Journal*, July 14, 2000, p. A10.

Deogun, Nikhil, and Jonathan Eig, "General Mills Agrees to Acquire Pillsbury," *Wall Street Journal*, July 17, 2000, p. 1.

Eig, Jonathan, "Forsaking the Fork: General Mills Intends to Reshape Doughboy in Its Own Image," *Wall Street Journal*, July 18, 2000, p. A1.

——, "General Mills Sets Agreement to Sell Pillsbury Operations," *Wall Street Journal*, February 6, 2001, p. B13.

Forster, Julie, "General Malaise at General Mills: Rivals Have Been Eating Lunch since the Pillsbury Deal," *Business Week*, July 1, 2002.

Fusaro, Dave, "The Doughboy Is Smiling Again," *Prepared Foods*, April 1994, p. 30.

Kuhn, Mary Ellen, "Pillsbury Plus Pet Looks Like a Winner," *Food Processing*, February 1995, p. 27.

"General Mills, Pillsbury Still Waiting," *Frozen Food Age*, July 2001, p. 10.

Gogoi, Pallavi, "Thinking Outside the Cereal Box: General Mills' Far-flung Search for Efficiency Ideas," *Business Week*, July 28, 2003.

Papa, Mary Bader, "Run, Doughboy, Run," *Corporate Report-Minnesota*, July 1990, p. 39.

"Pillsbury Acquires Rudi Baked Breads Producer," *Nation's Restaurant News*, July 11, 1994, p. 81.

"Pillsbury Buys Windmill Holdings Unit," *Nation's Restaurant News*, November 29, 1993, p. 30.

Riddle, Judith S., "McGlynn Brings Pillsbury Extra Dough," *Supermarket News*, July 20, 1992, p. 35.

Sidel, Robin, "General Mills Bought the Doughboy, but at What Price?," *Wall Street Journal*, October 17, 2002, p. C1.

St. Anthony, Neal, "The Soldier and the Salesman," *Star Tribune* (Minneapolis, Minn.), February 15, 2004, p. 1D.

Wieffering, Eric, "General Mills Faces More Fire from Analysts," *Star Tribune* (Minneapolis, Minn.), April 27, 2002, p. 1D.

Wiesendanger, Betsy, "Linda Keene: Making a Stale Business Poppin' Fresh," *Sales & Marketing Management*, April 1992, p. 38.

—updates: Beth Watson Highman and
Christina M. Stansell

Pleasant Holidays

Pleasant Holidays LLC

2404 Townsgate Road
Westlake Village, California 91361
U.S.A.
Telephone: (818) 991-3390
Fax: (805) 495-4972
Web site: http://www.pleasantholidays.com

Private Company
Incorporated: 1959 as Pleasant Travel Service
Employees: 710
Sales: $487 million (2002)
NAIC: 561520 Tour Operators

Pleasant Holidays LLC is a Westlake Village, California, company that offers wholesale tour packages to Hawaii, Australia, New Zealand, Mexico, Fiji, Tahiti, the Caribbean, and the Bahamas. Pleasant's tour packages are sold through travel agencies across the United States. In addition to its corporate headquarters, Pleasant maintains offices in Bakersville and San Diego, California, and Honolulu, Hawaii. Founded by Ed and Lynn Hogan, Pleasant is now owned by AAA (American Automobile Association); the Auto Club of Southern California holds a 95 percent interest, while the Auto Club of Northern New England controls a 5 percent stake.

Origins as a Travel Agency in 1959

Pleasant's founders, Ed and Lynn Hogan, met in a Newark, New Jersey, high school in 1943 and were married in 1951. During those intervening years, Ed learned how to fly during a stint in the Navy in the final year of World War II. He then put that training to use, earning a commercial pilot's license and going to work for a small airline called Sky Coach. A natural salesman, loquacious and enthusiastic, Hogan left the cockpit in the early 1950s to take a job with an unscheduled carrier, Transocean Air Lines. He was charged with selling seats on the first tourist flights from California to Hawaii in the days before jetliners, when it took 12 hours for propeller-driven airplanes to fly from the West Coast to the islands.

At Transocean, Hogan learned both the Hawaii area and how to assemble affinity groups. When the company failed, Hogan

began to look for a new job but decided to take the advice of a friend and start his own travel agency. While Ed was pioneering the Hawaiian tourist trade, his wife Lynn had earned a degree in graphic arts from Brooklyn's Pratt Art Institute, a highly regarded program at the time. After working for a New Jersey advertising agency, she became a flight attendant for a spell, and following her marriage she found employment at the Walt Disney Studios, doing some work on picture cells for the animated feature *Peter Pan*. In 1959, when Hawaii became the 50th state, the Hogans used $10,000 in savings to open a small travel agency in Point Pleasant, New Jersey. They decided to call it Pleasant Travel Service. Duties were divided between the couple: Ed sold the trips, and Lynn did the books. In addition, Ed wrote the ad copy, and Lynn provided the graphics and production expertise.

The first few years were difficult for the Hogans, but Ed began to join numerous local organizations, such as the Rotary Club and Chamber of Commerce, and used his charm to drum up business with the people he met. By 1962, Pleasant was able to show a $16,000 profit. Because of Ed Hogan's connections to Hawaii, the company had come to specialize in tours to the islands, and it soon became apparent that New Jersey was not an ideal location for the travel agency's business. It made more sense to relocate to the West Coast, and so in 1962 the Hogans and their four children moved to Panorama City, California, where they ultimately adopted the Pleasant Hawaiian Holidays moniker. As they reestablished the business, the Hogans relied on selling Hawaiian tours packaged by others. Ed attempted to strike deals with some of Hawaii's major hotels but found them reluctant to work with unproven companies. Pleasant's first major break came in 1967 when Ed was able to secure his first hotel wholesaling arrangement with Roy Kelley and his Waikiki hotels: Reef, Reef Towers, and Edgewater. Pleasant was then able to exploit its relationship with Kelley by growing along with his chain—Outrigger, now the largest in the Islands.

Pleasant Moves to Westlake Village in 1974

In 1974, the same year that Pleasant moved its corporate headquarters to Westlake Village, California, Ed Hogan found his attempts to package tours to the outer islands thwarted by hoteliers who remained unconvinced that Pleasant was a worthy

274

Pleasant Holidays—It's not just our name, it's our promise! Since 1959.

partner. Instead, Pleasant bought its own neighbor-island hotel, the $3.5 million Kahana Beach Resort on Maui. According to a 1989 article in *Hawaii Business,* "The purchase had two consequences. First, he [Ed Hogan] was able to expand his offerings to tourists, many of whom wanted to visit both Waikiki and the Neighbor islands. In addition, his outer-island business gave him stature in the eyes of the major hoteliers who had previously closed their doors to him. 'Once I broke the ice on the outer islands, people began to say, "This guy is not just a flash in the pan,"' says Hogan. Agreements with hotels and other tourists suppliers followed." Another major break in the 1970s was a switch from charters of United DC-8s to four DC-10s provided by Western Air. In the words of Ed Hogan, "That's when we really started moving." Another major factor in the evolution of Pleasant, was its decision to sell travel packages to agents rather than directly to consumers. This travel wholesale approach, according to company materials, "revolutionized the industry and put Pleasant Holidays on the map."

Another major factor in the growth of Pleasant was its relationship to American Express. Starting in 1978, American Express provided ground operations for Pleasant at destination sites (services such as contracting for hotel rooms and rental cars and staffing service desks). American Express had once been a major wholesaler of Hawaiian trips, from 1958 to the early 1970s. When, later in the 1970s, the company decided to augment what remained of its wholesaling business, it turned to ground operations. One of its first clients was Pleasant, which in 1976 was bringing more than 75,000 people a year to Hawaii. Pleasant was an attractive partner for American Express, as outlined by *Hawaii Business* in a 1986 article: "[Pleasant] was one of the fastest growing tour wholesalers to Hawaii, due to several factors. It was the first to get into packaging tours—bulk buying of hotel rooms and plane seats that allow lower prices for the wholesaler and consumer—in a big way. Hogan also invested heavily in computerization, and initiated the revolutionary marketing tactic of advertising packages directly to the masses instead of just travel agents." Pleasant's marketing savvy and the financial might of American Express "would be a powerful match."

In August 1980, after working together for three years, Pleasant and American Express signed a joint marketing agreement for a five-year term. The ability to use the advertising slogan "Pleasant Hawaiian Holidays with American Express" was of great help to Pleasant in cracking markets east of the Rockies, where the company had little name recognition, a feat accomplished without the expense of opening offices. The agreement called for American Express to receive a share of Pleasant tours booked on the East Coast, whether they were sold through America Express offices or independent travel agents. In addition, American Express shared in upgrades and additions that these customers might make during their stay on the islands. Pleasant, on the other hand, retained all revenues from orders placed west of the Rockies. Over the course of the five-

year deal, Pleasant grew at a rapid pace. In 1980, Pleasant brought 100,000 people to the islands, and by 1985 that number mushroomed to 335,000, representing roughly 10 percent of the market. Moreover, Pleasant gained a nationwide presence, opening sales offices around the country and using some of it increased earnings to beef up efforts to computerize its telephone and reservation system. Pleasant was also able to acquire more hotels. In 1981, it bought a 260-room hotel in Waikiki, followed the next year by the purchase of the 514-room Royal Lahaina Resort on Maui. In 1984, Pleasant added two more hotels: a 287-room hotel in Waikiki and the 452-room Kona Hilton Beach & Tennis Resort. The following year, Pleasant acquired the 309-room Sheraton Coconut Beach on Kauai. With a large number of hotel rooms at its disposal, Pleasant held a distinct advantage over many of its competitors. Another factor in Pleasant's growth during this period was the 1980 signing of its first long-term agreement with United Airlines.

When the agreement with American Express expired in 1985, both parties opted not to renew. The break was portrayed as amicable, although philosophical differences between the parties were admitted, and Ed Hogan insisted that only 5.4 percent of Pleasant's business came from American Express. Regardless, Pleasant took over its own Hawaiian ground operations in 1986, as the company continued its expansive ways. In that year, it spent $10 million on advertising and introduced a senior savings program. Also in 1986, Pleasant held the first of what would become an annual event, the Tournament of Centurions. The weekend retreat in Hawaii honored the company's 100 top-selling agents, ranging from small independents to multi-location operations.

In 1987, Pleasant sent its two-millionth customer to Hawaii, and in recognition of his contribution to the islands, Ed Hogan was named "Mr. Tourism Hawaii" by the Hawaii State legislature. Pleasant continued to expand its offerings over the next few years. In 1988, the company added United Express and Delta Connection flights, which brought the number of Mainland departure cities to more than 200. As a result, in 1991 Pleasant reached the three million customer mark in its Hawaii business. The recession of this period hurt but not to any lasting effect, since Pleasant was able to offer an assortment of tour packages that appealed to all sectors of the market. Traditionally aiming for the middle of the market, in the late 1980s Pleasant began to package tours for a more upscale clientele.

Pleasant continued to be dominated by the personality of Ed Hogan, but other family members in addition to his wife and co-founder were also playing key roles with the company as he entered his 60s. Ultimately four children and two in-laws held jobs at Pleasant. Son Brian Hogan, in his mid-30s, succeeded his father as president in 1990. His work experience with Pleasant was typical for the Hogan children. According to a 1992 *Los Angeles Business Journal* article, Brian "began working for the family business when he was 8 years old by stuffing brochures under the windshield wipers of automobiles. When he was 12, he moved into the office and began filing papers and doing other odd jobs. At 14, he began selling to consumers from behind a counter and at 16 he moved into the transportation department because by then he had a driver's license. . . . When Brian graduated from high school, he went to work full time at Pleasant Hawaiian, except for [a] goof-off year at age 19. During those years, he has been a mail room clerk, a tour escort in Hawaii, a reservationist, an operations planner, a computer programmer and marketing officer.'' He may have reached the presidency because of his parentage, but there was no guarantee that his father, who remained chairman of the board, would tolerate substandard performance. Ed Hogan, in fact, fired Brian's younger brother Glenn, although he eventually brought him back to head marketing and planning for Hawaii operations.

During the 1990s, Pleasant continued to nurture its Hawaiian tour business, while looking for new destinations to provide diversification and greater growth opportunities. In 1993, the company launched Pleasant Mexico Holidays. The next year, Pleasant added more than 500,000 seats to its inventory when it struck a deal with American Trans Air. In addition, the company introduced a new online reservations system. Pleasant sent it four-millionth customer to Hawaii in 1996, but the company continued to look beyond its core island business. In 1997, Pleasant acquired Japan & Orient Tours, a company founded in the 1950s, with the hope of eventually doing business in the Pacific, Asia, and Europe. During that same year, Pleasant Tahitian Holidays was launched and a new Web site went live. In addition, the company began to offer Pleasant Concierge Service, catering to upscale travelers interested in booking suites and requesting amenities. At the same time, Pleasant continued to package tours aimed at seniors, families, and couples looking for romantic getaways.

Ownership Change in 1998 Kept Secret

Control of Pleasant changed hands in 1998 when the Auto Club of Southern California bought a controlling interest, but news of the transaction was withheld until June 2001, at which point it caused a bit of a stir in the travel industry. Because of media attention paid to the matter, the California Attorney General's office ''looked into'' the sale and quickly concluded that there was no law requiring the disclosure of the deal. The office refused to even call its review an investigation or probe, language used in press reports. What made the acquisition so significant to the industry was that the seller was one of America's largest tour operators and the buyer, the Auto Club Southern California, with five million members, was the largest

AAA affiliate in the country. Hogan called the sale a strategic alliance that was beneficial to Pleasant, which in 1999 changed its name to Pleasant Holidays, in keeping with the company's diversification beyond Hawaii. He also admitted that he first negotiated with American Express about selling a controlling interest in the business but scuttled the deal because he would have to give up control. The auto club agreed to his terms, eager to find a reliable partner in the consolidating travel industry.

Hogan underwent bypass surgery in 1999, and, as he reached his mid-70s at the beginning of the new century, retained control of Pleasant for only two more years. On the last day of 2001, Hogan sold his remaining interest in the company he had founded with his wife more than 40 years earlier. He stayed on as chairman and remained involved in the business, but his role was more ceremonial than administrative. With the start of 2002, a new president took charge of Pleasant: Tim Irwin, the vice-president of travel for the Automobile Club of Southern California. Irwin quickly made it clear that the way Pleasant operated with independent travel agents would remain unchanged and that the auto club was to receive no special advantages. Given that the auto club provided only a modest amount of business to Pleasant, there was every incentive to continue good relations with travel agencies. Irwin soon oversaw the realization of a long-cherished dream of Ed and Lynn Hogan: serving the Caribbean from the West Coast. In April 2002, Pleasant announced that starting in January 2003 the company would begin to offer packaged tours to Aruba; Grand Cayman, Cayman Islands; Jamaica; Nassau/Paradise Island, Bahamas; Puerto Rico; and St. Lucia. Pleasant's entry into this new market promised to bring an entire new clientele to the Caribbean while adding a major new revenue stream to the company.

Principal Subsidiaries

Hawaii World; Air By Pleasant; Hotels By Pleasant; Pleasant Island Holidays; Pacific Destination Services.

Principal Competitors

Expedia/Classic Custom Vacations; Gogo Travel; Apple Vacations.

Further Reading

Chang, Diane, ''The Big Split,'' *Hawaii Business*, March 1986, p. 50.
Cogswell, David, ''The Hogan's Journey to Success: Pleasant All the Way,'' *Travel Weekly*, August 31, 2000, p. 12.
Deutsch, Martin B., ''Ed Hogan in Paradise Found,'' *Travel Agent*, February 19, 2001, p. 16.
Hooper, Susan, ''The Pleasant Principle,'' *Hawaii Business*, August 1989, p. 171.
Kristof, Kathy M., ''Hogan's Hard Work, Family and Blarney Create Hawaiian Empire,'' *Los Angeles Business Journal*, September 28, 1987, p. 1.

—Ed Dinger

Policy Studies, Inc.

1899 Wynkoop Street
Denver, Colorado 90202
U.S.A.
Telephone: (303) 863-0900
Toll Free: (800) 217-5004
Fax: (303) 295-0244
Web site: http://www.policy-studies.com

Private Company
Incorporated: 1984
Employees: 1,030
Sales: $128 million (2002)
NAIC: 541611 Administration Management and General
    Management Consulting Services

Policy Studies, Inc. (PSI) provides administration outsourcing, research, and consulting services to local, state and federal agencies in the areas of child support enforcement, health benefits administration, and judicial systems organization. The bulk of the company's business involves consulting and administration of child support enforcement, including payment collection and redisbursement, voluntary paternity establishment, backlog collections, review and adjustment, and other aspects of case management. In addition to providing research and consultation for specific aspects of case management for government agencies in all 50 states and administration outsourcing for specific programs in 21 states, PSI provides full-service child support enforcement administration for counties in Arizona, Colorado, Maryland, North Carolina, Oklahoma, Tennessee, Virginia, West Virginia, and Wyoming.

In the area of health care, PSI administers State Children's Health Insurance Programs (SCHIPs) and other health benefits programs. PSI Arista provides consulting and administration on healthcare-related issues, such as public policy research, public education campaigns, strategic planning, and technology. Other consulting and research services include judicial process assessment and recommendations for case flow management.

PSI Technologies specializes in the development and implementation of computer software systems that facilitate child support enforcement and health care enrollment and claims processing. Information technology services include web site development, call center customer service systems, and database development.

1980s Origins

Founded in 1984 by Robert Williams, David Price, and Betty Schulte, PSI originated with Williams's participation in a national study to determine the appropriate level of court-ordered child support payments. As the chief researcher for the U.S. Health and Human Services' Office of Child Support Enforcement (OCSE), Williams provided research and technical consulting for the Child Support Guidelines Project beginning in 1983. Williams initiated the formation of PSI to provide similar theoretical research to human services programs, primarily in the areas of food stamps and aid to families with dependent children.

Williams' work with the OCSE culminated in the 1987 publication *Development Guidelines for Child Support Orders,* a seminal work which recommended the Income Shares model to determine court-ordered child support for non-custodial parents. Williams based the model on the idea that children should be supported in the same manner as they would if living in the household of an intact family. A portion of the non-custodial parent's after-tax income therefore applied to children's support in a single household through payment to the primary parent. With the intention of preventing child poverty, the Income Shares model increased child support obligations by as much as triple original court-ordered arrangements. When the Family Support Act of 1988 required states to adopt uniform guidelines for determining child support, by tying it to eligibility for federal welfare funding, OCSE recommended the Income Shares model, thus assisting PSI's entry into child support consulting. Eventually, more than 30 states adopted the Income Shares model.

PSI's shift toward child support enforcement developed from its participation in the study. Government agencies faced an increasing backlog of uncollected child support in the aftermath of high divorce rates during the 1970s, and the situation

Company Perspectives:

PSI's commitment to improving performance distinguishes our work. We apply our deep understanding of policy, technology, and operations to help our clients solve problems, automate processes, and enhance performance.

demanded more effective methods of addressing child support enforcement. In partnership with state and local agencies, PSI developed efficient methods for administering larger caseloads, which involved using every legal step allowed under a particular jurisdiction. PSI consulted on the application of new computer technologies which began to play a significant role in administration. For instance, PSI initiated electronic funds transfer to facilitate collection and disbursement of child support payments and developed computer software to ease access to individual case information.

In 1991, as the company's innovations in child support collections came to national attention, PSI became the first company to be awarded a contract to provide child support enforcement administration. That year the Tennessee Tenth Judicial District hired PSI to handle cases for the cities of Cleveland and Athens and surrounding areas in southeast Tennessee. PSI received a fee, at 10 to 15 percent of money collected, declining over the term of the five-year contract (but not derived from child support funds).

PSI expanded as other county governments decided to outsource child support enforcement. PSI obtained a contract for the Tennessee 29th Judicial District for Dyer and Lake Counties in 1992. The following year Douglas County in Nebraska hired the company to manage its child support office for Omaha, the first urban program to be outsourced. In 1994 PSI obtained contracts for Fulton County, Georgia, covering the city of Atlanta, and for Yavapai and Santa Cruz Counties in Arizona.

Contracts effective January 1, 1995, covered Obion and Weakley Counties, and Union City, Tennessee. More than 5,000 cases accounted for potential collection of $2.5 million in court-ordered payments. In Wyoming PSI obtained contracts for the First, Second, and Third Judicial Districts, covering Cheyenne, Laramie, Green River, and Evanston. By the end of 1995 PSI operated with a staff of 280 lawyers, paralegals, clerks, and other employees. With outsourcing contracts in 5 states and consulting contracts in almost every state, PSI earned $12.9 million in revenues.

PSI had shown its child support enforcement methods to be effective by the end of 1995. During the first four years of its contract with the Tennessee Tenth Judicial District, from 1991 to 1995, PSI handled 130,000 cases of unpaid child support and alimony and increased collections 140 percent, a total of $63 million for all four years.

While child support services became the primary source of business, PSI continued to provide research and consulting services on other government issues. PSI conducted several studies on judicial process, involving structural and organizational assessment of judicial case flow. Landmark research resulted in

the 1992 publication of *An Approach to Long Range Strategic Planning in the Courts*, along with curriculum for judicial educators and trainers. In 1995 PSI released *Strategic Planning in the Courts, Implementation Guide,* describing the outcomes of strategic planning programs instituted in nine jurisdictions. PSI published research on *Representing Indigent Parties in Civil Cases: An Analysis of State Practices.* The study on *Culturally Responsive Alternative Dispute Resolutions for Latinos* utilized information PSI obtained from research in Maricopa County's judicial system in Phoenix, Arizona.

Mid-1990s Welfare Reform Creates New Demands

PSI's range of services within child support enforcement expanded with the Personal Responsibility and Work Opportunities Reconciliation Act of 1996. Also know as the Welfare Reform Act, the federal legislation allowed for government agencies to obtain overdue payments through federal income tax withholding, license restrictions, and other methods. The law required states to centralize case files for child support collection and disbursement, prompting PSI to increase its emphasis on high technology solutions to case management problems with the formation of PSI Technologies. For instance, the legislation required state participation in a National Directory of New Hires to assist in tracking delinquent child support obligors. The law required companies to report new employees within 20 days of hire. PSI implemented new-hire reporting systems for several states, primarily using electronic methods that easily transferred information to the national database.

Early paternity establishment became an essential aspect of rapidly initiating court-ordered child support for children of unwed mothers, in order to deter dependence on welfare. PSI instituted Paternity Opportunity Programs for state agencies in New Jersey, Iowa, Ohio, Massachusetts, and other states, involving both legal and technological solutions. The company emphasized obtaining voluntary acknowledgment. Approaching mothers in the maternity ward, they found fathers acknowledged paternity more readily at this time. PSI staff discovered they had more flexibility in this approach than a government agency, as hospital personnel perceived the company as a neutral third party. Technological concerns involved management of voluntary acknowledgments in a central database. PSI applied new software to provide imaging, storage, indexing, retrieval, and distribution of case file documents.

PSI continued to pursue child support enforcement outsourcing opportunities, bidding and winning several contracts during the late 1990s. PSI obtained child support enforcement contracts with Cobb County, Georgia, covering Marietta and Smyrna, and DeKalb County, covering cities east of Atlanta. A contract with Kanawha County in West Virginia covered the city of Charleston. The Tennessee 21st Judicial District, covering Franklin and Hohenwad, hired PSI to handle all aspects of child support enforcement. At the end of 1997 PSI operated 16 child support offices in five states. A five-year, $10 million contract with Chesapeake and Hampton Counties in Virginia, effective February 1, 1999, added two more offices.

PSI's research activities continued to focus on child support issues and judicial process. In 1997 PSI published its *Evaluation of the Child Access Demonstration Projects,* a report to the U.S. Congress which discussed and analyzed seven child support enforcement projects. Research conducted in four Wisconsin counties covered the judicial process in child abuse and neglect cases resulted in the 1998 publication *A Practical Guide to CHIPS Case Processing.* Other 1998 publications included *Continuous Quality Improvements in the Courts: A Practitioner's Handbook* and *A Judge's Guide to Culturally Competent Responses to Latino Family Violence.*

21st Century Technologies

As computer technology improved, PSI Technologies developed and adapted state-of-the-art systems to address the needs of child support administration. In 2000 the company obtained a contract to establish the New Mexico Child Support Information Center, which responds to inquiries about the status of particular child support cases. Using proprietary PSI-Link software, the system simplified and quickened access to information stored on mainframe computers, transferring only relevant data to desktop computers in a user-friendly format. PSI-Link provided a record of customer service calls, as well as related statistics. Effective technologies enabled customer service staff to handle 1,200 to 1,500 calls per day.

As organizations of all kinds began to use the Internet for information dissemination, PSI began to offer web site development to government agencies. In 2001 PSI developed a web site for the Colorado Department of Human Services to improve access to general information by parents, employers, and child support staff. PSI further improved the site in 2002 to allow parents access to case file status. Iowa's Bureau of Collections hired PSI to design and build a web site that provided employers direct access to child support forms online. The Employers Partnering in Child Support (EPICS) system was recognized by the Council of State Governments for its innovation in resolving bureaucratic problems in state government. PSI applied a similar system for the State of Vermont as well.

PSI obtained a contract with the state of Vermont's Office of Child Support to install an electronic document management

system that would facilitate access to case files from five regional offices, eliminating the need for mailing or faxing paper copies. PSI applied OnBase software solution, by Hyland Software, Inc., to provide imaging, storage, indexing, retrieval, and distribution of case file documents. The total system included Bar Code Recognition for indexing imaged documents and Applications Programming Interfaces for transferring data from the central system to staff desktop computers. Implementation of the system increased efficiency and improved customer service. Also, PSI transferred to the OnBase software documents for the state of New Jersey's Paternity Opportunity Program, implemented by PSI in 1995. OnBase allowed the documents to be accessed by a greater number of staff members at courts and human services agencies statewide.

PSI obtained successive contracts with the state of Michigan to overhaul its automated child support enforcement system to meet federal requirements. Contracts accumulated more than $200 million in revenues during the two-and-a-half year process. PSI converted nearly one million cases to the new system, involving offices of Family Independence Administration, prosecuting attorneys, and Friends of the Court in each of the state's 83 counties. The development, implementation, and federal certification process involved as many as 500 employees working in collaboration with state employees. The state of Michigan needed to implement the system rapidly, by September 30, 2003, in order to avoid several million dollars in federal penalties. PSI completed the system on time and the state received federal certification in November; however, several problems required high level of maintenance for which another company was hired at lower cost.

PSI continued to expand its child support reinforcement operations, obtaining contracts for the Eighth and Ninth Judicial Districts covering Douglas and Lander, Wyoming, in 2000. New contracts in 2001 involved jurisdictions covering Arlington and Alexandria, Virginia; Asheville, North Carolina, in Buncombe County; and neighboring Polk County. PSI obtained contracts with El Paso County in Colorado Springs and adjacent Teller County, both in Colorado, to collect back child support. The 5-year, $18.6 million contract with El Paso County involved hiring a staff of 22 employees who would operate the Parent Opportunity Program, providing job training and placement for unemployed and underemployed parents.

Job training and placement and parenting support developed as new subjects requiring study and solutions. Activities in this area included a study conducted for the Annie E. Casey Foundation, entitled *Low-Income Fathers: Starting Off on the Right Track.* The report recommended actions for improving the treatment of low-income fathers in the child support enforcement system.

PSI entered the field of health care administration, research, and consulting through acquisition. In April 2002 PSI acquired Child Health Advocates. That company administered the federal Child Health Plan Plus to provide health care for children of low-income families for the state of Colorado. (The state did not renew the contract in 2002, however.) Through the acquisition PSI obtained proprietary Child Health Administration Management Program System (CHAMPS) software. The technology facilitated qualification processing by transforming state regulations into a matching system, based on age, family income, and other factors, which could easily be adapted to changing regulations. CHAMPS processed four to five applications per hour, in contrast to about two per hour manually. The system was implemented in Colorado and Virginia.

Arista Associates, acquired by PSI in June, provided research, consulting, and marketing services to the state health agencies through offices in Charlotte, North Carolina, Washington, D.C., and Chicago, Illinois. Renamed PSI Arista, the subsidiary formulated health education campaigns in Maine and Massachusetts to encourage the general public to be tested for sexually transmitted diseases and hepatitis C, respectively.

Through the acquisition of Dental Health Administration and Consulting Services, Inc. (DHACS), PSI took over outsourcing contracts for administration of Georgia PeachCare for Kids and Florida KidCare, both health insurance programs for children of low-income families. The company also processed premiums for Indiana's Hoosier Healthwise and MedWorks programs. PSI transferred a call center operated by DHACS in Lisle, Illinois, to the Palm Beach area in Florida. The call center handled customer service inquiries for children's health plans in Georgia, Florida, Indiana, and Michigan.

In July 1, 2003, PSI began fulfillment of a contract to administer the state of Missouri's Managed Care Program for Medicaid recipients. PSI to implement a new information system that would ease enrollment and improve customer service through access to a database of participating health care providers.

A contract held jointly with Health Management Systems for the Colorado Department of Human Services involved enforcement of medical support orders, whereby parents are required to extend health insurance benefits to dependents. Under the contract, HMS would identify parents with health coverage and PSI matched data with the Child Support Enforcement Office files of non-custodial parents.

During 2002 PSI began fulfillment of child support enforcement contracts for Cochise County, Arizona; Horry Region, South Carolina; Haskell and Pittsburgh Counties in Oklahoma; and the Tennessee Sixth Judicial District, covering the city of Knoxville. These were followed in 2003 by contracts for Onslow County, North Carolina, and the Tennessee 20th Judicial District, covering Davidson County and the city of Nashville. The Davidson County contract for $28.4 million involved a fee of 9.82 percent of amount collected during the first year of the contract, and 6.22 percent in the fifth year. On January 2, 2004 PSI began administration of child support enforcement

programs for Baltimore City and Queen Anne's Counties, Maryland, contracts worth $10 to $15 million.

Principal Subsidiaries

Child Services of Arizona; Dental Health Administrative and Consulting Services, Inc.; Privatization Partners, Inc.; PSI Arista, Inc.; PSI Technologies, Inc.

Principal Competitors

DynTek, Inc.; Lockheed Martin Information Management Systems; Maximus, Inc.

Further Reading

Alligood, Leon, "Maximus Loses DHS Contract," *Tennessean,* May 22, 2003, p. 3B.
"Another Call Center Coming to St. Lucie," *Palm Beach Post,* November 24, 2003.
"Benefits Technology Could Help 1.7 Million Uninsured Children," *ManagedHealthcare.Info,* February 4, 2002, p. 4.
Cawley, Jim, "Private Firm to Run Child Support Div.," *Commercial Appeal,* November 16, 1994, p. B2.
Crowder, Carla, "Deadbeat Parents Have New Foes," *Rocky Mountain News,* September 9, 2000, p. 7A.
Dresser, Michael, "Maryland Board Grants Child-Support Enforcer Six-Month Contract Extension," *Baltimore Sun,* June 19, 2002.
Emerson, Adam, "Child Support Burdened by New System," *Lansing State Journal,* December 7, 2003.
Fischer, Howard, "State Privatizes the Processing of Child Support Checks," *Arizona Daily Star,* June 20, 1997, p. 1B.
"HMS Teams With Policy Studies, Inc. to Provide Medical Support Enforcement Services in Colorado," *PR Newswire,* July 8, 2003.
Kane, Arthur, "State's Choice of Firm Blasted; Conflict of Interest Alleged," *Denver Post,* November 1, 2002, p. B1.
Mook, Bob, "Reforms Might Benefit Child-Support Company," *Denver Business Journal,* June 27, 1997, p. 18A.
Olgeirson, Ian, "Policy Studies Collects From Deadbeat Fathers," *Denver Business Journal,* May 31, 1996, p. 3A.
Perrault, Michael, "Policy Studies Purchases Child Health Advocates," *Rocky Mountain News,* April 4, 2002, p. 16B.
"Private Consultant Paves the Way on Child Support," *Rocky Mountain News,* February 23, 1992, p. 2C.
Simpson, Elizabeth, "Privatization Put to the Test: 5-Year Child Support Collection Contract Awarded to Rival of Current Company," *Virginian Pilot,* December 26, 1998, p. B1.
Uhland, Vicky, "Partner in Service; Policy Studies Has Strong Commitment to Child Support Programs," *Rocky Mountain News,* October 3, 2003, p. 4B.
Zubeck, Pam, "Child Support Firm Opens After Winning Contract," *Colorado Springs Gazette,* January 3, 2001.

—Mary Tradii

Polo/Ralph Lauren Corporation

650 Madison Avenue
New York, New York 10022
U.S.A.
Telephone: (212) 318-7000
Toll Free: (888) 475-7674
Fax: (212) 888-5780
Web site: http://about.polo.com

Public Company
Incorporated: 1968 as Polo Fashions, Inc.
Employees: 11,000
Sales: $2.44 billion (2003)
Stock Exchanges: New York
Ticker Symbol: RL
NAIC: 315 Apparel Manufacturing; 54149 Other
   Specialized Design Services

The Polo/Ralph Lauren Corporation (RL) has become one of the best-known fashion design and licensing houses in the world. Founded by American designer Ralph Lauren in the late 1960s, the company boomed in the 1980s as Lauren's designs came to be associated with a sophisticated and distinctly American attitude. The company's first products were wide ties, but it soon designed and manufactured an entire line of menswear before entering the more lucrative women's fashion market as a designer and licenser. By the 1980s, the Polo/Ralph Lauren name helped sell a wide array of products, including fragrances and accessories for men and women, clothing for young boys and infants, and a variety of housewares, shoes, furs, jewelry, leather goods, hats, and eyewear. Menswear accounted for 42 percent of 2003 sales of $2.44 billion. Womenswear was the next largest segment (25 percent), followed by fragrances, accessories, children's, and home. Brands include Polo, Lauren, Chaps, and Club Monaco. The company licenses nearly 300 manufacturers and 100 retail outlets around the world. RL also runs 240 of its own stores in the United States.

Origins in the 1960s

Ralph Lifshitz was born on October 14, 1939 in the Bronx to a middle class Jewish family. Somewhere along the way he had his surname legally changed to "Lauren." His father was an artist and housepainter; his mother was reportedly disappointed Ralph did not become a rabbi.

The Polo empire began in the late 1960s, when Lauren, then a clothing salesman, got sick of selling other people's neckties and decided to design and sell his own. Lauren had no experience in fashion design, but he had grown up in the New York fashion world, selling men's gloves, suits, and ties. In 1967, he went to his employer, Abe Rivetz, with a proposal to design a line of ties, but Rivetz told him, "The world is not ready for Ralph Lauren." Lauren decided that it was, and he convinced clothier Beau Brummel to manufacture his Polo line of neckwear. "I didn't know how to make a tie," Lauren confessed to *Vogue* in 1982. "I didn't know fabric, I didn't know measurements. What did I know? That I was a salesman. That I was honest. And that all I wanted was quality." Lauren's ties were wider and more colorful than other ties on the market and they soon found a niche, first in small menswear stores and later in the fashionable Bloomingdale's department store.

Within a year, Lauren decided to form his own company with help from his brother Jerry and $50,000 in backing from Norman Hilton, a Manhattan clothing manufacturer. The company, Polo Fashions, Inc. (which changed its name to Polo/Ralph Lauren Corporation in 1987), expanded the Polo menswear collection to include shirts, suits, and sportswear, as well as the trademark ties. The company designed, manufactured, and distributed the Polo collection, which met with the approval of both the department stores that featured the clothes and the fashion critics who praised their style. Fashion critic Bernadine Morris was quoted in *Time* as saying, "He's acquired a certain reputation for clothes that are, you know, with it. But not too with it. Not enough to shock the boys at the bank." In 1970, Lauren received the coveted Coty Award for menswear. In a rare move, Lauren then began designing clothes for women as well as for men. His first designs—men's dress shirts cut for women—met with great success in 1971, and soon sales topped $10 million.

The rapid growth of Polo Fashions, Inc. proved hard to manage for the young entrepreneur, who had succeeded in crafting a brand identity but not in managing his business. By 1972, according to *Time*, "Lauren suddenly discovered that his enterprise was almost bankrupt because of poor financial management and the

Company Perspectives:

Polo has become a brand with unmatched recognition in the marketplace, offering the best of menswear, womenswear, childrenswear and home design. Polo's design excellence works in concert with its disciplined business approach, and these two traits together have allowed the Company to set the standard for the industry.

costs of headlong expansion." "I almost blew my business," Lauren told *Forbes*. "I wasn't shipping on time and had problems delivering." "It was probably . . . one of the darkest moments in my life," he remembered in New York. Scrambling to survive, Lauren invested $100,000 of his savings in the business and convinced Peter Strom to leave his job with Norman Hilton and become his partner. The arrangement gave Lauren 90 percent and Strom 10 percent ownership. Strom described their duties to the *New York Times Magazine:* "We divide the work this way: I do everything Ralph doesn't want to do; and I don't do anything he likes to do. He designs, he does advertising, public relations; I do the rest." The Lauren brothers and Strom soon made changes in the structure of the company that set the stage for more than two decades of unparalleled success.

During its first four years, Polo Fashions, Inc. had controlled each stage in the clothes making process, from design, to manufacture, to distribution. Their first step in reorganization was to concentrate on what they did best—design—and leave the rest to other companies. With this in mind, Polo Fashions, Inc. licensed the manufacture of Ralph Lauren brand womenswear to Stuart Kreisler, an experienced manufacturer who set out to build the reputation of the Lauren brand name. Under licensing agreements, the designer got a cut of wholesale revenues—usually between 5 and 8 percent for Polo, according to *Forbes*—and shared in advertising costs. Such agreements would be the basis for Polo's future business. Moreover, Strom insisted that those retailers who sold the company's clothes make a commitment to selling the entire line, which meant they had to carry the $350 Polo suit. "That eliminated two-thirds of our accounts," Strom told *Vogue*. "But those who stayed with us experienced our commitment to them, and it wasn't long before we felt their loyalty in return." With business once again secure, the company was able to turn its attention to crafting a brand image as distinctive as any in America.

1980s: The Decade of Polo

Beginning in the mid 1970s, Polo Fashions, Inc. entered a period of phenomenal growth that carried it through the late 1980s. From being a designer and licenser of limited lines of men's and women's clothing, the company expanded its products to include fragrances, eyewear, shoes, accessories, housewares, and a range of other products. Yet even as the number of products bearing the brand names "Polo" or "Ralph Lauren" expanded, the image of the company became more secure and more singular. Soon, people were speaking of the "Laurenification of America," crediting Ralph Lauren with creating a unique American aesthetic, and calling the 1980s the "decade of Ralph Lauren." The company's success in this period can be

credited to the design skills of Ralph Lauren and to the astute image-making and marketing skills of Lauren and his principal partner, Peter Strom.

Fashion critics and journalists used words like integrity, elegance, tradition, sophistication, WASPy, mannered, pseudo-English, and sporty to describe Lauren's many designs. Yet no single word could encompass the many themes—from the famous English Polo Club designs to the distinctly American western designs—with which Lauren experimented. Some critics complained that Lauren was a relentless borrower, possessed of no unique vision. Lauren himself stated in *New York* that he was interested in "style but not flamboyance, but sophistication, class, and an aristocratic demeanor that you can see in people like Cary Grant and Fred Astaire." And, as Lauren pointed out, "The things I do are not about novelty. They're things I love and can't get away from. There are some things in life that, no matter what the times are, keep getting better and better. That's really my philosophy."

Polo excelled at getting Lauren's distinctive design image across to consumers. From its very first advertisements in New York City newspapers in 1974, the company attempted to portray its products as part of a complete lifestyle. Polo pioneered the multi-page lifestyle advertisement in major magazines. These ads presented a world lifted out of time, where wealthy, attractive people relaxed in Polo products during a weekend at their country estate or on safari in Africa. *Vogue* described the ads as a kind of "home movie," with a cast of "faintly sorrowful but wildly attractive people. The women are always between childhood and thirty; the men are sometimes old." Polo lavished huge amounts of money on these ads, as much as $15 and $20 million a year, though its licensees shared some of the cost by returning 2 to 3 percent of sales into the advertising budget. An ad director for a major fashion magazine told *Time:* Polo "has some of the best advertising in the business because it sets a mood, it evokes a lifestyle."

Lauren's intuitive design sense and the company's ability to create an idealized image for its products provided the base for the company to expand the variety of products it marketed and attain greater control over retailing. From its first product lines—Polo by Ralph Lauren menswear and Ralph Lauren womenswear—the company introduced a variety of products: Polo by Ralph Lauren cologne and boys' clothing in 1978; a girlswear line in 1981; luggage and eyeglasses in 1982; home furnishings in 1983. Later brand extensions included shoes, furs, and underwear. The company introduced its collection of apparel for newborns, infants, and toddlers in 1994. These new product lines were accompanied by continual updating of the older brand names.

Although Polo retained control over the design and advertising of its products, the success or failure of Polo product expansion often depended upon its licensees, as Polo's experience with fragrances and its home collection indicated. Polo's fragrances became a major income producer only when it found a licensee who was willing to help develop and promote the products. Although Polo had marketed its fragrances—Polo by Ralph Lauren for men and Lauren for women—since 1978, they were not major sellers until the mid-1980s, when the company licensed fragrance production to Cosmair, Inc. In

Key Dates:

1968: Polo Fashions is created by tie salesman Ralph Lauren.
1974: The first ads appear in NYC newspapers.
1978: Polo cologne is introduced.
1983: An extensive, licensed home furnishings line debuts.
1986: The flagship store opens on Madison Avenue.
1997: Polo/Ralph Lauren goes public.
2003: The European headquarters moves from Paris to Geneva.

1990, Cosmair introduced Polo Crest for men and Safari for women, made to accompany a new line of clothing also bearing the Safari name. *Cosmetic Insiders' Report* called Safari the ''Fragrance of the Year'' after it recorded sales as high as $11,000 a day at Bloomingdale's flagship stores. Cosmair hoped to sell between $25 and $30 million wholesale by the end of the fragrance's first year. Two years later Polo and Cosmair launched Safari for Men, which they promoted in an uncharacteristic television commercial in which Ralph Lauren rode a horse bareback on a beach. According to *Women's Wear Daily,* Cosmair hoped to sell $28 million in wholesale at the end of six months, and to top $50 million by the end of two years.

Not all licensing arrangements worked so well. In 1983, Polo began to promote the introduction of its ''Home Collection,'' a line of products that Lauren had designed for the home. *House & Garden* called the collection, which numbered more than 2,500 items and included everything from sheets to furniture to flatware, ''the most complete of its kind conceived by a fashion designer.'' But the collection soon ran into serious trouble as the licensee, the J.P. Stevens Company, experienced difficulties getting the products to retail outlets on time. J.P. Stevens also had trouble maintaining quality control, having themselves licensed elements of the line to other companies. In addition, Stevens demanded that stores that wanted to show the collection construct $250,000 free-standing, wood-paneled boutiques to display the items—and stores balked at the price tag. Polo/Ralph Lauren Vice-Chairman Peter Strom told *Time* that the introduction was ''A disaster! Disaster!'' It took several years for Polo to get the collection back on track.

Over the years, Polo used a number of techniques to exert control over the way its merchandise was distributed and sold. Early on, the company insisted that retailers offer the entire product line instead of simply selecting items it wanted to carry, arguing that the lines had to stand as a coherent whole. Beginning in 1971, the company began to offer franchises as well, and it has franchised more than 100 Polo/Ralph Lauren stores worldwide since that time. Instead of charging a franchise fee, the company made money as the wholesaler for the clothing. These franchises allowed an entire store to concentrate on the Polo image. In 1982, Polo opened the first of its 50 outlet stores in Lawrence, Kansas. The outlet stores allowed the company to control the distribution of irregulars and items that had not sold by the end of each season, thereby preventing the company's products from appearing in discount stores. These outlet stores

were placed at a significant distance from the full-price retailers to ensure that they did not steal business. Such expansion occurred not only in America but around the world, as Polo opened shops in London, Paris, and Tokyo.

The flagship of the Polo/Ralph Lauren retail enterprise was the refurbished Rhinelander mansion on Madison Avenue in New York City. Opened in 1986, the 20,000-square-foot mansion featured mahogany woodwork, hand-carved balustrades lining marble staircases, and sumptuous carpeting. ''While men who look like lawyers search for your size shirt and ladies who belong at deb parties suggest complementary bags and shoes, you experience the ultimate in lifestyle advertising,'' wrote Lenore Skenazy in *Advertising Age.* Naomi Leff, who designed the interior of the Polo palace, called it ''a marker in retailing history. It tells manufacturers that if they're willing to put out, they'll be able to make their own statement, which is not being made in the department stores.''

Establishing brand-focused retail outlets made perfect sense for Polo/Ralph Lauren, for it allowed the company to increase profits by eliminating the middleman as well as to control the environment in which the products appeared. In fact, other designers have since followed Polo/Ralph Lauren's lead, including Calvin Klein, Liz Claiborne, Adrienne Vittadini, and Anne Klein. But the move caused tension between the designer and his traditional retailers, the large department stores. A *Forbes* feature on Lauren's strategy claimed that ''a lot of people in business think it is in bad taste to compete with your own customers. Lauren clearly does not agree. And such is his pull at the cash register that he may get away with this piece of business heresy.''

Public in 1997

The Polo/Ralph Lauren Corporation rode its expertly crafted brand image and astute retailing strategies to remarkable heights in the 1980s, as sustained economic growth and America's fascination with Lauren's image fueled an unparalleled expansion in products bearing the Ralph Lauren name. But retail expansion slowed dramatically with the economic downturn in the early 1990s, and some stores that once thrived on the sales of Ralph Lauren's high-priced products complained that the company was unable to adjust to changes in the market. Robert Parola, writing in the *Daily News Record* in 1990, noted that many clothing manufacturers had lifted their designs from Ralph Lauren and begun selling them for less. Polo/Ralph Lauren was hardly a company to be counted out in the 1990s, however. Successful fragrance introductions and the development of the popular Polo Sport active-sportswear and Double RL jeanswear lines promised to keep money rolling into the company coffers. The 1994 sale of 28 percent of the company to a Goldman Sachs & Co. investment fund for $135 million prompted speculation about the future of the company. *Wall Street Journal* reporter Teri Agins remarked that ''the company is at a crossroads as it embarks on a strategy to improve its retail operations and lure a younger generation'' to its products. In the short term, industry observers expected the company to use the cash influx to expand its retail stores. But observers also wondered whether this sale, the first in the company's history, indicated that the company would eventually go public or that Ralph Lauren was beginning to look toward life after designing.

The company did, in fact, go public on the New York Stock Exchange, on June 13, 1997. Founder and Chairman Ralph Lauren sold nearly 18 million of his own shares for $465.4 million. He retained 90 percent of voting rights, however, through his ownership of all outstanding class B stock.

Although the shares were trading at a premium, some analysts felt the stock had good growth potential due to relatively unexploited world markets and an underdeveloped women's line; two years earlier, Polo had regained the rights to it from its licensee, Biderman USA.

Polo had then brought out a moderately priced women's collection in collaboration with licensee Jones Apparel Group in the fall of 1996. (The more expensive Ralph line was then renamed ''RL.'') Within a couple of years, however, Polo would cancel the contract due to low sales volume, and Jones would take its case to court.

Polo rolled out a plethora of other brand extensions in the late 1990s, including shoes from Reebok and Rockport and a line of Polo-brand jeans. There was also more shifting of licensees: Corneliani S.p.A. of Italy won the right to produce RL's Blue Label clothing line for men. In 2001, WestPoint Stevens, which already made RL sheets and towels, took over the bedding license from Pillowtex Corp. The total number of licensees was soon approaching 300.

RL ended 1998 with announcements of 250 job cuts and nine store closings. At the same time, it was opening a flagship store in Chicago. An RL-branded restaurant opened next door a few months later. The company had about 200 outlets, half of them operated by licensees.

New Frontiers for the New Millennium

In March 1999, RL paid $80 million (C $80 million) for Club Monaco Inc., a chain of trendy clothing stores based in Toronto. It had 56 stores in Canada and 13 in the United States. Club Monaco attracted the younger, hipper clientele that Ralph Lauren had been unable to lure away from the likes of Tommy Hilfiger.

In 2000 the company formed a multimedia marketing joint venture with NBC and affiliates NBCi, CNBC, and ValueVision (operator of the Home Shopping Network). RL's first television advertising debuted soon after.

RL bought European licensee Poloco SA in 2000 for $230 million; Italian licensee PRL Fashions of Europe and a Belgian store were acquired in 2001. RL was able to quadruple European sales between 1999 and 2002, noted *Crain's New York Business,* but expansion was expensive. In Europe, clothing was typically sold in specialty shops, not giant department stores, such as the Big Three in the United States that made up more than a half of RL's wholesale revenues. RL moved its European operations from Paris to Geneva in 2003.

In February 2003, RL paid ¥5.6 billion ($47.6 million) for a 50 percent interest in the master license of the Polo Ralph Lauren men's, women's, and jeans business in Japan. Stores also were acquired from licensees in Germany and Argentina.

One employee at a San Francisco store sued RL for allegedly forcing its employees to buy its own pricey clothes to wear at work, and to update their wardrobes every season. Polo denied having such a uniform requirement, reported the *San Francisco Chronicle.* Ironically, a general return to dressier work clothes, a result of a tighter job market, was one good sign for the company entering 2004. RL assumed responsibility for its Lauren line for women from its former licensee, Jones Apparel Group.

Principal Subsidiaries

Acqui Polo, C.V. (Netherlands); Fashions Outlet of America, Inc.; PRL USA Holdings, Inc.; PRL International, Inc.; Ralph Lauren Media, LLC (50%).

Principal Operating Units

Polo Brands; Collection Brands.

Principal Competitors

Banana Republic; Liz Claiborne Inc.; Nautica Enterprises Inc.; Tommy Hilfiger Corporation.

Further Reading

Agins, Terry, ''Clothing Makers Don Retailers' Garb, Manufacturers Open Stores, Irk Main Outlets,'' *Wall Street Journal,* July 13, 1989.

——, ''Izod Lacoste Gets Restyled and Repriced,'' *Wall Street Journal,* July 22, 1991, p. B1.

——, ''Ralph Lauren Sells 28 Percent Stake in Polo Concern,'' *Wall Street Journal,* August 24, 1994, pp. A3, A10.

——, ''Retailing Executive Farah Is Said to be Discussing a Post with Ralph Lauren,'' *Wall Street Journal,* October 7, 1994, p. B10.

Aronson, Steven M.L., ''High Style in Jamaica,'' *House & Garden,* October 1984, pp. 127–37, 230.

Barns, Lawrence, ''J.P. Stevens Takes the Designer Route,'' *Business Week,* September 19, 1983, pp. 118–19.

''A Big Time Safari for Ralph Lauren,'' *Women's Wear Daily,* October 27, 1989, pp. 1, 14.

Born, Pete, ''Polo Crest Takes Fashion Approach to Fragrance,'' *Daily News Record,* July 26, 1991, p. 3.

——, ''Lauren Hits TV Trail for Men's Safari,'' *Women's Wear Daily,* August 21, 1992, p. 5.

Bounds, Wendy, ''Ralph Lauren Targets Younger Women with Hip Look,'' *Ottawa Citizen,* May 13, 1998, p. F5.

Brent, Paul, ''Why Ralph Lauren Looked North: Tommy, Do You Hear Me?,'' *National Post* (Canada), March 2, 1999, p. C1.

Curan, Catherine, ''Polo Goes Solo with Lauren Line,'' *Crain's New York Business,* June 16, 2003, p. 1.

——, ''Ralph Lauren Goes Nowhere,'' *Crain's New York Business,* May 13, 2002, p. 3.

Donaton, Scott, and Pat Sloan, ''Hearst, Lauren at Work on Lifestyle Magazine,'' *Advertising Age,* April 27, 1992, pp. 1, 54.

——, ''Ralph Lauren Sets Magazine Test,'' *Advertising Age,* November 2, 1992, p. 3.

Ettorre, Barbara, '' 'Give Ralph Lauren All the Jets He Wants','' *Forbes,* February 28, 1983, pp. 102–03.

Fallon, James, ''Ralph to Launch First TV Campaign Next Month,'' *DNR,* October 16, 2000, p. 6.

Ferretti, Fred, ''The Business of Being Ralph Lauren,'' *New York Times Magazine,* September 18, 1983, pp. 112+.

Gault, Ylonda, ''Wall St. Doesn't Begrudge Ralph Lauren Cashing Out,'' *Crain's New York Business,* April 14, 1997, p. 4.

Gross, Michael, ''The American Dream,'' *New York,* December 21–28, 1992, pp. 71–72.

Kaufman, Leslie, ''NBC Helps Ralph Lauren Fulfill a Multimedia Dream,'' *New York Times,* February 8, 2000, p. C13.

Koepp, Stephen, ''Selling a Dream of Elegance and the Good Life,'' *Time,* September 1, 1986, pp. 54–61.

Kornbluth, Jesse, ''Ralph Lauren: Success American Style,'' *Vogue,* August, 1982, pp. 263+.

Lafayette, Jon, ''Ralph Lauren Drops WRG,'' *Advertising Age,* September 18, 1989, pp. 1, 84.

''Lauren Price Cuts Don't Spark a Trend,'' *Women's Wear Daily,* June 14, 1991, p. 17.

Ling, Flora, ''Ralph Lauren's Polo Game,'' *Forbes,* June 26, 1978, p. 88.

Lockwood, Lisa, ''Ralph Lauren's Sales Go Up As Prices Fall,'' *Women's Wear Daily,* June 11, 1991, p. 1.

McMurdy, Deirdre, ''The Quest for Coolness,'' *Maclean's,* March 15, 1999, p. 38.

Parola, Robert, ''Polo/Ralph Lauren,'' *Daily News Record,* October 17, 1990, p. 3.

——, ''Polo/Ralph Lauren: At the Crossroads,'' *Daily News Record,* October 29, 1990, p. 10.

''Ralph Lauren: The Dream Maker,'' *U.S. News & World Report,* February 8, 1988, p. 78.

Rosen, Pat, ''Phony Pony? Polo Player Rides to Court in Logo Lawsuit,'' *Houston Business Journal,* May 6, 1991, p. 1.

Shaw, Hollie, and Serena French, ''Polo Cleaning House at Club Monaco,'' *National Post* (Canada), April 12, 2001, p. C3.

Skenazy, Lenore, ''Lauren Gets Honorable Mansion,'' *Advertising Age,* October 20, 1986, p. 56.

Sohng, Laurie, ''Polo Partners Ralph Lauren Footwear Always Plays to Win,'' *Footwear News,* October 14, 1991, p. S4.

Spevack, Rachel, ''Polo and Izod: Adding New Luster to Knit Logos,'' *Daily News Record,* March 12, 1991, p. 5.

Steinhauer, Jennifer, ''Ralph Lauren Learns Wall St. Is Fickle, Too,'' *New York Times,* August 5, 1997, p. D1.

——, ''Ralph Lauren's Stock: Why Has It Languished?,'' *New York Times,* January 30, 1998, p. D7.

Strasburg, Jenny, ''Polo Says Dress Code Not Forced,'' *San Francisco Chronicle,* November 6, 2002, p. B1.

Talley, Andre Leon, ''Everybody's All-American,'' *Vogue,* February 1992, pp. 203–10, 284.

Trachtenberg, Jeffrey A., ''You Are What You Wear,'' *Forbes,* April 21, 1986, pp. 94–98.

Valkin, Vanessa, ''Polo Plans Europe HQ in Geneva,'' *Financial Times* (London), November 7, 2002, p. 32.

Walsh, Sharon, ''Polo Ralph Lauren IPO Raises $767 Million,'' *Washington Post,* June 13, 1997, p. G2.

—Tom Pendergast
—update: Frederick C. Ingram

Quanex

Quanex Corporation

1900 West Loop South
Suite 1500
Houston, Texas 77027
U.S.A.
Telephone: (713) 961-4600
Toll Free: (800) 231-8176
Fax: (713) 877-5333
Web site: http://www.quanex.com

Public Company
Incorporated: 1927 as Michigan Seamless Tube Company
Employees: 3,153
Sales: $1.03 billion (2003)
Stock Exchanges: New York
Ticker Symbol: NX
NAIC: 331111 Iron and Steel Mills

Quanex Corporation is a leading U.S. manufacturer of engineered materials and components for the vehicular products and building products markets. Some of the items manufactured by its vehicular products division include carbon and hot-rolled steel bars, cold-finished steel bars, heat treated bars and tubes, and corrosion-resistant bars and tubes. These are used in engine and motor components, wheel assemblies, steering systems and drivetrain parts, air bags, and suspension parts. The company's buildings products segment serves the window and door industry. Quanex celebrated its 75th anniversary in 2002 with record sales and earnings.

Origins

Quanex was incorporated in 1927 in South Lyon, Michigan, as the Michigan Seamless Tube Company. Under the leadership of William N. McMunn, the fledgling start-up profited by reworking used boiler and condenser tubes for resale. Success in that business prompted the company to build a processing mill in 1929 that could produce seamless tubing from solid steel billets. Michigan Seamless managed to survive the 1929 stock market crash and even managed to increase its business during the Great Depression. Indeed, the enterprise began producing

tubing made from steel alloys in 1933 and by 1935 was generating more than $1 million in annual sales.

After the depression, Michigan Seamless enjoyed a sales boom as a result of U.S. government purchases during World War II. Founder McMunn died in 1941 and was replaced by board member W.A. McHattie, who oversaw the company's war effort and would lead the enterprise into the 1970s. Michigan Seamless was a major supplier to the armed forces during the war and was distinguished as the only company in the nation to be awarded five Army-Navy "E" awards for production and quality of aircraft tubing. Demand for the company's steel products temporarily declined immediately after the war. However, the postwar economic boom soon supplanted that market and Michigan Seamless resumed its hearty growth. In 1946, in fact, the company installed a new furnace and processing mill in anticipation of demand growth.

Postwar Growth

Throughout the 1950s and 1960s, Michigan Seamless enjoyed steady gains. Besides expanding its original South Lyon facilities, it also branched out into other regions and markets. In 1956, for example, Gulf States Tube Corporation, an affiliate of Michigan Seamless, was started in Rosenberg, Texas. That division would give Michigan Seamless an important foothold in the oil and gas tubing market. Importantly, Michigan Seamless acquired Standard Tube in 1965, an acquisition that gave Michigan Seamless new operations in Detroit and Shelby, Ohio. Shortly after the purchase, the company was listed on the New York Stock Exchange. Other acquisitions followed, including the purchase of U.S. Broach and Machine Company in 1968. By that time, Michigan Seamless was making and processing steel in several states and had diversified into a number of different industries.

During the early 1970s, Michigan Seamless began developing plans to build a state-of-the-art steel mill in Jackson, Michigan. The MacSteel mill, as it was called, would eventually become a model for other U.S. producers of high-grade engineered steel. Such steel was purchased by manufacturers for use in demanding applications like producing ball bearings and camshafts. MacSteel would also form the basis of what would become the company's primary operating division. In 1972, shortly after announcing construction of the MacSteel plant, McHattie died. He was replaced by Carl E. Pfeiffer, a Detroit native and a graduate of Michigan State University. An engineer by training, Pfeiffer joined Michigan Tubeless in 1953 and quickly worked his way to president of the company in 1971 before assuming the chief executive role in 1972.

Pfeiffer oversaw the opening of the MacSteel plant in 1974 and also helped to engineer the acquisition of Viking Metallurgical in 1976. Reflecting the company's growing market and product diversity, Pfeiffer changed the name of the company in 1977 from Michigan Seamless Tube Company to Quanex Corporation. Also in 1977, Quanex moved its headquarters from Michigan to Houston, Texas. Both the name change and the move mirrored the company's growing emphasis on the bustling oil and gas industry, which was demanding large amounts of tubing and other steel goods to build wells and other infrastructure. Indeed, during the energy crises of the late 1970s and early 1980s, consumption of steel by the energy industry boomed and producers like Quanex scrambled to keep pace with spiraling demand.

Encouraged by booming sales to the energy sector, Quanex set its sites on that market in the late 1970s. It purchased the operations of Acquired Pipe Specialties, Inc., of Houston in 1978, for example, before acquiring Leland Tube Company of New Jersey in 1979. At the same time, Quanex jettisoned its comparatively sluggish Standard Tube Division and the U.S. Broach and Machine Company, both of which did not complement the company's energy industry focus. As sales surged, Quanex expanded. It invested heavily to upgrade its MacSteel plant in Michigan and even constructed a new welded-oil-tubing manufacturing facility in 1980 in Bellmont, Texas—closer to its primary customer base. In 1981, Quanex completed construction of a heat treating facility in Indiana and announced an ambitious plan to build a second MacSteel plant in Arkansas. The MacSteel plant would be the centerpiece of Quanex's thriving energy-related steel business, which was accounting for about 50 percent of the company's total revenues by 1981.

Quanex rode into the 1980s on a wave of success that had buoyed the company for more than a decade. Indeed, during the 1970s Quanex achieved average annual sales gains of nearly 22

percent while earnings grew at a compounded rate of nearly 30 percent. Satisfied investors enjoyed fat stock price gains and hefty dividends, and it looked as though the expanding Quanex would continue to excel into the mid-1980s. In 1981, in fact, Quanex posted a record $31.4 million profit. Some of that excess cash was used in 1982 to purchase LaSalle Steel Company, an addition to the company's Indiana-based holdings. Meanwhile, plant expansions and construction of the new MacSteel plant continued.

Surviving a Collapse in the 1980s

To the surprise of executives at Quanex and many other companies, the energy industry collapsed in 1982, bringing down with it several other steel-consuming industries, including capital equipment and automotive businesses. Quanex managers were stunned. The company's total order backlog plunged from a whopping $139 million going into 1982 to about $60 million by the year's end. Surplus steel lay rusting on Quanex's lots, forcing Quanex to eventually take a $65 million write-off related to its oil-tubing inventories. The company finished the year with a depressing $34.5 million loss. Flustered Quanex executives quickly exited the depressed market for what is known as end-finished oil tubular goods and postponed construction on the new MacSteel plant for one year.

Quanex was faced with increasingly intimidating debt obligations as its profits plummeted. Under pressure from investors, the company reorganized and initiated an aggressive campaign to cut costs and reduce its dependency on gasping energy markets. Toward that end, Quanex halted operation at its Oil Country Tubular division late in 1984 and sold a fabricating unit, among other moves. Quanex did, however, resume construction of the Arkansas MacSteel plant in 1984 using funds gleaned from a February 1984 bond offering. Quanex floated $125 million worth of junk bonds in an effort to scale back its massive $176-million debt load. The MacSteel plant opened in 1985 but would operate in the red for a few years and drag down the company's bottom line.

As Quanex sold off divisions, revenues dropped—to about $400 million in 1984 and then to a low of $297 million in 1985. Despite major hurdles, however, the company continued to post profits during the mid-1980s, with the exception of 1986. It used the surplus to pay off its long-term debt, which shrank to about $40 million in 1988. Meanwhile, Pfeiffer and company slashed costs, reorganized to concentrate on specialty and high-margin steel products, and worked to diversify away from the oil business. The number of employees at the company's headquarters was cut from about 100 in the early 1980s to about 30 by the end of the decade, and the percentage of Quanex's sales attributable to the energy industry shrank from 50 percent to about 7 percent. Quanex made up for that lost market share by entering other markets, including construction, defense, agriculture, and transportation.

Besides expanding into new end markets, Quanex also diversified geographically with sales in Europe and Japan. Furthermore, to divert another inventory disaster such as that suffered in 1982, the company adopted a policy of holding almost no inventory; instead, almost every batch of steel was made to order and was even barcoded with the owner's name and

---

Key Dates:

1927: Michigan Seamless Tube Company is incorporated.
1933: Production on tubing made from steel alloys begins.
1956: The company expands into Texas.
1965: Standard Tube is acquired.
1974: The MacSteel plant is opened.
1977: The company changes its name to Quanex Corp. and moves its headquarters to Texas.
1989: Quanex buys Nichols-Homeshield.
1996: Piper Impact Inc. is acquired.
2003: North Star Steel and TruSeal Technologies Inc. are added to the company's arsenal.

---

address prior to delivery. Importantly, Quanex began to concentrate on efficiency and customer service as a means of capturing market share and increasing its competitiveness in the increasingly global steel industry. It installed state-of-the-art equipment in its processing mills and shaped its compensation system to promote quality and productivity; workers were paid a bonus according to how much steel they shipped out, less any defective steel that was returned.

Quanex's impressive productivity gains during the 1980s and early 1990s were made possible by its integration of mini-mill technology. During the 1980s, mini-mill steelmaking factories, which use scrap and such techniques as continuous casting, emerged as stellar performers in the steel industry. Indeed, the mini-mill process was used by industry powerhouses such as Nucor to undercut traditional steel manufacturers in commodity steel markets. Quanex added a twist to the mini-mill revolution when it utilized mini-mill techniques to create high-grade, engineered steel. The result was that Quanex was able to produce high-profit steel at a very low cost. By the early 1990s, in fact, Quanex was churning out nearly defect-free steel that required only 1.9 man-hours of labor per ton to produce, as compared to about four man-hours required to create a ton of steel in a traditional, or integrated, steel mill.

As Quanex implemented its unique new strategy, its financial performance rebounded. Sales shot up from $345 million in 1987 to $463 million in 1988, and then to $502 million in 1989. In 1990, moreover, Quanex generated $650 million in sales and nearly $30 million in net income. By that time, Quanex's debt burden had eased and several banks had even approached CEO Pfeiffer about the possibility of a leveraged buyout. Instead, Pfeiffer elected to pour the money back into the company to increase its diversity and to improve productivity. To that end, in 1989 Quanex purchased Nichols-Homeshield for $105 million. Nichols manufactured aluminum sheet for gutters, downspouts, and windows. Quanex invested $60 million to build a new plant for the company and expected to use the new division to penetrate the market for aluminum.

Success in the 1990s and Beyond

After elevating Quanex to a member of the Fortune 500 in 1991, Pfeiffer relinquished his chief executive duties in 1992 to Robert C. Snyder, an engineer. The 53-year-old Snyder had

been serving as president of Leland Tube Co. when it was acquired by Quanex in 1979. After filling key executive slots at several Quanex subsidiaries, he was tapped as Pfeiffer's successor. Snyder came into the job with goals similar to those established by his predecessor. Unfortunately, he also assumed the helm during an economic downturn that was suppressing the overall steel market. Quanex's sales slipped to $572 million in 1992, although the company continued to post relatively strong operating profits. Sales began to pick up the following year, however, and in 1994 reached the record level of $699 million. Earnings in that year reflected also big gains in the new Nichols-Homeshield division, as well as recovering steel prices.

Going into the mid-1990s, Quanex was serving four major markets: industrial machinery and capital equipment (32 percent of sales), transportation (29 percent), aluminum products (29 percent), and energy (9 percent). In addition, the company was operating its subsidiaries through four major divisions: hot-rolled steel bars; cold-finished steel bars; aluminum products; and steel tubing. Rising steel prices and increased market share in 1995 boded well for Quanex in the short term. Likewise, low debt, ongoing investments in productivity and quality initiatives, and geographic and product diversity suggested long-term growth and stability for the enterprise.

Indeed, Quanex continued to experience success into the late 1990s and beyond. During this time period, it began to restructure itself by divesting certain assets while purchasing others. In order to shore up funds for investments in high growth areas, the company sold off LaSalle Steel Co. in 1997. It also jettisoned Michigan Seamless Tube and Gulf States Tube. Meanwhile, the company made a string of acquisitions. Piper Impact Inc. was bought in 1996. Quanex added the Dutch limited partnership, Advanced Metal Forming C.V., to its arsenal in the following year. Decatur Aluminum Corp. was purchased in 1998 and renamed Nichols Aluminum Alabama. The firm bought Imperial Products Inc. and Temroc Metals Inc. in 2000.

The company reported profits in 1999 that were nearly four times higher than the previous year's results—a sure sign it was well positioned to enter the new century. To round out its restructuring process, Quanex launched a new business strategy in 2001 that clearly defined the company's focus on its role in the vehicular products and building products market segments. One of the main goals of the strategy was to shift its image from an aluminum or steel company into a market-driven manufacturing concern serving customers in its two main business areas. Its new corporate mantra adopted during this process was ''market-driven and process-based.''

Quanex celebrated its 75th anniversary in 2002 by securing record financial results. Sales increased to $994 million while net income jumped to $46.5 million—an increase of 59 percent over the previous year. The company acquired Colonial Craft in February 2002 and continued to bolster its Building Products division in 2003 by adding TruSeal Technologies Inc. to its holdings. Chairman and CEO Raymond Jean commented on the deal in a company press release, stating, ''Our purchase of TruSeal serves is an excellent example of the type of acquisition we will make as we profitably grow Quanex's core businesses.'' The firm also acquired North Star Steel that year, renaming it MacSteel Monroe.

While Quanex management remained optimistic about the company's future success, it nevertheless faced distinct challenges, including rising raw material costs. The firm's revenues also remained dependent on light vehicle builds, housing starts, and remodeling spending, which tended to fluctuate during times of economic uncertainty. Nevertheless, the restructuring over the past several years left it well positioned to compete in a challenging marketplace. With a solid business strategy in place, Quanex appeared to be on track for continued success in the years to come.

Principal Subsidiaries

Piper Impact, Inc.; Quanex Bar, Inc.; Quanex Steel, Inc.; Quanex Health Management Company, Inc.; Quanex Manufacturing, Inc.; Quanex Solutions, Inc.; Quanex Technologies, Inc.; Nichols Aluminum-Alabama, Inc.; Colonial Craft, Inc.; MAC-STEEL Monroe, Inc.; Nichols Aluminum-Golden, Inc.; Quanex Four, Inc.; Quanex Six, Inc.; Imperial Products, Inc.; Temroc Metals, Inc.

Principal Competitors

Alcoa Inc.; Commercial Metals Company; Republic Engineered Products LLC.

Further Reading

''Al Sheet Maker Quanex Sees Key Drivers Same in 2003,'' *Platt's Metals Week*, December 16, 2002, p. 10.

Byrne, Harlan S., ''A Specialty Rebound: Quanex Emerges from Steel Slump,'' *Barron's*, June 6, 1988, pp. 38–40.

Cleary, W.F., ''Quanex Announces Management Changes,'' *Business Wire*, September 2, 1992.

Cleary, W.F., and C.A. Meador, ''Quanex Corp. Announces Financial Results,'' *Business Wire*, May 30, 1990.

Galow, Jeff, ''Quanex Sells Bellville Tube Plant,'' *PR Newswire*, April 15, 1993.

Jacobs, Bill, ''Quanex Profits Get Boost from Q-C,'' *Quad-City Times*, December 10, 1994, p. M5.

''Nichols Sheet Demand Strong but Mill Sale Still Mulled,'' *Platt's Metals Week*, January 5, 2004, p. 5.

Nulty, Peter, ''The Less-Is-More Strategy,'' *Fortune*, December 2, 1991, p. 102.

''Profits Soar for Quanex in Fiscal '99,'' *American Metal Market*, December 13, 1999, p. 3.

''Quanex Completes Temroc Acquisition,'' *American Metal Market*, December 4, 2000, p. 8.

''Quanex Corp. of Houston Is Buying the North Star Steel Plant in Monroe, Mich.,'' *Purchasing*, December 11, 2003.

''Quanex Sells LaSalle Steel,'' *Iron Age New Steel*, June 1997.

''Quanex to Buy Dutch Company,'' *Wall Street Journal*, September 29, 1997, p. B8.

''US Sheet Makers Expect to Post Weaker 2001 Earnings,'' *Platt's Metals Week*, May 7, 2001, p. 13.

—Dave Mote
—update: Christina M. Stansell

Quantum.

Quantum Corporation

1650 Technology Drive, Suite 800
San Jose, California 95110
U.S.A.
Telephone: (408) 944-4000
Toll Free: (800) 677-6268
Fax: (408) 944-4040
Web site: http://www.quantum.com

Public Company
Incorporated: 1980
Employees: 2,000
Sales: $871 million (2003)
Stock Exchanges: New York
Ticker Symbol: DSS
NAIC: 334112 Computer Storage Device Manufacturing

Quantum Corporation is a leading supplier of digital linear tape (DLT) technology used to backup data. It has sold more than 100 million half-inch cartridge tapes for the two million DLT tape drives in use. Quantum was the largest hard disk drive manufacturer in the world before these operations were sold off to Maxtor. Quantum also produces disk-based data backup systems.

Origins

Quantum's first president was James L. Patterson, an experienced engineer with considerable business acumen. Making decisions based on a collegial rather than a hierarchical management model, Patterson inspired confidence and a hard work ethic. By 1984, four years after its incorporation, Quantum was leading the market in mid-capacity 5.25-inch disk drives, having jumped ahead of Priam Corporation, Micropolis Corporation, and Control Data. Nearly 20 percent of the 473,000 5.25-inch drives sold in 1985 were made by Quantum. The company's financial statement reflected its growing leadership position in the disk drive market. From 1984 to 1985, revenues increased from $106.2 million to $126.6 million, a growth of almost 20 percent, and earnings increased from $18.1 million to $21.5 million, a jump of over 18 percent. Without any long-term debt, the company was able to concentrate on developing a new line of 5.25-inch OEM (original equipment manufacturer) products.

The company's revenues remained at the same level in 1986, but production delays with its new generation of 3.5-inch disk drives led to a loss of all but two of its customers. Displeased with what they regarded as complacent management, Quantum's board of directors replaced Patterson with Stephen M. Berkeley, the head of the company's subsidiary, Plus Development Corporation. In addition to a new chief executive officer, the board also appointed David A. Brown, a former associate of Berkeley at Plus Development, as Quantum's new president.

Smaller Is Better in the Mid-1980s

Realizing that Quantum had fallen behind its competitors in the market for hard disk drives, Berkeley and Brown were determined that their company should take the lead in the industry-wide move toward smaller computers. This decision meant that Quantum would have to phase out its production of 5.25-inch disk drives in order to concentrate on the 3.5-inch disk drive market.

The two men immediately plotted a strategy that was unusual for companies within the disk drive industry. Ordinarily a firm either buys the components it uses to build disk drives or it manufactures its own. Either road has both benefits and liabilities: if a firm buys its components, it avoids high fixed costs but may run short of parts when demand increases; conversely, if a firm makes its own components, it can outfit production easily to meet an increase in demand, but if demand slows then high fixed costs take their financial toll. Having already established a working partnership with Matsushita Kotobuki Electronics Industries, Ltd., a Japanese firm that had grown into the largest manufacturer of videocassette recorders, Berkeley and Brown hired MKE to facilitate Quantum's entry into the 3.5-inch disk drive market. The two companies reached an agreement whereby Quantum took on the responsibility of designing and marketing new products while Matsushita manufactured them. Although the Japanese company had never built a disk drive before, its skills in manufacturing electromechanical equipment had already been proven.

Quantum's arrangement with Matsushita instantly led to benefits for both companies. Matsushita required Quantum to completely redesign and overhaul the manner in which it developed disk drives, which led to the implementation of design by robotic assembly. Although this redesign frustrated some of Quantum's engineers, the end result was more than the company could have hoped for. Since Matsushita spent nearly $150 million in developing automated plants, Quantum derived all the benefits of manufacturing in-house without any of the usual fixed costs. In contrast with most of Quantum's competitors, over 95 percent of all the disk drives built on Matsushita assembly lines needed no reworking. This efficiency meant that Quantum had one of the highest gross margins in the entire disk drive industry—even after what was paid to Matsushita.

Quantum's leadership was correct in anticipating a quick rather than slow transition toward more compact drives. Not surprisingly, the company's efforts to create the new generation of 3.5-inch disk drives resulted in record sales. In 1989, Quantum increased its revenues to $394.2 million and reported a net income of $41.3 million. These figures catapulted Quantum to the top of the compact drive market. The company's contract with Apple Computer Inc. significantly helped it achieve its leadership position. At the time, approximately 40 percent of company sales were going to Apple, which used Quantum's 3.5-inch ProDrive in its Macintosh SE30 and Macintosh Iicx computers. Other firms that bought Quantum disk drives included Sun Microsystems Inc., Hewlett-Packard, and Next Inc.

A $1 Billion Company in 1991

In 1991, Quantum passed one of its most important milestones—revenues of over $1 billion. Revenues increased an amazing 50 percent over the previous year, the amount totaling $1.07 billion. With its burgeoning revenues, its focus on quality control, and its efficient distribution network, Quantum was also listed in the ranks of the Fortune 500 for the first time during the same year. Quantum was Apple Computer's leading suppler of disk drives; Apple used the drives in its newly introduced Macintosh Classic and LC desktop computers. Even though the company continued to ship its disk drives to Apple at the same level through the entire year, sales to Apple actually fell as a percentage of Quantum's total sales, decreasing from 40 percent to 15 percent. Quantum's impressive revenue growth stood on a widening customer base.

Quantum's strong revenue growth was partially due to the introduction of new products and the upgrade of existing ones. The company brought out 11 new models of its 3.5-inch and 2.5-inch drives and improved its product line of Passport removable disk drives. The company also put a significant effort into reducing the amount of development time for a particular product, cutting the process from 24 months to 15. The most important element contributing to Quantum's revenue growth, however, was the company's expansion of its distribution network. Quantum signed agreements with Rein Elektronik, a leading distributor in Germany, and Inelco Peripheriques, one of the leading distributors in France. These two distributors provided Quantum with a reliable flow of cash from the European market. The company also merged its Plus Development Corporation subsidiary into its Commercial Products Division. Plus Development, a manufacturer of hard disks on adaptor cards, otherwise known as "hard cards," was reorganized to better serve the growing demands of the distribution network that included retail outlets and computer superstores.

In 1992, Quantum brought in new leadership. Berkeley and Brown, who had directed the company to unparalleled growth and record revenues, relinquished their day-to-day control of operations to the new chief executive officer William J. Miller, an 11-year management veteran from Control Data Corporation. The momentum that Berkeley and Brown had created continued under the new CEO. At the end of 1992, Quantum's revenues were reported at $1.54 billion, a whopping 43 percent increase over the previous year's figures. The company's increase in net income was even more impressive, from $49.6 million to $84.7 million—a leap of approximately 71 percent. Quantum appeared to be doing everything right.

Yet throughout 1992 and 1993, there were indications that Quantum's market share was eroding, and that companies such as Conner Peripherals Inc., Seagate Technology Inc., and even cash-strapped Maxtor Corp. were carving out a larger piece for themselves. In late 1992, Quantum sales nearly came to an abrupt halt, as the company found itself unprepared to meet the demand for its products. Matsushita, with whom Quantum had contracted to manufacture its product lines, was unable to build the required disk drives quickly enough for the company to maintain its share of the market. Thus, in spite of its increase in revenues, Quantum spent most of the latter part of 1992 and early 1993 expanding its production base in order to meet demand. The new management quickly entered into a long-term agreement with Matsushita that gave Quantum the right to design and market its product line worldwide and gave the Japanese company the right to worldwide manufacturing. The two companies also arranged for Matsushita to build a state-of-the-art plant in Ireland at a cost of $40 million to help Quantum quicken the pace of distributing products throughout its European network.

Quantum's management had corrected the incipient problems, and the company once again achieved record revenues—$1.7 billion by the end of fiscal 1993. Net income for the first nine months of the fiscal year rose an astonishing 128 percent. Sales to original equipment manufacturers, such as Apple, accounted for more than 33 percent of Quantum's total figures. Although Quantum was still heavily dependent on its business with Apple, the company had increased sales to other OEM customers, including AST Research, Dell Computers, Compaq, and Hewlett-Packard.

The company's strategy to increase its worldwide distribution network had also paid off handsomely. Sales from the

Key Dates:

1980: Quantum Corporation, headed by James Patterson, is incorporated.
1984: Quantum leads the market in mid-capacity 5.25-inch drives.
1986: Matsushita is contracted to produce 3.5-inch drives.
1989: Quantum leads the compact drive market.
1991: Revenues climb 50 percent in one year to exceed $1 billion.
1993: Matsushita opens a plant in Ireland to supply Quantum in Europe.
1994: Quantum buys hard disk, tape drive businesses from Digital.
1998: ATL, a tape-automation and library storage business, is acquired.
1999: Network-attached storage supplier Meridian Data is acquired.
2001: Quantum sells its hard drive business to Maxtor.
2002: Jabil Circuit buys Malaysian production facilities.

international sector accounted for over 45 percent of the company's total annual sales, and accounts with such well-known foreign firms as Fujitsu, ICL, Lucky Goldstar, NEC, Olivetti, Peacock, Philips, Sharp, and Siemens assured long-term financial stability. Quantum also decided to improve upon its burgeoning international operations by relocating its European headquarters to Neuchatel, Switzerland. With a new factory in Ireland and an expanding distribution network, Quantum had developed its operations to provide the best possible service and support to its multinational customers.

As of 1994, Quantum's continuing success depended on the development of its product line and its ability to bring these items to market in a timely manner. The company's ProDrive ELS, a low-priced disk drive targeted at entry-level systems, was doing very well, and the 240 ProDrive LPS 1-inch high-capacity disk drive was one of the best-selling products Quantum had ever introduced. Along with its Maverick 270 and 540 AT/S, a high-capacity disk drive for larger systems, and its Daytona and Go-Drive GLS drives for portable systems, primarily notebooks, Quantum was not only keeping abreast of the market in 1994 but continuing to position itself as one of the top companies in the industry.

Digital Businesses Bought in 1994

Quantum had sales of $2.1 billion in fiscal 1994, making it the third largest hard disk supplier behind Seagate and Conner Peripherals, two firms that later merged. Quantum acquired Digital Equipment Corp.'s disk drive business in July 1994 for $348 million, improving its position in the market for large capacity drives. An 81 percent stake in two-year-old recording head manufacturer Rocky Mountain Magnetics Inc. was included in the sale, as were production facilities in Massachusetts and Malaysia. The buy gave Quantum ownership of Digital's proprietary DLT tape drive.

Quantum posted a loss of $90 million in fiscal 1996. The company closed plants and cut more than 2,200 jobs as it

farmed out production of its most advanced disk drives to a joint venture with Matsushita-Kotobuki Electronics Industries called MKE-Quantum (MKQC). This partnership was ended in November 1998 due to losses.

Tape drive sales, oriented towards large companies with huge data storage needs, were growing ever more important. Focusing on this segment, rather than the low-margin hard drive business, in 1998 the company paid $300 million to buy Irvine, California-based ATL Products, which produced tape-automation and library storage equipment. Network-attached storage (NAS) supplier Meridian Data was acquired in 1999.

Quantum also licensed a Norwegian company to produce and sell tape drives for the European market. DLT drives accounted for a little over one-fifth of 1998's revenues of $6 billion.

Quantum's disk drives and storage systems units attracted different types of investors. Quantum inaugurated a unique scheme that allowed investors to buy shares in the two lines of business separately via "tracking stocks," which were issued on the New York Stock Exchange in July 1999. Quantum's original listing on the NASDAQ was phased out.

The company lost $30 million in fiscal 1999. Later that year, it laid off 800 employees as it reoriented its hard drive business towards low-cost PCs and consumer electronics such as digital TV recorders.

HDD Group Sold in 2001

Quantum's Hard Disk Drive Group lost $104.8 million on revenues of $3.31 billion in the fiscal year ended March 31, 2000. Quantum sold the unit to Maxtor in 2001 for about $1.3 billion worth of stock. The deal made Maxtor the largest producer of hard disk drives by volume and second only to Seagate in sales.

The sell-off of the hard disk drives division left Quantum with only the DLT & Storage Systems Group. This unit changed its name to Quantum Corporation while retaining its tracking stock symbol, DSS.

Since acquiring the tape drive business of Digital Equipment, Quantum's Colorado Springs operation had grown to occupy two buildings totaling almost 280,000 square feet and employing 1,700 people in mid-2001. While high-volume manufacturing had been shipped off to Malaysia, Colorado Springs remained an important strategic center for developing and producing new products, such as the Super DLT tape drive, which was twice as fast as the original. Quantum also had a 100-employee design center in Boulder.

Rick Belluzzo, formerly chief operating officer of Microsoft, became CEO in August 2002. He replaced Michael Brown, who had joined Quantum in 1984 and had become CEO in 1995 following the resignation of William Miller.

In September 2002, Jabil Circuit acquired Quantum's Malaysian facilities and was signed on as the company's new production partner. Quantum then laid off 1,100 workers, most of them at the factory in Malaysia, although it expected the majority of them to be rehired by Jabil Circuit.

The Storage Solutions and DLT Tape divisions were merged in 2003; at the same time, three business units—Storage Devices, Media, and Storage Systems—were created. With the amount of data used by business increasing and regulation and financial necessity compelling enterprises to back up their data, Quantum appeared to have ample opportunities ahead.

Principal Subsidiaries

ATL Products Vertriebs GmbH. (Germany); ATL Products UK Ltd.; ATL Products International Inc.; Benchmark Tape Systems Ltd (UK); Quantum Data Storage B.V. (Netherlands); Quantum Peripheral Products (Ireland) Ltd.; Quantum Peripherals (Europe) S.A. (Switzerland); Quantum Peripherals (Malaysia) Sdn. Bhd.; Quantum Storage GmbH (Germany); Quantum Storage Australia PTY, Ltd.; Quantum Storage Japan Corporation; Quantum Storage Singapore Pte. Ltd.; Quantum Storage UK Ltd.; Quantum Storage France; M4 Data (Holdings) Ltd. (UK); SANlight Inc.

Principal Divisions

Storage Devices; Media; Storage Systems.

Principal Competitors

Exabyte Corporation; Hewlett-Packard Company; International Business Machines Corporation; Seagate Technology; Sony Corporation; Storage Technology Corporation.

Further Reading

Abate, Tom, "Disk Drive Profits to Rise," *San Francisco Examiner*, December 13, 1995, p. B8.

Bean, Joanna, "Quantum Is Diversifying; Firm's Leap into Storage Systems Could Mean Expansion of Its Colorado Springs Operation," *Colorado Springs Gazette-Telegraph*, Bus. Sec., March 2, 1999, p. 1.

Bengali, Shashank, "Milpitas, Calif.-Based Tech Firm May Employ Stock Trick for Spin-offs," *San Jose Mercury News*, July 22, 1999.

Catalano, Frank, "James L. Patterson: The Drive to Succeed," *Electronic Business*, April 1, 1986, p. 50.

Einstein, David, "Quantum Buys Unit from DEC," *San Francisco Chronicle*, July 20, 1994, p. C1.

Gonzales, Lou, "Quantum Seals Deal for Market Expansion; Norwegian Company Will Make, Sell Tape Drives," *Colorado Springs Gazette-Telegraph*, Bus. Sec., September 10, 1998, p. 1.

Helft, Miguel, "Disk Drive Maker Quantum Corp. to Expand into Data Storage Systems," *San Jose Mercury News*, March 1, 1999.

Hof, Robert D., "Quantum Has One Tough Hurdle to Leap," *Business Week*, July 8, 1991, pp. 84–86.

Lindholm, Elizabeth, " 'Quantum Corporation,' The Datamation 100," *Datamation*, June 15, 1992, p. 86.

Newman, Cara, "Quantum Wins Round One," *Colorado Springs Business Journal*, November 9, 2001, p. 11.

Norr, Henry, "Quantum Corp. to Lay Off 600 in Milpitas," *San Francisco Chronicle*, August 20, 1999, p. B1.

——, "Maxtor Agrees to Buy Quantum's Hard-Disk-Drive Business," *San Francisco Chronicle*, October 5, 2000, p. B5.

"Quantum to Lay off 1,000 Workers," *Associated Press State & Local Wire*, September 9, 2002.

Rae-Dupree, Janet, "Bigfoot Disk Drive Packs More Data, Cuts Computer Cost," *San Jose Mercury News*, February 27, 1996.

Sanders, Edmund, "ATL Products Accepts Buyout by Quantum," *Orange County Register*, May 20, 1998, p. C1.

Sucharski, Karen, "Quantum Layoffs Reflect New Model," *Colorado Springs Business Journal*, February 18, 2000, p. 1.

Walsh, Chris, "Quantum Theory: Springs Operation Plays Bigger Strategic Role for Tape-Drive Maker," *Gazette* (Colorado Springs), Bus. Sec., May 6, 2001, p. 1.

—Thomas Derdak
—update: Frederick C. Ingram

The Quigley Corporation

The Kells Building
621 Shady Retreat Road
Doylestown, Pennsylvania 18901-2071
U.S.A.
Telephone: (267) 880-1100
Fax: (267) 880-1153
Web site: http://www.quigleyco.com

Public Company
Incorporated: 1989
Employees: 59
Sales: $29.4 million (2002)
Stock Exchanges: NASDAQ
Ticker Symbol: QGLY
NAIC: 325411 Medicinal and Botanical Manufacturing

Operating out of Doylestown, Pennsylvania, The Quigley Corporation makes over-the-counter homeopathic remedies. It is best known for its Cold-Eeze product, a zinc gluconate glycine combination that is taken to lessen the duration and severity of the common cold. Cold-Eeze is available in lozenge, tablet, nasal, and sugarless forms. Although there have been several conflicting studies concerning its effectiveness, all of the failed studies, as of 1994, did not utilize the Cold-Eeze patented formula. Cold-Eeze has no less than five positive clinically proven studies to its credit and is now established in the marketplace. In an attempt at diversification, Quigley has become involved in the development of other health and wellness products, through a wholly owned subsidiary based in Utah. In 2001, The Quigley Corporation established a second wholly owned subsidiary called Quigley Pharma Inc. In keeping with the company's quest to remain in the all-natural medication arena, the new research and development company has filed for and been issued several new patents, based on all-natural ingredients. The company has conducted initial double-blind studies, targeting such conditions as diabetic peripheral neuropathy, radiation dermatitis, and influenza. The company is also in the process of filing an NDA with the FDA seeking permission to conduct Phase 111 clinical trials on its diabetic peripheral neu-

ropathy topical application to establish the product as a prescription drug.

1970s Background and Company Origins

The Quigley Corporation was founded by Guy J. Quigley, who was born in Donegal, Ireland in 1941. He originally was involved in the thespian world, following the example of his father, a solo concert violinist, and his mother, an actress who performed on the Dublin and London stages. By college, however, Quigley switched his interest to business. He started a successful double-glazing window company in London, but in 1970 marriage took him to Zambia, Africa (formally Northern Rhodesia) where his wife was the sole heir destined to inherit a 100,000 acre-cattle ranch, founded by her American grandfather. He and his wife ran an adjacent 35,000 acre-spread, where he built the stock up to 10,000 head of cattle. Over the years, the timing proved unfortunate, as an independence movement was in the process of sweeping up neighboring Southern Rhodesia and all the liberation forces where housed in Zambia. Life in the independent Zambia became perilous for Europeans, who made residents of the host country an easy unarmed target. The ongoing liberation war eventually led to the establishment of present-day Zimbabwe. He stayed as long as he could, even making a business venture out of auctioneering and selling real estate of whites eager to flee the country. Quigley, his wife, and at that time their two daughters eventually moved back to London, where they were horrified to discovered that his wife's new stepmother had seized control of his wife's entire inheritance, leaving them only with the money Quigley had earned in cattle profits and deposited in European bank accounts.

With his wife's prompting, since her roots were American, Quigley next moved his family to Doylestown, a suburb of Philadelphia, Pennsylvania. There he launched a business producing resemblances of established French perfumes. When this business was acquired by a Canadian entity Quigley switched gears. In 1989 he formed The Quigley Corporation to become involved in the energy-bar business. What he marketed was an all-natural, easily digestible, high-energy product he named "Quigley's Alpha 1 Nurti-Bar." He and his close associate, Charles A. Phillips, worked out of a basement of a converted church in Doylestown, using second hand furniture. Despite his frugality, Quigley's new business was in a world of stiff competition and was not going anywhere. As he was self financing the entire operation, he managed to take the company public in 1991, selling 3 million shares at 15 cents apiece, netting $405,000. Nevertheless, he was forced him to empty his European accounts and ultimately sell his prized Rolls-Royces. His fortunes, however, would change one day when John Godfrey, an organic chemist who worked for Bristol Labs, Shell and Rorer, paid a visit, claiming he had a cure for the common cold in the form of a homemade zinc lozenge.

Focus on a Cold Remedy in the 1980s

Godfrey's zinc lozenge grew out of the discoveries of a Texan named George Eby, an urban planner by trade, who in 1979 was helping to nurse his daughter through leukemia. In order to keep her strong and able to fend off other illness, Eby fed her an array of vitamins and minerals. According to the lore surround the origins of Cold-Eeze, one night she was coming down with a cold, and because she was too weak to swallow a zinc pill, Eby simply allowed it to dissolve on her tongue. When the cold dissipated by morning, Eby sensed that he had stumbled upon something of importance and despite his lack of expertise in the medical field was able to arrange a clinical trial of zinc gluconate to treat colds. The results indicated that subjects taking zinc overcame their colds 64 percent faster than those who simply took placebos. The controversial results were published in a medical journal in 1984.

Godfrey came across the Eby-inspired zinc study and because his employers showed no interest, he began to devise different recipes in his home laboratory. An early lesson he learned was that too much zinc acted as an emetic and caused vomiting. Another issue was taste. Because of the heavy metallic taste of zinc, even when sweetened, most forms of zinc delivery relied on the common candy sweeteners of sorbitol, mannitol, and citric acid to act as a masking agent. But Godfrey believed that the reason zinc was effective on colds was because its ions bonded with cold virus particles, keeping them from settling in the nasal mucus membranes, and he wondered if the sweeteners might prevent this process. He then conducted an informal study, essentially a party, during which his guests sucked on zinc lozenges, which they spit out for analysis. Godfrey found no traces of zinc, thus verifying his theory. After some trial and effort, he settled on glycine as a proper substitute for candy sweeteners. Glycine was a basic amino acid that accounted for the sweetness found in meat. In 1987 Godfrey patented zinc gluconate glycine. He then mounted a clinical trial at Dartmouth College three years later. The results indicated that when subjects took zinc within a day of coming down with a cold, they exhibited 42 percent less cold symptoms.

Godfrey shared his product and studies with pharmaceutical firms, but they balked when he and his wife insisted on a performance clause, which would have required the company to actually produce a product. Their fear was that pharmaceuticals had an incentive to kill the idea, which threatened the billions of dollars the industry made each year on cold palliatives. There was also one more complication. A prospective manufacturer had to contend not only with Godfrey, who had the rights to the only palatable form of zinc, but also Eby, who held a patent on the use of zinc as a cold remedy.

When Godfrey turned to Quigley, because he basically had nowhere else to turn, he received very little encouragement. Quigley tried Godfrey's homemade zinc lozenges, which he describe as a culinary horror, "tasting like a ball of sawdust." Godfrey also showed Quigley his Dartmouth study, but Quigley said he would only be interested if the results were published somewhere. Godfrey left his office, Quigley forgot about him and his nasty tasting lozenges, but six months later turned up again at his office. This time he said the results of his study were about to be published and he left Quigley and Phillips a stack of documents for the partners to consider. Although neither man had a scientific background, they waded through the material and concluded that Godfrey had something worth pursuing. Because the corporation could not yet afford a lawyer, Quigley drew up a basic agreement for Godfrey to sign, offering a 3 percent royalty and a 2 percent consulting agreement. As for Eby, Quigley was prepared to pay a similar royalty should he ever sue. In time, Eby did sue and eventually settled for a 3 percent royalty.

Gaining Ground in the 1990s

After Quigley acquired the worldwide manufacturing and distribution rights to the zinc formulation, the company endured several leans years, as it prepared to market its zinc lozenge, which Quigley named and trademarked Cold-Eeze, while continuing to sell a meager number of nutri-bars. The company sent out free samples in hopes of getting free publicity and developing a word-of-mouth following, resulting in a few successes. Rodale Press listed Cold-Eeze in "Age Erasing for Men & Women," and in 1994 *McCall's* magazine printed Quigley's 800-number as part of an article titled, "How to Not Catch a Cold This Winter." To fuel interest further, as well as generate extra revenue, Quigley decided to price Cold-Eeze at $16.75 for a bag of 30 lozenges. Believing that he needed more scientific backing to properly market Cold-Eeze, Quigley approached the head of pediatrics at the Cleveland Clinic, Dr. Michael Macknin, who agreed to mount a double-blind study for free. In his career he had already disproved one cold cure, an Israeli-made inhaler of warm water vapor. This time, however, Macknin was surprised by the results of his study and became an enthusiastic backer of Cold-Eeze, so much so that in late 1994 he bought shares of stock in Quigley. When he announced the results, published in the *Annals of Internal Medicine* in July 1996, he was certain to hold up a bag of Cold-Eeze for the CNN crew covering the event. But negative publicity followed three weeks later when it was reported that Dr. Macknin had a financial interest in Quigley, although he maintained that he only purchased Quigley stock after his data had been gathered and that he had told his editors about his stock ownership before the results of the study were published. He then launched a second study of Cold-Eeze in the autumn of 1996.

Nevertheless, Macknin maintained his enthusiasm for the product in January 1997 when ABC's "20/20" program aired a report on the common cold, during which it declared Cold-Eeze to be the only effective product on the market. The "20/20" report only added fuel to a zinc craze that swept the country. Even before the show aired, the price of Quigley stock, which had been selling for less than a dollar six months earlier, soared to $37 a share. (By now, the company also had eased out of the nutri-bar business to focus all of its attention on Cold-Eeze.) With overnight success came problems. According to a *Philadelphia Magazine* article, "The day after the 20/20 report, however, a *Barron's* cover story asserted that some of the people involved in promoting Quigley stock were shady at best and mob-linked at worst." The stock fell to the teens. (The company's connections with those people never existed and was attributed to short selling of the stock in excess of one million shares.) Somebody released a damaging press release, on fake Quigley letterhead, and it actually ran on the Bloomberg wires, sending the value of the stock down even farther. "Someone," Guy Quigley warned darkly at the time, "is bent on the destruction of this company."

While the events surrounding Quigley stock were of interest to investors, in particular short-sellers, the general public was so enthused about Cold-Eeze that Quigley was unable to meet the surge in demand that began in the fall of 1996. The company tried to ramp up production but its manufacturers did not possess a metal die to stamp "Q" on each lozenge, as required by the FDA. The stamps, made in Italy, were delayed by weeks, while Quigley accumulated some $12 million in backorders. The shortage of Cold-Eeze spiked even greater interest in the product, as drug stores resorted to maintaining waiting lists and factory shipments were monitored by Internet groups. It was not until the spring of 1997 that Quigley was up to speed on production. But because customers stocked up for the following winter, which turned out to be mild, Quigley now faced a glut of inventory in the market, a situation that adversely impacted the price of its stock. Then, Macknin came out with his second study, this one targeting children, and the results were negative. Quigley disputed the methodology, claiming that a major portion of the subjects suffered from such ailments as asthma, bronchitis, and allergies. The company was kept in the dark during the peer review process, but ultimately the study was published in the *Journal of the American Medical Association*, in spite of last minute conversations by Quigley's general counsel with the editor of the publication. The company put on file

an independent audit of the published study, showing that an overwhelming number of participants were totally ineligible to be in the study in the first place. This document was available upon request from the company.

Diversification in the Mid-1990s

Despite scientific doubt about the efficacy of Cold-Eeze, the product was established enough in the marketplace that other zinc products soon emerged (at least 40 since 1996 according to Quigley). These products, according to Quigley, relied on zinc-acetate, which the company considered to be vastly inferior to its zinc gluconate glycine formulation. The company took one competitor to court, Dynamic Health Products Inc., whose Cold-Rid product was judged to mimic the Cold-Eeze packaging. There was enough legitimate competition that arose, however, to hurt Quigley's zinc franchise. The company began to diversify in two ways. First, it offered different forms of Cold-Eeze: sugar-free, bubblegum, and menthol. More important, Quigley already had taken steps to branch out beyond Cold-Eeze and escape investor criticism that it was just a one-hit wonder. In August 1998, after three years of research and development, the company announced the introduction of Bodymate, a weight-loss lozenge that was supposed to prevent the body from converting food energy into fat. The hope was that Bodymate would generate revenues for Quigley during the spring and summer months, the off-season for Cold-Eeze. Another effort to address the seasonal nature of Cold-Eeze was to expand internationally, in order to sell into southern hemisphere countries that experienced the cold season on an opposite schedule.

In 2000 Quigley formed a subsidiary, Darius International, Inc., to introduce new products into the marketplace, such as Beta-Eeze, a dietary supplement to support a health immune system; Ultra-Eeze, a dietary supplement for bones and joint; Vita-Eeze, a dietary supplement that combined vitamins, minerals, and an anti-oxidant; Ardor, a natural libido enhancer; and Nic-0-Time Gum, a smoking substitute. Today this wholly owned subsidiary has diversified into health and wellness and is a growing successful venture retailing its products through a network marketing system. In 2001, Quigley established its Ethical Pharmaceutical Unit, which was named Quigley Pharma Inc., to expand beyond over-the-counter products and direct marketing and move into the prescription drug market. The company also bought a controlling interest in Caribbean Pacific Natural Products in 2000 and in 2003 had sold its interest in favor of a spin-off as an independent public company with a stock dividend to Quigley Corporation shareholders.

The need for diversification was clear, given the company's financial results. Revenues that totaled $500,000 in 1995 grew to $5 million in 1996 and at the height of the Cold-Eeze craze in 1997 skyrocketed to $70.2 million, with a net profit of nearly $21 million. In 1998, however, sales dropped to $34.3 million and net income to $6.8 million, a drop-off that management attributed to a mild winter, high inventory levels, and the emergence of new herbal cold treatments that cut into business. Revenues fell further in 1999, totaling $21.6 million and resulting in a loss of $4.2 million. Again, heavy competition was the chief reason, with not only herbal sales cutting into business but also, according to management, the sale of ineffective zinc remedies that were discontinued during the course of the year and dumped onto the market.

Outlook for the 21st Century

Revenues continued to erode at a significant rate in 2000, totaling just $15.5 million, leading to a loss of another $5.2 million. In 2001, The Quigley Corporation made progress toward regaining and maintaining profitability as well as launching Quigley Pharma. The financial picture improved somewhat in 2001, as revenues improved to $22.7 million and the company posted a negligible profit of $216,000, due primarily to the addition of sales from Darius and Caribbean Pacific Natural Products (discontinued the following year). Although net sales showed improvement in 2002, totaling $29.4 million, Quigley again posted a net loss of nearly $6.5 million. The poor economy was certainly a factor, but it was likely that the future health of Quigley was very much dependent on its ability to develop and market new over-the-counter homeopathic products that found acceptance with consumers. Nevertheless, zinc cold remedies represented the fastest growing segment in the Cough/Cold over-the-counter category in 2002. Cold-Eeze was restaged in new packaging, and streamlined advertising campaigns as well as new clinical results regarding adolescents helped Cold-Eeze to begin the process of gaining back lost market share. Whether or not sales could approach those in 1997 remained to be seen.

Principal Subsidiaries

Darius International, Inc.; Quigley Pharma Inc.

Principal Competitors

Matrixx Initiatives, Inc.; NutraMax Products, Inc.; Perrigo Company.

Further Reading

Alpert, Bill, ''Research Questions Quigley's Miracle Pill—Barrons,'' *Dow Jones Commodities Service,* June 27, 1998.

Arroyo, Arnaldo, ''Quigley Is Becoming More Than a One-Trick Pony,'' *Equities,* March/April 1999, p. 36.

''Cough-Drop Maker Catches Wall Street Chill,'' *St. Louis Post-Dispatch,* March 15, 1998, p. E1.

Gifford, Bill, ''The Zinc Panther Strikes Again,'' *Philadelphia Magazine,* March 3, 1999.

Hollresier, Eric, ''Quigley Turns to TV Shopping to Sell Lozenges,'' *Philadelphia Business Journal,* April 21, 1995, p. 6B.

—Ed Dinger

Richardson Industries, Inc.

904 Monroe Street
Sheboygan Falls, Wisconsin 53085-1872
U.S.A.
Telephone: (920) 467-2671
Fax: (920) 467-2222
Web site: http://www.richardsonbrothers.com

Private Company
Incorporated: 1848 as Joseph Richardson Company
Employees: 700
Sales: $69.8 million (2002 est.)
NAIC: 337122 Non-Upholstered Wood Household
    Furniture Manufacturing; 321114 Wood Preservation;
    321918 Other Millwork (Including Flooring); 337110
    Wood Kitchen Cabinet and Counter Top
    Manufacturing

Located in Sheboygan Falls, Wisconsin, Richardson Industries, Inc., consists of several different divisions devoted to the various aspects of furniture and woodworking. In addition to its flagship division, furniture-maker Richardson Brothers, the company also owns Richardson Lumber, which sells building materials, produces custom architectural elements via a mill-work shop, designs homes, and develops real estate. Richardson Wood Preserving produces treated wood for outdoor use. Richco Structures manufactures both floor and roof trusses for new homes, as well as commercial buildings. Finally, Falls Dealer Supply is a wholesaler of building products, including glass block and treated lumber.

1841–75: Blazing the Trail

Richardson Industries' roots stretch back more than 150 years, when Joseph and Carolyn Richardson moved from New York to Roscoe, Illinois, in 1841. To fund the move, the couple borrowed $400 from Carolyn's father, Peter Burhans. By 1845, the Richardson family—which included three children—had relocated to what would become Sheboygan Falls, Wisconsin. There, the Richardsons purchased 200 acres of land for farming.

The early history of the company is chronicled in *The Richardson Story* by Jay Pridmore. In order to clear trees from his land, Richardson built a sawmill near the western shore of Lake Michigan on the Mullett River in 1848, with the help of his brother-in-law, Egbert Burhans. Wisconsin became a state that year, and Richardson's new sawmill represented the start of the Joseph Richardson Company. By 1871, Richardson had given the sawmill its first overhaul; the mill's water wheel and leather belts were replaced with turbines and gears.

Joseph Richardson's enterprise sold raw lumber processed at the mill, and eventually made available a growing selection of such wooden items as hayracks, water tanks, cheese boxes, and farm gates. According to the February 1997 issue of *Wood & Wood Products,* the sawmill became part of a larger operation that also included a planing mill and manufacturing division around 1868.

1876–1959: Growing With America

In 1876, the Joseph Richardson Company changed its name to Richardson Brothers Company. Joseph Richardson had retired, and his sons, William, Egbert, and Edward, took an ownership stake in the company. According to Pridmore's book, while Edward eventually relinquished his ownership so that he could to move west, he later returned and worked for his brothers.

By the later part of the decade, Richardson Brothers's offerings of wood products had expanded to include furniture. In 1881 the company produced its first chairs, and a factory was built for their manufacture the following year. Despite an economic depression that severely affected business, the company was able to persevere due to its broad offering of wood products. For example, while demand for chairs declined, the opposite was true of cheese boxes.

Several important developments took place during the first few decades of the 20th century. In 1910, Joseph Egbert Richardson, who went by the name Egbert, succeeded his uncle William Richardson as company president. In 1936, Jairus Richardson founded J.S. Richardson to design and produce woodworking equipment.

Early in the 1940s, many of Richardson Brothers's male employees left for World War II. As was the case in many industries across the nation, women assumed occupational roles previously performed by men. According to Pridmore, using machinery made by J.S. Richardson, Richardson Brothers shifted to wartime production. The company produced walnut handguards for M1 rifles, followed by rifle parts for NATO troops in later years. During the war, Richardson Brothers produced a newsletter called *Shop Shavings* to keep workers connected and informed about company news, even if they were stationed overseas. Only one Richardson Brothers employee was killed during combat.

Richardson Brothers increased its advertising and promotion efforts during the 1940s, using high-end photography and quality brochures to communicate the company's wide-ranging woodworking and manufacturing capabilities to consumers. In 1947, Lemont Richardson was named company president, succeeding Egbert. Also that year, Joe Richardson, Sr. (not the company founder, but rather the son of Egbert Richardson) separated Richardson Brothers from the rest of his family's operations. A new lumberyard was then constructed not far from the company's furniture mill.

Following the war, the company enjoyed renewed prosperity as the economy boomed. During this era, Richardson Brothers sold an expanded, modernized array of furniture, including cabinets and buffets produced in the Federal style. In 1952, a fourth generation of the family took the helm when Bill Richardson, son of Jairus, was named president. He was largely responsible for modernizing the company by working with well-known designers and increasing the company's marketing efforts. Despite his business acumen, according to Pridmore, ''Bill was a tinkerer at heart, and nothing pleased him more than devising new and sometimes homespun machines for cutting wood, building furniture and even plowing snow.''

Richardson Brothers had become a very self-sufficient enterprise by the 1950s. Pridmore summarized its operations, explaining that the company ''milled logs, generated power, devised many of its own tools and operated the business with a talented and motivated extended family whose roots went deep into the wood products business.''

The company concluded the decade by forming Richardson/Nemschoff in 1959. The new joint venture was established to produce and market high-fashion furniture. Expanding outside of Sheboygan Falls, Richardson Brothers placed a showroom in Chicago's Merchandise Mart, where it showcased pieces from its Peabody Collection, designed by Larry Peabody, a furniture designer from Boston.

1960–99: Expansion and Modernization

In 1960, Joe Richardson, Sr., made added prefabricated building trusses to the company's product offerings. Two years later, he succeeded his cousin, Bill Richardson, as president by purchasing a controlling interest in the firm. Another important development during this time was an increase in contract business. Richardson Brothers developed relationships with such clients as L.A. Period and California Furniture Shops on the West Coast, and Shelby Williams in Chicago. While this increased business made production more hectic, it also gave the company valuable experience in the area of high-volume manufacturing.

During the 1970s, less expensive furniture imports put pressure on companies like Richardson Brothers. These overseas competitors developed a knack for copying the Early American style that Richardson had begun producing again, as it moved away from the contemporary styles of the previous decade. Luckily, increased demand for high-quality oak furniture did not die, and the company was able to offset the effects of competition from imports.

A major development took place in 1973 when the company reorganized, forming Richardson Industries, Inc., as a holding company for its business segments, including furniture, lumber, and truss units. That same year, Marv Debbink was named general manager of the company's lumber business, as well as its truss unit, Richco Structures.

During the late 1970s, Joe Richardson III returned to his family's company as vice-president in charge of design and product development. He had first worked in the Richardson Brothers sawmill at the age of 16, and subsequently went on to learn the furniture plant's operations from top to bottom by gaining valuable experience in every department. He had then followed a varied path to become a furniture designer, including time at New York's Jiranek School of Furniture Design and Technology; coursework in both art and business; and employment in a furniture design studio, decorator showroom, factory, and retail furniture store. The company rounded out the 1970s by forming Richardson Wood Preserving in DePere, Wisconsin, located near one of the company's two Richco Structures sites.

In 1980, Joe Richardson III made an impression on the larger furniture industry when he designed a new line of bow-back chairs—a throwback to a style produced some 100 years before. The chair was a tremendous hit, and Richardson Brothers was besieged with orders from across the country, including many from new customers. This new product helped the company to expand its business in the West and Northwest.

In the June 1982 issue of *Wood & Wood Products*, Joe Richardson III commented on the success of his family's company and how he chose to become a part of it, explaining: ''I think many family businesses fail because they cater to the family, instead of people. I was raised to believe that whatever I wanted to do was fine.''

By the early 1980s, the Richardson Brothers division employed approximately 175 workers. Around this time, the company introduced a line of unfinished furniture that went on to become very profitable. Although Richardson Brothers would later scale back its presence in the unfinished market, in 1982

Key Dates:

1848: Joseph Richardson builds a sawmill on the Mullett River in Wisconsin, starting the Joseph Richardson Co.
1868: A planing mill and wood products manufacturing division are established.
1876: The Joseph Richardson Co. adopts the name Richardson Brothers.
1882: A factory is erected for manufacturing chairs.
1936: Jairus Richardson founds J.S. Richardson to design and produce woodworking equipment.
1942: The company engages in the wartime production of walnut handguards for M1 rifles.
1952: A fourth generation of the family takes the helm when Bill Richardson is named president.
1959: Richardson Brothers form a joint venture to produce and market high-fashion furniture.
1973: Reorganization creates Richardson Industries, with units devoted to furniture, lumber, and truss units.
1986: Glenn Dulmes is named president—the first non-family member to lead the enterprise.
1989: Joe Richardson III succeeds Dulmes as president.
1998: Richardson Industries celebrates 150 years of operation and is recognized as one of Wisconsin's oldest family-owned businesses.

Wood & Wood Products reported that unfinished furniture accounted for 20 percent of the company's shipments.

Also in 1982 a new manufacturing site was established in Haven, Wisconsin. The plant initially was used to make wall panels for Richardson Homes. Eventually, building trusses were also produced at this site for the Richco Structures unit.

While Richardson Brothers invested in new technology as appropriate, the company continued to use some pieces of equipment that had been in operation for several generations, including an eight-spindle boring machine. In addition, it also "rediscovered" equipment that had been dormant for a long time, including machinery that used steam to bend oak during the manufacture of bow-back chairs.

Computers had found their way into the Richardson Brothers plant by the early 1980s. While they were not widely used in the manufacturing process, computers helped improve several different business functions, including production data processing, costing, and inventory control. Computers were also employed at Richco Structures during the early 1980s. Around this time, as Pridmore explained in *The Richardson Story*, "computers and telecommunications, ploddingly slow by standards of a decade later, linked Richco with engineers at their supplier, Trusswall Corp. Richco personnel entered raw data on a screen, sent it to Trusswall by modem, and within a short period, they had engineered drawings for custom-made trusses." By 1983 Richco had decided to bring automated design in-house.

Two key leadership developments took place midway through the 1980s. First, the company suffered a loss in 1986 when Charles Richardson, Sr., formerly head of Richco Struc-

tures, died. The same year, Glenn Dulmes was named president of Richardson Brothers. This was a historic milestone in that Dulmes was the first person outside of the family to lead that enterprise. Dulmes's roots with the company stretched back to his teenage years. During the 1950s, Bill Richardson had increasingly given him greater—and unprecedented—amounts of operational responsibility, and he played an instrumental role in improving the company. In 1989, Joe Richardson III succeeded Dulmes as president, and a family member was once again at the organization's helm.

By 1996 Richardson Brothers had introduced a line of antique-finished furniture that was well received by many furniture dealers. Around the same time, a new 50-piece line of dining room and bedroom furniture was introduced. Named the Door County Collection, it was "the company's first major marketing effort outside oak in nearly 20 years," according to Pridmore. The March 25, 1996, issue of *HFN—The Weekly Newspaper for the Home Furnishing Network* explained how Richardson Brothers used consumer focus groups to gain valuable insight that affected the collection's design and price. The Door County Collection was highly successful, leading to first-year sales of several million dollars.

By the late 1990s, Richardson Brothers had a firmly established reputation for quality within the furniture industry, especially for long-lasting chairs. This reputation was communicated in the company's advertising, which displayed a Richardson family member standing on an inverted chair to promote its durability and strength.

In the February 1997 issue of *Wood & Wood Products*, Barbara Garet described the process used to make the sturdy chairs: "Steam bending makes chairs both durable and attractive. At Richardson Bros., bowbacks are hand bent from a solid piece of heated and pressurized wood. Fingerjoints are eliminated in continuous compound bent armchairs to create the strongest arm possible. Chair backs have doweled chuck joinery with reinforced screw plates. Legs and stretchers are double glued with compressed dowel construction."

A major milestone was reached in 1998, when Richardson celebrated 150 years of operation. In its July 5, 1999, edition, the *Wisconsin State Journal* reported that, according to a study conducted by Bryant College's Institute for Family Enterprise, Richardson Industries was perhaps the oldest family-owned business in the state of Wisconsin. By this time, the firm employed approximately 900 workers and was approaching annual sales of $100 million.

Despite years of tremendous success, the Richardson family had maintained a reputation for being approachable. In the same *Wisconsin State Journal* article, writer Jim Chilsen said that the residents of Sheboygan Falls described the family "as wealthy but down-to-earth—the kind who might slap you on the back if they see you at a local bar."

2000 and Beyond

As the 2000s arrived, although *Cabinet Maker* reported that Richardson Brothers had been able to drop the price of domestic goods twice in 18 months due to more efficient manufacturing processes, the company still faced a harsh economic climate and heightened foreign competition. Subsequently, layoffs occurred in the Richardson Brothers unit. The first workforce reduction took place in 2001, when 70 employees were let go. Although those workers eventually returned, 42 employees lost their jobs at the Richardson Brothers Sheboygan Falls plant in September 2002, followed by another 25 in April 2003. In the April 26, 2003, edition of the *Capital Times*, the company cited a need to "bring its production into line with customer demand and to reduce accumulating inventory."

Considering the sluggish economy of the early 2000s, the layoffs at Richardson Industries were not out of line with ones at countless other U.S. manufacturing companies. Backed by more than 150 years of success, the company was likely to weather the difficult times and continue its success in the 21st century.

Principal Divisions

Richardson Brothers; Richardson Wood Preserving; Richco Structures; Richardson Lumber; Falls Dealer Supply.

Principal Competitors

Ashley Furniture Industries Inc.; Hamel Forest Products Inc.; Hoida UBC; Midwest Manufacturing; Stan's Lumber Inc.

Further Reading

"CEO of Oldest Family-Owned Furniture Company to Chair IWF Design Competition," *Wood & Wood Products*, February 1994.

Chilsen, Jim, "Furniture Company May Be Oldest Family Outfit in State," *Wisconsin State Journal*, July 5, 1999.

Garet, Barbara, "Making Furniture With Geography In Mind," *Wood & Wood Products*, February 1997.

Gibson, Laureen, "Personal Profile: Joe Richardson III," *Wood & Wood Products*, June 1982.

"A Glow on Unfinished Furniture," *Business Week*, April 6, 1981.

"Home Made Solution to Imports," *Cabinet Maker*, October 25, 2002.

Pridmore, Jay, *The Richardson Story: A Family Enterprise At 150 Years*, Lyme, Conn.: Greenwich Publishing, 1998.

"Richardson Brothers Co. Expands Use of Antique Finish on Merchandise," *HFN—The Weekly Newspaper for the Home Furnishing Network*, January 1, 1996.

"Wood Products Firm Announces More Layoffs," *Capital Times*, April 26, 2003.

Wray, Christine L., and Jamie Sorcher, "Richardson Introduces 50-Piece Group," *HFN—The Weekly Newspaper for the Home Furnishing Network*, March 25, 1996.

—Paul R. Greenland

Ricola Ltd.

P.O. Box 130
CH-4242 Laufen
Switzerland
Telephone: (+41) 0 61 765 41 21
Fax: (+41) 0 61 765 41 22
Web site: http://www.ricola.ch

Private Company
Incorporated: 1930
Employees: 350
Sales: CHF 350 million ($171.00 million) (2003)
NAIC: 311330 Confectionery Manufacturing from
    Purchased Chocolate; 311311 Sugarcane Mills

Ricola Ltd. has been soothing the throats of over three generations of consumers. The family-owned company is based in Laufen, near Basel, Switzerland, where it produces its famous herb-based throat lozenges and related products. Ricola's flagship product remains its Ricola Swiss Herb Candy, a hard candy based on a blend of 13 herbs found in the Swiss mountains and created by company founder Emil Richterich. The company also produces two sugar-free variants, Fresh Pearls, a chewier version, and Lozenges, a hard-boiled drop candy. Each of these products is available in a range of flavors, including the original herb flavor, menthol-eucalyptus, lemon-mint, orange, and cherry mint, the last-named flavor having been developed specifically for the U.S. market. In the early 2000s, Ricola added new flavors based on elderberry flowers. It also extended its product offerings to include teas and other herbal preparations, such as the range of Ricola Herbal Health Dietary Supplements introduced at the turn of the century. Ricola's production remains focused at its Laufen facility, which employs nearly 400, and the company's candies and herbal products are sold in more than 50 countries worldwide. Raw materials come from some 200 farmers in Switzerland, who provide Ricola with organic herbs grown according to company specifications. Ricola remains wholly owned by the founding Richterich family and is led by Felix Richterich, grandson of the founder. In

2003, the company posted sales of approximately CHF350 million ($170 million).

Herbal Success in the 1940s

Ricola's success began with Emil Richterich, who acquired the Bleile bakery in the small town of Laufen, near the city of Basel, Switzerland, in 1924. Richterich carried on the bakery's candy making, cooking toffee candies in a kettle over a wood fire. He later expanded the business to include some 100 different confectionery types, including "fünfermocken," a traditional caramel candy that had long been popular in the region. Richterich himself handled sales and delivery, riding his bicycle throughout the local area to deliver candies to customers.

Richterich also began developing confectioneries based on herbs found in the mountainous region around Laufen, where herbal preparations and remedies had remained widely used. In the late 1920s, Richterich developed a cough drop, Hustenwohl, based on herbs.

The bakery's products gained increasing recognition in the region, and, with demand rising, Richterich turned to the full-time manufacture of candies and confectionery. In 1930, he created a new company, Confiseriefabrik Richterich & Co. Laufen, and added more modern production equipment, such as a coal-fired stove, cooling tables, presses, and molds.

Richterich continued working on new recipes and finally hit on the formula that was to turn the former bakery into a globally operating company. In 1940, he debuted his "Swiss Herb Candy"—a blend of 13 herbs, including peppermint, sage, thyme, as well as ribwort, horehound, burnet, mallow, yarrow, and others. The candy's unusual flavor, and its ability to soothe minor throat irritations (later proven clinically), quickly became a company flagship product.

The new drop, with its own distinctive shape, became a popular product in the region before spreading throughout much of Switzerland. In order to keep up with demand, Richterich built his first factory in 1950. Joining the company then was Richterich's son, Hans Peter, who recognized the potential for a new product line. Customers had taken to dissolving the Ricola

Company Perspectives:

Ricola believe that success is not an end in itself and takes its responsibilities to its employees, to society, and to the environment seriously. The corporate philosophy embraces both the economic and non-economic aspects of the company's operations. One way of making these aspects a reality is to maintain and foster cultural values. As a company with close ties to nature, Ricola assigns top priority to first-class raw materials. Ricola only uses herbs grown under controlled conditions which do no harm to the environment. Such herbs are not only more aromatic; they are also endowed with the inner vital force of nature.

Key Dates:

1924: Emil Richterich takes over a small bakery making candies and confectionery in Laufen, Switzerland.

1930: Increasing sales lead Richterich to found a dedicated candy business, Confizerie Richterich & Co. Laufen.

1940: Richterich develops a recipe for a new Swiss Herbal Candy, a throat and cough drop that features a blend of 13 herbs.

1950: The company builds its first factory in Laufen; Richterich's son Hans Peter Richterich joins the company and backs the launch of a new herbal tea based on its cough drop formula.

1960s: The company changes its name to Ricola, converts to a joint-stock company, and decides to focus on its herbal products, building a new factory and ending other candy and confectionery production; foreign sales to Germany, Italy, and France begin.

1976: Ricola launches new chewable Pearls candy based on its herbal candy formula.

1985: The company establishes a U.S. subsidiary.

1992: A subsidiary in Singapore is created to boost sales in the Asia Pacific region.

1997: The company launches a cough syrup.

1999: A new line of Herbal Health Supplements is introduced.

2002: Ricola launches a new line of elderberry flower-based lozenges.

drops in hot water, creating a herbal tea. In the 1950s, Richterich extended its product range with its own herbal tea blend based on the original Herb Candy formula.

During the 1960s, the Richterich family company remained focused on the Swiss market. When Hans Peter Richterich took over the company's leadership during that decade, he turned to conquering the international market. As part of that effort, the company changed its name, combining the first two initials of Richterich & Co. Laufen to form Ricola. The company also converted its status to that of a joint-stock company, although shares remained controlled by the Richterich family.

Whereas Emil Richterich had focused on inventing candies for the local market, Hans Peter Richterich's interests lay in developing the company's business and sales operations, turning the company toward the international market by launching sales initiatives in nearby Germany, Italy, and France.

Ricola now prepared to establish itself as a global brand. At the end of the 1960s, the company, which had continued to manufacture a wider assortment of candy and confectionery products, decided to focus its production around its herb-based flagship product. The company phased out its non-core products, then built a new factory just outside of Laufen. The expanded production enabled the company to enter new markets. Success in the German, Italian, and French markets came swiftly during the late 1960s, and by the early 1970s the company's 70 employees were producing more than 90 tons per year.

International Growth Continues: 1970s–1990s

The longstanding European interest in herbal products and remedies gave Ricola fertile ground to grow its sales throughout the 1970s. The popularity of herbal preparations in Asia also led the company to expand into that market during the decade. In the early 1970s, Ricola began selling its throat lozenges in Japan through a partnership with family-owned trading house Nisshoku. Hong Kong also became an important market for Ricola's products. At the same time, interest in herbal formulas had also been growing in the United States in the 1960s, and Ricola entered that market on a modest scale, with sales remaining limited to the health and natural foods retail channels.

Ricola's emphasis on its niche specialty led it to begin developing new herb-based products. In 1976, the company

released its first new major product line, the sugar-free Pearls. The new candy, which contained the same herbal formula as its predecessor, featured a gum arabic base, making it a chewy alternative to the Swiss Herbal Formula.

Ricola also began developing a wider assortment of flavors for its products. The original formula was soon joined by a range of flavors, including orange, menthol-eucalyptus, and, in support of the group's effort to increase its penetration of the U.S. market, cherry-mint.

Entry into the United States got underway in earnest during the mid-1980s. In 1986, the company decided to switch from its previous distributor, a specialty products group, to a more mainstream brokerage network with a commission-based sales force. Ricola also established a U.S. subsidiary in New Jersey in 1986. The company now expanded beyond the health foods retail channel to claim a position on the shelves and cashier counters of mainstream drugstore chains. By the beginning of the 1990s, Ricola had succeeded in placing its products in nearly all of the major drugstore groups in the United States. As in Europe, the company also began a drive to get its products into the still-broader supermaket channel.

Supporting the group's expansion efforts was a new line of herbal candy, a sugar-free lozenge, prepared using hard-boiled isomalt. That product was launched in 1988. In addition to the United States, the company also began targeting the wider market in the Asia Pacific, where consumption of herbal-based remedies had long been integral to the lifestyle of the region. In 1992, the company established a new sales subsidiary in Singapore to service its growing sales in this market. That initiative was taken by the group's new CEO, Felix Richterich, who took over from his father in 1991. By then, Ricola had succeeded in introducing its products in some 40 national markets. Felix Richterich now took the group's strategy a step further and began working on developing the company's name into a recognized specialty brand.

Global Brand Focus in the New Century

In support of its new strategy, the company built a new marketing office in its Laufen home base and also constructed a packaging plant in Brunstatt, in the French Alsace region, not far from the Swiss border. The company then began work on expanding its product range.

Ricola rolled out a new series of products during the second half of the 1990s, including a throat syrup based on its herbal formula. The company also debuted its own Ricola-branded line of breath mints. In 1998, the company added to its line of throat and cough products with the release of a new range of echinacea-based lozenges. In another extension of its reputation for quality herbal products, Ricola debuted its own line of Herbal Health Supplements in 1999.

Ricola's brand expansion continued into the 2000s with the introduction of sage-based drops in 2001 and, in 2002, a new line of lozenges based on elderberry flowers. As part of that launch, the company participated in the planting of some 5,000 new elderberry bushes near its home base in Laufen, Switzerland. Ricola had by then become one of the world's most recognized herbal specialists.

Principal Subsidiaries

Ricola Asia Pacific PTE Ltd (Singapore); Ricola USA Inc.

Principal Competitors

Warner Lambert Co.; Hershey Foods Corp.; Richardson-Vicks; Nestlé S.A.; Cadbury Schweppes PLC; CSM N.V.; Meiji Seika Kaisha Ltd.

Further Reading

"A Balanced Approach," *Supermarket Business*, December 15, 1999, p. 55.

Gold, Daniel, "Ricola Cough Drops Hack away at a Crowded Market," *Adweek's Marketing Week*, February 19, 1990, p. 24.

"Ricola Adds New Formula," *Chain Drug Review*, May 22, 2000, p. 19.

"Ricola Introduces Throat Syrup," *Chain Drug Review*, June 23, 1997, p. 86.

"A Swiss Alpine Meadow in Your Mouth," *Japan Times*, August 2, 2002.

—M.L. Cohen

RIDLEY Inc.

Ridley Corporation Ltd.

Level 10, 12 Castlereagh Street
Sydney
New South Wales 2000
Australia
Telephone: (+61) 02 82776100
Fax: (+61) 02 82276000
Web site: http://www.ridley.com

Public Company
Incorporated: 1987
Employees: 2,299
Sales: A$1.41 billion ($752.9 million) (2002)
Stock Exchanges: Australian
Ticker Symbol: RCL
NAIC: 311111 Dog and Cat Food Manufacturing; 212393
    Other Chemical and Fertilizer Mineral Mining;
    311119 Other Animal Food Manufacturing; 325998
    All Other Miscellaneous Chemical Product
    Manufacturing; 424910 Farm Supplies Merchant
    Wholesalers; 541710 Research and Development in
    the Physical Sciences and Engineering Sciences

Ridley Corporation Ltd. is Australia's leading manufacturer of salt and related products and animal feeds. Moreover, with its growing North American holdings, the company has claimed a place as one of the world's leading animal feeds producers. Ridley conducts its salt production operations through Cheetham Salt, the single-largest producer of food-grade salt in Australia. Cheetham Salt distributes its salt products throughout Australia, Southeast Asian, and Asian Pacific regions. Ridley also holds a 50 percent stake in Dominion Salt, based in New Zealand, one of that country's major salt producers. Yet animal feed is clearly the fuel for Ridley's growth. In Australia, the company operates in this sector under subsidiary Ridley Agri-products, producing a large variety of feed products for the country's livestock, as well as fish feeds and pet foods. In addition, Ridley develops and produces related animal health products, such as medications, disinfectants, and insecticides. In North America, the company operates through its 70 percent

holding in Canada-based Ridley Inc.—the remainder of that company's stock is listed on the Toronto Stock Exchange. Ridley Inc. operates through three primary divisions: Feed-Rite, based in Winnipeg, Manitoba, with 15 production plants; Hubbard Feeds, in the United States, with 26 production facilities; Ridley Block Operations; and Cotswold Swine Genetics, which produces genetically advanced pigs. Ridley Corporation is itself listed on the Australian Stock Exchange and is led by CEO Matthew Bickford-Smith.

From Salt to Feed in the 1990s

Ridley Corporation was founded in Australia in 1987 as a processor of bulk salt. A public company from the start, with a listing on the Australian Stock Exchange, Ridley quickly began expanding its salt operations, developing its own salt washing and refining facilities. By 1988, the company had launched the production of a complete line of washed and refined salt products for both the consumer and industrial foods markets. The company's success in this area led it to diversify.

By 1990, however, Ridley had decided to reorient itself as a specialty producer in two primary markets: salt and animal feed. Over the next year, the company sold off its non-core holdings and began developing a growth-through-acquisition strategy that was to last through much of the 1990s.

The company's first move into its new target sector came with the purchase of the feed operations of Goodman Fielder Wattie Limited, then in the midst of a drive to transform itself into a global prepared foods giant. That purchase brought Ridley several noted names in the Australian feedstock industry, including Barastoc, which was founded in 1938 and introduced the steamed pelleting process to the Australian market.

In 1987, Barastoc had joined the Goodman Fielder group, created in 1986 through a merger between New Zealand's Goodman and Australia's Fielder Gillepsie Davis, shortly joined by Australia's Allied Mills. Barastoc was merged into the Fielder and Allied Mills feed divisions. Two years later, that division grew again when Goodman Fielder purchased South Australia-based Milling Industries.

The acquisition of Goodman Fielder's feed business formed the basis of a new Ridley subsidiary, Ridley Agriproducts. The company next seized the opportunity to expand both of its core businesses when, in 1992, it purchased National Foods Limited Group's salt refinery, Cheetham Salt, the country's largest salt products brand, and its feedstock division, Cheetham Rural.

Ridley continued to build up its leadership position in both of its core Australian markets into the middle of the 1990s, notably with the acquisition of Aquafeed Products Australia. That purchase enabled the company to enter the fast-growing aquaculture market. In 1996, Ridley added to its dominant position in the region's salt market with the purchase of 50 percent of New Zealand's Dominion Salt.

By then, Ridley had already begun casting its eye on international expansion, especially an entry into the large North American market. The company's chance came in 1994, when it paid A$25 million to purchase Canada's Feed-Rite, which was founded in Winnipeg, Manitoba, in 1939 and had grown into one of the western Canada region's largest animal feed producers.

North American Expansion in the 1990s

The highly fragmented North American feed market remained the target of Ridley's acquisition drive through the mid-1990s. In 1995, the company purchased Lacombe, Alberta's Quality Feeds Alberta Ltd. Also in that year, the company added a breeding component when it acquired the exclusive rights to produce Cotswold genetically bred pigs in Canada.

In 1996, the company began to extend its Canadian operations nationwide, acquiring southern Ontario-based premix producer Fairmix. The company also strengthened its western Canadian base through the acquisition of the Green Valley Feed Service, which operated a feed mill as well as its own farm supply store. Not all of the company's expansion efforts met with success, however. In mid-1996, the company failed in its takeover attempt of Melbourne, Australia-based Joe White Maltings.

Instead, the company returned its focus to North America. In August 1996, Ridley made its first move into the U.S. market, acquiring, through Feed-Rite, Zip Feed Mills, which operated three integrated feed production plants in North and South Dakota. The move increased the company's North American production by 80,000 tons per year, with total production capacity of up to 150,000 tons per year. As then CEO Gary Busenhut told *The Advertiser:* "The acquisition of Zip Feeds will give Feed-Rite a strong presence in markets which are much larger than our traditional markets."

The purchase also whetted the company's desire for further expansion in North America, leading to its next major acquisition, of Hubbard Milling, in April 1997. For a price of $65 million, Ridley added 15 new production plants, more than doubling its North American production capacity to a total of more than one million tons annually, making the company a significant player in the North American market. The Hubbard acquisition also established Ridley as the leading producer of low-moisture supplement feed blocks in North America.

Following the Hubbard purchase, again made through Feed-Rite, Ridley renamed its Canadian operation as Ridley Canada. Hubbard itself was renamed as Hubbard Feeds, Inc., and absorbed the company's Zip Feed mills. Ridley Canada soon after added another acquisition, of Daco Laboratories, which produced concentrated nutritional base products. That purchase enabled the company to broaden its product range as well as extend its geographic reach. It also led Ridley Corporation to list its Canadian subsidiary on the Toronto Stock Exchange, selling a 40 percent stake and changing its name to Ridley Inc. Ridley Corporation later raised its shareholding in Ridley Inc. to 70 percent.

In the meantime, Ridley had not neglected its Australian business. In 1997, the company expanded by buying up six feed mills and a premix plant from Farmstock Stockfeed, strengthening its position in Queensland. Following that purchase, the company acquired Moloney's Stockfeed and Maffra Stockfeed, boosting its capacity in Australia's Western Districts.

Global Feed Producer for the 2000s

Ridley once again turned its attention to building up its North American holdings in 1998. In that year, the company acquired PM Ag Products, paying A$10 million to acquire that company's U.S.-based low-moisture feed block business. Also in 1998, the company bought up Iowa City, Iowa-based Gringer Feed and Grain Inc., which produced both concentrates and complete feed products. Further north, the company added to its Canadian base through the acquisition of Macleod Feed Mill, based in Alberta. At the same time, the company made its first move into Europe through its acquisition of Cotswold Pig Development Company Ltd. in the United Kingdom.

The economic collapse of much of the Asian Pacific region, combined with a soft market in its core Australian market, cut into Ridley's growth in the late 1990s. By 1999, Ridley was forced to restructure, shutting four of its production plants in Australia and centralizing the management of its remaining plants. At the same time, shrinking pork prices were hurting the company's Cotsworld subsidiary as well.

That operation was hit still harder in 2001, when an outbreak of foot-and-mouth disease in the United Kingdom brought about a freeze of the company's breeding stock and pig sperm exports into the company's main French and German market. The outbreak of the disease also had a negative impact on customer confidence in farther-flung markets, including Japan and the United States. By 2002, Ridley was forced to sell off the money-losing European Cotswold operations, keeping only its North American division, which was renamed Cotswold Swine Genetics.

Nevertheless, Ridley had not entirely abandoned external growth throughout this period. In 2000, the company achieved

Key Dates:

1987: The company incorporates as a bulk salt processor and is listed on the Australian Stock Exchange.

1988: Expansion into salt washing and refining commences.

1990: A new strategy focusing on salt and animal feed markets is adopted.

1994: The company acquires Feed-Rite of Canada in its first international expansion.

1997: Hubbard Milling in the United States is acquired; Ridley Canada is listed on the Toronto Stock Exchange.

2002: The company acquires U.S. equine feed and nutrition specialist McCauley Bros.

2003: Plans are announced to begin a new series of small-scale acquisitions in the United States as well as expansion of its salt business in Australia.

a significant advance in its U.S. position through the purchase of the Wayne Feeds Division from the American firm the ContiGroup. That operation, based in Chicago, expanded the company's feed production capacity and also gave it a solid base in such new market territories as Pennsylvania, Illinois, Kentucky, and North Carolina.

North America by then represented the largest share of the company's revenues, which topped A$1.4 billion in 2002. The region remained Ridley's growth market into the 2000s. In 2002, the company struck out in a new direction, aiming to develop a new business focused on the equine market. As the foundation of that business, the company made a new acquisition, of McCauley Bros., in April 2002. McCauley Bros. specialized in horse feeds and related nutritional products.

By the early 2000s, Ridley had grown into one of the world's major feeds producers, with an especially strong position in the North American market. The company showed no signs of loosening its growth-through-acquisition commitment, announcing in mid-2003 its intention to pursue a number of new, smaller acquisitions, particularly in North America. As new

CEO Matthew Bickford-Smith told *The Australian Financial Review*, "That's very much our preferred approach right now, basically gradual, bite-sized acquisitions in high value-added animal protein products, tending to be in the supplementary side." At the same time, Ridley reaffirmed its commitment to its salt division, announcing plans to expand its Cheetham Salt unit through a series of acquisitions and partnerships.

Principal Subsidiaries

Barastoc Stockfeeds Pty Ltd.; Cheetham Salt Ltd.; Cotswold Canada Ltd. (70%); Farmstock Pty Ltd.; Feed-Rite, Inc. (United States; 70%); Hubbard Feeds Inc. (United States; 70%); Ridley AgriProducts (NZ) Pty Ltd.; Dominion Salt Ltd. (New Zealand); Ridley AgriProducts Pty Ltd.; Ridley Argentina S.A.; Ridley Inc. (Canada; 70%); Wishbone Turkey Farm Ltd (Canada; 70%).

Principal Competitors

Cargill Inc.; Archer Daniels Midland Company; ConAgra Foods Inc.; Edison SpA; Eli Lilly and Company; President Enterprises Corporation; Land O'Lakes Inc.; Royal Cebeco Group Cooperative; Nutreco Holding N.V.

Further Reading

Archdall, Susan, "Ridley Expands North American Operations," *Advertiser*, May 30, 1997, p. 19.

Henley, Clive, "Farm Supplier in Good US Paddock," *Herald Sun*, August 6, 2001, p. 75.

McGuire, Michael, "Ridley Corp Buys US Feed Milling Firm," *Advertiser*, August 14, 1996, p. 35.

McMenemy, Lauren, "Price Dip Makes Ridley Squeal," *Advertiser*, July 22, 2000, p. 64.

"No Grain of Salt for Ridley," *Daily Telegraph* (Surrey Hills, Australia), October 29, 2002, p. 25.

Smith, Rod, "Ridley Building Company into 'Significant' Global Force," *Feedstuffs*, October 27, 1997, p. 6.

"Ridley Ready to Feed Again," *Australian Financial Review*, August 27, 2003.

Whyte, Jemima, "Investors Find Value in Ridley's Refocus," *Australian Financial Review*, April 30, 2002, p. 22.

—M.L. Cohen

Rostvertol plc

Ul. Novatorov 5
Rostov-Na-Donu 344038
Russia
Telephone: (+7) 8632 393 298
Fax: (+7) 8632 930 039
Web site: http://www.rostvertolplc.ru

State-Owned Company
Incorporated: 1939
Employees: 7,600
Sales: $1.92 billion (2002)
NAIC: 336411 Aircraft Manufacturing

Rostov, Russia-based Rostvertol plc is a major producer of helicopters, including its flagship Mi-26 heavy-lift helicopter. The company, which remains under state control, also produces a variety of other goods, including cargo trailers for automotive use, vans, foldable beds, telephones, stepladders, and even video cassettes. Nevertheless, helicopters remain the group's specialty. The Mi-26 has long held the world record for its lift capacity. The craft has climbed to 6,300 meters with a 10-ton load and higher than 4,000 meters with a 25-ton load. In addition to its military applications, the Mi-26 has been adapted for fighting forest fires and is also used extensively for difficult-to-reach construction projects. Another model, the Mi-24, is built for both transport and combat use, while the Mi-28 offers round-the-clock flying capability and the ability to fly at extremely low altitudes. Rostvertol also produces two lightweight helicopters, the Mi-2A and the Mi-60MAI. The company supports its aircraft sales through the production of main rotor blades, including replacement blades for its previous models. In 2003, Rostvertol set up a services subsidiary, Rostvertol Aviation Company Ltd., which provides air transport and fire fighting services as well as training and maintenance for the company's helicopters. Rostvertol is led by director general Boris Nikolayevich Slyusar and produces more than $1.9 billion in revenues per year.

Specializing in Helicopters in the 1950s

Rostvertol's origins lay in the build up to the "Great Patriotic War" (Russia's term for World War II). In 1939, a production complex was established in Rostov-on-Don, in southern Russia, in order to produce wooden propellers for civil and military aircraft in the Soviet Union. The outbreak of hostilities in western Europe forced the Soviets to step up their own armament campaign, and soon after its founding the Rostov site was expanded to include the production of entire craft, including engines.

Rostov first began production of the I-16 fighter plane during the period of truce between the Stalinist government and the Nazi regime. After Germany attacked the Soviet Union, the Rostov facility stepped up production. The plant began manufacturing the UT-2M airplane, then added production of the famous PO-2 in 1943. Originally designed by Polikarpov in the late 1920s, the PO-2, a wooden biplane with a five-cylinder piston engine, had long been outclassed by more modern fighter craft. Yet the PO-2 played a vital role as a night-time harassment bomber during World War II: capable of flying low and too small to be detected by radar, the PO-2 was easy to fly and cheap to build.

The Rostov plant continued to build the PO-2 into the late 1940s. By then, however, the site had begun to install metal-working capacity and in 1949 began to manufacture a new airplane type, the YAK-14 assault glider. Capable of carrying up to 25 people, the YAK-14 became the Rostov site's first all-metal aircraft. It was soon followed by the IL-10M, which was designed by Sergei Ilyushkin and debuted in 1952. That plane, which boasted plating capable of withstanding small arms and even rocket fire, earned the nickname the "Flying Tank." The IL-10M played an important role in both the Soviet and Allied air forces through the end of the Korean War. In the meantime, the Rostov plant had begun production of a successor plane, the IL-40, the plant's first to feature turbo-jet engines. The high-speed plane was also fitted out with small arms and rocket launchers, making it a potent attack craft.

In the early 1950s, The Rostov plant had become an important part of a new effort—the creation of the first Soviet helicopters. This initiative was being spearheaded by the government's Moscow-based Design Bureau, headed by Mikhail Mil. The Rostov site, as well as sister facilities in Kashov and elsewhere, began helicopter production with a light craft designated as the M-1. Mil then began working on a new type of helicopter capable of lifting heavy loads that could be used to

Key Dates:

1939: A plant in Rostov is constructed for the production of wooden airplane propellers.
1940: The Rostov site begins production of aircraft and aircraft engines, starting with the I-16 fighter plane.
1943: Production begins of PO-2 bomber.
1949: The company produces its first all-metal plane, the YAK-14 assault glider.
1954: The company's first turbo-jet plane, the Il-40 attack plane, goes into production.
1956: The company becomes a helicopter specialist with the launch of the first Soviet helicopter, the Mi-1.
1959: The company launches its first heavy-lift assault helicopter, the Mi-6, which remains in production for more than 20 years.
1973: Production of Mi-24 assault helicopters begins.
1980: Full-scale production of Mi-26 heavy-lift helicopter, which sets new worldwide lifting records, begins.
1992: Rostvertol becomes a public limited company under state control and diversification program begins.
2002: Production of Mi-26T helicopter begins.
2004: Rostvertol announces the start of full-scale production of a new generation Mi-28 combat helicopter for 2006.

support the country's large-scale construction and infrastructure projects. By 1959, the first Mi-6 heavy-lift helicopters went into production in Rostov.

During the 1960s, the Rostov plant converted its production to specialize in the manufacture of helicopters, especially heavy-lifting craft. The site then became known as the Rostov Helicopter Plant. The Mi-6 design proved highly successful, both within the Soviet Union and throughout the Soviet sphere of influence, and it remained in production for more than 20 years.

Setting New Lifting Records in the 1980s

The era of the helicopter began with the war in Vietnam, where the terrain hampered the operation of traditional fixed wing craft. The heavy-lifting helicopter segment had been developing especially rapidly. In the 1960s, the Rostov Plant set up the production technology for a new type of heavy lifter, the Mi-10. Production of that helicopter, capable of lifting as much as 15 tons, began at Rostov in 1964.

Although the Mi-10 set a number of lifting records, it did not attract the same level of international interest as its predecessor, and the model was dropped after 1969. In the mid-1970s, however, the Rostov plant adapted the Mi-10, producing the Mi-10K crane helicopter. This model featured a special cockpit beneath the fuselage that provided pilot controls and controls for operating a specially fitted crane. Limited run production began in 1974 and ended into the following year; the Mi-10K models nevertheless remained in service for many years thereafter.

The mid-1960s had seen the launch of a new assault and transport helicopter, the Mi-24, and production of the model (designated as the Mi-35 outside of the Soviet Union) began in 1969. Known as the Hind, the new design became the first Soviet helicopter to feature attack transport and gunship capacity and was said to outclass even its U.S. rivals. The M-24 Hind became an international success, and in 1973 the Rostov site began producing the craft in order to meet growing demand.

The Mil Design Bureau—named after Mikhail Mil after his death in 1970—began preparing a new generation of heavy-lifting craft during the 1970s. The role of the Rostov plant in the development of the new craft, which made its maiden flight in 1978, was particularly significant. By 1980, the new model went into full production. Dubbed the Mi-26, it once again established a new world's record for heavy lifting. In tests performed in 1982, the craft soared past 6,300 meters carrying a 10-ton load and passed the 4,000 meter mark with a 25-ton load, the heaviest load ever transported by helicopter.

Corporate Status in the New Century

With the launch of the Mi-26, Rostov ended production of the Mi-6. The plant became one of the primary building sites for the Mi-26 and participated in developing new variations of the design, including its adaptation as a fire fighting vehicle by the Belgian firm Skytech.

The uses of the Mi-26 continued to expand throughout the 1980s. The craft participated in the exploitation of the Siberian oilfields and provided support for the containment effort following the disaster at the Chernobyl nuclear power facility in the late 1980s. The Rostov facility later came to specialize in building the Mi-26T, which was designed for the transport of trucks and other vehicles as well as bulky cargo. Rostov also began producing a number of variations on the Mi-24 combat helicopter. These included the Mi-24D, a troop transporter and assault vehicle, and the Mi-24V, which featured a deadlier armament complement than the Mi-24D.

Following the breakup of the Soviet Union at the start of the 1990s, the Russian military complex went through a restructuring program. As part of that effort, the Rostov plant was reformed as a public limited company, Rostvertol, in 1992. Although still under state control, Rostvertol was now expected to compete as an independent company.

The end of the Soviet era helped open new markets for the company, such as Greece, which became an important Rostvertol customer, and Peru, which received its first Rostvertol helicopters in 1995. South Korea, India, China, Malaysia, and the United Arab Emirates were also added to Rostvertol's list of buyers. However, not all orders came from governments. In 1997, the company delivered an Mi-26 to Korea Samsung Aerospace and later to the Cyprus-based Nutshell Company. Rostvertol also began building lighter-weight helicopters, such as the Mi-2A light helicopter and the Mi-60 lightweight training helicopter. In addition, the company responded to the worldwide drop-off in military spending by expanding production into a variety of new, non-military areas. For this sector, the company began producing such varied goods as cargo trailers for automotive use, vans, foldable beds, telephones, stepladders, and video cassettes.

Rostvertol continued to attract new customers, including Mexico, which took delivery of its first helicopters in 2000. The company also worked on developing new variants of its core helicopter line, such as the Mi-26P, which was fitted out for round-the-clock use and went into production in 2002. The following year, the company began flight testing its all-weather variant, developed in conjunction with Mil MHP (the successor to the Mil Design Bureau), the Mi-24N. The company also developed another variant, the Mi-24PN, for the Russian government.

Rostvertol continued seeking new clients, such as Brazil, where the company found itself in head-to-head competition with the American firm of Sikorsky. Several days after tendering its bid, Rostvertol found itself blacklisted by the U.S. government for selling military equipment to countries accused of supporting international terrorism.

Undaunted, Rostvertol continued to develop new helicopter designs in conjunction with long-time partner Mil MHP. The company also moved to expand its service arm, forming new subsidiary Rostvertol Aviation Company Ltd. in 2003 to provide air cargo transportation and fire fighting and other services using the company's own helicopters, as well as providing maintenance, repairs, and support services for the company's sales. In February 2004, the company announced that it was preparing to launch a next-generation assault helicopter, the Mi-28N, capable of round-the-clock, all-weather operation. The new craft boasted superior plating for protection against increasingly deadly ground fire. The company expected full-scale production of the new model to begin in 2006 and had already filled its order book

into 2015. Rostvertol entered the 21st century as a leading specialist in the global helicopter industry.

Principal Subsidiaries

Rostvertol Aviation Company Ltd.; Rostvertol International NV/AG/SA (Belgium).

Principal Competitors

Bell Helicopter Textron Inc.; Sikorsky Aircraft Corporation; Aviation Industries Corporation of China; Boeing Company; EADS France S.A.S.; Lockheed Martin Corporation.

Further Reading

Karnozov, Vladimir, ''Russia Accepts First Upgraded Mi-24PN from Rostvertol,'' *Flight International*, January 20, 2004, p. 18.
Podshibiakin, Andrey, ''From the Banks of the Quiet Don,'' *Airfleet*, November/December 1998.
''Rostvertol Will Continue Mass Production of Mi-26 Halo Heavy Helicopters for at least 10 Years,'' *Inzhenernqaia Gazeta*, March 19, 2002, p. 4.
Sarsfield, Kate, ''Rostvertol to Retrofit Mi-2 Hoplite,'' *Airline Business*, December 3, 2002, p. 30.

—M.L. Cohen

Salvatore Ferragamo Italia S.p.A.

Via dei Tornabuoni 2
Firenze
I-50123 FI
Italy
Telephone: (+39) 055 33601
Fax: (+39) 055 336021
Web site: http://www.salvatoreferragamo.it

Private Company
Incorporated: 1927
Employees: 700
Sales: EUR584.7 million ($631 million)(2002)
NAIC: 316214 Women's Footwear (except Athletic)
Manufacturing; 315233 Women's and Girls' Cut and
Sew Dress Manufacturing; 315234 Women's and
Girls' Cut and Sew Suit, Coat, Tailored Jacket, and
Skirt Manufacturing; 315999 Other Apparel Acces-
sories and Other Apparel Manufacturing; 316213
Men's Footwear (except Athletic) Manufacturing;
316992 Women's Handbag and Purse Manufacturing

Salvatore Ferragamo S.p.A. has been synonymous with
Italian luxury for more than three-quarters of a century. The
Florence-based, family-owned company continues to produce
the shoes that once earned it the nickname ''Shoemaker to the
Stars,'' but also designs, produces, and distributes a full range of
men's and women's clothing and accessories. In addition, Ferragamo sells its own branded perfume lines, and, in a partnership
with another Italian company, Luxottica, a range of Ferragamo-
branded eyeglasses. Nevertheless, shoes remain at the heart of
the Ferragamo empire, and, while the company once focused on
custom-fitting such famous clients as Audrey Hepburn and Marilyn Monroe (who brought fame to the company's stiletto heels),
it now produces a wide range of sizes and shoe widths appealing
to a broader, yet still upscale market. Women's and men's
footwear represent more than 42 percent of the group's sales of
nearly EUR 600 million. Ferragamo's sales are made through a
global network of retailers, including most of the world's major
department stores, and through the company's own network of
nearly 450 retail Ferragamo stores, approximately half of which

are directly owned by Ferragamo. The Asian region, especially
Japan, accounts for the largest share of the company's sales at 45
percent. North America adds 31 percent to sales, while Europe
accounts for 23 percent. Ferragamo also owns French design
group Ungaro. Founded by Salvatore Ferragamo, the company
remains headed by his widow, Wanda, and their children. Eldest
son Ferruccio acts as CEO of the company, which remains 100
percent owned by the Ferragamo family.

Fitting the Walk of Fame in the 1920s

One of 14 children, Salvatore Ferragamo was born in Bonito, near Naples, in 1898. He began an apprenticeship with a
Naples shoemaker at the age of 11; two years later, he had set up
his own shoe shop in Bonito. A number of Ferragamo's older
brothers had traveled to the United States, and, when he was 14
years old, Ferragamo set out to join them.

Ferragamo at first went to Boston, where one of his brothers
worked at a large shoe manufacturer using industrialized shoemaking techniques—a far cry from Ferragamo's own commitment to traditional, quality craftsmanship. Ferragamo remained
in Boston for nearly a decade, but at the start of the 1920s he
decided to move closer to one of his other brothers, who lived in
Santa Barbara, California. There, Ferragamo opened his own
shoe shop, practicing traditional shoemaking techniques.

Ferragamo soon went to work for the film industry as a
designer and maker of boots and shoes. The quality of Ferragamo's costume shoes led actresses and actors to ask him to
make them footwear for off-screen as well, and Ferragamo
quickly established a reputation among people in the movie
business. In order to be in closer proximity to his new clientele,
Ferragamo moved his shop to Hollywood, where he opened the
Hollywood Boot Shop in 1923.

With customers such as Rudolph Valentino, Douglas Fair-
banks, Mary Pickford, and Gloria Swanson, Ferragamo quickly
earned the nickname ''Shoemaker to the Stars.'' In the meantime, Ferragamo enrolled at Los Angeles University, where he
studied human anatomy, mathematics, and chemical engineering, disciplines which he applied to the creation of his shoe
styles. Indeed, much of modern footwear, and especially
women's footwear, was to stem from Ferragamo's innovations.

Company Perspectives:

The values of the current company were translated by its founder Salvatore Ferragamo, who, with his life's experiences, guiding principles, creativity, and legendary success, bequeathed strong and distinctive ideals which were then carried on first by his wife, then by his children, and now with continuity in the third generation.

These included the open shoe and sandals for women. Over time, Ferragamo amassed a collection of some 300 patents, most, but not all, of which were for his shoes.

Ferragamo's popularity as a shoe designer rose steadily in 1920s, and his customer base spread beyond the acting world. By the middle of the decade, demand had risen beyond Ferragamo's capacity to complete the orders he received. Ferragamo now sought to expand his shop into a full-scale shoemaking business. However, unable to find qualified personnel in the United States, Ferragamo ultimately decided to return to Italy.

In 1927, Ferragamo set up a new business in Florence, a primary center for the Italian shoe industry, where the supply of trained workers was plentiful. While remaining committed to traditional handcrafted shoemaking techniques, Ferragamo was able to adapt them to modern production methods.

Expanding Production in the 1930s

Ferragamo began to establish his name as a preeminent Italian shoe manufacturer in Italy and elsewhere in Europe. Ferragamo's expanded operation also allowed him to continue to supply his loyal customers in the United States. However, following the Wall Street crash of 1929 and the resulting international depression, orders from overseas collapsed. Because Ferragamo's European sales were not yet sufficient to carry the company, he went bankrupt in 1930.

Faced with rebuilding his business, Ferragamo now focused exclusively on the Italian market. His inspired designs and quality craftsmanship quickly brought him a growing customer base, and by the mid-1930s Ferragamo was operating two workshops to supply his customers. In 1936, Ferragamo opened a new shop in Florence's famed Palazzo Spini Feroni.

The late 1930s were marked by a tightening supply of materials, such as leather and metal, that were essential to shoemaking, as the Mussolini-led government turned its attention to rebuilding the country's war machine. In response, Ferragamo began developing shoes based on a variety of other materials, such as felt, metallic threads, and raffia. These materials inspired Ferragamo to create new and innovative designs, and his popularity soared in Italy. A major success came with Ferragamo's inspired use of cork to create the so-called "wedge" heel, thereby overcoming the lack of materials needed to produce traditional heels.

The cork heel attracted customers and remained a company best-seller for years to come. Ferragamo's rising sales now allowed him to put down a down payment on the purchase of the Palazzo Spini Feroni building, which became the company's headquarters in 1938. Ferragamo's fortunes continued to rise despite the outbreak of World War II, and his company now owned the building outright. The 13th century landmark building remained the company's headquarters and later housed the Salvatore Ferragamo Museum.

The years following the end of World War II marked the period of Salvatore Ferragamo's greatest personal success, as his shoe designs became known throughout the world. In 1947, he released the so-called "invisible" sandal. That design received the prestigious Neiman Marcus Award, marking the first time this honor went to a footwear designer. Another significant innovation was Ferragamo's steel-reinforced stiletto heel, which became closely identified with Marilyn Monroe in the 1950s. Other important Ferragamo clients of the period were Sophia Loren, Greta Garbo, and Audrey Hepburn.

By 1950, Ferragamo employed some 700 workers, who produced just 350 handcrafted and for the most part custom-fitted shoes per day. During the 1950s, Ferragamo began mechanizing non-critical areas of the shoemaking process. However, the major part of his shoes remained fashioned by hand.

Toward the end of the 1950s, Ferragamo prepared to introduce a new generation into the family business. Married in 1940, Ferragamo was the father of six children, three boys and three girls. In the late 1950s, the oldest child, daughter Fiamma, joined the company and began learning design and shoemaking from her father.

Salvatore Ferragamo died in 1960, leaving the business to his family. Ferragamo's widow, Wanda, who had previously stayed at home to raise the couple's children, now took the lead of the company and quickly displayed her abilities as a businesswoman. The other Ferragamo children joined the company during the 1960s, each taking responsibility for a particular sphere of operation. Eldest son Ferruccio later took over as CEO, while Fiamma carried on the creative side of the business.

Within a year after her father's death, Fiamma Ferragamo had already debuted her first collection, in London, to great acclaim. She also became something of an ambassador for the company, personally making sales appearances at major clients throughout the world. By 1967, Fiamma was also recognized with the Neiman Marcus Award.

Diversified Luxury Goods Group in the New Century

Over the following decades, Ferragamo modernized its production methods, adding mechanized and automated production lines in order to meet the growing demand for its branded products. Where the company previously made at most 350 pairs of shoes each day, its capacity grew to as high as 11,000 pairs per day. The company shrewdly overcame the difficulty of maintaining its commitment to proper fit by developing an extensive range of sizes and shoe widths, with many sizes offered in up to six different widths.

Ferragamo also adapted to the rapidly changing luxury goods sector. The proliferation of designer lines in the late 1970s shifted the focus of the luxury footwear sector from a small, elite group of buyers to a larger, although still upscale

Key Dates:

1911: Apprenticed to a Naples shoemaker, Salvatore Ferragamo sets up his own shoe shop in Bonito.
1912: Ferragamo emigrates to the United States and begins working for a shoe manufacturer in Boston.
1920: Ferragamo moves to California, setting up his own shop in Santa Barbara.
1923: Ferragamo moves to Hollywood and opens the Hollywood Boot Shop, becoming known as the "Shoemaker to the Stars."
1929: Ferragamo declares bankruptcy; rebuilds his business, and focuses on the Italian market.
1947: Ferragamo wins Neiman Marcus Award for his "invisible" shoe design.
1959: Ferragamo's daughter Fiamma joins the company and begins training under her father.
1961: Fiamma Ferragamo presents her first collection in London.
1967: Fiamma Ferragamo wins Neiman Marcus Award.
1980: The company launches its first ready-to-wear clothing collection.
1996: Majority control of French design house Emanuel Ungaro is acquired.
2003: The company produces its first perfume, Incanta, and opens flagship stores in New York and Tokyo.

consumer market. Ferragamo responded by diversifying beyond footwear. After introducing an assortment of leather goods, including luggage, the company launched its own line of knitwear in the 1980s.

In 1980, Ferragamo added its first ready-to-wear clothing collection to complement its footwear, accessories, and knitwear, enabling the company to promote its "total look." The company, which relied on in-store boutiques in the world's department stores, also aimed to extend its vertical integration into the retail channel. During the 1980s, the company began opening its own stores, and by 1990 operated 18 stores in Italy, Zurich, and London. In the United States, Ferragamo had stores in New York and Palm Beach.

By then, exports represented 75 percent of Ferragamo's sales, while the United States alone accounted for some 48 percent of the group's total revenues. Yet the Far East represented perhaps the fastest-growing market for the company. At just over 11 percent of total sales at the start of the 1990s, the Asian region grew into the company's single largest market, accounting for more than 45 percent of sales by the opening years of the 21st century. Among Asian markets, Japan was Ferragamo's most lucrative.

By the mid-1990s, Ferragamo, which had weathered the worst of the recession of the early 1990s, prepared for further growth. As Ferruccio Ferragamo explained to *WWD*, "When you are confident in what you do, then a crisis is a moment of opportunity—shop space costs less to rent, supplies cost less, and new structures are cheaper to create."

Ferragamo's confidence allowed it to continue building up its retail network through the 1990s. By 2003, the company boasted more than 200 stores under its direct control and over 250 franchise operations in Asian markets. The company also rolled out its own outlet store format during the decade. By 1993, the company's sales had grown to more than $200 million worldwide.

Although hurt by the death of Fiamma Ferragamo in 1998, the company maintained its steady growth rate. This was aided in part by the group's first acquisition—that of majority control of the Paris-based fashion house of designer Emanuel Ungaro. The addition helped boost Ferragamo's presence in the ready-to-wear sector. That acquisition also gave the company its first introduction to the fragrance and beauty products market.

In the late 1990s, Ferragamo departed from its tradition of controlling its production. In 1998, the company signed a licensing deal with dominant Italian eyeglass manufacturer Luxottica to release a Ferragamo-branded line of eyeglass frames. The following year, the group debuted its own Ferragamo-branded perfume, Ferragamo pour Femme, produced under license by Bulgari SpA. The company also released a men's fragrance.

Two years later, however, Ferragamo ended the production license and instead brought its fragrance and beauty products operations in-house under subsidiary Ferragamo Parfums SA. Development began on a new line of fragrance and bath and beauty products which debuted in October 2003 under the name Incanta. In the meantime, Ferragamo continued its expansion, opening new flagship stores in New York and Tokyo in 2003. Even as it pursued its drive to become a leader in the global luxury fashion sector, Salvatore Ferragamo S.p.A. remained committed to the tradition of quality and innovation initiated by its founder more than 75 years before.

Principal Subsidiaries

Ferragamo Finanziaria SpA; Ferragamo Parfums s.p.a.; Palazzo Feroni Finanziaria SpA; Ungaro SA; ZeFer S.p.a. (50%).

Principal Competitors

LVMH Moet Hennessy Louis Vuitton S.A.; Prada Retail S.p.A.; C and J Clark Ltd.; Salamander AG; Donna Karan International Inc.; Gucci Logistica S.p.A.

Further Reading

"Ferragamo Designs Luminous Incanto," *Duty Free International*, October 1, 2003, p. 14.
Ferragamo, Salvatore, *Shoemaker of Dreams*, George G. Harrap & Co.: London, 1957.
Moin, David, "Reinvented Ferragamo Rides Luxe Boom," *WWD*, April 11, 2000, p. 20.
——, "Ferragamo's United Stand on Fifth," *WWD*, August 4, 2003.
Rachmansky, Anna, "Ferragamo Pushes Forward with Ambitious US Expansion Plan," *Footwear News*, September 8, 2003, p. 10.
Struensee, Chuck, "The New Ferragamo: Growing out of Its Shoes," *WWD*, July 18, 1990, p. 18.

—M.L. Cohen

Sberbank

19 Vavilova Street
117997 Moscow
Russia
Telephone: (+7) 095 957 58-62
Fax: (+7) 095 957 57-31
Web site: http://www.sbrf.ru

Public Company
Incorporated: 1991
Employees: 210,000
Total Assets: $34.2 billion (2003)
Stock Exchanges: Russian
Ticker Symbol: SBER
NAIC: 522110 Commercial Banking; 522120 Savings
    Institutions

Sberbank is Russia's oldest and largest bank. It is particularly dominant in the field of individual savings accounts, holding about 65 percent of household deposits nationwide. With more than 20,000 branches, its network pervades Russia's far-flung territory from the commercial center of Moscow to small provincial villages where it is often the only bank available for individual savers. Sberbank is the successor to the savings division of the Soviet central bank, which in turn traces its roots back to a network of private savings institutions that was created by tsarist decree in 1841. Sberbank was privatized in 1991 but retains close ties to the central government. Russia's Central Bank holds about two-thirds of its shares, and Sberbank is the only bank in Russia to benefit from a government guarantee on deposits. During the economic tumult of the 1990s, Sberbank's reputation for security and its ubiquitous branches made it the first choice for private savers in Russia, despite low interest rates that sometimes failed to keep up with inflation. More recently, Sberbank has been transforming itself into a universal commercial bank and a prime source of finance for Russia's large oil and natural resources enterprises. The bank now offers a full range of savings, investment, and lending services.

Savings Offices in Tsarist Russia

Tsar Nicholas I established the first private savings institutions in Russia in 1841 when he approved a statute "for the purpose of providing a means for people of every rank to save in a reliable and profitable manner." The next year, savings offices opened in the state treasury departments in Moscow and St. Petersburg. Over the next 20 years, about 45 such offices opened in nearly all of Russia's regional capitals. The State Bank of Russia, or Gosbank, was formed in 1860 and the savings offices were soon transferred under its jurisdiction.

Prior to 1861, the growth of private savings was limited by the fact that the majority of Russia's population was composed of serfs, agricultural laborers who were tied to the land and had few personal freedoms. The only people likely to take advantage of personal savings accounts came from a small class of urban merchants and craftsmen. In 1862, there were only 140,000 deposit accounts totaling 8.5 million rubles in a country of 70 million people. After the abolition of serfdom in 1861, savings accounts became more widespread. Growth was particularly rapid in the 1880s, when the central offices at Gosbank were supplemented by regional offices at local treasuries and telegraph stations. Savings offices opened in rural villages as well as urban centers, leading to a total of 4,000 branches and two million individual accounts in 1895.

Gosbank carried out a variety of lending activities using the funds deposited in savings accounts. To a greater degree than in other European countries, the state bank was used an as instrument to direct economic growth. Gosbank provided loans to the railroad and manufacturing industries under risky terms that were similar to state subsidies and occasionally waived repayment of loans for industries that were considered vital to the nation's economy. Other funds were directed toward war enterprises or used to prop up the failing system of aristocratic land ownership. The government's close control of the banking sector under the tsars foreshadowed the centrally controlled economy of the Soviet period.

The Russian Minister of Finance Sergei Witte carried out a monetary reform in 1895 that led to the adoption of the gold standard for the ruble. A special division, the Department of chervonets pushed out the old Soviet banknotes and became the sole currency.

Company Perspectives:

The Bank's mission is to meet requirements in banking services of high quality and reliability of each client, including private, corporate, and government entities, on the entire territory of Russia, ensuring stable functioning of the Russian banking system, public savings, and their investment into the real sector of the economy contributing to the development of the Russian economy. The Bank's motto is to be the "home bank" for the private depositor, respected by the corporate client, a reliable supporter and ally to the state, and a recognized authority on the international level.

State Savings Offices, was also established at Gosbank for individual savings accounts. Its first director was A. Nikolsky, a Senator, member of the State Council, and the head of Gosbank. Russia's stable currency attracted foreign investment, which led to economic growth and increased deposits in savings accounts. Total deposits were about 660 million rubles in 1900.

During the 1905 war with Japan, war expenses were primarily covered with the household savings deposits at Gosbank. World War I, on the other hand, was financed through the printing of money. The money supply in Russia grew ten times during the war, fueling hyperinflation and a severe devaluation of private savings. As public discontent grew, the Bolsheviks seized control in October 1917.

Centralized Banking in the Soviet Era

In Vladimir Lenin's view, banks were an important framework for the building of a socialist society. He believed the ready-made big banks of capitalism could be converted into an effective apparatus for state control of the economy. However, banking activities ground to a halt in the chaos of the years immediately following the revolution. All commercial banks closed down in October 1917. Their staff received salaries but were instructed not to perform any banking functions in the hope that economic paralysis would bring down the Bolshevik regime. Nevertheless, by the end of the year, the Bolsheviks had succeeded in nationalizing all commercial banks, sending armed detachments to occupy their offices in Petrograd. While business accounts were confiscated, private savings accounts were respected. Commissar of Finance V. Menzhinsky ordered the re-establishment of the Department of Savings Offices. However, his efforts to maintain the private savings system failed during the period of Revolution from 1918 to 1921. Throughout those years, farm and consumer goods were requisitioned, nearly all money was withdrawn from the economy, and the exchange of goods operated on a barter system.

In 1921, the New Economic Policy was implemented to normalize commodity exchange in the now ruined economy. The economists G. Sokolnikov and L. Yurovsky at the People's Commissariat for Finance carried out a monetary reform to replace the Soviet banknotes that had been massively overprinted in the preceding several years. Recalling the reliable gold chervonets of tsarist times, they introduced a new gold-backed chervonets as a parallel currency. By 1924, the

chervonets pushed out the old Soviet banknotes and became the sole currency. The State Bank of the USSR, or Gosbank, was established in 1923 and the network of savings banks was reconstituted. Encouragement of savings was a government priority in the late 1920s. The state targeted the general population with the magazine *Sberegatelnoe Delo*, or "Savings Business," which contained articles by leading government planners.

Control of savings banks was transferred to the People's Commissariat of Finance in 1929. The first Five-Year Plan of 1928–32 set ambitious targets for the promotion of personal savings, but the plan was only about 50 percent fulfilled since few people had any money to save. The situation improved under the second Five-Year Plan. Total deposits grew five times between 1935 and 1940 and reached prewar levels. Meanwhile, the Credit Reform of 1930–32 led to the formation of a system of specialized banks under Gosbank, each with a particular sphere of responsibilities. This system remained basically unchanged through most of the Soviet period.

The savings banks played a large role in funding Russia's involvement in World War II. Not only did they provide loans to the war effort, they also accepted donations from the populace for the defense effort and sold tickets for government-run lotteries that raised money for the war. A rationing system was in place during the war; in 1947, it was repealed and a money reform was carried out in which ten old rubles were exchanged for one new ruble. Those who put their money in savings banks, however, enjoyed a more favorable exchange rate. The network of savings bank branches, which had fallen by half during the war due to occupation of Russian territory, returned to prewar levels by 1952. There were about 42,000 branches in all. They remained under the jurisdiction of the Ministry of Finance, with soviet committees supervising local offices.

Savings offices were transferred to Gosbank, the state bank, in 1963. Gosbank now operated as simply an extension of the government's monetary and economic policy. It carried out all the functions of a central bank as well as a commercial bank: printing money, controlling the money supply, providing credit for industrial enterprises, operating private savings accounts for individuals, and taking care of the accounting and money transfer needs of the federal budget. Citizens brought their money to Gosbank's savings offices because they had no other option. In 1965, economic reforms were implemented to improve planning and make industry more responsive to demand, but the banking system remained fundamentally unchanged. Government funds were being drained by inefficient projects and military enterprises, so no amount of reform was able to significantly stimulate the economy. The years 1970 to 1985 were a period of economic stagnation, and personal savings stagnated as well.

In the mid-1980s, Mikhail Gorbachev launched programs of "perestroika," or restructuring, and "glasnost," or openness. Deposits at savings institutions began to increase and a major reorganization of the banking system was implemented in 1988. Gosbank was turned into a central regulatory institution, while five separate banks were created with specializations in particular economic spheres such as foreign trade, agriculture, and loans to industry. One of the newly created banks was Sberbank, whose responsibility was to operate a savings and loan system for workers and average citizens. Sberbank was structured as an umbrella institution for the 15 savings banks of the USSR's republics.

Other banking reforms were carried out at the same time. Commercial and cooperative banks were allowed for the first time. More than 200 were established in two years, although they attracted only a small number of depositors. Checks were introduced in 1987 but failed to catch on since stores would accept only hard cash for their scarce goods. Personal bank loans were also made available. At the time, however, the problem in the Soviet economy was not a shortage of cash but a shortage of goods on which to spend it.

Becoming a Joint Stock Company in the Early 1990s

In 1990, as the Soviet Union was falling apart, Boris Yeltsin, president of the Russian Republic, declared the Russian Republic Savings Bank (a unit of Sberbank) to be the property of the republic. Yeltsin worked with the bank's chairman, Pavel Zhikarev, to privatize the Russian Sberbank in 1991. It was organized as a joint stock company comprised of about 76 regional banks, each with its own particular way of operating. Price controls on consumer goods were removed in 1992, leading to rapid inflation; Sberbank froze depositors' accounts early that year to prevent further growth in the money supply. In 1993, Zhikarev, who had been the bank's chairman for 25 years, was replaced by the deputy chairman Oleg Yashin. The Russian Central Bank acquired a majority state in Sberbank by 1993. The Central Bank and the Finance Ministry made attempts to acquire nearly full control over Sberbank in the early years of its existence, but in the end parliament determined that it should remain an independent entity. Full privatization, however, was postponed indefinitely in 1995 when rumors surfaced that a Russian tycoon with a failed bank in his past was planning to gain control of Sberbank.

The newly privatized Sberbank was a sprawling entity with over 40,000 branches and nearly 90 percent of household savings. Even though it paid interest rates that were often lower than the rate of inflation, Russians who wanted a bank account continued to bring their money to the familiar Soviet institution. Many citizens preferred to keep their savings at home in dollars. Sberbank was saddled with some unprofitable operations, such as the processing of payments for public utilities and the operation of branches in provinces that were served by no other bank. Nevertheless, its dominance of the retail savings market allowed it to operate at a profit. Sberbank used its massive cash

reserves to make loans to smaller banks that lacked a substantial deposit base. It also invested heavily in government bonds, known as GKOs.

Smaller commercial banks, of which there were about 2,000 in the early 1990s, were more efficient and adaptable than Sberbank and more attractive to private businesses. In the early 1990s, only about two percent of deposits at Sberbank came from business enterprises. The commercial banks also started to attract more retail customers by paying higher interest rates. By 1995, Sberbank's share of household savings had fallen to about 60 percent. However, later that year savers poured their money back into Sberbank when a crisis of confidence shook the commercial banks. Interbank lending was suspended when some banks appeared to be insolvent. Even though its accounts offered less favorable terms, Sberbank was the only bank backed by a government guarantee on all deposits. Consumers chose stability over profit, and Sberbank's share of households deposits once again rose to over 70 percent.

Meanwhile, Sberbank was modernizing and adding services. It signed deals with Hewlett Packard and Unisys in 1994 to computerize all its branches and implement a central clearing system. Its first ATM opened that year at Moscow's Sheremetyevo airport. Sberbank was also remodeling some of its branches in marble and glass in order to dispel their reputation for dinginess. In the mid-1990s, the bank started construction on a lavish new headquarters in the center of Moscow.

Andrei Kazmin became the chairman of Sberbank in early 1995. As former deputy finance minister, he had close ties to the Central Bank. His vision for Sberbank was elaborated in the bank's four-year Concept of Development presented in 1996. Kazmin wanted to transform Sberbank into a universal commercial bank and expand services to corporate clients while maintaining a special focus on retail banking. At the time, Sberbank was heavily invested in treasury bonds, or GKOs, holding about 50 percent of them. The strategy was profitable for the time being but would be disastrous if the government changed its firm ruble policy. Sberbank's 1996 profit was estimated at $2.7 billion.

In early 1997, foreign investors took an interest in Sberbank as Russia seemed to be achieving economic stability. Sberbank's market capitalization was so low that, at $20 a share, an investor could buy the equivalent of a branch for $5,000. William Browder at the Russian investment company Hermitage Capital Management called attention to the company and shares rose to $323 in August 1997. A year later, an economic crisis struck Russia when the government allowed the ruble to be devalued. Once again, citizens' savings were made nearly worthless, and many commercial banks were wiped out. Sberbank, however, came through the crisis in good shape. Early in 1998, it had taken advantage of a government offer to swap ruble-denominated GKOs for dollar-denominated Eurobonds, even though returns were far lower. As a result, its financial condition was not severely damaged by the devaluation.

After the 1998 Crisis

Amid the 1998 crisis, the Russian government introduced a program allowing depositors at the largest banks, such as Inkombank, SBS-Agro, MOST-Bank, and Menatep, to transfer their accounts to Sberbank and take advantage of the government deposit guarantee. However, dollar accounts would be transferred at an unfavorable rate based on the pre-crisis value of the ruble. Sberbank gained about 440,000 new accounts, moving its share of individual accounts to about 85 percent and of corporate accounts to 20 percent. After the crisis, Sberbank continued to shift its focus away from GKOs and toward investment in the private sector of the economy. Its loan portfolio increased between two and three times in 1999 as it lent large amounts to oil, natural gas, and mining concerns. The International Monetary Fund (IMF) became concerned that Sberbank was making itself overly vulnerable to problems at any one of its major borrowers. The IMF asked Sberbank to allow a probe of its loan portfolio as a condition for further loans to the Russian government. In July 2000, Sberbank finally agreed to one of the IMF's demands and published results according to international accounting standards, reporting a 1999 profit of $285 million. However, the report failed to give the details that the IMF was seeking.

Over the past several years, Sberbank had been closing unprofitable branches in smaller communities and brought its total network to under 20,000 in 2001. Also that year, a controversial share issue led to a minority shareholder rebellion. William Browder of Hermitage Capital Management claimed that the proposed 35 percent capital increase would dilute shareholder value while offering shares far below book price. Nevertheless, Sberbank disregarded calls for an extraordinary general meeting and moved ahead with the issue.

Since 2000, the Central Bank had been discussing a bank reform that would institute deposit insurance for all banks, cutting back on Sberbank's powerful monopoly. Intense negotiations led to agreement by 2002 on how such a system would be organized, but the scheme failed to pass in the 2003 session of parliament. In 2003, a dispute erupted involving criticisms made by Vadim Kleiner, one of Sberbank's independent directors. Kleiner was the head of research for Hermitage Capital Management, which was known for an "activist" stance on corporate matters. In a presentation at a London banking conference, Kleiner claimed that Russian citizens were in effect subsidizing the country's wealthiest businesses, since Sberbank paid very low interest to account holders and then made loans to companies like Gazprom, Rosneft, Lukoil, and Russian Aluminum below the market rate. He also asserted that Sberbank was inefficient and overstaffed. Even though his comments were based on Sberbank's own reports, the bank sued Kleiner and the newspapers that published his comments. A higher court eventually ruled against Sberbank.

In late 2003, Sberbank placed a $1 billion Eurobond that was the first by a Russian company to receive an investment-grade rating. The bank's large cash reserves and government guarantee made an apparently reliable investment. Nevertheless, the makeup of Sberbank's loan portfolio remained the greatest concern for analysts as the bank entered 2004. *The Moscow Times* suggested that, due to its large number of private depositors, Sberbank had more money than it could lend responsibly and was pressured to make risky loans. The Central Bank pushed Sberbank to adhere to requirements related to diversification of its loan portfolio. Sberbank insisted that its loan portfolio was reasonable and that it had always followed diversification requirements. Russian citizens, meanwhile, were gradually putting more money in private banks even without a deposit guarantee, and Sberbank's share of household savings once again fell to under 70 percent. The bank's Concept of Development for 2000 to 2005 called for improvements in customer service.

Principal Competitors

Alfa Bank; Rosbank; MDM Bank; Deutsche Bank AG.

Further Reading

Aris, Ben, "Central Bank Cracks on with Sector Reform," *Banker*, December 2002, p. 43.

Belton, Catherine, "Sberbank's 1999 Profits Top $ 285M," *Moscow Times*, July 1, 2000.

——, "Sberbank Sues to Silence Its Critics," *The Moscow Times*, May 26, 2003.

——, "Too Much Cash Could Break the Bank," *Moscow Times*, May 27, 2003.

Bush, Jason, "A Renaissance in Retail Banking," *Business Week*, September 1, 2003, p. 45.

Clover, Charles, "Sberbank Agrees to Accounting Benchmark," *Financial Times* (London), July 11, 2000, p. 34.

Evans, Jules, "Vadim Kleiner: Director of Research, Hermitage Capital Management," *Euromoney*, March 2003, p. 30.

Fak, Alex, "Bank Insurance Bill in Danger of New Delay," *Moscow Times*, November 21, 2003.

Gall, Carlotta, "Sberbank Fights State Encroachment," *Moscow Times*, November 25, 1994.

Garvy, George, *Money, Financial Flows, and Credit in the Soviet Union*, Cambridge, Mass.: Ballinger Publishing Company, 1977.

"Into the Fray: Sberbank," *Economist* (U.S.), May 29, 1993, p. 86.

Jack, Andrew, "Russian Savers' Bank Accounts Unfrozen," *Financial Times* (London), December 5, 1998, p. 2.

——, " 'No Oligarch' at Sberbank," *Financial Times* (London), April 30, 2001, p. 17.

Korchagina, Valeria, "Court Backs Vocal Sberbank Director," *Moscow Times*, October 23, 2003.

Larsen, Poul Funder, "Sberbank Plans a More Aggressive Portfolio," *Moscow Times*, June 25, 1996.

Lascelles, David, "Curb on Soviet Commercial Banks," *Financial Times* (London), February 12, 1990, p. 24.

Lyons, Ronan, "Russia's Sleeping Giant," *Euromoney*, January 1998, pp. 94–96.

"A New Central Banker Could Revive Russia's Banks," *Business Week*, April 1, 2002, p. 29.

Peel, Quentin, "Soviet Citizens to Get Bank Loans," *Financial Times* (London), July 14, 1988, p. 2.

"The People's Plastic: Russian Credit Cards," *Economist* (U.S.), February 12, 1994, p. 82.

Roberts, Adrienne, "Sberbank Deal a First by Russian Borrower," *Financial Times* (London), October 16, 2003, p. 35.

Semenenko, Igor, "Sberbank Posts '98 Profit of $660M," *Moscow Times*, March 17, 1999.

Thornhill, John, "Nation's Piggy Bank Holds Up Russian System," *Financial Times* (London), March 27, 1996, p. 2.

——, "Bank Attracts Western Credit," *Financial Times* (London), October 4, 1997, p. 2.

—Sarah Ruth Lorenz

School-Tech, Inc.

745 State Circle
Box 1941
Ann Arbor, Michigan 48106
U.S.A.
Telephone: (734) 761-5690
Toll Free: (800) 521-2832
Fax: (800) 654-4321
Web site: http://www.school-tech.com

Private Company
Incorporated: 1953 as Champions on Film
Employees: 70
Sales: $12 million (2004 est.)
NAIC: 339920 Sporting and Athletic Goods
    Manufacturing; 454113 Mail-Order Houses

School-Tech, Inc. is a leading distributor of instructional videos and products for sports, science, and safety to schools and institutions across the United States. A number of its offerings, including gymnasium mats, safety patrol gear, and sports backstops, are manufactured at its Ann Arbor, Michigan, headquarters. The firm, which operates through divisions called School-masters, Wolverine Sports, Olympia Sports, and Champions on Film, is owned by founder/CEO Don Canham and his family.

Beginnings

School-Tech traces its origins to 1953, when University of Michigan track and field coach Don Canham started a business in Ann Arbor to sell film loops for use as coaching aids. Canham, born in 1918 in Oak Park, Illinois, had attended the University of Michigan beginning in 1938, where he had been a star on the track team. Following four years of army service and a brief stint as a high school teacher in Illinois, he had returned to Ann Arbor to take a job as assistant track coach at his alma mater, assuming the role of head coach in 1948. In his spare time, Canham pursued a number of other endeavors, including photographing sporting events and writing manuals on track techniques. In 1953, he sold an account of an informal meeting he had had with Russian athletes in Finland to *Sports Illustrated* magazine.

While in Finland, he had noticed coaches using 16 millimeter film loops to help athletes study a certain play or motion. Though the practice had arisen from a desire to conserve film, the loop configuration proved more convenient to use than a full reel of film, as it eliminated the need to rewind and re-thread for multiple viewings. At the time, the practice was not known in the United States.

Recognizing a business opportunity, Canham spent $250 to buy a negative of the public domain 1936 Berlin Olympics film, shot by Leni Riefenstahl, to use as the basis for a set of 16 different loops. The well-known film featured a number of athletic greats, including Jesse Owens. After advertising his new "Champions on Film" series via direct mail, Canham received orders from thousands of coaches around the United States. To manufacture the loops, he set up a production center in his basement and hired some of his student athletes to splice and package them.

Following up on this highly successful first series, Canham created a second group of more than 20 loop sets on subjects ranging from football to cheerleading. He used as their basis film he had shot at sporting events around the world, including the only footage taken of a record-setting long jump in Mexico City.

In 1955, Canham branched out into athletic goods and began to import Swiss stopwatches for sale in the United States. He also introduced another European training practice, that of using weighted ankle bands and jackets to boost performance. Canham contracted out production of these items to firms in nearby cities like Ypsilanti, Michigan, and they too soon proved popular with American coaches and athletes.

The new manufacturing endeavor, which he called Wolverine Sports, would later be expanded to produce such items as track hurdles, baseball backstops, and disposable sideline markers for football. Like the film unit, its sales were made via mail order, largely to educational accounts. When he began receiving inquiries from sporting goods stores, Canham added a wholesale division to service this sector, called Olympia Sports. In the latter half of the 1950s Canham also began distributing educational science equipment through another unit, which he named Schoolmasters Science.

Despite this growth, the firm's business remained small, with annual revenues estimated at less than $50,000 by the end of the 1950s. Canham continued to work as the head Michigan track coach, and he and a business partner, Phil Diamond, shared most of the firm's workload. In 1959, they hired 23-year-old Gail Green to take orders, and when Diamond retired three months later she became general manager of Don Canham Enterprises, as the firm was now known, and its sole employee. Her duties included creation and mailing of the company's catalogs, processing and fulfilling orders, billing, accounting, and even loading trucks.

Growth during the 1960s

The early 1960s saw the company continue its expansion. A new division, Schoolmasters Safety, was added to manufacture and market items like safety patrol belts and badges, and it would eventually become the U.S. leader in this niche category. During these years, the firm began hiring additional employees, and by the mid-1960s had moved into a new facility on 15 acres south of Ann Arbor. As the company continued to grow, this building would be expanded a number of times.

In 1968, legendary University of Michigan athletic director Fritz Crisler announced his impending retirement, and Don Canham was named to replace him. To avoid the appearance of conflict of interest, he placed his holdings in Don Canham Enterprises in a blind trust and renamed the firm School-Tech, Inc. He would remain involved only as a paid consultant.

By 1972, with Gail Green now serving as the firm's president, annual sales had grown to approximately $4 million. The company employed more than 60 workers and operated plastic, wood, and metal fabrication shops in its facility near Ann Arbor. In addition to items it manufactured, School-Tech distributed more than 6,000 products from other firms, which included such items as science experiments, text books, educational games, and trophies. School-Tech's catalog was mailed to 400,000 potential customers, which included every educational institution in the United States from preschool through college, every municipal recreation department, summer camp, and YMCA, and many other institutions such as churches, hospitals, and even nudist camps. The catalogs, a total of 15 different ones per year, were produced in-house.

School-Tech's strengths included its quick response time and its consistently low prices. Orders were shipped within 24 hours of receipt, and average turnaround time was just four hours. 1,000 orders per day could be processed using the company's manual fulfillment system, which increased after the adoption of computerization in the early 1970s. The operation was run in a spartan fashion, with no fancy offices or special perks, and this helped keep prices to a minimum. The company also took pride in keeping its customers satisfied and offered a no-questions-asked return policy.

School-Tech's personnel were allowed, and even encouraged, to take on different roles at the plant, which helped increase interest in their work and give the firm a more versatile staff. In the mid-1970s, an unsuccessful attempt at union organization by the United Auto Workers served to inspire the firm to improve its benefits package and develop a retirement plan for its workers.

Sewing Firm Acquired in 1970s

Growth continued during the 1970s with the acquisition of a small sewing company which manufactured gymnastic and tumbling mats and other products. In 1976, Don Canham's son Don H. Canham took over as president from Gail Green. Three years later, the company added a second wing to its manufacturing plant, and by 1985 annual sales had grown to $7 million.

During this time period, Don Canham was working hard to build up the University of Michigan athletic program, which featured one of the nation's most popular and successful college football teams. He put his marketing experience to work cutting deals to license the school's block "M" logo for use on clothing and souvenirs, and royalties from that and from selling the right to broadcast the team's games on television dramatically boosted revenues. He also worked on raising attendance, and by the end of his tenure the team routinely sold out its 100,000-plus seat stadium.

In 1988, after nearly 20 years in charge, Canham retired from the University of Michigan and returned to School-Tech, where he took the title of CEO. The 1990s saw the firm branch out into new areas with the acquisition of Wheelchair Carrier, Inc. of Waterville, Ohio, manufacturer of an automotive wheelchair carrying device, and Stage Stop, a Michigan-based maker of garden equipment such as wheelbarrows and benches. Canham increased the offerings of the former firm from one item to 25 but sold the company in 1997. Stage Stop was also sold after a few years. In both cases, Canham cited the inconvenience of managing a company distant from Ann Arbor as a primary reason for selling.

School-Tech in the 21st Century

In 2003, School-Tech completed another renovation of its manufacturing facility. At this time the company was offering more than 7,000 items in its catalogs and via the Internet. The latter outlet was proving a useful new sales tool, as it enabled the firm to take orders online and gave the flexibility to add new products as they became available, rather than when a new catalog was published. Direct-mail catalogs continued to be printed for a number of specific interest areas, including football, track and field, gymnastics, science, safety, children's videos, and marching band equipment. Some items, such as windbreakers, duffel bags, marker cones, and megaphones, appeared in several different catalogs, while many others were specific to a particular one, such as football line markers or vaulting poles. As it had done since its earliest days, the company used the firm's employees and their family members as models for photographs in its catalogs, which lent them a low-

Key Dates:

1953: University of Michigan track coach Don Canham begins selling film loops of athletes.
1955: Wolverine Sports is formed to distribute stopwatches and weighted athletic gear.
1960: The firm becomes known as Don Canham Enterprises.
1968: Canham puts the firm in trust to take a top job at the University of Michigan; Don Canham Enterprises changes its name to School-Tech.
1976: Canham's son is named president.
1988: After leaving the University of Michigan, Canham returns to School-Tech as CEO.
2003: School-Tech renovates its manufacturing plant and celebrates its 50th anniversary.

key ambience. A number of items that School-Tech manufactured had been developed by its staff, including a portable football helmet rack and an 11-man drinking station. The latter could be hooked up to a hose on the sidelines so that an entire football team could drink as soon as they left the field.

At age 85, Don Canham remained in the CEO position, while his son Don H. Canham served as president and his son-in-law, former University of Michigan football player Steve Eaton, filled the role of vice-president in charge of Wolverine Sports. Canham's daughter, Clare Canham-Eaton, was also on the company's board.

After a half-century in business, School-Tech, Inc. had established itself as a leading source for all manner of educational and institutional specialty items, from stopwatches and football line markers to marching band directors' towers and Magic Schoolhouse videos. Under the continuing leadership of members of the Canham family, the firm was set to serve its customers for many years to come.

Principal Divisions

Wolverine Sports; Olympia Sports; Schoolmasters; Champions on Film.

Principal Competitors

Goal Sporting Goods, Inc.; Jaypro Sports, Inc.; Cannon Sports; Toledo Physical Education Supply.

Further Reading

Barkholz, David, "A Heart of Blue, a Touch of Gold: Canham a Success in New Arena," *Crain's Detroit Business*, October 13, 1997, p. 1.
Huszczo, Adaline, "Gail Green Is the Company, and the Company Is Gail Green," *Ann Arbor News*, July 23, 1972, p. 13.
Spindle, Bill, "Don Canham—The Making of a Modern Athletic Director," *Ann Arbor News*, December 13, 1987, p. C1.

—Frank Uhle

THE SHARPER IMAGE®

The Sharper Image Corporation

650 Davis Street
San Francisco, California 94111
U.S.A.
Telephone: (415) 445-6000
Toll Free: (800) 344-5555
Fax: (415) 445-1588
Web site: http://www.sharperimage.com

Public Company
Incorporated: 1978
Employees: 1,600
Sales: $523.3 million (2003)
Stock Exchanges: NASDAQ
Ticker Symbol: SHRP
NAIC: 45411 Electronic Shopping and Mail-Order
    Houses; 45299 All Other General Merchandise Stores

The Sharper Image Corporation is a specialty retailer that sells apparel and gift items through catalogs, retail stores, and a Web site. Various editions of the catalogs are mailed to 16 million customers; these account for 25 percent of sales. Offering electronic and other unique and sometimes pricey products, the company grew rapidly in the 1980s, bolstered by a yuppie-driven demand for luxury goods. By 1990, however, the company's popularity and profitability dropped dramatically, prompting The Sharper Image to widen the scope of its retail operations to include less expensive merchandise that would appeal to a new, broader customer base.

Focusing on a more mainstream market paid off in 2000, when the company rode the Razor scooter craze to an outstanding year. Still, as founder and CEO Richard Thalheimer said in *Newsday,* "This is not the boy-toy company of 20 years ago. Today our best sellers are an air filter, an eyeglass cleaner and a nose-hair trimmer." Thalheimer remains the company's largest shareholder.

Founded in 1977

The Sharper Image was founded in 1977 by Richard Thalheimer. Thalheimer put himself through law school in San Francisco by selling office supplies, and three years after his

graduation he hit upon a potentially profitable marketing idea that led to a full-time career in retailing. An avid runner, Thalheimer speculated that high-tech stopwatches might prove popular among others who enjoyed the sport. After lining up a supplier, he invested $1,000 in a magazine ad offering digital wristwatches with a stopwatch mechanism for sale by mail. Thalheimer's venture coincided with the onset of a national jogging craze; he was able to sell out his entire stock of watches.

Realizing that a large American market existed for high-priced gadgetry, primarily among the country's growing yuppie community, of which he was a member, Thalheimer used his profits from the watch venture to run similar ads for telephones, miniature calculators, and other devices. In 1978, he incorporated his mail order business, calling it The Sharper Image, and the following year, he displayed his product line in a lavish, glossy mail order catalog.

Profits from The Sharper Image's mail order operations rose steadily throughout the early 1980s. Eschewing market research, Thalheimer based his product line on his own instincts about what people like himself might buy, and the company's catalogs featured pictures of Thalheimer using the items offered for sale. Product lines were expanded to include a wide variety of unique, often peculiar, items, including a $250 imitation Uzi submachine gun.

As a mail order operation, The Sharper Image was able to keep its overhead low. By purchasing its inventory on delayed credit and paying suppliers after collecting from customers, the company could maintain limited inventory and operate with relatively little ready cash. In 1981, the company reported revenues of $28 million and profits of $1.4 million. In 1982, revenues reached the $51 million mark, and three years later, The Sharper Image was issuing 42 million catalogs annually and reporting sales of $69 million. Quoted in a 1986 article in *Forbes* on the increasingly whimsical and non-utilitarian merchandise offered in the company's catalogs, Thalheimer remarked: "I think I got a little fixated on toys."

Mid-1980s Decline

In the mid-1980s, orders from The Sharper Image catalogs began to decline slightly, and the company explored new mar-

321

keting techniques. When The Sharper Image advertisements on cable television proved unsuccessful, the company focused on appealing to customers who preferred not to purchase items through mail order, opening The Sharper Image retail stores around the country. In 1985, 12 stores were introduced in such urban centers as New York, St. Louis, and Honolulu. Twenty more stores were opened the following year, primarily in affluent areas, including Beverly Hills and Stamford, Connecticut. The addition of in-store retailing involved a significant transformation of the company's business practices as well as increased costs for maintaining inventory and leasing store space. Nevertheless, the new Sharper Image stores contributed strong sales to the company's overall performance, and by the end of 1985 revenues from all operations had risen to $87 million.

Going Public in 1987

However, financial growth over the next two years stagnated. As new The Sharper Image retail outlets emerged, the costs they incurred, as well as markedly slower sales, contributed to a first quarter loss of $72,000 in 1987. To offset its lackluster performance, the company went public in April 1987, selling shares over the counter on the New York Stock Exchange. The Sharper Image raised $12 million by selling 1.4 million shares of stock. Thalheimer retained a 72 percent interest in the company, which immediately became worth millions. During this time, Thalheimer reduced his involvement in the company, gradually allowing management to oversee daily operations and make merchandising decisions.

With its infusion of capital, The Sharper Image forged ahead with plans for rapid expansion. The number of retail outlets was increased to 42 in 1987, and the company reported gains in the second and third quarters of the year. Moreover, after an extremely successful holiday season, the company finished 1987 with profits of $5.6 million on overall revenues of $161 million. Despite this strong finish to the year, The Sharper Image experienced losses again in 1988. While first quarter losses totaled $1.2 million, and were expected to continue for the next three months, the company continued its rapid expansion into conventional retailing, opening several more stores that year.

Increased competition from department and electronics stores, as well as an unfavorable currency exchange rate, which led to low profit margins on goods manufactured in Asia, contributed to the company's mounting losses, which were reported at $2 million in September 1988. Some analysts pointed out that

any growth reported on the part of The Sharper Image merely reflected the company's aggressive expansion policy and not higher sales at existing outlets. Sales at previously opened stores, in fact, dropped 7 percent between 1986 and 1987.

As a result, The Sharper Image set out to modify its product offerings. During this time, the company was known for its pricey gimmicks and gadgets, including a suit of armor that sold for $3,800, a collector's sport cars selling for $80,000, a $7,700 old-fashioned Coca-Cola vending machine, and a $649 toy model of a Ferrari. While such novelties drew people into The Sharper Image stores, the company began to rely on more practical, moderately priced products, such as briefcases and cordless telephones, for the bulk of its sales. Among its more popular items, for example, was a non-fogging shaving mirror for use in the shower, which retailed for $39; the company sold more than 70,000 of these mirrors.

In addition, the company focused on controlling costs and improving management relations, which reportedly suffered due to that fact many employees and executives found Thalheimer a difficult and demanding boss. In fact, The Sharper Image experienced a high degree of employee turnover and had gone nine months in 1988 without a chief financial officer due to disputes within the company. By providing a more cohesive managerial team, the company hoped to better control the costs incurred by its previously "loose" organization.

By the end of 1989, the company's earnings had fallen to $4.7 million, despite sales of $209 million that represented a 10 percent increase over the previous year. Having become closely associated with the yuppie generation, the company saw its profits decline as the yuppie ethic of consumerism declined. In an effort to bring new customers into its stores, The Sharper Image increased its catalog mailings to 39 million in 1989, incurring a cost of $25 million, or $6 million more than it had spent on promotional mailings the year before. With fewer people in the market for luxury gadgets, however, even this big push failed to significantly increase the company's sales, 80 percent of which now took place in retail stores.

New Markets in the 1990s

The Sharper Image introduced catalogs aimed at several new types of customers in 1990. Sharper Image Kids featured video games and other toys for children. Catalogs designed specifically for customers over the age of 50 were introduced, as were home furnishings catalogs, prompted by a perceived trend among Americans to spend more time at home. In a joint promotional venture, The Sharper Image began to feature celebrities on the cover of its catalogs in exchange for advertising tied in with movie ads. The company also planned to market more functional products, such as devices for measuring cholesterol levels in food. "We want to move away from the disposable glitz of the 80s," Thalheimer told *Business Week* in 1990.

During this time, the company sought to cut its spending on catalog operations, reducing its yearly mailings to 32 million and trimming its mailing list by dropping customers who had not recently made purchases. Cheaper catalogs, with fewer pages, were produced, and a practice of distributing a condensed version of the catalog through Sunday newspapers was

Key Dates:

1977: Richard Thalheimer peddles his first mail order product, a digital watch for runners.
1978: The Sharper Image is incorporated.
1982: Revenues exceed $50 million.
1985: The company's first 12 retail stores open.
1987: The company goes public on the New York Stock Exchange.
1990: Products for children and home living are featured.
2002: Circuit City begins stocking Sharper Image Design products.

established. Other cutbacks at The Sharper Image included a two-year freeze on salary increases, initiated in May 1990, and a lay off of 110 employees in September of that year.

Like most retailers, The Sharper Image suffered a heavy blow at the end of 1990, when holiday sales declined precipitously. The Sharper Image reported losses of $3.6 million, as sales dropped 13 percent to $181 million. In the spring of 1991, the company's merchandise buyer was let go, and Thalheimer returned to a more active role in the business. To cut costs, Thalheimer directed the renegotiation of some store leases during a time in which the real estate market was depressed. He also renewed the company's commitment to providing less expensive products, particularly those that could be sold for less than $50. Cutting down on the number of low-margin electronic products offered, he began exploring a new area of high margin goods: men's clothing. Since surveys indicated that 65 percent of the company's customers were men, and Thalheimer believed that most men preferred not to shop in department stores, The Sharper Image began to offer designer ties, silk shirts, leather jackets, and comfortable walking shoes for men. This simple selection of stylish goods soon accounted for more than 10 percent of Sharper Image sales. By the end of 1991, The Sharper Image was still struggling. Several banks refused to increase the company's credit lines, as sales fell to $142 million and losses reached $5.2 million during its second year of poor performance.

After this low point, the fortunes of The Sharper Image began to rebound slowly in 1992. The company began to run full-page promotional ads in local newspapers, and ads in two test cities—Kansas City, Missouri, and Buffalo, New York—prompted an 80 percent increase in foot traffic in The Sharper Image stores in one week. The company hoped that the ads, which were relatively inexpensive to run in major metropolitan areas, would familiarize more customers with its stores' new low-priced product offerings.

In April 1992, The Sharper Image began to market its products through mall carts—inexpensive, freestanding units that required only one employee. Offering a small selection of reasonably priced items, these were installed in 17 locations. "It's an easy way to expand the business without opening new stores," Thalheimer noted later that year in *Forbes*. Moreover, in August 1993, the company announced that it had finalized marketing deals with several department stores, including, most notably, Bloomingdale's, to sell its products at boutiques in their stores.

Later that year, The Sharper Image saw its stock price surge when it announced that it would market its wares through a cable television home shopping channel. During two hour-long promotions on the QVC network, the company sold as much merchandise as a small Sharper Image store typically sold in six months. Earnings from this endeavor were particularly high since most of the products marketed were manufactured by The Sharper Image, and those goods carried a 75 percent profit margin. In December 1993, The Sharper Image announced a second major department store deal, as it sealed an agreement with Dillard's, a department store chain with 200 outlets in the Midwest and Southwest, to sell The Sharper Image merchandise.

As a result of such innovative marketing strategies, The Sharper Image reported profits during 1992 and 1993. In January 1994, the company joined with five other retailers and media giant Time Warner Inc. to launch a new 24-hour cable shopping channel. With more functional and affordable merchandise, The Sharper Image had made strong strides in its effort to refashion itself for the 1990s. Future success would depend on its ability to adapt to changes in the marketplace through creative and aggressive marketing.

Refocusing in the Mid- and Late 1990s

This refashioning continued in 1995, when the company began targeting women through its Sharper Image SPA catalog and four SPA Collection stores. Men had accounted for an estimated 70 percent of sales. SPA products, including a face massager and calorie calculator, brought in about $10 million in their first year. However, the SPA Collection division was axed in 1997 after two years of increasing losses.

Sales were $188.5 million in 1995, producing a profit of $3.7 million. Sales increased to $204.2 million in 1996, while profits, hammered by rising paper costs, fell 88 percent to $444,000. The company was also marketing a line of furniture produced by Lexington Furniture. The Home Collection was pulling in $10 million a year by 1998.

Product selection attempted to track the interests of aging male baby boomers. At the same time, a $2 million print ad campaign took aim at the under-40 crowd. The company brought out more less-expensive, ostensibly useful items (like the electric nose hair trimmer) in order to widen its customer base. Designers also tried tweaking the interior design of the stores, replacing 1980s gray with beige, but this did not produce much measurable improvement.

There was also the old problem of inventory shortages for its unique items, which one executive blamed for stagnant same-store sales. Revenues in 1997 were $210 million, little changed from eight years earlier. To appease grumbling stockholders (though he was the largest), Thalheimer sold the company's corporate jet but continued to pilot a private plane for business travel.

At the same time, the company was developing an online version of its main catalog, which then had a circulation of 30 million. By 1998, online revenues were $5 million; significantly, most of these customers were new to the company. The Web site was revamped in 1999 to bring it more in line with the company's high tech image. It now included more futuristic photos of the merchandise, a 3-D section, and an auction feature for clearance items. Online sales reached $60 million in 2000. The Web business was expanded in 2002 with the addition of sites in Asia and Europe.

Beyond 2000

The Sharper Image rode the Razor scooter craze to one of the best years in its history in 2000. The scooter phenomenon helped the stores connect with mainstream shoppers. The company ended the year with 100 brick-and-mortar stores. An October 2002 tie-in placed 20 items from The Sharper Image's proprietary line of products in Circuit City's 600-plus U.S. stores.

Sales rose 32 percent to $523.3 million in 2002, producing a net profit of $15.9 million. The Sharper Image, once an icon of the 1980s, was finding its focus in the new century. Catalogs accounted for 25 percent of sales in 2002, when 78 million were mailed out to 16 million customers. There were 130 stores, and the company was experimenting with infomercials for its successful Ionic Breeze line of air purifiers.

The company's customers were tending to be younger and not quite as affluent as in the late 1990s. The latter attribute allowed The Sharper Image to open more stores in less upscale areas, such as malls in Milwaukee and Omaha that were far removed from the enterprise's home market in downtown San Francisco. The Sharper Image had more than 140 stores in 2003 and was opening two dozen stores a year. The company believed there was room for another 150 more in the United States.

Most products sold by The Sharper Image were from its more lucrative private label collection, which was by then accounting for three-quarters of sales. These were designed at a facility in Novato, California. New products in 2003 included an ionizing "Feel-Good Fan," a $700 massage chair, and a portable Personal Entertainment Center incorporating a DVD player, TV, and radio. Ionic Breeze air purifiers, which sold for $200 to $500, continued to be best sellers.

Principal Operating Units

The Sharper Image Stores; The Sharper Image Catalog & Direct Marketing; Internet Operations; Other Operations.

Principal Competitors

Brookstone, Inc.; Hammacher Schlemmer & Co., Inc.; Radio Shack Corporation; Relax the Back Corporation.

Further Reading

Angwin, Julia, "Sharper Takes on a New Edge," *San Francisco Chronicle*, May 17, 1996, p. B1.

Elliott, Stuart, "A New Campaign Is Trying to Restore Sharper Image's Edge," *New York Times*, September 6, 1996, p. D2.

Emert, Carol, "Sharper Gets Serious; After Years of Erratic Performances, Firm Buckles Down, Narrows Focus," *San Francisco Chronicle*, September 15, 1998, p. D1.

Gilligan, Gregory J., "Circuit City Adds Sharper Image Items to Its Stores," *Richmond Times-Dispatch*, October 11, 2002.

Goff, Leslie, "The Sharper Image," *Catalog Age i.merchant Supplement*, August 1999, p. S15.

Greenberg, Herb, "A Clearer Picture of Sharper Image," *San Francisco Chronicle*, January 24, 1994.

King, Ralph, Jr., "Richard Thalheimer's Toy Chest," *Forbes*, February 10, 1986.

Liedtke, Michael, "Sharper Image Hones Its Reputation," *San Diego Union-Tribune*, October 10, 2000, p. E2.

Morgenson, Gretchen, "The Sharper Image's Sharper Image," *Forbes*, October 26, 1992.

Peltz, James F., "Protecting a Sharper Image," *Los Angeles Times*, September 28, 2003, p. C1.

——, "Watching over a Sharp Image; Retailer Suing Consumer Reports," *Newsday*, October 17, 2003, p. A56.

Richards, Bill, "Sharper Image Is Dropping SPA Line, Focusing on Home-Furnishings Catalog," *Wall Street Journal*, March 7, 1997, p. A7.

Schwartz, Donna Boyle, "Sharper Image Widens Focus," *HFN*, June 17, 1996, p. 1.

Shao, Maria, "The Sharper Image May Need to Refocus," *Business Week*, November 21, 1988.

——, "Sharper Image: Where Have All the Yuppies Gone?," *Business Week*, July 23, 1990.

"Sharper Image Courting Women for Its High-Tech Toys," *Plain Dealer* (Cleveland, Ohio), August 15, 1995, p. 2C.

Shinkle, Kirk, "You're in a Bad Mood, So Turn on the Fan," *Investor's Business Daily*, August 5, 2003, p. A9.

Strasburg, Jenny, "Shifting Gears; Sharper Image Pitching a Line of More Practical Products That Are Designed to Appeal to Mainstream Shoppers," *San Francisco Chronicle*, March 9, 2003, p. I1.

Strom, Stephanie, "Sharper Image Begins Its First Campaign in Newspapers," *New York Times*, February 28, 1992.

—Elizabeth Rourke
—update: Frederick C. Ingram

Skyline Chili, Inc.

4180 Thunderbird Lane
Fairfield, Ohio 45014
U.S.A.
Telephone: (513) 874-1188
Fax: (513) 874-3591
Web site: http://www.skylinechili.com

Private Company
Incorporated: 1949
Employees: 800
Sales: $30 million (2003 est.)
NAIC: 722211 Limited Service Restaurants; 311412
    Frozen Specialty Food Manufacturing

Skyline Chili, Inc. is a regional family restaurant chain centered in the Ohio area. The company was founded in Cincinnati in 1949 by Greek immigrant Nicholas Lambrinides with a single restaurant. Skyline's unique chili recipe became a staple of Cincinnati cuisine. After cutting back on an earlier national expansion plan, the restaurant chain is now growing steadily within 500 miles of Cincinnati. It has more than 100 locations, most franchised. Skyline restaurants are found throughout Ohio and in Kentucky, Indiana, Michigan, and Florida. The company also sells frozen chili and other items from its restaurant menu in grocery stores in markets where it has a presence. The company makes its chili at a central commissary located outside Cincinnati, and ships fresh or frozen food to its chain outlets. The restaurants emphasize quick table service, and the average check is about $6.50. The company is privately owned by the investment firm Fleet Equity Partners.

Early Years in Cincinnati

Skyline Chili, Inc. began as a single chili parlor located on Cincinnati's Glenway Avenue. Its founder, Nicholas Lambrinides, grew up in the village of Kastoria, in Greece, where he learned to cook by watching his mother and grandmother. Lambrinides used his cooking skills to get a start in the United States. The restaurant he opened in 1949 looked out over the Cincinnati skyline, and so he took that as the name. He

worked the restaurant with his five sons. The chili Lambrinides developed was neither a traditional Greek dish nor the Mexican style of chili familiar in other regions of the United States. Using a blend of mild but flavorful spices, Lambrinides made a thin brown chili that was more a sauce than a meal in itself. The classic Skyline dish was a so-called ''three-way,'' which was a plate of spaghetti topped with chili topped with cheese. This was a distinctly Cincinnati way of eating chili, and the dish became something of a fetish with the natives. Cincinnati spawned many other chili restaurants, including Gold Star, another well-known regional chain.

The Lambrinides family ran the restaurant for years. The Lambrinides sons were entrusted with mixing the spices, and the exact blend was a closely guarded secret. In 1965, the business expanded when Skyline began packaging and selling frozen chili and chili with spaghetti to groceries. Skyline also opened new restaurants and franchised the Skyline concept in the Cincinnati area. The company built a central facility to make chili for its various locations. This kept the Skyline recipe consistent throughout the small chain. Skyline at times franchised to fellow Greek immigrants. Pete Perdikakis became the chain's youngest franchisee when he bought a Skyline franchise in 1974 when he was 22 years old. He was still running the restaurant in the early 2000s. Three of the Lambrinides brothers, Lambert, Christie, and William, remained closely involved in the management of the company from its inception through the mid-1990s. Skyline had become the chili champion of a self-professed chili town by the mid-1980s. At that time, the company began to consider expanding beyond its immediate environs.

First Expansion Wave in the 1980s

Almost all the stock in the privately held company was owned by Lambrinides family members until 1984. But in that year, the three Lambrinides brothers sold 4 percent of the company's stock to Thomas Bell, who became chief executive. Bell had been the head of accounting and auditing for the restaurant clients of management consultant firm Arthur Young & Co. He came into Skyline with bold plans for taking Cincinnati chili beyond Cincinnati. At that time, the company had fewer than 30 locations. Bell hoped to spend the next five years bringing the total to 200. His long-term goal was to roll out Skyline nationwide, with as many as a thousand stores. Bell was enthusiastic about Skyline's menu, and he was sure people outside Ohio could be convinced to enjoy Skyline's style of chili. He also thought the company had a great asset in its frozen food line. After the restaurants picked up in a new market, Skyline could then go in and sell the frozen entrees to area groceries. Initially, Bell hoped to bring off the nationwide rollout while keeping Skyline a private company.

Bell's plans took off quickly. Nearly 50 franchised Skylines opened, mostly in and around Ohio. But some new restaurants were as far away as West Virginia, Florida, and South Carolina. The company revamped the packaging for its frozen goods, now emphasizing that the chili was "Cincinnati-style." About 20 percent of Skyline's revenue came from frozen food sales by 1985, and total sales that year were $7.6 million. The company was profitable and growing, although there were some indications of problems. Several new franchises closed down because of lack of customer interest. The Hilton Head, South Carolina Skyline shut down, as did a location in Zanesville, Ohio and another in Tallahassee, Florida, where the restaurants seemed isolated from the parent company's regional reputation. Even so, Skyline kept two franchises in Florida and hoped to move into neighboring Georgia.

By 1986 Skyline had almost 50 franchised units in operation, along with nine company-owned restaurants. To fuel its growth and to pay down debt, which had risen to about $3 million by 1986, Skyline decided to sell shares to the public. The company launched a stock offering in December 1986, and raised $4.1 million. Family members and management held on to 60 percent of the stock. The company then worked on developing new menu items and opened more stores, both company-owned and franchised. Skyline revamped its strategy somewhat after the stock offering, opening much smaller restaurants. Whereas Cincinnati-area Skylines were about 3,000 square feet on average, the company began focusing on smaller buildings, from only 1,600 to 2,000 square feet. Skyline CEO Bell told the *Cincinnati Business Courier* (May 18, 1987) that this was the company's new "meager approach." Bell claimed large store size was cutting into profit margins, though he maintained that Skyline's restaurants outside Cincinnati were doing very well. By 1988, the chain had grown to 78 units, and Bell hoped to maintain slow and steady growth of some 15 to 20 new restaurants a year. Sales increased to $14.4 million for 1988, compared with $12.7 mil-

lion in 1987. But net income shrank slightly, and Skyline's national rollout seemed sluggish.

The company went to inventive lengths to promote new restaurant locations, especially those far from Cincinnati. When the first Skyline opened in 1989 in suburban Washington, D.C., the company contacted Cincinnati college alumni associations to locate former Cincinnatians in the capital. Skyline engineered a group of "chili fanatics," who camped out for days before the restaurant opened. When the ribbon was finally cut, more than a thousand people had shown up to indulge themselves in a hometown chili frenzy. At the time, Skyline's marketing director claimed he was afraid the chain would become too popular and grow too quickly along the East Coast. But soon after, Skyline CEO Bell resigned. Lambert Lambrinides, son of the founder and then chairman of the company, conceded that growth had been stagnant. Skyline picked its new CEO from the ranks of its board of directors, naming William G. Kagler to the post. Kagler had been president of the large grocery chain Kroger. Apparently Kagler's fiery personality had led to conflicts with Kroger's chairman, and Kagler had resigned from Kroger in 1986. Skyline was of course a much smaller company than Kroger, and unlikely to be able to compensate Kagler at the level to which he had been accustomed. But the little company must have appeared a challenge to Kagler. Lambert Lambrinides told the *Wall Street Journal* (May 24, 1989), "It was a surprise to us that he took the job." Kagler immediately announced that the company's growth was over-extended, and within months Skyline had closed a number of unprofitable restaurants.

Revamping in the Early 1990s

Skyline cut back, getting out of markets such as Washington, D.C. that proved insupportable far from where the chain was known. The company sold off some facilities and built a new commissary and warehouse, replacing the existing plant, which was 30 years old. Kagler upped advertising and promotions in markets closest to Cincinnati, hoping to revive the chain in the Ohio region before pushing again for a bigger national presence. And Skyline still reigned over Cincinnati chili parlors. A *New York Times* (September 5, 1990) food reviewer called a trip to Skyline "a rite of citizenship" for people new to the city. Although rival chili chain Gold Star had as many as 70 outlets within Cincinnati (compared with about 80 nationwide for Skyline), Skyline was still apparently what people thought of when they thought "Cincinnati chili."

After Kagler took over, Skyline had not opened new franchises, and the number of stores held steady through the mid-1990s. In 1993 the company began to look to expand again. It had continued to run outlets in Cleveland and Dayton, Ohio, and in Indianapolis, Indiana and Louisville, Kentucky. Skyline hoped to put more restaurants into those markets, which also would open the way for more sales of its frozen grocery items in those cities. Research had helped hone the Skyline formula. The company found that its restaurants with table service, rather than cafeteria-style service, tended to do better. The company decided to stay away from strip malls and mall food courts in favor of freestanding locations.

Then in 1994 the three Lambrinides sons all retired, along with William Kagler. Kagler stayed on as head of franchise

Key Dates:

1949: Nicholas Lambrinides and sons open the first Skyline restaurant in Cincinnati.
1965: The company moves into frozen grocery items.
1984: The company brings in Thomas Bell, begins expansion.
1986: A public stock offering is made.
1989: Bell resigns; former Kroger president William G. Kagler becomes CEO.
1994: Kagler and three founding Lambrinides sons retire.
1997: A management group and Fleet Equity take the company private.
2000: Skyline prepares for more concentrated regional expansion.

planning, but the chief executive position went to the former chief operating officer, Kevin McDonnell. Sales and earnings were on the rise by 1994, and McDonnell hoped that a cautious, less ambitious expansion plan would work this time around. The company seemed to have stabilized. By 1997, revenue had grown to $33 million, a new high, and Skyline pulled in $1.7 million in profit.

Acquisition Skirmish in 1997

In 1997 Skyline received an unsolicited buyout offer from a Michigan company called Meritage Hospitality Group, Inc. Skyline's board quickly refused Meritage's first offer, of about $25 million. Meritage was a publicly traded company that owned hotels and restaurant chains. It had recently taken on debt to buy a 26-chain franchise of the Wendy's hamburger restaurant in western Michigan. Meritage was not profitable and had little cash flow with which to pay its heavy debt load. Among Meritage's creditors was a well-known Cincinnati financier named Carl Lindner. Lindner was in a position to take over Meritage if it could not pay him back. Meritage made a second offer for Skyline shortly after its first was rejected. This aroused speculation that Lindner was trying to get hold of Skyline through Meritage. Meritage withdrew its second offer in April 1997.

Next, Skyline management got together with Fleet Equity Partners, a private, Rhode Island-based equity group, and put together a new buyout deal. The deal was worth about $24 million, and it left Kevin McDonnell and other senior managers in place. Despite noises from Meritage that it would make a third offer for Skyline, board members and stockholders quickly approved the Fleet Equity buyout. Skyline became a private company again in 1997, 11 years after it went public.

Regional Chain in the 2000s

By the late 1990s, Skyline had about 70 units in and around Cincinnati and 45 more in other nearby markets. Chainwide, sales had grown to $100 million. By 2000, the chain was ready to expand again. But it planned to move slowly, staying within 500 miles of its home base. Skyline's CEO McDonnell saw lots of room for more Skylines in cities near Cincinnati. The com-

pany hoped to put 40 Skylines in Columbus, Ohio over the early 2000s, and then to build up similar mass in other cities in its orbit, such as Indianapolis and Louisville. By that time, other companies had demonstrated that strong regional growth could be a winning formula. McDonnell compared Skyline to In-N-Out Burgers, a California-based hamburger chain, and the Southern charmer Krispy Kreme Donuts. Krispy Kreme had grown steadily within the Southeast in the late 1990s, and finally went public to much Wall Street admiration in 2000. Skyline was similar to these regional specialty chains in that it had intense customer loyalty.

Although it had not done well marching into unfamiliar territory like Washington, D.C., Skyline seemed loved and respected throughout its Ohio territory. When the original Skyline, on Glenway Avenue, closed in 2002, a civic group auctioned off 150 ladles that had been used there through the years. The auction, held on e-Bay, sparked a fervor, and bidding started at close to $20 (for a single ladle). But Skyline's vice-president for marketing told the *Cincinnati Post* (April 24, 2002): ''That Skyline has developed a cult following isn't news to us.'' Strong customer support seemed to be the key to Skyline's success. McDonnell hoped to be able to expand Skyline to ten times its current size by opening more units solely within a 500-mile ring around Cincinnati.

By 2004, Skyline's principal markets outside Ohio were Lexington and Louisville, Kentucky, and Indianapolis, where it had long had a presence. The company began to move into Michigan, and also looked for new opportunities in Florida. Skyline had six Florida outlets by 2004. Florida had strong ties to Ohio, as many Ohioans retired there. The manager of a Tampa-area Skyline claimed that about three-quarters of the restaurant's customers had some tie to Cincinnati. So even though geographically the Florida restaurants were far from the company's home base, it still fed off the reputation Skyline had built up in Ohio. Company revenue was estimated at about $30 million for 2003, and the outlook seemed good for a more controlled push into new markets.

Principal Competitors

Gold Star Chili, Inc.; Wendy's International, Inc.; Culver Franchising System, Inc.

Further Reading

Bertagnoli, Lisa, ''Strength Close to Home,'' *Chain Leader,* December 2000, p. 50.
Daumeyer, Rob, ''Skyline Revamps Strategy in Push to Go National,'' *Cincinnati Business Courier,* May 18, 1987, p. 1.
Jankowski, David, ''Skyline Public Offering to Bankroll National Expansion,'' *Cincinnati Business Courier,* October 13, 1986, p. 4.
Kaufman, Peter, ''At the Nation's Table: Cincinnati,'' *New York Times,* September 5, 1990, p. C3.
''Lindner in Position to 'Gobble' Skyline,'' *Cincinnati Business Courier,* April 21, 1997, p. 1.
''Meritage Withdraws Offer on Acquisition or Control,'' *Wall Street Journal,* April 24, 1997, p. B4.
Milstead, David, ''Skyline Eyes Slow, Steady Expansion,'' *Cincinnati Business Courier,* October 24, 1994, p. 1.

Monk, Dan, "Cash Might Be Cause of Scrap Over Skyline," *Business Courier Serving Cincinnati-Northern Kentucky,* April 13, 1998, p. 1.

Paeth, Greg, "A Bid for Nostalgia: Skyline Ladles Auctioned on Ebay," *Cincinnati Post,* April 24, 2002, p. 7B.

"Restaurant Concern Agrees to Buyout for $24 Million," *Wall Street Journal,* September 29, 1997, p. B6.

Sherman, Tiffani, "Bib Is Badge of Honor for Chili Lovers," *St. Petersburg (FL) Times,* June 17, 2003, p. 3.

Showalter, Kathy, "Homestyle Skyline Promo," *Business First-Columbus,* June 9, 2000, p. 14.

"Skyline Chili Inc.," *Wall Street Journal,* November 2, 1990, p. B4A.

Stercharchuk, Gregory, "Ex-Kroger Official Spices Up His Life with Chili-Firm Job," *Wall Street Journal,* May 24, 1989, p. B13.

Thomas, Paulette, "In a Move to Modernize, Search for a Good Fit," *Wall Street Journal,* August 13, 2002, p. B6.

"Unsolicited Offer Received and Rejected As Inadequate," *Wall Street Journal,* February 24, 1997, p. B4.

Walkup, Carolyn, "Skyline Chili Hits the Road," *Nation's Restaurant News,* October 11, 1993, p. 7.

——, "Skyline Chili Reaches for the Stars with Steady, Controlled Expansion," *Nation's Restaurant News,* August 1, 1988, p. 3.

——, "Skyline Chili Shifts Focus After Third-Quarter Loss," *Nation's Restaurant News,* October 9, 1989, p. 12.

Webb, John, "Skyline's March on Washington," *Adweek's Marketing Week,* February 20, 1989, p. 42.

—A. Woodward

SMORGON

Smorgon Steel Group Ltd.

G/F 650 Lorimer Street
Port Melbourne
VIC 3207
Australia
Telephone: (+61) 3 9673 0400
Fax: (+61) 3 9673 0450
Web site: http://www.smorgonsteel.com.au

Public Company
Incorporated: 1927
Sales: A$2.52 billion ($1.86)(2003)
Stock Exchanges: Australian Stock Exchange
NAIC: 331111 Iron and Steel Mills

Smorgon Steel Group Ltd. is Australia's second-largest steel and steel products manufacturer and distributor. An offshoot of Smorgon Consolidated Industries, once one of the largest private Australian companies before its breakup in 1995, Smorgon Steel is a vertically integrated company whose operations include one of the country's fastest-growing scrap metal collection and processing businesses. Smorgon's scrap metal division runs 39 facilities throughout Australia, as well as others in New Zealand and China. Smorgon's scrap metals are then recycled as raw materials for its steel production division, which manufactures steel and steel products using the electric-arc mini-mill process. The company's total annual steel production tops 900,000 tons, with an annual capacity of over one million tons. Smorgon Steel Distribution, the company's third core division, operates throughout Australia. Acquisitions have formed a major part of the group's growth in the early years of the 21st century; its purchases include Australian National Industries, Metalcorp Ltd., Sydney-based Chantlers Metal Recyclers, and a 50 percent stake share in Email Ltd. The founding Smorgon family retains a significant stake in the company, which went public in 1999.

Rags to Riches in the 1920s

Brothers Norman, Moses, and Abram Smorgon, along with their families, fled the Soviet Union in the 1920s. After living in conditions of appalling poverty, the Smorgons were determined to start a new life and traveled to Melbourne, Australia, aboard a converted cattle ship. The brothers, who spoke little English, set up a kosher butcher shop in 1927. The shop was a success, prompting the Smorgon to add a number of new butcher shops.

The Australian meat industry, like many of the country's industries at the time, was dominated by a very small number of businesses that held near-monopolies on the wholesale meat market. This did not deter Norman Smorgon's son, Victor, from branching out into a wholesale operation, setting a pattern of challenging monopolies that was to mark the group's rise in the Australian business world. Victor Smorgon's business started small, with a loan of just two pounds from his father, which he used to buy six chickens at the local market. The younger Smorgon quickly sold these chickens for three times his purchase price.

By the end of the 1930s, Smorgon had transformed his business into a small but growing wholesale meat and meat processing group. A decisive moment for the company came during World War II. Soon after the start of the war, Victor Smorgon went to see then Prime Minister Ben Chifley and related the story of how his family had escaped the Soviet Union during Stalin's purges of the middle class in the 1920s. He also told the prime minister of his plans for building his company, asking for a license to export meat to the United Kingdom. Smorgon's tale impressed Chifley, who helped Smorgon gain the export license.

The new market enabled the company to expand rapidly during the war years. In 1941, the Smorgon company, which included Victor's brother Eric, among others, built a new full-scale meat processing plant in West Footscray. The facility provided integrated operations, with a slaughterhouse, cannery, freezers, boilers, and boning rooms. There, the company inaugurated its patented Freezer Chain System, which set a meat industry standard for chain transport systems.

Diversified Conglomerate by the 1970s

At the end of World War II, the Smorgon family began to diversify. At first, the group remained close to its core meat business by extending into other food-processing areas. In the

Company Perspectives:

The Smorgon Way has been documented to ensure there is no mystery as to the Smorgon values and management style. These values are all about openness, honesty, group decision making, commitment, and a drive for continuous improvement. The company's way of doing things is characterized by energy, drive, and a sense of urgency. The following values are the cornerstone of The Smorgon Way and so the company's behavior must reflect them: two heads are better than one and therefore key issues will involve consultation and discussion; everyone has a right to be heard in a non-threatening environment and there is an expectation that the truth will be told. These key values are underpinned by the following: our word is our bond; we will demonstrate a high level of personal integrity; we are committed to satisfying customer needs and we expect to grow and develop the business, which in turn will increase shareholder value.

early 1950s, Smorgon added fruit canning and rabbit meat processing. The company now began to export to the United States as well, beginning with processed rabbit meat.

England's involvement in developing the European Common Market set the stage for the next evolution of the Smorgon group. Victor Smorgon recognized that England's participation in the European Common Market meant that the company would soon face intense competition from meat supplier in continental Europe. In response, Smorgon set out to diversify its operations in order to reduce its reliance on meat exports.

The company's diversification, launched at end of the 1950s, also provided the company with new opportunities for challenging some of Australia's other industrial monopolies. Victor Smorgon first focused on the paper and packaging industry, which also provided integration possibilities with the group's food businesses. The company launched production of paper and carton materials, as well as end products such as egg cartons produced from recycled paper. Following the death of his father, Victor Smorgon took over as head of the group's growing interests.

By the mid-1960s, the company had already succeeded in becoming a rising star on Australia's paper and packaging scene, defeating the monopoly long held by Australian Paper Manufacturers. The growth of this operation led the company to exit the fruit cannery business in 1967 in order to focus its growth, on the one hand, on its core meat business, and, on the other, its growing paper interests. This focus did not stop Smorgon from developing other business interests, however. Now known as Smorgon Consolidated Industries, the group continued to branch out in the 1970s and into the 1980s, developing a vast range of operations. Smorgon continued to target monopoly-dominated industries such as the glass industry, long controlled by ACI (Australian Consolidated Industries), which included glass and plastics manufacturing, forestry holdings, paper mills, and other interests such as clothing manufacture, retailing, and computer production.

By the early 1980s, the Smorgon group was Australia's largest diversified family-controlled business. Having success-

fully carved a place for itself in several formerly monopoly-controlled industries, Smorgon now set out to conquer another: the steel industry.

Australian Steel Magnates in the 1980s

Until the early 1980s, Australia's steel market had been entirely controlled by a single entity, Broken Hill Propriety Co., later known as BHP. Yet BHP had neglected a new and fast-developing steel market, that based on the "mini-mill." Rather than produce steel from raw ore using traditional blast furnace production methods, the new type of mill, which was much less expensive to build and operate, used a new type of electric-arc furnace in order to recycle scrap metals into usable steel products. In the meantime, BHP's control of the market had made it complacent in its relationship with its customers, who had to contend not only with the company's rigid pricing policies but also with its inability to offer flexible production schedules.

The seemingly daunting task of entering an entirely new industry did not dissuade Smorgon. As Victor Smorgon was quoted as saying: "Steel's nothing. It's an industrial process and we're good at processes. It's just like making sausages." In another statement at the time, Smorgon remarked: "The point is that as a family we're natural manufacturers. We understand production. We can get experts to work out the electronics and engineering. And if you ask 'Why steel?' the thinking is simple: go for the monopolies. Fight the monopolies. The bigger they are the better for us. They're easy. They're top heavy."

The lean, mean Smorgon organization began construction of an electric mini-mill in Laverton, near Melbourne, in 1981. Production at the mill was launched in 1983, fed by scrap metal bought from a nearby collector. Smorgon quickly imposed itself on the market, in part by offering lower prices but also by adapting its production schedules to customer needs. In order to maintain margins, the company also skirted the traditional steel distribution market in Australia and began distributing directly to customers. By 1984, the company had already begun to expand its steel operations, purchasing a used rolling mill from Pittsburgh's Jones & Laughlin Steel Corp. The group's initial investment in the steel industry stood at just A$60 million.

Smorgon's success in the steel industry led the company to begin acquiring and developing scrap metal collection and processing operations in the late 1980s and through the 1990s. A major moment in the development of the group's steel business came in 1987, when it agreed to sell its steel operations to Humes Ltd., which operated its own steel products production and distribution operation, called ARC. Humes was also Smorgon's largest customer. In exchange, Smorgon took a 46 percent stake in Humes.

Under Humes, Smorgon's steel interests grew strongly, including a major expansion of its steel mill's production capacity. In 1988, however, Smorgon launched a takeover offer for Humes itself, gaining complete control not only of its own steel interests but Humes's ARC business as well. That purchase set the stage for Smorgon's emergence as a regional steel power.

Steel Focus for the New Century

In 1994, Victor Smorgon, now in his 80s, stepped down as company chairman, turning over the reins of the group to

Key Dates:

1927: Russian immigrants Norman, Moses, and Abram Smorgon found a butcher shop in Melbourne.
1930: Victor Smorgon establishes a wholesale meat business.
1939: Smorgon is granted a license for exporting meat to the United Kingdom.
1958: After diversifying into canned fruits and other food processing markets, Smorgon launches paper and packaging manufacturing operations, becoming Smorgon Consolidated Industries.
1967: Smorgon sells its fruit canning business to focus on its meat and paper/packaging businesses, then further diversifies into glass and plastics manufacturing.
1981: The company begins the construction of an electric arc mini-mill in order to enter the steel industry.
1983: The company begins producing steel.
1984: A rolled steel facility is launched.
1987: Smorgon Steel is sold to Humes Ltd. in exchange for a 46 percent stake in Humes.
1988: Smorgon takes over Humes, including its ARC steel products and distribution businesses.
1994: Victor Smorgon steps down as chairman and is replaced by Graham Smorgon, who leads the breakup of Smorgon Consolidated Industries.
1999: Smorgon Steel goes public and acquires Australian National Industries.
2003: The company acquires 50 percent of Hartnell, in Hong Kong, forming Smorgon Hartnell Recyclers, the largest business of its kind in Southeast Asian

Graham Smorgon, grandson of Moses Smorgon. Under Graham Smorgon, Smorgon Consolidated Industries entered an entirely new phase in the company's history—that of its break up. By the mid-1990s, Smorgon family shareholders had swelled to some 100 family members representing seven distinct family groups. Recognizing that the shareholding structure had become increasingly unwieldy, Smorgon began plans to take the company public.

As part of that process, Smorgon decided to stake its future entirely on its steel business and began selling off and spinning off its other assets. Smorgon Steel Group, as the business was then renamed, became the single common holding among the family shareholders. The process leading to the company's public offering in 1999 offered a first glimpse at the family's financial arrangements and shareholding structure: the descendants of Norman Smorgon, including Victor and Eric Smorgon, controlled 75 percent of the company, compared to the Moses Smorgon wing, at 20 percent, and the Abram Smorgon branch, at 5 percent. Under a shareholder pact, the family agreed to maintain their shares for a two-year period following the public offering and to refrain from launching competing businesses. Family members were also barred from contributing their shares to takeover offers for the company.

The successful public offering put Smorgon on the map as Australia's leading vertically integrated steel business, valuing

Smorgon at more than A$1 billion. The company immediately began adding to its scale, buying up rival Australian National Industries (ANI) in 1999. Smorgon next targeted Metalcorp, the leading scrap metal recycler in New South Wales. That acquisition finally succeeded in 2000. The addition of Metalcorp, which processed nearly 600,000 tons of scrap metal each year, meant that Smorgon now covered nearly all of its steel production unit's own raw materials needs.

Smorgon made two more key purchases, buying up Palmer Tube, then joining with OneSteel in a partnership to acquire Email Ltd. in 2001. Smorgon continued looking for bolt-on acquisitions, such as its 2002 purchase of the Albion Steel group, which processed and distributed some 40,000 tons of steel products each year, much of which derived from Smorgon-produced steel. With the drop off in steel demand in Australia following the completion of the 2000 Olympic Games, Smorgon began developing itself as a steel exporter as well, particularly to China but also increasingly to other Southeast Asian markets. This development was followed by a move to extend the company's vertical integration onto the foreign stage as well. As part of that effort, the company acquired a 50 percent stake in Hong Kong-based Hartwell Pacific Ltd., which was then renamed Smorgon Hartwell Recycling in 2003. With operations in Hong Kong, Malaysia, Thailand, and the Philippines, the company's newest addition claimed a leading position in the Southeast Asian scrap market.

Closer to home, the company reached an agreement in September 2003 to buy up Chantlers Metal Recyclers, the second-largest non-ferrous scrap dealer in the Sydney area. In the meantime, parts of the Smorgon family had begun exercising their right to sell shares in the company, reducing their overall shareholding position. Nonetheless, Smorgon's continued leadership position remained a testament to the Smorgon family's heritage as one of Australia's true 20th century rags-to-riches stories.

Principal Subsidiaries

AB Metal Pty Ltd; ANI America Inc. (United States); ANI Ltd; Arnall Poland Sp. z.O.O. (Poland); Tube Mills Pty Ltd; Commonwealth Steel Company Ltd; Email Ltd.; Metalcorp Ltd; MI Steel (NSW) Pty Ltd; Ming Sing Electronics Ltd (Hong Kong); Ampy Holdings Ltd (England); Kelvinator Pty Ltd; TPS Holdings Pty Ltd.

Principal Divisions

Recycling; Distribution; Reinforcing and Steel Products.

Principal Competitors

Thompsons, Kelly and Lewis Proprietory Ltd.; BHP Steel Ltd.; Consolidated Manufacturing Industries Ltd.; Structural Systems Ltd.; Milnes Holdings Ltd.; National Forge Ltd.; Stokes Australasia Ltd.; United Group Ltd.; Nippon Steel Australia Proprietory Ltd.

Further Reading

Charles, Mathew, "Smorgon Meltdown," *Herald Sun*, October 30, 2003, p. 45.

Dodd, Andrew, ''Smorgon Steels Itself for a Bad Year,'' *Australian*, October 30, 2003, p. 21.

Henley, Clive, ''Hard Times but Smorgon Steels Itself for Change,'' *Herald Sun*, November 12, 2001, p. 66.

''Smorgon Steel Completes Buyout of 50 percent of Hartwell Pacific,'' *American Metal Market*, August 6, 2003, p. 7.

''Smorgon Steel Signs Agreement to Buy Nonferrous Scrap Dealer,'' *American Metal Market*, September 26, 2003, p.7.

Westfield, Mark, ''Art of a Survivor,'' *Australian*, August 26, 1999, p. M24.

Worden, Edward, ''Smorgon Steel Bid for Metalcorp Succeeds,'' *American Metal Market*, January 20, 2000, p. 10.

—M.L. Cohen

Standard Commercial Corporation

2201 Miller Road
Wilson, North Carolina 27893
U.S.A.
Telephone: (252) 291-5507
Fax: (252) 237-0018
Web site: http://www.sccgroup.com

Public Company
Incorporated: 1916 as Standard Commercial Tobacco
   Co.
Employees: 2,821
Sales: $993.7 million (2003)
Stock Exchanges: New York
Ticker Symbol: STW
NAIC: 422590 Other Farm Product Raw Material
   Wholesalers

Standard Commercial Corporation is involved in two main business segments—tobacco and wool. The company operates as one of the largest leaf tobacco dealers in the world and is a leading wool trading concern. It purchases, processes, stores, sells, and ships tobacco that is grown in over 30 countries and sells processed leaf tobacco to cigarette manufacturers in over 85 countries. Standard Commercial also trades greasy and scoured wool and operates processing facilities in Australia, Europe, and the United Kingdom.

Origins

Standard Commercial was founded in the early 1900s by Turkish immigrant Ery Kehaya, Sr., the son of a revered teacher of religion and ethics and his wife, also from a family of religious educators and prelates. Kehaya grew up in a tobacco-growing region of Turkey along the Black Sea. Although Kehaya was groomed for a role in the church, and educated by his uncle, an archbishop in a Macedonian diocese, the young man's interests soon lead him in other directions. After traveling extensively and studying at the Sorbonne in Paris, Kehaya arrived in the United States and became a U.S. citizen. He

initially found work as a waiter in a Greek-Turkish restaurant in New York City. However, the industrious young man had greater aspirations.

In New York at the time, several small factories had been established at which cigarettes were rolled by hand using imported tobaccos. Several tobacco importers frequented the restaurant at which Kehaya worked, and, having become acquainted with some of them, Kehaya was prevailed upon to help sell one importer's tobacco stock to the factories. Kehaya accepted the offer and received a commission for his sales. With the money he earned, he decided to leave the restaurant and get into the tobacco business himself.

The few thousand dollars Kehaya had earned by 1912 became the start-up capital for his new enterprise: Standard Commercial Tobacco Company. Garnering a solid reputation for the good quality of its imported Oriental tobacco, the company saw steadily increasing sales and was incorporated in Delaware in 1916. That year, as a testament to Kehaya's business acumen, Standard Commercial entered into a contract to provide Oriental leaf tobacco to R.J. Reynolds Tobacco Company. When offered a commission on the purchases, Kehaya said that he would prefer to be paid with interest in Reynolds, a company he believed offered tremendous opportunity for growth. He was right; his original shares in Reynolds would over the next ten years be worth about $5 million.

Overcoming Problems Leads to Expansion: 1917 to the 1920s

In 1917, Kehaya married Grace Whitaker, the daughter of a prominent North Carolina tobacco manufacturer. During this time, on the brink of U.S. involvement in World War I, Standard Commercial met with some misfortune. Kehaya had decided to diversify his interests, and his company had purchased two steamships, one of which was dubbed the Grace. However, that sideline business came to an abrupt end as Kehaya and Grace, on their honeymoon, learned that their two ships had been sunk by the Germans. Also during this time, as Bolshevik forces overthrew Kerensky's regime in Russia, Standard Commercial's large store of tobacco in Russia was threatened with

| | |

Company Perspectives:

Our mission is to be the most respected purchaser and processor of tobacco and wool products in the world.

---

confiscation. While U.S. businesses, investors, and banks with holdings in Russia were losing fortunes daily, Kehaya came up with a unique plan. Whereas other companies tried and failed to move merchandise out of Russia via railroads and established trade channels, he arranged for barges to move his tobacco up the Volga River to the White Sea and then on to the Arctic Ocean, on their way to the North Pole. Through this less traveled, and therefore unguarded, route, the tobacco reached its destination safely.

During the 1920s, Standard Commercial expanded the scope of its operations worldwide, purchasing a cigarette manufacturer in Hamburg, Germany, and establishing offices and processing plants in Korea. In fact, much of Kehaya's early work involved some real pioneering. For example, after securing a contract with a Japanese company for the export of tobacco grown in Korea, Kehaya and his wife lived in a railroad car in rural Korea for more than a year in 1922 to oversee the project, which involved teaching Korean farmers to grow tobacco.

By 1928, Standard's net worth had risen to $12 million and the company gained a listing on the New York Stock Exchange. However, the price of leaf tobacco had been depressed, and the United States was on the brink of a stock market crash that would result in the Great Depression. Having borrowed more than $15 million to purchase some Turkish tobacco, Standard was rocked soon thereafter when the bank was forced to request repayment of the loan at maturity. Kehaya was forced to choose between selling the tobacco at the current prices and losing millions of dollars or asking for an extension, risking the possibility of being denied further credit and potentially damaging Kehaya's reputation.

Kehaya opted to repay the loan, and toward that end he sold tobacco at record-low prices, divested many capital investments, and reduced his own salary significantly, asking his colleagues to do likewise. The depression thus hit Kehaya and Standard very hard. However, while the company founder lost much in the way of personal assets, Standard Commercial, unlike many larger corporations, survived.

The Axton-Fisher Purchase: 1930s and 1940s

As political and economic conditions overseas grew increasingly complex, Standard shopped stateside for opportunities in the 1930s. The company purchased a controlling interest in the Axton-Fisher Tobacco Company of Louisville, Kentucky, which produced the increasingly popular "Twenty Grand" cigarette brand for ten cents a pack, undercutting the more expensive brands of Camel, Lucky Strike, and Chesterfields. Standard also entered into an agreement with the Jas. I. Miller Tobacco Company, purchasing and processing some of that company's products.

Since Axton-Fisher continued to prosper in the mid-1930s, Standard borrowed money to buy up its remaining stock. How-

ever, the acquisition soon soured, when, in 1937, a devastating flood hit the Ohio Valley, submerging the warehouse in which Axton-Fisher stored its re-dried tobacco. Costly efforts were made to salvage the tobacco, but Standard's losses and debt load were mounting.

Standard Commercial and the once-promising Axton-Fisher eventually went into bankruptcy. At that point, the Bank of America came to the rescue, becoming Axton-Fisher's majority shareholder and taking over its management, while Standard Commercial tended to its own problems. In 1944, the Bank of America decided to sell Axton-Fisher's physical assets to Phillip Morris and to liquidate all assets. As the minority shareholder of Axton-Fisher, Kehaya found an interested buyer in the Jas. I. Miller Co., which paid a good price for the tobacco inventory and helped Standard Commercial to withstand the disaster, albeit so heavily scaled-down in size and scope that in the mid-1940s the company was not much more than a handful of employees and the founder's will to reemerge.

The onset of World War II also complicated matters for Standard Commercial. Greece, Bulgaria, and Turkey had been the company's major sources for tobacco leaf prior to the war, and when Greece and Bulgaria came under German occupation, they ceased shipments. Moreover, the company's Mediterranean ports serving Turkey were also disrupted by the war. With great effort, Standard managed to get some of its stores of tobacco out of Russia during this time and also received shipments of Oriental tobacco from Rhodesia.

By 1947, with continued assistance from the Bank of America, all of Standard's outstanding debts from the Axton-Fisher disaster were paid, and, with the end of the war, the company was ready to regain its momentum. By the end of the decade, the company had reestablished relations in the East and in Europe and had reinitiated trade with Greek and Turkish markets. Standard also formed a joint venture in Greece that was the largest of its kind at the time.

Postwar Growth

Establishment of Standard's foreign presence continued in the 1950s. In 1953, Standard formed a subsidiary in Valuz, called Eryka International, AG, to oversee purchases and sales of tobacco in the Eastern block countries, but many of Standard's dealing during this time took the form of partnerships, as had their 1955 venture to import tobacco from Thailand. With deals of such magnitude, Standard and its partners found that they needed to form a substantial subsidiary to oversee Far Eastern operations. In 1957, the Trans-Continental Leaf Tobacco Company (TCLTC) company was formed as a joint venture with the Elia Salzman Tobacco Co. Ltd. Elia Salzman, whose name the partner company bore, had founded his company in London, selling Indian tobacco in the United Kingdom and elsewhere. A formidable presence and an industry legend, Salzman could, according to Kehaya, "tear a thick phone book in half with his bare hands" and was fluent in Russian, German, French, Turkish, Greek, and English. Salzman's company oversaw TCLTC's Indian business, while Standard Commercial was responsible for its business in the Orient.

In the midst of these complex foreign affairs, Standard's founder suffered a stroke, and his son, Ery W. Kehaya, was named president. The younger Kehaya had been hard at work with the company since 1945, starting out on the docks and then helping with an ultimately unsuccessful tobacco farming project in California before becoming established in the company's sales force in the 1950s.

The late 1950s and early 1960s saw the rise to prominence of TCLTC. That company took over Salzman's tobacco interests in Rhodesia and then signed a ten-year contract with the Thailand Tobacco Monopoly for exclusive rights to the export of all surplus flue-cured tobaccos. The company was also contracting with the Japan Monopoly Corporation during this time for export of their burley to Europe. Moreover, having purchased tobaccos from Thai Company, Thapawong, Ltd. for some years, TCLTC signed with them in 1962 to form a joint company, Siam Tobacco Export Corporation, which built a factory and over time bought out curing stations in order to produce and acquire its own tobaccos as security against years of small crops. TCLTC entered the Philippines in the late 1950s, exporting that country's first shipments of flue-cured tobaccos, and entered Taiwan in 1960, striking a deal with the Taiwanese Monopoly to export surplus tobaccos in Europe, Indonesia, and the United States. Business with India was ceased for some years after the death of Salzman in 1963 but would later be reestablished with the acquisition of Siemssen Threshie & Co. in the 1970s. By the mid-1960s, TCLTC had accounts in Mexico, Brazil, Argentina, and Europe, as well as smaller operations in Pakistan, Ceylon, Ghana, and Indonesia.

Meanwhile, Standard Commercial explored untapped sources such as Uganda and Tanzania in 1964. While Uganda's potential exports were ceased under the Amin regime, Tanzania proved a particularly prosperous exporter for Standard Commercial. In the late 1960s, Standard became interested for the first time in cigar tobacco and began buying it in Paraguay, Mexico, Brazil, and the Philippines, delegating responsibility for the cigar business to the German subsidiary Werkhof GmbH. However, Standard Commercial soon became dissatis-

fied with the operation, which proved too small to handle all of the business demands, and a more suitable arrangement was found in partnering Werkhof with the East Asiatic Co. of Copenhagen. Standard would later reacquire these cigar interests, which became known as LEAFCO, in 1982 and relocate all such operations as a division in Copenhagen.

After years of global expansion and a slowdown in the early 1970s, Standard Commercial decided to enhance its presence in the United States. In 1974, they engaged with Imperial Tobacco in establishing facilities in Wilson, North Carolina. The company also established a branch office in Richmond, Virginia. Moreover, Standard Commercial acquired the outstanding shares of its former joint venture, TCLTC, in 1975, making it a wholly owned subsidiary.

Acquisitions in the 1970s included Andrew Chalmers International, Ltd., which was eventually merged with Siemssen to form Standard Commercial (UK). Standard also acquired a 51 percent interest in Swiss company Spierer Frères, which moved Oriental leaf out of markets in Turkey and Greece. Jas. I. Miller Tobacco Company, Standard's frequent partner in deals, was purchased in 1978. This North Carolina-based company gave Standard a firmer presence in the United States, adding a processing factory and some great employees to the company. In 1981, Marvin Coghill was named president of Standard Commercial, as Kehaya ascended to the position of chairman.

When sanctions against Rhodesia, which had since become known as Zimbabwe, were lifted in 1979, Standard reviewed its options and decided to acquire a 49 percent interest in a plant called Tobacco Packers. Toward that end, Standard partnered with Zimbabwe's largest locally owned public company, T.A. Holdings. In 1984, Standard acquired British Leaf Tobacco Co. of Canada Ltd., which would later be merged with Standard Commercial Co. of Canada Ltd. Moreover, the company also solidified its stateside presence during this time, buying up the remaining land and buildings of Jas. I. Miller's Springfield, Kentucky, facilities after a fire destroyed most of the processing machinery there. Standard installed all new equipment at the Springfield facility in time for the 1983 burley processing season. The facility secured Standard's place in Kentucky's burley markets. That year, the company's net profit was $11.4 million.

A Change in Focus in the Late 1980s

Standard Commercial's focus changed drastically in the late 1980s. Though there had always been a need for leaf dealing, the U.S. cigarette market was shrinking as increasingly health-conscious Americans began kicking the smoking habit. In fact, cigarette consumption domestically had been dwindling since 1981. Standard had to either downsize accordingly or widen its interests.

One of Standard's closest competitors in leaf dealing during this time, Dibrell Brothers, had diversified into the manufacturing of ice cream freezers. Standard took another direction. Beginning in 1986, the company spent $35 million for acquisitions in the wool industry, adding four wool trading and processing companies in 1987 alone, and the company began buying and processing wool for a long list of customers, primarily overseas. By 1988, wool accounted for 44 percent of the company's sales. Standard's global contacts in banks and business helped guide this growth.

Wool trading in the late 1980s was similar to tobacco trading in the 1950s—very fragmented. No single company owned more than 10 percent of the wool business in the free world. Nevertheless, Standard had plants in Australia, France, and Argentina by 1988, and by 1990 had acquired seven wool dealers and processors to become one of the largest entities in that market. Wool accounted for half of its $936 million in revenues in fiscal 1989.

However, just as its production was soaring, the demand for wool plunged. Prices collapsed globally and Standard was in a position similar to the one its founder had faced in the Great Depression. Stuck with a surplus of wool, few buyers and bad prices, Standard had to devise a plan. Although the company tended to avoid retaining large inventories, it waited out the depressed prices, and by 1991 was able to move from a $4.3 million loss in 1991 to $6.2 million in operating profits in 1992.

Luckily, the company's tobacco business was reviving at the same time. Tobacco was then accounting for two-thirds of Standard's revenues. Foreign sales, particularly of American blends and low-tar products, increased so much that Standard's tobacco revenues increased 140 percent between 1990 and 1992. In fact, American blends represented about 30 percent of tobacco consumed worldwide in 1991, and Standard was one of that product's major exporters.

Facing Difficulties in the Mid-1990s and Beyond

Early 1993 saw competitor Dibrell Brothers seek a merger with Standard Commercial; any tentative agreements reached, however, were scrapped the next year by Standard. Dibrell maintained a 9.9 percent stake in Standard but opted to explore mergers with other companies instead. Also during this time, the domestic cigarette market was suffering as U.S. legislators debated enacting laws to regulate tobacco content and impose federal excise taxes on cigarettes and other tobacco products. Moreover, an oversupply of tobacco hurt everyone in the industry in 1993 and 1994, and Standard joined its competitors when it sold its inventory at a loss to manufacturers. Referring to 1994 as a "year of unprecedented difficulty," President and CEO J. Alec G. Murray pledged to divest those interests not crucial to Standard's role as wool and tobacco. However, in March 1995, Standard announced that was going to sell off its wool trading and processing business. Given the severe state of flux in the tobacco trade in the United States, the future seemed uncertain for the company, but Standard vowed to focus on improving risk management, reducing inventory, improving profitability, and strengthening its management structure in hopes of a turnaround.

The company planned to sell its wool operations to competitor Chargeurs SA for $51 million. The deal failed to meet regulatory requirements, however, and never reached fruition. By December 1995, Standard Commercial decided to forgo a sale altogether and instead began to restructure its existing wool businesses. The company commented on its change of direction in a December 1995 *Wall Street Journal* article, claiming, "Despite the fact that the sale of the wool business would have resulted in a reduction of debt, management believes that ade-

quate credit facilities will continue to be available to conduct both the tobacco and wool businesses."

Standard Commercial continued to face challenges during the late 1990s. Market conditions in both the tobacco and wool sectors faltered, forcing the company to deal with weak demand for wool and slowing tobacco sales. To make matters worse, the tobacco industry as a whole was surrounded by negative sentiment as a result of tobacco-related litigation in the United States. The deteriorating economies of Asia and Eastern Europe also began to affect the firm's bottom line. Another factor that threatened to lower sales revenue for the company came when U.S. cigarette manufacturers began contracting directly with farmers for product in 2000, which differed from the traditional auction-style of selling.

Despite the difficult operating environment, Standard Commercial forged ahead. In September 1999, the company opened a raw tobacco processing facility in St. Petersburg, Russia. The company also made several acquisitions including the processing assets of Export Leaf Tobacco, which was a subsidiary of Brown and Williamson Tobacco Co. As a result of the 2003 deal, Standard Commercial secured a contract which gave it exclusive rights to process all of Brown and Williamson's U.S. tobacco. The firm also added the processing arm of Argentina-based Nobleza Picardo—a subsidiary of British American Tobacco—to its holdings.

As market conditions in the tobacco sector began to even out, the company's wool operations were negatively influenced by an outbreak of hoof and mouth disease in Europe and drought conditions in Australia. These factors caused a shortage in the wool supply, which drove prices up. As a result, demand for wool fell as the spinning and weaving industries began to use substitutes for wool in their manufacturing processes. In response to these challenges, Standard Commercial closed four of its facilities and exited the Argentina, South Africa, and New Zealand wool markets. The company also shuttered its specialty fibers business in Holland.

Sales and net income rose in 2003, a sign that the company was taking in stride increased competition in its markets. It was also able to put the DeLoach class action litigation behind it, having settled the case in 2003. According to the company, the DeLoach suit was a "class action claim brought on behalf of U.S. tobacco growers and quota holders alleging that defendants violated antitrust laws by bid-rigging at tobacco auctions." While Standard Commercial continued to revamp its business structure to keep pace with changes in its business sectors, management remained optimist about its future.

Principal Subsidiaries

Standard Commercial Tobacco Co. Inc.; Standard Commercial Services Inc.; Standard Commercial SA (Switzerland); Standard Commercial Tobacco Company of Canada Ltd.; Standard Commercial Tobacco Company (UK) Ltd.; Standard Commercial Tobacco Services (UK) Ltd.; Werkhof GmbH (Germany); Standard Wool Inc.; Standard Wool France S.A.; Standard Wool South Africa (Pty.) Ltd.; Standard Wool Australia (Pty.) Ltd.; Standard Wool (New Zealand) Limited (New Zealand); Standard Wool (UK) Ltd.

Principal Competitors

Chargeurs; DIMON Inc.; Universal Corp.

Further Reading

Bruno, Joe Bel, "Tobacco Leaf Company Promotes Deal," *High Yield Report*, March 15, 2004.

Cone, Edward, "Turning over a New Leaf," *Forbes*, April 4, 1988, p. 87.

Cochran, Thomas, "Hardly a Wool Gatherer," *Barron's*, January 22, 1990, p. 42.

Dubashi, Jagannath, "Standard Commercial: Investing Without Getting Fleeced," *FW*, August 4, 1992, p. 14.

"The First Tobacco Processing Factory 'Cress Neva' Opened in St. Petersburg," *Banks and Exchanges Weekly*, September 20, 1999, p. 14.

Nivens, David, "Future Looks Grim for Winston-Salem, N.C., Tobacco Auctions," *High Point Enterprise*, August 2, 2001.

"Standard Commercial Corporation Reports Third Quarter and Nine Months Results," *PR Newswire*, February 8, 1995.

"Standard Commercial Corp.: Plan to Sell Wool Unit to Chargeurs Is Dropped," *Wall Street Journal*, December 19, 1995, p. B4.

"Standard Commercial Co.: Soft Sales of Wool, Tobacco Will Hurt Fiscal '99 Earnings," *Wall Street Journal*, January 14, 1999.

"Standard Commercial Reports Solid Performance in Difficult Conditions," *PR Newswire*, June 8, 1999.

"Standard Commercial Settles Tax Dispute, Pays IRS $1.3 Million," *Wall Street Journal*, January 3, 1985, p. 2.

—Carol I. Keeley
—update: Christina M. Stansell

The Staubach Company

15601 Dallas Parkway, Suite 400
Addison, Texas 75001
U.S.A.
Telephone: (972) 361-5000
Fax: (972) 361-5912
Web site: http://www.staubach.com

Private Company
Incorporated: 1977 as Holloway-Staubach Corporation
Employees: 1,200
Sales: $225 million (2002 est.)
NAIC: 531210 Offices of Real Estate Agents and
    Brokers; 531312 Nonresidential Property Managers

The Staubach Company is one of the leading providers of corporate real estate services in the United States. The firm specializes in helping tenants negotiate leases and offers a host of related services, including site selection, financing, acquisition, disposition, design and construction, and property management. Staubach has more than 50 offices in North America and works with affiliates in more than 40 countries to negotiate leases worth upwards of $13 billion annually. Its clients include major corporations like JPMorgan Chase, Burlington Northern Santa Fe Corporation, Texas Instruments, and ExxonMobile. Company namesake and CEO Roger Staubach, a former football star, owns a majority stake in the firm.

Late 1970s Origins

The Staubach Company was founded in Dallas, Texas, by Roger Staubach, a quarterback for the National Football League's Dallas Cowboys. Born in 1942 near Cincinnati, Ohio, Staubach was a natural athlete who had excelled in baseball, basketball, and football. He played all three sports at the U.S. Naval Academy, where he won college football's prestigious Heisman Trophy in 1963. After graduating in 1965 with an engineering degree, he spent four years as an officer in the U.S. Navy. He joined the Cowboys after completing his tour of duty and went on to lead them to four Super Bowls and two national championships.

In the days before athletes' salaries hit the stratosphere, Staubach was paid just $25,000 a year to start, and he sought a job in the off-season to better support his wife and three young daughters. In 1970, he began working for the Henry S. Miller Company as an insurance salesman but soon switched to being a commercial real estate broker. He became one of the firm's top salesmen and was eventually named a vice-president. In 1977, he and fellow broker Robert Holloway left to form a real estate company, which they called Holloway-Staubach Corporation. Their first project was developing the Hillcrest Oaks office complex in Dallas, where the new firm also located its headquarters. The company had a staff of six.

After an outstanding career that included leading his team to more victories than any quarterback in NFL history, Staubach retired from football after the 1979 season to devote himself full-time to real estate. The early 1980s saw Dallas in the midst of a building boom, and the company grew rapidly. In 1982, Staubach bought out Holloway, who wanted to concentrate on property development, and the firm became known as the Staubach Company. The following year the firm's first major tenant representation transaction, for Commercial Metals, was completed.

Roger Staubach, whose football persona had been one of taking risks, never giving up and of diving into oncoming tacklers to get an extra yard rather than stepping safely out of bounds, was conversely a cautious and conservative businessman. He preferred to avoid risk, disdaining speculative development projects in favor of concentrating his firm's energies on the less glamorous work of brokering leases for tenants. A deeply religious, highly principled man, he was committed to his employees and clients and preferred to build the company carefully to assure its financial health over the long term. Unlike most real estate brokers, his firm's employees were paid with salaries and bonuses rather than commissions. Because Staubach represented the lessee, rather than the property owner, his clients were put at ease by the knowledge that the broker did not have a personal stake in the deal, as commissions were paid by the landlord.

By 1985 the firm had 120 employees and was taking in more than $5.4 million annually, up from just over a million in 1983.

Company Perspectives:

Operating Principles: We will adopt the objectives of our clients, the users of space, and dedicate ourselves to the achievement of their goals. We strive to understand our clients' long-term operational objectives and to orient our work to achieve these objectives, rather than simply fulfill a short-term real estate need. . . . If at any time our clients are not completely satisfied with the services we have provided, they have the unilateral right to adjust our fee.

It was now performing national work for such accounts as AT&T. The company was organized into four divisions—office and industrial leasing, commercial real estate brokerage, investment, and property management. The first of these units, which produced 85 percent of the firm's revenues, had grown from negotiating leases worth $6 million in 1982 to $100 million in 1985. In addition to helping tenants secure the best possible rental rates, the division also assisted with site selection and provided other consulting services. Staubach's property management unit handled some 75,000 square feet of commercial building space, a figure that had more than doubled in a year's time. This rapid growth helped place the firm on *Inc.* magazine's list of the 500 fastest-growing firms in the United States.

The company's business was largely centered in Dallas, but Staubach had plans to expand, and the firm was already doing work as far away as San Francisco, Phoenix, and Denver and had formed an association with a British agency, Weatherall-Green. Roger Staubach also helped operate and was a one-third stockholder in SBC Development Corporation, which had grown from putting $4 million into construction projects in 1982 to $40 million in 1985. It was run by Bob Breunig, a former Cowboy linebacker who had roomed with Staubach on road trips and also served as executive vice-president of Staubach Company.

The mid-1980s saw office leasing opportunities in the Dallas market began to decline, and in the fall of 1986 Staubach added new divisions to handle leasing of retail properties and design and construction consulting services. Also during that year, the company opened its first satellite office, in Atlanta, where it was helping develop a 430-acre site with wealthy Dallas businessman H. Ross Perot.

In May 1987, Staubach opened an East Coast office near Washington D.C., and the next year won a major assignment from the U.S. General Services Administration to handle leases for federal offices in Texas, Oklahoma, Louisiana, and New Mexico. In 1988, the company also opened a new office in Newport Beach, California, which joined other recent additions in Boca Raton, Florida, and Nashville. In November of that year, Roger Staubach sold a 20 percent stake in his company to Robert Rainwater, a Fort Worth, Texas-based financier. The new capital was used to help fund the company's ongoing national expansion. By now, Staubach's annual revenues had grown to $12.7 million. Major clients included CompUSA and GTE.

The early 1990s saw the company complete a number of major assignments; these included helping United Parcel Ser-

vice and MCI find new headquarters. The firm also formed a financial services division, which secured one of the first so-called ''synthetic leases'' in the industry for Sun Microsystems. During this period, Staubach opened offices in Houston, San Francisco, Detroit, and Denver. Its clients now included such top corporations as Barnes & Noble, Toyota, and Kmart.

Expansion Abroad in Mid-1990s

As Staubach gained more work from multinational corporations, it began to enlarge its international capabilities. Beginning in late 1994, new alliances were formed with complementary firms in Hong Kong and Mexico. With its foreign partners—First Pacific Davies in Asia and Corporacion Mexicana de Inmuebles in Mexico, as well as Weatherall Green in Britain—it could offer leasing, purchasing, and construction services for corporations looking for office space on three continents.

In March 1996, Roger Staubach appointed company veteran James Leslie to the posts of president and chief operating officer, retaining for himself the CEO and board chairman roles. Freed from the demands of day-to-day management, he would focus on gaining new clients and promoting the firm's services. By now, Staubach Company had offices in 11 U.S. cities and employed 235. Annual revenues topped $54 million, and the firm handled transactions worth an estimated $2 billion. Its recent growth had been helped by expansion into the industrial, retail, and financial services areas, a move necessitated by the firm's increasing competition, as well as pressure from property owners to lower commissions on lease renewals.

The year 1997 saw Staubach open its first New York office and also add an international real estate division in Cupertino, California, that would serve companies seeking quarters abroad. One of its first clients was Netscape Communications, which hired the firm to make all of its international real estate deals. Staubach was now able to perform complete oversight of a company's real estate operations, which served to aid growing firms that could not assemble an experienced staff quickly enough to execute expansion plans. The company also continued to be active in other areas of real estate, including land acquisition, construction management, and facility management.

In 1998, the firm opened an office in Cleveland with four former brokers recruited from Ostendorf-Morris Company. As was the arrangement with the managers of Staubach's other regional offices, they would also be co-owners of the agency with Staubach Company. The year 1999 saw Staubach form a partnership to handle the $80 million conversion of a Denver hospital into a mixture of housing and businesses. The firm also took over management of the 1,200 facility real estate portfolio of New Century Energies of Denver, as well as working to broker the sale of $135 million worth of retail properties, most of which had been used as drugstores by the CVS chain. They were eventually sold and then leased back to CVS.

Staubach expanded to Canada in 1999 when it formed a partnership with Tenant Resource Corporation of Toronto, Canada, which changed its name to Staubach Canada, Inc. It had additional offices in Ottawa and Montreal. Staubach's sales hit $130 million for the year, and its employee ranks grew to 700. It now had offices in 29 cities, the most recent U.S. addition being

Key Dates:

1977: Roger Staubach and Robert Holloway form Holloway-Staubach Corporation.
1982: Staubach buys out his partner's interest to create Staubach Company.
1986: The company's first regional office is opened in Atlanta.
1988: A 20 percent stake in the firm is sold to Robert Rainwater.
1994–96: European, Asian, and Mexican partnerships are formed.
1997: New York and Silicon Valley International offices are opened.
1999: The company opens a Canadian branch, forms a partnership with DTZ Debenham Tie Leung, and moves to new headquarters.
2000: A sales division is formed.
2001: Staubach wins a commission to help develop a new Penn Station in New York.

Chicago, which came via a merger with the brokerage half of Tanguay-Burke-Stratton LLC. Its client list had grown to include IBM, AMC Theatres, Mobil, and Home Depot, along with Lincoln Financial Services and Blockbuster, whose national real estate portfolios the firm managed.

In December 1999, Staubach formed a joint venture with Singapore-based DTZ Debenham Tie Leung to offer real estate services in 33 countries under the name DTZ Staubach Tie Leung. Staubach would own a third of the operation, with DTZ's European and Asian entities each holding another third. Plans for Staubach to build more than 1,000 homes in southern Dallas were dropped late in the year after a request for $7.6 million in public assistance caused controversy.

In January 2000, Staubach announced it was forming a new division to handle sales of commercial real estate, primarily industrial and retail properties. The move came as the firm found increasing numbers of its leasing clients requesting help selling property they needed to dispose of. During the year, the company also formed eStaubach Partners, based in Virginia, which would develop Web-based real estate products and services, and formed two new partnerships in South America, Herzog Staubach and Staubach Spanish Americas and Caribbean (SAC), Ltda., with offices slated to open in Santiago, Chile, and Panama City, Panama.

By now, Staubach had 800 employees and was taking in an estimated $165 million. Many of its regional offices that had started with just a handful of employees had grown exponentially, as typified by the Denver agency, which now employed 25. At this time, the company's business was increasingly derived from high tech, Internet, and telecommunications companies, which accounted for more than a third of its total work.

Penn Station Contract Awarded in 2001

Staubach won a major contract in March 2001 when it was selected, along with Frankfurt Airport Services Group World-

wide of Germany, to develop and manage the $788 million Penn Station redevelopment project in New York City. The two firms would oversee the work, which involved converting a historic post office near Madison Square Garden by building a new structure on top of it as well as adding a sizable retail complex. Staubach would manage the development of the project and design and implement the retail component.

The year 2001 also saw Staubach and Washington Group International Inc. of Boise, Idaho, team up to take over management of the airport at Addison, Texas, in which city the firm was now headquartered. They would keep 18 percent of the gross revenues in exchange for Staubach's managing its leasing and real estate operations, while Washington Group's handled flight operations and development. The firm also opened a new office in Fort Worth, Texas, to oversee its work for Burlington Northern Santa Fe Corporation, one of Staubach's largest clients, which had more than 10,000 active leases. The company also finalized another major sale/leaseback deal for CVS properties worth $288 million.

In 2002, Staubach linked up with Davaco, Inc. of Dallas, a retail fixture design and service company, and Buxton Company of Fort Worth, a direct marketing research firm, to offer their services in conjunction with its own. The year also saw Roger Staubach partner with former Dallas Cowboy quarterback Troy Aikman to form Hall of Fame Racing, which would sponsor a NASCAR racing team. In 2003, Staubach Company formed a unit to provide lease negotiation and development consulting for the automotive sector, including dealerships and manufacturers. The company had already been working with such firms in this area as BMW, Honda, Alamo Rental Car, and AutoNation. Though the economic downturn of the early 2000s had caused considerable turmoil in the real estate business, during 2002 Staubach negotiated leases valued at $13.7 billion, which made it the fourth-largest firm of its kind in the United States.

In January 2003, Staubach named Elysia Ragusa president and chief operating officer. She had worked with the firm for 14 years, most recently heading its real estate services division. In March, an office was opened in Tallahassee, Florida, to serve the northern part of that state, and in October the firm partnered with MetaPartners of Cary, North Carolina, to offer tenant representation services there under the Staubach name. In December, the company also hired a Washington-based lobbying firm to help bring it more government work. Roger Staubach, a staunch Republican, had been friends with President George W. Bush for many years. By now, the firm had more than 50 offices and 1,200 employees.

In 2004, Staubach was hired to sell or lease major facilities owned by OfficeMax, Inc. in Cleveland and by Texas Instruments, Inc. in Massachusetts. The latter firm sought to dispose of a 261 acre site where more than 2,000 workers had staffed a 1.1 million square foot building complex.

After more than 25 years, The Staubach Company had grown to become one of the largest tenant-representation real estate firms in the United States, as well as offering a wide range of other services. It continued to be led by namesake and founder Roger Staubach, whose fame as a football great had helped open doors but whose principled leadership and carefully chosen team of skilled professionals had established a solid reputation for service.

Principal Subsidiaries

Staubach Global Services; Staubach Retail Services; Wolverine Equities Company; Staubach Canada, Inc.

Principal Competitors

Julien J. Studley, Inc.; Cushman & Wakefield, Inc.; Trammell Crow Company; CRESA Partners LLC; Jones Lang LaSalle, Inc.; Grubb & Ellis Company.

Further Reading

Aldrich, Nelson W., Jr., "#91: The Staubach Co., (Inc. 500)," *Inc.*, December 1, 1985, p. 66.

Bistritz, Nancy, "Going Head to Head with Roger Staubach," *National Real Estate Investor*, October 30, 1999.

Brown, Steve, "Staubach Co. Reshuffles Administration," *Dallas Morning News*, November 21, 1986, p. 2D.

——, "Rainwater Invests in Staubach Co.," *Dallas Morning News*, November 11, 1988, p. 3D.

——, "Staubach Forms 2nd International Alliance," *The Dallas Morning News*, January 13, 1995, p. 2D.

——, "Staubach Passes Duties," *The Dallas Morning News*, March 27, 1996, p. 3D.

——, "Dallas Real Estate Firm Staubach Co. to Try Hand at Property Sales," *Texas*, January 26, 2000.

Bullard, Steve, "Teaming up with Staubach Proves to Be Touchdown for Great Lakes Firm," *Crain's Cleveland Business*, August 21, 2000, p. 19.

Cannon, Steve, "Realty Gets Big Name," *News & Observer*, October 14, 2003, p. D1.

Chapman, Parke, "Staubach Wins Penn Bowl," *Real Estate Weekly*, March 21, 2001, p. 1.

Corfman, Thomas A., "Staubach Makes Local Brokerage Play," *Crain's Chicago Business*, October 4, 1999, p. 1.

Halliday, Jean, "Staubach Is Quarterback for Real-Estate Tenants Now," *Crain's Detroit Business*, October 15, 1990, p. 5.

Harris, Mike, "Aikman, Staubach Co-Owners of NASCAR Team," *AP Online*, January 16, 2003.

Ingrassia, Robert, "Former NFL Star's Real-Estate Firm Halts Plans on Project in Dallas," *Dallas Morning News*, September 18, 1999.

McLinden, Steve, "Dallas-Based Commercial Real Estate Firm Opens Office in Fort Worth, Texas," *Knight Ridder Tribune Business News*, March 30, 2001.

——, "Fort Worth, Texas-Based Retail Research Firm Partners with Dallas Companies," *Fort-Worth Star-Telegram*, May 28, 2002.

McPherson, David, "Texas Instruments Hires Firm to Plan Attleboro, Mass., Redevelopment," *Providence Journal*, February 18, 2004.

Mullins, Brody, "Staubach Takes Game to D.C.," *Roll Call*, December 1, 2003.

Murray, Michael, "Staubach Co. to Manage Lincoln Financial's Real Estate Portfolio," *Real Estate Finance Today*, December 3, 1999, p. 14.

——, "Ex-Quarterback Excels in Competition," *Real Estate Finance Today*, January 24, 2000, p. 3.

Quinn, Steve, "Addison, Texas Strikes Deal with Independent Operators to Run Airport," *Knight Ridder Tribune Business News*, February 12, 2001.

Rebchook, John, "Real Estate Game's Careful Cowboy Roger Staubach's Keen Attention to Detail Making Him a Winner in Commercial Property," *Denver Rocky Mountain News*, May 18, 2000, p. 2B.

Rutledge, Tanya, "Staubach Tackles the Silicon Valley," *Business Journal*, October 6, 1997, p. 9.

Schwanhausser, Mark, "Staubach Co.'s Latest Play in Silicon Valley," *Dallas Morning News*, August 11, 1990, p. 7H.

Steinhart, David, "Football's Staubach to Announce Drive into Canada," *National Post*, April 20, 1999, p. C1.

Templin, Neal, "Gridiron Fame Dazzles Real-Estate Clients," *Wall Street Journal*, October 18, 1996, p. B1.

Zuckerman, Steve, "Staubach Seeks Stardom in Commercial Real Estate Leasing," *Dallas Business Courier*, August 26, 1985, p. 7.

——, "Staubach Co. Moves into Retail Leasing and Looks to Expand outside of Texas," *Dallas Business Courier*, July 28, 1986, p. 17.

—Frank Uhle

Stirling Group plc

Atlantic Street, Broadheath
Altrincham
WA14 5FY
United Kingdom
Telephone: +44 161 926 7000
Fax: +44 161 926 7029
Web site: http://www.stirlinggroup.com

Private Company
Incorporated: 1973 as Stirling Knitting Group
Employees: 1,824
Sales: £170 million ($285 million) (2003)
NAIC: 315230 Women's and Girls' Cut and Sew Apparel
Manufacturing; 315220 Men's and Boys' Suit and
Sew Apparel Manufacturing; 423220 Home
Furnishing Merchant Wholesalers; 423920 Toy and
Hobby Goods and Supplies Merchant Wholesalers;
423940 Jewelry, Watch, Precious Stone, and Precious
Metal Merchant Wholesalers; 423990 Other
Miscellaneous Durable Goods Merchant Wholesalers

Stirling Group plc provides clothing design and manufacturing services, as well as sourcing services for a variety of goods to retailers, especially department store groups. Stirling's clothing design and manufacturing operation, Bentwood, has long specialized in contract production of lingerie and swimwear, but also outerwear and other clothing items. After more than 50 years working in the shadows as a leading clothing supplier to the Marks & Spencer department store group—which for some time was Stirling's only customer—Stirling has begun to emerge into the spotlight through a two-pronged strategy. On the one hand, the company has begun to acquire its own range of clothing brands, although remaining close to its core specialty of lingerie and swimwear. As such, the group has targeted the swim and surf market, acquiring popular ''board'' brand Headworx (Europe) and the ''women-only'' surf brand Voodoo Dolls, together with its younger variants V Dolls and iDolls. The company also owns the Over The Top lingerie brand. The second prong of the company's strategy has been to expand into the sourcing market—that is, acting as a go-between for

Western retailers for their Asian purchasing and contract-manufacturing needs. As part of this effort, Stirling owns Tamarind International, based in Hong Kong and Shanghai, which sources a variety of goods, including luggage, toys, and other items, in addition to providing support for the group's Bentwood division. Formerly a publicly listed company, Stirling was taken private in a management-led buyout in 2003. Steven Bentwood is company CEO. In 2003, Stirling's revenues reached £170 million ($285 million).

Partnering for Growth in the 1950s

By the middle of the 20th century, Marks & Spencer had already established its reputation as one of the United Kingdom's top retailers. Founded by Michael Marks in 1884 as a simple stall at the Leeds market, the business moved into its first retail shop in 1893. The following year, Marks teamed up with partner Tom Spencer, creating British retailing history.

Originally based on a five-and-dime style concept, Marks & Spencer added textile sales—starting with hosiery—in the early 1920s. By the end of the decade, Marks & Spencer had begun developing a full range of goods. This led the company, then under the leadership of Marks's son Simon Marks, to launch its own brand, St. Michael, in honor of the company's founder, in 1928. The first St. Michael-branded products were pajamas and other knitwear. With its offering of quality goods at discounted prices, Marks & Spencer had revolutionized British consumer retail. In the 1920s, Marks & Spencer revolutionized the business end of the sector as well, launching a policy of buying directly from manufacturers.

This new policy led to the growth of a new class of clothing manufacturers dedicated to supplying Marks & Spencer as it expanded throughout the United Kingdom and into other parts of the world. Among these partner manufacturers was Stirling Knitting, launched in the 1950s by George MacDonald. Based in Southport, Stirling specialized in producing women's and children's knitted clothing, such as jumpers (sweaters) and cardigans. The majority of Stirling's production was specifically for Marks & Spencer, and sold under the St. Michael label.

Marks & Spencer did not simply place orders with manufacturers. The retailer took an active interest in the production

Company Perspectives:

Stirling Group Plc has shown its commitment to expanding its product base this past year with the acquisition of exciting, vibrant brands that bring a whole new dimension to this highly focused forward-thinking organization. While the Group's core values stay focused firmly on innovation, excellence of service, and enduring business partnerships, Stirling has made a significant step towards embracing new opportunities in both its manufacturing sectors and also its move towards the consumer. Its vision, which combines multi-disciplinary capabilities in a wide range of international markets and operating environments, is to continue this expansion and acquisition objective. At the same time, quality service remains a crucial factor, and the Group will work even more closely with its long term business partners to ensure outstanding customer service and profile our unique capacity for business innovation.

process itself, encouraging manufacturers to adopt the latest production techniques in an effort to increase quality and decrease cost. Marks & Spencer also worked with its suppliers in the introduction of new fabrics and prints. Stirling Knitting itself expanded from its clothing production to add its own fabric manufacturing operation. This expansion led the group to go public, with an offering in 1960.

Stirling Knitting remained a small company through the 1960s—by 1970, its revenues were less than £500,000. The company's intimate relationship with Marks & Spencer left it vulnerable to downturns at the retailer, and in the early 1970s, Stirling itself faced a number of difficulties, including slipping sales. By 1971, the company's revenues had dropped to just £436,000.

Acquisitions in the 1970s

Despite its problems, compounded by the loss of George MacDonald, who had served as company chairman, Stirling began to expand its operation at the start of the decade. In 1971, the company built an extension to its factory in order to expand its production capacity. The following year, the company acquired additional facilities by paying £75,000, as well as granting shares, to H&T Miller. That acquisition was followed up by the purchase of the Bodycote Knitwear Division from Bodycote Plc.

In that year, MacDonald's widow sold off the family's 56 percent stake in the business to Maurice Goldstone, who headed another fabric group, Kerrybrook Knits, in a deal that valued the entire company at £350,000. Goldstone then bought up the remainder of the company's shares, de-listing it from the London stock exchange.

Under Goldstone, Stirling continued to expand, notably through the acquisition of Bentwood Bros., owned by Peter and Henry Bentwood, for a cash and shares consideration worth nearly £600,000. Manchester-based Bentwood Bros. added to Stirling's operation by extending its range of goods to include Bentwood's women's outerwear specialty. The purchase also brought the Bentwood family into Stirling's management for the first time.

Stirling now went on an acquisition spree, starting with the purchase of Standard Knitting Company in 1973. That company, which had been in receivership, gave Stirling additional fabric knitting capacity at a cost of £100,000. Yet that acquisition proved to be only the first of many that year, as the company sought out a number of new, small-scale textile manufacturers, including Weston Street Mills, Rossiter Knitwear, Henshaw Knitwear, Gee Knitwear, Aeros Textile Exports, Rellimac, and others.

In this way, Stirling sought to reduce its costs, in part by boosting its bulk purchasing power, in part by rationalizing the production and distribution process among its new acquisitions. The series of acquisitions also allowed Stirling to reposition itself as a provider of a complete range of knitwear to retailers and wholesalers. At the same time, the company reduced its dependence on Marks & Spencer, attracting a new range of customers among department stores and mail-order businesses. Nonetheless, Marks & Spencer remained Stirling's primary customer.

Following its buying spree, the larger Stirling returned to the stock market, re-listing its shares on the London exchange, while changing its name to Stirling Knitting Group. Yet Goldstone, who had transformed the company from a small-scale operation to a full-scale and internationally operating business—including manufacturing operations in Canada—was himself forced to resign in a management shakeup at the end of 1973. Goldstone sold off his shares, which were acquired by Peter Bentwood and other members of the management team.

Stirling exited fabric manufacturing in 1974 in order to concentrate on building its clothing manufacturing operation. In support of this, the company made a new acquisition of textiles group D. Verblow, in 1978. Stirling's growth continued through the 1970s. By 1974 the company posted revenues of £4.6 million, which more than doubled to move past £10 million at the start of the 1980s. By then, the Bentwood family continued to acquire shares in Stirling and by the middle of the 1980s had gained effective control of the company.

Adding Brands for the New Century

Marks & Spencer's strong growth—which included its move into the United States with the acquisition of Brooks Brothers—in the 1980s encouraged Stirling to hitch its own growth more firmly on the retail group. In 1985, the company launched a new acquisition drive, this time targeting other manufacturers in the Marks & Spencer supplier pool. The first of these came that same year, with the purchase of B. Fortster & Co., for £3.5 million. That acquisition added a new range of women's and children's clothing and sales of nearly £10 million to Stirling. Another significant purchase came with the addition of Ritz Design—that acquisition helped transform Stirling's focus away from the general textiles market to a greater focus as a specialist in lingerie and swimwear. By the middle of the 1990s, Stirling had emerged as one of the top three suppliers to Marks & Spencer.

Yet like much of the British clothing sector, Stirling suffered through the recession of the 1990s and its extended effect on the British economy through much of the first half of the decade. After slipping into losses during the first half of the decade, the company managed to pull back into profitability by 1996. Yet

---

Key Dates:

1950s: Stirling Knitting forms as supplier of knitwear to the Marks & Spencer retail group.
1960: Stirling lists on the London Stock Exchange.
1972: Stirling acquires H&T Miller for £75,000; Bodycote Knitwear Division is acquired.
1973: Maurice Goldstone buys control of the company and launches it on an acquisition spree that includes Bentwood Bros.
1974: Goldstone sells his stake in Stirling to Peter Bentwood and others.
1978: The company acquires D. Verblow.
1985: Controlled by the Bentwood family, Stirling begins a new acquisition drive targeting other Marks & Spencer suppliers, such as B. Fortster & Co.
1999: Stirling acquires Tamarind International.
2003: Steven Bentwood leads a management buyout of Stirling, de-listing the company from the London Stock Exchange.

---

its low share price exposed it to possible takeover. Instead, the Bentwood family, now represented by Steven Bentwood, bought up additional shares in the company, shielding it from unwelcome bids.

Stirling's troubles nonetheless continued through the end of the decade. Marks & Spencer's own problems cast a shadow over Stirling, as the retailer found itself confronted with a rising number of new and more aggressive retailers, both from U.K.-based groups, and from fast-rising international businesses such as Zara, Benneton, H&M, and others. Meanwhile, Marks & Spencer's international division was failing, leading the company to exit a number of markets, such as Paris, by the beginning of the 2000s.

Stirling itself bore the brunt of much of Marks & Spencer's problems. At the same time, the company found itself under growing pressure to follow the U.K. textiles sector trend in de-localizing its production base to lower-cost marks in Asia and elsewhere. Stirling attempted to resist at first, asserting its commitment to maintaining its production in the United Kingdom, and even set out to buy up factories that had been abandoned by other manufacturers.

Yet at the end of the decade, Stirling became threatened by the loss of part of its business with Marks & Spencer. The retailer, in an effort to revitalize its operation, had decided to drop its St. Michael label—or rather, convert it as a "quality guarantee"—and instead began adopting a designer brand focus in line with the prevailing retail and consumer trend. As part of that process, Stirling found its role within the Marks & Spencer supply network reduced to just the lingerie, underwear, and nightwear sections in 1999.

In response, Stirling set out to transform its own business. The company's first move was to increase its ability to provide products from Asian markets, and in 1999 the company paid nearly £12 million to acquire Tamarind International, a sourcing group based in Hong Kong. Tamarind provided intermediary services, acting as a liaison between Asian contract manufacturers and Western wholesalers and retailers. The acquisition of Tamarind, owned by Joe Lewis, the fourth richest person in the United Kingdom, also gave Lewis a stake in Stirling. Following the acquisition, Stirling began an effort to increase Tamarind's margins by transferring the bulk of its operations to the Chinese mainland in Shanghai.

While the Tamarind acquisition enabled Stirling to reduce its reliance on its U.K. manufacturing park—the company began shutting down most of its U.K. plants in 2002—the company also had begun plotting a second prong to its future growth strategy: the acquisition and development of its own branded clothing.

The company's first brand acquisitions came in 2001, with the purchase of noted Australian surf and "board" brands, the sport-oriented Headworx and the "women-only" surf and swimwear brand Voodoo Dolls, previously owned by Mecca Group Pty Ltd. The following year, Stirling added another line, the high-end lingerie, nightwear, and swimwear brand Over The Top, which was placed under a newly formed subsidiary, O.T.T. International.

By the end of 2003, Stirling's sales were showing new growth, rising from less than £160 million to more than £170 million. Yet the company's share price remained depressed as part of an overall investor disaffection for textile stocks. In response, Stirling decided to remove its listing from the London stock exchange for a second time. In September 2003, Steven Bentwood and the management members formed a new company, Potter Acquisitions, and, backed by LDC and the Bank of Scotland, bought out the company in a deal valued at some £60 million. Free from shareholder demands, Stirling now prepared to continue its transformation into a branded products group in the new century.

Principal Subsidiaries

Bentwood Ltd.; Headworx (Europe) Limited; O.T.T. International; Tamarind International Inc. (Hong Kong).

Principal Competitors

Central Group of Cos.; Liz Claiborne Inc.; ECOTEX; Blue Bell Commodities Inc.; South African Clothing Industries; Fruit of the Loom Inc.; Hering Textil S.A.; Nile Clothing Co.; Sunflag Tanzania Ltd.

Further Reading

Burney, Ellen, and Sarah Harris, "Surfin' UK," *WWD*, August 7, 2003, p. 36S.
"Clothing Group Stirling Considers Going Private As It Sinks into the Red," *Independent*, December 5, 2002, p. 25.
Feddy, Kevin, "Stirling Put Up for Sale at BP 60m," *Manchester Online*, September 23, 2003.
Rivlin, Richard, "Joe Lewis Takes Stirling Stake," *Financial Times*, July 14, 1999, p. 20.
Robert, Patricia, "Stirling Stuff in the Lingerie Department," *Manchester Online*, February 10, 2004.
"Stirling Plans Life After M&S," *Financial Times*, December 10, 1999, p. 26.

—M.L. Cohen

TaKaRa

Takara Holdings Inc.

Karasuma-Higashiiru
Shijodori, Shimogyo-ku
Kyoto, 600-8688
Japan
Telephone: (+81) 75-241-5130
Fax: (+81) 75-241-5127
Web site: http://www.takara.co.jp

Public Company
Incorporated: 1925
Sales: ¥187.39 billion ($1.57 billion) (2003)
Stock Exchanges: Tokyo Osaka
Ticker Symbol: 2531
NAIC: 312140 Distilleries; 312120 Breweries; 541710
    Research and Development in the Physical Sciences
    and Engineering Sciences; 551112 Offices of Other
    Holding Companies

Takara Holdings Inc. is the new holding company created from the breakup of the former Takara Shozu into its two core operations: drinks maker Takara Shozu Co. and fast-growing biotech and pharmaceutical company Takara Bio Inc. Takara Shozu, which traces its operations back to the mid-19th century, is one of Japan's leading producers and distributors of alcoholic beverages, including its market-leading *shochu* (a distilled liquor) range, sake, the sweet cooking wine *mirin,* and other traditional Japanese alcoholic beverages and alcohol-based seasonings. Takara Shozu also produces soft drinks and Scotch whisky, the latter through its ownership of Scotland's Tomatin Distillery, the largest distiller in that country, as well as bourbon whisky, through its ownership of Age International and its Blanton's brand. In China, the company operates production and sales subsidiaries for its *shochu,* sake, and other products. The flipside of Takara Holdings is its Takara Bio subsidiary, which is one of Japan's leading biotechnology firms and a pioneer in the genetic engineering field. That company is involved in a variety of research and development areas within the biotech sector, including the development of reagents, manufacturing of DNA chips, and DNA base sequencing—in part through subsidiary Dragon Genomics Center—and development of gene therapies. While Takara Bio represents less than 8 percent of Takara Holdings' total sales—Takara Shozu generated more than 89 percent of the group's ¥187.39 billion ($1.57 billion) in sales in 2003—the division held strong promise amid expectations that the Japanese biotech sector will expand by a factor of 25 by the end of the 2000s. Listed on the Tokyo Stock Exchange, Takara is led by president Hisashi Ohmiya.

Building a Beverage Business in the 20th Century

What scotch is to Scotland, *shochu* was to Japan after a Fushimi area merchant began producing it as a distilled variant of sake, a fermented liquor, in 1842. The distillery operations grew strongly into the next century, and in 1925 the company was incorporated as Takara Shuzo. Co. Ltd. Takaro Shuzo grew into Japan's leading maker of *shochu* and *mirin,* a sweet wine used for cooking, as well as a prominent maker of sake. In that latter category, the company especially became known for its so-called "celebration sake," a special category of sake typically used for gifts and celebrations. The company launched that range in 1933 under subsidiary Sho-Chiku-Bai Shuzo Co.

Takara Shuzo went public in 1949, and the following year opened a research and development center in order to produce new fermentation techniques and agents. The company then attempted to leverage its growing fermentation expertise with an entry into a new beverage category, beer, in the mid-1950s. In 1957, the company launched its own beer brand, Takara Beer, which met with only limited success. Ten years later, Takara exited that market. The company continued developing new alcoholic beverages, however, and in 1977 launched Takara Shochu Jun, a "white" *shochu.* That product was credited transforming shochu's traditional image and creating an entirely new market. Backed by the strong sales of Shochu Jun, Takara Shuzo joined the ranks of Japan's top alcoholic beverage companies.

That market enjoyed a high degree of protectionism into the 1990s, with foreign alcohol types, especially whisky, taxed heavily—boosting their prices by as much as six times those for sake and *shochu.* Nonetheless, Takara Shuzo developed a wider portfolio, beginning a distribution relationship in 1971 with Tomatin Distillery, the largest in Scotland and one of the largest in the

Company Perspectives:

The Takara Group is committed to contributing to healthy, fulfilling living by seeking out new possibilities in culinary culture, cultural life, and the life sciences and by continuing to create new value. This commitment is underpinned by our fermentation technologies for traditional Japanese sake brewing and our innovative, cutting-edge biotechnologies. A precise vision bolsters value and leads to growth and development into the future. The Takara Group is engaged in business activities based on the Takara Evolution-100 (TE-100) long-term business concept, which covers the ten-year period from 2001 to 2010. We are dedicated to the vision laid out in TE-100, working to increase real corporate value by enhancing both the economic and cultural value of the Group through evolution in five areas: business results, business operations, management, corporate culture and human values, and social and environmental actions. Realizing this vision will fuel the growth and development of the Takara Group into the future.

world, to introduce that company's Speyside whiskies in Japan. Takara Shuzo also began importing a bourbon brand, Blanton's, through a relationship with Age International, operators of one of Kentucky's largest distilleries. In the early 1970s, the company started marketing alcoholic beverages in China as well.

In the late 1980s, Takara Shuzo moved to become a full-range beverage supplier. In 1984, the group launched its hugely successful line of Takara Can Chu-Hi, a *shochu*-based light alcoholic beverage, then added Takara Barbican, a non-alcoholic beer in 1986. In that year, also, Takara acquired 80 percent of Tomatin, later boosted to 100 percent, marking the first time a Japanese company had acquired a Scottish distillery. By then, the group had entered the United States, setting up Takara Sake USA to take advantage, on the one hand, of the rising Japanese population in the United States and, on the other, of the increasing interest in that market for the traditional rice-based Japanese drink. The company's U.S. interests were strengthened in 1991 when it acquired a strategic stake in Age International, before gaining full control of the bourbon maker and adding its Ancient Age, Ancient Ancient Age, and Blanton's brands to its drinks portfolio.

Biotech Diversification for the New Century

Into the 1990s, Takara Shuzo continued introducing new beverage products, including fruit juices and a new line of health food drinks, starting with Calcium Parlor in 1993. In 1995, the company turned to the Chinese market, establishing a subsidiary in Beijing for the production of beverages and alcohol-based seasonings for that country. In the late 1990s, Takara Shuzo sought to diversify its beverage operations into the wider foods category, starting with the launch of a new seasoning, Cookin' Good, in 1997. The success of that product led the company to extend the Cookin' Good brand to include a full line of seasonings and cooking products. The following year, the group extended its beverage portfolio by adding imported California wines.

Takara continued expanding its range of beverage products into the 2000s, adding a new organic *mirin*, Tokusen Takara Yuki Hon Mirin, in 2000, Schucho Zipang in 2001, and the "self care" line of Tencha & Shiso health drinks in 2002. The company also built a new brewery, Shirakabegura at its Nada facility, which began producing specialty sakes in 2002. With the launch of government campaigns against drunk driving, the company moved to extend its non-alcoholic beverage line with the addition of Barbican Ginger in 2003. The company also launched Takara Can Chu-Hi Sukish that year, using a special heat-free process in the preparation of fruit.

By then, Takara faced the deregulation of the Japanese drinks industry. The company braced itself for the lowering of trade barriers and the expected flood of foreign brands into the country. With the leading *shochu* and *mirin* brands, and a significant place in the sake market as well, Takara remained confident of its position. Nonetheless, in 2001, the company decided to reorganize its operation in order better to meet the coming competition, and, at the same time, to recognize the company's diversified operations. Indeed, by the beginning of the 2000s, Takara Shuzo had also become one of the clear leaders in Japan's biotech sector.

Takara's entry into biotechnology came in the late 1960s, when the company recognized the it could turn the fermentation expertise gained at its research and development center to a new and fast growing sector, that of bio-engineering. In 1970, Takara founded a new, central research and development facility in Otsu and began work on developing new reagents needed for the research sector. At the same time, and in direct relationship with the group's fermentation operations, the company's research and development efforts had been working on inventing new fungal strains, and in 1970 launched a patented method for artificially cultivating Shimeji mushrooms.

Takara's break in the biotech sector came in 1979, when it became the first in Japan to produce restriction enzyme products. The company quickly developed its own production methods and was able to start exporting its own range of reagent kits for the genetic engineering sector in 1982.

The company began adding new products and technologies, such as PCR products for DNA amplification in 1988, and developed its own gene transfer method by 1995. In 1996, the company added a dedicated agribusiness subsidiary, Takara Agri Co, and then began manufacturing DNA chips in 1998.

By then, the company had launched a new research and development laboratory in China, established in 1993. The division's international expansion continued with the creation of a European subsidiary in Paris in 1995 and a subsidiary in Seoul, Korea, that same year. It acquired Korea's ViroMed in 2000.

By the end of the 1990s, Takara had already become one of Japan's biotech stars and a sought-after partner in the global biotech industry. In 2000, the company began a partnership with the United States' Lynx Therapeutics to develop new DNA microbeads array technologies. The following year, the company began working with Italy's MolMed, which licenses Takara's patented RecroNectin gene therapy technology. These alliances were complemented with a partnership with Nanosphere Inc., based in the United States, and, in South Korea, growth in the coming years. In Japan alone, where biotechnology had been slow in taking off, this sector was expected to expand by as much as 25 times by the end of the new century's first decade. Takara, which already held the position as the country's market leader, decided that, in the face of the future prospects of its biotech operations and the coming competition in its core beverages businesses, the time was right to restructure its operations.

In 2002, Takara restructured as Takara Holdings Inc., spinning off its operations into two new companies, Takara Shuzo, which inherited the company's larger drinks business, and Takara Bio, which took over its fast-growing biotech division. The new structure promised to enable each division greater operational focus and shortened decision-making times. Takara Bio got off with a bang, making its first acquisition, that of Dragon Genomics Co, an operator of a high-throughput genomic sequence analysis center. Revitalized after more than 160 years in operation, Takara Holding planned to remain a leader in both of its core businesses in the new century.

Key Dates:

- **1842:** A Fushimi-area merchant begins distilling Shochu.
- **1925:** The distilling business is incorporated as Takara Shozu.
- **1933:** A sake subsidiary and brand Sho-Chiku-Bai Shuzo are established.
- **1949:** Takara Shuzo goes public on the Tokyo Stock Exchange.
- **1950:** The company opens a fermentation research and development center.
- **1970:** A central research and development facility is established in order to begin production reagents and other biotech research.
- **1977:** The company launches its new ''white'' Shucho, Takara Shochu Jun.
- **1979:** Takara becomes the first Japanese company to develop restrictive enzymes.
- **1982:** The company begins the export of genetic engineering reagents.
- **1983:** A U.S. sake brewing and sales subsidiary is established.
- **1984:** Takara Can ChuHi light alcoholic beverage is launched.
- **1988:** The company begins sales of DNA amplification products.
- **1993:** Takara begins production of fruit juice and establishes a biotech research and development and production facility in China.
- **1995:** A European subsidiary in Paris and Takara Korea Biomedical in Seoul are opened.
- **1997:** The company launches its patented RetroNectin reagent; begins production of DNA chips the following year.
- **2000:** ViroMed of Korea is acquired and organic *mirin* is launched.
- **2002:** Takara Holdings is established and two new subsidiaries, Takara Shuzo and Takara Bio, are created.

a joint-venture with Pulmuone to develop and distribute mushrooms in that market, both in 2002. The following year, MolMed granted Takara the exclusive Asian rights for the Italian company's suicide gene and other gene therapies for cancer and AIDS treatment.

With the mapping of the human genome completed in the early 2000s, the biotechnology sector promised explosive

Principal Subsidiaries

AADC Holding Company, Inc. (United States); Age International, Inc. (United States); Beijing Takara Shuzo Brewery Co., Ltd., (China); Dragon Genomics Co. Ltd.; J&W Hardie Ltd. (United Kingdom); Leo Lab Co., Ltd.; Luc Corp. Ltd.; Shanghai Takara Shuzo International Trading Co., Ltd.(China); Singapore Takara Pte. Ltd.; Takara Bussan Co., Ltd.; Takara Butsuryu System Co.,Ltd.; Takara Holding Company (United States); Takara Marketing Business Co., Ltd.; Takara Sake USA Inc.; Takara Yoki Co., Ltd.; Thai Takara Co., Ltd.; The Tomatin Distillery Co., Ltd. (United Kingdom).

Principal Competitors

Asahi Breweries Ltd.; Sichuan Yibin Wuliangye Distillery; Mercian Corporation; Oenon Holdings Inc. Bayer AG; Bristol-Myers Squibb Company; Eli Lilly and Company; Pharmacia and Upjohn Inc.; Novartis Corporation; Clariant International AG; Pfizer Incorporated; Daiichi Pharmaceutical Company Ltd.; Rhodia Recherches; Genentech Inc.

Further Reading

Asayama, Sho, ''Shochu Maker Betting on Biotech,'' *Nikkei Weekly*, September 18, 1995, p. 10.
Chiba, Hitoshi, ''Fermenting Takara Shuzo,'' *Look Japan*, October 2001, p. 24.

—M.L. Cohen

Tamfelt Oyj Abp

PB 427
Tampere
FIN-33101
Finland
Telephone: +358 3 363 91 11
Fax: +358 3 356 01 20
Web site: http://www.tamfelt.com

Public Company
Incorporated: 1942 as Tampereen Verkatehdas Oy –
    Tammerfors Klädesfabriks Ab
Employees: 1,384
Sales: EUR 126 million ($135 million) (2003)
Stock Exchanges: Helsinki
Ticker Symbol: TAF
NAIC: 313210 Broadwoven Fabric Mills

One of Finland's oldest companies, Tamfelt Oyj Abp is also a major European producer of technical and industrial textiles. The company's core product line focuses on producing a full range of paper machine clothing. These products are used to transport paper web during the production process, offering ''dewatering'' and forming functions, as well as protection for the paper-making machinery itself. The company's products including forming fabrics, press felts, shoe press belts, and dryer fabrics. Tamfelt products are marketed under several branded lines, including Transmaster Open, Ecostar, Tambelt, Tamfil, Silverstar, Unistar, among others. Tamfelt operates two plants in Finland, the 60,000-square-meter mill at Tampere, producing press felts, dryer fabrics, belts, filter fabrics, and carrier ropes; and the 20,000-square-meter mill in Juankoski, focused on the production of forming fabrics. Tamfelt's international operations include plants in Portugal, through subsidiary Fanafel, which is Europe's leading producer of laundry felts with an 80 percent market share; in Brazil, where the company specializes in wet filtration products for the mining industry; and through its joint venture plant in Tianjin, China. Finland accounts for the largest share of the group's sales, at more than 38 percent, while the other Scandinavian countries add 10 percent. The rest of Europe

contributes nearly 29.5 percent of group sales, while the North American market adds 9.5 percent to sales. Tamfelt is listed on the Helsinki stock exchange. In 2003, the company posted sales of EUR 126 million ($135 million).

Founding Finnish Industry in the 19th Century

The invention of the first weaving machines in England at the end of the 18th century, coupled with the development of the steam engine, introduced the first modern manufacturing techniques and inaugurated the Industrial Revolution of the 19th century. Finnish manufacturing, as in much of the Scandinavian region, remained mostly undeveloped until then, with the production of goods restricted to craftsmen within the guild system.

The late 18th century, however, saw the emergence of a new type of ''manufacturer,'' in which the owner of a mill was not necessarily a craftsman, or even directly involved in the production process itself. The new manufacturing class evolved in part from the noble class, itself under threat from new democratic and revolutionary ideas. In Finland, then under the control of the Swedish monarchy, a number of the manufacturing groups that appeared during this period grew into dominant positions, both within their markets and in the country's economy as a whole. Such was the case with the Fiskars and Hackman groups, and with a maker of textiles based in Turku province that formed the basis of the later Tamfelt group.

The origin of Tamfelt traced back to 1797, when Ernst Gustaf von Willebrand, then governor of Turku province under the Swedish monarchy, was given permission to set up a water-driven textile mill on his estate in Jokioinen. Willebrand sought to take advantage of the large sheep herd on the estate, producing wool using the new machinery being developed in England at the time. Willebrand installed two of the English-type weaving looms on the estate and production began that year.

Willebrand's factory burned down in its second year. Yet by 1800 the mill had been rebuilt and re-equipped, with new weaving looms and a carding machine, which represented an important advance for the nascent textile manufacturing industry. The mill continued production through the first decade of the 19th century, but faded with Willebrand's death in 1809. Soon after, Finland came under Russian control.

The Jokioinen site was revived in 1838 by Axel Wilhelm Wahren, who went on to become one of Finland's most noted industrialists. By the middle of the 1840s, the Jokioinen mill had become one of the largest in the country. The mill's growth, however, was hampered by inadequate water supply, a situation that led Wahren into dispute with local authorities. Wahren left the company in 1852, having by then founded a new cotton mill in the town later known as Forssa.

Operation of the Jokioinen site was leased to Axel Israel Frietsch, who began looking for a means of overcoming the mill's water shortage problem. By then, the town of Tampere had become an important industrial center in Finland. Tampere had two important features attracting industry: located between the Nasijarvi and Pyhajarvi lakes, the rapids ran right through the city, offering a good supply of water power. In addition, Tampere was a ''free'' city, having been granted an exemption from import duties under Swedish rule. Frietsch began building a new mill in Tampere, which opened in 1859 as AI Frietsch & Co.

The United States had by then become the world's major supplier of cotton. Yet the Civil War severely disrupted cotton imports. Cotton prices shot up as only small quantities of cotton, chiefly from Egypt and India, remained available to the Finnish market. By 1863, Frietsch had declared bankruptcy and the mill was taken over by the Bank of Finland. In 1869, the mill was sold to a group of prominent Tampere-based industrialists, including Axel Wilhelm Wahren and Carl Zuhr.

Zuhr became the mill's manager, and the company was renamed as Tampereen Verkatehdas Osakeyhtiö, Finnish for Tampere Woollen and Worsted Mill. The company remained one of the country's most prominent wool and textiles mills. Yet, Zuhr's interest increasingly turned toward a newly developing Finnish industry, paper.

That industry had been undergoing its own revolution since the mid-19th century with the development of the first papermaking machinery, which used wood instead of cotton or cotton rags as primary material. Finland's large forests made it ideally suited for paper production, and Tampere had boasted a modern paper mill since the 1840s. The rise of the industry, and the increasing sophistication of papermaking machinery created a need for support materials, especially felts, used both as a protective layer between the paper and the machinery, and as means of ''de-watering'' the paper. Zuhr became interested in reorienting the company's production toward machine felts in the late 1870s.

Zuhr was succeeded by Carl Gustaf Angonius Dahlbom, a Swedish native, who became determined to carry out the reorientation envisaged by Zuhr. Dahlbom found an ally in Axel Wahren and together they convinced the company's other

shareholders that the company's future best lay in developing itself as a manufacturer of specialist products, starting with technical felts. The board agreed, and production of felts for paper industry started in 1882. In 1887, that operation became a separate division, Tammerfors Kaldesfabrik.

The initial years of production were fraught with technical and other difficulties. As reported in Tamfelt's 2000 Annual Report, ''The new product line, in itself one of the toughest within the weaving industry, was the source of great trouble for many years. Products that turned out badly, claims and heavy damages, before even a satisfactory manufacturing skill was achieved. In spite of many hardships Mr. Dahlbom continued to develop the product with admirable energy. He took advantage of the experiences gained, and by investigating the way foreign mills made their felts he enhanced his own knowledge and the skill of the workers. Thus the machine felts of the company started slowly to gain foothold in the domestic market.''

The company faced a number of other difficulties in the decades to come. A second fire destroyed the mill in 1888. Although it was rebuilt soon after, the mill once again suffered damage by a flood in 1889. The company made it through World War I; in 1918, during the civil war that followed the Soviet revolution, Tampere became the site of the final battle between the White and Red armies. Although Finland gained its independence as a result, the company's warehouse was destroyed.

Felt Force in the 1950s

Wool, yarn, and textiles remained the company's chief product focus into the second half of the 20th century. Nonetheless, the company's felt production began to grow steadily, boosted by the construction of a new, dedicated plant in 1936. The company was once again hit hard by war, when bombing raids caused heavy damage to its plants. The shortage of raw materials also cut into the company's production. During this period, the company listed its shares on the Helsinki Stock Exchange, taking on the name Tampereen Verkatehdas Oy – Tammerfors Klädesfabriks Ab.

Emerging from World War II, Tammeren now found itself confronted with new competition, in the form of cheaper, foreign-produced wools and a steady stream of new types of textile materials. Yet the strong growth of the Finnish paper industry helped counterbalance the group's dwindling wool sales, as demands for its technical felts and other textiles increased steadily through the 1950s.

The other Scandinavian markets were experiencing a similar boom in paper demand, and by 1956, Tammeren was able to begin exporting its technical textiles for the first time. Soon after, the company began exporting its felts into the rest of Europe and elsewhere in the world.

By the early 1960s, felt production had overtaken the company's wool and consumer textiles operations. The growing focus on technical textiles was highlighted by an extension of the original felt mill at this time. Meanwhile, the company had begun seeking new outlets for its technical expertise and in 1965 began producing filter fabrics as well. By the end of the decade, the company had outgrown its original location.

Key Dates:

1797: Governor Ernst Gustaf von Willebrand begins wool manufacture on his estate at Jokioinen, Finland.
1938: The mill is acquired by Axel Wilhelm Wahren.
1852: Wahren rents the mill to Axel Israel Frietsch, who moves the mill to Tampere in 1859 and renames it AI Frietsch & Co.
1863: The mill defaults to the Bank of Finland, which sells it to a group of investors who change the name to Tampereen Verkatehdas Osakeyhtiö.
1882: Tampere mill launches production of industrial felts for the paper industry.
1936: A new production plant is built for industrial felts.
1942: The company is listed on the Helsinki Stock Exchange as Tampereen Verkatehdas Oy – Tammerfors Klädesfabriks Ab.
1956: The company begins exports of technical felts.
1965: The company begins production of filtering fabrics.
1981: A new technical textiles production facility is introduced, ending production of consumer grade wool and textiles.
1984: Tamfelt acquires Viira Oy.
1986: Tamfelt enters the United States with the acquisition of Draper Felt Company of Massachusetts.
1989: Tamfelt establishes Formtec Inc. in Georgia and begins producing forming fabrics for the U.S. market.
1998: A filter fabrics production subsidiary is established in Brazil.
2000: A joint venture subsidiary begins production in Tianjin, China.
2002: Tamfelt establishes U.S. distribution agreement with Andritz-Ahlstrom.

Construction of a new facility took more than a decade to complete, but by 1981, the company had shifted its machinery and employees to its new and larger manufacturing plant. Not all of the company survived the move, however—at that time, the company decided to leave behind its wool production and transform itself into a focused technical textiles group. As part of that process, the company changed its name to Tamfelt in 1981.

Focused Technical Textiles Group in the New Century

The newly focused Tamfelt now began to expand its operations. In 1984, the company acquired Viira Oy, based in Juankoski, adding that company's forming fabrics capacity. The move helped Tamfelt develop into a full-line paper machine clothing group.

Tamfelt next turned to the United States, where it bought Draper Felt Company, based in Canton, Massachusetts in 1986. The acquisition gave Tamfelt a new felt production facility as well as a springboard into the U.S. market. In 1989, the company extended its U.S. production to include forming fabrics

when it established a second subsidiary, Formtec Inc., in Peachtree, Georgia.

Tamfelt also sought expansion in Europe, and in 1990 the company bought a majority share of Portugal's Fanafel Ltda. The addition of Fanafel not only added to the group's technical textiles capacity, but also brought it new operations in the production of laundry felts, giving Tamfelt the position of European leader for that product segment.

Tamfelt's international extension continued into the turn of the century. In 1998 the company established a new subsidiary in Brazil, Tamfelt Tecnologia em Filtraçao Ltda. That company began producing filtration fabrics specifically for the Brazilian mining industry.

The following year, Tamfelt formed a joint venture with Tianjin Paper Net in Tianjin, China, called Tamfelt-GMCC Paper Machine Clothing Co. Ltd. Production at the new facility began the following year, giving Tamfelt entry into the fastgrowing Chinese paper industry. In 2001, the company acquired full control of Fanafel.

Not all of the group's effort went toward expanding its operations. In 1997 the company shut down Formtec's Georgia site and moved that operation to its Juankoski facility, in part in response to shrinking paper industry demand. In 2002, however, the company strengthened its U.S. presence again through a distribution agreement with Andritz Ahlstrom Inc. While not the largest in its field, Tamfelt remained an important Scandinavian technical textiles producer and one of Finland's historic industrial groups.

Principal Subsidiaries

Fanafel Ltda. (Portugal); Tamfelt – GMCC (Tianjin) Paper Machine Clothing Co, Ltd. (China); Tamfelt Corporation Juankoski Mill; Tamfelt PMC, Inc. (United States); Tamfelt Tecnologia em Filtraçao Ltda. (Brazil).

Principal Competitors

E.I. du Pont de Nemours and Co.; Saint-Gobain SA; ESTAR OU; Toray Industries Inc.; Kanebo Ltd.; Collins and Aikman Corporation; InterTech Group Inc.

Further Reading

''Andritz-Ahlstrom in New Partnerships,'' *Solutions–for People, Processes and Paper,* January 2002, p. 9.
''Tamfelt Corp.,'' *Pulp & Paper,* August 1995, p. 114.
''Tamfelt Oyj Cuts Nine Jobs,'' *Nordic Business Report,* March 12, 2003.
''Tamfelt Reports Net Sales of EUR 131m,'' *Nordic Business Report,* February 13, 2002.
''Tianjin Paper Net,'' *Pulp & Paper International,* December 1999, p. 12.
Toland, Justin, ''Pressing Issues,'' *Pulp & Paper International,* March 2003.

—M.L. Cohen

Tarrant Apparel Group

3151 East Washington Boulevard
Los Angeles, California 90023
U.S.A.
Telephone: (323) 780-8250
Fax: (323) 780-0751
Web site: http://www.tags.com

Public Company
Incorporated: 1988 as Fashion Resource, Inc.
Employees: 6,990
Sales: $347.4 million (2002)
Stock Exchanges: NASDAQ
Ticker Symbol: TAGS
NAIC: 315999 Other Apparel Accessories and Other
Apparel Manufacturing

Los Angeles-based Tarrant Apparel Group designs and manufactures private label women's jeans and other moderately prices casual apparel for women, men, and children. Major customers include such retailers as Abercrombie and Fitch, Chicos, Federated, Kohl's, The Limited, Mervyn's, JC Penney, Kmart, Sears, Target, and Wal-Mart. The publicly-traded company also helps customers to market-test new designs. In recent years, Tarrant has attempted to become a vertically integrated manufacturer. Rather than outsource manufacturing to the Far East, the company acquired a number of facilities in Mexico. The transition prove to be more difficult than anticipated, and in 2003 Tarrant elected to reverse course and return to its previous strategy of acting as a trading company offering design services. In addition to its Los Angeles offices, the company maintains a New York City showroom and customer service offices in Ohio and Arkansas. Tarrant operations are also found in Mexico and Hong Kong.

Tarrant Founder Breaks Away from Sasson in 1985

Tarrant was founded by its chairman, Gerard Guez, younger brother of Paul Guez, who was credited with launching the craze for women's designer jeans. Paul Guez emigrated to the United States from Tunisia in 1976, bringing with him a mere $51 in cash and a bag of tight-fitting, French-cut jeans. Despite his inability to speak English, Guez was able to talk Bloomingdale's into carrying his jeans bearing the label of Sasson (the name of an Israeli partner he soon bought out). Sasson experienced tremendous growth, and soon Guez licensed the Sasson name to any number of products, including watches, eyeglasses, luggage, boots, and even cassette players. In 1981, he brought Gerard and two other brothers into the business, the four of them sharing an equal portion of Sasson Jeans, L.A.—the flagship licensee, selling Sasson women's jeans and pants. It was also in 1981 that Paul Guez reportedly first tried cocaine, and within a matter of years the Sasson empire was in turmoil. According to *The Wall Street Journal,* by 1984 ''family feuding and litigation were burdening the business, Money had stretched the bond between Mr. Guez and his brothers to the breaking point. Never meticulous in corporate bookkeeping, they had treated Sasson as a personal piggybank, sometimes withdrawing large sums as 'officer loans' to avoid income taxes; then they fell out over who owed what to whom.'' Guez would eventually check himself into a drug rehabilitation program and after lapsing into bankruptcy, Sasson Jeans would be dissolved and its trademark sold in 1988. Long before the end, however, Gerard left to launch his own business.

Company Incorporated in 1988

In 1985, Gerard Guez and partner Todd Kay founded what would become Tarrant Apparel Group. A year later they introduced their own brand of designer jeans—NO! Jeans. They enjoyed modest success with this brand line, sold in a variety of retailers, but when they realized that one private label line of seven-button ''flip top'' jeans, produced for The Limited's Express boutiques, generated most of the company's business, the partners decided to enter the women's private label denim market. In 1988, they incorporated the business as Fashion Resource, Inc. The timing proved to be fortuitous, as designer jeans began to lose favor, and less expensive, private label jeans began to pick up in sales. Embracing private label apparel made sense to retailers because the items cost less at wholesale and offered much higher margins than their brand name counterparts. According to *Forbes,* between 1990 and 1998 the private

---

Company Perspectives:

Tarrant is a value-added supplier. We have an in-depth understanding of the fashion and pricing strategies of our customers, which we support with our own teams of expert designers, our sample-making capability, and our ability to assist customers in market-testing designs with quick-turn-around production of "test-order" products.

---

label share of the $18 billion U.S. jeans market grew from 3 percent to 20 percent.

Fashion Resource added customers and supplemented its product line to include casual pants, blouses, shorts, and dresses. In 1991, the company reached $80 million in annual sales, and by 1995 topped $205 million. During this period, the product mix was also diversified. Bottoms accounted for more than 80 percent of sales in 1991 but dropped to just 34 percent in 1995. It was also in 1995 that Fashion Resource changed its name to Tarrant Apparel Group and the company taken public. With Prudential Securities Inc. acting as underwriter, Tarrant raised $16.7 million. Guez continued to own a 46.2 percent stake, Kay 23.1 percent, and The Limited Inc., Tarrant's largest customer, held a 10 percent stake in the business. According to 1994 numbers, The Limited accounted for 61.1 percent of all sales, followed by Target with 14.8 percent and Kmart with 4.7 percent.

In 1996, Guez began to think about returning to the brand apparel business—four years after NO! Jeans were discontinued. The purpose was to broaden the company's distribution mix. Tarrant apparel was already well represented in mass chains and specialty stores, but Guez was eager to break into the department store tier, where brand names were still all important. In addition, designer names such as Calvin Klein, Donna Karan, and Tommy Hilfiger were also thriving during the mid-1990s, adding renewed luster to the brand label business. Moreover, adding brand names would hopefully boost the anemic performance of Tarrant's stock, which had been stagnant since it began to trade a year earlier. A further goal for Tarrant at this stage was to add young men's clothing as part of an effort to create a full casual sportswear line. In August 1997, after searching for more than a year, Tarrant appeared to have acquired a brand, agreeing to pay $23.8 million for bankrupt B.U.M. International Inc., but the deal fell through when the courts rejected the offer.

Tarrant was more successful in its efforts to broaden its product line. In February 1998, it bought assets from Marshall Gobuty International and GBI International Limited, both men's and boy's private label providers. In addition, the acquisitions achieved the goal of adding another big retail account, JC Penney Co. Later in 1998, Tarrant bolstered its men's business with the acquisition of New York-based Rocky Apparel, which manufactured both men's and women's denim wear. Rocky's added about $50 million in annual sales and was expected to greatly help Tarrant reach a target of becoming a $500 million company by the end of decade. An important component in this effort was a major change in strategy for the company, which launched a four-year plan to become a vertically integrated apparel manufacturer.

Rather than outsource to Hong Kong, Tarrant decided to establish its own manufacturing and distribution facilities in Mexico. One of the benefits was a significant increase in delivery time. Items that took 30 days to be shipped from the Far East could now be trucked from Mexico to U.S. customers in 30 hours. In addition, Tarrant could warehouse undyed jeans and hold onto them until retailers could determine which shades were selling the best before placing an order. The items could then be dyed and shipped in two weeks, a month sooner than jeans produced from scratch. Owning its own facilities would also cut Tarrant's costs, thereby improving gross margin. Furthermore, it was expected to more than double the company's revenues in just three to five years. Wall Street took notice, bidding up the price of Tarrant shares from around $8.00 to more than $48, making it one of the fastest growing stocks in the country.

To achieve its vertical integration plan, in April 1999 Tarrant paid $45.3 million in cash and stock for a denim mill located in Puebla, Mexico. Then, in August of that year, the company acquired Industrial Exportadora Famian, S.A. de C.V. and Coordinados Elite, S.A. de C.V. for a total consideration of $10 million. In the deal, Tarrant picked up seven apparel production facilities situated in the Tehuacan, Mexico, area. Subsequent investments of $6 million greatly expanded these operations. In June 2000, Tarrant procured additional manufacturing capabilities by signing an exclusive production agreement with Manufactures Cheja. A major sewing facility located in Ajalpan, Mexico, was then bought for $11 million in March 2001. Finally, in December 2002, Tarrant, through subsidiaries, added an denim and twill manufacturing plant in Tlaxacala, Mexico. As a result of these transactions, Tarrant completed its plan to vertically integrate its business. Company-owned facilities could now provide cutting, sewing, washing, finishing, packing, shipping, and distribution functions. Tarrant also had fabric production capabilities.

Major Losses in 1999

Tarrant's ambitious plan was not without risk, however. The company was saddled with a large amount of fixed costs that it had previously avoided by outsourcing to the Far East, and it now faced the necessity of keeping both equipment and personnel in use. The loss of a major customer could prove problematic, and indeed that is exactly what occurred in 1999 when the Limited turned to Taiwan and South Korean manufacturers, costing Tarrant $80 million in business. The Limited accounted for 66 percent of Tarrant's business in 1998 but now fell to about 40 percent. Even as the company doggedly pursued the implementation of its strategy of vertical integration, investors began to back off. The price of Tarrant's stock tumbled to the $5.00 range and some Wall Street analysts stopped following the company. In addition to the loss of The Limited's business, Tarrant's management also found that the process of reinvention was difficult to balance with the day-to-day running of the business. The transition cost more money than expected and assimilating the new operations was arduous and time consuming. An earthquake that hit Mexico in June 1999 caused further mischief, impacting shipments and contributing to lower-than-expected earnings.

In 1998, Tarrant posted net sales in excess of $378 million and net income of $24.7 million. While revenues improved to

Key Dates:

1985: Company is founded.
1988: The business is incorporated as Fashion Resource, Inc.
1995: The company is taken public as Tarrant Apparel Group.
1998: The company initiates a vertical-integration strategy.
2003: Mexican manufacturing facilities are leased to a third party.

$395.3 million in 1999, net income declined by close to 50 percent, to $12.9 million, due in large part to write-offs involving inventory, debt, and computer upgrades. The financial picture worsened in 2000, as net sales receded slightly, to $395.2 million, and the company recorded a $2.5 million loss. A shakeup in management did not help matters. Barry Aved was appointed president in the fall of 1999 and suddenly resigned several months later, citing personal reasons. Guez and the rest of the management team attempted to stay the course, continuing to pursue its Mexican initiative, but the company lost ground on its stated goal of becoming a $500 million company. Net sales fell to $330.3 million in 2001, as the company lost another 2.8 million.

In October 2001, Guez relinquished the role of chief executive officer to Eddy Tak Yu Yuen, who had been with the company from the start and had most recently served as the president of Tarrant Mexico. However, Guez retained the chairmanship, vowing to remain "as active as ever, opening new markets for the company and finding strategic deals." Nevertheless, business did not improve in 2002. Although Tarrant rebounded on the revenue side to $347.4 million, the company's losses grew in excess of $6 million. Guez replaced Yuen as CEO, and Yuen was dispatched to his native Hong Kong to take charge of subsidiary Tarrant's Fashion Resources Inc. The reshuffling of the top ranks continued when later in the year Barry Aved was called back to once again assume the presidency.

In 2003, Tarrant faced labor problems in Mexico and was criticized by labor rights organizations for firing some 200 workers at its Pubela plant. The company, already changing its tack, elected to lease three of its Mexican manufacturing facilities to an outside party. Tarrant would now devote its resources to once again acting as a trading company, taking advantage of its strong design capabilities. It launched a number of private brand initiatives with major retailers. Newly formed Tarrant subsidiary Private Brands, Inc. acquired a 50 interest in American Rag CIE II and received a long-term exclusive license to design, manufacture, distribute, and sell apparel under the American Rag label. American Rag had something of a cult following for its vintage apparel and portfolio of labels that included Deisel, Ruth, Paper Denim & Cloth, and Marc Jacobs. American Rag also ran stores in Los Angeles and San Francisco, as well as nine franchised stores in Japan. More outlets were planned for Japan and flagship stores were targeted for such U.S. markets as New York and South Beach, Florida.

In exiting its Mexican manufacturing initiative, Tarrant was hit with restructuring costs, but Guez insisted that the company was now on the right track. His view was bolstered to some extent by the company's ability in early 2004 to raise $4 million in a secondary offering of stock.

Principal Subsidiaries

Tarrant Company Limited; Rocky Mexico, Inc.; Tag Mex, Inc.; Industrial Exportadora Famian, S.A. de C.V.; Coordinados Elite, S.A. de United Apparel Ventures.

Principal Competitors

Avondale Incorporated; Cone Mills Corporation; Kellwood Company.

Further Reading

Brinsley, John, "Tarrant's Fortunes Unravel Amid Manufacturing Move," *Los Angeles Business Journal*, April 3, 2000, p. 35.

Kanter, Larry, "Ooh la la . . . Tarrant?," *Los Angeles Business Journal*, November 25, 1996, p. 14.

Medina, Hildy, "Mutating Jeans," *Forbes*, August 23, 1999, p. 88.

Moore, Brenda L., "Clothes Call: Why Analysts Are Enthusiastic Over Tarrant Apparel," *Wall Street Journal*, June 3, 1998, p. CA2.

Sarkisian-Miller, Nola, "Tarrant Gets American Rag Label," *WWD*, April 2, 2003, p. 3.

Sobol, Shayna, "Tarrant Apparel Group Designs Its Own Success," *Apparel Industry Magazine*, June 1997, p. 8.

Wilkinson, Peter, "Storm Swirls Around Brothers Guez," *Daily News Record*, May 3, 1985, p. 11.

—Ed Dinger

Taser International, Inc.

7860 East McClain Drive, Suite 2
Scottsdale, Arizona 85260
U.S.A.
Telephone: (480) 991-0797
Toll Free: (800) 978-2737
Fax: (480) 991-0791
Web site: http://www.taser.com

Public Company
Incorporated: 1993 as Air Taser, Inc.
Employees: 130
Sales: $24.5 million (2003)
Stock Exchanges: NASDAQ
Ticker Symbol: TASR
NAIC: 332995 Other Ordnance and Accessories
   Manufacturers

Taser International, Inc. is a leading manufacturer of stun guns. Its weapons, which it describes as "less lethal," are used by law enforcement officers across the United States and Canada. The company markets its Taser brand stun guns in some 60 other countries as well. While law enforcement and the military make up most of its customers, Taser has also developed models designed for consumers. United Airlines made a major purchase of Tasers to protect its airplane cockpits, and Taser International has a potential wide market among other airlines, pending federal regulation. Unlike other stun guns, the Taser can operate from a distance. It fires small barbs into an attacker, and electrical charges travel along wires through the barbs, delivering incapacitating electronic pulses. The company was founded by two brothers, Patrick and Thomas Smith, and is chaired by their father, Phillips W. Smith. The Smith family owns roughly one-third of the stock of the publicly traded company.

Reinventing an Idea from the 1970s

Taser International, Inc. manufactures and markets several styles of stun guns under the brand name Taser. The word

"taser" apparently originated in a Tom Swift adventure book, part of a ghostwritten series of books about a boy inventor that ran from 1910 through the 1970s. Taser stands for "Thomas A. Swift Electric Rifle." Jack Cover, a NASA scientist, invented and patented the electronic stun gun in 1974, naming it for the invention he recalled from his childhood reading. Cover's original Taser resembled a large flashlight. It used gunpowder to blast two wires at its target. When probes attached to the wires connected to the target's body, the Taser delivered massive but short-lived electrical bursts. These bursts overrode the target's neuromuscular system. Ideally, the target collapsed instantly and remained incapacitated—but essentially unharmed—long enough for the Taser's wielder to escape. Cover marketed his invention through a company called Taser Systems. Taser Systems went into bankruptcy, and it was then sold to an investor who operated it under the name Tasertron. Tasertron was a small business which marketed its products to police departments. The Los Angeles Police Department used Tasertron's Tasers, most publicly in 1991 in the notorious Rodney King case. Police officers fired a Taser at King, but it failed to incapacitate him. The officers then beat King in a videotaped attack that prompted much outrage.

Patrick "Rick" Smith was earning a master's degree in business administration at the time of the Rodney King incident. That same year, two of Smith's friends were shot to death during an angry altercation with a motorist. Smith wanted his mother to have a gun at home, to defend herself, but she would not accept one. Smith brooded over the problem of self-defense, wondering why the public could not buy something less dangerous than a gun for protection. He researched the stun gun used in the King incident, which had evidently failed to work because of a battery problem. As a classroom project, Smith developed a business plan for a new and improved stun gun. When he graduated in 1993, Smith brought his academic project to life. He contacted inventor Jack Cover, and the two began to tinker with the stun gun design. With an investment put up by his brother Tom and other family members, Smith bought the rights to the Taser and made a significant change. Cover's Taser fired its barbs using gunpowder. Because of that, it was classified as a firearm and was subject to all the laws and regulations that governed guns. The Smiths adapted the firing mechanism so that it used a compressed air cartridge. This changed the weapon's classification so that consumers would be able to buy it without a license.

Initial Marketing in the Early 1990s

The Smith brothers incorporated Air Taser, Inc. in Scottsdale, Arizona in 1993. They hired an electrical engineer to design a prototype, and by the end of the year they had a model to show the Bureau of Alcohol, Tobacco, and Firearms. The bureau approved the Air Taser for consumer use, and the new company began selling its product at the 1995 Consumer Electronics Show. Though Air Taser did little advertising, there was enough interest in its product line to give it sales of several million dollars in its first year. Air Taser grew from seven employees to 25, and it began selling through the electronic gadget retailer Sharper Image. Air Taser employed a lobbyist and public relations man to handle regulatory and safety concerns. While stun guns were outlawed in several states, 43 states allowed their sale without the licensing and waiting period that burdened other weapon transactions.

All Air Taser's marketing was initially directed at consumers. It produced a video to show people how the Taser worked, and the brothers demonstrated the Taser at trade shows. However, though the company had strong initial sales, its costs were high, and Air Taser was far from profitable. The Smiths frequently scrambled to meet the payroll of their assemblers and other employees. Air Taser hoped it could reach a broader market by selling to law enforcement agencies, but there were several roadblocks. The Taser still had some operational flaws. Rick Smith showed the product to the Czech National Police Academy in Prague in 1995, when to his mortification the Taser failed to stop a volunteer. This police cadet was able to keep going despite the pain of the Taser attack, and Smith's demonstration came to a humiliating end with the cadet locking him in a wrestling hold. The company went back to the drawing board, developing a different model that set off severe muscle contractions in the target body. This meant that even if a person was impervious to pain—because of rage, psychosis, or whatever reason—the Taser's shock would nevertheless be debilitating. The next step was to sell the Taser to police forces. In this endeavor, Air Taser was blocked by an existing licensing agreement between Jack Cover and the earlier Taser manufacturer Tasertron. Tasertron filed suit against Air Taser, claiming it had the exclusive rights to market Cover's invention to police and military. While Air Taser believed its agreement with Cover let

it sell to the military and police as well, the company did not have the finances to fight the case in court. Consequently, Air Taser settled with Tasertron, agreeing to market only to private consumers until February 1998.

Air Taser thought its consumer sales would jump if ordinary people could see and hear about police using the weapons. Bound by Tasertron's suit, however, the company instead tried to reach consumers with a different product line. The company made an anti-theft device for cars which debuted in 1997. The Auto Taser was similar to a popular anti-theft device called The Club, a metal bar that locked the steering wheel. Car thieves had figured out how to get past The Club by sawing through the steering wheel or by picking the lock. The Auto Taser was a locking metal bar with the addition of a motion sensor. Any movement of the steering wheel activated an alarm. This set off electrical waves that shocked or stunned a would-be thief. Air Taser began selling the Auto Taser through Sharper Image, which ran both retail stores and a mail order catalog. However, the Auto Taser never took off. "No one bought it," Tom Smith told the *Los Angeles Times* (March 21, 2002). "My brother started calling it the Bearded Lady: Everyone wanted to look at it and no one would take it home."

Going Public in 2001

The company was close to bankruptcy several times, but it kept going. In 1998, Air Taser was legally free to market its products to law enforcement agencies. By that year, it had sold more than 100,000 Tasers in the United States and had exported the weapon to some 60 countries abroad. The company began to develop a more powerful Taser and to show prototypes to the law enforcement community. Air Taser used a former Marine, Hans Marrero, to demonstrate the effects of the new model. Marrero had been the Hand-to-Hand Combat Chief of the U.S. Marine Corps, and he had the physical strength and willpower to fight off the effects of the first Air Taser. The new Advanced Taser knocked down even the formidable Marrero in under two seconds. In 1998, the company changed its name to Taser International, Inc., reflecting its growing overseas sales and its development past the Air Taser to more advanced models. In 1999, Taser International demonstrated its new model at the U.S. Marine Corps headquarters and then at a meeting of the International Association of Chiefs of Police. The company got permission to sell its products in Canada in 1999, though stun guns had previously been banned in that country. Taser International began to make sales of its Advanced Taser to police forces and correctional facilities throughout the United States by the end of 1999.

Taser International quickly gained sales in the law enforcement market, and by 2000 more than 500 law enforcement agencies were either using or testing the company's Advanced Taser. Police guarding both the Republican and the Democratic National Conventions in 2000 were equipped with Tasers. The company took in several large orders, including 500 Advanced Tasers for the police force of Albuquerque, New Mexico, and 400 for police in Sacramento, California. Taser still did not turn a profit, despite growing sales. The company needed an infusion of capital in order to keep up with its burgeoning markets. The

Smiths considered selling the company but decided instead to sell shares to the public.

Taser arranged its initial public offering (IPO) with an underwriting firm that had handled several other law enforcement-related businesses, Paulson Investment Company. The firm was to debut on the NASDAQ, and the stock sell-off was intended to raise about $11 million. Unfortunately, the timing of the offering was bad. Many small high-tech companies traded on the NASDAQ, and these stocks had been flying high through the late 1990s into 2000. The stock market started to contract in 2000, and the NASDAQ was particularly hard hit. Over 400 companies went public in 2000, the last good year of the 1990s bull market, compared to only 91 for 2001. Financing was hard to find, and investors were wary of once-hot small cap stocks. Tom Smith, in the *Los Angeles Times* interview cited above, claimed that the IPO market was so poor that "we had to pull brokers from under desks to talk to us."

Taser International went public in May 2001, pricing its shares at $13. The price dropped from there, making the deal a modest success, not one of the eye-popping instant-millionaire IPOs of a few years earlier. However, conditions soon changed drastically. The terrorist attacks on September 11, 2001 jolted the United States into a mode of heightened security. Barely two months after the attacks, United Airlines announced that it was buying Tasers for all its 600 plus planes. Other airlines soon followed suit. This action was taken by the airlines despite the fact that the Federal Aviation Administration (FAA) did not allow arming of pilots. The airlines believed Tasers were the appropriate choice for its cockpit crews for two principal reasons: first, unlike a gun, a Taser did not have the potential of puncturing the aircraft and possibly causing a dangerous loss of pressure; second, the Taser was designed to immobilize its target, not to kill. While the FAA mulled over allowing the defensive weapons on board planes, Taser sales took off. The company's stock price began to rise, and orders poured in from all sides. Taser International finished 2001 in the black, making a profit for the first time since its founding. Revenue stood at $6.8 million.

Wider Markets in the 2000s

The tragedy of September 11 stimulated Taser sales to law enforcement groups, airlines at home and abroad, and to consumers. Since 1998, Taser International had focused its sales on the police and military. Tasers were available in fewer than 100 retail stores. In 2002, the company brought out a model designed specifically for the consumer market. Some 500 retailers were expected to carry the consumer model Taser by the end of 2002. More than a thousand police departments in the United States were using Tasers by that year. Revenue doubled, and the company's long struggle to keep going finally seemed to be paying off. Tasers were also increasingly in the news. *Time* magazine, *Business Week*, the *New York Times* and the *Wall Street Journal* all wrote about the company in 2002 or 2003. There were some cases of deaths of people stunned with Tasers, though the company claimed that medical examinations in every case pointed to another underlying cause for the fatality.

In 2003, Taser International bought out its rival Tasertron. The company spent $1 million to acquire Tasertron's assets and patents. This gave Taser International undisputed rights to the underlying technology and left the company the unquestioned leader in the stun gun market. Taser International also took over Tasertron's pending government contracts. The acquisition gave Taser International new access to some military markets and put an end to the legal squabbling between the two companies. Several months later, the company announced it was spending $2.9 million to build new facilities in Scottsdale. The company brought out a new model that year, the X26, and needed the new plant to meet its growing orders. Law enforcement sales were increasing. Many of Taser's customers were small police departments, but in 2003 the company sold 200 stun guns to the Chicago Police Department, one of the largest police departments in the country. Taser hoped that might lead to more orders from major metropolitan law enforcement bureaus.

Taser International hoped to break $20 million in sales for 2003. The company had phenomenal sales in its fourth quarter and finished the year at $24.5 million. Its stock price took a run, hitting $135 per share in February 2004. The stock had sold a year earlier for only $4. Investors clearly believed the company had bright prospects. Taser's stun guns seemed to be gaining acceptance as standard police equipment, and the company had still not fully tapped the law enforcement market. It also had no serious domestic rivals in its particular market niche. The Smith brothers had run the company at a loss for seven years. By the early 2000s, their persistence seemed to have been well worth it.

Principal Competitors

Talon Self Defense Products; Black Cobra Stun Guns.

Further Reading

Blackwood, Alisa, "Response to Terror: New Taser Guns Aim for Bigger Things," *Los Angeles Times*, November 18, 2001, p. A21.
Coppola, Chris, "Taser Still Awaits Federal Approval for Pilots," *Tribune* (Mesa, Arizona), September 9, 2002.
Eiserer, Tanya, "Police Increasingly Adding Tasers to Arsenal," *Knight Ridder/Tribune News Service*, January 26, 2003.
"For Taser, Sky Could Be the Limit," *Business Week*, March 25, 2002, p. 118.
Gonderinger, Lisa, "Solid Plan Is Firm's Best Defense," *Business Journal Serving Phoenix and the Valley of the Sun*, January 5, 1996, p. 1.
Hamilton, Anita, "Stun Guns for Everyone," *Time*, February 4, 2002, p. 50.
Lunsford, J. Lynn, "Taser Expects Its Sales to Surge Amid More Interest in Stun Guns," *Wall Street Journal*, January 8, 2002, p. B6.

Mungin, Lateef, ''Jail Inmate Subdued with Stun Gun Dies,'' *Atlanta Journal-Constitution*, September 30, 2003, p. B1.

Riordan, Teresa, ''New Taser Finds Unexpected Home in Hands of Police,'' *New York Times*, November 17, 2003, p. C4.

''Scottsdale, Ariz.-Based Stun-Gun Devices Maker Gets Big Deal with Airline,'' *Knight Ridder/Tribune Business News*, November 16, 2001.

''Scottsdale, Ariz.-Based Stun Gun Maker Continues to See Growth,'' *Knight Ridder/Tribune Business News*, September 23, 2003.

''Smaller Deal Size Could Help Taser IPO, Says Analyst,'' *Corporate Financing Week*, May 14, 2001, p. 5.

Spors, Kelly K., and Jonathan Weil, ''Moving the Market—Tracking the Numbers,'' *Wall Street Journal*, February 3, 2004, p. C5.

''Taser International, Inc. Announces Land Purchase for New Corporate Headquarters,'' *PR Newswire*, August 22, 2003, p. 1.

—A. Woodward

Teledyne Technologies Inc.

12333 West Olympic Boulevard
Los Angeles, California 90064-1021
U.S.A.
Telephone: (310) 893-1600
Fax: (310) 893-1669
Web site: http://www.teledyne.com

Public Company
Incorporated: 1999
Employees: 5,300
Sales: $840.7 million (2003)
Stock Exchanges: New York
Ticker Symbol: TDY
NAIC: 333319 Other Commercial and Service Industry
    Machinery Manufacturing; 334511 Search, Detection,
    Navigation, Guidance, Aeronautical, and Nautical
    System and Instrument Manufacturing; 335999 All
    Other Miscellaneous Electrical Equipment and
    Component Manufacturing; 336412 Aircraft Engine
    and Engine Parts Manufacturing; 541710 Research
    and Development in the Physical, Engineering, and
    Life Sciences

Teledyne Technologies Inc. owns a number of aerospace and electronics businesses. Its Continental Motors unit is as leading engine manufacturer for private planes. Spun off from Allegheny Teledyne in 1999, Teledyne Technologies has since sought to widen its focus by buying companies making such high tech products as fuel rods and environmental and industrial sampling equipment. However, the U.S. government continues to be an important customer, accounting for about 40 percent of sales in 2002.

1960s Origins

Ever since he was a boy, Henry A. Singleton wanted to build a large corporation, declaring, "A company like GM, AT&T, Dupont—I want to build a company like that." In 1960, after earning three degrees from MIT and rising to vice-president and general manager of Litton, Singleton decided the time was right. He quit his $35,000 a year job and convinced his assistant and old friend, George Kozmetsky, who had earned a doctorate in commercial science from Harvard, to join him in a new business venture.

Singleton, who in five years had helped raise Litton Industries Inc.'s electronics equipment division to $80 million in sales, decided that success lay in the semiconductor business. Despite an already crowded market, he nevertheless believed that producing semiconductors, the "basic building block of electronics," would lead to other high-technology and high-growth inventions.

Using the money they earned from their Litton stock options, Singleton and Kozmetsky each invested $225,000 to start their business. Singleton became chairman and president of the company they named Teledyne, and Kozmetsky became executive vice-president. Their backgrounds in high technology and innovative ideas quickly paid off. The company achieved first year sales of $4.5 million and employed nearly 450 people. Second year sales of $10.5 million confirmed their success. Sales continued on an upward trend when the company embarked on a series of acquisitions, first in electronics and then in geophysics, to increase the company's strength in businesses related to semiconductors. In 1966, Teledyne bought Vasco Metals Corporation, which started a third wave of acquisitions, in specialty metals. Vasco, with sales of $43 million, specialized in titanium, molybdenum, beryllium, and vanadium alloys.

Later that year, Kozmetsky, whose 130,000 shares of Teledyne were by then worth well over $20 million, retired from the company to become dean of the College of Business Administration at the University of Texas. George A. Roberts, formerly president of Vasco, replaced him as president of Teledyne. Singleton continued on as chairman and chief executive officer. By the end of 1966, Teledyne broke into the 293rd spot in the Fortune 500 ranking with sales of more than $256 million—nearly triple the total of just one year before.

1960s–70s: Acquisitions and Growth

In 1967, Teledyne continued its impressive growth. The company's 16,000 employees were busily making microelec-

358

Company Perspectives:

We serve niche market segments where performance, precision, and reliability are critical. Our customers include major industrial and communications companies, government agencies, aerospace prime contractors, and general aviation companies. We have developed strong core competencies in engineering, software development, and manufacturing that we can leverage both to sustain and grow our current niche businesses and to become an innovator in related higher-growth markets. We seek to grow in niche market segments where we have a strong competitive position, both by development of new products and services and by acquiring businesses that are highly complementary to our current product lines.

tronic integrated circuits, microwave tubes, aircraft instruments, miniature television camera transmitters, hydraulic systems, computers, seismic measuring devices, specialty alloys, and a large variety of other sophisticated products. More good news arrived when the company bettered IBM and Texas Instruments in a government defense contract contest and became the prime contractor for the development of the Integrated Helicopter Avionics System (IHAS). The IHAS was a helicopter control system that used computers to provide "precise navigation, formation flight, terrain following, and fire control" in virtually any kind of weather. Also that year, in a move *Business Week* magazine called a "coup," Teledyne purchased the Wah Chang Corporation, a leading producer of tungsten and columbium and the world's top producer of hafnium, zirconium, and other exotic metals. In addition, to increase the company's assets and provide it with more leverage for future acquisitions, Teledyne moved into the insurance business by purchasing 21 percent of United Insurance Company for $40 a share.

In 1969, Teledyne's sales surpassed the $1 billion mark. The company subsequently stopped its aggressive acquisition program and paid off its short term debts. Wall Street analysts predicted that the acquisition phase was over and that Singleton was turning Teledyne into an operating company. Teledyne's financial condition was quite strong. For the ten years previous to 1971, the company led the Fortune 500 ranking in earnings and earnings per share growth. In the early 1970's, while many conglomerates were experiencing financial difficulties, Teledyne weathered the recession well. Sales increased somewhat with inflation, but net profits remained near $60 million.

In 1972, Argonaut, one of Teledyne's six financial companies, decided to expand from the worker's compensation field into the medical malpractice insurance business. At the same time, the frequency and size of malpractice claims were growing—but premiums did not keep pace. By 1974, Argonaut took a $104 million pretax write-off, resulting in a $31.2 million net loss in insurance operations and a reduction of Teledyne's net profit for the year to $31.5 million. Nine of Argonaut's 11 top officers were fired, and Singleton began running the operations from the company's headquarters in Los Angeles. Argonaut, one of the last large companies in the malpractice market, discontinued underwriting individual policies for the 20,000 physicians it covered. It continued to offer coverage to the 25 percent of the nation's hospitals it covered, but at higher rates and covering fewer risks. In the meantime, the company collected $170 million in reserves against malpractice cases.

Teledyne's problems were compounded in 1973 when the consumer products division lost $1.8 million, mostly because of its Packard-Bell television production unit's failure to capture a large enough share of the West Coast television market. Teledyne reduced production and narrowed the loss to $500,000 the next year.

With the insurance unit and consumer unit problems solved, Teledyne's outlook had improved markedly. Net income soared to $101.7 million on sales of $1.71 billion in 1974. The largest share of profit came from industrial products such as diesel and gasoline engines and machine tools. Insurance operations had improved and were contributing $19 million. The consumer products division showed a healthy profit of $13.1 million because of Water Pik, which had sold a million shower heads at $25 to $40 each. The closing of the Packard Bell television unit had little effect on earnings; it was accomplished so successfully that no final write-down was taken.

In 1976, the company attempted, for the sixth time since 1972, to buy back its stock in order to eliminate the possibility of a takeover attempt by someone eager for the cash reserves the company had accumulated. Altogether, Teledyne spent $450 million buying back its stock, leaving $12 million outstanding, compared to $37.4 million at the close of 1972. With many of the company's divisions showing stronger results and fewer shares outstanding, Teledyne's stock increased from a low of $9.50 per share to $45 per share, becoming the largest gainer on the New York Stock Exchange. Singleton was not content to buy back his own stock, however. Teledyne then purchased 12 percent of Litton's stock, becoming that company's largest shareholder.

By 1978, Singleton's strategy of bringing in new management to replace underachievers appeared to be working. Only one of the 130 profit centers into which the company was divided was losing money. Without a single acquisition, company sales had soared to $2.2 billion, the result of internal growth at an annual rate of 7 percent. Nearly all of Teledyne's units were reporting continued growth and strong positioning in the marketplace. Sales from the company's offshore drilling rig had grown to $80 million from $10 million in 1966. Water Pik's sales reached $130 million, up from $8 million in 1966. Teledyne had also become an important producer of specialty metal. Allvac, which vacuum-melts metals, had surpassed $40 million in sales compared with $1.5 million in 1964. Furthermore, Merla Manufacturing, purchased for only $80,000 with monthly sales of $30,000, had grown to $7 million in sales. Chang had grown from near bankruptcy in 1967 to over $100 million in sales in 1977, and Packard Bell's business was greater than when it sold televisions.

In the meantime, over a two-year period, Singleton took advantage of the company's regained financial strength and used $400 million of the company's earnings to purchase surprisingly large stakes in 11 companies. By 1978, through Teledyne, Singleton had gained effective control of five other companies, owning 22 percent of Litton's common stock, 28.5 percent of Curtiss-Wright, nearly 20 percent of Walter Kidde, 22 percent of Brockway Glass, and 20 percent of Reichhold Chemicals. In addition, he purchased 8 percent of GAF, 5.5 percent of Rexnord, 7 percent of Federal Paper Board, 5 percent of Colt Industries, and 8 percent of Eltra.

Most of the money for these purchases was funneled through Unicoa and Argonaut. Almost all insurance companies keep some of their assets in stock, but most have stock holdings less than their net worth. Argonaut, on the other hand, had accumulated seven times its net worth in stock holdings, which is very unusual in the insurance business. Singleton's action quickly caught the attention of the business press and of the management of the companies whose stock he purchased. Rumors abounded about his possible intentions, some of which speculated that he wanted to merge the companies into Teledyne, particularly his former employer, Litton.

In the end, the merger attempts never materialized. What soon became apparent was that Singleton had actually purchased a number of difficulties. As earnings were being channeled into the stock market, Teledyne was putting only 1.5 percent of manufacturing sales back into research and development and plant and equipment maintenance, more than 25 percent below the average industry investment. Manufacturing operations, cut off from corporate resources, started to lose competitiveness. As a result, Teledyne's divisions lost market shares, contracts, and technological advantages.

Trouble in the 1980s

One of the worst problems the company was confronted with occurred in 1980. Until then, its Continental Motors division in Muskegon, Michigan, supplied diesel engines to all U.S. military tanks, an important contributor to Teledyne's earnings. When the turbine-powered M1 was introduced that year, however, Continental was relegated to the replacement-engine market for existing tanks.

In addition, Wah Chang, which had once enjoyed a virtual monopoly on the free-world production of zirconium, a crucial metal in building nuclear reactors, had lost a large portion of its market share to French companies, which controlled 40 percent of the market. Moreover, Westinghouse Electric Corporation's completion of a new plant threatened to reduce Chang's market share to less than half of the $150 million free-world output. In 1981, the insurance operations, which contributed 25 percent of Teledyne's total revenue, were once again in trouble. These companies, which were not performing well within their industry, lost $79.2 million before taxes.

The stock portfolio, which had been built up at the expense of the rest of the company, was also in trouble during 1982. Overall, Teledyne's stock portfolios had dropped $380 million during the previous year. That unreported loss almost matched the company's earnings of $412 million on sales of $4.3 billion. Part of Teledyne's stock problems were due to its 16 percent investment in International Harvester, which over the previous year and a half had lost $100 million on paper.

The manufacturing plants and service companies continued to perform poorly in several important markets. Water Pik was showing a profit but only by reducing product development, advertising, and marketing expenditures drastically. Ryan Aeronautical, formerly the premier producer of robot aircraft used for military target practice and reconnaissance, lost most of its market share. Ryan's Firebee model controlled 75 percent of the market in the early 1970's, but Teledyne's emphasis on accumulating cash opened the field to more innovative competitors. Northrop Corporation, for instance, introduced less expensive and easier to launch alternatives that used sophisticated electronics to match the Firebee's capabilities.

With the company financially weakened, Teledyne management appeared to adopt a more aggressive strategy in 1982 by making its first large acquisition bid in 13 years. Continental tried to purchase Chrysler's tank division, which was the prime contractor for the M-1 tank. However, General Dynamics Corporation won the bid with a $336 million offer, exceeding Teledyne's offer by $36 million. According to *Business Week,* Pentagon officials were relieved that Continental lost the bid because they considered Continental to be "stagnating."

In 1983, Teledyne's sales fell from $3.24 billion to $2.86 billion, while net profit fell 37 percent to $248.7 million. That same year, Teledyne took a $49.1 million loss on its stake in GAF, and in December 1985 the company sold its 6.7 percent share in GAF.

With Teledyne's financial troubles fully apparent, discord also began to appear in management. High level executives complained increasingly that Singleton, who once claimed to have no specific business plan for the company, was only involved in management when problems developed. Due to the rumbling in management ranks, and because he was increasingly out of touch with the demands of strategic corporate planning, Singleton remained chairman but handed over the day-to-day management operations to George Roberts in 1986. Roberts, formerly the head of Vasco Metals and part of the company's specialty metals business, jumped in as chief executive officer and attempted to right Teledyne's financial difficulties.

Downsizing a Conglomerate in the 1990s

Teledyne seemed to rebound almost immediately under Roberts' leadership. In 1986, the company spun off Argonaut Insurance and began to divest some of the numerous operations it had acquired over the previous 15 years. By 1988, Teledyne was back on track when it reported a profit of $392 million on revenues of $4.5 billion—an impressive return on equity of nearly 20 percent. In 1990, the company spun off its Unitrin insurance group to shareholders and then disposed of its industrial rubber and oilfield equipment units. Even though the employee count had been reduced from 43,000 to 24,000, Roberts was a long way from completing the company's restructuring. In 1991, he announced that Teledyne planned to either close or sell 24 of its facilities.

Mounting legal problems, however, began at this stage to undermine the company's reputation, reduce profits, and interfere with its restructuring strategy. Numerous lawsuits were filed against Teledyne, including accusations of falsifying test results on missile relays, selling defective equipment, lying to cover up commissions on sales of military goods to Taiwan, and bribing both Saudi Arabian and Egyptian officials to procure contracts. Due to a U.S. government investigation into its Relays Division, the company was temporarily prohibited from bidding for any government contracts. Although Teledyne denied most of these charges, the sheer number of them indicated something was wrong with company management.

While continuing with his plans to restructure the company, Roberts also began to deal straightforwardly with Teledyne's legal woes. After 1992, Teledyne pled guilty to many accusations cited in the lawsuits brought against it and paid nearly $30 million to settle charges. The settlement of a federal probe into its Relays Division significantly reduced profits in 1992, but management thought this move was necessary because the U.S. government accounted for more than one-third of Teledyne's business that year. In short, Teledyne did not want to take any chances of losing any future government contracts, especially with the economic upheaval in the defense industry signaled by the end of the Cold War.

In 1993, Roberts retired and was replaced by William P. Rutledge. The new chairman and chief executive officer was from FMC Corporation and had worked at Teledyne in specialty metals since 1986. Rutledge brought in Donald Rice, a former secretary of the U.S. Air Force, to serve as president and chief operating officer. Immediately, the two men set out to repair Teledyne's damaged reputation. While Rutledge began to speed up the final phases of Teledyne's restructuring, Rice supervised the company's internal probe of ethical compliance. Under Rutledge and Rice, Teledyne's operations were consolidated from 65 units into 21 companies, reduced from a high of 130 in 1990. Wholesale layoffs of 1,200 executives followed, which brought the payroll down to almost 22,000.

Going into the middle 1990s, forecasts by Wall Street analysts for Teledyne's consumer products line, commercial use of specialty metals, industrial factory systems, and aviation electronics were very positive, as were conjectures that Teledyne could survive its legal problems. They also warned that Teledyne must repair its reputation, restore its credibility, and narrow its corporate focus.

Teledyne posted net income of $162 million on revenues of $2.57 billion in 1995. It had 18,000 employees at the time. Though Teledyne was profitable, conglomerates were finding themselves out of fashion on Wall Street in the 1990s. Cuts in military spending had given TeleDyne's defense-related units no room to grow.

In August 1996, Teledyne, Inc. was acquired by Allegheny Ludlum Corp., a Pittsburgh-based producer of stainless and specialty steels. The two companies each became wholly owned subsidiaries of Allegheny Teledyne Inc., a nearly $4 billion business with a total of 24,000 employees. WHX Corp., a producer of carbon steel, had launched a hostile takeover attempt but was outbid. According to the *Pittsburgh Post-Gazette,* Ludlum had been interested in Teledyne's specialty metals business since the mid-1980s.

Teledyne Tech Spun off in 1999

In 1999, Allegheny Teledyne spun off two divisions in order to focus on its specialty metals business. The consumer division became Water Pik Technologies. At the same time, three aerospace and electronics businesses were spun off into the newly created Teledyne Technologies, Inc. After the spin-off, Allegheny Teledyne itself was renamed Allegheny Technologies.

The businesses that formed Teledyne Technologies included Electric Technologies, Brown Engineering, Continental Motors, and Cast Parts. Their combined 1998 revenues were $800 million.

Teledyne Technologies was based in Century City, California, and headed by Robert Mehrabian, formerly president of Pittsburgh's Carnegie Mellon University and a professor of metallurgy and mechanical engineering. Shortly after the spin-off, Teledyne completed a secondary public offering that brought in a net of about $90 million. In 1999, government work had accounted for 40 percent of revenues. Developing products for the commercial marketplace was then a priority.

The company invested $20 million in fiber optics in a bid to enter the then booming broadband communications business. It had already been producing fiber-optic components for the military. Teledyne was also developing wireless applications.

Fuel cells were another area of interest. In 2001, Teledyne combined its energy systems business with that of Energy Partners, Inc., a Florida company dedicated to commercializing proton exchange membrane (PEM) fuel cell components and systems.

Teledyne then deepened its involvement in the growing environmental monitoring and pollution control market by acquiring Advanced Pollution Instrumentation (API) and Monitor Labs. API alone had sales of about $16 million a year. Teledyne CEO Robert Mehrabian described its business as highly complementary to Teledyne's precision electronics line.

Defense Fuels Growth after 9/11

The defense electronics business grew, fueled by the F-22 fighter and Comanche helicopter programs. New military applications, such as monitoring submarines, were developed for the company's Geophysical Instruments line.

The Systems Engineering Solutions segment was chosen as a subcontractor for Boeing's Ground-based Midcourse Defense (GMD) missile and continued Teledyne's near 50-year relationship with NASA by winning prime contractor status for microgravity science payloads for the International Space Station.

Teledyne's commercial aviation business suffered to an extent along with the rest of the industry. However, Teledyne was able to adapt some of its commercial avionics for military use. Continental Motors was experiencing several years of growth on the wings of aircraft manufacturers such as the highly successful Cirrus Design.

Sales were $840.7 million in 2003, up $68 million from the previous year. Net income rose from $25.4 million to $29.7 million. The company benefited from the post-9/11 increase in defense spending as well as a recovery in some of its commercial electronics businesses.

In 2003, Teledyne had acquired Aviation Information Solutions, a $17 million producer of flight deck and cabin displays, from Spirent plc for $6.85 million. In February 2004, the company announced it was buying assets of Leeman Labs, Inc., a producer of spectrometers used for environmental and quality control sampling, for $8 million.

Principal Subsidiaries

Advanced Pollution Instrumentation Inc.; Aerosance Inc.; Teledyne Brown Engineering Inc.; Teledyne Continental Motors Inc.; Teledyne Controls; Teledyne Electronic Technologies; Teledyne Electronic Technology; Teledyne Energy Systems Inc.

Principal Divisions

Aerospace Engines and Components; Electronics and Communications; Energy Systems; Systems Engineering Solutions.

Principal Competitors

Lockheed Martin Corporation; Northrup Grumman Corporation; Raytheon Company.

Further Reading

Belgum, Deborah, "Teledyne Tops List Thanks to Spinoff Circumstances," *Los Angeles Business Journal*, May 1, 2000, p. 15.

Biddle, RiShawn, "A Renewed Focus on Aviation Helps to Give Teledyne a Lift," *Los Angeles Business Journal*, December 8, 2003, p. 25.

Boselovic, Len, "Allegheny Teledyne Splits Up," *Pittsburgh Post-Gazette*, September 15, 1999, p. F1.

Brinsley, John, "Fiber-Optic Future Seen as Good Strategy for Teledyne," *Los Angeles Business Journal*, December 25, 2000, p. 34.

"Let's Make a Deal," *Pittsburgh Post-Gazette*, April 2, 1996, p. A1.

Mehta, Seema, "Allegheny Spinoffs Will Create L.A. Company," *Los Angeles Times*, January 20, 1999, p. C2.

Norman, James R., "A New Teledyne," *Forbes*, September 27, 1993.

Peltz, James F., "Requiem for a Conglomerate," *Los Angeles Times*, August 15, 1996, pp. D1ff.

"Teledyne, Energy Partners Combine Units," *Fuel Cell Technology News*, August 2001.

—updates: Thomas Derdak and Frederick C. Ingram

Tilia Inc.

303 Second Street, North Tower, Floor 5
San Francisco, California 94107
U.S.A.
Telephone: (415) 371-7200
Toll Free: (800) 777-5452
Fax: (415) 896-6469

Wholly Owned Subsidiary of Jarden Corp.
Incorporated: 1990
Employees: 150
Sales: $184 million (2001)
NAIC: 333319 Other Commercial and Service Industry
    Machinery Manufacturing

Tilia Inc. is a manufacturer and distributor of vacuum packaging systems used to store food. Tilia's kitchen appliances are sold under the names FoodSaver and FreshSaver. The company also sells a variety of accessory products intended for use with its vacuum packaging systems, including bags, canisters, and jar sealers. Tilia's products are sold in warehouse retail outlets, discount stores, grocery stores, through a company-operated Web site, and through infomercial programs aired on television. Acquired by Jarden Corp. in 2002, Tilia also markets its products overseas through partnership agreements.

Origins

Tilia began with an innovation, a vacuum packaging system developed by a German inventor named Hanns Kristen. Kristen's experimentations were driven by his belief that the vacuum systems in existence fell short of being true to their name. He surveyed the products on the market in the mid-1980s and discovered that most of the vacuum systems available sealed bags without first removing all the air from the bags. In 1987, Kristen succeeded in developing what would become known as the ''FoodSaver,'' a product with impressive capabilities whose success was stalled by the absence of effective marketing support.

The advantages afforded to the consumer by the FoodSaver family of products were enticing, but relatively few consumers were aware of the novel product until years after Kristen's pioneering work. It took roughly a decade before FoodSaver was able to shed its anonymity and draw the attention of U.S. consumers. The person responsible for igniting the interest in Kirsten's invention joined Tilia about three years after the introduction of the FoodSaver on the market. In 1993, Linda Graebner was named president and chief executive officer of Tilia, the parent company of Nationwide Marketing, which was directly involved with marketing the unique vacuum packaging system developed by Kristen.

Graebner was responsible for broadcasting the merits of the FoodSaver to consumers in the United States. She joined Tilia after vacating her post as vice-president of marketing for the Dole Food Company. At the time of her arrival, Nationwide Marketing sold three different models of the FoodSaver: the FoodSaver II, the FoodSaver Professional, and the Food Saver Compact. Although there were features that distinguished each model, all three included two-way cutting blades, jar-sealing attachments, and instructional videos. Additionally, the company marketed the VacuSave Commercial Vacuum Packaging System, which was designed for food sealing and storage for institutional users. Aside from equipment, Tilia, through Nationwide Marketing, offered a variety of accessories that included the company's patented VacLoc bags, canisters, and jar sealers.

The company and the products Graebner took charge of in 1993 possessed qualities that were sufficient, in retrospect, to attract customers. The FoodSaver family of counter-top products employed powerful piston pumps to remove air from Tilia's VacLoc bags, enabling food to remain fresh three to five times longer than if the food were refrigerated in a conventional manner. The reusable bags, which were boilable, microwaveable, and washable, featured a nylon layer that provided a complete oxygen, moisture, and odor barrier. As opposed to canning, vacuum packing did not sterilize food, thereby making it shelf-stable, but by removing air, vacuum packaging dramatically slowed the deterioration of food caused by air. For the consumer, vacuum packaging promised a savings of time and money, enabling users to buy in bulk quantities and retain freshness far longer than traditional food storage methods offered.

Graebner realized the strengths of Tilia's vacuum packaging system when she took the helm in 1993. Shortly after her appointment, she agreed to an interview with *HFD—The Weekly Home Furnishings Newspaper* that revealed her thoughts about her new company. In the June 14, 1993 interview, she said: "With my background, clearly my arrival is a commitment to build the business and to increase our marketing efforts. I have quite a bit of advertising experience through doing a lot of television commercials at Dole. My view of this opportunity is that FoodSaver is clearly the premier product in this category, and we want to create more awareness about its superiority. Our machine is patented and the only true vacuum saving product and we want to create some more awareness about it."

Graebner realized the importance of delineating the strengths of the Food Saver family of products from the beginning of her tenure at Tilia. It would take several years, however, before she could broadcast the marketable qualities of a genuine vacuum packaging system to the public to an extent that could foster significant sales growth. A private company backed by venture capital, Tilia lacked the financial resources to deliver an effective, broadly based message to the public. In time, once the financial resources were available, Graebner's vision was manifested in an effective marketing campaign that vaulted FoodSaver onto the national stage, thereby delivering exponential sales growth to Tilia.

Tilia generated less than $10 million in annual sales when Graebner assumed responsibility for spearheading FoodSaver's marketing campaign. The company's revenue volume did not increase substantially in the years immediately following Graebner's arrival, but the momentum toward greater growth began to build not long after she joined the company. Historically, Tilia had garnered the bulk of its sales from distributing FoodSaver models to club stores, the membership discount stores frequented by consumers who preferred to buy in bulk quantities. To a lesser extent, the company advertised FoodSaver on cable television shopping channels. The breadth of distribution began to widen in 1995, however, when a new vice-president of sales, Jim Schnabel, joined Tilia. The team of Graebner and Schnabel began to plan for FoodSaver's introduction into department stores. For the most expensive models of the company's vacuum packaging system, retail prices were reduced from $300 to $230. The financial goal, as articulated by Schnabel in 1995, was to increase sales 15 percent for the year and between 15 percent and 20 percent for 1996.

Rapid Growth in the Late 1990s

Despite the efforts to broaden distribution, annual sales did not increase with the percentage gains that later confirmed FoodSaver's maturation into a product of national recognition.

The foray into department stores failed to capture the interest of consumers. FoodSaver was a product whose novelty proved to be its own undoing. "It is a product that doesn't sell itself," Graebner explained in an October 11, 1999 interview with *HFN—The Weekly Newspaper for the Home Furnishing Network*. "It needs description and education," she added. Patrons of department stores looked at the FoodSaver and, presumably, were confronted by a product whose value they little understood. A different way of effectively delivering the value of FoodSaver needed to be found to unlock the potential of vacuum packaging to the public. Toward the end of her fifth year in charge of Tilia, Graebner found the ideal way to relate FoodSaver's worth.

During the late 1990s, no better format existed to describe and to demonstrate the capabilities of a product to a mass audience than an infomercial. Tilia aired its first infomercial in December 1998, a program that featured the FoodSaver Compact II, one of three models offered by the company. At the time of the infomercial's debut, Tilia was ending a year during which it collected $18.5 million in sales. From this point forward, the company began to record robust financial growth, as it at last found a way to preach to potential customers. During the first six months of 1999, Tilia sold more FoodSaver vacuum packaging systems than it did during the previous year. The broadcast of the infomercial was part of an aggressive marketing campaign unleashed in 1999, an advertising program that also included marketing FoodSaver through print catalogs and through traditional retail advertising methods. Infomercials were the deciding factor in the ascendance of FoodSaver, however, injecting Tilia's signature product line with unprecedented vitality. The effectiveness of the company's infomercials also had a beneficial effect on the retail success of the FoodSaver line. "It [the infomercial] is clearly driving retail business," Graebner explained in her October 11, 1999 interview with *HFN-The Weekly Newspaper for the Home Furnishing Network*. "Because when you promote it on television," she added, "the subsequent retail business is strong. Consumers are seeing the infomercial and walking into their retailer and purchasing the product."

Fueled by the aggressive marketing campaign, Tilia's revenue volume swelled dramatically as the company ended its first decade of existence. Sales increased from less than $20 million in 1998 to more than $80 million in 1999. By 2000, when infomercials accounted for one-quarter of the company's sales, the effect of the marketing campaign on Tilia's retail business was evident, its growth sparked by the increased awareness of FoodSaver. Between 1998 and 2000, the company's retail distribution quadrupled, confirming Graebner's belief that the infomercials would not only add another source of revenue but also spur growth in Tilia's retail sales. "We had the products, but the biggest challenges for us was educating consumers," Graebner explained in an October 27, 2000 interview with *San Francisco Business Times*. "The cable shows created a wide audience and brought us new accounts such as Wal-Mart and Kmart."

While in the midst of watching the company expand at a rapid pace, Graebner began to pay increasing attention to Tilia's presence overseas. At the end of 2001, when the company recorded $184 million in sales, Tilia signed an agreement with Sanyo to help bring FoodSaver to the Japanese market. The agreement, which gave responsibility to Sanyo for the distribution and marketing of the vacuum packaging appliance in Japan, was not the first international partnership Tilia forged but it was the most important overseas deal the company made. In an interview with *HFN-The Weekly Newspaper for the Home Furnishing Network*, Graebner marked the occasion by articulating her commitment to the further development of Tilia's international business. "A big part of our message," she said, "is we're continuing to look for strong partners to broaden our base, and we really want them to be partners, not just distributors. Right now we're really focusing on international growth and looking for potential candidates."

Buyout in 2002

Graebner's efforts to orchestrate Tilia's international expansion soon were overshadowed by events on the company's domestic front. During the spring of 2002, merger negotiations were underway that would lead Graebner to forsake Tilia's independence for the benefits of joining another company. The discussions sprang from a relationship with Alltrista Corp., the dominant player in the home-canning business. Tilia had used Alltrista's Ball brand of jars to demonstrate the advantages of using FoodSaver's vacuum packing system in home canning, which led the two companies to entertain the idea of merging their operations. The central figure leading the negotiations was Alltrista's chief executive officer, Martin Franklin, who assumed control over the company in September 2001 and immediately began to make sweeping changes at the company. Franklin moved the company's headquarters to Rye, New York, trimmed its involvement in the industrial market, and focused Alltrista's effort on the consumer market. In a March 29, 2002 interview with the *San Francisco Chronicle*, Franklin explained his reasoning behind the interest in Tilia. "We looked at the home preservation industry," he said, "and really the market leader that's carved out an entire sector on their own is Tilia."

There were benefits for each company in the corporate union. Franklin expected the acquisition of Tilia to immediately increase Alltrista's earnings and double the size of its consumer business. For Tilia, there were several advantages to be gained by being absorbed by Alltrista, which possessed a much bigger distribution network than Tilia's. Alltrista's distribution network included a strong presence in grocery store chains, an area of the retail sector where Tilia enjoyed little exposure. Furthermore, the deal promised to give Tilia greater access to capital. Alltrista agreed to pay $145 million for Tilia and assume responsibility for $15 million of Tilia's debt, as well as to award Tilia as much as $25 million in cash or stock during the ensuing three years provided certain profit requirements were met. The merger, which combined Tilia's $184 million in sales with Alltrista's $241 million in sales, was completed in April 2002. "This is the marriage of a sales- and marketing-strong company [Tilia] with a manufacturing- and distribution-strong company [Alltrista]," Franklin remarked in an April 8, 2002 interview with *HFN-The Weekly Newspaper for the Home Furnishing Network*.

Several weeks after the merger was completed, Alltrista changed its name to Jarden Corp., a change in identity meant to signal the company's emphasis on the consumer market. Under the control of Jarden, Tilia retained much of its independence, operating as separately managed subsidiary within a decentral-

ized organizational structure. Graebner kept her titles as the company's leader, presiding over a new era of Tilia's existence.

As Tilia moved forward, the company was expected to benefit from the support of Jarden. One significant change to Tilia's operations that occurred under Jarden's control was the company's partnership with a leader in the food preparation market. In late 2003, Jarden acquired VillaWare Manufacturing, a maker of small electric kitchen appliances, cookware, and kitchen tools such as waffle makers and panini grills. Jarden combined VillaWare's and Tilia's marketing and operations functions, although the two companies' sales forces remained independent of each other. In the years ahead, as Tilia attempted to capitalize on the spreading awareness of its product, the exploitation of Jarden's distribution network promised to deliver robust growth. At the time of its acquisition by Jarden, Tilia had reached only 3.5 percent of the nation's households, a percentage figure that Graebner hoped to significantly increase in the future.

Principal Subsidiaries

Tilia Direct, Inc.

Principal Competitors

American Household, Inc.; Conair Corporation; Newell Rubbermaid Inc.

Further Reading

"Alltrista to Acquire Tilia International, Inc.," *Gourmet Retailer*, May 2002, p. 20.

Cariaga, Vance, "Jarden Corp.," *Investor's Business Daily*, September 6, 2002, p. A7.

"Foodstuff," *Houston Chronicle*, August 29, 2001, p. 2.

Ginsberg, Steve, "Food Rapper Tilia Zips up Revenue with Road Show," *San Francisco Business Times*, October 27, 2000, p. 19.

Hill, Dawn, "Schnabel Steers Tilia's FoodSaver," *HFN-The Weekly Newspaper for the Home Furnishing Network*, October 2, 1995, p. 68.

"More Tilia Vac Packaging Lines," *HFN-The Weekly Newspaper for the Home Furnishing Network,* January 12, 1998, p. 118.

Porter, Thyra, "Tilia Vacuums up Market; Informercial Educates Consumers about Packaging Food," *HFN-The Weekly Newspaper for the Home Furnishing Network*, October 11, 1999, p. 82.

Quail, Jennifer, "Sanyo to Distribute Tilia's Line of FoodSaver Appliances in Japan," *HFN-The Weekly Newspaper for the Home Furnishing Network*, December 17, 2001, p. 46.

——, "Sealing the Deal; Alltrista's Acquisition of Tilia Is Expected to Create a New Force in Food Preservation," *HFN-The Weekly Newspaper for the Home Furnishing Network*, April 8, 2002, p. 50.

——, "Jarden Acquires Villaware, Combines It with Tilia Inc.," *HFN-The Weekly Newspaper for the Home Furnishing Network*, October 27, 2003, p. 3.

Renstrom, Roger, "Alltrista Pays $160 Million to Acquire Tilia," *Plastics News*, May 6, 2002, p. 9.

Sarkar, Pia, "Alltrista to Acquire San Francisco's Tilia," *San Francisco Chronicle*, March 29, 2002, p. B2.

Thomas, Laura, "Taking the Bad Air Out," *San Francisco Chronicle*, October 6, 2001, p. WB2.

"Tilia and VillaWare Join Forces," *Gourmet Retailer*, December 2003, p. 8.

"Tilia Taps Graebner for President, CEO," *HFD-The Weekly Home Furnishings Newspaper*, June 14, 1993, p. 59.

—Jeffrey L. Covell

Tong Yang Cement Corporation

Tongyang Security Building, 23-8 Ye
Seoul
South Korea
Telephone: (+82) 2 3770 3000
Fax: (+82) 2 3770 3305
Web site: http://www.tongyangmajor.com

Wholly Owned Subsidiary of Tong Yang Major Co.
Incorporated: 1957 as Tong Yang Cement Industrial Co.
   Ltd.
Employees: 1,460
Sales: KW 524.16 billion ($1.25 billion)(2002)
NAIC: 327310 Cement Manufacturing; 327320 Ready-
   Mix Concrete Manufacturing

Tong Yang Cement Corporation is one of South Korea's two leading cement producers and is among the world's largest specialized cement manufacturers, with a total production capacity of close to 14 million tons per year. The company's primary production facility is in Samchok, which churns out more than ten million tons of cement per year. With seven fully automated kilns, the Samchok site claims to be the world's largest single cement production facility. Tong Yang also operates plants at Donghae and Kwangyang, which each produce more than one million tons per year. The company specializes in the production of slag cement (which uses waste materials from iron production to produce a fortified cement), producing more than 1.1 million tons per year. Tong Yang's cement production is backed by limestone quarries with reserves of some 100 years. The company also operates cement silos in Busan, Ulsan, Changwon, Yosu, Gunsan, and Incheon, giving it full coverage of the national market. Tong Yang pioneered cement exports from Korea, operating a fleet of bulk carriers to supply the Japanese, Chinese, and U.S. markets. In addition to production, Tong Yang has its own research and development center where it develops new cement production technologies. Tong Yang Cement forms the core of a diversified *chaebol,* or conglomerate, Tong Yang Major, through which it is listed on the Korea Stock Exchange. Tong Yang Cement is led by CEO Roh Young-in.

Rebuilding Korea in the 1950s

Tong Yang Cement Industrial Co. Ltd. was founded in 1957 as part of South Korea's efforts to rebuild following the devastation of the Korean War. Headquartered in Seoul, the company began construction of its factory in Samchok in order to take advantage of the region's extensive limestone deposits. The Samchok plant launched operation with a production capacity of just 80,000 tons per year.

Yet the company quickly began expanding the facility, and in 1959 the enlarged plant reached production levels of more than 180,000 tons. Tong Yang moved its headquarters to Samchok in 1961, and, backed by a government loan of more than $2 million, completed its second expansion that year. By the end of 1961, production had risen to 380,000 tons.

Korea's industrial development in the 1960s and 1970s created a steady demand for cement, and Tong Yang responded by continuing to expand its production capacity. By 1967, as its annual production topped one million tons, Tong Yang became Korea's largest private cement producer. The group continued its expansion into the 1970s, boosting capacity at the Samchok site to three million tons after a fourth major extension of the facility in 1975.

Tong Yang went public in 1976 with a listing on the Korea Stock exchange, anticipating the coming boom in the Korean economy with still more dramatic plans to increase capacity, while at the same time extending its operation to a national scale. In 1978, the company completed the fifth extension to the Samchok site, where capacity reached four million tons. The following year, a new production facility was opened at Bukpyung. At the same time, Tong Yang expanded its product range, and, in addition to raw cement, began offering ready-mix concrete (RMC) with the construction of an RMC plant in Seoul. These installations were complemented with the opening of a production facility in Yeosu in 1980.

Diversification in the 1980s

Tong Yang continued to add production sites, constructing facilities in Anyang and Jinju in 1983 and in Juju, Daejeon, and Gimje in 1984. The company also expanded its RMC production, building two new plants in Jumunjin and Iksan. The Samchok plant nevertheless remained Tong Yang flagship, and, after completing a new expansion in 1985, boosted its capacity to five million tons per year. Also in 1985, the company changed its name to Tong Yang Cement Co.

With business booming in the 1980s, Tong Yang continued adding to its production capacity. By 1990, the Samchok plant's capacity topped eight million tons. In 1993, the Samchok site featured seven fully automated kilns, enabling the plant to pass the 11 million tons per year mark, making it the world's single largest cement production site. In the meantime, Tong Yang had continued to extend its national network of cement silos, RMC plants, and related production sites. In 1985, the company included among these new facilities a plant in Kwangyang that produced specially reinforced slag cement using waste products from iron producers. The following year, Tong Yang opened its Institute of Technology, adding research and development capabilities.

By then, the company's operations had become increasingly diversified, as Tong Yang added production of industrial machinery and a shipping department. The company also began manufacturing home appliances, starting with gas ovens, under the Tong Yang Magic name, as well as developing interests in confectionery. By then, Tong Yang had moved into the financial markets with the 1984 acquisition of Ilkook Securities, which was renamed to Tong Yang Securities. That subsidiary was then listed on the Korean Stock Exchange in 1987.

Tong Yang was well on its way to becoming another of Korea's *chaebols.* The company launched assets management operations, as Tong Yang Capital Management Co., in 1988, then became a venture capital provider through new subsidiary Tong Yang Venture Capital in 1989. The following year, the company acquired Daewoo Investment & Finance, which was then renamed Tong Yang Investment & Finance. Also in 1990, Tong Yang launched a commodities trading subsidiary, Tong Yang Futures America, in Chicago.

During the 1990s, the company began to spin off a number of its diversified operations into independent subsidiaries. In this way, the company created Tong Yang Shipping Co. in 1991 and Tong Yang Machinery & Engineering Co in 1992. In the latter year, the company also launched Orion Asset Management Co., based in New York City, which complemented its new European operations, Tong Yang Securities Europe, based in London. In other diversification moves, the company entered the information technology market in 1991 and launched a construction division in 1992. Another subsidiary, Tong Yang Industrial Machine, took over the group's growing appliance business, and, in 1996, was renamed Tong Yang Magic Co.

Specialized Cement Producer in the New Century

Despite its diversification, cement and concrete production remained Tong Yang's largest business. In the late 1980s, increases in the company's production levels enabled it to begin exports, starting with Japan, where the company opened a subsidiary in 1988. Mainland China also became a major export market for the company, prompting Tong Yang to open a subsidiary in Beijing in 1993. By 1996, the company had built its own Chinese production facilities, including raw cement and RMC plants in Beijing. The group's investment in bulk carriers later enabled it to become a low-cost shipper, leading Tong Yang to enter the U.S. market in the 1990s as well. By 1995, Tong Yang had recorded a new production milestone—100 million tons per year.

Hit hard by the economic crisis of the late 1990s, especially the collapse of the Korean construction market, Tong Yang was forced to restructure. Leading the group was newly appointed CEO Roh Young-in. Roh moved quickly to reorganize the group, slashing its executive team from 23 to just 9. Roh also began selling off a large number of the group's properties, including a number of its plants, helping to raise cash to pay down its debt. In addition, Roh began lobbying the Korean government to change its regulations so that the country's *chaebols* could reform under a holding company structure.

Roh's efforts were successful, and in 2000 the company reorganized, creating a new holding company, Tong Yang Major Co. Nevertheless, the large cement backlog built up at the end of the previous decade forced the company to seek added cash. The company stepped up its export efforts and by 2003 had increased that part of its sales to more than one million tons per year.

In 2001, Tong Yang Major announced its interest in selling part of Tong Yang Cement. By November 2001, the company had reached an agreement to sell 25 percent of the cement business to France's Lafarge Group in a deal worth KW 137.5 billion (U.S.$116 million). The company was then spun off into a new joint-venture, Tong Yang Cement Corporation. The agreement to sell the stake in its core business was seen as a prelude to an eventual complete takeover of the Korean cement business by Lafarge, especially since Tong Yang Major announced its intention to redevelop itself as a leading e-business group.

With the construction sector once again on the rise, and with its increasing export business, Tong Yang Cement had once again become profitable in the early 2000s, posting a net profit of KW 72 billion (U.S.$55 million) in 2002. By the end of 2003, the company was able to buy out its joint venture partner, paying Lafarge $138 million to complete the transaction. As Roh told *JoongAng Daily,* "Since the 1997–98 financial crisis, numerous companies have been taken over by foreign capital due to financial difficulties. But we will be a rare case to have regained the stake we had sold after only two years. I think the ruthless restructuring and export-centered strategy have worked. The timely boom in the construction business also helped." After nearly 50 years as a major cement supplier to Korea, and the world, Tong Yang had laid a strong foundation for its future.

Principal Competitors

Kumgang Korea Chemical Company Ltd.; Ssangyong Cement Industrial Company Ltd.; Sung Shin Cement Manufacturing Company Ltd.; Hyundai Cement Company Ltd.; Asia Cement Manufacturing Company Ltd.; Hanil Cement Company Ltd.; Koryo Cement Manufacturing; Union Corp.

Further Reading

Hong, Seung-il, "Cement Company CEO Proud of Turnaround," *JoongAng Daily,* December 15, 2003.

"Tong Yang Cement Changes Name to Tong Yang Major," *Korea Herald,* July 17, 2000.

"Tong Yang Major Forms Joint Venture with Lafarge," *Korea Times,* November 30, 2001.

"Tong Yang Major to Spin off Cement Division," *Korea Herald,* November 10, 2001.

"Tong Yang's 2.5 Million Ton Kiln on Stream," *World Cement,* March 1991, p. 11.

"Tong Yang Will Be 1st Chaebol with Holding Company," *Korean Industry,* December 1, 1999.

—M.L. Cohen

The Topaz Group, Inc.

126/1 Krungthonburi Road
Banglampoo Lang
Klogsarn
Bangkok, 10600
Thailand
Telephone: (+66) 24394621
Fax: (+66) 24378814
Web site: http://www.topazgroup.com

Public Company
Incorporated: as H&H Energy Corporation
Employees: 1,750
Sales: $22.9 million (2002)
Stock Exchanges: American
Ticker Symbol: TPZ
NAIC: 339911: Jewelry (Except Costume Manufacturing)

The Topaz Group, Inc., a vertically integrated manufacturing company based in Bangkok, Thailand, is engaged in the production and selling of jewelry and such gemstones as amethysts, emeralds, rubies, sapphires, and topaz. The company is comprised of three Thailand-based subsidiaries: Creative Gems & Jewelry Co., LTD; Advance Gems and Jewelry Co., LTD; and Advance Manufacturing Co., LTD. Because the United States is its major market, accounting for 80 percent of all sales, Topaz maintains an operation in Issaquah, Washington, which combines marketing with a customer service and distribution center. The company also has offices in Canada and Brazil. By merging with an obscure U.S. corporation, Topaz has been able to gain a listing on the American Stock Exchange, a first for a Thai country. As a result, Topaz has gained access to America capital markets as part of a plan to become a major international player in the jewelry industry.

Although it is positioned to produce jewelry using any gem stone, the company concentrates on topaz stones, primarily because it is able to control the entire manufacturing process. Topaz has ties to mines in Brazil, Africa, India, and Sri Lanka, giving it a steady source of the highest quality rough stones. It also has mass production capabilities for cutting and polishing the stones cut from this material. Finally, the company has a long-term, exclusive agreement to use the nuclear research reactor at the University of Missouri to treat the cut gemstones with an irradiation process, which turns them to their signature blue color. When mined, topaz stones are white. To make them blue, they may be subjected to intense heat, but this process merely affects the surface and a scratch will reveal a white core. An accelerator process may also be used, but results are unreliable and only lighter shades of blue are attained. The only drawback to the irradiation method is that the stones must be stored until a requisite half-life has elapsed, and they are able to be safely handled. Half lives vary according to the depth of color. Baby Blues are the lightest in color and have a half-life around 120 days. Swiss Blues are slightly darker and have a half-life of 180 days. The darkest stones are the London Blues, with a half-life as long as 240 days. These topaz stones are then shipped to Creative Gems & Jewelry, where they are either sold to the industry or incorporated into the company's own jewelry.

The company product design draws its inspiration from the European and Asian jewelry making school of the 19th century, but Topaz is also keen to adapt to changing trends and fashions, and it sells jewelry that caters to all markets, from $10 silver items to platinum jewelry that might retail in excess of $10,000. Topaz sells to more than 350 customers. Accounting for approximately 46 percent of net sales are Goldmine Enterprises, Colibri, Sears Roebuck, and Wal-Mart. In addition, the company sells to Helen Andrews, the wholesale distributor to Kmart, television marketer QVC, and T.J. Maxx.

Roots of Company Date to Early 1970s

The origins of The Topaz Group are traced back to the early 1970s when several family-run Thai goldsmith operations joined forces to open a jewelry store in Bangkok. Through joint ventures with other companies, these families branched into a variety of jewelry making activities. In 1993, all of these ventures were organized under three companies: Creative Gem and Jewelry Co., Advance Gems and Jewelry Co., and Well Gems and Jewelry Co. The three entities were incorporated into a holding company named Topaz Gem Group, Inc., which as a result represented a fully integrated jewelry production and sales operation, controlling the process from the purchase of rough stones to the sale of fine finished jewelry. Over the next three years, the company took advantage of the thriving economy of the Pacific Rim and the stability of the Thai *baht* currency to enjoy solid growth. Topaz also benefited from the growth of the American and Japanese jewelry markets, the company's top export countries. Its largest customers during this period were Wal-Mart and Sears.

The fortunes for Topaz changed dramatically in 1997, when the *baht* was devalued and the Thai economy collapsed, resulting in widespread failures in every industry. Topaz was better off than most Thai companies because it had no debt, was not involved in any outside businesses, and received U.S. dollars for its exports. Nevertheless, the company was unable to receive funding from Thai financial institutions and faced the possibility that overseas customers would pull their business, fearing that Topaz, like many Asian suppliers, might be an unreliable partner because it could be adversely impacted by the devaluation of the bhat. Topaz was able, however, to convince customers that its worldwide activities were in fact based on the dollar. As a result, there was no interruption in the company's strong flow of orders. However, Topaz continued to face difficulty in arranging the financing needed to maintain inventory and provide a timely response to order placement. Because so much of the company's business involved topaz stones, which had to be stored for extended periods of time due to the irradiation process, Topaz had a need for financing to cover this period when its investment in rough stones was held in abeyance.

Economic conditions in Thailand continued to be poor in 1998 with little signs of recovery. A number of jewelry operations shut down, and the recession spread to other Asian countries. Moreover, many American buyers elected to cut back on buying trips to the region. To counteract this trend, Topaz began to actively attend jewelry shows in Hong Kong and the United States. It also cut prices on certain merchandise for over-the-counter delivery and instituted a policy of taking orders for stones and jewelry for later delivery. As a result, Topaz was able to land three new major accounts and realize growth in net income in 1998. In the meantime, the Thai government put pressure on Thai commercial banks to return to the lending market. While this action was helpful, Topaz was still frustrated by the restricted credit situation which prevented it from expanding its offerings and customer base.

Reverse Merger Engineered in 1998

Topaz now looked to its largest market, the United States, in hopes of tapping the equity markets to gain access to the kind of funding that would allow the company to realize its potential. Unable to secure an underwriter, Topaz found another way to achieve its aims by engineering a reverse merger with little-known Chancellor Corporation, which was trading on an over-the-counter basis. The company was originally incorporated in Utah as H&H Energy Corporation. After a number of name changes, it merged into a Nevada corporation, Technivision, Inc., which in 1996 became Chancellor. At this point in its meandering search for a viable business, the company was looking to mainland China, where it was involved in an attempt to establish a ''Welfare Lottery'' in Beijing and a world-class horse racing track and horse training facility. In spite of these grand plans, in November 1998 Chancellor agreed to the Topaz transaction, which was structured as an acquisition of Topaz by Chancellor. In reality, Topaz received enough shares of stock in the deal to gain control of Chancellor, which was subsequently renamed the Topaz Group, Inc. A month later, Chancellor's chairman, Ronald Sparks, stepped down, and interests in the social welfare lottery and race track were subsequently divested. In April 1999, Topaz Group completed a transaction that brought the three Thai subsidiaries—Creative Gems and Jewelry, Advance Gems and Jewelry, and Well Gems and Jewelry—into the fold. In the meantime, Topaz began trading on the NASDAQ bulletin board under the ticker symbol TOPZ. The company also began reporting its financial results to the SEC. For 1998, Topaz recorded sales of $18.9 million and net income of $4.64 million.

In 1999, Topaz initiated a number of moves. In September, it elected Jeremy F. Watson as chairman of the board. Watson had spent more than 20 years with The Singer Company, rising to the position of managing director of China operations. He then became regional vice-president for Fritz Gegauf, A.G., another sewing machine company, before joining Topaz. A few weeks after assuming the chairmanship, Watson announced that Topaz was entering into a joint venture with jewelry maker K PI TAK to launch a new high-end jewelry line, operating as the Thunder Jewelry Co. Ltd. and targeting affluent customers in the United States and the Middle East. It was an important step for Topaz because it completed its jewelry lineup, which for the first time extended to the upscale market, and also provided a way to enter the Middle East market. Another important development in 1999 was an agreement that subsidiary Creative Gems & Jewelry signed with the largest ruby mine in Nairobi, Kenya, to take its entire production. Topaz was now positioned to become the world's largest supplier of rubies.

Topaz began to increase its presence in the United States, announcing in early 2000 that it planned to move more of its operations to Washington state in order to better serve the all-important U.S. market, as well as to streamline administrative functions. The company's desire to take advantage of its new status as a publicly traded American company, however, was proving problematic. By this point, management felt it needed to hire an American who could help them in the transformation. The company was referred to Timothy Matula, a Seattle resident with several years of experience with Smith Barney and Prudential Securities. Under his guidance, along with colleague Terrance C. Cuff, Topaz retained Grant Thornton as its auditor and Parker Chapin as it legal counsel to provide the due diligence necessary in gaining a U.S listing. This process took close to two years to complete, at which time Topaz applied to be listed on the American Stock Exchange. During this period, Matula and Cuff became so convinced about the potential for

Key Dates:

1993: Topaz Gem Group is formed.
1998: Reverse merger with Chancellor Group leads to the creation of The Topaz Group.
2001: Aphichart Fufuangvanich is named president.
2002: Topaz gains a listing on the American Stock Exchange.

Topaz that in May 2001 they decided to stay on. Matula became treasurer and a director of the company, while Cuff became a director and the chief financial officer.

Dr. Aphichart Fufuangvanich Named Chairman and CEO in 2002

Another major addition to the ranks of management at this time was the appointment of Dr. Aphichart Fufuangvanich to be president of Topaz. He brought with him a great deal of expertise in the jewelry industry. A Thai native, he began working with jewelry at the age of three. By the age of 19, he opened his own jewelry shop and grew to become an expert in the field. He was responsible for a number of firsts in Thailand. He was the first to introduce calibration of stones to the country's gem cutting industry, resulting in larger gems that could be mass-produced. He was also the first Thai to turn to Africa for a variety of gem stones, a step that transformed the reputation of Thailand, helping to make it known as a top gem center on the world stage. For his many years of service to the industry, he was awarded an honorary doctoral degree in marketing from Ramkamhang University. It 2002 he took on additional responsibilities with Topaz, becoming chief executive officer and chairman of the board.

In March 2002, Topaz made an offering of stock, six million shares priced at $3 each. A month later, it became the first Thai company to gain a listing on the American Stock Exchange, making it only the second Thai company to be listed on a major U.S. stock exchange. The hope was that by being able to tap the U.S. equity market, Topaz would be able to dominate the U.S. manufacturing sector and entirely bypass wholesalers in the industry. The goal was to also be in a position to become a rollup vehicle, acquiring smaller companies in the highly fragmented jewelry industry. While many companies were suffering from difficult economic conditions, Topaz was poised to take advantage of the situation and pick up valuable assets at reasonable prices. Already a dominant player in the topaz market, the company held ambitious plans for other areas of the jewelry industry.

Principal Subsidiaries

Creative Gems & Jewelry, Ltd.; Advance Gems & Jewelry Manufacturing Company; Advance Gems & Jewelry Co., Ltd.

Principal Competitors

LJ International Inc.; M Fabrikant & Sons, Inc.; Michael Anthony Jewelers, Inc.

Further Reading

Gomelsky, Victoria, "Thai Gem Manufacturer Lists on AMEX," *National Jeweler*, April 16, 2002, p. 6.

Polkuamdee, Nuntawun, "Bangkok, Thailand-Based Jeweler Hopes Listing Will Bring Sparkling Returns," *Bangkok Post*, May 6, 2002.

——, "Topaz Supplier Becomes First Thai Firm Listed on American Stock Exchange," *Bangkok Post*, April 12, 2002.

Wilhelm, Steve, "Building Stones," *Puget Sound Business Journal*, August 24, 2001, p. 1.

—Ed Dinger

Unifi, Inc.

7201 West Friendly Road
Greensboro, North Carolina 27410
U.S.A.
Telephone: (910) 294-4410
Fax: (910) 316-5422
Web site: http://www.unifi-inc.com

Public Company
Incorporated: 1969
Employees: 4,500
Sales: $849.12 million (2003)
Stock Exchanges: New York
Ticker Symbol: UFI
NAIC: 313111 Yarn Spinning Mills; 313112 Yarn
    Texturizing, Throwing, and Twisting Mills

Unifi, Inc. is one of the largest manufacturers of textured polyester and nylon in the world. The company also produces various natural and blended materials. From its high-tech production facilities in the United States and Ireland, Unifi exports its output to more than 40 different countries. Unifi increased its revenues more than three-fold during the early 1990s by merging with several other companies to form Unifi Spun Yarns, Inc.

Before the turn of the 21st century, Unifi's world began to change. Although recognized as a leader in innovation in the industry, the company found itself compelled to make several changes to adapt to the new global marketplace. It hired its first marketing staff, entered new markets and territories via partnerships, and scaled back its workforce, while continuing to develop new products.

Origins

The Unifi (rhymes with butterfly) story is one of spectacular triumph over adversity. The company started its operations in 1971, manufacturing polyester yarn that was popular with the textile industry at the time. When Unifi opened its doors, there were already more than 50 other companies competing in the United States. Unfortunately, demand for Unifi's product col-

lapsed during the 1970s and 1980s. Indeed, the industry's production capacity plummeted during those two decades from 2.5 billion pounds to only 700 million pounds as the number of competitors shrank to only three by the late 1980s. Despite the shakeout, Unifi prospered. Through grit, determination, and savvy business strategies, Unifi's management team was able to grow the company's revenues from $21 million in 1971 to $300 million by 1988, and then to more than $1 billion a few years later. "Unifi is one of the great American success stories," observed analyst Michael Hopwood in the April 5, 1988 *Financial World,* noting that "through that entire bloodbath, it never posted a loss once."

Unifi's miraculous success is largely attributable to Allen Mebane, chairperson and founder of Unifi. Mebane was born in 1924 and raised in Greensboro, North Carolina. Although his father was an insurance salesman, Mebane's great-great-grandfather had owned a cotton mill, and Mebane himself was intrigued with the textile industry. His father sent him to Davidson College, but Mebane transferred to the Philadelphia College of Textiles and Science to learn more about the industry. Immediately after graduating in 1950, he went to work with Sale Knitting Company in Martinsville, Virginia.

Mebane started in manufacturing, working long hours and gaining valuable knowledge about the production side of the business. However, it did not take him long to realize that he was in the wrong place. "I was there at six o'clock in the morning, and I was there at eight or nine at night," Mebane recalled in the November 1993 *Business North Carolina,* "and the fellows selling the yarn would come in and they'd have a suit on and they'd have a car and could take people out to lunch and have an expense account, and I said, 'I'm doing the wrong thing here.' " Mebane left his job to serve in the army during the Korean War, and when he returned in 1954 he took a job as a sales trainee at American & Efird Inc., a fiber manufacturer.

Mebane soon left American & Efird for a better job. Between 1957 and 1964, he sold yarn for Burlington Industries. At Burlington, Mebane benefited from being able to meet and talk with the people who owned and ran the textile companies. By observing their different strategies and styles, he was able to determine which methods did and did not work. "The ones that

Company Perspectives:

OUR MISSION: Provide Innovative Fibers and Competitive Solutions. Unifi's long-standing reputation for manufacturing excellence rests on our ability to supply innovative and consistently high-quality polyester and nylon textured yarns, worldwide. Positioned at the beginning of the supply chain, Unifi typically sells directly to fabric and thread makers, who in turn supply products for a wide variety of end uses. In addition to the texturing of polyester and nylon, we provide package dyeing of both textured and spun yarns, covering of elastomeric and other yarns, conventional and warp draw beaming, and the twisting of yarns. Unifi products are often specified by downstream manufacturers, brands, and retailers for the unique qualities they bring to finished products. As one of the world's largest processors of synthetic yarns, our products can be readily found in home furnishings, apparel, industrial, automotive, hosiery, sewing thread, military, and medical applications.

were successful were the ones that were innovative, moving all the time,'' he noted in the *Business North Carolina* article. ''The ones that weren't successful were the status-quo boys.'' By that time, the 40-year-old Mebane was eager to make his mark on the industry with his own textile operation.

He got his chance to run a textile company in 1964, when he was hired by Throwing Corporation of America to serve as the manufacturer's president. Confident in his ability to improve Throwing's performance, Mebane bought 20 percent of the company for $10,000. He was only at Throwing for a short time, though, before becoming a partner at Universal Textured Yarns. Mebane made his move to Universal at an opportune time. Universal was getting in on the ground floor of the burgeoning polyester texturing industry. Through the texturing process, producers like Universal were able to heat raw polyester fibers and manipulate them to generate different characteristics and qualities. Because the polyester could be converted into stronger fibers with the look and feel of natural materials, it was viewed as a wonder fabric. Not only was it was durable, inexpensive, and versatile, but it never had to be ironed.

Unifi Begins Operations 1971

As the popularity of textured polyester surged, Universal thrived. Mebane and his fellow top managers sold their shares in the company for $1 million in 1971. They immediately invested that money, along with a $6 million dollar bank loan, into their own operation—Unifi. The strategy employed by Mebane and his fellow managers during Unifi's start-up was one that they would continue to employ throughout the 1970s, 1980s, and into the mid-1990s: they invested in cutting edge manufacturing equipment that would give them a long-term cost and quality advantage over competitors. They first purchased 32 high-tech English machines, which were considered state-of-the-art in the early 1970s. As their competitors adopted similar technology in the mid-1970s, Unifi upped the ante. In 1975, the company invested heavily in new German-built equipment that could make better yarn at a faster rate.

Unifi prospered during the early and mid-1970s and quickly established itself as a low-cost provider of high-quality polyester yarns. Although Unifi's business strategy was impressive, the same could not be said for the popularity of polyester by the late 1970s. Dismissed by many retailers and consumers as a fad, polyester's appeal waned as markets renewed their desire for natural fibers such as cotton, silk, and wool. While polyester leisure suits and dresses, for example, had been a hit in the mid-1970s, they had become a fashion joke by the late 1970s and early 1980s. As a result, domestic polyester production plunged. Manufacturing overcapacity quashed price growth, and many producers were forced out of business.

In order to stay afloat, Mebane and company knew that they were either going to have to find new markets for their polyester or vastly increase their share of the market. Ultimately, they did both. At home, Unifi benefitted from its manufacturing prowess. Because its operations were so advanced, it was able to undercut its less efficient competitors and rapidly steal market share. Unifi management understood early that it was operating in a commodity business; if one of its competitors was forced to charge even a slightly higher price, Unifi knew that it was only a matter of time until that company folded. So, despite dying demand, Unifi continued to risk hefty capital investments in new production facilities and techniques. And it was able to keep its selling and administrative costs to an industry low of 3 percent throughout the late 1970s and 1980s. As its rivals struggled and failed to keep up, Unifi bought them out or simply took on their customers when they went out of business.

International in the 1980s

However, leadership in U.S. markets was not enough to keep Unifi profitable during the lean late 1970s and early 1980s. To buoy profits, Unifi aggressively pursued foreign business. Importantly, Unifi was among the first U.S. companies to begin selling to China when the People's Republic opened its doors to exports in 1980. The emerging, yet massive, Chinese market proved a boon for Unifi during the early 1980s. As demand soared, so did Unifi's overseas sales. At one point, Unifi trucks were literally blocking the road to the port as they waited to unload tons of commodity yarns for export to China. By 1983, Unifi was garnering about one-quarter of its $176 million in annual revenues from sales in China, and shipments to the country were topping one million pounds per week. Unfortunately, the China boom was short-lived. China and several other Asian countries, particularly Taiwan, soon built their own texturing facilities. Besides costs related to shipping, Asian producers also benefited from advantages like cheap labor and loose environmental regulations. Asian demand for U.S. polyester faded quickly after 1983, but Mebane and his fellow executives were undaunted. They mimicked their domestic strategy by purchasing the polyester operations of another major U.S. polyester supplier to China, Macfield Inc., in 1986. More importantly, Unifi continued to search for new international customers in Latin America, South America, Australia, Israel, Africa, and the Far East.

Vital to Unifi's international strategy was its 1980 entrance into Europe. After only two years of exporting to that region, Unifi had captured a healthy 6 percent share of the western European polyester market. However, Unifi's success in that

Key Dates:

1971: Unifi begins producing polyester yarn.
1980: The company enters the Chinese and European markets.
1984: A polyester plant in Ireland is opened.
1986: The polyester business of Macfield Inc. is acquired.
1991: The remainder of Macfield and Vintage Yarns is acquired.
1992: Sales pass $1 billion.
1993: Unifi merges with the Pioneer Corporations.
1999: Unifi Technology Group is spun off; Brazil's Fairway Poliester is acquired.
2001: The company's technical fabrics division is sold off.
2003: Several hundred jobs are cut in restructuring.

region was hampered by European Economic Community charges that the company was dumping polyester into Europe at prices below cost. Unifi was eventually cleared of the allegations, and it elected to pursue a different strategy in that heavily protected market. In 1984, it purchased a former Courtaulds plant in Ireland and spent $50 million making it into one of the most efficient and technologically advanced facilities of its kind in the world. By the early 1990s, Unifi's Irish operations were supplying 20 percent of European demand (measured in sales volume). In 1984, Unifi also acquired the former ICI Fibers plant near Manchester, England.

As Unifi expanded globally, the U.S. polyester markets continued to deteriorate. Demand for filament poly (used to make polyester yarn) collapsed from 1.4 billion pounds in 1975 to 650 million in 1985. ''The market went to hell in a handbasket,'' Mebane confirmed in the January 24, 1994 *Fortune*. However, Unifi continued to boost domestic market share during the mid- and late 1980s through its aggressive high-tech, low-cost operating strategy. In addition, Unifi diversified into nylon and began cultivating new markets for its polyester fibers. Most notably, Unifi was successful in marketing its polyester and nylon products to the automobile industry for the production of seat covers and vehicle interiors. The company also developed a large niche in the hosiery business. One of its largest customers, in fact, became Sara Lee, a leading supplier of women's hosiery.

By 1988, Unifi had become one of the largest manufacturers of polyester and nylon in the world. It was controlling about 40 percent of the U.S. market and had a strong toehold in Europe and several other export regions. Unifi's total revenues had swelled to $275 million in 1987, up from $248 million the previous year. Similarly, net income had grown steadily from $5.6 million in 1985, to $10.4 million in 1986, and then to $12 million during 1987. Moreover, Unifi achieved those gains as it steadily shrunk its long-term debt to $1 million by early 1988.

Unifi's long-term outlook seemed bright. Domestic demand for polyester seemed to have stabilized, and the company was making massive capital investments in cutting edge technology, including the purchase of new Japanese texturing equipment in 1988. Much of Unifi's success during the late 1980s was credited to William Kretzer, who had assumed the president's

slot in 1985. Kretzer controlled day-to-day operations, while chairperson Mebane retained his strategic role.

Expanding in the 1990s

While Unifi's gains throughout the 1980s had wowed observers, the company experienced even greater expansion and profitability during the early 1990s. Unifi's success during that period was simply more evidence of Mebane's emphasis on long-term growth. For example, since deciding to go global in the late 1970s, Unifi's managers had determined that they would stick with the markets that they entered, even when performance in a particular region waned. By contrast, many of Unifi's competitors had simply bailed out of ailing markets, ceding their share to Unifi. As a result, Unifi was invariably positioned to take advantage of different recovering markets. ''They are the first in the gate when the rebound starts,'' explained industry specialist Bill Dawson in the November 1993 issue of *Business North Carolina*.

Unifi's gains during the early 1990s were also the result of major acquisitions. In 1991, for example, Unifi acquired the remaining operations of Macfield, as well as a company called Vintage Yarns. Macfield had been Unifi's largest competitor, and the two mergers literally doubled Unifi's size. The buyouts gave Unifi a dominant presence in the U.S. nylon industry and extended its reach into profitable market niches like hosiery and vehicle interiors. By 1993, Unifi was employing 5,000 workers in its various manufacturing plants, increasing its work force while also working to make operations more efficient. For example, Unifi's major Pennsylvania facility generated about 3.2 million pounds of nylon per week in 1981 with about 1,300 employees. In 1993, the same plant was pumping out about twice as much material with only 1,000 workers.

Due largely to the mergers, Unifi's sales suddenly escalated past the $1 billion mark in 1992, and net income leapt to a record $63 million. Then, in 1993, Unifi merged again. This time it effectively absorbed Pioneer Yarn Mills, Pioneer Spinning, Edenton Cotton Mills, and Pioneer Cotton Mill— companies merged into a single entity, the Pioneer Corporations, and subsequently acquired by Unifi. Unifi formed a subsidiary for the division called Unifi Spun Yarns, Inc. The acquisition was important because it represented Unifi's move into the natural fibers industry; the former Pioneer companies' primary products were spun yarns made of cotton but also some cotton/synthetic blends. During 1994 (fiscal year ended June 26), Unifi achieved sales of $1.38 billion, about $76.5 million of which was netted as income.

Going into the mid-1990s, Unifi was controlling a full 70 percent of the U.S. polyester market and was selling about $500 million worth of nylon annually. It was serving 20 percent of demand in Europe and planned to boost that share to at least 30 percent by the late 1990s. As a result of the mergers, its work force had grown to 6,000 employees in 15 U.S. production facilities, one plant in Ireland, and sales offices in England, France, and Japan. The company spent nearly $400 million between 1991 and 1993 to ensure that its plants would continue to be among the most advanced in the world.

Furthermore, Unifi's three most influential executives— Mebane, Kretzer, and William J. Armfield, all of whom had been with the company since the early 1970s—were still at the helm, suggesting continued innovation and dominance of Unifi's key markets throughout the decade. ''Its hard to bet against Unifi,'' said textile industry analyst Lorraine Miller in the *Business North Carolina* article, who added that ''come hook or by crook, whether it's through acquisition or by adding on to their own facilities, they're going to be positioned to take market share.''

Sales reached $1.6 billion in fiscal 1995. After selling off a small French factory, Unifi would spend the next couple of years acquiring and upgrading its facilities in the western hemisphere. In October 1995, the company agreed to buy nylon yarn texturing equipment from Glenn Raven Mills, Inc., another North Carolina textile firm.

Unifi acquired Spanco Yarns in 1997, adding four North Carolina plants. Two of these, in Graham and Lincolnton, were closed in 1998. The remaining covered yarns plants in Raeford and Sanford were phased out the next year as production shifted to a new facility in Madison, North Carolina.

In the spring of 1999, Unifi acquired a leading Brazilian producer of textured polyester, Fairway Poliester LTDA. The following year, Unifi acquired Intex Yarns Limited, a 200-person firm in Manchester, England. Renamed Unifi Dyed Yarns Limited, this became the basis of Unifi's European dyed yarns business.

After developing considerable expertise in factory automation, Unifi in 1999 formed a spin-off company to apply these skills to other textile firms and other industries. The new subsidiary, which employed 110 people, was called Unifi Technology Group LLC.

Other areas of research were aimed at keeping the company competitive through innovation. Unifi was researching ways to dye fabric using carbon dioxide, rather than water, as a medium. Envisioned benefits were water conservation and reduced pollution. The company was also studying the possibility of using carbon dioxide to replace solvents in dry cleaning.

Beyond 2000

Brian R. Parke was named CEO of Unifi in January 2000. Parke, a native of County Sligo, Ireland, had begun working for the company in 1985 as a manager at its Irish plant and had led the creation of Unifi do Brasil. Six months later, G. Allen Mebane announced he was stepping down as chairman, to be succeeded by Donald. F. Orr, a board member since 1988.

Parke took the helm at a difficult time. Asian yarn producers were flooding the market. Unifi lost some U.S.-based textile-producing clients when competition from abroad put them out of business; it was able to supply others who shifted their manufacturing to the Caribbean Basin. Asian imports were also hurting Unifi's business in Europe. The company would post losses in the 2001, 2002, and 2003 fiscal years.

Unifi sought to enter new markets through partnerships. In the United States, the company was forming a polyester filament yarn manufacturing alliance with DuPont. Another partnership extended Unifi's involvement in Asia. Unifi offered South Korean volume manufacturer Hankook Synthetics its expertise in producing premium polyester yarns in exchange for a share of profits.

Still another partnership, also announced in 2000, brought Unifi into the industrial yarn market. South African company SANS Fibres agreed to supply equipment for a plant in Madison, North Carlina, and market the fabric. SANS was also buying Solutia, Inc., an industrial yarn supplier in Greenwood, South Carolina.

More casual business dress codes had hurt Unifi's business as the top U.S. supplier of nylon yarn for pantyhose. Unifi addressed this trend by processing a fine yarn for use in ''seamless'' underwear, as found in Victoria's Secret's ''Body by Victoria'' undergarments, designed to complement tight-fitting fashions.

The company had more difficulty smoothing out its own bottom line, thanks to a slow economy, price competition from Asia, and the decline in professional dress. Durable goods such as automobiles and furniture—other industries that used Unifi's yarns—were also suffering. The company laid off 750 workers in 2001.

Unifi sold its technical fabrics division to an Israeli company, Avgol Nonwovens Industries, in May 2001. In the spring of the year, Unifi began leasing an automotive yarn processing plant from Glen Raven, signaling a shift into a more promising area than apparel.

The company boosted its Asian presence by establishing a sales office in Hong Kong. It also formed a joint venture with Tuntex (Thailand) PCL, which was partly owned by the Tuntex Group of Taiwan. At the end of 2003, Unifi was finalizing a partnership with a Chinese company, Kaiping Polyester Enterprises Group Company.

Research on new products continued. These included odor-fighting, anti-microbial yarn and hollow polyester fiber for insulating clothing. Unifi was also involved in texturing Cargill Dow's new NatureWorks fiber, which was made from corn. Another ecologically friendly Unifi yarn was made from recycled soda bottles.

Unifi was also embracing the art of branding. As the Greensboro *News & Record* reported, the company formed its first marketing department, which replaced such lackluster names as ''single 70 34 semi-dull'' with ''Sparkle,'' ''Sultra,'' and ''Sorbtek.'' The latter was picked up by Nike and JC Penney as a wicking material for sport socks.

Unifi enlisted the aid of employees in a cost-cutting program called ''Project Paragon,'' the aim of which was to discover inefficiencies throughout the production process. Ensuing consultations resulted in the company embracing a more entrepreneurial culture that entrusted employees with more front-line decisions. Layoffs continued in 2003, as Unifi eliminated several hundred jobs in North Carolina. The company ended the year with 4,500 employees.

Principal Subsidiaries

Unifi Asia Ltd. (Hong Kong); Unifi do Brasil; Unifi Dyed Yarns Limited (UK); Unifi GmbH (Germany); Unifi Italia, S.r.l.; Unifi

International Services, Inc.; Unifi International Services Europe (France); Unifi Manufacturing, Inc.; Unifi Sales & Distribution, Inc.; Unifi Technical Fabrics, LLC; Unifi Technology Group, LLC; Unifi Textured Yarns Europe, Ltd. (Ireland); Unifi-SANS Technical Fiber, LLC.

Principal Divisions

Nylon; Polyester.

Principal Competitors

Dillon Yarn Company, Inc.; McMichael Mills, Inc.; Sapona Manufacturing Company, Inc.; Spectrum Dyed Yarns, Inc.; Worldtex, Inc.

Further Reading

Bailey, David, "Getting His Irish Up: Faced with EC Protectionism, Unifi's Allen Mebane Decided the Way to Beat the Europeans Was to Join Them," *Business North Carolina*, November 1993, p. 26.

Barkley, Meredith, "Unifi Planning Job Cuts," *News & Record* (Greensboro, NC), April 15, 2003, p. B7.

Bartholomew, Doug, "Automations Advance," *Industry Week*, Manufacturing 2020 Sec., May 15, 2000, p. 27.

Craver, Richard, "400 Jobs to Be Lost in Unifi Shake-Up," *Winston-Salem Journal*, April 17, 2003, p. A1.

Daniel, Fran, "Greensboro, NC , Textured Yarn Producer to Close Nylon Plant," *Winston-Salem Journal*, November 8, 2002.

"DuPont and Unifi Form Polyester Manufacturing Alliance," *HFN*, April 10, 2000, p. 23.

Heisler, Eric, "Unifi Forms Asian-Market Partnership," *News & Record* (Greensboro, NC), July 25, 2000, p. B8.

——, "Unifi, South Africa Firm Plan Venture," *News & Record* (Greensboro, NC), September 19, 2000, p. B6.

——, "Tracking Fashion's Moving Target; Unifi Takes Aim at the Panty Line," *News & Record* (Greensboro, NC), October 8, 2000, p. E1.

——, "Unifi Plans to Cut 590 Jobs in Triad," *News & Record* (Greensboro, NC), March 15, 2001.

——, "Unifi Leases Yarn Plant," *News & Record* (Greensboro, NC), May 23, 2001, p. B8.

——, "Corny Alternative to Polyester," *News & Record* (Greensboro, NC), July 8, 2001, p. E1.

——, "Unifi Develops Two New Yarns," *News & Record* (Greensboro, NC), August 22, 2001, p. B8.

——, "Emphasis on Marketing Paying Off," *News & Record* (Greensboro, NC), March 3, 2002, p. E1.

——, "Unifi Close to Deal with Tuntex," *News & Record* (Greensboro, NC), July 9, 2002, p. B8.

Kritzer, Jamie, "Unifi Seeks Expansion Incentives," *News & Record* (Greensboro, NC), September 30, 1998, p. B3.

Krouse, Peter, "Unifi, chief Ponder Separate Paths," *News & Record* (Greensboro, NC), January 13, 1999, p. B4.

——, "Dying for a New Alternative," *News & Record* (Greensboro, NC), February 16, 1999, p. A1.

——, "Yarn Maker Spins off Tech Venture," *News & Record* (Greensboro, NC), May 21, 1999, p. B8.

McAllister, Isaacs III, "Unifi Tops the Sales Yarn Market and Is Still Moving," *Textile World*, August 1993, p. 33.

McMillan, Alex Frew, "When Irish Eyes," *Business North Carolina*, April 1995, p. 40.

Patterson, Donald W., "Unifi's China Deal up in Air," *News & Record* (Greensboro, NC), December 30, 2003, p. B5.

Patterson, Donald W., and Scott Michels, "Blaming Economy, Unifi Announces More Layoffs," *News & Record* (Greensboro, NC), September 9, 2003, p. A1.

Serwer, Andrew S., "Business Is Bad? It's Time to Grow!," *Fortune*, January 24, 1994, p. 88.

Sykes, Jeffrey, "Unifi Workers Asked to Assist in Cutting Costs," *Winston-Salem Journal*, January 11, 2003, p. D1.

"Synthetics Prove to Be the Real Thing for Unifi," *Business North Carolina*, January 1988, p. 57.

Wrubel, Robert, "Unifi: The Next Textile Takeover," *Financial World*, April 5, 1988, p. 16.

—Dave Mote
—update: Frederick C. Ingram

United States Pipe and Foundry Company

3300 First Avenue North
Birmingham, Alabama 35222
U.S.A.
Telephone: (205) 254-7000
Toll Free: (866) 347-7473
Fax: (205) 254-7165
Web site: http://www.uspipe.com

Wholly Owned Subsidiary of Walter Industries, Inc.
Incorporated: 1899 as United States Cast Iron Pipe and
    Foundry Company
Sales: $457 million (2002)
NAIC: 331210 Iron and Steel Pipe and Tube
    Manufacturing from Purchased Steel

The United States Pipe and Foundry Company (U.S. Pipe) is one of the nation's leading manufacturers of ductile iron pipe. Ductile iron pipe is used principally to carry water and wastewater. The company also manufactures pipe fittings, valves, joints, and hydrants. U.S. Pipe operates manufacturing plants in Bessemer and North Birmingham, Alabama; Chattanooga, Tennessee; Burlington, New Jersey; and Union City, California. In 2003, the company closed its U.S. Castings division plant in Anniston, Alabama. U.S. Pipe also operates many regional sales offices and is involved in markets in all sectors of the United States. The company also sells to an international market. Early in its history, U.S. Pipe brought in new pipe casting technology, which for the first time made uniform mass production a possibility in the industry. Since 1969, the company has been wholly owned by Walter Industries, Inc., formerly known as the Jim Walters Corp. Walter Industries is a $1.3 billion conglomerate with interests in home building, home financing, mineral, and industrial products. U.S. Pipe is the key component of Walter Industries's industrial products division.

Big Combination at the Turn of the Century

U.S. Pipe was founded in 1899 as the United States Cast Iron Pipe and Foundry Company. This new company put together 12 existing companies spread across eight states. This was a time of massive consolidation in the pipe industry, which had grown up over the previous 40 or so years, mostly in the South. The Alabama Consolidated Coal and Iron Company and the Tennessee Coal and Iron Company were already vigorous rivals by 1899, and that year also saw the formation of another large combination of iron and steel companies, Sloss-Sheffield Steel and Iron, which would become a part of U.S. Pipe in 1942.

The iron industry was booming at the turn of the century, with high demand at home and in Europe. The Birmingham, Alabama, region led the country in iron production, putting out over three times the tonnage of the Pennsylvania region. United States Cast Iron Pipe and Foundry, however, put together companies operating in different regions of the country. Its plants were in Bessemer and Anniston, Alabama, in Chattanooga, Tennessee, in Pittsburgh, Pennsylvania, and in Buffalo, New York, and as far west as Ohio and Wisconsin. Some of the companies that made up the original U.S. Pipe had long histories of their own. The Chattanooga Foundry and Pipe Company dated to 1882. It was the first pit cast pipe maker in the South. It began with one pit and had eight by the time it was bought up by U.S. Pipe. The McNeal Pipe and Foundry Company was even older, founded in 1866 by Andrew McNeal. This was a large industrial complex built along the Delaware River in Burlington, New Jersey. McNeal also built a significant mansion adjoining the plant. U.S. Pipe acquired the mansion in its 1899 takeover, and this graceful building served as its corporate headquarters until 1953. The mansion is now on the National Register of Historic Places.

All the 12 plants in the original corporation manufactured cast iron pipe using a method known as pit casting. Pit casting was essentially a medieval process, dating back 300 years. Workers produced pipes by pouring molten iron into vertical molds lined with sand. This was highly skilled work producing satisfactory pipe, though shifting sand often resulted in variation in the thickness of the pipe wall. Some of U.S. Pipe's plants produced hundreds of tons of pipe a day by this method. The company made cast iron pipe in various diameters, from half an inch to 60 inches, and later also made valves, fittings, and hydrants. Most of the pipe was used for municipal water works. As the nation's population surged in the early part of the 20th century, the demand for pipe was constant, and U.S. Pipe did well. In 1911, it bought another manufacturer, the Dimmick Pipe Company, in North Birmingham, Alabama. Dimmick was already producing from 150 to 175 tons of pipe per day. U.S. Pipe soon added another pit casting facility at the plant, which made larger diameter pipes at a rate of some 125 tons daily.

In 1921, U.S. Pipe introduced a new way of making pipe, called centrifugal casting. This method was developed by a French engineer living in Brazil, Dimitri Sensaud deLavaud. The company bought rights to the method from deLavaud and set new standards for its competitors to follow. U.S. Pipe first introduced centrifugal casting at its North Birmingham plant. Using this method, workers poured molten iron into a rotating steel mold. The centrifugal force of the rotating mold spread the iron evenly around the inside of the form, so the resulting pipe was completely uniform in thickness. At last pipe manufacturing had become a real mass production process.

The company did well throughout the 1920s, paying healthy dividends to its stockholders. It paid out over $8 a share in 1924. U.S. Pipe seemed strong financially, with very little debt, and by the end of the 1920s it was indisputably the largest iron pipe producer in the East. It had set the standard for manufacturing, and other companies hurried to catch up. U.S. Pipe made improvements to the deLavaud process, which allowed it to cut costs and raise quality. At first, the new process limited the diameter of pipes made this way. Eventually, however, the company worked this out and was able to make any diameter pipe in this new way.

Depression and Postwar Years

In 1929, the company changed its name from United States Cast Iron Pipe and Foundry to simply United States Pipe and Foundry. U.S. Pipe had shown solid earnings all through the 1920s and into 1930. Nevertheless, the company soon felt the effects of the Great Depression. U.S. Pipe depended largely on municipal spending on public works projects, and with high unemployment in the depression years, municipal budgets were severely strained. Many cities were hard pressed to meet payrolls for their workers and had to manage relief for the unemployed and hungry. The result was that cities deferred building projects, and pipe companies competed fiercely for whatever work was available. U.S. Pipe reduced its operating expenses in the early 1930s, when the demand for its products was very low. The company posted a net loss of over $1 million for 1932. By 1934, the company's prospects brightened with the addition of government-funded public works projects.

As in many other industries, sales did not pick up in the 1930s until the start of World War II. U.S. Pipe's sales for 1935

troughed at $8.2 million, but by 1942 the company was bringing in over $29 million. That year, U.S. Pipe made a significant acquisition, buying up just over 50 percent of the shares of a principal rival, Sloss-Sheffield Steel and Iron. Sloss-Sheffield was the second largest cast iron pipe producer in the South, and the third largest in the nation. U.S. Pipe spent $5.4 million on the acquisition, taking on debt to swing the deal. By the war's end, U.S. Pipe had a healthy backlog of orders. The company formed a joint operating agreement with a French company to develop concrete pipe, which was becoming increasingly common in large waterworks. The two companies formed a subsidiary called Pontusco Corp., which built a concrete pipe plant in Cuba.

In 1951, U.S. Pipe moved into West Coast markets, building a new manufacturing plant from scratch in Union City, southeast of Oakland, California. This plant would help the company handle new orders as the population west of the Rocky Mountains began to swell. The next year, U.S. Pipe completed its acquisition of Sloss-Sheffield. This gave it control of that company's vast resources of coke, pig iron, and coal, as well as its pipe manufacturing facilities. In 1953, the company abandoned its historic headquarters in Burlington, New Jersey, and moved its offices to the heart of the iron industry, Birmingham, Alabama. It also spent money updating many of its facilities. Sales rose precipitously through the early 1950s. Sales in 1950 stood at $41.2 million, and then more than doubled the next year, to $90 million. Increasing sales allowed the company to pay down debt. U.S. Pipe had over $12 million in long-term debt in 1951, taken on when it purchased Sloss-Sheffield and added to with subsequent expansion. By the mid-1950s, however, long-term debt had dropped to some $5.4 million.

Changes in the 1960s

U.S. Pipe made several more acquisitions in the 1960s, and at the end of the decade it was itself bought. In 1961, it increased its holdings in Alabama by acquiring the T.C. King Pipe and Fittings Company, of Anniston, Alabama. The plant expanded in the 1970s, and in the late 1980s became U.S. Pipe's U.S. Castings division. In 1966, U.S. Pipe made another significant acquisition, this time on the East Coast, when it bought an East Orange, New Jersey, manufacturer of valves, hydrants, and related parts called the A.P. Smith Manufacturing Company. Over the next four years, U.S. Pipe moved A.P. Smith's production lines to its existing plant in Chattanooga. In 1967, U.S. Pipe made one more major purchase, buying the Irondale, Alabama, company Southern Precision, Inc. Southern Precision was not a pipe maker but a pattern and specialized tooling business. It was a major producer of specialized tooling used in the foundry business.

After expanding through the 1950s and making large acquisitions in several markets in the 1960s, U.S. Pipe was bought out by a young company whose principal business was home building. The Jim Walter Corporation was founded in 1946 in Tampa, Florida, by an enterprising 23-year-old builder who discovered a new way to sell houses. Walter's company specialized in building so-called shell homes, which were unfinished on the inside. Because they were unfinished, they were relatively inexpensive to buy, since the new homeowners would complete the interior work themselves. These sold well, especially in the South, and by 1960 Jim Walter was a na-

Dates:

1899: A manufacturing concern is formed out of 12 previously existing companies.

1921: The deLavaud centrifugal casting method is introduced.

1951: The company builds a new West Coast plant in Union City, California.

1961: T.C. King Pipe and Fittings Co. is bought.

1969: Jim Walter Corp. acquires U.S. Pipe.

1987: U.S. Pipe's parent company is taken private in a leveraged buyout.

1997: The company goes public, trading on the New York Stock Exchange.

2003: U.S. Pipe closes its U.S. Castings division.

tionally known businessman. Jim Walter Corp. began a rapid expansion in 1962, buying up a fiberboard manufacturer, Celotex Corp. In 1964, the company went public, and in 1969 it acquired U.S. Pipe. That year Jim Walter Corp. ranked number 287 on the Fortune 500 list of the nation's top companies, with annual sales of $623 million. U.S. Pipe became one division of a classic 1970s conglomerate, which had dozens of subsidiaries in a host of different industries. Jim Walter began developing coal mines in the 1970s on land it had acquired from U.S. Pipe. Walter Corp. also moved into the aluminum industry in 1980. In the early 1980s, Walter's pipe division accounted for 16 percent of sales and about 17 percent of profits. U.S. Pipe's sales rose and fell with the housing industry, though they depended more on the building of subdivisions rather than on individual homes.

Leveraged Buyout of the Parent Company in 1987

By the late 1980s, parent company Jim Walter's interests included carpet manufacturing, paper, jewelry, industrial products and building materials, as well as home building and financing and pipe manufacturing. U.S. Pipe was the second-largest division of Jim Walters Corp. By the late 1980s, the piping division's sales were estimated at more than $400 million. Operating profits at the division were estimated at around $57 million, about half that of the company's homebuilding and financing division. By the mid-1980s, it was clear that Jim Walter was a candidate for takeover. A wave of mergers and acquisitions swept the country in the 1980s, fueled in part by Michael Milken's proselytizing of the junk bond from the California offices of Drexel Burnham Lambert. Public companies like Jim Walter were taken private in leveraged buyouts, meaning the new owners put up very little cash but raised financing from unrated or "junk" bonds. Prime targets of the takeover wars were manufacturing companies with good cash flow and lots of subsidiaries that could be sold off. Jim Walter Corp. fit the pattern, and in 1987 it was taken private by one of the best-known takeover groups, Kohlberg Kravis Roberts (KKR). The deal, valued at $2.4 billion, was a small one for KKR. The year before, it had raised $8.7 billion to buy out Beatrice Foods. In 1988, it made the record-breaking $25 billion buyout of RJR Nabisco, a deal so momentous it inspired not only a book but a movie, *Barbarians at the Gate*.

After the buyout, Jim Walter Corp. sold off assets, though the pipe division was not affected. Company documents claim Jim Walter Corp. was still a profitable company, but in 1989 it filed for bankruptcy, brought down by a huge class action lawsuit relating to the company's former Celotex subsidiary. At the time, this was the biggest financial collapse of a company taken private in a leveraged buyout. The U.S. Pipe division had its own legal problems. The city of Atlanta complained that U.S. Pipe and another Alabama pipe company had conspired to fix prices on municipal contracts dating back to 1972. A federal judge ruled in 1989 that the city could ask to recover payments it made to U.S. Pipe reaching back to the early 1970s.

New Developments in the 1990s and After

Parent company Jim Walter Corp. changed its name to Walter Industries, Inc. in 1991. It settled its legal problems in 1994, and in 1995 it emerged from bankruptcy. In 1997, Walter Industries became a public company again, traded on the New York Stock Exchange. By the mid-1990s, U.S. Pipe was still a leading iron pipe manufacturer and remained a division of Walter Industries. It ran six manufacturing plants at that time and had 35 sales offices across the United States. Though the company had regional rivals, U.S. Pipe stood out as the pipe manufacturer with the broadest market coverage in the industry. For 1997, revenue at U.S. Pipe stood at $420 million, a little higher than a decade earlier.

U.S. Pipe's youngest plant dated to 1951. Three of its plants had been in operation since the company was formed in 1899. These old facilities were expensive. In 2000, U.S. Pipe spent some $20 million to upgrade its Chattanooga plant. Despite this heavy investment, two years later the company announced that it had to trim its Chattanooga workforce by 20 percent. Orders had slowed, and the company also faced steep competition from foreign manufacturers. Sales at the company's U.S. Castings division, which ran out of the company's Anniston plant, were so poor that U.S. Pipe was forced to close the plant completely in 2003. The company blamed heavy competition from both foreign and domestic rivals. The Anniston plant had been acquired from the T.C. King Pipe and Fittings Co. in 1961, and the facility had been built in the 1930s. Given the low profitability of the plant, U.S. Pipe announced that it could not afford to modernize it, and so shut it down.

The generally sluggish U.S. economy dampened the company's sales in the early 2000s. However, U.S. Pipe believed it had promising business in replacing older pipe systems, especially in light of new environmental regulations. Many municipalities with aging water systems would need to upgrade their pipes soon. U.S. Pipe believed it was well situated to supply major municipal markets in the Northeast. The company was also in a good position to supply markets on the West Coast from its Union City plant. The West Coast had chronic water shortages, and the company anticipated future municipal water projects in that region.

Principal Competitors

American Cast Iron Pipe Company; Griffin Ductile Iron Pipe Company; McWane Corporation.

Further Reading

Bass, George G., "U.S. Pipe & Foundry: The Home Building Boom Gives It a Steady Profit Flow," *Barron's*, September 26, 1955, p. 17.

"Beneficiary of Public Works," *Barron's*, January 15, 1934, p. 15.

Engardio, Pete, "Why Jim Walter Is Ripe for the Picking," *Business Week*, August 3, 1987, pp. 31–34.

Gordon, Mitchell, "Rebuilding Profits," *Barron's*, May 30, 1983, pp. 38–39.

"Great Iron Combination," *New York Times*, August 10, 1899, p. 9.

"New Ideas Keep Flowing at U.S. Pipe," *Water Engineering & Management*, March 1994, p. 6.

"Pipe & Foundry Doing Better," *Barron's*, July 21, 1930, p. 17.

"Record Sales Restore U.S. Pipe's Profit Margin," *Barron's*, January 12, 1948, p. 34.

"Two Major Chattanooga, Tenn., Employers to Cut Jobs Despite Recent Expansion," *Knight Ridder/Tribune Business News*, May 24, 2002.

"U.S. Pipe Ordered to Cool It after Blasts Hurt 12 Workers," *American Metal Market*, December 13, 2000, p. 16.

"U.S. Pipe Shutters Anniston, Ala. Castings Plant," *Contractor*, May 2003, p. 28.

—A. Woodward

United States Playing Card Company

4590 Beech Street
Cincinnati, Ohio 45212
U.S.A.
Telephone: (513) 396-5700
Toll Free: (800)863-1333
Fax: (513) 396-5878
Web Site: http://www.usplayingcard.com

Wholly Owned Subsidiary of Bicycle Holding, Inc.
Incorporated: 1894
Employees: 750
Sales: $130 million (2003 est.)
NAIC: 323119 Other Commercial Printing; 339932
 Game, Toy, and Children's Vehicle Manufacturing

The United States Playing Card Company (USPC) is the largest manufacturer of playing cards in the world and sells more than 100 million decks of playing cards per year, including more than 20 million decks to casinos. The company's long-lived brands include Bicycle, Bee Club Cards, Aviator, Aristocrat, and Hoyle, each with a distinctive card back design. Through licensing agreements, USPC can produce cards carrying back designs of consumer product brands (such as Coca-Cola and Harley Davidson), cartoon characters (such as Mickey Mouse and Scooby-Doo), and characters from children's stories and products (such as Harry Potter and Mr. Potato Head). Moreover, the company's custom playing cards can be uniquely designed and produced for promotional purposes. USPC products are distributed worldwide under brand names that vary according to local markets. Specialized decks of playing cards include those for playing the games of euchre, which uses nines, tens, and royal cards, and bridge, which calls for a slightly narrower sized deck. The company also licenses the Bicycle and Hoyle brands to software companies for computer-based card and board games. Under the organizational umbrella of Bicycle Holding, Inc., USPC agreed to be acquired by New York-based Jarden Corporation in 2004.

Late 19th Century: Origins and Early Success

The United States Playing Card Company began as an offshoot of a printing business founded in Cincinnati in 1867 by four men named Russell, Morgan, Armstrong, and Robinson. Named for the two printers in the group, Russell, Morgan and Company purchased some office space from the *Cincinnati Enquirer* newspaper and began printing promotional posters for theatrical performances and circuses, as well as placards and labels. The company's growth soon necessitated a move to larger facilities nearby.

In 1880 Russell, Morgan and Company decided to enter the playing card business, then an industry dominated by companies on the East Coast. The company's first deck of playing cards was produced on June 21, 1881. Soon thereafter, the company was employing 20 people for the operation and producing 1,600 decks of playing cards per day.

Russell, Morgan's first brand of playing cards was called Congress. By 1885 the company had begun to produce the Bicycle brand. Over the years Bicycle card back designs featured various images of a bicycle in a mirror image so that the card never appeared upside down. The ''rider back'' deck pictured the front view of a cherub riding a bicycle in a mirror image, with Florentine decorations framing the card.

In 1891 Russell, Morgan and Company was renamed The United States Printing Company, and three years later, the successful new playing card business segment was incorporated separately as the United States Playing Card Company. Acquisitions followed, most notable, perhaps, being that of New York Consolidated Cards, known for its Bee brand of playing cards introduced in 1892. Having outgrown its facilities in downtown Cincinnati, USPC moved five miles south to Norwood, in 1900. The 30-acre site provided ample space for offices and production and warehouse facilities, as well as for expansion. A public company, USPC operated profitably and paid dividends on a regular basis.

Continued Growth Amidst Depression and War

USPC expanded internationally in the 1910s, establishing the International Playing Card Company in 1914, initially for product distribution to Canada. Successful sales in that country led the company to establish a manufacturing facility in Windsor, Ontario, in 1928. Among the unique brands marketed to Canadian customers was Texan 45, a style popular in Quebec since its introduction in the 1930s.

In 1922, to promote card playing, particularly bridge, USPC established a radio station called WSAI. Housed at the company's Norwood facilities, WSAI featured the show "Bridge by Radio" which provided bridge instruction from experts actually playing the game on the air. USPC operated WSAI until 1930. As contract bridge became increasingly popular in the decade that followed, the company's Congress brand emerged as a favorite brand of card for bridge.

USPC expanded its sales network during the 1930s, acquiring other selling agencies to promote certain brands of playing cards to different markets. The company sold its products through wholesalers, jobbers, cigar stores, and department stores. Playing card brands at the time included Tally-ho, Blue Ribbon, and Aristocrat, as well as the standards Bee, Bicycle, and Congress. The Aviator brand, introduced in 1927, honored Charles Lindberg for his historic flight across the Atlantic Ocean.

With the legalization of gambling in Las Vegas in 1931, casinos provided a new base of business. As one of a few companies licensed to provide cards to casinos, USPC garnered a large portion of the casino market. A majority of casinos preferred its Bee brand playing cards as characteristics of the product addressed the requirements of casino gaming, such as durability and good "slip" for ease in shuffling and dealing. "Snapback" flexibility allowed the cards to bend without creating identifying creases.

Despite the failed economy in the United States at the time, sales at USPC increased substantially during the 1930s, from less than $700,000 in 1933, to $6.9 million in 1935. In 1936 the company purchased more production machinery and equipment from another playing card manufacturer that had gone out of business. By 1940 sales at USPC had increased to $8.3 million, with net earnings of $1 million. At this time the company produced about 75 percent of cards sold in the United States and was the largest manufacturer of playing cards in the world.

USPC filled several different roles in supporting the U.S. war effort during World War II. Most of its production facility was converted for the assembly of parachutes used to carry antipersonnel fragmentation bombs. In collaboration with the U.S. government, the company also developed playing cards that aided the war effort. USPC's "spotter cards" featured illustrations of tanks, ships, and aircraft used by enemy forces, helping military personnel identify the enemy. USPC also produced special decks of playing cards for American troops that featured the latest military intelligence. The cards concealed maps printed between the two layers of the cards; moisture loosened the glue to reveal escape routes from prisoner of war camps. At home the company advertised card playing as a good way to relax at home, thereby conserving gas rations.

USPC continued to grow as it returned to normal business in the postwar era. In this period, the South American game Canasta became very popular in the United States. To promote the game as well as sell more playing cards, USPC offered a free booklet on how to play Canasta, receiving some 600,000 requests for the booklet in the first month. Bicycle cards produced for Canasta featured the Fan Back design, a mirrored image of a fan decorated in a Spanish-style motif. The popularity of the game resulted in a spike in sales in 1950 to $21.3 million. Sales returned to the $17 to 19 million range through most of the 1950s. In 1959 sales increased to $21.5 million, and the company reported net income of $2.2 million.

In 1966, during the Vietnam War, USPC responded to a request for packs of cards containing only the Bicycle Ace of Spades, considered a portent of death and suffering by the Viet Cong. The Viet Cong had apparently been exposed to the idea from French fortune-telling during France's occupation of Indo-China. USPC contributed thousands of decks of the "Bicycle Secret Weapon" to troops in Vietnam. Strewn in jungles and villages, the Bicycle Ace of Spades may or may not have frightened Viet Cong during military raids, but it boosted the morale of the troops.

1970s–80s: Reorganizations and New Directions

USPC experienced several ownership changes during the late 20th century. In 1969 Diamond International Corporation, a forest products manufacturer, acquired the company, attracted by its profitability and an annual cash flow of $11 million. USPC became a largely neglected part of Diamond International's Specialty Printing Division and lost market share to low-price competitors, such as Hoyle Products. In response, a new marketing strategy was developed in which special back designs were offered to appeal to diverse consumer interests. For example, in 1978 the company issued cards with backs featuring a depiction of King Tut's exotic, black and golden tomb, commemorating the special exhibit of Egyptian treasures on tour in the United States. Moreover, the company won rights to use the official logo of the Olympics to produce and distribute souvenir playing cards during the 1980 Winter Olympics.

Diamond International installed new manufacturing technology and equipment to improve efficiency. One machine rapidly packaged, grouped, and shrink-wrapped cards. A five-color sheet-fed, offset press, installed in early 1981, improved the quality of the company's major brands of playing cards and provided more flexibility in production.

A victim of a corporate raider in 1982, Diamond International's holdings were sold off, with USPC going to Jesup and Lamont for $5 million. While Howard Curd, chairman of Jesup and Lamont, was interested in the company for its large market share, USPC continued to flounder under his leadership. The

Key Dates:

1881: Russell, Morgan and Company prints its first deck of playing cards.
1885: Production of the Bicycle brand of playing cards begins.
1894: The United States Playing Card Company (USPC) is established.
1922: Company establishes a radio station to broadcast lessons on how to play bridge.
1950: The craze for the South American card game Canasta boosts sales.
1969: Diamond International acquires USPC.
1984: Museum opens at Norwood facility displaying company's collection of playing cards.
1994: USPC is acquired from Frontenac by management and private investors.
2001: The company acquires Hoyle Products and its Hoyle brand playing cards.
2004: USPC accepts acquisition offer from Jarden Corporation.

company's near monopoly on the wholesale casino business suffered when Las Vegas authorities loosened licensing requirements for playing card manufacturers and the new Atlantic City casinos sought secondary suppliers. George Matteson Company's GEMACO brand became an important new competitor in the Atlantic City casino market during this time.

Curd initiated a sales and marketing program to recapture market share, and in January 1983, with the expectation of increased sales and economic recovery, USPC increased production. In addition to rehiring laid-off employees, the company invested some $16 million in automated production, including laser scanners to check for defects and equipment capable of cutting and packing 65 decks of cards per minute.

USPC faced a decline in interest in card playing during the 1980s. Video games were garnering the attention of children and adults were drawn to other activities. To address these trends the company sponsored canasta and euchre tournaments on college campuses. Advertising in consumer magazines, such as *Modern Maturity* and *Readers' Digest*, sought to retain the loyalty of its older card-playing customers. To compete with cheap imports the company introduced the inexpensive Metro brand of playing of cards.

In 1984 USPC opened a museum at the Norwich headquarters to display its collection of European and American playing cards, a collection begun in 1900 and featured in a book on the history of playing cards in 1931. The museum curator and historian traveled and gave lectures to promote the museum and card playing. The company's promotional efforts resulted in increased sales, from $40 million in 1982 to $54.9 million in 1984. After a loss in 1983, the company was able to realize net income of $3.5 million in 1984.

USPC coped with several labor challenges during the 1980s, including several protracted strikes, one that lasted for three months during the summer of 1983. In 1985 a five-month labor

strike ended with the company able to realize a 34 percent wage cut. In 1987 the company's skilled printers went on strike only to be replaced permanently by non-union workers. Curd hired Ronald Rule as chief executive officer in 1985. Rule made several changes to improve operations, such as eliminating excess inventory. The combination of reduced inventory and automation increased gross profit margins, from 21 percent to 30 percent. Rule reduced the company's sales force by nearly one-half and reorganized to better serve the casinos and retail chain stores.

USPC expanded through acquisition in the mid-1980s. In 1986 the company acquired an 87 percent interest in Heraclio Fournier S.A. of Spain, the largest manufacturer of playing cards in Europe and a family operation since 1868. The $7 million acquisition added $22 million in sales. In 1987 USPC acquired the Arrco Playing Card Company, a competitor in the Las Vegas market and the third largest playing card company in the United States, for $5 million.

The company diversified its product line with the introduction of several new games, some of which used playing cards. Under the newly created Bicycle Games Division, eight board games designed for pre-teens were introduced. Other games aimed at an older market included Pyramid Po-Ke-No, in which players formed a pyramid of ten poker hands, and The Headline Game, in which players made up media headlines based on predetermined letters of the alphabet and topics. A 1990 public relations program, the Most Outrageous Tabloid Headline (MOTH) awards, attracted attention to the game and gained coverage in *Newsweek*, the *Los Angeles Times*, the *Detroit Free Press*, and on television's *Joan Rivers Show*.

USPC underwent several organizational changes in the late 1980s and early 1990s before becoming an independent company again. In 1988 the company was merged into the Jesup Group then sold to Frontenac in 1989 for $95 million. After a four-year bidding war for ownership of the company, in January 1994 a group of investors led by Ronald Rule acquired USPC for $140 million, establishing Bicycle Holding Inc., as a corporate umbrella company.

1990s: Changing Consumer Interests

During the 1990s USPC directed its marketing efforts to appeal to diverse and changing consumer interests. Through several licensing agreements the company sought to attract children, boys in particular. For example, in 1991 the company released Major League Aces, featuring the best players from Major League Baseball, and in 1993 released Ditka's Picks, cards featuring players from the National Football League chosen by Hall of Fame player Mike Ditka. Other license agreements for card back designs included characters from Batman, Mighty Morphin Power Rangers, and Marvel Comics.

As personal computers in the home became widespread, the company licensed the Bicycle brand trademark design for use on computer games. In August 1991 SWFTE International (acquired by Expert Software in 1992) released the Bicycle Solitaire Game Pack which offered seven versions of solitaire for the PC. Other software games released during this time included cribbage and poker. In 1996 Expert Software released

Bicycle Hearts & Spades and Bicycle Pinochle. The Bicycle series quickly became the top selling card game software. Beginning in October 1998, Bicycle card games reached players worldwide via Microsoft's Internet Gaming Zone, which offered poker, bridge, rummy, blackjack, and euchre for multiple players on the network.

During the late 1990s sales increased as card playing enjoyed a rebirth in popularity. Consumer advertising in magazines supported the trend as did a radio advertising campaign that touched on the nostalgia of card playing with the sound of shuffling cards, resulting in significant sales increases in the major metropolitan areas where it aired. Gift tins of playing cards enjoyed brisk sales; USPC sold more than 400,000 units of a set with the Harley Davidson insignia between 1996 and 1998. In 1999 USPC obtained an important new contract when it received manufacturing and distribution rights for the Pokemon Rummy Game for children.

Also during this time, USPC introduced its first educational games for children. Licensing agreements in 1996 allowed the company to produce cards based on such educational programs as The Brain Quest, The Magic School Bus, and Bill Nye the Science Guy. In 1999 the company introduced Bicycle Kids, card games designed to encourage learning in mathematics, memory, and storytelling.

New Applications in a New Century

The January 2001 acquisition of Hoyle Products further enhanced USPC's market share. In addition to the popular Hoyle brand of playing cards and the Uno card game, the acquisition brought with it licensing agreements for computer products using the Hoyle brand. Moreover, in November of that year, Microsoft Games Division licensed the Bicycle brand to provide new game titles for its computer software.

USPC renewed its attention to the casino market by creating products that addressed the particular concerns of casino managers worldwide. In 2001 the company introduced tamper resistant cards; the following year the company began marketing cards that incorporated an anti-fraud technology developed by LaserLock Technology. Through this innovation, a visible band on a box of cards would indicate whether someone had tampered with the deck.

American politics provided another profitable venue for USPC during this time. USPC's Patriotic Tribute cards featured photographs of active servicemen and women. In 2003 the company manufactured cards for PlayingPolitics2004.com, featuring prominent politicians. Garnering perhaps the most media attention, however, was the April 2003 introduction by the U.S. Defense Intelligence Agency (DIA) of playing cards to help troops identify prominent members of Saddam Hussein's regime. These Iraq's Most Wanted cards featured the trademarked Hoyle joker, to which USPC maintained trademark rights. Companies that wanted to reproduce the deck with the Hoyle joker had a legal obligation to obtain licensing rights from the company. GreatUSAflags.com obtained exclusive distribution rights to the deck as originally produced by the DIA (with the Hoyle joker) and received orders online for 750,000 decks worldwide within the first week.

In February 2004, USPC braced for another reorganization as an acquisition bid from New York-based Jarden Corporation was accepted. Under the agreement, Jarden would pay $232 million for USPC and the other Bicycle holdings, including European player Heraclio Fournier S.A. and the International Playing Card Company of Canada. Management at Jarden expected to maintain USPC's Cincinnati headquarters. In addition to gaining a company Jarden management referred to in a 2004 *New York Times* article as "the quintessential dominate player in a niche market," the prospective new parent vowed to focus on the company's profitable licensing agreements and non-card game segments as well.

Principal Competitors

Gemaco Playing Card Company; Liberty Playing Card Company.

Further Reading

"The Bicycle Games Division of U.S. Playing Card Presents an Adult Party Game Called The Headline Game," *Playthings,* February 1989, p. 103.

Blankenhorn, Dana, "New for PC: Bicycle Solitaire game pack debuts," *Newsbytes,* August 14, 1991.

Boyer, Mike, "Playing Card to Deal with Dispute," *Cincinnati Enquirer,* December 4, 1999, p. 14C.

"Card Company Reaches for Younger Generations," *Cincinnati Enquirer,* August 22, 1999.

Carlson, Scott, "St. Paul, Minn.-Based Brown & Bigelow Sells Playing-Card Unit to Ohio Company," *Saint Paul Pioneer Press,* January 17, 2001.

Croft, Tara, "Four of a Kind for Jarden," *Daily Deal,* February 27, 2004.

"'Dealing' in Education," *Science Activities,* Fall 1996, p. 36.

"Expert Software and Microsoft Corp. to Bring Bicycle Card Games to the Internet Gaming Zone," *Business Wire,* July 29, 1998.

Feldman, Amy, "Rule Rules," *Forbes,* July 3, 1995, p. 16.

Hannon, Kerry, " 'We're Finally Playing with a Full Deck'," *Forbes,* April 18, 1988, p. 35.

"Independence MO Firm Playing Its Cards Right," *St. Louis Post-Dispatch,* March 19, 1995, p. 8E.

"Local Firm Big Winner in Pokemon Card Game," *Cincinnati Enquirer,* August 22, 1999.

"Morehead, Albert H., "Rummy From Argentina," *New York Times,* August 28, 1949, p. SM22.

"The Most Outrageous Tabloid Headline," *Adweek's Marketing Week,* March 12, 1990, p. R16.

Raines, Halsey, "Playing Cards and Their History," *New York Times,* February 8, 1931, p. 66.

"Rosenthal Named Chairman of U.S. Playing Card Co.," *Wall Street Journal,* February 3, 1937, p. 3.

Solomon, Jolie B., "U.S. Playing Card, Hit by Video Games, Bids for a Fresh Deal," *Wall Street Journal,* January 18, 1984, p. 1.

Sorkin, Andrew Ross, "A Deal that Involves Playing with Far More Than a Full Deck," *New York Times,* February 26, 2004, p. C4.

Symons, Allene, "Manufacturers and Chains Deal a New Hand for Playing Cards," *Drug Store News,* March 2, 1998, p. 35.

"U.S. Playing Card Acquires Company," *Wall Street Journal,* September 28, 1929, p. 6.

Wood, Roy, "Norwood Firm Plays its Cards Right," *Cincinnati Post,* January 15, 2002, p. 7B.

—Mary Tradii

USAA

9800 Fredericksburg Road
San Antonio, Texas 78288
U.S.A.
Telephone: (210) 498-2211
Toll Free: (800) 531-8722
Fax: (210) 498-9940
Web site: http://www.usaa.com

Private Company
Incorporated: 1922 as United States Army Automobile
    Association
Employees: 22,000
Total Assets: $9.22 billion (2002)
NAIC: 522120 Savings Institutions; 522210 Credit Card
    Issuing; 523920 Portfolio Management; 524210
    Insurance Agencies and Brokerages; 524113 Direct
    Life Insurance Carriers; 524114 Direct Health and
    Medical Insurance Carriers; 524126 Direct Property
    and Casualty Insurance Carriers

USAA is a diversified insurance and financial services company patronized primarily by U.S. military personnel and their dependents. It is considered to be the first "one-stop" retail financial services company in the United States. Since most of its business is conducted via mail, telephone, and the Internet, *Best's Review* calls USAA the country's largest direct mail company.

The country's fourth largest auto insurer and fourth largest home insurance company, USAA was founded in Texas in the 1920s as a mutual association, so that military officers, who moved frequently, could obtain automobile insurance. Led by a series of retired officers, who managed its assets and operations conservatively, USAA grew steadily throughout the century, as successive wars and military build-ups increased its pool of eligible members.

In the 1970s and 1980s, USAA began to branch out into additional financial services related to its insurance business, and with its customer base of loyal and reliable members, the company grew rapidly in size and financial strength. A banking subsidiary, USAA Federal Savings Bank, was established in 1983; in 2002, this unit had assets of $12.5 billion. Altogether, USAA owned or managed more than $71 billion in assets.

Origins

USAA was founded in 1922, when Major William Henry Garrison called together 24 of his fellow army officers at the Gunter Hotel in San Antonio, Texas. The purpose of the meeting was to discuss solutions to the problem of automobile insurance for army officers. Because of their frequent moves, officers often found that their policies were extremely expensive and prone to cancellation. Moreover, many insurance companies were unreliable and failed with some regularity, leaving their former policyholders without insurance.

The 25 men present at Garrison's meeting decided to form a mutual company and thereby would insure one another. They took as their model the Army Cooperative Fire Insurance Company—based at Fort Leavenworth since 1887—and called the new enterprise the United States Army Automobile Association. An agreement was signed, and a president, vice-president, and board of directors were established, all of whom were active duty army officers. Shortly thereafter, a manager named Harold Dutton was also hired, and he set up an office at Kelly Field in San Antonio. The new firm issued its first policy to Major Walker Moore for his 1922 Elcar. He was charged $114.47.

Within two months, USAA had enrolled 142 members, and proceeds from their policies totaled $820. Ten months later, however, USAA had a deficit of more than $3,000, caused by its failure to accurately estimate the cost of an insurance policy. In an effort to compensate for the shortfall in funds, USAA's board voted at its first annual meeting in 1924 to extend membership to all active duty and retired officers of the U.S. Navy and Marine Corps. The company's name was changed to reflect this broader constituency, becoming the United Services Automobile Association.

The 1924 annual meeting also resulted in a vote to adopt an industry standard for insurance premiums, minus a discount of 20 percent. In addition, the company's leaders applied for a

Company Perspectives:

The mission of USAA is to facilitate the financial security of its members, associates, and their families through provision of a full range of highly competitive financial products and services; in so doing USAA seeks to be the provider of choice for the military community.

Texas license, declared an 8 percent dividend, and established a reserve for losses. By the end of the year, the company had more than 3,300 members and assets exceeding $85,000.

Two years later, in an effort to foster growth, USAA's board designated funds for advertising. With $1,500, the company mailed a flier to all eligible officers and put an ad in the *Service Journal.* In addition, the company bought 6,000 company emblems which it sold to members for display on the hoods of their cars. These symbols soon became popular among members and served to promote the company.

By 1927, USAA's business was thriving. Its management, however, was in chaos. The board of directors had split, and a breakaway group had begun meeting in secret, plotting to overthrow the company. At the same time, USAA's secretary-treasurer and general manager were engaged in a struggle for control of the company. After a six-hour board meeting, during which power changed hands repeatedly, it was determined that a new leader was needed from outside the company to restore members' faith in USAA's leadership. Thus, on January 1, 1928, Major General Ernest Hinds, commanding general of Fort Sam Houston in Texas, became both the general manager and secretary-treasurer of USAA. Assured that he would have complete control of the company, Hinds took over. The company then had 7,500 members and more than $300,000 in assets.

Less than two years after Hinds assumed command, the crash of the stock market plunged the United States into the Great Depression. Under Hinds' leadership, USAA invested its money in government securities early on in the financial crisis. These safe bonds prevented the company from losing large sums of money in the volatile financial markets. When USAA did invest in the stock market, it did so conservatively, limiting its exposure to $20,000.

An unexpected side effect of the depression was that cars bearing the USAA hood emblem became the special targets of thieves, causing the company to discontinue distribution of the symbols. USAA adopted another preventive measure in 1938, introducing its first Safe Driver Reward Plan, which enrolled a majority of the company's members.

By 1941, the year the United States entered World War II, USAA's membership exceeded 22,000, and its assets had increased five-fold over the previous decade. The company continued to grow throughout the war and instituted a practice of sending telegrams and updating policies when soldiers who had been declared missing in action or had been taken prisoner resurfaced. As a result of the war, and the vast number of men conscripted into the military, the number of potential USAA members grew exponentially. By 1947, the company's annual business was double what it had been six years earlier, and its membership had increased by more than a third.

Postwar Growth

In 1948, USAA opened its first office outside San Antonio, in New York City. This step was taken in order to qualify the company to write insurance policies for people who lived in New York. Even further afield, USAA opened an office in Frankfurt, Germany, to serve members of the American occupation forces in Europe.

During the late 1940s, USAA's business grew rapidly, aided by the Cold War and compulsory ROTC programs on the campuses of land-grant colleges. The company's revenues doubled between 1948 and 1949, and then doubled again by 1952.

The following year, when the company's offices on Grayson Street in San Antonio had become badly overcrowded, USAA's board of directors agreed to spend $6 million to construct a new facility in the city. Containing such amenities as an employee cafeteria, the facility was designed in the hopes of lessening the company's employee turnover rate of more than 100 percent a year. By 1956, the new building on Broadway was complete, and the company's 802 employees, nearly all of whom were female, had been installed.

That year, USAA's bylaws were altered to modernize the company's corporate structure. The company's general manager was named president, and his assistants were named vice-presidents. This change was made to accommodate USAA's ever-expanding operations, since the company's business had doubled again between 1952 and 1955. In 1957, USAA installed an IBM 650 computer, the first move in the drive to automate its cumbersome operations.

Within five years, the company's new facilities were again deemed inadequate. In 1962, USAA added 110,000 more square feet to its San Antonio building and began conversion to a newer, larger computer system, the IBM 7074-1041. Also during this time, the board of directors amended the bylaws to enable the company to offer life insurance, along with property and casualty insurance. With $5 million in seed money, the company began to organize the USAA Life Company.

By 1967, USAA's assets had reached $206 million, and its membership topped 650,000, a rapid rate of growth attributed to the mass mobilization of troops to fight in Vietnam. In 1969, the company's presidency was assumed by Robert F. McDermott, a retired Air Force brigadier general who had previously been Dean of the Faculty at the Air Force Academy. McDermott set out to reform the company, instituting more modern, streamlined procedures to improve employee morale and customer service.

Such reform was necessitated largely by USAA's failure to implement adequate computer systems. For example, in the late 1960s, the company was still keeping separate claims and underwriting files on each of its members. In order for a new insurance policy to be issued, 55 steps had to be performed in 32 different locations spread across four separate floors. Files piled up on employees' desks and were continually misplaced. The company hired dozens of college students to come to its offices every night to search, often in vain, for missing folders.

Key Dates:

1922:	USAA is established in San Antonio to provide auto insurance for Army officers.
1941:	Membership in the association exceeds 22,000.
1948:	A New York office is opened.
1956:	A new headquarters is completed in San Antonio.
1973:	Membership opens to National Guard and Reserves.
1983:	USAA Federal Savings Bank and USAA Brokerage Services are established.
1997:	Membership extended to enlisted personnel.
1999:	A Web site is launched.

Moreover, the many separate units of USAA had poor lines of communication, and personnel problems at the company were rampant. Managers were promoted solely on the basis of seniority, which often caused friction, and many jobs were regarded as repetitious and boring, as some people were assigned such tasks as unsealing envelopes and pulling staples. Not surprisingly, the annual turnover rate stood at 43 percent.

Restructuring for the 1970s

Under McDermott, numerous changes were made. The company reduced its number of employees by more than 800 through attrition by the end of 1969. Those employees who remained were given much broader job descriptions in an effort to increase their interest in their work. To make sure they were able to perform new tasks, USAA inaugurated a program of extensive employee training.

In addition, USAA invested heavily in computers and telecommunications to improve service to its members. With new computers, USAA was able to make several important changes. Instead of writing a separate insurance policy for each car, for instance, the company began to write multi-car policies. With this shift, USAA was able to eliminate hundreds of employee slots and also reduce the cyclical nature of its business, spreading its workload more evenly throughout the year.

Furthermore, USAA restructured its organization, dividing members by geography rather than by type of policy issued. Under this new structure, company leaders devised a 20-year plan for growth prompted by the results of a member survey, which asked whether a more diverse line of services would be appreciated. Respondents to the survey indicated that they would be interested in several additional financial services, including mortgage loans, auto financing and leasing, mutual funds, and a bank. Car-related services, such as an auto travel club, were also deemed desirable. This data paved the way for USAA's eventual diversification into several fields outside the insurance business. However, development of these new fields would not begin for several years, since the company's board of directors balked at this radical revision of the company's scope.

In 1973, USAA bylaws were revised to allow officers in the National Guard and the military reserves to be eligible for membership, as well as military dependents. Members from these groups soon made up a large part of the company's

business. A centralized training and education facility was developed during this time, and the company moved from its overcrowded offices to a new building, situated on 286 acres in northwest San Antonio. This facility became the world's largest private office building. With tennis courts, picnic tables, four cafeterias, and a company store, it was designed to enhance employee satisfaction on the job. The company also instituted a four-day work week to provide its workers with more flexible hours.

Along with the main San Antonio facility, USAA opened several smaller, satellite offices in areas around the country with large concentrations of military personnel, including Sacramento, Seattle, Colorado Springs, Tampa, and the Virginia cities of Norfolk and Reston. A second overseas office was opened in London.

Expanding Services for the 1980s and 1990s

After an amendment in the company's bylaws, USAA finally moved to provide a greater number of services for its members. Organizing new functions under subsidiaries, the company added the USAA Life Insurance Company and the USAA Investment Management Company, or IMCO, which managed a number of mutual funds. USAA also began to offer a discount brokerage service.

In the 1980s, the USAA Federal Savings Bank was founded, establishing lucrative Visa and MasterCard operations, mortgage and home equity loans, deposit services, and consumer loans. USAA also set up a travel agency and began to offer real estate investment opportunities. The move directly into the real estate market was realized with the completion of USAA Towers, a 23-story retirement community, and USAA Parklane West, a medical care facility. Each of these new enterprises made a broader range of services available to USAA members and also contributed to the company's overall net worth.

By the early 1990s, USAA's diversified business lines were thriving. The Life Insurance Company, carrying policies totaling more than $46 billion, was the country's 43rd largest life insurance company; within three years, it ranked 37th on the list, with $57.4 billion worth of policies written. The company's bank, USAA Federal Savings Bank, reported over $3.5 billion in assets, had issued more than 1.5 million credit cards, and had become one of the five largest savings and loan institutions in the United States. In addition, USAA had also inaugurated a joint program with Sprint to provide discount telephone services to its customers.

By 1993, USAA's owned and managed assets had reached $33 billion as the company, in its broadened guise, became the 21st largest American diversified financial services company in the Fortune Service 500. USAA's attention to employee morale and training had also won praise, and it was named one of the ten best companies to work for in America. With a loyal and well-trained corps of employees, and a smooth-running operation that ran with precision, USAA appeared well situated to continue its growth and solid financial success well into the 21st century under the leadership of new chairman and CEO, Robert T. Herres, a retired U.S. Air Force general.

Developments in the 1990s and Beyond

A new building for USAA's mid-Atlantic regional center in Norfolk, Virginia, was completed in 1992. It featured contemporary architecture and high-tech security.

By the mid-1990s, USAA had nearly three million members and 16,000 employees. About 95 percent of active-duty military officers were customers, and in 1996 USAA opened up its auto insurance to enlisted personnel. Revenues were $6.8 billion in 1996. USAA had a greater than average exposure to weather-related catastrophes due to its retired members moving to coastal areas.

A new product, retirement and estate planning, was added in 1998. The success of cross selling led to expansion and to a need to upgrade both USAA's facilities and its computer networks. From 1995 to 1998, the company spent $100 million upgrading its network infrastructure (Cisco Systems was the vendor) for its regional offices and its headquarters, which, according to the *San Antonio Business Journal,* processed 16 million computer transactions a day. USAA's document imaging system, one of the world's largest, also required sophisticated data handling capabilities. According to *Forbes,* USAA scanned 65,000 documents, or 650,000 pages, a day, and sent out 5,000 faxes a day without producing hard copies for them. USAA saved 35,000 square feet of office space by going paperless.

USAA's relationship with its employees continued to draw positive press. It consistently landed a spot in *Fortune*'s "100 Best Companies to Work for in America" on the strength of such benefits as college tuition reimbursement ($2.7 million worth per year, according to *Fortune*), a childcare center, and recreational facilities. It also offered a four-day, 38-hour work week. Dress was business casual, with jeans allowed on Fridays. A one million square-foot expansion to the company's 4.5 million square-foot San Antonio headquarters was begun in 1998.

Robert G. Davis became chairman, president, and CEO of USAA in June 1999, succeeding Robert Herres. Davis had formerly led several of the group's subsidiaries. Before joining USAA, he had worked for a number of investment companies and banks. Davis succeeded Herres as chairman as well in 2002.

There were considerable layoffs in 2000 and 2001, and the number of regional offices was also reduced. Offices in Reston, Virginia, and Seattle were closed and about 800 of their personnel relocated to Norfolk, Virginia, and Colorado Springs. USAA had 24,000 employees at the time; 17,000 of these were in San Antonio, Texas. By July 2002, though, the company was hiring again for 100 customer service positions for its San Antonio office. Another 500 positions were added there in March 2004; regional offices were hiring as well.

The end of the bull market of the 1990s affected USAA's investment income, but the insurer was still able to post a profit (unlike its larger rival State Farm, which was losing money by the billions). Consolidated net income fell 17 percent to $500 million in 2002.

In 2003, USAA was preparing to make all of its core processing transactions accessible through the Internet. The Web already handled most of USAA's non-insurance transactions and half of its insurance transactions, such as rate inquiries, reported *American Banker.*

Principal Subsidiaries

USAA Alliance Services Company; USAA Federal Savings Bank; USAA Investment Management Company; USAA Property and Casualty; USAA Real Estate Company.

Principal Competitors

AIG; Allstate; MetLife; Nationwide; State Farm.

Further Reading

"Banking Veteran Moves to Top Job at USAA," *American Banker,* February 10, 1999.

Chordas, Lori, "The Ultimate Niche," *Best's Review,* November 2002, pp. 30ff.

Clark, Michael, "Is This the Ideal Place to Work? Fostering Employee Loyalty Is a Business Strategy at USAA," *Virginian-Pilot,* February 1, 1998, p. D1.

"Customer-Focused Culture Gives USAA Edge, Chief Says," *Best's Review,* April 2002, p. 112.

Freiberg, Kevin, and Jackie Freiberg, *GUTS! Companies That Blow the Doors Off Business-as-Usual,* New York: Doubleday Publishing, 2003.

Henkoff, Ronald, "Growing Your Company: Five Ways to Do It Right!," *Fortune,* November 25, 1996, pp. 78ff.

Levering, Robert, and Milton Moskowitz, *The 100 Best Companies to Work for in America,* New York: Doubleday, 1993.

Mack, Toni, "They Have Faith in Us," *Forbes,* July 25, 1988, pp. 181f.

Poling, Travis E., "USAA Employees Brace for Layoffs; Firm Seeks Changes in Tough Times," *San Antonio Express-News,* July 13, 2001.

Rifkin, Glenn, "USAA: Conquering a Paper Mountain," *Forbes,* October 9, 1995.

Santosus, Megan, "USAA: Document Imaging," *CIO,* April 1, 1993, pp. 32f.

Shean, Tom, "USAA Plans to Interlink Its Services," *Virginian-Pilot,* Bus. Sec., October 11, 1993.

——, "Area to Gain 500 USAA Employees," *Virginian-Pilot,* June 21, 2001, p. D1.

——, "Respected Insurer Not Immune to Difficult Times," *Virginian-Pilot,* June 15, 2003, p. D1.

Sidime, Aissatou, "Following Big Layoffs, USAA Is Hiring," *San Antonio Express-News,* July 12, 2002.

Wade, Will, "Already a Maverick, USAA Shifting Online with Insurance Menu," *American Banker,* January 16, 2003, p. 12.

Weiss, Sebastian, "USAA Nears Completion of $100 Million Network Upgrade," *San Antonio Business Journal,* December 5, 1997.

——, "One-Stop Model Fuels USAA's Fast Growth, McDermott Says," *San Antonio Business Journal,* April 27, 1998.

—Elizabeth Rourke
—update: Frederick C. Ingram

Windswept Environmental Group, Inc.

100 Sweeneydale Avenue
Bay Shore, New York 11706
U.S.A.
Telephone: (631) 434-1300
Toll Free: (800) 282-8701
Fax: (631) 435-4337
Web site: http//:www.tradewindsenvironmental.com

Public Company
Incorporated: 1986 as International BankCard Service
   Corp.
Employees: 101
Sales: $32.9 million (2002)
Stock Exchanges: Over the Counter (OTC)
Ticker Symbol: WEGI
NAIC: 3344512 Automatic Environmental Control
   Manufacturing for Residential, Commercial, and
   Appliance Use

Windswept Environmental Group, Inc., operating out of Bay Shore, New York, is a holding company whose subsidiaries offer a wide range of environmental services, including emergency response and catastrophe restoration; site restoration; mold contamination remediation; commercial drying; wetlands restoration; asbestos abatement; fire and flood restoration; lead abatement; underground storage tank removal; spill remediation; oil spill response; chemical spill response; duct cleaning; microbial remediation; and environmental services. Approximately one-fifth of Windswept's revenues are derived from insurance customers.

1980s Origins

The origins of Windswept date back to 1986 and the incorporation of International BankCard Service Corporation, which marketed credit card and consumer services to financial institutions. Over the next few years the company also became involved in a number of divergent businesses, such as video advertising and gaming machine manufacturing. To reflect this diversity, the company changed its name to Integrated Resource

Technologies (IRT) in July 1992. During the course of fiscal 1993 it divested itself of its financial services assets. In fiscal 1994 IRT completed several acquisitions to move into the environmental cleanup business, focusing initially on asbestos remediation, transportation, and disposal. In October 1993 it acquired a 51 percent stake in Dicar Asbestos, followed a month later by the purchase of Phoenix Dismantling, a hazardous waste transporter operating in Queens, New York. Then, in December 1993, IRT used stock to acquire Trade-Winds Environmental Restoration, Inc., the subsidiary that today provides the bulk of Windswept's revenues and brought with it the company's current chief executive, Michael O'Reilly.

O'Reilly studied marine biology in college in Puerto Rico while he worked for the family's charter boat operation. He also worked as a diver on marine salvage crews as well as on some marine cleanup jobs. He then moved his family to Long Island and launched Branch Services, Inc. to provide environmental cleanup services. In 1990 he went to work for North Shore Environmental Remediation, Inc., serving as a vice-president for the company, which was involved in environmental cleanup services and lead and asbestos removal. O'Reilly next established Trade-Winds Environmental Restoration in 1993 and was soon approached by IRT to sell the business in exchange for stock and a seat on the board. Trade-Winds proved to be a solid source of profits for IRT over the next two years. IRT then completed a number of other acquisitions between 1993 and 1995 as part of an effort to achieve vertical integration in the environmental industry. The company bought a controlling stake in Kimberlyn Trading Inc., a start-up commodity brokerage that dealt in environmental paints and crumb rubber. In early 1994 IRT bought Eastgate Removal Inc., and in 1995 acquired New York Testing Laboratories Inc., which permitted the company to perform in-house and third-party testing, of blood lead levels for lead-abatement workers. Despite these advances, the parent company, renamed Comprehensive Environmental Systems in 1995, posted overall losses, a situation that prevented O'Reilly's Trade-Winds from fully investing in its expansion, and also put it in arrears with vendors.

O'Reilly joined forces with other unhappy shareholders to buy out the contracts of senior management, spending more than $1 million drawn from operating funds. Although it may

Company Perspectives:

When a catastrophe of any kind occurs, whether it is fire, smoke, water, wind, oil/chemical spill, biological hazard, explosion or radiological release, Trade-Winds is committed to providing the highest quality, immediate response, remediation, and restoration services. Our goal is simple: To significantly reduce an owner's loss. Trade-Winds knows that it is essential to have a complete understanding of what the owner and the insurance company require—complete restoration of facilities and equipment to productivity with minimal down time. Our hands-on approach is what sets us apart.

have simply appeared that the management team was incompetent, O'Reilly, and the world at large, would soon learn that, in fact, the officers were engaged in criminal activity and had essentially hijacked the corporation in order to bilk unsuspecting investors. Three weeks after O'Reilly appointed himself president of Comprehensive Environmental, members of previous management were indicted and charged with securities fraud, the result of an investigation that originally focused on the conduct of Dan Dorfman, a CNBC financial commentator and writer for *Money* magazine.

Roots of Stock Fraud Scheme Dating to 1993

Comprehensive's connection to a massive stock fraud scheme began in mid-1993 when Leo J. Mangan was named the company's chief operating officer. What investors did not know, and what should have been revealed in SEC filings, was that Mangan had a criminal record, including eight arrests, the earliest dating to 1972 and the most recent in 1991. Most of the arrests involved drug possession and distribution. Mangan's two colleagues, Grant Curtis and Timothy Masley, had their own questionable backgrounds. Curtis had been convicted of bank fraud in 1994 and, according to *Business Week,* Masley was a "former broker with North American Investment Corporation, a controversial Hartford brokerage firm that ceased operation in 1988 amid stock-manipulation investigations and a class action by investors. ... his record with the National Association of Securities Dealers shows disciplinary problems, including a suspension." According to the *Wall Street Journal,* the three men controlled Comprehensive, as well as Alter Sales Co., a Florida auto parts company, by issuing stock to "bogus companies around the world that were allegedly created by co-conspirators Ray Irangy and Pedro Gomez to hide the group's control of the two companies, the indictment says. The phony foreign companies purportedly rendered services in exchange for the stock, but the indictment says they never did."

In essence, the scheme called for a reverse split of the company's stock, which reduced the number of shares in the marketplace, thus raising its price. The group then issued millions of shares of stock to themselves for little or no consideration, some of which were used to procure favorable television coverage to pay brokers to tout the stock. "But investors didn't learn about the new shares until months later, when the moves showed up in the company's quarterly SEC reports," reported the *Wall Street Journal.* According to *Business Week,* "Mangan

hired stock-promoter Donald Kessler, an acquaintance, who was reputed to have an ability to get plugs from his close friend Dan Dorfman. On April 18, [1995,] Dorfman gave a positive CNBC report on Alter. ... About that time, Kessler became CEO of Comprehensive."

Another member of the scheme that enveloped Comprehensive was a rogue SEC enforcement attorney named James W. Nearen. *Business Week* reported that, according to a federal indictment, in 1994, "Nearen began looking for work in the private sector. He approached a brokerage, which sources say was Chatfield Dean & Co., an Englewood (Colo.) penny-stock firm that then was the target of an SEC probe. To ingratiate himself, Nearen allegedly fraternized with the 'lead target' at the firm and disclosed nonpublic information to help the target firm defend the SEC action. That same year, Nearen became involved with the probe of Comprehensive Environmental." In 1995 he left the SEC to work with Comprehensive as "a special regulatory consultant." In February 1995 Comprehensive completed a 1-for-10 stock split. Then in June 1995 the little-known company caught the attention of the press when the price of its stock increased by 50 percent over the course of two trading sessions on heavy volume. The company issued no news to account for the sudden interest, although Mangan noted that "business is booming," and the chairman maintained that Comprehensive was "the most undervalued stock on the exchange." It was later determined that from 1994 until October 1996, when O'Reilly succeeded in taking control of the company, Comprehensive issued more than four million shares of stock to participants in the stock manipulation scheme. Ultimately, seven people pleaded guilty and were imprisoned for their role in the fraudulent activities surrounding the company, with the various charges including stock fraud, income tax evasion, insider trading, and money laundering. Dorfman was never charged with a crime.

O'Reilly may have succeeded in removing Comprehensive's management team, but he had no idea what had been going on in the shadows. O'Reilly told *Long Island Business News,* "I learned about the charges from the papers. ... One of the people indicted was a former enforcement agent for SEC. There was just no reason to suspect anything was off-color." With the company already strapped for cash because of the management contract buyouts, O'Reilly now faced a long-term effort to rebuild the company's tarnished reputation and answer charges leveled at the company. The price of its stock dropped precipitously, and because of the indictments of Mangen and Nearen the company was delisted by NASDAQ. Reduced to penny stock status, Comprehensive now traded over-the-counter. A name change to Windswept Environmental Group in 1997 was of limited help, and certainly did nothing to end three federal investigations into the company's fiscal operations during the Mangan-Kessler-Nearen era. It was not until June 1999 that the company reached a settlement, which did not include any fines or penalties.

New Management Team Following the 1996 Indictments

In the wake of the 1996 indictments, O'Reilly installed a new management team, oversaw the election of a new board of directors, instituted better internal control procedures, and es-

<table>
<tr><td colspan="2">

Key Dates:

</td></tr>
<tr><td>**1986:**</td><td>International BankCard Service Corporation is founded.</td></tr>
<tr><td>**1992:**</td><td>To reflect its divergent businesses, the company changes its name to Integrated Resource Technologies.</td></tr>
<tr><td>**1993:**</td><td>Company enters the environment cleanup business through several acquisitions, including Trade-Winds Environmental Restoration, Inc.</td></tr>
<tr><td>**1995:**</td><td>The company is renamed Comprehensive Environmental Systems.</td></tr>
<tr><td>**1996:**</td><td>Company is taken private through a management-led buyout.</td></tr>
<tr><td>**1997:**</td><td>The company's name is changed again, to Windswept Environmental Group.</td></tr>
<tr><td>**2001:**</td><td>Revenues improve as the company transforms itself into a full-service emergency response provider.</td></tr>
<tr><td>**2002:**</td><td>Sales total $32.9 million, a 34 percent increase over the previous year.</td></tr>
</table>

tablished an audit committee. Operating under a cloud, however, proved difficult. Spending some $2 million in legal and accounting fees was burdensome enough, but he also had to deal with the loss of Windswept's $10 million bonding capacity, which prevented the company from bidding on major contracts. To guarantee $2 million in bonding O'Reilly had to put up his own assets—essentially everything he owned, including his house. In addition to money problems, he had to deal with what he called soft costs. According to a 1999 profile of Windswept in *Crain's New York Business,* "It is the soft costs—all of the time he has had to spend away from operations defending himself—that Mr. O'Reilly terms 'devastating.' He estimates that nearly half of his time and that of other key executives was spent not on getting the business done but in desperately trying to keep it from fleeing. 'We also had to take on lower-quality work and become more aggressive in our pricing in order to show the industry as a whole that we're not going to go out of business,' says Mr. O'Reilly."

Despite a lack of resources, Comprehensive was able to achieve some external growth through an acquisition in 1997. It paid $1.5 million in cash and stock for North Atlantic Laboratories, Inc., which served the New York metropolitan area offering certified environmental training, laboratory testing, and consulting services. But Comprehensive continued to struggle. Because working capital was limited, in the first quarter of 1998, O'Reilly had to lay off about 20 percent of his 100-person workforce. In September 1999 O'Reilly gained some financial cushion by selling a controlling interest in the company to Australia-based Spotless Plastics for $2.5 million. In addition, Spotless lent the company $2 million. As a result of this change in ownership, O'Reilly stepped down as chairman, replaced by Peter A. Wilson, a director of Spotless's parent company, Spotless Group Limited.

With this infusion of cash, O'Reilly was able to broaden Windswept's emergency response and disaster recovery services and invest in the equipment needed to perform wildlife

rehabilitation and wetland restoration. According to *Long Island Business News,* "Using a portable lab, company technicians are now able to do wildlife blood work-ups in the field, to allow for better triage efforts. The company also specializes in the area known as hazing: preventively driving wildlife out of a distressed area."

A major development in 1998 that helped Windswept a great deal was the opening of a second operation, located in Brooklyn within the Bayside Fuel Oil terminal near the East River, at a cost less than the market rate. Not only did the site allow Windswept to better serve Bayside Fuel, a new client, but it also acted as an operational hub for oil spill cleanup projects. The metropolitan area included some 30 tank farms, which offered the potential for a lucrative revenue stream. The second office was especially useful because Windswept had recently signed four new oil spill response agreements with area companies: Castle Oil, Staten Island Ferry, Northrop Grumman Corporation, and Warex Terminal Corporation.

In 1998 Windswept recorded revenues of nearly $12 million and a net loss of more than $5.6 million, but the company appeared to be turning the corner. In 1999 revenues grew to nearly $14 million and the loss was trimmed to $1.3 million. Unfortunately, in 2000 Windswept suffered a setback. A drop in asbestos and construction/renovation projects had an adverse impact of the balance sheet, leading to a falloff in sales, which totaled less than $12.9 million in 2000 and a net loss of more than $2.25 million. On a positive note, the company saw an increase in emergency response and environmental remediation/compliance projects, a development that reinforced management's decision to de-emphasize asbestos abatement and to transform Windswept into a full-service emergency response provider. The success of this strategy was established in 2001, as the company saw revenues improve to $22 million and it turned a profit in excess of $1 million.

The tragic events of September 11, 2001, when terrorists leveled the twin towers of the World Trade Center, provided a major boost to Windswept's business. The company's largest project to this point had been a 600-worker toxic mold cleanup assignment. Now Windswept put together a team of 2,000 workers to clean a number of corporate offices and the New York City mayor's office. For fiscal 2002, which ended July 31, 2002, the company enjoyed a 34 percent increase in sales over the previous year, totaling $32.9 million. Net income grew to $3.5 million.

A sound business model, as well as the confluence of world events, allowed Windswept to overcome the shadow cast upon it in the mid-1990s, but perhaps the company's greatest asset was its CEO, O'Reilly. Chris Seniuk, a principal at a consulting firm that did business with Windswept, told *Long Island Business News,* "There are a lot of what are called shirt-and-tie companies who come in (to a waste spillage situation) and will give you a plan of action. Mike, he gets his fingernails dirty. He doesn't just give you a plan of action. He gets it done."

Principal Subsidiaries

Trade-Winds Environmental Restoration, Inc.; North Atlantic Laboratories Inc.

Principal Competitors

CET Environmental Services, Inc.; Clean Harbors, Inc.; Professional Service Industries, Inc.

Further Reading

McMorris, Francis A., "Ex-SEC Lawyer, 5 Others Are Indicted for Fraud, Following Dorfman Probe," *Wall Street Journal,* October 7, 1996, p. B12.

Schroeder, Michael, "Caveat Entrepreneur," *Business Week,* October 14, 1996, p. 114.

Shane, Alice, "Windswept Finds a Better Climate," *Crain's New York Business,* October 26, 1998, p. 17.

Strugatch, Warren, "Fraud Flurries Clear for Windswept," *Long Island Business News,* July 2, 1999, p. 1A.

—Ed Dinger

Woolrich Inc.

1 Mill Street
Woolrich, Pennsylvania 17779
U.S.A.
Telephone: (570) 769-6464
Toll Free: (800) 995-1299
Fax: (570) 769-6470
Web site: http://www.woolrich.com

Private Company
Incorporated: 1830
Employees: 660
Sales: $200 million (2003 est.)
NAIC: 313210 Broadwoven Fabric Mills; 314129 Other
Household Textile Product Mills; 315225 Men's and
Boys' Cut and Sew Work Clothing Manufacturing;
315228 Men's and Boys' Cut and Sew Other
Outerwear Manufacturing

Woolrich Inc. calls itself "The Original Outdoor Clothing Company." The wool hat and red-and-black plaid hunting coat that one associates with New England hunters have been staples at Woolrich since the 19th century. The company is headquartered in the small village of the same name in Clinton County, Pennsylvania. As the oldest vertically integrated woolen mill in the United States, Woolrich handles manufacturing "from sheep to shirt." However, it has followed the lead of other outerwear manufacturers in becoming more of a marketing operation; many of its products are produced overseas from U.S.-spun cloth or simply bought finished from other manufacturers. With a history dating back to 1830, Woolrich is one of the most venerable brands in the United States. In the last half of the 1990s, the company began licensing its trademark in earnest, extending the brand into hosiery, boys' clothing, footwear, home furnishings, and other areas.

Origins

The company's first mill was founded in 1830 in Plum Run, Pennsylvania, by English immigrants John Rich and Daniel McCormick. They sold woolen yarn and fabric to families of loggers and trappers. Rich bought out his partner in 1845, when the operation was expanded and moved to the town that would become known as Woolrich. Rich took one of his sons into the business seven years later.

Woolrich made army blankets during the Civil War. (It later offered reproductions of these and fabric for making uniforms to Civil War reenactors and film production companies.) Other Rich family members bought and sold shares in the business. By 1888, when it became a partnership of three brothers, the town surrounding the mill was known as Woolrich, rather than Richville, according to an account in *Shooting Industry*.

The company spun off into leisure wear in the late 1920s, producing woolen bathing suits and golf pants. In 1939, the company outfitted Admiral Byrd's expedition to Antarctica.

The company grew in the 1950s, though at the end of the decade its product line remained exclusively wool-based. Woolrich benefited from the 1960s and 1970s boom in camping and focused on capturing general recreational users rather than sportsmen. Roswell Brayton, Sr. was company president from 1968 to 1985, when he became chairman, a post he held for another eleven years. Woolrich began marketing a line of boys' wear called Prep Sizes in the 1960s but dropped it in the early 1980s to focus on the rapidly expanding adult business.

Down in the 1970s

Woolrich established a down-filled garment operation in Alliance, Nebraska in 1971. In 1974, the company acquired Down Products Corp. of Denver. Down Products had been established five years earlier by former Eddie Bauer production manager Bob Lamphere.

Employment peaked at 3,000 in 1988, when revenues approached $200 million. The company had ten plants in the United States and opened one near Montreal in 1989. By this time, Woolrich had begun marketing synthetic fabrics such as Endurich Cloth, a fast-drying safety orange fabric. Having acquired the Malone brand, which dated back to the 1890s, Woolrich incorporated a machine washable wool fabric in its

Malone Hunting Pants. The company was already selling integrated outwear systems featuring weatherproof shells with zip-in, insulated jackets.

Marketing-Driven in the 1990s

Woolrich laid off about 1,500 of its 2,600-strong workforce in October 1990 due to a shortage of orders. According to company president S. Wade Judy, the company was falling by the wayside in the outdoor clothing market, which was becoming crowded with brands.

Woolrich then operated ten plants, half of them in Pennsylvania, the others in Georgia, Colorado, and Nebraska. Woolrich's factories in north central Pennsylvania accounted for more than three-quarters of its domestic production. Customers included catalog retailers such as L.L. Bean, Eddie Bauer, Recreational Equipment Inc. (REI), Eastern Mountain Sports, and Land's End.

The Down Products Division of the company produced down coats and vests in Broomfield, Colorado, and Alliance, Nebraska. Employment in this division increased to 500 workers in 1989, and the company invested in state-of-the-art equipment to increase capacity. The Denver plants were shut down in August 1991. Their production was shifted to the Nebraska site, and in 1993 employment there jumped from 90 workers to 150. However, the Nebraska plant, too, closed in July 1995.

Company officials scrapped a plan to build an outlet mall in 1993 when village residents objected over quality-of-life issues. Woolrich then focused on boosting wool production, expanding two of its Clinton County, Pennsylvania mills. Also in 1993, H. Varnell Moore, a former Wrangler executive, came out of retirement to take the position of president at Woolrich. Moore was responsible for introducing tags proclaiming the Woolrich brand on the outside of its garments. He also endeavored to make the company less dependent on the fall season by introducing more warm weather garments. During this time, Woolrich was expanding its distribution beyond traditional sporting goods stores to department store chains.

As more marketing-savvy companies like Columbia and Timberland began to source their products in Asia, Woolrich risked being priced out of the market. By 1995, the company had closed six of its plants in the United States. It shifted much assembly work to Mexico, while continuing to produce fabric and some finished items domestically.

The venerable firm's business was changing as it never had before. The company went from being manufacturing-oriented to being a marketer, distributor, and brand-builder. By the end of the decade, only 20 percent of its products were assembled by Woolrich from start to finish. Forty percent were produced entirely by other manufacturers, and the remaining 40 percent were produced abroad. Revenues were between $150 million and $200 million a year. Roswell Brayton, Jr. a sixth-generation descendant of company founder John Rich, became company president in May 1996 (he had first started working for Woolrich in 1977).

Licensing in the Late 1990s and Beyond

In 1996, Woolrich was licensing Seneca Knitting Mills to produce hosiery and a Japanese company to produce camping gear for that market. Woolrich was also strong in Italy. The Canadian market was a natural one for the company, due to its emphasis on cold weather apparel.

With the help of IMG, the agency known for promoting sports figures and other celebrities, Woolrich aggressively extended its brand. According to the trade journal *DNR*, it signed licensing deals with F&M Hat Company, L.B. Evans (slippers), A.V. Sportswear (children's clothing), Rocking Horse (gloves), Stagg Industries (belts), and Chadwick Footwear. The company also licensed Italy's W.P. Lavori to produce sportswear for the European market under the Woolrich brand.

Though well-known to older users, Woolrich needed to attract 20- to 30-year-olds, reported the *Pittsburgh Gazette*. Woolrich produced its first television advertising in 1997. The $2 million campaign emphasized the company's heritage as the "Original Outdoor Clothing Company." It was also promoting its wholesale woolen fabrics line, particularly to men's wear manufacturers.

Besides pitching its products on cable TV stations such as the Discovery Channel, Woolrich acquired print advertising space in outdoors publications such as *Outside* and *Men's Journal*. Prominent product placement in Robert Redford's feature film *The Horse Whisperer* gave the brand a dose of Hollywood hipness. Woolrich provided producers more than 300 articles of women's outdoor clothing, which happened to be a very fast-growing segment at the time.

Woolrich was updating its styles, incorporating the increasingly ubiquitous Polartec polyester fleece in its performance-oriented jackets. The company's venerable Arctic parka remained a best seller and was particularly popular in Italy and Germany. A blanket division was organized in 1997, and Babyrich clothing for infants and toddlers debuted. A line of golf clothing was introduced a few years later.

Woolrich ended 1998 with 1,400 employees. It was profitable again, reported the Associated Press, after several years of losses. However, it continued to downsize in the United States. The sewing plant in Macon, Georgia, which had 115 employees, closed in 1999. Most of its capacity was outsourced abroad.

Taking a page from its competitors, Woolrich began producing a catalog for the first time in 2000. Advertising spread to general interest magazines like *People* and *Self* in 2000. Woolrich had developed a new fabric, called TechnoWool, with different versions emphasizing different properties, such as breathability and insulation; one type was washable. New tech-

---

<table>
<tr><td colspan="2">Key Dates:</td></tr>
<tr><td>1830:</td><td>John Rich and Daniel McCormick establish a woolen mill in Clinton County, Pennsylvania.</td></tr>
<tr><td>1845:</td><td>Rich buys out McCormick.</td></tr>
<tr><td>1852:</td><td>The business becomes known as John Rich & Son.</td></tr>
<tr><td>1939:</td><td>The company outfits Admiral Byrd's Antarctic expedition.</td></tr>
<tr><td>1971:</td><td>A down garment operation is opened in Nebraska.</td></tr>
<tr><td>1974:</td><td>Denver's Down Products Corp. is acquired.</td></tr>
<tr><td>1988:</td><td>Employment peaks at 3,000.</td></tr>
<tr><td>1991:</td><td>The Denver Down Products plant is closed.</td></tr>
<tr><td>1994:</td><td>The Pennsylvania plants are consolidated.</td></tr>
<tr><td>1995:</td><td>The Nebraska plant is closed.</td></tr>
<tr><td>1996:</td><td>The company achieves visible product placement in the feature film The Horse Whisperer.</td></tr>
<tr><td>1997:</td><td>The company's first TV ads appear.</td></tr>
<tr><td>2003:</td><td>Licensing deals continue to proliferate.</td></tr>
</table>

nologies for spinning yarn more finely than had been possible in the past allowed for the creation of this fabric.

Woolrich continued to sign licensing deals, including two aimed at sportsmen. Clothing lines were developed for the National Wild Turkey Federation in 1997 and Ducks Unlimited in 2000. Woolrich also contracted Badger Sportswear to produce corporate and promotional apparel under the Woolrich brand.

After a 20-year absence, Woolrich reentered the boys' wear market in 2001 by licensing production to Rays Apparel, Inc. of Costa Mesa, California. (Ray's also manufactured boys' clothing under the Op brand.) Towards the end of the year, Woolrich announced Tandy Brands Accessories would be producing Woolrich-branded luggage and handbags.

In 2002, Woolrich licensed Elan-Polo of St. Louis to produce a wide range of footwear under the Woolrich brand. At the same time, Nester Hosiery was contracted to produce outdoor socks under license. Finally, Woolrich teamed with the Discovery Channel to develop a line of co-branded apparel for the spring 2003 season.

Home after 2000

In the opening years of the 21st century, Woolrich's began devoting a great deal of attention to home furnishings. The company opened a 2,500-square-foot home store towards the end of 2001. Woolrich soon partnered with Target Stores to produce a line of bedding. The company aimed to bring an outdoor feeling inside, and its rustic furnishings were often decorated with animal motifs. In the fall of 2003, Woolrich licensed lighting production to Shady Lady, furniture to Lexington Home Brands, soft goods to Fallani and Cohn and Southern Textiles, and area rugs to Oriental Weavers of America.

Principal Subsidiaries

Woolcan Inc. (Canada).

Principal Competitors

Columbia Sportswear Company; Eddie Bauer, Inc.; L.L. Bean Inc.; Pendleton Woolen Mills; The Timberland Company.

Further Reading

"Badger Sportswear Lands Licensing Deal for Woolrich Corporate Apparel," *Wearables Business*, September 2000, p. 8.

Beauge, John, "Woolrich to Consolidate Sewing Operations in Central Pennsylvania," *Patriot-News* (Harrisburg, Pa.), October 24, 1996.

——, "Pennsylvania-Based Clothing Firm Woolrich Inc. Relishes Movie Role," *Knight Ridder/Tribune Business News*, May 17, 1998.

——, "Woolrich Starts Marketing Products in Catalog," *Patriot-News* (Harrisburg, Pa.), November 19, 2000, p. D10.

——, "Outdoor Clothier Woolrich Moves into Furniture; Line to Be Released Next Month," *Patriot-News* (Harrisburg, Pa.), September 5, 2003.

Brant, Howard, "Woolrich: A Name in Outdoor Clothing That Continues to Remain a Tradition," *Shooting Industry*, January 1989, pp. 8f.

Clack, Erin E., "Woolrich Re-Enters Kids,' " *Children's Business*, March 2001.

Davis, Skippy, "Georgia Woolrich Plant Closing; 115 Workers to Lose Jobs," *Macon Telegraph*, April 29, 1999.

Dodd, Annmarie, "IMG Positions Itself to Be a Player in Apparel Licensing," *DNR*, November 23, 1998, p. 7.

Emling, Shelley, "Guatemala Apparel Sourcing Show a Good Place to Make US Contacts," *Journal of Commerce*, February 28, 1992, p. 5A.

Eshleman, Russell E., Jr., "Woolrich: It's a Company Town of Yesteryear," *Patriot-News* (Harrisburg, Pa.), Bus. Sec., January 2, 1989, p. 7.

Friedman, Arthur, "Seasoned Labels Win Laurels," *Women's Wear Daily Fairchild 100 Supplement*, November 1997, p. 38.

Gallagher, Leigh, "Shear Logic," *Sporting Goods Business*, April 14, 1997, p. 42.

Genn, Adina, "Charting a Better Retail Space," *Long Island Business News*, September 22, 2000, p. 27A.

Griffin, Cara, "Woolrich Flies into Fall with Ducks Unlimited Apparel Line," *Sporting Goods Business*, May 15, 2000, p. 14.

Henricks, Mark, "Woolrich Leverages a Venerated Brand," *Apparel Industry*, August 1995, pp. 18ff.

——, "The Licensing Explosion," *Apparel Industry*, June 1998, pp. 50ff.

Jordon, Steve, "Alliance, Neb. Losing Woolrich Plant, 93 Jobs," *Omaha World-Herald*, Bus. Sec., July 1, 1995, p. 14.

Kinney, David, "Woolrich Markets Its Brand," *Associated Press State & Local Wire*, Bus. News, January 2, 1999.

——, "Red and Black and Worn All Over; Woolrich Is Back in the Pink After Nearly a Decade of Shrinking Sales and Soul-Searching," *Pittsburgh Post-Gazette*, January 5, 1999, p. E1.

——, "Woolrich Out of the Cold; Leaner Company Again Profitable," *Chicago Sun-Times*, Financial Sec., February 10, 1999, p. 12.

Leand, Judy, "Woolrich Ads Go Outside the Boundaries," *Brandmarketing*, February 2000, p. 14.

Leib, Jeffrey, "Woolrich to Close Denver Plants, Blames Foreign Textile Competition," *Denver Post*, May 1, 1991, p. C2.

——, "Woolrich's Success Creating Colo. Jobs," *Denver Post*, August 24, 1988, p. D1.

McGovern, J. Michael, "Woolrich Licenses Footwear, Sock Lines for 2002," *Outdoor Retailer*, January 2002, p. 48.

Mackinnon, Jim, "Woolrich Outerwear Plant to Close; 75 Jobs Lost in Centre County, Pa.," *Centre Daily Times* (State College, Pa.), October 23, 1996.

Mintz, Steven, "Weaves Style with Tradition," *Sales & Marketing Management*, October 12, 1981, pp. 40ff.

"Performance Wool Innovations from Woolrich," *DNR*, February 5, 2001, p. 76.

Romero, Elena, "Boys' Is in Again at Woolrich," *DNR*, February 9, 2001, p. 24.

"Shady Lady and Woolrich Team Up," *Home Accents Today*, July 2003, p. 14.

Spevack, Rachel, "After 166 Years, Woolrich Is Learning Some New Tricks; Roswell Brayton Jr. Hastens Evolution of Family Business into Marketing-Driven Entity," *Daily News Record*, December 30, 1996, pp. 6f.

Walsh, Lawrence, "Small Town Says No to a Plan for Outlet Mall; Woolrich Residents Fear Shops Will Harm Their Quality of Life," *Pittsburgh Post-Gazette*, May 30, 1993, p. B1.

——, "Woolrich Abandons Plan for Outlet Mall But Residents Still Wary, *Pittsburgh Post-Gazette*, June 20, 1993, p. B1.

"Woolrich: Brings Nature's Beauty Indoors in Renowned Textiles Line," *Home Accents Today*, September 2002, p. 56.

"Woolrich Embraces Home with New Store in a Store," *HFN*, November 26, 2001, p. 15.

"Woolrich Establishes Home Division, Licensing," *Home Accents Today*, May 2003, p. 52.

"Woolrich to Lay Off Half of Work Force," *New York Times*, Sec. 1, October 6, 1990, p. 33.

—Frederick C. Ingram

The Yates Companies, Inc.

1 Gully Avenue
Philadelphia, Mississippi 39350
U.S.A.
Telephone: (601) 656-5411
Fax: (601) 656-8958
Web site: http://www.yatescompanies.com

Private Company
Incorporated: 1964 as W.G. Yates & Sons Construction
Employees: 3,000
Sales: $1 billion
NAIC: 233310 Manufacturing and Industrial Building
Construction; 233320 Commercial and Institutional
Building Construction

With its headquarters in Philadelphia, Mississippi, The Yates Companies, Inc. is a holding company whose subsidiaries are involved in virtually every area of construction: commercial, heavy, electrical, highway, hospitality, industrial, institutional, marine, and multi-family/condominium. In addition, Yates maintains in-house operations, such as asphalt, civil, concrete, drywall, electrical, heavy, instrumentation, marine, millwright, painting, steel fabrications, and steel erection construction capabilities. The main Yates subsidiaries include W.G. Yates & Sons Construction Company and JESCO Inc., both Mississippi based; Blaine Construction Company, operating out of Tennessee; and the Yates Electrical Division, comprised of Merit Electrical, EEC, Edwards Electric Service, and MEI Electrical. In addition to its Philadelphia headquarters, Yates maintains branch offices in Jackson and Biloxi, Mississippi; Memphis, Tennessee; Mobile, Alabama; and Destin, Florida. Yates primarily serves the central and southern United States, plus Oklahoma and Texas, although it was involved in the construction of a major Atlantic City hotel and casino in the early 2000s. The private company is owned and operated by the second and third generations of the Yates family.

1960s Origins

W.G. Yates & Sons Construction was incorporated in 1964 by 51-year-old William Gully Yates, his wife Opal, and their sons, William Gully Yates, Jr., and Andrew Yates. The family's ties to construction actually stretched back another generation, as the founder's father was a builder in Neshoba County, Mississippi. Yates himself started up W.G. Yates & Sons by selling his interest in another Mississippi construction company. Gully, as he was known to his friends, had a reputation for hard work and honesty.

His younger namesake, known to everyone as Bill, would prove an ambitious businessmen with a knack for surrounding himself with talented people. Bill Yates was not able to join the family business until 1967. First he had to complete a law degree at the University of Mississippi, where he also received an ROTC commission in 1965. He then served a two-year stint in Germany in the U.S. Army Corps of Engineers, rising to the rank of captain, as well as being named Engineering Plans and Services Division chief at the U.S. Army's largest NATO training center. When Bill joined W.G. Yates & Sons, it was just a 15-employee operation, generating 200,000 in annual sales. His brother Andrew ultimately decided not to devote himself to the construction business.

Gully Yates was very much in charge of the company for close to 30 years. The company grew steadily during most of this time, taking on larger and larger jobs, and adding to its capabilities in order to offer a complete package of construction services, rather than rely on subcontractors. It was the unreliability of subcontractors, in fact, that led Yates to branch out. Moreover, Yates was able to distinguish itself from typical general contractors who were subjected to the conventional bid process. By becoming more of a full-service operation, the company was able to negotiate bids. Over the years, Yates established in-house divisions to handle sand and gravel and asphalt operations, and opened a ready-mix concrete plant as well as a building supply store. In addition, the company added a complete line of construction services, including preliminary cost feasibility studies, project management, design engineering and construction, equipment installation, site and foundation work, off-site utility work, electrical, plumbing, heavy piping, mechanical services, and refurbishing capabilities. Yates was also able to erect pre-engineered metal buildings.

Nevertheless, it appeared that Yates had reached a level in the late 1980s that was the limit for a business located in Philadelphia, Mississippi, with its population of less than 6,500. In 1989, Yates began to operate in the larger market of Jack-

Company Perspectives:

The Yates family of construction companies prides itself on producing the highest quality work in the areas of: General Construction, Construction Management, Design/Build, Engineering, Electrical, Forest Products, Marine, Industrial, Heavy Commercial, Retail, Processing, Hospitality, Utility, Resort, Casino, Medical, Corporate, Institutional, Renovation, and Environmental.

son—Mississippi's capital city. This move provided Yates with greater visibility and allowed it to more efficiently compete in the central Mississippi region. In less than two years the company landed such major projects as the Madison County Detention Center; Laird Hospital in Union, Mississippi; an expansion and renovation project for First Mississippi Corporation; the electrical work and stainless steel process piping for a Borden's plant in Jackson; and an expansion and renovation project at Mississippi Baptist Medical Center. Yates also won a number of projects from the University of Mississippi, including the university medical center's Computer Services Center, a baseball stadium, the M Club, the Raspet Flight Research Laboratory, and the Research Center for Advanced Scientific Computing.

By the start of the 1990s Yates was a $70 million company, employing approximately 1,500 people. More branch offices would follow: Butler, Alabama, in 1991 and Mobile, Alabama, in 1994.

Gully Yates died in 1992, leaving the business in the hands of son Bill and grandson, William Gully Yates III. William III had joined the firm after graduating summa cum laude from the University of Mississippi and earnings master's degree from Arizona State University in construction management. What really provided the spark that took Yates to an entirely new level was the decision by the Mississippi State Legislature in 1990 to legalize dockside gambling on the Mississippi River and along the Gulf Coast. Bill Yates told *South Central Construction* in a 2003 company profile, ''Casinos changed everything.'' In order to comply with the law, the casinos had to be constructed on top of floating barges, requiring specialized construction. Yates personnel developed a unique way to offset tidal surge fluctuations. Yates' chief financial officer, Marvin Blanks, offered *The Mississippi Business Journal* his analysis of Yates' exceptional growth during the 1990s: ''First, we began to get a lot of repeat business, which builds momentum, then we self-performed lot of phases, so when the casinos boomed in Mississippi, we were able to get things done on time—which was very important to them—and didn't have to rely on others. And last, we were able to hire some of the best managers in the industry.'' The largest of these projects was a casino in Biloxi, Mississippi, and an accompanying 1,780-room hotel, the Beau Rivage, which opened in 1999.

1999: Yates Merges with JESCO and Blaine

In 1999 W.G. Yates took the most important step in its 35-year history when late in the year it agreed to merge with JESCO Inc., based in Tupelo, Mississippi, and its sister com-

pany Blaine Construction of Knoxville, Tennessee, both of which were owned by Memphis, Tennessee-based Eagle Ventures. The three companies became part of a holding company named The Yates Companies, creating the largest construction company in Mississippi. With more than 2,000 employees and annual revenues in excess of $600 million, the company instantly cracked the top 50 of the 400 largest contractors in the United States, according to industry journal *Engineering News Record.* The three companies enjoyed different strengths: Yates was primarily a commercial general contractor while JESCO concentrated on industrial projects. Blaine was the second largest pre-engineered metal building contractor in America. Together, they created a formidable company, diverse, able to share expertise, capable of taking on bigger projects, and able to realize a variety of growth opportunities.

JESCO boasted a history even longer than W.G. Yates. It was founded in 1941 by Joseph E. Staub in Fulton, Mississippi. Staub left the family hardware business to launch a remodeling business, a partnership called J.E. Staub & Co. (It was not incorporated until 1958.) Grossing just $3,000 in the first year, the company struggled for a number of years as it grew into a general contracting company. Joe Staub, who never went to college, was eventually joined by his son Travis, who studied construction engineering at Auburn University and learned the practical side of the business during summer vacations. However, business was so lean in the late 1950s that Travis recalled having to wait on his own paycheck at times because there was only enough funds available to cover the employees, not family members. Just to stay afloat the Staubs had to take out a small business loan and even put a second mortgage on their houses. The company's big break came in 1959. Travis told *The Mississippi Journal* in a 1988 profile, ''I was in my office one day in 1959, when Daddy came in and said, 'We've got a tire plant to build in Tupelo,' I asked him where the plans and specifications were and about the price. He said, 'Well, I just agreed to build it for this price.' And he had it on a napkin. I said, 'I don't know anything about a tire plant.' We started from scratch and did it.''

The Penn Tire plant spurred JESCO's growth in a number of ways. With an increased work force from the job, the company was able to take on larger jobs, many of which it designed itself. Moreover, Penn Tire provided JESCO with an opportunity for diversification. At the time, Penn Tire was a non-union business, but it had a major need for millwrights to move around a vast amount of equipment. The only available millwrights, located in Memphis and New Orleans, were all unionized. Instead, Penn Tire turned to JESCO who bid on the business and won.

Branching out in all directions continued to be the pattern for JESCO during the ensuing years. In the 1970s it launched its own mechanical and electrical divisions, and when pre-engineered metal buildings became a viable alternative to general construction, the company created its own metal buildings subsidiary. It was because of the growing number of subsidiaries that JESCO Inc. was formed to serve as a parent company. In 1978 Joe Staub retired and because older stockholders wanted to cash in, JESCO was sold to AMCA International Corporation, a Charlotte, North Carolina, company involved in the non-residential construction, energy, and industrial markets. It turned out to be a fortuitous change in ownership, because AMCA was able to bring the kind of administrative structure

Key Dates:

1964: W.G. Yates & Sons Construction established by William Gully Yates and family.
1989: Yates opens Jackson, Mississippi, office.
1994: Gully Yates dies.
1999: The Yates Companies are formed following merger with JESCO Inc. and Blaine Construction Company.

that JESCO needed in order to continue its strong growth. According to Travis Staub, "We used to shoot from the hip. (AMCA taught us how to do strategic planning." JESCO also expanded beyond its Mississippi market. At the time of the sale, the company had gross sales in the $20 million range, with 95 percent of that amount derived from Mississippi. Ten years later—after opening offices in Montgomery, Alabama, in 1981 and Atlanta, Georgia, in 1986—annual sales were in the $120 million range, just 40 percent of which came from business in the state.

In 1995 ownership of JESCO changed hands, when AMCA's successor, United Dominion Industries, elected to sell the company to the privately held investment group Eagle Ventures. Eagle was headed by Jack Hatcher, a former UDI corporate officer who had been president of AMCA when it acquired JESCO in 1978. In addition to JESCO, UDI also sold Blaine Construction Company to Eagle. Blaine was a full-service general contractor founded in 1969. Four years after buying the businesses Eagle merged them with W.G. Yates.

2000 and Beyond

The Yates Companies was involved in a number of major projects following the 1999 merger. It landed one of the largest construction projects in the history of Mississippi, a $930 million Nissan auto plant, located near Canton, Mississippi, completed in 2003. The company was contracted by Boyd Gaming Corporation along with partner Tishman Construction of New Jersey to build the first hotel casino in Atlantic City in 13 years. The $1 billion 40-story tower featured more than 2,000 hotel rooms, 11 restaurants, and ten retail shops, numerous entertainment venues, and a 225,000-square-foot gaming area in the casino, plus a 5,000-car parking garage. In the fall of 2002 Yates completed the first phase of a Toyota assembly plant in San Antonio, Texas, which involved the construction of a 2.6 million-square-foot plant. Before that work was even completed, Yates was named the general contractor and construction manager for phase II of the project, which would increase the size of the plant by another 40 percent. Clearly, Yates, now generating annual revenues in excess of $1 billion, had transcended its regional roots. At the same time, the company, still very much controlled by the Yates family, adhered to a commitment to excellence espoused by Gully Yates 40 years earlier.

Principal Subsidiaries

W.G. Yates & Sons Construction Company; JESCO Inc.; Blaine Construction Company.

Principal Divisions

Yates Electrical Division.

Principal Competitors

Fluor Corporation; Jacobs Engineering Group Inc.; The Turner Corporation.

Further Reading

Cotton, C. Richard, "Yates Construction Steps to Forefront of Mississippi Construction Industry," *South Central Construction,* July 2003.

Dale, Nicholas Jan, "A Bid Scrawled on a Napkin Was the Making of Jesco," *Mississippi Business Journal,* February 1988, p. 30.

Fortson, Sanna, "Building a Better Construction Company," *Mississippi Business Journal,* February 4, 1991, p. 14.

Gillette, Becky, "Very Big Deal," *Mississippi Business Journal,* November 29, 1999, p. 1.

Holliday, Karen Kahler, "State's 2nd Largest Construction Company Sold," *Mississippi Business Journal,* July 24, 1995, p. 1.

Wilton, J. "Bill" Johnson Jr., "A Five-Letter Word for Omnipresent—Yates," *Mississippi Business Journal,* August 20, 2001, p. 3.

—Ed Dinger

INDEX TO COMPANIES

Index to Companies

Listings in this index are arranged in alphabetical order under the company name. Company names beginning with a letter or proper name such as Eli Lilly & Co. will be found under the first letter of the company name. Definite articles (The, Le, La) are ignored for alphabetical purposes as are forms of incorporation that precede the company name (AB, NV). Company names printed in bold type have full, historical essays on the page numbers appearing in bold. Updates to entries that appeared in earlier volumes are signified by the notation **(upd.)**. Company names in light type are references within an essay to that company, not full historical essays. This index is cumulative with volume numbers printed in bold type.

Aquarium Supply Co., **12** 230
Aquarius Group, **6** 207
Aquatech, **53** 232
Aquila Energy Corp., **6** 593
Aquila, Inc., **IV** 486; **50 37–40 (upd.)**
Aquitaine. *See* Société Nationale des
  Petroles d'Aquitaine.
AR Accessories Group, Inc., **23 20–22**
AR-TIK Systems, Inc., **10** 372
ARA Services, **II 607–08**; **21** 507; **25** 181
Arab Japanese Insurance Co., **III** 296
Arab Petroleum Pipeline Co., **IV** 412
Arab-Israel Bank Ltd., **60** 50
Arabian American Oil Co., **I** 570; **IV** 386,
  429, 464–65, 512, 536–39, 552, 553,
  559; **7** 172, 352; **14** 492–93; **41** 392.
  See also Saudi Arabian Oil Co.
Arabian Gulf Oil Co., **IV** 454
Arabian Investment Banking Corp., **15** 94;
  26 53; **47** 361
Arabian Oil Co., **IV** 451
Aracruz Celulose S.A., **57 45–47**
Aral AG, **62 12–15**
ARAMARK Corporation, **13 48–50**; **16**
  228; **21** 114–15; **35** 415; **41 21–24**
Aramco. *See* Arabian American Oil Co.;
  Saudi Arabian Oil Company.
Aramis Inc., **30** 191
Arandell Corporation, **37 16–18**
Arapuã. *See* Lojas Arapuã S.A.
Aratex Inc., **13** 49
Aratsu Sekiyu, **IV** 554
ARBED S.A., **IV 24–27**, 53; **22 41–45**
  (upd.); **26** 83; **42** 414
Arbeitsgemeinschaft der öffentlich-
  rechtlichen Rundfunkanstalten der
  Bundesrepublick. *See* ARD.
The Arbitron Company, **10** 255, 359; **13**
  5; **38 56–61**
Arbor Acres, **13** 103
Arbor Drugs Inc., **12 21–23**. *See also*
  CVS Corporation.
Arbor International, **18** 542
Arbor Living Centers Inc., **6** 478
Arbuthnot & Co., **III** 522
Arby's Inc., **II** 614; **8** 536–37; **14 32–34**,
  351; **58** 323
ARC. *See* American Rug Craftsmen.
ARC International Corporation, **27** 57
ARC Ltd., **III** 501
ARC Materials Corp., **III** 688
ARC Propulsion, **13** 462
ARCA. *See* Appliance Recycling Centers
  of America, Inc.
Arcadia Company, **14** 138
Arcadia Group plc, **28 27–30 (upd.)**,
  95–96
Arcadia Partners, **17** 321
Arcadian Corporation, **18** 433; **27** 317–18
Arcadian Marine Service, Inc., **6** 530
Arcadis NV, **26 21–24**
Arcata Corporation, **12** 413
Arcata National Corp., **9** 305
Arcelik, **I** 478
ARCH Air Medical Service, Inc., **53** 29
Arch Mineral Corporation, **IV** 374; **7
  32–34**
Arch Petroleum Inc., **39** 331
Arch Wireless, Inc., **39 23–26**; **41** 265,
  267
Archbold Container Co., **35** 390
Archbold Ladder Co., **12** 433
Archer-Daniels-Midland Co., **I 419–21**;
  IV 373; **7** 432–33, 241 **8** 53; **11 21–23**

(upd.); **17** 207; **22** 85, 426; **23** 384; **25**
  241; **31** 234; **32 55–59 (upd.)**
Archer Drug, **III** 10
Archer Management Services Inc., **24** 360
Archibald Candy Corporation, **36** 309
Archipelago RediBook, **48** 226, 228
Archstone-Smith Trust, **49 27–30**
Archway Cookies, Inc., **29 29–31**
ArcLight, LLC, **50** 123
ARCO. *See* Atlantic Richfield Company.
ARCO Chemical Company, **IV** 376–77,
  456–57; **10 110–11**
ARCO Comfort Products Co., **26** 4
Arco Electronics, **9** 323
Arco Pharmaceuticals, Inc., **31** 346
Arco Societa Per L'Industria Elettrotecnica,
  II 82
Arcon Corporation, **26** 287
Arctco, Inc., **12** 400–01; **16 31–34**; **35**
  349, 351
Arctic, **III** 479
Arctic Alaska Fisheries Corporation, **14**
  515; **50** 493–94
Arctic Cat Inc., **40 46–50 (upd.)**
Arctic Enterprises, **34** 44
Arctic Slope Regional Corporation, **38
  62–65**
ARD, **41 25–29**
Ardal og Sunndal Verk AS, **10** 439
Arden Group, Inc., **29 32–35**
Ardent Computer Corp., **III** 553
Ardent Risk Services, Inc. *See* General Re
  Corporation.
Ardent Software Inc., **59 54–55**
Areal Technologies, **III** 715
Argbeit-Gemeinschaft Lurgi und
  Ruhrchemie, **IV** 534; **47** 342
Argenbright Security Inc. *See* Securicor
  Plc.
Argentaria Caja Postal y Banco
  Hipotecario S.A. *See* Banco Bilbao
  Vizcaya Argentaria S.A.
Argentine National Bank, **14** 46
Argo Communications Corporation, **6** 300
Argon Medical, **12** 327
Argonaut, **10** 520–22
Argos, **I** 426; **22** 72; **50** 117
Argos Retail Group, **47** 165, 169
Argos Soditic, **43** 147, 149
Argosy Gaming Company, **21 38–41**
Argosy Group LP, **27** 197
Argus Chemical Co., **I** 405
Argus Corp., **IV** 272, 611
Argus Energy, **7** 538
Argus Motor Company, **16** 7
Arguss Communications, Inc., **57** 120
Argyle Television Inc., **19** 204
Argyll Group PLC, **I** 241; **II 609–10**,
  656; **12** 152–53; **24** 418. *See also*
  Safeway PLC.
Aria Communications, Inc. *See* Ascend
  Communications, Inc.
Ariba, Inc., **38** 432; **57 48–51**
Ariel Capital Management, **28** 421
Ariens Company, **48 32–34**
Aries Technology, **25** 305
Aris Industries, Inc., **15** 275; **16 35–38**
Arista Laboratories Inc., **51** 249, 251
Aristech Chemical Corp., **12** 342
Aristocrat Leisure Limited, **54 14–16**
The Aristotle Corporation, **62 16–18**
Arizona Airways, **22** 219
Arizona Daily Star, **58** 282
Arizona Edison Co., **6** 545

Arizona Growth Capital, Inc., **18** 513
AriZona Iced Tea. *See* Ferolito, Vultaggio
  & Sons.
Arizona One, **24** 455
Arizona Public Service Company, **6**
  545–47; **19** 376, 412; **26** 359; **28**
  425–26; **54** 290
Arizona Refrigeration Supplies, **14** 297–98
Arjo Wiggins Appleton p.l.c., **13** 458; **27**
  513; **34 38–40**
Ark Restaurants Corp., **20 25–27**
Ark Securities Co., **II** 233
Arkansas Best Corporation, **16 39–41**;
  19 455; **42** 410
Arkansas Breeders, **II** 585
Arkansas Chemicals Inc., **I** 341
Arkansas Louisiana Gas Company. *See*
  Arkla, Inc.
Arkansas Power & Light, **V** 618
Arkay Computer, **6** 224
ARKE, **II** 164
Arkia, **23** 184, 186–87
Arkla, Inc., **V 550–51**; **11** 441
Arla Foods amba, **48 35–38**
Arlington Corporation, **6** 295
Arlington Motor Holdings, **II** 587
Arlington Securities plc, **24** 84, 87–89
Arlon, Inc., **28** 42, 45
Armani. *See* Giorgio Armani S.p.A.
Armaturindistri, **III** 569
Armco Inc., **III** 721; **IV 28–30**, 125, 171;
  10 448; **11** 5, 255; **12** 353; **19** 8; **26**
  407; **30** 282–83; **41** 3, 5; **54** 247–48
Armement Sapmer Distribution, **60** 149
Armin Corp., **III** 645
Armin Poly Film Corp., **III** 645
Armitage Shanks, **III** 671
Armor All Products Corp., **12** 333; **15**
  507; **16 42–44**; **22** 148; **26** 349; **47** 235
Armor Elevator, **11** 5
Armor Holdings, Inc., **27 49–51**
Armour. *See* Tommy Armour Golf Co.
Armour & Company, **8** 144; **12** 198; **13**
  21, 506; **23** 173; **55** 365
Armour-Dial, **8** 144; **23** 173–74
Armour Food Co., **II** 494, 518; **12** 81, 370;
  13 270; **42** 92
Armour Pharmaceutical Co., **III** 56
Armstrong Air Conditioning Inc. *See*
  Lennox International Inc.
Armstrong Autoparts, **III** 495
Armstrong Communications, **IV** 640
Armstrong Nurseries, **I** 272
Armstrong Rees Ederer Inc., **IV** 290
Armstrong-Siddeley Co., **III** 508
Armstrong Tire Co., **15** 355
Armstrong World Industries, Inc., **III
  422–24**; **9** 466; **12** 474–75; **22 46–50
  (upd.)**, 170–71; **26** 507; **53** 175–76; **59**
  381–82
Armtek, **7** 297
Army and Air Force Exchange Service,
  39 27–29
Army Cooperative Fire Insurance
  Company, **10** 541
Army Ordnance, **19** 430
Army Signal Corps Laboratories, **10** 96
Arndale, **IV** 696
Arno Press, **IV** 648; **19** 285
Arnold & Porter, **35 42–44**
Arnold Clark Automobiles Ltd., **60
  39–41**
Arnold Communications, **25** 381

Brown & Brown, Inc., **41** 63–66
Brown & Haley, **23** 78–80
Brown & Root, Inc., **III** 498–99, 559; **13** 117–19; **25** 190–91; **37** 244; **38** 481; **55** 192. *See also* Kellogg Brown & Root Inc.
Brown & Sharpe Manufacturing Co., **23** 81–84
Brown and Williamson Tobacco Corporation, **I** 426; **14** 77–79; **15** 72; **22** 72–73; **33** 80–83 (upd.)
Brown Bibby & Gregory, **I** 605
Brown Boveri. *See* BBC Brown Boveri.
Brown Brothers Harriman & Co., **45** 64–67
Brown Co., **IV** 289
Brown Cow West Corporation, **55** 360
Brown Drug, **III** 9
Brown-Forman Corporation, **I** 225–27; **10** 179–82 (upd.); **12** 313; **18** 69; **38** 110–14 (upd.)
Brown Foundation, **III** 498
Brown Group, Inc., **V** 351–53; **9** 192; **10** 282; **16** 198; **20** 86–89 (upd.)
Brown Institute, **45** 87
Brown Jordan Co., **12** 301
Brown Oil Tools, **III** 428
Brown Paper Mill Co., **I** 380; **13** 379
Brown Printing Company, **26** 43–45
Brown-Service Insurance Company, **9** 507
Brown Shipbuilding Company. *See* Brown & Root, Inc.
Brown, Shipley & Co., Limited, **II** 425; **13** 341; **45** 65
Brown Shoe Co., **V** 351–52; **14** 294
Browne & Nolan Ltd., **IV** 294; **19** 225
Browning-Ferris Industries, Inc., **V** 749–53; **8** 562; **10** 33; **17** 552; **18** 10; **20** 90–93 (upd.); **23** 491; **33** 382; **46** 456; **50** 13–14
Browning International, **58** 147
Browning Manufacturing, **II** 19
Browning Telephone Corp., **14** 258
Broyhill Furniture Industries, Inc., **III** 528, 530; **10** 183–85; **12** 308; **39** 170, 173–74
BRS Ltd., **6** 412–13
Bruce Foods Corporation, **39** 67–69
Bruce Power LP, **49** 65, 67
Bruce's Furniture Stores, **14** 235
Bruckmann, Rosser, Sherill & Co., **27** 247; **40** 51
Bruegger's Bagel Bakery, **29** 171
Brufina, **II** 201–02
Brugman, **27** 502
Brummer Seal Company, **14** 64
Bruno's Inc., **7** 60–62; **13** 404, 406; **23** 261; **26** 46–48 (upd.)
Brunswick Corporation, **III** 442–44, 599; **9** 67, 119; **10** 262; **17** 453; **21** 291; **22** 113–17 (upd.), 118; **30** 303; **40** 30; **45** 175
Brunswick Pulp & Paper Co., **IV** 282, 311, 329; **9** 260; **19** 266
The Brush Electric Light Company, **11** 387; **25** 44
Brush Electrical Machines, **III** 507–09
Brush Moore Newspaper, Inc., **8** 527
Brush Wellman Inc., **14** 80–82
Bryan Bros. Packing, **II** 572
Bryant Heater Co., **III** 471
Bryce Brothers, **12** 313
Brylane Inc., **29** 106–07
Brymbo Steel Works, **III** 494

Bryn Mawr Stereo & Video, **30** 465
Brynwood Partners, **13** 19
BSA. *See* The Boy Scouts of America.
BSB, **IV** 653; **7** 392
BSC. *See* Birmingham Steel Corporation; British Steel Corporation.
BSkyB, **IV** 653; **7** 392; **29** 369, 371; **34** 85
BSN Groupe S.A., **II** 474–75, 544; **22** 458; **23** 448. *See also* Groupe Danone
BSN Medical, **41** 374, 377
BSR, **II** 82
BT Group plc, **49** 69–74 (upd.)
BTG, Inc., **45** 68–70; **57** 173
BTI Services, **9** 59
BTM. *See* British Tabulating Machine Company.
BTR Dunlop Holdings, Inc., **21** 432
BTR plc, **I** 428–30; **III** 727; **8** 397; **24** 88
BTR Siebe plc, **27** 79–81. *See also* Invensys PLC.
Bublitz Case Company, **55** 151
Buca, Inc., **38** 115–17
Buchanan, **I** 239–40
Buchanan Electric Steel Company, **8** 114
Buck Consultants, Inc., **32** 459; **55** 71–73
Buck Knives Inc., **48** 71–74
Buckaroo International. *See* Bugle Boy Industries, Inc.
Buckbee-Mears Company. *See* BMC Industries, Inc.
Buckeye Business Products Inc., **17** 384
Buckeye Technologies, Inc., **42** 51–54
Buckhorn, Inc., **19** 277–78
The Buckle, Inc., **18** 84–86
Buckler Broadcast Group, **IV** 597
Buckley/DeCerchio New York, **25** 180
BUCON, Inc., **62** 55
Bucyrus Blades, Inc., **14** 81
Bucyrus-Erie Company, **7** 513
Bucyrus International, Inc., **17** 58–61
Bud Bailey Construction, **43** 400
Budapest Bank, **16** 14
The Budd Company, **IV** 222; **8** 74–76; **20** 359
Buderus AG, **III** 692, 694–95; **37** 46–49
Budgens Ltd., **57** 257; **59** 93–96
Budget Group, Inc., **25** 92–94
Budget Rent a Car Corporation, **6** 348–49, 393; **9** 94–95; **22** 524; **24** 12, 409; **25** 143; **39** 370; **41** 402
Budgetel Inn. *See* Marcus Corporation.
Budweiser, **18** 70
Budweiser Budvar, National Corporation, **59** 97–100
Budweiser Japan Co., **21** 320
Buena Vista Distribution, **II** 172; **6** 174; **30** 487
Buena Vista Music Group, **44** 164
Bufete Industrial, S.A. de C.V., **34** 80–82
Buffalo Forge Company, **7** 70–71
Buffalo Mining Co., **IV** 181
Buffalo News, **18** 60
Buffalo Paperboard, **19** 78
Buffalo Wild Wings, Inc., **56** 41–43
Buffets, Inc., **10** 186–87; **22** 465; **32** 102–04 (upd.)
Bugaboo Creek Steak House Inc., **19** 342
Bugatti Industries, **14** 321
Bugle Boy Industries, Inc., **18** 87–88
Buhrmann NV, **41** 67–69; **47** 90–91; **49** 440
Buick Motor Co., **III** 438; **8** 74; **10** 325
Build-A-Bear Workshop Inc., **62** 45–48
Builders Emporium, **13** 169; **25** 535

Builders Square, **V** 112; **9** 400; **12** 345, 385; **14** 61; **16** 210; **31** 20; **35** 11, 13; **47** 209
Building Materials Holding Corporation, **52** 53–55
Building One Services Corporation. *See* Encompass Services Corporation.
Building Products of Canada Limited, **25** 232
Buitoni SpA, **II** 548; **17** 36; **50** 78
Bulgari S.p.A., **20** 94–97
Bulgarian Oil Co., **IV** 454
Bulgheroni SpA, **27** 105
Bulkships, **27** 473
Bull. *See* Compagnie des Machines Bull S.A.
Bull-GE, **III** 123
Bull HN Information Systems, **III** 122–23
Bull Motors, **11** 5
Bull Run Corp., **24** 404
Bull S.A., **III** 122–23; **43** 89–91 (upd.)
Bull Tractor Company, **7** 534; **16** 178; **26** 492
Bull-Zenith, **25** 531
Bulldog Computer Products, **10** 519
Bulley & Andrews, LLC, **55** 74–76
Bullock's, **III** 63; **31** 191
Bulolo Gold Dredging, **IV** 95
Bulova Corporation, **I** 488; **II** 101; **III** 454–55; **12** 316–17, 453; **13** 120–22; **14** 501; **21** 121–22; **36** 325; **41** 70–73 (upd.)
Bumble Bee Seafoods, Inc., **II** 491, 508, 557; **24** 114
Bunawerke Hüls GmbH., **I** 350
Bundall Computers Pty Limited, **56** 155
Bundy Corporation, **17** 62–65, 480
Bunge Ltd., **62** 49–51
Bunte Candy, **12** 427
Bunzl plc, **IV** 260–62; **12** 264; **31** 77–80 (upd.)
Buquet, **19** 49
Burbank Aircraft Supply, Inc., **14** 42–43; **37** 29, 31
Burberry Ltd., **41** 74–76 (upd.); **47** 167, 169
Burberrys Ltd., **V** 68; **10** 122; **17** 66–68; **19** 181
Burda Holding GmbH. & Co., **20** 53; **23** 85–89
Burdines, Inc., **9** 209; **31** 192; **60** 70–73
Bureau de Recherches de Pétrole, **IV** 544–46, 559–60; **7** 481–83; **21** 203–04
The Bureau of National Affairs, Inc., **23** 90–93
Bureau Veritas SA, **55** 77–79
Burelle S.A., **23** 94–96
Burger and Aschenbrenner, **16** 486
Burger Boy Food-A-Rama, **8** 564
Burger Chef, **II** 532
Burger King Corporation, **I** 278; **II** 556–57, 613–15, 647; **7** 316; **8** 564; **9** 178; **10** 122; **12** 43, 553; **13** 408–09; **14** 25, 32, 212, 214, 452; **16** 95–97, 396; **17** 69–72 (upd.), 501; **18** 437; **21** 25, 362; **23** 505; **24** 140–41; **25** 228; **26** 284; **33** 240–41; **36** 517, 519; **56** 44–48 (upd.)
Burgess, Anderson & Tate Inc., **25** 500
Bürhle, **17** 36; **50** 78
Burhmann-Tetterode, **22** 154
Buriot International, Inc., **53** 236
Burke Scaffolding Co., **9** 512
BURLE Industries Inc., **11** 444

29 375, 407–08; 34 133–35, 303; 36 32,
240–44 (upd.), 298; 38 86, 458, 461; 43
319; 45 142, 170; 50 197, 376; 51 34;
55 326; 56 284; 57 92, 189; 59 393,
395–96; 62 180–81
**General Nutrition Companies, Inc., 11
155–57;** 24 480; 29 210–14 (upd.); 31
347; 37 340, 342; 45 210
General Office Products Co., 25 500
General Packing Service, Inc., 19 78
General Parts Inc., 29 86
General Petroleum and Mineral
Organization of Saudi Arabia, IV
537–39
General Petroleum Authority. *See* Egyptian
General Petroleum Corporation.
General Petroleum Corp., IV 412, 431,
464; 7 352
General Physics Corporation, 13 367
General Portland Cement Co., III 704–05;
17 497
General Portland Inc., 28 229
General Precision Equipment Corp., II 10;
30 418
General Printing Ink Corp. *See* Sequa
Corp.
General Property Trust, IV 708
General Public Utilities Corporation, V
629–31; 6 484, 534, 579–80; 11 388; 20
73
General Radio Company. *See* GenRad, Inc.
General Railway Signal Company. *See*
General Signal Corporation.
General Re Corporation, III 258–59,
276; 24 176–78 (upd.); 42 31, 35
General Rent A Car, 6 349; 25 142–43
General Research Corp., 14 98
General Seafoods Corp., II 531
General Sekiyu K.K., IV 431–33, 555; 16
490. *See also* TonenGeneral Sekiyu K.K.
General Signal Corporation, III 645; 9
250–52; 11 232
General Spring Products, 16 321
General Steel Industries Inc., 14 324
General Supermarkets, II 673
General Telephone and Electronics Corp.,
II 47; V 295, 345–46; 13 398; 19 40;
25 267
General Telephone Corporation, V 294–95;
9 478, 494
General Time Corporation, 16 483
General Tire, Inc., 8 206–08, 212–14; 9
247–48; 20 260, 262; 22 219; 56 71; 59
324
General Transistor Corporation, 10 319
General Turbine Systems, 58 75
General Utilities Company, 6 555
General Waterworks Corporation, 40 449
Generale Bank, II 294–95
Générale Biscuit S.A., II 475
Générale de Banque, 36 458
Générale de Mécanique Aéronautique, I 46
Générale de Restauration, 49 126
Générale des Eaux Group, V 632–34; 21
226. *See* Vivendi Universal S.A.
Generale du Jouet, 16 428
Générale Occidentale, II 475; IV 614–15
Générale Restauration S.A., 34 123
Generali. *See* Assicurazioni Generali.
Génération Y2K, 35 204, 207
GenerComit Gestione SpA, II 192
Genesco Inc., 14 501; 17 202–06; 27 59
Genesee & Wyoming Inc., 27 179–81
Genesee Brewing Co., 18 72; 50 114

Genesee Iron Works. *See* Wickes Inc.
Genesis, II 176–77
**Genesis Health Ventures, Inc., 18
195–97;** 25 310
Genesse Hispania, 60 246
Genetic Anomalies, Inc., 39 395
Genetic Systems Corp., I 654; III 18; 37
43
Genetics Institute, Inc., 8 215–18; 10 70,
78–80; 50 538
Geneva Metal Wheel Company, 20 261
Geneva Pharmaceuticals, Inc., 8 549; 22
37, 40
Geneva Rubber Co., 17 373
Geneva Steel, 7 193–95
Geneve Corporation, 62 16
Genex Corp., I 355–56; 26 246
GENEX Services, Inc., 52 379
GENIX, V 152
Genix Group. *See* MCN Corporation.
Genmar Holdings, Inc., 45 172–75
Genoc Chartering Ltd, 60 96
Genosys Biotechnologies, Inc., 36 431
Genovese Drug Stores, Inc., 18 198–200;
21 187; 32 170; 43 249
Genpack Corporation, 21 58
GenRad, Inc., 24 179–83
GenSet, 19 442
Genstar, 22 14; 23 327
Genstar Gypsum Products Co., IV 273
Genstar Rental Electronics, Inc., 58 110
Genstar Stone Products Co., III 735; 15
154; 40 176
GenTek Inc., 37 157; 41 236
Gentex Corporation, 26 153–57; 35
148–49
Gentex Optics, 17 50; 18 392
GenTrac, 24 257
Gentry Associates, Inc., 14 378
Gentry International, I 497; 47 234
Genty-Cathiard, 39 183–84; 54 306
Genuardi's Family Markets, Inc., 35
190–92
Genuin Golf & Dress of America, Inc., 32
447
Genuine Parts Company, 9 253–55; 45
176–79 (upd.)
Genung's, II 673
Genus, 18 382–83
Genzyme Corporation, 13 239–42; 38
203–07 (upd.); 47 4
Genzyme Transgenics Corp., 37 44
Geo. H. McFadden & Bro., 54 89
GEO SA, 58 218
Geo Space Corporation, 18 513
GEO Specialty Chemicals, Inc., 27 117
geobra Brandstätter GmbH & Co. KG,
48 183–86
Geodynamics Oil & Gas Inc., IV 83
Geographics, Inc., 25 183
Geomarine Systems, 11 202
The Geon Company, 11 158–61
Geon Industries, Inc. *See* Johnston
Industries, Inc.
Geophysical Service, Inc., III 499–500; IV
365
GeoQuest Systems Inc., 17 419
Georesources, Inc., 19 247
Georg Fischer AG Schaffhausen, 38 214;
61 106–09
George A. Hormel and Company, II
504–06; 7 547; 12 123–24; 18 244. *See
also* Hormel Foods Corporation.
George A. Touche & Co., 9 167

George Booker & Co., 13 102
George Buckton & Sons Limited, 40 129
The George F. Cram Company, Inc., 55
158–60
George Fischer, Ltd., III 638
George H. Dentler & Sons, 7 429
The George Hyman Construction
Company, 8 112–13; 25 403
George J. Ball, Inc., 27 507
George K. Baum & Company, 25 433
George Kent, II 3; 22 10
George Newnes Company, IV 641; 7 244
George P. Johnson Company, 60 142–44
George R. Rich Manufacturing Company.
See Clark Equipment Company.
George S. May International Company,
55 161–63
George Smith Financial Corporation, 21
257
George Weston Limited, II 631–32; 36
245–48 (upd.); 41 30, 33
George Wimpey plc, 12 201–03; 28 450;
51 135–38 (upd.)
Georges Renault SA, III 427; 28 40
Georgetown Group, Inc., 26 187
Georgetown Steel Corp., IV 228
Georgia Carpet Outlets, 25 320
Georgia Cotton Producers Association. *See*
Gold Kist Inc.
Georgia Credit Exchange, 6 24
Georgia Federal Bank, I 447; 11 112–13;
30 196
Georgia Gulf Corporation, IV 282; 9
256–58, 260; 61 110–13 (upd.)
Georgia Hardwood Lumber Co., IV 281; 9
259
Georgia Kraft Co., IV 312, 342–43; 8
267–68; 19 268
Georgia Natural Gas Corporation, 6
447–48
Georgia-Pacific Corporation, IV 281–83,
288, 304, 345, 358; 9 256–58, 259–62
(upd.); 12 19, 377; 15 229; 22 415, 489;
31 314; 44 66; 47 145–51 (upd.); 51
284; 61 110–11
Georgia Power & Light Co., V 621; 6 447,
537; 23 28; 27 20
Georgia Power Company, 38 446–48; 49
145
Georgia Railway and Electric Company, 6
446–47; 23 28
Georgie Pie, V 35
GeoScience Corporation, 18 515; 44 422
Geosource Inc., 21 14; 22 189
Geotec Boyles Brothers, S.A., 19 247
Geotecnia y Cimientos SA, 55 182
Geotek Communications Inc., 21 238–40
GeoTel Communications Corp., 34 114
Geothermal Resources International, 11
271
GeoVideo Networks, 34 259
Geoworks Corporation, 25 509
Geraghty & Miller Inc., 26 23
Gerald Stevens, Inc., 37 161–63
Gérard, 25 84
Gerber Products Company, II 481; III
19; 7 196–98, 547; 9 90; 11 173; 21
53–55, 241–44 (upd); 25 366; 34 103;
36 256
Gerber Scientific, Inc., 12 204–06
Gerbes Super Markets, Inc., 12 112
Gerbo Telecommunicacoes e Servicos
Ltda., 32 40
Gerdau S.A., 59 200–03

Henry L. Doherty & Company, **IV** 391; **12** 542

Henry Lee Company, **16** 451, 453

Henry, Leonard & Thomas Inc., **9** 533

Henry Meadows, Ltd., **13** 286

Henry Modell & Company Inc., 32 263–65

Henry Pratt Company, **7** 30–31

Henry S. King & Co., **II** 307

Henry S. Miller Companies, **21** 257

Henry Schein, Inc., 29 298; **31 254–56**

Henry Telfer, **II** 513

Henry Willis & Co. *See* Willis Corroon Group Plc.

HEPCO. *See* Hokkaido Electric Power Company Inc.

Hepworth plc, **44** 438

Her Majesty's Stationery Office, 7 215–18

Heraclio Fournier S.A., **62** 383–84

Heraeus Holding GmbH, IV 98–100, 118; **54 159–63 (upd.)**

Herald and Weekly Times, **IV** 650, 652; **7** 389, 391

Herald Publishing Company, **12** 150

Heralds of Liberty, **9** 506

Herbalife International, Inc., 17 226–29; **18** 164; **41 203–06 (upd.)**

Herbert Clough Inc., **24** 176

Herbert W. Davis & Co., **III** 344

Herby's Foods, **36** 163

Herco Technology, **IV** 680

Hercofina, **IV** 499

Hercules Filter, **III** 419

Hercules Inc., I 343–45, 347; **19** 11; **22 260–63 (upd.); 28** 195; **30** 36

Hercules Offshore Drilling, **28** 347–48

Hereford Paper and Allied Products Ltd., **14** 430

Herff Jones, **II** 488; **25** 254

Heritage Bankcorp, **9** 482

Heritage Communications, **II** 160–61

Heritage Federal Savings and Loan Association of Huntington, **10** 92

Heritage House of America Inc. *See* Humana Inc.

Heritage Media Group, **25** 418

Heritage National Health Plan, **III** 464

Heritage Springfield $$Heritage Springfield, **14** 245

Heritage 21 Construction, **60** 56

Herley Industries, Inc., 33 187–89

Herman Goelitz, Inc., 28 186–88

Herman Miller, Inc., 8 251–52, **255–57;** **39** 205–07

Herman's World of Sports, **II** 628–29; **15** 470; **16** 457; **43** 385

Hermann Pfauter Group, **24** 186

Hermès International S.A., 34 211–14 (upd.); 49 83

Hermès S.A., 14 238–40

Hermosillo, **51** 389

Herrburger Brooks P.L.C., **12** 297

Herrick, Waddell & Reed. *See* Waddell & Reed, Inc.

Herring-Hall-Marvin Safe Co. of Hamilton, Ohio, **7** 145

Hersey Products, Inc., **III** 645

Hershey Bank, **II** 342

Hershey Foods Corporation, II 478, 508, **510–12,** 569; **7** 300; **11** 15; **12** 480–81; **15** 63–64, **219–22 (upd.),** 323; **27** 38–40; **30** 208–09; **51 156–60 (upd.);** **53** 241

F.N. Herstal. *See* Groupe Herstal S.A.

Hertel AG, **13** 297

Hertford Industrial Estates, **IV** 724

Hertie Waren- und Kaufhaus GmbH, V 72–74; 19 234, 237

Herts & Beds Petroleum Co., **IV** 566

Herts Pharmaceuticals, **17** 450; **41** 375–76

The Hertz Corporation, I 130; **II** 90; **6** 129, 348–50, 356–57, 392–93; **V** 494; **9 283–85; 10** 419; **11** 494; **16** 379; **21** 151; **22** 54, 56, 524; **24** 9, 409; **25** 143; **33 190–93 (upd.); 36** 215

Hertz-Penske Leasing. *See* Penske Corporation.

Hervillier, **27** 188

Heska Corporation, 39 213–16

Hespeler Hockey Inc., **22** 204

Hess. *See* Amerada Hess Corporation.

Hess Department Stores Inc., **16** 61–62; **19** 323–24; **41** 343; **50** 107

Hessische Landesbank, **II** 385–86

Hessische Ludwigs-Eisenbahn-Gesellschaft, **6** 424

Hesston Corporation, **13** 17; **22** 380

Hetteen Hoist & Derrick. *See* Polaris Industries Inc.

Heublein Inc., I 226, 246, 249, **259–61,** 281; **7** 266–67; **10** 180; **14** 214; **21** 314–15; **24** 140; **25** 177; **31** 92; **34** 89

Heuer. *See* TAG Heuer International SA.

Heuga Holdings B.V., **8** 271

Hewitt & Tuttle, **IV** 426; **17** 355–56

Hewlett-Packard Company, II 62; **III 142–43; 6** 219–20, 225, **237–39 (upd.),** 244, 248, 278–79, 304; **8** 139, 467; **9** 7, 35–36, 57, 115, 471; **10** 15, 34, 86, 232, 257, 363, 404, 459, 464, 499, 501; **11** 46, 234, 274, 284, 382, 491, 518; **12** 61, 147, 162, 183, 470; **13** 128, 326, 501; **14** 354; **15** 125; **16** 5, 139–40, 299, 301, 367, 394, 550; **18** 386–87, 434, 436, 571; **19** 515; **20** 8; **25** 96, 118, 151–53, 499, 531; **26** 177, 520; **27** 221; **28 189–92 (upd.); 33** 15; **36** 3, 81–82, 299–300; **38** 20, 187, 417–19; **41** 117, 288; **43** 294; **50 222–30 (upd.); 51** 150

Hexalon, **26** 420

Hexatec Polymers, **III** 742

Hexcel Corporation, 11 475; **27** 50; **28 193–95**

Heyer-Schulte, **26** 286

Heytesbury Party Ltd., **34** 422

HFC. *See* Household Finance Corporation.

HFS Inc., **21** 97; **22** 54, 56; **53** 275

HG Hawker Engineering Co. Ltd., **III** 508

HGCC. *See* Hysol Grafil Composite Components Co.

HH Finch Ltd., **38** 501

HI. *See* Houston Industries Incorporated.

Hi-Bred Corn Company, **9** 410

Hi-Lo Automotive, Inc., **26** 348–49

Hi-Mirror Co., **III** 715

Hi Tech Consignments, **18** 208

Hi-Tek Polymers, Inc., **8** 554

Hibbett Sporting Goods, Inc., 26 189–91

Hibernia Corporation, 37 187–90

Hickman Coward & Wattles, **24** 444

Hickory Farms, Inc., 12 178, 199; **17 230–32**

Hickorycraft, **III** 571; **20** 362

Hicks & Greist, **6** 40

Hicks & Haas, **II** 478

Hicks, Muse, Tate & Furst, Inc., **24** 106; **30** 220; **36** 423; **55** 202

Hicksgas Gifford, Inc., **6** 529

Hidden Creek Industries, Inc., **16** 397; **24** 498

HiFi Buys, **30** 465

Higgs International Ltd., **51** 130

High Integrity Systems, **51** 16

High Point Chemical Corp., **III** 38

High Retail System Co., Ltd., **V** 195; **47** 391

Highgate Hotels, Inc., **21** 93

Highland Distillers Ltd., **60** 355

Highland Superstores, **9** 65–66; **10** 9–10, 304–05, 468; **23** 51–52

Highland Telephone Company, **6** 334

Highlander Publications, **38** 307–08

Highlands Insurance Co., **III** 498

Highmark Inc., I 109; **27 208–11**

Highsmith Inc., 60 167–70

Highteam Public Relations Co. Ltd., **60** 143

Highveld Steel and Vanadium Corporation Limited, 59 224–27

Hilbun Poultry, **10** 250

Hildebrandt International, 29 235–38

Hilex Poly Co., Inc., **8** 477

Hill & Knowlton Inc. *See* WPP Group PLC.

Hill Publishing Co., **IV** 634

Hill-Rom Company, **10** 349–50

Hill's Pet Nutrition, Inc., 14 123; **26** 207; **27 212–14,** 390. *See also* Colgate-Palmolive Company.

Hillard Oil and Gas Company, Inc., **11** 523

Hillards, PLC, **II** 678

Hillenbrand Industries, Inc., 6 295; **10 349–51; 16** 20

Hiller Aircraft Company, **9** 205; **48** 167

Hiller Group, **14** 286

Hillerich & Bradsby Company, Inc., 24 403; **51 161–64**

The Hillhaven Corporation, III 87–88; **6** 188; **14 241–43; 16** 57, 515, 517; **25** 307, 456

Hillin Oil, **IV** 658

Hillman, **I** 183

Hillos GmbH, **53** 169

Hills & Dales Railway Co. *See* Dayton Power & Light Company.

Hills Brothers Inc., **II** 548; **7** 383; **28** 311

Hills Pet Products, **III** 25

Hills Stores Company, 11 228; **13 260–61; 21** 459; **30** 57

Hillsborough Holdings Corporation. *See* Walter Industries, Inc.

Hillsdale Machine & Tool Company, **8** 514

Hillsdown Holdings, PLC, II 513–14; 24 218–21 (upd.); 28 490; **41** 252

Hillshire Farm, **II** 572

Hillside Industries Inc., **18** 118

Hilo Electric Light Company, **9** 276

Hilti AG, 53 167–69

Hilton Athletic Apparel, **16** 296–97

Hilton Group plc, 49 191–95 (upd.), 449–50

Hilton Hotels Corporation, II 208; **III** 91–93; **IV** 703; **6** 201, 210; **9** 95, 426; **19 205–08 (upd.); 21** 91, 93, 182, 333, 363; **23** 482; **27** 10; **54** 345–46; **62 176–79 (upd.).** *See also* Hilton Group plc.

Hilton International Co., **6** 385; **12** 489

Himley Brick, **14** 248

Janus Capital Group Inc., 6 401–02; **26** 233; **57 192–94**
Japan Acoustics, II 118
Japan Advertising Ltd., **16** 166
Japan Air Filter Co., Ltd., III 634
Japan Airlines Company, Ltd., I 104–06; **6** 70–71, 118, 123, 386, 427; **24** 399–400; **27** 464; **32 288–92 (upd.); 49** 459
Japan Brewery. *See* Kirin Brewery Company, Limited.
Japan Broadcasting Corporation, I 586; **II** 66, 101, 118; **7 248–50; 9** 31
Japan-California Bank, II 274
Japan Commerce Bank, II 291
Japan Creative Tours Co., I 106
Japan Credit Bureau, II 348
Japan Dairy Products, II 538
Japan Day & Night Bank, II 292
Japan Development Bank, III 300, 403
Japan Dyestuff Manufacturing Co., I 397
Japan Elanco Company, Ltd., **17** 437
Japan Electricity Generation and Transmission Company (JEGTCO), V 574
Japan Energy Corporation, **13** 202; **14** 206, 208; **59** 375
Japan Food Corporation, **14** 288
Japan Iron & Steel Co., Ltd., IV 157; **17** 349–50
Japan Leasing Corporation, 8 278–80; **11** 87
Japan Medico, **25** 431
Japan National Oil Corp., IV 516
Japan National Railway, V 448–50; **6** 70
Japan Oil Development Co., IV 364
Japan Petroleum Development Corp., IV 461
Japan Petroleum Exploration Co., IV 516
Japan Pulp and Paper Company Limited, IV 292–93, 680
Japan Reconstruction Finance Bank, II 300
Japan Telecom, **7** 118; **13** 482
Japan Telegraphic Communication Company (Nihon Denpo-Tsushin Sha), **16** 166
Japan Tobacco Inc., V 403–04; **30** 387; **46 257–60 (upd.)**
Japan Trust Bank, II 292
Japan Trustee Services Bank Ltd., **53** 322
Japan Try Co., III 758
Japan Vilene Company Ltd., **41 170–72**
Japanese and Asian Development Bank, IV 518
Japanese Electronic Computer Co., III 140
Japanese Enterprise Co., IV 728
Japanese National Railway, I 579; III 491; **43** 103
Japanese Victor Co., II 118
Japex Oman Co., IV 516
Japonica Partners, 9 485
Jara Enterprises, Inc., **31** 276
Jarden Corporation, **62** 365, 381
Jardinay Manufacturing Corp., **24** 335
Jardine Matheson Holdings Limited, I **468–71,** 577, 592; II 296; IV 189, 699–700; **18** 114; **20 309–14 (upd.); 47** 175–78
Jartran Inc., V 505; **24** 410
Järvenpään Kotelo Oy, IV 315
Jarvis plc, 39 237–39
Jas, Hennessy & Co., I 272
Jas. I. Miller Co., **13** 491
JASCO Products, III 581

Jason Incorporated, 23 299–301; 52 138
Jasper Corporation, III 767; **22** 546. *See also* Kimball International, Inc.
JAT, **27** 475
Jato, II 652
Jauch & Hübener, **14** 279
Java-China-Japan Line, 6 403–04; **26** 242
Java Software, **30** 453
Javelin Software Corporation, **10** 359
Javex Co., IV 272
Jax, 9 452
Jay Cooke and Co., **9** 370
Jay Jacobs, Inc., 9 243–45
Jay-Ro Services, III 419
Jay's Washateria, Inc., **7** 372
Jayco Inc., 13 288–90
Jazz Basketball Investors, Inc., 55 237–39
Jazzercise, Inc., 45 212–14
JB Oxford Holdings, Inc., 32 293–96
JB Pawn, Inc., **57** 139
JBA Holdings PLC, **43** 184
JBL, **22** 97
JCB, **14** 321
JCJL. *See* Java-China-Japan Line.
JCT Wireless Technology Company, **61** 233
JD Wetherspoon plc, 30 258–60
JDS Uniphase Corporation, 34 235–37
The Jean Coutu Group (PJC) Inc., 46 261–65
Jean-Jacques, **19** 50
Jean Lassale, III 619–20; **17** 430
Jean Lincet, **19** 50
Jean Nate, I 695
Jean Pagées et Fils, III 420
Jean-Philippe Fragrances, Inc. *See* Inter Parfums, Inc.
Jean Prouvost, IV 618
Jeanmarie Creations, Inc., **18** 67, 69
Jeanne Piaubert, III 47
Jeanneau SA, **55** 56
Jefferies Group, Inc., 25 248–51
Jefferson Bancorp, Inc., **37** 201
Jefferson Chemical Co., IV 552
Jefferson National Life Group, **10** 247
Jefferson-Pilot Corporation, 11 213–15; **29 253–56 (upd.)**
Jefferson Properties, Inc. *See* JPI.
Jefferson Smurfit Group plc, IV 294–96; **16** 122; **19 224–27 (upd.); 49 224–29 (upd.).** *See also* Smurfit-Stone Container Corporation.
Jefferson Standard Life Insurance, **11** 213–14
Jefferson Ward, **12** 48–49
Jefferson Warrior Railroad Company, III 767; **22** 546
Jeffery Sons & Co. Ltd., IV 711
Jeffrey Galion, III 472
JEGTCO. *See* Japan Electricity Generation and Transmission Company (JEGTCO).
Jeld-Wen, Inc., 33 409; **45 215–17**
Jell-O Co., II 531
Jem Development, **17** 233
Jenaer Glaswerk Schott & Genossen, III 445, 447
Jenn-Air Corporation, III 573; **22** 349
Jennie-O Foods, II 506; **54** 166–67
Jennifer Convertibles, Inc., 31 274–76
Jenny Craig, Inc., 10 382–84; 12 531; **29 257–60 (upd.)**
Jeno's, **13** 516; **26** 436
Jenoptik AG, 33 218–21; 53 167

Jensen Salsbery, I 715
Jenson, Woodward & Lozier, Inc., **21** 96
JEORA Co., IV 564
Jeppesen Sanderson, Inc., IV 677; **17** 486
Jepson Corporation, 8 230
Jeri-Jo Knitwear, Inc., **27** 346, 348
Jerome Foods, Inc., **54** 168
Jerome Increase Case Machinery Company. *See* J.I. Case Company.
Jerrico Inc., **27** 145
Jerrold Corporation, **10** 319–20
Jerry Bassin Inc., **17** 12–14
Jerry's Famous Deli Inc., 24 243–45
Jerry's Restaurants, **13** 320
Jersey Central Power & Light Company, **27** 182
Jersey European Airways (UK) Ltd., 61 144–46
Jersey Paper, IV 261
Jersey Standard. *See* Standard Oil Co. of New Jersey.
Jerusalem Post Publications Limited, **62** 188
Jervis B. Webb Company, 24 246–49
JESCO Inc. *See* The Yates Companies, Inc.
Jesse Jones Sausage Co. *See* GoodMark Foods, Inc.
Jessup & Moore Paper Co., IV 351; **19** 495
Jet America Airlines, **6** 67, 82
Jet Petroleum, Ltd., IV 401
Jet Research Center, III 498
Jet Set Corporation, **18** 513
JetBlue Airways Corporation, 44 248–50
Jetro Cash & Carry Enterprises Inc., 38 266–68
Jetway Systems, III 512
Jeumont-Industrie, II 93
Jeumont-Schneider Industries, II 93–94; **9** 10; **18** 473
Jevic Transportation, Inc., **45** 448
Jewel Companies, Inc., II 605; **6** 531; **12** 63; **18** 89; **22** 38; **26** 476; **27** 291
Jewel Food Stores, **7** 127–28; **13** 25
Jewell Ridge Coal Corp., IV 181
JFD-Encino, **24** 243
JG Industries, Inc., 15 240–42
Jheri Redding Products, Inc., **17** 108
JHT, Inc., **39** 377
Jiamusi Combine Harvester Factory, **21** 175
Jiangsu General Ball & Roller Co., Ltd., **45** 170
JIB Group plc, **20** 313
Jiffee Chemical Corporation, III 21; **22** 146
Jiffy Auto Rental, **16** 380
Jiffy Convenience Stores, II 627
Jiffy Lube International, Inc., IV 490; **21** 541; **24** 339; **25** 443–45; **50** 353
Jiffy Mixes, **29** 109–10
Jiffy Packaging, **14** 430
Jiji, **16** 166
Jil Sander A.G., **45** 342, 344
Jillian's Entertainment Holdings, Inc., 40 273–75
Jim Beam Brands Co., 14 271–73; 29 196
Jim Beam Brands Worldwide, Inc., 58 194–96 (upd.)
Jim Cole Enterprises, Inc., **19** 247
The Jim Henson Company, 23 302–04; **45** 130
The Jim Pattison Group, 37 219–22

National Realty Trust. *See* NRT Incorporated.
National Record Mart, Inc., 29 348–50
National Register Publishing Co., **17** 399; **23** 442
National Reinsurance Corporation. *See* General Re Corporation.
National Rent-A-Car, **6** 392–93
National Research Corporation, **8** 397
National Restaurants Management, Inc., **38** 385–87
National Revenue Corporation, **22** 181
National Rifle Association of America, 37 265–68
National Rubber Machinery Corporation, **8** 298
National Sanitary Supply Co., 13 149–50; **16 386–87**
National Satellite Paging, **18** 348
National School Studios, **7** 255; **25** 252
National Science Foundation, **9** 266
National Sea Products Ltd., 14 339–41
National Security Containers LLC, **58** 238
National Semiconductor Corporation, II 63–65; III 455, 618, 678; **6** 215, **261–63; 9** 297; **11** 45–46, 308, 463; **16** 122, 332; **17** 418; **18** 18; **19** 312; **21** 123; **26 327–30 (upd.); 43** 15
National Service Industries, Inc., 11 336–38; 54 251–55 (upd.)
National Shoe Products Corp., **16** 17
National Slicing Machine Company, **19** 359
National-Southwire Aluminum Company, **11** 38; **12** 353
National Stamping & Electric Works, **12** 159
National Standard Co., IV 137; **13 369–71**
National Starch and Chemical Company, II 496; **IV** 253; **17** 30; **32** 256–57; **49 268–70**
National Steel and Shipbuilding Company, **7** 356
National Steel Car Corp., **IV** 73; **24** 143–44
National Steel Corporation, I 491; **IV** 74, 163, 236–37, 572; **V** 152–53; **7** 549; **8** 346, 479–80; **11** 315; **12 352–54; 14** 191; **16** 212; **23** 445; **24** 144; **26** 527–29; **28** 325. *See also* FoxMeyer Health Corporation.
National Student Marketing Corporation, **10** 385–86
National Supply Co., **IV** 29
National System Company, **9** 41; **11** 469
National Tanker Fleet, **IV** 502
National Tea, **II** 631–32
National Technical Laboratories, **14** 52
National TechTeam, Inc., 41 280–83
National Telecommunications of Austin, **8** 311
National Telephone and Telegraph Corporation. *See* British Columbia Telephone Company.
National Telephone Co., **7** 332, 508
National Thoroughbred Racing Association, 58 244–47
National Trading Manufacturing, Inc., **22** 213
National Transcontinental, **6** 360
National Tube Co., **II** 330; **IV** 572; **7** 549
National Union Electric Corporation, **12** 159

National Utilities & Industries Corporation, **9** 363
National Westminster Bank PLC, II 237, **333–35; IV** 642; **13** 206
National Wine & Spirits, Inc., 49 271–74
Nationale Bank Vereeniging, **II** 185
Nationale-Nederlanden N.V., III 179, 200–01, **308–11; IV** 697; **50** 11
Nationar, **9** 174
NationsBank Corporation, 6 357; **10 425–27; 11** 126; **13** 147; **18** 516, 518; **23** 455; **25** 91, 186; **26** 348, 453. *See also* Bank of America Corporation
NationsRent, **28** 388
Nationwide Cellular Service, Inc., **27** 305
Nationwide Credit, **11** 112
Nationwide Group, **25** 155
Nationwide Income Tax Service, **9** 326
Nationwide Logistics Corp., **14** 504
Nationwide Mutual Insurance Co., **26** 488
NATIOVIE, **II** 234
Native Plants, **III** 43
NATM Buying Corporation, **10** 9, 468
Natomas Company, **IV** 410; **6** 353–54; **7** 309; **11** 271; **61** 28
Natref. *See* National Petroleum Refiners of South Africa.
Natrol, Inc., 49 275–78
Natronag, **IV** 325
Natronzellstoff-und Papierfabriken AG, **IV** 324
NatSteel Electronics Ltd., **48** 369
NatTeknik, **26** 333
Natudryl Manufacturing Company, **10** 271
Natural Alternatives International, Inc., 49 279–82
Natural Gas Clearinghouse, **11** 355. *See also* NGC Corporation.
Natural Gas Corp., **19** 155
Natural Gas Pipeline Company, **6** 530, 543; **7** 344–45
Natural Gas Service of Arizona, **19** 411
Natural Selection Foods, 54 256–58
Natural Wonders Inc., 14 342–44
NaturaLife International, **26** 470
The Nature Company, **10** 215–16; **14** 343; **26** 439; **27** 429; **28** 306
The Nature Conservancy, 26 323; **28 305–07**, 422
Nature's Sunshine Products, Inc., 15 317–19; 26 470; **27** 353; **33** 145
Nature's Way Products Inc., **26** 315
Naturipe Berry Growers, **62** 154
Natuzzi Group. *See* Industrie Natuzzi S.p.A.
NatWest Bancorp, **38** 393
NatWest Bank, **22** 52. *See also* National Westminster Bank PLC.
Naugles, **7** 506
Nautica Enterprises, Inc., 16 61; **18 357–60; 25** 258; **27** 60; **44 302–06 (upd.)**
Nautilus International, Inc., bf]XIII 532; **25** 40; **30** 161
Nautor Ab, **IV** 302
Navaho Freight Line, **16** 41
Navajo LTL, Inc., **57** 277
Navajo Refining Company, **12** 240
Navajo Shippers, Inc., **42** 364
Navan Resources, **38** 231
Navarre Corporation, 22 536; **24 348–51**
Naviera Vizcaina, **IV** 528
Navigant International, Inc., 47 263–66
Navigation Mixte, **III** 348

Navire Cargo Gear, **27** 269
Navisant, Inc., **49** 424
Navistar International Corporation, I 152, 155, **180–82**, 525, 527; **II** 330; **10** 280, **428–30 (upd.); 17** 327; **33** 254. *See also* International Harvester Co.
Navy Exchange Service Command, 31 342–45
Navy Federal Credit Union, 33 315–17
Naxon Utilities Corp., **19** 359
Naylor, Hutchinson, Vickers & Company. *See* Vickers PLC.
NBC **24** 516–17. *See also* National Broadcasting Company, Inc.
NBC Bankshares, Inc., **21** 524
NBC/Computer Services Corporation, **15** 163
NBD Bancorp, Inc., 9 476; **11 339–41**, 466. *See also* Bank One Corporation.
NBTY, Inc., 31 346–48
NCA Corporation, **9** 36, 57, 171
NCB. *See* National City Bank of New York.
NCB Brickworks, **III** 501; **7** 207
NCC Industries, Inc., **59** 267
NCC L.P., **15** 139
NCH Corporation, 8 385–87
Nchanga Consolidated Copper Mines, **IV** 239–40
nChip, **38** 187–88
NCNB Corporation, II 336–37; 12 519; **26** 453
NCO Group, Inc., 42 258–60
NCR Corporation, I 540–41; **III 150–53; IV** 298; **V** 263; **6** 250, **264–68 (upd.)**, 281–82; **9** 416; **11** 62, 151, 542; **12** 162, 148, 246, 484; **16** 65; **29** 44; **30 336–41 (upd.); 36** 81
NCS. *See* Norstan, Inc.
NCTI (Noise Cancellation Technologies Inc.), **19** 483–84
nCube Corp., **14** 15; **22** 293
ND Marston, **III** 593
NDB. *See* National Discount Brokers Group, Inc.
NDL. *See* Norddeutscher Lloyd.
NEA. *See* Newspaper Enterprise Association.
NEAC Inc., **I** 201–02
Nearly Me, **25** 313
Neatherlin Homes Inc., **22** 547
Nebraska Bell Company, **14** 311
Nebraska Cellular Telephone Company, **14** 312
Nebraska Furniture Mart, **III** 214–15; **18** 60–61, 63
Nebraska Light & Power Company, **6** 580
Nebraska Power Company, **25** 89
Nebraska Public Power District, 29 351–54
NEBS. *See* New England Business Services, Inc.
NEC Corporation, I 455, 520; **II** 40, 42, 45, 56–57, **66–68**, 73, 82, 91, 104, 361; **III** 715; **6** 101, 231, 244, 287; **9** 42, 115; **10** 257, 366, 463, 500; **11** 46, 308, 490; **13** 482; **16** 139; **18** 382–83; **19** 391; **21 388–91 (upd.); 25** 82, 531; **36** 286, 299–300; **47** 320; **57 261–67 (upd.)**
Neches Butane Products Co., **IV** 552
Neckermann Versand AG, **V** 100–02
Nedcor, **61** 270–71

University Microfilms, **III** 172; **6** 289
University of Phoenix, **24** 40
Univisa, **24** 516
Univision Communications Inc., **IV** 621; **18** 213; **24 515–18**; **41** 150–52; **54** 72–73, 158
Unix System Laboratories Inc., **6** 225; **25** 20–21; **38** 418
UNM. *See* United News & Media plc.
Uno-e Bank, **48** 51
Uno Restaurant Corporation, **16** 447; **18** 465, **538–40**
Uno-Ven, **IV** 571; **24** 522
Unocal Corporation, **IV** 508, **569–71**; **24 519–23 (upd.)**
UNR Industries, Inc. *See* ROHN Industries, Inc.
Unterberg Harris, **25** 433
UNUM Corp., **13 538–40**
UnumProvident Corporation, **52 376–83 (upd.)**
Uny Co., Ltd., **II** 619; **V** 209–10, 154; **13** 545; **36** 419; **49 425–28 (upd.)**
UOB. *See* United Overseas Bank Ltd.
UPC. *See* United Pan-Europe Communications NV.
UPI. *See* United Press International.
Upjohn Company, **I** 675, 684, 686, 700, **707–09**; **III** 18, 53; **6** 42; **8 547–49 (upd.)**; **10** 79; **12** 186; **13** 503; **14** 423; **16** 440; **29** 363. *See also* Pharmacia & Upjohn Inc.
UPM-Kymmene Corporation, **19 461–65**; **25** 12; **30** 325; **50 505–11 (upd.)**
UPN. *See* United Paramount Network.
Upper Deck Company, LLC, **34** 448; **37** 295
Upper Peninsula Power Co., **53** 369
UPS. *See* United Parcel Service of America Inc.
UPS Aviation Technologies, Inc., **60** 137
UPSHOT, **27** 195
Urban Investment and Development Co., **IV** 703
Urban Outfitters, Inc., **14 524–26**
Urban Systems Development Corp., **II** 121
Urbaser SA, **55** 182
Urenco, **6** 452
URS Corporation, **45 420–23**
Urwick Orr, **II** 609
US. *See also* U.S.
US Airways Express, **32** 334; **38** 130
US Airways Group, Inc., **28 506–09 (upd.)**; **33** 303; **52** 24–25, **384–88 (upd.)**
US Industrial Chemicals, Inc., **I** 377; **8** 440
US Industries Inc., **30** 231
US Monolithics, **54** 407
US 1 Industries, **27** 404
US Order, Inc., **10** 560, 562
US Repeating Arms Co., **58** 147
US Sprint Communications Company, **V** 295–96, 346–47; **6** 314; **8** 310; **9** 32; **10** 543; **11** 302; **12** 136, 541; **14** 252–53; **15** 196; **16** 318, 392; **25** 101; **29** 44; **43** 447. *See also* Sprint Communications Company, L.P.
US Telecom, **9** 478–79
US West Communications Services, Inc., **19** 255; **21** 285; **29** 39, 45, 478; **37** 312, 315–16. *See also* Regional Bell Operating Companies.
USA Cafes, **14** 331

USA Floral Products Inc., **27** 126
USA Interactive, Inc., **47 418–22 (upd.)**; **58** 117, 120
USA Networks Inc., **25** 330, 411; **33** 432; **37** 381, 383–84; **43** 422
USA Security Systems, Inc., **27** 21
USA Truck, Inc., **42 410–13**
USAA, **10 541–43**; **62 385–88 (upd.)**
USAir Group, Inc., **I** 55, **131–32**; **III** 215; **6** 121, **131–32 (upd.)**; **11** 300; **14** 70, 73; **18** 62; **21** 143; **24** 400; **26** 429; **42** 34. *See also* US Airways Group, Inc.
USANA, Inc., **27** 353; **29 491–93**
USCC. *See* United States Cellular Corporation.
USCP-WESCO Inc., **II** 682
Usego AG., **48** 63
USF&G Corporation, **III 395–98**; **11** 494–95; **19** 190
USFL. *See* United States Football League.
USFreightways Corporation, **27** 475; **49** 402
USG Corporation, **III 762–64**; **26 507–10 (upd.)**
USH. *See* United Scientific Holdings.
Usines Métallurgiques de Hainaut, **IV** 52
Usinger's Famous Sausage. *See* Fred Usinger Inc.
Usinor SA, **42 414–17 (upd.)**
Usinor Sacilor, **IV** 226–28; **22** 44; **24** 144; **26** 81, 84; **54** 393
USLD Communications Corp. *See* Billing Concepts Corp.
USM, **10** 44
USO. *See* United Service Organizations.
Usource LLC, **37** 406
USPS. *See* United States Postal Service.
USSC. *See* United States Surgical Corporation.
USSI. *See* U.S. Software Inc.
UST Inc., **9 533–35**; **42** 79; **50 512–17 (upd.)**
UST Wilderness Management Corporation, **33** 399
Usutu Pulp Company, **49** 353
USV Pharmaceutical Corporation, **11** 333
USWeb/CKS. *See* marchFIRST, Inc.
USX Corporation, **IV** 130, 228, **572–74**; **7** 193–94, **549–52 (upd.)**. *See also* United States Steel Corporation.
UT Starcom, **44** 426
UTA, **I** 119, 121; **6** 373–74, 93; **34** 397
Utag, **11** 510
Utah Construction & Mining Co., **I** 570; **IV** 146; **14** 296
Utah Federal Savings Bank, **17** 530
Utah Gas and Coke Company, **6** 568
Utah Group Health Plan, **6** 184
Utah International, **II** 30; **12** 196
Utah Medical Products, Inc., **36 496–99**
Utah Mines Ltd., **IV** 47; **22** 107
Utah Oil Refining Co., **IV** 370
Utah Power and Light Company, **9** 536; **12** 266; **27 483–86**. *See also* PacifiCorp.
UTI Energy, Inc. *See* Patterson-UTI Energy, Inc.
Utilicom, **6** 572
Utilicorp United Inc., **6 592–94**. *See also* Aquila, Inc.
UtiliTech Solutions, **37** 88
Utility Constructors Incorporated, **6** 527
Utility Engineering Corporation, **6** 580
Utility Fuels, **7** 377

Utility Line Construction Service, Inc., **59** 65
Utility Service Affiliates, Inc., **45** 277
Utility Services, Inc., **42** 249, 253
Utility Supply Co. *See* United Stationers Inc.
AB Utra Wood Co., **IV** 274
UUNET, **38 468–72**
UV Industries, Inc., **7** 360; **9** 440
Uwajimaya, Inc., **60 312–14**

V&S Variety Stores, **V** 37
V.A.W. of America Inc., **IV** 231
V.L. Churchill Group, **10** 493
VA Linux Systems, **45** 363
VA TECH ELIN EBG GmbH, **49 429–31**
VA Technologie AG, **57** 402
Vabis, **I** 197
Vacheron Constantin, **27** 487, 489
Vaco, **38** 200, 202
Vaculator Division. *See* Lancer Corporation.
Vacuum Metallurgical Company, **11** 234
Vacuum Oil Co., **IV** 463–64, 504, 549; **7** 351–52
Vadic Corp., **II** 83
Vadoise Vie, **III** 273
VAE AG, **57** 402
VAE Nortrak Cheyenne Inc., **53** 352
Vail Associates, Inc., **11 543–46**; **31** 65, 67
Vail Resorts, Inc., **43 435–39 (upd.)**
Vaillant GmbH, **44 436–39**
Val Corp., **24** 149
Val-Pak Direct Marketing Systems, Inc., **22** 162
Val Royal LaSalle, **II** 652
Valassis Communications, Inc., **8 550–51**; **37 407–10 (upd.)**
Valcambi S.A., **II** 268; **21** 145
Valcom, **13** 176
ValCom Inc. *See* InaCom Corporation.
Valdi Foods Inc., **II** 663–64
Valdosta Drug Co., **III** 9–10
Vale do Rio Doce Navegacao SA— Docenave, **43** 112
Vale Harmon Enterprises, Ltd., **25** 204
Vale Power Company, **12** 265
Valenciana de Cementos, **59** 112
Valentine & Company, **8** 552–53
Valeo, **III** 593; **23 492–94**
Valero Energy Corporation, **IV** 394; **7 553–55**; **19** 140; **31** 119
Valhi, Inc., **10** 435–36; **19 466–68**
Valid Logic Systems Inc., **11** 46, 284; **48** 77
Vality Technology Inc., **59** 56
Valke Oy, **IV** 348
Vallen Corporation, **45 424–26**
Valley Bank of Helena, **35** 197, 199
Valley Bank of Maryland, **46** 25
Valley Bank of Nevada, **19** 378
Valley Crest Tree Company, **31** 182–83
Valley Deli Inc., **24** 243
Valley East Medical Center, **6** 185
Valley Fashions Corp., **16** 535
Valley Federal of California, **11** 163
Valley Fig Growers, **7** 496–97
Valley Media Inc., **35 430–33**
Valley National Bank, **II** 420
Valley-Todeco, Inc., **13** 305–06
Valleyfair, **22** 130
Vallourec SA, **IV** 227; **54 391–94**

Zellstoffabrik Waldhof AG, **IV** 323–24
Zellweger Telecommunications AG, **9** 32
Zeneca Group PLC, 21 544–46. *See also* AstraZeneca PLC.
Zengine, Inc., **41** 258–59
Zenit Bank, **45** 322
Zenith Data Systems, Inc., II 124–25; **III** 123; **6** 231; **10 563–65; 36** 299
Zenith Electronics Corporation, II 102, **123–25; 10** 563; **11** 62, 318; **12** 183, 454; **13** 109, 398, **572–75 (upd.); 18** 421; **34 514–19 (upd.)**
Zenith Media, **42** 330–31
Zentec Corp., **I** 482
Zentralsparkasse und Kommerzialbank Wien, **23** 37
Zentronics, **19** 313
Zep Manufacturing Company, **54** 252, 254
Zeppelin Luftschifftechnik GmbH, **48** 450
Zerex, **50** 48
Zergo Holdings, **42** 24–25
Zero Corporation, 17 563–65
Zero First Co Ltd., **62** 245
Zero Plus Dialing, Inc. *See* Billing Concepts Corp.
Zetor s.p., **21** 175
Zeus Components, Inc., **10** 113; **50** 43
Zewawell AG, **IV** 324
ZF Friedrichshafen AG, 48 447–51
Zhenjiang Zhengmao Hitachi Zosen Machinery Co. Ltd., **53** 173
Zhong Yue Highsonic Electron Company, **62** 150
Zhongbei Building Material Products Company, **26** 510
Zhongde Brewery, **49** 417
Ziebart International Corporation, 30 499–501
The Ziegler Companies, Inc., 24 541–45
Ziff Communications Company, 7 239–40; **12** 359, **560–63; 13** 483; **16** 371; **17** 152, 253; **25** 238, 240; **41** 12
Ziff Davis Media Inc., 36 521–26 (upd.); 47 77, 79. *See also* CNET Networks, Inc.
Ziff-Davis Publishing Co., **38** 441
Zijlker, **IV** 491
Zila, Inc., 46 466–69
Zilber Ltd., **13** 541
Zildjian. *See* Avedis Zildjian Co.
Zilkha & Company, **12** 72
Zilog, Inc., 15 543–45; 16 548–49; **22** 390
Zimbabwe Sugar Refineries, **II** 581
Zimmer AG, **IV** 142
Zimmer Holdings, Inc., 45 455–57
Zimmer Inc., **10** 156–57; **11** 475
Zinc Products Company, **30** 39
Zindart Ltd., 60 370–72
Zinsser. *See* William Zinsser & Company, Inc.
Zion Foods, **23** 408
Zion's Cooperative Mercantile Institution, 33 471–74
Zions Bancorporation, 12 564–66; 24 395; **53 375–78 (upd.)**
Zippo Manufacturing Company, 18 565–68
Zipps Drive-Thru, Inc., **25** 389
Zippy Mart, **7** 102
Zircotube, **IV** 174
Zodiac S.A., 36 527–30
Zody's Department Stores, **9** 120–22
Zolfo Cooper LLC, **57** 219

Zoll Foods, **55** 366
Zoll Medical, **18** 423
Zoloto Mining Ltd., **38** 231
Zoltek Companies, Inc., 37 427–30
Zomba Records Ltd., 52 428–31
The Zondervan Corporation, **51** 131
Zondervan Publishing House, 14 499; **24 546–49**
Zoom Technologies, Inc., 53 379–82 (upd.)
Zoom Telephonics, Inc., 18 569–71
Zortech Inc., **10** 508
Zotos International, Inc., **III** 63; **17** 110; **22** 487; **41** 228
ZPT Radom, **23** 427
ZS Sun Limited Partnership, **10** 502
Zuari Cement, **40** 107, 109
Zuellig Group N.A., Inc., **46** 226
Zuivelcooperatie De Seven Provincien UA, **59** 194
Zuka Juice, **47** 201
Zumtobel AG, 50 544–48
Zurich Financial Services, 40 59, 61; **42 448–53 (upd.)**
Zurich Insurance Group, **15** 257; **25** 154, 156
Zürich Versicherungs-Gesellschaft, III 410–12. *See also* Zurich Financial Services
Zurn Industries, Inc., **24** 150
Zvezda Design Bureau, **61** 197
Zwarovski, **16** 561
Zweckform Büro-Produkte G.m.b.H., **49** 38
Zycad Corp., **11** 489–91
Zycon Corporation, **24** 201
Zygo Corporation, 42 454–57
ZymoGenetics Inc., **61** 266
ZyMOS Corp., **III** 458
Zytec Corporation, 19 513–15. *See also* Artesyn Technologies Inc.

INDEX TO INDUSTRIES

Index to Industries

ACCOUNTING

American Institute of Certified Public
  Accountants (AICPA), 44
Andersen Worldwide, 29 (upd.)
Automatic Data Processing, Inc., 47 (upd.)
Deloitte Touche Tohmatsu International, 9;
  29 (upd.)
Ernst & Young, 9; 29 (upd.)
Grant Thornton International, 57
KPMG International, 33 (upd.)
L.S. Starrett Co., 13
McLane Company, Inc., 13
NCO Group, Inc., 42
Paychex, Inc., 46 (upd.)
PricewaterhouseCoopers, 9; 29 (upd.)
Robert Wood Johnson Foundation, 35
Univision Communications Inc., 24

ADVERTISING & OTHER BUSINESS SERVICES

A.C. Nielsen Company, 13
ABM Industries Incorporated, 25 (upd.)
ACNielsen Corporation, 38 (upd.)
Acsys, Inc., 44
Adecco S.A., 36 (upd.)
Adia S.A., 6
Administaff, Inc., 52
Advo, Inc., 6; 53 (upd.)
Aegis Group plc, 6
Affiliated Computer Services, Inc., 61
AHL Services, Inc., 27
Alloy, Inc., 55
Amdocs Ltd., 47
American Building Maintenance Industries,
  Inc., 6
The American Society of Composers,
  Authors and Publishers (ASCAP), 29
Amey Plc, 47
Analysts International Corporation, 36
The Arbitron Company, 38
Ariba, Inc., 57
Armor Holdings, Inc., 27
Ashtead Group plc, 34
The Associated Press, 13
Bain & Company, 55
Barrett Business Services, Inc., 16
Barton Protective Services Inc., 53
Bates Worldwide, Inc., 14; 33 (upd.)
Bearings, Inc., 13
Berlitz International, Inc., 13
Big Flower Press Holdings, Inc., 21
Boron, LePore & Associates, Inc., 45
The Boston Consulting Group, 58
Bozell Worldwide Inc., 25
BrandPartners Group, Inc., 58
Bright Horizons Family Solutions, Inc., 31
Broadcast Music Inc., 23
Buck Consultants, Inc., 55
Bureau Veritas SA, 55
Burns International Services Corporation,
  13; 41 (upd.)
Cambridge Technology Partners, Inc., 36

Campbell-Mithun-Esty, Inc., 16
Career Education Corporation, 45
Carmichael Lynch Inc., 28
CDI Corporation, 54 (upd.)
Central Parking Corporation, 18
Century Business Services, Inc., 52
Chancellor Beacon Academies, Inc., 53
ChartHouse International Learning
  Corporation, 49
Chiat/Day Inc. Advertising, 11
Chicago Board of Trade, 41
Chisholm-Mingo Group, Inc., 41
Christie's International plc, 15; 39 (upd.)
Cintas Corporation, 21
COMFORCE Corporation, 40
Command Security Corporation, 57
Computer Learning Centers, Inc., 26
Corporate Express, Inc., 47 (upd.)
CORT Business Services Corporation, 26
Cox Enterprises, Inc., 22 (upd.)
Creative Artists Agency LLC, 38
Cyrk Inc., 19
Dale Carnegie Training, Inc., 28
D'Arcy Masius Benton & Bowles, Inc., 6;
  32 (upd.)
Dawson Holdings PLC, 43
DDB Needham Worldwide, 14
Deluxe Corporation, 22 (upd.)
Dentsu Inc., I; 16 (upd.); 40 (upd.)
Deutsch, Inc., 42
Deutsche Post AG, 29
DoubleClick Inc., 46
Drake Beam Morin, Inc., 44
The Dun & Bradstreet Corporation, 61
  (upd.)
Earl Scheib, Inc., 32
EBSCO Industries, Inc., 17
Ecology and Environment, Inc., 39
Edelman, 62
Edison Schools Inc., 37
Education Management Corporation, 35
Electro Rent Corporation, 58
Employee Solutions, Inc., 18
Ennis Business Forms, Inc., 21
Equifax Inc., 6; 28 (upd.)
Equity Marketing, Inc., 26
ERLY Industries Inc., 17
Euro RSCG Worldwide S.A., 13
Expedia, Inc., 58
Fallon McElligott Inc., 22
FileNet Corporation, 62
Fiserv, Inc., 33 (upd.)
FlightSafety International, Inc., 29 (upd.)
Florists' Transworld Delivery, Inc., 28
Foote, Cone & Belding Communications,
  Inc., I
Forrester Research, Inc., 54
Frankel & Co., 39
Franklin Covey Company, 37 (upd.)
Frost & Sullivan, Inc., 53
Gage Marketing Group, 26
The Gallup Organization, 37
George P. Johnson Company, 60
George S. May International Company, 55

GfK Aktiengesellschaft, 49
Glotel plc, 53
Grey Advertising, Inc., 6
Group 4 Falck A/S, 42
Groupe Jean-Claude Darmon, 44
GSD&M Advertising, 44
Gwathmey Siegel & Associates Architects
  LLC, 26
Ha-Lo Industries, Inc., 27
Hakuhodo, Inc., 6; 42 (upd.)
Hall, Kinion & Associates, Inc., 52
Handleman Company, 15
Havas SA, 33 (upd.)
Hays Plc, 27
Headway Corporate Resources, Inc., 40
Heidrick & Struggles International, Inc., 28
Hildebrandt International, 29
IKON Office Solutions, Inc., 50
IMS Health, Inc., 57
Interep National Radio Sales Inc., 35
International Brotherhood of Teamsters, 37
International Management Group, 18
International Total Services, Inc., 37
The Interpublic Group of Companies, Inc.,
  I; 22 (upd.)
Ipsos SA, 48
Iron Mountain, Inc., 33
ITT Educational Services, Inc., 33
J.D. Power and Associates, 32
Jackson Hewitt, Inc., 48
Japan Leasing Corporation, 8
Jostens, Inc., 25 (upd.)
JOULÉ Inc., 58
JWT Group Inc., I
Katz Communications, Inc., 6
Katz Media Group, Inc., 35
Keane, Inc., 56
Kelly Services Inc., 6; 26 (upd.)
Ketchum Communications Inc., 6
Kinko's Inc., 16; 43 (upd.)
Kirshenbaum Bond + Partners, Inc., 57
Kohn Pedersen Fox Associates P.C., 57
Korn/Ferry International, 34
Kroll Inc., 57
Labor Ready, Inc., 29
Lamar Advertising Company, 27
Learning Tree International Inc., 24
Leo Burnett Company Inc., I; 20 (upd.)
Lintas: Worldwide, 14
Mail Boxes Etc., 18; 41 (upd.)
Manpower, Inc., 30 (upd.)
marchFIRST, Inc., 34
Maritz Inc., 38
MAXIMUS, Inc., 43
Mediaset SpA, 50
MPS Group, Inc., 49
Mullen Advertising Inc., 51
National Equipment Services, Inc., 57
National Media Corporation, 27
Neopost S.A., 53
New England Business Services, Inc., 18
New Valley Corporation, 17
NFO Worldwide, Inc., 24
Nobel Learning Communities, Inc., 37

ENGINEERING & MANAGEMENT SERVICES

FINANCIAL SERVICES: BANKS

FOOD SERVICES & RETAILERS

HEALTH & PERSONAL CARE PRODUCTS

HEALTH & PERSONAL CARE PRODUCTS (continued)

Shionogi & Co., Ltd., III
Shiseido Company, Limited, III; 22 (upd.)
Slim-Fast Nutritional Foods International, Inc., 18
Smith & Nephew plc, 17
SmithKline Beecham PLC, III
Soft Sheen Products, Inc., 31
STAAR Surgical Company, 57
Sunrise Medical Inc., 11
Tambrands Inc., 8
Terumo Corporation, 48
Tom's of Maine, Inc., 45
The Tranzonic Companies, 37
Turtle Wax, Inc., 15
United States Surgical Corporation, 10; 34 (upd.)
USANA, Inc., 29
Utah Medical Products, Inc., 36
VHA Inc., 53
VIASYS Healthcare, Inc., 52
VISX, Incorporated, 30
Vitamin Shoppe Industries, Inc., 60
Water Pik Technologies, Inc., 34
Weider Nutrition International, Inc., 29
Wella AG, III; 48 (upd.)
West Pharmaceutical Services, Inc., 42
Wright Medical Group, Inc., 61
Wyeth, 50 (upd.)
Zila, Inc., 46
Zimmer Holdings, Inc., 45

HEALTH CARE SERVICES

Acadian Ambulance & Air Med Services, Inc., 39
Adventist Health, 53
Advocat Inc., 46
Alterra Healthcare Corporation, 42
Amedysis, Inc., 53
The American Cancer Society, 24
American Lung Association, 48
American Medical Association, 39
American Medical International, Inc., III
American Medical Response, Inc., 39
American Red Cross, 40
AmeriSource Health Corporation, 37 (upd.)
AmSurg Corporation, 48
Applied Bioscience International, Inc., 10
Assisted Living Concepts, Inc., 43
Beverly Enterprises, Inc., III; 16 (upd.)
Bon Secours Health System, Inc., 24
Caremark Rx, Inc., 10; 54 (upd.)
Children's Comprehensive Services, Inc., 42
Children's Hospitals and Clinics, Inc., 54
Chronimed Inc., 26
COBE Laboratories, Inc., 13
Columbia/HCA Healthcare Corporation, 15
Community Psychiatric Centers, 15
CompDent Corporation, 22
CompHealth Inc., 25
Comprehensive Care Corporation, 15
Continental Medical Systems, Inc., 10
Continuum Health Partners, Inc., 60
Coventry Health Care, Inc., 59
Easter Seals, Inc., 58
Erickson Retirement Communities, 57
Express Scripts Incorporated, 17
Extendicare Health Services, Inc., 6
FHP International Corporation, 6
Fresenius AG, 56
Genesis Health Ventures, Inc., 18
GranCare, Inc., 14
Group Health Cooperative, 41
Hazelden Foundation, 28
HCA - The Healthcare Company, 35 (upd.)

Health Care & Retirement Corporation, 22
Health Management Associates, Inc., 56
Health Risk Management, Inc., 24
Health Systems International, Inc., 11
HealthSouth Corporation, 14; 33 (upd.)
Highmark Inc., 27
The Hillhaven Corporation, 14
Hooper Holmes, Inc., 22
Hospital Central Services, Inc., 56
Hospital Corporation of America, III
Howard Hughes Medical Institute, 39
Humana Inc., III; 24 (upd.)
Intermountain Health Care, Inc., 27
Jenny Craig, Inc., 10; 29 (upd.)
Kinetic Concepts, Inc. (KCI), 20
LabOne, Inc., 48
Laboratory Corporation of America Holdings, 42 (upd.)
Lifeline Systems, Inc., 53
Lincare Holdings Inc., 43
Manor Care, Inc., 6; 25 (upd.)
March of Dimes, 31
Matria Healthcare, Inc., 17
Maxicare Health Plans, Inc., III; 25 (upd.)
Mayo Foundation, 9; 34 (upd.)
Memorial Sloan-Kettering Cancer Center, 57
Merit Medical Systems, Inc., 29
National Health Laboratories Incorporated, 11
National Medical Enterprises, Inc., III
New York City Health and Hospitals Corporation, 60
NewYork-Presbyterian Hospital, 59
NovaCare, Inc., 11
Option Care Inc., 48
Orthodontic Centers of America, Inc., 35
Oxford Health Plans, Inc., 16
PacifiCare Health Systems, Inc., 11
Palomar Medical Technologies, Inc., 22
Pediatric Services of America, Inc., 31
Pediatrix Medical Group, Inc., 61
PHP Healthcare Corporation, 22
PhyCor, Inc., 36
Primedex Health Systems, Inc., 25
Quest Diagnostics Inc., 26
Ramsay Youth Services, Inc., 41
Res-Care, Inc., 29
Response Oncology, Inc., 27
Rural/Metro Corporation, 28
Sabratek Corporation, 29
St. Jude Medical, Inc., 11; 43 (upd.)
Salick Health Care, Inc., 53
Sierra Health Services, Inc., 15
Smith & Nephew plc, 41 (upd.)
The Sports Club Company, 25
SSL International plc, 49
Stericycle Inc., 33
Sun Healthcare Group Inc., 25
SwedishAmerican Health System, 51
Tenet Healthcare Corporation, 55 (upd.)
Twinlab Corporation, 34
U.S. Healthcare, Inc., 6
Unison HealthCare Corporation, 25
United HealthCare Corporation, 9
United Nations International Children's Emergency Fund (UNICEF), 58
United Way of America, 36
Universal Health Services, Inc., 6
VCA Antech, Inc., 58
Vencor, Inc., 16
VISX, Incorporated, 30
Vivra, Inc., 18
WellPoint Health Networks Inc., 25
YWCA of the U.S.A., 45

HOTELS

Amerihost Properties, Inc., 30
Aztar Corporation, 13
Bass PLC, 38 (upd.)
Boca Resorts, Inc., 37
Boyd Gaming Corporation, 43
Bristol Hotel Company, 23
The Broadmoor Hotel, 30
Caesars World, Inc., 6
Candlewood Hotel Company, Inc., 41
Carlson Companies, Inc., 22 (upd.)
Castle & Cooke, Inc., 20 (upd.)
Cedar Fair, L.P., 22
Cendant Corporation, 44 (upd.)
Choice Hotels International Inc., 14
Circus Circus Enterprises, Inc., 6
Club Méditerranée S.A., 6; 21 (upd.)
Doubletree Corporation, 21
Extended Stay America, Inc., 41
Fibreboard Corporation, 16
Four Seasons Hotels Inc., 9; 29 (upd.)
Fuller Smith & Turner P.L.C., 38
Gables Residential Trust, 49
Gaylord Entertainment Company, 11; 36 (upd.)
Granada Group PLC, 24 (upd.)
Grand Casinos, Inc., 20
Grand Hotel Krasnapolsky N.V., 23
Grupo Posadas, S.A. de C.V., 57
Helmsley Enterprises, Inc., 9
Hilton Group plc, III; 19 (upd.); 49 (upd.)
Hilton Hotels Corporation, 62 (upd.)
Holiday Inns, Inc., III
Hospitality Franchise Systems, Inc., 11
Howard Johnson International, Inc., 17
Hyatt Corporation, III; 16 (upd.)
Interstate Hotels & Resorts Inc., 58
ITT Sheraton Corporation, III
JD Wetherspoon plc, 30
John Q. Hammons Hotels, Inc., 24
The La Quinta Companies, 11; 42 (upd.)
Ladbroke Group PLC, 21 (upd.)
Las Vegas Sands, Inc., 50
Madden's on Gull Lake, 52
Mandalay Resort Group, 32 (upd.)
Manor Care, Inc., 25 (upd.)
The Marcus Corporation, 21
Marriott International, Inc., III; 21 (upd.)
Mirage Resorts, Incorporated, 6; 28 (upd.)
Motel 6, 13; 56 (upd.)
Omni Hotels Corp., 12
Park Corp., 22
Players International, Inc., 22
Preussag AG, 42 (upd.)
Prime Hospitality Corporation, 52
Promus Companies, Inc., 9
Real Turismo, S.A. de C.V., 50
Red Roof Inns, Inc., 18
Resorts International, Inc., 12
Ritz-Carlton Hotel Company L.L.C., 9; 29 (upd.)
Santa Fe Gaming Corporation, 19
The SAS Group, 34 (upd.)
SFI Group plc, 51
Showboat, Inc., 19
Sonesta International Hotels Corporation, 44
Starwood Hotels & Resorts Worldwide, Inc., 54
Sun International Hotels Limited, 26
Sunburst Hospitality Corporation, 26
Thistle Hotels PLC, 54
Trusthouse Forte PLC, III
Vail Resorts, Inc., 43 (upd.)
WestCoast Hospitality Corporation, 59
Westin Hotels and Resorts Worldwide, 9; 29 (upd.)

LEGAL SERVICES

MANUFACTURING

TOBACCO

TRANSPORT SERVICES

UTILITIES

WASTE SERVICES

GEOGRAPHIC INDEX

Geographic Index

United States

Venezuela

Vietnam

Virgin Islands

Wales

Zambia

NOTES ON CONTRIBUTORS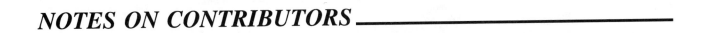

Notes on Contributors

BRENNAN, Gerald E. California-based writer.

CAPACE, Nancy K. Detroit-based writer, editor, researcher, specializing in history and biography.

COHEN, M. L. Novelist and business writer living in Paris.

COVELL, Jeffrey L. Seattle-based writer.

DINGER, Ed. Bronx-based writer and editor.

GREENLAND, Paul R. Illinois-based writer and researcher; author of two books and former senior editor of a national business magazine; contributor to *The Encyclopedia of Chicago History* and *Company Profiles for Students.*

HALASZ, Robert. Former editor in chief of *World Progress* and *Funk & Wagnalls New Encyclopedia Yearbook;* author, *The U.S. Marines* (Millbrook Press, 1993).

HAUSER, Evelyn. Researcher, writer and marketing specialist based in Arcata, California; expertise includes historical and trend research in such topics as globalization, emerging industries and lifestyles, future scenarios, biographies, and the history of organizations.

INGRAM, Frederick C. Utah-based business writer who has contributed to *GSA Business, Appalachian Trailway News,* the *Encyclopedia of Business,* the *Encyclopedia of Global Industries,* the *Encyclopedia of Consumer Brands,* and other regional and trade publications.

KEPOS, Paula. Manhattan-based editor and writer.

LEMIEUX, Gloria A. Researcher and writer living in Nashua, New Hampshire.

LORENZ, Sarah Ruth. Minnesota-based writer.

ROTHBURD, Carrie. Writer and editor specializing in corporate profiles, academic texts, and academic journal articles.

STANSELL, Christina M. Writer and editor based in Farmington Hills, Michigan.

TRADII, Mary. Writer based in Denver, Colorado.

UHLE, Frank. Ann Arbor-based writer; movie projectionist, disc jockey, and staff member of *Psychotronic Video* magazine.

WOODWARD, A. Wiconsin-based business writer.